Hillier
THE GARDENER'S GUIDE TO
TREES & SHRUBS

Hillier
THE GARDENER'S GUIDE TO
TREES & SHRUBS

EDITOR JOHN KELLY
CONSULTANT EDITOR JOHN HILLIER

David & Charles

A DAVID & CHARLES BOOK

David & Charles is a subsidiary of F&W (UK) Ltd.,
an F&W Publications Inc. company

First published in the UK in 1995
Reprinted 2004
First paperback edition 2004

ISBN 0 7153 0130 6 hardback
ISBN 0 7153 2021 1 paperback

Acknowledgements
The inspiration for this book was the catalogue of plants prepared by Sir Harold Hillier,
Desmond Clarke, Roy Lancaster and Mr P. H.B. Gardner and first published in 1972 as
the *Hillier Manual of Trees and Shrubs*. The original text was revised, edited and updated
for *The Hillier Gardener's Guide to Trees and Shrubs* and contains a substantial amount of
new material.

Book design by Michael Whitehead and Ian Muggeridge
Cover design by Lisa Forrester and Jodie Lystor
Line illustrations by Coral Mula
Printed in China by SNP Leefung
for David & Charles
Brunel House   Newton Abbot   Devon

Visit our website at www.davidandcharles.co.uk

David & Charles books are available from all good bookshops; alternatively you can
contact our Orderline on (0)1626 334555 or write to us at FREEPOST EX2 110,
David & Charles Direct, Newton Abbot, TQ12 4ZZ (no stamp required UK mainland).

CONTENTS

HOW TO USE THE GUIDE

DESCRIPTIONS

The descriptions in the guide have, where possible, been based on typical plants growing in the United Kingdom. Because of natural variations in species and varieties, however, such characteristics as leaf shape, colour and texture, flower colour, occurrence of flower and fruit, habit of growth and autumn colour may differ (within the limitations of the species) from those described. Autumn colours are particularly influenced by local and seasonal conditions, but some clones of a species are more reliable than others.

Genus descriptions The genus heading provides the genus name, family name and common name (where it applies to the whole genus) in the following style:

Acer *Aceraceae*
Maple

The genus description sets out distinctive generic characteristics including size, period of bloom, flower and leaf characteristics, hardiness tolerance, soil preferences, pruning advice and the region of origin. Where no information is given on a particular subject, it may be assumed that no relevant information exists on that topic for that plant.

Plant descriptions The plant heading may describe a species, subspecies, variety, form, cultivar or hybrid. It includes the common name in parentheses where specific to the species in the following style:

A. saccharum (Sugar maple)

Where a plant has been granted Plant Breeder's Rights (a procedure which is becoming recognized internationally and seeks to prevent propagation of the plant without permission from, and a royalty to, the rights holder) PBR names and numbers are included in the heading, as are any synonyms (see page 9). The plant description details the characteristics for which the plant is renowned and any special growing descriptions which differ from those of the genus (in the case of a species) and from those of the species (in the case

The superb flaming orange-reds of this *Rhododendron* 'Balzac' are typical of many of the Exbury Azaleas

of subspecies, varieties, forms, cultivars and hybrids). The plant is denoted as deciduous or evergreen only where the genus comprises a mix of evergreen and deciduous specimens; refer otherwise to the genus description. Region of origin and date of introduction into western gardens are given where known; where this information is not available, the guide gives the earliest known date of cultivation. Finally, the plant description includes an RHS hardiness zone rating and, where applicable, the RHS Award of Garden Merit symbol together with the year in which it was awarded. Both of these are explained overleaf.

Heights The ultimate height of a tree or shrub is dependent on a number of factors including soil, aspect, and local weather conditions and seasonal variations. The following scale defines the terms large, medium and small as used throughout the guide and indicates the probable range of heights for each plant grown under average conditions in the United Kingdom. Allowances must be made for specimens growing in shade, against walls and in any other exceptional conditions.

TREES
Large	over 18m (over 60ft)
Medium	10 to 18m (35 to 60ft)
Small	up to 10m (up to 35ft)

SHRUBS
Large	over 3m (over 10ft)
Medium	1.5 to 3m (6 to 10ft)
Small	1 to 1.5m (3 to 5ft)
Dwarf	0.3 to 0.75m (1 to 2½ft)
Prostrate	creeping

Seasons and months Even within the relatively small area of the British Isles, each region experiences spring and first frosts at slighty different times of the calendar year. For this reason, the guide employs the widely used seasonal system which requires the reader to apply experience gained from knowledge of local weather patterns and seasonality to roughly allocate a period of the calendar year to each of the four seasons, and within those seasons to subdivide further into early, mid and late. Once understood, this system allows the most accurate application of seasonally relevant information over the widest area.

Award of Garden Merit ♛ The Award of Garden Merit (AGM) is given by the Royal Horticultural Society to recognize plants of outstanding excellence for garden use, whether grown in the open or under glass. The AGM is of practical value for gardeners in that it highlights exceptional plants among the tens of thousands currently offered in the international horticultural trade.

Hardiness The hardiness of plants is a subject full of pitfalls, surprises, disappointments and exceptions to the rule. In Britain, and in many other parts of the world in which a temperate climate applies, the term 'hardy' is used to describe a plant's ability to survive cold. The guide employs the Royal Horticultural Society's definitions of hardiness which divide plants grown in the United Kingdom into four categories:

H4 = plants which are hardy when grown outside
H3 = plants which are hardy outside in some regions and/or particular situations, or plants which may usually be grown outside in summer but require frost-free overwintering
H2 = plants which require the protection of unheated glass
H1 = plants which require the protection of heated glass

Every plant in the guide is given a hardiness rating which indicates its ability to survive in a particular environment given average conditions. Exceptional weather conditions or unusual sites may cause discrepancies. For example, a plant in category 4 which is perfectly hardy may be encouraged into growth during mild periods in spring only to be attacked by late frosts which will have a particularly destructive effect on tender new growth. On the other hand, plants that fall into categories 1, 2 and 3 can often be accommodated outside throughout the year by siting them in positions that offer a favourable microclimate, such as against a wall or among other trees and shrubs.

NOMENCLATURE AND CLASSIFICATION

Plant nomenclature is controlled by two internationally accepted codes. The botanical names of plants (necessary for both wild and cultivated plants) are covered by the International Code of Botanical Nomenclature, while the use of cultivar and group epithets as well as the names of graft hybrids (required only for cultivated plants) are covered by the International Code of Nomenclature for Cultivated Plants.

As our knowledge of both plant variation and plant relationships has developed, so we have been forced to review the earlier classification of many plants. This, along with the application of the 'Rule of Priority' (that is, the obligatory use of the earliest legitimate name), has necessitated a number of name changes over the years. Not all of these changes are accepted in the guide, but where a plant has been re-named it also appears under its old name with a cross-reference referring the reader to the new name for full information. The old name is generally included as a synonym (see opposite) after the new name.

USE OF BOTANICAL NAMES IN THE GUIDE

The conventions governing the naming of plants may appear complex but they are in fact extremely logical and intuitive once some basic principles are grasped. A full treatment of the subject can be found on page 80; for now, however, it will suffice to understand the significance of the various elements of a given plant name.

Plants are referred to scientifically by at least two names, generally written in italics. The first name, which is always written with an initial capital, is that of the genus (plural *genera*), a group of related species which share various characteristics. The second is the species name, or specific epithet. Members of a species are closely related and often very similar.

Genera are themselves classified into groupings called families on the basis of botanical similarities which are often not immediately apparent to the gardener. Indeed, some families contain genera with quite different external characteristics: the *Caprifoliaceae*, for example, includes such outwardly dissimilar plants as *Abelia*, *Lonicera* and *Viburnum*.

Throughout the guide, certain typestyles have been used consistently to denote the hierarchical ordering of plant name elements, and these are reproduced below:

Acer	genus name
Aceraceae	family name
Maple	genus common name
Acer saccharum	species
(Sugar maple)	species common name

Subspecies, varietas and forma In nature, species often show greater or lesser degrees of variation in character, and these variants are denoted by a third scientific name. The botanically recognized subdivisions of a species (that is, distinct forms occurring in the wild) are: the **subspecies (subsp.)**, the **varietas (var.)** and the **forma (f.)**, denoted in the guide in the following style:

Acer saccharum subsp. *grandidentatum*   subspecies

Acer grosseri var. *hersii*   varietas

Acer rufinerve f. *albolimbatum*   forma

(Note: Although varietas is a recognized botanical category, the term 'variety' is often used to refer to a varietas or cultivar, and by the same token the botanical category forma is not to be confused with the term 'form', often used colloquially to refer to a variety, subspecies or cultivar.)

Groups, cultivars and specific crosses In status, the group falls somewhere between the botanical subdivisions of the species and the cultivar. Whereas a cultivar (from *cultiv*ated *var*iety) should show little or no variation from plant to plant, the members of a group can vary considerably. Cultivars are distinct forms often with considerable horticultural merit for their flower colour, attractive leaf form or some other garden-worthy characteristic. Selected either from the wild or from garden plants, they are grown in cultivation and their characteristics are maintained by controlled propagation. Neither groups nor cultivars are considered distinct enough to warrant full botanical recognition. The product of inter-breeding between two species of the same genus is called a specific hybrid or specific cross, and the resulting offspring normally shows characteristics from both parents. The hybrid plant is given a new Latin name preceded by 'x' (cross); for example, *Gleditsia* x *texana* is a specific hybrid of *Gleditsia aquatica* and *Gleditsia triacanthos*. These subdivisions are indicated in the following style:

Acer saccharinum Laciniatum Group   group

Acer saccharinum 'Lutescens'   cultivar

Acer × *hillieri*   specific hybrid

Synonyms One consequence of the continuing reclassification of plants is that many names by which they were previously known are now no longer valid. These old names, together with names not accepted in the guide, are shown in italics after the accepted name and prefixed by the abbreviation syn.:

Acer maximowiczianum, syn. *A. nikoense*   synonym

ABBREVIATIONS

Genus and species names These are abbreviated to an initial capital (for the genus) and lowercase letter (for the species) after their first mention; in order to establish the full name refer back to the first preceding generic or specific name beginning with that letter. For example:

Paeonia *Paeoniaceae*
Peony

P. × *lemoinii* **'Chromatella'**
(the *P.* refers to the generic name *Paeonia*)

P. × *l.* **'Souvenir de Maxime Cornu'**
(the *P.* refers to the generic name *Paeonia* and the *l.* to the specific name *lemoinii*)

General abbreviations and codes

c	circa
m	metre
cm	centimetre
mm	millimetre
yd	yard
ft	foot
in	inch
sp	species (singular)
spp	species (plural)
var	variety
cv	cultivar
f	form

Specific abbreviations used in the guide

AGM	Award of Garden Merit
H	Hardiness

GLOSSARY

Acicular Needle-shaped

Acuminate Tapering at the end, long-pointed

Acute Sharp-pointed

Adpressed Lying close and flat against

Alternate (Leaves) borne singly at each node on opposite sides of the stem

Anther Pollen-bearing part of the stamen

Aristate Bearded, bristle-tipped

Articulate Jointed

Ascending Rising somewhat obliquely and curving upwards

Auricle Ear-shaped projection or appendage

Auriculate Shaped like an ear

Awl-shaped Tapering from the base to a slender and stiff point

Axil Angle formed by a leaf or lateral branch with the stem, or that formed by a vein with the midrib

Axillary Produced in the axil

Bearded Furnished with long or stiff hairs

Berry Strictly a pulpy, normally several-seeded, indehiscent fruit

Bifid Divided in two by a deep cleft

Bipinnate Twice pinnate

Bisexual Both male and female organs in the same flower

Blade Expanded part of a leaf or petal

Bloom A fine powder-like, waxy deposit

Bole Trunk, of a tree

Bract Modified, usually reduced leaf at the base of a flower-stalk, flower-cluster or shoot

Bullate Blistered or puckered

Calcareous Containing carbonate of lime or limestone, chalky or limy

Calyx Outer part of a flower, the sepals

Campanulate Bell-shaped

Capitate Head-like, collected in a dense cluster

Capsule Dry, several-celled pod

Catkin Normally dense spike or spike-like raceme of tiny, scaly-bracted flowers or fruits

Ciliate Fringed with hairs

Cladode Flattened leaf-like stem

Clone Group of individuals derived originally from a single specimen and maintained in cultivation by vegetative propagation. All cloned specimens are exactly alike and identical to the original. The majority of cultivars are clonal in origin and are normally propagated vegetatively

Columnar Tall and cylindrical or tapering

Compound Composed of two or more similar parts

Compressed Flattened

Conical Cone-shaped

Cordate Shaped like a heart (leaf base)

Coriaceous Leathery

Corolla Inner, normally conspicuous, part of a flower, the petals

Corymb Flat-topped or dome-shaped flowerhead with the outer flowers opening first

Corymbose Having flowers in corymbs

Crenate Toothed with shallow, rounded teeth, scalloped

Crenulate Minutely crenate

Cultivar Distinct form not considered to warrant full botanical recognition, selected either from garden or wild plants and maintained in cultivation by propagation

Cuneate Wedge-shaped

Cuspidate Abruptly sharp-pointed

Cyme Flat-topped or dome-shaped flowerhead with the inner flowers opening first

Cymose Having flowers in cymes

Deciduous (Of tree or shrub) that sheds its leaves each year at the end of the period of growth; not persistent

Decumbent Reclining, the tips ascending

Decurrent Extending down the stem

Deltoid Triangular

Dentate Toothed with teeth directed outward

Denticulate Minutely dentate

Depressed Flattened from above

Diffuse Loosely or widely spreading

Digitate With the members arising from one point like fingers (as in a digitate leaf)

Dioecious Bearing male and female flowers on different plants

Dissected Divided into many narrow segments

Distichous Arranged in two vertical ranks

Divaricate Spreading far apart

Divergent Spreading

Divided Separated to the base

Double (Flowers) with more than the usual number of petals, often with the style and stamens changed to petals

Doubly serrate Large teeth and small teeth alternating

Downy Covered with soft hair or down

Elliptic Widest at or about the middle, narrowing equally at both ends

Elongate Lengthened

Emarginate With a shallow notch at the apex

Entire Undivided and without teeth

Evergreen Remaining green during winter

Exfoliating Peeling off in thin strips

Falcate Sickle-shaped

Fascicle Dense cluster

Fastigiate With branches erect and close together

Ferruginous Rust-coloured

Fertile Of stamens producing good pollen or fruit containing good seeds, or of stems with flowering organs

Filament Stalk of a stamen

Filiform Thread-like

Fimbriate Fringed

Flexuous Wavy or zigzag

Floccose Clothed with flocks of soft hair or wool

Florets Small, individual flowers of a dense inflorescence

Floriferous Flower-bearing, usually used to indicate profuse flowering

Gibbous Swollen, usually at the base (as in corolla)

Glabrous Hairless

Glandular With secreting organs

Glaucous Covered with a bloom, bluish-white or bluish-grey

Glutinous Sticky

Hastate Shaped like a spearhead

Hermaphrodite Bisexual, bearing both male and female organs in the same flower

Hirsute With rather coarse or stiff hairs

Hispid Beset with rigid hairs or bristles

Hoary Covered with a close whitish or greyish-white pubescence

Hybrid Plant resulting from a cross between different species

Imbricate Overlapping, as tiles on a roof

Impressed Sunken (as in veins)

Incised Sharply and usually deeply and irregularly cut

Indehiscent Said of fruits which do not (burst) open

Indumentum Dense hairy covering

Inflorescence Flowering part of the plant

Internode Portion of stem between two nodes or joints

Involucre Whorl of bracts surrounding a flower or flower cluster

Keel Central ridge
Lacerate Torn, irregularly cut or cleft
Laciniate Cut into narrow-pointed lobes
Lanceolate Lance-shaped, widening above the base and long-tapering to the apex
Lanuginous Woolly or cottony
Lateral On or at the side
Lax Loose
Leaflet Part of a compound leaf
Linear Long and narrow with nearly parallel margins
Lip One of the parts of an unequally divided flower
Lobe Any protruding part of an organ (as in leaf, corolla or calyx)
Lustrous Shining
Membranous Thin and rather soft
Midrib Central vein or rib of a leaf
Monoecious Bearing male and female flowers separately, but on the same plant
Monotypic Of a single species (genus)
Mucronate Terminated abruptly by a spiny tip
Nectary Nectar-secreting gland, usually a small pit or protuberance
Node Point on the stem where the leaves are attached, the 'joint'
Nut Non-splitting, one-seeded, hard or bony fruit
Oblanceolate Inversely lanceolate
Oblique Unequal-sided
Oblong Longer than it is broad, with nearly parallel sides
Obovate Inversely ovate
Obtuse Blunt (as in apex of leaf or petal)
Opposite (Leaves) borne two to each node, opposite each other
Orbicular Almost circular in outline
Oval Broadest at the middle
Ovary Basal 'box' part of the pistil, containing the ovules
Ovate Broadest below the middle
Ovule Female germ cell in flowering plant
Palmate Lobed or divided in hand-like fashion, usually five- or seven-lobed
Panicle Branching raceme
Paniculate Bearing flowers in panicles
Parted Cut or cleft almost to the base
Pea-flower Shaped like a sweet-pea blossom
Pectinate Comb-like (of leaf margin)
Pedicel Stalk of an individual flower in an inflorescence
Peduncle Stalk of a flower cluster or of a solitary flower
Pellucid Clear, transparent (as in gland)
Pendulous Hanging, weeping
Perfoliate Of leaves in pairs fused at the base whose stem appears to pass through them
Perianth Calyx and corolla together; also commonly used for a flower in which there is no distinction between corolla and calyx
Persistent Remaining attached
Petal One of the separate segments of a corolla

Petaloid Petal-like (as in stamen)
Petiole Leaf-stalk
Pilose With long, soft straight hairs
Pinnate With leaflets arranged on either side of a central stalk
Pinnatifid Cleft or parted in a pinnate way
Pistil Female organ of a flowering plant comprising ovary, style and stigma
Plumose Feathery, as the down of a thistle
Pollen Spores or grains contained in the anther, containing the male element
Polygamous Bearing bisexual and unisexual flowers on the same plant
Procumbent Lying or creeping
Prostrate Lying flat on the ground
Pruinose Bloomy
Puberulent Minutely pubescent
Pubescent Covered with short, soft hairs, downy
Punctate With translucent or coloured dots or depressions
Pungent Ending in a stiff, sharp point, also acid (to the taste) or strong-smelling
Pyramidal Pyramid-shaped (broad at the base and tapering to a point)
Raceme Simple elongated inflorescence with stalked flowers
Racemose Bearing flowers in racemes
Rachis Axis bearing flowers or leaflets
Recurved Curved downward or backward
Reflexed Abruptly turned downward
Reniform Kidney-shaped
Reticulate Like a network (as in veins)
Retuse Round-ended with central notch
Revolute Rolled backwards, margin rolled under (as in leaf)
Rib Prominent vein in a leaf
Rotund Nearly circular
Rufous Reddish-brown
Rugose Wrinkled or rough
Runner Trailing shoot taking root at the nodes
Sagittate Shaped like an arrowhead
Scabrous Rough to the touch
Scale Minute leaf or bract, or a flat gland-like appendage on the surface of a leaf, flower or shoot
Scandent With climbing stems
Scarious Thin and dry, not green
Semi-evergreen Normally evergreen but losing some or all of its leaves in a cold winter or cold area
Sepal One of the segments of a calyx
Serrate Saw-toothed (teeth pointing forward)
Serrulate Minutely serrate
Sessile Attached without a stalk
Setose Clothed with bristles
Sheath Tubular envelope
Shrub Woody plant which branches from the base with no obvious trunk
Simple Said of a leaf that is not compound or an unbranched inflorescence
Sinuate Strongly waved (as in leaf margin)
Sinus Recess or space between two lobes or divisions of a leaf, calyx or corolla

Spathulate Spoon-shaped
Spicate Flowers in spikes
Spike Simple, elongated inflorescence with sessile flowers
Spine Sharp-pointed end of a leaf or branch
Spur Tubular projection from a flower, or a short, stiff branchlet
Stamen Male organ of a flowering plant comprising filament and anther
Staminode Sterile stamen, or structure resembling a stamen, sometimes petal-like
Standard Largest, normally uppermost petal in a pea-flower; tall, clear-stemmed young tree; shrub (often rose) trained in this fashion
Stellate Star-shaped
Stigma Summit of the pistil which receives the pollen, often sticky or feathery
Stipule Appendage (normally two) at the base of some petioles
Stolon Shoot at or below the surface of the ground which produces a new plant at its tip
Striate With fine, longitudinal lines
Strigose Clothed with flattened, fine, bristle-like hairs
Style Middle part of the pistil, often elongated between the ovary and stigma
Subulate Awl-shaped
Succulent Juicy, fleshy, soft and thickened in texture
Suckering Producing underground stems; also the shoots from the stock of a grafted plant
Tendril Twining thread-like appendage
Tepal Subdivision of a perianth that cannot be clearly differentiated into sepal or petal
Ternate In threes
Tessellated Mosaic-like (as in veins)
Tomentose With dense, woolly pubescence
Tomentum Dense covering of matted hairs
Tree Woody plant that normally produces a single trunk and an elevated head of branches
Trifoliate Three-leaved
Trifoliolate Leaf with three separate leaflets
Truncate Cut short (of leaf base)
Turbinate Top-shaped
Type Strictly the original (type) specimen, but often used in a general sense to indicate the typical form in cultivation
Umbel Normally flat-topped inflorescence in which the pedicels or peduncles all arise from a common point
Umbellate Flowers in umbels
Undulate With wavy margins
Unisexual Of one sex
Urceolate Urn-shaped
Velutinous Clothed with a velvety indumentum
Venation Arrangement of veins
Verrucose Having a wart-like or nodular surface
Verticillate Arranged in a whorl or ring
Villous Bearing long and soft hairs
Viscid Sticky
Whorl Three or more flowers or leaves arranged in a ring

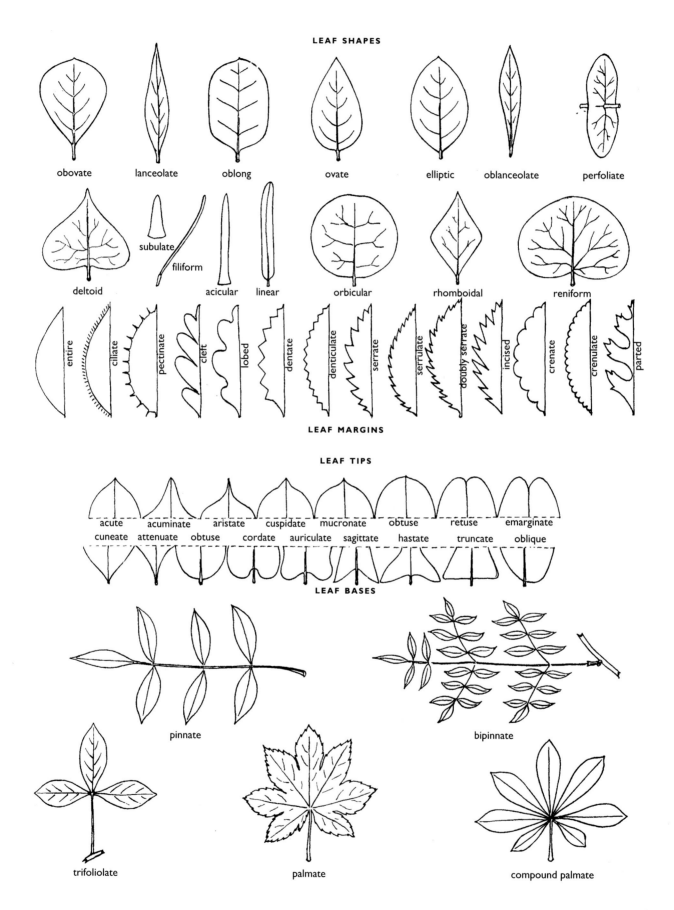

LEAF SHAPES

obovate   lanceolate   oblong   ovate   elliptic   oblanceolate   perfoliate

deltoid   subulate   filiform   acicular   linear   orbicular   rhomboidal   reniform

entire   ciliate   pectinate   cleft   lobed   dentate   denticulate   serrate   serrulate   doubly serrate   incised   crenate   crenulate   parted

LEAF MARGINS

LEAF TIPS

acute   acuminate   aristate   cuspidate   mucronate   obtuse   retuse   emarginate

cuneate   attenuate   obtuse   cordate   auriculate   sagittate   hastate   truncate   oblique

LEAF BASES

pinnate   bipinnate

trifoliolate   palmate   compound palmate

INFLORESCENCES (SIMPLIFIED)

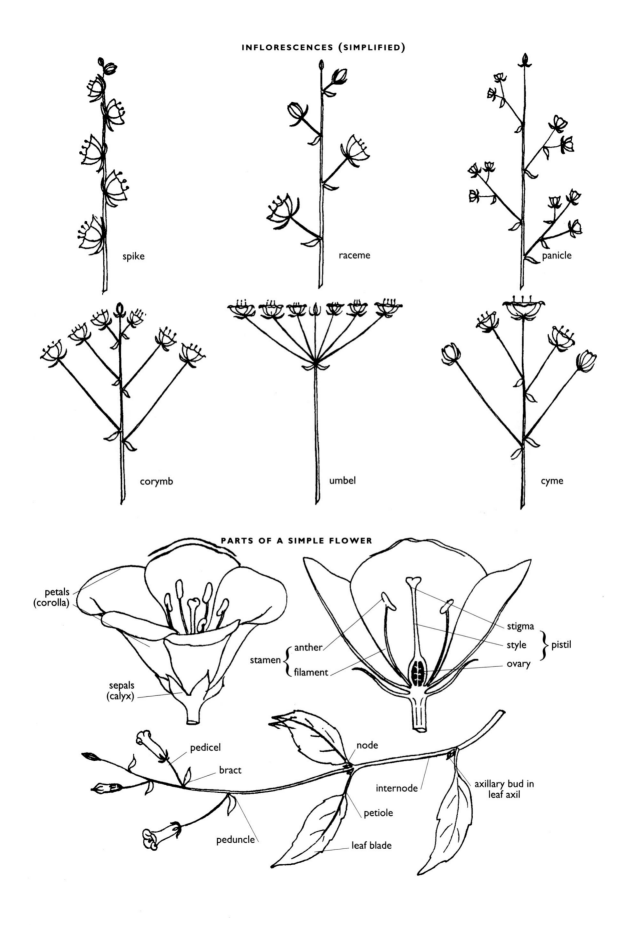

spike

raceme

panicle

corymb

umbel

cyme

PARTS OF A SIMPLE FLOWER

petals
(corolla)

sepals
(calyx)

stamen { anther
         filament

stigma
style   } pistil
ovary

pedicel

bract

peduncle

node

internode

petiole

leaf blade

axillary bud in
leaf axil

PRACTICALITIES

INTRODUCTION

If you want to create a garden for a year, then fill the borders with flowers, but if you want to create a garden for a lifetime, then plant it with trees and shrubs. One of the delights of trees and shrubs is that they make a garden develop from year to year rather than merely repeat itself. As a leaf canopy fills out or a tree gains in height, new focal points appear, views change and the character of the garden matures. Trees and shrubs add a new dimension to the garden, allowing leaves, flowers and fruit to be carried far above the heights that can be reached by the soft stems of herbaceous perennials, and lift the garden from the limitations of the flower border.

The characteristic woodiness of trees and shrubs, which allows these plants to remain above ground long after herbaceous plants have retreated, provides a garden with its permanent framework not only from year to year but also throughout the year. In a bare winter garden the mere presence of the tree skeleton – perhaps with elegant boughs or brilliant bark – is pleasure enough but there is also a host of bonuses. Long-lived woody plants provide the garden with an enormous range of interest throughout the year from the wonderful scent of the winter flowers of witch hazel borne on naked stems, through the flamboyant blooms of spring viburnum and summer hydrangea, to the dazzling leaf displays of Japanese maple as nature completes her autumnal clean-up.

Woody plants – trees and shrubs – dominate and control the garden. On gaining maturity they often define it much more surely than the shape of the land itself and may encompass the garden so thoroughly that an entirely new, private world is created. To a large extent they determine the climate of the garden and, to an overwhelming degree, its microclimates. By affording shelter from wind they allow a wider range of plants to be grown and also dominate by casting shade in varying degrees, from the dense shadow of a holly or rhododendron to the dappled shade found under an oak tree.

The qualities of atmosphere and mood created by trees and shrubs are almost infinitely variable, not least because of the effect upon them of such things as the weather, the season and the time of day. Gardeners should be as aware of the intangible, mood-creating attributes of woody plants as they are of their tangible ones and plan for these effects. It is only with trees and shrubs that such long-term considerations come into play, so the gardener needs to spend some time learning about the characteristics of individual plants.

Above The bare outline of a well-established oak makes a powerful impact when little other plant life is above ground on a foggy winter's day. *Opposite* When summer is over, this *Betula pendula* 'Youngii' will still provide a focal point of interest on account of its magnificent framework and bark

Having evolved for over 100 million years and adapted to a variety of different habitats, trees and shrubs provide today's gardeners with an unbelievable selection of plants drawn from all over the world. Their evolution to produce wood tissue within their cells has enabled trees and shrubs to reach high above other plants to compete for sunlight. All green plants produce their own food by taking energy from sunlight, carbon dioxide from the air, and water and nutrients from the soil. Then within the chlorophyll, a green pigment found in leaves, they produce carbohydrates, giving off oxygen as a by-product. This self-contained factory has enabled plants to colonize all but the harshest regions of the world and it has enabled trees, in particular, to excel in the art of survival. Trees and shrubs have the unique ability to produce a living framework of wood tissue, where energy produced throughout the growing season can be stored, enhancing survival throughout severe climatic conditions. This stored energy is also used for the formation of trunks, branches, stems, shoots, new leaves, roots and, on reaching sexual maturity, flowers.

Our gardens today are a mix of plants which have been collected from many regions of the world, and today's gardeners owe much to the plant collectors who scoured the earth in search of nature's treasures. From the early 1600s until the mid-1900s plant collectors, funded by botanical gardens or famous nurseries, actively sought plants from the temperate zones of the world. Dedicated plant collectors, such as Robert Fortune, Sir Joseph Hooker, Ernest Wilson, George Forrest and Frank Kingdon-Ward, enhanced the reputation of England as a nation of gardeners. China and the Himalayas have yielded a tremendous volume of new plant material. Other countries have also offered great treasures, as expeditions widened to the United States, Japan, Chile, Korea, Europe and Russia, adding plants to produce the almost unbelievable range that we see today. Modern plant collectors are constantly exploring new areas in search of garden-worthy plants. New acquisitions are strengthened by new forms produced by plant breeders throughout the world, creating a supply of plants that is truly global. Garden centres and nurseries now have the ability, skill, and systems, to supply a diverse and breathtaking supply of high-quality and affordable plants virtually to our doorsteps.

TREE AND SHRUB DEFINITIONS

The principal difference between a tree and a shrub is that the former has a distinct main stem, or trunk, branching some significant distance from the ground, while the latter consists of a number of stems arising at or close to ground level. Apart from this formal definition, the word 'tree' has other implications. It suggests an altogether larger plant, evoking a mental picture of a certain massiveness of structure – a thick, more or less tapering, tall trunk, heavy load-bearing branches and a high, substantial canopy of foliage.

For most of us, 'tree' means a big, leafy, imposing presence, while

Opposite Forsythia exhibits the classic shrub-like shape with a number of stems rising from close to ground level. *Above* A rhododendron illustrates how some shrubs develop the height and trunk-like stems that give them tree-like proportions

the words 'shrub' and 'scrub' are not very far apart. For a great many of us, the climates in which we have been raised have encouraged the development of large forest trees on the one hand and short, scrubby shrubs on the other. It is important to remember, however, that our garden plants are gathered from all over the world; in some places shrubs grow as large as many of our native trees, while in others there are trees that are not just small but quite dwarf. Large rhododendrons with multiple stems can easily grow as big as small trees, such as the mountain ash, and demonstrate that the difference between a tree and a shrub is not necessarily one of size. Differences in garden climates also induce changes of habit; what might be thought of as a tree in one garden may be considered to be a shrub rather further north.

Generally speaking, we use the terms 'tree' and 'shrub' in a practical sense, sometimes with little regard to their strict definitions. Thus, in anything but the very smallest garden, trees are the largest plants that dominate the rest and form the uppermost canopy of the garden, while shrubs, occupying a lower level, complement them. In fact, they fulfil subtly different roles.

TREES AND SHRUBS IN SMALL GARDENS

To an extent, all gardens are 'small', especially in the light of the enormous number of plants available to gardeners. In recent years the choice of plants has greatly increased, as we have experienced a new age of plant hunters and witnessed great advances in the techniques of hybridization and propagation. For example, in its first four editions during the 1970s, *The Hillier Manual of Trees & Shrubs* listed – fairly comprehensively – about 30 cultivars of the Japanese maple *Acer palmatum*. By 1995, *The RHS Plant Finder* (which did not exist in those earlier years) cited an incredible 185.

The gardener is faced with an overwhelming problem of choice. Even the largest garden can hold only a small proportion of the plants available; for the owner of a small garden, selection can seem quite impossible. A good way of setting about the task is to look for plants with more than one main feature. A plant in a small garden needs to give the best account of itself for as much of the year as possible. Anything with pretty flowers for a month or so but ordinary foliage and a dumpy shape should be left for those with more space.

It is, however, too much to hope for – and actually not really desirable – that every plant should live up to the ideal of beautiful flowers, lovely foliage, striking bark, long-lasting berries and a sweet scent. In practice, two or possibly three attractive features are enough. If there are too many stars, none of them will shine and the garden will become a muddle with too many accents, contrasts and focal points all defeating one another. For this reason, plain green foliage should not be considered a deficiency. As long as it is combined with an interesting shape or an intangible quality, such as elegance, it will play an important supporting role.

In the small garden, statements should be simple and not repeated too often. Purple foliage, for example, is all too easily overdone; one 'purple' accent is usually enough. Even in a large garden, three may be one too many. The use of plants with variegated foliage should be similarly restrained. A single variegated plant combined with plants of differing shades of solid green will provide an accent without losing the restfulness for which any garden, but especially a small one, should be designed.

The best possible combination of features is at its most important when choosing trees. Most small gardens have room for very few trees and some may be restricted to one. Something like the Japanese cherry *Prunus* 'Kanzan', which so often appears in gardens far too small for it and has but one short season of stardom, is far from ideal. It would be much better to plant a cherry with the versatility of *Prunus sargentii*, which has daintier flowers and a shining, rich chestnut bark. Its foliage starts by being bronze-red, becomes green, and then flames into orange and crimson in early autumn. It is the smallest of trees, but it is beautiful throughout the year and takes a long time to become at all large.

Finally, the overall shape and outline of a tree or a shrub is as important as any of its other characteristics. For much of the time we see plants in silhouette and a series of formless shapes can be most uninteresting. The interplay of domed crowns, flat heads of branches, the cones and cylinders of conifers and the skeletal outlines of deciduous trees in winter can be effectively achieved on any scale from the intimate to the grand.

TREES AND SHRUBS IN THIS BOOK

The range of trees and shrubs that can be found in gardens, parks and arboreta in cool temperate regions is extensive. However, many are found only in large collections and a number of woody plants are of more academic than horticultural interest. Some, while beau-

tiful and highly desirable, are of such marginal hardiness that they may be destroyed by weather, even in the mildest areas, before they reach the stage at which their aesthetic qualities have properly developed. Of course, such trees and shrubs should be grown, but their inclusion is justified only in very large or academically oriented gardens. This book is concerned primarily with those woody plants that appeal to gardeners, bearing in mind that the selection is inclined towards those that offer the most beauty for the greatest possible part of the year.

Many of the plants in this book have received awards for their garden-worthiness, while those that have not are nevertheless recognized as deserving space in gardens. There are evergreen and deciduous trees and shrubs, climbers, conifers and bamboos. There are mighty oaks and dwarf conifers that make less than a metre of growth in 30 years. You will find trees and shrubs suitable for the seaside, industrial areas, cold places and areas deep in shade. There are brilliantly coloured leaves, vivid berries, beautiful barks and sweet, subtle fragrances. Whether you garden in the deepest, best loam or battle with a scrape of soil over Hampshire chalk, the peats of the Atlantic fringe or even the Pine Barrens of New Jersey, you will find more than enough choice of woody plants with which to create a garden that is truly individually yours.

Prunus sargentii is an excellent tree for the small garden with its dainty spring flowers *(below left)* followed in autumn by striking red and orange foliage *(below right)*. Popular for its autumn foliage and graceful leaf shape, the number of available varieties of *Acer palmatum (opposite)* increases yearly

BASIC BIOLOGY

AN UNDERSTANDING OF THE BIOLOGICAL CHARACTERISTICS OF TREES AND SHRUBS AND OF HOW THEY GROW CAN ONLY ENHANCE OUR CULTIVATION SKILLS AS WE MANIPULATE PLANTS AWAY FROM their native environments. All plants are native to at least one part of the globe and to cultivate them successfully we must know where this is and what sort of environment it offers in order to satisfy the plant's growing requirements in our own gardens.

THE ORIGINS OF PLANTS

All plants are autotrophs or 'self-feeders'; in other words, they (along with algae and some bacteria) manufacture their own food or energy by the process of photosynthesis. Once they have converted water and carbon dioxide into sugar using the sun's energy, it is then available to other organisms, called heterotrophs, which depend on plants for their energy; humans, animals and fungi are typical examples. The first fossil evidence shows that 'self-feeders' colonized the oceans 3.4 billion years ago, but it is possible that primitive organisms with the ability to photosynthesize appeared much earlier. It was not until around one hundred million years ago that the first flowering plants began to appear. Once flowering plants colonized the soil, the great diversity that we witness today began to evolve.

FIG.·I   HOW TREES AND SHRUBS WORK

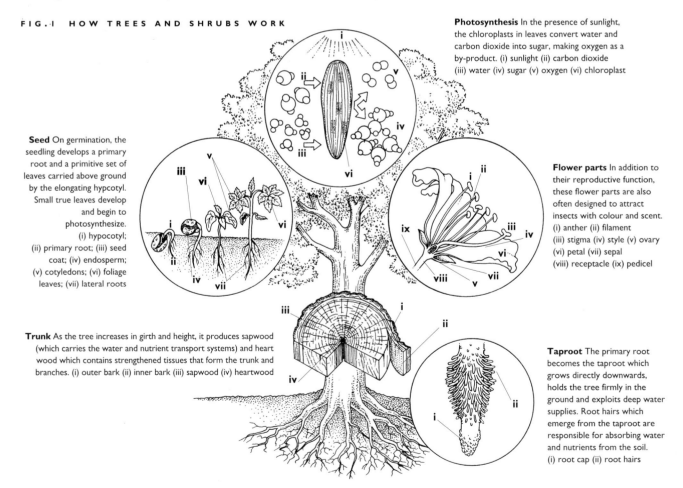

Photosynthesis In the presence of sunlight, the chloroplasts in leaves convert water and carbon dioxide into sugar, making oxygen as a by-product. (i) sunlight (ii) carbon dioxide (iii) water (iv) sugar (v) oxygen (vi) chloroplast

Seed On germination, the seedling develops a primary root and a primitive set of leaves carried above ground by the elongating hypcotyl. Small true leaves develop and begin to photosynthesize. (i) hypocotyl; (ii) primary root; (iii) seed coat; (iv) endosperm; (v) cotyledons; (vi) foliage leaves; (vii) lateral roots

Flower parts In addition to their reproductive function, these flower parts are also often designed to attract insects with colour and scent. (i) anther (ii) filament (iii) stigma (iv) style (v) ovary (vi) petal (vii) sepal (viii) receptacle (ix) pedicel

Trunk As the tree increases in girth and height, it produces sapwood (which carries the water and nutrient transport systems) and heart wood which contains strengthened tissues that form the trunk and branches. (i) outer bark (ii) inner bark (iii) sapwood (iv) heartwood

Taproot The primary root becomes the taproot which grows directly downwards, holds the tree firmly in the ground and exploits deep water supplies. Root hairs which emerge from the taproot are responsible for absorbing water and nutrients from the soil. (i) root cap (ii) root hairs

How trees and shrubs work

As gardeners we need to understand how plants germinate, develop and reproduce in order to care for them effectively. The following section is a brief look at the parts and processes that make woody plants work (*Fig. 1*).

Germination Most woody plants begin their lives as seeds, which require water, oxygen and warmth to germinate. They do not usually require sunlight, because at this stage a new plant is not photosynthesizing but rather using stored reserves of sugar within its seed to develop.

On germination, the seedling develops a root and then a primitive set of leaves, which for the first time allows it to produce its own energy. These first 'leaves' are then followed by small true leaves. As the plant develops, so do the transport systems for energy and water. These develop from single cells into a series of tubes running the whole length of the plant. The water and nutrients are transported from the roots to the leaves in the xylem (water transport system), and the energy produced by photosynthesis is transported to the growing points of the plants by the phloem (energy transport system).

Photosynthesis Using solar power to convert the sun's energy into electricity is probably the closest people will ever come to reproducing photosynthesis. Just as we harvest crops, plants harvest water and carbon dioxide in the presence of sunlight converting them into sugar. The energy state of these compounds is changed so that the chemical bonds are broken and the ions reformed into new molecules. This final sugar produced is the plant's food.

Photosynthesis can be broken down into two separate areas: 'light reaction' and 'carbon dioxide fixation'. The first of these occurs when light enters the chloroplast (a single unit of chlorophyll) through the surface of the leaf, creating energy that is used to split water molecules into hydrogen and oxygen to create simple sugars. The oxygen is released back into the atmosphere.

Carbon dioxide fixation is the process by which carbon dioxide is absorbed into the leaf through small openings called stomata. The carbon dioxide then bonds with the processed sugar to make more elaborate molecules, such as glucose and starch, which are used to feed the growing plant.

Leaves Leaves are the factories of food production in which the plant makes maximum use of the raw materials of sunlight, water and carbon dioxide. The production of a growing structure above ground enables woody plants to hold their leaves high above competitors and take the lion's share of sunlight.

The shape, size and foliage pattern of leaves are carefully considered by gardeners in terms of their ornamental value but the characteristics of leaves are often also the means by which they survive. The needle-shaped leaves of conifers are small, compared to the leaves of deciduous trees, and covered with a tough cuticle to keep water loss to a minimum. This is especially important in winter when frozen ground may make water replacement difficult

In the uncultivated environment of a beech wood, fallen leaves replenish the soil with nutrients and organic matter ready for the coming year

or even impossible. Their leaf shape also minimizes the harsh effects of cold winds and sheds snow more easily than broader leaves. Furthermore, the stomata of conifers are deeply set into the underside of the leaf, again minimizing moisture loss. These simple factors have enabled conifers to survive within harsh environments. These same harsh environments also explain the evergreen nature of most conifers. Quite simply they are indigenous to regions in which a yearly loss of leaves is pointless as by the time new ones have grown, summer has ended.

Deciduous plants lose their leaves as a response to falling temperatures and lower light levels in order to minimize moisture loss in winter. As their growth slows, the green pigment remaining in the leaves breaks down, leaving the autumnal tints. Once the leaves have fallen, soil organisms break down the remaining tissues into the soil, providing recycled nutrients for our trees and shrubs. In spring, deciduous trees grow new green leaves whose characteristics enable them to excel at photosynthesis and make the most of the long hours of sunshine.

Wood production At the end of the first season following germination, growth begins to slow and energy is stored in the stems and roots. At this point, the inner, actively dividing cambium meristem – the tissue located directly below the bark on trees and shrubs – divides to produce wood on the inner side and bark on the outer side. The wood is made up of fibres called lignin; this strengthens the stem or trunk and creates the woody framework. Bark is developed from fibres of cork, which protect the stem of trees and shrubs from damage and reduce water loss from the stem. As the tree or shrub ages, the cork will split and be replaced by a new layer, giving bark its familiar knobbly texture.

With future development, the tree or shrub will increase in girth and height. In doing so it will produce sap wood (which contains the cambium and the transport systems) and heartwood (which contains strengthened tissues that form the trunk, stems and branches). This is known as secondary thickening, and can be thought of

FIG. 2 WOOD PRODUCTION

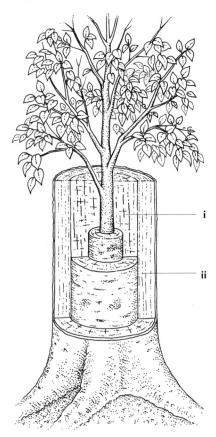

Every growth period, a tree develops new heartwood (i) and sapwood (ii) which envelops the tree like a new skin

as the woody plant growing a new layer of skin over its entirety, including the roots. It can be clearly seen in the annual rings of temperate woody plants, which display two distinct growth rings: one large ring in the spring and one smaller in autumn as the growth slows down and finally stops.

Water Trees and shrubs have certain growth requirements. Gardeners can help with some of these, such as in the provision of water and nutrients.

Water is used in many ways within a plant. It keeps the living cells turgid so that they can carry out their function of producing energy. It also keeps the leaves cool during hot, summer days. Water movement within the stems and leaves reduces the risk of damage from freezing because as water moves out of the plant cells, the remaining sap thickens and has a lower freezing point.

It is estimated that a mature beech tree can absorb 900-1,200 litres (200-300 gals) of water per day. This water is transported by the underground system which is made up of two different types

A tree depends on its roots for anchorage and for the uptake of water and nutrients to the stems, branches and leaves

of roots. The big structural roots anchor the plant into the soil. At their ends and along their length are tiny absorption roots, called root hairs. These are delicate and brittle and are constantly broken off as the root cap grows through the soil. Root hairs absorb water and nutrients, which are essential to a plant's healthy growth. Once water has been absorbed into the main root system, it moves up the stem into the leaves through the xylem, aiding in the production of energy. Excess water is carried on to the surface of the leaf, where it evaporates and cools the leaf. This process is known as transpiration and the transpiration stream created between the roots and shoots draws more water through the system.

The ability to recognize a plant in water stress is important when transplanting or planting. If a plant cannot replace lost water, it will die. During transplanting, particularly of evergreens, it is important to spray the foliage at regular intervals to cool down the leaves until damaged roots hairs have re-grown. When planting, it is important to prevent dehydration of both the compost into which the plant has been established and the surrounding soil. Leaves should always feel cool during the growing season; if they feel warm, the plant is suffering water stress.

Roots The leaves, branches and stems of all plants depend upon the roots for anchorage, the uptake of water and nutrients and the storage of food reserves. The extent of the root system depends on the type of plant, its growing environment and its management through cultivation. The root systems of most plants grow mainly within the first metre (3ft) of soil, with the majority of the absorption roots within the first 15cm (6in). The depth of roots is influenced by the availability of water, oxygen, nutrients and ease of soil penetration. On heavily compacted soils, the lack of oxygen to the roots will force them to grow near to the surface, whereas deeply cultivated soils with a high organic content will allow a much deeper root system.

The roots of individual specimen trees may grow two or three times further than the edge of the leaf canopy. Trees grown in groups, on the other hand, may compete with each other, decreasing the overall extent of the root system. If competition is reduced, roots grow wherever there is sufficient oxygen, moisture, temperature and nutrients, invariably in directions in which there is least resistance to the advancing root system.

Tree and shrub root systems are often misunderstood. Willows, poplars and alders, in particular, are often blamed for developing massive root systems which block up drains, lift paving slabs or cause problems with the foundations of nearby buildings. In fact, tree root systems will only stray where they are not wanted when they are not provided with satisfactory conditions in their normal root zone. When roots enter a land drain which carries water, grow under a paving slab on which water condenses or against a building beneath which water collects, they are suddenly provided with perfect conditions. Inevitably, roots exploit this by growing rapidly and, therefore, split or block the drainage pipe, lift the paving slab and exert pressure on the side of a building. If the roots are severed, the new developing roots will soon find their way back to their oasis. The way to prevent problems of this sort is to make the conditions within the normal root zone as inviting as possible, by irrigation, aeration and fertilization.

The root to shoot balance The roots, stems, branches and leaves of healthy trees and shrubs grow in harmony; there is enough energy being produced by the leaves to support the whole plant, while the root system absorbs sufficient water to support the above-ground tissues. After transplanting shrubs, it is advisable to reduce the leaf area in proportion to the damaged root system (*see page 49*). Remember to water the plant thoroughly a few weeks before lifting and after transplanting.

Trees react dramatically to damage suffered by roots and shoots. If a tree is damaged in a storm or even heavily pruned, it will use stored energy to replace lost leaf area as quickly as possible. The resulting mass of new shoots arising from the stem are called epicormic or adventitious shoots. Removing these important new shoots will only stimulate the growth of replacements. If the tree does not recreate the balance of shoot to root successfully, areas of the root system may die until the balance is recovered.

Sexual maturity Both trees and shrubs have a period of non-flowering growth before reaching sexual maturity. Some of the tree magnolias, such as *Magnolia campbellii*, may take up to 30 years from seed to flower. This period allows the tree time to attain sufficient height so that it can display its flowers high above its competitors.

Plants consume massive amounts of energy stored within the stems, roots and shoots in order to produce their flowers. Even during periods of drought, when trees and shrubs may drop some of their flowering buds in order to preserve their energy balance, they will always produce some flowers. This is typical of camellias, which produce thousands of flower buds, some of which simply fail to open and drop to the ground. This is perfectly healthy and gardeners should simply regard it as a sign of the plant restoring its natural balance. Many species are pruned directly after flowering. This allows the maximum amount of time for the production of more vegetative shoots, thus increasing the area available to store energy for the following season's blooms.

Flowers Living things naturally seek to perpetuate themselves and plants use up considerable energy to ensure that their species survives. The flowers of some trees are wind-pollinated and these are usually quite insignificant blooms. However, the majority of trees and shrubs that we cultivate in our gardens carry bold attractive flowers. These have evolved not to attract gardeners but pollinators. The brightly coloured petals of these flowers serve as an advertisement to the right pollinator, whose reward for pollen collection is supplied in the form of nectar.

Flowers are highly complex with a huge number of individual characteristics. The nature and arrangement of their various parts have enabled botanists to select common features which can be used to place closely related plants into families. While the individual characteristics of a flower vary from species to species, the main parts of a flower are common to all species and serve roughly similar functions.

The flower is connected to the stem by the pedicel or flower stalk, which holds it above the foliage. Before the flower opens, it is protected by the sepals or flower buds. When these open they reveal the brightly coloured petals – the plant's attraction to pollinators. On entering the flower the pollinator must take pollen from the male parts (the stamens which comprise anthers and filament) and pass on the pollen it is already carrying to the female parts (the stigma and style) in order to fertilize the ovary. Once fertilization is complete, the seeds will develop and the plant has ensured its survival by perpetuating its species.

Seeds In the same way that flower production costs the plant dearly in reserves of stored energy, so seed production eats into the plant's energy store. All the elements that the offspring needs to survive until it germinates are present in each seed. As the seed develops on the parent plant it builds up a store of food within the seed leaves, or cotyledons, which surround the embryo. The seed may be covered in a fruit, which is itself no more than a mechanism to ensure efficient dispersal. In the case of the cherry, for example, the fruits containing the seeds are carried away from the plant by birds. They are eaten, pass unharmed through the host's digestive system, and are then excreted, returning to the soil where, if conditions are right, they will germinate. From the earliest stage of germination until it develops leaves, the embryonic plant relies totally on reserves of stored energy.

UNDERSTANDING INDIVIDUAL REQUIREMENTS

While an understanding of how plants work botanically is a good starting point, clearly their individual requirements of light and shade, water, nutrients, soil and shelter vary enormously from genus to genus and, indeed, within a particular genus. Today, our gardens play host to millions of plants from all areas of the world. A garden plant is often selected for its ornamental value alone with little consideration given to the its native habit. Ideally, plant selection should include other considerations if the specimens are to thrive. Fortunately, most of the trees and shrubs available in garden centres and nurseries have been in cultivation for a long time and are tried and tested.

However, new introductions have not endured the test of time and may require careful siting. For example, *Choisya ternata* 'Sundance' is a recently introduced yellow-leafed form of the Mexican orange blossom. Its cultivar name suggests that it likes to 'dance' in the sun. However, its lack of chlorophyll means that it scorches if placed in direct sunlight, an environment in which the green-leafed form thrives. A poorly sited, stressed plant will succumb to pests and diseases and be a poor addition to the garden. Therefore, it is important to understand your garden's different habitats and microclimates and plant appropriately.

The flamboyant, colourful blooms of deciduous azaleas appeal to many gardeners and also attract insects for pollination

THEORY
& PRACTICE

IT IS TEMPTING TO CONSIDER ONLY THE AESTHETIC VALUES OF TREES AND SHRUBS WHEN USING THEM IN THE GARDEN LANDSCAPE, LOOK- ING NO FURTHER THAN ATTRACTIVE LEAVES, BEAUTIFUL FLOWERS, intricate bark patterns and a fascinating variety of fruit and seed shapes. However, this is a very small part of the overall picture, as a well-designed and clearly thought out garden will do much more than simply look pretty. Trees and shrubs within a garden control the prevailing climate by creating a unique microclimate. This may be achieved quite simply by protecting the garden from cold wind or by cooling the area by providing shade. They also have positive effects on atmospheric pollution and noise, provide increased secu- rity and define boundaries. The first part of this chapter considers the ways in which trees and shrubs contribute in physical ways to our local environment; the second part shows how practical con- siderations often merge into aesthetics; and the third part focuses on two key practical considerations prior to planting - hardiness and soil requirements.

PHYSICAL BENEFITS OF TREES AND SHRUBS

How many of us stop and think about the shelter and shade that our plants give us, how they improve our soils by simply stopping erosion or what happens to all the dust and pollutants which float about in the atmosphere? Just imagine how unbearable life in our cities and towns would be if there were no trees or shrubs.

Pollution We tend to think of trees as the lungs of the planet: most of the oxygen in our atmosphere is a by-product of photo- synthesis, and huge volumes of the greenhouse gas carbon dioxide are absorbed in the process. But trees contribute in other ways to the cleaning-up of the air we breathe.

In tree-less cities, the annual dust fall may be as high as 850 mg per square metre per day. A one-hectare plantation of spruces can intercept as much as 32 tonnes of dust in a year. A thick foliage screen, such as a copse or woodland planting, will also effectively fil- ter the air for atmospheric pollutants, accumulating particulate or gaseous material on and sometime in their leaves.

Temperature Trees and shrubs cool the air; think of the dif- ference in temperature between a busy city street and a nearby park, which can be several degrees cooler than the surrounding urban environment. This is due not only to a reduction in sun- light, but also to increased transpiration. All plants absorb heat as

they transpire, and this brings about significant temperature reduction even at relatively low planting densities: it is estimated that a 30 per cent cover of vegetation will give two-thirds of the cooling effect of complete plant cover. This natural air-condition- ing property is an often overlooked benefit of tree planting.

The lowering of temperatures is accompanied by a rise in relative humidity as water vapour is transferred from the leaf surface to the surrounding atmosphere. The air in towns and cities is often uncom- fortably dry; wooded parks and tree-lined streets can increase rela- tive humidity in their immediate vicinity by 18 per cent or more, thus contributing to the local environment as well as providing bet- ter air quality and pleasantly cool surroundings in summer.

Noise reduction Noise is not significantly reduced by the foliage and trunks of trees: the actual amount of sound energy absorbed will cause a reduction of only a few decibels. Where they can help is in concealing the source of the sound which may bring some relief. In addition the movements of leaves and branches can disguise other sounds simply by raising the background level of noise: trees such as *Populus tremula* (Aspen) may be used to help mask the rush of traffic by the rustling of their leaves.

Trees improve the quality of our environment in all sorts of ways including provision of shade and reduction of atmospheric pollution

Soil erosion Large quantities of soil can be eroded if exposed to rain, running water or wind. Water erosion accounts for the highest loss of topsoil, something which few of us can spare. Trees and shrubs influence soil erosion in two main ways. First, the foliage can intercept raindrops and reduce their impact on the soil. Second, the root systems of trees and shrubs can physically bind the soil together, stopping or reducing the run-off caused by particles of soil being picked up by the rainwater.

Drainage and nutrients The consistency and moisture content of garden soil are profoundly affected by the trees and shrubs planted in it. On a warm summer's day hundreds of litres of water are transferred from the soil via the systems of a large tree to the air by transpiration. This means that a dry soil may become drier but, more importantly, it also means that wet soils are rendered less wet. It does not imply, however, that trees by themselves can convert bad drainage to good.

The fall of deciduous leaves is, in part, nature's way of returning nutrients to the soil. In larger plantings the soil will gradually be changed by annual mulches of leaves falling from above. In the garden this hardly happens simply because the quantity of leaves involved is so much smaller, but if you gather up the fallen leaves and compost them, the return of this material to the ground will be highly beneficial.

Protection An immediately apparent effect of trees and shrubs is that they provide protection from wind, although exactly how the wind is affected by them is not quite so obvious as it might first seem. Fences and walls offer shelter from wind only within a short distance from their base. Further away they create violent swirls and eddies that can cause severe damage to plants and also make the garden less than comfortable for the gardener.

A 50 per cent permeable screen capable of filtering the wind creates virtually no swirling and provides effective protection over a distance of ten times its own height. However, at the further reaches this is afforded only close to ground level and the maximum protection is of an area about six times its height. The wind speed returns to its original velocity after 30 times the height of the screen.

The very best permeable screens consist of trees and shrubs. Ideally, a windy site is best protected by a shelter belt 20m (65ft) deep, but this is obviously practicable only on large estates. Nevertheless, the average garden will receive more than adequate protection from hedges or even simply from ornamental planting of trees and shrubs. In this case, there should be a good balance between deciduous and evergreen subjects so that enough protection is given in winter.

In really windy gardens, hedges can be planted so that they reinforce one another. For example, a hedge 2m (6ft) high will provide excellent protection for 12m (40ft) downwind. If a second hedge of the same height is planted at this distance from the first, maximum protection is provided over 24m (80ft). In practice, such perfect solutions are seldom sought and the spacing of hedges can be considerably greater. Where more than the prevailing wind gives trouble, a system of boundary and internal hedges or plantings of trees and shrubs can be devised relatively easily.

Screening The use of trees and shrubs for visual screening should not be forgotten. Whereas a fence or wall may well shut out an offensive view or provide much-needed privacy, it always introduces strong, straight lines which, in an urban environment, merely add to the sort of unsightliness you are trying to exclude. Trees and shrubs introduce natural lines with flowing shapes and tend to soften urban geometry or to blend in with country landscapes.

Remember that the closer the screen is to you, the more effectively you are screened. A tree or shrub planted close to your viewpoint can be quite small but still highly effective. If you are overlooked by another house, for example, a small tree with a fairly open structure, such as the autumn cherry (*Prunus subhirtella* 'Autumnalis'), will protect you from curious eyes when planted just a few metres away as effectively as a much larger, denser tree at the bottom of the garden.

Unlike tree flowers which are admired at some distance for the combined effect of many blooms, shrub flowers are encouraged to bloom at a height at which they can be appreciated at close quarters

Opposite The trim symmetrical outline of *Carpinus betulus* 'Fastigiata' complements a formal garden. *Right above* Trees comprise the top layer and shrubs the middle layer of the garden with bulbs, perennials and annuals filling the bottom storey. *Right below* Scented flowering shrubs are particularly suited to seating areas where one stops to relax and enjoy the garden

AESTHETIC CONSIDERATIONS

Shrubs are appreciated primarily for their flowers which are near to the eye, while trees often appeal mainly for their foliage. There are, of course, exceptions to this: the larger magnolias, for example, are worth growing for their flowers alone, and there are many shrubs grown mainly for their foliage. Nevertheless, it can be said that the higher the tree, the less important its flowers, and the lower the shrub, the more significant its flowers.

It is the whole mass of the foliage, rather than the individual leaves of a large tree that is effective. This is because the eye's ability to distinguish individual leaves diminishes with distance. The higher the tree and the longer the clean length of its trunk, the more important the general shape and overall colour and character of the foliage become. Shrubs, on the other hand, have foliage at about eye level and each leaf, therefore, has greater significance. Shrubs with foliage that relies on mass effect are worthy of space in larger gardens, where they are seen from a greater distance, but are not a wise choice for smaller ones.

Trees with interesting, arresting or beautiful leaves should not be planted closely. If they are, the outcome will be long trunks and high, distant crowns and the leaf characteristics will be lost. The variegated tulip tree (*Liriodendron tulipifera* 'Aureomarginata'), for example, has beautifully sculpted leaves with yellow margins. When planted in an open position so that it is furnished with foliage almost to ground level, it is quite magnificent. Grown too close to other trees, however, it ultimately forms a long, leafless bole, above which is carried a head of branches whose leaves can be appreciated individually only with the aid of binoculars.

Gardening in layers There are three distinct layers in a mature garden: the tree canopy at the top, the middle foliage layer composed partly of the lower foliage of trees but mainly of shrubs and small trees, and below that a layer largely inhabited by a mixture of herbaceous perennials, evergreen perennials, shorter-lived plants, bulbs and small shrubs.

For successful gardening, it is more profitable to think in terms of plants that are suitable for the three layers than to become over concerned with the academic distinctions between a tree and a shrub. In this book, therefore, a 'large shrub' or a 'small tree' is used to describe a plant suitable for the middle foliage layer.

Tree and shrub outlines The outline of a tree or a shrub is an important quality, too. The shape of plants can be thought of as natural sculptures, which can be used to hide, frame or create focal points. Upright, fastigiate, or tapering trees have many uses. For example, an upright conifer, such as *Cupressus sempervirens*

'Green Pencil', can be used to hide a street light or frame a view. Contorted trees or shrubs make an interesting feature within a garden. The twisted hazel (*Corylus avellana* 'Contorta') makes an intricate sculpture in the winter, especially if illuminated at night. Weeping or pendulous trees are important, allowing for the under canopy to be planted with contrasting plants or features.

HARDINESS

The word 'hardy' has many shades of meaning between two extremes. At one extreme is the Australian interpretation in which a plant's hardiness relates to its ability to withstand heat; at the other is the interpretation common in most other parts of the English-speaking world which indicates resistance to freezing conditions.

Provenance – the wild locality from which it was introduced –

Garrya elliptica, from California and Oregon, performs best given the protection of a north- or north-east-facing wall which will greatly enhance the production of decorative catkins in late winter

may be a major factor in determining the hardiness of a woody plant. For many species it is not very important, but for others, those from large areas with considerable differences in climate, it can be, horticulturally speaking, vital. For example, from the late 1980s the number of eucalyptus species that could be grown in Britain increased dramatically. This was largely as a result of work done at the Australian National Botanic Gardens, Canberra, in developing a bank of seeds collected from the coldest provenance. Consequently, a species such as *Eucalyptus nicholii*, previously thought of as one of the more tender, was found to be capable of surviving severe frosts for short periods better than the then current prove-

nance of the Mountain Snow Gum, *E. pauciflora* subsp. *niphophila*, supposedly one of the hardiest.

Hardiness can be considered as a form of environmental stress. To understand it, you must comprehend the growing conditions native to plants and then manipulate these within the garden landscape. The British climate is equable but, within its limits, highly variable, and gardens within the British Isles exhibit a diverse array of the world flora. For example, the west coast of Scotland is affected by the warm Gulf Stream and plants grown there are not hardy in more central locations. There is much we still do not understand about whether a certain plant will survive and, more importantly, flourish. Even so, many plants described in this book can be grown with a fair degree of success outside such favoured areas as well as within them.

The hardiness of plants is also related to the amount of sun they receive and the wetness of the soil in winter. Thus, two identical plants situated at the same altitude but on opposing sides of a range of coastal hills might exhibit quite different hardiness characteristics. The one on the side receiving the incoming, moisture-laden, prevailing wind will experience more rain and less sun. The other, on the rain-shadow side, will be subject to less rain and more sun and is likely to appear to be appreciably hardier. Altitude, of course, makes a significant difference. All things being equal, a plant growing at 150m (500ft) experiences an average temperature about 1.5°C (3°F) lower than one at sea level.

Wind-chill – the lowering of the effective temperature below the reading obtained by a screened thermometer – is a major factor in determining the hardiness of plants in any given situation. Many trees and shrubs can tolerate very low temperatures in still air, whereas in a wind of force 5 on the Beaufort scale they may perish, even when the screened temperature is not much below freezing. In other words, a plant which survives in a sheltered garden in Edinburgh could be killed by cold in a windy one in Lincolnshire.

MICROCLIMATES

Microclimate is an often misunderstood concept. It is not the climate of a particular river valley or the surroundings of a specific village, but that of an area so small that there may be several microclimates within a single garden. An individual plant can be supplied with its own microclimate simply by giving it a hessian or netting shelter against wind. A valuable microclimate can be provided at the foot of a warm wall, where the extra heat will help plants to ripen their wood. A small barrel, sunk in the soil and kept full of water, will provide increased humidity. A slight fall in level, even over just a few metres, may be sufficient to allow frozen air to flow downward letting warm air take its place. A sandy strip passing naturally through a clay garden allows drainage and proves a haven for plants on the margin of local hardiness.

Exploring the variables Plants often set puzzles for gardeners in their resistance to winter weather. You may find, for instance, that a shrub such as *Convolvulus cneorum*, whose home is in the Mediterranean, will survive a winter that kills a nearby weigela. Alternatively, you may note that New Zealand shrubs have shrugged off conditions that would have destroyed them a few years before. Hardiness is subject to so many variables that experimen-

For the beautiful *Camellia japonica* 'Lady Vansittart' (below right), as for all camellias, avoid a site that gets the early morning sun as this causes damage during thawing to blooms caught by the night frost

tation should be encouraged. There is science enough; if gardeners cannot be romantic, then who can? Nevertheless, 'science' simply means 'knowledge'; who cares how we come by it as long as it is truthful? If you want to experiment, go ahead. Other gardeners will be the first to offer you their congratulations.

SOIL

Land plants are remarkable organisms in that they inhabit two different environments; one above and one below ground. The conditions affecting the aerial parts of plants have a profound effect on the roots and vice versa. It is essential that you understand your growing medium before buying or planting.

The term soil means many different things to people, reflected in the various words used to describe it: earth, ground, dirt and mud. As growers of plants, our main concern is always the care and management of what we seek to cultivate. However, it is extremely important to understand and respect the most important factor – the soil. It is, perhaps, best regarded as shorthand for 'an environment that teems with life'.

In looking at the components of soil and how each contributes to plant growth, bear in mind that the nature and proportion of the components varies greatly from one area to another. No two soils are identical. This makes generalization difficult. Similarly, always remember that soil structure is much easier to destroy than to restore.

Structure Soils differ in their make-up and behaviour depending on the underlying geology of the area and on its cultivation history. They are composed of minute particles of weathered rock of different types and sizes together with accumulated organic material and micro-organisms. In gardening when we talk of soil types we are mainly interested in a relatively shallow band of soil where the plant roots will grow, and this is referred to as topsoil.

Most soil is classified into approximate groups according to the varying proportions of each of three components, clay, silt and sand, present in the mix. The size of these mineral particles varies widely, from coarse grits up to 2mm ($\frac{1}{8}$in) in diameter to clay particles too small to be visible to the naked eye, and their relative proportions determine the physical and chemical characteristics of the soil, from drainage to fertility.

Types of soils Clay soils are defined as those with more than 25 per cent clay particles; soils with fewer than 8 per cent clay are classified as silt or sandy, depending on the predominant mineral. Soils with a good balance of gravel, sand, silt and clay particles are known as loams. Where clay particles predominate, we speak of a clay loam and where sand is the dominant mineral, a sandy loam.

Sandy loams have a poor water-holding capacity, which means that nutrients are quickly leached from the soil. This has lead to them being known as 'hungry soils'. However, sandy loams drain freely, so they warm up quickly in spring; they also cool down quickly in winter. They are easily worked at any time of year but require frequent supervision and, because they are less fertile than

clays, copious amounts of organic matter. A sandy loam can contain up to 75 per cent sand, with the remainder made up of silt and clay in approximately equal proportions.

Silt loams have a high water-retaining capacity, although the very fine particles (several hundred times smaller than sand grains) tend to compact and may cause the surface to cap and puddle easily. They warm up and cool down relatively slowly, and are prone to erosion by water and wind, especially when dry. A silt loam may contain up to 80 per cent silt, 5 per cent sand and 15 per cent clay.

Clay loams are very sticky when wet. They compact easily and, once dry, can crack and become almost impenetrable. They may have serious drainage problems, making them cool down and warm up slowly. However, clay particles are chemically charged so they hold nutrients and organic matter. Both clay and silt loams can present serious problems to the gardener as both require the installation of adequate drainage systems to remove surface water. Following this, the soil particles should be held open by adding quantities of coarse sand or grit, which allows frost action to aid particle separation. Only once this has been achieved should organic matter be added. Digging in well-rotted farmyard manure first will just serve to bind the soil tighter.

Soil pH The acidity or alkalinity of soil is measured on a scale of 1-14. Neutral soil has a pH of 7; values below this are considered acidic and values above, alkaline. The reason soil pH is so important is that it directly affects the solubility of certain soil minerals, and hence their availability to plants. These nutrients, essential for healthy growth, fall into two groups.

There are nine so-called macronutrients, all of which plants need in relatively large quantities. Carbon, hydrogen and oxygen are obtained from air and water, while nitrogen, phosphorus, potassium, calcium, magnesium and sulphur are normally absorbed through the roots. Macronutrients are present in most soils, but their levels require careful management as deficiencies do sometimes occur.

The seven micronutrients – iron, manganese, zinc, boron, molybdenum, copper and chlorine – are required in smaller quantities. Soils are rarely deficient in micronutrients, but they may occur in forms that make them unusable to plants.

When the pH of a soil falls below 4.5, aluminium, iron and manganese dissolve readily and occur in such concentrations that they become toxic to certain plants. The activity of bacteria, earthworms and fungi is also greatly decreased as soil pH drops. As soil pH rises, ions of aluminium, iron and manganese precipitate out of solution and become less available, which may lead to a deficiency in these elements at a pH of 7 and above.

A soil which falls between a pH of 6.5 and 7.5 is favourable for most plant growth. Within this range, the essential nutrient elements are readily available to most plants, the micro-organisms of the soil can carry on their beneficial functions and aluminium toxicity is not a problem. However some species of plants grow best under acid conditions (calcifuges), while others grow best under alkaline conditions (calcicoles).

This delightful garden with its inventive and varied planting is achieved on chalky soil demonstrating that a soil characteristic does not have to be regarded as a soil problem

Modifying soil pH The biggest single determinant of soil pH is its calcium level. Calcium is a strongly alkaline element which occurs naturally in chalk and limestone. Because it is readily soluble, however, it tends to leach out (wash away in water) of many types of free-draining soil, especially sandy soils, causing these to turn gradually more acidic.

If the soil pH is too low for optimum plant growth, it can be raised by applying calcium in the form of one of the calcium compounds known as limes. How much lime to add depends on the amount of change required, soil texture, organic-matter content and the form in which it is added. Sulphur may be used to lower the pH of an alkaline soil. Aluminium sulphate may also be used for this purpose, but it is only suitable for use on small areas.

It is possible to grow plants outside their pH range by treating the deficiency directly. The commonest example is the use of chelated iron compounds to prevent chlorosis (calcium-induced iron deficiency) on lime-rich land. It is generally more effective to manipulate the pH for a particular crop in a confined area than to attempt large-scale treatment. This may be done by using raised beds, containers or other methods of creating small pockets which can then be filled with acid soils. On more neutral soils, organic matter, nitrogen fertilizer or flowers of sulphur have been successfully used to lower the pH.

Growing rhododendrons on top of high pH soils is not generally recommended; a plastic liner may be used to separate the soils. It is, however, far wiser to select the right plant for the right location, as opposed to fighting nature and keeping your plants alive by the use of artificial fertilizers. If you wish to grow plants not suited for your soil type, then using ornamental containers could provide a solution.

SELECTION & PURCHASE

IT IS VERY COMMON TO APPROACH GARDEN PLANNING BY DECID-ING, APPARENTLY FOR NO REAL REASON, TO HAVE A TREE HERE AND A GROUP OF SHRUBS THERE. THE THOUGHT PROCESS LEADING to this decision may have been complex or subconscious but quite possibly are also accurate. However, whether you plan 'properly' or allow your intuition some sway, the next questions carry the real weight. Which tree? What kind of shrubs?

The key is to ask yourself, 'What do I want the tree/shrubs for?' A tree is planted for one or, more likely, several reasons. You may want to plant a tree in that position because it will eventually screen your living room from the neighbours' view, to give a vertical component to an otherwise horizontal landscape or to cast some welcome shade in summer. These considerations involve matters of height, spread, shape, density of foliage and whether your tree should be deciduous or evergreen. Immediately your attention should turn to what is culturally possible – climate, soil and drainage.

Just by thinking about what you want the tree for, you have begun to describe it. Now ask yourself the same question – 'What do I want the tree for?' – but, this time, in terms of its perfor-mance as an object of splendour. Is your first priority beauty of foliage or the need for an all-year-round grace and presence? Perhaps you feel a garden tree should have a spectacular display of flowers. Maybe you have already gone through this process when selecting other plants and you want a tree that will complement them, contrast with them or relate to them in some other way.

This sort of process brings to bear the knowledge you have gained from garden visits, reading and chatting to other gardeners. As you think about each criterion, different kinds of trees come to mind. Foliage? Acers! Flowers? Magnolias! Coloured stems? Birches! And so on. You can then start to shop around to find the best all-round performers. White stems, graceful branches, pretty foliage, good autumnal colour, not too large: the birch *Betula utilis jacque-montii* 'Doorenbos'. Pretty foliage for spring and summer, the finest red autumnal colour, the longest-lasting berries for winter: the moun-tain ash *Sorbus hupehensis*.

Asking yourself these questions leads to clear thinking and gar-dening is generally a matter of thinking in a fairly logical way while still allowing your imagination to exercise itself.

SPACING TREES AND SHRUBS

Knowing the ultimate sizes of the trees and shrubs will save you time, trouble and money later on. If you can visualize their height and spread in about 20 years' time and plant accordingly, you will avoid a great deal of disappointment. It is helpful, too, to know roughly what they will be like after five, ten and 15 years, but 20 should be the benchmark for deciding on the location and spacing of woody plants. By visiting gardens and arboreta and becoming

Sorbus hupehensis boasts pretty foliage on purple-brown branches in spring and summer *(below left)* followed by a striking autumnal display *(below right)*. *Opposite* Care with spacing allows each plant to develop its natural shape and individual character

reasonably familiar with trees of different sizes, you will soon be able to translate general descriptions, such as 'small to medium-sized tree', into these sorts of terms.

Trees and shrubs are often planted too close together to achieve a short-term effect, which ultimately leads to their removal. Many plants can be pruned to prevent their growth becoming too rampant, untidy or unbalanced and, even to some extent, to slow down the rate at which they occupy space. However, the time will come when further pruning begins to spoil them and they become overclipped, overcrowded and unhealthy. Flowering ceases except on patchy groups of branches, leaf formation stops where the shrubs meet and the ground beneath them becomes worn out and starved of moisture. Over-restricting growth on such a scale is desirable only in the formation of hedges and topiary features.

If the trees and shrubs intended to form the framework of your garden are planted at their proper spacing, they must be looked on as a long-term investment. Proper spacing means something like their approximate 20-year span plus about 10 per cent for trees. The space between them may, of course, be used while you are still allowing for the annual increase in size. For example, you may interplant with shrubs that are naturally short-lived but which give

Opposite Interplanting with suitable shrubs and underplanting with perennials, annuals and bulbs provides interest in the garden while young trees develop to fill their intended space. *Below* Although largely determined by climate, a good balance of deciduous and evergreen plants brings great rewards, particularly in autumn

good accounts of themselves in their early years. Brooms provide quick growth and flower in their youth. Cultivars of *Cytisus scoparius* are among the many shrubs that can be used for short-term height. Others, such as daphnes, ceanothus, cistus, genistas, halimiums and hebes, will do a similar job. Meanwhile, some of the framework shrubs of medium longevity, such as forsythias, spiraeas, cotoneasters, laburnums, hydrangeas and hypericums, begin to occupy their permanent spaces. They may, if necessary, be sacrificed later. You may also complement the scheme with perennials, bulbs and annuals, creating what is, in effect, a mixed border.

The advantages of this system are that you can reduce the area covered by a particular herbaceous perennial merely by splitting it up and replanting fewer pieces. Eventually you can move it to somewhere else entirely; the same thing goes for bulbs. What is clear, however, is the wrong-headedness of the piece of advice concerning a shrub (not so often a tree) that goes, 'Of course, you can always move it later'. Often this is next to impossible (many magnolias), dependent on fairly precise timing (hollies and many other evergreens), a back-breaking job needing many fit assistants (the majority) or lethal to the plant (brooms, ceanothus, evergreen oaks and others). The question also arises of where to move it to. If everything else has also grown and you have not suffered any major losses, there will be no room.

DECIDUOUS AND EVERGREEN

The proportion of evergreen to deciduous trees and shrubs in your garden will be partly determined by climate. In very cold areas,

the number of broad-leaved evergreens will have to be fewer than where it is warmer, and in really mild areas they may constitute a high proportion of the woody plants. The evergreen component in cold gardens will necessarily contain a higher level of conifers with foliage developed to tolerate frosty and windy conditions. An evergreen tree or shrub will lose far more water in winter through wind and wind-frost than a deciduous one. This may be difficult to replace, especially when the soil is frozen. Conifers reduce the water lost from their leaves through having needle-like foliage or tiny leaves closely pressed to the stems, giving them an advantage over broad-leaved evergreens (see page 23).

The balance between deciduous and evergreen is also a matter of taste and design, governing the mood and atmosphere of the garden. Try to make the plantings relate to one another. A dark blob of green is an anomaly among the bare twigs of deciduous shrubs unless there is a specific reason for it to be there. Perhaps the new red growths of the evergreen *Photinia* x *fraseri* 'Red Robin' are complimented by the rosy-pink bark of the beautiful Chinese birch *Betula albo-sinensis* var. *septentrionalis*. It may be that the neatly shaped cone of the blue Lawson cypress *Chamaecyparis lawsoniana* 'Pembury Blue' is placed to give background and substance to a group of deciduous azaleas, while leading you to anticipate the gorgeous bright flowers against its steely blue foliage. Whatever valid and valuable links, contrasts and comparisons are made, they will create a planting that holds together in a balanced and interesting way.

BUYING TREES AND SHRUBS

The first approach for most gardeners is to visit a local garden centre. There you will find interesting species and cultivars with excellent qualities and the additional advantage that it caters for local conditions. Looking through their stock will provide a good survey of the plants that do well in your area. Even so, this may represent only a small proportion of the trees and shrubs that you might be able to grow; you may need to look further afield for a wider interest and variety. Larger garden centres carry a wide selection of both garden plants and sundries. They also display plants pleasingly, with suggestions for companion plants. These displays are thought through carefully to provide maximum interest. They may been seen as a starting point to plant selection. Before any on-the-spot purchase make sure that you check the compatibility with your site and its requirements; a garden centre bookshop is a good place to do this.

Buying by mail order These days, nurserymen send plants great distances in the knowledge that their skill in preparing and packing, allied to the efficiency of the handling services, make the transportation of plants safe within and between most countries. Well-established nursery firms can be relied upon to provide well grown, disease-free plants. Their quality control is usually first class, as it is altogether bad for business if plants have to be replaced because of complaint. It is common sense for them to dispatch plants in the best of condition; those who fail to do so will not last long. Mail order nurseries tend to carry more specialized plants and some

Above A nursery presents a magnolia for sale 'balled', that is with its roots surrounded by the soil in which it was grown, and wrapped in hessian. *Below* A bare-rooted specimen is literally that and must be quickly planted or heeled in *(see page 43)*

concentrate on a particular range of plants. There are nurseries that specialize in bamboos, Japanese maples, oaks and even architectural foliage plants.

If you do have difficulty in locating a certain plant, it is worth consulting the *RHS Plant Finder*, produced in association with the Royal Horticultural Society. It lists thousands of plants and the nurseries that sell them.

When trees and shrubs arrive, they will be containerized, bare-rooted or balled (the latter have their roots in much of the original soil ball in which they were grown in the field, and are usually wrapped in hessian or something similar). Those in containers are easily dealt with on arrival, they can be watered and sheltered until you are ready to plant them. Balled and bare-rooted trees and shrubs may be planted straightaway if the conditions are right, or heeled in (see page 43).

WHAT TO LOOK FOR WHEN BUYING

It is important to select quality grown plants, as this could mean the difference between success and failure within the garden. The most important places to look at are the root and shoot areas.

Appearance A well-developed and healthy root system is essential to the survival of a plant. Watch out for roots that appear out of the surface of the growing medium at acute angles; this is an indicator of two evils. First, the plant may have be grown in too small a container for too long, causing the root system to grow unnaturally. Second, if a root girdling the stem was not noticed and removed when young, it will place great pressure on the stem. Both will result in problems after planting, causing the tree or shrub to be unstable.

In particular, neglect shows when plants have a mass of root fibres emerging through the drainage holes at the bottom of the pot, especially when this is combined with major shrinkage of the compost. Small plants in large pots are equally suspect, as they have probably been potted on very recently to make them look better value for money.

The presence of a few weeds on the surface of the compost is excusable – there has to be a reasonable interval between weeding in the best-run establishments – but copious weed growth, especially if they are perennial, flowering and seeding, should be enough for you to reject the plant.

Trees should have a clear taper along the stem, that is, the top of the trunk should be much thinner than the base. Trees naturally produce reaction timber on load-bearing areas, the main one being the base of the trunk at soil level. This allows stress within the trunk to be evenly distributed along the lower two-thirds of the stem, so reducing the risk of breakage or cracking. Trees without a clear taper should be avoided. Trees which have been permanently staked along their trunks do not generally produce reaction timber, so once the stake is removed they have difficulty in supporting themselves and are vulnerable to breakage.

Vigour is a good guide to the health and well-being of a tree or shrub. Check this by looking at the extension growth. The current and previous season's growth are good indicators of health. The spacing between nodes should be equal along the stem, regardless of species. The plants should look healthy and well grown. They should be free from pests and diseases; always look for insect pests on the underside of leaves and around soft new tips. Inspect areas of the trunk, stems and branches for any visual damage.

Foliage Green foliage should be green. It may be a light, yellowish green, but the colour should be appropriate to the variety and should look healthy. Foliage that has turned yellow through starvation or deficiency looks distinctly ill. The veins may remain green and the rest of the leaf is bright, or the leaf may be patchy yellow and green. Unseasonal leaf drop may be a sign that all is not well. Remember, however, that evergreens shed some leaves in summer. More than just a very few fallen leaves means that the plant has not been properly watered.

Labelling If you ask for a specific tree or shrub, you cannot complain later that you really meant something else. On the other hand, you have the right to expect that the label means what it says. Commonsense checks can be made easily in many cases. A plant called 'Goldleaf' should not have blue foliage, for instance, or one called 'Variegata' should not have plain green foliage. The best course of action with flowering trees and shrubs is to go and see the plant when it is in flower. If you are still in doubt, ask; a good garden centre will have knowledgeable and reliable staff.

Healthy foliage, absence of weeds from the soil surface and suitable sized containers indicate that these rhododendrons are acceptable candidates for purchase

Clear labelling of these *Choisya ternata* 'Sundance' specimens leaves customers with no doubt about what they are buying. The reverse of the label carries useful facts on care and planting

CARE & MAINTENANCE

Woody plants contribute greatly to our living environment, providing endless hours of pleasure as we cultivate them. Cultivation is the art of manipulating plants by providing them with the most suitable growing conditions so that they perform to their utmost potential. Gardeners require the appropriate knowledge so that they can preserve and care for the well-being of their garden plants and provide the conditions they require. The following chapter contains information for doing just that, through planting, staking, pruning and correct aftercare.

HEELING-IN AND PLANTING

Heeling-in is a simple procedure for holding plants for a very short period before proper planting. Bare-rooted trees and shrubs should be soaked thoroughly first. Make a trench in a shady part of the garden, preferably where the soil is light and free draining. 'Plant' the plants in it very lightly, laying their roots in the trench and covering them with soil, peat, garden compost or whatever suitable material you have to hand – even moist sand will do. This

Opposite Trees and shrubs are a long-term commitment bringing years of pleasure if they are well looked after. *Above* If you do not wish to plant bare-rooted specimens immediately, they may be heeled in to prevent damage from cold or dehydration

method allows you to delay planting for two to three weeks and protects the fragile roots from frost and dehydration.

Planting is a very different matter from heeling-in. By this stage, you should have acquired adequate knowledge about the plant, its height and spread and, of course, its growing requirements. The most important factors to consider before planting are the condition of the plant, its requirements and the current weather.

Plant bare-rooted deciduous trees and shrubs in the open ground during the dormant season (i.e. after leaf fall and before spring leaf growth). Plant balled evergreen trees and shrubs either between early and mid-autumn or between mid- and late spring; they will establish more effectively during the spring period, once the threat of desiccation to their foliage by winter wind is removed. Newly planted evergreens should always be given wind protection while they establish, regardless of planting season (*Fig. 10*). Well-established containerized plants can be planted at any time, other than in frosty conditions or during a drought, although even then they can be planted if adequate water can be artificially supplied. In sandy soils which warm up quickly there are advantages to be gained in planting from mid- to late spring, however, as sandy soils drain freely some experts favour autumn planting. Experts recommend mid- to late autumn planting in heavier soils which warm up late in the year but retain their heat longer into autumn.

Container-grown plants are the most difficult to establish after planting. The pot soils contain optimum levels of nutrients and a medium that supplies little resistance to developing roots, making it difficult for the plant to establish into the surrounding soil . This is especially problematic on heavy clay soils, where the sides of the planting hole can smear easily and create an almost impenetrable barrier against developing roots. Bare-rooted trees and shrubs do not suffer in quite the same way because there is little of their native soil remaining. All new roots will develop in the new soil. On easy to cultivate soils, a conventional planting hole may be sufficient, but on heavier clay soils, a wider planting area may be adopted.

Prepare the planting hole Remove any perennial weed cover before planting. This may involve applying a herbicide or digging out deep-rooted weeds. The next step is to prepare a planting site well in advance.

On light sandy soils, dig in organic matter at a rate of 9-15kg per m² (20-30lb per square yard). This may include spent compost, leafmould, farmyard manure, green manure or spent hops to

FIG. 3   PREPARING THE PLANTING HOLE

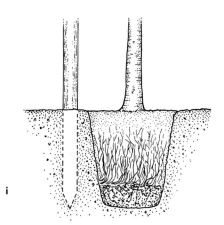

i

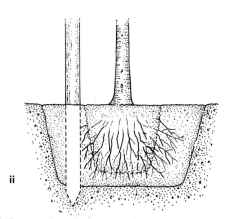

ii

Prepare the planting hole by cultivating a sufficiently large area for the roots to become established. In figure (i) the roots have been unable to force their way through the glazed sides of the hole

Figure (ii) illustrates how the roots are able to make headway in a well-prepared planting hole, exploiting the larger area of well turned soil to develop rapidly outwards

enhance the depth of the soil for root exploration.

On heavy clay soils, first improve the drainage problems before adding material to improve the fertility of the soil, such as leaf mould, old grow bag compost, spent hops and garden compost. Add this at a rate of 2-3kg per m² (4-6lb per square yard), preferably in late autumn, allowing it until spring to break down. Letting the soil settle will improve its aeration and texture.

Once these preparations have been completed, dig a planting hole three times the width and twice the depth of the existing root system. Although this may not always be practical, it is worth getting close to this as the rapid establishment of your tree or shrub will most certainly depend on the quality of the planting hole.

Staking Almost all trees and a few shrubs need to be staked. This is primarily to allow the roots to become established as anchors. Once they have gained a firm hold in the soil, the chances of the plant being blown over are slender. Until then, however, the constant movement of the stem under the influence of even light breezes will prevent the roots from growing into the surrounding soil.

Until experiments showed the importance of movement to stem development, tree stakes had always extended to just below the head of branches. Many people still use long stakes, but increasingly the short stake, 50cm (20in) in height, has been adopted. A long stake immobilizes the tree stem throughout its length. This does not inhibit growth but encourages the stem to develop a tube-like shape. If a short stake is used, the upper portion of the stem moves and in doing so produces reaction timber which reinforces the trunk *(see page 41)*. Single short stakes can be used for bare-rooted plants, but you can also use a short stake, consisting of two uprights and a crossbar, for containerized trees and shrubs and large specimen shrubs.

Tall or slender shrubs and those that move readily with the wind will also need staking. A short, angled stake is best as shrubs have many stems and often there is not a straight one among them. If you use a short stake and drive it in at an angle that nei-

ther interferes with the root ball nor chafes any branches, you will achieve sufficient stability for the shrub to become anchored.

One or more proper tree ties should always be used when staking trees and shrubs. It is a false economy to use strips of old pantyhose or tyre inner-tubes. Not only do they look ugly and untidy but they are also inefficient, causing damage to the stem leading to the entry of disease organisms. A purpose-made tree tie costs only pennies and may well make the difference between success and failure. It should consist of a strap with a buckle and one or more buffer blocks. It should grip the stem and the stake snugly. You can fasten it into the stake with a light nail to prevent it sliding down.

Very large tree specimens are difficult to establish because of anchorage problems and even expert growers may fail. Specialized systems of guying are best used. In most cases, three guy ropes, passing through rubber anti-friction tubes, are fastened to strong posts driven into the ground.

Stakes are frequently left in the ground and attached to the plants they are supporting for far too long. You should check them at least twice a year and be prepared to remove the stakes from established and independent trees and shrubs after two years. The majority of trees, except perhaps those bought as large specimens, should be capable of standing alone after three years.

Neglecting the tree-tie can easily lead to the formation of a groove in the stem and this 'tight collar' effect often leads to the stem's snapping later on. It is especially easy to forget that you staked a shrub, as the stake may become hidden. It is an unpleasant reminder to find a fine camellia in full flower, for example, suddenly reduced to half its height.

Planting bare-rooted trees and shrubs Bare-rooted trees and shrubs should have been properly packed and the roots safely protected by the nursery immediately upon lifting from the open ground. You should either keep the roots moist within their

FIG. 4 STAKING METHODS

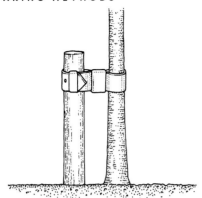

Short stakes allow the upper portion of the tree or shrub stem to move producing reaction timber which reinforces the trunk

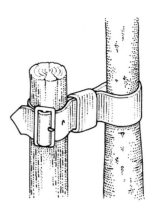

Purpose-made tree ties not only look more professional but also prevent chafing which may provide an entry point for pests and diseases

Short stakes and crossbar Two short stakes linked with a crossbar which is tied to the tree trunk is particularly useful with container-grown specimens to prevent damage to the rootball

Guy-rope staking Purpose-made guying systems are recommended for the staking of large tree specimens

wrappings or heel them in immediately upon receipt.

After preparing the soil, make a hole wide enough to accommodate the roots without their being bent or forced. It is a good idea make a firmed cone of soil in the bottom. The stem can rest on the apex of this as the roots fan downwards. An excellent precaution is to provide yourself with an assistant, as it is very difficult to ensure that the tree or shrub is planted upright when you are also concerned with filling in the hole properly.

Find the point where the roots end and the stem or stems begin on each tree or shrub you plant. This is called the 'nursery mark' – a dark band across the bottom of the stem where the soil level was. You should also look for any graft union and make sure it is not buried but remains 5-6cm (2-2¹/₂in) above soil level. (The opposite is true for roses, where the graft union would have been below ground level at the nursery and should remain so when you plant.) The way to ensure that the mark stays at the right level is to place a batten of wood across the hole and align the mark with its lower

edge. It is part of your assistant's job to see that it is still aligned at the end of the planting process.

Before putting the tree in the hole, position the stake and drive it into the bottom of the hole. Next, have your assistant hold the stem (let us assume it is a tree) while you check the alignment. As you backfill the hole, she or he should give the tree a vertical shake from time to time to help settle the soil around the roots. It is most important not to allow air pockets to form and this action, in concert with your use of feet, hands and spade, will ensure that they do not occur.

Bad planting often occurs when the soil around the roots of a plant is firmed with the heel, as the pressure through this small area is great enough to break roots. The sole, having a larger area, transmits less pressure and tends to firm rather than ram the soil. However, as the hole is further filled and the cushion of soil between the foot and the roots deepens, then the full pressure of body weight can be applied through the heel. This firming is essential, as with-

FIG. 5 HOW TO PLANT A BARE-ROOTED TREE OR SHRUB

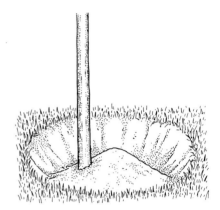

2 Line up the nursery mark using a wooden batten or cane to ensure that the tree is planted at the correct level

3 Remove the tree. Position the stake and drive it into the bottom of the hole

I Make a firm pyramid of soil at the bottom of the hole and rest the tree on top to make sure that the height is sufficient for the roots to fan down unrestricted

4 With stake in position, replace the tree and begin backfilling the hole giving the tree an occasional vertical shake to settle the soil around its roots

5 Firm the soil around the trunk of the tree first with the sole of your boot, then with the heel

out it the soil will sag into the hole, leaving a water-bearing depression which will cause the top of the root system to be exposed.

Planting balled trees and shrubs Shrubs and trees with masses of fibrous root are often delivered with their root balls intact and tied up or 'balled' in netting made of hessian or some other material. You need to know what the material is, as only a bio-degradable substance can be allowed to remain on the root ball; non-degradable plastics must be removed. Even hessian should be untied and loosened from the top of the root ball.

Use the crossbar method for staking *(Fig. 4)* because you do not want to damage the root ball by driving a stake through it. Alternatively, large trees can be guyed at three points or double staked. Double staking *(Fig.6)* is the only method that allows the use of flexible ties, such as strips of rubber, because the two strips oppose one another and keep the trunk firm but allow it to sway.

The stakes are driven in opposite one another and to the sides of the root ball. The rubber strips form an alternative to attaching a crossbar and using a tree tie, a method that may not be practicable in the case of heavier trees with thicker stems.

Planting container-grown trees and shrubs In many ways it is much easier to plant a containerized tree or shrub than one grown in the field. It is important to soak the root ball thoroughly before planting, as peat and several peat substitute composts are extremely reluctant to take up water once they have dried out. To ensure that the centre of the root ball is wet, sink the container in a bucket or bath of water and leave it to soak for an hour or two – certainly until the very last bubbles have finished rising. Let it drain properly before you remove the pot, otherwise a rush of water might disturb the root ball and cause damage.

Placing the nursery mark correctly is important and it is still a

FIG. 6 DOUBLE STAKING

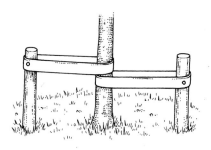

With this method, the stakes are linked by looped strips of rubber which hold the tree firm but allow it to sway. It is particularly suitable for heavy, thick-stemmed trees unsuited to the short stake and crossbar technique

FIG. 7 THE NURSERY MARK

The nursery mark on container-grown trees and shrubs is level with the soil surface

good idea to have an assistant when planting large specimens. It is essential that the soil should be part of a properly cultivated and enriched area around the planting hole. Containerized trees and shrubs are entirely unforgiving towards gardeners who expect them to force their way through inhospitably resistant soil. Firm the soil thoroughly around the root ball.

Planting formal and informal hedges It is often asserted that planting containerized plants is safe at any time of year but the dangers from drought are ever present. Where just a few trees or shrubs are planted in late spring or summer, it is no great problem to keep an eye on them and water when necessary. Hedges, which consist of quite large numbers of young plants, are often situated away from water supplies and located at the boundaries of the garden. Unless you are particularly vigilant, they are best planted between autumn and spring, even when container grown. Plant bare-rooted, deciduous hedging plants after leaf fall and before spring is properly under way. Plant evergreens in mid-autumn or late spring, when the soil is warm enough for the roots to replenish water lost by the leaves.

You can plant in dry conditions as long as the plant roots are soaked prior to planting and generously watered in. It is often supposed that because hedges are generally the best defences against wind, they need no protection when young. Nothing could be further from the truth, especially as hedges are often planted in exposed positions. Lack of protection during the first three or four winters is one of the commonest causes of losses, with resultant gaps which have to be filled with replacement plants. Plastic netting, which provides protection from the wind, pays dividends in terms of the speed of growth, quality and economy of the hedge. In addition, make sure when planting that you have firmed the soil well around the roots. Check the plants after strong winds for soil movement throughout their first year.

TRANSPLANTING

Transplanting is simply a matter of moving trees and shrubs from one place to another within the garden. In practice it is almost entirely confined to smaller shrubs and young, small trees, as anything large becomes a matter for professional skill and machinery.

The root hairs – the part of the root system that absorbs nutrients and water from the soil – are easily damaged and only rapidly repaired or replaced when the soil is warm and moist. The younger the root, the more root hairs it bears and the younger the root system, the more young roots it has. Therefore the younger the plant, the better its chance of surviving a move. It follows, too, that the greater the proportion of the root system you manage to transplant intact, the more likely it is that the plant will be relatively unaffected.

Plants, such as rhododendrons, that have closely massed, highly fibrous roots can be moved at almost any time of the year apart from during periods of drought or when soil is frozen.

Deciduous trees and shrubs can be moved during their dormant season – between leaf fall and bud-break. The earlier part of that season is better; to plant at rather than after leaf fall allows damaged roots to re-grow while the soil is still warm. Transplantation late in the dormant season may lead to trouble when icy or drying winds blow in early spring. There is often a short spell after the dormant season during which soft showers fall and the soil has warmed up enough to activate the roots. This provides an extension to the transplanting season for deciduous subjects. The few tricky ones, including the deciduous magnolias, may be moved with the greatest safety at this time.

Evergreen trees and shrubs, with few exceptions, are not so easily moved, as the leaves lose water during the winter and a damaged root system cannot replace it. No matter how careful you are to retain the root balls intact, you will always fail to some degree and this will adversely affect the water balance. Evergreens are best moved just after the autumn equinox in milder areas and just before where it is colder. In places where spring is characterized by early spells of dry, cold winds, transplanting should be delayed until warmer, moister weather arrives. In regions where spring is short and swift, action is demanded as soon as the soil warms up. No matter when evergreen trees or shrubs are moved, they should, if possible, be protected from wind for the first season or two.

Hedges are often planted in exposed wind-blown positions at the boundaries of gardens, so particular care with watering is required while the young plants are getting established

How to transplant *(Fig. 8)* To lift a tree or shrub, drive your spade into the soil at a good distance from it. The exact position depends on the size of the plant, but may be rather further than you might expect to come into contact with the root system. A general guide is to use the drip line, an imaginary line drawn from the outer edge of the canopy to soil level. Tie a line to the base of the plant to locate the distance to the drip line and, using this as a guide, mark out a circle around the plant with a spade. Insert the spade one spade's width outside the marked circle. Rock the spade backwards and forwards without loosening the root ball. Continue around the plant and then cut out a trench using the inner edge as a guide. Cut through any exposed roots with an old, but sharp saw. Finally, undercut the root ball to free it.

Tie a stout pole to the bottom of the main stem, with a loop of rope for the stem and another for the pole so that the pole is horizontal. Lift the shrub onto a sheet of strong sacking or plastic and carry it by the four corners of this support to the planting site. Then follow Fig. 5.

In practice, no matter how careful you are in transplanting a tree shrub, you are almost certain to cause some root damage. Even when this is not apparent, it is still a good idea to reduce the head of branches to balance the loss of roots. Otherwise the plant may not be able to balance water loss from the foliage and die-back may occur. A reduction of up to one-third of the head is possible in many cases; simply remove all crossing branches, open it up a little and cut back the main branches by a relatively small amount. Take care, however, to maintain the leader.

TREE SHELTERS AND GUARDS

Tree shelters improve the establishment of whips and are commonly used by landscape companies. They not only protect the plant from grazing animals, but also provide a microclimate within a tube, which if properly used, can increase the establishment of trees and shrubs. Newly planted trees in forestry and parkland plantations may be subject to damage by browsing animals – cattle, horses and deer – and need robust protection from them. They are also vulnerable to smaller animals, such as rabbits and squirrels, which strip or otherwise injure the bark.

Rabbits, squirrels and occasionally roe deer can quickly ruin garden trees, too. Tree guards made of plastic mesh are the best defence

FIG. 8 TRANSPLANTING

1 Having established the outer edge of the root system, mark out a circle and then cut a trench using the inner edge of the circle as a guide

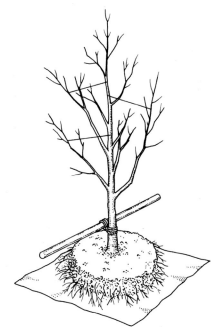

2 Tie a stout pole to the bottom of the main stem so that the pole is horizontal. With at least one assistant, lift the pole at each end and carry the plant onto a sheet of strong sacking or polythene. With a helper at each corner of the sheet, the plant may now be carried to its pre-prepared planting site

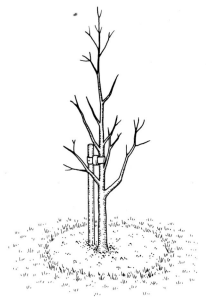

3 To counteract root damage which is almost inevitable during transplanting, reduce the plant's head of branches by up to one-third. Remove damaged and crossing branches but retain the leader

FIG. 9 TREE GUARDS

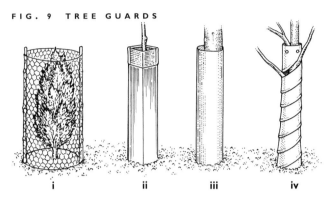

i   **ii**   **iii**   **iv**

The following defences offer some degree of protection against animals:
(i) Home-made bamboo and chicken wire fence which extends to a depth
of 30cm (12in) below the soil surface to deter rabbits (ii) Purpose-made,
flat-sided plastic tube available in a range of lengths (iii) Purpose-made,
cylindrical, plastic tube available in a range of lengths (iv) Purpose-made
spiral wrap

FIG. 10 PROTECTION FROM WIND

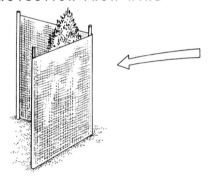

For the first few winters after planting, erect a V-shaped shelter which
points into the wind allowing the young trees to shelter behind it

against rabbits and deer. They are available in different heights and
diameters. For rabbits 60cm (2ft) is high enough, but for roe deer
they should be 2m (6ft) tall. Where rabbits and deer are a persistent nuisance, however, and given to destroying shrubs, more expensive alternatives, such as double deer and rabbit fences, leaning or
electric fences may be required.

PROTECTION FROM WIND

Many hardy adult trees and shrubs are susceptible to cold during
their first few winters. The still air temperature rarely poses a danger, but the wind can produce a temperature many degrees lower.

Winter protection should, therefore, be on two fronts. Temper
the prevailing cold wind by erecting a V-shaped shelter *(Fig. 10)*,
consisting of close plastic mesh or a material such as hessian, with
the angle of the V pointing into the wind and the plant snugly
behind it. Alternatively, use purpose-made tree and shrub shelters.
Protect the soil from freezing with a generous mulch of a material such as composted forest bark over the root area. Alternatively,
porous matting may be used where winters are less severe.

WATERING

It is a mistake to think that a light watering is adequate after planting. One of the purposes of watering is to get the soil into contact
with the roots and the water must reach to the very lowest of them
for this to happen. Furthermore, water should move down through
the soil below the bottom of the planting hole. Also make sure that
watering is not limited to the immediate spread of the roots. A thor-
ough, copious watering will go a long way towards ensuring that
no air pockets lie in wait to discourage questing roots. This is, of
course, especially important in spring, when planting in warm soil
and when there may be the possibility of a dry spell.

This generous watering is often described as essential for the
establishment of certain plants, such as clematis, but it is a good
idea to make it standard practice for all of them. All trees and shrubs
should be carefully monitored during the first three years after planting and watered when necessary. Thereafter, you should need to
water only in periods of prolonged drought.

WEED CONTROL

Pay special attention to weed control around newly planted trees
and shrubs. Some compete better than others. For example, young
oaks will grow strongly where there is a cover of grass, whereas
birches will not. Nevertheless, garden plants should not have to
put up with the sort of competition they may encounter in nature,
so good practice dictates that you should keep weeds down.

Grasses and weeds make strong demands on moisture and
nutrients, especially the nitrogen that a young tree or shrub needs
so much. Routine use of herbicides near young trees may be unde-
sirable in a small garden, although it is likely to be inevitable in
larger areas. Hand weeding or hoeing is environmentally friendly
and safer. However, the efficient use of herbicides is more effective
if they are used with care.

Keeping weeds hoed from the root areas of trees and shrubs is
neither a heavy nor a time-consuming job on small areas, as long
as it is done fairly frequently. If you hoe quite often, you do not
need to hoe roughly or deeply and risk damaging the roots of the
plants. Furthermore, you can stop hoeing at the onset of dry weather. The loose soil on top dries quickly, making it unsuitable for weed
seed germination; it also forms an insulating mulch to the soil
beneath it. If you stir it up during dry weather, you bring moist
soil to the surface, where it dries out. Weed germination is unlikely during dry spells and if you have prepared the ground properly, there will be no up-growth of perennial weeds.

MULCHES

Any material placed on the surface of the soil is classed as a mulch.
It may be organic, such as pine needles, composted bark chips, grass
clippings or leaf mould, or inorganic, such as old newspapers, old
carpets, black polythene or purpose-made mulch mats. Applied correctly, mulches conserve moisture within the soil, reduce soil erosion and suppress the growth of annual weeds. Organic mulches
also improve fertility and increase the temperature under the mulch.
Inorganic mulches can inhibit water penetration but still suppress ·

FIG. 18 CLEMATIS VARIETIES WHICH FLOWER ON OLD WOOD

Remove all flower stems immediately after flowering

FIG. 19 CLEMATIS VARIETIES WHICH FLOWER ON NEW WOOD

Prune to within 30cm (12in) of the ground in early spring

FIG. 20 WISTERIA

For maximum flower production, prune in summer the current year's growth on wisteria back to 2-3 buds from the main stem

spurs will develop flower buds and the plants will flower much more profusely and all along the main stems *(Fig. 20).*

Renewal pruning There is one type of shrub pruning, however, that can be carried out without concern for the loss of a season's flowers. This is renewal pruning – a drastic measure taken when a shrub has become old, unsightly or so lanky that the number of flowers it carries is of no great decorative value *(Fig. 21).* It usually applies to evergreens.

If shrubs have been dealt with properly from the start and given good light and adequate space, few really need renewal pruning, but it is occasionally necessary even in the best regulated gardens. The beautiful Moroccan broom, *Cytisus battandieri*, is a good example of a deciduous shrub that benefits from this treatment from time to time. At its simplest, the entire shrub is cut down by half or even more, and weak or badly crossing branches can be removed at the same time. Do not be afraid to cut back hard, as new growth usually starts from just below the cut and not all the way up a bare stem. As the plant will put so much energy into growth during the following year, flowers are unlikely anyway. Nevertheless, the best time to carry out this operation is in late winter. It is worth noting that many shrubs, including several other brooms, cannot be treated in this way as they will not 'break' into new growth from old wood. Rhododendrons, on the other hand, will break from buds that have been concealed beneath their bark.

Pruning evergreens The reasons for pruning evergreens are almost always to do with shape and size and as such decisions about when and how much are largely up to the individual. Renewal pruning may also be required from time to time. All pruning of evergreens should be carried out in late winter or early spring, as this gives the maximum length of growing season during which they can make new leaves.

Pruning deciduous shrubs Generally speaking, pruning deciduous shrubs depends on when they flower and whether they do so on wood made in the previous or current year. Those that flower earlier usually do so on the previous year's wood; there is no new wood on which to flower. Those that flower later do so on wood made in the current year. The best rule to observe is always to prune to provide the longest possible period of growth between pruning and flowering.

Shrubs that flower on new wood It makes sense to prune shrubs that flower on new wood *(Fig. 22)* in late winter or early spring for two reasons. The first is because winter pruning is for growth, and it is on new growths that flowers will be borne. The second is that this gives them the longest period of growth before flowering, which is late in the summer or in autumn. Pruning immediately after flowering has little point, as no growth is made during the winter and they are also rendered liable to die-back caused by frost, so that another pruning might well be necessary.

Pruning does not need to be severe; just enough to stimulate good

FIG. 21 RENEWAL PRUNING

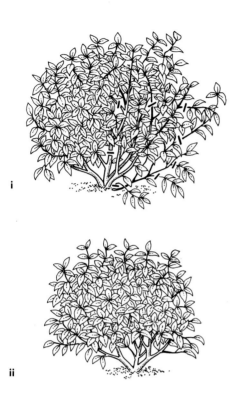

Remove all dead, diseased and crossing branches (i) and cut back the remainder by half (ii). This operation may be carried out at any time of year but is best done in late winter

FIG. 22 SHRUBS THAT FLOWER ON NEW WOOD

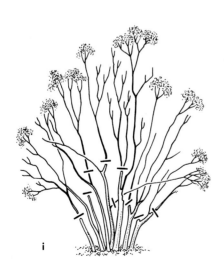

Prune shrubs that flower on new wood in late winter or early spring (i) to maximize growth and resultant flowering (ii)

quantities of new shoots for bearing the best possible crop of flowers. Exactly how hard you cut back depends on the particular shrub. However, once you step on to the treadmill of keeping the shrub to a set size by hard pruning, you may end up producing an ugly duckling that will take months to turn into a swan again. A typical shrub to which this happens is *Hydrangea paniculata*, which is all too often reduced to a tangle of shorn stumps in the mistaken idea that this is necessary annually for it to put on a good show of flower. (The correct pruning method is illustrated in Fig. 23.) Forms of *Buddleja davidii*, on the other hand, really do need to be cut back drastically each year *(Fig. 24)*. They are best grown where their pollarded stumps are hidden but where their stems, which grow well over 2m (7ft) in a season, can reach into the light and put on their show for you and the butterflies.

Shrubs that flower later on new wood but which partly renew themselves from the base each year can be pruned in late winter or early spring in a somewhat different manner. Mophead and lacecap hydrangeas, for example, are best pruned first from the bottom upwards, with old, weak or overcrowded stems being removed entirely at ground level. This stimulates strong, straight growths which will grow right up through the bush in the first year. The second step is to prune from the top downwards, an operation consisting of cutting back the old flowering growths to the first strong pair of buds.

Shrubs that flower on old wood The majority of shrubs that flower on the wood of the previous year are pruned immediately after flowering to allow the longest period of growth before the next flowering. However, those that flower in early spring are pruned differently from those that flower later. This is because the early ones flower before the formation of any new wood and, there-

FIG. 23 HYDRANGEA PANICULATA

i

ii

Less vigorous shrubs that flower on new wood, like *H. paniculata*, should be pruned carefully in late winter or early spring. First remove all old, weak and overcrowded growth from the base; then cut back flowered growths to the first pair of strong buds (i). Careful pruning will result in good flowering and a compact shape (ii)

FIG. 24 BUDDLEJA DAVIDII

i

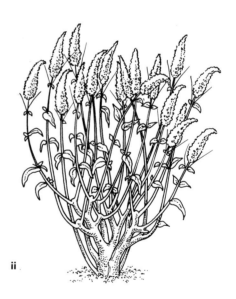

ii

Vigorous shrubs that flower on new wood, like *B. davidii*, should be pruned hard in early spring. Remove the entire length of the previous year's flowering shoot (i) to achieve good flowering at an attractive height in the summer (ii).

fore, can be cut back with only the old flowering wood being removed. This stimulates the formation of new wood and leads to a better crop of flowers the following year. It is the method used for forsythias.

If simple cutting back is performed directly after flowering on shrubs that flower later, when formation of new wood is under way, the new wood will be removed or badly shortened and the next flowering will be more or less severely curtailed. They should, therefore, be much more selectively pruned, so that just the old flowering stems are cut away. At the same time, any crossing or overcrowded branches can be removed at their points of origin. If this regime is used on philadelphus and deutzias, for example, they will be greatly improved.

Clipping formal hedges The object of clipping hedges is to create a neat, attractive barrier but patience is essential. If the hedge is allowed to grow too quickly in height, it will become thin and gappy. It may require clipping when young, sacrificing height for the formation of a dense, wide base. Once established, a hedge may require only one or two cuts each year. There are

FIG. 25 SHRUBS THAT FLOWER EARLY ON OLD WOOD

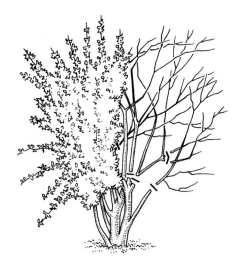

i

ii

Shrubs, such as forsythia, which flower early in the year on wood produced the previous year, should be pruned immediately after flowering. As no

new growth will have formed, simply remove the old flowered stems (i) to maintain a good shape and flowering for the following year (ii)

FIG. 26 SHRUBS THAT FLOWER LATE ON OLD WOOD

i

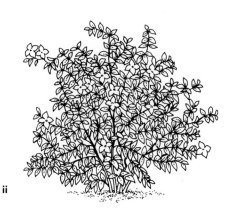

ii

Shrubs, such as philadelphus, which flower later in the year on wood produced the previous year, should have flowered stems, crossing branches and overcrowded branches removed carefully immediately

after flowering, avoiding the current year's growth (i). This procedure will ensure that the wood is retained in good shape to maximize flowering the following year (ii)

exceptions, however, such as *Lonicera nitida*, which needs clipping every few weeks.

All clipping should be delayed until early summer and should be completed by late summer. This allows spring growth to take place and permits a little growth before winter sets in. Hedges such as hornbeam and beech that need only one clipping should be trimmed in late summer. Those, such as caryopteris, that flower late on wood of the current year should be clipped in early to mid-spring. With several kinds of flowering hedges a different pruning regime may be necessary. For example, pyracanthas may be clipped any time after spring, but flowering will be cut short. If you want to enjoy the decorative effect of the fruits, you should prune with secateurs just after flowering, allowing chosen clusters of young berries to remain, and then clip between with hand shears.

Young hedges should be clipped with hand shears, while secateurs may well prove to be the best tool for early shaping. Power hedge trimmers may be used on strong, mature hedges that are not required to flower or fruit.

Additional problems – snow Although most trees and shrubs are tough and capable of standing up to the rigours of winter, they still repay vigilance after heavy snow falls. Evergreens, and particularly conifers, may be 'opened up' by snow – a process by which heavily laden branches are torn from the main body of the plant. If this occurs, it will be necessary to neaten the tear by means of a clean pruning cut in order to avoid any potential problems with pests and diseases. However, it is preferable to prevent the possibility of such damage by gently shaking snow off affected plants.

PROPAGATION

THE METHODS USED TO INCREASE THE NUMBER OF PLANTS DESCRIBED IN THIS CHAPTER CAN BE EMPLOYED BY THE GARDENER USING READILY AVAILABLE EQUIPMENT. MOST GARDENS TODAY HAVE a greenhouse, conservatory, cold frame or at least a vacant kitchen window that can be used for the propagation of plants. All the methods covered are widely used for the production of plants by vegetative propagation or cloning. The latter is the method by which plants are rooted either by being removed or by remaining attached to the parent or stock plant. Because they involve material from a parent plant there is no change in the genetic make-up of the plant, so these methods are described as asexual propagation. The methods covered by this chapter are propagation of plants by cuttings and by layering and represent the most effective ways of raising modest numbers of new plants for the garden.

CUTTINGS

It is important that the material selected for any method of vegetative propagation is true to type, free from pests and diseases and

Cornus alba (Red-barked dogwood) is grown for its rich-red stems which develop into small thickets and may be propagated by taking hardwood cuttings

Populus nigra 'Italica' (Lombardy poplar) forms an effective screen and its rustling leaves are beneficial to disguise traffic noise. It may be propagated by taking root cuttings

FIG. 27 HARDWOOD CUTTINGS

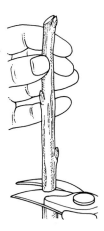
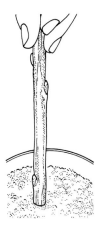

1 Take hardwood cuttings between late autumn and late winter

2 Select well-ripened, vigorous pencil-thick shoots

3 At the top of the cutting, make a sloping cut just above the proposed top bud

4 Then make a flat cut 15cm (6in) below the top cut

5 Dip the cutting base into hormone rooting powder

6 Bundle the cuttings together and place into a sand box with top third above the surface

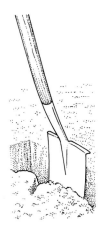

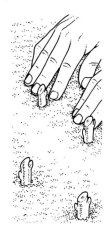

7 In spring, before bud break, prepare 12cm (5in) trench in propagation bed or grow on in cold frame

8 Plant cuttings vertically in the trenches at 10-15cm (4-6in) intervals

9 Leave 30-45cm (12-18in) between rows in open ground and 10cm (4in) in the cold frame

10 Firm down the soil allowing 2cm (1in) of cutting exposed

11 In autumn, lift the rooted cuttings and plant in final site

not flowering. If flowering material is selected, all flower buds must be removed as the plant will use energy to produce them rather than develop a new root system.

In cutting propagation a portion of stem, root or leaf is cut from the parent or stock plant and induced to form roots and shoots. Taking cuttings, in all its variations, is the most widely practised method of vegetative propagation. The list of plants that can be propagated by cuttings is endless and the method has many advantages. First, many cuttings can be taken from a single parent and propagated in a small area. They can be rooted quickly and inexpensively and do not require complicated equipment. Plants raised by vegetative propagation exhibit greater uniformity, something that is not present in seed propagation.

It is important that the medium for rooting cuttings is firm and dense so it will hold the cuttings upright. Its volume must be fairly constant, whether wet or dry, although it must retain enough moisture not to need constant watering. It must also be sufficiently porous to allow excess water to drain freely so that oxygen can

FIG. 28 SEMI-HARDWOOD CUTTINGS

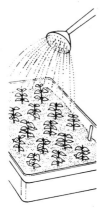

I Cut off a shoot with all its current season's growth in late summer

2 Make a flat cut at the bottom of the shoot below a leaf node and wound (Fig. 29) if the bark is thick

3 Dip cuttings into hormone rooting powder and insert into a tray. Water well and spray with fungicide

FIG. 29 WOUNDING

Making a heavy single slice wound on a semi-hardwood cutting

reach the roots. Finally, it must be free from pests and diseases. Commonly used mixes for cutting propagation medium are as follows: 50 per cent pulverized bark (fine grade) and 50 per cent perlite (fine); 50 per cent sharp sand or silver sand and 50 per cent peat or coir; 50 per cent peat or coir and 50 per cent pulverized bark; and equal parts peat, bark and perlite. All these mix ratios are by volume and not by weight.

Rooting hormones Cuttings are treated with a rooting hormone (auxin) to increase their propensity to form roots, to hasten root initiation and to increase the uniformity of rooting. Plants that root easily do not benefit from an external supply of auxin. It is best to save rooting hormones for those that are difficult to root. In the late 1930s the substance now known as auxin was identified as indole acetic acid. Of simple formation, it was soon being artificially manufactured. Today the most reliable rooting agents contain indolebutyric acid (IBA) or naphthalenacetic acid (NAA), both available in liquid and powder form.

Deciduous hardwood cuttings *(Fig. 27)* are taken through the winter from matured material. The aim of this method is to induce the cutting to produce roots before the buds grow in spring. As they have no leaves when the cutting is taken, water loss is greatly reduced. Hardwoods are the easiest and least expensive method of cutting propagation. The range of plants successfully propagated by deciduous hardwood cuttings is smaller than those by softwood or semi-hardwood propagation, but includes the following: *Laburnum, Platanus, Populus, Prunus cerasifera, Salix, Metasequoia glyptostrobioides, Buddleja davidii, Clematis montana, Cornus alba, Lonicera periclymenum, Cornus stolonifera, Polygonum, Deutzia, Euonymus, Vitis, Forsythia, Hibiscus, Hypericum, Kerria japonica, Philadelphus, Physocarpus,*

Rosa rugosa, Sambucus, Spiraea, Symphoricarpos and *Weigela.*

Take cuttings from well-ripened, vigorous, one-year-old shoots of roughly pencil thickness. Discard weak and bent shoots along with the shoot tip. Begin at the top of the cutting by making a sloping cut away from the bud, then make a flat cut at the bud closest to 15cm (6in) from the top of the cutting. Bundle the cuttings together and tie with string or an elastic band. The cuttings may then be heeled into the ground, placed in a cold frame or in a bucket of sand with the top third above the surface. Placing them in a cold frame or a container of sand allows them to pre-callus before planting out in spring. Allow the cuttings to over-winter; then in spring, carefully lift them, separate the individual specimens out and plant in a propagation bed or cold frame prior to planting in their final locations in autumn.

The final planting depth varies for trees and shrubs. For trees,

The *Deutzia* species, including *Deutzia scabra* 'Punctata' illustrated here, are suitable for propagation by taking softwood cuttings

FIG. 30 SOFTWOOD CUTTINGS

1 Cut off the soft tip in the early morning when the cells are fully turgid

2 Trim the stem at 2mm (¹/₈in) below the leaf node using a sharp knife

3 Remove the lower third of leaf cover and dip stem into hormone rooting powder

4 Insert the cuttings into potting compost up to the lowest leaves

5 Label clearly and water

6 Spray with a liquid fungicide at least once a week

insert the cutting so only one or two buds are left above soil level. For shrubs, leave two to four buds to create a multi-stemmed specimen.

Semi-hardwood cuttings *(Fig. 28)* are taken from evergreens once they have started to build up wood tissue towards the end of the growing season. Material is collected between late summer and mid-winter. Some of the plants commonly propagated using this method are listed here: *Calocedrus decurrens, Abelia, Aucuba, Akebia trifoliata, Cephalotaxus fortunei, Berberis, Buxus, Clematis armandii, Chamaecyparis, Calycanthus floridus, Camellia, Cryptomeria japonica, Elaeagnus, Euonymus, Hedera, Cupressus, Ilex, Garrya elliptica, Jasminum, Juniperus, Microbiota decusata, Kalmia latifolia, Mahonia, Lapageria rosea, Picea, Podocarpus, Nandina domestica, Osmanthus, Pileostegia hydrangoides, Taxus, Thuja, Pieris, Pittosporum, Smilax, Torreya californica, Prunus laurocerasus, Trachelospermum jasminoides, x Cupressocyparis laylandii, Rhododendron, Sarcococca* and *Skimmia.*

Cut off a shoot with all its current season's growth in late summer. Because the stems have begun to produce bark some semi-hardwood cuttings may require wounding *(Fig. 29)*. Greater emphasis is placed on the use of hormone rooting powders, too. The optimum cutting size is 10-17cm (4-7in). Remove the lower foliage so that it does not come into contact with the cutting compost. Make a flat cut below a node. If the bark is thick, wound the specimen, then apply the rooting hormone. Insert cuttings into seed trays, label, water well, spray with a fungicide and place in a

A nodal cutting is taken by cutting the soft tip just below a leaf node

An internodal cutting is taken by cutting the soft tip halfway between two leaf nodes

closed case environment or in a cold frame and cover with polythene.

Softwood cuttings *(Fig. 30)* are taken from very soft growth between mid-spring and midsummer in the early morning when the cells are still turgid. The cuttings are extremely soft so they must be taken quickly and placed in a humid environment before they wilt.

Listed here are some of the plants propagated in this way: *Acer, Buddleja, Cornus, Actinidia kolomikta, Catalpa, Cotinus, Deutzia, Campsis radicans, Magnolia, Forsythia, Fuchsia, Clematis, Stewartia, Hebe, Hydrangea, Hypericum, Lonicera, Kolkwitzia amabilis, Parthenocissus, Perovskia, Potentilla, Schisandra, Philadelphus, Schizophragma hydrangoides, Pyracantha, Ribes, Vitis, Spiraea, Syringa, Wisteria* and *Viburnum.*

Softwood cuttings can be divided into two groups: those taken nodally and those taken internodally. Nodal – cutting the soft tip just below a leaf node – is the commonest method. The optimum cutting length is 5-10cm (2-4in). Strip or cut off the leaves from the cutting and remove the top rosette of leaves at the soft tip to prevent wilting. Make a clean cut just below a node with a sharp knife.

Internodal cuttings are used for plants, such as *Buddleja davidii,* that have large internodal spacing. If nodal cuttings were used, then the rooted cutting would develop with a clear, short stem, whereas taking the cutting internodally allows shoots to break close to the base. The method is identical to that for nodal cuttings, apart from the fact that the cut is made at a point roughly halfway between two nodes.

FIG. 31 ROOT CUTTINGS

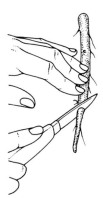

I Lift the plant from mid- to late winter

2 Carefully wash the roots and then with a sharp knife remove pencil-thick ones close to the crown

3 Return the plant to its position in the garden

4 Remove any fibrous laterals from the root cuttings

5 Make a flat cut at the top of the root (the end nearest to the stem)

6 Make a sloping cut at the bottom of the root

Root cuttings *(Fig. 31)* are taken less often commercially as a result of the advances and economics of softwood and semi-hardwood propagation. It remains, however, a suitable method for the domestic gardener. Listed here are some of the plants that can be raised by this method: *Ailanthus altissima, Amelanchier, Aralia, Bignonia capreolata, Albizia, Chaenomeles, Campsis radicans, Catalpa, Cladrastis lutea, Daphne, Gymnocladus dioica, Decaisnea fargesii, Koelreuteria paniculata, Embothrium coccineum, Paulownia tomentosa, Indigofera, Phellodendron amurense, Rhus, Rosa, Populus, Rubus, Sambucus, Robinia, Syringa, Sassafras albidum* and *Xanthoceras sorbifolium*.

Take root cuttings from mid- to late winter while the plant is dormant. First, lift the parent plant, expose and carefully wash some of the roots. Remove pencil-thick roots to make into cuttings 5cm (2in) long. Make a sloping cut at the bottom of the cutting, the distal end (the end furthest away from the stem) and a flat cut at the top, the proximal end. Dip the prepared cuttings into a fungicide; there is no need for a hormone rooting treatment. Insert the distal end into the medium until the tip is covered. The cuttings may also be laid flat and lightly covered with compost. Label and water well. Place the cuttings in a cold frame or a greenhouse or just cover in polythene. Do not for-

Prunus cerasifera 'Nigra' makes an excellent dense hedging shrub and is suitable for propagation by layering

7 Insert the bottom end of the root cutting into a compost-filled seed tray so that the top

of the root cutting is level with the surface of the compost
8 Label and water regularly

get to replant the parent plant returning it to its position in the garden.

LAYERING

Propagation by means of layering differs from other methods of asexual propagation in that the 'new addition' is induced to produce new roots while it is still attached to the parent plant. Once rooted, this 'new' plant is then severed from its parent or stock plant and allowed to grow on its own roots unaided. The easiest plants to produce by this method are those that naturally produce suckers. Many, such as *Rubus fruticosus* (blackberry), naturally reproduce themselves by this method. In fact, tip layering is the only method of propagation for the blackberry.

Layering is first recorded as having been used in 1608, but was probably practised much earlier. During the 18th, 19th and early 20th centuries, layering was widely used and, in many cases, was the primary method of propagation. The main problem with layering as a commercial production method is the amount of space occupied by the stock plants. However, it remains an excellent way to raise small numbers of plants for the gardener.

The following factors are required if the layer is to succeed. In all methods of layering the plant being layered is attached to the parent plant during the production of roots. This produces a larger plant in a much shorter time compared with other methods of propagation. Constriction must be induced within the stem to

FIG. 32 SIMPLE LAYERING

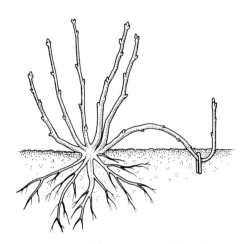

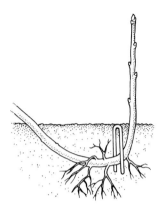

I Take a stem and pin it down just below the surface of the soil

2 Sufficient root development to allow the layer to be severed from the parent plant will usually have been made after one year

restrict the natural flow of auxin which acts as a rooting hormone at the point of restriction. The exclusion of light is thought to speed up the production of wound tissue and hence increase the speed of rooting.

Simple layering *(Fig. 32)* There are three main periods when simple layering can be undertaken: autumn, late winter and early spring. Spring and summer may be used when the stems of some

FIG. 33 STEM CONSTRICTION

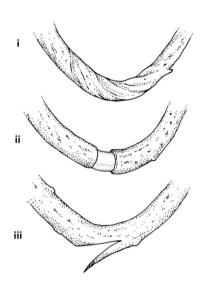

Methods of stem constriction required for simple, serpentine and air layering: (i) twisting is achieved by rotating each end of the stem in opposite directions and pinning down; (ii) girdling involves removing the top layer of bark as shown with a sharp knife; (iii) create a tongue by making an incision to a third of the thickness of the stem

plants, such as the flowering dogwoods (*Cornus kousa*, *C. nuttallii* and *C. florida*), may be too brittle during the winter months.

The method involves bending a stem and pegging it just below the surface of the soil. A mixture of peat and sand is often used as a rooting medium although just peat, sand, sawdust, coir or even the native soil can also be used. The stem is then constricted and staked; this can take the form of twisting the stem, girdling it or creating a tongue *(Fig. 33)*.

The constricted stem is pegged down into the soil; a cane may be used to keep it vertical. The developing layer should produce sufficient root growth within a year although, in some cases, two years may be required. The layer can be severed from the stock plant, as close to the parent as possible. After four to six weeks carefully lift it. The layer can either be placed in its permanent location or containerized and grown on.

Mound or stool layering *(Fig 34)* is undertaken during late winter. The stem of the parent plant is cut back hard to within 2.5cm (1in) of the soil to encourage shoots to develop near the base. Mounding-up is normally undertaken in two or three stages to avoid suffocating the parent plant. When the stems reach 15-20cm (6-8in), soil is mounded-up to approximately 5-7.5cm (2-3in). This is repeated in midsummer, mounding-up to half the height of the stem. Another mounding can be undertaken in late summer so that the total depth of the mound is approximately 15-20cm (6-8in). The first layers are severed from the parent plant two years after mounding, during late winter.

French or continuous layering *(Fig. 35)* is often used if more than one plant is required. Selected shoots of the parent plant

Cornus florida Rubra group is grown for its beautiful rosy-pink flower bracts which are carried in late spring. Layering is best carried out in spring and summer when the plant stems are less brittle

FIG. 34 MOUND OR STOOL LAYERING

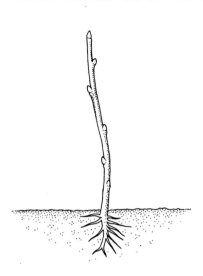

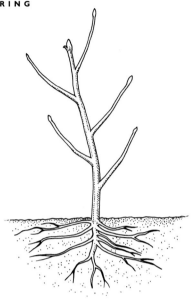

1 Plant the parent plant in winter and allow to establish during spring and summer

2 A substantial root system will have developed by one year after planting

3 In late winter, a year after planting, cut the stem back to 2.5cm (1in) above soil level to encourage shoots to develop at the base of the stem

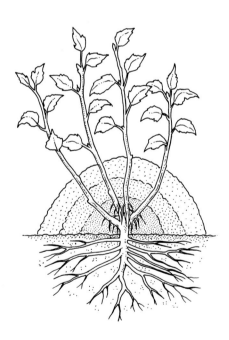

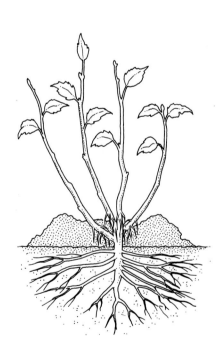

4 Mound the soil up in three stages: when the shoots are 15-20cm (6-8in) tall; in midsummer; in late summer

5 The first crop of layers are ready for harvesting one year after planting the parent plant

6 A single layer is removed ready for planting in a new site

FIG. 35   FRENCH OR CONTINUOUS LAYERING

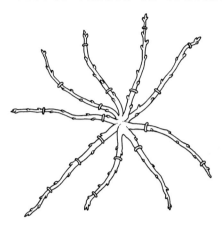

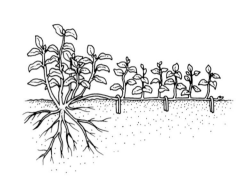

1 Select shoots of the parent plant and peg down during winter

2 New growth will develop uniformly along the pegged-down stem

3 When new growth reaches 10cm (4in) high, remove peg

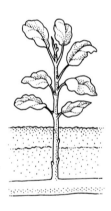

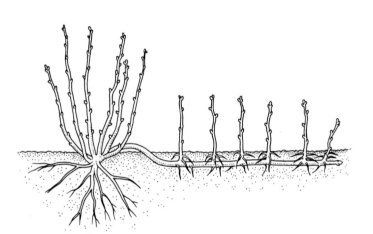

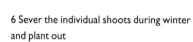

4 Mound up the developing shoots first in early summer and again in midsummer

5 Substantial root growth will have developed by the end of the growing season

6 Sever the individual shoots during winter and plant out

FIG. 36   SERPENTINE LAYERING

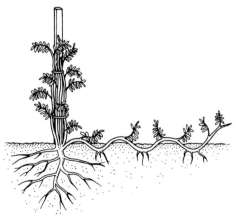

Suitable for climbers like clematis and wisteria, sufficient roots will have developed after one year from layering to allow the stem(s) to be severed from the parent plant for lifting and replanting the following autumn or winter

FIG. 37 AIR LAYERING

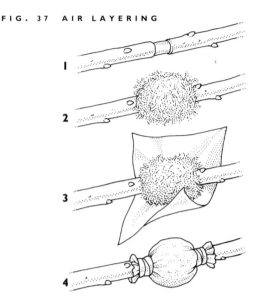

1 Girdle the stem or constrict it using an alternative method (Fig. 33).
2 Apply a powdered rooting compost to the cut surface and cover with damp sphagnum moss. 3 Wrap a square of black or opaque polythene around the sphagnum moss. 4 Secure the polythene at either end to the stem

are pegged down into the soil during winter. New growth develops along the stem. It should be uniform in habit and once it has reached a height of 10cm (4in), the pegs may be removed. The developing plants are then layered from side to side into shallow trenches. Developing shoots are mounded during early summer and again in midsummer. Substantial root growth should have developed on the layer by the end of the growing season. The horizontal stem is

Perhaps the most spectacular of all vines, *Vitis coignetiae* gives a magnificent autumn display. Propagation is best achieved by serpentine layering

then severed from the parent plant during winter and the individual layers can be potted up or field grown.

Serpentine layering *(Fig. 36)* was once widely used in the commercial production of climbing plants, such as wisteria and clematis and remains a valuable technique for the domestic gardner. It looks similar to the French layering, but multiple layers are produced without burying all the stem. This method is carried out during spring or autumn. The stems are girdled, twisted or tongued *(Fig 33)* before bending and are often laid in a circular pattern to save space. The constricted parts are then staked and buried in the ground. The stem is severed from the parent plant after one year for lifting and replanting the following autumn or winter.

Air layering *(Fig. 37)* was popular 4,000-5,000 years ago and is one of the oldest methods of vegetative propagation; it is also known as Chinese layering. It differs from other methods of layering as plants may be propagated in a glasshouse. It should be carried out between mid-spring and late summer. A constriction is made 12-30cm (5-12in) from the tip *(Fig. 33)* and a rooting hormone is applied to the cut surface to encourage root production (a powdered, semi-ripe hormone is commonly used). This area is then covered with damp sphagnum moss. Finally, wrap a square of black or opaque polythene around the moss to conserve moisture and improve humidity and secure on either side of the stem. Rooting may take up to two years out of doors. The layer can then be removed from the parent plant.

The following is a list of plants that can be propagated using different methods of layering:

SIMPLE LAYERING			
Amelanchier	Hamamelis	Pterocarya	Viburnum
Arbutus	Ilex	Rhododendron	
Azara	Kalmia	Syringa	**SERPENTINE LAYERING**
Camellia	Laurus	Tilia	Celastrus
Carpenteria	Liquidambar		Clematis
Chimonanthus	Magnolia	**CONTINUOUS LAYERING**	Lapageria
Corylopsis	Nothofagus	Acer cappadocicum	Jasminum
Corylus	Parrotia	Acer rubrum	Smilax
Daphne	Photinia	Acer saccharinum	Vitis
Davidia	Pieris	Alnus	Wisteria
Disanthus	Rhododendron	Amelanchier	
Distylium	Schizophragma	Cercidiphyllum	**AIR LAYERING**
Drimys	Syringa	Cornus	Daphne
Enkianthus		Cotinus	Drimys
Erica	**MOUND LAYERING**	Hoheria	Ficus
Eucryphia	Castanea	Hydrangea	Hamamelis
Fothergilla	Chaenomeles	Prunus	Magnolia
Halesia	Daphne	Stachyurus	Rhododendron
	Prunus	Syringa	

PESTS & DISEASES

TREES AND SHRUBS ARE CONSTANTLY AT RISK FROM ORGANISMS – ANIMAL, FUNGAL, VIRAL OR BACTERIAL – THAT CAUSE DAMAGE OR DISEASE. TO UNDERSTAND AND SO CONTROL THEM, THE GARDENER must first recognize the symptoms that betray their presence, and often these are all he or she has to go on. Most pathogens (disease-causing agents) are invisible to the naked eye, and insect pests rapidly move on once the damage is done.

Even if you were to keep your plants in optimum conditions they would still be attacked. So should pests and diseases be clinically eradicated at first sight? No, for this would harm the many beneficial organisms that co-exist with the plant. The key to successful control is an integrated system, whereby the cause is identified, monitored and dealt with in a measured way when visible damage begins to occur. At the same time control measures should be put in place to prevent a repeat invasion, identifying the conditions that create the opportunity and acting accordingly. Here, as elsewhere, prevention is better than cure. This chapter covers all the major pest and disease problems commonly associated with trees and shrubs, with information on identification and control.

PESTS

The term 'pest' encompasses all animals that cause damage to plants, including vertebrates, such as rabbits, deer, mice, moles and birds, as well as invertebrates, such as mites, snails, slugs, aphids and eel-worms. If a pest is seen causing damage to a plant, then identification is fairly easy. Very often, especially with smaller pests such as mites and eelworms, it is the symptoms which identify a problem. These symptoms vary from plant to plant, but are generally related to the damage they cause.

Insects, such as aphids, have needle-like mouthparts which they push into the soft tissues of the plant and use very much like straws to suck sugars from the living plant. Generally insects feed on the undersides of leaves and on the stems of soft growth. Many insects inject fluid into the plant which may transmit virus disorders. In this case the pest is known as a vector. Eelworms are virus vectors and in many cases deal the plant a double blow, as they not only live in the tissue and feed on the sap but also introduce a disease and reduce its vigour. The final group of pests have mouthparts that bite or rasp at plant foliage. These include caterpillars, slugs, snails, and many of the beetles and they may cause a lot of local-ized and conspicuous damage. It is generally either the adults or the larvae that cause most serious damage to woody plants.

Rabbits, squirrels and other small rodents can cause a great deal of damage to trees and shrubs. Deer may be a serious problem in larger gardens. Unfortunately, the various counter-measures usu-ally recommended are largely of mythical success. Bundles of human or lion hair, lights, music and soap, for example, may put off deer for a short while, but that is all. Other similar traditional deter-rents are equally ineffective. The only defences which work are an electric fence or a high deer fence (2m/6ft) and cattle grids in any gaps, such as a driveway. Rabbits can be excluded by a fence of similar height made of wire netting and dug into the ground to a depth of about 30cm (1ft) (see page 50).

Aphids Aphids are small sap-feeding insects which can be found feeding on soft stems and on the undersides of leaves. Their pres-ence weakens and distorts growth, resulting in loss of vigour. There are more than 500 species of aphid native to the British Isles and Europe, many of which are restricted to just a few host plants. It is possible to control aphids, even on large trees, but it is particularly important on a young plant whose development may be affected. If young trees and shrubs are attacked, use a systemic insecticide, insecticidal soap or hand pick every three weeks from early spring to midsummer and you will escape serious damage. Beneficial insects, such as ladybirds, may have limited effect.

Larger trees can also be treated with systemic insecticide, as it will be translocated throughout the tissues, but this is expensive. Applying insecticides to medium or large trees is a specialized job; contact your local arborist for advice.

Adelgids are sap-sucking insects 1-2mm ($^1/_{16}$-$^1/_8$in) long and cov-ered with a woolly, waxy, usually white substance. They are seri-ous pests on larches, spruce and silver firs. They also occur on Scots pines and some other members of the genus but do less damage: on dwarf pines they merely look unsightly. They can be treated by spraying with malathion or a systemic insecticide in spring.

Spruce gall adelgids produce small galls on Norway spruce, which may persist for many years. These interfere with normal growth and produce misshapen trees. In North America, control of the Hemlock adelgid, which is a serious pest of *Tsuga canadensis*, has been controlled using horticultural oils and insecticidal soaps.

Caterpillars

Generally speaking, the best method of dealing with caterpillars within reach is to pick them off, together with any eggs, and crush them or drop them into alchohol or paraffin, but any short-term contact insecticide, including derris, will kill them. Systemic insecticides are not particularly effective. While every effort should be made to control caterpillars on young or small plants, there is not much you can do when they occur on larger trees. Sometimes, however, natural control will take place, as with the oak tortrix moth, which has several predators.

Vine weevil Vine weevils are small, black beetles with fine yellow speckles. The larvae eat the roots of a wide range of plants and the adults make notches in the edges of leaves. The adults are active by night in late spring and early summer, hiding in the ground by day. Spray with a contact insecticide if they are visible. The larvae produce symptoms of apparently inexplicable wilt during summer. Closer inspection reveals that the plant's roots have been completely eaten and plump, white grubs with copper-coloured heads can be seen.

Control of the adults is by systemic pesticides, whereas the larvae can be controlled using a worm-like predatory nematode, which 'swims' through the soil and attacks the grubs. The nematode can be used outdoors only during summer.

DISEASES

Diseases are caused by parasitic organisms, including fungi, bacteria and viruses. Many of them are secondary pathogens, that is, they require an entry point, such as a wound or tissue damaged by an aphid (primary pathogen).

The most important secondary pathogens are fungi. They do not have chlorophyll (the green energy producing pigment found in plants), so they must find their food from another source – by breaking down plant tissues. Fungi absorb plant nutrients through their thread like 'roots' called hyphae (in mass they are termed mycelium). The mushrooms or toadstools which are produced are the fruiting bodies; it is these we use to help identify the pathogen.

Fungi are divided into two groups: obligate parasites which develop specialized hyphae able to drain nutrients from plant cells without killing the host; and facultative parasites which are far more destructive and grow into and between the plant cells. These produce toxic enzymes which seriously damage plant tissues.

Honey fungus, phytophthora root rot, mildews, rusts, blights, and wilts are examples of fungi pathogens.

Honey fungus (*Armillaria*) This attacks and kills a wide range of trees and shrubs and is common in old orchards or where tree stumps have not been removed. The fungus spreads by means of black, thread-like rhizomorphs, which can grow a considerable distance through the soil. They infect other plants that are either under stress or have been damaged. The fungus produces fruiting bodies (toadstools), growing on the bark of dead trees or shrubs. They are easily identified by the collar around the stem just under the hood. Honey fungus is very difficult to control; removal of infected wood, including the stumps, is imperative. Chemical or mechanical methods (laying of plastic boundaries) seem to have little effect, but forking over the soil will help to break up the rhizomorphs. Do not replant susceptible trees or shrubs. These include maple, birch, cedar, cypress, walnut, privet, apple, pine, cherry, rhododendron, willow, lilac, hemlock and elm.

Phytophthora root rot (*Phytophthora cinnamomi*)

This is a major cause of rot in conifers, heathers, rhododendrons, maples, chestnuts, lilacs, camellias and other woody plants. Phytophthora is a soil-borne fungus transmitted through soil water. The fungi infect roots and quickly disturb the water supply to the plant, resulting in foliage wilt, loss of normal colour and desiccation, causing the foliage to turn rusty brown. This colour change is most commonly seen during hot, dry, windy or freezing conditions, when plants are under water stress. The disease is prevalent on soils which waterlog easily and where plants are suffering for other reasons. Infected plants should be removed and so, too, should any plants showing symptoms.

Beech bark disease Caused by the fungus *Nectria coccinea* this is a serious disease of young and mature beech trees. It follows infestation by the felted beech coccus, a white, woolly, scale insect which feeds on the bark and leaves of beech trees. The feeding holes create a wound through which the fungus gains access to the tree's sap wood. Initially the wounds around the feeding insects exude sap and weep. Larger areas of bark and cambium die, resulting in yellowing of the foliage. In severe infestation small red or black bumps may develop on the bark, followed by further infection by decay fungi and boring insects. In the early stages the insect can be controlled by chemical sprays and this is best done during late spring. Large, heavily infected trees should be felled, as they quickly become unstable.

Rose rust and blackspot This disease has become more prevalent over recent years and is now a major debilitating fungal disease of roses. Orange pustules develop on the leafy stalks and particularly on the undersides of the leaves. Bushes can die quite rapidly. The pustules turn black in autumn and emit countless spores.

Blackspot is a fungal disease most prevalent where the air is clean. It rapidly defoliates roses, but is relatively easily kept in check by a regular spray programme and by mulching in winter. This prevents the spores from the previous year being splashed up on to the stems by rain.

Verticillium wilt This fungal disease causes die-back in spring. The foliage suddenly collapses and turns brown and the tree or shrub may suffer a severe setback to growth. It is spread in infected soil and penetrates the slightest wounds in the fine roots, such as those caused by the entry of eelworms. It persists in the tissues for only one year, so an older plant that has survived stands a reasonable chance of recovering. Young plants, however, are usually killed because their conducting tissues become totally blocked by the fungus. The organism may persist in the soil in the form of spores. Avoid planting susceptible plants in the same location.

Treatment is difficult but a systemic fungicide, made up in sufficient quantities to apply as a root drench, may alleviate the problems. The most frequently affected woody plant genera are *Acer*, *Catalpa*, *Tilia* and *Syringa*. It does not affect conifers.

BACTERIA

Bacteria are much smaller than fungi. Each one normally comprises a single, microscopic cell which may be rod-shaped, spherical or thread-like. They reproduce by simple division and can multiply rapidly, especially under warm conditions. They can cause high levels of damage to certain crops. Symptoms are very similar to that of fungal infection. It is worth stressing that bacterial infections are very difficult to control for few chemicals are effective against them.

Bacteria are responsible for diseases such as fireblight, canker, die-back, gall and leaf curl.

Fireblight (*Erwinia amylovora*) This is a serious disease of apples, hawthorns, cotoneasters, pyracanthas, pears, photinias, whitebeams and mountain ash. The bacterium usually enters the plant via the flowers or through open wounds. The infected branch then dies, with the leaves turning brown and remaining on the branch, looking as though they have been burned. In severe cases, re-infection occurs, leading to the death of the entire plant. Cut out infected material immediately by removing the entire branch. Seriously infected shrubs or trees should be removed completely and burned. Any equipment used in such an operation must be sterilized afterwards.

VIRUSES

Viruses and virus-like microscopic organisms are responsible for a wide range of diseases and disorders, such as cucumber mosaic, but also are responsible for creating aesthetic effects on ornamental plants, such as variegation, mottles, flower breaking and the production of green blooms.

Viruses are difficult to trace as they can mask themselves within the plant; the virus is present, but no obvious symptoms exist. It may be that the plant has reduced vigour. They are easily transported by propagation or by virus vectors.

It is important to keep your tools clean, particularly those with which you prune, trim or take cuttings. A virus that occurs among camellias – yellow mottle virus – produces irregular yellow patches on the leaves. It is known that it is not carried by insects in Europe, and the same is probably true in the United States and Australia. It is, however, easily transmitted on garden tools. Some people have propagated it for ornament, but this is a mistake, as an infected knife or secateurs can set up yellow mottle virus in healthy, green cuttings.

Examples of virus diseases are mosaic virus, malformation, ring spots, necrosis, leaf pucker, dwarfing and green flower.

PEST AND DISEASE CONTROL

Integrated pest management (IPM) This is the control of pests and diseases to keep them at an acceptable or threshold level above which visible damage occurs. It involves understanding the pest, its host range and the most effective methods of control. Control may be cultural, chemical and pesticidal, physical by means of the introduction and increase of natural predators or involve the use of biological control agents.

Cultural control Good cultural control practices lead to healthier plants. These include correct planting methods, adequate watering, using organic or inorganic fertilizers, mulching and removing dead and diseased material. Hygiene is also of the utmost importance; the removal of weeds, infected material and general cleanliness all help to reduce the level of pest infestation.

Chemical control No one wants to use more chemicals in the garden than absolutely necessary and of all garden chemicals, pesticides are the ones most people aim to cut down on. Used in moderation they can be manipulated to control a wide variety of pests. They are relatively easy to use and the success rate of control is very high. Since their introduction people have used them to control virtually everything that crawls or grows in the wrong place. Unfortunately, the over-use of certain pesticides has lead to an alarming increase in resistant strains of both pests and diseases.

It is always necessary to follow the manufacturer's instructions when using chemicals. Use a little common sense, too. Remember to store them away from children and pets and to keep them in their original containers under lock and key. To reduce the risk of promoting resistance use pesticides in rotation. Never use the same sprayer for herbicides and pesticides and always clean equipment thoroughly. Avoid mixing pesticides to create 'cocktails' to control a wider range of pests.

Physical or mechanical control This involves the use of mechanical traps and fencing or the physical removal of pests from a plant. For example, you may remove the small clusters of caterpillar eggs and destroy them. Later you may pick off caterpillars and drop them into alcohol or paraffin. Yellow sticky traps may be used to help control whitefly on a small scale.

Encouraging natural predators Before you can encourage natural predators, you have to establish whether they are friends or foes. Generally, insect pests move slowly because they do not require speed to catch their food – plants. Insect predators move quickly because they have to hunt their prey. Good examples of a gardener's friend are dragonflies, ladybirds, ground beetles and hoverflies, which eat large numbers of insect pests.

Biological control Probably the best known example of biological control is the destruction of the prickly pear (*Opuntia*) in eastern Australia during the first half of the twentieth century. The first, but unsuccessful attempt at biological control was in 1903. By 1925 this cactus weed had covered more than 20 million hectares of farmland. Research into the prickly pear in its native habitat led to the discovery of some 160 species of insects associated with it. Of these, 51 were imported into Australia between 1921 and 1935, and 13 became established. One species, the cactoblastis moth, was successful and caused the collapse of vast areas of prickly pear by 1940.

There are currently several biological control agents available. The commonest include *Encarsia formosa* against whitefly, *Phytoseulis persimilis* against red spider mite, *Cryptolaemus montrouzieri* against mealy bug, *Amblyseius cucumeris* against western flower thrip and *Bacillus thuringiensis* against caterpillars. Many of these are commonly used within a controlled environment, such as a glasshouse, although they could be used outdoors during the warmer months.

Biological control does not completely eradicate a pest, but keeps it below threshold level. If the pest were completely controlled, the predator would perish from lack of food.

Good cultivation and all-round hygiene make an enormous difference to the health of garden plants of all kinds, especially woody plants. Pests and diseases are the main subjects of questions asked by gardeners and cause a great deal of anxiety. This is entirely natural, but if you apply the same degree of concern to good cultivation and acute observation, you will find plant ailments much less threatening. When trouble occurs, prompt – even immediate – action is vital. Pests are pests and diseases are diseases largely because they share reproduction rates that verge on the incredible; early action pays true and lasting dividends.

Although generally easy and rewarding to cultivate, the acers are susceptible to attack by pests and diseases, the most serious of which is the honey fungus, causing sudden death

Pests and Diseases of Woody Plants

Genera	Pest or disease	Symptoms
Acer	Yellow aphids infest leaves during spring	Leaf curl, loss of vigour. Honeydew and sooty mould present
	Gall mites (summer)	Small red pimples on the upper leaf surface
	Coral spot	Die-back of branches. Small pink pimples appear on dead branches
	Honey fungus	Sudden death. Black thread-like rhizomorphs present near the trunk
	Phytophthora root rot	Foliage wilts, becomes brown and dies. Sudden death of tree
	Powdery mildew (summer)	White powdery coating on leaves and stems
	Verticillium wilt	Sudden wilting, withering and die-back of stems. Wood stained greenish-brown
Aesculus	Scale insect (summer)	White egg masses on the bark during summer. Adults brown 4mm long
	Bleeding canker of the stems	Stems ooze a yellow-brown black liquid which dries brown black
	Coral spot	Die-back of branches. Small pink pimples appear on dead branches
Amelanchier	Fireblight (summer)	Entire branch dies, with brown shrivelled leaves still attached
Berberis	Honey fungus	Sudden death. Black thread-like rhizomorphs present near the trunk
Betula	Aphids (summer)	Discoloration and distortion of leaves. Honeydew and sooty mould present
Buxus	Box sucker (summer)	Pale green insects suck sap from tips causing distorted growth
	Rust	Dark brown, powdery spots appear on both leaf surfaces
Camellia	Scale insect (summer)	Scale insect found on the large veins on the under leaf. Scale is yellow-brown
	Leaf blotch	Dull brown leaf blotch near the margin of the leaf. May feel bumpy (1-2cm wide)
	Twig blight	Young shoots wilt and die suddenly. Dead leaves turn dark brown or black
	Canker	Depressed canker growth often found on stems
	Die-back	Canker growth girdles the stem resulting in rapid death
	Phytophthora root rot	Foliage wilts, becomes brown and dies. Sudden death of tree
Caryopteris	Capsid bug (spring-summer)	Causes holes in foliage, which looks tattered by many small holes
Castanea	Phytophthora root rot	Foliage wilts, becomes brown and dies. Sudden death of tree
Ceanothus	Scale insect (summer)	Brown scale 6mm long. Willow scale 3mm long on underside of leaf
	Honey fungus	Sudden death. Black thread-like rhizomorphs present near the trunk
	Verticillium wilt	Sudden wilting, withering and die-back of stems. Wood stained greenish-brown
Cercis	Verticillium wilt	Sudden wilting, withering and die-back of stems. Wood stained greenish-brown
Chaenomeles	Fireblight (summer)	Entire branch dies, with brown shrivelled leaves still attached
Clematis	Vine weevil (spring-summer)	Sudden wilting caused by white, plump, copper headed larvae feeding on roots
	Clematis wilt (spring-summer)	Shoots die back rapidly often at the base of the plant. Stems turn black and rot
Conifers	Butt rot	Pustules appear near the base of plant which are reddish-brown with white margin
	Needle blight	Fungus causes foliage to yellow, then turn brown leading to die-back or death
	Phytophthora root rot	Foliage wilts, becomes brown and dies. Sudden death of tree
	Conifer spinning mite (summer)	Orange-red mites spin webs between needles which slowly turn yellow and fall
	Juniper scale	Small, white scale cover the needles and stems
	Juniper webbing moth (summer)	Small, brown caterpillars bind shoots together and feed. Needles turn brown
	Red spider mite	Needles turn brown
	Spruce aphid	Small, green-eyed aphid feeds on needles causing yellowing and leaf drop
	Pineapple gall adelgid	Causes pineapple-shaped galls on Picea abies
	Woolly aphid	White, woolly insects cover the shoots and needles of plants, causing yellowing
Cotinus	Powdery mildew (summer)	White, powdery coating appears on new leaves, causing distortion
	Verticillium wilt	Sudden wilting, withering and die-back of stems. Wood stained greenish-brown
Cotoneaster	Hawthorn webbing moth (spring)	Reddish-brown caterpillar spins a fine web. Feeding caterpillars turn leaves brown
	Fireblight (summer)	Entire branch dies, with brown shrivelled leaves still attached
	Honey fungus	Sudden death. Black thread-like rhizomorphs present near the trunk
	Silver leaf	Foliage silver in appearance, bracket-shaped fungus emerges out of dead branches
Crataegus	Hawthorn webbing moth (spring)	Reddish-brown caterpillar spins a fine web. Feeding caterpillars turn leaves brown
	Fireblight (summer)	Entire branch dies, with brown shrivelled leaves still attached
Daphne	Crown Gall	Swellings develop at intervals along stems and roots
	Leaf spots	Causes loss of vigour and defoliation
Euonymus	Black bean aphid (summer)	Aphids feed on foliage causing distortion and curling of foliage
	Scale insect (summer-autumn)	2mm long whitish-brown scale on stems and leaves causing loss of vigour
Fagus	Beech bark disease (summer)	Large areas of bark lift off the stem. Branches die, tree becomes unstable
	Beech scale (summer)	White powdery insect inhabit natural cracks in the trunk and branches
	Woolly aphid (summer)	Greyish-white, powdery insect on underside of leaves and shoot tips
	Phytophthora root rot	Foliage wilts, becomes brown and dies. Sudden death of tree
	Coral spot	Die-back of branches. Small pink pimples appear on dead branches
Forsythia	Bullfinches (winter-spring)	Eat flower buds during winter, resulting in shoots with no flowers
	Honey fungus	Sudden death. Black thread-like rhizomorphs present near the trunk
Heathers	Needle blight	Fungus causes foliage to yellow, then turn brown leading to die-back or death
	Phytophthora root rot	Foliage wilts, becomes brown and dies. Sudden death of plant
Hebe	Downy mildew (summer)	White mildew appears on the underside, with pale white blotches on upper foliage
	Phytophthora root rot	Foliage wilts, becomes brown and dies. Sudden death of tree
Hydrangea	Red spider mite (summer)	Foliage speckled with small, white blotches. Characteristic webbing on top leaves
	Powdery mildew (summer)	Brown spots with white coating on upper and lower surface of leaves
	Honey fungus	Sudden death. Black thread-like rhizomorphs present near the trunk
Hypericum	Rust	Orange pimples on underside of foliage, turn reddish brown
Ilex	Leaf miner	Irregular, purple-yellow blotches on leaves. Maggots feed inside leaf
Laburnum	Leaf miner	Irregular, purple-yellow blotches on leaves. Maggots feed inside leaf
	Silver leaf (spring)	Foliage silver in appearance, bracket-shaped fungus emerges out of dead branches
	Honey fungus	Sudden death. Black thread-like rhizomorphs present near the trunk
Laurus	Bay sucker (summer)	Greyish insects suck the sap of leaves causing curl, and resulting in brown spots

Genera	Pest or disease	Symptoms
Lavendula	Froghoppers (summer)	Juvenile stage feeds below 'cuckoo spit' on stems and flowers
	Shab	Young shoots loose vigour during late spring, wilting then death
Ligustrum	Thrips (summer)	2mm long yellow or brown-black. Feed on upper leaf causing a dull silver sheen
	Honey fungus	Sudden death. Black thread-like rhizomorphs present near the trunk
Lonicera	Aphid (spring-summer)	Grey-black aphids feed on shoots and flowers in summer. Can cause shoot death
	Whitefly (summer)	White-winged insects 1mm long cause leaf discoloration
Magnolia	Honey fungus	Sudden death. Black thread-like rhizomorphs present near the trunk
	Squirrels (Grey)	Bite into unopened flowers causing them to fall early
Mahonia	Powdery mildew (summer)	White powdery coating on young leaves
	Rusts	Red pimples appear on upper surface, powdery, brown spots on under surface
Malus	Canker	Sunken zones of bark around branches and stems, occasional death of branches
	Coral spot	Die-back of branches. Small pink pimples appear on dead branches
	Fireblight (summer)	Entire branch dies, with brown shrivelled leaves still attached
	Honey fungus	Sudden death. Black thread-like rhizomorphs present near the trunk
	Powdery mildew (summer)	White powdery coating on young leaves
	Scab (summer-autumn)	Fruits become spotted and distorted
	Apple replant disease	Greatly reduced root system results in loss of vigour. Avoid planting in area
Photinia	Powdery mildew (summer)	White powdery coating on young leaves
Pieris	Phytophthora root rot	Foliage wilts, becomes brown and dies. Sudden death of tree
Platanus	Anthracnose	Failure of buds to open in spring, stem death, wood stained orange-yellow
Populus	Leaf spots	Small, blackish brown spots on foliage which fall prematurely
	Rusts	Yellow-orange pimples on foliage which falls prematurely
	Honey fungus	Sudden death. Black thread-like rhizomorphs present near the trunk
	Silver leaf	Foliage silver in appearance, bracket-shaped fungus emerges out of dead branches
	Yellow leaf blister	Foliage bears bright yellow blisters, which cause distortion
Prunus	Bacterial canker	Cankers ooze gum-like liquid causing death of branches which may look flattened
	Peach leaf curl (spring-summer)	Young foliage is thick and tinged orange, old leaves are distorted, red and white
	Silver leaf	Foliage silver in appearance, bracket-shaped fungus emerges out of dead branches
	Powdery mildew (summer)	White powdery coating on young leaves
	Cherry replant disease	Plants grown in soil where other cherries were once grown lose vigour
	Shothole	Holes appear in foliage, ragged edge in deciduous spp, round edge in evergreen
Pyracantha	Fireblight (summer)	Entire branch dies, with brown shrivelled leaves still attached
Quercus	Gall wasps	Small galls on roots, shoots and acorns
	Powdery mildew	White powdery coating on young leaves
Rhododendron (inc. Azalea)	Lace bug (summer)	4mm yellow-brown insects feed on foliage causing yellow mottling
	Leafhopper (summer)	6mm metallic-green insects with orange stripes feed on foliage. Eggs laid in buds
	Bud blast (summer-autumn)	Infected buds turn black, brown or silver, covered in black pimples, flower aborts
	Whitefly (summer)	White-winged insects 1mm long cause leaf discoloration
	Weevils	Feed on foliage producing notches along the leaf edge
	Powdery mildew (summer)	White powdery coating on young leaves
	Honey fungus	Sudden death. Black thread-like rhizomorphs present near the trunk
	Phytophthora root rot	Foliage wilts, becomes brown and dies. Sudden death of tree
	Leaf spot and stem die-back	Silver-grey lesions on leaves, which form rings of dead tissue causing die-back
Rosa	Aphids (summer)	Green or pink aphids cause reduced vigour and leaf and flower disfiguration
	Red spider mite (summer)	Leaves become bronze, mottled yellow and fall prematurely
	Leafhopper (summer)	Pale yellow 3mm insects cause loss of colour to foliage
	Thrips (summer)	2mm long yellow to brown insects cause brown mottling to upper leaf surface
	Leaf rolling sawfly (summer)	Leaves become tightly rolled, small green caterpillars feed on leaves
	Slug Sawfly (summer)	Slug-like insect larvae, white-green with brown heads graze on leaves
	Capsid bugs (summer)	Pale green insects cause leaves to develop numerous small holes
	Blackspot (summer-autumn)	Fungus causes round, black spots to appear on the leaves
	Powdery mildew (summer)	White powdery fungal growths on new stems, leaves and flowers
	Rusts	Orange pimples appear on leaves, followed by brown ones in late season
	Honey fungus	Sudden death. Black thread-like rhizomorphs present near the trunk
	Verticillium wilt	Sudden wilting, withering and die-back of stems. Wood stained greenish-brown
Salix	Large willow aphid (summer-autumn)	Dark brown aphid forms dense colonies on the stems. Produce honeydew
	Scale (summer)	Greyish-white, pear-shaped scale insects 3mm long cover the bark
	Sawflies (summer)	Caterpillars completely defoliate willows
	Anthracnose (spring)	Fungus causes small brown spots on foliage and black cankers on stems
	Honey fungus	Sudden death. Black thread-like rhizomorphs present near the trunk
Senecio (*Bracyglotis*)	Phytophthora root rot	Foliage wilts, becomes brown and dies. Sudden death of tree
Sorbus	Blister mite (summer)	Microscopic mites cause pale green blotches on leaves which slowly turn brown
	Fireblight (summer)	Entire branch dies, with brown shrivelled leaves still attached
	Silver leaf	Foliage silver in appearance, bracket-shaped fungus emerges out of dead branches
Syringa	Leaf mining moth (summer)	White larvae feeds inside mines within the leaf, roll up the tips to pupate
	Blight (spring-summer)	Brown spots develop on leaves, causing blackening and death of shoots
	Honey fungus	Sudden death. Black thread-like rhizomorphs present near the trunk
	Phytophthora root rot	Foliage wilts, becomes brown and dies. Sudden death of tree
Tilia	Aphids (summer)	Infest underside of leaves causing honeydew and sooty mould
	Nail gall mite (summer)	Cause 3mm tall, red upright structures on upper leaf surface, in which mites live
	Coral spot	Die-back of branches. Small pink pimples appear on dead branches
	Verticillium wilt	Sudden wilting, withering and die-back of stems. Wood stained greenish-brown
Vaccinium	Phytophthora root rot	Foliage wilts, becomes brown and dies. Sudden death of tree
Viburnum	Aphids (spring-summer)	Cause leaf curling in spring and summer
	Viburnum beetle	7mm, grey-brown beetles - 7mm yellow larvae with black marking damage leaves
	Viburnum whitefly	Small, white insects feed on *V. tinus*, white, waxy fringed scale over winter
	Honey fungus	Sudden death. Black thread-like rhizomorphs present near the trunk

Control of Pests and Diseases

Pest/Disease	Chemical Control-Frequency	Mechanical	Biological/natural
Adelgid	Malathion, dimethoate, permethrin 7-14 days	remove infected foliage	
Anthracnose	Bordeaux mixture 14 days	collect infected leaves, burn	
Aphids	Malathion, dimethoate, permethrin 7-14 days	remove or wash off	ladybirds, hoverflies
Apple/Cherry replant	Do not plant back into the same location	remove infected plants	
Beech scale	Malathion, permethrin, dimethoate 14 days	wash off with pressurized water	
Blackspot	Benomyl, Bordeaux mixture, captan 10-14 days	remove infected plants/leaves	
Box sucker	Malathion, permethrin, dimethoate 14-21 days	remove infested leaves	
Canker	Benomyl, Bordeaux mixture 14-21 days	remove infected branches	
Capsid bugs	Dimethoate, malathion, formothion 14-21 days	remove old foliage in winter	
Caterpillars	Permethrin, trichlophon, carbaryl 7-14 days	remove, grease bands	Bacillus thuringiensis
Clematis wilt	Benomyl, Bordeaux mixture 14-21 days	plant deeper to protect stems	
Conifer butt rot	Treat cut stumps with urea	remove infected stumps/plants	Peniophora antagonistic fungi
Coral spot	Spray infected plants with thiophanate-methyl 7 days	remove infected branches/plants	
Crown Gall		prune to healthy wood	
Downy mildew	Zineb, mancozeb 14 days	remove infected leaves	
Fireblight	Remove infected branches 60cm below visual signs of infection	remove completely infected plants	
Froghoppers	Dimethoate, malathion 14-21 days	spray with water under pressure	Birds
Honey fungus		remove stumps/infected plants	
Lace bug	Dimethoate, malathion, formothion 14-21 days	remove eggs from young leaves	
Leaf hopper	Malathion, dimethoate, formothion 7 days	remove infected buds	
Leaf miner	Malathion, dimethoate, formothion (adults)	remove infested leaves	
Leaf spots	Benomyl, Bordeaux mixture 14 days	remove infected leaves	
Mites	Malathion, dimethoate, demeton-S-methyl 7-14 days	spray foliage with water	
Needle blight	Benomyl 14 days	remove infected plants	
Peach leaf curl	Bordeaux mixture 14 days	collect infected and fallen leaves	
Phytophthora root rot		remove infected plants/ improve drainage	
Powdery mildew	Benomyl, carbendazim, thiram 10-14 days	remove infected leaves	
Red spider mite	Dimethoate, permethrin 10-14 days	spray with water	Phytoseulis persmilis in summer
Rusts	Benodanil, maneb, zineb 10-14 days	remove infected leaves	
Sawflies	Malathion, permethrin, dimethoate 14-21 days	remove infested leaves	
Scab	Benomyl, captan, mancozeb 14 days	remove infected fruits	
Scale insect	Dimethoate, diazinon, deltamethrin 14-21 days	paint with methylated spirit	
Shab	Bordeaux mixture, thiram 14 days	remove infected stems/plants	
Shothole	Bordeaux mixture, benomyl, captan 14 days	collect infected leaves	
Silver leaf	Wound dressing containing thiophanate-methyl	prune in summer	rub wound with garden soil- may contain Trichoderma
Stem die-backs/ twig blight	Bordeaux mixture, benomyl, captan 14 days	prune out infected parts	
Thrips	Malathion, carbaryl, cypermethrine 7-14 days	blue sticky traps	Amblyseius (predator)
Verticillium wilt	Benomyl, thiram, carbendazim 10-14 days	remove infected plants	
Viburnum beetle	Malathion, permethrin, dimethoate 14-21 days	remove infested leaves	
Vine weevil (adults)	Chlorpyrifos, gamma HCH	trap adults in grease traps	
Vine weevil (larvae)	Gamma HCH	remove dead leaves	Heterorhadbitis (parasite)
Whitefly	Malathion, dimethoate, demeton-S-methyl 7-14 days	remove leaves, yellow traps	Encarsia formosa
Woolly aphid	Malathion, permethrin, dimethoate 14 days	remove infected leaves	
Yellow leaf blister	Bordeaux mixture 14 days	collect infected leaves and burn	

The vigorous Hydrangea macrophylla 'Blue Wave' is generally trouble free although it is vulnerable to powdery mildew and the more serious honey fungus

PLANT NAMES

SHAKESPEARE WOULD HAVE UNDERSTOOD THOSE WHO SHY AWAY FROM BOTANICAL NAMES. IN PART II OF HENRY VI, JACK CADE EXCLAIMS, 'AWAY WITH HIM! AWAY WITH HIM! HE SPEAKS LATIN!' It is a sentiment you might find yourself directing against botanists when the Latin names of plants seem to get longer and appear constantly to be changing. Indeed, botanical Latin is regarded by many people as consisting of long, eminently forgettable words coined by cryptographers with a strong streak of sadism. Nothing, however, could be further from the truth.

There are exceptions of course. Even if you sympathized with the reasons for the change, you might find it hard to understand why the creeping dogwood *Cornus canadensis* has also been known as *Chamaepericlymenum canadense*. Nevertheless, the botanical names of plants are there to help everyone, and when changes occur they usually (but not quite always) do so in the interests of knowledge and understanding.

WHY NOT USE COMMON NAMES?

Our garden plants are trawled from all corners of the world, in relatively few of which is the English language traditional or even current. Those who demand 'English' or 'common' names for plants will find themselves up against more than one obstacle, not the least of which is the fact that botany and horticulture are international and other people have proper, legitimate common names in their own vernaculars. In Mexico, for example, there is a tree whose botanical name is *Cheirostemon platanoides*. It has no English equivalent to its Mexican name, as its relatives Cacahuatl (cacao) and Xocoatl (chocolate) have. This is not entirely surprising, as the only vernacular name it possesses is Macpalxochitlquahuitl. Would you not agree that the Latin is a positive relief?

English itself should not be regarded as one vernacular. There are several, as anyone who has crossed the Atlantic can certify. In North America, wake robin is *Trillium grandiflorum*; in Britain it is *Arum maculatum*; in North America the sycamore is a plane, *Platanus occidentalis*, in Britain it is a maple, *Acer pseudoplatanus*. Even within Britain itself, one vernacular cannot be said to exist as far as plant names are concerned. *Arum maculatum* has many 'common' names besides wake robin – among which are lords and ladies, stallions and mares, priest in the pulpit, priest's pintle and cuckoo pint (pronounced with a short i) to name but a few.

Beyond mere names, you run into all sorts of complications when you try to be specific about plants. For instance, the bloody cranesbill is a species of geranium native to Europe. In one locality on the coast of Lancashire, England, it is light pink instead of magenta-pink. The botanical name of this form is *Geranium sanguineum* var. *lancastriense*. Something of a mouthful, you might say. But then, how do you define the plant otherwise? Any such attempt would produce a sentence such as: 'The light pink form of the bloody cranesbill that grows almost exclusively on Walney Island, near Barrow-in-Furness, Lancashire, England' – because it is not the only lightly coloured form, but a specific one.

By using one word – *lancastriense* – we define not only the plant but its specific place of origin, and imply its colour. Similarly, in using the Latin name of the birch *Betula albosinensis* var. *septentrionalis*, we define it as the northern form of this Chinese species, but also imply by definition that it is the form with matt instead of glossy leaves and bark which is more peachy-coppery-pink than just coppery-pink.

THE BINOMIAL SYSTEM

Prior to the great Linnaeus (1707-78), botanists struggled in much the same way to describe plants using Latin, the language of herbalists and botanists since ancient times. You would perhaps have had some justification for complaint at having to find labels long enough for *Tulipa globosa serotina aureo-colore punctata* or *Hyacinthus stellatus Aquitanicus coeruleo flore* – and those are mild examples.

The triumph of Linnaeus was to reduce plant names such as *Ranunculus seminibus aculeatis foliis superioribus decompositis linearibus* to two basic components, in this case *Ranunculus arvensis*. These are perhaps analogous to forename and surname. Provided that a recognized and authoritative description of the plant concerned was published in a proper manner this 'binomial', followed by the name of the author, would refer to that species and to that only and, moreover, to the 'type' the specific specimen described.

Family and Genus Biological classification is a system of sorting organisms into related groups of ever-decreasing sizes. You start, for example, with two Kingdoms, Animal and Plant. The largest groupings that really concern gardeners are families. The term 'family' is often used mistakenly by non-botanists. For example, you will quite often hear gardeners saying something like, 'It is a member of the cotoneaster family', when there is actually no such thing. In fact, cotoneasters belong to the rose family, which is properly called Rosaceae, but it does not mean that they are roses. The grouping they really mean is the *genus*. Cotoneasters belong to the genus *Cotoneaster* and roses to the genus *Rosa*: both *genera* belong to the Family Rosaceae, because in scientific terms their flowers, seeds and so on are similar in composition.

In this book, you will find that the general entry for *Cotoneaster* begins with its generic name, followed by the name of the family. The first specific entry after this general one is for *Cotoneaster adpressus*. The generic name constitutes in effect the surname, while the specific epithet (in this case *adpressus*) plays the part of the forename (but comes second, as in Chinese usage) and closely defines the species, whose species name is *Cotoneaster adpressus*. Generic names are always spelt with capital initial letters and specific epithets with lower-case ones.

Species The concept of species is not always an easy one to grasp and is often misunderstood by gardeners. A species is an assemblage of individuals that have the same constant and distinctive characters. However, this is not to say that every member of a species is identical with any other: there is a degree of variation, be it ever so small. In the colour blue, for example, there is a wide range of blueness, although blue as a definitive characteristic of the flowers of a species may always be present. Were there no variation of characteristics within a species, there would be no evolution and neither you nor I would be here.

Within a species, the grading of characteristics may be infinitesimal, but individuals at the extremes may seem so different as not to be the 'same plant'. 'Educated' gardeners may be heard at shows murmuring that such-and-such is not 'true to type' – a phrase that reveals a world of misapprehension. This is one of the main sources of friction between gardeners and botanists: gardeners, whose 'common sense' tells them that two 'species' are self-evidently distinct, cannot understand why the botanists declare that they are in fact one and the same. Unfortunately, they do not see the whole picture, and the expert on the genus (who does) is in a much better position to judge.

Subspecies, Varietas and Forma If you stick strictly to binomials you fail to take account of the minor classifications that can be bolted on, as it were, to the species. These subordinate divisions are, in order of descent, subspecies, varietas and forma. Thus, in the species *Cornus kousa*, there is an assemblage of individuals that are taller than the typical form and have somewhat larger leaves. The differences are within the range of variation within the species, but are regarded as worth recognizing as distinct. These plants are given the rank of variety as *Cornus kousa* var. *chinensis*. As *Cornus kousa* covers both the typical form and var. *chinensis*, plants which do not belong to this variety should technically be referred to as *C. kousa* var. *kousa*, a practice which is rarely adopted in horticulture.

Subspecies is the next division down from species. Varietas (not to be confused with the loosely used variety, which often does duty for cultivar) comes next, while forma is the last refuge into which botanists can place plants which they think are sufficiently distinct.

'Think' is the operative word. Subspecies, varietas and forma are, ultimately, matters of opinion. However, we should by no means dismiss them, as the differences even at the level of forma, while relatively insignificant to a scientist, may be of considerable importance to a gardener, especially where such matters as habit and flower colour are involved. For example, *Indigofera decora* f. *alba* has white flowers rather than the pink of the species, but is not significantly different from it in other ways. *Stuartia pseudocamellia* var. *koreana* comes from a Korean population of the species characterized by better autumn colour and wider-opening flowers – sufficiently different from the Japanese population to warrant its rank. *Rhododendron fortunei* – the typical form of the species – has bell-shaped, lilac-pink flowers in trusses and flowers in late spring. *R. fortunei* subsp. *discolor* has funnel-shaped, pink flowers in very much larger trusses and flowers in early to midsummer. These, along with differences in habit, have influenced the balance of respected opinion to place it, for now at any rate, in the rank of subspecies.

The bolting-on of subdivisions of a species does not invalidate the binomial system. Species are designated by generic name and species epithet, but the minor categories are a little like the Welsh habit of defining people with the same name, as in Thomas Jones Cefn Mawr and Thomas Jones Cefn Bach. Their Thomas-Jones-ness is not changed by the bolted-on reference to their respective farms.

When it comes down to it, you are unlikely either to remember or to care whether it is subspecies (subsp.), variety (var.) or forma (f.) that is involved in a particular case, and we usually write *Cornus kousa chinensis* on our labels. This looks very much like a trinomial – but so what? As long as we have a working understanding of the system it matters little.

Garden Varieties, Cultivars and Clones It does matter, however, that we should firmly distinguish between variety in the botanical sense and in its purely colloquial, gardening use. Perhaps it is better to stick to the formal Latin varietas for the former. Be that as it may, the word variety has another meaning entirely, but one that is not recognized by botanists, when applied to those plants that have a fancy name in a vernacular tongue added on to the species name.

For example, *Cornus kousa* 'Satomi' is a garden variety of the species we have been discussing. You will note that, whereas the Latin components of this and every other name are written in italics, and that everything below genus has a lower-case initial, this vernacular name is in Roman letters, has an upper-case initial, and is between single inverted commas. This convention should be followed closely by gardeners, as it avoids a great deal of unnecessary confusion. The correct term for a garden variety of this sort, is 'cultivar'.

A clone is an individual grown from a piece of a parent plant by means other than seed, and is not only identical to its parent but also in reality the same plant. A tree or shrub cultivar does not actually have to be a clone but almost always is, and you can take it that if you purchase or are given a tree or shrub with a cultivar name it will have been propagated vegetatively – from cuttings, root cuttings, layering, budding or grafting – and will be identical to any other correctly labelled tree or shrub carrying the same cultivar (garden variety) name.

The difference between a botanical variety and a cultivar is that whereas a botanical variety is distinguished from the typical form by botanical characters which may or may not be relevant to gardeners, a cultivar has been selected by man either from the wild or from a garden, for a feature or features that make that plant worth maintaining in cultivation by vegetative propagation. These features, for example, variegated foliage, larger, differently coloured or double flowers, or a variation in habit giving a weeping, prostrate or upright plant, distinguish the cultivar from the form or forms normally found in gardens. Here, though, opinion comes in, and many gardeners will be found who tend strongly to prefer the simpler, wild forms to those that may be larger, more brightly coloured, double or 'improved'.

HYBRIDS

A hybrid is a cross between two species. A cross may produce many individual plants, all of which are different from one another. They are all indicated by one name, which is in Latin and contains the symbol 'x'. This name includes back-crosses. Thus, *Viburnum* x *burkwoodii* is the name for all hybrids between *V. carlesii* and *V. utile*. The plant that bears the name *V.* x *burkwoodii* 'Park Farm Hybrid' is a particular, rather more spreading form, while *V.* x *b.* 'Anne Russell' and 'Fulbrook' are back-crosses with *V. carlesii*.

Most hybrids are between plants in the same genus. Hybrids involving different genera occur infrequently in woody plants but examples include x *Cupressocyparis* (*Chamaecyparis* x *Cupressus*) and x *Fatshedera*, (*Fatsia* x *Hedera*). These take the equivalent of specific epithets, as in x *Fatshedera lizei* and cultivar names, such as x *F.l.* 'Annemieke'.

NAME CHANGES

Nothing annoys gardeners more than name changes. They are not the currency of an amateur gardener's working life and are thus an unwanted complication of a leisure pursuit. However, most name changes result from a better understanding of the plants involved and give gardeners a better idea of their relationships. It was not that long ago that *Mahonia* was included in *Berberis* but today, most gardeners and botanists accept that, although closely related, they are quite distinct genera.

Of course, these changes do mean that we can occasionally lose a familiar name or gain an unfamiliar one. For example, William Fox-Strangways, fourth Earl of Ilchester (1793-1865), was honoured during the nineteenth century by the naming of the shrub genus *Stranvaesia*. During the latter part of the twentieth it was absorbed into *Photinia* and the Fox-Strangways family lost their foothold in botanical nomenclature for good and sufficient scientific reasons. It is most unlikely that *Stranvaesia* will ever be resurrected and with good reason, as there is really nothing to separate it as a genus from *Photinia*.

We can rest happy with the fact that the trend in both botany and horticulture is now very much away from unnecessary name changes and is focusing strongly on the stability of plant names.

Although name changes will always be with us, they are likely to be less frequent than in the past.

Reasons for change There are several broad reasons for name changes, often based on new methods of diagnosis, such as chromosome analysis, but sometimes on pure academic research. Scientific advance may reveal that a plant simply cannot any longer be regarded as belonging to the genus or species in which it has been included. It may show that a genus is too varied and that it should be split into smaller ones – or conversely, opinion may converge on the view that several others have hitherto been separated by considerations that are more nit-picking than scientific.

It happens more than occasionally that the laws governing the naming of plants have been breached in the case of a particular plant or plant grouping. In this case, as long as its naming was post-Linnaeus, the matter must be rectified. For example, if a name was published for plant X by John Doe, it would not matter that it had become universally accepted if it were later discovered that Richard Roe had published the same name for plant Y one year previously. A new name for X would have to be found.

Fancy, or cultivar names, cannot be changed frivolously. They have to be properly published in an article or a nursery catalogue. Translation is permitted, as when 'Neige de Juillet' might become 'July Snow'; but you cannot change it to 'Summer White'. We are no longer allowed to use honorifics such as 'Mrs', 'Madame' and 'Professor-Doktor', and similar modesty should prevail whenever we imagine we have developed a new, improved cultivar. The chances are that there are better ones around already.

PRONUNCIATION

The most self-confident people fall prey to all sorts of fears when faced with pronouncing botanical names. There is no need. The purpose of botanical names is to identify plants, not to impress others; as long as you get across what you mean, it matters not one whit how you do so – clarity and precision are what count.

Botanical Latin is not a classical language; nor is it a dead one. It is the living language of the herbalists and botanists and has been so continuously since Classical Latin died after giving birth to the Romance languages. Besides, the Latin of ordinary people was as varied in its pronunciation as English is today.

Academic Latin has three systems of pronunciation. There is the English system (Giulius Seezer), the Reformed Academic (Yewlius K-eye-sar), and Church Latin, which is characterized by elements of modern Italian speech, such as 'ch' as in *Citrus*. For example, the first two allow *caespitosa* (growing in short tufts) to be pronounced either as sea-spit-oh-sa or as k-eye-spit-oh-sa, while a Roman Catholic cleric might be tempted towards chay-spit-oh-sa. The whole thing falls down with a satisfying thud, though, when an Edinburgh graduate says cess-pit-oh-sir and frees you to do as you please.

Plants which are apparently unrelated in practical gardening terms have botanical characteristics drawing them into the same family. For example, *Cotoneaster* 'Hybridus Pendulus' is in the rose family, *Rosaceae*

PLANT SELECTOR

MANY FACTORS INFLUENCE PLANT CHOICE BUT SUCCESS IN THIS FIELD IS STRONGLY LINKED TO THE ATTENTION PAID TO SITUATION AND SOIL CHARACTERISTICS. THIS CHAPTER AIMS TO PROVIDE A selection of recommended trees and shrubs for particular sites and specific effects. It is neither comprehensive nor does it necessarily recommend that a particular specimen be planted only in the situation within which it is listed: a great many plants grow happily in a wide range of locations.

Plants for Clay Soils

Clay soils are sticky and unworkable when wet and can set like concrete when dry. On the other hand, they tend to be fertile and, if sympathetically worked, can be among the most satisfactory of garden soils. If attention is given to providing the best drainage possible, a very wide range of trees and shrubs can be grown even on dense clays.

Abies lasiocarpa 'Compacta', grown for its attractive grey-green leaves, is a conifer suitable for clay soils

TREES
Acer (all)
Aesculus (all)
Alnus (all)
Betula (all)
Carpinus (all)
Crataegus (all)
Eucalyptus (all)
Fraxinus (all)
Ilex (all)
Laburnum (all)
Malus (all)
Platanus (all)
Populus (all)
Prunus (all)
Quercus (all)
Salix (all)
Sorbus (all)
Tilia (all)

SHRUBS
Abelia (all)
Aralia elata and cvs
Aronia (all)

Aucuba japonica and cvs
Berberis (all)
Chaenomeles (all)
Choisya (all)
Colutea (all)
Cornus (all)
Corylus (all)
Cotinus (all)
Cotoneaster (all)
Cytisus (all)
Deutzia (all)
Escallonia (all)
Forsythia (all)
Genista (all)
Hamamelis (all)
Hibiscus syriacus and cvs
Hypericum (all)
Lonicera (all)
Mahonia (all)
Magnolia (all)
Osmanthus (all)
Philadelphus (all)
Potentilla (all)
Pyracantha (all)

Rhododendron Hardy Hybrids
Ribes (all)
Rosa (all)
Senecio 'Sunshine'
Skimmia (all)
Spiraea (all)
Symphoricarpos (all)
Viburnum (all)
Weigela (all)

CONIFERS
Abies (all)
Chamaecyparis (all)
Juniperus (all)
Larix (all)

Pinus (all)
Taxodium (all)
Taxus (all)
Thuja (all)

BAMBOOS
Fargesia
Phyllostachys (all)
Pleioblastus (all)
Pseudosasa japonica
Sasa (all)
Sinarundinaria (all)
Thamnocalamus
Yushania (all)

Plants for Dry, Acid Soils

Dry, acid soils, like those that occur in light, sandy heathland, can be greatly improved by the incorporation of organic material. They are, however, difficult to manage in drought and tend to be among the less fertile.

Many plants are perfectly adapted to dry, acid conditions and some of the great nurseries were founded on them. Such soils are easy to work and warm up early in the year. Select plants from the following list to begin with and then expand to include other trees and shrubs after a few seasons of soil improvement. When planting, water in well and mulch heavily.

TREES

Acer negundo and cvs
Ailanthus altissima
Betula (all)
Castanea (all)
Cercis (all)
Gleditsia
Ilex aquifolium and cvs
Populus alba
   tremula
Robinia (all)

SHRUBS

Acer ginnala
Berberis (all)
Calluna vulgaris and cvs
Caragana arborescens
Cistus (all)
Colutea arborescens
Cotoneaster (all)
Elaeagnus angustifolia
   commutata
Erica (all)

Genista (all)
Halimodendron halodendron
Helianthemum (all)
Hibiscus (all)
Ilex crenata and cvs
Indigofera (all)
Kerria japonica and cvs
Lonicera (all)
Lycium barbarum
Pernettya mucronata and cvs
Physocarpus opulifolius and cvs
Rosa pimpinellifolia and cvs
Salix caprea
   cinerea
   repens var. *argentea*
Tamarix (all)
Ulex (all)

CONIFERS

Cupressus glabra and cvs
Juniperus (all)
Pinus (all)

This garden-worthy selection of plants includes, from the top: *Acer negundo* 'Flamingo', *Pinus mugo* 'Winter Gold' and *Hibiscus syriacus* 'Pink Giant'. All are suitable for dry acid soils

Plants for Shallow Soil Over Chalk

Chalk is a form of soft, porous limestone. It is highly calcareous and so harmful to many trees, shrubs and other plants. However, calcium and magnesium limestone support an extraordinarily rich flora in nature, so do not be put off by them. They are more difficult when there is only a shallow layer of soil above the rock; the problem then is more a result of heat and dryness than the calcareous environment itself. Where many gardeners go wrong is to persist in trying to grow favourites, such as rhododendrons and azaleas, which will not thrive in such soils. It is far better to garden using plants that will.

Incorporating organic matter will improve this kind of soil, although the chalk does, in fact, retain moisture itself, acting like blotting paper. This helps established plants to survive better than on dry soils. It is also possible, because of the soft nature of the rock and the excellent drainage, to increase the depth of the soil by making occasional excavations in the chalk.

TREES

Acer campestre
  negundo and cvs
  platanoides and cvs
  pseudoplatanus and cvs
Aesculus (all)
Carpinus betulus and cvs
Cercis siliquastrum
Crataegus laevigata and cvs
Fagus sylvatica and cvs
Fraxinus excelsior and cvs
Fraxinus ornus
Morus nigra
Populus alba
Prunus (Japanese cherries)
Sorbus aria and cvs
  hybrida and cvs
  intermedia

SHRUBS

Aucuba japonica and cvs
Berberis (all)
Buddleja davidii and cvs
Buxus sempervirens and cvs
Caragana arborescens and cvs
Ceanothus (all)
Cistus (all)
Colutea (all)
Cornus mas and cvs
Cotoneaster (all)
Cytisus nigricans
Deutzia (all)
Dipelta floribunda
Elaeagnus (deciduous species)

Euonymus (all)
Forsythia (all)
Fuchsia (all)
Hebe (all)
Hibiscus syriacus and cvs
Hypericum (all)
Laurus nobilis
Ligustrum (all)
Lonicera (all)
Mahonia aquifolium and hybrids
Olearia (all)
Paeonia delavayi
  lutea
Philadelphus (all)
Phillyrea (all)
Photinia × fraseri cvs
  serratifolia
Potentilla (most)
Rhus (most)
Rosa (most)
Rosmarinus (all)
Rubus tricolor
Sambucus (all)
Sarcococca (all)
Senecio (all)
Spartium junceum
Spiraea japonica and cvs
  nipponica and forms
Stachyurus (all)
Symphoricarpos (all)
Syringa (all)
Vinca (all)
Weigela (all)
Yucca (all)

CONIFERS

Juniperus communis and cvs
  × media and cvs
Pinus mugo and forms
  nigra
Taxus baccata and cvs
Thuja occidentalis and cvs

Thuja plicata and cvs
Thujopsis dolabrata and cvs

BAMBOOS

Pseudosasa japonica
Sasa ramosa

Plants for Damp Sites

Generally speaking, trees and shrubs require good drainage and locations where soil is not waterlogged. Some, however, are adapted to living in conditions of permanent dampness or even wetness. In well-aerated soils oxygen levels rarely fall below 15 per cent, whereas in wet sites they may be as low as one per cent. Trees such as the swamp cypress (Taxodium distichum) can survive this for many months. On the other hand, trees and shrubs without special adaptations to such environmental conditions may live no longer than a few weeks if flooded during the growing season.

Where damp places are associated with water movement they may be rich in oxygen. Plants that have evolved in such conditions thrive where the majority of trees and shrubs would fail.

TREES

Alnus (all)
Amelanchier (all)
Betula nigra
  pendula and cvs
  pubescens
Crataegus laevigata and cvs
Magnolia virginiana
Mespilus germanica cvs
Populus (all)
Pterocarya (all)
Pyrus betulifolia
  communis cvs
Quercus palustris
Salix (all)
Sorbus aucuparia and cvs

SHRUBS

Amelanchier (all)
Aronia (all)
Calycanthus floridus
Clethra (all)
Cornus alba and cvs
  stolonifera and cvs
Gaultheria shallon
Hippophae rhamnoides
Lindera benzoin
Myrica gale
Neillia thibetica

Photinia villosa
Physocarpus opulifolius and cvs
Prunus spinosa and cvs
Salix caprea
  purpurea and cvs
  repens and cvs
  many other bush species
Sambucus (all)
Sorbaria (all)
Spiraea × vanhouttei
  veitchii
Symphoricarpos (all)
Vaccinium (all)
Viburnum opulus and cvs

CONIFERS

Metasequoia glyptostroboides
Picea sitchensis
Taxodium ascendens and forms
  distichum

BAMBOOS

Phyllostachys (all)
Pleioblastus (most)
Pseudosasa japonica
Sasa (all)
Sinarundinaria (all)
Thamnocalamus (all)
Yushania anceps

Plants for Industrial Areas

The air of industrial areas is cleaner now than it was during the first half of the twentieth century, when soot and sulphuric acid, among other injurious substances, greatly reduced the range of plants that could be grown in cities and large towns. Although the situation has improved, pollution from industry still occurs and affects the growth of plants. In general, though, the range of trees and shrubs that can be grown in industrial areas is very much more extensive than you might have thought; only relatively few, such as the Japanese maples, cannot tolerate modern levels of pollution.

TREES

Acer (many, but not Japanese
    maples)
Aesculus (all)
Ailanthus altissima
Alnus cordata
    glutinosa and cvs
    incana and cvs
Amelanchier (all)
Betula papyrifera and forms
    pendula and cvs
    pubescens
Carpinus betulus and cvs
Catalpa bignonioides and cvs
Crataegus (all)
Davidia (all)
Eucalyptus (most)
Fagus (all)
Fraxinus (all)
Ilex × altaclerensis and cvs
    aquifolium and cvs
+ Laburnocytisus adamii
Laburnum (all)
Ligustrum lucidum and cvs
Liriodendron tulipifera and cvs
Magnolia denudata
    kobus
    × loebneri and cvs
    × soulangeana and cvs
Malus (all)
Mespilus germanica cvs
Morus nigra
Platanus (all)
Populus (most)
Prunus × amygado-persica 'Pollardii'
    avium
    cerasifera and cvs
    dulcis cvs
    Japanese cherries
    padus and cvs
Pterocarya (all)
Pyrus (all)
Quercus ilex
    × turneri
Rhus (most)
Robinia pseudoacacia and cvs
Salix (most)
Sorbus aria and cvs
    aucuparia and cvs
Tilia × euchlora
    × europaea and cvs
    platyphyllos and cvs

SHRUBS

Amelanchier (all)
Aralia elata
Arbutus unedo and cvs
Aucuba japonica and cvs
Berberis (all)
Buddleja davidii and cvs
Buxus sempervirens and cvs
Camellia japonica and cvs
    × williamsii cvs
Ceratostigma willmottianum
Chaenomeles (all)
Cistus (all)
Clethra (all)
Colutea arborescens
Cornus alba and cvs
Cotoneaster (most)
Cytisus (most)
Daphne mezereum
Deutzia (many)
Elaeagnus × ebbingei and cvs
    pungens and cvs
Escallonia (all)
Euonymus fortunei and cvs
    japonicus and cvs
Fatsia japonica
Forsythia (all)
Garrya (all)
Genista (many)

Hibiscus sinosyriacus and cvs
    syriacus and cvs
Hydrangea macrophylla and cvs
Hypericum (all)
Ilex aquifolium and cvs
    cornuta and hybrids
Kerria japonica and cvs
Leycesteria formosa
Ligustrum japonicum
    ovalifolium
Lonicera pileata
Lycium barbarum
Magnolia grandiflora and cvs
    × soulangeana and cvs
    stellata and cvs
Mahonia aquifolium and hybrids
    japonica
    lomariifolia
    × media and cvs
    pinnata
    repens 'Rotundifolia'
Olearia × haastii
Osmanthus (all)
Pernettya mucronata and cvs
Philadelphus (all)
Phillyrea (all)
Photinia davidiana
Physocarpus (all)
Prunus laurocerasus and cvs
Pyracantha (all)
Rhododendron Hardy Hybrids
    Knap Hill azaleas
    luteum
    ponticum
Rhodotypos scandens
Rhus glabra
    typhina
Ribes (all)

Rosa (most)
Salix (most)
Sambucus canadensis 'Maxima'
    nigra and forms
Sarcococca (many)
Senecio monroi
    'Sunshine'
Skimmia japonica and cvs
Sorbaria (all)
Spartium junceum
Spiraea (all)
Staphylea (all)
Symphoricarpos (all)
Syringa (all)
Tamarix tetranda
Ulex (all)
Viburnum (many)
Vinca major and cvs
    minor and cvs
Weigela florida and cvs
    hybrids

CLIMBERS

Ampelopsis (most)
Hedera (all)
Parthenocissus (all)

CONIFERS

Cephalotaxus fortunei and cvs
    harringtonia and forms
Fitzroya cupressoides
Ginkgo biloba
Metasequoia glyptostroboides
    and cvs
Taxus baccata and cvs
    × media and cvs
Torreya californica

Plants for Cold, Exposed Areas

Cold is one thing, but a cold wind is quite different. A plant's tolerance to cold is meaningless if it is expressed in terms merely of temperature in still air, as the degree of chilling is directly proportional to wind speed. A plant in an exposed, windy position may experience wind-chill equivalents many degrees lower than the temperature prevailing in a sheltered spot.

Furthermore, when the soil is cold – or worse, frozen – and the roots of plants are almost dormant, winds cause loss of water from the leaves which cannot be replaced by the roots. The result is physiological drought, wilting, defoliation and possible death. However, some evergreens are adapted to extreme cold and exposure and many deciduous trees and shrubs are notably tolerant of bitter winter blasts.

TREES

Acer pseudoplatanus and cvs
Betula (most)
Crataegus monogyna and cvs
Fagus sylvatica and cvs
Fraxinus excelsior and cvs
Laburnum (all)
Populus × canadensis 'Robusta'
    tremula
Quercus robur and cvs
Sorbus aria and cvs
    aucuparia and cvs
    intermedia and cvs
Tilia cordata and cvs

SHRUBS

Arctostaphylos uva-ursi
Calluna vulgaris and cvs
Cornus alba and cvs
    stolonifera and cvs
Cotinus coggyria and cvs
Elaeagnus commutata
Euonymus fortunei and cvs
× Gaulnettya cvs
Gaultheria shallon
Hippophae rhamnoides
Hydrangea paniculata 'Grandiflora'
Kalmia angustifolia and cvs
    latifolia and cvs
Kerria japonica 'Variegata'
Lavatera thuringiaca cvs
Ledum groenlandicum
Leucothoë fontanesiana

Lonicera pileata
Mahonia aquifolium
Myrica gale
Pachysandra terminalis
Pernettya mucronata and cvs
Philadelphus (many)
Prunus spinosa
Rhododendron Hardy Hybrids
    ponticum
    yakushimanum
Salix (most)
Spiraea (most)
Tamarix (all)
Ulex (all)
Viburnum opulus and cvs

CONIFERS

Chamaecyparis nootkatensis
    and cvs
    obtusa and cvs
    pisifera and cvs
Cryptomeria japonica and cvs
Ginkgo biloba
Juniperus communis and cvs
    × media and cvs
Larix decidua
Picea abies and cvs
Pinus nigra and forms
    ponderosa
    sylvestris and cvs
Taxus baccata and cvs
Thuja occidentalis and cvs
Tsuga canadensis and cvs

From the top: Betula utilis var. jacquemontii 'Doorenbos' is good for cold, exposed sites, Pinus radiata will flourish in seaside gardens and Skimmia japonica subsp. reevesiana 'Robert Fortune' tolerates heavy shade

Plants for Seaside Areas

Wind is a major factor in gardens near the sea and temperatures are often higher than those inland. What distinguishes seaside gardens is the prevalence of salt in the air, which can be carried 24 km (15 miles) inland during a storm. It can also accumulate in the soil. The salt makes it harder for plants to take up water, as there is insufficient difference between the concentration of salts in the soil water and those in the root cells. Plants with tough, waxy leaves and grey foliage often withstand seaside conditions well.

TREES

Acer pseudoplatanus
Arbutus unedo and cvs
Castanea sativa
Crataegus (all)
Eucalyptus (many)
Fraxinus angustifolia and cvs
   excelsior and cvs
Griselinia littoralis
Ilex × altaclerensis and cvs
   aquifolium and cvs
Laurus nobilis and cvs
Phillyrea latifolia
Populus alba
   tremula
Quercus cerris
   ilex
   petraea
   robur
   × turneri
Salix (most)
Sorbus aria and cvs
   aucuparia and cvs

SHRUBS

Atriplex halimus
Bupleurum fruticosum
Cassinia fulvida
Chamaerops humilis
Choisya (all)
Colutea (all)
Cordyline australis and cvs
Corokia cotoneaster
   × virgata and cvs
Cotoneaster (many)
Cytisus (many)
Elaeagnus × ebbingei and cvs
   pungens and cvs
Erica arborea var. *alpina*
   lusitanica
   × veitchii
Escallonia (most)

Euonymus fortunei and cvs
   japonicus and cvs
Fabiana imbricata 'Prostrata'
Fuchsia magellanica and cvs
Garrya elliptica and cvs
Genista (most)
Halimium (all)
Halimodendron halodendron
Hebe (all)
Helianthemum (most)
Helichrysum (many)
Hippophae rhamnoides
Hydrangea macrophylla and cvs
Ilex aquifolium and cvs
Lavandula (all)
Lavatera thuringiaca cvs
Leycesteria formosa
Lonicera pileata
Lycium barbarum
Olearia (most)
Ozothamnus (many)
Parahebe (all)
Phlomis (most)
Phormium (all)
Pittosporum (most)
Prunus spinosa
Pyracantha (all)
Rhamnus alaternus and cvs
Rosa (many species)
Rosmarinus officinalis and cvs
Salix (many)
Sambucus racemosa and cvs
Santolina (all)
Senecio (most)
Spartium junceum
Spiraea (many)
Tamarix (all)
Ulex (all)
Viburnum (many, especially evergreen spp.)
Yucca (all)

CLIMBERS

Fallopia baldschuanica
Muehlenbeckia complexa

CONIFERS

× Cupressocyparis leylandii
Cupressus (many)
Juniperus (most)
Pinus contorta
   mugo and forms
   muricata
   nigra

Pinus nigra subsp. *laricio*
   pinaster
   pinea
   radiata
   thunbergii
Podocarpus alpinus
   nivalis

BAMBOOS

Pleioblastus (many)
Sasa (all)

Plants Tolerant of Heavy Shade

It is unnatural for most trees to tolerate shade, but some shrubs tolerate the reduced light under dense tree canopies. In nature, shrubs usually appear towards the edges of the forest, either where it begins to give way to high moorland or, as with *Arbutus unedo*, on lakesides. Trees and shrubs that are adapted to dense shade are of great value in the garden. Many, such as *Fatsia japonica*, the hollies and the mahonias, are notable for their foliage, while others, for example, the camellias are grown for their spectacular flowers.

TREES AND SHRUBS

Arctostaphylos uva-ursi
Aucuba japonica and cvs
Buxus sempervirens and cvs
Camellia japonica and cvs
   × williamsii and cvs
Cornus canadensis
Daphne laureola
   pontica
Elaeagnus (evergreen)
Euonymus fortunei and cvs
× Fatshedera lizei
Fatsia japonica
Gaultheria (all)
Hypericum androsaemum
   calycinum
Ilex × altaclerensis and cvs
   aquifolium and cvs
Leucothoë fontanesiana and cvs
Ligustrum (many)
Lonicera nitida cvs
   pileata
Mahonia aquifolium and cvs
Osmanthus decorus
   heterophyllus and cvs
Pachysandra terminalis
Prunus laurocerasus and cvs
   lusitanica and cvs

Rhododendron Hardy Hybrids
   ponticum
Rhodotypos scandens
Ribes alpinum
Rubus odoratus
   tricolor
Ruscus (all)
Sarcococca (all)
Skimmia (all)
Symphoricarpos (all)
Vaccinium vitis-idaea
Viburnum davidii
Vinca (all)

CONIFERS

Cephalotaxus (all)
Juniperus × media 'Pfitzeriana'
Podocarpus alpinus
   andinus
   nivalis
Taxus (all)

BAMBOOS

Fargesii (all)
Phyllostachys (most)
Pleioblastus (most)
Sasa (all)

Plants for Shady Walls

Plants that succeed on north-facing walls must be able to tolerate almost unbroken shade, while those facing east will receive sunshine only in the mornings. In addition, they may be further shaded from what sun there is by other plants that are further to the east.

Another factor that comes into play is frost. If flower buds formed the previous autumn become frozen, they will be killed by any sudden thawing caused by the sun's rays falling on them in the morning. This applies particularly to camellias.

In Britain, easterly winds in the winter and spring are usually dry and often bitingly cold. Where the wall affords them no protection, care should taken even with the following plants: *Azara* species, *Drimys winteri*, *Crinodendron* species and *Osmanthus yunnanensis*.

SHRUBS

Azara microphylla
Berberis × stenophylla
Camellia (north walls only)
  'Inspiration'
  japonica and cvs
  reticulata
  sasanqua
  × *williamsii* and cvs
Chaenomeles (most)
Choisya ternata
Crinodendron hookerianum
  patagua
Daphne × hybrida
  odora
Desfontainia spinosa
Drimys winteri
Eriobotrya japonica
Eucryphia cordifolia
  × *intermedia* cvs
  × *nymansensis* and cvs
Euonymus fortunei and cvs
Garrya elliptica and cvs
Grevillea rosmarinifolia
Ilex latifolia
Illicium anisatum
Jasminium humile and forms
  nudiflorum

Kerria japonica 'Pleniflora'
Lomatia myricoides
Mahonia japonica
  lomarifolia
  × *media* and cvs
Mitraria coccinea
Osmanthus yunnanensis
Photinia × fraseri and cvs
  serratifolia
Piptanthus nepalensis
Pyracantha (all)
Ribes laurifolium
Schima argentea
Viburnum foetens

CLIMBERS

Akebia quinata
Celastrus orbiculatus
Hedera colchica and cvs
  helix and cvs
Hydrangea petiolaris
Muehlenbeckia complexa
Parthenocissus (all)
Pileostegia viburnoides
Rubus henryi var. *bambusarum*
Schizophragma hydrangeoides
  integrifolium

Plants for Ground Cover

Gardeners have a saying that unless you cover the ground, nature will cover it for you. Bare soil soon becomes a mass of weeds. If you are a good gardener, you will want to prevent this happening and also, perhaps, to make the site as ornamental as possible consistent with the minimum expenditure of labour.

'Ground-cover' plants have gained something of a bad name in the past because of a relatively unimaginative approach involving a fairly hackneyed selection of rapidly growing carpeters such as ivies (*Hedera*) and periwinkles (*Vinca*). While these are of great value, they are only a few of the many interesting and exciting shrubs that can cover your ground in a way that is far from being merely utilitarian.

SHRUBS

Arctostaphylos uva-ursi
Artemisia 'Powis Castle'
Aucuba japonica 'Nana
  Rotundifolia'
Berberis tsangpoensis
  wilsoniae
Buxus microphylla
Calluna vulgaris and cvs
Ceanothus prostratus
  thyrsiflorus var. *repens*
Cornus canadensis
Cotoneaster: several, including:
  'Coral Beauty'
  dammeri
  'Gnom'
  horizontalis and cvs
  nanshan
  'Skogholm'
Cytisus × beanii
  scoparius subsp. *maritimus*
Daboecia cantabrica and cvs
Erica (most)
Euonymus fortunei and cvs
Gaultheria (most)
× *Gaulnettya* cvs
Halimiocistus 'Ingwersenii'
  sahucii
Hebe: many, especially
  albicans
  pinguifolia 'Pagei'
  rakaiensis
  'Youngii'
Hedera (most)
Helianthemum (all)
Hypericum calycinum
  moserianum
Jasminium nudiflorum
  parkeri
Leptospermum humifusum
Leucothoë fontanesiana and cvs
Lonicera pileata
Mahonia aquifolium 'Apollo'
  nervosa

Pachysandra terminalis
Pernettya mucronata cvs
Pimelea prostrata
Potentilla 'Abbotswood'
  'Longacre'
Rhododendron: many, especially
  members of the Subsections
  Lapponica and Saluenensia
  and most evergreen azaleas
Ribes laurifolium
Rosa 'Max Graf'
  nitida
  'Paulii'
  wichuraiana
Rosmarinus officinalis 'Prostratus'
Rubus calycinoides
  tricolor
Salix: several, including:
  × *cottetii*
  repens and cvs
  uva-ursi
Santolina (all)
Sarcococca hookeriana var. *humilis*
Stephanandra incisa 'Crispa'
Symphoricarpos × chenaultii
  'Hancock'
Vaccinium: many, especially
  delavayi
  glauco-album
  vitis-idaea
Viburnum davidii
Vinca (all)

CONIFERS

Cephalotaxus fortunei 'Prostrate
  Spreader'
Juniperus communis: several
  forms, including:
  'Hornibrookii'
  'Repanda'
  conferta
  horizontalis and cvs
  × *media* (several cvs)
  sabina var. *tamariscifolia*

Podocarpus alpinus
   nivalis
Taxus baccata 'Repandens'
   'Repens Aurea'
Tsuga canadensis 'Bennett'

BAMBOOS
Indocalamus tessellatus
Sasa veitchii
Shibataea kumasaca

Plants of Pendulous Habit

Trees vary greatly in shape and habit, but most of them share the general configuration of a trunk topped by a head of branches. Garden design depends a great deal on contrasts, comparisons and accents and often just one or two trees that depart radically from the norm will make their neighbours look all the more interesting. Pendulous or weeping trees perhaps provide the strongest contrasting accents, with their downward sweeps often hiding their trunks and providing foliage where in other trees it is absent. Deciduous trees make firm architectural statements in winter and there are many more available than the ubiquitous weeping willow.

TREES

Acer saccharinum f. *laciniatum*
Betula pendula 'Dalecarlica'
   'Tristis'
   'Youngii'
Cercidiphyllum japonicum
   'Pendulum'
Fagus sylvatica 'Aurea Pendula'
   'Pendula'
   'Purpurea Pendula'
Fraxinus excelsior 'Pendula'
Malus 'Red Jade'
Populus tremula 'Pendula'
Prunus subhirtella 'Pendula Rubra'
   × *yedoensis* 'Shidare Yoshino'
Pyrus salicifolia 'Pendula'
Robinia pseudoacacia
   'Rozynskyana'
Salix babylonica 'Pendula'
   × *sepulcralis* 'Chrysocoma'
   'Erythroflexuosa'
Sophora japonica 'Pendula'
Tilia tomentosa 'Petiolaris'
The ultimate height of the following trees is largely dependent on the stem height at which they are grafted or to which they are trained.
Caragana arborescens 'Pendula'
   'Walker'
Cotoneaster 'Hybridus Pendulus'
Ilex aquifolium 'Argentea
   Marginata Pendula'

Ilex aquifolium 'Pendula'
Laburnum alpinum 'Pendulum'
Malus 'Royal Beauty'
Morus alba 'Pendula'
Prunus 'Cheal's Weeping'
   × *yedoensis* 'Ivensii'
Salix caprea 'Kilmarnock'
   purpurea 'Pendula'

CONIFERS

Cedrus atlantica 'Glauca Pendula'
   'Pendula'
Chamaecyparis nootkatensis
   'Pendula'
Cupressus lusitanica 'Glauca
   Pendula'
Dacrydium franklinii
Fitzroya cupressoides
Larix kaempferi 'Pendula'
Picea abies 'Inversa'
   breweriana
   omorika 'Pendula'
   smithiana
Taxus baccata 'Dovastoniana'
   'Dovastonii Aurea'
Tsuga canadensis 'Pendula'
   heterophylla 'Greenmantle'

Plants of Upright or Fastigiate Habit

'Fastigiate' means 'having branches erect and close together'. 'Upright' is a non-botanical term that covers trees and shrubs with ascending branches, such as several hollies and conifers, but, for design purposes, it also includes fastigiate trees and shrubs.

Single upright accents are not quite as strong as pendulous ones, but repeated or in groups they are powerful design features. A group of strongly upright trees with broad crowns, such as *Fagus sylvatica* 'Dawyck', is highly effective. On a much smaller scale, a group of the diminutive *Juniperus communis* 'Compressa' can lend definitive character to a rock garden. A repeated vertical accent, such as that given by *Juniperus scopulorum* 'Skyrocket', can transform a large border which might otherwise lack effectiveness because of its unbroken horizontal line. Trees such as fastigiate oaks, beeches and Japanese cherries can be very useful by driveway entrances and streets, providing height without too much width.

TREES AND SHRUBS
Acer × *lobelii*
   platanoides 'Columnare'
   pseudoplatanus 'Erectum'
   rubrum 'Scanlon'
   saccharinum 'Pyramidale'
Betula pendula 'Fastigiata'
Carpinus betulus 'Fastigiata'
Corylus colurna
Crataegus monogyna 'Stricta'
Fagus sylvatica 'Cockleshell'
   'Dawyck'
   'Dawyck Gold'
   'Dawyck Purple'
Ilex aquifolium 'Green Pillar'
Liriodendron tulipifera 'Fastigiatum'
Malus tschonoskii 'Van Eseltine'
Populus alba 'Pyramidalis'
   nigra 'Italica'
Prunus 'Amanogawa'
   lusitanica 'Myrtifolia'
   'Pandora'
   × *schmittii*
   'Snow Goose'
   'Spire'
Pyrus calleryana 'Chanticleer'
Quercus castaneifolia 'Green Spire'
   frainetto 'Hungarian Crown'
   petraea 'Columna'
   robur f. *fastigiata* 'Koster'
Robinia pseudoacacia 'Pyramidalis'
Sorbus aucuparia 'Fastigiata'
   'Sheerwater Seedling'
   commixta
   'Joseph Rock'

Sorbus aucuparia × *thuringiaca*
   'Fastigiata'
Tilia cordata 'Greenspire'
Ulmus × *hollandica* 'Dampieri
   Aurea'

CONIFERS
Calocedrus decurrens
Cephalotaxus harringtonia
   'Fastigiata'
Chamaecyparis lawsoniana
   'Alumii'
   'Columnaris'
   'Ellwoodii'
   'Erecta'
   'Kilmacurragh'
   'Pottenii'
   'Wisselii'
   'Witzeliana'
× *Cupressocyparis leylandii* and cvs
Cupressus glabra 'Pyramidalis'
   sempervirens and cvs
Ginkgo biloba 'Tremonia'
Juniperus chinensis 'Pyramidalis'
   communis 'Compressa'
   'Hibernica'
   'Sentinel'
   scopulorum (several cvs)
Pinus sylvestris 'Fastigiata'
Taxus baccata 'Fastigiata'
   'Standishii'
   × *media* 'Hicksii'
Thuja occidentalis 'Malonyana'
   plicata 'Fastigiata'

Plants with Ornamental Bark and Twigs

Many trees and shrubs have coloured, patterned or attractively peeling bark on their trunks and major branches. Others have coloured smaller branches and twiggy branchlets. An example of the former is the shining white trunk of *Betula utilis* var. *jacquemontii* 'Jermyns', while *Acer palmatum* 'Senkaki' with its branches of bright coral typifies the latter.

In general, ornamental barks have their greatest effect among deciduous trees and shrubs, as they are prominent features in the garden in winter. However, many evergreens have strikingly beautiful bark and are outstanding throughout the year. Among these are *Eucalyptus*, *Arbutus × andrachnoides* and *Myrtus luma*.

TREES
Acer capillipes
   davidii 'George Forrest'
   griseum
   grosseri var. *hersii*
   negundo var. *violaceum*
   palmatum 'Senkaki'
   pensylvanicum and cvs
Arbutus × andrachnoides
   menziesii
Betula (most)
Carya ovata
Eucalyptus (most)
Fraxinus excelsior 'Jaspidea'
Myrtus luma
Parrotia persica
Platanus (all)
Prunus maackii 'Amber Beauty'
   × *schmittii*
   serrula
Salix acutifolia 'Blue Streak'
   alba 'Britzensis'
   var. *vitellina*
   babylonica 'Tortuosa'
   daphnoides and cvs
   × *sepulcralis* 'Chrysocoma'
   'Erythroflexuosa'
Stuartia (most)
Tilia platyphyllos 'Aurea'
   'Rubra'

SHRUBS
Abelia triflora
Arctostaphylos (most)
Clethra barbinervis
Cornus alba and cvs
   officinalis
   stolonifera 'Flaviramea'
Corylus avellana 'Contorta'

Deutzia (several spp.)
Dipelta floribunda
Euonymus alatus
   phellomanus
Hydrangea aspera and forms
   heteromalla 'Bretschneideri'
Kerria japonica and cvs
Leycesteria formosa
Philadelphus (several)
Rhododendron barbatum
   thomsonii
Rosa sericea f. *pteracantha*
   virginiana
Rubus cockburnianus
   phoenicolasius
   thibetanus
Salix irrorata
   moupinensis
Stephanandra tanakae
Vaccinium corymbosum

CONIFERS
Cryptomeria japonica
Pinus bungeana
   sylvestris
Sequoia sempervirens
Sequoiadendron giganteum

Plants with Bold Foliage

Texture and contrast have a foremost role among design elements and can be richly provided by the foliage of trees and shrubs. Very large or interestingly shaped leaves draw the eye irresistibly and make strong and often exotic contrasts to the smaller, more tightly massed leaves of the majority of woody plants.

There is a great variety of types of bold leaves, each creating a different texture or accent. The spear-shaped clusters of the Torbay palm (*Cordyline australis*), for example, share a somewhat jungle-like character with the widely lobed *Fatsia japonica*, but each strikes a very different note. Bold or architectural foliage can have the greatest influence on the general atmosphere of your garden.

TREES
Ailanthus altissima
Aralia (all)
Catalpa (all)
Cordyline australis
Gymnocladus dioica
Idesia polycarpa
Kalopanax pictus
Magnolia hypoleuca
   macrophylla
   officinalis var. *biloba*
   tripetala
Meliosma veitchiorum
Paulownia (all)
Platanus (all)
Populus lasiocarpa
   szechuanica var. *tibetica*
Pterocarya (all)
Quercus frainetto 'Hungarian
   Crown'
   velutina 'Rubrifolia'
Sorbus insignis
   thibetica 'John Mitchell'
   vestita
Toona sinensis
Trachycarpus fortunei

SHRUBS
Acer japonicum 'Vitifolium'
   macrophyllum
Aralia (all)
Chamaerops humilis
Eriobotrya japonica
× *Fatshedera lizei*
Fatsia japonica
Hydrangea quercifolia and cvs
   aspera subsp. *sargentiana*
Ilex latifolia

Magnolia delavayi
   grandiflora and cvs
Mahonia japonica
   lomariifolia
   × *media* and cvs
Melianthus major
Osmanthus armatus
   yunnanensis
Phormium (all)
Rhododendron: several, including
   macabeanum
   rex and forms
   sinogrande
Sambucus canadensis 'Maxima'
Sorbaria (all)
Viburnum rhytidophyllum
Yucca gloriosa
   recurvifolia

CLIMBERS
Actinidia chinensis
Ampelopsis megalophylla
Aristolochia macrophylla
Hedera algeriensis and cvs
Vitis 'Brant'
   coignetiae

BAMBOOS
Indocalamus tessellatus

Plants for Autumn Colour

Autumn foliage can be a truly spectacular sight in the garden. It varies from place to place, is better on some soils than others and has good and bad years, but it is generally worth bearing in mind when you are planning the garden. The fiery combinations of glowing crimson, blazing scarlet and orange and rich gold so typical of picture-book autumns are attainable if you choose carefully. Try to find room, even in a small garden, for one or two of these plants, particularly those that have interest in other seasons as well. With judicious planning, a larger garden can provide a succession of changing hues over several weeks.

TREES

Acer: many, including
  capillipes
  maximowiczianum
  platanoides and cvs
  rubrum and cvs
  triflorum
Aesculus: several, including
  glabra
Amelanchier laevis
  lamarckii
Betula (most)
Carpinus (all)
Carya (all)
Cercidiphyllum japonicum
Cercis canadensis
Cladrastis (all)
Cornus controversa
Crataegus: many, especially
  crus-galli
  pinnatifida var. *major*
  prunifolia
Fagus (most)
Fraxinus angustifolia 'Raywood'
  excelsior 'Jaspidea'
Gymnocladus dioica
Liquidambar (all)
Malus: several, including
  coronaria 'Charlottae'
  transitoria
  trilobata
  tschonoskii
Nothofagus antarctica
Nyssa (all)
Parrotia persica
Phellodendron (all)
Photinia beauverdiana
  villosa
Picrasma quassioides
Populus: several, including

Populus alba
  × *canadensis* 'Serotina Aurea'
  tremula
  trichocarpa
Prunus: many, including
  'Hillieri'
  sargentii
  verecunda 'Autumn Glory'
Quercus: many, including
  coccinea 'Splendens'
  palustris
  phellos
  rubra
Rhus trichocarpa
Sassafras albidum
Sorbus: many, including
  alnifolia
  commixta
  'Embley'
  'Joseph Rock'
  scalaris
Stuartia (all)
Toona sinensis

SHRUBS

Acer: many, especially
  ginnala
  japonicum and cvs
  palmatum and cvs
Aesculus parviflora
Amelanchier canadensis
Aronia (all)
Berberis: many, including
  dictyophylla
  × *media* 'Parkjuweel'
  thunbergii and cvs
  wilsoniae
Callicarpa (all)
Ceratostigma willmottianum
Clethra (all)

Cornus alba
  'Eddie's White Wonder'
  florida and cvs
  officinalis
Corylopsis (all)
Cotinus (all)
Cotoneaster: many, including
  bullatus
  divaricatus
  horizontalis
  nanshan
  splendens
Disanthus cercidifolius
Enkianthus (all)
Eucryphia glutinosa
Euonymus: many, including
  alatus and cvs
  europaeus and cvs
  latifolius
  oxyphyllus
  planipes
Fothergilla (all)
Hamamelis (all)
Hydrangea quercifolia
  serrata 'Preziosa'
Lindera (most)
Prunus: several, including
  glandulosa and cvs
  incisa
  pumila var. *depressa*
Ptelea trifoliata
Rhododendron: several, including
  arborescens
  calendulaceum
  'Coccineum Speciosum'
  'Corneille'
  luteum
  'Nancy Waterer'
  quinquefolium
Rhus: several, especially
  copallina
  glabra and cvs
  typhina and cvs
Ribes odoratum
Rosa nitida
  rugosa and cvs
  virginiana
Sorbaria aitchisonii
Spiraea thunbergii
Stephanandra (all)
Vaccinium: several, including
  corymbosum
  praestans

Viburnum: many, including
  carlesii and cvs
  furcatum
  × *hillieri* 'Winton'
  opulus and cvs
  plicatum cvs
Zanthoxylum piperitum

CLIMBERS

Ampelopsis (all)
Celastrus (all)
Parthenocissus (all)
Vitis (all)

CONIFERS

Ginkgo biloba
Larix (all)
Metasequoia glyptostroboides
  and cvs
Pseudolarix amabilis
Taxodium (all)

Plants with Red or Purple Foliage

'Purple', in foliage terms, defines a group of plants with dark leaf tones from copper and mahogany to near-black. Trees and shrubs with such foliage provide very strong contrasts and should be used judiciously. Just one purple-leaved subject is likely to be enough in a small garden and it is easy to overdo dark foliage in gardens of any size.

These coloured leaves are often at their most dramatic when backlit by the sun. It is worth finding a site for them where they will be between you and the sun as you walk along a path or relax in a sitting area.

TREES

Acer campestre 'Schwerinii'
   platanoides 'Crimson King'
   'Deborah'
   'Schwedleri'
Betula pendula 'Purpurea'
Catalpa × erubescens 'Purpurea'
Fagus sylvatica 'Dawyck Purple'
   Purpurea group
   'Purpurea Pendula'
   'Riversii'
   'Rohanii'
Malus 'Lemoinei'
   'Liset'
   'Profusion'
   'Royal Beauty'
   'Royalty'
Prunus × blireana
   cerasifera 'Nigra'
   'Pissardii'
   'Rosea'
   padus 'Colorata'
   virginiana 'Schubert'
Quercus petraea
   robur 'Atropurpurea'

SHRUBS

Acer palmatum: many, including
   Atropurpureum group
   'Bloodgood'
   'Crimson Queen'
   'Dissectum Atropurpureum'
   'Hessei'
   'Red Pygmy'
Berberis × ottawensis 'Superba'
   thunbergii: many, including
   Atropurpurea group
   'Atropurpurea Nana'
   'Red Chief'
   'Rose Glow'

Cercis canadensis 'Forest Pansy'
Corylopsis willmottiae 'Spring
   Purple'
Corylus maxima 'Purpurea'
Cotinus coggygria 'Royal Purple'
   'Velvet Cloak'
   'Grace'
Phormium tenax 'Purpureum'
   and others
Pittosporum tenuifolium
   'Purpureum'
   'Tom Thumb'
Prunus cistena
Salvia officinalis 'Purpurascens'
Sambucus nigra 'Guincho Purple'
Weigela florida 'Foliis Purpureis'

CLIMBERS

Vitis vinifera 'Purpurea'

Plants with Golden or Yellow Foliage

Restraint with golden or yellow foliage is almost as important as it is with purple-leaved trees and shrubs. Too much brightly coloured foliage is trying on the eyes in sunlight and can produce a rather tawdry effect. On the other hand, one or two well-placed, well-chosen subjects, especially in a dull corner, can have a wonderfully cheerful, lightening effect on the garden. It is advisable to avoid strong yellows, such as that of *Robinia pseudoacacia* 'Frisia', in smaller gardens or where there is a lot of red brick. It is highly attractive in a larger setting and among greens or set against grey stone, but where it is too strident a greener, softer tone, such as that of *Gleditsia triacanthos* 'Sunburst', may be more fitting.

TREES

Acer cappadocicum 'Aureum'
   negundo 'Auratum'
   pseudoplatanus 'Worleei'
Alnus incana 'Aurea'
Catalpa bignonioides 'Aurea'
Fagus sylvatica 'Aurea Pendula'
   'Zlatia'
Gleditsia triacanthos 'Sunburst'
Laurus nobilis 'Aurea'
Liquidambar styraciflua
   'Moonbeam'
Populus alba 'Richardii'
   × canadensis 'Serotina Aurea'
Quercus robur 'Concordia'
   rubra 'Aurea'
Robinia pseudoacacia 'Frisia'
Sorbus aria 'Chrysophylla'
Tilia × europaea 'Wratislaviensis'
Ulmus × hollandica 'Dampieri
   Aurea'

SHRUBS

Acer shirasawanum 'Aureum'
Berberis thunbergii 'Aurea'
Calluna vulgaris 'Beoley Gold'
   'Gold Haze'
   'Joy Vanstone'
   'Orange Queen'
   'Robert Chapman'
   'Sir John Charrington'
Choysia ternata 'Sundance'
Cornus alba 'Aurea'
   mas 'Aurea'
   'Aurea Elegantissima'
Corylus avellana 'Aurea'
Erica carnea 'Ann Sparkes'
   'Aurea'
   'Foxhollow'

Erica carnea 'Golden Drop'
   'Golden Hue'
   × darleyensis 'Jack H.
   Brummage'
   vagans 'Valerie Proudley'
Euonymus japonicus 'Ovatus
   Aureus'
Ligustrum ovalifolium 'Aureum'
   'Vicaryi'
Lonicera nitida 'Baggesen's
   Gold'
Philadelphus coronarius 'Aureus'
Physocarpus opulifolius 'Dart's
   Gold'
Pittosporum tenuifolium
   'Warnham Gold'
Ptelea trifoliata 'Aurea'
Ribes alpinum 'Aureum'
   sanguineum 'Brocklebankii'
Sambucus nigra 'Aurea'
   racemosa 'Plumosa Aurea'
   'Sutherland Gold'
Viburnum opulus 'Aureum'
Weigela 'Looymansii Aurea'
   'Rubidor'

CLIMBERS

Hedera helix 'Buttercup'
Humulus lupulus 'Aureus'
Jasminum officinale 'Fiona
   Sunrise'

CONIFERS

Abies nordmanniana 'Golden
   Spreader'
Calocedrus decurrens 'Berrima
   Gold'
Cedrus atlantica 'Aurea'
   deodara 'Aurea'

Chamaecyparis lawsoniana:
  many cvs, including
  'Aurea Densa'
  'Lane'
  'Minima Aurea'
  'Stardust'
  'Stewartii'
  'Winston Churchill'
  obtusa: several cvs, including
  'Crippsii'
  'Fernspray Gold'
  'Nana Aurea'
  'Tetragona Aurea'
  pisifera: several cvs, including
  'Filifera Aurea'
  'Gold Spangle'
  'Golden Mop'
  'Plumosa Aurea'
Cryptomeria japonica 'Sekkan-sugi'
× *Cupressocyparis leylandii*
  'Castlewellan Gold'
Cupressus macrocarpa: several
  cvs, especially
  'Donard Gold'
  'Goldcrest'
Cupressus sempervirens 'Swane's
  Golden'

Juniperus chinensis 'Aurea'
  communis 'Depressa Aurea'
  × *media*: several, including
  'Gold Coast'
  'Old Gold'
  'Pfitzeriana Aurea'
  'Plumosa Aurea'
  'Sulphur Spray'
Picea orientalis 'Aurea'
Pinus sylvestris 'Aurea'
Taxus baccata: several cvs,
  including
  'Adpressa Variegata'
  'Dovastonii Aurea'
  'Elegantissima'
  'Standishii'
  'Summergold'
Thuja occidentalis: several cvs,
  especially
  'Europe Gold'
  'Rheingold'
  orientalis: several cvs,
  especially
  'Aurea Nana'
  plicata 'Aurea'
Thujopsis dolabrata 'Aurea'

From top: The deep red foliage of *Acer palmatum* 'Bloodgood' holds its
colour well; the leaves of *Sambucus racemosa* 'Plumosa Aurea' are
graceful as well as being a beautiful golden-yellow; and *Vitis vinifera*
'Purpurea' turns from claret red to vinous purple through the autumn

Plants with Grey or Silver Foliage

Grey, silver and blue foliage does not have to be treated with quite the same degree of caution with which you should approach other coloured leaves. The subtle grading into shades of green makes for a much softer, quieter range of tones and the contrasts are more gentle.

Many woody plants with silver or grey foliage are adapted to withstand drought. The hairs or waxy coatings that give them their colour are usually there to minimize water loss.

TREES

Eucalyptus: many, including
    coccifera
    gunnii
    pauciflora subsp. *niphophila*
Populus alba
    canescens
Pyrus: several, especially
    nivalis
    salicifolia 'Pendula'
Salix alba var. *sericea*
    exigua
Sorbus aria 'Lutescens'

SHRUBS

Artemisia (all)
Atriplex halimus
Berberis dityophylla
    temolaica
Buddleja: several, including
    alternifolia 'Argentea'
    fallowiana
Calluna vulgaris 'Silver Queen'
    'Sister Anne'
Caryopteris × *clandonensis* cvs
Cassinia vauwilliersii var. *albida*
Cistus 'Peggy Sammons'
    'Silver Pink'
Convolvulus cneorum
Cytisus battandieri
Elaeagnus: several, including
    angustifolia
    commutata
    macrophylla
Erica tetralix 'Alba Mollis'
Euryops acraeus
    pectinatus
Feijoa sellowiana
Halimiocistus wintonensis
Halimium lasianthum
    ocymoides
Halimodendron halodendron

Hebe: several, including
    albicans
    pimeleoides 'Quicksilver'
    pinguifolia 'Pagei'
Helianthemum: several cvs,
    including
    'Rhodanthe Carneum'
    'Wisley Pink'
    'Wisley White'
Helichrysum (all)
Hippophae rhamnoides
Lavandula angustifolia: several
    cvs, including
    'Grappenhall'
    'Hidcote'
    'Vera'
    stoechas and forms
Leptospermum lanigerum
Olearia: several, including
    × *mollis*
    × *scilloniensis*
Perovskia atriplicifolia 'Blue Spire'
Potentilla arbuscula 'Beesii'
    'Vilmoriniana'
Romneya (all)
Rosa glauca
Ruta graveolens and cvs
Salix elaeagnos
    exigua
    gracilistyla
    lanata
    repens var. *argentea*
Salvia officinalis
Santolina chamaecyparissus
    pinnata subsp. *neapolitana*
Senecio: several, especially
    'Sunshine'
Teucrium fruticans and cvs
Zauschneria cana

CLIMBERS

Lonicera caprifolium and cvs
Vitis vinifera 'Incana'

CONIFERS

Abies concolor 'Candicans'
    'Compacta'
    pinsapo 'Glauca'
Cedrus atlantica Glauca group
Chamaecyparis lawsoniana: many
    cvs, including
    'Columnaris'
    'Ellwoodii'
    'Fletcheri'
    'Pembury Blue'
    'Triomf van Boskoop'
    'Van Pelt'
    pisifera 'Boulevard'
Cupressus cashmeriana
    glabra 'Pyramidalis'
    lusitanica 'Glauca Pendula'
Juniperus chinensis (several cvs)
    'Grey Owl'

Juniperus horizontalis and cvs
    especially:
    'Bar Harbor'
    'Wiltonii'
    × *media* 'Blaauw'
    'Pfitzeriana Compacta'
    procumbens
    scopulorum: several cvs,
    including:
    'Blue Heaven'
    'Skyrocket'
    'Springbank'
    squamata 'Blue Carpet'
    'Blue Star'
    'Meyeri'
    virginiana 'Glauca'
Picea pungens Glauca group
Pinus koraiensis 'Compacta
    Glauca'
    sylvestris 'Edwin Hillier'
    wallichiana

Plants with Variegated Foliage

Opinions on the value of variegated foliage vary. Some gardeners will not entertain variegation at any price while others actively collect plants with variegated leaves. There are so many kinds of variegation and individual tastes vary so greatly that it is impossible to generalize. What can be said is that coloured foliage tends to be rewarding in direct proportion to the restraint applied to its use.

Trees with variegated foliage are at their most effective when grown apart from others so that their canopies are low and not too far from eye level. If they are overcrowded, their variegation may be rendered all but invisible. Variegated shrubs are objects of contrast and accent and should be positioned with this in mind.

TREES

Acer negundo 'Elegans'
    'Flamingo'
    'Variegatum'
    platanoides 'Drummondii'
    pseudoplatanus 'Leopoldii'
    'Nizetti'
Castanea sativa 'Albomarginata'
Cornus controversa 'Variegata'
Crataegus monogyna 'Variegata'
Fagus sylvatica 'Albovariegata'
Fraxinus pennsylvanica 'Variegata'
Ilex × *altaclerensis*: several cvs,
    including

Ilex altaclarensis × 'Belgica
    Aurea'
    'Golden King'
Ligustrum lucidum 'Excelsum
    Superbum'
    'Tricolor'
Liquidambar styraciflua 'Silver
    King'
    'Variegata'
Liriodendron tulipifera 'Aureo-
    marginatum'
Platanus × *hispanica* 'Suttneri'
Populus × *candicans* 'Aurora'
Quercus cerris 'Variegata'

SHRUBS

Acer palmatum: several cvs,
    especially
    'Butterfly'
    'Kagiri Nishiki'
    'Ukigumo'
Aralia elata 'Aureovariegata'
    'Variegata'
Aucuba japonica: several cvs,
    especially
    'Crotonifolia'
    'Gold Dust'
    'Variegata'
Azara integrifolia 'Variegata'
    microphylla 'Variegata'
Berberis thunbergii 'Pink Queen'
    'Rose Glow'
Buddleja davidii 'Harlequin'
Buxus sempervirens
    'Elegantissima'
Cleyera japonica 'Tricolor'
Cornus alba 'Elegantissima'
    'Spaethii'
    alternifolia 'Argentea'
    florida 'Rainbow'
    'Welchii'
    mas 'Variegata'
    stolonifera 'White Gold'
Coronilla valentina 'Variegatus'
Daphne × burkwoodii 'Carol
    Mackie' and similar cvs
    cneorum 'Variegata'
    longilobata 'Peter Moore'
    odora 'Aureo-marginata'
Elaeagnus × ebbingei 'Gilt Edge'
    'Limelight'
    pungens 'Dicksonii'
    'Frederici'
    'Maculata'
    'Variegata'
Euonymus fortunei 'Emerald
    Gaiety'
    'Emerald 'n' Gold'
    'Silver Pillar'
    'Silver Queen'
    'Variegatus'
    japonicus: especially
    'Aureus'
    'Latifolius Albomarginatus'
    'Microphyllus Pulchellus'
    'Microphyllus Variegatus'
× Fatshedera lizei 'Annemieke'
    'Variegata'

Fatsia japonica 'Variegata'
Feijoa sellowiana 'Variegata'
Fuchsia magellanica 'Sharpitor'
    'Variegata'
    'Versicolor'
Griselinia littoralis 'Dixon's
    Cream'
    'Variegata'
Hebe × andersonii 'Variegata'
    × franciscana 'Variegata'
    glaucophylla 'Variegata'
    'Purple Tips'
Hypericum × moserianum
    'Tricolor'
Ilex aquifolium: many cvs,
    especially
    'Argentea Marginata'
    'Golden Milkboy'
    'Golden Queen'
    'Handsworth New Silver'
    'Silver Milkmaid'
Kerria japonica 'Variegata'
Leucothoë fontanesiana 'Rainbow'
Ligustrum sinense 'Variegatum'
Myrtus communis 'Variegata'
Myrtus luma 'Glanleam Gold'
Osmanthus heterophyllus
    'Aureomarginatus'
    'Goshiki'
    'Variegatus'
Pachysandra terminalis
    'Variegata'
Philadelphus coronarius 'Variegatus'
Phormium (many)
Photinia davidiana 'Palette'
Pieris japonica 'Little Heath'
    'Variegata'
Pittosporum eugenioides
    'Variegatum'
    'Garnettii'
    tenuifolium: several cvs,
    including
    'Irene Paterson'
    'Silver Queen'
    tobira 'Variegatum'
Prunus laurocerasus 'Marbled
    White'
    lusitanica 'Variegata'
Rhamnus alaternus
    'Argenteovariegata'
Rhododendron ponticum
    'Variegatum'
Rubus microphyllus 'Variegatus'

Salvia officinalis 'Icterina'
    'Tricolor'
Sambucus nigra
    'Aureomarginata'
    'Pulverulenta'
Symphoricarpos orbiculatus 'Foliis
    Variegatis'
Viburnum tinus 'Variegatum'
Vinca major 'Variegata'
    minor 'Argenteo-variegata'
Weigela florida 'Variegata'
    praecox 'Variegata'
Yucca filamentosa 'Bright Edge'
    'Variegata'
    flaccida 'Golden Sword'
    gloriosa 'Variegata'

CLIMBERS

Actinidia kolomikta
Ampelopsis brevipedunculata
    'Elegans'
Hedera algeriensis 'Gloire de
    Marengo'
    'Margino-maculata'
    colchica 'Dentata Variegata'
    'Sulphur Heart'
    helix: several cvs, including
    'Adam'
    'Cavendishii'
    'Glacier'
    'Goldchild'
    'Goldheart'
    'Harald'
    'Kolibri'
    'Little Diamond'
    'Sagittifolia Variegata'
    'Sicilia'
Jasminum officinale
    'Argenteovariegatum'
    'Aureum'
Kadsura japonica 'Variegata'
Lonicera japonica
    'Aureoreticulata'
Trachelospermum jasminoides
    'Variegatum'

CONIFERS

Calocedrus decurrens
    'Aureovariegata'
Chamaecyparis lawsoniana
    'Pygmaea Argentea'
    'White Spot'

Chamaecyparis pisifera 'Nana
    Aureo-variegata'
    'Snow'
Thuja plicata 'Irish Gold'
    'Zebrina'

BAMBOOS

Pleioblastus auricoma
Pleioblastus variegatus
Sasa veitchii

Plants with Ornamental Fruits

When botanists speak of fruits they mean seed vessels in general, rather than just the fleshy, edible ones. There are many trees and shrubs whose fruits – in this broad sense – are highly ornamental and valuable in the autumn garden.

If you have a small garden, it is important to choose from the quite wide selection of trees and shrubs whose fruits last well into winter or even as far as the following spring, as those of pyracanthas do. Yellow or amber berries often last longer then red ones, as they are not as attractive to birds. White fruits, such as those of *Sorbus hupehensis*, are often the longest lasting of all.

It helps to prolong the lives of fruits if the trees and shrubs bearing them are planted close to a frequently used area, as this tends to discourage birds. In contrast, trees and shrubs that attract wildlife have tasty, fleshy fruits or regularly attract insects which birds feed on.

TREES

Ailanthus altissima
Arbutus (all)
Catalpa bignonioides
Cercis siliquastrum
Crataegus: many, including
    laciniata
    mollis
    prunifolia
Diospyros kaki
Fraxinus ornus
Halesia (all)
Ilex: all females, including
    'Camelliifolia'
    'Wilsonii'
    aquifolium 'J.C. van Tol'
    latifolia
Koelreuteria paniculata
Magnolia: several, including
    campbellii subsp. *mollicomata*
    hypoleuca
    officinalis var. *biloba*
    tripetala
Malus: many, including
    'Crittenden'
    'Golden Hornet'
    hupehensis
    'John Downie'
    'Red Jade'
    'Red Sentinel'

Malus transitoria
Pterocarya (all)
Sorbus: most, including
    aucuparia and cvs
    commixta
    'Joseph Rock'
    × *kewensis*
    scalaris
    vilmorinii
    'Winter Cheer'
Tetradium daniellii

SHRUBS

Aucuba japonica (female cvs)
Berberis (most, especially
    deciduous)
Callicarpa (all)
Chaenomeles (most)
Citrus 'Meyer's Lemon'
Colutea (all)
Coriaria (all)
Cornus: many, especially
    amomum
    mas
    'Variegata'
    'Porlock'
Cotinus (all)
Cotoneaster (all)
Daphne mezereum
    tangutica

From top: Malus 'Golden Hornet' is a good example of fruiting crab apple; *Rosa moyesii* 'Geranium' has the bonus of smooth scarlet fruits after flowering; and *Hamamelis mollis* 'Pallida' is known for its scent

Decaisnea fargesii

Euonymus: many, including
  europaeus 'Red Cascade'
  hamiltonianus 'Coral Charm'
  latifolius
  oxyphyllus
  planipes

× Gaulnettya cvs

Gaultheria: many, including
  cuneata
  miqueliana
  procumbens

Hippophae rhamnoides

Ilex: females, including
  aquifolium 'Amber'
  'Bacciflava'
  'Pyramidalis'
  'Pyramidalis Fructu Luteo'
  cornuta 'Burfordii'

Leycesteria formosa

Mahonia aquifolium
  japonica
  lomariifolia

Mespilus germanica cvs

Pernettya mucronata and cvs

Photinia davidiana and forms

Poncirus trifoliata

Prunus laurocerasus and cvs

Ptelea trifoliata

Pyracantha (all)

Rosa: many, including
  'Arthur Hillier'
  'Highdownensis'
  macrophylla and cvs
  moyesii and forms
  rugosa and cvs
  webbiana

Rubus phoenicolasius

Ruscus aculeatus

Sambucus (most)

Skimmia japonica (female forms)
  subsp. reevesiana

Staphylea (all)

Symphoricarpos (most)

Symplocos paniculata

Vaccinium: several, including
  corymbosum and cvs
  cylindraceum
  vitis-idaea

Viburnum: many, including
  betulifolium
  opulus and cvs
  setigerum

Viburnum wrightii 'Hessei'

CLIMBERS

Actinidia chinensis

Akebia quinata
  trifoliata

Ampelopsis: several, especially
  brevipedunculata

Billardiera longiflora

Celastrus (all)

Clematis: several, especially
  tangutica
  tibetana subsp. vernayi

Parthenocissus (several)

Passiflora caerulea
  edulis

Schisandra

Stauntonia hexaphylla

Vitis: several, especially
  'Brant'

CONIFERS

Abies: many, including
  forrestii
  koreana
  procera

Picea: many, including
  abies 'Acrocona'
  likiangensis
  purpurea
  smithiana

Pinus: many, including
  wallichiana

Taxus baccata 'Lutea'

Plants with Fragrant Flowers

Many trees and shrubs have fragrant flowers. In addition, it is worth noting that a high proportion of those that flower in winter are scented, so if you plan to have flowers in winter, you are almost certain to enjoy scent as well.

It is possible to plant nothing but scented plants and have a diverse and interesting garden. In practice, however, you are more likely to select comparatively few, so it is important that they are sited to the best advantage. This means planting them near paths or sitting areas. It is a good idea to put scented plants towards the boundary of the garden from which the prevailing wind comes, otherwise their fragrance will be wafted into neighbouring gardens rather than your own. Alternatively, they may be located in a sheltered area near a kitchen window or walkway.

TREES

Acacia dealbata

Aesculus hippocastanum

Azara microphylla

Cladrastis lutea
  sinensis

Crataegus monogyna

Drimys winteri

Eucryphia × intermedia 'Rostrevor'
  lucida

Fraxinus mariesii

Laburnum alpinum
  × watereri 'Vossii'

Magnolia hypoleuca
  kobus
  macrophylla
  salicifolia

Malus baccata var. mandshurica
  coronaria 'Charlottae'
  floribunda
  'Hillieri'
  hupehensis
  'Profusion'
  × robusta

Michelia doltsopa

Myrtus luma

Prunus 'Amanogawa'
  'Jo-nioi'
  lusitanica and cvs
  × yedoensis and cvs

Robinia pseudoacacia and cvs

Styrax japonica

Tilia × euchlora
  oliveri
  platyphyllos
  tomentosa and cvs

SHRUBS

Abelia chinensis
  × grandiflora
  triflora

Abeliophyllum distichum

Berberis buxifolia
  sargentiana

Brugmansia suaveolens

Buddleja: many, including
  alternifolia
  crispa
  davidii and cvs
  fallowiana
  'Lochinch'

Buxus sempervirens and cvs

Camellia sasanqua cvs

Ceanothus 'Gloire de Versailles'

Chimonanthus praecox and cvs

Chionanthus virginicus

Choisya 'Aztec Pearl'
  ternata

Citrus 'Meyer's Lemon'

Clerodendrum bungei

Clethra alnifolia and cvs
  barbinervis
  fargesii

Colletia hystrix 'Rosea'
  paradoxa

Corokia cotoneaster

Coronilla valentina subsp. glauca

Corylopsis (all)

Cytisus battandieri
  'Porlock'
  × praecox and cvs

Daphne: many, including
  bholua 'Jacqueline Postill'
  blagayana

Plants with Fragrant Flowers (continued)

Daphne × burkwoodii and cvs
  cneorum and forms
  collina
  × hybrida
  × mantensiana 'Manten'
  mezereum and cvs
  × napolitana
  odora and cvs
  pontica
  tangutica
Deutzia compacta and cvs
  × elegantissima and cvs
Edgeworthia chrysantha
Elaeagnus (all)
Erica arborea var. alpina
  × darleyensis and cvs
  lusitanica
  × veitchii
Eucryphia glutinosa
  milliganii
Euonymus planipes
Fothergilla gardenii
  major
Genista aetnensis
Hamamelis × intermedia cvs
  mollis and cvs
Hoheria glabrata
  lyallii
Itea ilicifolia
  virginica
Jasminum humile 'Revolutum'
Ligustrum: all, including
  quihoui
  sinense
Lomatia myricoides
Lonicera fragrantissima
  × purpusii
  'Winter Beauty'
  standishii
  syringantha
Luculia gratissima
Lupinus arboreus
Magnolia denudata
  grandiflora and cvs
  × loebneri and cvs
  sieboldii
  sinensis
  × soulangeana and cvs
  stellata and cvs
  × thompsoniana

Magnolia virginiana
  × wieseneri
  wilsonii
Mahonia japonica
Myrtus communis and cvs
Oemleria cerasiformis
Olearia × haastii
  ilicifolia
  macrodonta and cvs
Osmanthus (all)
Paeonia × lemoinei and cvs
Philadelphus: many, including
  'Belle Etoile'
  'Bouquet Blanc'
  coronarius and cvs
  'Erectus'
  microphyllus
  'Sybille'
  'Virginal'
Pimelea prostrata
Pittosporum tenuifolium
  tobira
Poncirus trifoliata
Prunus mume and cvs
Ptelea trifoliata
Pterostyrax hispida
Pyracantha (all)
Rhododendron: many, including
  Albatross group
  arborescens
  auriculatum
  calophytum
  'Countess of Haddington'
  decorum
  fortunei
  'Fragrantissimum'
  loderi and cvs
  luteum
  'Polar Bear'
  roseum
  viscosum
  deciduous azaleas: many, especially
  'Daviesii'
  'Exquisitum'
  'Irene Koster'
Ribes alpinum
  gayanum
  odoratum
Romneya (all)
Rosa: many, including
  'Albert Edwards'
  'Andersonii'

Rosa 'Anemonoides'
  banksiae (single forms)
  bracteata
  filipes 'Kiftsgate'
  helenae
  mulliganii
  'Macrantha'
  moschata
  primula
  rugosa and cvs
  wichuraiana
Sarcococca (all)
Skimmia × confusa and cvs
  japonica
  'Rubella'
Spartium junceum
Syringa: many, including
  × chinensis 'Saugeana'
  × josiflexa 'Bellicent'
  julianae
  × persica and cvs
  sweginzowii 'Superba'
  vulgaris cvs
Ulex europaeus
Viburnum: many, including
  × bodnantense cvs
  × burkwoodii and cvs
  × carlcephalum
  carlesii and cvs
  'Chesapeake'
  farreri

Viburnum japonicum
  × juddii
Yucca filamentosa
Zenobia pulverulenta

CLIMBERS

Actinidia chinensis
Akebia quinata
Clematis armandii and cvs
  cirrhosa var. balearica
  flammula
  montana and forms
  rehderiana
Decumaria sinensis
Dregea sinensis
Jasminum azoricum
  beesianum
  officinale and cvs
  polyanthum
  × stephanense
Lonicera × americana
  caprifolium and cvs
  etrusca
  japonica and cvs
  periclymenum and cvs
Mandevilla laxa
Stauntonia hexaphylla
Trachelospermum (all)
Wisteria (all)

Plants with Aromatic Foliage

Aromatic plants and those with scented foliage or wood may give off their aroma freely or as a result of gentle bruising. In both cases, they contribute much to the immediate environment. Again, it is advantageous to site such plants near paths or frequently used areas, but on a warm, still summer's day the air of the entire garden will be subtly but unmistakably aromatic.

TREES

Cercidiphyllum japonicum (in autumn)
Clerodendrum (all)
Eucalyptus (all)
Juglans (all)
Laurus nobilis and cvs
Phellodendron amurense
Populus balsamifera
  trichocarpa
Salix pentandra

Sassafras albidum

SHRUBS

Aloysia triphylla
Artemisia 'Powis Castle'
Caryopteris (all)
Cistus: many, including
  × cyprius
  ladanifer
  × loretii
  palinhae

Cistus × purpureus
Clerodendrum bungei
Comptonia peregrina
Elsholtzia stauntonii
Escallonia (many)
Gaultheria procumbens
Hebe cupressoides
Helichrysum italicum subsp.
    serotinum
Illicium (all)
Lavandula angustifolia and cvs
Lindera (all)
Myrica (all)
Myrtus communis and cvs
Olearia illicifolia
    mollis
Perovskia (all)
Prostanthera (all)
Ptelea trifoliata
Rhododendron: many, including
    augustinii
    cinnabarinum forms and

hybrids
Mollis azaleas
'Pink Drift'
    saluenense
Ribes sanguineum and cvs
Rosmarinus officinalis and cvs
Ruta graveolens
Salvia (all)
Santolina (all)
Skimmia: all, particularly
    anquetilia
    × confusa and cvs

CONIFERS
Most conifers, particularly
Calocedrus decurrens
Chamaecyparis (all)
Cupressus (all)
Juniperus (all)
Pseudotsuga menziesii and forms
Thuja (all)

Flowering Plants for Every Season

It is possible to have woody plants in flower during every month of the year in many parts of the temperate world. It is all too easy when buying plants to be carried away by them when they are in flower, and as most people visit nurseries and garden centres during the warmer months this tends to create a concentration of flowering in the summer.

The gardening year is much longer than many people realize, and the plants that flower in autumn, winter and early spring are often among the most interesting. There is nothing quite so cheering, for example, as the golden flowers of the Chinese witch hazel *Hamamelis mollis*, or the airy clouds of white blooms borne on leafless branches in the depths of winter by the cherry *Prunus subhirtella* 'Autumnalis'.

The following lists will enable you to plan a balanced garden in which each month is given its due weight and each year merges seamlessly with the next.

Mid-winter

TREES
Acacia dealbata

SHRUBS
Camellia sasanqua cvs
Chimonanthus praecox and cvs
Erica carnea and cvs
    × darleyensis and cvs

Garrya elliptica
Hamamelis (many)
Jasminum nudiflorum
Lonicera fragrantissima
    × purpusii and cvs
    standishii
Sarcococca (several)
Viburnum × bodnantense and cvs
    farreri
    tinus

Late Winter

TREES
Acacia dealbata
Magnolia campbellii and forms
Populus tremula
Prunus incisa 'Praecox'
    mume and cvs
Rhododendron arboreum & forms
Sorbus megalocarpa

SHRUBS
Camellia sasanqua cvs
Cornus mas
    officinalis
Daphne mezereum
    odora and cvs
Erica carnea and cvs
    × darleyensis and cvs
Garrya elliptica
Hamamelis (many)
Jasminum nudiflorum
Lonicera fragrantissima
    × purpusii and cvs
    setifera
    standishii
Mahonia japonica
Pachysandra terminalis
Rhododendron dauricum
    'Midwinter'
Sarcococca (several)
Ulex europaeus
Viburnum × bodnantense and cvs
    farreri
    tinus and cvs

Early Spring

TREES
Acer opalus
    rubrum
Magnolia (several)
Maytenus boaria
Prunus (several)
Rhododendron (several)
Salix (many)
Sorbus megalocarpa

SHRUBS
Camellia japonica (several cvs)
    sasanqua and cvs
Chaenomeles (several)

Corylopsis pauciflora
Daphne mezereum
Erica carnea and cvs
    × darleyensis cvs
    erigena and cvs
    lusitanica
    × veitchii cvs
Forsythia (several)
Lonicera setifera
Magnolia stellata
Mahonia aquifolium
    japonica
Osmanthus (several)
Pachysandra terminalis
Prunus (several)
Rhododendron (several)
Salix (many)
Stachyurus praecox
Ulex europaeus
Viburnum tinus and cvs

Mid-spring

TREES
Acer platanoides
Amelanchier (several)
Magnolia kobus
    × loebneri and cvs
Magnolia salicifolia
Malus (several)
Prunus (many)

SHRUBS
Amelanchier (several)
Berberis darwinii
Camellia japonica and cvs
    × williamsii and cvs
Chaenomeles (many)
Corylopsis (several)
Cytisus (several)
Daphne (several)
Erica (several)
Forsythia (many)
Kerria japonica and cvs
Magnolia × soulangeana and cvs
    stellata
Mahonia aquifolium
    pinnata
Osmanthus × burkwoodii
    decorus
    delavayi
Pieris (most)

Flowering Plants for Every Season (continued)

Prunus (many)
Rhododendron (many)
Ribes (many)
Spiraea 'Arguta'
  thunbergii
Viburnum (many)

CLIMBERS
Clematis alpina
  armandii
Holboellia coriacea

Late Spring

TREES
Aesculus (many)
Cercis (many)
Cornus nuttallii
Crataegus (many)
Davidia involucrata
Embothrium coccineum and cvs
Fraxinus ornus
Halesia (all)
Laburnum anagyroides
  watereri 'Vossii'
Malus (many)
Paulownia tomentosa
Prunus (many)
Pyrus (all)
Sorbus (many)

SHRUBS
Camellia japonica cvs (several)
Ceanothus (several)
Chaenomeles (many)
Choisya (all)
Cornus florida and cvs
Cotoneaster (many)
Crinodendron hookerianum
Cytisus (many)
Daphne (many)
Dipelta floribunda
Enkianthus (all)
Erica (several)
Exochorda (all)

Genista (many)
Halesia (all)
Helianthemum (all)
Kerria japonica and cvs
Kolkwitzia amabilis
Ledum (all)
Lonicera (many)
Magnolia liliiflora
  × *soulangeana* cvs
Menziesia (all)
Paeonia (many)
Piptanthus nepalensis
Potentilla (many)
Pyracantha (many)
Rhododendron (many)
Rosa (many)
Xanthoceras sorbifolium

CLIMBERS
Clematis (many)
Lonicera (many)
Schisandra (all)
Wisteria (all)

Early Summer

TREES
Aesculus (several)
Crataegus (many)
Embothrium coccineum and forms
Laburnum alpinum
  × *watereri* 'Vossii'
Magnolia: several, including
  hypoleuca
Malus trilobata
Robinia (several)
Styrax (several)

SHRUBS
Abelia (several)
Buddleja globosa
Cistus (many)
Colutea (all)
Cornus kousa
  'Porlock'
Cotoneaster (many)
Cytisus (many)
Deutzia (most)

The pure pink flowers of *Viburnum* × *bodnantense* 'Charles Lamont' appear in late winter; *Jasminum nudiflorum* flowers in late winter; and *Pieris japonica* 'Blush' carries deep-pink inflorescences in mid-spring

Erica ciliaris and cvs
    cinerea and cvs
    tetralix and cvs
Escallonia (many)
Genista (many)
Halimiocistus (all)
Halimium (all)
Hebe (many)
Helianthemum (all)
Hydrangea (several)
Kalmia (all)
Kolkwitzia amabilis and cvs
Lonicera (several)
Magnolia: several, including
    × *thompsoniana*
    virginiana
Neillia (several)
Olearia (several)
Ozothamnus (all)
Paeonia (all)
Penstemon (several)
Philadelphus (many)
Potentilla (all)
Rhododendron (many)
Rosa (many)
Rubus (many)
Spartium junceum
Spiraea (many)
Staphylea (several)
Syringa (many)
Viburnum (many)
Weigela (all)
Zenobia pulverulenta

CLIMBERS

Clematis (many)
Jasminum (several)
Lonicera (many)
Schisandra (several)
Wisteria (all)

Midsummer

TREES

Aesculus indica
Castanea sativa
Catalpa (all)

Cladrastis sinensis
Eucryphia (several)
Koelreuteria paniculata
Liriodendron tulipifera
Magnolia delavayi
    grandiflora and cvs
Stuartia (several)

SHRUBS

Aster albescens
Buddleja davidii and cvs
Calluna vulgaris and cvs
Cistus (many)
Colutea (all)
Daboecia cantabrica and cvs
Desfontainia spinosa
Deutzia setchuenensis
Erica ciliaris and cvs
    cinerea and cvs
    tetralix and cvs
    vagans and cvs
Escallonia (many)
Fuchsia (many)
Grevillea juniperina 'Sulphurea'
Halimodendron halodendron
Hebe (many)
Hoheria (several)
Holodiscus discolor
Hydrangea (many)
Hypericum (many)
Indigofera (several)
Lavandula angustifolia and cvs
Magnolia virginiana
Olearia (several)
Penstemon (several)
Philadelphus (several)
Phygelius (all)
Potentilla (many)
Rhododendron (several)
Romneya (all)
Yucca (several)
Zenobia pulverulenta

CLIMBERS

Clematis (many)
Eccremocarpus scaber
Fallopia baldschuanica

From top: *Kerria japonica* 'Variegata' flowers in late spring; *Halesia monticola* var. *vestita* has large white flowers in late spring; and *Trachelospermum asiaticum* is an evergreen climber for midsummer flowering

Flowering Plants for Every Season (continued)

Jasminum (several)
Lonicera (many)
Mutisia oligodon
Passiflora (several)
Schizophragma (all)
Solanum (all)
Trachelospermum (all)

Late Summer

TREES

Catalpa bignonioides
Eucryphia (several)
Koelreuteria paniculata
Ligustrum lucidum and cvs
Magnolia delavayi
    grandiflora and cvs
Oxydendrum arboreum
Stuartia (several)

SHRUBS

Buddleja (many)
Calluna vulgaris and cvs
Caryopteris (several)
Ceanothus (several)
Ceratostigma willmottianum
Clerodendrum (all)
Clethra (several)
Colutea (all)
Daboecia cantabrica and cvs
Desfontainia spinosa
Deutzia setchuenensis
Elsholtzia stauntonii
Erica ciliaris and cvs
    cinerea and cvs
    tetralix and cvs
    vagans and cvs
Fuchsia (many)
Genista tinctoria and cvs
Grevillea juniperina 'Sulphurea'
Hibiscus (several)
Hydrangea (many)
Hypericum (many)
Indigofera (several)
Itea ilicifolia
Lavandula angustifolia
    (several cvs)
Leycesteria formosa
Myrtus (several)

Olearia (several)
Perovskia (all)
Phygelius (all)
Potentilla (all)
Romneya (all)
Rosa (many)
Yucca (several)
Zenobia pulverulenta

CLIMBERS

Campsis (all)
Clematis (many)
Eccremocarpus scaber
Jasminum (several)
Lonicera (many)
Lapageria rosea cvs
Mutisia oligodon
Passiflora (several)
Pileostegia viburnoides
Fallopia (all)
Solanum (all)
Trachelospermum asiaticum

Early Autumn

TREES

Eucryphia × nymanensis and cvs
Magnolia grandiflora and cvs
Oxydendrum arboreum

SHRUBS

Abelia chinensis
    × grandiflora
    schumannii
Aralia elata
Buddleja (several)
Calluna vulgaris and cvs
Caryopteris (several)
Ceratostigma griffithii
    willmottianum
Clerodendrum bungei
Colutea (several)
Daboecia cantabrica and cvs
Elsholtzia stauntonii
Erica ciliaris and cvs
    cinerea (several cvs)
    terminalis
    tetralix and cvs
    vagans and cvs
Fuchsia (several)
Genista tinctoria and cvs
Grevillea juniperina 'Sulphurea'

Hebe (several)
Hibiscus (several)
Hydrangea (several)
Hypericum (several)
Indigofera (several)
Lespedeza thunbergii
Leycesteria formosa
Perovskia (all)
Potentilla (most)
Romneya (all)
Vitex (all)
Yucca gloriosa
Zauschneria

CLIMBERS

Campsis (all)
Clematis (several)
Eccremocarpus scaber
Fallopia baldschuanica
Jasminium (several)
Lapageria rosea cvs
Mutisia oligodon
Passiflora (several)
Pileostegia viburnoides
Solanum crispum 'Glasnevin'

Mid-autumn

TREES

Magnolia grandiflora and cvs

SHRUBS

Abelia × grandiflora
Calluna vulgaris (several cvs)
Ceratostigma griffithii
    willmottianum
Erica carnea 'Eileen Porter'
    vagans (several cvs)
Fatsia japonica
Fuchsia (several)
Hibiscus (several)
Hydrangea (several)
Hypericum (several)
Lespedeza thunbergii
Mahonia × media and cvs
Potentilla (several)
Vitex (all)
Zauschneria (all)

CLIMBERS

Clematis (several)
Eccremocarpus scaber

Lapageria rosea cvs

Late Autumn

TREES

Prunus subhirtella 'Autumnalis'

SHRUBS

Erica carnea 'Eileen Porter'
Jasminum nudiflorum
Lonicera standishii
Mahonia × media and cvs
Viburnum × bodnantense cvs
    farreri

Early Winter

TREES

Prunus subhirtella 'Autumnalis'
    'Autumnalis Rosea'

SHRUBS

Erica carnea (several cvs)
    × darleyensis 'Silberschmelze'
Hamamelis × intermedia (some)
    mollis
Jasminum nudiflorum
Lonicera fragrantissima
    × purpusii and cvs
    standishii
Mahonia × media and cvs
Viburnum × bodnantense and cvs
    farreri
    foetens
    tinus and cvs

Plants for Hedging

Hedges are invaluable for screening unsightly areas beyond the garden boundary and for reducing traffic noise. Inside the garden, they can be used to create 'rooms', providing separate areas with a considerable degree of privacy or, if they are low, breaking up the eyeline and adding interest. A hedge gives an air of tradition to a garden, and topiary, employed selectively, adds grandeur too; on the down side, hedges cast a good deal of shade and also draw up a lot of moisture from the soil, necessitating more frequent watering of borders.

TREES
Acer campestre
Carpinus betulus
Crataegus monogyna
Fagus sylvatica
Ilex (many)
Laurus nobilis
Quercus ilex

SHRUBS
Berberis (several)
Buxus sempervirens
Caryopteris × *clandonensis* and cvs
Cotoneaster (several)
Elaeagnus (several)
Escallonia
Euonymus japonicus
Griselinia littoralis
Hebe (many)
Hippophae rhamnoides
Lavandula (most)
Ligustrum ovalifolium
   vulgare
Lonicera nitida
   'Baggesen's Gold'
   'Ernest Wilson'
   pileata
Myrtus communis
Olearia haastii
Osmanthus × *burkwoodii*
   delavayi
Phillyrea angustifolia
Pittosporum tenuifolium
Potentilla (many)
Prunus cerasifera 'Nigra'
   'Pissardii'
   × *cistena*

   laurocerasus and cvs
   lusitanica
   spinosa
Pyracantha (most)
Rhododendron ponticum
Rosmarinus officinalis
   'Miss Jessop's Upright'
Rosa (many)
Symphoricarpos Doorenbos
   Hybrids 'White Hedge'
Tamarix gallica
   ramosissima

CONIFERS
Chamaecyparis lawsoniana and
   several cvs
× *Cupressocyparis leylandii* and cvs
Cupressus macrocarpa
   sempervirens
Taxus (several)
Thuja occidentalis
   plicata
   'Fastigiata'
Tsuga heterophylla

From top: Solanum crispum 'Glasnevin' flowers from midsummer to early autumn; *Oxydendrum arboreum* flowers in late summer; *Rosa* 'Canary Bird' can be trained to make an attractive, informal hedge

Guide to Plant Characteristics

TREES

Key to symbols & abbreviations

☐ Suitable for conditions or having marked characteristics listed in column headings

▨ Suitable for extreme conditions or having indicated characteristic to an intense degree

S Semi-evergreen

Flowering time is indicated using the following convention:
1 = mid-winter, 2 = late winter, 3 = early spring, and so on

∗ Acid soil only

Column headings (left to right): CLAY · DRY · CHALK · MOIST/BOGGY · COLD EXPOSED INLAND · COASTAL · EVERGREEN (S=Semi) · DECIDUOUS · LARGE · MEDIUM · SMALL · WEEPING HABIT · UPRIGHT NARROW HABIT · RED OR PURPLE FOLIAGE · GOLD OR YELLOW FOLIAGE · GREY OR SILVER FOLIAGE · VARIEGATED FOLIAGE · AUTUMN COLOUR · BOLD ARCHITECTURAL FOLIAGE · AROMATIC FOLIAGE · ORNAMENTAL FRUIT · ORNAMENTAL BARK · FLOWERING TIME · FRAGRANT FLOWERS · HEDGING/SCREENING · SOUTH/WEST WALLS · SHADE TOLERANT

Tree	Evergreen/Semi	Flowering time
ACER campestre & cultivars (Field maple)		
ACER capillipes & other Snake-barks		
ACER griseum (Paperbark maple)		
ACER negundo & cultivars (Box elder)		
ACER platanoides & cultivars (Norway maple)		4
ACER pseudoplatanus & cultivars (Sycamore)		
ACER rubrum & cultivars (Red maple) ∗		
ACER saccharinum & cultivars (Silver maple)		
AESCULUS (Horse chestnut)		5/6
AILANTHUS altissima (Tree of heaven)		
ALNUS (Alder)		3
AMELANCHIER (Snowy mespilus)		4/5
ARBUTUS (Strawberry tree)		10/11
BETULA (Birch)		
CARAGANA (Pea tree)		5/6
CARPINUS (Hornbeam)		
CARYA (Hickory)		
CASTANEA (Sweet chestnut)		7
CATALPA (Bean tree)		7
CELTIS (Hackberry)		
CERCIDIPHYLLUM		
CERCIS (Judas tree)		5
CLADRASTIS		6/7
CORNUS (Dogwood)		5/6/7
CORYLUS colurna (Turkish hazel)		
COTONEASTER	S	6
CRATAEGUS (Thorn)		5
DAVIDIA (Pocket handkerchief tree)		5
DIOSPYROS (Persimmon)		7
EMBOTHRIUM (Chilean fire bush) ∗		5/6
EUCALYPTUS (Gum)		
EUCRYPHIA ∗		7/8/9
FAGUS (Beech)		
FRAXINUS (Ash)		5/6
GLEDITSIA		
GYMNOCLADUS		
HALESIA (Snowdrop tree) ∗		5
IDESIA		6
ILEX (Holly)		
JUGLANS (Walnut)		
KOELREUTERIA (Pride of India)		7/8
LABURNUM		6
LIGUSTRUM (Privet)		8
LIQUIDAMBAR ∗		
LIRIODENDRON (Tulip tree)		6/7

TREES

Key to symbols & abbreviations

☐ Suitable for conditions or having marked characteristics listed in column headings

▓ Suitable for extreme conditions or having indicated characteristic to an intense degree

S Semi-evergreen

Flowering time is indicated using the following convention:
1 = mid-winter, 2 = late winter, 3 = early spring, and so on

* Acid soil only

	CLAY	DRY	CHALK	MOIST/BOGGY	COLD EXPOSED INLAND	COASTAL	EVERGREEN (S=Semi)	DECIDUOUS	LARGE	MEDIUM	SMALL	WEEPING HABIT	UPRIGHT NARROW HABIT	RED OR PURPLE FOLIAGE	GOLD OR YELLOW FOLIAGE	GREY OR SILVER FOLIAGE	VARIEGATED FOLIAGE	AUTUMN COLOUR	BOLD ARCHITECTURAL FOLIAGE	AROMATIC FOLIAGE	ORNAMENTAL FRUIT	ORNAMENTAL BARK	FLOWERING TIME	FRAGRANT FLOWERS	HEDGING/SCREENING	SOUTH/WEST WALLS	SHADE TOLERANT
MAACKIA			☐					☐		☐									☐				7/8				
MAGNOLIA [Some *]	☐		☐	☐		☐		☐		☐									☐			☐	8/9	☐		☐	
MALUS (Flowering crabs)	☐		▓		☐			☐		☐				☐				☐			☐		4/5	☐			
MORUS (Mulberry)			☐					☐		☐	☐										☐						
NOTHOFAGUS (Southern beech) *				☐		☐		☐	☐									☐									
NYSSA *				☐				☐		☐	☐							▓									
OSTRYA (Hop hornbeam)			☐					☐		☐								☐									
PARROTIA			☐					☐		☐								▓				☐					
PAULOWNIA			☐					☐		☐									☐				5	☐			
PHELLODENDRON (Amur cork tree)	☐		☐					☐		☐								☐	☐		☐						
PHILLYREA	☐		☐			☐	☐				☐												5	☐			
PLATANUS (Plane)	☐		☐					☐	☐										☐			☐					
POPULUS (Popular)	▓	☐	☐	☐	☐	☐		☐	☐	☐		☐	☐		☐	☐	☐	☐							☐		
PRUNUS (Almond, cherry, peach, etc.)	☐		▓			☐		☐		☐	☐			☐				☐			☐	☐	2 to 12	☐	☐		
PTEROCARYA	☐		☐	☐				☐	☐						☐			☐	☐				6				
PYRUS (Pear)	☐		☐			☐		☐		☐		☐				▓							4				
QUERCUS (Oak) [Some *]	☐		☐			☐	☐	☐	☐	☐				☐				☐	☐								☐
RHUS (Sumach)			☐					☐			☐			☐				☐	☐								
ROBINIA (False acacia)		▓	☐					☐	☐				☐		☐								6	☐			
SALIX (Willow)	▓		☐	▓		☐		☐	☐	☐	☐	☐			☐	☐						☐	3				
SASSAFRAS *				☐				☐		☐								☐	☐								
SOPHORA			☐					☐		☐																	▓
SORBUS (Mountain ash/Whitebeam)	☐		☐		☐	☐		☐		☐	☐		☐			☐		☐			☐		5/6	☐			
STUARTIA *				☐				☐		☐								☐				☐	7/8				
STYRAX (Snowbell)				☐				☐		☐	☐												6	☐			
TETRACENTRON			☐					☐		☐								☐	☐				6	☐			
TETRADIUM			▓					☐		☐								☐	☐				6	☐			
TILIA (Lime)	☐		☐					☐	☐			☐											6				
TOONA	☐		☐		☐			☐	☐				☐	☐				☐					7/9	☐			
TRACHYCARPUS	☐	☐				☐	☐			☐									☐				6				
ZELKOVA	☐		☐		☐			☐	☐									☐									

Guide to Plant Characteristics

CONIFERS AS TREES

Key to symbols & abbreviations

□ Suitable for conditions or having marked characteristics listed in column headings

▓ Suitable for extreme conditions or having indicated characteristic to an intense degree

Flowering time is indicated using the following convention:
1 = mid-winter, 2 = late winter, 3 = early spring, and so on

∗ Acid soil only

	CLAY	DRY	CHALK	MOIST/BOGGY	COLD EXPOSED INLAND	COASTAL	EVERGREEN	DECIDUOUS	LARGE	MEDIUM	SMALL	WEEPING	UPRIGHT NARROW HABIT	GOLD OR YELLOW FOLIAGE	GREY OR SILVER FOLIAGE	VARIEGATED FOLIAGE	AUTUMN COLOUR	AROMATIC FOLIAGE	ORNAMENTAL CONES	ORNAMENTAL BARK	HEDGING/SCREENING	SHADE TOLERANT
ABIES (Silver firs) [Some ∗]	□		□	□	□	□	□		□	□	□			□					□			
ARAUCARIA (Monkey puzzle)	□		□	□		□	□		□	□												
CALOCEDRUS (Incense cedar)	□		▓			□	□		□	□			□	□		□		□				
CEDRUS (Cedar)	□		▓			□	□		□	□					□					□		
CHAMAECYPARIS lawsoniana & cultivars (Lawson cypress)	□	□	▓			□	□		□	□		□	□	□	□	□					□	
CHAMAECYPARIS nootkatensis (Nootka cypress)	□	□	□	□	□	□	□		□	□		□							□	□		
CHAMAECYPARIS obtusa & cultivars (Hinoki cypress)	□	□	□	□		□	□			□	□			□		□						
CHAMAECYPARIS pisifera & cultivars (Sawara cypress)	□		□			□	□			□	□			□		□						
CRYPTOMERIA (Japanese cedar)	□		□			□	□		□	□							□		□			
CUNNINGHAMIA (Chinese fir)	□		□				□		□	□												
X CUPRESSOCYPARIS (Leyland cypress)	□	□	□			□	□		□				□	□							□	
CUPRESSUS (Cypress)	□	▓	□			□	□		□	□			□	□					□			
GINKGO (Maidenhair tree)	□	□	□		□	□		□	□	□							□					
JUNIPERUS (Juniper)	□	▓	▓		□	□	□			□	□	□	□	□	□	□		□	□			
LARIX (Larch)	□		□	□	□	□		□	□			□		□			□		□			
METASEQUOIA (Dawn redwood)	□	□	□	▓				□	□				□				□			□		
PICEA (Spruce)	□		□	□	□		□		□	□	□	□			□				□			
PINUS (Pine)	□	▓	□		□	□	□		□	□	□			□	□				□	□	□	
PSEUDOTSUGA (Douglas fir) ∗	□		□		□		□		□									□				
SEQUOIA (Californian redwood)	□	▓	□			□	□		□											□		
SEQUOIADENDRON (Wellingtonia)	□		□		□		□		□											□		
TAXODIUM (Swamp cypress) ∗	□		▓	▓				□	□								□			□		
TAXUS (Yew)	□	□	▓		□	□	□			□	□	□	□	□		□				□	□	□
THUJA (Arborvitae)	□	□	□	□	□	□	□			□	□		□	□	□	□		□			□	
THUJOPSIS	□	□	□			□	□			□	□					□						
TORREYA	□	□	▓			□	□			□	□											□
TSUGA (Hemlock)	□		▓	□		□	□		□	□												□

SHRUBS

Key to symbols & abbreviations

☐ Suitable for conditions or having marked characteristics listed in column headings

▨ Suitable for extreme conditions or having indicated characteristic to an intense degree

S Semi-evergreen

Flowering time is indicated using the following convention:
1 = mid-winter, 2 = late winter, 3 = early spring, and so on

✳ Acid soil only

	CLAY	DRY	CHALK	MOIST/BOGGY	COLD EXPOSED INLAND	COASTAL	EVERGREEN (S=Semi)	DECIDUOUS	LARGE	MEDIUM	SMALL	DWARF	GROUND COVER	RED OR PURPLE FOLIAGE	GOLD OR YELLOW FOLIAGE	GREY OR SILVER FOLIAGE	VARIEGATED FOLIAGE	AUTUMN COLOUR	BOLD ARCHITECTURAL FOLIAGE	AROMATIC FOLIAGE	ORNAMENTAL FRUIT	ORNAMENTAL BARK	FLOWERING TIME	FRAGRANT FLOWERS	HEDGING/SCREENING	NORTH/EAST WALLS	SOUTH/WEST WALLS	SHADE TOLERANT
ABELIA							S																6/9					
ABELIOPHYLLUM																							2					
ABUTILON																							5/9					
ACACIA (Wattle)																							1/2					
ACER japonicum, palmatum & cultivars (Japanese maples)																												
AESCULUS (Horse chestnut)																							5/7					
ALOYSIA (Lemon plant)																							8					
AMELANCHIER (Snowy mespilus)																							4/5					
ANDROMEDA ✳																							5/6					
ANTHYLLIS																							6/7					
ARALIA																							7/9					
ARBUTUS (Strawberry tree)																							10/11					
ARCTOSTAPHYLOS ✳																							4/5					
ARONIA (Chokeberry)																							4					
ARTEMESIA																												
ATRIPLEX							S																					
AUCUBA																												
AZARA																							3					
BALLOTA																							7					
BERBERIS (Barberry)																							4					
BUDDLEJA																							5/6 & 8/9					
BUPLEURUM																							7					
BUXUS (Box)																												
CALLICARPA																							8					
CALLISTEMON (Bottle brush)																							7					
CALLUNA (Ling) ✳																							7/10					
CALYCANTHUS (Allspice)																							7					
CAMELLIA ✳																							2/5					
CARAGANA (Pea tree)																							5					
CARPENTERIA																							7					
CARYOPTERIS																							8					
CASSINIA																							7					
CASSIOPE ✳																							4					
CEANOTHUS (Californian lilac)																							5 & 8					
CERATOSTIGMA (Plumbago)																							8/10					
CERCIS (Judas tree)																							5					
CHAENOMELES (Japonica)																							3/4					
CHAMAEROPS (Fan palm)																												
CHIMONANTHUS (Winter sweet)																							1					
CHIONANTHUS (Fringe tree)																							6/7					
CHOISYA (Mexican orange)																							5/6					
CISTUS (Sun rose)																							6/7					
CLERODENDRUM																							8/9					
CLETHRA ✳																							7/8					

Guide to Plant Characteristics

SHRUBS

Key to symbols & abbreviations

☐ Suitable for conditions or having marked characteristics listed in column headings

▣ Suitable for extreme conditions or having indicated characteristic to an intense degree

S Semi-evergreen

Flowering time is indicated using the following convention:
1 = mid-winter, 2 = late winter, 3 = early spring, and so on

* Acid soil only

Column headings (left to right): CLAY · DRY · CHALK · MOIST/BOGGY · COLD EXPOSED INLAND · COASTAL · EVERGREEN (S=Semi) · DECIDUOUS · LARGE · MEDIUM · SMALL · DWARF · GROUND COVER · RED OR PURPLE FOLIAGE · GOLD OR YELLOW FOLIAGE · GREY OR SILVER FOLIAGE · VARIEGATED FOLIAGE · AUTUMN COLOUR · BOLD ARCHITECTURAL FOLIAGE · AROMATIC FOLIAGE · ORNAMENTAL FRUIT · ORNAMENTAL BARK · FLOWERING TIME · FRAGRANT FLOWERS · HEDGING/SCREENING · NORTH/EAST WALLS · SOUTH/WEST WALLS · SHADE TOLERANT

Shrub	Flowering Time
CLIANTHUS (Lobster's claw)	6
COLLETIA	7/8
COLUTEA (Bladder senna)	6/8
COMPTONIA (Sweet fern) *	3
CONVOLVULUS	5
CORNUS (Dogwood) [Some *]	2/5/6
COROKIA	5/6
CORONILLA	5/7
CORYLOPSIS	3/4
CORYLUS (Hazel)	2
COTINUS (Smoke tree)	6/7
COTONEASTER	6
CRINODENDRON *	5
CYATHODES *	5
CYTISUS (Broom)	5/7
DABOECIA (Irish heath) *	6/8
DANAE (Alexandrian laurel)	
DAPHNE	2/6
DECAISNEA	5
DESFONTAINIA *	7/9
DEUTZIA	6/7
DIERVILLA	6/7
DIPELTA	5
DIPTERONIA	
DISANTHUS *	10
DISTYLIUM	4
DRIMYS	4/5
ELAEAGNUS	5/6 & 10
ENKIANTHUS *	5
ERICA, tall forms (Heath) *	3/5
ERICA canea, mediterranea, terminalis and x daryleyensis	4/5 & 9
ERICA, others *	6/10
ERIOBOTRYA (Loquat)	
ESCALLONIA	6/7
EUONYMUS	5/6
EXOCHORDA	5
FABIANA	5/6
X FATSHEDERA	
FATSIA	10
FORSYTHIA	3/4
FOTHERGILLA *	4
FREMONTODENDRON (FREMONTIA)	6/8
FUCHSIA	7/9
GARRYA	1/2

SHRUBS

Key to symbols & abbreviations

☐ Suitable for conditions or having marked characteristics listed in column headings

▨ Suitable for extreme conditions or having indicated characteristic to an intense degree

S Semi-evergreen

Flowering time is indicated using the following convention:
1 = mid-winter, 2 = late winter, 3 = early spring, and so on

* Acid soil only

Column headings:
CLAY · DRY · CHALK · MOIST/BOGGY · COLD EXPOSED INLAND · COASTAL · EVERGREEN (S=Semi) · DECIDUOUS · LARGE · MEDIUM · SMALL · DWARF · GROUND COVER · RED OR PURPLE FOLIAGE · GOLD OR YELLOW FOLIAGE · GREY OR SILVER FOLIAGE · VARIEGATED FOLIAGE · AUTUMN COLOUR · BOLD ARCHITECTURAL FOLIAGE · AROMATIC FOLIAGE · ORNAMENTAL FRUIT · ORNAMENTAL BARK · FLOWERING TIME · FRAGRANT FLOWERS · HEDGING/SCREENING · NORTH/EAST WALLS · SOUTH/WEST WALLS · SHADE TOLERANT

Name	Flowering Time
X GAULNETTYA *	5/6
GAULTHERIA *	5/6
GENISTA (Broom)	5/9
GREVILLEA *	6/7
GRISELINIA	
x HALIMIOCISTUS (Sun rose)	5/9
HALIMIUM (Sun Rose)	5/6
HALIMODENDRON (Salt tree)	6/7
HAMAMELIS (Witch hazel)	12/3
HEBE (Veronica)	6/10
HEDYSARUM	7/9
HELIANTHEMUM (Rock rose)	5/9
HELICHRYSUM	7
HIBISCUS	7/10
HIPPOPHAE (Sea buckthorn)	
HOHERIA	6/7
HOLODISCUS	7
HYDRANGEA	6/9
HYPERICUM	6/10
ILEX (Holly)	
ILLICIUM	5/6
INDIGOFERA	6/9
ITEA ilicifolia	8
JASMINUM (Jasmine)	11/12 & 6/7
KALMIA *	4/6
KERRIA	4/5
KOLKWITZIA (Beauty bush)	5/6
LAURUS (Sweet bay)	
LAVANDULA (Lavender)	7
LAVATERA (Mallow)	6/10
LEDUM *	4/6
LEIOPHYLLUM *	5/6
LEPTOSPERMUM	5/6
LESPEDEZA	8/9
LEUCOTHOE *	5/8
LEYCESTERIA	6/9
LIGUSTRUM (Privet)	6/9
LINDERA *	
LOMATIA *	7
LONICERA (Honeysuckle)	1/3 & 5/6
MAGNOLIA [Some *]	7/9 & 3/4
X MAHOBERBERIS	4
MAHONIA	11/4
MENZIESIA *	5

Guide to Plant Characteristics

SHRUBS

Key to symbols & abbreviations

☐ Suitable for conditions or having marked characteristics listed in column headings

▨ Suitable for extreme conditions or having indicated characteristic to an intense degree

S Semi-evergreen

Flowering time is indicated using the following convention:
1 = mid-winter, 2 = late winter, 3 = early spring, and so on .

* Acid soil only

	CLAY	DRY	CHALK	MOIST/BOGGY	COLD EXPOSED INLAND	COASTAL	EVERGREEN (S=Semi)	DECIDUOUS	LARGE	MEDIUM	SMALL	DWARF	GROUND COVER	RED OR PURPLE FOLIAGE	GOLD OR YELLOW FOLIAGE	GREY OR SILVER FOLIAGE	VARIEGATED FOLIAGE	AUTUMN COLOUR	BOLD ARCHITECTURAL FOLIAGE	AROMATIC FOLIAGE	ORNAMENTAL FRUIT	ORNAMENTAL BARK	FLOWERING TIME	FRAGRANT FLOWERS	HEDGING/SCREENING	NORTH/EAST WALLS	SOUTH/WEST WALLS	SHADE TOLERANT
MYRICA																							6/7					
MYRTUS (Myrtle)		☐	☐			☐	☐			☐							☐			☐			7/8	☐			☐	
NANDINA (Sacred bamboo)		☐					☐			☐				☐									6/7					
NEILLIA	☐		▨					☐		☐													5/6					
OLEARIA (Daisy bush)		☐	☐			▨	☐			☐						☐				☐			5/8	☐				
ONONIS		☐	☐					☐			☐												6/7					
OSMANTHUS		☐	☐				☐			☐							☐						4/5 & 9	☐				
X OSMAREA		☐	☐				☐			☐													4/5	☐				
OZOTHAMNUS		☐				☐	☐			☐										☐			7	☐				
PACHYSANDRA		☐	☐				☐				☐		☐				☐						2/3					☐
PAEONIA (Tree paeony)		☐	▨					☐		☐									☐				5/6					
PARAHEBE	☐	☐	☐				☐					☐											7/8					
PARROTIA		☐	☐					☐		☐								☐				☐	3					
PERNETTYA *		☐		☐			☐				☐									☐			5/6					☐
PEROVSKIA		☐	☐					☐		☐						☐				☐			8/9					
PHILADELPHUS (Mock orange)	☐	☐	▨					☐		☐					☐								6/7	☐				
PHILESIA *				☐			☐				☐												6/7					
PHILLYREA		☐	☐				☐			☐													5	☐				
PHLOMIS		☐	☐				☐				☐					☐				☐			6					
PHORMIUM	☐					☐	☐			☐				☐			☐		☐				7/9					
PHOTINIA	☐		☐				☐			☐				☐									5/6					
PHYGELIUS (Cape figwort)	☐		☐					☐			☐												7/9					
PHYLLODOCE *				☐	☐		☐					☐											5/6					
PHYLLOSTACHYS (Bamboo)		☐					☐			☐												☐						
PHYSOCARPUS	☐		☐					☐		☐					☐								6					
PIERIS *				☐			☐			☐				☐			☐						3/5					☐
PIPTANTHUS (Evergreen laburnum)	☐		☐			S				☐													5			☐	☐	
PITTOSPORUM	☐	☐	☐			☐	☐			☐							☐			☐			5/6	☐	☐			
PLEIOBLASTUS (Bamboo)	☐	☐	☐			☐	☐				☐						☐											
POLYGALA *				☐			☐					☐											4/6					
PONCIRUS (Bitter orange)		☐						☐		☐										☐			5	☐				
POTENTILLA	☐	▨	☐					☐			☐												6/11					
PRUNUS	☐	☐	▨				☐			☐				☐				☐					3/6		☐			
PTELEA (Hop tree)	☐							☐		☐					☐					☐			6	☐				
PTEROSTYRAX	☐	☐						☐		☐										☐			6/7					
PUNICA (Pomegranate)		☐	☐					☐		☐					☐			☐					9/10				☐	
PYRACANTHA (Firethorn)	☐		☐				☐			☐										☐			6		☐	☐		
RHAMNUS (Buckthorn)	☐	☐					☐			☐							☐			☐								
RHAPHIOLEPIS		☐	☐				☐				☐												6					
RHODODENDRON *	☐			☐			☐			☐									☐				1/8					☐
RHODODENDRON AZALEA, deciduous *	☐			☐				☐		☐								☐					5/6					
RHODODENDRON AZALEA, evergreen *	☐			☐			☐				☐												4/5					
RHODOTYPOS	☐	☐	▨					☐		☐										☐			5/7					
RHUS (Sumach)	☐	☐	▨					☐		☐								▨										
RIBES (Currants and Gooseberries)	☐	☐	▨					☐		☐							☐			☐			2/5					

SHRUBS

Key to symbols & abbreviations

☐ Suitable for conditions or having marked characteristics listed in column headings

▨ Suitable for extreme conditions or having indicated characteristic to an intense degree

S Semi-evergreen

Flowering time is indicated using the following convention:
1 = mid-winter, 2 = late winter, 3 = early spring, and so on

✳ Acid soil only

Plant	Flowering Time
ROMNEYA (Tree poppy)	7/10
ROSA (Rose species)	5/7
ROSE (Shrub roses)	6/9
ROSMARINUS (Rosemary)	5
RUBUS (Brambles)	5/8
RUSCUS (Butcher's broom)	
RUTA (Rue)	6/8
SALIX (Willow)	2/3
SALVIA	8/9 (evergreen = S)
SAMBUCUS (Elder)	6
SANTOLINA (Lavender cotton)	7
SARCOCOCCA (Christmas box)	2
SASA (Bamboo)	
SENECIO	6/7
SKIMMIA	4/5
SORBARIA	6/8
SORBUS reducta	5
SPARTIUM (Spanish broom)	6/8
SPIRAEA	4/8
STACHYURUS	3
STAPHYLEA (Bladder nut)	5/6
STEPHANANDRA	6
SYCOPSIS	2/3
SYMPHORICARPOS	
SYRINGA (Lilac)	5/6
TAMARIX (Tamarisk)	3 & 7/9
TELOPEA (Waratah) ✳	6
TEUCRIUM	6/8
TROCHODENDRON ✳	5/6
ULEX (Gorse)	3/5 & 8/10
VACCINIUM ✳	5/6
VIBURNUM	11/3 & 4/6
VINCA (Periwinkle)	4/6
VITEX (Chaste tree)	9/10
WEIGELA	5/6
YUCCA	7/8
ZENOBIA ✳	6/7

Column headings: CLAY · DRY · CHALK · MOIST/BOGGY · COLD EXPOSED INLAND · COASTAL · EVERGREEN (S=Semi) · DECIDUOUS · LARGE · MEDIUM · SMALL · DWARF · GROUND COVER · RED OR PURPLE FOLIAGE · GOLD OR YELLOW FOLIAGE · GREY OR SILVER FOLIAGE · VARIEGATED FOLIAGE · AUTUMN COLOUR · BOLD ARCHITECTURAL FOLIAGE · AROMATIC FOLIAGE · ORNAMENTAL FRUIT · ORNAMENTAL BARK · FLOWERING TIME · FRAGRANT FLOWERS · HEDGING/SCREENING · NORTH/EAST WALLS · SOUTH/WEST WALLS · SHADE TOLERANT

Guide to Plant Characteristics

CONIFERS AS SHRUBS

Key to symbols & abbreviations

☐ Suitable for conditions or having marked characteristics listed in column headings

▨ Suitable for extreme conditions or having indicated characteristic to an intense degree

Flowering time is indicated using the following convention:
1 = mid-winter, 2 = late winter, 3 = early spring, and so on

* Acid soil only

	CLAY	DRY	CHALK	MOIST/BOGGY	COLD EXPOSED INLAND	COASTAL	EVERGREEN	LARGE	MEDIUM	SMALL	DWARF	GROUND COVER	UPRIGHT, NARROW	GOLD OR YELLOW FOLIAGE	GREY OR SILVER FOLIAGE	VARIEGATED FOLIAGE	AUTUMN COLOUR	AROMATIC FOLIAGE	ORNAMENTAL CONES	SHADE TOLERANT
ABIES (Silver fir)	☐		☐		☐		☐	☐							☐					
CEDRUS (Cedar)	☐	☐					☐	☐												
CEPHALOTAXUS	☐		▨				☐		☐										☐	
CHAMAECYPARIS lawsoniana & cultivars	☐		▨		☐		☐	☐						☐		☐				
(Lawson cypress)																				
CHAMAECYPARIS obtusa & cultivars	☐	☐	☐				☐		☐	☐				☐		☐				
(Hinoki cypress)																				
CHAMAECYPARIS pisifera & cultivars	☐		☐				☐	☐						☐		☐				
(Sawara cypress)																				
CHAMAECYPARIS thyoides & cultivars	☐		☐	☐			☐									☐				
(White cypress)																				
CRYPTOMERIA (Japanese cedar)	☐		☐	☐			☐	☐									☐			
JUNIPERUS (Juniper)	☐	▨	☐		☐	☐	☐		☐	☐		☐	☐	☐	☐	☐			☐	
PICEA (Spruce)	☐		☐	☐	☐		☐	☐							☐					
PINUS (Pine)	☐	▨	☐		☐	☐	☐	☐												
PODOCARPUS	☐		☐			☐	☐		☐										☐	
PSEUDOTSUGA (Douglas fir) *	☐			☐			☐	☐							☐		☐			
TAXUS (Yew)	☐	☐	▨		☐	☐	☐		☐	☐		☐	☐	☐		☐				☐
THUJA (Arborvitae)	☐	☐	▨	☐	☐		☐	☐		☐				☐		☐		☐		
TSUGA (Hemlock)	☐		☐		☐		☐	☐		☐		☐								☐

CLIMBERS

Key to symbols & abbreviations

☐ Suitable for conditions or having marked characteristics listed in column headings

■ Suitable for extreme conditions or having indicated characteristic to an intense degree

S Semi-evergreen

Flowering time is indicated using the following convention:
1 = mid-winter, 2 = late winter, 3 = early spring, and so on

✳ Acid soil only

	CLAY	DRY	CHALK	COASTAL	EVERGREEN (S=Semi)	DECIDUOUS	VIGOROUS	MEDIUM	GROUND COVER	TWINING	SELF CLINGING	RED OR PURPLE FOLIAGE	GOLD OR YELLOW FOLIAGE	VARIEGATED FOLIAGE	AUTUMN COLOUR	BOLD ARCHITECTURAL FOLIAGE	ORNAMENTAL FRUIT	FLOWERING TIME	FRAGRANT FLOWERS	NORTH/EAST WALLS	SOUTH/WEST WALLS	SHADE TOLERANT
ACTINIDIA																		7/8				
AKEBIA					S													4				
AMPELOPSIS																						
ARISTOLOCHIA																		6				
BERBERIDOPSIS																		7/8				
CAMPSIS (Trumpet vine)																		8/9				
CELASTRUS																						
CLEMATIS																		4/10				
FALLOPIA (Russian vine)																		7/9				
HEDERA (Ivy)																						
HUMULUS (Hop)																						
HYDRANGEA, climbing																		6				
JASMINUM (Jasmine)																		8/9				
LONICERA (Honeysuckle)																		5/10				
PARTHENOCISSUS																						
PASSIFLORA (Passion flower)																		6/9				
PILEOSTEGIA																		8/9				
RUBUS (Bramble)																						
SCHISANDRA																		5 & 8/9				
SCHIZOPHRAGMA																		7				
SENECIO					S													9/11				
SOLANUM					S													7/10				
TRACHELOSPERMUM																		7/8				
VITIS (Vine)																						
WISTERIA																		5/6				

PLANT DIRECTORY

A

Abelia *Caprifoliaceae*

A genus of about 30 species of evergreen and deciduous shrubs native to eastern Asia and Mexico. Their profusely borne, funnel-shaped or tubular flowers often have persistent calyces that remain attractive long after the rest of the flower has fallen. They are easily grown in any average soil and perform best in full sun.

Abelia chinensis

A. chinensis A small deciduous shrub with fragrant, rose-tinted white flowers, usually borne in pairs and freely produced from midsummer to mid-autumn. C and E China. In cultivation 1844.
H4

Abelia 'Edward Goucher'

A. 'Edward Goucher' (*A. × grandiflora × A. schumannii*) A small, semi-evergreen shrub with glossy, bright green leaves that are bronze when young. The lilac-pink flowers are borne for a long period in summer and autumn. A first-class shrub for the small garden. Raised 1911 in the United States.
H4 ♔ 1993

A. floribunda A medium-sized evergreen or semi-evergreen shrub producing an abundance of tubular, brilliantly cherry-red flowers, each 5cm (2in) long, in early summer. Best against a warm wall. Mexico. Introduced 1841.
H3 ♔ 1993

Abelia × grandiflora

A. × grandiflora (*A. chinensis × A. uniflora*) A vigorous, arching, medium-sized, semi-evergreen shrub with glossy, dark green leaves. The slightly fragrant flowers appear from midsummer to mid-autumn, and may be borne singly or in clusters of up to four. They are white, tinged with pale pink, as are the persistent sepals. Raised before 1866 in Italy and possibly elsewhere.
H4 ♔ 1993

A. × g. 'Francis Mason' A form with dark green leaves with a golden-yellow margin, the best variegation being obtained in full sun and a dry soil. Originated early 1950s as a sport at Mason's Nurseries, New Zealand, and itself frequently sports to a form with all-gold leaves, which has been called 'Goldsport', 'Goldspot' and 'Goldstrike'.
H4 ♔ 1993

A. schumannii During late summer and well into autumn this small deciduous shrub gives a continuous display of slightly fragrant pink flowers, prettily blotched with

Abelia schumannii

orange. It is very hardy and only damaged in the most severe winters. W China. Introduced 1910 by Ernest Wilson.
H4

Abelia triflora

A. triflora A large, erect deciduous shrub of graceful habit with white, pink-tinged, exquisitely scented flowers produced in dense clusters in early summer. NW Himalaya. Introduced 1847.
H4

Abeliophyllum *Oleaceae*

A genus of one deciduous species. It is related to Forsythia *but has white flowers. Although hardy, it will not thrive unless it has hot sun, but requires only ordinary soil. The flowers should be protected from severe frost. It does best against a warm, sheltered wall.*

A. distichum A small, slow-growing shrub with fragrant, white flowers tinged with

Abeliophyllum distichum

pink. They appear on the purplish, leafless stems in late winter. The leaves sometimes turn purple in autumn. Korea, introduced 1924.

H4

Abies *Pinaceae*
Silver fir

A genus of more than 50 species of evergreen conifers from the northern hemisphere, reaching as far south as Central America and Taiwan. Many of them attain great sizes, particularly in the wild. Most are conical when young. The linear leaves are usually flattened, with greyish or white lines on their lower surfaces and in some species on the upper surfaces as well. The cones are borne on the upper sides of the branchlets and are often an attractive blue-purple or violet when young.

The firs need a deep, moist soil for their best development. Most of them dislike industrial atmospheres and shallow chalk soils, the chief exceptions among those listed being A. cephalonica *and* A. pinsapo *'Glauca'.*

A. alba 'Pyramidalis' A form of the European silver fir, the common species of the mountains of France, Switzerland and Germany but an unsatisfactory garden tree. 'Pyramidalis' is a medium-sized, conical tree, narrow when young, with crowded, ascending branches with short, dark, shining green leaves. In cultivation 1851.

H4

A. balsamea 'Hudsonia' A dwarf shrub of dense and compact habit, with a flattish top and short leaves densely arranged on the branches. A specimen at the Hillier

Abies balsamea 'Hudsonia'

Gardens and Arboretum reached 0.75 × 1.2m (2½ × 4ft) in about 30 years. The typical form, the balsam fir of North America, is a medium-sized tree and a lime-hater, but this dwarf is more lime-tolerant. Introduced before 1810.

H4 ♔ 1993

A. brachyphylla See *A. homolepis*.

A. cephalonica (Greek fir) A large, handsome tree to 30m (100ft) in the wild. The leaves are rigid, sharp-pointed, shining green, up to 2.5cm (1in) long, white beneath and spreading more or less round the branchlets. It is one of the best species for chalky soils and is relatively free from disease, but it breaks into growth early and should not therefore be planted in frost pockets. Mountains of S Greece. Introduced 1824.

H4

Abies cephalonica 'Meyer's Dwarf'

A. c. 'Meyer's Dwarf', syn. *A. c.* 'Nana' A dwarf cultivar with horizontally spreading

branches, rigid branchlets and shorter leaves. In cultivation 1963.

H4

A. c. 'Nana' See *A. c.* 'Meyer's Dwarf'.

A. concolor (Colorado white fir) A very beautiful, large tree with smooth, grey bark that is grooved and scaly on old trees. The leaves are up to 6cm (2½in) long, thick, attractively blue-green or grey-green and arranged in two ranks. The cones are up to 14cm (5½in) long, pale green when young and sometimes purplish-bloomy. SW United States. Introduced 1873.

H4 ♔ 1993

Abies concolor 'Candicans'

A. c. 'Candicans' A striking tree with vivid grey or silvery-white leaves. Introduced before 1929.

H4

A. c. 'Compacta', syn. *A. c.* 'Glauca Compacta' A dwarf shrub of compact but irregular habit and attractive, greyish-blue leaves. It is a wonderful plant, the most outstanding dwarf silver fir, and is suitable for the large rock garden or as an isolated lawn

Abies concolor 'Compacta'

specimen. A specimen at the Hillier Gardens and Arboretum has exceeded 2m (6ft) in height and width. In cultivation 1891.
H4 ⚱ 1993

A. c. 'Glauca Compacta' See *A. c.* 'Compacta'.

A. c. 'Violacea' A form with glaucous blue leaves. In cultivation 1875.
H4 ⚱ 1993

A. fargesii A strong-growing, splendid, medium-sized tree with glossy, purple young shoots. The leaves are loosely two-ranked, up to 5cm (2in) long, notched, dark green above and with two whitish-bloomy bands beneath. Unfortunately, the climate of the British Isles does not suit it and it is not long-lived here. N China. Introduced 1901 by Ernest Wilson.
H4

A. forrestii A distinct, beautiful, small to medium-sized tree. Its leaves are variable but are usually 2–4cm (³/₄–1¹/₂in) long, dark green above and conspicuously silvery-white beneath. The barrel-shaped cones are up to 15cm (6in) long and sloe-black. It is similar to *A. fargesii* in its dislike of the climate of the British Isles. China, Tibet. Introduced c1910 by George Forrest.
H4

A. grandis (Giant fir) A remarkably fast-growing tree, rapidly attaining large size. The leaves are 2–6cm (³/₄–2¹/₂in) long, dark shining green above and with two glaucous-grey bands beneath, horizontally arranged on either side of the shoot. The cones are up to 10cm (4in) long and bright green when young. It grows best in areas with heavy rainfall and prefers a moist but well-

Abies grandis

drained soil. It is a good shade-bearing species and moderately lime-tolerant, and the leaves are delightfully aromatic when crushed. W North America. Introduced 1830 by David Douglas.
H4 ⚱ 1993

A. homolepis, syn. *A. brachyphylla* (Nikko fir) A large, splendid tree, very tolerant of atmospheric pollution. The leaves are up to 3cm (1¹/₄in) long, green above, with two chalk-white bands beneath, and are crowded on the upper sides of the branchlets. The cones are up to 10cm (4in) long, purple when young. Japan. Introduced 1861.
H4

A. koreana A small, slow-growing, neat tree with leaves 1–2cm (¹/₂–³/₄in) long, dark green above, gleaming white beneath, radially arranged on strong shoots, loosely arranged on others. It produces its violet purple, cylindrical cones, which are 5–7.5cm (2–3in) long, even on specimens 50cm (20in) high. However, this description by no means applies to a great many of the

Abies koreana

plants in cultivation, which are of a tall-growing but very poor form, and plants of the more desirable kind are hard to come by. S Korea. Introduced 1905.
H4

Abies koreana 'Silberlocke'

Abies lasiocarpa 'Compacta'

A. k. 'Silberlocke' A slow-growing small tree with the leaves twisted upwards to

reveal their white undersides. Raised before 1979 in Germany.
H4 🏆 1993

A. lasiocarpa arizonica 'Compacta' See *A. l.* 'Compacta'.

A. l. 'Compacta', syn. *A. l. arizonica* 'Compacta' A slow-growing compact form of the cork fir, conical in habit and with leaves of an eye-catching, silvery blue-grey and small purple cones. It is moderately lime-tolerant. SW United States. In culitvation 1927.
H4 🏆 1993

Abies nordmanniana

A. nordmanniana (Caucasian fir) A large to very large noble tree of great ornamental value, with tiered branches that sweep downwards. The leaves are densely arranged on the branchlets, 2–3cm (³⁄₄–1¹⁄₄in) long, shining green above, and marked with two white bands beneath. The cones are 15–20cm (6–8in) long, greenish when young. It is a very satisfactory, generally disease-free species, now being used as

Abies nordmanniana 'Golden Spreader'

a Christmas tree. W Caucasus. Introduced 1840.
H4 🏆 1993

A. n. 'Golden Spreader' A slow-growing dwarf shrub of compact habit. The leaves are 1–2.5cm (¹⁄₂–1in) long, light yellow above, pale yellowish-white beneath. In cultivation 1960.
H4 🏆 1993

A. pinsapo 'Glauca' A form of the Spanish fir selected for its strikingly blue-grey rigid leaves, which are up to 2cm (³⁄₄in) long and radiate from all sides of the branchlets. It is a large tree. Good on chalk. In cultivation 1863.
H4 🏆 1993

Abies procera

A. procera (Noble fir) A most beautiful, large to very large tree with leaves 2.5–3.5cm (1–1¹⁄₂in) long that are bluish green above with two narrow, bloomy bands beneath. They are crowded on the upper sides of the branchlets. The magnifi-

cent, cylindrical cones are 16–25cm (6–10in) long, green when young. W United States. Introduced date 1830 by David Douglas.
H4 🏆 1993

Abies procera 'Glauca'

A. p. 'Glauca' A large tree with blue-grey leaves. In cultivation 1863.
H4

A. spectabilis (Himalayan fir) A magnificent large tree with reddish brown young shoots and densely two-ranked leaves, up to 5cm (2in) long or a little more, that are shining dark green above and gleaming silvery-white beneath. The cones are cylindrical, 14–18cm (5¹⁄₂–7in) long, violet-purple when young. Unfortunately this striking species is susceptible to spring frosts. Himalaya. Introduced 1822.
H4

A. veitchii A beautiful, large, fast-growing tree. The densely arranged, upcurved leaves, 1–2.5cm (¹⁄₂–1in) long, are glossy dark green above and silvery-white beneath. The cones are 5–7.5cm (2–3in) long and are bluish-purple when young. It does not thrive on limy soils. First discovered 1860 by John Gould Veitch on Mt Fuji and introduced 1879 by Charles Maries.
H4 🏆 1993

Abutilon *Malvaceae*

There are more than 100 species of deciduous trees, shrubs and herbaceous plants in this genus, occurring in the tropical and subtropical regions of both hemispheres. Those described below are small to large shrubs with conspicuous, brightly coloured flowers borne over long periods: you can have abutilons in bloom from late spring to mid-autumn. The flowers are large, bell- or open saucer-shaped, or in some species more like dainty Chinese lanterns. They are mainly suitable for a warm wall, cold greenhouse or conservatory, although A. suntense, A. vitifolium and their forms will grow as freestanding specimens in sheltered, sunny sites. Abutilons do well in any average, dryish soil.

Abutilon 'Ashford Red'

A. 'Ashford Red' A medium-sized shrub with large, apple-green leaves and bell-shaped flowers of good texture, size and substance in a deep shade of crushed strawberry in summer and autumn.
H2 ♛ 1993

Abutilon 'Canary Bird'

A. 'Canary Bird' This medium-sized shrub is similar to 'Ashford Red' in form and size, has excellent lush green foliage and is grown for its clear lemon-yellow bell-shaped flowers which it bears throughout

the summer and into early autumn.
H2 ♛ 1993

A. 'Cannington Carol' A dwarf shrub with golden-variegated foliage. The bell-shaped flowers are a vivid, flaming orange in summer and early autumn.
H2 ♛ 1993

Abutilon 'Cannington Peter'

A. 'Cannington Peter' A medium-sized shrub with very dark red bell-shaped flowers, which are carried throughout the summer and into early autumn, and yellow-variegated foliage.
H2 ♛ 1993

Abutilon 'Kentish Belle'

A. 'Kentish Belle' A small to medium-sized shrub with purplish stems and dark green, long-pointed, triangular leaves. The flowers are bell shaped, 4cm (1½in) long, with a red calyx and soft apricot petals faintly veined red and make a spectacular display. They are borne through most of the summer season and into early autumn.

It does best supported against a warm wall.
H3 ♛ 1993

A. 'Louise Marignac' A hybrid medium-sized shrub which is similar to 'Ashford Red' in form and size but with pale pink bell-shaped flowers which are carried throughout the summer and into early autumn.
H2

Abutilon megapotamicum

A. megapotamicum A small to medium-sized shrub with lantern-shaped flowers borne from summer into autumn. They are pendulous and conspicuous, with a red calyx, bright yellow petals and purple anthers. Best against a warm wall, not least because the plant displays its flowers to greatest advantage when given support. Brazil. Introduced 1804.
H3 ♛ 1993

A. m. 'Variegatum' This form differs from the above in having leaves with mottled yellow variegation.
H3

Abutilon × milleri 'Variegatum'

A. × *milleri* A medium-sized shrub with bell-shaped blooms in soft orange with crimson stamens. Again, best when supported against a warm wall, where it will flower continuously and generously throughout the summer and well into autumn.

H2 🏆 1993

A. × *m.* **'Variegatum'** A form differing from the above in having mottled yellow leaves.

H2

A. **'Nabob'** Similar in habit to 'Ashford Red', this medium-sized shrub is a sumptuous combination of dark green leaves and large burgundy flowers tinted plum-purple which are carried throughout the summer and into early autumn.

H2 🏆 1993

Abutilon 'Patrick Synge'

A. **'Patrick Synge'** A vigorous, medium-sized shrub similar to 'Ashford Red' in form and size but with flame-red bell-shaped flowers which are carried throughout the summer and into early autumn.

H2

A. **'Souvenir de Bonn'** A tall, vigorous, upright shrub up to 3.5m (11ft). The leaves are maple-like and grey-green, with edgings and marblings in creamy-white. The bell-shaped flowers, which are carried throughout the summer and into early autumn, are large, salmon-orange, and veined in darker orange.

H2 🏆 1993

A. × *suntense* (A. ochsenii × A. vitifolium) A large, fast-growing shrub that bears its saucer-shaped flowers between late spring

Abutilon × suntense

and midsummer. Raised 1967 intentionally by Hillier Nurseries' propagator Peter Dummer, and also accidentally by Richard Gorer of Sunte House, after which it is named. The flower colour varies. The following clones are available.

H3

A. × *s.* **'Jermyns'** A large shrub with saucer-shaped flowers of lavender to dark

Abutilon × suntense 'Jermyns'

mauve selected from the cross made in the Hillier nursery. The pollen parent was *A. vitifolium* 'Veronica Tennant', which is described below.

H3 🏆 1993

A. × *s.* **'Violetta'** A large shrub with deep violet-blue to indigo saucer-shaped flowers.

H3

A. × *s.* **'White Charm'** A large shrub with

Abutilon vitifolium

Abutilon × suntense 'Violetta'

Abutilon vitifolium 'Veronica Tennant'

pure white flowers and yellow stamens. A chance seedling, 1975.

H3

A. vitifolium A large, handsome shrub with downy, grey-green, vine-shaped leaves and saucer-shaped flowers of pale violet to deep purple-blue. Flowering is from late spring to midsummer, and the shrub should be given a sheltered, sunny position to perform well. A selection of particularly recommended garden-worthy clones are listed given below. Chile. Introduced 1836.

H3

Abutilon vitifolium 'Tennant's White'

A. v. 'Tennant's White' A particularly free-flowering large shrub with very large blooms of pure white.

H3 ♔ 1993

A. v. 'Veronica Tennant' This large shrub was selected for its abundant flowering and large lavender blooms. It is the pollen parent of A. × s. 'Jermyns'.

H3 ♔ 1993

Acacia *Leguminosae*
Wattle

This genus of evergreens should not be confused with the trees and shrubs commonly known as acacia, which belong to the genus Robinia. These are entirely different and consist of some 1,000 species found throughout tropical and subtropical regions, particularly of Africa and Australia. Australian species are known as wattles because their timber was used by early settlers in the wattle-and-daub method of house-building. The leaves are usually bipinnate, often filigree-feathery, but sometimes reduced to phyllodes — expanded, flattened leaf stalks that perform the functions of true leaves. Acacia species are mostly winter- or spring-flowering, cool greenhouse or conservatory shrubs, but some species grow rapidly to tree size outdoors in mild, sheltered areas. The flowers are usually yellow, borne in small, rounded or bottlebrush heads, and made up mainly of stamens. Most are unsuitable for shallow chalk soils, on which their foliage becomes chlorotic yellow. Best grown in neutral or acid soil which is on the dry side.

A. armata (Kangaroo thorn) A prickly large shrub with a dense, bushy habit and small, narrow, dark green phyllodes. In spring the branches are covered all along their length with masses of yellow flowers. Introduced 1803.

H2

A. baileyana (Cootamundra wattle) A large shrub or small tree with attractively

Acacia baileyana 'Purpurea'

Acacia armata

Acacia baileyana

feathery, very blue-green, bipinnate leaves and freely produced clusters of bright yellow flowers which are borne from late winter to early spring. New South Wales. Introduced 1888.
H2 ♛ 1993
A. b. 'Purpurea' A spectacular large shrub or small tree whose young foliage is deep

Acacia dealbata

purple and contrasts well with the blue-green, older leaves.
H2 ♛ 1993
A. dealbata (Silver wattle) The florists' golden mimosa, this is a large shrub or small tree with silvery-green, fern-like leaves and fluffy, golden, fragrant flowers from late winter to early spring. Suitable for a sheltered position in mild areas. SE Australia, Tasmania. Introduced 1820.
H2 ♛ 1993
A. longifolia (Sallow wattle, Sydney golden wattle) A large shrub with long, lance-shaped, dark green phyllodes and bright yellow flowers in spikes 4–8cm (1½–3in) long which are borne in mid or late winter. One of the hardier species, and fairly lime tolerant. Australia, Tasmania. Introduced 1792.
H2–3

Acacia mucronata

A. mucronata (Variable sallow wattle) A large shrub, related to and resembling A. *longifolia* but with much narrower, although variable, phyllodes carrying bright yellow flowers in spikes which are 4–8 cm (1½–3in) long throughout their flowering period from mid to late winter. SE Australia, Tasmania.
H2
A. pravissima (Oven's wattle) The phyllodes of this large shrub or small tree are quite distinctive being triangular, two-veined, blue-green on both sides and with a single spine on the lower side of the broad apex. The plant is attractive on account of its slender arching shoots along with the yellow flowers which are borne in small

Acacia pravissima

Acacia rhetinodes

clusters in early spring. SE Australia.
H2–3
A. rhetinodes (Four-seasons mimosa) A small tree with its main flowering season in summer, although it bears its conspicuous clusters of yellow pompoms freely for most of the year. The foliage consists of narrow, grey-green, willow-like simple phyllodes. It is one of the most lime-tolerant species in the genus. SE Australia, Tasmania. Introduced 1871.
H2 ♛ 1993
A. riceana (Rice's wattle) A graceful large shrub or small tree with slender, weeping shoots and dark green, sharp-pointed phyllodes. The flowers are pale yellow and borne in spring in drooping clusters. Tasmania.
H2

Acanthopanax

See **Eleutherococcus.**

ACER

Aceraceae Maple

The genus *Acer* earns a prime position in gardens largely on account of its autumn foliage

FOR MANY PEOPLE, the term 'acer' has come to mean merely the Japanese maples – the many beautiful forms of *Acer palmatum* and *A. japonicum* (particularly the former). Perhaps 'merely' is the wrong word to use for a large and rapidly increasing group of shrubs and small trees that offer such a variety of foliage, but there is much more to the genus than just the two species, however distinguished they may be.

Acer is also the genus of the sycamore (*A. pseudoplatanus*), the box elder (*A. negundo*) and many other sorts of maples, including the sugar (*A. saccharum*), silver (*A. saccharinum*), red (*A. rubrum*) and Norway maples (*A. platanoides*). Its species are found throughout the northern hemisphere, especially in eastern Asia and North America, and most of them are hardy, adaptable trees in cultivation.

The most recognizable characteristic of acers is the leaf, which is usually lobed like the palm of a hand and either entire (all in one piece) or compound (consisting of several separate leaflets). The sycamore and the field maple (*A. campestre*) are as immediately identifiable as acers as the North American sugar maple – the source of

maple syrup – or the snake-bark maple *A. grosseri* var. *hersii* from central China. Beautiful bark is also found in many species, the most outstanding in this respect being *A. palmatum* 'Senkaki', the coral-barked maple, and the snake-barked maples. These comprise a group of acers, occurring naturally in eastern North America as well as eastern Asia, of which the bark is marked with a reticulate pattern or marbling of cream or white on a green or russet ground quite like the markings on the skin of a python.

However, the genus as a whole probably owes its prime position in gardens to its autumn foliage colour. Acers are magnificent in this respect, colouring well even in climates and conditions that militate against the development of autumn colours. Nevertheless, it is a mistake to latch on to just one quality of any group of plants, and acers are among the ones that readily take their places in the front rank of trees and shrubs because of the great many different ways in which they are beautiful.

SHAPES AND SIZES

Some acers are large, imposing trees, while

others may take a century to attain a height and spread of 3m (10ft). In between are many small to medium-sized trees, and the genus offers a wide choice to owners of small gardens.

At the upper end are the Norway maple and the sycamore. The latter, *A. pseudoplatanus*, is not a good garden tree in itself but comes into its own in a handful of forms with coloured leaves, such as 'Atropurpureum' and 'Brilliantissima'. The common species is dogged by disadvantages which include martyrdom to honeydew-producing aphids and a propensity for germinating its deep-rooted seedlings in the most inconvenient places. The Norway maple (*A. platanoides*) suffers from aphid attacks in North America but is relatively immune in Europe. It is a fine, big tree with clear yellow, occasionally red, autumn colour. The purple-leaved form, *A. p.* 'Crimson King', is magnificent but should be used sparingly, while *A. p.* 'Drummondii' can be the best of all variegated trees in an open situation, although its leaves are inclined to revert to green. Any such growths should be cut back immediately they are seen.

The smallest acers are among the varieties of *A. palmatum* (Japanese maple), some of which make mounds of foliage that, from a distance, look more like silky-haired animals than woody plants. Some of the Dissectum Group are small enough for the larger rock garden, while other forms of the species eventually grow to be trees of 4.5m (15ft) or more.

Between the largest and the smallest is a wealth of trees and shrubs that share the distinction of never being coarse and always displaying elegance. They are aristocrats among the deciduous elements of the garden, whether in full leaf or displaying traceries of fine branches in winter.

FOLIAGE

The typical palmate leaf of the acer can be bold in its effect or, in its smaller version, dainty. How it behaves in a breeze depends on the length of its stalk and the speed with which it twitches to turn its edge to the wind. It can be cut (dissected) to a greater or lesser degree so that the lobes, which may number as many as nine, are finely pinnate, making a soft pelt of foliage in green, bronze-red, or purple; or at the other extreme it can be three-lobed and striking in its simplicity, as in the Nikko maple, *A. maximowiczianum.*

The season for autumn colour among acers starts with the American *A. rubrum* 'October Glory' which, provided the soil is acid or reasonably neutral, turns to flame before any other tree. The others follow either canary yellow as in *A. pensylvanicum* or brilliant red like *A. p.* 'Osakazuki'. The paperbark maple, *A. griseum,* of which the leaves turn red and blackish crimson like dying embers, boasts a peeling, mahogany-orange bark that would warrant the tree's place in gardens were it never to change from green.

CULTIVATION

Acers as a whole are easily grown and most are very hardy. However, other than *A. campestre, A. negundo, A. platanoides* and *A. pseudoplatanus,* it is advisable to plant them where they can be sheltered from wind. The reason for this is two-fold. In the first place, trees that are valued for autumn colour should not be subjected to having their leaves stripped prematurely by wind, and in the second, several species are damaged by cold winds. This applies particularly to *A. palmatum* and its varieties and to *A. japonicum,* a species that also dislikes strong sunlight. It is advisable to avoid sites in which they may suffer from late frosts followed by early morning sun.

A few species, including the field maple, *A. campestre,* positively enjoy a calcareous soil, while most will grow in almost any soil from stiff clay to sand and from limestone to one acid enough for rhododendrons. The main requirement is that it should be rich, moisture-retentive, but at the same time well-drained.

A. buergerianum A small, bushy deciduous tree with three-lobed, ivy-like, persistent leaves that often turn red or orange in autumn. E China, Korea. In cultivation 1890.
H4

A. campestre (Field maple, hedge maple) A picturesque, medium-sized deciduous tree frequently used in rustic hedges. In autumn the foliage turns clear yellow, and may sometimes be flushed with red. Europe (including Britain), W Asia.
H4 ♛ 1993

A. c. 'Elsrijk' A Dutch selection of dense, conical habit. A small tree good for streets. In cultivation 1953.
H4

A. c. 'Postelense' A large shrub or mop-headed small tree with red-stalked leaves that are yellow when young and then turn yellow-green. In cultivation 1896.
H4

A. c. 'Pulverulentum' The leaves of this

Acer buergerianum

Acer campestre 'Pulverulentum'

medium-sized tree are thickly speckled and blotched with white. In cultivation 1859.
H4

A. c. 'Schwerinii' A medium-sized tree with purple leaves. In cultivation 1897.
H4

A. capillipes A small deciduous tree with coral-red young shoots and green-brown bark striated with white. The bright green, three-lobed leaves turn attractive tints of orange and red in autumn. Japan. Introduced 1892 by Charles Sargent, Director of the Arnold Arboretum, Massachusetts, while collecting with James Veitch.
H4 ♛ 1993

A. cappadocicum A medium-sized to large deciduous tree with broad, five- to seven-lobed, glossy leaves, turning rich butter-yellow in autumn. Caucasus, W Asia to the Himalaya. Introduced 1838.
H4Z6

A. c. 'Aureum' A striking small tree with red young leaves soon turning yellow and

Acer capillipes

Acer cappadocicum 'Aureum'

remaining so for many weeks into the summer, then becoming bright green by late summer, followed by yellow again in the autumn. In cultivation 1914.

H4 ♔ 1993

A. c. 'Rubrum' A most attractive medium-sized to large tree in which the young growths are blood-red. The leaves are green in summer and yellow in autumn. Introduced 1838.

H4 ♔ 1993

Acer carpinifolium

A. carpinifolium (Hornbeam maple) A small to medium-sized deciduous tree with leaves remarkably like those of the common hornbeam, but opposite rather than alternately arranged. They turn gold and brown in autumn. Japan. Introduced 1879 by Charles Maries.

H4

Acer circinatum

A. circinatum (Vine maple) A large decidu-ous shrub or occasionally a small tree, with

Acer crataegifolium 'Veitchii'

almost circular leaves that are prettily tinted in summer and turn orange and crimson in autumn. The contrast between the white petals and red bud scales makes for a very pretty floral display in mid-spring. Grows well even in dry, shady positions. W North America. Introduced 1826 by David Douglas.

H4 ♔ 1993

A. crataegifolium 'Veitchii' A large

deciduous shrub or small tree with prettily marked bark and small leaves of variable shape, which are heavily mottled with white and pink and turn brilliant pink and purple in autumn. The flowers are mustard-yellow and borne in slender racemes in spring. In cultivation 1881.

H4

A. dasycarpum See *A. saccharinum*.

A. davidii A small deciduous tree with attractively striated, green and white 'snake-bark' and shining, dark green, ovate leaves that colour richly in autumn. The green fruits are often brightly suffused with red and enhance the autumn effect when hanging all along the branches. C China. Introduced 1879 by Charles Maries.

H4

A. d. 'Ernest Wilson' A form that is rare in cultivation and a more compact tree, with 'snake-bark' trunk and branches that ascend and then arch over. The leaves, which are somewhat cup shaped at the base, have pink stalks and are pale green,

Acer davidii

turning orange-yellow in autumn. This is the form originally introduced by Maries and later by Ernest Wilson and Frank Kingdon-Ward.
H4

Acer davidii 'George Forrest'

A. d. 'George Forrest' The form most commonly met with in cultivation, this is a small, open, 'snake-bark' tree of loose habit with vigorous, spreading branches and large, dark green leaves with rhubarb-red stalks turning orange-red in autumn. Introduced 1921–2 by George Forrest.
H4 ♕ 1993

A. d. 'Serpentine' A small tree with an upright habit, smaller leaves, purple shoots and very good striped bark.
H4 ♕ 1993

A. distylum A medium-sized deciduous tree with undivided, glossy green leaves, something like those of a lime, which are attractively tinted cream and pink when unfolding and provide rich autumn colours. Japan. Introduced 1879 by Charles Maries.
H4

A. forrestii A most beautiful small deciduous tree with striated 'snake-bark', and young stems and leaf stalks of a pretty coral-red. It is not very tolerant of chalky soils. China. Introduced 1906 by George Forrest.
H4

A. f. 'Alice' A small tree with red young shoots and leaves tinged with red, pink and white in summer.
H4

A. ginnala (Amur maple) A large deciduous shrub or small tree of vigorous, spreading, but bushy habit with bright green,

three-lobed leaves that turn orange and vivid crimson in autumn. The yellowish-white flowers, borne in late spring, are fragrant. Manchuria, China and Japan. Introduced 1860.
H4 ♕ 1993

Acer griseum

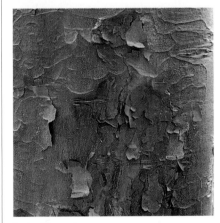

Bark of Acer griseum

A. griseum (Paperbark maple) This is one of the most beautiful of all small trees. The deciduous leaves are each made up of three

leaflets and are dark green, turning the most gorgeous shades of crimson and scarlet in autumn. The bark is rich mahogany, and where it is older – on the trunk and primary branches – it peels in flakes that show orange in the sunlight and reveal the cinnamon-coloured new bark underneath. C China. Introduced 1901 by Ernest Wilson.
H4 ♕ 1993

Acer grosseri var. hersii

A. grosseri var. hersii, syn. *A. hersii* A superb small deciduous tree with wonderfully marbled bark. It bears fruits in long, conspicuous racemes and has rich autumn colour. C China. Introduced 1921.
H4 ♕ 1993

A. heldreichii A very handsome medium-sized deciduous tree, distinctive because of its deeply cleft three-lobed leaves. SE Europe. Introduced 1879.
H4

A. henryi A small to medium-sized, spreading but quite slow-growing deciduous tree with stems marked with bluish striations. The young, beautifully tinted leaves

Acer henryi

have three leaflets, each drawn out into a slender point. As the leaves unfold, they coincide with the slender, drooping catkins of yellow flowers. This tree provides brilliant red autumn colour. C China. Introduced 1903 by Ernest Wilson.
H4

A. hersii See *A. grosseri* var. *hersii*.

Acer japonicum

A. japonicum A large shrub or small

deciduous tree with soft green leaves on downy stalks that turn excellent autumn colours of yellow-orange to red. The flowers are red with yellow anthers and appear in delicate, drooping clusters at the same time as the young leaves. This and the selected forms do best in moist, well-drained soil in a position sheltered from cold winds. Japan. Introduced 1864.
H4

Acer japonicum 'Aconitifolium'

A. j. 'Aconitifolium', syn *A. j.* 'Filicifolium', *A. j.* 'Laciniatum' The leaves of this large shrub or small tree are deeply lobed and cut, and colour a rich ruby-crimson in autumn. In cultivation 1888.
H4 ♆ 1993

A. j. 'Aureum' See *A. shirasawanum* 'Aureum'.

A. j. 'Filicifolium' See 'Aconitifolium'.

A. j. 'Laciniatum' See 'Aconitifolium'.

Acer japonicum 'Vitifolium'

A. j. 'Vitifolium' This large shrub or small

tree has broad, fan-shaped leaves with 10–12 lobes which colour brilliant yellow-orange and red in autumn. In cultivation 1882.
H4 ♆ 1993

Acer lobelii

A. lobelii A fast-growing, medium-sized to large deciduous tree, related to *A. cappadocicum*. It has bloomy young shoots and wavy-edged, dark green leaves with taper-pointed lobes. The branches ascend sharply to form a compact, columnar head that broadens with age. A good tree for growing in restricted spaces. S Italy. Introduced 1683.
H4

A. macrophyllum (Oregon maple) A large deciduous tree with very big, handsome, dark green, shining leaves that turn bright orange in autumn. The drooping clusters of fragrant yellow flowers are also large, and the bristly fruits that follow are very ornamental. It is best planted where there is shelter from high wind. W North America.

Acer macrophyllum

Introduced 1826 by David Douglas.
H4

Acer maximowiczianum

A. maximowiczianum, syn. *A. nikoense* (Nikko maple) A very hardy and beautiful small to medium-sized deciduous tree. The hairy leaves, each consisting of three leaflets, are blue-green beneath and turn glorious orange and flame-red in autumn. In its native ranges it is now rare. Japan, C China. Introduced 1881.
H4

A. maximowiczii Any confusion between this and the last may be dispelled if it becomes confirmed as a subspecies of *A. pectinatum*. It is an attractive small deciduous tree with purplish-red stems that gradually take on the 'snake-bark' striation. The leaves are tinted red throughout the growing season, a colour that becomes richer as autumn approaches. C China. Introduced 1910 by Ernest Wilson.
H4

Acer micranthum

A. micranthum The small, prettily cut, five-lobed leaves of this large deciduous shrub or small tree are beautifully tinted throughout the season and turn bright red in autumn. Japan. Introduced 1879.
H4 🏆 1993

A. negundo (Box elder) A fast-growing, bushy-headed deciduous tree of medium to large size, and not an elder at all. The young shoots are bright green and the leaves are pinnate, with 3–5 and sometimes 7–9 leaflets, which are bright green above and paler underneath. Variegated forms are inclined to revert, producing all-green shoots that should be removed as soon as possible. North America. In cultivation 1688.
H4

A. n. 'Argenteovariegatum' See *A. n.* 'Variegatum'.

Acer negundo 'Auratum'

A. n. 'Auratum' A small tree with leaves of a bright golden-yellow when young, which gradually pale to cream with age.
H4

A. n. 'Elegans', syn. *A. n.* 'Elegantissima' The young leaves of this small tree have bright yellow marginal variegation, paling with age, and the shoots are covered with a white bloom. In cultivation 1885.
H4

A. n. 'Elegantissima' See *A. n.* 'Elegans'.

Acer negundo 'Flamingo'

A. n. 'Flamingo' The young leaves of this attractive form have a broad, soft pink margin that changes to white, often green at first. The shoots have a glaucous bloom. Left to itself it will reach small tree size, but if pruned hard each winter it will make a bushy shrub and the colour will be more effective.
H4 🏆 1993

A. n. 'Variegatum', syn. 'Argenteovariegatum' A form whose leaves have broad, irregular, white margins. An effective small tree, but keep a careful watch for reversion.
H4

Acer negundo var. violaceum

A. n.* var. *violaceum A medium-sized tree most attractive in spring, when it is draped with long, pendulous, reddish-pink flower tassels, and also in winter, when its purple or violet shoots, covered with a white, powdery bloom, are at their most conspicuous. H4 🏆 1993

A. nikoense See *A. maximowiczianum*.

A. oliverianum A handsome species, forming a large deciduous shrub or small tree. The leaves are deeply five-lobed and resemble those of *A. palmatum*, but are more cleanly cut, taking on subtle shades of orange, red and purple over a long period in autumn. C China. Introduced 1901 by Ernest Wilson. H4

A. opalus (Italian maple) A slow-growing deciduous tree, eventually of medium size. It has a rounded habit and shallowly five-lobed leaves that are glabrous above and downy beneath. The yellow flowers appear in conspicuous, crowded clusters on the leafless stems in early spring. S Europe. Introduced 1752. H4

Acer palmatum

A. palmatum (Japanese maple) Generally a large deciduous shrub or small tree with a low, rounded head and five- or seven-lobed leaves that are bright green in spring, turning to lovely colours in autumn. It is very variable, and has given rise to many cultivars, which exhibit a wide range of habits and leaf shapes. Most of them grow to be large shrubs, while some are small trees. They are rightly renowned for their gorgeous red, orange or yellow autumnal colours. Although the typical form and certain stronger ones will tolerate chalk soils, the Japanese maples are at their best in a moist but well-drained loam, sheltered from cold winds. Japan, C China, Korea. Introduced 1820. H4

Acer palmatum 'Asahi Zuru'

***A. p.* 'Asahi Zuru'** A large, fast-growing, spreading shrub with leaves variably blotched with white. When young they are sometimes nearly all white, or they may be pink. One of the best variegated forms. H4

Atropurpureum group The most popular of the Japanese maples, these have leaves that are bronze-crimson throughout the summer and brilliant red in autumn. A number of selections have been named. In cultivation 1857. H4

Acer palmatum 'Beni Maiko'

***A. p.* 'Beni Maiko'** A small, bushy shrub with brilliant red young foliage which later turns pink and then greenish-red. H4

***A. p.* 'Beni Schichihenge'** A striking and rare small shrub, whose blue-green leaves have 5–7 deep lobes margined with pinkish-white or almost entirely bright orange-pink. H4

Acer palmatum 'Bloodgood'

***A. p.* 'Bloodgood'** (Atropurpureum group) The leaves of this large shrub are a very deep reddish-purple and hold their colour well. The foliage turns red in autumn, when the red fruits are also attractive. H4 🏆 1993

***A. p.* 'Burgundy Lace'** A small, spreading tree with richly wine-red leaves, divided to the base into narrow, sharply toothed lobes. H4 🏆 1993

Acer palmatum 'Butterfly'

***A. p.* 'Butterfly'** A medium-sized, upright shrub whose rather small, deeply cut leaves

are grey-green margined with cream, tinged with pink when young. The margins turn red in autumn.
H4 ♈ 1993

A. p. **'Chitoseyama'** A superb clone with deeply cut, greenish-bronze leaves that colour richly in autumn. A medium-sized shrub, old specimens forming dense mounds with gracefully drooping branches.
H4 ♈ 1993

Acer palmatum 'Corallinum'

A. p. **'Corallinum'** A rarely seen, slow-growing, compact dwarf shrub. The young stems are soft coral-pink and the five-lobed leaves, which are usually less than 5cm (2in) long, are bright shrimp pink when unfolding, turning a pale, mottled green by mid-summer.
H4

Acer palmatum 'Crimson Queen'

A. p. **'Crimson Queen'** (Dissectum group) The leaves of this small shrub are a very long-lasting, deep reddish-purple and

divided into slender, finely cut lobes.
H4 ♈ 1993

A. p. **'Deshojo'** An upright shrub of medium size, with leaves with slenderly pointed lobes that are brilliant red when young, and later turn bright green.
H4

Dissectum group A group of Japanese maples with leaves divided to the base into five, seven or nine lobes. The individual lobes are themselves cut almost to their midribs and are thus pinnatifid, rather like the fronds of some ferns. Their general habit is shrubby, and they are somewhat mushroom-shaped when young, eventually making dense, rounded, small or medium-sized bushes with the branches falling from a high crown. They can be trained carefully when young to produce standards.
H4

Acer palmatum 'Dissectum'

Acer palmatum 'Dissectum Atropurpureum'

A. p. **'Dissectum'** The leaves of this small to medium-sized shrub are green in spring

and summer, turning red in autumn.
H4 ♈ 1993

A. p. **'Dissectum Atropurpureum'** A small shrub with deep reddish-purple foliage. For similar clones see 'Crimson Queen', 'Garnet' and 'Inaba Shidare'.
H4

Acer palmatum 'Dissectum Nigrum'

A. p. **'Dissectum Nigrum'**, syn. *A. p.* 'Ever Red' A small shrub with a dense habit, and deep, bronze-red leaves turning red in autumn.
H4

Acer palmatum 'Dissectum Ornatum'

A. p. **'Dissectum Ornatum'** A small shrub with bronze-tinted leaves turning rich red in autumn.
H4

Elegans group A group of Japanese maples previously known as the Heptalobum or Septemlobum group, consisting of shrubs which are large leaved and usually seven-lobed, with the lobes finely double-

toothed and broadest about the middle.
H4

A. p. 'Elegans Purpureum' See *A. p.* 'Hessei'

A. p. 'Ever Red' See *A. p.* 'Dissectum Nigrum'

Acer palmatum 'Garnet'

A. p. 'Garnet' (Dissectum group) A strong-growing small shrub with large, deep garnet-red leaves with finely cut lobes. Raised in Holland. In cultivation 1960.
H4 ♔ 1993

A. p. 'Hessei', syn. *A. p.* 'Elegans Purpureum' (Elegans group) A large shrub with dark bronze-crimson leaves.
H4

Acer palmatum 'Inaba Shidare'

A. p. 'Inaba Shidare' (Dissectum group) A small, strong-growing shrub with large, red-stalked leaves that are deeply divided into finely pointed, deep purplish lobes and turn crimson in autumn. It retains its colour well.
H4 ♔ 1993

A. p. 'Kagiri Nishiki', syn. *A. p.* 'Roseomarginatum' A charming medim-sized shrub with pale green leaves irregularly edged with coral-pink, but not constant in its variegation and liable to revert.
H4

A. p. 'Karasugawa' The leaves of this medium-sized shrub are deeply five- to seven-lobed, pink when young and becoming streaked and speckled with white and pink.
H4

A. p. 'Koreanum' The leaves of this medium-sized shrub or small tree become rich crimson in autumn and last longer than most. As this plant has been raised for many years from seed, there is a small degree of variation.
H4

A. p. 'Linearilobum' A medium-sized shrub with leaves that are divided to the base into long, narrow lobes that bear widely separated teeth.
H4 ♔ 1993

Acer palmatum 'Osakazuki'

A. p. 'Osakazuki' (Elegans group) Probably the most brilliant of the Japanese maples, the green leaves of this large shrub turning the most vivid, fiery scarlet in autumn. There are some poor seedling forms available.
H4 ♔ 1993

A. p. 'Red Pygmy' A slow-growing, small shrub resembling 'Linearilobum' but with reddish-purple leaves and less than 2m (6ft) tall. The colour is held well, and the leaves are often divided to the base into very long, slender lobes, although in some the lobes

are broader. Selected before 1969 in Holland.
H4 ♔ 1993

A. p. 'Reticulatum' The leaves of this large shrub are soft yellow-green with green margins and dark veins.
H4

A. p. 'Ribesifolium', syn. *A. p.* 'Shishigashira' A slow-growing large shrub of distinctive, dense, upright habit. It is not quite fastigiate, as the crown is broad. The leaves are dark green, deeply cut, and turn old gold to orange-red in autumn.
H4

A. p. 'Roseomarginatum' See *A. p.* 'Kagiri Nishiki'.

A. p. 'Sango Kaku' See *A. p.* 'Senkaki'.

Acer palmatum 'Seiryu'

A. p. 'Seiryu' (Dissectum group) An unusual, upright form with bright green leaves, tinged red when young. The lobes are finely cut, and in autumn turn orange-yellow splashed with crimson. It becomes a large shrub.
H4 ♔ 1993

A. p. 'Senkaki', syn. *A. p.* 'Sango Kaku' (Coral-bark maple) This large shrub or small tree is one of the most valuable and dramatic for winter effect. All the young branches are of a conspicuous, highly attractive coral-red. The leaves turn soft canary-yellow in autumn.
H4 ♔ 1993

A. p. 'Shishigashira' See *A. p.* 'Ribesifolium'.

A. p. 'Shishio Improved' A bushy, medium-sized to large shrub with leaves that are small and brilliantly red when

Acer palmatum 'Senkaki'

young, turning green with maturity.
H4

A. p. 'Trompenburg' A large shrub with leaves a deep purplish-red becoming green, and then red in autumn. They are divided to the base and the lobes are narrow, with the margins rolled under. An outstanding plant. Raised in Holland.
H4

A. p. 'Ukigumo' A striking variegated, small to medium-sized shrub with deeply five-lobed leaves, heavily mottled ` and edged with white and pink. The name means 'passing cloud'.
H4

Acer pensylvanicum

A. pensylvanicum A small tree with green young stems that are beautifully striped, 'snake-bark' fashion, with white and pale jade-green. Its leaves are up to 18cm (7in) across, three-lobed, and turn an attractive bright, rich yellow in autumn. *A. pensylvanicum* is not very tolerant of chalk soils. E

Acer pensylvanicum 'Erythrocladum'

North America. Introduced 1755.
H4 ♛ 1993

A. p. 'Erythrocladum' A lovely form in which the young shoots are brilliant candy-pink, with white striations in winter. Attractive when young, it is best grown as a large shrub, although it will also make a small tree.
H4 ♛ 1993

A. platanoides (Norway maple) A handsome, fast-growing large tree. The large, five-lobed leaves turn clear, bright yellow, occasionally red, in autumn. The yellow flowers are borne in conspicuous clusters on the bare stems in mid-spring. Europe, Caucasus. Long cultivated.
H4 ♛ 1993

A. p. 'Cleveland' A large tree with a strong, upright habit, making an oval head of branches with large, deep green leaves.
H4

Acer platanoides 'Columnare'

A. p. 'Columnare' A large, erect tree of

columnar habit. Raised 1855 in France.
H4

Acer platanoides 'Crimson King'

A. p. 'Crimson King' A large, handsome tree with leaves of deep crimson-purple. The flowers are deep yellow, tinged with red. A seedling of *A. p.* 'Schwedleri'. In cultivation 1946.
H4 ♛ 1993

A. p. 'Crimson Sentry' A dense, narrowly columnar medium-sized tree with reddish-purple leaves, not as dark as 'Crimson King'.
H4

A. p. 'Deborah' A medium-sized tree that is a seedling of *A. p.* 'Schwedleri'. The young leaves are brilliant red, turning dark green, and have wavy margins. Raised in the United States.
H4

Acer platanoides 'Drummondii'

A. p. 'Drummondii' A very striking medium-sized to large tree bearing leaves

with a broad marginal band of creamy-white. Remove any reverting shoots. In cultivation 1903.
H4 ♛ 993

A. p. **'Emerald Queen'** A vigorous large tree with glossy, dark green leaves, upright when young and broadening with age. Raised 1959.
H4

Acer platanoides 'Globosum'

A. p. **'Globosum'** An eye-catching small tree, with short branches forming a dense, mop-shaped head. In cultivation 1873.
H4

A. p. **'Schwedleri'** A large tree with rich crimson-purple young growths and leaves, at its most effective when pruned hard every other autumn.
H4 ♛ 1993

A. pseudoplatanus (Sycamore) This large tree has long been planted in the British Isles, where it has become naturalized. It is a picturesque tree and one of the best for exposed situations in any soil. Europe, W Asia.
H4

A. p. **'Atropurpureum'**, syn. *A. p.* 'Purpureum Spaethii' A selected form reaching large tree size with leaves that are dark green above and purple beneath. In cultivation 1883.
H4 ♛ 1993

A. p. **'Brilliantissimum'** A distinctive small tree of slow growth. The young spring leaves are a glorious shrimp-pink that later changes to pale yellow-green before finally becoming green. In cultivation 1905.
H4 ♛ 1993

Acer pseudoplatanus 'Brilliantissimum'

A. p. **'Erectum'** A large tree with erect branches. In cultivation 1935.
H4

Acer pseudoplatanus 'Leopoldii'

A. p. **'Leopoldii'** The leaves of this large tree are yellowish-pink at first, later becoming green, speckled and splashed with yellow and pink.
H4 ♛ 1993

A. p. **'Nizetii'** This large tree has leaves which are heavily blotched and streaked with pale green and white, their undersides tinged with purple. In cultivation 1887.
H4

A. p. **'Purpureum Spaethii'** See *A. p.* 'Atropurpureum'.

A. p. **'Prinz Handjery'** A small, slow-growing tree similar to 'Brilliantissimum', but slightly larger and with its leaves purple-tinged beneath.
H4

A. p. **'Simon-Louis Frères'** The leaves of this large tree are pink when young and

Acer pseudoplatanus 'Simon Louis Frères'

then become blotched and streaked with green and white, but are plain green beneath. In cultivation 1881.
H4

Acer pseudoplatanus 'Worleei'

A. p. **'Worleei'** (Golden sycamore) A medium-sized tree with leaves that are soft yellow-green at first, then golden, and finally green. Raised before 1893 in Germany.
H4 ♛ 1993

A. rubrum (Canadian maple, red maple) A free-growing tree, ultimately of large size, whose palmate leaves are dark green above and bluish beneath. It is one of the earlier trees to take on its autumn colour, becoming rich scarlet-red. Although fairly lime-tolerant, it rarely colours well on chalk. E North America. In cultivation 1656.
H4

A. r. **'October Glory'** The leaves of this medium-sized tree turn colour quite early in the autumn, becoming brilliant red and

Acer rubrum

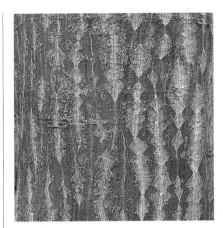

Acer rufinerve

A. rufinerve A medium-sized deciduous tree with bluish young stems, while the older ones and the trunk have 'snake-bark' patterning of white striations on a green background. This is not unlike the bark of *A. pensylvanicum*, and the three-lobed leaves also recall that species. It has bright red and yellow autumn colours. Japan. Introduced 1879.

H4 🏆 1993

Acer rufinerve f. albolimbatum

Acer rubrum 'October Glory'

Acer rubrum 'Scanlon'

remaining so for a comparatively long time. In cultivation 1964.

H4 🏆 1993

A. r. 'Red Sunset' A medium-sized tree with upswept branches and particularly good orange-red to red autumn colour. In cultivation 1968.

H4

A. r. 'Scanlon' A medium-sized, columnar

tree which takes on rich autumn colour. In cultivation 1948.

H4 🏆 1993

A. r. 'Schlesingeri' A medium-sized tree notable for its outstanding, very early autumn colour which is a rich, deep scarlet, but with an untidy habit. In cultivation 1888.

H4

A. r. f. albolimbatum The leaves of this medium-sized tree are mottled and margined with white, turning brilliant red and purple in autumn. In cultivation 1869.

H4

A. saccharinum, syn. *A. dasycarpum* (Silver maple) A large, fast-growing deciduous tree with deeply five-lobed leaves that are silvery-white beneath. The foliage creates a delightful effect when it is ruffled by breezes, but care must be taken to protect the tree from high winds, which can often cause damage.

Acer saccharinum

The foliage provides attractive autumn tints. E North America. Introduced 1725.
H4 ♈ 1993

A. s. 'Fastigiatum' See *A. s.* 'Pyramidale'.
A. s. f. *laciniatum* See Laciniatum group.
Laciniatum group This name covers medium-sized or large trees with deeply cut leaves. See *A. s.* 'Wieri'.
H4

Acer saccharinum 'Lutescens'

A. s. 'Lutescens' The leaves of this large tree are orange-yellow when young and yellow-green in summer. In cultivation 1881.
H4

A. s. 'Pyramidale', syn. *A. s.* 'Fastigiatum' A large tree with upright growth. In cultivation 1885.
H4

A. s. 'Wieri' (Laciniatum group) A large tree with pendulous lower branches and leaves deeply divided into sharply cut lobes. Found in 1873.
H4

A. saccharum (Sugar maple) An ornamental, ultimately large deciduous tree, not to be confused with *A. saccharinum*. It resembles the Norway maple and is one of America's finest autumn-colouring trees, with different individuals displaying orange, gold, scarlet or crimson tints. In the British Isles it does not colour as well, nor can maple syrup be made satisfactorily from the sap, as it is so successfully in North America. C and E North America. Introduced 1735.
H4

Acer shirasawanum

Acer shirasawanum 'Aureum'

A. shirasawanum This relative of *A. japonicum* is an elegant large deciduous shrub or small tree. It has bloomy shoots, and the rounded, bright green leaves with smooth stalks usually have 11 sharply toothed lobes. The leaves turn a rich orange and red in autumn. The flowers, which have pink calyces and cream petals, are held in spreading or almost upright clusters.

Japan. In cultivation 1888.
H4

A. s. 'Aureum', syn. *A. japonicum* 'Aureum' A well-known, slow-growing large shrub or small tree with soft yellow leaves. It should be positioned in part shade, as the foliage is liable to scorching in hot sun.
H4 ♈ 1993

A. 'Silver Vein' A strong-growing 'snakebark' maple, with arching branches conspicuously patterned and striated in green and white. The leaves of this small deciduous tree are large, three-lobed above the middle and tapered at the point. They are rich green on the upper sides, carried on long red stalks, and turn butter-yellow in autumn. Raised by Hillier Nurseries from a cross made in 1961.
H4

A. trautvetteri A small to medium-sized deciduous tree with large, deeply five-lobed leaves that turn deep-golden yellow in autumn. Its flowers are borne in upright panicles and are followed in late summer by fruits with showy, broad red wings. A handsome foliage tree, it is conspicuous when the bright red buds open in spring. Caucasus, SW Asia. Introduced 1866.
H4

A. triflorum A very rare, slow-growing, small tree related and similar to *A. maximowiczianum* but with characteristically pale grey-brown, flaking bark. The leaves have three leaflets and are bluish underneath. One of the most consistent trees for brilliance of autumn colour. Manchuria, Korea. Introduced 1923.
H4

Acer × zoeschense

A. × zoeschense This hybrid between *A. campestre* and (probably) *A. cappadocicum* is of garden origin and is a medium-sized tree with five-lobed, dark green leaves, somewhat tinged with purple.
H4

Acradenia *Rutaceae*

There are just two species in this genus of evergreens, which will grow well in any average, well-drained soil. A. euodiiformis, the second species in the genus, occurs in eastern Australia.

Acradenia frankliniae

A. frankliniae This small to medium-sized shrub of upright habit succeeds well in mild areas. It is grown for its aromatic leaves, which are dark green, and for its flat clusters of white flowers in late spring. W Tasmania. Introduced 1845.
H2–3

Actinidia *Actinidiaceae*

A genus of about 30 species of deciduous climbers, natives of eastern Asia. They are vigorous, generally hardy, twining plants with simple leaves which sometimes bear edible, juicy fruits. (Those grown for fruits are best planted in pairs.) They are excellent for covering old walls or tall stumps and flourish in most fertile soils in sun or semi-shade.

A. chinensis, syn. *A. deliciosa* (Chinese gooseberry, kiwi fruit). A large, vigorous climber reaching a height of 9m (28ft), with shoots densely covered with reddish hairs and large, heart-shaped leaves 15–23cm

Actinidia chinensis

(6–9in) long and up to 20cm (8in) wide. The 4cm (1¹/₂in) wide, fragrant flowers are cream turning buff-yellow, and are produced in clusters in late summer. The edible fruits are green then brown, resembling large, elongated gooseberries, and having a similar flavour. To obtain fruit it is necessary to plant both sexes, though worthwhile fruit are rarely produced in cool-temperate climates unless the plants are grown on a warm sunny wall or under glass. Selected clones are cultivated for fruiting, notably 'Hayward' (female) and 'Tomuri' (male). The main commercial sources of the fruits are New Zealand, Kenya and Israel. China. Introduced 1900 by Ernest Wilson.
H4

A. deliciosa See *A. chinensis*.

Actinidia kolomikta

A. kolomikta A striking, large, slender climber reaching 4–6m (12–20ft). It is remarkable for the tricoloured variegation of many of its leaves, in which the terminal

half is cream, flushed with pink. There is no variegation on young plants, however. The flowers are small, white and slightly fragrant, opening in early summer. The form in gardens appears to be a male, so the yellowish, sweet fruits are very rarely seen. Japan, N China, Manchuria. Introduced c1855.
H4 ♈ 1993

Aesculus *Hippocastanaceae*
Buckeye, horse chestnut

This genus of around 13 deciduous species native to North America, south-eastern Europe and eastern Asia includes some of the most ornamental of the larger trees that flower in late spring and early summer. All of them have compound, palmate leaves and flowers borne in showy panicles. They are easily grown and thrive in any soil. Buckeye is an American vernacular name, dating from the eighteenth century, and refers to the glossy brown seed with its pale hilum, which reminded settlers of the eye of a buck. Harmful if eaten.

Aesculus californica

A. californica A low-growing, wide-spreading tree or large shrub. Its leaves are relatively small, with 5–7 blue-green leaflets. The fragrant, white or pink-tinted flowers are borne in summer in dense, erect panicles up to 20cm (8in) long. California. Introduced c1850 by William Lobb.
H4

A. × carnea *(A. hippocastanum × A. pavia)* (Red horse chestnut) A medium-sized to large tree frequently used for avenues and parks. The flowers are rose-pink and borne in panicles up to 20cm (8in) long in late spring. It

Aesculus × carnea

Aesculus flava

is similar to *A. hippocastanum* but generally smaller and more compact, with smaller, darker green leaflets. In cultivation 1820. H4

Aesculus × carnea 'Briotii'

A. × *c.* **'Briotii'** A compact medium-sized to large tree with deeper-coloured flowers. Raised 1858.
H4 ♔ 1993

A. × *c.* **'Plantierensis'** *(A. × carnea × A. hippocastanum)* Perhaps the best form, this is a large tree resembling *A. hippocastanum* but with pale pink flowers. Being a back cross that does not set seed, it is no good for conkers. Raised c1894 in France.
H4

A. × *dallimorei* A graft hybrid that makes a medium-sized tree with dark green leaves that turn orange and red in autumn. The flowers are cream red flares and spots.
H4

A. flava, syn. *A. octandra* (Sweet buckeye) A medium-sized to large tree with flowers that are the nearest thing to yellow in the genus. They are borne from late spring to early summer. The leaves have 5–7 leaflets and colour well in autumn. SE United States. Introduced 1764.
H4 ♔ 1993

A. georgiana, syn. *A. neglecta* var. *georgiana* A large shrub or small tree with dense panicles of orange-red flowers borne in late spring/early summer. SE United States. Introduced 1905.
H4

A. glabra (Ohio buckeye) A small to medium-sized tree with rough bark. Its leaves usually have five leaflets and turn orange-yellow in autumn. The flowers, borne in late spring, are yellow-green, have protruding stamens and are followed by prickly fruits. C and SE United States. In cultivation 1809.
H4

A. hippocastanum (Common horse chestnut) One of the most beautiful of large, flow-

Aesculus hippocastanum

ering trees. It is exceptionally attractive when covered in late spring with its stout candles of flowers, which are white with a yellow blotch that later turns red. Its seeds provide the conkers with which European children have played for centuries. Greece, Albania, now rare in the wild. Introduced 1576.
H4 ♔ 1993

Aesculus hippocastanum 'Baumannii'

A. h. **'Baumannii'**, syn. *A. h.* 'Flore Pleno' In time becomes a large tree with double white flowers that does not set seed.
H4 ♔ 1993

A. h. **'Flore Pleno'** See *A. h.* 'Baumanii'.

A. indica (Indian horse chestnut) A magnificent large tree, with panicles of pink-flushed flowers from early to midsummer that are as much as 40cm (16in) long and 13cm (5in) wide. The leaves have seven leaflets and are bronze when young, before becoming glossy, dark green and then eventually turning orange or yellow in autumn. A splendid specimen grows on chalk soil on the site of Hilliers' West Hill Nursery in Winchester, where it was 15m (50ft) tall in

Aesculus indica

1994. NW Himalaya. Introduced 1851.
H4 ♆ 1993

A. i. 'Sydney Pearce' A free-flowering large tree of upright habit with dark olive-green leaves. Its flowers are borne in large panicles and individual blossoms are up to 2.5cm (1in) across, with white petals marked with yellow and prettily suffused with pink. Raised 1928 at Kew, England.
H4

A. × mutabilis 'Induta', syn. *A. × m.* 'Rosea Nana' A large shrub or small tree bearing apricot flowers with yellow markings in summer. In cultivation 1905.
H4 Z5

A. × m. 'Rosea Nana' See *A. × m.* 'Induta'.

Aesculus × neglecta 'Erythroblastos'

A. × neglecta 'Erythroblastos' A spectacular though rather slow-growing hybrid that eventually makes a medium-sized tree. Its flowers, borne from late spring to early summer, are pale yellow, and it has rich autumn colour, but the main attraction is the young leaves, which are brilliant shrimp-pink, changing to a pale yellow-green later in the season. In cultivation 1935.
H4 ♆ 1993

A. × n. var. georgiana See *A. georgiana*.
A. octandra See *A. flava*.

Aesculus parviflora

A. parviflora A suckering medium-sized to large shrub which flowers freely from mid- to late summer, bearing white flowers with protuberant red anthers in slender panicles 20–30cm (8–12in) long. The leaves are bronze when young and attractively coloured yellow in autumn. SE United States. Introduced 1785.
H4 ♆ 1993

A. pavia (Red buckeye) A beautiful and rewarding medium-sized to large shrub or small tree. Its leaves have five glossy green leaflets, and its striking crimson flowers which are borne in panicles 15cm (6in) long, open in early to midsummer. SE

Aesculus pavia 'Atrosanguinea'

United States. Introduced 1711.
H4 ♆ 1993

A. p. 'Atrosanguinea' A form with flowers of a little deeper red than those of the species.
H4

A. splendens This large shrub with long panicles of scarlet flowers in late spring is perhaps the most handsome of the buckeyes. Botanists now consider that it should be included in *A. pavia*.
H4

A. turbinata (Japanese horse chestnut) A large tree with outsize foliage – on young trees a leaf and its stalk may be more than 65cm (26in) long – attractively veined and tinted in autumn. Its flowers are borne in long panicles, being yellowish-white with a red spot, and appear in late spring or early summer, a little later than *A. hippocastanum*. The fruits are large, pear-shaped and not spiny. Japan. Introduced before 1880.
H4

Ailanthus *Simaroubaceae*

A genus of about five deciduous species from eastern Asia to Australia. Handsome, fast-growing trees with large, pinnate leaves, they are extremely tolerant of atmospheric pollution and grow well in most soils.

Ailanthus altissima

A. altissima (Tree of heaven) A large, imposing tree with distinct, ash-like leaves which can be up to 1m (3ft) long on young specimens. Female trees produce large, conspicuous bunches of reddish fruits rather like ash keys in mid or late summer.

N China. Introduced 1751 by Peter Collinson.
H4 ♇ 1993

Akebia *Lardizabalaceae*

A genus of five species of vigorous, hardy, semi-evergreen, twining climbers with attractive foliage and flowers. They succeed in most soils in sun or shade and are excellent for growing over hedges, low trees, bushes or stumps, though they can sometimes be a little over-vigorous in mild climates. A mild spring is necessary for the flowers and the conspicuous and unusual fruits are produced only after a long, hot summer.

Akebia quinata

A. quinata A large climber reaching up to 9–12m (28–40ft) in a tree. The leaves have five notched leaflets and the flowers are spicily fragrant, red-purple and borne on racemes in mid-spring. The male and female flowers are separate but carried on the same inflorescence, the females at the base and the males at the tip. The fruits are sausage-shaped, 5–10cm (2–4in) long, dark purple, and contain black seeds embedded in a white pulp. Japan, Korea, China. Introduced 1845 by Robert Fortune.
H4

A. trifoliata A large and elegant plant, climbing to 9m (28ft) in a tree. The leaves have three shallowly lobed leaflets and the flowers are dark purple, borne on racemes in mid-spring. The sausage-shaped fruits, 7.5–13cm (3–5in) long and often in groups of three, are pale violet. Japan, China. Introduced 1895.
H4

Akebia trifoliata

Alangium *Alangiaceae*

A genus of about 20 species of deciduous trees, shrubs and climbers mainly from warm regions of the Old World. The following species is an attractive foliage plant. Plant it in full sun or partial shade and any type of well-drained, reasonably fertile soil.

A. platanifolium A large shrub with leaves that have 3–5 and sometimes 7 lobes and clusters of white flowers like miniature lilies in early to midsummer. Taiwan to Manchuria. Introduced 1879.
H4

Albizia *Leguminosae*

A genus of deciduous, mimosa-like shrubs or small trees with handsome foliage and attractive, fluffy heads of flowers borne in early or midsummer. There are about 150 species, mainly native to the Old World tropics and South America and preferring any average, dryish soil.

A. julibrissin 'Rosea' The hardiest form of the hardiest species, this is a small, spreading, graceful tree with dense heads of bright pink flowers in late summer. To flower it requires a sheltered position in full sun. Korea. Introduced 1918 by Ernest Wilson.
H3 ♇ 1993

Alnus *Betulaceae*
Alder

A genus of about 35 species of fast-growing

deciduous trees and shrubs native mainly to northern temperate regions. They will grow in most soils, even those that are infertile, but with very few exceptions, which include A. cordata and A. glutinosa, they do not thrive on shallow soils over chalk. They are especially valuable in damp or even wet situations, although A. cordata and A. incana will do well on drier soils. A. glutinosa can grow in very wet conditions, even where there is standing water. Male and female flowers are borne in spring on the same plant: the male catkins are long and drooping, while the females are short and become woody cones.

Alnus cordata

A. cordata (Italian alder) A splendid, medium-sized to large, conical tree for all types of soil, including chalk, on which it grows rapidly. It is notable for its bright green, glistening foliage and yellow catkins borne in late winter or early spring. Corsica, S Italy. Introduced 1820.
H4 ♇ 1993

A. glutinosa (Common alder) A small to

Alnus glutinosa

Alnus glutinosa 'Imperialis'

Alnus incana 'Pendula'

Alnus incana aurea

Aloysia triphylla

medium-sized, bushy tree with sticky young growths and yellow catkins in early spring. It was once extensively used for making clogs in the north of England. W Asia, N Africa, Europe.
H4

A. g. **'Imperialis'** An attractive and very graceful small tree with deeply and finely cut leaves. In cultivation 1859.
H4 ♔ 1993

A. g. **'Laciniata'** This medium-sized tree is similar to 'Imperialis', but stronger growing and with a stiffer habit. Its leaves are not as finely divided. Arose before 1819 in France.
H4

A. g. **'Pyramidalis'** The branches of this medium-sized tree grow at an acute angle, making a narrow, conical form.
H4

A. incana (Grey alder) An exceptionally hardy, large shrub or small tree with grey undersides to its leaves. Yellow/brown catkins are borne in late winter or early spring. Ideal for cold and wet situations. Europe, Caucasus. Introduced 1780.
H4

A. i. **'Aurea'** The young shoots and foliage of this small tree are yellow, and the catkins are conspicuously tinted red.
H4

A. i. **'Pendula'** A handsome small, weeping tree forming a large mound of pendulous branches and grey-green leaves. It Originated before 1900 in Holland.
H4

A. rubra This medium-sized, large-leaved tree is very fast growing. It has a graceful habit and in spring is festooned with male catkins 10–15cm (4–6in) long. W North America. Introduced before 1880.
H4

A. × *spaethii* A fast-growing tree of medium size, with large leaves that are purplish when young. An outstanding tree when bearing its 15cm (6in) long catkins in early spring. In cultivation c1908.
H4 ♔ 1993

Aloysia *Verbenaceae*

A genus of about 35 species of evergreen and deciduous aromatic shrubs, native to the southwestern United States and Central and South America, of which only one species is commonly grown. They will grow in any average, dryish soil.

A. triphylla, syn. *Lippia citriodora* (Lemon verbena) A medium-sized to large deciduous shrub with lanceolate, lemon-scented leaves normally in whorls of three. The tiny, pale purple flowers are profusely borne in late summer in panicles at the ends of the branches. Best against a warm wall. Chile. Introduced 1784.

H3

Amelanchier *Rosaceae*
June berry, serviceberry, snowy mespilus

A genus of about 10 species of beautiful and very hardy, small, deciduous trees or shrubs, which are natives mainly of North America but are also found in Europe and Asia, although those growing wild in Europe are naturalized American species which probably spread when their dried fruits were used as currants. The ones described below thrive in moist, well-drained, lime-free soils. The abundant white flowers are produced in racemes in spring before the leaves are fully developed. The foliage is often richly coloured in autumn.

A. **'Ballerina'** A vigorous, large shrub or small tree with finely toothed leaves that are bronze when young and colour well in autumn. The large, white flowers are profusely borne. Probably a hybrid of *A. laevis*. Selected 1970 in Holland from plants sent from Hillier Nurseries.

H4 ♔ 1993

Amelanchier laevis

A. **canadensis** The true species is rare. It is a medium-sized to large, suckering shrub with tall, erect stems and erect racemes of flowers. Unfortunately, its name is often

Amelanchier canadensis detail

attached to *A. laevis* and *A. lamarckii*, which are better garden plants and can be distinguished from it by their lax or pendulous racemes. It grows well in moist situations. North America.

H4

A. × **grandiflora** A large, spreading shrub with bronze young leaves and profuse clusters of large white flowers. This hybrid has originated in the wild as well as in cultivation. The best clones are as follows. See also *A. lamarckii*.

H4

A. × *g.* **'Robin Hill'** A large shrub or small tree of dense, upright habit with flowers which are pink in bud, open pale pink, and then become white.

H4

A. × *g.* **'Rubescens'** An attractive large shrub or small tree with pale pink flowers that are deep pink in bud. Raised before 1820 in New York.

H4

A. **laevis** A small tree, or occasionally a large

Amelanchier laevis in flower

shrub, which is usually wrongly grown under the name of *A. canadensis*. It is a picture of striking beauty towards the latter part of mid-spring, when the white flowers, profusely borne in pendulous racemes, contrast prettily with the delicately pink young foliage. In autumn the leaves take on orange and red tints. North America. In cultivation 1870.

H4

A. lamarckii This is the plant often incorrectly known as *A. canadensis*, and is the best species for general planting. It is a large shrub or small tree with a bushy, spreading habit and oval to oblong leaves, coppery-red and silky when young, that colour richly in autumn. The flowers are borne in lax, ample racemes, scattered along the branches as the young leaves unfold, and a tree in full flower is most beautiful spectacle. The fruits which follow are black. Naturalized Belgium, Holland, NW Germany, England.
H4 ♛ 1993

Amorpha *Leguminosae*

A genus of about 15 species of deciduous, sun-loving shrubs or sub-shrubs native to North America and Mexico, with pinnate leaves and dense, spiky heads of small flowers that are usually blue or violet. They are recognizably pea-flowers, but are unusual in having only one petal.

A. fruticosa (False indigo) A variable, medium-sized to large shrub with pinnate leaves and slender racemes of purplish-blue flowers which are borne in midsummer. It will grow in any well-drained soil in sun. S United States. Introduced 1724.
H4

Ampelopsis *Vitaceae*

A genus of about 20 species of deciduous ornamental vines that climb by means of curling tendrils. They are natives mainly of North America and eastern Asia excellent for covering walls and fences, and with initial support, clambering into trees. Ampelopsis are vigorous and not suitable for small gardens. They are grown for their attractive foliage and for their fruits which, however, need a long, hot summer and a mild autumn if they are to develop. They will grow in any ordinary soil and in sun or semi-shade, but for those species with attractive fruits a warm, sunny, sheltered position is best. See also Parthenocissus *and* Vitis.

Ampelopsis brevipedunculata

A. brevipedunculata A luxuriant large climber with three- or occasionally five-lobed, heart-shaped leaves up to 15cm (6in) wide, rather like those of the hop. After a hot summer the masses of small fruits vary between verdigris (copper-rust blue) and deep blue but in the mass are Wedgwood blue and very attractive indeed. NE Asia. In cultivation 1870.
H4

***A. b.* 'Elegans'**, syn. *A. b.* 'Tricolor' The leaves are densely mottled with white and tinged with pink. It is a weak grower and can be planted where space is restricted. It is sometimes seen in florists' shops as a house plant.
H4

***A. b.* 'Tricolor'** See *A. b.* 'Elegans'.

A. megalophylla A large, strong but rather slow-growing climber of considerable quality, reaching to 9m (28ft) or more in a suitable tree. The leaves are bipinnate, 30–60cm (1–2ft) long, with leaflets 5–15cm (2–6in) long. The loose bunches of top-shaped fruits are purple at first and finally black. W China. Introduced 1894.
H4

Andromeda *Ericaceae*

A genus of only two species of low-growing, slender-stemmed, evergreen shrubs for leafy, damp, acid soils or peat walls.

A. polifolia (Bog rosemary) A charming dwarf shrub. Its slender stems bear narrow, glaucous-green leaves whose undersides are smooth and white. It carries clusters of soft

Amelanchier lamarckii

Andromeda polifolia

pink, pitcher-shaped flowers at the ends of the branches in late spring and early summer. Andromeda is widely distributed in N Hemisphere. In cultivation 1768.
H4

Andromeda polifolia 'Compacta'

A. p. 'Compacta' A gem for a cool, peaty bed, which bears clusters of bright pink flowers from late spring onwards. As its name suggests, it is of compact habit.
H4 ♛ 1993

A. p. 'Compacta Alba' Another compact plant suitable for small gardens, this dwarf form has white flowers.
H4 ♛ 1993

A. p. 'Macrophylla' A low-growing form with relatively broad leaves and deep pink flowers.
H4 ♛ 1993

A. p. 'Nikko' Another neat, compact form, which some consider an improvement on 'Compacta'.
H4

Anthyllis *Leguminosae*

A genus of around 20 species of annual and perennial, evergreen and deciduous shrubs and herbaceous plants, which usually have pinnate leaves and clustered, pea-like flowers. They are natives of Europe, western Asia and North Africa and will grow in any average, well-drained soil.

A. hermanniae An attractive, deciduous dwarf shrub for the rock garden with small, narrow leaves, all of which have three leaflets but sometimes appear to consist of one only, as the side leaflets are reduced practically to nothing. The flowers are freely borne in clusters of two to eight from early to midsummer and are small, pea shaped and yellow, with orange markings on the standard petals. Mediterranean. Introduced early 1700s.
H4

Aralia *Araliaceae*

A genus of more than 35 species of perennials, deciduous shrubs and one or two climbers native to parts of America and Asia, chiefly grown for the great beauty of their large, compound leaves. They will grow in any average soil.

Aralia elata

A. elata (Japanese angelica tree) This species is usually seen as a large, suckering shrub but occasionally makes a small, sparsely branched tree. The stems are often spiny. The huge leaves are doubly pinnate; in other words, they are divided, fern-like, into several leaflets on each side of the midrib, and then each leaflet is itself divided. They are gath-

ered mainly in ruff-like arrangements at the tips of the stems and often colour well in autumn. The flowers are white and borne in autumn in large panicles that are branched from the base. Japan. Introduced 1830.
H4 ♛ 1993

Aralia elata 'Aureovariegata'

A. e. 'Aureovariegata' A large shrub with its leaflets irregularly margined and splashed with yellow. This is noticeable in spring, but later in summer the variegation becomes silvery-white.
H4

Aralia elata 'Variegata'

A. e. 'Variegata' A highly desirable large shrub with its leaves irregularly blotched and edged with creamy-white, which changes to silvery-white in summer. Both variegated forms are difficult to propagate, as they have to be grafted and produce little in the way of material for scions. Be prepared for prices that justifiably reflect this. Introduced 1865.
H4 ♛ 1993

Araucaria *Araucariaceae*

A genus of about 18 species of evergreen conifers from Oceania, Queensland and South America. Apart from the following, the only nearly hardy species is A. heterophylla, *the Norfolk Island Pine, which is a popular conservatory plant, although it will attain heights of around 30m (100ft) in a favourable climate.*

Araucaria araucana detail

Araucaria araucana

A. araucana (Chile pine, monkey puzzle) A medium-sized to large tree unique in appearance, with long, spidery branches and densely overlapping, rigid, spine-tipped, dark green leaves. The cones are globular, up to 18cm (7in) long and take three years to mature. They break up while still on the tree and the sharp scales can be hazardous on lawns. It is one of the few South American trees hardy in the British Isles, where it resists wind very well. It grows best in a moist, loamy soil. In industrial areas it loses its lower branches and becomes ragged. Chile, Argentina. Introduced first 1795 by Archibald Menzies and then 1844 by William Lobb. H4

Arbutus *Ericaceae*
Strawberry tree

A genus of around 15 species which are among the most ornamental and highly prized of small evergreen trees. They are found in both the New and Old Worlds and with few exceptions attain 3–6m (10–20ft) – but see A. unedo *below. The glossy, dark green leaves, panicles of white, pitcher-shaped flowers and strawberry-like fruits are all most attractive. Apart from those mentioned below, species can also be found in the Canary Islands, south-west United States, Mexico and Central America.*

Arbutus × andrachnoides

A. × andrachnoides, syn. *A. × hybrida (A. unedo × A. andrachne)* This hybrid small tree has inherited its late-flowering tendency from the first parent and its beautiful cinnamon-red branches from the latter. The flowers are white and borne in late autumn and early winter. It is lime tolerant and quite hardy. Greece. In cultivation 1800. H4 🏆 1993

A. × hybrida See *A. × andrachnoides.*

Arbutus menziesii

A. menziesii (Madrona) This medium-sized tree occasionally reaches 18m (60ft) in cultivation. It has beautiful, smooth, reddish-brown bark that peels in late summer to reveal the young, green bark beneath. The flowers are borne in conspicuous panicles in late spring and are followed by small, orange-yellow fruits. Hardiness depends to a large extent on how it is sited; it requires acid soil. W North America. Introduced 1827 by David Douglas. H3 🏆 1993

Arbutus unedo

A. unedo (Killarney strawberry tree) A large shrub or small, gnarled tree in cultivation, but there is a specimen in the Killarney National Park that is well over 12m

(40ft) high, with the appearance of an old evergreen oak. The bark of this species is deep brown and shredding and the white flowers and red fruits are produced simultaneously in autumn. It is perfectly hardy, withstanding gales in coastal districts, and is unusual among ericaceous plants for its lime tolerance, growing well in gardens on chalk downland. Mediterranean, SW Ireland.
H4 ♇ 1993

A. u. 'Elfin King' A bushy form that eventually makes a medium-sized shrub. It is free flowering and fruits when small.
H4

Arbutus unedo 'Rubra'

A. u. 'Rubra' A choice form with pink-flushed flowers and abundant fruits, still to be found wild in Ireland. It makes a large shrub or small tree. In cultivation 1835.
H4 ♇ 1993

Arctostaphylos *Ericaceae*

A genus of around 50 species native to western North America and Mexico. These distinctive evergreens vary from prostrate shrubs to small trees, and in the larger species usually have attractive bark. The small, nodding flowers are white to pink, borne in clusters and followed by berry-like fruits. They are allied to Rhododendron *and succeed in the same sorts of conditions, including acid soil, although they love the sun.*

A. manzanita (Common manzanita) This species is anything but common in gardens. It is a beautiful, tall-growing shrub with extremely attractive red-purple, peeling

bark, sea-green leaves and spikes of pink or white, pitcher-shaped flowers borne in early or mid spring. California. Introduced 1897.
H4

A. uva-ursi (Red bearberry) An interesting, creeping, alpine shrub with white, pink-tinged flowers borne in early or mid-summer and red fruits. A good plant for sandy banks. Cool-temperate regions of northern hemisphere.
H4

Aristolochia *Aristolochiaceae*

This is a genus of about 300 species of evergreen and deciduous shrubs, climbers and herbaceous plants, mainly from warmer regions. They have more or less heart-shaped leaves and oddly shaped flowers.

A. macrophylla (Dutchman's Pipe) A large, vigorous deciduous climbing species, reaching 9m (28ft) in a suitable tree. Its leaves are heart- to kidney-shaped and up to 30cm (1ft) long. The flowers are tubular and bent in the lower half like a siphon or calabash pipe, and are 2.5–4cm (1–1¹/₂in) long, yellowish green, and with a brownish purple, flared mouth. They are produced in pairs in early summer. E United States. Introduced 1763.
H4

Aristotelia *Elaeocarpaceae*

A genus of about five species of mainly evergreen shrubs from Australasia and South America that need some protection in cold districts. Male and female flowers often occur on separate plants. They will grow in any average soil.

A. chilensis 'Variegata' A graceful, medium-sized to large shrub whose leaves, 13cm (5in) long, are conspicuously variegated with yellow. It is an interesting evergreen for mild areas and does well in exposed places near the sea. From Chile.
H3

Arctostaphylos uva-ursi

Aronia *Rosaceae*
Chokeberry

A genus of three species of attractive deciduous shrubs related to Pyrus *and* Sorbus. *They have white flowers in spring followed by conspicuous clusters of red or black fruits, and brilliant autumn colours. They are not recommended for shallow chalk soils.*

A. arbutifolia (Red chokeberry) A medium-sized shrub with narrow, dark green leaves, grey felted beneath. It is grown for its bright red fruits and exceptionally brilliant autumn colours. E North America. The following forms are particularly recommended for their garden-worthy characteristics. In cultivation 1700. H4

Aronia arbutifolia 'Brilliant'

A. a. 'Brilliant' This form was selected for its vivid red, long-lasting fruit which are carried during the summer months. It has apparently been raised from seed and several forms may be grown under this name or under 'Brilliantissima'. H4

A. a. 'Erecta' A compact, erectly branched medium-sized shrub, arching with age, which has fine rich autumn colour. H4

A. melanocarpa (Black chokeberry) A small shrub with glossy, dark green leaves that colour brilliantly in autumn. It bears white, hawthorn-like flowers in spring that are followed by lustrous black fruits. E North America. Introduced 1700. H4

Aronia melanocarpa

Artemisia *Compositae*

A genus of about 300 species of perennials and evergreen and deciduous shrubs and sub-shrubs with attractive, often aromatic, green or grey foliage and relatively insignificant yellow flowers. The shrubby species are suitable as wall shrubs and in mixed borders. They are mainly natives of the temperate northern hemisphere, but are also found in South Africa and South America. They prefer a dry, well-drained soil in full sun.

A. abrotanum (Lad's love, southernwood) A small, erect, grey-downy deciduous shrub with a bushy habit and sweetly aromatic, finely divided leaves, traditional in cottage gardens. Dull yellow flowers are borne in panicles from midsummer to early autumn.

Artemisia 'Powis Castle'

Artemisia abrotanum

S Europe. In cultivation in England since the sixteenth century.

H4

A. 'Powis Castle' A beautiful small deciduous shrub with deeply cut, silvery-grey leaves. Almost fully hardy, it is superior to other artemisias as a foliage shrub as it does not flower, and thus retains its compact habit. The best one for general garden use and excellent groundcover. Originated at the National Trust Garden at Powis Castle, Wales.

H3–4 ♛ 1993

Arundinaria

Originally a genus of about 50 species of bamboo of tufted growth or with creeping underground stems now split and re-classified under a variety of genera as listed below.

A. a anceps See *Yushania anceps*.
A. auricoma See *Pleioblastus auricomus*.
A. 'Gauntletti' See *Pleioblastus humilis* 'Gauntetti'.
A. fortunei See *Pleioblastus variegatus*.
A. hindsii See *Pleioblastus hindsii*.
A. japonica See *Pseudosasa japonica*.
A. murielae See *Thamnocalamus spathaceus*.
A. nitida See *Sinarundinaria nitida*.
A. pygmaea See *Pleioblastus pygmaea*.
A. simonii See *Pleioblastus simonii*.
A. spathiflora See *Thamnocalamus spathiflorus*.
A. viridi-sriata See *Pleioblastus auricomus*.

Astelia *Asteliaceae*

There are 25 species in this small genus of evergreen, clump-forming perennials which are native to the Pacific Islands, Australia and New Zealand. They will grow in any average, well-drained soil.

A. nervosa (Kakaha) Technically not a shrub, but a perennial with tufts of long, sword-shaped leaves which are reminiscent of those of a *Phormium* species. They are sage-green and conspicuously veined. The flowers are very small but sweetly scented and borne in dense, branching panicles in late summer. There are male and female plants, the latter bearing orange berries. New Zealand.

H2–3

Aster *Compositae*

Most of the 250 species in this genus are herbaceous perennials, but there are a small number of deciduous shrubs which are suitable for any average well-drained soil.

A. albescens A small shrub up to 1m (3ft) tall, producing its pale lilac-blue, daisy-like flowers in terminal clusters in mid- to late summer. Best in full sun. Himalaya, China. Introduced 1840.

H4

Asteranthera *Gesneriaceae*

A genus of one evergreen species that climbs with aerial roots. It needs a cool, leafy soil, preferably neutral or acid, and grows well in milder areas in a sheltered site or against a north-facing wall.

A. ovata A beautiful medium-sized trailing creeper that will climb up the trunks of trees or the surface of a wall. It can also make charming ground cover being more of a scrambler than a true climber. The leaves are small, more or less rounded, and the flowers are tubular, two-lipped, 5cm (2in) long and appear in early summer arising in the leaf axils. They are red with a white throat and closer examination reveals the similarities which make this plant's close relationship with *Saintpaulia* less unexpected. Chile. Introduced 1926 by Harold Comber.

H2–3

Atherosperma *Monimiaceae*

There is only one evergreen species in this genus.
A. moschatum An interesting small tree with lanceolate leaves that are downy beneath. The whole plant is highly aromatic and yields an essential oil. The solitary cream flowers are 2.5cm (1in) across and are borne in late spring or early summer. Requires an acid soil. Tasmania, SE Australia. Introduced 1824.

H2–3

Athrotaxis *Tasmanian cedar*

A genus of three Tasmanian conifers needing warm, sheltered positions in cultivation, although the following species is hardy and long-lived once established.

Athrotaxis laxifolia

A. laxifolia (Summit cedar) A small to medium-sized tree with a domed crown and brown, furrowed bark. The leaves are only 5mm (¼in) long, partly adpressed to the branchlets and partly spreading. Its small cones, often profusely borne, are bright green, changing through orange to brown. It is found in the wild in West Tasmania together with its two genus relatives, *A. cupressoides* and *A. selaginoides*. Introduced 1857.

H4

Atriplex *Chenopodiaceae*

There are more than 100 species of annuals,

perennials and evergreen or semi-evergreen shrubs in this genus. They are widely distributed, especially in deserts and salt marshes. The flowers are inconspicuous.

A. halimus (Tree purslane) A salt-marsh plant, making a medium-sized, semi-evergreen shrub with silvery-grey leaves, ideal for seaside areas. Good in poor, dry soils. S Europe. In cultivation since the early seventeenth century.
H4

Aucuba *Cornaceae*

A genus of evergreen, shade-loving shrubs with the male and female flowers on separate plants. They form dense, rounded bushes 2–3m (6–10ft) tall and thrive in almost any soil or situation, however sunless. They are very handsome when well grown, especially the variegated forms (which retain their colour best in open positions) and the berrying clones. There are three species, found in the Himalaya and eastern Asia.

A. japonica (Spotted laurel) A medium-sized shrub with green leaves, often referred to as *A. concolor* or *A. viridis*. The small, reddish-purple flowers, the males of which have conspicuous, creamy-white anthers, are produced in mid-spring. The male plant is the more common in cultivation. The following forms are available. Japan. Introduced 1783.
H4

Aucuba japonica 'Hillieri'

Aucuba japonica 'Crotonifolia'

A. j. 'Crotonifolia' A medium-sized shrub with large leaves, boldly spotted and blotched with gold. The best golden-varie-

Aucuba japonica 'Gold Dust'

gated aucuba. Female.
H4 🏆 1993

A. j. 'Gold Dust' The leaves of this medium-sized shrub are brightly speckled and blotched with gold. Female.
H4

A. j. 'Golden King' This medium-sized shrub is similar to 'Crotonifolia' but with a more striking variegation comprising bold

blotches. Best in semi-shade. Male.
H4

A. j. 'Hillieri' A noble medium-sized shrub with large, lustrous, dark green leaves and pointed fruits. Female.
H4

Aucuba japonica 'Lance Leaf'

A. j. 'Lance Leaf' A striking, sculptural medium-sized shrub with polished, deep

green, lance-shaped leaves. This is the male counterpart to 'Longifolia'.
H4

Aucuba japonica 'Longifolia'

A. j. 'Longifolia' The leaves of this medium-sized shrub are long, lanceolate and bright green. Female.
H4 AGM 1993

A. j. 'Maculata' See *A. j.* 'Variegata'.

A. j. 'Marmorata' The leaves of this form are heavily spotted and blotched with yellow. Female.
H4

A. j. 'Nana Rotundifolia' A small, freely berrying form whose small, rich green leaves have an occasional spot and are sharply toothed in the upper half. Its stems are an unusual shade of sea-green. Female.
H4

Aucuba japonica 'Picturata'

A. j. 'Picturata' The leaves of this form have a large central yellow blotch and are yellow-spotted within the margin. How-

Aucuba japonica 'Variegata'

ever, it reverts so badly that it is hardly worth growing. Male.
H4

A. j. 'Rozannie' A medium-sized shrub with broad, dark green leaves, toothed above the middle. It is compact and bears its large red fruits freely and reliably. Female. In cultivation 1984.
H4

A. j. 'Salicifolia' A free-berrying medium-sized shrub that differs from 'Longifolia' in its narrower leaves and sea-green stems. Female.
H4

A. j. 'Sulphurea Marginata' A distinct form with sea-green stems and green leaves with a pale yellow margin. A medium-sized shrub, in shade it is inclined to revert. Usually grown under the name 'Sulphurea'. Female.
H4

A. j. 'Variegata', syn. *A. j.* 'Maculata' A medium-sized shrub with yellow-speckled leaves, this is the form that was first intro-

Aucuba japonica 'Sulphurea Marginata'

duced and gave rise to the common name of the species. Japan. Introduced 1783.
H4

Austrocedrus *Cupressaceae*

A genus of one evergreen species of conifer with small, solitary cones. The leaves are scale-like and borne is unequal opposite pairs.

Austrocedrus chilensis

Azara serrata

A. integrifolia 'Variegata' The (non-variegated) species is quite tall and has oval leaves; in this form the leaves are smaller and rounder and prettily variegated in pink and cream. Yellow spikes of flowers are borne in spring. Raised at Kew c1870. H3

A. lanceolata A medium-sized or large shrub with attractive bright green leaves and small, fragrant, mustard-yellow flowers from mid- to late spring. Chile, Argentina. Introduced 1926 by Harold Comber. H3

A. microphylla An elegant small tree with large sprays of dainty foliage and yellow, vanilla-scented flowers that appear on the undersides of the twigs in early spring. The hardiest species. Chile, Argentina. Introduced 1861 by Richard Pearce. H3 ♛ 1993

A. m. 'Variegata' The leaves of this small tree are prettily margined with cream. It is notably slow-growing. In cultivation 1916. H3

A. serrata A large shrub of upright habit which is most suitable for a wall or sheltered site and has particularly distinctive oval, shiny, serrate leaves and conspicuous clusters of attractive orange-yellow flowers in midsummer. Small, white berries are produced in hot summers. Hardier than most other species. Chile. H3

A. chilensis (Chilean cedar) A remarkably beautiful species. It is slow growing but hardy and makes a small columnar tree. The branchlets are flattened and divided so as to appear beautifully moss-like or ferny. The sea-green leaves are in V-shaped pairs. This tree grew successfully at the Hillier Gardens and Arboretum for more than 40 years, but is sensitive to cold, dry winds. It also dislikes dryness, and a moisture-retentive soil is necessary, although it must also be well drained. Chile, Argentina. Introduced 1847. H3–4

Azara *Flacourtiaceae*

A genus of around 10 species of evergreen shrubs or small trees from Chile and Argentina. Except in mild areas, need to be grown in sheltered positions. They have accessory leaves at the bases of the true leaves, giving them an unusual 'herringbone' appearance. The orange-yellow, fragrant flowers are made up principally of stamens.

Azara microphylla

B

Baccharis *Compositae*

A genus of 350 evergreen and deciduous species in all, consisting of small trees, shrubs and herbaceous plants from North and South America. Their flowers are held in small heads and the following is a fast-growing shrub for any soil. It is resistant to salt spray.

B. patagonica A medium-sized deciduous shrub with red shoots and short, stalkless, evergreen, dark glossy green, polished leaves. The flower heads are yellowish-white and appear singly in the upper leaf axils in late spring. Patagonia. H3–4

Ballota *Labiatae*

A genus of about 35 species of herbaceous

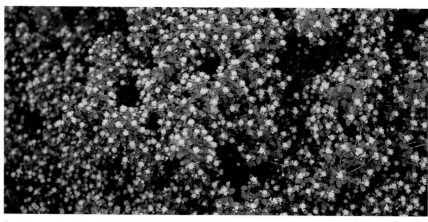

Baccharis patagonica

perennials and deciduous sub-shrubs, mainly from the Mediterranean region and western Asia. The following requires a sunny, well-drained position but is otherwise tolerant of poor soils.

B. pseudodictamnus A dwarf sub-shrub for a sunny, well-drained position. The whole plant, including the rounded, slightly heart-shaped leaves, is covered with a dense, greyish-white wool, and it is a most effective foliage plant, particularly if pruned back each spring. An excellent addition to grey border schemes, with lilac-pink flowers in midsummer. Mediterranean region. H3-4 ♔ 1993

Berberidopsis *Flacourtiaceae*

A genus of one species that requires an open or sandy, loamy, preferably acid or neutral, moist soil and a sheltered position in shade. In the right conditions it is moderately hardy.

Berberidopsis corallina

B. corallina (Coral plant) A beautiful medium-sized evergreen plant with climbing stemsl. The leaves are thick and leathery, set with spiny teeth, and the flowers are deep crimson, quite small, but strikingly eye-catching. They are borne singly on slender stalks or in dangling clusters in late summer. Chile. Introduced 1862. H3

Ballota pseudodictamnus

BERBERIS

Berberidaceae Barberry

Berberis georgei

BERBERIS is a very large genus of shrubs (about 450 species and as many cultivars and hybrids) which are often referred to as 'barberries'. The derivation of this name is uncertain, but probably has to do with the spines that are borne, usually in threes, by most of them.

It is not only the spines that make berberis highly distinctive plants, but also their foliage, which is often spiny in a holly-like way and in many cases covered with a waxy, powdery bloom; their flowers vary from pale yellow to orange and appear during spring.

There are evergreen and deciduous berberis, of which the latter contribute greatly to the autumn colour scene in the garden, while the former are a major asset during winter. Then, too, the conspicuous and often showy crops of berries help to make them indispensable for anyone who wishes to make the garden attractive all year round. The berries of deciduous plants are usually red, while those of the ever-greens are predominantly blue-black.

Berberis vary from quite large shrubs, such as the 3m (10ft) tall *B. julianae*, to dwarf ones, such as the dense, compact *B. ×stenophylla* 'Corallina Compacta', which is dwarf enough for a small rock garden or even a large trough. The majority, however, are of medium size, often building up to impenetrable barriers with great potential as hedges.

Once you have looked closely at the flowers of a berberis, you will always know them again. They have a button-like appearance, with their parts always in multiples of three – six stamens, six petals, and six or nine sepals. If the base of a stamen is touched with the point of a pin, it and its fellows will bend sharply inwards towards the pistil – the reaction to the sharp proboscis of pollinating insects. The flowers are sometimes borne singly, but are often carried in conspicuous clusters (racemes).

CARE AND CULTIVATION

Berberis are not difficult to grow. The deciduous ones are on the whole better in sun, where autumn colour in both leaf and berries is produced to best effect, while the evergreens prefer the dappled shade of trees. There is no hard-and-fast rule about this, however, and in Britain both kinds tolerate shade. In nature their role is as 'pioneer' plants, and as a result they will thrive on most soils, even dry, thin ones over chalk. However, they will not stand water-logging – good drainage is as important for them as for the majority of shrubs.

Few shrubs are so little affected by atmospheric pollution, and there are numerous examples of clipped berberis being used as anti-dazzle barriers on central reservations. They will grow and flower happily in the most heavily industrialized towns and their spines provide some discouragement to unwanted intruders.

Other than for formal hedges, little pruning is required. Trimming of evergreen berberis should be carried out immediately after flowering, while that of deciduous kinds should be carried out in late summer and early autumn.

Berberis *Berberidaceae*
Barberry

B. × antoniana *(B. buxifolia × B. darwinii)* The dark green leaves of this small, rounded, evergreen bush are almost spineless, and it is most attractive when bearing its single, long-stalked, deep yellow flowers and dark, purplish berries. Arose at Daisy Hill Nursery, Northern Ireland.
H4

Berberis 'Bountiful'

B. 'Bountiful' A small, spreading deciduous bush which is very decorative in autumn, when laden with clusters of coral-red berries on arching branches. Pale yellow flowers are borne in late spring or early summer.
H4

B. × bristolensis *(B. calliantha × B. verruculosa)* A small, densely rounded, evergreen shrub with small, prickly leaves that are glossy dark green on the upper sides and

Berberis 'Buccaneer'

bloomy-white beneath. Yellow flowers are borne in late spring. It makes an excellent dwarf hedge if clipped. Garden origin.
H4

B. 'Buccaneer' An erect-branched small deciduous shrub notable for the large size of its deep red berries, which are carried in large clusters and last until early winter. It has good autumn colour.
H4

Berberis buxifolia 'Nana'

B. buxifolia 'Nana' A slow-growing, dense, evergreen mound about 50cm (20in) high with rounded leaves, and virtually thornless. It rarely flowers. In cultivation 1867.
H4

B. cabrerae A large deciduous shrub remarkable for the large size of its flowers, which are yellow and pale orange. The berries are black. Some plants grown as *B. montana* really belong to this species. Argentinian Andes. Introduced 1925–7 by Harold Comber.
H4

B. calliantha A small, evergreen shrub with small, holly-like leaves that are waxy-white beneath, and crimson young stems. It bears its pale yellow, comparatively large flowers either singly or in pairs in late spring, followed by blue-black fruits. SE Tibet. Introduced 1924 by Frank Kingdon-Ward.
H4 ♛ 1993

B. candidula A small, dense, dome-shaped, evergreen bush, with small, shining, dark green leaves that are silvery-white beneath. The flowers are single, and bright yellow. W China. Introduced 1895 by Père Farges.
H4

Berberis darwinii

B. darwinii This early-flowering, medium-sized, evergreen species is one of the finest of all flowering shrubs. Its leaves are three-pointed with shining, dark green upper sides, and its flowers are bright orange tinged with red, borne in drooping clusters over a long period in spring. Chile and Argentina. First discovered 1835 by Charles Darwin on the voyage of the Beagle. Introduced 1849 by William Lobb.
H4 ♛ 1993

Berberis dictyophylla

B. dictyophylla, syn. *B. dictyophylla* 'Albicaulis' A graceful deciduous shrub up to about 2m (6ft) with good autumn colour. The young stems are red and covered with a white bloom, and the leaves are chalk-white underneath. Solitary pale yellow flowers are borne in late spring. The large, solitary, red berries are also covered with a white bloom. W China. Introduced 1916.
H4 ♛ 1993

B. d. 'Albicaulis' See *B. dictyophylla*.

B. × **frikartii** *(B. candidula × B. verruculosa)* A small evergreen shrub of dense habit with angled shoots and glossy, dark green, spiny leaves that are waxy-white beneath. The relatively large, pale yellow flowers are borne singly or in pairs and are followed by blue-black berries. It is available in the following clones.
H4

Berberis × frikartii 'Amstelveen'

B. × **f. 'Amstelveen'** A small, dense evergreen shrub with attractively drooping shoots and glossy green leaves that are white on their lower surfaces. Raised c1960 in Holland.
H4 ♔ 1993

Berberis × frikartii 'Telstar'

B. × **f. 'Telstar'** Similar to 'Amstelveen' but taller, growing to as much as 1.2m (4ft). At the same time, though, it is more compact in habit. Raised c1960 in Holland.
H4 ♔ 1993

B. **gagnepainii** A small evergreen shrub that makes a dense thicket of erect stems, closely set with narrow leaves with undulating margins. The yellow flowers are borne in clusters of between six and 12 and are followed by black berries covered in a blue bloom. Suitable for making an impenetrable hedge. W China. Introduced c1904 by Ernest Wilson.
H4

Berberis georgei

B. **georgei** A rare and attractive deciduous shrub of medium height, with arching branches. It flowers in late spring, with yellow blooms borne in hanging, red-stalked clusters. The toothed leaves colour well in autumn, when the profusion of crimson berries in large, pendulous clusters are at their most showy. Origin uncertain.
H4

B. **'Goldilocks'** *(B. darwinii × valdiviana)* A large, vigorous, evergreen shrub with upright but arching branches and spiny, glossy, dark green leaves. The deep golden yellow flowers are profusely borne in hanging, red-stalked clusters over a long period in spring. Raised 1978 by Hillier Nurseries' propagator, Peter Dummer.
H4 ♔ 1993

B. **hypokerina** (Silver holly) An outstanding small, evergreen shrub that forms a thicket of purple stems, with holly-like leaves as much as 10cm (4in) long with silvery-white undersides. Yellow flowers are borne in clusters in midsummer. Its berries are dark blue and have a white bloom. This species does not thrive on shallow, chalky soils. It is unfortunately not as hardy as most berberis. Upper Burma. Discovered

and introduced 1926 by the plant hunter Frank Kingdon-Ward.
H3–4

B. × **interposita 'Wallich's Purple'** A small, dense, evergreen bush with arching shoots. Its leaves are bronze-red when young and turn glossy green later. Their undersides are tinted with blue.
H4

B. × **irwinii** See *B.* × *stenophylla* 'Irwinii'.

Berberis stenophylla 'Corallina Compacta'

B. × **i. 'Corallina Compacta'** See *B.* × *stenophylla* 'Corallina Compacta'.

B. **julianae** An excellent dense, evergreen shrub growing up to 3m (10ft) tall with strong, spiny stems and clusters of stiff, narrow, spine-toothed leaves that are copper tinted when young. The yellow flowers, which are slightly scented, are borne in dense clusters of as many as 15. A good screening or hedging plant. China. Introduced 1900 by Ernest Wilson.
H4

Berberis linearifolia 'Jewel'

B. linearifolia An erect, medium-sized, evergreen shrub with a rather ungainly habit of growth and narrow, glossy, dark green, spine-tipped leaves. The orange-red flowers are produced early in spring and sometimes again in autumn, and are the richest coloured in the genus. It is available in the following clones. Argentina, Chile. Introduced 1927 by Harold Comber. H4

B. l. **'Jewel'** A splendid medium-sized shrub and possibly the best berberis of all for flowers, which are larger than average, scarlet in bud and bright orange when open. In cultivation 1937. H4

Berberis linearifolia 'Orange King'

B. l. **'Orange King'** A medium-sized shrub with rich orange flowers larger than those of the species. H4

B. × *lologensis* (*B. darwinii* × *B. linearifolia*) A very beautiful, medium-sized, evergreen

Berberis × *lologensis* 'Apricot Queen'

Berberis × *lologensis*

shrub and the offspring of two superb species. Its leaves are variable in shape, with entire and spiny ones on the same bush. A natural hybrid found 1927 with the parents near Lake Lolog, Argentina, by Harold Comber. It is available in the following clones. H4

B. × *l.* **'Apricot Queen'** This broadly upright shrub bears a profusion of pale orange flowers. H4 ♔ 1993

B. × *l.* **'Mystery Fire'** A vigorous, upright shrub with a profusion of deep orange flowers. H4

B. × *l.* **'Stapehill'** A free-flowering shrub with rich orange flowers. H4

B. × *media* (*B.* × *chenaultii* × *B. thunbergii*) An evergreen hybrid, represented in gardens by the following forms. H4

B. × *m.* **'Parkjuweel'** A small, dense,

Berberis × *media* 'Parkjuweel'

prickly shrub with leaves that are widest above the middle, almost spineless and colour richly in autumn, occasionally remaining until the following spring. The yellow flowers are single or borne in clusters of 2–4 in late spring. Garden origin c1956 in Holland. H4 ♔ 1993

B. × *m.* **'Red Jewel'** A small, dense shrub

similar to 'Parkjuweel', of which it is a sport, but with somewhat broader leaves that become a deep, metallic purple.
H4 ♔ 1993

***B.* × *ottawensis* 'Purpurea'** See *B.* × *o.* 'Superba'.

Berberis × *ottawensis* 'Superba'

***B.* × *o.* 'Superba'**, syn. *B.* × *o.* 'Purpurea' A vigorous, medium sized to large deciduous shrub, and a really first-class plant with rich, wine-purple foliage, yellow flowers borne in late spring and red berries.
H4 ♔ 1993

B. panlanensis See *B. sanguinea* 'Panlanensis'.

***B.* 'Pirate King'** A small, dense but vigorous shrub with yellow flowers and fiery, orange-red berries.
H4

Berberis x ottawensis 'Rubrostilla'

***B.* 'Rubrostilla'** A beautiful small deciduous shrub that is very showy in autumn when it bears oblong, coral-red berries

which are among the largest in the genus. Pale yellow flowers are borne in racemes 3cm (1¹/₂in) long in late spring or early summer. Possibly a hybrid of *B. wilsoniae*. Garden origin.
H4 ♔ 1993

***B. sanguinea* 'Panlanensis'**, syn. *B. panlanensis* This is the form of the species that is most usually grown: a charming, medium-sized, compact, evergreen shrub of very neat growth. Its leaves are linear, sea-green and spine-toothed, and it makes an excellent hedging plant. W China. Introduced 1908.
H4

B. sargentiana A hardy medium-sized species up to 2m (6ft) tall with leathery, evergreen, net-veined leaves up to 13cm (5in) long. It has yellow flowers and blue-black berries. W China. Introduced 1907 by Ernest Wilson.
H4

B. sieboldii A small, compact, suckering deciduous shrub with oval leaves that colour richly in autumn. The clusters of pale yellow flowers are followed by round, shining orange berries. Japan. Introduced 1892.
H4

B.* × *stenophylla *(B. darwinii* × *B. empetrifolia)* An indispensable, evergreen bush that ultimately becomes a graceful, medium-sized shrub. In mid-spring its long, arching branches are wreathed with yellow flowers. In cultivation 1860.
H4 ♔ 1993

Berberis × *stenophylla* 'Claret Cascade'

***B.* × *s.* 'Claret Cascade'** A medium-sized

shrub with rich orange flowers flushed with red on the outside and foliage tinged purple making a striking display.
H4

***B.* × *s.* 'Corallina Compacta'**, syn. *B.* × *irwinii* 'Corallina Compacta' A dwarf shrub suitable for the rock garden and seldom exceeding 30cm (12in) in height. The buds are coral-red and open to yellow. In cultivation 1930.
H4 ♔ 1993

Berberis × *stenophylla* 'Crawley Gem'

***B.* × *s.* 'Crawley Gem'** A small shrub forming a dense mound of arching stems that in spring become covered with orange flowers with red-tipped buds. In cultivation 1930.
H4

***B.* × *s.* 'Cream Showers'** An unusual but garden-worthy medium-sized shrub with creamy-white flowers.
H4

***B.* × *s.* 'Irwinii'**, syn. *B.* × *irwinii* A small, compact shrub with deep yellow flowers. In cultivation 1903.
H4

B. temolaica One of the most striking of the barberries, this is a vigorous deciduous shrub up to 3m (10ft) tall, with stout, erectly spreading branches. The young shoots and leaves are conspicuously glaucous, the shoots becoming a dark, bloomy purple-brown with age and the leaves having bloomy-green upper sides and strikingly white undersurfaces. Pale yellow flowers are borne in late spring or early summer. The red berries are egg-shaped and covered with bloom. SE Tibet. Introduced

Berberis thunbergii

1924 by Frank Kingdon-Ward.
H4

B. thunbergii An invaluable small deciduous shrub of dense and compact habit, unsurpassed in the brilliance of its autumn foliage and bright red berries. Small, pale yellow flowers tinged with red in mid- or late spring. Japan. Introduced c1864.
H4 ♛ 1993

Berberis Atropurpurea group

B. t. **Atropurpurea group** A small shrub which has rich, reddish-purple foliage in spring, summer and autumn that increases in intensity of colour as winter approaches. In cultivation 1913.
H4

Berberis thunbergii 'Atropurpurea Nana'

B. t. **'Atropurpurea Nana'**, syn. *B. t.* 'Crimson Pygmy' A charming dwarf form, suitable for the rock garden and making a fine, purple-foliaged dwarf hedge. Raised 1942 in Holland.
H4 ♛ 1993

Berberis thunbergii 'Aurea'

B. t. **'Aurea'** A small shrub with bright yellow leaves that become pale green by late summer. It tends to burn in sun and does best in a moist atmosphere. In cultivation 1950.
H4

B. t. **'Bagatelle'** (*B.t.* 'Atropurpurea Nana' × *B.t.* 'Kobold') This cultivar is similar to *B. t.* 'Atropurpurea Nana' but is much more compact. Raised 1971 in Holland.
H4 ♛ 1993

B. t. **'Crimson Pygmy'** See *B. t.* 'Atropurpurea Nana'.

Berberis thunbergii 'Dart's Red Lady'

B. t. **'Dart's Red Lady'** A small shrub with very deep purple leaves that turn brilliant red in autumn.
H4

Berberis thunbergii 'Golden Ring'

Berberis thunbergii 'Kelleriis'

B. t. 'Erecta' A small, compact, fastigiate shrub that forms a close clump and has superb autumn colours. It is good as a low hedge but tends to fall open with age.
H4

B. t. 'Golden Ring' The leaves of this small shrub are reddish-purple with a narrow gold margin. By sowing seed of forms of the Atropurpurea group, similar variega-

tions can be produced. In cultivation 1950.
H4

B. t. 'Harlequin' A small shrub similar to 'Rose Glow' but with smaller leaves heavily mottled with pink. In cultivation 1969.
H4

B. t. 'Helmond Pillar' A narrow, upright small shrub with rich purple foliage.
H4

B. t. 'Kelleriis' A compact, spreading small bush with leaves which are mottled with creamy-white. In autumn the white portion of the leaf turns through shades of pink to a rich deep crimson. Raised in Denmark.
H4

B. t. 'Kobold' A free-fruiting, dwarf form of very dense, rounded habit. Raised c1960 in Holland.
H4

B. t. 'Pink Queen' A small shrub which is the best pink-variegated form, with reddish leaves heavily flecked with grey and white. Raised before 1958 in Holland.
H4

Berberis thunbergii 'Harlequin'

Berberis thunbergii 'Helmond Pillar'

Berberis thunbergii 'Red Chief'

B. t. 'Red Chief' A small, upright shrub with branches that arch as it gets older. Its stems are bright red and its narrow leaves deep red. Selected 1942 in Holland.
H4 ♛ 1993

B. t. 'Red Pillar' A most attractive form of

Berberis thunbergii 'Red Pillar'

'Erecta'. It, too, falls open as it ages.
H4

Berberis thunbergii 'Rose Glow'

B. t. 'Rose Glow' A small, very striking, colourful shrub. The leaves of the young shoots are purple, mottled with silver, pink and bright rose, later becoming purple. Selected in Holland c1957.
H4 ♡ 1993

B. t. 'Silver Beauty' This form is similar to *B. t.* 'Kelleriis' but somewhat less vigorous.
H4

B. tsangpoensis A most interesting deciduous species that forms a dwarf, widespreading mound with slender, yellow stems often extending for a considerable distance along the ground. Deep yellow flowers are borne in clusters in late spring. It has attractive autumn colour and red berries. SE Tibet. Introduced 1925.
H4

B. valdiviana This large, stately, ever-

Berberis valdiviana

green species is like a smooth-leaved holly and has distinctive large, leathery, polished, almost spineless leaves. Its flowers are saffron-yellow and borne in long, drooping clusters. This is a first-class hardy shrub that deserves wider planting, but is scarce because it is difficult to propagate. Chile. Introduced 1902.
H4

B. veitchii An evergreen shrub up to about 2m (6½ft) tall with long, lance-shaped, spine-toothed leaves and red young shoots. The flowers are bronze-yellow, long-stalked, and borne in axillary clusters o0f up to eight. The berries are black. C China. Introduced 1900 by Ernest Wilson.
H4

B. verruculosa A very pleasing, compact, slow-growing, evergreen shrub, about 1.5–2m (5–6½ft) tall, with rough, minutely warty, drooping stems densely covered with small, glossy, dark green leaves that are white beneath. The flowers are usually solitary and golden yellow. China. Introduced 1904 by Ernest Wilson.
H4 ♡ 1993

B. wilsoniae A splendid small deciduous shrub that forms dense mounds of thorny stems. The leaves are small, sea-green and turn to attractive autumn shades that blend with the coral of the fruit clusters. The true plant can be perpetuated only by seed obtained from the wild or by cuttings. W

Berberis wilsoniae

China. Introduced c1904 by Ernest Wilson and named after his wife.
H4 ♛ 1993

B. yunnanensis An attractive, medium-sized, rounded deciduous shrub with comparatively large, golden yellow flowers, brilliant autumn colours and bright red berries. W China. Introduced 1885 by Delavay.
H4

Beschorneria *Agavaceae*

A genus of about 10 evergreen shrubs and perennials related to Agave *and natives of Mexico.*

Beschorneria yuccoides

B. yuccoides A striking, yucca-like plant that is not strictly a shrub, but an evergreen perennial with a semi-woody stem. The flower stems reach about 2m (6½ft) in height and carry drooping racemes of bright green flowers with red bracts in mid- or late summer. This remarkable plant flourished in Hilliers' Winchester nursery on chalk at the foot of a south-facing wall for more than 20 years. Requires full sun and a well-drained position. Mexico. Introduced before 1859.
H2 ♛ 1993

Betula *Betulaceae*
Birch

A genus of about 60 deciduous species, some of which are among the most beautiful of garden trees. Birches are grown for their generally graceful habit, lightness of foliage and often for their singularly decorative bark, which in some is startlingly white and in many cases peels attractively. Their flowers consist of male and female catkins borne on the same tree; the males are pendulous and elongate in spring, while the females are shorter and erect. Many birches display bright yellow autumn colour. They succeed on most soils, both damp and dry, but do not reach maximum size on shallow soils over chalk.

B. alba See *B. pendula, B. pubescens.*

Betula albo-sinensis

B. albo-sinensis A beautiful, medium-sized species with glossy green leaves on slightly rough shoots. The attractive, peeling bark is pinkish to coppery-red and cream when first exposed. W China. Introduced 1901 by Ernest Wilson.
H4 ♛ 1993

Betula albo-sinensis var. septentrionalis

B. a. var. septentrionalis This splendid medium-sized variety has strikingly grey-pink bark that is coppery-pink on the main branches. Its leaves are matt rather than glossy. Introduced 1908 by Ernest Wilson.
H4 ♛ 1993

B. alleghaniensis, syn. *B. lutea* A medium-sized tree with smooth, shining, amber-coloured or golden-brown bark that peels prettily. Its leaves are oblong and broadest above the middle, downy, and turn rich yellow in autumn. E North America. Introduced c1767.
H4

Betula costata

B. costata The true *B. costata* is rare in cultivation, and plants grown under this name are sometimes a form of *B. ermanii*, as described below.
H4

Betula ermanii

B. ermanii A very graceful, vigorous large tree with rough shoots and bright green, often heart-shaped leaves with conspicuous veining. The bark is creamy-white and pinkish, and fawn when first exposed by

Bark of *Betula ermanii*

peeling. It has many lenticels (raised pores on the surface) that are pale brown on the trunk and brown to red-brown on the branches. NE Asia.
H4

Betula ermanii 'Grayswood Hill'

B. e. 'Grayswood Hill' A particularly fine form, and the tree usually offered as *B. costata*.
H4 ♔ 1993

B. 'Fetisowii' A hybrid forming a graceful, medium-sized, narrow-headed tree notable for its peeling, chalk-white bark that extends up the trunk to the branches. Plants grown under this name are probably seedlings of the original. C Asia.
H4

B. jacquemontii See *B. utilis* var. *jacquemontii*.

B. lenta (Cherry birch) This tree can grow to 25m (80ft) tall in its native land, but the tallest in cultivation tend to be around 14m (46ft). Its trunk is smooth, dark and reddish-brown or purple. The bark does not peel

Betula lenta (Cherry birch)

and, when young, is sweetly aromatic. The leaves turn rich yellow in autumn. E North America. Introduced 1759.
H4

B. lutea See *B. alleghaniensis*.

B. mandshurica var. szechuanica See *B. szechuanica*.

Betula maximowicziana

B. maximowicziana (Monarch birch) This form has the largest leaves of all the

birches and is a fast-growing, wide-headed tree of medium height except in its native habitat, where it is taller. Its trunk is orange-brown, becoming grey and pinkish but coppery on the branches and peeling in narrow strips. The leaves are heart-shaped, and up to 15cm (6in) long; they turn a lovely shade of butter-yellow in autumn. Japan. Introduced 1893.
H4

Betula medwedewii

B. medwedewii A large shrub or small, shrubby tree with stout, erect branches. It can be distinguished from other birches by its large terminal buds and particularly by its fine autumn foliage, in which the large, corrugated leaves turn bright yellow. Caucasus, NW Iran, NE Turkey. Introduced 1897.
H4 ♔ 1993

Betula nana

B. nana (Dwarf birch) A dwarf or small shrub, 0.5–1m (20in–3ft) high, with tiny rounded leaves. Sub-arctic Europe (includ-

ing some mountains of Scotland and N England), Asia, Greenland.
H4

Betula nigra

B. nigra (Red birch, river birch) A beautiful, fast-growing medium-sized tree, remarkable for its shaggy, pinkish-orange bark that becomes brown and ridged on old trees. As its common name suggests, it is one of the finest trees for planting on damp ground. The soft green, diamond-shaped leaves are covered on their undersides with a bluish bloom. C and E United States. Introduced 1736 by Peter Collinson.
H4 ♛ 1993

Betula papyrifera

B. papyrifera (Canoe birch, paper birch) A striking, large tree with white, papery bark and yellow autumn foliage. North America. Introduced 1750.
H4

B. p. var. kenaica A medium-sized tree with characteristic white bark tinged with

Betula pendula

orange. Alaskan coast. Introduced 1891.
H4

B. pendula, syn. *B. alba*, *B. verrucosa* (Silver birch) Often described as 'the lady of the woods', this is a medium-sized, white-stemmed tree that thrives on drier soils than *B. pubescens* (white birch), from which it is distinguished by its rough, warty shoots and sharply cut, diamond-shaped leaves. Its young twigs are generally pendulous, as opposed to those of *B. pubescens* and, unlike that species, old specimens develop rough, black bark at the base. N Asia, Europe (including Britain and Ireland).
H4 ♛ 1993

B. p. 'Dalecarlica' Hort. (Swedish birch) A tall, slender, graceful tree with drooping branches and prettily cut leaves. The plant commonly grown under its name should correctly be known as 'Crispa' or 'Laciniata'. The true plant is rare, and differs in its leaves being more deeply cut and its branches not as weeping. Discovered 1767 in Sweden.
H4 ♛ 1993

B. p. 'Fastigiata' An erect form of medium size and rather stiff habit. 'Obelisk' is similar but perhaps not becoming as wide. In cultivation 1870.
H4

B. p. 'Golden Cloud' A small tree with yellow leaves that tends to burn badly and suffer from birch rust, a disease causing premature leaf loss.
H4

B. p. 'Purpurea' (Purple-leaved birch) A slow-growing small tree with purple leaves, drooping branches, and a rather weak con-

Betula pendula 'Tristis'

stitution. In cultivation 1872.
H4

B. p. 'Tristis' A tall, graceful tree of outstanding merit, with slender, pendulous branches, forming a symmetrical head. In cultivation 1867.
H4 ♛ 1993

B. p. 'Youngii' (Young's weeping birch)

Betula pendula 'Youngii'

This form ultimately becomes a beautiful small, dome- or mushroom-headed, weeping tree, ideal for smaller gardens.
H4 ♔ 1993

Betula pubescens

B. pubescens (White birch) A medium-sized tree that thrives on a variety of soils and especially in damp places. It is distinguished from *B. pendula* by its less weeping, more upright habit, smooth, downy shoots, more rounded leaves, and its bark being white to the base. The twigs are generally of a richer, mahogany-brown. N Europe (including Britain and Ireland), N Asia.
H4

Betula szechuanica

B. szechuanica A vigorous, medium-sized tree with glossy, blue-green leaves and chalk-white, peeling bark. W China, SE Tibet. Introduced 1908 by Ernest Wilson.
H4

B. 'Trost's Dwarf' A small shrub with slender, arching branches and small, finely

cut leaves. Although superficially attractive, it is a weak grower and susceptible to birch rust.
H4

Betula utilis var. *jacquemontii* in summer

B. utilis (Himalayan birch) In its typical form this is an attractive, medium-sized tree with orange-brown or dark, coppery-brown, peeling bark, often bloomed grey-

pink. However, the most sought-after forms are those with white barks, which are among the most beautiful of all the birches. SW China to Nepal. Introduced 1849 by Sir Joseph Hooker.
H4

Betula utilis var. *jacquemontii* in winter

B. u. var. jacquemontii This medium-sized tree differs from the typical form in its

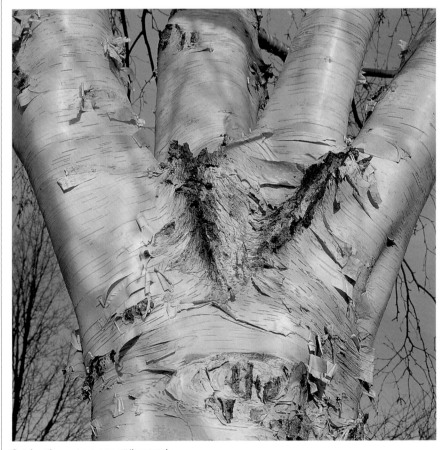

Betula utilis var. *jacquemontii* 'Jermyns'

white bark. However, contrary to popular belief it is not the one that is most usually grown, although the best forms are too often grown under its name.

H4

B. u. var. j. 'Doorenbos' The medium-sized Dutch clone that is readily available as *B. jacquemontii*. The striking white peeling bark is pale orange when freshly exposed.

H4 ♔ 1993

B. u. var. j. 'Jermyns' A very vigorous form, making a medium-sized, broadly conical tree, whose very fine white bark is retained into maturity. Its catkins are showy and up to 17cm (7in) in length. Selected in Hillier Nurseries from plants received from Belgium, it had reached 14m (46ft) in the Hillier Gardens and Arboretum by 1990.

H4 ♔ 1993

Betula utilis var. jacquemontii 'Silver Shadow'

B. u. var. j. 'Silver Shadow' One of the loveliest birches, with dazzlingly white stems. It is a very distinct form of *B. utilis* var. *jacquemontii* and grows into a small to medium-sized tree whose large, drooping, dark green leaves contrast dramatically with its unmarked, pure white bark. The original tree grew for many years in Hillier West Hill Nurseries in Winchester, England, and was previously distributed as *B. jacquemontii*.

H4 ♔ 1993

B. verrucosa See *B. pendula*.

Bignonia *Bignoniaceae*

This is now a genus of one evergreen or semi-evergreen species.

B. capreolata A large, vigorous plant that climbs with twining leaf tendrils. Each leaf consists of two fairly slender leaflets up to 13cm (5in) long. The tubular flowers, about 5cm (2in) long, are orange-red, paler within, in clusters in early summer. It is a rampant climber for a sunny, sheltered wall or a tree, but only in mild locations or where there are good amounts of sun to ripen the wood. SE United States. In cultivation 1653.

H3

Billardiera *Pittosporaceae*

A genus of about eight species of low-growing evergreen twining plants from Australia. The following is suitable for a warm, sunny position in milder areas and makes an unusual conservatory plant.

Billardiera longiflora

B. longiflora A slender climber up to 2m (6ft) high. It has lance-shaped leaves and solitary, bell-shaped flowers that hang from slender stalks in summer and autumn. They are greenish yellow, 2cm (¾in) long and are followed by brilliantly deep blue, oblong fruits up to 2.5cm (1in) long. Tasmania. Introduced 1810.

H2–3

Broussonetia *Moraceae*

A genus of seven or eight species of deciduous shrubs and trees from eastern Asia and Polynesia. The male flowers are in catkin-like spikes, while the female ones are in round heads. They grow in any ordinary soil in a warm, sunny spot in a mild area.

B. papyrifera (Paper mulberry) A large shrub or small tree with unusually and variably lobed hairy leaves. The male and female flowers borne in early summer are on the same tree, the males in catkins and the females in round heads that give rise to the decorative, orange-red fruits. In Japan, paper is made from its bark. Will grow on soils that are quite poor but prefers a well-drained, warm, sunny site. E Asia, naturalized in USA. Introduced early eighteenth century.

H4

Bruckenthalia *Ericaceae*

A genus of only one evergreen species, related to Erica *and requiring acid soil.*

B. spiculifolia A dwarf, heath-like, lime-hating plant up to 25cm (10in) high, with terminal clusters of rose-pink, bell-shaped flowers in early summer. E Europe, Asia Minor. Introduced 1888.

H4

Brugmansia *Solanaceae*
Angel's trumpet

A genus of five species of highly attractive deciduous shrubs and trees native to South America, particularly the Andes. They have large, hanging, trumpet-shaped flowers and have hitherto been included in Datura, *which is now restricted to annual species with upright flowers. They require a light, fertile soil which is moisture-retentive and can be grown outdoors only in mild places that are virtually frost-free, but are*

Brugmansia × candida 'Grand Marnier'

eminently suitable for the conservatory. It is a useful patio tub plant. Harmful if eaten.

B. × candida A splendid hybrid with yellow or pink flowers borne from early summer to early autumn. The following forms are grown in gardens.
H2

B. × c. 'Grand Marnier' A large shrub with large, dangling, fragrant, trumpet-shaped flowers in a beautiful peach colour, with the lobes ending in long, tail-like points.
H2 ♛ 1993

Brugmansia × candida 'Knightii'

B. × c. 'Knightii' A large shrub with large, hanging, double white flowers.
H2 ♛ 1993

Brugmansia sanguinea

B. sanguinea, syn. *Datura sanguinea* A tree-like shrub up to 3m (10ft) tall, or more where it is ideally sited. It has large, softly hairy leaves, toothed on young plants, and

large, orange-red trumpets hanging from the branches in late spring and early summer. Colombia to N Chile.
H2 ♛ 1993

Brugmansia suaveolens

B. suaveolens, syn. *Datura suaveolens* A large shrub or small tree whose untoothed leaves have something of the consistency of flannel. The very large, white flowers are pendulous, trumpet-shaped and highly fragrant, and are borne from early to late summer. An excellent subject for the conservatory. Brazil.
H2 ♛ 1993

Buddleja *Loganiaceae*

A genus of about 100 evergreen and deciduous species occurring in Africa, Asia and both American continents, many of them being first-rate garden plants that thrive in almost any soil and revel in full sun. Most flower from midsummer to early autumn and many are fully hardy, although

Buddleja alternifolia

a few need the protection of a warm wall, against which many species, hardy or otherwise, can readily double their size. Buddlejas are grown mainly for their massed clusters of tubular, nectar-rich, often fragrant flowers that in some species attract butterflies and day-flying moths from miles around. With the single exception of B. alternifolia, all have opposite leaves.

B. alternifolia A large deciduous shrub or occasionally a small tree, with graceful, arching branches and long, narrow, dark green leaves. In early summer the branches are wreathed all along their length with dense clusters of delicately fragrant, lilac flowers. China. Introduced 1915.
H4 ♛ 1993

Buddleja alternifolia 'Argentea'

B. a. 'Argentea' An uncommon medium-sized shrub with leaves covered by closely laid, silky hairs that give them a silvery sheen.
H4

Buddleja asiatica

B. asiatica A large deciduous shrub or small tree with long, lax stems, narrowly lance-shaped evergreen leaves and drooping, cylindrical panicles of sweetly scented white flowers during winter. E Asia from Nepal to the Philippines. Introduced 1876. H2 ♀ 1993

Buddleja auriculata

B. auriculata A medium-sized, open evergreen shrub with white felting on the undersides of the leaves. The strongly fragrant flowers are borne in long, cylindrical panicles and are creamy-white with a yellow throat. It flowers in winter and is suitable for a warm wall. Southern Africa, from Zimbabwe to the Cape. H2

Buddleja colvilei 'Kewensis'

B. colvilei 'Kewensis' A vigorous, large deciduous shrub with outstandingly large, rich red flowers in terminal, drooping panicles in early summer. Although it is tender when young, mature specimens have with-

Buddleja crispa

stood zero temperatures at Hilliers' West Hill Nursery, Winchester, Hampshire and survived all winters there since 1925. E Himalaya. Introduced 1849. H3

B. crispa A medium-sized to large deciduous shrub with deeply toothed leaves and stems covered with a dense, white felt. Its fragrant flowers are lilac with an orange throat, and produced in terminal panicles in late summer. N India. Introduced 1850. H3

B. davidii This deciduous species is rather weedy and seeds itself abundantly, but its cultivars are the superb medium-sized shrubs that you expect when buddleias are mentioned. Their fragrant flowers, borne in long racemes from mid- to late summer, are

Buddleja davidii

Buddleja davidii 'Black Knight'

highly attractive to butterflies. They do well in maritime areas and give the best results when pruned hard in early spring. The following are among the best garden selections. China, Japan. Introduced c1890. H4

B. d. 'Black Knight' A medium-sized shrub with long trusses of deep violet flowers. In cultivation 1959.
H4 ♛ 1993

B. d. 'Dartmoor' A vigorous medium-sized to large shrub with drooping branches and large, dense, widely branched panicles up to 60cm (2ft) long of fragrant magenta flowers. Found 1957 near Yelverton on Dartmoor, Devon, England by Mr Hayles.
H4 ♛ 1993

Buddleja davidii 'Empire Blue'

B. d. 'Empire Blue' A medium-sized shrub with rich violet-blue flowers with an orange eye. In cultivation 1941.
H4 ♛ 1993

B. d. 'Fascinating' A medium-sized shrub with wide, full panicles of vivid lilac-pink flowers. In cultivation 1940.
H4

B. d. 'Harlequin' A sport of 'Royal Red' and lower growing than most. The leaves are brightly variegated with creamy white and the flowers are reddish-purple. In cultivation 1964.
H4

B. d. 'Ile de France' A medium-sized shrub with long, elegant clusters of rich violet flowers. In cultivation 1930.
H4

B. d. 'Masquerade' (*B. d.* 'Notbud' PBR 4657) Large panicles of scented purple-red

Buddleja davidii 'White Bouquet'

flowers. Conspicuous bright cream and yellow, broad, irregularly variegated leaves. Bred at East Halling Research Station. Protected by Plant Breeders' Rights.
H4

B. d. var. nanhoensis An elegant medium-sized shrub with slender branches, narrow leaves and long, narrowly cylindrical panicles of mauve flowers. Found in

Buddleja davidii 'Peace'

Kansu Province, China, by Reginald Farrer. Introduced 1914.
H4

B. d. 'Nanho Blue' The pale blue flowers of this medium-sized form are very prone to reversion.
H4

B. d. 'Nanho Purple' A medium-sized form with violet-purple flowers with an orange centre, but it, too, reverts. In cultivation 1980.
H4

B. d. 'Peace' A form with large panicles of white, orange-eyed flowers. In cultivation 1945.
H4

B. d. 'Royal Red' A medium-sized shrub with massive panicles of red-purple flowers. In cultivation 1941.
H4 ♛ 1993

B. d. 'White Bouquet' A medium-sized shrub with large panicles of fragrant, white, yellow-eyed flowers. In cultivation 1942.
H4

Buddleja davidii 'White Cloud'

B. d. 'White Cloud' A medium-sized shrub with pure white flowers borne in large panicles.
H4

B. d. 'White Profusion' A very fine medium-sized shrub with large panicles of pure white, yellow-eyed flowers. In cultivation 1945.
H4 ♕ 1993

B. fallowiana A medium-sized to large deciduous shrub whose stems and leaves are white-woolly. Its flowers are very fragrant, pale lavender-blue, and borne in large panicles from mid- to late summer. Requires a sheltered position. N Burma and SW China. In cultivation 1921.
H3

B. f. var. alba The flowers of this medium-sized shrub are creamy-white, with an orange eye.
H3 ♕ 1993

B. globosa (Orange ball tree) A striking, medium-sized, erect, arching deciduous

Buddleja globosa

shrub with handsome foliage. In early summer it becomes laden with orange-yellow, ball-like flower clusters which make a bold statement. Andes of Chile, Peru, Argentina. Introduced 1774.
H4 ♕ 1993

Buddleja lindleyana

B. lindleyana A medium-sized deciduous shrub with long, slender, curved racemes of violet-purple flowers, each one of which is strikingly beautiful. The flowers are borne from mid- to late summer. China, Japan. Introduced 1843 by Robert Fortune.
H4

B. 'Lochinch' *(B. davidii × B. fallowiana)* A medium-sized, compact, bushy deciduous shrub with grey-pubescent young stems and leaves. Later the leaves become green and smooth above but retain a white woolliness beneath. The flowers are scented, violet-blue with a deep orange eye, and borne in dense, conical panicles from mid- to late summer.
H3-4 ♕ 1993

B. 'Pink Delight' A recent hybrid making a medium-sized deciduous shrub with long panicles of bright pink flowers.
H4 ♕ 1993

B. salviifolia (South African sage wood) This medium-sized deciduous shrub is hardy only in mild, sheltered places. It has sage-like leaves and fragrant, white or pale lilac flowers with an orange eye which are borne from

Buddleja 'Pink Delight'

Buddleja × weyeriana

early to mid-spring. In cultivation 1783.
H2-3

B. × *weyeriana* A deciduous hybrid with orange-yellow flowers borne from mid- to late summer in long panicles of individual, ball-shaped flowerheads. The following are the two most popular clones.
H4

B. × *w*. 'Golden Glow' A medium-sized shrub with orange-yellow flowers flushed with lilac.
H4

B. × *w*. 'Sungold' A beautiful sport of 'Golden Glow' that makes a medium-sized shrub with deep orange flowers. In cultivation 1966.
H4 ♛ 1993

Bupleurum *Umbelliferae*

A genus of about 75 evergreen and deciduous species, mostly herbs and sub-shrubs, from Europe, Asia, North Africa and North America. The

Bupleurum fruticosum

following is the only woody species normally cultivated in the open in Britain. It will grow in all types of soil.

B. *fruticosum* One of the best medium-sized evergreen shrubs for exposed coastal locations. It has sea-green foliage and yellow flowers from early to late summer. H4

Buxus *Buxaceae*
Box

A genus of about 30 species of well-known evergreen shrubs and small trees with opposite, leathery leaves and inconspicuous male and female flowers on the same plant. The boxes grow well on a wide range of soils in sun or shade, although they prefer sun for at least part of the day. Often used for hedges and topiary specimens.

B. *balearica* (Balearic Islands box) A large shrub or small tree with comparatively large, leathery, bright green leaves, 4cm

Buxus balearica

($1\frac{1}{2}$in) long by 2cm ($\frac{3}{4}$in) wide. Balearic Isles, SW Spain. Introduced before 1780.
H4

B. *microphylla* This species is a dwarf to small, dense, rounded shrub with thinly textured, narrowly oblong leaves up to 1.5cm ($\frac{1}{2}$in) long. Originated in Japan, but unknown in the wild. Introduced 1860.
H4

Buxus sempervirens 'Gold Tip'

B. sempervirens (Common box) A large shrub or small tree with luxuriant masses of small, dark green leaves. It has given rise to many forms several of which are suitable for hedging and topiary. S Europe, N Africa, W Asia, naturalized and possibly wild on calcareous soils in England. H4 ♔ 1993

B. s. 'Aurea Maculata' See *B. s.* 'Aureovariegata'.

B. s. 'Aureovariegata' syn. *B. s.* 'Aurea Maculata' A medium-sized to large, dense, bushy shrub with green leaves that are variously striped, splashed and mottled with creamy-yellow. H4

Buxus sempervirens 'Elegantissima'

B. s. 'Elegantissima' A small to medium-sized, dense, compact, dome-shaped shrub. Its small leaves are often misshapen, but pleasantly so, and have irregular, creamy-white margins. It makes an attractive specimen shrub and is the best silver-variegated box. H4 ♔ 1993

B. s. 'Gold Tip' This small to medium-sized shrub is one of the most common forms of box in commercial horticulture. The upper leaves of the terminal shoots are often tipped with yellow. H4

B. s. 'Handsworthensis' This form is erect at first but more spreading when mature. It is a large shrub with leathery, thick, dark green, rounded or oblong leaves and is excellent as a tall hedge or screen. In cultivation 1872. H4

Buxus sempervirens 'Handsworthensis'

B. s. 'Japonica Aurea' See *B. s.* 'Latifolia Maculata'.

B. s. 'Latifolia Maculata', syn. *B. s.* 'Japonica Aurea' Dense and compact when young, eventually forming a medium-sized shrub, this box has leaves that are irregularly blotched with yellow. When grown in the open, its bright yellow young growths are attractive in spring. Makes a slow-grow-

Buxus sempervirens 'Suffruticosa'

ing but otherwise excellent, dense hedge. H4 ♔ 1993

B. s. 'Suffruticosa' (Edging box) A dwarf to small shrub commonly used as an edging to paths and flowerbeds, especially formal ones. The leaves are of medium size, broadest below the middle, and bright, shining green. In cultivation for many centuries. H4 ♔ 1993

Buxus sempervirens 'Latifolia Maculata'

C

Caesalpinia *Leguminosae*

A genus of about 100 species of evergreen and deciduous trees, shrubs and climbers with showy flowers and leaves that are bipinnate (divided or cut into rows of leaflets that are themselves divided). They are spectacular shrubs for sunny, sheltered sites and are found throughout tropical and subtropical regions of the world.

Caesalpinia japonica

C. japonica A large, handsome deciduous shrub, quite viciously armed with prominent spines. Its leaves are pinnate, acacia-like and a refreshing shade of soft green. In midsummer it bears racemes of 20–30 bright yellow, pea-shaped flowers with scarlet stamens. Requires a sunny, sheltered position. Japan. Introduced 1881.
H3

Calceolaria *Scrophulariaceae*

A genus of about 300 species of shrubs and herbaceous perennials, including some popular greenhouse plants and alpines. The shrubby members are sun-loving evergreen plants with pouch-shaped flowers in terminal panicles. The following requires a well-drained position at the foot of a sunny wall.

C. integrifolia A small, shrubby member of the genus with clusters of large yellow flowers in late summer. Prefers a well-drained position at the foot of a sunny wall.

Calceolaria integrifolia

Chiloe area of Chile. Introduced 1822.
H3 ♔ 1993
C. i. var. angustifolia A small shrub with narrow leaves.
H3 ♔ 1993

Callicarpa *Verbenaceae*

A genus of about 140 species of deciduous shrubs and small trees, found mainly in tropical and subtropical regions, among which are one or two that are particularly notable for their soft rose-madder autumn colour and conspicuous clusters of small, rounded fruits that look as if they were made from violet or lilac-purple steel. They are freely produced, particularly where several specimens are grown together. The flowers are clustered and small.

Callicarpa bodinieri var. giraldii

C. bodinieri var. giraldii A medium-sized to large shrub with long-pointed leaves and lilac flowers that appear in late summer, followed by small fruits ranging

from purple-red through dark lilac to pale violet. The best selection is described below. China. In cultivation 1900.
H4

Callicarpa bodinieri 'Profusion'

C. b. 'Profusion' A medium-sized to large shrub on which the dense clusters of steely-violet fruits are remarkably freely borne. It has bronze-purple young foliage.
H4 ♔ 1993

Callicarpa japonica 'Leucocarpa'

C. japonica 'Leucocarpa' A small, compact shrub with oval leaves, white to pale pink flowers and unusual white fruits.
H4

Callistemon *Myrtaceae*
Bottlebrush

A genus of about 25 species of shrubs and small trees which are found only in Australia and Tasmania. They are magnificent, sun-loving evergreens, but suited only to the mildest districts.

In summer, cylindrical spikes of flowers are formed, of which the most colourful parts are the tufts of long stamens. The branches continue to grow beyond the ends of the spikes. Callistemons are not successful on shallow, chalky soils.

C. citrinus 'Splendens' A graceful medium-sized shrub with dense spikes of brilliant scarlet flowers and narrow, rigid leaves that are lemon scented when crushed. It flowers throughout the summer and thrives in the open in mild areas. E Australia. Introduced 1788.
H3 ♔ 1993

Callistemon linearis

C. linearis A species with small, narrow leaves and long, cylindrical spikes of scarlet flowers in summer. It is hardy in sheltered, maritime locations. New South Wales. Introduced 1788.
H3 ♔ 1993

Callistemon salignus

C. salignus One of the hardiest of the bottlebrushes. In a favourable spot it can grow to as much as 2.5m (8ft) high and wide. The leaves are narrow and willow-like, and the summer flowers are usually pale yellow. SE Australia. Introduced 1788.
H3 ♔ 1993

Callistemon sieberi

C. sieberi (Alpine bottlebrush) A medium-sized shrub with small, narrow, densely arranged leaves and pale yellow flowers in short spikes in summer. This is the hardiest species and has survived many hard winters outdoors in the Hillier Gardens and Arboretum. SE Australia.
H3 ♔ 1993

C. viminalis 'Captain Cook' A low-growing, spreading form of the weeping bottlebrush, with large clusters of deep crimson flowers in summer.
H3 ♔ 1993

Calluna *Ericaceae*

A genus of just one species which is however of great importance to gardeners with lime-free soils. See also Erica.

C. vulgaris (Heather, ling) A dwarf to small shrub occurring widely on the mountains and moorland in the northern and western parts of the British Isles. It differs from *Erica* species in that the petals are concealed by the coloured sepals. It is rarely grown as the typical form but in its many cultivars. Europe and Asia Minor.
H4

Cultivars of *C. vulgaris* are all small shrubs, so the size of each is given below as an average for a mature plant that is well cultivated and trimmed back after flowering. They are all H4 and evergreen. Flowering times are indicated as follows:

Early season   Mid- to late summer
Mid-season   Late summer to early autumn
Late season   Mid- to late autumn

Calluna vulgaris 'Alba Plena'

C. v. 'Alba Plena' A popular, free-flowering, mid-season cultivar with double white flowers. 50cm (20in).

C. v. 'Alba Rigida' An attractive plant with distinctive, horizontal branching and mid-season white flowers. 15cm (6in).

C. v. 'Alexandra' (PBR 5793) In this unusual and remarkable form the profusely borne deep dusky pink pointed flower buds do not open fully but remain conspicuous for several months during autumn to early winter.

C. v. 'Allegro' A neat heather with red flowers in mid- to late season. 50cm (20in).
♔ 1993

C. v. 'Annemarie' This excellent cultivar is an improvement on 'H. E. Beale'. Double flowers open light purple, deepening to carmine rose. It has a compact habit and dark green foliage. 50cm (20in).
♔ 1993

C. v. 'Anthony Davis' An attractive plant with silvery-grey foliage, which bears its mid-season white flowers in profusion. 45cm (18in).

C. v. 'Battle of Arnhem' Interesting over a long period with light purple-red flowers in late season and dark green foliage, turn-

Calluna vulgaris 'Beoley Gold'

ing bronze in winter. 60cm (24in).
♉ 1993

C. v. 'Beoley Gold' A strong-growing form which is grown for its bright yellow foliage and short sprays of white flowers in mid-season. 50cm (20in).
♉ 1993

C. v. 'Blazeaway' A startling plant with

Calluna vulgaris 'Blazeaway'

Calluna vulgaris 'Boskoop'

green foliage that changes to orange and rich red in winter. Its mid-season flowers are lilac-mauve. 50cm (20in).

C. v. 'Boskoop' A rewarding form grown for its rich gold foliage that turns orange-red in winter, and delicate lilac-pink flowers in mid-season. 30cm (12in).

C. v. 'County Wicklow' A dwarf but spreading plant with double, shell-pink

Calluna vulgaris 'County Wicklow'

flowers in mid-season. 25cm (10in).
♉ 1993

C. v. 'Cuprea' A cultivar with long shoots that are golden in summer and turn ruddy-bronze in winter. Its mid-season flowers are pale mauve. In cultivation before 1873. 30cm (12in).

C. v. 'Darkness' A dense bush with bright green foliage and short, dense clusters of dark purplish-pink flowers in mid-season. 30cm (12in).
♉ 1993

C. v. 'Dark Star' A shrub of neat, dense habit and dark green foliage. The semi-double crimson flowers are borne from mid- to late season.
♉ 1993

C. v. 'Drum-ra' A pretty plant which bears white flowers in mid-season. Raised 1960 in Scotland. 30–45cm (12–18in).

C. v. 'Elsie Purnell' A sport from 'H. E. Beale' grown for its double flowers of a lively silvery-pink which are more deeply coloured in the bud. It blooms from mid- to

Calluna vulgaris 'Darkness'

Calluna vulgaris 'Elsie Purnell'

late season. 60–80cm (24–32in).
♔ 1993

C. v. **'Finale'** A spreading plant with fresh green foliage and amethyst flowers from mid- to late season. 30cm (12in).
♔ 1993

C. v. **'Firefly'** The foliage of this cultivar is reddish-brown, turning to deep orange-red in winter, and the mid-season flowers are deep lilac. 45cm (18in).
♔ 1993

Calluna vulgaris 'Gold Haze'

C. v. **'Gold Haze'** A white-flowered, mid-season cultivar, with bright gold foliage. 50–60cm (20–24in).
♔ 1993

C. v. **'Golden Carpet'** A low-growing plant with orange-yellow foliage and short racemes of purplish-pink flowers in mid-season. 8cm (3in).

C. v. **'Golden Feather'** A most attractive cultivar with feathery, golden foliage that changes to a gentle orange in winter. It

bears mauve flowers in mid- to late season. 50cm (20in).

C. v. **'Hammondii Aureifolia'** A dense-growing plant that carries white, mid-season flowers and the tips of its young shoots coloured golden-yellow in spring. 50–60cm (20–24in).

Calluna vulgaris 'H. E. Beale'

C. v. **'H. E. Beale'** A highly popular cultivar with long racemes of double, bright rose-pink flowers in mid- to late season. It is excellent for cutting, but has nevertheless been improved upon (see 'Annemarie'). 60cm (24in).

C. v. **'J. H. Hamilton'** A pretty, dwarf heather with large, double, clear fuchsia-pink flowers in early season. Perhaps the finest double. 25cm (10in).
♔ 1993

C. v. **'Jimmy Dyce'** A somewhat prostrate form with dark green foliage. Double lilac pink flowers are borne from mid- to late season. 20cm (8in).
♔ 1993

C. v. **'Joy Vanstone'** This cultivar bears orchid-pink, mid-season flowers over golden foliage, which deepens in winter to rich orange. 50cm (20in).
♔ 1993

C. v. **'Kinlochruel'** This sport of 'County Wicklow' is grown for its double white flowers which it bears in mid-season, and bright green foliage. 25cm (10in).
♔ 1993

C. v. **'Mair's Variety'** A tall heather with white flowers in mid-season that are especially suitable for cutting. 80cm (32in).
♔ 1993

Calluna vulgaris 'Kinlochruel'

C. v. **'Marleen'** A similar plant to 'Alexandra' but with purple-pink buds white at the base during autumn and early winter.

C. v. **'Melanie'** A similar plant to 'Alexandra' but pure white.

Calluna vulgaris 'Mullion'

C. v. **'Mullion'** A semi-prostrate, well-branched heather with densely packed racemes of deep pink flowers in mid-season. 15–25cm (6–10in).
♔ 1993

C. v. **'Orange Queen'** The young foliage of this cultivar is golden in spring, turning deep orange as the season advances. The mid-season flowers are pink. 60cm (24in).
♔ 1993

C. v. **'Peter Sparkes'** A good heather for cutting on account of its double, deep pink flowers which are carried in long racemes from mid- to late season. 50cm (20in).

C. v. **'Radnor'** A very compact plant, popular for its bright green foliage and mid-season, double, pale lilac-pink flowers with

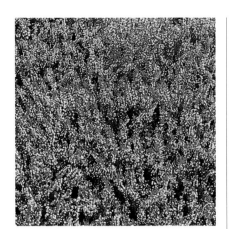
Calluna vulgaris 'Radnor'

Calluna vulgaris 'Silver Knight'

Calluna vulgaris 'Spitfire'

Calluna vulgaris 'Spring Cream'

Calluna vulgaris 'Serlei'

Calluna vulgaris 'Sunrise'

white inner petals. 25cm (10in).
♛ 1993

C. v. **'Red Star'** A shrub of pleasing open habit which bears the reddest flowers of all the double-flowered red cultivars, from mid- to late season.
♛ 1993

C. v. **'Robert Chapman'** The foliage of this cultivar is golden in spring and changes during the winter months, first to orange and finally to red. The mid-season flowers are soft purple. The heights of the individual growths vary from 30–60cm (12–24in), producing a most pleasant effect.
♛ 1993

C. v. **'Roland Haagess'** A bushy plant with pale purple flowers mid-season and bronze-yellow foliage, turning orange- to bronze-red in winter. 30cm (12in).
♛ 1993

C. v. **'Romina'** A similar plant to 'Alexandra' but of distinctly upright habit with white buds tipped deep pink.

C. v. **'Serlei'** An erectly growing heather with late-season white flowers carried in long racemes and distinctive dark green foliage. 60cm (24in).

C. v. **'Serlei Aurea'** This cultivar is similar to 'Serlei' but has bright golden foliage. 60cm (24in).
♛ 1993

C. v. **'Silver Knight'** An upright heather with grey foliage and mauve-pink flowers in mid-season. 30cm (12in).

C. v. **'Silver Queen'** A very beautiful plant with silvery-grey foliage and pale mauve flowers in mid-season. 60cm (24in).
♛ 1993

C. v. **'Silver Rose'** A cultivar with bright rose-pink flowers in mid- to late season and silvery foliage on upright shoots. The combination of flower and foliage is delightful. 40cm (16in).
♛ 1993

C. v. **'Sir John Charrington'** A vigorous, spreading heather with yellow leaves, tinged with red in summer, that become reddish all over in winter. Its early-season flowers are lilac-pink. 40cm (16in).
♛ 1993

C. v. **'Sister Anne'** A dwarf plant which makes compact mounds of pretty, grey foliage. Its flowers borne during mid-season are pink. 8-10cm (3-4in).
♛ 1993

C. v. **'Spitfire'** The golden foliage of this cultivar turns bronze-red in winter. Its flowers are pink and borne in mid-season. 25–30cm (10–12in).

C. v. **'Spring Cream'** A very vigorous heather with dark green foliage tipped with cream in spring. The long spikes of white flowers are produced in abundance during mid-season. 50cm (20in).
♛ 1993

C. v. **'Sunrise'** A heather whose golden-yellow foliage turns orange-red in winter. It

Calluna vulgaris 'Sunset'

has purple, mid-season flowers. 30cm (12in).
C. v. 'Sunset' The foliage of this cultivar is variegated in yellow, gold and orange, and has the benefit of taking on deep orange-red tints in winter. The mid-season flowers are pink. 25–30cm (10–12in).
♔ 1993

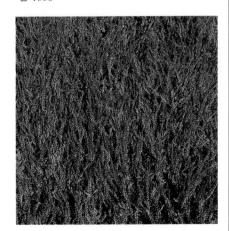

Calluna vulgaris 'Tib'

C. v. 'Tib' A lovely, floriferous plant, blooming in early season with double flowers in rosy-red. 30–60cm (12–24in).
♔ 1993
C. v. 'Underwoodii' The buds of this mid- to very late season cultivar do not open to form flowers but remain closed, and change from pale mauve to a silvery-white colour that lasts well into winter. 30cm (12in).
♔ 1993.
C. v. 'White Lawn' A prostrate plant with deep green foliage and white flowers in mid-season. 10cm (4in).
♔ 1993

Calluna vulgaris 'Wickwar Flame'

C. v. 'Wickwar Flame' This cultivar has bright orange and yellow summer foliage that turns copper and gold in winter. The mid-season flowers are mauve-pink. Raised by George Osmond, nurseryman, of Avon, England. 30cm (12in).
♔ 1993

Calluna vulgaris 'Winter Chocolate'

C. v. 'Winter Chocolate' A cultivar with

greenish-yellow and orange summer foliage that in winter becomes dark chocolate, tipped with red. It has lilac-pink flowers mid-season. 30cm (12in).

Calocedrus *Cupressaceae*

A genus of three species of evergreen coniferous trees from South-East Asia and North America. The

Calocedrus decurrens detail

branchlets are in broad, flattened sprays and the leaves are scale-like, flattened, and densely borne in opposite pairs. Ordinary soil.

Calocedrus decurrens

C. decurrens (Incense cedar) A large tree with a conical head of spreading branches in the wild. In cultivation, most trees belong to the form 'Columnaris' (syn. 'Fastigiata'), and its characteristically columnar habit renders it unmistakable among cultivated trees and ideal for growing as a single specimen or to add height in a group of trees

Calycanthus floridus

and shrubs. The dark green leaves are crowded into dense, fan-like sprays. W North America. Introduced 1853.
H4 🏆 1993

C. d. 'Aureovariegata' Sprays of golden leaves occur irregularly spaced about the branches. This is an attractive, slow-growing, medium-sized tree.
H4

Calocedrus decurrens 'Berrima Gold'

C. d. 'Berrima Gold' A slow-growing form with orange bark and pale yellow-green foliage tipped with orange in winter. Introduced 1976 from an Australian nursery by Sir Harold Hillier. Its ultimate height is not yet known.
H4

Calycanthus *Calycanthaceae*
Allspice

Four species of deciduous, medium-sized North American shrubs with aromatic bark. They are easily grown and have striking, red-brown flowers consisting of numerous sepals and petals. They are borne in summer and early autumn.

C. floridus (Carolina allspice) A medium-sized shrub with aromatic, glossy, dark green leaves. The brownish-red flowers, which consist of many strap-shaped petals, are borne over a long period in summer. SE United States. Introduced 1726.
H4

CAMELLIA

Theaceae

Camellia japonica 'Coquettii'

MORE THAN any other shrubs, camellias are redolent of romance and firmly associated with thoughts of the exotic. The leafy, glossy evergreen bushes, covered with large, stemless blooms like masterpieces of the confectioner's art, suggest the tropics and make them seem as if they surely belong in the sultry atmosphere of the greenhouse or conservatory.

When they were first introduced to western gardens from China and Japan they were indeed believed to need heat, so much so that many were eventually lost because the stove conditions given to them were entirely unsuitable. However, enlightened owners of gardens in the milder parts of south-west England planted them in sheltered places out of doors and found that they grew beautifully and with little attention. As time went by, it was discovered that the majority of camellia species were as hardy as laurels and that with a little care over positioning so that the flowers were not damaged by weather (particularly morning frosts) camellias could become firmly established as shrubs for growing and flowering out of doors in climates that were quite cold.

Today, there is a wealth of camellias from which to choose. They are derived mainly from four species: *Camellia japonica, C. saluenensis, C. reticulata* and C. *sasanqua*, of which the first two constitute the parents of the Williamsii camellias, *C. × williamsii.* Other species increasingly play their part, and the prospect of flowers in yellow and apricot shades, derived from *C. chrysantha*, is an exciting one.

C. sasanqua and its cultivars flower freely in autumn and winter and therefore require protection from frost. They are best grown in a cool greenhouse. The flowers are usually scented. *C. reticulata* is becoming a much more significant feature in the open garden as time goes by and its hardiness is more fully understood. Many of its cultivars and hybrids have withstood severe winter conditions much more readily than had been anticipated, and the generally large but beautifully proportioned blooms are within the reach of most of us who can grow other camellias.

Meanwhile, the mainstays of the garden camellias are the cultivars of *C. japonica* and *C.× williamsii.* To say that their colour range – white, pink and red – is limited is to mislead, as the infinite permutations of subtle shading, delicate tinting and glorious flamboyance are one of the great spectacles of gardening. These, combined with the diverse array of flower shapes, are a never failing source of fascination.

CAMELLIA FLOWERS
Flower shapes:
Single One row of not more than eight regular, irregular or loose petals and conspicuous stamens.

Semi-double Two or more rows of regular, irregular or loose petals and conspicuous stamens.

Anemone form One or more rows of large outer petals lying flat or wavy; the centre a convex mass of intermingled petaloids and stamens.

Peony form A deep, rounded flower consisting of a convex mass of petals, petaloids and sometimes stamens.

Double Imbricated petals (laid like roof tiles) showing stamens in a concave centre when open.

Formal double Fully imbricated, with many rows of petals with no stamens.

Flower sizes:

Very large Over 12.5cm (5in) across.

Large 10–12.5cm (4–5in) across.

Medium 7.5–10cm (3–4in) across.

Small 5–7.5cm (2–3in) across.

Flower size and form are subject to some variation in certain cultivars. Soil, aspect and general cultivation can all play a part, and can also occasionally cause some variation in colour.

CULTIVATION

Although the great majority of camellias are hardy and capable of standing up to remarkably low temperatures, their buds and flowers are vulnerable to certain combinations of conditions.

For them to be formed in the first place, which happens in late summer and early autumn, they need warmth and sunlight. The warmer the climate, the less direct sun they need, and the more they can be grown in shade. Conversely, the cooler it is, the more sun they need. However, there comes a point where the sun may scorch the leaves without there being enough general warmth to induce flower-bud formation. This happens, for example, with cultivars of *C. japonica* in Scotland north of Edinburgh, but luckily the requirements of the Williamsii hybrids are not as exacting in this respect and they flower well in the cooler climate.

Camellia flower buds are highly susceptible to the disruption of their cells by the action of sunlight while they are frozen. This is most likely to happen if they are planted facing east, as the early morning sun will strike before the temperature has risen enough to thaw the ice in the tissues (the sun does not heat the air, but does heat solid objects on to which its light falls). The effects of frost are greatly reduced if camellias are never allowed to face the morning sun. They are modified, too, by the shelter of overhead tree canopies, which reduce radiation frost, and greatly alleviated by shelter from winds which, when it is cold, have a chilling effect which is equivalent to exposing the plants to temperatures many degrees below the still-air temperature. Mulching is beneficial, too, as it can make the difference between the soil's freezing profoundly enough to deprive the leaves of water to replace that which they are losing to the air and allowing a life-saving degree of root activity and sap flow.

Camellias in containers – pots, tubs and so on – are especially vulnerable, as death ensues if the soil ball is allowed to freeze solid. If the pots are small enough, plunging them in soil or sand will help greatly; if not, then they can be lagged with some material that insulates without being very water-absorbent.

Camellias dislike lime in the soil and will not grow in shallow soils over chalk. In good soils in which lime is present, chlorosis (yellowing of the leaves but with the veins remaining green) will always win the battle against remedial treatment and the plant will inevitably die. A lime-free soil, as leafy and crumbly as possible, is the ideal medium. However, if your soil is limy you can grow camellias in tubs of lime-free compost. The necessity for rainwater collection is a myth; container-grown camellias watered with tap water heavily charged with lime will thrive perfectly well as long as the compost is sufficiently acid to start with and they are allowed out of doors for at least five months of the year. The planting area should be well prepared, and you should dig in as much organic matter as possible. Planting should be firm, but the soil should not be stamped on, as the fibrous roots do not appreciate compaction of the soil.

Pruning is not required, other than an occasional shaping. Pests and diseases do not present major problems, but black sooty mould in the open and red spider mite under glass can sometimes be troublesome. Yellowing of the leaves at the ends of the branches or in patches on the shrubs can mean an attack by a virus, transmitted by insects (rarely) or secateurs and the propagating knife (frequently). In this yellowing, the whole leaf, veins and all, eventually becomes mottled or entirely yellow.

Although camellias can eventually attain the size of small or even medium-sized trees, it is many decades before they are more than medium-sized to tall shrubs, and most remain below the height of an average man for as much as 20 years.

Certain camellia cultivars that are hardy throughout the British Isles and might be expected to carry a hardiness rating of H4 have been rated H2, because their flowers are so large that they become badly damaged by weather and are best flowered under glass. Examples are *Camellia* 'Dr Clifford Parks' and *C. japonica* 'Drama Girl'.

Despite their exotic appearance camellias flourish outdoors in quite cool climates if sited with care

C. **'Barbara Hillier'** *(C. japonica × C. reticulata)* A first-class, beautiful, large shrub with big, handsome, polished leaves and large, single, satin-pink flowers. Originated at Embley Park, near Romsey, Hants. H4

C. **'Cornish Snow'** A delightful, free-growing, medium-sized to large hybrid that bears masses of small, single white flowers along the branchlets. Garden origin c1930. H4 ♔ 1993

C. **'Cornish Spring'** A medium-sized shrub of upright habit with small, single pink flowers. In cultivation 1972. H4 ♔ 1993

C. **'Dr Clifford Parks'** A large, vigorous, upright camellia grown for its very large, semi-double to peony or anemone form flowers that are red with an orange cast. In cultivation 1971. H2 ♔ 1993

C. **'Fortyniner'** A bushy, vigorous, upright plant with glossy foliage that may occasionally be flecked with white. Its flowers are peony form and rich red, measuring up to 15cm (6in) across. H2–3 ♔ 1993

C. **'Francie L'** A vigorous shrub grown for its very large, semi-double, rose-pink blooms with wavy petals. It is good on a wall, but the foliage is sparse, over-slender, and rather poor. H3

C. **'Inspiration'** A medium-sized shrub with large, semi-double, deep pink flowers. An excellent, reliable hybrid. H4 ♔ 1993

C. japonica A large shrub or small tree. The species is virtually never seen in cultivation except as its many cultivars, which are highly bred and very unlike the typical form. Japan, China. Introduced 1739. H4

C. j. **'Adolphe Audusson'** A first-class, well-proven medium-sized shrub of vigorous but compact growth with large, semi-double, blood-red flowers featuring a conspicuous central boss of yellow stamens. H4 ♔ 1993

C. j. **'Akashi-gata'** See *C. j.* 'Lady Clare'.

C. j. **'Alba Plena'** An erect, bushy, medium-sized shrub with large, formal double, white flowers. Probably the best

Camellia 'Barbara Hillier'

Camellia 'Cornish Snow'

Camellia 'Dr Clifford Parks'

Camellia 'Inspiration'

Camellia japonica 'Adolphe Audusson'

double white camellia for general planting.
H4 🏆 1993

Camellia japonica 'Alba Simplex'

C. j. 'Alba Simplex' The most reliable white single, with large flowers with conspicuous stamens.
H4

Camellia japonica 'Alexander Hunter'

C. j. 'Alexander Hunter' A medium-sized shrub grown for its large, bright crimson, single to semi-double flowers with golden stamens.
H4 🏆 1993

C. j. 'Apollo' A vigorous shrub with medium-sized blooms, semi-double and rose-red, occasionally blotched with white. It is often confused with 'Jupiter', but has a larger number of petals and deeper colour. The leaves are longer, too, and have characteristically twisted, pointed tips.
H4 🏆 1993

C. j. 'Apple Blossom', syn. *C. j.* 'Joy Sander' A medium-sized shrub with

medium-sized, semi-double, pale pink flowers, deepening at the margins.
H4 🏆 1993

Camellia japonica 'Ballet Dancer'

C. j. 'Ballet Dancer' A compact, upright shrub with medium-sized, peony form, cream flowers shading to coral-pink at the margins. In cultivation 1960.
H4 🏆 1993

Camellia japonica 'Berenice Boddy'

C. j. 'Berenice Boddy' A vigorous, erect shrub grown for its medium-sized, semi-double, light pink flowers that are deeper pink beneath the petals.
H4 🏆 1993

C. j. 'Betty Sheffield Supreme' A medium-sized shrub with medium-sized to large, semi-double to loose peony form white flowers, each petal bordered deep pink to red. It is a lovely shrub but tends to sport badly.
H4

C. j. 'Blood of China' A vigorous, com-

Camellia japonica 'Blood of China'

pact shrub with deep salmon-red, large, semi-double to loose peony form flowers.
H4

C. j. 'Bob Hope' Just about the darkest red camellia, approaching black-red. The large, semi-double blooms are borne on compact medium-sized bushes. In cultivation 1972.
H4 🏆 1993

Camellia japonica 'Bob's Tinsie'

C. j. 'Bob's Tinsie' A compact, medium-sized, upright shrub grown for its small, brilliant red flowers of anemone form. In cultivation 1962.
H4 🏆 1993

C. j. 'C. M. Hovey' A vigorous, compact, medium-sized plant with medium-sized, formal double, carmine flowers.
H4 🏆 1993

C. j. 'C. M. Wilson' A slow-growing, spreading, medium-sized sport of *C. j.* 'Elegans' with very large, anemone form, light pink flowers that are prone to weather dam-

Camellia japonica 'C.M. Wilson'

age and best flowered under protection.
H4 🏆 1993

***C. j.* 'Carter's Sunburst'** A compact medium-sized shrub with large to very large flowers, pale pink and striped and otherwise marked with pink of a deeper shade. They are semi-double to peony form, or even formal double. In cultivation 1958.
H4 🏆 1993

***C. j.* 'Chandleri Elegans'** See *C. j.* 'Elegans'.

***C. j.* 'Clarise Carlton'** A vigorous, upright, medium-sized bush with large to very large, semi-double red flowers. In cultivation 1955.
H4

***C. j.* 'Contessa Lavinia Maggi'** See *C. j.* 'Lavinia Maggi'.

***C. j.* 'Coquettii'** A slow-growing, erect and compact medium-sized shrub, with flowers a bright Delft-rose, medium-sized and double.
H4 🏆 1993

***C. j.* 'Devonia'** A vigorous, erect shrub

Camellia japonica 'Donckelaeri'

with medium-sized, white, rather cup-shaped single flowers. It blooms very early and is prone to frost damage.
H4

***C. j.* 'Donckelaeri'** A slow-growing, medium-sized bushy shrub with large, semi-double red flowers, often marbled with white. A first-class plant for the open garden. Introduced before 1834.
H4 🏆 1993

Camellia japonica 'Drama Girl'

***C. j.* 'Drama Girl'** A vigorous shrub of open growth with very large flowers: almost too much so, as they tend to drag the semi-pendulous branches down and are easily damaged by weather. The blooms are semi-double and deep salmon-rose-pink.
H2 🏆 1993

***C. j.* 'Dr Tinsley'** A compact, upright, medium-sized bush with medium-sized, semi-double flowers that are pale pink, shading to deep pink at the margins.
H4 🏆 1993

Camellia japonica 'Elegans'

***C. j.* 'Elegans'**, syn. *C. j.* 'Chandleri Elegans' A medium-sized cultivar that has been well proven as suitable for general cultivation, with very large, deep pink flowers of anemone form. In cultivation 1822.
H4 🏆 1993

***C. j.* 'Gloire de Nantes'** A splendid, early-flowering, well-proven cultivar with erect, compact growth and large, semi-double, rose-pink flowers.
H4 🏆 1993

Camellia japonica 'Grand Prix'

***C. j.* 'Grand Prix'** A vigorous, upright, medium-sized shrub with very large, semi-double, brilliant red flowers with irregular petals. In cultivation 1968.
H4 🏆 1993

Camellia japonica 'Grand Slam'

***C. j.* 'Grand Slam'** A vigorous, open and upright medium-sized bush with large to very large, brilliant dark red, semi-double to anemone form flowers. The shrub itself is hardy enough; it is, however, best flowered

under protection. In cultivation 1962.
H2 🏆 1993

Camellia japonica 'Guilio Nuccio'

***C. j.* 'Guilio Nuccio'** A vigorous, erect, medium-sized shrub with pointed leaves. The flowers are very large, semi-double and coral-pink.
H4 🏆 1993

Camellia japonica 'Haku-rakuten'

***C. j.* 'Haku-rakuten'** A vigorous, erect but neat camellia grown for its large, white, semi-double to loose peony form flowers, with curved and fluted petals and some petaloid stamens.
H4 🏆 1993

***C. j.* 'Hawaii'** A sport of 'C. M. Wilson', this camellia is particularly useful for its late flowering. The blooms are medium to large, pale pink, peony form with fringed petals. In cultivation 1961.
H4

***C. j.* 'Jingle Bells'** A vigorous, upright sport of 'Tinker Bell', with small red flowers

of anemone form. In cultivation 1959.
H4

***C. j.* 'Joy Sander'** See *C. j.* 'Apple Blossom'.

***C. j.* 'Jupiter'** One of the best camellias for general planting, this is a medium-sized bush with medium-sized, single to semi-double, bright scarlet flowers, sometimes blotched with white and with a conspicuous bunch of stamens.
H4 🏆 1993

***C. j.* 'Konron-koku'**, syn. *C. j.* 'Kouron-jura' A very reliable camellia with exceptionally dark, almost black-red, medium-sized, formal double flowers – one of the darkest-coloured of all camellias. The growth of this medium-sized bush is fairly vigorous and semi-erect.
H4 🏆 1993

***C. j.* 'Kouron-jura'** See *C. j.* 'Konron-koku'.

Camellia japonica 'Lady Clare'

***C. j.* 'Lady Clare'**, syn. *C. j.* 'Akashi-gata' A vigorous and spreading medium-sized shrub with large, semi-double, deep, clear peach-pink flowers. It is still one of the best camellias. Introduced 1887.
H4 🏆 1993

***C. j.* 'Lady de Saumarez'** This is an excellent, vigorous, compact, medium-sized cultivar. A sport of 'Tricolor', it has medium-sized, semi-double, bright red flowers spotted with white.
H4 🏆 1993

***C. j.* 'Lady Vansittart'** This is not the most reliable of camellias, as its medium-sized, semi-double flowers, which are white striped with rose-pink, revert badly. It

reaches medium height. Introduced 1887 from Japan.
H4

Camellia japonica 'Latifolia'

***C. j.* 'Latifolia'** A broad-leaved, very hardy medium-sized cultivar with vigorous, bushy growth, which succeeds well in open situations. The flowers are medium-sized, rose-red and semi-double.
H4

***C. j.* 'Lavinia Maggi'**, syn. *C. j.* 'Contessa Lavinia Maggi' A medium-sized shrub with large, formal double flowers that are white or pale pink and have broad, rose-cerise stripes, splashes and blotches.
H4 🏆 1993

***C. j.* 'Magnoliiflora'** A medium-sized,

Camellia japonica 'Magnoliiflora'

compact camellia with blush-pink flowers with forward-pointing petals, rather like the expanding buds of *Magnolia stellata*. The blooms are medium-sized and semi-double.
H4 🏆 1993

Camellia japonica 'Margaret Davis'

C. j. 'Margaret Davis' A medium-sized shrub which is grown for its medium-sized, peony-form, white flowers that are streaked rose-red and edged with deep vermilion. In cultivation 1961.
H4

Camellia japonica 'Mars'

C. j. 'Mars' This camellia is often confused with both 'Apollo' and 'Mercury'. A medium-sized shrub, it has an open, loose habit and the flowers are large, turkey-red and semi-double, with a conspicuous bunch of stamens.
H4 ♛ 1993

C. j. 'Mathotiana Alba' A first-class camellia, though not recommended for an exposed position, with large, formal double, white flowers, just occasionally with a pink spot.
H4 ♛ 1993

C. j. 'Mercury' A compact medium-sized shrub with large, semi-double flowers in a deep, soft crimson with slightly darker veins.
H4 ♛ 1993

C. j. 'Miss Charleston' A neat, medium-sized, upright bush with very large, high-centred, deep red, semi-double to peony form flowers with golden stamens.
H4 ♛ 1993

Camellia japonica 'Mercury'

C. j. 'Mrs D. W. Davis' The very large, semi-double, light blush-pink flowers of this medium-sized camellia are so large that they are easily damaged by weather. It needs shelter, but its vigorous though compact growth helps to make it an excellent conservatory plant.
H4 ♛ 1993

C. j. 'Nagasaki' A spreading medium-sized shrub with large, semi-double, rose-pink flowers marbled with white.
H4

Camellia japonica 'Nobilissima'

C. j. 'Nobilissima' A fairly erect medium-sized shrub with medium-sized, peony form, white flowers. Prone to frost damage.
H4

C. j. 'Nuccio's Gem' A compact and upright medium-sized camellia grown for its purest white, medium-sized to large flowers of perfect formal double formation. In cultivation 1970.
H4 ♛ 1993

C. j. 'Nuccio's Jewel' A bushy medium-sized shrub with medium-sized, peony form flowers which are white, delicately and irregularly flushed with orchid-pink. In cultivation 1977.
H4 ♛ 1993

C. j. 'Nuccio's Pearl' A compact, upright medium-sized bush which is grown for its medium-sized, formal double, white flowers that are washed with the palest pink and shaded orchid-pink on the outer petals. A beautiful, delicately coloured camellia. In cultivation 1977.
H4

C. j. 'Preston Rose' A vigorous shrub with medium-sized, peony form, salmon-pink flowers.
H4

Camellia japonica 'R.L. Wheeler'

C. j. 'R. L. Wheeler' A beautiful, vigorous, large camellia with large to very large, rose-pink flowers of semi-double to anemone form. Raised by Wheeler's Nurseries, Georgia, United States.
H4 ♛ 1993

C. j. 'Rubescens Major' An old, reliable cultivar with large, double crimson flowers, veined in a darker tone. The plant is compact, medium-sized and bushy. In cultivation 1886.
H4 ♛ 1993

C. j. 'Scentsation' A compact, vigorous,

upright bush with sweetly scented, medium to large pink, peony form flowers.
H4

Camellia japonica 'Rubescens Major'

Camellia japonica 'Scentsation'

Camellia japonica 'Silver Anniversary'

C. j. 'Silver Anniversary' Vigorous, shrub with large, white, semi-double flowers, irregular petals and golden stamens.
H4

C. j. 'Souvenir de Bahuaud Litou' A sport of 'Mathotiana Alba' grown for its large, light peach-pink, formal double flowers which may suffer weather damage. It reaches medium size, its growth vigorous and erect.
H4 ♔ 1993

C. j. 'Tinker Bell' A vigorous, upright shrub grown for its small, anemone form, white flowers that are striped with red and rose-pink. A delightful, justifiably popular form In cultivation 1958.
H4

Camellia japonica 'Tricolor'

C. j. 'Tricolor' A compact, medium-sized camellia with distinctive crinkled leaves. The flowers are medium-sized, very variable single to semi-double, and striped with carmine and pink on a white ground.
H4 ♔ 1993

C. 'Lasca Beauty' A vigorous and beautiful shrub with very large, semi-double, soft pink flowers with yellow anthers. Introduced at Los Angeles State and County Arboretum (LASCA) by Dr Clifford Parks.
H2–3 ♔ 1993

C. 'Leonard Messel' *(C. reticulata × C. × williamsii* 'Mary Christian'*)* A very beautiful, large shrub. The flowers are large, semi-double and rich, clear pink, and the dark green leaves incline, like the flowers, towards *C. reticulata*. Originated at Nymans, Sussex, England, where it proves hardy.
H4 ♔ 1993

C. 'Mandalay Queen' A *C. reticulata* seedling, probably a hybrid, with very large, rich rose-pink, semi-double flowers with yellow anthers and variegated

Camellia 'Leonard Messel'

petaloids. Its habit is vigorous and upright.
H2 ♔ 1993

C. 'Michael' A beautiful, medium-sized to large shrub, similar to 'Cornish Snow' but with larger, single, white flowers.
H4

Camellia reticulata 'Arch of Triumph'

C. reticulata One of the most beautiful of all flowering shrubs. It makes a large, compact shrub of much better constitution than the more popular named cultivars, and it is hardy in all but the coldest and most exposed gardens. The two forms described below will grow and flower outdoors in mild areas, but elsewhere are magnificent plants for the conservatory. Thesemidouble 'Captain Rawes', introduced by Robert Fortune in 1820, was for one hundred years regarded in the West as the type plant, until the great plant collector George Forrest sent home the single wild form from China in 1924.
H4

C. r. 'Arch of Triumph' A seedling of *C. reticulata* (wild type) with a vigorous, upright habit and very large, deep pink to wine-red flowers of loose peony form. In cultivation 1970.
H3 ♛ 1993

C. r. 'Captain Rawes' A large, magnificent shrub of open, rather spreading habit with very large, semi-double, carmine-rose-pink flowers.
H3 ♛ 1993

C. sasanqua A delightful species, flowering generally from late winter to early spring. The flowers require protection from frost. In cold areas it is best grown in a cool greenhouse or conservatory. The flowers are often fragrant. The two described below are reliable and free-flowering.
H3

Camellia sasanqua 'Crimson King'

C. s. 'Crimson King' This medium-sized camellia is proving to be one of the most reliable and prolifically flowering of all, with small, single, bright red flowers. It is often in full flower at Christmas in the Hillier Gardens and Arboretum under dappled shade. Because of its colour frost damage is not very noticeable.
H3 ♛ 1993

C. s. 'Narumi-gata' Another of the most reliable forms of the species, this is a medium-sized bush with large, single, fragrant white flowers with pink edging.
H3 ♛ 1993

C. 'Satan's Robe' A vigorous, upright shrub with large, semi-double, oriental-red flowers with a satin sheen to the petals.
H2–3 ♛ 1993

Camellia sasanqua 'Narumi-gata'

Camellia 'Spring Festival'

C. 'Spring Festival' The narrow, upright, fastigiate habit of this large shrub is most unusual among camellias. The flowers are pink, fading to light pink, miniature and double. Raised before 1975 in California.
H4 AGM 1993

C. 'Tristram Carlyon' A vigorous, upright, medium-sized bush with medium-sized, rose-pink flowers of peony form.
H4

C. tsaii A tender, very graceful, large shrub. The single white flowers are small but numerous, and the foliage is copper-coloured when young. W China, Burma, N Vietnam. Introduced 1924 by George Forrest.
H2 ♛ 1994

C. × williamsii One of the most valuable hybrid shrubs ever produced and perhaps the best camellia for general planting. This medium-sized to large bush does not require as much heat for the production of flower buds as does *C. japonica* and is highly

cold resistant. The cultivars originating from the cross are exquisitely beautiful and flower extremely freely over a long period from late autumn to late spring. They tend towards *C. japonica* in their foliage and *C. saluenensis* in their flowers. The following are among the best garden forms. Original cross made 1925 by J. C. Williams at Caerhays Castle, Cornwall, England.
H4

Camellia × williamsii 'Anticipation'

C. × w. 'Anticipation' An upright medium-sized shrub with large, deep rose flowers of peony form. In cultivation 1962.
H4 ♛ 1993

Camellia × williamsii 'Bowen Briant'

C. × w. 'Bowen Briant' A vigorous, upright bush with large, semi-double, deep pink flowers. In cultivation 1960.
H4 ♛ 1993

C. × w. 'Brigadoon' A compact, upright, medium-sized camellia with medium-sized, semi-double, rose-pink flowers with slightly

Camellia × williamsii 'Brigadoon'

Camellia × williamsii 'Debbie'

Camellia × williamsii 'Donation'

Camellia 'E. T. R. Carlyon'

Camellia × williamsii 'Daintiness'

Camellia × williamsii 'Elsie Jury'

Camellia × williamsii 'Glenn's Orbit'

darker veining. In cultivation 1960.
H4 ♔ 1993

C. × w. 'China Clay' An open medium-sized shrub with white flowers that are medium sized and semi-double. In cultivation 1972.
H4 ♔ 1993

C. × w. 'Daintiness' The *C. japonica* parent of this open medium-sized shrub was 'Magnoliiflora'. The salmon-pink flowers are large and semi-double. In cultivation 1975.
H4 ♔ 1993

C. × w. 'Debbie' One of the most popular of all camellias with large, peony form, clear pink flowers with a hint of blue – its colour requires careful placing. In cultivation 1965.
H4 ♔ 1993

C. × w. 'Donation' A large camellia, arguably the most beautiful raised during the twentieth century. The flowers are semi-double and orchid-pink, with slightly darker veining, and the growth is vigorous and erect. The *C. japonica* parent was 'Donckelaeri'. Originated at Borde Hill, Sussex, England just before World War II.
H4 ♔ 1993

C. × w. 'Elsie Jury' An open, spreading shrub with large, peony form flowers of clear pink, shaded to orchid-pink. In cultivation 1964.
H3 ♔ 1993

C. 'E. T. R. Carlyon' (*C. × williamsii* 'J. C. Williams' × *C. japonica* 'Adolphe Audusson'). A vigorous, upright, medium-sized shrub with medium-sized, semi-double to double, white flowers. In cultivation 1972.
H4 ♔ 1993

C. × w. 'Galaxie' An open, upright bush with medium-sized to large, semi-double to rose-form double flowers which are white striped deep pink with cupped and twisted upright petals. The first striped *williamsii* hybrid, it tends to be slow growing because of its free flowering.
H4 ♔ 1993

C. × w. 'George Blandford' A very early-flowering camellia with medium-sized, semi-double to peony form flowers of pinkish-mauve, and a stiffly spreading habit.
H4 ♔ 1993

C. × *w.* **'Glenn's Orbit'** A seedling of 'Donation' with large, deep orchid-pink, semi-double to loose peony form flowers on a vigorous, upright, medium-sized shrub. H4 ♔ 1993

Camellia × *williamsii* 'Golden Spangles'

C. × *w.* **'Golden Spangles'** A sport of 'Mary Christian' with unusually variegated foliage. The flowers are small, single and phlox-pink, and each leaf has a central yellow-green blotch. Found 1957 at RHS Wisley, England. H4 ♔ 1993

C. × *w.* **'Hiraethlyn'** A vigorous, erect, large shrub with narrow, matt leaves and perfect large, single, orchid-pink flowers. In cultivation 1950. H4 ♔ 1993

C. × *w.* **'J. C. Williams'** It has medium-sized, single, phlox-pink flowers and is one of the most beautiful of all camellias. It makes a medium-sized bush. H4 ♔ 1993

Camellia × *williamsii* 'Jermyns'

C. × *w.* **'Jermyns'** A selection made at Hillier Nurseries which is grown for its broad-petalled, clear peach-pink flowers. H4

C. × *w.* **'Joan Trehane'** A shrub with a dense, spreading habit grown for its very large rose-form double to formal double clear, rose-pink flowers carrying thirty-five petals and a few petaloids among the cream stamens. H4 ♔ 1993

C. × *w.* **'Julia Hamiter'** A seedling of 'Donation' with medium-sized, semi-double to double, white flowers and a compact habit. In cultivation 1964. H4 ♔ 1993

C. × *w.* **'Jury's Yellow'** A compact, medium-sized upright shrub grown for its medium-sized, anemone form, white flowers that have wavy petals and a distinctive central mass of creamy-yellow petaloids. In cultivation 1976. H4

C. × *w.* **'Mary Christian'** A medium-sized shrub which is one of the earliest of the Williamsii hybrids to flower, with small, single, clear pink flowers of fine quality. H4 ♔ 1993

Camellia × *williamsii* 'Muskoka'

C. × *w.* **'Muskoka'** A superb medium-sized to large shrub with medium-sized, semi-double, deep pink flowers with darker stripes. H4 ♔ 1993

C. × *w.* **'Rose Parade'** A vigorous, upright, yet compact shrub. The flowers are medium-sized, deep rose-pink and peony form to formal double. In cultivation 1969. H4 ♔ 1993

Camellia × *williamsii* 'St Ewe'

C. × *w.* **'St Ewe'** Named for a Cornish saint of the early Celtic church, this medium-sized camellia has medium-sized, cup- to bell-shaped, single flowers of bright rose-pink. H4 ♔ 1993

Camellia × *williamsii* 'Water Lily'

C. × *w.* **'Water Lily'** A graceful, vigorous, slender and beautiful camellia with medium to large, formal double flowers. The pink petals are lavender-tinted and have a darker rim. In cultivation 1967. H4 ♔ 1993

C. **'Winton'** A medium-sized to large shrub similar to 'Cornish Snow' but with large, single, soft almond-pink flowers. H4

Campsis *Bignoniaceae*

A genus of two species of attractive, deciduous shrubs with long, climbing stems, related to Bignonia *and equally brilliant in flower. Both require a position in full sun to ripen growth and produce flowers, although they are hardy – particularly so in the case of* C. radicans. *They are excellent when trained over tree stumps, walls and roofs of outhouses. If they become too large or tangled, they may be pruned in late winter or early spring. They prefer a moist, well-drained soil.*

Campsis grandiflora

C. grandiflora This large and beautiful oriental climber will reach a height of 6m (20ft) or more. Its leaves are pinnate, with 7–9 leaflets, and the deep orange and red flowers are trumpet-shaped, up to 9cm (3½in) long, and carried in drooping panicles from the tips of the current year's growths in late summer and early autumn. China. Introduced 1800.
H4

C. radicans (Trumpet vine) A tall, strongly growing species - rampant in good conditions - that climbs by aerial roots but should still be given some support at first. The leaves have 9–11 leaflets, and the brilliant orange and scarlet flowers are trumpet-shaped, up to 8cm (3in) long, and produced in clusters at the ends of the current year's growths in late summer and early autumn. SE United States. In cultivation 1640.
H4

C. r. 'Flava', syn. *C. r.* 'Yellow Trumpet' A most attractive large climber grown for its rich yellow flowers.
H4 ♛ 1993

C. r. 'Yellow Trumpet' See *C. r.* 'Flava'.

C. × tagliabuana 'Madame Galen' (*C. grandiflora × C. radicans*) A vigorous large climber with panicles of salmon-red flowers that are borne in late summer. Provide the

Campsis radicans

Campsis × tagliabuana 'Madame Galen'

plant with support. In cultivation 1889.
H4 ♛ 1993

Cantua *Polemoniaceae*

A genus of six species of shrubs and trees found in the northern Andes of South America. The genus as nowadays defined consists of semi-evergreen to evergreen, perennial shrubs and trees.

Cantua buxifolia

C. buxifolia (Magic tree) A little known but very beautiful small shrub which bears graceful, drooping corymbs of bright cherry-red, tubular flowers in mid-spring. It is semi-evergreen in mild areas and is best grown against a warm wall if it is to flower successfully. Bolivia, Peru, Chile. Introduced 1849.
H2–3

Caragana *Leguminosae*

A genus of about 80 species of deciduous shrubs or small trees that are usually spiny and found mainly in Central Asia. The leaves are evenly pinnate, with the terminal leaflet reduced to a spine, although the reduction of one of the leaflets at the base of the spine can make them appear oddly pinnate. The pea-like flowers are normally yellow and are borne in early summer. These are plants that do well in dry soils.

Caragana arborescens

C. arborescens A small, shrubby tree with yellow flowers. It is valuable as one of the toughest and most accommodating of all plants, succeeding in the most exposed areas on all types of soil. Siberia and Manchuria. Introduced 1752.
H4

Caragana arborescens 'Lorbergii'

C. a. 'Lorbergii' An extremely graceful, medium-sized shrub with narrow, almost grass-like leaflets and much smaller flowers.

In cultivation from around 1906.
H4 ♆ 1993

Caragana arborescens 'Pendula'

C. a. 'Pendula' A very attractive weeping form, making a medium-sized shrub. In cultivation 1856.
H4

C. a. 'Walker' (*C. a.* 'Lorbergii' × *C. a.* 'Pendula') The foliage of this form is similar to 'Lorbergii' but the growth is prostrate and it is usually top-grafted to produce a small, narrow, weeping standard with hanging branches. Raised in Canada.
H4

Carpenteria *Philadelphaceae*

A genus of only one evergreen species, for warm, sunny sites.

Carpenteria californica

C. californica (Tree anemone) A beautiful medium-sized shrub whose large, white flowers with golden anthers are produced in

midsummer. It should be given a warm, sunny position, preferably backed by a wall. California. Introduced c1880.
H3 ♆ 1993

C. c. 'Bodnant' A vigorous, large-flowered, medium-sized shrub. Selected during the 1960s at Bodnant, N Wales, by Charles Puddle.
H3

Carpinus *Carpinaceae*
Hornbeam

A genus of more than 30 species of picturesque, easily grown, deciduous trees, mainly from China but widely distributed in northern temperate regions as far as South America. They are suitable for all soils, including clay and chalk, and are very attractive when laden with their hop-like fruit clusters.

Carpinus betulus

Carpinus betulus 'Fastigiata'

C. betulus (Common hornbeam) A medium-sized to large tree with a characteristically grey, fluted trunk and toothed, ribbed leaves. It is also used for hedging. Europe (including Britain and Ireland), Asia Minor.

H4 ♔ 1993

***C. b.* 'Fastigiata'**, syn. *C. b.* 'Pyramidalis' A medium-sized tree of erect, conical habit. It is quite narrow as a young tree but broadens as it matures. In cultivation 1883.

H4 ♔ 1993

***C. b.* 'Frans Fontaine'** A fastigiate medium-sized form that retains its habit with age. Selected from trees growing in a street in Eindhoven, Holland.

H4

***C. b.* 'Pyramidalis'** See *C. b.* 'Fastigiata'.

Carpinus caroliniana

C. caroliniana (American hornbeam, blue beech) A beautiful small tree with grey fluted bark among its many attractive features. It is not as tall as *C. betulus* and has spreading branches that arch at their tips. The leaves are a polished apple-green and become red-orange as autumn approaches. E North America. Introduced 1812.

H4

C. japonica A very beautiful, spreading, large shrub or small tree, with prominently corrugated leaves and conspicuous fruiting catkins in spring. Japan. Introduced 1895.

H4

C. laxiflora A medium-sized tree with rather drooping branches, ovate-oblong, slenderly pointed leaves and loose clusters of bright green fruiting 'keys' that are a particularly attractive feature of the tree in autumn. Japan, Korea. Introduced 1914.

H4

Carpinus laxiflora

Carya *Juglandaceae*
Hickory

A genus of about 17 species of fast-growing, stately, large, deciduous trees allied to the walnuts (Juglans). They are mainly to be found in eastern North America but also occur in Mexico and South-East Asia. The large, compound leaves, often over 30cm (12in) long, turn clear yellow before falling, and the grey trunks become even more striking in winter. As they are difficult to transplant, they are best planted when small. The nuts are contained in the four-valved fruit, but in moister climates with cool summers, such as that of Britain and Ireland, they are seldom if ever properly formed.

C. cordiformis (Bitter nut) Eventually a large tree with thin, scaly, brown bark and characteristic yellow winter buds. The leaves usually have seven lanceolate leaflets, but may occasionally have five or nine. Probably the best hickory for general planting. E North America. Introduced 1766.

H4 ♔ 1993

C. ovata (Shagbark hickory) The most valuable nut-producing species in the United States, with several cultivars grown for their heavy cropping. As an ornamental, it is a handsome tree of medium to large size with leaves consisting of five long-pointed leaflets, of which the two lower ones are rounder and shorter than the other

Carya cordiformis

Carya ovata

Caryopteris × clandonensis 'Heavenly Blue'

three. The foliage turns rich yellow in autumn. It may fruit occasionally in the British Isles following a hot summer. E North America. In cultivation 1629. H4 ⚱ 1993

Caryopteris *Verbenaceae*

A genus of about six species of small, showy deciduous shrubs with aromatic leaves, flowering in late summer. They grow best in well-drained soil and full sun and are excellent for chalk soils. They may be found in the wild in an area from the Himalayas to Japan.

C. × clandonensis A variable hybrid between two of the species which was raised by Arthur Simmonds, perhaps the greatest secretary ever to have served the Royal Horticultural Society. It makes a small shrub. The plant usually seen in gardens under this name is C. × c. 'Arthur Simmonds' *(see below).*
H4
C. × c. 'Arthur Simmonds' This is an attractive hybrid that thrives almost anywhere, producing its blue flowers in late summer and early autumn. It is an ideal subject for mass effect and can be kept to a height of about 60cm (24in) by pruning back in early spring. Rightly one of the most popular of all small hybrid shrubs. Raised 1933 by Arthur Simmonds.
H4
C. × c. 'Heavenly Blue' This is by a considerable margin the best of the clones and certainly better than either 'Ferndown' or 'Kew Blue', which are hardly different from

'Arthur Simmonds'. It is a compact, free-flowering small shrub and has the deepest blue flowers.
H4 ⚱ 1993

Caryopteris × clandonensis 'Worcester Gold'

C. × c. 'Worcester Gold' Although becoming reasonably well known, this small shrub with leaves flushed golden-yellow has a tendency, on occasion, to look somewhat chlorotic even when quite healthy.
H4

Cassinia *Compositae*

A genus of about 28 species of evergreen, heath-like shrubs found in Australia, New Zealand and South Africa. Those listed below are from New Zealand, of dense habit, and grown mainly for foliage effect. They are best given full sun and good drainage. In non-continental climates they pass through all but the severest winters unharmed.

C. fulvida (Golden cottonwood, golden

heather) A small, erect, dense shrub with small, crowded leaves that give a golden effect. The flowers are white and are borne in dense terminal heads in midsummer. The young growths are sticky to the touch.
H4
C. vauvilliersii var. albida (Silver heather) This is similar to *C. fulvida*, but taller and more upright and with larger leaves which, along with the stems, are white and hoary.
H4

Cassiope *Ericaceae*

A genus of about 10 species of attractive dwarf shrublets, related to Calluna *and* Erica, *with tiny, densely overlapping leaves and solitary, bell-shaped flowers. They are natives of arctic and northern mountain regions, and require a moist, peaty, lime-free soil and conditions like those of open moorland. All are evergreen.*

Cassiope 'Edinburgh'

C. 'Edinburgh' A hybrid with slender, dark green stems up to 18cm (7in) high, which in spring bear white flowers with the green calyx edged in red. It is perhaps the most easily grown of a fairly pernickety genus. A chance seedling raised at the Royal Botanic Garden, Edinburgh.
H4 ⚱ 1993
C. lycopodioides This species forms a prostrate mat or shallow bun of thread-like branches, above which little white bells dangle from the slenderest of stalks in spring to summer. NE Asia, NW North America.
H4 ⚱ 1993
C. 'Muirhead' A tiny shrublet with char-

Cassiope 'Muirhead'

Castanea sativa 'Albo marginata'

often. A valuable timber tree, useful for coppicing, and has been in cultivation for a very long time. S Europe, N Africa, Asia Minor. H4 ♛ 1993

C. s. **'Albo marginata'** A large tree bearing leaves with a creamy-white margin. H4

C. s. **'Marron de Lyon'** A cultivar selected for its large nuts, and the best fruiting clone, fruiting at an early age. H4

Catalpa *Bignoniaceae*

A genus of about 11 species of beautiful, late-summer-flowering deciduous trees, mostly of low, spreading habit. The foxglove-like flowers, which are not produced by young plants, are borne in conspicuous panicles and are followed by slender seedpods. Do not plant them in exposed positions where their large, usually heart-shaped leaves might become tattered. Catalpas are suitable for all types of well-drained soils and tolerate pollution. They are natives of North America and China.

acteristically curved, repeatedly forked shoots and small, nodding, white flowers which are borne in spring. H4 ♛ 1993

C. **'Randle Cooke'** A mat-forming shrublet with stems up to 15cm (6in) tall. The white, bell-shaped flowers appear along the stems in mid-spring. Originated in a garden in Northumberland, England, 1957. H4 ♛ 1993

Castanea *Fagaceae*
Chestnut

A genus of about 12 species of deciduous trees and shrubs found in temperate parts of the northern hemisphere. They are long-lived, drought resistant plants that thrive on well-drained, preferably rather light soils. They are moderately lime tolerant and may be grown with a fair degree of success over chalk as long as the soil is deep. Take care on shallow soils of this type, however, as they may become chlorotic.

C. sativa (Spanish chestnut, sweet chestnut) A fast-growing tree. A large specimen can be extremely ornamental, particularly at midsummer, when its large, sharply toothed leaves contrast with its yellowish male and female catkins. Hotter than average summers are generally required to produce good crops of nuts, although in sunnier areas with lower rainfall they occur more

Catalpa bignonioides

Castanea sativa

Catalpa bignonioides flower detail

C. bignonioides (Indian bean tree) The name of this medium-sized tree refers to American Indians. It has leaves up to 20cm (8in) long and wide, and attractive, scented white flowers with yellow and purple markings, borne in candelabras from mid- to late summer. E United States. Introduced 1726. H4 ♆ 1993

Catalpa bignonioides 'Aurea'

C. b. 'Aurea' (Golden Indian bean tree) An outstanding large shrub or small tree with large, velvety, soft yellow leaves that are almost green by the time the flowers open. In cultivation 1877.
H4 ♆ 1993

C. b. 'Variegata' A large shrub or small tree with leaves variegated creamy-yellow.
H4

C. × erubescens 'Purpurea' A medium-sized tree with broad leaves of which some are entire and some three-lobed, and mid-summer flowers like those of *C. bignonioides* but smaller and more numerous. The

Catalpa speciosa

Catalpa bignonioides 'Variegata'

young leaves and shoots are dark purple, almost black, and gradually become dark green. In cultivation 1886.
H4 ♆ 1993

C. fargesii f. duclouxii A fine, midsummer-flowering medium-sized tree with leaves smaller than those of *C. bignonioides*. The flowers are foxglove-like, lilac-pink with red-brown spots and stained with yel-

low, and are borne in clusters of 7–15. China. Introduced 1907 by Ernest Wilson. H4

C. speciosa (Western catalpa) A tall tree with large, heart-shaped leaves and purple-spotted flowers, slightly larger but fewer in the cluster than those of *C. bignonioides*. C United States. Introduced 1880.
H4

Catalpa × erubescens 'Purpurea'

CEANOTHUS

Rhamnaceae Californian lilac

The exquisite colour and density of a mature ceanothus contribute to the success of this underplanting beneath three elegant birches

THE CALIFORNIAN LILACS – which are not lilacs at all, but are reminiscent of them when bearing their panicles of blue or occasionally pink or white flowers – include some 55 species of evergreen and deciduous shrubs and trees that are widely distributed over the United States, southern Canada, and Mexico south to Guatemala. As the name suggests, however, they occur mainly in California.

Ceanothus range from the small-tree size of *C. arboreus* (attained only in very mild areas) to prostrate, carpeting shrubs such as *C. prostratus* and *C. thyrsiflorus* var. *repens*. There are evergreens, of which these two are examples, and deciduous ceanothus, among which are 'Gloire de Versailles' and 'Topaz', hybrids between the very hardy *C. americanus* from New Jersey and a Mexican species.

Ceanothus do well, perhaps surprisingly so, in climates that are less Mediterranean in nature than their own, and this is probably due to their native habit being chaparral – bushy brushwood at elevations where the climate is considerably chillier than on the coastal plain below. When asked to thrive in the cool, moist, maritime climate of the British Isles they respond bravely, flowering profusely and growing quickly, but they are not long-lived and, although widely grown outdoors in the milder regions, are not fully hardy. On the other hand, their beauty is such that gardeners will find it worth trying very hard to find somewhere in their gardens for one or more of these delectable shrubs.

The deciduous ceanothus are hardier than the evergreens, and among the latter those with smaller leaves (less than about 2.5cm/1in long) are usually, but not always, hardier than those with leaves on the large side. Although you might imagine that the deciduous kinds would be more popular because of their greater hardiness, it is not so, and the evergreens, which are most attractive even when out of flower, are much more sought after.

CARE AND CULTIVATION

Plant ceanothus in a sunny position and a well-drained soil, and try to make sure that they are sheltered from cold, drying winds, especially the evergreens. It is as well to take a little extra care about placing them, as although the deciduous kinds can be transplanted with care, the evergreens resent being moved once they begin to become established. In cooler climates they benefit from being planted against or in the shelter of a warm wall, but failing that the sunny side of a belt of evergreen shrubs will provide shelter.

Ceanothus are reasonably lime tolerant, although they do not thrive on hot, shallow soils over chalk. Most are resistant to salty, seaside conditions.

Deciduous ceanothus can have their laterals pruned in early spring to within 8–10cm (3–4in) of the previous year's growth. Other than removing dead wood in spring, evergreens are best not pruned at all if possible – another reason for ensuring that they are planted in the place that you want them and in which they can flourish from the start. If they are adequately spaced, there should be no need for pruning which, if repeated regularly, shortens the lives of the shrubs. Any light trimming that may be necessary should be carried out immediately after flowering.

Ceanothus may be propagated by taking semi-hardwood cuttings in summer.

C. **arboreus 'Trewithen Blue'** A vigorous, large, spreading evergreen shrub or small tree with large, ovate leaves. The big panicles of vivid, deep blue, slightly scented flowers are borne in spring. It is better grown and tied back against a wall, as it can become top-heavy.
H3 ♚ 1993

C. **'A. T. Johnson'** A vigorous and free-flowering evergreen hybrid with rich blue flowers in spring and again in autumn. The leaves of this medium-sized shrub are ovate, glossy green and grey-downy on their undersides.
H3

C. **'Autumnal Blue'** Of the evergreen hybrid ceanothus, this medium-sized shrub is possibly the hardiest. It bears abundant panicles of sky-blue flowers in late summer, autumn, and often spring as well. The leaves are broadly ovate, three-veined and a bright, glossy green.
H3 ♚ 1993

C. **'Blue Jeans'** A small to medium-sized shrub making a dense mound of arching branches with glossy dark green, holly-like, spine-toothed leaves. The massed clusters of deep lavender-blue flowers are so prolific as to almost completely hide the foliage in mid- to late spring.
H3

C. **'Blue Mound'** A dense, bushy, small to medium-sized, evergreen shrub with dense clusters of bright blue flowers in late spring, early summer and usually again in late summer and autumn. The leaves are glossy green and wavy edged. Raised at Hillier Nurseries.
H3 ♚ 1993

C. **'Burkwoodii'** A medium-sized, rounded, dense, evergreen shrub with rich dark blue flowers throughout summer and autumn and oval, glossy leaves.
H3 ♚ 1993

C. **'Cascade'** A lovely hybrid of the evergreen, spring-flowering group, bearing its bright blue flowers in elongated clusters. It makes a medium-sized shrub.
H3 ♚ 1993

C. **'Concha'** A dense, medium-sized, evergreen shrub, broader than it is tall, with profuse clusters of deep blue flowers emerging from red buds in late spring to early

Ceanothus arboreus 'Trewithen Blue'

Ceanothus 'Blue Mound'

Ceanothus 'Burkwoodii'

Ceanothus 'Cascade'

Ceanothus 'Concha'

summer. It has arching branches and narrow, dark green leaves.
H3

C. 'Dark Star' An arching medium-sized evergreen shrub bearing small ovate leaves up to 8mm (³/₈in) long with deeply impressed veins. Deep purplish-blue, honey-scented flowers are borne in clusters in early spring.
H3

Ceanothus 'Delight'

C. 'Delight' A splendid evergreen hybrid, and one of the hardiest. It is a medium-sized shrub with rich blue flowers borne in long panicles in spring.
H4 ♔ 1993

Ceanothus 'Edinburgh'

C. 'Edinburgh' A dense, medium-sized, evergreen shrub with large, olive-green leaves and rich blue flowers in spring and early summer. Originated at the Royal Botanic Gardens, Edinburgh, Scotland.
H3 ♔ 1993

Ceanothus 'Gloire de Versailles'

C. 'Gloire de Versailles' This is the most popular deciduous ceanothus. It is a medium-sized shrub bearing large panicles of powder-blue flowers in summer and autumn.
H4 ♔ 1993

C. gloriosus 'Emily Brown' A dwarf shrub making a low mound with arching shoots and holly-like leaves. Clusters of violet-blue flowers are borne in mid- to late spring.

C. griseus 'Yankee Point' This compact medium-sized shrub is frequently grown for its very dark, evergreen leaves and deep blue flowers, but it is killed at Hillier Nurseries by winters during which most others have survived.
H2–3

Ceanothus impressus

C. impressus (Santa Barbara ceanothus) A small to medium-sized deciduous shrub with deep blue flowers in spring. It is very distinct in its small leaves, which have deeply impressed veins, and is among the

hardiest of the evergreen ceanothus.
H3

Ceanothus 'Italian Skies'

C. 'Italian Skies' A vigorous, medium-sized, densely branched, evergreen shrub with deep blue flowers in late spring and small, dark green leaves.
H3 ♔ 1993

Ceanothus 'Marie Simon'

C. 'Marie Simon' A medium-sized, deciduous shrub with pink flowers borne in panicles on the young growths in summer.
H4

C. papillosus subsp. roweanus A narrow-leaved form of the species, this medium-sized to large, evergreen shrub gives a brilliant display of rich blue flowers in late spring. The leaves are notable for the slightly sticky, glandular papillae on their upper surfaces.
H3

C. 'Perle Rose' A medium-sized, bushy, deciduous shrub with bright rose-carmine

to strawberry-pink flowers in summer.
H4

C. prostratus (Squaw carpet) A creeping evergreen, making a dense mat up to 1.5m (5ft) wide, with bright blue flowers in spring. Its leaves are opposite, leathery, dark green and toothed.
H3

Ceanothus 'Puget Blue'

C. 'Puget Blue' This magnificent dense, medium-sized, evergreen shrub is possibly a hybrid between *C. impressus* and *C. papillosus*. It bears deep blue flowers over a long period during late spring and early summer. Raised before 1945 at the Washington Arboretum, Seattle, USA.
H4 ♛ 1993

C. 'Southmead' A dense-growing, evergreen shrub of medium size with very dark, rich blue flowers in late spring and early summer. The small, oblong leaves are glossy, dark green on their upper sides.
H3 ♛ 1993

C. thyrsiflorus (Blue blossom) A large shrub and one of the hardiest evergreen species. It bears bright blue flowers in early summer and has broadly elliptic, dark green, three-veined leaves.
H3

C. t. 'Millerton Point' A vigorous, medium-sized shrub with fresh green leaves and white flowers in late spring and early summer.
H3

C. t. 'Skylark' A medium-sized evergreen shrub with glossy green leaves to 5cm (2in) long. Clusters of deep blue flowers are profusely borne over a long period during late

spring and early summer.
H3

Ceanothus thyrsiflorus var. repens

C. t. var. repens (Creeping blue blossom) A vigorous, comparatively hardy, mound-forming variety, rather variable in habit, that produces generous quantities of Cambridge-blue flowers in spring and early summer.
H3 ♛ 1993

Ceanothus 'Topaz'

C. 'Topaz' A medium-sized to large deciduous shrub renowned for its light indigo-blue flowers borne in summer.
H4 ♛ 1993

C. × veitchianus A large evergreen shrub with deep blue flowers in late spring and early summer and small, glossy green, wedge-shaped leaves. It is deservedly popular, as it is free flowering, rich in colour, and comparatively hardy. A naturally occurring hybrid discovered and introduced 1853 by William Lobb.
H3

Cedrela

C. sinensis See *Toona sinensis*.

Cedrus *Pinaceae*
Cedars

A genus of four species of evergreen coniferous trees, the true cedars. They are renowned for their grandeur and their longevity. Young trees are conical, often developing massive trunks and large, horizontal branches as they age. The narrow, needle-like leaves are in sparse spirals on terminal shoots and in rosettes on the spur-like side growths. Good drainage is essential, but cedars will grow on all kinds of soil from acid sands to clays and chalk.

C. atlantica (Atlas cedar) A large or very large tree that grows rapidly when it is young. The leaves are 2–3.5cm ($^3/_4$–$1^1/_2$in) long, green or grey-green, and cover the young branches thickly. The species is very similar to *C. libani* and is now considered by some authorities to be one of its subspecies. N Africa. Introduced c1840.
H4

C. a. 'Aurea' A medium-sized tree with shorter leaves that are distinctly golden-yellow. It does not always grow satisfactorily. In cultivation 1900.
H4

Cedrus atlantica 'Fastigiata'

C. a. 'Fastigiata' A large, densely branched, erect tree with sharply ascending branches and short, erect branchlets. The leaves are bluish green. In cultivation 1890.
H4

Glauca Group (Blue cedar) Perhaps the

Cedrus atlantica Glauca Group

most spectacular of all blue conifers and a very popular tree for specimen planting. The leaves are silvery blue and have a highly effective shimmering quality.
H4 🏆 1993

C. a. 'Glauca Pendula' A superb small tree with weeping branches and blue-bloomy leaves. In cultivation 1900.
H4

C. a. 'Pendula' A small, weeping tree dis-

Cedrus deodara

tinguishable by its green or greyish-green leaves. In cultivation 1875.
H4

C. brevifolia (Cyprian cedar) A rare, slow-growing tree, eventually reaching medium size. The leaves are much smaller than those of *C. libani*, of which some consider it to be a subspecies. Mountains of Cyprus. Introduced 1879.
H4 🏆 1993

C. deodara (Deodar) A most beautiful, large, somewhat pendent tree with leaves that are bluish-bloomy when young but soon become deep green. It is readily distinguished from all other cedars by its drooping leader and its longer leaves, which are sometimes as much as 5cm (2in) long. W Himalayas. Introduced 1831.
H4 🏆 1993

Cedrus deodara 'Aurea'

C. d. 'Aurea' (Golden deodar) The leaves of this large tree are golden yellow in spring, becoming greenish yellow later in the year. In cultivation 1866.
H4 🏆 1993

C. d. 'Golden Horizon' A large, spreading bush with golden-yellow foliage. Raised in Holland.
H4

C. d. 'Karl Fuchs' Very hardy, with good silvery blue foliage. Its ultimate height is as yet uncertain. Raised c1979 in Germany from seed collected in Afghanistan.
H4

C. libani (Cedar of Lebanon) A large, wide-spreading tree, slower growing than *C. atlantica* and also conical when young, gradually assuming the familiar, pic-

Cedrus libani

turesque, flat-topped and tiered arrangement of a mature tree. The leaves are green or greyish green, 2–3.5cm (³⁄₄–1¹⁄₂in) long. This interesting tree has innumerable scriptural and historical associations. Asia Minor, Syria, Lebanon. Introduced c1645.
H4 🏆 1993

C. l. 'Comte de Dijon' A slow-growing, conical form of dense, compact growth, eventually a medium-sized shrub. In cultivation 1867.
H4

Cedrus libani 'Sargentii'

C. l. 'Sargentii' A slow-growing, small shrub with a short trunk and dense, weeping branches with blue-green leaves. It is ideal for the rock garden.
H4

Celastrus *Celastraceae*

A genus of around 30 species of vigorous deciduous climbers whose main attraction is their seed capsules and autumn leaves. *The flowers have only one sex on each specimen, so unless a hermaphrodite form (which has flowers of both sexes) is grown, it is advisable to grow more than one plant for a display of capsules.*

Celastrus orbiculatus

C. orbiculatus A strong-growing climber for sun or shade and any reasonably fertile soil, capable of growing to 12m (40ft) or more in a tree. The twining young shoots have a pair of spines at each bud, and the leaves are up to 13cm (5in) long and turn clear yellow in autumn. In autumn, too, the brownish capsules split open to reveal a yellow lining, against which the bright red seeds show brilliantly. It is a most spectacular garden plant for autumn. NE Asia. Introduced 1860.

H4 ♛ 1993 *(to a hermaphrodite form)*

Celtis *Ulmaceae*
Hackberry, nettle tree

A genus of 60 or more species of medium-sized, deciduous trees allied to the elms and occurring in northerly temperate regions and the tropics. On the whole they require consistently warm summers and are not at their best in cooler, maritime climates. They will grow in most types of soil and tolerate dryness.

C. australis A small to medium-sized tree with characteristically broad, lance-shaped leaves that are rough to the touch on their upper surfaces. S Europe, North Africa, Asia Minor. In cultivation in England since the sixteenth century.
H4

Celtis occidentalis

C. occidentalis (Hackberry) A medium-sized tree of which mature specimens have rough, warted, corky bark. It rarely produces its black fruits in Britain. North America. Introduced 1656.
H4

Cephalanthus *Rubiaceae*

A genus of about six species of evergreen and deciduous trees found in North and Central America, eastern Asia and Africa.

Cephalanthus occidentalis

C. occidentalis (Button bush) An easily cultivated but rarely grown, medium-sized, deciduous shrub with ovate leaves 5–15cm (2–6in) long and creamy-white fragrant flowers produced in small, globular heads in late summer. It will grow in moist soils that are rich in organic matter and does best in an open position. E and S United States. Introduced 1735.
H4

Cephalotaxus *Cephalotaxaceae*

A genus of four species of evergreen coniferous shrubs or shrubby trees, in effect large-leaved yews, natives of the Himalayas and eastern Asia. Like the yews, they grow well in shade, in the drip of other trees, and thrive on calcareous soils. The female plants produce large, olive-like fruits that ripen in their second year. The leaves have two broad, silvery bands beneath.

Cephalotaxus fortunei

C. fortunei 'Prostrate Spreader' A low-growing shrub with wide-spreading branches and large, deep green, lanceolate leaves 6–9cm (2½–3½in) long, arranged spirally in two opposite rows along the branches. It is a superb ground-cover plant that bears shade very well and eventually covers several yards. It originated at Hillier Nurseries before the First World War as a side cutting from the species and the original plant reached 0.8m (32in) high by 5m (15ft) across.
H4

Cephalotaxus harringtonia 'Fastigiata'

C. harringtonia var. drupacea A dense, compact, medium-sized shrub rarely higher than 3m (10ft), with ascending leaves 2–5cm (³⁄₄–2in) long. Large plants make beautiful large mounds with elegant, drooping branchlets. The olive-green fruits are 2–3cm (³⁄₄–1¹⁄₄in) long. C China, Japan. H4

C. h. 'Fastigiata' An erectly branched, medium to large shrub, resembling the Irish yew in habit. Its leaves are almost black-green and spread all round the shoots. Garden origin in Japan. Introduced 1861. H4

C. h. 'Gnome' A dwarf form of the shrub with short ascending stems and radially arranged leaves, forming a flat-topped dome. A sport from 'Fastigiata'. Raised 1970 by Hillier Nurseries. H4

Ceratostigma *Plumbaginaceae*

A genus of about eight deciduous species found in east Asia and east Africa. The cultivated species are small, ornamental shrubs often referred to as hardy plumbago. They bear blue flowers over a long period during early autumn and are suitable for dry, well-drained soil, preferably in full sun. For the best effect, cut back the old flowering growths in spring.

Ceratostigma griffithii

C. griffithii A beautiful, low-growing semi-evergreen species with deep blue flowers and leaves that turn bright red in late autumn, often persisting well into winter. Although it has survived the more severe winters experienced at the Hillier Nurs-

eries, it is reluctant to flower well and is not fully hardy. H3–4

Ceratostigma willmottianum

C. willmottianum A deciduous shrub about 1m (3ft) high with rich blue flowers appearing in midsummer and continuing until autumn, when the foliage becomes red tinted. Ideal for either the shrub or herbaceous border. W China. Introduced 1908 by Ernest Wilson. H3-4 ♔ 1993

Cercidiphyllum *Cercidiphyllaceae*

A genus of one species of deciduous tree from east Asia, grown for its autumn colour. The tiny red flowers emerge with the young leaves, with males and females on separate plants.

Cercidiphyllum japonicum

C. japonicum (Katsura tree) An attractive tree with leaves similar to the Judas tree (*Cercis siliquastrum*), but opposite and

smaller. Its growth rate varies with the climate; in Britain and Ireland it forms a small to medium-sized tree whose foliage, in favourable seasons, turns pale yellow or smoky pink and scents the air with the aroma of burnt sugar, accentuated when crushed. It can be grown in any deep, fertile soil. Japan, China. Introduced 1881. H4 ♔ 1993

C. j. var. magnificum A rare, medium-sized tree with smoother bark and larger, more heart-shaped leaves with coarser serrations than the species. Its autumn colour is a lovely yellow. Japan. H4 ♔ 1993

C. j. 'Pendulum' An unusual form of medium height with long, pendulous branches. Japan. H4

Cercis *Leguminosae*

A genus of about six species of small, deciduous trees with broad, rounded, heart-shaped leaves and beautiful pea flowers in spring, widely distributed in temperate regions of the northern hemisphere. Their apparently simple leaves are in fact formed by fusion of the leaflets of pinnate leaves. Cercis require full sun and good drainage. Pruning is rarely required.

C. canadensis (American redbud) A small tree with a broad, round head. In its native range it flowers extremely freely, covering its branches with pale rose flowers before the foliage appears, but in Britain and Ireland it is often shy-flowering. The following form is recommended. SE Canada, E

Cercis canadensis 'Forest Pansy'

United States, NE Mexico. Introduced 1730.

H4

***C. c.* 'Forest Pansy'** A splendid large shrub or small tree grown for its deep reddish-purple foliage, for a better display of which it can be grown as a stooled specimen. It does flower, but inconspicuously in late spring and early summer.

H4 ♛ 1993

Cercis siliquastrum

C. siliquastrum (Judas tree) The branches and even the trunk of this medium-sized tree or large shrub become wreathed in rosy lilac flowers in late spring, making a unique display, often followed by purple-tinted seed pods from midsummer onwards. Legend has it that this was the tree from which Judas Iscariot hanged himself, but the name may also derive from its having once been common in the hills of Judaea. E Mediterranean region.

H4 ♛ 1993

Cercis siliquastrum 'Bodnant'

***C. s.* 'Alba'** A large shrub (more usually in cooler climates) or medium-sized tree with pale green foliage and white flowers borne in late spring.

H4

***C. s.* 'Bodnant'** A clone that is primarily grown for its deep purple flowers borne in late spring.

H4

Cestrum *Solanaceae*

A large genus of around 200 species of evergreen and deciduous shrubs and small trees native to Central and South America and the West Indies. The cultivated species are showy, medium-sized flowering shrubs suitable for a warm wall or conservatory. They will grow in any well-drained friable soil.

Cestrum elegans

C. elegans A small to medium-sized evergreen shrub with large, startling clusters of bright red flowers over a long period in summer and autumn. It usually needs some support. Mexico. Introduced 1840.

H2 ♛ 1993

***C.* 'Newellii'** An evergreen seedling very much like *C. elegans* in habit, but with large, orange-red flowers in midsummer. Requires support.

H2 ♛ 1993

C. parqui (Willow-leaved jessamine) A small to medium-sized shrub with yellowish-green flowers, fragrant at night, borne from early to midsummer. It is hardy in sunny, sheltered places where frost is slight and infrequent and, although it may be cut to the ground in such situations, it can

Cestrum parqui

quickly recover. Chile. Introduced 1787.

H3 ♛ 1993

Chaenomeles *Rosaceae*
Japonica, quince

Old names for this genus of three species of deciduous shrubs from eastern Asia are still sometimes familiarly but mistakenly used. Whereas you will hear them called japonicas, japonica merely means 'from Japan' and is applied to many plants. Cydonia is now the genus of the true quinces only, and the name has not applied to these Japanese quinces for many years. Chaenomeles are among the most beautiful and easily grown of early-flowering spring shrubs and have saucer-shaped flowers in shades of red, pink, orange and white followed by large, yellow, aromatic quinces. They will thrive in an open border or against a wall, even when shaded, although in general they flower better in sun. They will grow in any well-drained friable soil. When treated as wall shrubs, they can be cut back

Chaenomeles japonica

immediately after flowering, leaving a framework of main branches and reducing the shoots of the previous year's growth to two or three buds. Freestanding shrubs need not be pruned unless their branches become overcrowded.

C. japonica A small, thorny shrub with bright flame-orange flowers followed by rounded, yellow, fragrant fruits. Japan. Introduced c1869.
H4

C. speciosa This species is represented in gardens mainly by its cultivars, which are the well-known, early-flowering japonicas. It is a much-branched, spreading, thorny, medium-sized shrub, seed-raised plants bearing flowers in mixed colours, though predominantly red. The following forms are recommended. China. Introduced 1869 by Sir Joseph Banks.
H4

Chaenomeles speciosa 'Geisha Girl'

C. s. 'Geisha Girl' A medium-sized shrub with double, deep apricot-peach flowers.
H4

C. s. 'Moerloosei' Sometimes wrongly named 'Apple Blossom', this medium-sized cultivar bears delicate pink and white flowers in thick clusters. In cultivation 1856.
H4 ♛ 1993

C. s. 'Nivalis' A medium-sized shrub grown for its large, pure white flowers. In cultivation 1881.
H4

C. s. 'Simonii' An exceptionally beautiful, dwarf, spreading shrub with blood red, flat, semi-double flowers. In cultivation 1882.
H4

Chaenomeles speciosa 'Simonii'

C. × superba *(C. japonica × C. speciosa)* Small to medium-sized shrubs with slender thorns and a vigorous habit. The following are recommended.
H4

Chaenomeles × superba 'Crimson and Gold'

C. × s. 'Crimson and Gold' A medium-sized shrub bearing flowers that have deep crimson petals and distinct golden anthers, a bold combination. In cultivation 1939.
H4 ♛ 1993

C. × s. 'Fire Dance' *(C. speciosa 'Simonii' × C. × superba)* A back-cross, with signal-red flowers and a spreading habit, making a medium-sized shrub. In cultivation 1953.
H4

C. × s. 'Jet Trail' A medium-sized, spreading shrub with few thorns and profusely borne pure white flowers.
H4

C. × s. 'Knap Hill Scarlet' This medium-sized hybrid bears its bright orange-scarlet flowers profusely throughout spring and

Chaenomeles × superba 'Knap Hill Scarlet'

early summer. In cultivation 1891.
H4 ♛ 1993

C. × s. 'Nicoline' A medium-sized shrub with scarlet-red flowers and a spreading habit. In cultivation 1954.
H4 ♛ 1993

Chaenomeles superba 'Pink Lady'

C. × s. 'Pink Lady' This spreading shrub has clear rose-pink flowers opening from darker buds, produced profusely and early. In cultivation 1946.
H4 ♛ 1993

C. × s. 'Rowallane' A medium-sized shrub with large, blood-crimson flowers. In cultivation 1920.
H4 ♛ 1993

Chamaecyparis *Cupressaceae*
False cypress

A genus of about seven species of evergreen trees, natives of North America, Japan and Taiwan. They are distinguished from Cupressus chiefly by their flattened, frond-like branches. Young trees are conical and broaden as they mature. The leaves are opposite, densely arranged, awl-shaped in seedling plants and then becoming small and scale-like. They thrive best in moist, well-drained soils and on dry, chalky (soft limestone) ones they are slower growing. Unlike Cupressus, *they do not resent disturbance and may be moved even as small specimen trees. Although there are few species, they have given rise to an astonishing number of cultivars that cover a wide range of shapes and sizes, with foliage varying greatly in form and colour. A few are really dwarf, others are merely slow-growing, while many are as vigorous as their typical form.*

C. lawsoniana (Lawson cypress) A large, conical tree with drooping branches and broad, fan-like sprays of foliage that are arranged in drooping horizontals. It is a most useful and ornamental tree and makes an excellent hedge or screen even in exposed positions and shade. Its numerous

Chamaecyparis lawsoniana 'Albospica'

cultivars range from dwarf shrubs suitable for the rock garden to stately, columnar trees in many shades of green, grey, blue and yellow, including a number of variegated forms. Native to SW Oregon and NW California, where trees 60m (200ft) high have been recorded. In cultivation in Britain, 35m (120ft) is seldom exceeded. Introduced 1854.
H4

***C. l.* 'Albospica'** A slow-growing, small, conical tree with green foliage, speckled white and with the tips of scattered shoots cream. In cultivation 1884.
H4

***C. l.* 'Alumii'** A medium-sized, columnar tree with its branches dense, compact and ascending. The foliage is blue-grey, soft, in large, flattened sprays. A popular and commonly planted conifer. In cultivation 1891.
H4

***C. l.* 'Alumigold'** A sport of 'Alumii' of more compact habit, with the young foliage tipped with golden yellow.
H4

Chamaecyparis lawsoniana 'Aurea Densa'

***C. l.* 'Aurea Densa'** A small, slow-growing, conical, compact bush, eventually up to 2m (6ft) high. The foliage is golden yellow and arranged in short, flattened, densely packed sprays that are stiff to the touch. It is one of the best golden conifers for the rock garden.
H4 ♟ 1993

***C. l.* 'Backhouse Silver'** See *C. l.* 'Pygmaea Argentea'.

***C. l.* 'Bleu Nantais'** A slow-growing, small, conical shrub with striking, silvery-

blue foliage useful in the rock garden.
H4

***C. l.* 'Broomhill Gold'** A small, upright tree with golden yellow young foliage that later turns green.
H4

Chamaecyparis lawsoniana 'Chilworth Silver'

***C. l.* 'Chilworth Silver'** A slow-growing, broadly columnar medium-sized bush, with densely-packed, silvery blue juvenile foliage. Until 1968 recognized as a sport of *C. l.* 'Ellwoodii'.
H4 ♟ 1993

Chamaecyparis lawsoniana 'Columnaris'

***C. l.* 'Columnaris'** A small, narrow, conical tree with densely packed, ascending branches and flattened sprays that are bloomy beneath and at the tips. It is one of the best narrow conifers for the small garden, but see also *C. l.* 'Van Pelt'. Raised c1940 by Jan Spek of Boskoop.
H4

***C. l.* 'Elegantissima'** A beautiful, small,

broadly conical tree with pale yellow shoots and broad, flattened, drooping sprays of silvery grey or greyish cream foliage. Raised before 1920 in the Hillier Nurseries.
H4

Chamaecyparis lawsoniana 'Ellwoodii'

C. l. 'Ellwoodii' A slow-growing, columnar bush of medium to large size. The short, feathery sprays of grey-green foliage are densely arranged and become steel blue in winter. It is a deservedly popular and commonly planted conifer. Raised before 1929 in Swanmore Park, Bishops Waltham, England.
H4 ♔ 1993

C. l. 'Ellwood's Gold' A neat, compact, columnar, slow-growing medium-sized bush. The tips of the sprays are tinged with yellow, which gives the whole bush a warm glow. In cultivation 1968.
H4 ♔ 1993

C. l. 'Ellwood's Pillar' A narrow and compact medium-sized form of 'Ellwoodii'

with attractive, feathery, blue-grey foliage.
H4

C. l. 'Ellwood's Silver' A medium-sized shrub similar to 'Ellwoodii' but with intensely silvery-grey foliage.
H4

Chamaecyparis lawsoniana 'Ellwood's White'

C. l. 'Ellwood's White' A slow-growing medium-sized sport of 'Ellwoodii' with cream or pale yellow patches of foliage. In cultivation 1965.
H4

C. l. 'Erecta', syn. *C. l.* 'Erecta Viridis' A medium-sized to large tree of dense, compact growth, columnar when young and broadening in maturity. The foliage is bright, rich green, arranged in large, flattened, vertical sprays. It normally forms numerous, long, erect branches that should be tied in to prevent damage being done by heavy snow.
H4

C. l. 'Fletcheri' A well-known conifer,

Chamaecyparis lawsoniana 'Fletcheri'

forming a dense column up to 5m (15ft) or more. It is usually a broad, columnar bush with several main stems. The semi-juvenile foliage, feathery like that of 'Ellwoodii', is greyish green and becomes bronzed in winter. It is slow growing but becomes much too large for the rock garden. Introduced by Fletcher Bros.
H4 ♔ 1993

Chamaecyparis lawsoniana 'Forsteckensis'

C. l. 'Forsteckensis' A dwarf, slow-growing, dense, globular bush with short branchlets in congested, fern-like sprays and greyish-blue-green foliage. A specimen at Hillier Nurseries reached 0.9 × 1.2m (3ft × 4ft) after 30 years. Raised before 1891 at Forsteck, near Kiel, Germany.
H4

C. l. 'Fraseri' A medium-sized tree of narrowly conical or columnar habit. Its erect branches have grey-green foliage in flattened, vertically arranged sprays. It is similar to *C. l.* 'Alumii' but has greener foliage and a neater base.
H4

C. l. 'Gimbornii' A dwarf, dense, globular bush of slow growth with bluish-green foliage that is tipped with mauve. It is eminently suitable for the rock garden. In cultivation before 1938.
H4 ♔ 1993

C. l. 'Golden Pot' A small, narrow, conical tree with soft, bright golden yellow foliage that retains its colour well. Its name derives from its being a sport of 'Pottenii'.
H4

C. l. 'Golden Wonder' A medium-sized, broadly conical tree with bright yellow

Chamaecyparis lawsoniana 'Gimbornii'

foliage. Raised c1955 in Holland.
H4

C. l. **'Grayswood Feather'** A small, slender, columnar tree with upright sprays of dark green foliage.
H4

C. l. **'Grayswood Pillar'** A medium-sized, narrowly columnar tree with tightly packed, ascending branches and grey foliage. The original tree reached about 9 × 0.5m (28ft × 20in) after 16 years.
H4 ♛ 1993

C. l. **'Green Globe'** A very dense, dwarf, rounded bush that becomes more irregular with age. The foliage is deep, bright green in short, tightly congested sprays. It tends to revert, with larger, coarser branches emerging. These should be cut out. Raised before 1973 in New Zealand.
H4

C. l. **'Green Hedger'** An erect, medium-sized to large tree of dense, conical habit with branches from the base and rich green

Chamaecyparis lawsoniana 'Green Hedger'

foliage. It is excellent for hedges and screens. Raised before 1949 by Jackman's.
♛ 1993

C. l. **'Green Pillar'** A conical, upright medium-sized tree with ascending branches clothed in bright green foliage that is lightened even further with a tint of gold in early spring. In cultivation 1940.
H4

C. l. **'Intertexta'** A superb large, open tree of ascending habit. The branches are loosely borne, with widely spaced, drooping branchlets and large, thick, flattened, fan-like sprays of dark, bloomy, green foliage. A most attractive conifer that resembles *Cedrus deodara* from a distance. Raised c1869 at Lawson's nursery, Edinburgh.
H4 ♛ 1993

C. l. **'Kilmacurragh'** A medium to large, dense, narrowly columnar tree. The short, ascending branches have irregular sprays of dark green foliage. It is a superb tree, similar in effect to the Italian cypress and perfectly hardy. It is remarkably resistant to snow damage because of the angle of branching. Raised before 1951 at Kilmacurragh, Co Wicklow.
H4 ♛ 1993

C. l. **'Lane'**, *syn. C. l. 'Lanei'* A medium-sized, columnar tree with thin, feathery sprays of golden-yellow foliage. One of the best golden cypresses. In cultivation 1938.
H4 ♛ 1993

C. l. **'Little Spire'** A slow-growing, small, narrowly conical tree with the distinctive foliage of *C. l.* 'Wisselii'.
H4

C. l. **'Lutea'** A medium-sized, broadly

Chamaecyparis lawsoniana 'Lutea'

columnar tree with a narrow, drooping top. The foliage is golden yellow and arranged in large, flattened, feathery sprays. This is a long-standing cultivar which has been well-tried and is deservedly popular.
H4 ♛ 1993

C. l. **'Lutea Nana'** A small, slow-growing, narrowly conical bush, eventually 2m (6ft) high. Foliage is golden and arranged in flattened sprays. In cultivation 1930.
H4 ♛ 1993

Chamaecyparis lawsoniana 'Minima Aurea'

C. l. **'Minima Aurea'** A densely growing, dwarf, conical bush with vertically held sprays of golden yellow foliage that is soft to the touch. One of the best golden conifers for the rock garden. In cultivation 1929.
H4 ♛ 1993

C. l. **'Minima Glauca'** A dense, globular, dwarf bush of slow growth. The foliage is sea-green, borne in short, densely packed, often vertically arranged sprays. A specimen at Hillier Nurseries reached 1 × 1.2m (3 × 4ft) in 25 years. In cultivation 1863.
H4 ♛ 1993

Chamaecyparis lawsoniana 'Minima Glauca'

C. l. **'Naberi'** A medium-sized, conical tree. The green foliage is distinctive on account of its sulphur-yellow tips that pale to creamy blue during winter. In cultivation 1929.

H4

C. l. **'Pembury Blue'** A medium-sized, conical tree with sprays of silvery blue foliage. A very striking cultivar and perhaps the best blue Lawson cypress.

H4 ♛ 1993

C. l. **'Pottenii'** A medium-sized, columnar tree of dense, slow growth. The sea-green foliage is partly juvenile and is in soft, crowded, feathery sprays. A very decorative conifer.

H4

C. l. **'Pygmaea Argentea'**, syn. *C. l.* 'Backhouse Silver' A dwarf, slow-growing, rounded bush with dark bluish green foliage and silvery white tips. It is suitable for the rock garden and perhaps the best dwarf, white-variegated conifer. Raised before 1891 by James Backhouse and Son of York.

H4 ♛ 1993

C. l. **'Silver Threads'** A large shrub or small tree with foliage marked in cream and silver. A sport of 'Ellwood's Gold'.

H4

C. l. **'Snow White'** (PBR 2753) A dwarf, compact shrub with juvenile foliage tipped with white.

H4

C. l. **'Stardust'** An outstanding columnar or narrowly conical medium-sized tree with yellow foliage with bronze at the tips.

H4 ♛ 1993

C. l. **'Stewartii'** A medium-sized to large, elegant, conical tree with slightly erect branches that have large, flattened sprays of golden yellow foliage that change to yellowish green in winter. A very hardy, popular conifer and one of the best golden Lawsons. In cultivation 1890.

H4

C. l. **'Summer Snow'** A small, bushy shrub with white young growth.

H4

C. l. **'Tamariscifolia'** A slow-growing, eventually medium to large bush with several ascending and spreading main stems. It is flat-topped and spreading when young becoming umbrella-shaped. Foliage is sea-green and in horizontally arranged, flattened, fan-like sprays. In cultivation 1923.

H4

Chamaecyparis lawsoniana 'Treasure'

C. l. **'Treasure'** A large, narrowly upright shrub with blue-green juvenile foliage heavily flecked with creamy yellow.

H4

C. l. **'Triomf van Boskoop'** This was once a very popular conifer, growing into a large, open, conical tree with bloomy-blue foliage in large, flat sprays. It needs to be trimmed if it is to be at all dense. Raised c1890 in Holland.

H4

Chamaecyparis lawsoniana 'Pembury Blue'

Chamaecyparis lawsoniana 'Stardust'

C. l. **'Van Pelt'** A narrowly conical small tree with deep blue-grey foliage that later becomes blue-green. An improvement on *C. l.* 'Columnaris', itself a very fine conifer. H4 ♛ 1993

C. l. **'Westermannii'** A medium-sized, broadly conical tree with loose, spreading branches. The foliage is in large sprays, light yellow when young and becoming yellowish green. Raised c1880 in Holland. H4

C. l. **'White Spot'** The foliage of this small tree is grey-green and the young growth is flecked with cream. H4

Chamaecyparis lawsoniana 'Winston Churchill'

C. l. **'Winston Churchill'** A dense, broadly columnar, small to medium-sized tree with foliage that is rich yellow all year round. One of the best Lawsons although it can be difficult to establish. Raised before 1945. H4

Chamaecyparis lawsoniana 'Wissellii'

C. l. **'Wisselii'** A most distinct and attractive, fast-growing tree of medium to large size. It is slenderly conical with widely spaced, ascending branches, and the stout, upright branchlets bear short, crowded, fern-like sprays of bluish-green foliage. The rather numerous, red, male cones are most attractive in spring. In cultivation 1888. Raised by F. van der Wissel of Epe, Holland. H4 ♛ 1993

C. l. **'Witzeliana'** A small, narrow, columnar tree with long, ascending branches and vivid green, crowded sprays. A most effective conifer, like a slender green flame. In cultivation 1931. H4

C. l. **'Yellow Transparent'** The young foliage is yellowish and in summer is transparent with the sun behind it. It turns bronze in winter. Slow-growing. Raised c1955 at Boskoop, Holland. H4

C. nootkatensis (Nootka cypress) A large, conical tree with drooping branchlets and coarser, more strongly smelling, duller green foliage than *C. lawsoniana* that is rough to the touch due to sharp-pointed scale-like leaves. The male cones are yellow. Following forms are recommended. W North America. Introduced c1853. H4

C. n. **'Lutea'** A medium-sized, conical tree with foliage that is yellow when young and gradually becomes yellowish green as the tree matures. In cultivation 1891. H4

Chamaecyparis nootkatensis 'Pendula'

C. n. **'Pendula'** A superb specimen tree of medium to large size with branchlets hanging vertically in long, graceful streamers. There are two forms of this tree in cultivation. In cultivation 1884. ♛ 1993

C. obtusa (Hinoki cypress) A large, broad, conical tree with horizontally spreading

branches. The foliage is deep, shining green in thick, horizontally flattened sprays. The garden cultivars of this species, which include many of Japanese origin, are almost as numerous as those of *C. lawsoniana* and include several excellent dwarf or slow-growing forms. The following are recommended. Japan. Introduced 1861 by P. F. von Siebold and J. G. Veitch.
H4

Chamaecyparis obtusa 'Chabo-yadori'

***C. o.* 'Chabo-yadori'** A dwarf or small, dome-shaped or conical bush. Both juvenile and adult foliage are present in irregular, fan-like sprays. A most attractive conifer.
H4

***C. o.* 'Coralliformis'** A small to medium-sized bush with densely arranged, twisted cord-like, brown branchlets. The foliage is dark green. A specimen in the Hillier Gardens and Arboretum in Hampshire has reached 2.5 × 2.5m (8 × 8ft). In cultivation 1903.
H4

***C. o.* 'Crippsii'** A small, slow-growing, loosely conical tree with spreading branches and broad, frond-like sprays of rich golden yellow foliage. It is one of the loveliest and most elegant of small golden conifers. Raised before 1899 by Thomas Cripps and Sons of Tunbridge Wells.
H4 ♛ 1993

***C. o.* 'Fernspray Gold'** A small to medium-sized shrub with golden-yellow foliage in fern-like sprays.
H4

***C. o.* 'Kosteri'**, syn. *C. o.* 'Nana Kosteri' A dwarf bush that is intermediate in growth

Chamaecyparis obtusa 'Crippsii'

between 'Nana' and 'Pygmaea'. It is conical, with flattened and mossy sprays of bright green foliage that become bronze in winter. Suitable for the rock garden. In cultivation 1915.
H4

Chamaecyparis obtusa 'Mariesii'

***C. o.* 'Mariesii'** A small, slow-growing,

cone-shaped bush of open growth. The foliage is in loose sprays, cream or pale yellow during summer and yellowish green in winter. In the Hillier Gardens and Arboretum it has reached 1.7m (5½ft) high and 1.5m (5ft) wide. In cultivation 1891.
H4

***C. o.* 'Nana'** A miniature, flat-topped

Chamaecyparis obtusa 'Nana'

Chamaecyparis obtusa 'Nana Aurea'

fro1
c18
H4

Cha

C.
of s
for1
spe
tu1
yea
H4
C.
ical
soft
plu
H4
C.
dw:
gre
pur
and
ver
H4

Cl
Lea

A ge
rela

C.
whi
arcl
ica,
H4
C.
tive
H4

dome, consisting of tiers of densely packed, cup-shaped fans of black-green foliage. It is one of the best dwarf conifers for the rock garden. A specimen at Hilliers attained 0.75m (30in) high by 1m (3ft) wide at the base in 40 years. The stronger growing plant found in many collections under this name is 'Nana Gracilis'. Japan. Introduced c1861 by Philip von Siebold.
H4 🏆 1993

***C. o.* 'Nana Aurea'** A looser, slightly taller plant than 'Nana', with golden yellow foliage. It is perhaps the best dwarf golden conifer and is ideal for the rock garden. Japan. Introduced by J. G. Veitch. In cultivation 1867.
H4 🏆 1993

Chamaecyparis obtusa 'Nana Gracilis'

***C. o.* 'Nana Gracilis'** A conical bush or eventually a small tree of dense, compact habit. The foliage is dark green, in short, shell-like sprays. It is perhaps the most commonly planted 'dwarf' conifer but ulti-

Chamaecyparis obtusa 'Pygmaea'

mately reaches a height of several metres. In cultivation 1874.
H4 🏆 1993

***C. o.* 'Nana Kosteri'** See *C. o.* 'Kosteri'.

***C. o.* 'Pygmaea'** A small, wide-spreading bush with loose sprays of bronze-green foliage that is tinged with reddish bronze in winter and arranged in flattened tiers. Japan. Introduced 1861 by Robert Fortune.
H4

***C. o.* 'Tempelhof'** A dense, conical, small to medium-sized bush with deep green foliage in broad, dense, shell-like sprays.
H4

Chamaecyparis obtusa 'Tetragona Aurea'

***C. o.* 'Tetragona Aurea'** An unusual large shrub or small tree of distinctive angular appearance. The branches are sparse, usually wide-spreading, and thickly covered with golden yellow, moss-like sprays of foliage. It is a very distinct and attractive conifer that associates well with heathers.

Japan. Introduced around 1870.
H4 🏆 1993

***C. o.* 'Tonia'** A dwarf sport of 'Nana Gracilis', making a dense, small bush of irregular habit with the shoots occasionally tipped with white. Raised c1928 in Holland.
H4

C. pisifera (Sawara cypress) A large, broadly conical tree with spreading branches and horizontally flattened sprays of dark green foliage, which consists of sharply pointed, scale-like leaves that have white markings below. It has given rise to many cultivars, several of which have soft, juvenile foliage. The following are recommended. Japan. Introduced 1861 by Robert Fortune.
H4

***C. p.* 'Boulevard'** An outstanding medium-sized bush of dense, conical habit. The steel-blue foliage is soft to the touch and becomes attractively purple-tinted in winter. It is a juvenile form and one of the most popular of all conifers. It tends to burn in full sun.
H4 🏆 1993

Chamaecyparis pisifera 'Filifera Aurea'

***C. p.* 'Filifera Aurea'** A medium-sized to large bush with string-like sprays of attractive, golden yellow foliage. It can burn in full sun. See also *C. p.* 'Sungold'. In cultivation 1889.
H4 🏆 1993

***C. p.* 'Filifera Nana'** A dense, rounded, flat-topped, dwarf bush with long, string-like branchlets. Suitable for the rock garden. In cultivation 1897.
H4

C. praecox A medium-sized, easily grown, winter-flowering deciduous shrub best planted against a sunny wall to ripen the growth, unless in an area where the summers are warm and sunny. It succeeds in any well-drained soil and is excellent on chalk. If grown on a wall, the long growths can be cut back immediately after flowering. The sweetly scented, pale waxy-yellow, purple-centred flowers are not produced on young plants. The cultivars described below are both grafted and flower at an early age. China. Introduced 1766.
H4

Chimonanthus praecox 'Grandiflorus'

C. p. **'Grandiflorus'** A medium-sized form with deeper yellow flowers conspicuously stained with red.
H4 ♔ 1993

C. p. **'Luteus'** This medium-sized shrub is distinct from other forms because of its rather large flowers that do not have a purple stain but are a clear waxy-yellow and

Chimonanthus praecox 'Luteus'

open rather later than the typical form.
H4 ♔ 1993

Chionanthus *Oleaceae*
Fringe trees

A genus of about 120 deciduous species, of which two are hardy. They are both easily grown in any reasonable garden soil and are best in full sun. They flower in midsummer, and the blooms are unusual in their 4–5 narrow, strap-shaped petals.

C. retusus (Chinese fringe tree) Given a continental climate, this is one of the most handsome large shrubs, with a profusion of snow-white flowers borne in erect panicles in midsummer, followed by damson-like fruits. China. Introduced 1845 by Robert Fortune.
H4

Chionanthus virginicus

C. virginicus (North American fringe tree) Ultimately a large shrub with larger and more noteworthy leaves than its Chinese counterpart. The flowers are white, slightly fragrant, and held in pendent panicles. Good bright yellow autumn foliage. E North America.
H4

Choisya *Rutaceae*

A genus of seven species of evergreen, aromatic flowering shrubs, natives of Mexico and the southwest United States. They will grow in any well-drained friable soil.

C. **'Aztec Pearl'** (*C. arizonica* × *C. ternata*)

Choisya 'Aztec Pearl'

The first hybrid in the genus and an elegant, small shrub, whose aromatic leaves are attractively divided into 3–5 slender, bright green leaflets. The almond-scented flowers are like those of *C. ternata* but larger and pink-flushed in the bud, opening white with a pink flush on the backs of the petals. They are profusely borne in late spring and again in summer and appear in clusters of 3–5 in the leaf axils. Raised 1982 by Hillier Nurseries' propagator Peter Moore.
H4 ♔ 1993

Choisya ternata

C. ternata (Mexican orange blossom) A medium-sized shrub of rounded habit with shining, dark green leaves aromatic when crushed. The flowers are white, sweetly scented, and borne in clusters of up to six from the leaf axils during late spring and early summer, and usually again in autumn. Thrives in sun or shade. Mountains of SW Mexico. Introduced 1825.
H4 ♔ 1993

Choisya ternata 'Sundance'

Chusquea culeou

C. t. 'Sundance' (*C. t.* 'Lich' PBR 3106) A striking small to medium-sized shrub of which the young foliage is bright yellow. H3 ♀ 1993

Chordospartium *Leguminosae*

A genus of only one deciduous species, related to Carmichaelia.

Chordospartium stevensonii

C. stevensonii (Weeping broom) A medium-sized, broom-like, leafless shrub, bearing racemes of white, lavender-pink-tinged flowers in summer and looking very much like a miniature weeping willow in habit. The stems of young plants appear brown and lifeless for the first three or four years. It is scarce in cultivation, and rare in the wild. It will grow in any well-drained friable soil. South Island of New Zealand. Introduced 1923.
H3–4

Chusquea *Gramineae*

A genus of graceful, mainly South American, evergreen bamboos, distinct in their numerous, densely clustered branches and solid stems. They are useful for cutting, as their leaves do not flag as easily as those of hollow-stemmed bamboos.

C. culeou A hardy species, forming broad, dense clumps. The deep olive green canes, 2.5–3.5m (8–11ft) high or occasionally up to 9m (28ft), produce dense clusters of slender, short, leafy branches along their whole length, giving them a characteristic bottle-brush effect. The first-year canes have conspicuous white sheaths at each node. The graceful leaves are 2.5–7.5cm (1–3in) long and 6–10mm ($^1/_4$–$^1/_2$in) wide with a slenderly pointed shape. Chile. Introduced 1926 by Harold Comber.
H4

Cistus *Cistaceae*
Sun rose

A genus of about 20 species of evergreen, usually small shrubs found in the wild from the Canary Islands throughout the Mediterranean region to the Caucasus. There are many hybrids that have originated either in the wild or in cultivation. They revel in full sun and are ideal for dry banks, rock gardens and similar positions. Although the flowers are individually short-lived, they are very freely produced. From early to midsummer, and sometimes for longer, there is a long succession of bloom, so much so that the short life of the individual, papery flowers does not matter at all. Most cistus resent severe frost but are remarkably wind-tolerant and are ideal shrubs for gardens near the sea, on chalk, or where the soil is shallow or on the poor side. They are usually about 1m (3ft) tall and exceptions are noted in the individual descriptions.

Cistus resent pruning, which should be confined to cutting away any dead wood, although young plants can be pinched out to promote bushiness. Take care to plant them in the right places from the start, as they are very difficult to transplant resenting the disruption.

Cistus × aguilari 'Maculatus'

C. × *aguilari* 'Maculatus' The white flowers of this most handsome small shrub have a central ring of crimson blotches. H3 ♛ 1993

Cistus 'Chelsea Bonnet'

C. 'Chelsea Bonnet' A small shrub with narrow dark green leaves. Pure white, lightly scented flowers with five notched

Cistus × cyprius

petals and a yellow centre are profusely borne in early summer.
H3

C. × *corbariensis* See *C. × hybridus*.

C. × *cyprius* *(C. ladanifer × C. laurifolius)* Vigorous hybrid about 2m (6ft) tall, bearing white flowers 8cm (3 in) wide with crimson blotches at the petal base. France, Spain.
H4 ♛ 1993

Cistus 'Elma'

C. × *dansereaui* 'Decumbens' A small shrub growing to 1.2m (4ft) or more wide and 0.6m (2ft) tall, with lance-shaped, dark green, sticky, wavy-edged leaves and large white flowers with crimson basal blotches.
H4 ♛ 1993

C. 'Elma' *(C. laurifolius × C. palhinhae)* The beautifully formed, extra-large, pure white flowers of this hybrid contrast well with the deep green, polished, lanceolate leaves that are bloomy beneath. The shrub is sturdy, bushy, and grows to 2m (6ft).
H3 ♛ 1993

C. 'Grayswood Pink' A dwarf shrub with soft grey-green leaves complimented by clear pink flowers.
H4

C. × *hybridus*, syn *C. × corbariensis* A dense, spreading small shrub and one of the hardiest, with crimson-tinted buds that open to pure white.
H4 ♛ 1993

C. *ladanifer* (Gum cistus) A tall, erect shrub growing to over 2m (6ft) with lance-

Cistus laurifolius

Cistus ladanifer

Cistus 'Peggy Sammons'

Cistus × pulverulentus

Cistus × purpureus

shaped, dark green leaves. The flowers are up to 10cm (4in) across, and white with a distinctive chocolate basal blotch and rumpled petals. SW Europe and North Africa. In cultivation 1629.
H3 ♚ 1993

C. laurifolius This is the hardiest species of all, sometimes exceeding 2m (6ft) in height, and has leathery, bloomy dark green leaves and white flowers with yellow centres. SW Europe to C Italy. Introduced 1731.
H4 ♚ 1993

Cistus × loretti

C. × loretii A dwarf hybrid with large white flowers with crimson basal blotches. It occurs naturally in the wild. S Europe and North Africa.
H3

C. palhinhae This strikingly handsome and distinct species is low growing, compact and has glossy leaves and pure white flowers that are nearly 10cm (4in) across. SW

Portugal. Introduced 1939 by Capt Collingwood Ingram.
H3

C. 'Peggy Sammons' A small to medium-sized hybrid shrub of erect habit, with grey-green, downy stems and leaves and flowers in a delicate shade of pink. Raised in 1955 by J. E. Sammons.
H3 ♚ 1993

Cistus populifolius var. lasiocalyx

C. populifolius var. lasiocalyx An erect shrub up to 2m (6ft) tall with smallish, hairy, poplar-like leaves and large, wavy, white flowers with a conspicuously inflated calyx. A rewarding cistus and one of the hardiest. S Spain, S Portugal, Morocco.
H3 ♚ 1993

C. × pulverulentus, syn. *C.* 'Sunset' A dwarf shrub of compact habit, with sage-green, wavy leaves and vivid cerise flowers. SW Europe. In cultivation 1929.
H3 ♚ 1993

C. × purpureus A small shrub with reddish stems and narrow, rather wavy-edged, dark green leaves. The flowers are large and rosy crimson, with a dark maroon blotch at the base of each petal, contrasting with the central cluster of yellow stamens. Occurs naturally in the wild. S Europe. Introduced 1790.
H3 ♚ 1993

Cistus 'Silver Pink'

C. **'Silver Pink'** An exceptionally hardy small cistus with flowers in a lovely shade of silver-pink carried in long clusters. Originated as a chance hybrid of *C. laurifolius* at Hillier Nurseries c1910.
H4

Cistus × skanberghii

C. × *skanberghii* A small shrub, one of the most beautiful of all cistus, with stems whitened by down and silky-petalled, clear pink flowers. Occurs naturally in the wild. Greece.
H3 🏆 1993

C. **'Sunset'** See *C.* × *pulverulentus.*

Citrus *Rutaceae*

A genus of around 15 species of semi-evergreen trees and shrubs from South-East Asia, encompassing the oranges, lemons, grapefruits and other citrus fruits. They will grow in any well-drained oil ideally in a conservatory or against a sunny wall in a very warm sheltered garden.

Citrus 'Meyer's Lemon'

Cladrastis lutea

C. **'Meyer's Lemon'** The hardiest lemon is a medium-sized to large shrub with short-stalked, large, dark green leaves and clusters of fragrant white flowers that are followed by freely produced, large, yellow lemons. Best grown in a conservatory.
H2

Cladrastis *Leguminosae*

A genus of around six species of deciduous trees with pinnate leaves, native to east Asia but with one species from the south-east United States. The flowers, similar to those of Robinia pseudoacacia *are not produced by young trees. They will grow in any well-drained friable soil.*

C. lutea (Kentucky yellow wood) A very handsome, medium-sized tree producing long, drooping, wisteria-like panicles of fragrant white flowers in early summer. The leaves turn clear yellow before falling. SE United States. Introduced 1812.
H4 🏆 1993

Cladrastis sinensis

C. sinensis (Chinese yellow wood) A remarkably beautiful medium-sized tree, flowering in midsummer. The compound leaves are soft green above and bloomy beneath, and the pink-tinged, white, slightly fragrant flowers are borne in large panicles. The plant is scarce and not easily obtained. China. Introduced 1901 by Ernest Wilson.
H4

CLEMATIS

Ranunculaceae

Clematis 'Dawn'

THERE CAN BE LITTLE doubt that clematis are the most popular climbers of all. They are unsurpassed for variety of colour and flower shape, for the lengths of their flowering seasons, and in many cases for the sheer power of their display. They can be modest and understated, flamboyant and dramatic – or somewhere between these extremes. There are clematis for spring, summer, autumn and even winter. They can climb trees, sprawl elegantly over shrubs, allow themselves to be trained neatly on walls, drape themselves nonchalantly over your porch, and always look as if they belong.

Garden clematis divide themselves fairly neatly into two main groups. The first consists of species clematis and their primary hybrids (which is to say hybrids between two species or at any rate very few, rather than the products of complex breeding). These are in general more on the modest side than the other group, the large-flowered garden clematis, and are also more varied in habit, form of flowers, size and general impact. A few species, such as *C. flammula*, are very pleasantly scented. Interestingly, they are for the most part easier to establish than their larger-flowered counterparts and a few are indeed sometimes a little overwhelming in their ability to cover anything in their path with tangles of stems that can in time become heavy and unstable, and need to be pruned simply to keep them within bounds.

Among the species are the renowned *C. montana*, queen of the spring clematis, and its forms; *C. alpina*, which is never too large even for the smallest garden; and for the purposes of this book the utterly delightful small-flowered forms of *C. viticella*, thought by many gardeners to be the most desirable of all. If you are looking for an evergreen climber to flower in winter, seek no further than *C. cirrhosa* var. *balearica*, and if you want a display in autumn, the informal drapery of *C. tangutica* 'Aureolin', studded with yellow lanterns and silky-mop seed heads, is irresistible and entirely reliable.

The large-flowered garden clematis present such a wide choice that it can be difficult to know where to begin. Perhaps the best way is to try to establish the longest possible succession of flowering. Many come into flower in late spring and early summer, after *C. montana* and alongside *C. macropetala*, and several of them flower again in early autumn. Sometimes the flowers produced in the different seasons by the same plant are of different kinds. 'Vyvyan Pennell', for example, has double flowers from late spring to midsummer and single blooms in autumn. Others occupy the mid- to late season; 'Ascotiensis' is one example, flowering from midsummer to early autumn, and another is 'Daniel Deronda', which starts a month or so earlier. October sees the end of the season for these wonderful flowers, but a full six months of colour is easy to provide with just a few well chosen cultivars.

CARE AND CULTIVATION

Clematis are successful in a wide range of soils, from acid to chalky. They are in the main long-lived plants, likely to remain for many years, and this means that the preparation of the soil is of the first importance. A hole at least 45cm (18in) square should be dug as deeply as the depth of topsoil will

Clematis 'Ville de Lyon'

allow, the bottom should be well broken up, and then a mixture of good topsoil and its own volume of well-rotted manure or leaf-mould should be used to back-fill the hole. A handful or two of bonemeal can be added as well.

The clematis should be planted in this mixture, and large-flowered forms should have at least 2.5cm (1in) and as much as 7.5cm (3in) of soil above the level of the container's compost level. This encourages growth buds at the base and also helps to prevent the occurrence of the disease clematis wilt, which is one of the main causes of disappointment for gardeners who want to enjoy clematis. The hole should be made well away from the feeding roots of any tree or shrub up which the clematis is to grow, but it should not be so close to the trunk as to be difficult to plant. A cane can be placed at a slant so as to encourage the clematis to grow towards and eventually onto the trunk. If it is to grow on a wall, do not dig the hole too close to it, as the soil at the bottom of a wall is often in a rain shadow, and clematis do not enjoy dry conditions. You should water the plants while they are still in their containers and then again as soon as planting is complete – copiously. Spring-planted clematis should be monitored very carefully until autumn and watered well whenever they appear dry.

Clematis will grow in heavy soils as long as they are well drained but cannot tolerate sticky soils that remain wet or waterlogged. In general they prefer to have their roots shaded but to grow their stems up into the sunlight. Some pale-coloured large-flowered cultivars are, however, best grown so that they flower in shade, otherwise their flowers fade badly. The most popular clematis of all, 'Nelly Moser', is one such.

The large-flowered clematis are listed below with a letter following the name: F = Florida, J = Jackmanii, L = Lanuginosa, P = Patens, T = Texensis and V = Viticella. Although this may seem of academic interest, it helps when you are trying to decide when and how to prune. There are two main concentrations of these groups for pruning purposes: (a) The Florida, Lanuginosa and Patens groups, which flower on the previous year's wood. They normally flower in late spring and early summer and the only pruning required is to trim back the old flowering growths immediately after flowering. Old, dense plants may also be hard pruned in late winter, but the first crop of flowers will be lost; (b) The Jackmanii, Texensis and Viticella groups, which flower on the current year's shoots. These normally flower in late summer and autumn and may be hard pruned to within 30cm (12in) of the ground in late winter or early spring. Old, unpruned plants will become bare at the base.

C. aethusifolia A slender-stemmed climber about 2m (6½ft) high, with deeply divided leaves and late-summer flowers that are bell-shaped, 2cm (¾in) long with turned-back lobes, pale primrose-yellow and fragrant, nodding on slender stems. N China. Introduced c1875.
H4

C. akebioides A relative of *C. tibetana*, growing to about 4m (12ft). It has pinnate leaves with up to seven leaflets, and bell-shaped, yellow flowers that may be green or purple-tinged on the outside, borne on long stalks in summer and early autumn. W China.
H4

C. alpina A lovely species with slender stems to 2.5m (8ft) long and leaves with nine leaflets. The flowers are solitary, blue or violet-blue with a central tuft of white, petaloid stamens (staminodes). They open in mid- to late spring and are followed by silky seed heads. It is superb when growing over a low wall, a large rock or small bush. Europe, C Asia. Introduced 1792.
H4

***C. a.* 'Columbine'** A medium-sized clematis with pale lavender, bell-shaped flowers with taper-pointed sepals and white staminodes.
H4

Clematis alpina 'Frances Rivis'

***C. a.* 'Frances Rivis'** A vigorous, free-flowering medium-sized form with larger flowers and a contrasting sheaf of white stamens and staminodes in the centre.
H4 ♆ 1993

C. a. **'Frankie'** A medium-sized form with a profusion of rich blue flowers, similar to but an improvement upon 'Frances Rivis'. H4

C. a. **'Helsingborg'** A medium-sized form with deep blue flowers.
H4 🏆 1993

C. a. **'Pamela Jackman'** A medium-sized clematis with large, rich blue flowers. The outer staminodes are tinged with blue and the inner ones are tinged with white. In cultivation 1960.
H4

Clematis alpina 'Ruby'

C. a. **'Ruby'** A medium-sized clematis bearing rose-red flowers with creamy staminodes. Raised 1935 by Ernest Markham. H4

C. a. **'White Columbine'** A medium-sized clematis grown for its white flowers on upright shoots.
H4 🏆 1993

C. a. **'White Moth'** See *C. macropetala* 'White Moth'.

C. a. **'Willy'** A medium-sized form bearing mauve-pink flowers that have a distinctive deep pink blotch at the base of each sepal. In cultivation 1971.
H4

C. armandii A strongly growing, evergreen climber with stems 4–6m (12–20ft) long. The leaves have three long, leathery, glossy dark green leaflets and the creamy flowers, 5–7cm (2–3in) across, are borne in clusters in mid- or late spring. It is a beautiful species but subject to injury in severe winters and best planted on a warm, sunny wall. There are from time to time seedling

plants that may be offered from certain sources and these usually produce smaller, inferior flowers. China. Introduced 1900 by Ernest Wilson.
H3

Clematis armandii 'Apple Blossom'

C. a. **'Apple Blossom'** The true plant is a superb medium-sized clematis with broad sepals that are white, shaded with pink, especially on the reverse. The true plant is scarce and a poor form that is easy to propagate has appeared on the market.
H3

Clematis armandii 'Snowdrift'

C. a. **'Snowdrift'** A medium-sized form with pure white flowers. Beautiful although it is, this plant is scarce in cultivation.
H3

C. **'Bill MacKenzie'** *(C. tangutica × C. tibetana* subsp. *vernayi)* A vigorous, free-flowering medium-sized climber with bright green leaves made up of sharply toothed leaflets. The flowers are long-stalked, up to

6cm (2¹⁄₂in) across, with four widely spreading, rather thick, bright yellow sepals with purple filaments. You should make sure to obtain the true plant, as there are many seedlings about that are poor. Introduced before 1976 by Valerie Finnis.
H4

C. **'Blue Bird'** *(C. alpina × C. macropetala)* A vigorous small hybrid between two popular species, both of which it resembles. The flowers are 7.5cm (3in) wide, purple-blue and semi-double. In cultivation 1965.
H4

C. **campaniflora** A vigorous climber up to 6m (20ft) with pinnate leaves and leaflets in groups of three. Its small, bowl-shaped, blue-tinted flowers, borne profusely from midsummer to early autumn, are most effective in the mass. Portugal, S Spain. Introduced 1810.
H4

C. **chrysocoma** Hort. This very beautiful plant, whose name is in doubt, resembles *C. montana*, though less rampant. The trifoliate leaves, shoots and flower-stalks are covered with a thick yellowish down. The soft pink flowers, 4–6cm (1¹⁄₂–2¹⁄₂in) across, are borne in profusion in early summer and spasmodically into late summer on young growths. The true plant has recently been rediscovered in China.
H4

C. c. **var. sericea** A very attractive variety with white flowers produced singly or in pairs on older growths in late spring.
H4 🏆 1993

C. **cirrhosa var. balearica** (Fern-leaved clematis) An elegant, evergreen climber

Clematis cirrhosa var. *balearica*

with slender stems up to 4m (12ft) long. The leaves are prettily divided into several segments, becoming bronze-tinged in winter. The flowers are pale yellow, spotted with reddish purple on the inside. They reach up to 5cm (2in) across and are produced freely throughout the winter. Balearic Isles. Introduced before 1783.
H3 ♔ 1993

Clematis cirrhosa 'Freckles'

C. c 'Freckles' A medium-sized evergreen climber bearing flowers very heavily spotted and streaked with red.
H3 ♔ 1993

C. c. 'Wisley Cream' A medium-sized evergreen climber with large, creamy white, unspotted flowers.
H3

C. × durandii A lovely hybrid up to 3m (10ft). The leaves are simple and up to 15cm (6in) long, and the dark blue, four-sepalled flowers are sometimes more than 10cm (4in) across. They have a central cluster of yellow stamens and appear from early summer to early autumn. Garden origin c1870.
H4 ♔ 1993

C. × eriostemon 'Hendersonii' A beautiful, semi-herbaceous clematis. Each year it throws up slender stems of 2–2.5m (6–8ft) in length with simple or pinnate leaves. The flowers are deep bluish purple, widely bell-shaped, slightly fragrant, up to 7cm (3in) across, nodding, and borne singly on slender stalks from midsummer to early autumn. It is best given some support. Raised c1830 by Messrs Henderson of St John's Wood, London.
H4

Clematis × eriostemon 'Hendersonii'

Clematis flammula

C. flammula A strong-growing climber, 4–5m (12–15ft) high, that forms a dense tangle of stems, clothed with bright green, bipinnate leaves. From late summer to mid-autumn, the loose panicles of small, white, sweetly scented flowers are abundantly scattered over the whole plant and are followed by silky seed heads. It is an ideal climber for clothing unsightly walls and hedges. S Europe. In cultivation in Britain since the late sixteenth century.
H4

C. florida An elegant species with wiry stems 3–5m (10–15ft) long and glossy, compound leaves. The flowers are creamy white, up to 10cm (4in) across and open in early to midsummer. A parent of many hybrids. The following forms are recommended. China, Japan. Introduced 1776.
H3

C. f. 'Alba Plena' In this striking medium-sized form each flower is fully double, a dense mass of greenish white sepals. These

Clematis florida 'Alba Plena'

flamboyant flowers are long-lasting and borne over a long period.
H3

Clematis florida 'Sieboldii'

C. f. 'Sieboldii' A beautiful medium-sized form reminiscent of a passion flower. The flowers are white, 8cm (3in) wide, with a central boss of violet-purple petaloid stamens. Japan. Introduced before 1836.
H3

C. forsteri A scrambling species of clematis with bright apple-green leaves composed of three leaflets, each of which is lobed or prettily cut. The flowers are verbena-scented and star-like. The males are up to 4cm (1½in) across with 5–8 white to creamy yellow sepals and the females are smaller. New Zealand.
H3

C. × jackmanii A spectacular hybrid, 3–4m (10–12ft) high, with pinnate leaves and flowers 10–13cm (4–5in) across with four rich purple-violet sepals. They are

Clematis forsteri

Clematis × jackmanii

borne in great profusion either singly or in threes from midsummer to mid-autumn, on the current year's growth. Many clones have been named and some are listed among the large-flowered garden clematis on page 228. Raised 1858 by Messrs Jackman of Woking, England.
H4 ♛ 1993

Clematis × jouiniana

C. × jouiniana A somewhat shrubby climber that reaches up to 3.5m (11ft) high. Its leaves have 3–5 coarsely toothed leaflets and its small, white, lilac-tinted flowers are borne very freely in autumn. The following forms are recommended. Garden origin before 1900.
H4

C. × j. 'Cote d'Azur' A charming medium-sized form with azure blue flowers, excellent for covering low walls, mounds or tree stumps.
H4

C. × j. 'Praecox' A vigorous, early flowering medium-sized form with slightly larger, pale blue flowers.
H4 ♛ 1993

C. macropetala A slender-stemmed climber up to 2.5m (8ft) with prettily divided leaves. The flowers are up to 7.5cm (3in) across, violet blue, with conspicuously paler petaloid stamens that give the effect of doubling. Flowering is from late spring or early summer onwards. The seedheads are silky and become fluffy and grey with age. A beautiful species for a low wall or fence. N China, Siberia. Introduced 1910 by William Purdom.
H4

Clematis macropetala 'Jan Lindmark'

C. m. 'Jan Lindmark' This clematis is a small to medium-sized form with pale purple flowers.
H4

C. m. 'Lagoon', syn. *C. m.* 'Blue Lagoon' A small to medium-sized climber similar to 'Maidwell Hall' but with slightly deeper blue flowers. It is considered to be the best

clone. In cultivation 1959.
H4 ♛ 1993

C. m. 'Maidwell Hall' A small to medium-sized climber with deep lavender-blue flowers. In cultivation 1956.
H4

Clematis macropetala 'Markham's Pink'

C. m. 'Markham's Pink' A lovely small to medium-sized form with flowers the shade of crushed strawberries.
H4 ♛ 1993

C. m. 'White Moth', syn. *C. alpina* 'White Moth' A small to medium-sized climber grown for its pure white flowers. In cultivation 1955.
H4

C. m. 'White Swan' See *C.* 'White Swan'.

C. montana A popular species, usually grown in one of the forms listed below. They are of good constitution and may verge on being rampant. Their stems are 6–9m (20–30ft) long with leaves that consist of three leaflets. The flowers are borne in great profusion in late spring. They are lovely climbers for any aspect and excellent for growing into trees and over walls, outhouses and arbours, especially where there is a shady aspect. Himalaya. Introduced 1831 by Lady Amherst.
H4

C. m. 'Alexander' A lovely large form with creamy white, scented flowers. N India. Introduced by Col R. D. Alexander.
H4

C. m. 'Elizabeth' A most beautiful large form with large, slightly fragrant, soft pink flowers in late spring and early summer.
H4 ♛ 1993

Clematis montana 'Elizabeth'

C. m. 'Freda' A large climber bearing deep cherry-pink flowers with darker edges and bronze young foliage.
H4 ⚱ 1993

C. m. f. grandiflora A strong-growing variety, occasionally up to 12m (40ft), with an abundance of white flowers in late spring and early summer. A particularly valuable characteristic of this clematis is its ability to flourish on a north-facing wall.
H4 ⚱ 1993

C. m. 'Marjorie' A large plant with semi-double, creamy pink flowers with a salmon-pink centre.
H4

Clematis montana 'Pink Perfection'

C. m. 'Pink Perfection' A large climber with fragrant flowers similar to 'Elizabeth' but slightly more deeply coloured.
H4

C. m. var. rubens A beautiful large variety with bronze-purple shoots and leaves and rose-pink flowers up to 7.5cm (3in)

Clematis montana var. rubens

across in late spring and early summer. Hillier Nurseries' clone of this plant was selected best in trials in 1990. China. Introduced 1900 by Ernest Wilson.
H4 ⚱ 1993

Clematis montana 'Tetrarose'

C. m. 'Tetrarose' An excellent large form with bronze foliage and lilac-rose flowers up to 7.5cm (3in) across that are borne in late spring and early summer.
H4 ⚱ 1993

C. m. var. wilsonii A large form with masses of fragrant, rather small, white flowers in early summer.
H4

C. orientalis The true species is rare in cultivation. For the plant commonly grown under this name see *C. tibetana* subsp. *vernayi*.

C. pitcheri A climber of about 3–4m (10–12ft) with leaves that have up to nine leaflets. The flowers are pitcher-shaped, purplish blue, deeper inside. The sepals are curved backwards and the flowers are solitary on long stalks. The name refers to its discoverer, Zina Pitcher, and not to the shape of the flowers. C United States. Introduced 1878.
H4

C. rehderiana A charming species that reaches 8m (25ft) in a tree. The leaves are pinnate or bipinnate and the nodding, bell-shaped flowers are soft primrose yellow and have a delicious cowslip scent. They are in

Clematis rehderiana

erect panicles up to 23cm (9in) long in late summer and autumn. Introduced 1898. H4 ♛ 1993

C. 'Rosy O'Grady' (*C. alpina* × *C. macropetala*) A successful small hybrid with large, rose-pink, semi-double flowers. In cultivation 1967. H4

C. serratifolia A slender species up to 3m (10ft) with prettily divided green leaves. The flowers are 2.5cm (1in) long, yellow with purple stamens, borne most profusely in late summer and early autumn and followed by silky seed heads. Korea, China, C Asia. Introduced c1918. H4

Clematis tangutica

C. tangutica A dense climber up to 5m (15ft) with prettily divided, sea-green leaves and yellow flowers that are usually lantern-like. It is a fine species, probably the best with yellow flowers, and ideal for low walls, fences, trellises, large boulders and banks,

but it is very variable when grown from seed. The following form is recommended. China. Introduced 1908 by Ernest Wilson. H4

Clematis tangutica 'Aureolin'

C. t. 'Aureolin' A medium-sized form specially selected for its large, nodding, bright yellow flowers with sepals to 4cm (1½in) long, often opening widely. H4 ♛ 1993

C. terniflora A vigorous species up to 10m (30ft), often forming a dense tangle of growth. The leaves have 3–5 long-stalked leaflets and the hawthorn-scented white flowers are in panicles on the current year's growth in autumn. It needs a long, hot summer to induce flowering. Korea, China, Japan. Introduced c1864. H4

Clematis tibetana subsp. *vernayi*

C. tibetana subsp. *vernayi* This is the form of the species that is grown in gardens: the type is not in cultivation. It is a vigorous

and graceful medium-sized climber with finely divided, blue-bloomy leaves. The flowers are nodding, yellow to greenish yellow or purple-flushed, with purple stamens. It is remarkable in its thick, spongy sepals that have earned it the name of 'orange-peel clematis'. Nepal, Tibet. Introduced 1947 by Ludlow & Sherriff. H4 ♛ 1993

C. × **triternata 'Rubromarginata'** A vigorous climber to 5m (15ft) with pinnate or bipinnate leaves and terminal panicles of fragrant flowers that are white, margined with reddish violet, and borne in such masses in late summer that they give the effect of dark, billowing clouds. H4 ♛ 1993

C. vitalba (Old man's beard, traveller's joy). An extremely rampant, European native that is a nuisance in gardens, where it can seed itself and rapidly invade trees and shrubs with its rope-like stems that form dense columns or curtains. In extensive, wild gardens it has a place. H4

C. viticella A slender climber up to 3.5m (11ft) with pinnate leaves. Some truly delightful, small-flowered hybrids of it are recommended below.

Clematis viticella 'Abundance'

C. v. 'Abundance' Delicately veined, soft purple to red flowers. H4

C. v. 'Alba Luxurians' White flowers, tinted mauve. H4 ♛ 1993

C. v. 'Kermesina' Crimson. H4

Clematis viticella 'Alba Luxurians'

C. v. 'Minuet' Flowers are erect and cream with a broad band of purple at the end of each sepal.
H4 🏆 1993

Clematis viticella 'Purpurea Plena Elegans'

C. v. 'Purpurea Plena Elegans' Double flowers up to 6cm (2½in) across, with many sepals. Lilac purple, paler in the centre.
H4 🏆 1993

C. v. 'Royal Velours' Deep velvety purple.
H4 🏆 1993

C. 'White Swan', syn. *C. macropetala* 'White Swan' A small hybrid with pure white, double flowers up to 12cm (5in) across. Raised 1961 in Canada.
H4

LARGE-FLOWERED GARDEN CLEMATIS

All the following are H4 and medium-sized climbers. The letters in parentheses after the names indicate the groups to which the cultivars belong (page 222).

Clematis 'Asao'

C. 'Asao' (P) Large flowers with 6–7 broad, rose-carmine sepals.

C. 'Ascotiensis' (V) Azure-blue flowers up to 13cm (5in) across. Very free-flowering, midsummer to early autumn. In cultivation 1871.
🏆 1993

C. 'Barbara Dibley' (P) Pansy-violet flowers 20cm (8in) or more across, with a deep carmine stripe along each sepal. They appear in late spring to early summer and again in early autumn.

Clematis 'Barbara Jackman'

C. 'Barbara Jackman' (P) Deep violet flowers striped with magenta, up to 15cm (6in) wide. They have cream stamens, and are borne from late spring to early summer. In cultivation 1952.

C. 'Beauty of Worcester' (L) Blue-violet flowers, occasionally double, with contrasting creamy white stamens, up to 15cm (6in) across. They are borne from late spring to late summer. In cultivation 1900.

Clematis 'Bee's Jubilee'

C. 'Bee's Jubilee' (P) Renowned for its blush pink flowers banded with carmine to make a striking display, up to 18cm (7in) across. In cultivation 1958.
🏆 1993

C. 'Belle of Woking' (F) Pale mauve, double flowers, 10cm (4in) across, borne in late spring and early summer.

C. 'Carnaby' (L) Deep raspberry pink flowers with a deeper bar. Good in shade. In cultivation 1983.

Clematis 'Comtesse de Bouchaud'

C. 'Comtesse de Bouchaud' (J) Beautiful, soft rose-pink flowers with yellow stamens, up to 15cm (6in) across. Vigorous and free-flowering. Early to late summer. In cultivation 1903.
🏆 1993

C. 'Countess of Lovelace' (P) Double and single flowers, bluish lilac with cream anthers, 15cm (6in) wide, borne in late spring to midsummer. In cultivation 1876.

C. 'Daniel Deronda' (P) Large, violet-

Clematis 'Daniel Deronda'

Clematis 'Duchess of Edinburgh'

plant. The flowers are nodding, bell-shaped, 5cm (2in) long, deep cherry-purple with a silvery pink margin. Summer.

Clematis 'Etoile Violette'

blue flowers, paler at the centre, up to 20cm (8in) across with creamy stamens. The flowers are often double and appear in early summer to early autumn.
🏆 1993

C. 'Dawn' (L/P) Pale pink flowers shading white towards the base, 15cm (6in) across with conspicuous red anthers. Best in shade. Late spring to early summer. In cultivation 1969.

Clematis 'Dr Ruppel'

C. 'Dr Ruppel' (P) Deep pink flowers with a carmine bar and yellow stamens, up to 20cm (8in) across. In cultivation 1975.
🏆 1993.

C. 'Duchess of Albany' (T) Tubular, nodding flowers, bright pink, shading to lilac-pink at the margins. Midsummer to early autumn.
🏆 1993

C. 'Duchess of Edinburgh' (F) Large, double, rosette-like, white flowers with green shading, scented, up to 10cm (4in)

across. Late spring to early summer. In cultivation 1875.

C. 'Duchess of Sutherland' (V) Petunia-red flowers with a darker bar on each tapered sepal, up to 15cm (6in) across, often double. Mid- and late summer.

C. 'Edith' (L) Similar to 'Mrs Cholmondeley', of which it is a seedling, but the flowers are white with red anthers.
🏆 1993

Clematis 'Elsa Späth'

C. 'Elsa Späth' (P) Popular for its large, lavender-blue flowers with red stamens, up to 20cm (8in) wide. Late spring/early summer and early autumn.
🏆 1993

C. 'Ernest Markham' (V) Glowing petunia-red flowers with a velvety sheen and rounded sepals, up to 15cm (6in) across. Early summer to early autumn. Best in a sunny position. In cultivation 1938.
🏆 1993

C. 'Etoile Rose' (T) A semi-herbaceous

C. 'Etoile Violette' (V) A vigorous and free-flowering clematis, with deep purple flowers up to 10cm (4in) across with 4–6 sepals. Midsummer to early autumn. In cultivation 1885.
🏆 1993

C. 'Fair Rosamond' (L/P) Fragrant flowers up to 15cm (6in) across, pale blush pink with a carmine bar, fading to white. The anthers are purple. Late spring and early summer. In cultivation 1871.

C. 'Fireworks' (L) Violet flowers, striped with red; long, slender, twisted sepals.
🏆 1993

Clematis 'Fujimu-Sumi'

C. 'Fujimu-Sumi' (L) Deep lavender-blue flowers with, six pointed sepals with a white bar on the reverse and a centre composed of green-white stamens.

C. **'General Sikorski'** (L) Mid-blue flowers, reddish at the bases of the sepals, up to 15cm (6in) across. Early to midsummer.
🏆 1993

C. **'Gillian Blades'** (J) Very large, pure white flowers up to 22cm (9in) across with frilled edges appear in midsummer. Little or no pruning is required.
🏆 1993

C. **'Gipsy Queen'** (J) Rich, velvety violet-purple flowers, up to 12cm (5in) across, with broad, rounded sepals. Vigorous and free-flowering. Midsummer to early autumn. In cultivation 1871.
🏆 1993

Clematis 'Gravetye Beauty'

C. **'Gravetye Beauty'** (T) The cherry-red flowers of this clematis are bell-shaped at first, the sepals later spreading. Midsummer to early autumn.

C. **'H. F. Young'** (P) Flowers of a good blue, up to 20cm (8in) across, with broad, overlapping sepals and white stamens. Late

Clematis 'Hagley Hybrid'

spring/early summer and early autumn. In cultivation 1962.
🏆 1993

C. **'Hagley Hybrid'** (J) Shell-pink flowers with contrasting, chocolate-brown anthers, up to 15cm (6in) across, free-flowering, early summer to early autumn. In cultivation 1956.

Clematis 'Henryi'

C. **'Henryi'** (L) Large, creamy white flowers up to 18cm (7in) across, with pointed sepals and dark stamens. Late spring/early summer and again in late summer/early autumn. In cultivation 1858.
🏆 1993

C. **'Horn of Plenty'** (L) Cup-shaped, rose-purple flowers with darker stripes and a centre of plum stamens in early summer.
🏆 1993

C. **'Huldine'** (V) Pearly white flowers with a mauve bar on the reverse. Requires full sun. Midsummer to mid-autumn.

C. **'Jackmanii Alba'** (J) White flowers

Clematis 'Jackmanii Alba'

veined with blue, up to 13cm (5in) wide, early flowers double, later ones single. Very vigorous. In cultivation 1878.

Clematis 'Jackmanii Superba'

C. **'Jackmanii Superba'** (J) Large, rich violet-purple flowers with broad sepals; vigorous and free-flowering, midsummer to early autumn.

C. **'John Huxtable'** (J) An excellent, late-flowering white, a seedling of 'Comtesse de Bouchaud', which it resembles in all but colour. Mid- to late summer.

C. **'John Warren'** (L) Pinkish lilac flowers with a deeper bar and margins and red stamens, the bar fading as the flower opens to 25cm (10in) across.

C. **'Kathleen Wheeler'** (P) Deep mauve-blue flowers up to 18cm (7in) across. The prominent stamens have lilac filaments. Late spring and early summer with smaller flowers in autumn. In cultivation 1967.

C. **'Ken Donson'** (P) Blue flowers with golden anthers in late summer.
🏆 1993

C. **'Lady Betty Balfour'** (V) Deep, velvety purple flowers, 12cm (5in) across, with golden stamens. Very vigorous, best in full sun. Late summer to mid-autumn. In cultivation 1910.

C. **'Lady Londesborough'** (P) Flowers pale mauve at first, becoming silvery grey. To 15cm (6in) wide with dark stamens and broad, overlapping sepals. Free-flowering, late spring and early summer.

C. **'Lady Northcliffe'** (L) Rich violet-blue flowers with broad, wavy sepals and cream stamens, up to 15cm (6in) wide. Early summer to early autumn and later.

Clematis 'Lasurstern'

C. **'Lasurstern'** (P) Deep lavender-blue flowers up to 18cm (7in) wide with white stamens and broad, tapering, wavy-margined sepals. Late spring/early summer and again in early autumn.
♇ 1993

Clematis 'Lincoln Star'

C. **'Lincoln Star'** (P) Brilliant raspberry-pink flowers, 15cm (6in) across, with dark red stamens. Late spring and early summer. Flowers borne during a second flush in early autumn are paler and have a deep pink bar. In cultivation 1954.
C. **'Lord Nevill'** (P) A vigorous plant with bronze young foliage. The flowers are deep purplish blue, up to 18cm (7in) across, and have darker veins. Early summer and early autumn. In cultivation 1878.
♇ 1993
C. **'Mme Baron Velliard'** (J) A vigorous plant with pale lilac-pink flowers 13cm (5in) wide with six sepals. Midsummer to early autumn. In cultivation 1885.

Clematis 'Mme Baron Velliard'

C. **'Mme Edouard André'** (J) Rich crimson flowers up to 12cm (5in) wide, with yellow stamens. Very free-flowering, early to late summer. In cultivation 1893.
♇ 1993

Clematis 'Mme Grangé'

Clematis 'Mme Julia Correvon'

C. **'Mme Grangé'** (J) Grown for its velvety, deep purplish red flowers up to 12cm

(5in) wide. Midsummer to early autumn. In cultivation 1873.
♇ 1993
C. **'Mme Julia Correvon'** (V) Rose-red flowers up to 13cm (5in) across, with cream stamens. Free flowering, midsummer to early autumn. In cultivation 1900.
♇ 1993
C. **'Margot Koster'** (V) A delightful clematis with flowers deep rose pink, up to 10cm (4in) across, with up to six reflexed sepals. Midsummer to early autumn.
C. **'Marie Boisselot'** (P) Large flowers, up to 20cm (8in) wide, pure white, with cream stamens and broad, rounded, overlapping sepals. Vigorous and free-flowering. Late spring to mid-autumn. In cultivation 1900.
♇ 1993

Clematis 'Miss Bateman'

C. **'Miss Bateman'** (P) White flowers, 15cm wide, banded with pale green when first open. Late spring to early summer. In cultivation 1869.
♇ 1993
C. **'Mrs Cholmondeley'** (J) Pale blue flowers up to 20cm (8in) wide with long-pointed sepals. Vigorous and free-flowering, late spring to late summer.
♇ 1993
C. **'Mrs George Jackman'** (P) White flowers, up to 18cm (7in) wide, with broad, overlapping petals. It is similar to 'Marie Boisselot' but the sepals have a cream bar and the darker anthers are more prominent. Late spring/early summer and early autumn. In cultivation 1873.
♇ 1993
C. **'Mrs N. Thompson'** (P) Violet flowers

up to 12cm (5in) across, with a scarlet bar. Late spring/early summer and early autumn. In cultivation 1961.

C. **'Multi-Blue'** (P/L) Deep violet-blue, fully double flowers with a centre of blue and white staminodes. Late spring/early summer and again in autumn.

Clematis 'Nelly Moser'

C. **'Nelly Moser'** (L) One of the most popular clematis of all. Large, pale mauve-pink flowers up to 20cm (8in) across, each sepal with a carmine central bar. Very free-flowering but best on a north-facing wall or other shady position in order to prevent bleaching. Late spring/early summer and again in late summer/early autumn. In cultivation 1897.
♔ 1993

Clematis 'Niobe'

C. **'Niobe'** (J) The best red. Deep red flowers up to 15cm (6in) wide, with yellow anthers. In cultivation 1975.
♔ 1993

C. **'Perle d'Azur'** (J) Light blue flowers with broad sepals account for this plant's popularity. Vigorous and free-flowering early to late summer. In cultivation 1885.
♔ 1993

C. **'Pink Champagne'** (P) Large, rich pink flowers in early summer.

C. **'Polish Spirit'** (V) A fast-growing viticella bearing rich purple flowers with deep red stamens from July to November. It requires hard pruning.
♔ 1993

C. **'Proteus'** (F) Deep mauve-pink flowers up to 15cm (6in) wide, double with many sepals. The later flowers are single. Early summer and early autumn.

C. **'Richard Pennell'** (P) Lavender flowers flushed with white, up to 20cm (8in) across, with wavy-margined sepals, red stamen filaments and cream anthers. Late spring/early summer and again in early autumn. In cultivation 1974.
♔ 1993

Clematis 'Rouge Cardinal'

C. **'Rouge Cardinal'** (J) Crimson velvet flowers, up to 15cm (6in) wide, with brown anthers. Early to late summer. In cultivation 1968.

C. **'Royalty'** (P) A vigorous and compact plant with double flowers, single in autumn. Similar to 'Vyvyan Pennell' but darker blue-purple.
♔ 1993

C. **'Silver Moon'** (L) A vigorous and bushy plant with large, pale lavender flowers borne over a long period. Good on a north-facing wall.
♔ 1993

C. **'Star of India'** (J) Red-purple flowers becoming violet-purple with a redder central bar, up to 16cm (6in) across, with broad sepals. Early summer to early autumn.
♔ 1993

C. **'Sylvia Denny'** (F) Pure white, semi-double, rosette-like flowers with pink stamens in late spring and summer.

Clematis 'The President'

C. **'The President'** (P) A popular clematis with deep purple blue flowers that are silver on the reverse and measure 18cm (7in) across. Free-flowering from early summer to early autumn.
♔ 1993

C. **'Venosa Violacea'** (V) A very distinct hybrid of *C. viticella* which develops flowers up to 10cm (4in) wide. They have 5–6 boat-shaped sepals, a white centre, and are veined and edged with purple. The anthers are blackish purple. Early summer to early autumn. In cultivation 1910.
♔ 1993

Clematis 'Victoria'

C. **'Victoria'** (J) Rose-purple flowers with three darker ribs on each sepal, up to 15cm (6in) wide, with white stamens. Vigorous and free-flowering, blooms are borne from early summer to early autumn.
C. **'Ville de Lyon'** (V) Bright carmine-red flowers, deeper at the margins, with golden stamens. Midsummer to mid-autumn.
C. **'Vyvyan Pennell'** (P) Its raisers describe it as the best double clematis. The flowers are deep violet-blue, suffused with purple and carmine in the centre, to 15cm (6in) wide, fully double and produced from late spring to midsummer. In autumn, single, lavender-blue flowers are produced. In cultivation 1959.
♛ 1993
C. **'Wada's Primrose'** (P) Pale creamy yellow flowers, best in shade.Late spring and early summer. In cultivation 1979.
C. **'Will Goodwin'** (P) Large, pale lavender flowers with broad, overlapping, wavy-edged sepals and a centre of golden stamens. Late spring to early autumn.
♛ 1993
C. **'William Kennet'** (L) Lavender-blue flowers with dark stamens, and sepals with crimped margins. Early to late summer.

Clerodendrum *Verbenaceae*

A large genus of about 400 species of deciduous trees, shrubs and climbers with opposite leaves and showy flowers. They are found mainly in tropical regions and, apart from the hardy species, many are grown for greenhouse decoration. They will grow in sun or shade and in any well-drained friable soil.

Clerodendrum bungei

C. **bungei** A remarkable, suckering shrub of medium height that makes a thicket of dark-coloured, erect stems that bear large, heart-shaped leaves and large, terminal flowerheads. These are borne from late summer to early autumn and consist of fragrant rosy-red flowers which, superficially, look something like those of a mophead hydrangea. The plant grows and flowers well in the shade of large shrubs or trees. In contrast to the sweet scent of the flowers, the leaves are foetid when disturbed so the plant requires careful siting. China. Introduced 1844 by Robert Fortune.
H4 ♛ 1993

Clerodendrum trichotomum var. fargesii

C. **trichotomum** var. **fargesii** A strong-growing, large shrub that comes into its own in late summer and early autumn with its very fragrant white flowers, enclosed in maroon calyces, which are followed by bright blue berries that look like jewels in the contrasting setting of the persistent calyces. This variety flowers with greater freedom than the species, but shares its tendency to succumb to unusually cold winters and so requires careful siting. W China. Introduced 1898 by Père Farges.
H4 ♛ 1993

Clethra *Clethraceae*

This genus is now considered to include around 60 species of evergreen and deciduous shrubs and trees native to the southern United States, Central and South America, South-East Asia and Madeira. Their flowers are small, white and fragrant, and are produced in long clusters from mid- to late

summer. Several of them have attractive, peeling bark and all require a lime-free soil. Although routine pruning is not required, the older wood of established shrubs can be thinned out to improve their shape and, particularly with C. alnifolia, any growths from the base can be removed in the winter. Really old specimens can be renewed by cutting them back hard in spring and then feeding.

Clethra alnifolia

C. **alnifolia** (Sweet pepper bush) A deciduous shrub seldom more than 2m (6½ft) tall with white or nearly white flowers borne in erect, terminal panicles in late summer. The following forms are recommended. E North America. Introduced 1731.
H4
C. a. **'Paniculata'** A superior small to medium-sized form, recommended for planting in preference to the species.
H4 ♛ 1993
C. a. **'Rosea'** Also recommended in preference to the species, this lovely small to medium-sized clone has glossy leaves and

Clethra barbinervis

buds and flowers tinged pink. 'Pink Spire' is similar. Introduced 1906.
H4

C. barbinervis A handsome, medium-sized deciduous species with long racemes of fragrant white flowers and leaves that turn red and yellow in autumn. Japan. Introduced 1870.
H4 ♛ 1993

C. delavayi A magnificent large deciduous shrub of great beauty, needing a sheltered site. Its long, broad, many-flowered racemes of white, lily-of-the-valley-like flowers are borne at the ends of branchlets all over the plant and, instead of being erect, take up a more or less horizontal position. In milder areas it is damaged only by the most severe frosts, but it is not hardy everywhere. W China. Introduced 1913.
H3 ♛ 1993

C. fargesii A very beautiful deciduous species about 2.5m (8ft) tall that produces pure white, fragrant flowers in panicles up to 25cm (10in) long in midsummer. Its leaves turn rich yellow in autumn. C China. Introduced 1900 by Ernest Wilson.
H4

Cleyera *Theaceae*

A genus of around 18 species of evergreen trees and shrubs, mostly from Mexico and Central America but with one species in eastern Asia.

Cleyera japonica 'Tricolor'

C. japonica 'Tricolor' A slow-growing shrub, eventually about 3m (10ft) high, with its branches rigidly spreading and densely leafy. The foliage is shining dark green,

marbled grey, and has a cream margin that is flushed deep rose when the leaves are young. In favoured places it is a most attractive shrub. Japan. Introduced 1861.
H3

Clianthus *Leguminosae*

A genus of two species of semi-evergreen shrubs, of which the species described requires a hot, sunny position in a well-drained soil. Pruning may be carried out in early summer when flowering finishes and is mainly a matter of removing any dead wood and preventing the plant from shading itself too much, thus inhibiting flowering.

C. puniceus (Lobster claw, parrot's bill) A vigorous semi-evergreen shrub with climbing stems. It is medium-sized and has attractive pinnate leaves 8–15cm (3–6in) long, composed of 11–25 oblong leaflets. The claw-like flowers, which are really very large, long, pointed pea flowers, are brilliant red and carried in bright, showy clus-

ters during early summer. When grown outside it succeeds best against a warm, sunny wall, but this is only possible in the mildest areas; elsewhere, it is ideal as a dramatic conservatory shrub. Extremely rare in the wild. North Island of New Zealand. Introduced 1831.
H2 ♛ 1993

C. p. 'Albus' This medium-sized form has

Clianthus puniceus 'Albus'

Clianthus puniceus

white flowers with a slight green tint.
H2 ♛ 1993

***C. p.* 'Flamingo'** A medium-sized shrub with deep rose pink flowers.
H2

***C. p.* 'White Heron'** This medium-sized cultivar has pure white flowers, delicately flushed with green.
H2

Colletia *Rhamnaceae*

A genus of five species of deciduous shrubs native to southern South America. Those described are very distinct among cultivated plants in being entirely or almost leafless and bearing very prominent spines. The attractive, small, honey-scented flowers are usually produced in late summer and autumn. Pruning is not for the faint-hearted but luckily is seldom necessary, apart from tip-pinching young plants to promote bushiness. Up to a point, the poorer the soil, the hardier they are and the sunnier their position, the more profusely they flower.

C. armata See *C. hystrix.*
C. cruciata See *C. paradoxa*

Colletia armata

C. hystrix, syn. *C. armata* This robust shrub up to 2.5m (8ft), has strong, stout, rounded spines. In late summer and autumn the branches are crowded with small, fragrant, pitcher-shaped white flowers. Chile, N Argentina. Introduced c1882.
H3–4

***C. h.* 'Rosea'** A delightful medium-sized shrub with white flowers pink in bud.
H3–4

Colletia hystrix 'Rosea'

C. paradoxa, syn. *C. cruciata* A remarkable, rather slow-growing medium-sized shrub, with branchlets transformed into formidable, flat, triangular spines making it a suitable boundary plant. It is covered with small, white, pitcher-shaped flowers in late summer and early autumn. E Argentina, Uruguay, S Brazil. Introduced 1824.
H3–4

Colquhounia *Labiatae*

A genus of three species of evergreen sub-shrubs from the Himalaya and South-East Asia. They will grow in any well-drained friable soil.

Colquhounia coccinea

C. coccinea A showy, medium-sized shrub with large, downy leaves and scarlet, tubular flowers borne in autumn. It needs a sunny site, preferably against a wall, where it will reach a height of 2.5m (8ft). It is occasionally cut back by sharp frost but usually shoots again in early summer, although it

cannot be grown outdoors in really cold areas. Himalaya. Introduced before 1850.
H3 ♛ 1993

Colutea *Leguminosae*
Bladder senna

A genus of around 25 species of deciduous shrubs, ranging from southern Europe to North Africa and the western Himalayas. They are easily grown shrubs with pinnate leaves and eye-catching pea flowers throughout the summer, and are made distinct by their inflated seed pods. Prune hard in early spring if they are getting in the way of other plants or generally becoming out of hand, although in poorish soils this is unlikely to happen.

Colutea arborescens

C. arborescens A vigorous shrub up to 4m (12ft) high with yellow flowers. British gardeners may sometimes see it naturalized on railway embankments. Mediterranean region. Introduced in the sixteenth century.
H4

***C. × media* 'Copper Beauty'** A strong-growing, medium-sized shrub with blue-green leaves and an abundance of bright orange flowers.
H4

Comptonia *Myricaceae*

A genus of only one deciduous species, related to and once included in Myrica.

C. peregrina (Sweet fern) A small, suckering, aromatic shrub with downy stems rather like the fronds of a small spleenwort fern, and small, glistening, brown catkins in spring. It requires a lime-free soil and is best in full sun provided the soil is sufficiently moisture retentive. E North America. Introduced 1714.

H4

Convolvulus *Convolvulaceae*

This genus is widely distributed, mainly in temperate regions and with many of the 200 species occurring in the Mediterranean area. It is probably best known for its many trailing perennials, but there are also several evergreen and deciduous shrubby species.

Convolvulus cneorum

C. cneorum A very beautiful, evergreen, rock-garden shrub with silvery, silky leaves and large, pale pink and white, funnel-shaped flowers borne mainly in late spring, although if the plant is well suited they may be produced off and on for several months. Flowering and hardiness are greatly enhanced in a gritty, really well-drained soil and in a site which gets full sun. SE Europe. In cultivation 1640.

H3 ♛ 1993

Coprosma *Rubiaceae*

A genus of around 90 species of evergreen shrubs or small trees, mainly from New Zealand. Flowers are small but fruits are attractive.

C. × kirkii 'Variegata' A pretty dwarf spreading shrub. The small, narrow leaves are pale green with white margins. It is good ground cover in mild areas.

H2–3

Cordyline *Agavaceae*

A genus of 15 species of evergreen trees and shrubs native to New Zealand, Australia, India, South America and Polynesia.

Cordyline australis

C. australis (New Zealand cabbage tree) A small to medium-sized tree, usually forming a single trunk, and bearing several stout, ascending branches, each one crowned with a large, dense mass of long, sword-like leaves. The flowers are small, creamy white and fragrant, and are produced in large terminal panicles in early summer. It makes a striking feature in gardens in mild areas, although its survival may even so depend on small variations in temperature and wind direction in winter. New Zealand. Introduced 1823.

H3 ♛ 1993

C. a. 'Purpurea' A small to medium-sized tree with purple leaves.

H3

C. a. 'Red Star' A selected purple-leaved form with deeply coloured foliage.

H3

C. a. 'Sundance' A small tree bearing yellow leaves with midribs and bases attractively flushed deep pink.

H3

C. a. 'Torbay Dazzler' A small form with leaves margined with creamy white.

H3

Coriaria *Coriariaceae*

An interesting genus, of which about 80 species in all are now recognized, including some deciduous, shrubby members suitable for cool-temperate gardens. Their foliage is frond-like and the flower petals, borne in late spring, persist, becoming thick and fleshy, to enclose the fruits in autumn. They will grow in any well-drained friable soil.

Coriaria japonica

C. japonica A pleasing, small, low-growing shrub with arching stems, making good ground cover. Eye-catching red fruits and good autumn foliage which is attractively tinted. Japan. Introduced before 1893.

H4

C. myrtifolia A graceful shrub up to 1.5m (5ft) tall with four-angled, curving branches and glistening black fruits. Both the leaves and fruits of this plant are poisonous. Mediterranean region. Introduced 1629.

H4

C. terminalis var. **xanthocarpa** An attractive, small sub-shrub with frond-like leaves that give rich autumn colours. Its fruits are translucent yellow. Sikkim, E Nepal.

H4

CORNUS

Cornaceae Cornel, dogwood

Cornus alba 'Sibirica'

THIS IS A GENUS of some 50 mainly deciduous species, ranging from creeping ground cover to beautiful trees and shrubs, collectively called dogwoods. Perhaps they should not be, as the word derives from the use made, centuries ago, of the tough, hard wood of the cornelian cherry, *Cornus mas*, a species that has been in cultivation in Europe for centuries. It was used for making small domestic tools and also for daggers. The wood was called dag-wood, which in turn became dogwood as its origin faded from memory. Parkinson, who wrote in 1640 that the name originated because the berries were not fit to be given to a dog, was romancing a little.

Cornus, however, is a genus with a distribution far wider than Europe, and includes species with great differences in their structure and appearance. Botanists have from time to time advocated that it be divided into up to four new genera, one of which would have included just *C. mas* and its close relative *C. officinalis*, shrubs with winter flowers on the bare branches and red, cherry-like fruits. Another that was proposed consisted of the group that includes shrubs making thickets of brilliantly coloured stems, often osier-like and happy in wet places, and sometimes bearing handsomely variegated foliage. This would have taken in the magnificent *C. controversa*, the slow-growing, variegated form of which is one of the best trees of all for small gardens.

FLOWERING DOGWOODS

Perhaps the showiest and most captivating dogwoods of all are the species that some botanists would distinguish because of the beautiful floral bracts that surround and support their otherwise inconspicuous, tight heads of minute, dark flowers. These, and their hybrids and cultivars, are among the most beautiful of all garden shrubs and trees, flowering in late spring and summer and then providing in many cases a feast of scintillating autumn colour.

This group comes from North America and the Far East, and its members vary considerably in their suitability for gardens in differing climates. *C. kousa*, for example, is a better garden plant in Britain and Ireland than the American *C. florida*, *C. nuttallii* and their hybrids, whereas they in turn are naturally suited to American gardens.

Hybrids between these two species are some of the best of all, especially the renowned 'Eddie's White Wonder', one of a superb series raised by the Eddie nursery in British Columbia, several of which were tragically lost in a flood.

If only the sumptuous *C. capitata* had the hardiness of its fellow-asiatic *C. kousa*, it would be one of the wonders of cool-temperate gardens, like large, billowing cushions of green embroidered with a lacework of bright creamy yellow. Nevertheless, it is capable of growing to a large size and flowering regularly and abundantly – in mild areas, certainly, where gardens may be frost-bitten but never frost-bound.

Cornus alba

Cornus capitata

C. alba (Red-barked dogwood). This well-known deciduous species, succeeding in wet or dry soils, forms a thicket of stems up to 3m (10ft) high, with the young branches glowing rich red in winter and the leaves colouring well in autumn. The fruits, when borne, are white to light blue. Siberia to Manchuria, N Korea. Introduced 1741. H4

Cornus alba 'Aurea'

GROWING DOGWOODS

The thicket-making species that are mainly grown for their beautifully coloured stems – C. alba, sanguinea, stolonifera and others – can be grown in just about any soil, no matter whether it is poor, thin, shallow, chalky, dry or wet. C. mas and C. officinalis are very nearly as tolerant, drawing the line only at wet soils, but in general all of them are plants for places where the rich soil is better appreciated by others. While all these shrubs are happiest in full sun, they will also tolerate some shade, although under these conditions the colours of the stems might not be as bright.

Those grown for their coloured stems give the best displays if they are pruned hard back every year to within a few inches of the ground, or at least every other year, in early spring. If this is not done, the result tends to be a somewhat straggly clump of woody stems of indeterminate colour, with short, brilliantly but apparently anomalously coloured branchlets sprouting here and there. Proper pruning should produce a fairly dense thicket of whippy, upright, evenly bright stems.

The remainder of the genus are best grown on a deeper, neutral to acid soil as, while not precisely lime-hating, they thrive less as the soil becomes more alkaline or shallow over limestone or chalk. As a great deal of their beauty is in their form – some have gracefully drooping branches, while others are horizontally tiered – they should always be placed, and above all spaced, with a good deal of care. Shaping by pruning should be hardly necessary, unless in the very early years, and apart from that they should be left unpruned and certainly never subjected to the stooling process meted out to those above.

Although the bract-forming species and hybrids from America and the asiatic C. capitata present difficulties in some climatic conditions – the former in climates with cool summers and the latter where winters are less than mild – you should not think of them as particularly tricky. It is true that the wetter and more equably cool the climate the worse the American species will do, but the converse also applies, and they react favourably to quite small increases in overall sunshine and warmth.

C. a. 'Aurea' A charming medium-sized form with leaves suffused with soft yellow. H4

C. a. 'Elegantissima' The leaves of this medium-sized shrub are broadly margined and mottled with white. 'Sibirica Variegata' is similar. In cultivation 1900. H4 ♈ 1993

C. a. 'Gouchaltii' Although often confused with 'Spaethii', the leaves of this medium-sized shrub are dull by comparison, with a pink tinge. In cultivation 1888. H4

Cornus alba 'Elegantissima'

C. a. 'Kesselringii' The stems of this very striking medium-sized shrub are almost black-purple making the plant a suitable winter focal point. The leaves open brown. In cultivation 1907.
H4

C. a. 'Sibirica', syn. *C. a.* 'Westonbirt' This is less robust than some other forms, but is nevertheless an excellent medium-

sized shrub with brilliant coral-crimson winter shoots.
H4 ♔ 1993

Cornus alba 'Sibirica Variegata'

C. a. 'Sibirica Variegata' A medium-sized shrub with leaves with a broad, creamy white margin turning interesting shades in autumn. The winter shoots are deep red. It is similar to 'Elegantissima' but

not as vigorous and therefore more useful in the smaller garden.
H4

C. a. 'Spaethii' A superb medium-sized shrub with conspicuously golden-variegated leaves.
H4 ♔ 1993

C. a. 'Westonbirt' See *C. a.* 'Sibirica'.

C. alternifolia A large deciduous shrub or occasionally a small tree, with horizontally spreading branches. The leaves are alternate and give rich autumn tints in a good season. The following form is recommended as particularly rewarding. E North America. Introduced 1760.
H4

Cornus alternifolia 'Argentea'

C. a. 'Argentea', syn. *C. a.* 'Variegata' This is one of the best of all silver-variegated shrubs, forming a bush about 2.5–3m (8–10ft) high. Its leaves are small with a regular, creamy white margin.
H4 ♔ 1993

C. a. 'Variegata' See *C. a.* 'Argentea'.

C. amomum A medium-sized shrub notable for its blue fruits and purple winter shoots. The leaves turn red in autumn. E North America. Introduced 1683.
H4

C. 'Ascona' *(C. florida × C. nuttallii)* A wide-spreading, large deciduous shrub. The flowerheads are freely borne in mid-spring even when the shrub is young and measure, with their four-pointed white bracts, up to 7.5cm (3in) across. The leaves colour well in autumn.
H4

C. canadensis (Creeping dogwood) This is

Cornus alba 'Gouchaltii'

not strictly a shrub but a herbaceous perennial with a creeping, woody rootstock and annually renewed, 15 cm (6in) shoots that form attractive carpets, starred in summer with white flowers that are succeeded by tight heads of vivid red fruits. It does best in a sandy but peaty or leafy soil in light shade. North America. Introduced 1774.
H4 ♛ 1993

C. capitata In the mildest gardens this beautiful, evergreen species is a small tree. From early to midsummer, the button-like flowerheads are surrounded by lovely, sulphur-yellow bracts, which are followed in autumn by large fruits that look just like very large raspberries. Himalaya, China. Introduced 1825.
H3

Cornus controversa

Cornus controversa 'Variegata'

C. controversa A magnificent medium-sized or large deciduous tree with alternate leaves and sweeping, layered branches clothed in late spring with broad, flat clus-

ters of cream-coloured flowers. In autumn, small black fruits are produced and at the same time the foliage often turns rich purple-red. Japan, China, Taiwan. Introduced before 1880.
H4

C. c. 'Variegata' One of the best and most ornamental of small trees. It has the same horizontal, tiered branching as the species but is considerably slower growing and has narrower, more pointed leaves, variegated with silver margins. In cultivation 1890.
H4 ♛ 1993

C. 'Eddie's White Wonder' *(C. florida ×* *C. nuttallii)* A superb large deciduous shrub or small tree of compact, upright habit. Flowering is in spring, and the rounded bracts that surround the flowerheads give the appearance of perfectly round, white flowers wreathing the branches. The leaves colour brilliant orange in autumn. The expectations of its American raisers have been more than fulfilled, and it is reliable as well as ornamentally first-rate.
H4 ♛ 1993

C. florida (Eastern dogwood, flowering dogwood) This large deciduous shrub or small tree, usually represented in gardens by its cultivars, has its flowerbuds enclosed during winter by bracts which enlarge and turn white, so that each button-like flowerhead has four showy, petal-like bracts in late spring. The leaves turn orange or red in autumn, sometimes with a violet flush. It does not succeed on shallow soils over chalk. The following forms are recommended. E United States. In cultivation 1730.
H4

Cornus florida 'Cherokee Chief'

C. f. 'Cherokee Chief' A large shrub or small tree with bracts of a bright, deep rose-red. In cultivation 1958.
H4 AGM 1993

C. f. 'Cloud Nine' A cultivar with large, showy white bracts, free flowering even when young.
H4

C. f. 'First Lady' This plant is considered by many to be an improvement on 'Rainbow', with leaves which are variegated with yellow.
H4

Cornus florida 'Rainbow'

C. f. 'Rainbow' A large shrub or small tree with a dense, upright habit and leaves margined with deep yellow, turning in autumn to deep red-purple margined with scarlet. The bracts are large and white. In cultivation 1967.
H4

C. f. Rubra Group These are large shrubs or small trees in which the bracts are pink

Cornus florida Rubra Group

to red; they may be offered for sale as *C. f.* 'Rubra'. The best and most beautiful forms should have fully rosy-pink – not washed-out pink – bracts and the young leaves are usually reddish (see 'Cherokee Chief'). In cultivation 1889.
H4

C. f. **'Tricolor'** See *C. f.* 'Welchii'.

C. f. **'Welchii'**, syn. *C. f.* 'Tricolor' A superb but slow-growing, medium-sized variegated shrub whose green leaves have an irregular, creamy white margin, flushed rose, and turning to bronze-purple edged with rosy red in autumn.
H4

C. f. **'White Cloud'** This large shrub or small tree has bronze young foliage in the spring and is notable for its freedom of flowering and the whiteness of its large floral bracts. In cultivation 1946.
H4

C. kousa A large, elegant deciduous shrub or small tree. The abundant flowers, of which the white bracts are the showy part, are poised on slender, erect stalks covering the spreading branches in early summer, and are followed by fruits like small strawberries. The leaves turn rich bronze and crimson in autumn. Not recommended for shallow chalk soils. Japan, Korea. Introduced 1875.
H4

Cornus mas

Cornus kousa var. chinensis

C. k. **var. *chinensis*** This is the more usually grown form. It is taller, more open, slightly larger-leaved and if anything more beautiful. China. Introduced 1907.
H4 ♔ 1993

C. k. **'Gold Star'** This large shrub or small tree has leaves with a large central blotch of golden yellow. In autumn the centre turns red and the margin of the leaf, purple. Introduced 1977.
H4

C. k. **'Satomi'** A recently introduced Japanese selection with pink bracts and leaves that turn deep purple-red in autumn. It makes a large shrub or small tree.
H4 ♔ 1993

C. k. **'Snowboy'** A form that has turned out to be a great disappointment. Although young plants look attractive with their grey-green, broadly white-margined leaves, they grow very weakly and sometimes hardly at all. It can make a large shrub or small tree. In cultivation before 1977.
H4

C. mas (Cornelian cherry) A large shrub or small, densely branched deciduous tree that produces an abundance of small yellow flowers on the naked twigs in late winter. These are followed by bright red, cherry-

Cornus mas flower detail

like, edible fruits. The leaves turn reddish-purple in autumn. C and S Europe. Long cultivated.
H4 ♔ 1993

C. m. **'Aurea'** A large shrub with leaves suffused yellow. In cultivation 1895.
H4

C. m. **'Aurea Elegantissima'**, syn. *C. m.* 'Tricolor' A notably slow-growing medium-sized shrub with leaves variegated yellow and flushed with pink. Shelter from strong sun. Originated c1869.

H4

C. m. 'Tricolor' See *C. m.* 'Aurea Elegantissima'.

Cornus mas 'Variegata'

C. m. 'Variegata' An outstanding, variegated, free-fruiting large shrub or small tree with its leaves brightly margined with white. In cultivation 1838.

H4 🏆 1993

Cornus 'Norman Hadden'

C. 'Norman Hadden' *(C. kousa × C. capitata)* A beautiful, graceful, spreading, small deciduous tree that develops peeling bark with age. The small flowerheads have four taper-pointed, creamy white bracts that open in early summer and turn deep pink about a month later. Large crops of long-lasting, strawberry-like fruits are borne in autumn. In mild areas the foliage is retained until spring; where it is colder,

some leaves may persist over winter while others turn red and fall. It is a seedling that arose in the garden of Norman Hadden near Porlock, Somerset, England, in the late 1960s. See also 'Porlock'.

H4 🏆 1993

Cornus nuttallii

C. nuttallii (Western dogwood) A noble medium-sized deciduous tree. Its flowers appear in late spring, often after a few have expanded in autumn, and the heads are furnished usually with six large, white floral bracts that sometimes become flushed with pink. The flowerheads are not enclosed by bracts in winter; the foliage turns yellow or sometimes red in autumn. It is not recommended for poor, shallow, chalk soils. Be sure to obtain the true species from the nursery, as many plants have turned out to be hybrids with *C. florida.* W North America. Introduced 1835.

H4

C. n. 'Colrigo Giant' A vigorous large

Cornus nuttallii 'Colrigo Giant'

shrub or medium-sized tree with large leaves and very large flowerheads up to 15cm (6in) across the bracts, and an upright habit. It was found in the Columbia river gorge after which it is named.

H4

C. n. 'Gold Spot' A large shrub with its leaves splashed, spotted and mottled yellow; perhaps the same as *C. n.* 'Eddiei'. This plant sometimes produces many of its flowers in autumn.

H4

C. n. 'North Star' A large shrub or medium-sized tree with strong, vigorous growth, dark purple young shoots and large flowerheads.

H4

Cornus nuttallii 'Portlemouth'

C. n. 'Portlemouth' A large shrub or medium-sized tree selected for its large bracts and good autumn colour.

H4

C. officinalis A large deciduous shrub or

Cornus officinalis

small tree with attractive, peeling bark and clusters of yellow flowers on the naked twigs in late winter. It bears red fruits and rich autumn leaf colour. Closely related to *C. mas*, it is coarser and earlier flowering, and the individual flowers have longer stalks. Japan, Korea. Introduced c1870.
H4

Cornus 'Ormonde'

C. 'Ormonde' *(C. florida × C. nuttallii)* A large deciduous shrub similar to 'Eddie's White Wonder' but of a spreading habit. The large white bracts have pink tips. It flowers in mid-spring. Its origin is unknown, but it grew at Kew Gardens for many years as *C. nuttallii*.
H4

C. 'Porlock' A small, spreading, beautiful deciduous tree similar, if not just about identical, to 'Norman Hadden'. It, too, occurred as a seedling in Norman Hadden's Somerset garden, but in 1958.
H4 ♔ 1993

Cornus sanguinea 'Winter Beauty'

C. sanguinea 'Winter Beauty', syn. *C. s.* 'Winter Flame' A striking Dutch selection of the European common dogwood, a deciduous species with greenish, red-flushed stems and rich purple autumn colour. In this medium-sized shrub the stems are bright orange-yellow and red in winter, the autumn colour is orange-yellow, and the habit is compact. 'Midwinter Fire' is very similar, if not the same clone.
H4

C. s. 'Winter Flame' See *C. s.* 'Winter Beauty'.

Cornus stolonifera 'White Gold'

C. stolonifera A rampant, suckering deciduous shrub with vigorous shoots up to 2.5m (8ft) which, in suitable situations, forms a dense °thicket of dark red stems. The fruits are white. The following forms are recommended. North America. Introduced 1656.
H4

C. s. 'Flaviramea' A highly effective

Cornus stolonifera 'Flaviramea'

medium-sized winter shrub with ochre-yellow to olive-green young shoots, particularly dramatic when planted with the red-stemmed dogwoods and ideal for moist or wet places. In cultivation 1899.
H4 ♔ 1993

C. s. 'Kelsey Dwarf' See 'Kelseyi'.

Cornus stolonifera 'Kelseyi'

C. s. 'Kelseyi', syn. *C. s.* 'Kelsey Dwarf' A somewhat unexciting, dwarf, dense form, with small, crowded leaves and yellowish green winter shoots, red towards the tips.
H4

C. s. 'White Gold', syn. *C. s.* 'White Spot' The leaves of this medium-sized shrub have a white margin, resembling those of *C. alba* 'Elegantissima'.
H4

C. s. 'White Spot' See *C. s.* 'White Gold'.

Corokia *Cornaceae*

A genus of three species of interesting, evergreen shrubs or small trees native to New Zealand. In mild areas, the cultivated species make medium-sized to large shrubs with small, starry, yellow flowers and often very showy red or orange fruits. They will grow in any well-drained friable soil. Pruning is not necessary.

C. cotoneaster (Wire-netting bush) A curiously attractive, small to medium-sized shrub, with a tortuous, tangled tracery of wiry stems that looks rather like crumpled wire netting. It has sparse foliage, tiny yellow flowers in late spring, and orange fruits. Introduced 1875. North and South Islands.
H3

Corokia × virgata

C. × virgata A medium-sized, erect shrub with sparse leaves that are white beneath and broadest above the middle. It bears its mid-spring yellow flowers and bright orange fruits freely. The following forms are grown much more frequently and make excellent and unusual hedges in mild places. Introduced 1907.

Corokia × virgata 'Red Wonder'

C. × v. 'Red Wonder' A medium-sized shrub with masses of deep red berries. H3

C. × v. 'Yellow Wonder' This cultivar is similar to 'Red Wonder' but more vigorous, and with larger leaves and equally profuse, bright yellow fruits. H3

Coronilla *Leguminosae*

A genus of about 55 species of evergreen and deciduous shrubs and herbaceous plants with pinnate leaves, native to central and southern

Europe, the Mediterranean, Africa, northern Asia and China. Those described are free-flowering shrubs, grown for their umbels of bright yellow, fragrant pea flowers that are often produced right through the growing season. Light, well-drained soils in full sun are preferred. In late winter, dead or weak growth can be pruned away, and old specimens whose flowering is declining can be renewed by being cut back to near ground level.

Coronilla emereus

C. emerus (Scorpion senna) A hardy, medium-sized, elegant deciduous shrub with clusters of yellow flowers in the leaf axils and seedpods that are like a scorpion's tail. C and S Europe. Long cultivated. H4

Coronilla valentina

C. valentina A small evergreen shrub with slightly bloomy leaves and rich yellow, scented flowers. The forms described below are the ones most usually grown. Mediterranean region. In cultivation 1596. H2–3

Coronilla valentina subsp. glauca

C. v. subsp. glauca A small to medium-sized shrub suitable for growing against a warm wall or in a sheltered position. It has bloomy leaves and masses of rich yellow flowers with a scent of peaches. Its main burst of flower is in mid-spring, but it carries on intermittently throughout most of the year. S Europe. Introduced 1722. H2–3 ♛ 1993

Coronilla valentina 'Citrina'

C. v. 'Citrina' A small to medium-sized form with lemon-yellow flowers. H2–3 ♛ 1993

C. v. 'Variegata' A small form of subsp. *glauca* with leaves prettily variegated with creamy white. H3

Correa *Rutaceae*

A small genus of about 10 species of evergreen shrubs, native to Australia and Tasmania and suitable only for mild gardens or greenhouse cultivation. The attractive, showy and usually bell-shaped flowers are regularly and abundantly produced in late winter under glass. They enjoy a well-drained, preferably sandy soil and can be pruned after flowering to keep them neat.

C. backhousiana Capable of becoming a medium-sized shrub, this species bears clusters of drooping, tubular, greenish white flowers. Tasmania.
H2 ♔ 1993

C. 'Harrisii' See *C.* 'Mannii'.

C. 'Mannii', syn. *C.* 'Harrisii' A beautiful, early-flowering, small hybrid shrub with rose-scarlet flowers about 2.5cm (1in) long.
H2 ♔ 1993

Corylopsis *Hamamelidaceae*

A genus of seven species of deciduous shrubs from the eastern Himalayas, China and Japan. They are easily grown, exquisitely beautiful and should be much more widely planted. Just before the leaves appear in spring, the plants are bedecked with drooping catkins of fragrant, primrose-yellow, cup-shaped flowers. They thrive on acid or neutral soil and, with the exception of C. pauciflora, *will grow indefinitely in chalk soil as long as there is a minimum depth of 60cm (2ft). They are hardy, but at the limit of their hardiness (about −15°C/59°F) they may need protection from cold, drying winds which can cause dieback. Prune only to remove dead wood.*

Corylopsis glabrescens

C. glabrescens A wide-spreading, medium-sized to large shrub with rounded leaves that are slightly bloomy on their

undersides. The primrose-yellow flowers are freely borne in slender tassels. Japan. Introduced 1905.
H4

C. gotoana For the plant previously named *C. gotoana*, see *C. sinensis* var. *calvescens*.

Corylopsis pauciflora

C. pauciflora A densely branched shrub with slender stems, slowly growing to 2m (6½ft) high and wide. The rounded, bristle-toothed leaves, 4–6cm (1½–2½in) long, are the smallest in the genus and are pink when young. The flowers are primrose-yellow, cowslip scented, and borne in short tassels of two or three blooms each, opening in early spring, usually before the other species. It requires an acid soil. Japan, Taiwan. Introduced c1860 by Robert Fortune.
H4 ♔ 1993

Corylopsis sinensis

C. sinensis A large shrub or small tree 4-5m (12-15ft) tall with slightly bloomy leaves that are densely downy on their undersides.

The flowers are lemon-yellow. C and W China. Introduced c1901.
H4

C. var. calvescens This large shrub differs from the species mainly in the characteristics of its leaves, which may be considerably larger and more rounded, smooth and sometimes chalk-white on the undersides, and pink-flushed when young. W China. Introduced 1907.
H4

Corylopsis spicata

C. spicata A spreading, hazel-like, medium-sized shrub with soft down on the young shoots and the undersides of the leaves. The flowers, borne in spring, are in rather narrow clusters about 15cm (6in) long, with long, bright yellow petals and dark purple anthers. Japan. Introduced c1860 by Robert Fortune.
H4

Corylopsis veitchiana

C. veitchiana A very distinct, large, erect-

growing shrub with characteristically elongated, bright green leaves, edged with incurved teeth and purplish when young. The primrose-yellow flowers have conspicuous, brick-red anthers and are borne in large racemes. W China. Introduced 1900 by Ernest Wilson.
H4 ♔ 1993

Corylopsis willmottiae

C. willmottiae A medium-sized to large shrub with variable leaves, generally purple or reddish purple when young. The flowers are soft yellow and borne in dense, showy racemes. Fruits are glabrous. W. China. Introduced 1909 by Ernest Wilson.
H4 ♔ 1993

Corylopsis willmottiae 'Spring Purple'

C. w. 'Spring Purple' This garden-worthy plant is a medium-sized to large shrub with most attractive, plum-purple young growths. Raised at Hillier Nurseries before 1969.
H4

Corylus avellana 'Contorta'

Corylus *Betulaceae*
Hazel

A genus of around 10 species of deciduous large shrubs or small trees from temperate regions of the northern hemisphere. Their flowers are borne in catkins, the males of which are pendulous and elongate to make an endearing feature in late winter and early spring. The female catkins are

Corylus avellana

little tufts of bright red stigmas. Many hazels are grown for their edible nuts, while others are purely ornamental. They do well in almost any garden soil, especially loams, and are excellent on chalk. Most can be pruned regularly to prevent their becoming too large.

C. avellana (Cobnut, European hazel) A large shrub or small, many-stemmed tree, impressive when draped with its long, yellow lamb's tails in late winter. It is useful in larger gardens as a tall, screening shrub. The leaves turn yellow in autumn. Europe, W Asia, North Africa.
H4

C. a. 'Aurea' A large shrub or small tree with soft yellow leaves, excellent when used to contrast with *C. maxima* 'Purpurea'. In cultivation 1864.
H4

C. a. 'Contorta' (Corkscrew hazel) The branches of this shrub are curiously twisted in spirals and it is slow growing, eventually reaching about 3m (10ft). In order to create

a strong garden feature rather than an unattractive tangle, it should be pruned to a few main stems so that their sinuous twists, which can make a most interesting architectural focal point, can be outlined clearly. Its winter catkins play their part, too. Discovered c1863 in a hedgerow in Gloucestershire, England.
H4 ♔ 1993

Corylus colurna

C. colurna (Turkish hazel) A remarkable, large tree of very symmetrical, pyramidal form, with striking, corky furrows in the bark that make an attractive feature. It is the only commonly grown hazel with a straight, single trunk. SE Europe, W Asia. Introduced 1582.
H4 ♔ 1993

C. maxima **'Purpurea'** (Purple-leaved filbert) A large shrub grown for its large, rounded, purple leaves that rival the purple beech in the intensity of their colouring.
H4 ♔ 1993

Cotinus *Anacardiaceae*
Smoke tree

A genus of three species that used to be included in Rhus, *and are among the most attractive of the large summer-flowering shrubs. They are deciduous and come from a wide range of habitats in the temperate parts of the northern hemisphere. Grown mainly for their fine autumn effects, they are content in any well-drained soil in full sun – too rich a diet can inhibit the development of autumn colours and make the shrubs too coarse and sappy. Prune only to remove dead wood or, in spring, to shorten any growths that have become too long.*

Cotinus coggygria

C. coggygria (Smoke tree, Venetian sumach) This species grows to 2.5–4m (8–12ft) and has smooth, rounded, green leaves that colour well in autumn. The fawn-coloured, plume-like inflorescences, 15–20cm (6–8in) long, which are borne in profusion from early to midsummer, are persistent and by late summer will have turned smoky-grey. Europe to the Himalaya, China. In cultivation 1656.
H4 ♔ 1993

C. c. **'Atropurpureus'** See *C. c.* f. *purpureus.*

Cotinus coggygria 'Foliis Purpureis'

C. c. **'Foliis Purpureis'**, syn. *C. c.* 'Rubrifolius' The leaves of this medium-sized shrub, especially when young, are rich plum-purple, changing to light red shades in autumn.
H4

C. c. f. *purpureus*, syn. *C. c.* 'Atropurpureus' (Burning bush) In this medium-sized shrub it is the large panicles of purplish grey flowers, which from a distance resemble puffs of pink smoke, to which the common name refers. The leaves are green and colour well in autumn.
H4

Cotinus coggygria 'Royal Purple'

C. c. **'Royal Purple'** A selected form with deep wine-purple leaves, translucent in sunshine and with the colour reddening as autumn approaches. It makes a medium-sized shrub. 'Notcutt's Variety' is similar.
H4 ♔ 1993

C. c. **'Rubrifolius'** See *C. c.* 'Foliis Purpureis'.

Cotinus coggygria 'Velvet Cloak'

C. c. **'Velvet Cloak'** The leaves of this medium-sized shrub are deep red-purple, almost black in some lights, and retain their colour well into autumn, when they eventually turn red. Found as a seedling in the United States before 1962.
H4

C. **'Flame'** A large shrub resembling *C.*

Cotinus 'Flame'

Cotinus obovatus

C. adpressus A dwarf, wide-spreading deciduous shrub, a gem for the larger rock garden, with white flowers, bright red fruits and small, wavy-edged leaves that turn scarlet in autumn. Interesting all the year round. W China. Introduced 1896. H4 ♛ 1993

C. a. var. *praecox* See *C. nanshan*.

Cotoneaster amoenus

coggygria but more vigorous and tree-like, with larger leaves in younger plants or on strongly growing shoots. Its autumn colour is truly splendid, with the leaves turning brilliant orange-red before they fall. Large, pink flower clusters are borne in summer. Almost certainly a hybrid between *C. coggygria* and *C. obovatus*.
H4 ♛ 1993

Cotinus 'Grace'

C. **'Grace'** *(C. obovatus* × *C. coggygria* 'Velvet Cloak', Dummer Hybrids)* A vigorous, tall shrub with large, soft purplish red leaves that turn scarlet in autumn, and large, conical, purplish pink flower clusters in summer. Raised late 1970s by Hillier Nurseries' propagator, Peter Dummer, as part of the series from the same cross known as Dummer Hybrids.
H4 ♛ 1993

C. obovatus (Chittamwood) A rare large shrub or small tree which, in favourable seasons and situations, is one of the most

brilliantly coloured of autumn shrubs. Its leaves are much larger than those of *C. coggygria* and turn to shades of orange, red and purple. SE United States. Introduced 1882.
H4 ♛ 1993

Cotoneaster *Rosaceae*

Botanical authorities vary in their estimate of how many species there are in this far-flung and indispensable genus of ornamental shrubs. Some would say there are about 200, others twice that many, while still more reduce the genus to just 70 species. Whatever the case may be, cotoneasters range from prostrate mats to small trees, most of which are deciduous, though some are evergreen. Their great variety of habit makes them suitable for many purposes in the garden, from hedging and border plants to specimen and wall shrubs, ground cover, and even for quite modest rock gardens. They are grown chiefly for their brilliant autumn colour and bright, showy berries, although their white or pink-tinged flowers often smother the branches in early summer and are very attractive to bees.

Cotoneasters will grow in almost any soil, but will not tolerate a bog or bad drainage. They can be grown in sun or part shade, though the best ornamental results are often obtained in full sun. They are hardy shrubs and tolerate quite severe levels of atmospheric pollution.

Pruning requirements vary but are essentially a matter of removing dead wood and branches that are growing in unwanted directions, although old, overgrown shrubs can be renewal pruned by cutting them hard back in late winter. This is also the time for trimming cotoneaster hedges informally.

Cotoneasters are, unfortunately, highly susceptible to fireblight.

C. amoenus A pretty, semi-evergreen shrub resembling *C. franchetii* but with smaller leaves and of a more compact, bushy habit. The fruits are bright red and the flowers white. Yunnan Province, China. Introduced 1899 by Ernest Wilson.
H4

Cotoneaster bullatus

C. bullatus A large deciduous shrub with broad, handsome, noticeably corrugated leaves that colour richly in autumn, white flowers and clusters of large, bright red fruits early in the season. One of the finest species in cultivation. See also *C. rehderi*. W

China. Introduced 1898.
H4 ⚲ 1993

C. cashmiriensis A prostrate evergreen shrub making a low mound with small, glossy dark green leaves. White flowers are followed by small, bright red berries. It makes good ground cover and will tumble over a rock or low wall. This plant is also sometimes grown as *C. mircrophyllus* var. *cochleatus*. Kashmir.
H4 ⚲ 1993

C. cavei A small, semi-evergreen, thicket-forming shrub with red shoots and rounded, glossy dark green leaves. White flowers tinged with pink are followed by bright red berries which persist for a long period during autumn and winter. Himalayas, W China.
H4

Cotoneaster cochleatus

Cotoneaster congestus

C. cochleatus This charming, slow-growing, prostrate evergreen shrub is related to *C. microphyllus*, but with paler,

duller green, broader leaves. It has small, bright red berries and white flowers. W China, SE Tibet, E Nepal.
H4

C. congestus A dense-habited, creeping evergreen shrub, forming a series of mole-hill-like mounds of small, bluish green leaves. It is mentioned here mainly as a warning that it does not bear its red fruits at all freely. The form described here is often referred to as 'Nanus'. Introduced 1868.
H4

Cotoneaster conspicuus in flower

Cotoneaster conspicuus in fruit

C. conspicuus **'Decorus'** A free-fruiting, low-growing but widely spreading evergreen shrub which is ideal for covering banks. Its white flowers cover the plant in early summer and are followed by large numbers of bright red berries that persist for many months. Although the name is not botanically accurate, it is the one universally used in gardens.
H4 ⚲ 1993

C. **'Coral Beauty'** A very dense, small evergreen shrub with arching branches. The leaves are glossy green, ovate-elliptic, and up to 2cm (³⁄₄in) long. White flowers are followed in autumn by abundantly borne bright orange-red berries. It makes excellent ground cover, and is sometimes available as a small, top-worked, weeping tree. In cultivation 1967.
H4

Cotoneaster 'Cornubia'

C. **'Cornubia'** A vigorous semi-evergreen shrub growing to 6m (20ft) or more. Among the tall-growing cotoneasters its red fruits are probably the largest, and are borne so profusely after the white flowers that they weigh down the branches. It is often available as a standard tree. Raised at Exbury, Hampshire, England, 1930.
H4 ⚲ 1993

C. dammeri A prostrate evergreen shrub with long, trailing shoots studded in autumn with fruits of sealing-wax red, following generously borne, white flowers with purple anthers. The leaves are oval or obovate, prominently veined and 2.5–4cm (1–1¹⁄₂in) long. It is an ideal shrub for covering banks and as ground cover beneath other shrubs. See also *C. radicans*. China. Introduced 1900 by Ernest Wilson.
H4 ⚲ 1993

C. divaricatus A medium-sized deciduous shrub, one of the best and most reliable for autumn fruits and foliage. The berries are dark red and the flowers a bright, rosy red. Excellent for hedging. W China. Introduced 1904 by Ernest Wilson.
H4

C. **'Exburiensis'** A large deciduous shrub with white flowers followed by apricot-yellow fruits that become pink-tinged in winter. Almost identical to 'Rothschildianus'. Raised 1930 at Exbury.
H4

Cotoneaster franchetii

C. **franchetii** A very graceful, medium-sized, semi-evergreen shrub, with sage-green foliage. The flowers are white, with erect petals that become flushed with pink and are succeeded by ovoid, orange-scarlet fruits. One of the most popular species. China. Introduced 1895.
H4

C. **frigidus** The true plant, which is a variable, fast-growing, large deciduous shrub or small spreading tree with large, broad elliptic, magnolia-like leaves and large, heavy clusters of orange to crimson fruits in autumn and throughout the winter, is now seldom seen, and *C. frigidus* of the trade is a form of the Watereri group of hybrids. Himalayas. Introduced 1824.
H4

C. **glabratus** A medium-sized evergreen shrub with purple arching shoots and glossy dark green leaves, blue-white beneath, becoming purple-tinged in winter. The white flowers are followed by small, bright red fruits in broad clusters. W China. Introduced 1906 by Ernest Wilson.
H4

C. **'Gnom'** A dwarf, evergreen shrub with slender, purplish, arching shoots making a low, wide mound. The leaves are lance-shaped, up to 3 × 1cm (about 1 × ½in), glossy dark green and bronze-tinged in win-

ter. It makes excellent ground cover despite the fact that the small, bright red berries that ripen in late autumn following the white flowers are not freely borne. Raised c1938 in Germany.
H4

C. **hjelmqvistii** This recently described deciduous species is, in effect, a large version of *C. horizontalis*, with which it has been confused. It makes a small, spreading shrub with arching branches and glossy green leaves which turn red in autumn. White flowers tinged with pink are followed by red berries. W China.
H4

Cotoneaster horizontalis

C. **horizontalis** A low-growing deciduous shrub of spreading habit, with branches of characteristically herringbone pattern, invaluable for shady walls or covering banks. The flowers are red with white stamens, the fruit are orange-red, and the foliage becomes richly coloured in autumn.

Cotoneaster horizontalis 'Variegatus'

W China. Introduced c1870 by Père David.
H4 ♔ 1993

C. h. **'Variegatus'** This prostrate form is especially pleasing in the autumn, when the small, cream-margined leaves are suffused with red. In cultivation 1922.
H4 ♔ 1993

C. **'Hybridus Pendulus'** A very striking evergreen or semi-evergreen with glossy leaves, white flowers and long, prostrate branches that carry an abundance of brilliant red fruits in autumn and winter. When grown on a stem it makes an attractive small weeping tree. Bush specimens are very prone to fireblight, standards less so. Garden origin.
H4

Cotoneaster hylmoei

C. **hylmoei** A medium-sized evergreen shrub with arching branches, related to *C. salicifolius* but with broader, darker leaves that are deeply veined above and white-woolly beneath. The white flowers are larger and pink in the bud, and the fruits persist for a long time on the branches. One of the most ornamental species.
H4

C. **integrifolius** A dwarf, mound-forming evergreen shrub with small, glossy dark green leaves. The small white flowers are followed by relatively large deep reddish pink fruits. It is commonly grown as *C. microphyllus* and is useful for ground cover and for growing over low walls. Himalayas, W China. Introduced 1824.
H4 ♔ 1993

C. **lacteus** A medium-sized, evergreen shrub with large, oval, leathery leaves that

Cotoneaster lacteus

Cotoneaster nanshan

Cotoneaster 'Pink Champagne'

are grey-woolly beneath and quite unlike any other species. The flowers are milky white and followed by red fruits that are rather small but carried in broad clusters, ripening late in the year and lasting well into midwinter. China. Introduced 1913 by George Forrest.
H4 ♔ 1993

C. meiophyllus A medium-sized ever-

Cotoneaster microphyllus

green shrub with oval leaves that are blue-white beneath. White flowers are followed by small red berries which ripen late in autumn and persist providing colour throughout winter. This species is frequently grown as *C. serotinus*. China.
H4 ♔ 1993

C. microphyllus A dwarf, stiffly branched, spreading evergreen shrub forming a low mound. The leaves are more or less elliptic, usually less than 1cm (½in) long, and rounded or notched at the apex. Tiny, white flowers are succeeded by small, deep reddish pink berries. Several other plants are grown under this name (see *C. cashmiriensis* and *C. integrifolius*). Himalayas.
H4 ♔ 1993

C. nanshan A vigorous, dwarf to small deciduous shrub with arching branches, related to *C. adpressus* but growing up to 1m (3ft) high and 2m (6½ft) across and with larger leaves. The flowers are pink, the fruits extra large and orange-red, and the autumn colour red. It was previously grown

as *C. adpressus* var. *praecox*. W China. Introduced 1905.
H4

C. 'Pink Champagne' A large, vigorous, dense-growing deciduous shrub with slender, arching branches and narrow leaves. The white flowers with a pink tinge are insignificant. The fruits are small but plentifully produced, at first creamy yellow and then becoming tinged with pink.
H4

C. radicans A prostrate evergreen shrub related to *C. dammeri*, with which it is sometimes confused. Its leaves, however, are smaller and longer stalked without the deep veins of *C. dammeri*, and its white flowers are usually in pairs instead of solitary. The berries are bright red. *C. dammeri* 'Oakwood' and 'Eichholz' are very similar if not identical. China.
H4

C. rehderi A very handsome, medium-

Cotoneaster rehderi

sized to large deciduous shrub of open habit, with large, dark green, deeply veined leaves. White flowers with a rosy flush are followed by a profusion of deep red berries. It is often listed as a form of *C. bullatus*. W China. H4

C. 'Rothschildianus' A large deciduous shrub with a distinctive, spreading habit

Cotoneaster 'Rothschildianus'

Cotoneaster salicifolius

when young. Large, creamy yellow fruits follow the white flowers, and a mature shrub fully laden with the almost luminescent berries is a fine sight. Similar to 'Exburiensis', both being raised at Exbury, Hampshire, England.
H4 ♔ 1993

C. salicifolius A tall, variable, evergreen shrub, bearing heavy crops of red fruits in autumn and parent of many hybrids. Unfortunately, it and its varieties and cultivars are very susceptible to fireblight. See *C. hymoei*. China. Introduced 1908.
H4

Cotoneaster serotinus

C. serotinus A vigorous deciduous shrub up to 5m (15ft) tall or more, with blue-green, oval to elliptic leaves that are woolly beneath. It bears its white flowers in great numbers in midsummer, and it is early winter before the berries take on their red colour. See also *C. meiophyllus*. W China. Introduced 1907 by George Forrest.
H4

C. simonsii A well-known, erectly growing, semi-evergreen medium-sized shrub, much used in plantations and for hedges, and given to seeding itself around. The flowers are white with pink stamens and the fruits are large and scarlet. Himalaya. Introduced 1865.
H4 ♔ 1993

C. 'Skogholm' A dwarf evergreen shrub of wide, spreading habit, with small leaves and tear-drop, coral-red berries in autumn that are not, however, freely produced. The white flowers with a pink tinge borne in spring are insignificant. A hybrid of *C.*

dammeri, selected 1941.
H4

C. splendens A handsome deciduous species up to 2m (6½ft) tall. The arching shoots, with small, greyish green, rounded leaves, are studded with large, bright orange fruits in autumn, following pink flowers with red margins. The seedling 'Sabrina' appears identical. Introduced 1934.
♔ 1993 H4

Cotoneaster sternianus

C. sternianus An excellent medium-sized shrub of arching habit that is more or less evergreen and one of the best of all cotoneasters. It has sage-green leaves with silvery white undersides, pink flowers and large, round but slightly flattened, bright orange-red berries produced in very large numbers. A rewarding garden plant. S Tibet, N Burma. Introduced 1913.
H4 ♔ 1993

C. × watereri A group of variable, semi-evergreen, complex hybrids. All of them are hardy, medium-sized to large shrubs or occasionally small trees of strong, vigorous growth, with long leaves and heavy crops of fruits that are normally red or orange-red. The white flowers with a pink tinge are insignificant. In the trade they tend to stand in for *C. frigidus*, which was but one of the several parents of the cross. There are many named clones.
H4

C. × w. 'John Waterer' A large, semi-evergreen shrub with long, spreading branches laden with bunches of red fruits in autumn. In cultivation 1928.
H4 ♔ 1993

Crataegus *Rosaceae*
Hawthorn, thorn

These are among the hardiest and most adaptable of deciduous trees and are found throughout the temperate parts of the northern hemisphere. Although until quite recently there were thought to be as many as 1000 species from North America alone, many of them are now regarded as hybrids or forms of variable species, and the true number in the genus may now be between 100 and 200.

They are grown for their impenetrability as hedges, for their flowers, which are usually white but may be pink or red and sometimes double, and for their berries, which are usually red but sometimes yellow and occasionally blue or black. The flowers are intensely fragrant, but it is a scent that is not found pleasant by everyone. Many will grow where there is industrial pollution, salt-laden seaside gales, limy soils, drought and even a degree of waterlogging, but generally any reasonable soil will suit them, preferably in full sun.

Any pruning should be done after flowering; hedges that are intended to bear flowers and fruits should also be trimmed after flowering, but only then. An annual trim is sufficient.

Crataegus crus-galli

C. crus-galli (Cockspur thorn) This widespreading small tree, with thorns up to 8cm (3in) long, has attractive leaves, white, pink-tinged flowers in late spring and long-lasting berries, but is often confused with *C. prunifolia*. E and C North America. Introduced 1691.
H4

C. durobrivensis A large shrub, and one of the most ornamental of the North American thorns, with white flowers that are

Crataegus durobrivensis

probably the largest in the genus and open from late spring to early summer, followed by large red fruits that remain until midwinter. New York State. Introduced 1901.
H4

C. × grignonensis A small tree, late in bearing its white flowers and in ripening its large, bright red, grey-speckled fruits. The leaves remain green until winter. Introduced c1873.
H4

Crataegus laciniata

C. laciniata, syn. *C. orientalis* A beautiful, small, not very thorny tree with deeply cut, downy leaves that are dark green above and grey beneath. The flowers are white and borne in clusters of 12 or more in late spring, and the fruits are large and coral-red or yellowish red. SE Europe to SW Asia. Introduced 1810.
H4

C. laevigata, syn. *C. oxyacantha* The clones described below, often listed under this

species, are more probably hybrids between it and *C. monogyna*; both species are also known by the common name, English hawthorn. They are all large shrubs or small trees and are very showy when covered with flowers in late spring. Europe.
H4

Crataegus laevigata 'Paul's Scarlet'

C. l. 'Paul's Scarlet' A sport of 'Rosea Flore Pleno' with double scarlet flowers and deep red fruits. Introduced 1858.
H4 ♛ 1993

C. l. 'Plena' A form with double white flowers and deep red fruits. In cultivation 1770.
H4

C. l. 'Punicea' This form has single scarlet flowers with a pronounced white eye and deep red fruits. This is the same plant as 'Crimson Cloud'. In cultivation 1828.
H4

Crataegus laevigata 'Rosea Flore Pleno'

C. l. 'Rosea Flore Pleno' An attractive

Crataegus laevigata 'Punicea'

form with double pink flowers.
H4 ♛ 1993

C. × lavallei 'Carrièrei' A small, dense-headed tree, distinguished by its long, glossy, dark green leaves that often remain until midwinter. The flowers are white with pink anthers and the berries are orange-red, persist throughout the winter, and are very colourful against the dark foliage. Garden origin c1870.
H4 ♛ 1993

C. mollis (Red haw) One of the best of the American species, forming a wide-spreading tree 10–12m (30–50ft) tall, with downy leaves, white flowers, and showy fruits like red cherries carried in large clusters. C United States. Long cultivated.
H4

Crataegus monogyna

C. monogyna (Common hawthorn, may, quick) In Britain, this is a familiar native, grown for hedges throughout the country and called 'may' because of its spectacular

flowering in late spring, when a tree in full flower is the equal of any other species. In autumn the branches are often laden with red fruits (haws), and the flowers are white and strongly fragrant. It makes a large shrub or small tree. It is a bad fireblight host, but if hedges are kept trimmed, thereby removing the flowering wood, it should not occur. Europe, North Africa, W Asia.
H4

C. m. 'Biflora' (Glastonbury thorn) This medium-sized or large shrub (occasionally a tree) produces leaves earlier than normal and occasionally an early crop of white flowers in winter, but these are smaller than in those that flower in late spring. The fruits are dark red. In cultivation 1770.
H4

C. m. 'Stricta' An excellent, tough, small tree, with erect branches, which is particularly suited to exposed places.
H4

C. m. 'Variegata' The leaves of this large shrub or small tree are splashed and mottled with creamy white.
H4

C. orientalis See *C. laciniata*.

C. oxyacantha See *C. laevigata*.

Crataegus phaenopyrum

C. phaenopyrum (Washington thorn) A striking, round-headed, slender tree. To 10m (30ft). It has glossy, maple-like leaves that turn bright orange in autumn. White flowers with pink anthers precede a profusion of small, dark crimson, long-lasting fruits. SE United States. Introduced 1738.
H4

C. pinnatifida var. major One of the most ornamental of the thorns, with large, conspicuously lobed leaves, white flowers with pink anthers, and glossy, crimson fruits almost 2.5cm (1in) across. It is among the best small trees for rich red autumn colour. N China. In cultivation 1880.
H4

Crataegus prunifolia

C. prunifolia An excellent small, compact, broad-headed tree notable for its persistent, showy fruit, which are green flushed with purple, then becoming dark red and glossy. The flowers are white with red anthers, and the tree provides rich autumn colour. Origin unknown: possibly a hybrid between two North American species. In cultivation 1797.
H4 ♛ 1993

C. tanacetifolia (Tansy-leaved thorn) A small, usually thornless, slow-growing tree with grey, downy leaves, fragrant white flowers with red anthers, and fruit which are like small yellow apples. Asia Minor. Introduced 1789.
H4

Crinodendron *Elaeocarpaceae*

Both species of this evergreen genus come from Chile, and one in particular is of the greatest value for gardens in milder areas. Crinodendrons require lime-free soil, partial shade and protection from wind. No pruning is necessary.

C. hookerianum (Chilean lantern tree) This shrub is one of the shining gems of the mild garden. The flowers, like long-stalked,

Crinodendron hookerianum

Cryptomeria japonica

Cryptomeria japonica 'Bandai-Sugi'

Cryptomeria japonica 'Compressa'

Cryptomeria japonica 'Elegans'

crimson lanterns, hang thickly along the branches in late spring to early summer and contrast beautifully with the dark green foliage. It is a large, dense shrub that can sometimes withstand surprisingly low temperatures. Chile. Introduced 1848 by William Lobb.

♔ 1993 H3 LS E A

C. patagua A strongly growing large shrub or small tree with white, slightly fragrant, bell-shaped flowers in late summer. It is not as hardy as the above species and requires wall protection or a conservatory. It can be a disappointment and may even err on the dull side. Chile. Introduced 1901.

H2–3

Cryptomeria *Taxodiaceae*

A genus of one evergreen coniferous species.

C. japonica (Japanese cedar). A large, fast-growing, broadly columnar tree with reddish, shredding bark and spreading or decurved branches. The leaves are awl-shaped and densely crowded on the long, slender branchlets. In some ways it resembles the Wellingtonia (*Sequoiadendron giganteum*) but its leaves are longer and the bark does not have the spongy thickness of the American tree. It is easily cultivated and thrives best in moist soils. Japan (var. *japonica*, China (var. *chinensis*). Introduced 1842.

H4 ♔ 1993

C. j. 'Bandai-Sugi' A small, slow-growing, compact bush that becomes more irregular in old age. The foliage is in congested, moss-like clusters with intermittent normal growth, turning bronze in very cold weather. In cultivation 1939.

H4 ♔ 1993

C. j. 'Compressa' This is a very slow-growing, dwarf bush, and is similar to 'Vilmoriniana', forming a compact, rather flat-topped globe. The foliage, which is densely crowded, turns reddish purple in winter. It is eminently suitable for a rock garden or scree.

H4

C. j. 'Elegans' A beautiful, tall, bushy form that eventually makes a small tree. The soft, feathery, juvenile foliage is retained throughout life and turns to an attractive red-bronze in autumn and winter. Introduced 1854 by Thomas Lobb.

H4

C. j. 'Elegans Compacta' A slower-growing, smaller shrub than 'Elegans', with even softer, more feathery foliage, forming a medium-sized, billowy bush. The leaves turn an attractive rich purple in winter. In cultivation 1881.

H4 ♔ 1993

C. j. 'Elegans Nana' A very dense, slow-growing small shrub with juvenile foliage that turns bronze in winter. The foliage is fairly stiff to the touch. In cultivation 1923.

H4

Cryptomeria japonica 'Elegans Nana'

C. j. 'Lobbii' A most desirable, medium-sized to large, conical tree, differing from the type in its longer branchlets that are more clustered at the ends of the shorter branches. The leaves are deep, rich green and more adpressed to the shoots. Introduced c1850 by Thomas Lobb.
H4

C. j. 'Nana' A small, slow-growing, compact bush with slender branchlets that end in recurved tips. In cultivation 1850.
H4

Cryptomeria japonica 'Sekkan-Sugi'

C. j. 'Sekkan-Sugi' A small tree with pale creamy yellow young foliage. It is liable to burn in full sun. Introduced 1930.
H4

C. j. 'Spiralis' (Grannies' ringlets) Although this can very occasionally grow to be a large tree, it is usually a small to medium-sized, slow-growing bush of dense, spreading habit with the leaves spirally twisted round the stem. The whole plant is

Cryptomeria japonica 'Vilmoriniana'

a pleasant bright green. Introduced 1860.
H4

C. j. 'Vilmoriniana' An exceedingly slow-growing dwarf bush with very small, crowded branchlets and leaves, forming a dense globe that turns reddish purple in winter. It is one of the most popular dwarf conifers for the rock garden, very similar to 'Compressa', but with leaves a little shorter and more congested on the branchlets. A specimen at the Hillier Gardens and Arboretum reached 0.6 × 1m (2 × 3 ft) in about 30 years. Raised 1890 in France by M. de Vilmorin.
H4 ♔ 1993

Cunninghamia *Taxodiaceae*

A small genus of probably just two species of very distinct evergreen coniferous trees that recall Araucaria. They are fairly hardy but thrive best in a sheltered position in a mild area. The whorled branches are densely clothed with spirally arranged

Cunninghamia lanceolata

leaves that are twisted so as to seem to be organized in two ranks.

C. lanceolata (Chinese fir) A small to medium-sized, exotic-looking tree. The lance-shaped leaves, 3–7cm (1¼–3in) long, are irregularly arranged, emerald- to blue-green above with two white bands beneath. They become dark and bronzed by autumn. Not for a windswept site. China. Introduced 1804 by William Kerr.
H3–4

× Cupressocyparis *Cupressaceae*

These interesting hybrids between Cupressus *and* Chamaecyparis *have all arisen in cultivation. They are extremely fast-growing evergreen trees with many uses and are by far the most commonly planted conifers. They need much the same conditions as* Chamaecyparis.

× C. leylandii (*Cupressus macrocarpa* × *Chamaecyparis nootkatensis*) (Leyland cypress) A large, noble, extremely vigorous, densely columnar tree. The foliage is in flattened or irregular, slightly drooping sprays and in general the tree looks more like its *Chamaecyparis* parent. In Britain at least it is the fastest growing conifer and also, with the exception of some eucalypts, the fastest growing evergreen. Even on poor sites plants have reached a height of 15m (50ft) in 16 years from cuttings. It is unsurpassed for tall screens but is generally too vigorous for hedging in the small garden. When trimming it is important to avoid cutting into any but the young growth. It is tolerant

× Cupressocyparis leylandii 'Castlewellan Gold'

of a wide range of conditions including coastal areas and chalk soils. May cause skin allergy.

H4

× *C. l.* **'Castlewellan Gold'** The young foliage is golden yellow on small plants and tends to become bronze-green with age. It can make a large tree, but is slower growing and more suitable for hedging than the green forms. Raised 1962 at Castlewellan, Co Down.

H4

× *Cupressocyparis leylandii*

× *C. l.* **'Gold Rider'** A large tree with yellow foliage, this is the best form.
H4 ⬛ 1993

× *C. l.* **'Haggerston Grey'** A large and common clone in cultivation, whose foliage is green or has a slight pale grey cast, arranged in dense, irregular sprays. Raised 1888 at Leighton Hall, Powys, Wales.
H4 ⬛ 1993

× *C. l.* **'Hyde Hall'** This dwarf cultivar is often recommended for small gardens but is not a good plant.
H4

× *C. l.* **'Robinson's Gold'** Similar to 'Castlewellan Gold' but of a better colour. Raised c1962 at Belvoir Castle, Co Down.
H4 ⬛ 1993

× *C. l.* **'Silver Dust'** The foliage of this large tree is conspicuously blotched with cream. Introduced 1966.
H4

× *Cupressocyparis notabilis*

× *C.* **notabilis** *(Chamaecyparis nootkatensis × Cupressus glabra)* An attractive, medium-sized tree with sinuous, upswept branches draped with flattened sprays of dark grey-green foliage. The crown is broader and more open than that of × *C. leylandii*. Raised 1956 by the Forestry Commission.
H4 ⬛ 1993

Cupressus *Cupressaceae*
Cypress

A genus of around 20 species of evergreen coniferous trees, mostly of conical or columnar habit. The globular cones become woody and often remain on the trees for several years. Cypresses do not take kindly to clipping and thus do not make good hedges. They are on the whole less hardy than Chamaecyparis. *They do not transplant easily, which is why young trees are always pot-grown. They tolerate a wide range of soils with the exception of wet ones, and several species will grow well even in shallow chalk soils.*

Cupressus cashmeriana

C. cashmeriana (Kashmir cypress) One of the most graceful and beautiful of all conifers, making a small to medium-sized tree of conical habit. The branches are ascending and draped with long, pendulous branchlets. The foliage is blue-grey and arranged in flattened sprays. This conifer will grow out of doors in the mildest areas and elsewhere is a fine specimen for a large conservatory. Its exact origin is unknown, but some authorities consider it a form of *C. torulosa*, a species from the Himalaya. It is quite possible that it does not come from Kashmir at all. Introduced 1862.
H2 ⬛ 1993

Cupressus glabra

Cupressus glabra

C. glabra (Smooth Arizona cypress) A small to medium-sized tree with attractive peeling, red bark and greyish green or grey foliage. It is common in cultivation but usually grown under the name *C. arizonica*, which is a rarer species with green foliage and less attractive bark. Some authorities now classify it as *C. arizonica* var. *glabra*. The

Cupressus glabra 'Aurea'

following forms are recommended. Introduced 1907.
H4

C. g. 'Aurea' A broadly conical small to medium-sized tree with leaves suffused with yellow in summer, paling towards winter. Raised 1957 in Australia.
H4

C. g. 'Blue Ice' A small, slow-growing, conical tree with striking blue-grey foliage. Originated c1984 in New Zealand.
H4

C. g. 'Pyramidalis' A dense, compact, conical tree of medium size, with blue-grey foliage. In late winter the branches are dotted with yellow male cones. It is one of the best formal blue conifers in cultivation. In cultivation 1928.
H4 ♀ 1993

C. lusitanica (Mexican cypress) A medium to large, graceful tree with rich brown, peeling bark. The branches are spreading, with pendulous branchlets and greyish green foliage. Although surprisingly hardy, it cannot be recommended for cold areas. NE Mexico, Guatemala, Honduras. In cultivation 1682.
H3

C. l. 'Glauca Pendula' A beautiful form, selected by Edwin Hillier, with a spreading crown and graceful, drooping, glaucous blue branchlets. It makes a small, wide-spreading tree. In cultivation 1925.
H3

Cupressus macrocarpa

C. macrocarpa (Monterey cypress) A popular, very fast-growing tree of medium to large size, conical or broadly columnar

when young, becoming broad-crowned with age and resembling a Lebanon Cedar. The foliage is bright green, in densely packed sprays. It is a valuable shelter tree in coastal districts but young plants are subject to damage in cold areas. The forms with yellow foliage colour best in open positions and become green in shade. California. Introduced c1838.
H3–4

C. m. 'Donard Gold' A conical or broadly columnar tree of medium size. The foliage is rich, deep golden yellow and is an improvement on 'Lutea'. Raised 1935 in the Slieve Donard Nursery.
H3 ♀ 1993

Cupressus macrocarpa 'Goldcrest'

C. m. 'Goldcrest' This is a medium-sized, narrowly columnar, dense, compact tree and has rich yellow, feathery juvenile foliage. It is one of the best of its colour. Raised c1948 by Messrs Treseder of Truro, Cornwall.
H3 ♀ 1993

C. m. 'Golden Pillar' A small, narrow tree with golden yellow foliage. Raised before 1955 in Holland.
H3

C. m. 'Gold Spread' A very distinct and ornamental, compact, wide-spreading form about 1m (3ft) tall, with bright golden yellow foliage. It is excellent ground cover except in the coldest areas.
H3–4 ♀ 1993

C. m. 'Lutea' A tall tree with yellow foliage that turns green. Now superseded by 'Donard Gold'. In cultivation before 1893.
H3–4

Cupressus sempervirens 'Green Pencil'

C. m. 'Wilma' A small, narrow tree with bright yellow spring and summer foliage. H3

C. sempervirens (Italian cypress) A medium-sized, narrowly columnar tree with steeply ascending branches and dark green foliage. It is familiar in the Mediterranean region and young plants are susceptible to injury in cold areas. This form, sometimes known as 'Fastigiata' or 'Stricta', is unknown in the wild. H3 ♛ 1993

C. s. 'Green Pencil' A very slender, medium-sized form with bright green foliage. Hardier than most *sempervirens* forms. It was selected at Hillier Nurseries. The original plant in the Hillier Gardens and Arboretum was 10.5m (32ft) high and only 80cm (32in) wide in 1990. H3–4

Cupressus sempervirens 'Swane's Golden'

C. s. 'Swane's Golden' A compact, columnar form with gold-tinted foliage. It is one of the best medium-sized golden conifers for the small garden. H3 ♛ 1993

Cyathodes *Epicradaceae*

A genus of around 15 species of heather-like evergreen shrubs from New Zealand and Australia with tiny, white, pitcher-shaped flowers in spring and very attractive foliage. These shrubs require a lime-free soil with some shelter and are especially suitable for rock gardens.

C. colensoi A small, decumbent, sometimes prostrate shrub with narrow, unstalked glaucous leaves and white or red fruits. It is a beautiful small shrub and proving quite hardy. New Zealand. H3

Cydonia *Rosaceae*
Quince

A genus of one deciduous species that is a small to medium-sized tree with attractive fruits and related to Chaenomeles.

Cydonia oblonga

Fruit of Cydonia oblonga

C. oblonga (Common quince) Native, unarmed tree up to 6m (18ft) high.
C. oblonga 'Vranja' A named clone of the common quince, forming a small, picturesque lawn tree and selected for its well-flavoured, fragrant, large golden fruits, highly prized in the kitchen. The flowers are white. H4 ♛ 1993

Cytisus & Genista

Leguminoseae Broom

GARDENERS, generally speaking, know a broom when they see one. They expect a whippily branched shrub with apparently few leaves and branchlets that themselves may be green, lending an evergreen appearance even to the deciduous species. Brooms have pea-like flowers, usually but not invariably yellow, and they may be anything from prostrate mats to medium-sized shrubs or even small trees.

Botanists, however, distinguish between two main broom genera – *Cytisus* (preferably pronounced 'sitissus') and *Genista*. They do this on grounds that might seem piffling – a minute but constant difference in the seed and in the notching of the calyx – but it is not for them to retreat from proper knowledge, and these two genera are truly different from one another. On the other hand, they are alike enough for gardeners to think of them together.

There are about 50 species of *Cytisus* and 80 of *Genista*, and their wild distribution is very roughly the same, with brooms of both genera found in Europe, western Asia and North Africa. While what a gardener might recognize as the 'typical' broom characteristics are found throughout the range, occasionally a shrub of such idiosyncratic appearance occurs that it is hard to guess its identity. One such is the stunning *Cytisus battandieri*, a native of North Africa with quite broad, trifoliate leaves of a lustrous and intense silveriness and large, packed heads of brilliantly summer-yellow flowers whose delectable scent of pineapples gives it the common name of pineapple broom. In complete contradistinction is *Genista aetnensis*, an entirely leafless small tree with branches like whipcord and massed yellow flowers in summer. Because it occurs on the slopes of Sicily's famous volcano (among other places) it is called the Mount Etna broom.

Cytisus × beanii

Their wide range of sizes and forms means that the brooms are highly versatile. There are several that are neat enough for a small rock garden, a few that will be unlikely to become too large for a trough, some that need to be kept in bounds even in a large garden, and still others that are ideal for short-term planting in new gardens where some initial height and quick flowering are required.

CARE AND CULTIVATION

Members of both genera are tolerant of a wide range of soils. Dry, poor, stony soils, gravels and clays are all the same to them, although *Cytisus* will not succeed on poor, shallow soils over chalk (soft limestone) and, strangely enough, fails on those that are excessively acid. Both genera, on the other hand, may be thought of as lime tolerant as long as the soil is reasonably deep.

Pruning is slightly tricky. Where *Genista* species depend for much of their attractiveness on their shape or characteristics such as elegance (*G. aetnensis* is a good example), pruning should be avoided, although training to establish a good stem is sometimes necessary. Other *Genista* species and cultivars can be tipped back each year in order to preserve bushiness, but never cut into the old wood. As far as *Cytisus* goes, the rules are the same, although those that flower on the wood of the previous year – most of them, in fact – should have that wood cut back by a little more than half after flowering. The great exception is *C. battandieri*, which benefits greatly from renewal pruning every few years. This means cutting back deeply into the old wood, in which are buds that rapidly renew the shrub, reducing legginess and instability and greatly increasing the spectacle. This treatment would spell death to most other brooms.

Perhaps the two most important factors in growing brooms are to plant them in the right place from the beginning, and to make certain that the drainage is as good as it can be. They resent root disturbance (this applies especially to *Cytisus*), and cannot safely be moved once planted. Their natural habitats dictate their preference for sun and a well-drained soil, and they benefit from shelter from wind. There is no sadder sight in gardening than the slow death of a fine broom whose roots have been wrenched by a gale.

Geoffrey, Count of Anjou, soon to be the father of the future King Henry II of England, reached down from his saddle one day in the early twelfth century and plucked a sprig of broom, adopting it as his badge. Plant names change, of course, but in Plantagenet, the dynastic name of a succession of 14 kings, *Planta genista* has been immortalized.

C. *ardoinii* A miniature, mat-forming deciduous alpine shrub with bright yellow flowers from mid- to late spring. Maritime Alps of France. Introduced 1866.
H4 ♀ 1993

C. *battandieri* A tall deciduous shrub with silvery grey, silky, laburnum-like leaves and cone-shaped clusters of bright yellow, pineapple-scented flowers in midsummer. An excellent shrub for a high wall, but one that is surprisingly hardy for a plant from its native range and capable of surviving in open positions in many places. Morocco. Introduced c1922.
H4 ♀ 1993

C. *b.* 'Yellow Tail' A form with flower clusters 15cm (6in) long or more. Selected before 1975 at Hillier Nurseries.
H4 ♀ 1993

C. × *beanii* A charming, dwarf deciduous shrub up to 35cm (14in) in height, with golden yellow flowers in late spring. Garden origin 1900.
H4 ♀ 1993

C. 'Boskoop Ruby' A small, rounded deciduous shrub with deep crimson flowers borne very profusely in mid- to late spring. One of the most striking red hybrids. Raised in Holland.
H4 ♀ 1993

C. 'Burkwoodii' A vigorous medium-sized deciduous hybrid with cerise flowers, the wings of which are deep crimson edged with yellow, borne from late spring to early summer.
H4 ♀ 1993

C. 'Cottage' A small deciduous hybrid similar to *C. × kewensis* in its pale, creamy, late-spring flowers, but of upright habit.
H4

C. *decumbens* A prostrate, deciduous rock-garden shrublet with bright yellow flowers in late spring and early summer. S Europe. Introduced 1775.
H4

C. *demissus* A prostrate deciduous shrub no more than 10cm (4in) high. It is a gem for the rock garden and has exceptionally large yellow flowers with brown keels in late spring. Found on Mount Olympus, Greece, at about 2,300m (7,500ft).
H4 ♀ 1993

C. 'Dukaat' A small, deciduous, erectly

Cytisus battandieri

Cytisus battandieri 'Yellow Tail'

Cytisus 'La Coquette'

Cytisus 'Burkwoodii'

Cytisus 'Hollandia'

branched, F$_1$ hybrid shrub of dense habit, with silky-hairy young shoots and small, narrow leaves. The flowers, borne in late spring, are small and golden yellow. In cultivation 1965.
H4

C. 'Goldfinch' A compact medium-sized deciduous shrub grown for its creamy yellow flowers flushed with pink and red in mid- to late spring.
H4

C. 'Hollandia' A medium-sized deciduous shrub, similar to *C. × praecox*. The flowers appear from late spring to early summer and are pale cream, with the back of the standard petal cerise and the wings dark cerise.
H4 ♔ 1993

Cytisus 'Johnson's Crimson'

C. 'Johnson's Crimson' A fine medium-sized deciduous hybrid, in habit resembling *C. multiflorus*, with clear crimson flowers in mid- to late spring.
H4

Cytisus × kewensis

C. × kewensis Sheets of cream-coloured flowers are borne in late spring on this semi-prostrate deciduous shrub. Raised 1891 at Kew, England.
H4 ♔ 1993

C. × k. 'Niki' A prostrate form grown for its golden yellow flowers. Found as a sport 1984 in Holland.
H4

C. 'Killiney Red' A medium-sized deciduous broom of the *C. scoparius* type, with flowers produced from late spring to early summer. These are rich red, with darker red, velvety wings.
H4

C. 'La Coquette' A medium-sized deciduous hybrid in which the standard of the late-spring flowers is rose-red but yellow inside, and the wings are deep orange-yellow, veined with brick red. The keel is pale yellow, faintly marked with rose-red.
H4

Cytisus 'Lena'

C. 'Lena' A vigorous, compact, medium-sized deciduous shrub that flowers freely in mid- to late spring. The standard is deep red, the wings red margined with yellow, and the keel pale yellow. Raised at Kew.
H4 ♔ 1993

C. 'Luna' A medium-sized deciduous hybrid with large, late-spring flowers in which the standard petal is broad, pale creamy yellow and tinged red on the back and inside, the wings are rich yellow and the keel pale yellow. In cultivation 1959.
H4 ♔ 1993

C. 'Maria Burkwood' A vigorous medium-sized deciduous shrub. Large red

flowers with coppery wings are an attractive spectacle in late spring.
H4

Cytisus 'Minstead'

C. 'Minstead' A charming medium-sized deciduous hybrid derived from *C. multiflorus*. It produces multitudes of small flowers from late spring to early summer that are white flushed with lilac, and darker on the wings and in bud.
H4 ♔ 1993

Cytisus multiflorus

C. multiflorus (White Spanish broom) An erect deciduous shrub of medium size whose stems are studded with small white flowers in late spring and early summer. A parent of many hybrids, it should be given a soil on the acid side of neutral. Spain, Portugal, North Africa.
H4 ♔ 1993

C. nigricans A most useful and elegant small, late-flowering deciduous shrub that produces its long, terminal clusters of yel-

Cytisus 'Porlock'

low flowers continuously during late summer. C and SE Europe to C Russia. Introduced 1730.
H4

***C.* 'Palette'** A vigorous medium-sized shrub with large flowers in late spring. The standard shades from cerise-pink at the tip to orange-yellow at the base, with rich vermilion wings and pale yellow tips to the pink keel. In cultivation 1959.
H4

***C.* 'Porlock'** A hybrid that quickly forms a large, semi-evergreen bush. The flowers are golden yellow, very fragrant and borne in racemes, and appear in mild weather between autumn and spring. It is hardy in milder areas, especially on a sunny wall, and is also a lovely conservatory shrub. Raised c1922.
H3 🏆 1993

C.* × *praecox A group of small or medium-sized deciduous hybrids. The following are recommended, and the original form previously listed under this name and known as the Warminster broom has been given the cultivar name 'Warminster' (*see below*).
H4

Cytisus × *praecox* 'Albus'

***C.* × *p.* 'Albus'** A small or medium-sized white-flowered selection with the compact habit and profuse flowering that are typical of the group. It flowers in mid- to late spring.
H4

Cytisus × *praecox* 'Allgold'

***C.* × *p.* 'Allgold'** An outstanding small shrub with arching sprays of long-lasting yellow flowers in mid- to late spring.
H4 🏆 1993

Cytisus × *praecox* 'Warminster'

***C.* × *p.* 'Warminster'** A spectacular, smallish shrub, forming a tumbling mass of rich cream flowers in late spring. Garden origin c1867.
H4 🏆 1993

C. procumbens A dwarf deciduous shrub with prostrate branches. The flowers are formed in the leaf axils in late spring and early summer. SE Europe.
H4

***C. purpureus* 'Albus'** A pretty, low-growing deciduous shrub about 45cm (18in) high with white flowers produced in late spring. In cultivation 1838.
H4

***C. p.* 'Atropurpureus'** A superb dwarf shrub with deep purple flowers.
H4 🏆 1993

Cytisus × praecox 'Warminster'

C. 'Red Wings' A vigorous but compact deciduous shrub. The flowers, profusely borne in mid- to late spring, are deep, velvety red with a yellow keel flushed with bright red.
H4

Cytisus scoparius

C. scoparius (Common broom) A medium-sized deciduous shrub as conspicuous as gorse (*Ulex europaeus*) but spineless. It has rich butter-yellow flowers in late spring. The following forms are recommended. Europe, including Britain.
H4

C. s. 'Andreanus' A medium-sized form in which the flowers are attractively marked with brown-crimson. Found wild in Normandy c1884.
H4 ♛ 1993

C. s. 'Cornish Cream' A most attractive medium-sized form with cream flowers.
H4 ♛ 1993

C. s. 'Fulgens' A late-flowering small to medium-sized clone of dense, compact habit. The flowers are brownish red in the bud and open to orange-yellow with deep crimson wings. Raised c1906.
H4

C. s. 'Golden Sunlight' A strong-growing medium-sized form with rich yellow flowers. In cultivation 1929.
H4

Cytisus × spachianus

C. s. subsp. maritimus A nearly prostrate, spreading shrub with large yellow flowers. Found in the wild on sea cliffs in a few places in Cornwall and Channel Isles.
H4

C. × spachianus A medium-sized evergreen shrub with arching shoots and long clusters of fragrant yellow flowers in late winter and early spring. It is not hardy and is often grown under protection in a conservatory or as a houseplant.
H2 ♛ 1993

C. 'Windlesham Ruby' A medium-sized deciduous form of upright habit grown for its striking coloured flowers of a rich mahogany-crimson.
H4

C. 'Zeelandia' This medium-sized deciduous hybrid produces its flowers from late spring to early summer. The standard petal is lilac outside and cream inside; the wings are pinkish and the keel cream. An elegant plant deserving of a place in the garden.
H4 ♛ 1993

Cytisus 'Zeelandia'

D

Daboecia *Ericaceae*

There are only two species in this genus of low-growing, lime-hating, evergreen shrubs that are related to Erica but they are distinct in their large flowers and broader, elliptic leaves. They do best in a thoroughly peaty or leafy, acid soil; sandy soils to which large quantities of organic material have been added are close to the ideal. As with other heathers, an open position is preferred, but daboecias grow and flower well in part shade where there is less danger of damage by drought.

In shady situations, however, they tend to be less compact. This is not the drawback it might be with most other heathers, which cannot safely be cut back into the old wood, and plants that become old and leggy can be pruned back drastically and thus renewed.

D. cantabrica (Connemara heath). This species is one of the most charming of dwarf shrubs, producing long racemes of very showy, rose-purple, pitcher-shaped flowers from early summer to late autumn. The following forms are recommended. Coastal strip of Portugal and NW Spain, Connemara (a mountainous, boggy area NW of Galway, Ireland). In cultivation 1800. H4

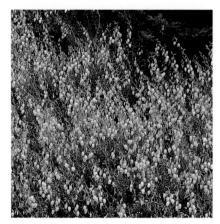

Daboecia cantabrica 'Alba'

D. c. 'Alba' A dwarf shrub with long racemes of white flowers. H4

D. c. 'Atropurpurea' The pitcher-shaped flowers of this dwarf shrub are rose-purple, darker than the type. H4

Daboecia cantabrica 'Bicolor'

D. c. 'Bicolor' A dwarf cultivar with white, rose-purple and striped flowers often in the same cluster. H4 ♔ 1993

D. c. 'David Moss' A dwarf shrub with white, freely borne flowers and glossy, dark green foliage. H4 ♔ 1993

Daboecia cantabrica 'Praegerae'

D. c. 'Praegerae' A dwarf, spreading shrub with rich pink flowers, curiously narrowed. Connemara. Found wild c1932. H4

D. c. 'Waley's Red' A form with deep, glowing magenta-coloured flowers with a bluish tinge. H4 ♔ 1993

D. × scotica A group of hybrids between *D. cantabrica* and the other species in the genus,

Daboecia cantabrica 'Waley's Red'

D. azorica. Like *D. cantabrica*, they flower over a long period from early summer to late autumn. The following forms are recommended. Garden origin, Glasgow, Scotland, c1953.

D. × s. 'Jack Drake' A dwarf shrub 25cm (10in) high with ruby-red flowers. H4 ♔ 1993

D. × s. 'Silverwells' A dwarf shrub up to about 15cm (6in) with white flowers. H4 ♔ 1993

D. × s. 'William Buchanan' A form with deep purple flowers on a dwarf shrub 45 cm (18in) high. H4 ♔ 1993

Dacrydium *Podocarpaceae*

A genus of about 25 species of evergreen coniferous trees and shrubs, related to Podocarpus.

Dacrydium franklinii

D. franklinii (Huon pine) In mild areas this forms a large, graceful shrub or small, conical tree. The slender, drooping branches are clothed in bright green, scale-like leaves. It is subject to injury in cold winters. Tasmania.

H3

Danaë *Ruscaceae*
Alexandrian laurel

A genus of one species of evergreen shrub, which is related to Ruscus *(butcher's broom) but has hermaphrodite flowers in short, terminal panicles as opposed to male and female flowers on separate plants. As in* Ruscus, *the leaves are in fact flattened stems.*

D. racemosa A charming small shrub with arching sprays of narrow, polished, green 'leaves' and cream flowers in early summer followed by orange-red fruits if the summer has been hot. Suitable for growing in moisture-retentive soil in sun or part shade, and excellent for cutting. SW Asia to N Iran. Introduced 1713.

H4 ♛ 1993

Daphne *Thymelaeaceae*

A genus of around 50 species of evergreen and deciduous shrubs from Europe, Asia and North Africa, a remarkably high proportion of which are desirable garden plants. Daphnes are justifiably renowned for their beauty and particularly for their scent, which can often be detected at a distance of several metres, and it is well worth planting them where you are likely to pass by frequently.

Daphnes are mostly small, but vary from prostrate plants eminently suitable for the rock garden to quite large shrubs. Their flowers are cylindrical tubes that flare suddenly outward into four lobes, so that the bloom looks flat when viewed directly head-on. Colours vary from mauve or purple to white and greenish yellow and are enhanced by a luminescent, frost-sprinkled appearance. Attractive but poisonous seeds sometimes follow.

The best sorts of soils are loamy, moisture retentive, but above all well drained. Some alpine species, including D. cneorum *and* D. retusa, *are happy in a scree, but it must be a rich one.*

Daphnes are excellent for cutting, but you should be a little careful, as the exquisite daphne scent can be too much of a good thing in the home.

CAUTION: toxic if eaten.

D. alpina A dwarf deciduous species, suitable for a rock garden, with grey-green leaves and terminal clusters of fragrant white flowers showing from late spring to early summer, followed by orange-red fruits. Mountains of S and C Europe. In cultivation 1759.

H4

Daphne arbuscula

D. arbuscula A dwarf, rounded, evergreen alpine shrublet with crowded, narrow leaves and rose-pink, fragrant flowers in late spring to early summer, followed by brownish yellow fruits. Carpathian Mountains of C Europe.

H4 ♛ 1993

D. bholua A deciduous or semi-evergreen shrub up to 2m (6½ft) high with stout, erect branches and oblanceolate leaves. The large, sweetly scented flowers are deep reddish mauve in bud, opening white, with reddish mauve reverse. They are borne in terminal clusters from mid- to late winter.

Daphne bholua

The fruits are black. The following forms are recommended. Himalayas. In cultivation 1938.

H3

Daphne bholua 'Gurkha'

D. b. 'Gurkha' A very hardy deciduous form of this highly variable medium-sized shrub which, in its best forms, is simply stunning. With a height of up to 2m (6½ft) and a long succession of large, richly scented, purplish pink flowers with white insides, borne in clusters of up to 20 from mid- to late winter, this plant has greatly increased the popularity of the species. E Nepal. Introduced 1962.

H3 ♛ 1993

Daphne bholua 'Jacqueline Postill'

D. b. 'Jacqueline Postill' Another very hardy, evergreen or semi-evergreen medium-sized form, which flowers when in full leaf. The flowers, borne from mid- to late winter, are larger and more showy than those of 'Gurkha' and have an equally powerful fragrance. Raised 1982 as a seedling of the latter by Hillier Nurseries' propagator Alan Postill.

H3 🏆 1993

D. blagayana A dwarf deciduous shrub with prostrate branches, at the ends of which are bunches of oval leaves and clusters of richly scented, creamy white flowers from early to mid-spring. The fruits are whitish. It is not one of the easiest plants, succeeding best in deep leaf mould and semi-shade. Mountain forests of SE Europe. Introduced c1875.

H4

Daphne × burkwoodii

D. × burkwoodii A group of deciduous or semi-evergreen hybrids, including some of the most popular and easily grown plants in the genus. The plants listed under this name are usually the seedlings 'Albert Burkwood' and 'Somerset'.

H4 🏆 1993

D. × b. 'Albert Burkwood' A fast-

Daphne × burkwoodii 'Albert Burkwood'

growing, semi-evergreen shrub up to 1m (3ft) high with pale pink, deliciously fragrant flowers borne in clusters on short, leafy shoots all along the branches from late spring to early summer and often again in autumn. Raised 1931.

H4 🏆 1993

D. × b. 'Carol Mackie' A small semi-evergreen form with leaves with a golden yellow margin that becomes creamy white. Named for the raiser, in whose garden in New Jersey it originated as a sport. Previously distributed as 'Variegata'. Introduced 1962.

H4

Daphne × burkwoodii 'Somerset'

D. × b. 'Somerset' A sister seedling to 'Albert Burkwood', slightly larger, more upright, and with paler flowers.

H4 🏆 1993

Daphne cneorum

D. cneorum (Garland flower) A prostrate deciduous shrub that is a great favourite because of its fragrance and the clusters of

rose-pink flowers that are borne on the prostrate branches from mid- to late spring. The occasional fruits are brownish yellow. Most gardeners find it difficult to establish, although it usually grows away well at first; but if you work peaty or leafy soil among and over its branches, leaving the leafy tips unburied, it will root widely and lead a long life. C and S Europe.

H4

D. c. 'Eximia' An even more prostrate form with larger leaves and flowers. The buds are crimson and open to rich pink.

H4 🏆 1993

Daphne cneorum 'Ruby Glow'

D. c. 'Ruby Glow' A prostrate form with very deep pink flowers.

H4

Daphne cneorum 'Variegata'

D. c. 'Variegata' A vigorous prostrate form with dark green leaves attractively margined with cream.

H4

Daphne collina

Daphne retusa

D. collina A first-rate evergreen dwarf shrub for the rock garden, forming a shapely bush only 25–35cm (10–14in) high. Each shoot is clothed with blunt, deep green leaves and in late spring ends in a cluster of fragrant, rose-purple flowers. This most rewarding of daphnes is now regarded by many as synonymous with or a form of *D. sericea*. S Italy. In cultivation 1752.
H4 ♛ 1993

D. genkwa There can be few lovelier shrubs than this oriental species, but it is difficult to grow and establish. It is a small deciduous shrub with lilac-like and lilac-coloured flowers all along the leafless branches from mid- to late spring. Maximum summer warmth, perfect drainage and summer watering probably afford the best chances of success, although it is a scarce plant and not easy to obtain. Winter cold is not a problem. China, Taiwan. Introduced 1843 by Robert Fortune.
H4

D. × houtteana A small, semi-evergreen, erect shrub with more or less oblong, pointed, purplish leaves and dark red-purple flowers in mid-spring. Stocks were subject to virus but new, clean material has been obtained through micropropagation. In cultivation 1850.
H4

D. × hybrida This charming small evergreen shrub with dark glossy leaves has the beauty and fragrance of *D. odora* and is hardier. Reddish purple, highly scented flowers are produced from late autumn through winter. Raised c1820.
H4

D. jasminea A dwarf, cushion-forming shrublet with small, narrow, glaucous, evergreen leaves. The flowers are rose-pink in the bud, opening white in spring, and deliciously fragrant. It is a rare alpine gem and requires winter protection, preferably in an alpine house. Cliffs and rocks in Greece (notably at Delphi). Introduced 1954. There is also an upright form that stands about 45cm (18in) high and is from other Greek locations.
H2–3

D. jezoensis A dwarf shrub with pale green young leaves that emerge in autumn. They are dark blue-green when mature and fall in early summer (summer-deciduous). In winter it bears dense clusters of fragrant, golden yellow, green-tinged flowers with protruding stamens. Best in a moist but well drained, peaty soil in a bright but not exposed position. Japan. Introduced c1960.
H4

D. laureola subsp. **philippi**. A dwarf

Daphne laureola subsp. philippi

form of the spurge laurel, this is an evergreen shrub ideal for the shady side of a rock garden, with fragrant, yellow-green flowers in dense clusters beneath the leathery, glossy, green leaves in late winter to early spring. May cause skin allergy. Pyrenees. In cultivation 1894.
H4

D. longilobata 'Peter Moore' A strikingly variegated, small to medium-sized, erect, deciduous or semi-evergreen shrub with grey-green leaves margined with creamy white. White flowers in summer are followed by red berries. A seedling found 1980 by Hillier Nurseries' propagator Peter Moore.
H4

Daphne × mantensiana 'Manten'

D. × mantensiana 'Manten' A dwarf evergreen shrub of dense, rounded habit with glossy dark green leaves up to 3.5cm (1½in) long. The strongly scented flowers are deep rose-purple outside, deep lilac within, and borne in dense clusters at the ends of the branches from mid- to late spring, usually with a second flush in summer and autumn. Raised 1941.
H4

D. mezereum (Mezereon) The well-known, sweet-scented daphne of cottage gardens. A small, twiggy deciduous shrub, it flowers in late winter and early spring; the purple-red flowers, which cover the previous year's shoots, are followed by scarlet, poisonous fruits. It thrives on chalky soils. Unfortunately virus is all too common in this species and shows itself in poor, yellowish foliage. May cause skin allergy. Europe

Daphne mezereum

(including England), Asia Minor, Siberia. In cultivation 1561.
H4

D. m. f. alba A form in which the branches are more upright. The flowers are white and the fruits translucent amber.
H4

D. × napolitana This is the correct spelling

Daphne × napolitana

Daphne odora

for a beautiful, dwarf, evergreen, hardy shrub rarely more than 1m (3ft) high, with blunt, ash green leaves. Clusters of fragrant, rose-pink flowers are borne profusely from mid-spring to very early summer. In cultivation 1823.
H4 ♔ 1993

D. odora This small evergreen shrub flowers in winter and early spring. It should be given some protection, although it is hardy enough to withstand reasonably severe frost if sheltered. It makes a bush 1.2–2m (4–6½ft) tall with dark green leaves and highly fragrant, reddish purple and white flowers. It and its forms are prone to virus infection. China, Japan. Introduced 1771.
H3

D. o. f alba A form with white flowers.
H3

Daphne odora 'Aureo-Marginata'

D.o. 'Aureo-Marginata' The leaves of this form have a narrow yellow margin that becomes creamy white with age. It is hardier than the typical species.
H3

D. petraea 'Grandiflora' A tiny, evergreen, alpine gem only 5–7.5cm (2–3in) high with small, linear leaves and rosy pink, fragrant flowers produced in clusters at the ends of the branches in early summer. A choice, gnarled little shrublet best grown in the alpine house but possible on a well-made scree. Not easily obtained. N Italy. Collected 1914 from the wild.
H2–4

D. pontica A small, free-growing, widespreading evergreen shrub that will thrive under the drip of trees and in heavy soil. It

Daphne pontica

has glossy bright green leaves and loose clusters of elusively fragrant, spidery, yellow-green flowers from mid- to late spring. The fruits are black. SE Bulgaria, N Iran, N Turkey. Introduced 1752.
H4 ♔ 1993

D. retusa A slow-growing, dwarf, evergreen shrub with stout, stiff branches. It bears clusters of fragrant, deep rose-purple flowers from late spring to early summer and often again in autumn. Some authorities include it in *D. tangutica*; both are variable and could be extremes within the same species. In gardens, *D. retusa* has shorter, more glossy leaves and is even slower growing. W China, Himalaya. Introduced 1901 by Ernest Wilson.
H4 ♔ 1993

Daphne tangutica

D. tangutica A dwarf evergreen shrub bearing clusters of fragrant flowers from early to mid-spring. These are white with a purple tinge on the inside and rose-purple

on the outside. China. Introduced early 1900s by Ernest Wilson.
H4 🏆 1993

Daphne 'Valerie Hillier'

D. **'Valerie Hillier'** A dwarf, spreading, evergreen shrub with downy shoots and narrowly oblong, glossy green leaves up to 5cm (2in) long. Its fragrant flowers are borne in terminal clusters on the young growths continuously from late spring to autumn. They are purplish pink in bud, opening to pale pink, fading nearly to white with pink-edged lobes, and the tube of the flower is pale pink, shading to green at the base. A splendid hybrid. Raised 1984 by Hillier Nurseries' propagator Alan Postill and named after the wife of John Hillier, elder son of Sir Harold Hillier.
H4

Daphniphyllum *Daphniphyllaceae*

A genus of 10 species of evergreen trees and shrubs

Daphniphyllum macropodum

from east and South East Asia to Australia. These aristocratic-looking shrubs have leaves recalling Rhododendron decorum *but the flowers are not conspicuous. They thrive in part shade and a neutral, loamy soil, but are nevertheless lime-tolerant.*

D. **macropodum** A large, striking shrub with large leaves that are pale green above, with bloomy undersides. The flowers are borne in late spring in clusters beneath the leaves and have no petals, but contribute a pungent scent. The fruits are blue-black and shaped like peas. It is remarkably hardy but should be sheltered from cold, drying winds. Prune to open up the centre of the shrub, or cut back old specimens really hard. China, Japan. Introduced 1879 by Charles Maries.
H4

Datura

D. **sanguinea** See *Brugmansia sanguinea*.
D. **suaveolens** See *Brugmansia suaveolens*.

Davidia *Davidiaceae*

A genus of medium-sized deciduous trees with something of the appearance of limes. Authorities differ as to whether there are two species or just one, but gardeners agree that whatever their botanical status, davidias are extremely beautiful in a haunting way when in flower. A deep, moist but well-drained, loamy soil is best, though they tolerate chalk well. They should be planted with some shelter from wind. As broad-headed trees, and because their beauty is best appreciated from a

Davidia involucrata

little distance, they should always be given enough room. No pruning required.

D. **involucrata** (Dove tree, ghost tree, pocket handkerchief tree) This sublimely beautiful tree is outstanding in late spring when draped with its large bracts, which give the impression of a flight of doves or a scattering of pure white pocket handkerchiefs. The leaves are smooth on young plants but become densely hairy on their undersides. C and W China. First introduced 1869 by Père David, reintroduced 1904 by Ernest Wilson.
H4 🏆 1993

Davidia involucrata var. vilmoriniana

D. *i.* var. **vilmoriniana** This form is very similar to *D. involucrata*, but with the leaves smooth underneath. For garden purposes this and the typical form are both of equal merit, and most plants that are grown as *Davidia involucrata* belong in fact to this variety. China. Introduced 1897.
H4 🏆 1993

Decaisnea *Lardizabalaceae*

A genus of two species of deciduous shrubs from western China and the Himalaya.

D. **fargesii** A most interesting shrub up to 3m (10ft) high, with large, bold, pinnate leaves 60cm–1m (2–3ft) long, blue-tinged when young. The yellow-green flowers, in clusters up to 45cm (18in) long, are borne in late spring and are followed by remarkable, metallic-blue pods much like those of broad beans. It will grow in sun or semi-shade and

Decaisnea fargesii

in a moist but well-drained soil. W China. Introduced 1895.

H4

Decumaria *Hydrangeaceae*

A genus of two hardy semi-evergreen or evergreen species of shrubs that climb by means of aerial roots. They are related to Hydrangea *but all their flowers are fertile. Like the climbing hydrangeas and schizophragmas, they succeed in sun or shade on a wall or tree trunk in any soil.*

D. barbara A semi-evergreen climber up to 9m (28ft). The small, sweetly scented white flowers are borne in small clusters from early to midsummer. In the wild it climbs the trunks of trees. SE United States. Introduced 1785.

H4

D. sinensis A rare evergreen species up to 5m (15ft) with a profusion of small green and white flowers in clusters in late spring. They are deliciously honey-scented. China. Introduced 1908 by Ernest Wilson.

H4

Dendromecon *Papaveraceae*

A genus of two species of evergreen shrubs, native to California and related to Romneya, *but with entire leaves and smaller, yellow flowers.*

D. rigida A large, frost-tender shrub, worth trying in mild areas against a warm, sunny wall and in an extremely well-drained, loamy soil. The leaves are narrow, rigid and bloomy, and the flowers are

Dendromecon rigida

poppy-like, four-petalled, bright buttercup yellow and produced over a long period in summer. Prune out weak branches. It has now become scarce. California, United States. Introduced c1854 by William Lobb.

H2–3

Desfontainia *Potaliaceae*

A genus of one, somewhat variable evergreen species, found in South America, mainly in the Andes but always in cool, moist places. It does not succeed on shallow soils over chalk (soft limestone) or any that are very limy. Requires a sheltered position.

D. spinosa A most beautiful shrub, slowly growing to 1.8–2m (5–6½ft). The leaves are small and easily mistaken for those of a holly. The flowers, borne in late summer, are tubular, and scarlet with a bright yellow mouth. Prune for shape only if necessary. Costa Rica to Cape Horn. Introduced c1843 by William Lobb.

H3 ♥ 1993

Desfontainia spinosa

Desmodium *Leguminoseae*

A genus of about 300 species of herbaceous perennials and deciduous shrubs, related to Lespedeza *and widely distributed in tropical and sub-tropical regions.*

D. tiliifolium A small to medium-sized, semi-woody shrub with erect stems and

Desmodium tiliifolium

leaves with three leaflets. Massed, large panicles of pale lilac pea flowers appear in summer, followed by flattened and lobed pods. It will grow in any good, well-drained soil in sun. Himalaya. Introduced 1879. H4

Deutzia *Philadelphaceae*

A genus of about 70 species of deciduous shrubs native to the Himalayas and south and east Asia. They are mainly easy to grow in all types of fertile soil, usually reaching 1.2–2m (4–6½ft). Flowering is in early summer. Thin out the shoots that have finished flowering and cut them back to within a short distance of the old wood. Flowering is prolonged and colour better preserved if there is a little shade during the hottest part of the day.

D. chunii A very beautiful and remarkable medium-sized shrub, blooming in mid-summer. The flowers are 12mm (½in) across with white or pink petals, reflexed to expose the yellow anthers, and are borne all along the branches in panicles up to 10cm (4in) long. This plant, in both its pink and white forms, is sometimes seen under the name *D. ningpoensis*. E China. Introduced 1935. H4

D. c. 'Pink Charm' A pink-flowered form selected at Hillier Nurseries. H4

D. compacta 'Lavender Time' A medium-sized shrub with flowers that are lilac at first, turning to pale lavender in mid-summer. A very distinct shrub collected from the wild by Frank Kingdon Ward

which, in fact, may be a new species. H4

Deutzia × elegantissima

D. × elegantissima A medium-sized hybrid with clusters of fragrant flowers, tinted with rose-pink. Garden origin, 1909. H4

D. × e. 'Rosealind' A lovely clone with

Deutzia × elegantissima 'Rosealind'

Deutzia gracilis

clusters of flowers in deep carmine-pink. In cultivation 1962.
H4 🏆 1993

D. gracilis An elegant, white-flowered species, parent of many good hybrids. It was previously much used for forcing and needs protection from late spring frosts. Japan. Introduced c1840. H3

D. × hybrida A group of hybrids of identical parentage, all of which are extremely free-flowering. The following are recommended. H4

Deutzia × hybrida 'Magicien'

D. × h. 'Magicien' This medium-sized form has large flowers, mauve-pink edged with white and tinted purple on the reverse. H4

Deutzia × hybrida 'Mont Rose'

D. × h. 'Mont Rose' A very free-flowering medium-sized form which has rose-pink flowers with darker-coloured tints borne in

large clusters. Raised c 1925.
H4 🏆 1993

D. × h. 'Pink Pompon' A medium-sized shrub with dense heads of double flowers, pink at first and then becoming white.
H4

D. × h. 'Strawberry Fields', syn. *D. × magnifica* 'Rubra' A medium-sized shrub with large flowers that are deep crimson outside and white flushed with pink within.
H4

Deutzia × kalmiiflora

D. × kalmiiflora A charming, medium-sized free-flowering shrub with large, white flowers flushed with carmine. The leaves are purple in autumn. Garden origin, 1900.
H4

Deutzia longifolia 'Veitchii'

D. longifolia 'Veitchii' A handsome, medium-sized shrub with long, narrowly lance-shaped leaves and large clusters of rich lilac-pink-tinted flowers from early to midsummer. The most aristocratic of this

genus. The species itself introduced from W China 1905 by Ernest Wilson.
H4 🏆 1993

D. × magnifica A vigorous, medium-sized shrub with large panicles of double, white flowers. Garden origin 1909.
H4

D. × m. 'Rubra' See *D. × hybrida* 'Strawberry Fields'.

D. monbeigii A slenderly branched small shrub with distinctly small leaves with white undersides. It bears a profusion of white, starry flowers rather late for the genus. China. Introduced 1921 by George Forrest.
H4

D. 'Nikko' This shrub, welcomed for its dwarf, compact habit, has proved less than worthy of its reception. Its small, white flowers, said to have been profusely borne, are rarely produced with any freedom. In cultivation 1975.
H4

D. pulchra A magnificent, hardy shrub of medium size. The clusters of white flowers are like drooping spikes of lily-of-the-valley. Philippines, Taiwan. Introduced 1918 by Ernest Wilson.
H4

Deutzia × rosea 'Campanulata'

D. × rosea 'Campanulata' An erect medium-sized shrub bearing bell-shaped flowers whose white petals contrast with the purple calyx. In cultivation 1899.
H4

D. × r. 'Carminea' A very attractive small to medium-sized shrub with flowers flushed with rose-carmine. In cultivation 1900.
H4 🏆 1993

Deutzia × rosea 'Carminea'

Deutzia scabra 'Candidissima'

D. scabra 'Candidissima' A medium-sized to large shrub with large clusters of double pure white flowers from early to midsummer. In cultivation 1867.
H4

D. s. 'Plena' The double white flowers of this medium-sized to large shrub are suffused with rose-purple on the outside.

Deutzia scabra 'Punctata'

Introduced 1861 by Robert Fortune.
H4

D. s. 'Punctata' A form in which the leaves are dotted with white.
H4

Deutzia setchuenensis var. corymbiflora

D. setchuenensis var. corymbiflora A charming, slow-growing shrub up to 2m (6½ft) high, producing its dome-shaped heads of small, white, star-like flowers very freely from mid- to late summer. One of the best summer-blooming shrubs. Some shelter from the coldest winds is advisable.
H4 🏆 1993

Diervilla *Caprifoliaceae*

A genus of three species of easily grown, small, summer-flowering deciduous shrubs from North America. They are allied to Lonicera. *They are sometimes confused with* Weigela *but have small, yellow, two-lipped flowers. They will grow in any well-drained friable soil.*

Diervilla sessilifolia

D. sessilifolia A small shrub with narrow pointed leaves which are often copper-tinted when young, and sulphur-yellow flowers borne in short panicles from early to late summer. SE United States. Introduced 1844.
H4

D. × splendens A small hybrid shrub with short-stalked leaves and sulphur-yellow flowers in summer. Introduced c1850.
H4

Diospyros *Ebenaceae*

*There are almost 500 species of evergreen and deciduous trees and shrubs in this genus, which is best known worldwide for ebony (*D. ebenum*) and other decorative striped, banded or otherwise patterned woods, as well as for fruits such as date-plums and persimmons. Most are native to tropical regions and very few are hardy.*

Diospyros kaki

D. kaki (Chinese persimmon) A large deciduous shrub or small tree long culti-vated in the East for its edible fruits and in gardens chiefly for the glorious orange-yel-low to orange-red and plum-purple autumn colour of its large, lustrous leaves. The orange-yellow, tomato-like fruits are borne in most summers in temperate regions. They are edible, but unless fully ripe are made unacceptably bitter by high concen-trations of tannin. China. Introduced 1796.
H3

Dipelta *Caprifoliaceae*

A small genus of four species of tall shrubs,

bearing a general resemblance to Weigela. *The difference is mainly in their showy, winged fruits.*

D. floribunda A first-class large shrub with fragrant, weigela-like flowers produced in great quantities in late spring. They are pink, flushed yellow in the throat. Propaga-tion is extremely difficult, hence the plant is somewhat scarce. It is a most amenable shrub, tolerating chalk and poor soils, and should be pruned after flowering to remove old and crowded branches. C and W China. Introduced 1902 by Ernest Wilson.
H4

Dipteronia *Aceraceae*

A genus of two species of large deciduous shrubs from central and south China, allied to Acer, *and the only other member of the family. They differ from* Acer *in having the fruits winged all round instead of down one side.*

Dipteronia sinensis

D. sinensis A large shrub with bold, pin-nate leaves. The insignificant flowers are followed in autumn by large clusters of pale green seeds, later red, and rather like those of the wych elm (*Ulmus glabra*) but more eye-catching. China. Introduced c1900.
H4

Disanthus *Hamamelidaceae*

A genus of one deciduous species related to Liquidambar.

D. cercidifolius A medium-sized shrub like a witch hazel (*Hamamelis*) in habit and a

Disanthus cercidifolius

Judas tree (*Cercis siliquastrum*) in leaf, highly valued for its beautiful, soft crimson and claret-red autumn tints. The tiny, purplish flowers are produced in mid-autumn. It requires a moist but well-drained, acid soil in semi-shade and protected from wind. Japan, SE China. Introduced 1893. H4 ♔ 1993

Distylium *Hamamelidaceae*

A genus of about 12 species of evergreen shrubs and trees native to east and South East Asia and Central America. They do best in conditions suitable for Hamamelis.

D. racemosum A wide-spreading but slow-growing medium-sized to large shrub that reaches tree size in the wild. It has glossy, leathery leaves and its flowers, which have no petals, consist of bright red stamens and are produced in clusters from mid- to late spring. The plant is similar to *Sycopsis*, to which it is related. It prefers an acid soil

Distylum racemosum

in part shade. S Japan, Taiwan, Korea, China. Introduced 1876. H4

Dorycnium *Leguminoseae*

A genus of about 12 species of deciduous sub-shrubs and herbaceous perennials from the Mediterranean region and the Canary Islands.

The leaves usually have five leaflets and the flowers are borne in tight, clover-like heads.

Dorycnium hirsutum

D. hirsutum A charming, dwarf sub-shrub with erect annual stems and terminal heads of pink-tinged, white pea flowers from late summer into autumn. The whole plant is silvery-hairy and a pleasant foil for the red-tinted fruit pods. It is suitable for a dry position in full sun which is as well-drained as possible, perhaps on a rock garden. Mediterranean region, S Portugal. In cultivation 1683. H3

Dregea *Asclepiadaceae*

A genus of three species of deciduous climbers from warm regions of the Old World. The following one can be grown out of doors in mild areas on a warm, sheltered wall or in a conservatory.

Dregea sinensis

D. sinensis A moderately hardy species

with slender stems up to 3m (9ft) long that need some support. The ovate leaves are grey-felted beneath and the deliciously scented flowers, very much like those of a hoya, are white with a central zone of red spots. They are borne in long-stalked, downy umbels in summer. China. Introduced 1907 by Ernest Wilson.
H2–3

Drimys *Winteraceae*

The estimates of species in this genus of evergreen trees and shrubs vary from around 10 to about 30. They are native to Malaysia, eastern Australia, New Guinea, and Central and South America. The cultivated species are fine, handsome plants for milder places.

D. lanceolata A medium-sized to large, aromatic, slender, upright shrub with purplish red shoots and dark green leaves that are light green beneath. It has attractive, copper-tinted young growths and bears numerous small, creamy white flowers from mid- to late spring. Male and female flowers are on separate plants. Tasmania, SE Australia. Introduced 1843.
H3

Drimys winteri

D. winteri (Winter's bark) A large shrub or small tree with large, leathery leaves with bloomy undersides. The ivory-white flowers are fragrant and borne in loose umbels in late spring. It can be encouraged to form a tree by training when it is young. It does well against a wall. C Chile. Introduced 1827.
H3

Dryas *Rosaceae*

A genus of two species of carpeting plants with small, evergreen, oak-like leaves that are shining dark green above and startlingly white beneath. They are natives of northern temperate and arctic regions and are suitable for screes, wall-tops, paving or the rock garden. Flowering is at its best and the plants are more compact if they are grown in a poor, gravelly, but quite moist soil.

Dryas octopetala

D. octopetala (Mountain avens) The white flowers of this prostrate mat-forming species are like little dog roses, with a mass of yellow stamens in the centre. It is a suitable plant for the rock garden. Each flower is carried separately on 7.5cm (3in) stalks which rise above the fans of distinctive oak-like leaves that are dark green on top and grey-green beneath. Each has a mass of golden stamens and is clasped by long, green sepals. In ideal conditions the flowers cover the whole plant during late spring and early summer and are followed by silky tassels of seedheads that change to balls of down. It is rarely seen in the wild but favours the rocky ledges of Scotland, Ireland, Canada and other circumpolar regions. In cultivation 1750.
H4

D. × suendermannii This is a rather uncommon hybrid that is very similar to *D. octopetala* but with rather larger, more erect leaves and creamy white flowers, ivory in bud, that are nodding when open. They appear in late spring or early summer. In cultivation 1750.
H4

E

Eccremocarpus *Bignoniaceae*

A genus of about five species of evergreen or nearly evergreen plants that climb by means of coiling leaf tendrils. The following is hardy in a sheltered corner in milder gardens and can be grown in colder areas in the conservatory or, as it is easy and quick from seed and grows quickly to flowering in the same year, it can be treated as a half-hardy annual. It will grow in any soil.

Eccremocarpus scaber

E. scaber A vigorous, fast-growing climber that quickly covers a support with its angular stems that are up to 5m (15ft) long. The leaves are bipinnate and end in a slender tendril. The scarlet to orange or yellow, tubular flowers, 2.5cm (1in) long, are in clusters that are continually produced throughout summer and autumn. Chile. Introduced 1824.
H3 ♛ 1993

Edgeworthia *Thymeleaeaceae*

A genus of two species of semi-evergreen or deciduous shrubs, related to Daphne *and native to the Himalayas and China.*

E. chrysantha This deciduous species grows to 1.2–1.5m (4–5ft) and in late winter bears dense, nodding, terminal clusters of fragrant yellow flowers clothed on the outside with silky hairs. It requires a sheltered spot in a mild area and will not tolerate hot,

Edgeworthia chrysantha

dry summers. The soil should be well drained and organic. It is used in Japan for high-grade banknote paper. China. Introduced 1845.

H3

Elaeagnus *Elaeagnaceae*
Oleaster

There are around 40 evergreen and deciduous species in this genus. 'Oleaster' means 'lesser olive' or almost 'tries hard to be an olive'. These are not olives at all, but evergreen and deciduous, fast-growing shrubs or small trees native to southern Europe and Asia, with one species in North America. They are grown chiefly for their lustrous foliage, which is doubly welcome when standing up to wind, especially in maritime and other exposed locations. The white or off-white flowers, though small, are pleasantly scented and abundantly produced, although they are often hidden by the leaves when the plant is evergreen. They will thrive in any fertile soil except very shallow ones over chalk.

E. angustifolia This species, to which the term 'oleaster' properly belongs, is a large, spiny deciduous shrub or small tree with silvery grey, willow-like leaves and fragrant flowers in early summer. The fruits are silvery amber, oval, and 12mm (¹/₂in) long. It is easily mistaken for the willow-leaved pear, *Pyrus salicifolia*. Temperate W Asia, widely naturalized in S Europe. In cultivation in England in the sixteenth century.

H4

E.a. var. caspica See *E.* 'Quicksilver'.

E. commutata (Silver berry) A medium-sized deciduous shrub, spreading by underground shoots, with intensely silver leaves and fragrant flowers in late spring. The fruits are small, egg-shaped and silvery. Good on poor soils. North America. Introduced 1813.

H4

Elaeagnus × ebbingei

Elaeagnus × ebbingei 'Gilt Edge'

E. × ebbingei A large, hardy, fast-growing, evergreen shrub, splendid for creating shel-

ter, even near the sea. The large, glossy dark green leaves are silvery beneath, and the silvery-scaly, fragrant flowers are borne in autumn, followed by silver-speckled orange fruits in spring. Garden origin 1929.

H4

E. × e. 'Gilt Edge' The leaves of this large shrub are margined with golden yellow. In cultivation 1961.

H4 ♛ 1993

Elaeagnus × ebbingei 'Limelight'

E. × e. 'Limelight' A large shrub on which the leaves are green above at first with silvery scales, developing a broad blotch of deep yellow and pale green, silvery beneath. Liable to revert.

H4

Elaeagnus macrophylla

E. macrophylla The broad, rounded leaves of this evergreen species are silvery on both surfaces, becoming glossy dark green above as the season advances. It eventually forms a large, spreading shrub. The fragrant

flowers are borne in autumn. Korea, Japan. Introduced 1879 by Charles Maries.
H4

E. parvifolia A large deciduous shrub with arching branches and bronze-scaly shoots that are silvery when young. The leaves are elliptic-lanceolate, scaly above when young and then becoming glossy bright green. Fragrant, creamy white flowers in spring and early autumn are followed by red fruits. Himalaya, W China.
H4 ♔ 1993

E. pungens A large, vigorous, spreading evergreen shrub reaching 5m (15ft) in height and excellent for creating shelter. The leaves are shiny dark green above, dull white speckled brown beneath. It has fragrant flowers, which are borne in autumn. The following forms are recommended. Japan. Introduced 1830.
H4

E. p. 'Dicksonii' A rather slow-growing medium-sized shrub. The upper sides of the leaves are green with a wide, irregular margin of golden yellow.
H4

Elaeagnus pungens 'Frederici'

E. p. 'Frederici' A slow-growing medium-sized shrub, with narrow leaves mainly pale, creamy yellow with a narrow, bright green border. In cultivation 1888.
H4

E. p. 'Goldrim' A large, striking shrub with glossy deep green leaves margined with bright yellow. The margin is brighter than that of 'Variegata' and narrower than 'Dicksonii'. A sport of 'Maculata'
H4

Elaeagnus pungens 'Goldrim'

Elaeagnus pungens 'Maculata'

E. p. 'Maculata' The leaves of this large shrub have a central splash of gold, giving a very bright effect. This is a very handsome shrub of moderate growth, but a close watch needs to be kept for any signs of reversion, to which it is prone.
H4 ♔ 1993

E. p. 'Variegata' A large shrub on which the dark green leaves are brightened with a thin, creamy yellow margin.
H4

E. 'Quicksilver' An oustanding large deciduous shrub or small tree with narrowish leaves that are exceptionally silvery, especially when young. Until fairly recently it was grown under the name *E. angustifolia* var. *caspica*. Caucasus.
H4 ♔ 1993

Eleutherococcus *Araliaceae*

A genus of about 50 species of deciduous trees and shrubs, sometimes climbing, related to Fatsia *and* Aralia, *and natives of east and South East Asia. Until recently this genus was known as* Acanthopanax.

E. sieboldianus 'Variegatus' A medium-sized shrub with numerous erect, cane-like stems and clusters of large leaves parted into three or five leaflets and edged with creamy white, each cluster with a small curved prickle at its base. The small greenish white late-spring flowers form in umbels and are followed by clusters of black fruits. It tolerates poor soils but should be sheltered from cold winds.
H4

Elsholtzia *Labiatae*

A genus of about 30 species of aromatic herbs and deciduous sub-shrubs from Asia, Europe and Ethiopia. The following species is valued for its early flowering.

E. stauntonii A small sub-shrub with rounded stems and lance-shaped leaves that are mint-scented when crushed. Lilac-purple flowers are freeely borne from late summer to mid-autumn and make a splendid splash of late colour. The stems may be cut to the ground by frosts, especially in cold districts, but they usually regrow the following spring. It is easily grown in any fertile soil in an open position in full sun. N China. Introduced 1909.
H4

Embothrium *Proteaceae*

A genus of eight species of evergreen trees or shrubs, native to the Andes of South America. Their ideal situation is in a sheltered border or woodland clearing in a deep, moist but well-drained, lime-free soil. They are particularly suitable for cool, moist, equable climates.

E. coccineum (Chilean fire bush) This glorious species, with its profusion of brilliant orange-scarlet flowers in late spring and early summer, is one of the most desirable garden treasures. The blooms are long, tubular, and borne in clusters of several. Normally it is an erect, slender, semi-

Embothrium coccineum

evergreen tall shrub or small tree, but it is capable of extremely rapid growth and long life particularly in south-west Ireland, where many very large specimens can be seen. Chile. Introduced 1846.
H3

Embothrium coccineum Lanceolatum Group

E. c. Lanceolatum Group These forms are the least evergreen and by far the most hardy, with linear-lanceolate leaves rather than broad, paddle-shaped ones. The best is 'Norquinco Form', in which the flower clusters touch one another so that each whole branch is clad in scarlet in late spring to early summer.
H3 ♔ 1993 (*E. coccineum* Lanceolatum group 'Norquinco Form')

Empetrum *Empetraceae*

A genus of about five species of dwarf, carpeting, heath-like evergreen shrubs, that are natives of moors and mountains and other wild, windswept

Empetrum nigrum

places in the northern hemisphere, southern Andes and Falkland Islands.

E. nigrum (Crowberry) A very widely distributed, procumbent shrub that forms wide-spreading, dense carpets. The purple-red flowers, borne in spring, are not very significant, but are followed by glossy black fruits. Requires a moist, peaty, lime-free soil. High northern latitudes, including moors in Scotland and England.
H4

Enkianthus *Ericaceae*

A genus of about 10 species of outstanding deciduous shrubs ranging in the wild from the Himalayas to Japan. They all require lime-free soil and flower in late spring, producing clusters of drooping, cup- or urn-shaped, prettily veined blooms. Their autumn foliage is almost unrivalled.

E. campanulatus A species with erect branches, growing to 2.5–3m (8–10ft). It is a

Enkianthus campanulatus

splendid, somewhat variable shrub with subtle qualities and is one of the easiest to grow of this lovely genus. The flowers are cup-shaped, sulphur to rich bronze, and carried in great profusion for about three weeks. They last well when cut. The autumn foliage is in every shade from yellow to red. Japan. Introduced 1880 by Charles Maries.
H4 ♔ 1993

E. c. **Albiflorus group** The flowers of this group are creamy white.
H4

E. c. **'Red Bells'** A medium-sized shrub of compact, upright habit and flowers richly streaked with red.
H4

Enkianthus cernuus var. rubens

E. cernuus **var.** *rubens* A very choice, small to medium-sized shrub noteworthy for its deep red, fringed flowers and brilliant, reddish purple autumn colour. Japan.
H4 ♔ 1993

Enkianthus chinensis

E. chinensis A beautiful small tree or tall, narrow shrub that reaches 6m (20ft) under favourable conditions. The flowers are yellow and red with darker veins, and are borne in many-flowered umbels. The leaves are comparatively large, usually with red stalks, and are attractively tinted in autumn. W China, Upper Burma. Introduced 1900.
H4

Enkianthus perulatus

E. perulatus A densely leafy, slow-growing, compact shrub up to 2m (6½ft) high. Masses of urn-shaped white flowers appear with the leaves in spring. It is one of the most consistently good shrubs for the intensity of its scarlet leaves in autumn. Japan. Introduced c1870.
H4 ♔ 1993

Ephedra *Ephedraceae*

A genus of about 40 species of curious, evergreen shrubs with slender, rush-like, green stems and leaves reduced to tiny scales. They make good ground cover, especially in dry soils; if male and female plants are grown together, fruits are produced. They are of great botanical interest, providing a link between flowering plants and conifers, and are widely distributed in North and South America and Eurasia.

E. gerardiana **var.** *sikkimensis* A dwarf shrub with slender, erect many-branched stems forming large, creeping patches. The leaves are scale-like and the flowers insignificant. Although useful for ground cover, this plant is of more interest than ornament. Himalayas. Introduced 1915.
H4

Ercilla *Phytolaccaceae*

This is a genus of two species of evergreen climbers that support themselves with aerial roots and are grown particularly for their neat, green leaves, which densely cover the stems. These plants are quite frost-hardy and may be successfully grown either on a wall in sun or shade, also making attractive ground cover in any ordinary well-drained soil.

E. volubilis This self-clinging climber is medium-sized with rounded, leathery leaves and bears dense spikes of small, purplish white flowers in spring. It is hardy as long as it is sheltered from cold winds. Chile. Introduced 1840.
H4

ERICA

Ericaceae Heaths and heathers

Erica arborea 'Albert's Gold' is vigorous, with bright yellow foliage

HEATHERS are immensely popular shrubs, and with good reason. Few other groups of plants are so large and varied or go so well together as the heathers and those of their number that are often referred to as heaths. Their long succession of flowering is unsurpassed, and there is hardly a week in the year when there is no heather in bloom. What is more, their great variety of foliage makes it possible to create an undulating carpet of golds, silvers, greys, reds and an almost infinite range of greens, from bronze to youthful brightness.

The heathers-with-conifers garden, so fashionable a few years ago, is now slightly passé, and there are better ways of deploying heathers than with geometrically shaped conifers thrusting through them at intervals. Conifers, particularly the large dwarf and slow-growing forms, do indeed go well with heathers, but in the main are better as a backdrop or as a feature from and around which the heathers can flow.

'Heath' and 'heather' are neither scientific nor truly horticultural terms, but are somewhat loosely (although occasionally pedantically) used to distinguish the species of *Erica* on the one hand from that of *Calluna* on the other. However, *Erica cinerea* is always known as bell heather, while *Calluna vulgaris* grows on many a heath. Originally, the plants of the heaths – tracts of land deemed useless for agriculture – were called heathers, and the inhabitants – the poor and the dispossessed for whom there was no church – were termed heathens. Thus, as we are but gardeners after all, we may legitimately use the term 'heathers' for ericas and callunas alike, and by extension for closely related plants such as the daboecias.

Erica is a genus of more than 500 evergreen species from dwarf shrubs to small trees, native to Europe, Turkey and Africa, with by far the largest number of species occurring in South Africa. The latter, although often staggeringly beautiful, are rarely possible in even the mildest of temperate gardens. *Erica* is distinguished botanically from *Calluna* in that it is the corolla (petals) of the flower that bear the colour, rather than the calyx (sepals).

At the upper end of the height range in *Erica* are the tree heaths. They can be magnificent shrubs, fully 5m (15ft) high and wide, and often growing to great ages in the wild. In gardens they are imposing all-year features and ideal architectural accents

Erica carnea 'Aurea' with a purple-flowered calluna

among the carpeting heathers. At the other end are truly dwarf shrubs, under 30cm (12in) high, forming dense mounds of weed-suppressing foliage which is often sufficiently ornamental of itself, but more usually bursting into generous and prolific flower for long periods.

In winter and early spring, cultivars of *Erica carnea* provide drifts of bright flowers, along with those of *E.* × *darleyensis*. At the same time, the taller *E. erigena* forms stand sentinel over them and, if your climate is kind, they may be joined by the magnificent tree heath, *E. lusitanica*. This early pageant is joined by what is perhaps *the* tree heath, *E. arborea*, hardy forms of which are daunted only by the severest winters, and continues as cultivars succeed one another until the early days of summer, when *E. cinerea* and *E. tetralix* begin their display, to be joined later by *E. cinerea*, *E. vagans* and a few other species. Unique among summer heathers are the daboecias, whose relatively large flowers and distinct appearance add to the already clamorous versatility of a planting of heathers.

The callunas, the 'true' heathers as some

would have it, start their long march down from midsummer into autumn. *Erica* species will continue to flower into autumn as well and almost link up with the first flushings of *E. carnea*, but the great tide of cultivars of *Calluna vulgaris* presents one of the great spectacles of cool-temperate gardening – something not to be missed as a show, and to be embraced as a fascinating aspect of gardening by those who can provide the right conditions.

CARE AND CULTIVATION

The majority of heaths and heathers demand soils that are lime-free. Many of them grow on sand in nature, but it is always well charged with organic matter. That is the most important consideration of all, as the fibrous roots of the plants never run very deep and need the soil to be moisture-retentive, open and well drained, and it is organic matter that makes such a combination possible.

In general, therefore, the plants are unsuccessful on shallow soils over chalk (soft limestone), although *Erica terminalis* is a significant exception. They are by no means

all lime-haters, though, and you can grow *E. carnea*, *E. erigena* and *E.* × *darleyensis* on limy soils as long as they are deep and not thin layers above the rock.

Heathers should be planted so that, rather than creating a spotty effect, they join up to make a carpet. This applies as much to just a few plants as it does to many, and you should choose the planting distances accordingly. How far 'apart' is a misleading measure, as it depends on the sizes and ages of the plants. To plant at an average of 45cm (18in) centres will, however, be correct for most, but with really dwarf plants, such as the forms of *Erica mackayana*, 35cm (14in) is enough. *Calluna vulgaris* cultivars mostly need 90cm (36in) centres, with the exception of dwarf forms which can be planted at double the density. During the initial preparation of the ground, dig copious amounts of well-rotted organic matter into the soil and ensure that the ground is completely free of perennial weed roots.

You will have to give care and attention to a heather planting for the first three years or so, after which the plants should have closed together to form a weed-suppressing mass. Vigilance against weeds must be kept up and, until the plants have made a continuous carpet, keen attention needs to be given to watering, as the soil between heathers easily dries out in hot weather.

Callunas must be clipped back every year, otherwise bare lengths of stem appear where previously there were flowers, and the planting will look scruffy and neglected. Ericas need such treatment much less frequently, but it nevertheless helps them to be more bushy, less leggy, and not as coarsely woody –in fact, it is a good idea to clip them more than is strictly necessary for their long-term health. Old plants can be cut back hard, and new shoots will form from their bases. Use secateurs for this, but all other clipping operations can be done with shears.

A mulch of peaty material, given in spring, is an excellent measure to ensure healthy plants and strong growth, and you can also give the plants an annual feed of a balanced general fertilizer. Garden compost, on the other hand, should not be used, unless you can be absolutely certain that it contains no weed seeds.

E. arborea (Tree heath) The cultivars of this species are medium-sized to large shrubs with fragrant white flowers being produced very profusely in early spring. The following forms are recommended. S Europe, Caucasus, North and E Africa. Introduced 1658.
H4

E. a. **'Albert's Gold'** A vigorous, hardy form with bright yellow foliage.
H4 ♔ 1993

E. a. **var. *alpina*** A more hardy form, which is less tall, but more erect and with brighter green foliage. Mountains of Spain. Introduced 1899.
H4 ♔ 1993

E. a. **'Estrella Gold'** A slow-growing, very hardy form with bright yellow young foliage. Portugal. Found wild 1972.
H4 ♔ 1993

E. australis (Spanish heath) A medium-sized shrub with fragrant rose-purple flowers from mid- to late spring. It is one of the showiest of the tree heaths and very hardy, but not recommended for the coldest areas. Spain, Portugal. Introduced 1769.
H4 ♔ 1993

E. a. **'Mr Robert'** A beautiful white-flowered form. Found in Spain, 1912.
H3 ♔ 1993

E. a. **'Riverslea'** A lovely cultivar with flowers of fuchsia-purple.
H4 ♔ 1993

E. canaliculata This beautiful tree heath has reached a height of 5.5m (17ft) in the mildest parts of Britain, but elsewhere is best grown in a conservatory. The fragrant flowers are white or pink-tinged with protruding brown anthers, and appear from midwinter to early spring. S Africa. In cultivation c1802.
H2

E. carnea One of the most widely planted dwarf shrubs in cultivation, forming dense hummocks and mats, whose cultivars have flowers in a wide selection of shades in the white-purple-pink range. They are all lime-tolerant but nevertheless are not recommended for shallow chalk soils. All are H4 and, unless otherwise stated, grow 15–23cm (6–9in) high. Flowering times are indicated as follows:

Early season: late autumn to midwinter.

Erica arborea

Erica australis 'Riverslea'

Erica arborea var. *alpina*

Erica australis

Erica canaliculata

Mid-season: midwinter to early spring.
Late season: mid-spring.

E. c. 'Adrienne Duncan' A form with dark bronze-green foliage and mid-season, carmine-red flowers.
🏆 1993

Erica carnea 'Ann Sparkes'

E. c. 'Ann Sparkes' A slow-growing, spreading form with golden foliage and rich purple flowers in late season.
🏆 1993

E. c. 'Aurea' A form with bright gold foliage during spring and early summer. Deep pink flowers, paling almost to white, are produced from mid- to late season.

E. c. 'Challenger' A form with mid-season magenta flowers with crimson sepals and dark green foliage.
🏆 1993

E. c. 'December Red' This form has deep green foliage and strong spikes of rose-red flowers from mid- to late season.

E. c. 'Eileen Porter' A low-growing

Erica carnea 'Eileen Porter'

form with rich carmine-red flowers from mid-autumn to mid-spring. The dark corollas and pale calyces give a delightful, bicoloured effect. In cultivation 1934.

E. c. 'Foxhollow' The yellowish green foliage of this form becomes rich yellow tinged red in winter. Pale pink flowers appear in late season. In cultivation 1970.
🏆 1993

Erica carnea 'Golden Starlet'

E. c. 'Golden Starlet' The foliage of this form is bright yellow in winter, becoming lime-green in summer. White flowers appear in mid-season.
🏆 1993

E. c. 'Heathwood' A form with dark green foliage which turns bronze in winter. Bright rose-purple flowers appear in late season.

Erica carnea 'King George'

E. c. 'King George' There is very little difference between this plant and 'Winter Beauty'. In bud, however, the sepals are

pale green and the corolla pale mauve. Flowering begins in early winter.

Erica carnea 'Loughrigg'

E. c. 'Loughrigg' A form with mid-season, rose-purple flowers and dark green foliage.
🏆 1993

E. c. 'March Seedling' A spreading form with dark green foliage and rich red-purple flowers in late season.

Erica carnea 'Myretoun Ruby'

E. c. 'Myretoun Ruby' An excellent plant with deep green foliage and masses of deep rose-pink flowers in late season. Raised 1965 at Myretoun House, Scotland.
🏆 1993

E. c. 'Pink Spangles' An improvement on 'Springwood Pink', with pink flowers profusely produced in mid-season.
🏆 1993

E. c. 'Praecox Rubra' A form with deep rose-red flowers in early to mid-season.
🏆 1993

Erica carnea 'Pink Spangles'

Erica carnea 'R. B. Cooke'

E. c. 'R. B. Cooke' The clear pink flowers of this form are produced over a long period from mid- to late season. 20cm (8in). ♔ 1993

E. c. 'Ruby Glow' A form with large, rich dark red flowers produced in late-season and bronzed foliage.

E. c. 'Snow Queen' In this form the large,

Erica carnea 'Snow Queen'

pure white, mid-season flowers are held well above the foliage. In cultivation 1934.

E. c. 'Springwood Pink' This form has clear rose-pink, mid-season flowers, plus a good habit and foliage, but has now been superseded by 'Pink Spangles'.

Erica carnea 'Springwood White'

E. c. 'Springwood White' Still one of the finest white cultivars. Its strong, trailing growths are packed with long, urn-shaped flowers in mid-season. ♔ 1993

E. c. 'Sunshine Rambler' A form with clear yellow foliage, becoming bronze-yellow in winter. Pink flowers appear in late season. In cultivation 1971. ♔ 1993

Erica carnea 'Vivellii'

E. c. 'Vivellii' A superb cultivar with deep, vivid carmine flowers in mid-season which develops bronze-red foliage in winter. In cultivation 1919. ♔ 1993

Erica carnea 'Westwood Yellow'

E. c. 'Westwood Yellow' A compact form with golden-yellow foliage and deep pink flowers in late season. ♔ 1993

E. c. 'Whitehall' A compact, bushy form with bright green foliage and large, pure white flowers, profusely borne in mid-season. Some experts believe it to be an improvement on 'Springwood White'.

E. c. 'Winter Beauty' This cultivar has been confused with 'King George'. It has bright rose-pink flowers with the sepals and corolla red-tinged in the bud. Flowering starts in early winter.

E. ciliaris (Dorset heath) A low, spreading species up to 80cm (32in) high. The flowers are comparatively large, rosy-red, and borne in short, terminal clusters from mid-summer to mid-autumn. The following forms are recommended. It requires a lime-free soil. SW Europe, including SW England and the Connemara, Ireland. H4

E. c. 'Corfe Castle' This dwarf form has leaves which turn bronze in winter and salmon-pink flowers. 30cm (12in). H4 ♔ 1993

E. c. 'David McClintock' A dwarf form with grey foliage and white flowers, tipped with mauve-pink. Found wild in Brittany by David McClintock. 40cm (16in). H4 ♔ 1993

E. c. 'Mrs C. H. Gill' A dwarf cultivar with dark green foliage and freely produced, clear red flowers. 30cm (12in). H4 ♔ 1993

E. c. 'Stoborough' A dwarf form with long racemes of white flowers. Found in

Dorset. 50–60cm (20–24in).
H4 ♛ 1993

E. cinerea (Bell heather) This common native species forms mats of wiry stems and produces its red-purple flowers from early summer to early autumn. It and its cultivars require a lime-free soil. The latter are all H4 and, unless otherwise stated, grow to 25–30cm (10–12in) high. The following are recommended. W Europe, including Britain and Ireland.
H4

Erica cinerea 'Alba Minor'

***E. c.* 'Alba Minor'** A compact, white-flowered form. 15cm (9in).
♛ 1993

Erica cinerea 'C. D. Eason'

***E. c.* 'C. D. Eason'** A form with glowing, deep pink flowers. In cultivation 1931.
♛ 1993

***E. c.* 'Cevennes'** This cultivar produces its lavender-rose flowers over a long period.
♛ 1993

Erica cinerea 'C. G. Best'

***E. c.* 'C. G. Best'** A form with soft salmon-pink flowers. In cultivation 1931.
♛ 1993

***E. c.* 'Cindy'** A cultivar with large, pure pink flowers and bronze-green foliage.
♛ 1993

Erica cinerea 'Domino'

***E. c.* 'Domino'** A charming form with white flowers with ebony calyces.

***E. c.* 'Eden Valley'** A cultivar with soft lilac-pink flowers which are paler at the base. 15cm (6in). In cultivation 1926.
♛ 1993

***E. c.* 'Fiddler's Gold'** A compact, vigorous form with pale green foliage, flushed with yellow and red when young. The flowers are deep mauve.
♛ 1993

***E. c.* 'Foxhollow Mahogany'** This form has dark green foliage and bears its deep wine-red flowers in profusion. 30cm (12in).

***E. c.* 'Golden Drop'** The summer foliage of this form is golden copper, turning to

Erica cinerea 'Golden Drop'

rusty-red in winter. The pink flowers are rarely produced. 15cm (6in).

***E. c.* 'Golden Hue'** A most effective plant, with golden foliage turning red in winter. 50cm (20in).

***E. c.* 'Hookstone White'** A form with bright green foliage and large white flowers borne in long clusters. 35cm (14in).
♛ 1993

***E. c.* 'Knap Hill Pink'** A vigorous form, producing long trusses of pure carmine-pink flowers. 30cm (12in).
♛ 1993

***E. c.* 'My Love'** The striking, mauve-blue flowers of this cultivar contrast effectively with the foliage. 25–30cm (10–12in).

***E. c.* 'Pentreath'** A delightful form with rich purple flowers.
♛ 1993

Erica cinerea 'Pink Ice'

***E. c.* 'Pink Ice'** A compact, vigorous form with distinctively bright deep green leaves, bronzed in winter and when young. The

flowers are clear, pale pink.
♔ 1993

Erica cinerea 'P. S. Patrick'

E. c. 'P. S. Patrick' This form produces long sprays of bright purple flowers. In cultivation 1928.
♔ 1993

Erica cinerea 'Purple Beauty'

E. c. 'Purple Beauty' A form with deep rose-purple flowers and dark green foliage.

E. c. 'Sherry' This form has glossy green foliage and produces its clear, dark red flowers in abundance. 30cm (12in).

E. c. 'Stephen Davis' A compact form with dark green foliage and vivid, deep pink flowers. 20cm (8in).
♔ 1993

E. c. 'Velvet Night' A form with flowers in a most unusual shade of blackish purple.
♔ 1993

E. c. 'Windlebrooke' A vigorous cultivar with golden yellow foliage that turns orange-red in winter while the flowers pro-

Erica cinerea 'Stephen Davis'

duced are a pretty shade of mauve.
♔ 1993

E. × darleyensis A most useful hybrid in its various forms, and a natural companion for *E. carnea*. The following recommended cultivars average 50–60cm (20–24in) in height unless otherwise stated, and flower throughout the winter. They are all H4 and are lime-tolerant, but they are not recommended for shallow chalk soils. See also 'Darley Dale'.
H4

E. × d. 'Ada S. Collins' The white flowers of this form contrast well with the attractive, dark green foliage. 20cm (8in).

E. × d. 'Arthur Johnson' This form produces long, dense sprays of magenta flowers, which are good for cutting.
♔ 1993

E. × d. 'Darley Dale' This form produces its pale pink flowers over a long period and is one of the most popular of all ericas. Originally catalogued as *E. × darleyensis*, it is the original of the hybrid, which arose in the Darley Dale Nurseries, Derbyshire, England, c1890.

E. × d. 'Furzey' A vigorous, compact form with dark green foliage. The flowers, borne over a long period, are deep rose-pink.
♔ 1993

E. × d. 'George Rendall' A superb form with rich pink flowers over a long period.

E. × d. 'Ghost Hills' A sport of 'Darley Dale'with bright green foliage, tipped with cream in spring, and pink flowers with deeper pink tips.
♔ 1993

E. × d. 'J. W. Porter' A form with mauve-

pink flowers and shoots which are reddish when young in spring.
♔ 1993

E. × d. 'Jenny Porter' A vigorous, upright form with soft pink flowers.
♔ 1993

E. × d. 'Jack H. Brummage' The pale yellow foliage of this form turns golden with a red tinge in winter. The flowers are deep pink and borne in short spikes.
H4

E. × d. 'Kramer's Rote' A cultivar with deep magenta flowers and bronze-green foliage. 35cm (14in).
♔ 1993

E. × d. 'Margaret Porter' This form has glossy green foliage, tipped with cream when young. The flowers are clear rose and borne in short, curving racemes.

Erica × darleyensis 'Silberschmeltze'

E. × d. 'Silberschmeltze' Until recently, this was considered the best white form, but has now been superseded by 'White Perfection'. Its sweetly scented flowers are produced over a long period.

E. × d. 'White Perfection' A form with bright green foliage and white flowers.
♔ 1993

E. erigena, syn. *E. mediterranea* This species is a dense, small to medium-sized shrub, covered from early to late spring with particularly fragrant, rose-red flowers. It and its cultivars are lime-tolerant but are not recommended for shallow soils over chalk. The following are recommended. S France, Spain, W Eire.
H4

E. e. 'Brian Proudley' A vigorous,

upright form growing up to 90cm (3ft) tall, with bright green foliage and long racemes of white flowers.
H4 ♔ 1993

Erica erigena 'Brightness'

E. e. 'Brightness' A low-growing form with bronze-red buds that open to rose-pink. 60–90cm (2–3ft). In cultivation 1925. H4

Erica erigena 'Golden Lady'

E. e. 'Golden Lady' A compact form with golden-yellow foliage and white flowers. 30cm (12in)
H4 ♔ 1993

E. e. 'Irish Dusk' A compact form with dark green foliage and salmon-pink flowers. 45cm (18in).
H4 ♔ 1993

E. e. 'Superba' This is a fine pink-flowered form, growing to a size of 2m (6½ft) or more.
H4

E. e. 'W. T. Rackliff' A charming, dense,

Erica erigena 'Superba'

Erica erigena 'W.T. Rackliff'

compact plant with dark green foliage and pure white flowers with noticeably brown anthers. 1–1.2m (3–4ft).
H4 ♔ 1993

Erica lusitanica

E. lusitanica (Portugal heath) A fine tree heath, resembling *E. arborea* but earlier flowering. The large, pale green, feathery stems

are crowded with tubular, fragrant white flowers that are pink in bud and borne over a very long period from late autumn to early spring. It requires a lime-free soil. Portugal.
H3 ♔ 1993

Erica lusitanica 'George Hunt'

E. l. 'George Hunt' A form with golden yellow foliage.
H3

Erica mackayana

E. mackayana A rare, dwarf species, up to about 15cm (6in). Flowers rose-crimson, in umbels, from midsummer to early autumn. Requires lime-free soil. Following forms are recommended. N and W Ireland, Spain.
H4

E. m. 'Dr Ronald Gray' A form with white flowers.
H4

E. m. 'Maura' An upright form growing to 25cm (10in). Grey-green foliage and semi-double, purple flowers profusely borne.
H4 ♔ 1993

E. m. 'Plena' A form with double, rose-crimson flowers. Found in W Galway.
H4

E. m. 'Shining Light' A form with a profusion of large, white, freely borne flowers and dark green foliage.
H4 ♔ 1993

E. manipulifera 'Heaven Scent' A vigorous, small, upright shrub up to 1m (3ft) high, with dark grey-green foliage. It has long sprays of fragrant, lilac-pink flowers over a long period from summer to autumn. Lime-free soil.
H4 ♔ 1993

E. mediterranea See *E. erigena*.

E. × stuartii A group of hybrids requiring lime-free soil. They flower over a very long period from late spring to early autumn. The following are recommended.
H4

E. × s. 'Irish Lemon' A form with bright pink flowers. The young foliage is lemon-yellow in spring. 30cm (12in).
H4 ♔ 1993

Erica × *stuartii* 'Irish Orange'

E. × s. 'Irish Orange' The flowers of this form are deep pink, and the young foliage orange-tipped. 30cm (12in)
H4

E. terminalis (Corsican heath) A bushy, medium-sized shrub with erect branches. The rose-coloured flowers, borne in late summer in terminal heads, fade to warm brown and remain throughout the winter. It is excellent on chalk soils. W Mediterranean. Introduced 1765.
H4 ♔ 1993

E. tetralix The species grows from 20–50cm (8–20in) high and usually produces its rosy flowers in terminal clusters from early summer to mid-autumn. It and its cultivars require a lime-free soil. The following are recommended. N and W Europe, including Britain and Ireland.
H4

Erica tetralix 'Alba Mollis'

E. t. 'Alba Mollis' A form making 30cm (12in) in height with pretty grey foliage and white flowers.
H4 ♔ 1993

E. t. 'Con Underwood' A form making hummocks of grey-green foliage studded with crimson flower clusters. 20cm (8in). In cultivation 1938.
H4 ♔ 1993

Erica tetralix 'Hookstone Pink'

E. t. 'Hookstone Pink' A vigorous form with silvery grey foliage and pale pink flowers. 30cm (12in). In cultivation 1953.
H4

E. t. 'L. E. Underwood' A form making

20cm (8in) high mounds of silver-grey foliage with pale pink flowers, strikingly terracotta in bud. In cultivation 1937.
H4

Erica tetralix 'Pink Star'

E. t. 'Pink Star' An interesting and unusual form in which the lilac-pink flowers are held erect on the stems. The foliage is grey-green and the plant is only 20cm (8in) high and spreading in habit. Found in the wild in Cornwall, England.
H4 ♔ 1993

E. vagans (Cornish heath) A vigorous dwarf, spreading shrub, with long sprays of pink or purple-pink flowers from midsummer to mid-autumn and mid-green foliage. It and its cultivars require a lime-free soil. All are H4. The following are recommended. SW Europe, including Cornwall, England, and Fermanagh, N Ireland.
H4

E. v. 'Birch Glow' A form with bright green foliage and glowing rose-pink flowers.

Erica vagans 'Fiddlestone'

Grows to a height of 45cm (18in)
🏆 1993

E. v. 'Cornish Cream' The creamy white flowers of this cultivar are borne in slender racemes. Found in Cornwall. 50cm (20in).
🏆 1993

E. v. 'Diana Hornibrooke' A compact form with red flowers and dark green foliage. 30cm (12in).

E. v. 'Fiddlestone' A superb form, throwing up long racemes of rose-cerise flowers over a long period. 50–60cm (20–24in).
🏆 1993

Erica vagans 'Holden Pink'

E. v. 'Holden Pink' A compact, mound-forming plant with dark green foliage. The flowers are white, flushed with mallow-purple at the tips. 35cm (14in).

E. v. 'Kevernensis Alba' A compact form with small racemes of white flowers. 30cm (12in).
🏆 1993

E. v. 'Lyonesse' A form with pure white

Erica vagans 'Lyonesse'

flowers with protruding brown anthers. 50cm–1m (20in–3ft). In cultivation 1925.
🏆 1993

Erica vagans 'Mrs D. F. Maxwell'

E. v. 'Mrs D. F. Maxwell' A superb cultivar with deep cerise flowers . 50cm (20in).
🏆 1993

E. v. 'Pyrenees Pink' This form bears long clusters of pink flowers. 50cm (20in)

E. v. 'St Keverne' A form with clear, rose-pink flowers, but unfortunately liable to revert back to the usual wild form. Found in Cornwall, England. 50cm (20in).

Erica vagans 'Valerie Proudley'

E. v. 'Valerie Proudley' A dwarf bush 20cm (8in) high with bright yellow foliage and white flowers. It has won RHS awards for both summer and winter foliage.
🏆 1993

E. × veitchii Tree heath hybrids reaching 2.2m (7ft) and requiring lime-free soil. The following are recommended.

H3–4

E. × v. 'Exeter' A beautiful, medium-sized shrub, with attractive, bright green foliage and great plumes of fragrant white flowers in spring. Not recommended for the coldest areas. Raised before 1900 by Messrs Veitch in Exeter, England.

H3–4

E. × v. 'Gold Tips' The young foliage of this medium-sized shrub is bright yellow, becoming dark green.

H4 🏆 1993

Erica × watsonii 'Dawn'

E. × watsonii 'Dawn' A spreading plant with young foliage yellow in spring and terminal clusters of large, rose-pink flowers from midsummer to mid- or even late autumn. 23cm (9in). It requires a lime-free soil. Found 1923 in Dorset.

H4 🏆 1993

E. × williamsii 'P D Williams' A pretty, late-flowering heath. The young growths are tipped with yellow in spring and become bronze in winter. The rose-pink flowers are borne in umbels from midsummer to early autumn and the plant grows to 30–60cm (12–24in). It requires a lime-free soil. This is the original clone found in the wild in Cornwall 1910.

H4 🏆 1993

Erinacea *Leguminosae*
Blue broom, hedgehog broom

A genus of one species of deciduous shrubs related to Genista *and* Spartium.

E. anthyllis A dwarf, slow-growing, spiny shrub that makes a very dense, rigid hum-

Erinacea anthyllis

mock. It requires a well drained position in full sun and a very gritty soil. The flowers, borne from late spring to early summer, are bright, slaty blue. SW Europe, North Africa. Introduced 1759.
H4 ♛ 1993

Eriobotrya *Rosaceae*

A genus of about 27 species of evergreen trees and shrubs native to the Himalayas and east Asia. They will grow in any well-drained friable soil. No pruning is required.

Eriobotrya japonica

E. japonica (Loquat) An architectural plant normally seen as a large shrub in cool temperate gardens such as in the British Isles (a small tree in Mediterranean-type climates) and best grown against a wall. It is one of the most striking evergreens by virtue of its firm, leathery, corrugated leaves that are often 30cm (12in) long. The clusters of white, strongly fragrant,

hawthorn-like flowers, produced only after a hot summer, open intermittently from late autumn to mid-spring and are only very occasionally followed by globular or pear-shaped, yellow fruits 4–5cm (1¹/₂–2in) across. It is commonly cultivated in warmer countries for its edible fruits, but is a first-class foliage shrub. Introduced 1787.
H3 ♛ 1993

Erythrina *Leguminosae*

A genus of over 100 species of mainly tropical deciduous trees and shrubs with trifoliate leaves and often prickly stems. They are natives of tropical and sub-tropical regions of the world. They will grow in any well-drained friable soil.

Erythrina crista-galli

E. crista-galli (Coral tree) A very beautiful, semi-woody plant of which the leaves have three leaflets. The flowers are like deep scarlet, waxen sweet peas, and are borne in large, terminal clusters in late summer. It barely succeeds on a warm, sunny wall in the mildest places, and even then the crown needs to be protected. It is much better as a conservatory plant, grown in a tub and moved outside in summer. Brazil. Introduced 1771.
H2 ♛ 1993

Escallonia *Escalloniaceae*

A genus of about 40 species of shrubs and small trees, mainly evergreen, all natives of South America and mostly from the Andes. They rank high among flowering evergreens and are all the more valuable for putting on their display in

summer and early autumn. Not all of them are hardy inland, but most can be grown successfully near the sea, where they make excellent hedges and windbreaks. They average 1.5–2.5m (5–8ft) in height, but can be a good deal taller in mild, maritime areas. With rare exceptions, escallonias are lime-tolerant and drought-resistant, thriving in all types of well-drained soil. None of them have large leaves or large flowers; reference to size is merely comparative within the genus itself. Immediately after flowering, cut back the old flowering growths and prune large, unwieldy plants hard at the same time.

Escallonia 'Apple Blossom'

E. 'Apple Blossom' A very attractive, slow-growing evergreen small to medium-sized shrub with pink and white flowers.
H4 ♛ 1993

Escallonia 'C. F. Ball'

E. 'C. F. Ball' A vigorous evergreen shrub up to 3m (10ft) tall, excellent for maritime exposure, it has large leaves which are aromatic when bruised, and crimson flowers.

Raised 1912 at Glasnevin, Scotland.
H4

E. **'Donard Beauty'** A graceful evergreen shrub to about 1.5m (5ft), with large leaves that are aromatic when bruised and rich rose-red, freely borne flowers.
H4

E. **'Donard Radiance'** A magnificent, strong-growing but compact evergreen

Escallonia 'Donard Radiance'

shrub of medium size. It has large, brilliant, soft rose-red, chalice-shaped flowers and large, shining, deep green leaves.
H4 ♔ 1993

E. **'Donard Seedling'** A vigorous evergreen hybrid up to 3m (10ft) tall. The flowers are flesh-pink in bud and open white, and the leaves are large.
H4

E. **'Donard Star'** A medium-sized, compact, upright evergreen shrub with large leaves and lovely rose-pink, large flowers.
H4

E. **'Edinensis'** A neat, bushy evergreen shrub which grows to 2–2.5m (6–8ft) high, with small bright green leaves. The flowers are carmine in bud, opening to clear shell-pink. Raised at Edinburgh Botanic gardens, Scotland, before 1914.
H4 ♔ 1993

E. **'Gwendolyn Anley'** A small, very hardy, bushy evergreen shrub with small leaves and flesh-pink flowers.
H4

Escallonia 'Iveyi'

E. **'Iveyi'** A large, vigorous evergreen hybrid with large, handsome, glossy leaves that are aromatic when bruised, and large panicles of white flowers in autumn. It is not hardy very far inland.
H3 ♔ 1993

E. **'Langleyensis'** A hardy, graceful evergreen shrub up to 2.5m (8ft) tall, with small leaves and rose-pink flowers that wreathe the arching branches.
H4 ♔ 1993

E. macrantha See *E. rubra* var. *macrantha*.

Escallonia 'Peach Blossom'

E. **'Peach Blossom'** An attractive medium-sized evergreen shrub, similar in growing habit to 'Apple Blossom' but with flowers of clear peach-pink.
H4 ♔ 1993

E. **'Pride of Donard'** The flowers of this medium-sized evergreen shrub are large, brilliant rose, somewhat bell-shaped, and carried in terminal clusters from early summer on. The leaves are large with polished

Escallonia 'Donard Star'

Escallonia 'Pride of Donard'

dark green upper surfaces.
H4 ♔ 1993

E. **'Red Dream'** A compact small shrub with reddish young shoots and small glossy green leaves. The relatively large, clear pinkish red flowers open over a long period during summer. An excellent plant for a container or garden with limited space.
H4

E. **'Red Elf'** A vigorous, medium-sized evergreen shrub with glossy dark green leaves and freely borne deep crimson flowers. In cultivation 1970.
H4

E. **'Red Hedge'** A vigorous, erect, medium-sized to large shrub with dark glossy leaves and vivid crimson flowers.
H4

E. rubra **'Crimson Spire'** A strong-growing evergreen shrub of erect growth up to 2m (6½ft) tall. The leaves are large and glistening dark green, and the flowers are bright crimson, appearing throughout the

Escallonia × *virgata*

summer. An excellent hedging shrub.
H4 ♔ 1993

E. r. **var. *macrantha***, syn. *E macrantha* A strong-growing shrub up to 4m (12ft) tall, and one of the best hedging plants for withstanding sea gales. It has rose-crimson flowers, set among large, glossy, aromatic leaves. Chile. Introduced 1848.
H4

Escallonia rubra 'Woodside'

Escallonia rubra 'Slieve Donard'

E. r. **'Woodside'** A small, neat shrub, the product of a witches' broom that occurred in Ireland. It is small enough for a large rock garden, although its branches spread over a considerable area. The flowers are small and crimson.
H4

E. **'Slieve Donard'** A medium-sized, compact evergreen shrub with small leaves and large panicles of apple-blossom-pink flowers. Very hardy.
H4

E. × *stricta* 'Harold Comber' A clone of a natural hybrid and one of the hardiest of the family. This is a dense shrub which grows up to 1.5m (5ft) tall, the slender stems become crowded with small leaves and small white flowers.
H4

E. × *virgata* A graceful, small-leaved, deciduous shrub with arching branches and white flowers. Not suitable for chalky soils, but very hardy. Chile. Introduced 1866.
H4

EUCALYPTUS

Myrtaceae Gum tree

EUCALYPTUS IS A GENUS of more than 400 species of fast-growing, evergreen trees that resemble no other trees seen in temperate gardens. The individual species often have very wide distributions in the wild, and by selecting seed from trees from the more southerly parts of their ranges and from the greatest altitude, a wider range of species, all of which are natives of Australia and Tasmania, can be made possible for our gardens.

The lush foliage, multi-stamened flowers and outstandingly attractive stems and trunks of the eucalypts provide an impressive, sub-tropical effect. The leaves of adult trees, often very different from those of young specimens, are usually more or less sickle-shaped and hang edge-downwards so as to minimize the incidence of their native sun. The juvenile leaves, by contrast, are usually rounded. Either type, when cut, makes superb foliage for flower arrangements. In the British Isles the seed capsules are very insignificant.

CARE AND CULTIVATION

Eucalypts will grow in a great variety of soils and many are tolerant of wet sites, but some species tend to suffer from chlorosis (yellowing of the leaves followed by death) in shallow soils over chalk. *E. parvifolia* is the only species that can be relied upon in such soils. They are best planted as small, pot-grown plants in early summer and not staked. Larger plants (which must be staked) are best cut down to about 25cm (10in) from the ground in spring, whereupon several new shoots will appear, the strongest of which can be selected for the new main stem. If you prefer a bushy plant, retain all the shoots rather than just the one. Cold, strong winds are a greater danger to most eucalypts than frosts, and you should

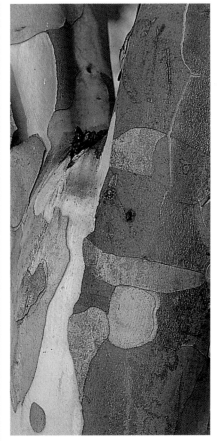

Eucalyptus parvifolia

always provide them with shelter.

Pruning is generally unnecessary. Eucalypts that are apparently dead after a severe winter should be left severely alone until at least the latter part of early summer, when new shoots may grow from any part of the tree, including from ground level. Those higher up will soon establish a new branch structure and the dead wood can then be cut back to them; ground-level shoots can be treated in the same way as those on specimens cut down early for stability.

All of the species described below have multi-stamened white flowers.

E. citriodora (Lemon-scented gum) In the wild, this makes a large tree with smooth, white bark and very slender adult leaves. It is mainly grown in the juvenile stage as a medium-sized shrub for its lemon-scented foliage, which is best enjoyed in a conservatory, especially as it is not hardy out of doors even in the mildest areas. It is widely planted in warm countries. Queensland. H2

Eucalyptus coccifera

E. coccifera (Mount Wellington peppermint) A large tree with strikingly bloomy leaves and stems, not apparent in young plants. In all but the severest winters it comes through undamaged in south-east England. Tasmania. Introduced 1840. H3 ♆ 1993

E. dalrympleana (Mountain gum) A most attractive, very fast growing, medium-sized to large tree and one of the hardiest. Its attractive patchwork bark becomes white, and its handsome, grey-green leaves are bronze when young. A specimen at the Hillier Gardens and Arboretum was 22m (75ft) high in 1995. New South Wales, Tasmania, Victoria. H3 ♆ 1993

Eucalyptus dalrympleana

Eucalyptus pauciflora **subsp.** niphophila

E. globulus (Tasmanian blue gum) In the very mildest areas this species will make a large, noble tree, but it is more usually seen as a sparsely branched shrub in tropical bedding schemes. The large leaves are almost silvery on young specimens, turning blue-green with age. Tasmania, Victoria. In cultivation 1829.
H2 ♛ 1993

E. gunnii (Cider gum) The best-known species in cultivation and one the hardiest. It is a fine tree with juvenile leaves that are rounded and startlingly silver-blue, becoming sickle-shaped with maturity. It can reach large tree size or remain as a most attractive bush if regularly pruned. Tasmania. In cultivation 1853.
H3 ♛ 1993

E. johnstonii (Yellow gum) One of the hardier species, this is a large tree with red-dish peeling bark and bright, glossy, apple-green leaves. In 1995 a specimen in the Hillier Gardens and Arboretum was found to be an impressive 23m (over 75ft) high. Tasmania. In cultivation 1886.
H3

E. parvifolia An exceptionally hardy

Eucalyptus gunnii

Eucalyptus johnstonii

Eucalyptus parvifolia

species that will survive relatively hard winters, this is a handsome, medium-sized tree with attractively peeling bark. It tolerates chalk soils. The mature leaves are on the small side, narrow and blue-green. New South Wales.
H4 ♛ 1993

E. pauciflora subsp. *niphophila* (Snow gum) This beautiful small tree of comparatively slow growth has large, leathery, grey-green leaves. The trunk is a lovely patchwork of green, grey and cream and has been likened, not too inaccurately, to the skin of a python. A tree in the Hillier Gardens and Arboretum sustained no damage over three decades, but in an even milder garden in the next county another, perhaps not of such a hardy provenance, was killed outright. Queensland to S Australia and Tasmania.
H3–4 ♛ 1993

E. perriniana (Spinning gum) A small tree which has silver leaves and white, dark-blotched stems. The juvenile leaves are

Eucalyptus perriniana

Eucalyptus urnigera

Eucryphia cordifolia

round (perfoliate); the mature leaves are oblanceolate and bloomy. New South Wales, Tasmania, Victoria.
H3

E. urnigera (Urn gum) This species makes a fairly hardy, small to medium-sized tree with greyish, peeling bark and dark green leaves. Its urn-shaped fruits are distinct from all others. In cultivation 1860.
H3

Eucommia *Eucommiaceae*

A genus of one deciduous species, which is perfectly hardy and thrives in all types of fertile soil.

E. ulmoides The only hardy tree known to produce rubber. It is a vigorous and ornamental tree up to 9m (28ft) or more, with rather large, leathery, glossy, elm-like leaves which, on gently tearing, will display fine strands of latex. Introduced 1896 from cultivation in China but not known in the wild.
H4

Eucryphia *Eucryphiaceae*

A genus of five species of highly ornamental evergreen and deciduous shrubs or trees that flower from midsummer to early autumn once they are a few years old. They all have white flowers with conspicuous stamens. They thrive best in sheltered positions and in moist loam, preferably lime-free, but provided large amounts of organic matter are added, they can be grown on soils a little on the alkaline side of neutral. The roots should be shaded from hot sun, and this can be done by growing low plants such as Erica carnea that do not rob the soil unduly. Pruning is generally unnecessary.

E. cordifolia (Ulmo) A very beautiful, large evergreen shrub or, in favoured areas, a broad columnar tree of 9–12m (28–40ft). Its leaves are oblong, wavy-edged and often heart-shaped at the base. The flower is like a white Rose of Sharon (*Hypericum calycinum*). This species is reasonably lime-tolerant. Chile. Introduced 1851.
H3

Eucryphia glutinosa

E. glutinosa This is one of the most glorious of woody plants. It makes a large, deciduous shrub or small tree (although evergreen in the wild) with erect branches, pinnate leaves, and white flowers 6cm (2.5in) across, borne profusely in mid- to late summer. The leaves have beautiful autumn tints. Chile. Introduced 1859. H4 ♔ 1993

E. × hillieri 'Winton' A medium-sized evergreen shrub bearing pinnate leaves with 3–7 leaflets and beautifully formed, cup-shaped, white flowers like those of *E. lucida*. This interesting hybrid originated as a self-sown seedling in one of the Hillier Nurseries. H3

Eucryphia × intermedia 'Rostrevor'

E. × intermedia 'Rostrevor' A lovely, fast-growing, small evergreen tree of compact, broadly columnar habit. On the same plant there will be simple leaves and others with three leaflets. The fragrant white flowers are each 2.5–5cm (1–2in) across and smother the branches in late summer and early autumn. Raised at Rostrevor, Co. Down, Ireland. H3 ♔ 1993

Eucryphia lucida

E. lucida A delightful, densely leafy, large evergreen shrub or small tree with simple, oblong leaves that are bloomy on their undersides. The charming, fragrant, pendulous flowers, up to 5cm (2in) across, appear in early to midsummer. Tasmania. Introduced 1820. H3

E. l. 'Pink Cloud' The margins of the petals of this form are pale pink shading to white, and the petals are red at the base. Found as a single 20m (70ft) tree in a remote area of NW Tasmania. H3

E. milliganii A delightful and very hardy miniature species, eventually a small, usually slender, shrubby deciduous tree. The tiny, neat leaves are shining dark green and bloomy beneath and the buds are exceptionally sticky. The flowers are cup-shaped and similar to those of *E. lucida* but somewhat smaller. This species flowers freely, even as a small shrub. Tasmania. Introduced 1929 by Harold Comber. H3

Eucryphia × nymansensis 'Nymansay'

E. × nymansensis 'Nymansay' A magnificent, small to medium-sized, densely columnar evergreen tree of rapid growth, with both simple and compound leaves on the same plant. The flowers are fully 6cm (2½in) across, wreathing the branches in bridal white in late summer and early autumn. It tolerates a little lime in the presence of large quantities of organic matter. Raised 1915 at Nymans, Sussex, England. H3 ♔ 1993

Euodia

E. danielli See *Tetradium danielli*.

EUONYMUS

Celastraceae

THE 170 SPECIES of evergreen and deciduous shrubs that make up the genus *Euonymus* have a major part to play in our gardens, though it is often not recognized just how valuable they can be.

The genus is extremely versatile, encompassing dwarf shrubs, creepers, climbers and small trees, which can be found in Europe, North America, Asia, Africa and Australia. The deciduous species are grown mainly for their brilliant autumn colour and for their dangling, brightly coloured winter fruits that make every branch look as though it has been bedecked with jewellery. The evergreen ones are valued for their foliage, and the many coloured forms contribute bright, sunny accents, not only in winter but also during summer, when their showiness is no less impressive in the face of greater competition from other plants.

These are plants that can be put to many uses, including ground cover, hedging, edgings, screens, or as attractive freestanding specimens. The evergreens are all highly resistant to salt-laden winds and are excellent for planting near the sea; and in general the genus as a whole is tolerant of conditions that you might expect to be most unpromising.

The flowers, borne in early summer and normally green or purplish, are not very significant, and it is the brightly coloured fruits, which open to reveal equally showy seeds, that are the main attraction. Sometimes the fruit, seeds and aril (a fleshy attachment to the seeds) will all be of different colours in the red/pink/orange part of the spectrum. However, fruits will not occur in the majority of cases unless more than one specimen is grown to ensure cross-pollination. *Euonymus alatus* is something of an exception, but even so it is better grown as a small group, in which case there is a

Euonymus phellomanus has attractive pink fruits

much better chance of all four of the fruits in each cluster being fertilized and eventually displaying the orange seeds against the vermilion of the opened fruit. On single specimens the fruits tend to ripen in twos instead of fours.

All species are harmful if eaten.

CARE AND CULTIVATION

Euonymus are remarkably lacking in fussiness about soil. They will grow in poor places and are excellent in shallow, dry soils over chalk, where the value of the deciduous species for autumn colour is exceptional. If you have an area of dry shade and find, as most people do, that it is difficult to persuade most things to grow in it, euonymus should be the first shrubs you consider, especially the brightly variegated forms of *E. fortunei* and *E. japonicus*. They are also unusually tolerant of compaction of the soil and grow well near to paths.

There is little need to prune euonymus; just cut away dead or damaged branches, and remove any occasional reversion to green in a variegated evergreen as soon as you see it.

Although this is a genus of plants that are on the whole easy to grow, pests can be a problem, particularly the black bean aphid. Euonymus (particularly *E. europaeus*) are winter hosts, carrying the autumn-laid eggs near their buds. The eggs hatch in midspring just as the buds are opening, and the aphids proceed to multiply rapidly. In late spring the females fly off to beans and other plants, where they start new infestations from which, in autumn, a new generation of females flies to the winter hosts. It is therefore a good idea to spray euonymus with a systemic insecticide in early spring and again in early autumn.

E. alatus A slow-growing, many-branched, medium-sized shrub, distinguished by the broad, corky wings that develop on the branchlets in favourable conditions. It is one of the finest and most reliable of all deciduous shrubs for autumn colour, with the leaves turning brilliant crimson-pink. The fruits are reddish purple, opening to reveal bright orange-coated seeds. China, Japan. Introduced 1860. H4 ♔ 1993

E. a. **'Compactus'** A dense, small, compact form that colours equally well; ideal for a low hedge. Raised before 1928 in the United States. H4 ♔ 1993

E. europaeus (Spindle) The wood of this shrub, which is a familiar sight in many European hedgerows, was used for making spindles for spinning. A vigorous deciduous shrub with an abundance of brilliant red capsules that open to show vivid orange seeds, it grows especially well on chalk soils. It is usually grown in one of its forms or cultivars. Europe, W Asia. H4

E. e. **f.** *albus* A white-fruited form, showy in winter. At 3m (10ft), it is about half the height of the usual wild form. H4

E. e. **'Red Cascade'** A selected form which eventually makes a small tree with arching branches made pendulous by the weight of the rosy-red fruits. The leaves turn rich scarlet in autumn. H4 ♔ 1993

E. fortunei A very hardy, trailing evergreen species good for ground cover in shade or sun. It will also climb without assistance. It seldom flowers or fruits and then only on adult stems. Many cultivars have arisen from *E. f.* var. *radicans*. The following forms are recommended. H4

E. f. **'Canadale Gold'** This cultivar is a small shrub with green leaves broadly edged with deep yellow. H4

E. f. **'Coloratus'** A trailing or climbing form reaching 8m (25ft) with support. Its leaves are beautifully coloured sanguineous purple throughout the winter, especially when the roots are starved or controlled.

Euonymus europaeus

Euonymus alatus 'Compactus'

Euonymus europaeus

Euonymus europaeus 'Red Cascade'

Euonymus fortunei 'Canadale Gold'

An interesting feature is that the leaves may resume their green colour in spring.
H4

E. f. 'Dart's Blanket' An improvement on 'Coloratus', selected in Holland, where it is widely planted as ground cover. The leaves are deep green, and turning bronze-red in autumn. In cultivation 1969.
H4

Euonymus fortunei 'Emerald Gaiety'

E. f. 'Emerald Gaiety' A small, compact, bushy shrub which has deep green leaves with an irregular white margin that becomes attractively tinged with pink in winter. Raised in the United States.
H4 ♛ 1993

Euonymus fortunei 'Emerald 'n' Gold'

E. f. 'Emerald 'n' Gold' A very striking, dense, dwarf bush with deep green leaves that are broadly margined in bright gold. The margin becomes cream flushed with pink in winter. This cultivar will also climb if it is provided with support. Raised prior

to 1967 in the United States.
H4 ♛ 1993

E. f. 'Gold Tip' A small, compact shrub of broadly upright habit with golden-yellow-margined leaves.
H4

Euonymus fortunei 'Harlequin'

E. f. 'Harlequin' A recently introduced dwarf shrub with leaves heavily mottled with white. It may be some time before judgement can properly be made on its value as a garden plant.
H4

Euonymus fortunei 'Kewensis'

E. f. 'Kewensis' A dainty form with slender, prostrate stems and minute leaves, suitable for the rock garden. It will climb if support is available. Introduced 1893.
H4

E. f. 'Silver Pillar' A shrub of erect habit with narrow leaves with a broad marginal white variegation.
H4

Euonymus fortunei 'Silver Queen'

E. f. 'Silver Queen' A small, compact shrub, although it can reach 2.5–3m (8–10ft) against a wall. The unfolding leaves in spring are rich creamy yellow, later becoming green with a broad, creamy white margin. It is one of the loveliest variegated shrubs and has the added bonus of occasionally producing pale green flowers which are followed by pink fruits. In cultivation 1914.
H4 ♛ 1993

Euonymus fortunei 'Sunspot'

E. f. 'Sunspot' A compact shrub with deep green leaves with a central golden blotch, tinged red beneath in winter. The stems are yellowish. In cultivation 1980.
H4

E. f. 'Variegatus' This medium-sized trailing or climbing form has greyish green leaves margined white and often tinged with pink. It has now effectively been superseded by other selections.
H4

Euonymus grandiflorus

E. grandiflorus An erect, slow-growing semi-evergreen shrub reaching 4m (12ft) high. It bears conspicuous, comparatively large, straw-yellow flowers and yellow capsules with scarlet seeds. The leaves give rich wine-purple autumn colour. Himalaya, W China, introduced 1824.
H4

E. hamiltonianus A large semi-evergreen or deciduous shrub or small tree bearing pink fruits with orange or red seeds. This is a particularly variable species, the typical form of which is thought not to be in cultivation. The following forms are recommended. Himalayas.
H4

Euonymus hamiltonianus 'Coral Charm'

E. h. 'Coral Charm' This large shrub or small tree of spreading habit has pale yellow leaves that are green in autumn; the freely borne fruits are pale pink and the seeds have red arils. A Hillier selection.
H4

E. h. 'Coral Chief' This cultivar is similar to 'Coral Charm' but upright, with pink fruits showing red arils. A Hillier selection.
H4

Euonymus hamiltonianus subsp. sieboldianus

E. h. subsp. sieboldianus This large shrub or small tree has dull green leaves that turn yellow, pink or red in autumn. The showy fruits are rose-pink, and often abundantly borne. Japan, E China, Korea. Introduced 1865.
H4

E. japonicus A large, densely branched, evergreen shrub with glossy dark green leathery leaves. It is one of the best evergreens for coastal or town planting and succeeds in sun or shade. China, Japan, Korea.
H4

E. j. 'Aureopictus' See *E. j.* 'Aureus'.
E. j. 'Aureovariegatus' See *E. j.* 'Ovatus Aureus'.
E. j. 'Aureus', syn. *E. j.* 'Aureopictus' A large shrub on which the leaves have a

Euonymus japonicus 'Aureus'

golden centre and a broad green margin. It is liable to revert.
H4

Euonymus japonicus 'Duc d'Anjou'

E. j. 'Duc d'Anjou' A large shrub with dark green leaves with a central splash of pale or yellowish green.
H4

Euonymus japonicus 'Latifolius Albomarginatus'

E. j. 'Latifolius Albomarginatus', syn. *E. j.* 'Macrophyllus Albus' The leaves of this large shrub have an eye-catching broad white margin. The showiest of the variegated forms.
H4

E. j. 'Macrophyllus Albus' See *E. j.* 'Latifolius Albomarginatus'.
E. j. 'Marieke' With its creamy yellow-margined foliage, this is very similar to *E. j.* 'Ovatus Aureus' but with smaller leaves.
H4

E. j. 'Microphyllus Aureus' See *E. j.* 'Microphyllus Pulchellus'.

Euonymus japonicus 'Marieke'

E. j. 'Microphyllus Pulchellus', syn. *E. j.* 'Microphyllus Aureus' A small, slow-growing form of dense, compact habit with small, narrow green leaves suffused with gold. It has something of the appearance of box (*Buxus*).
H4

E. j. 'Microphyllus Variegatus' A similar plant to the above with green leaves margined with white.
H4

Euonymus japonicus 'Ovatus Aureus'

E. j. 'Ovatus Aureus', syn. *E. j.* 'Aureo-variegatus' The leaves of this medium-sized shrub are margined and suffused with creamy yellow, particularly when young; growth is rather slow and compact. It requires a sunny site if it is to retain its colour but is the most popular golden euonymus.
H4 ♛ 1993

E. latifolius Growing to 3.5–5m (11–15ft) high, this deciduous species has larger scar-

Euonymus latifolius

let fruits and more brilliant autumn foliage than the common spindle tree. It is similar to, and has been confused with, *E. planipes* but differs in the sharp-edged wings of the fruit. Europe. Introduced 1730.
H4

E. nanus A useful, procumbent, semi-evergreen shrub with narrow leaves and tiny, brown-purple flowers. Ideal as ground cover and for banks. Caucasus to China. Introduced 1830.
H4

E. n. var. turkestanicus A semi-erect variety up to 1m (3ft), with longer leaves. It is the commonest form in cultivation and has bright pink fruits with orange seeds. C Asia. In cultivation 1883.
H4

Euonymus oxyphyllus

E. oxyphyllus A slow-growing, medium-sized to large deciduous shrub with leaves that turn rich shades of red and purple-red in the autumn, when the branches are

strung with rich carmine-red capsules. Japan, Korea and China. Introduced 1892.
H4

E. phellomanus A large shrub with conspicuously corky-winged shoots, oval to obovate leaves and four-lobed pink fruits.
H4

Euonymus planipes

E. planipes A large, handsome deciduous shrub, similar to *E. latifolius* and equally colourful in autumn. The large and showy scarlet fruits are freely borne. NE Asia.
H4 ♛ 1993

Eupatorium *Compositae*

A genus of around 500 species of evergreen and deciduous trees, shrubs and herbaceous perennials, widely distributed for the most part in tropical America.

Eupatorium ligustrinum

E. ligustrinum An evergreen shrub producing large, flat heads of small, white, fra-

grant flowers in late summer and autumn. In the mildest areas it grows to 2.5m (8ft). It thrives in most soils but needs shelter from wind. No pruning is necessary.
H3

Euphorbia *Euphorbiaceae*
Spurge

The spurges make up a very large genus of more than 1500 species. There are many excellent herbaceous perennials and a large number of spiny, cactus-like succulents, sometimes growing to be large trees. Among these mainly subtropical and tropical plants are some hardy, evergreen sub-shrubs with flowers that, while not very showy individually, are highly effective in the typical euphorbia clusters. They grow in any ordinary garden soil and do not require pruning. Of those below, only the first is fully hardy. They are harmful if eaten and are skin and eye irritants.

E. amygdaloides var. robbiae, syn. *E.*

Euphorbia characias

robbiae (Mrs Robb's bonnet) This is a dwarf evergreen sub-shrub that spreads rapidly by underground stems. Its deep glossy green, leathery leaves are broadest above the middle, and are arranged in dense rosettes at the tips of the stems. Eye-catching greenish yellow flowerheads are borne over a long period during late winter and early spring. It spreads to make excellent ground cover in the shade. Turkey. Introduced early 1890s by Mrs Robb.
H4 ♆ 1993

E. characias A small, evergreen sub-shrub which displays erect, unbranched stems, each of which lives for two years; the downy, bluish green linear leaves are held in dense clusters at the ends of the shoots. The flowers are in terminal panicles with striking, yellowish green bracts and reddish purple glands, and are attractive for several months during spring and summer. Mediterranean region.
H3 ♆ 1993

Euphorbia characias subsp. *wulfenii*

Euphorbia characias 'John Tomlinson'

E. c. subsp. wulfenii This differs from the typical form in the yellowish green glands of the flower cluster.
H3 ♆ 1993

E. c. 'John Tomlinson' The flowers of this form are borne in large heads, with long upper rays making the inflorescence almost rounded. The bracts are yellow-green. Found 1966 in the wild in former Yugoslavia.
H3 ♆ 1993

Euphorbia characias 'Lambrook Gold'

E. c. 'Lambrook Gold' A form with columnar inflorescence and bright golden-green bracts.
H3 ♆ 1993

Euphorbia × martinii

E. × martinii (*E. amygdaloides × E. characias*) A clump-forming evergreen sub-shrub, producing tufts of dark green leaves flushed purple when young. Green flowers, tinged purple, appear over a long period in spring.
H3 ♆ 1993

E. mellifera A small to medium-sized, dense, rounded evergreen shrub with stout shoots and narrowly oblong leaves up to 20cm (8in) long. The brown, intensely honey-scented flowers are borne in late spring; round, hard, warty fruits follow. In the very mildest places, especially near the sea, it can grow in the open, but otherwise is best under glass. Madeira and Canary Isles, now very rare.
H2

E. robbiae See *E. amygdaloides* var. *robbiae*.

Euptelea *Eupteleaceae*

A genus of two or perhaps three species of large deciduous shrubs or small trees with petal-less flowers made up of dense bunches of red-anthered stamens, borne in dense clusters all along the bare branches in spring. It does well in full sun in any reasonably moisture-retentive soil and pruning is not necessary.

E. polyandra This is a large shrub or small tree, attracting attention in spring when crowded with flowers consisting of clusters of red anthers. The young growths are copper- tinted, and the narrow, oval, long-stalked coarsely and irregularly toothed leaves turn red and yellow in autumn. Japan. In cultivation 1887.
H4

Euryops *Compositae*

A genus of around 100 species of evergreen shrubs with bright yellow, daisy flowerheads. They are natives mainly of South Africa but extend north

Euryops acraeus

into *Arabia. The following need a warm, sunny position and a well-drained soil.*

E. acraeus A dwarf shrub of neat, domed habit when well grown, forming a compact mound of grey stems and narrow, silver-grey leaves. The canary-yellow flowers (strictly flowerheads), 2.5cm (1in) across, cover the plant entirely during late spring and early summer. It is ideal for the rock garden or scree, but the drainage must be near-perfect. Unaccountable failures and spasmodic attacks of rust are experiences to be balanced against those of the many growers for whom this is one of the best shrubs of its size. Drakensberg Mountains of South Africa.
H4 ♛ 1993

E. chrysanthemoides A small, tender shrub with purplish stems and leaves deeply divided into oblong lobes that become linear towards the base. The solitary, yellow, daisy flowerheads are deeper coloured in the centre and 6cm (2½in) across. They are borne on long, erect stalks from mid-summer onwards. South Africa.
H2

Euryops pectinatus

E. pectinatus A small shrub up to 1m (3ft), with erect, greyish, downy shoots. The leaves are 5–7.5cm (2–3in) long, deeply lobed like the teeth of a comb (pectinate), and grey-downy. The flowerheads are rich yellow, 4cm (1½in) across and carried on long, slender, erect stalks in late spring and early summer. If it is cut back by about 15cm (6in) after the main flush of flowers, it is likely to flower again almost as freely and

to continue right through the winter. It flowers best on a fairly poor soil in full sun. It will survive and flower through frosty winters in mild areas and is superb in the conservatory. South Africa.
H2–3 ♛ 1993

Exochorda *Rosaceae*

There are four or five species of these beautiful and showy deciduous shrubs. Their long, arching branches are festooned in late spring with impressive racemes of comparatively large, paper-white flowers. Preferring full sun, they grow on almost all garden soils but are inclined to become chlorotic on very shallow ones over chalk. Pruning, where necessary in order to reduce overcrowding and remove weak stems, can be carried out after flowering has finished.

Exochorda giraldii var. *wilsonii*

E. giraldii var. wilsonii An excellent, large, free-flowering shrub producing the largest flowers in the genus at 5cm (2in)

Exochorda × macrantha 'The Bride'

across. C China. Introduced 1907.
H4

Exochorda korolkowii

E. korolkowii A vigorous species exceeding 4.5m (13ft) in height and one of the best for growing on chalky soils. Turkestan. Introduced 1881.
H4

E. × macrantha 'The Bride' This is a small to medium-sized, dense bush with an elegant weeping habit and highly attractive when the arching branches are wreathed in large, white flowers in mid- or late spring. In cultivation 1938.
H4 ♔ 1993

Exochorda racemosa

E. racemosa This is the best-known species. It is a large, rather spreading shrub with upright clusters of white flowers in late spring and oblong, deep blue-green leaves. It is not suitable for chalky soils. China. Introduced 1849.
H4

F

Fabiana *Solanaceae*

A genus of around 25 species of evergreen, heath-like shrubs, belonging to the potato family and most closely related to Cestrum *among hardy plants. For the most part they are natives of temperate regions of South America. Just one species is in general cultivation, and it succeeds best in a mild area in a sunny position and in moist, well-drained, neutral or acid soil, although it is lime-tolerant enough to be well worth growing in all but very shallow soils over chalk. Prune lank older plants for shape in spring.*

Fabiana imbricata

Fabiana imbricata f. violacea

F. imbricata The branches of this charming, medium-sized shrub are transformed in early summer into plumes of white, tubular flowers. Chile. Introduced 1838.
H3

F. i. 'Prostrata' A small shrub, hardier than the typical form, forming a dense, rounded mound of feathery branchlets that are usually covered with small, pale, mauve-tinted flowers in late spring and early summer. Ideal for large rock gardens or the top of walls.
H3

F. i. f. violacea A medium-sized shrub that is similar to the typical form but with lavender-mauve flowers.
H3 ♔ 1993

Fagus *Fagaceae*
Beech

There are only about 10 species of beeches, which are deciduous trees of the north temperate regions. They are best grown in a deep, well-drained soil and sunny position. Where summers are cool, the European species perform best, with Asiatic beeches close behind. American species require the warmer summers of their homeland.

F. engleriana A rare, medium-sized tree with bloomy, sea-green foliage. China. Introduced 1907 by Ernest Wilson.
H4

Fagus sylvatica

F. sylvatica (Common beech) This is undoubtedly the most noble large tree for limy soils and is also excellent for hedge-making. The rich golden copper of the autumn foliage is not bettered by any other tree. Given a well-drained soil, there is perhaps no other tree that will survive in such extremes of acidity and alkalinity. There are very many named cultivars. Europe,

including Britain and Ireland.
H4 ♔ 1993

F. s. 'Albovariegata' A large tree with leaves margined and streaked with white. In cultivation 1770.
H4

Fagus sylvatica 'Aspleniifolia'

F. s. 'Aspleniifolia' (Cut-leaved beech, fern-leaved beech) The leaves of this large tree are relatively narrow and deeply cut into slender lobes.
H4 ♔ 1993

F. s. 'Aurea Pendula' An elegant, tall, slender form with branches hanging down almost parallel with the main stem. The golden yellow leaves will sometimes scorch in full sun, and in deep shade they lose their rich colour. Originated 1900 as a sport.
H4

F. s. 'Cockleshell' A tall, columnar form with small, rounded leaves. Raised 1960 by Hillier Nurseries.
H4

Fagus sylvatica 'Dawyck'

F. s. 'Dawyck' (Dawyck beech) A stately tall, columnar tree with erect branches which broadens in maturity. This species is sometimes incorrectly known by the name of 'Fastigiata'. Originated before 1850 at Dawyck, Scotland.
H4 ♔ 1993

F. s. 'Dawyck Gold' A dense, tall, colum-

Fagus sylvatica 'Dawyck Gold'

nar tree with bright yellow young foliage turning pale green in summer. A seedling of 'Dawyck'. Raised 1969 by J. R. P. van Hoey-Smith.
H4 ♔ 1993

F. s. 'Dawyck Purple' A tall, splendid, narrowly columnar tree with deep purple foliage. It is narrower than 'Dawyck Gold' and not as dense.
H4 ♔ 1993

Heterophylla group The plant previously grown under this name is *F. s.* 'Aspleniifolia'.

Fagus sylvatica 'Pendula'

F. s. 'Pendula' (Weeping beech) A rather spectacular, large, weeping tree that takes on various forms. Sometimes the enormous branches hang close and perpendicular to the main stem like elephants' trunks, while in other specimens some primary branches are almost horizontal and draped with long, hanging branchlets. In cultivation 1836.
H4 ♔ 1993

Fagus sylvatica 'Riversii'

***F. s.* 'Purple Fountain'** A seedling of 'Purpurea Pendula', this is a large, narrowly upright tree with purple leaves and weeping branches. Raised 1975 in Holland.
H4 ♛ 1993

Purpurea group This name refers to purplish-leaved forms normally selected from among plants raised from seed. They are best used for hedging only.

Fagus sylvatica 'Purpurea Pendula'

***F. s.* 'Purpurea Pendula'** (Weeping purple beech) A superb, small, weeping tree with dark leaves. It is usually grafted high to make a small, mushroom-headed tree. In cultivation 1865.
H4

***F. s.* 'Purpurea Tricolor'**, syn. *F. s.* 'Roseomarginata' A large, attractive but not very constant cultivar with purple leaves edged with an irregular pale pink border. In cultivation 1888.
H4

***F. s.* 'Riversii'** (Purple beech) A large tree

Fagus sylvatica 'Rohanii'

with large, dark purple leaves. 'Atropurpurea', 'Atropurpurea Macrophylla', 'Norwegiensis' and 'Purpurea Latifolia' are similar. In cultivation 1880.
H4 ♛ 1993

***F. s.* 'Rohanii'** A remarkably beautiful, slow-growing, medium-sized to large tree that is a purple-leaved form of the fern-leaved beech. In cultivation 1894.
H4

***F. s.* 'Roseomarginata'** See *F. s.* 'Purpurea Tricolor'.

Fagus sylvatica 'Zlatia'

***F. s.* 'Zlatia'** A slow-growing, medium-sized tree. The leaves are soft yellow at first, becoming green in late summer. Originally a wild form from former Yugoslavia. In cultivation 1890.
H4

Fallopia *Polygonaceae*

A genus of nine species of herbaceous perennials and deciduous woody climbers, native to north temperate regions.

F. baldschuanica, syn. *Polygonum baldschuanicum* (Russian vine) A rampant climber with stems up to 12m (40ft) long and more or less heart-shaped, pale green leaves. The pinkish flowers are individually small but are borne in large, crowded panicles throughout summer and autumn. It is not a plant for a small garden being very fast-growing and large, but can be kept within bounds by being severely pruned in late winter, after which new growth will arise from the old wood. It will grow in any

soil. Tadzhikistan. In cultivation 1883.
H4 ♛ 1993

Fascicularia *Bromeliaceae*

A genus of about five species of stemless plants that form dense clumps of evergreen, strap-shaped, spiny leaves not unlike many of the tropical bromeliads. They are all natives of Chile. They require a warm, sunny, sheltered position in a well-drained soil or rock fissure and are hardy only in the mildest places.

Fascicularia bicolor

F. bicolor The leaves of this evergreen perennial are long, narrow and spine-toothed, sage green above and bloomy beneath. They are produced in dense, tufted rosettes. The shorter, central leaves are rich crimson, giving a delightful effect. The sky-blue, tubular flowers are gathered into a dense, sessile head in the centre of the rosette. While in bud, the flowerhead is concealed by showy, ivory-coloured bracts. It is hardy in mild climates and is best with winter protection. Alternatively, it makes a striking specimen for a container which can be put outside in summer.
H2–3

× Fatshedera *Araliaceae*

This splendid, shade-bearing evergreen plant is a hybrid between the two genera Fatsia *and* Hedera. *It is excellent ground cover for all but the coldest places as long as it is sheltered from wind. It tolerates maritime exposure and pollution, grows in all types of soil and does well even in dry shade. It is in demand as a house plant.*

× *Fatshedera lizei* 'Variegata'

× *F. lizei* A small to medium-sized shrub of loose or sprawling habit, forming a mound of branches clothed with large, leathery, palmate leaves. Spherical heads of white flowers are borne in autumn. Garden origin, 1910.
H3 ♈ 1993

× *F. l.* **'Annemieke'** The leaves of this small to medium-sized shrub have a central botch of bright yellow-green.
H2–3 ♈ 1993

× *F. l.* **'Variegata'** A small to medium-sized shrub of which the grey-green leaves have an irregular, creamy white margin.
H3 ♈ 1993

Fatsia *Araliaceae*

A genus of just one evergreen species. It thrives on any kind of well-drained soil.

F. japonica A bold, handsome, medium-sized to large dense shrub, tending to be

Fatsia japonica

wider than it is high. The very large, polished, dark green, palmate leaves produced on stout shoots give a subtropical effect and are an admirable foil to the panicles of milk-white, globular flowerheads that appear at the ends of the branches in mid-autumn. It succeeds in sun or semi-shade and is excellent for seaside gardens. It is proving much hardier than has been generally believed. Japan. Introduced 1838.
H4 ♈ 1993

Fatsia japonica 'Variegata'

F. j. **'Variegata'** A highly attractive and eye-catching medium-sized to large shrub. The lobes of the leaves are white at the tips.
H3 ♈ 1993

Feijoa *Myrtaceae*

A genus of two species of evergreen shrubs with opposite leaves and solitary flowers in the leaf joints. They are natives of South America and closely related to guavas.

Feijoa sellowiana

F. sellowiana (Pineapple guava) A large shrub, grown commercially for its fruit in warm countries and as an ornamental in temperate ones. It requires a warm and sheltered position and soil that is on the light side. Its leaves are grey-green, white-felted on the undersides, and the fleshily textured flowers are crimson and white, with a central bunch of long, crimson stamens. The large, egg-shaped fruits are sometimes produced after a long, hot summer. The petals and fruits are both edible and have a rich, aromatic flavour. Brazil, Uruguay. Introduced 1898.
H3

Feijoa sellowiana 'Variegata'

F. s. **'Variegata'** The leaves of this large shrub are margined with cream and white.
H3

Ficus *Moraceae*

The fig genus is a very large one and includes over 800 species of evergreen and deciduous trees, shrubs and woody vines from all over the tropical and subtropical regions of the world. Only a few can be grown outside in cool-temperate gardens, but many are popular as conservatory plants.

F. carica **'Brown Turkey'** The most popular fruit-producing form of the common fig, making a large deciduous shrub, or a small tree where the climate is on the mild side. Its handsome, lobed leaves and delicious fruits are an object of interest throughout the year, especially when it is grown against a warm, sunny wall. It is remarkably resistant to salt spray. Skin irri-

Ficus carica

tant in sunlight. The species from W Asia has been in cultivation in Britain since the early sixteenth century.

H4

Ficus pumila

F. pumila (Climbing fig) In its native habitat, this species scrambles up the trunks of trees much as ivy does. The juvenile growths have small, neat, ovate or heart-shaped leaves, and in time growths are formed that produce much larger leaves, up to 10cm (4in) long, and bear flowers and fruits if conditions are suitable. It is a tender plant for the conservatory, where it can cover walls or be used in hanging baskets. In the very mildest districts it may be grown out of doors in a sheltered corner. Far East. Introduced 1721.

H1 🏆 1993

Fitzroya *Cupressaceae*

A genus of one evergreen coniferous species.

F. cupressoides A beautiful, cypress-like, graceful large shrub or small dense tree shaped like a vase with scale-like, white-lined, dark green leaves on drooping branchlets. Chile, Argentina. Introduced 1849 by William Lobb.

H4

Forsythia *Oleaceae*

These highly colourful, spring-flowering deciduous shrubs are very easy to grow. There are seven species, six in east Asia and one in south-east Europe. The bell-shaped flowers that wreathe the branches are golden yellow in most cases. Any ordinary garden soil suits them. As soon as flowering is finished, thin out and cut back the old flowering shoots, making sure to cut back to within a short distance of the old wood.

Forsythia 'Beatrix Farrand'

F. 'Beatrix Farrand' The deep canary-yellow, nodding flowers of this upright, dense bush are exceptionally large – well over 2.5cm (1in) wide when fully expanded. It is named after the renowned American garden designer whose work was influenced by Gertrude Jekyll.

H4

F. 'Golden Nugget' A vigorous, medium-sized shrub with large, golden yellow flowers. There are occasional flowers with six corolla lobes instead of the usual four. Cross made 1964 by Alf Alford.

H4

F. × intermedia There are several named clones of a vigorous, medium-sized to large hybrid, flowering in late winter and spring.

H4

F. × i. 'Fiesta' A medium-sized shrub of compact habit bearing large golden yellow flowers in spring. The leaves are green with cream and gold variegation.

H4

Forsythia × intermedia 'Lynwood'

F. × i. 'Lynwood' A lovely medium-sized to large shrub with large, broad-petalled, rich yellow flowers profusely borne all along the branches in mid-spring. This is one of the most spectacular of the forsythias.

H4 🏆 1993

F. × i. 'Minigold' A compact, upright, medium-sized shrub with deep yellow, small, broad-lobed flowers borne in abundance in mid-spring.

H4

Forsythia × intermedia 'Spectabilis'

F. × i. 'Spectabilis' This is one of the most popular of the many shrubs that flower in early spring deserving of its name. The blooms on this medium-sized to large shrub are so generously borne that they create a

mass of yellow. Garden origin, 1906.
H4

Forsythia × intermedia 'Spring Glory'

F. × i. 'Spring Glory' A large-flowered, floriferous medium-sized to large shrub. It flowers in mid-spring. Found c1930 in a garden in Ohio.
H4

F. × i. 'Tremonia' A small, compact shrub that is made distinct by its very deeply toothed leaves. The large and freely borne mid-spring flowers are pale yellow, with broad petals lightly saw-toothed at the apex. A hybrid of 'Beatrix Ferrand'. In cultivation 1963.
H4

Forsythia ovata 'Tetragold'

F. ovata 'Tetragold' A small, dense shrub with amber-yellow flowers produced in late winter. It associates well with heaths and *Rhododendron* 'Praecox'. In cultivation 1963.
H4

F. suspensa A rambling shrub to about 3m (10ft) but much higher against a wall, with slender, interlacing branches. It is excellent on north- and east-facing walls. The deep yellow flowers on slender stalks are produced from early to mid-spring. The leaves often have three lobes. China. Introduced 1833.
H4 ♔ 1993

F. s. f. atrocaulis The young stems of this medium-sized to large shrub are almost black-purple, contrasting with the comparatively large, pale yellow flowers.
H4

F. s. 'Nymans' A large shrub with bronze-purple branches and large, primrose-yellow flowers. A sport of *F. spectabilis* f. *atrocaulis*. In cultivation 1951.
H4

Forsythia viridissima 'Bronxensis'

F. viridissima 'Bronxensis' A dense, compact, slow-growing shrub only about 30cm (1ft) high with masses of twiggy branches and abundant bright yellow, slightly green-tinged flowers. Best in a sunny position. Garden origin, 1928.
H4

Fothergilla *Hamamelidaceae*
Witch alder

There are two species in this genus, both deciduous and both native to the south-eastern United States. They have two seasons when they are outstanding: spring for their bottle-brush flower spikes and autumn for the rich colouring of their leaves. They need lime-free soil. No pruning is necessary.

F. gardenii A pretty small shrub, usually

Fothergilla gardenii

less than 1m (3ft) high, notable for its erect, fragrant flower clusters made up of clusters of white stamens which are borne in mid- to late spring, and its crimson autumn leaf colour. 'Blue Mist' is a form with particularly blue-green leaves. N Carolina to S Alabama. Introduced 1765.
H4

Fothergilla major

F. major, syn. *F. monticola* A slow-growing, medium-sized shrub with fragrant white flower clusters borne before the leaves emerge. The leaves are bloomy beneath and change colour beautifully in autumn. Allegheny Mountains. Introduced 1780.
H4 ♔ 1993
F. monticola See *F. major*.

Franklinia *Theaceae*

A genus of just one species. This is a gorgeous, autumn-flowering shrub or small tree as long as it has a hot, continental summer, when its ripened growth will stand a zero winter. It is not, however, generally suitable for cool, moist climates such as that of Britain or Ireland, but may be tried there in the warmest places on a hot, sunny wall.

F. alatamaha A remarkable and rare shrub or small tree. It has large, lustrous, green, oblong leaves that turn crimson in autumn. The large, cup-shaped, white flowers are like those of a stuartia but only open after a long, hot summer. It is tolerant of slightly alkaline soils. Georgia, USA, but not found in a wild state since the 18th century. Introduced 1770.
H4

Fraxinus *Oleaceae*
Ash

There are 65 deciduous species of ash – mainly hardy, fast-growing trees that thrive in almost any soil. They are tolerant of windswept and coastal positions and of industrial pollution. Their leaves

Fraxinus americana 'Autumn Purple'

are pinnate. Those of the section Ornus are attractive flowering trees.

F. americana 'Autumn Purple' A noble, broadly conical tree with dark green leaves that are reddish purple in autumn. An American selection of the white ash.
H4

Fraxinus angustifolia 'Raywood'

F. angustifolia 'Raywood', syn. *F. oxycarpa* 'Raywood' A large, fast-growing, dense, fairly upright tree that is especially attractive in autumn, when its dark green leaves turn plum-purple. An excellent tree of relatively compact habit. In cultivation 1928.
H4 ♔ 1993

Fraxinus chinensis

F. chinensis (Section Ornus) (Chinese ash) A freely growing, medium-sized tree with attractive leaves that sometimes turn wine-purple in autumn. The winter buds are conspicuously grey and the off-white flow-

ers, borne in spring, are sweetly scented. China. Introduced 1891.
H4

Fraxinus excelsior

F. excelsior (Common ash) A large, magnificent tree and one of the most valuable for timber. The winter buds are black. Europe (including Britain and Ireland), Caucasus.
H4 ♔ 1993

Fraxinus excelsior 'Jaspidea'

F. e. 'Jaspidea' A large, vigorous clone with golden yellow young shoots and yellowish branches, making a fine show in winter. The leaves are clear yellow in autumn. It is often mislabelled 'Aurea', a dwarf, slow-growing tree. In cultivation 1873.
H4 ♔ 1993

F. e. 'Pendula' (Weeping ash) A large, strongly growing tree, forming an attractive, widespreading mound of divergent, weeping branches.
H4 ♔ 1993

Fraxinus excelsior 'Pendula'

F. e. 'Westhof's Glorie' A vigorous, medium-sized to large tree, narrowly upright when young, later developing a more spreading habit. The leaves are dark green and open late. It is a commonly found street tree in continental Europe. In cultivation 1947.
H4 ☙ 1993
F. mariesii (Section Ornus) The most beautiful flowering ash, with fragrant, creamy white flowers in handsome panicles in early summer. It is slow-growing, with a compact head, and is usually seen as a medium to large shrub. C China. Introduced 1878 by Charles Maries.
H4

Fraxinus ornus

F. ornus (Section Ornus) (Manna ash) A pretty round-topped tree of medium size with scented, off-white flowers abundantly borne in late spring. This is the type species of the Section Ornus, popularly known as the flowering ashes. S Europe, SW Asia.

Introduced before 1700.
H4 ☙ 1993
F. oxycarpa 'Raywood' See *F. angustifolia* 'Raywood'.
F. pennsylvanica 'Summit' A broadly conical form of the red ash (also known as the green ash). It is a medium-sized, fast-growing tree with large, glossy leaves that

Fraxinus pennsylvanica 'Summit'

Fraxinus sieboldiana

turn golden yellow in autumn. Selected in the United States.
H4
F. p. 'Variegata' A medium-sized tree, with silver-grey leaves, brightly margined and mottled with creamy white.
H4
F. sieboldiana (Section Ornus) A medium-sized tree of which the leaves have five or sometimes seven leaflets, often colouring well in autumn. The white flowers are borne in panicles at the ends of the branchlets in late spring. Japan, Korea. Introduced 1894.
H4
F. velutina (Arizona ash) A neat and pretty tree of 9–12m (28–40ft), remarkable for its leaves and shoots, which are densely clothed in grey, velvety down. The winter buds are brown. Arizona, New Mexico. Introduced 1891.
H4

Fremontodendron *Sterculiaceae*

A genus of two species of tall, evergreen shrubs best grown on a sunny wall in all but the mildest places. The flowers have no petals but have large, coloured calyces. They require full sun and good drainage, and are excellent on chalk soils. Too rich a soil may well encourage growth at the expense of flowers. Pruning is largely unnecessary. Skin and eye irritant.

Fremontodendron 'California Glory'

F. 'California Glory' A floriferous, vigorous, medium-sized large shrub or small tree that is a hybrid between the two species that make up the genus. The yellow flowers are up to 6cm (2½in) across and are borne over a long period from summer to autumn. H3 ♔ 1993

Fremontodendron californicum

F. californicum A beautiful large shrub or small tree bearing yellow flowers throughout summer and autumn. It is still widely grown but is effectively superseded by 'California Glory', which is not only even more spectacular but also a little hardier. California, Arizona. Introduced 1851.
H3

Fuchsia *Onagraceae*

There are about 100 species of Fuchsia, including shrubs, small trees and climbers. All deciduous, they are mainly natives of Central and South America, but there are outlying species in Tahiti and New Zealand. The flowers are usually pendulous and showy and have often been likened to earrings.

The fuchsias listed here are those that have passed successfully through many winters at the Hilliers Nurseries in the south of England. Although the tender forms, and even the hardiest, may be cut to ground level by winter cold, they usually shoot up again rapidly in spring to flower freely throughout summer and autumn. They are remarkable in thriving in sun or shade and in any well-drained soil.

The pruning of outdoor fuchsias is a matter of prevailing circumstances. Where outdoor specimens are subject to cut-back by frost they can be pruned back to good wood in spring, and a reduction of top growth by about one-third preserves their bushiness after mild winters. F. magellanica and its forms and cultivars can be allowed to grow

large and untrammelled in mild areas, where they will flower from mid-spring until late autumn, or they can be controlled by pruning and clipping, especially if used for hedging.

F. 'Alice Hoffman' A small shrub with small, purple-tinged leaves in dense clusters. The flowers are small, with scarlet calyces and white petals.
H3

F. 'Blue Gown' A dwarf, free-flowering, compact shrub. The flowers are double, with a deep purple corolla and scarlet calyx.
H3

F. 'Chillerton Beauty' A beautiful small shrub with medium-sized flowers. The calyx is white, flushed rose; the petals are a soft, clear violet.
H3 ♔ 1993

F. 'Corallina' A strong, robust small shrub with large, deep green leaves and scarlet and violet flowers. Raised 1914.
H3 ♔ 1993

Fuchsia 'Corallina'

Fuchsia 'Garden News'

F. 'Garden News' A vigorous, hardy, upright small shrub with large double flowers; the calyx and tube are pale pink, the corolla magenta-rose. In cultivation 1978.
H3

Fuchsia 'Genii'

F. 'Genii' A dwarf, upright shrub with red shoots and attractive, lime-yellow leaves, richer yellow in sun. The small flowers have a corolla that is violet and then reddish purple, and the calyx is cerise.
H3

F. 'Hawkshead' A very hardy (for a fuchsia) small shrub with small leaves and an upright habit. The slender flowers have pure white petals and the calyx is white tinged with green.
H3

Fuchsia 'Lady Thumb'

F. 'Lady Thumb' A dwarf shrub. Semi-double flowers with light red calyx and red-veined white corolla. In cultivation 1966.
H3 ♔ 1993

Fuchsia 'Lena'

F. 'Lena' The flowers of this small cultivar are semi-double, with pale pink calyces and corollas of rosy magenta flushed with pink. This is a lax shrub but is a good fuchsia for training as a standard.
H3 ♛ 1993

F. 'Madame Cornelissen' A small hybrid of *F. magellanica* bearing large flowers

Fuchsia 'Madame Cornelissen'

Fuchsia magellanica var. gracilis

with red calyces and white petals.
H3 ♛ 1993

F. magellanica A graceful shrub of medium size, with long, slender flowers with scarlet calyces and violet petals. The leaves are generally held in whorls of three. The following forms are recommended. South America.
H3

F. m. var. gracilis A beautiful, slender, medium-sized shrub with leaves generally held in pairs. The small, freely borne flowers are scarlet and violet.
H3 ♛ 1993

F. m. var. molinae The flowers of this medium-sized form are shorter and white, faintly blushed with mauve.
H3

F. m. 'Riccartonii' See *F.* 'Riccartonii'.

F. m. 'Sharpitor' A small form of var. *molinae* with grey-green leaves margined with white. In cultivation 1973.
H3

Fuchsia magellanica 'Thompsonii'

Fuchsia magellanica 'Variegata'

F. m. 'Thompsonii' A small to medium-sized form with flowers smaller and more profusely borne than the typical species.
H3 ♛ 1993

F. m. 'Variegata' A striking medium-sized form with green leaves margined creamy yellow flushed pink, against which the small scarlet and purple flowers are most effective. It is less hardy, however, than the green form.
H3 ♛ 1993

Fuchsia magellanica 'Versicolor'

F. m. 'Versicolor' A small, spreading shrub with slender stems sporting strikingly grey-green leaves that are rose-flushed when young and irregularly variegated with cream and white when mature. A lovely foliage shrub.
H3 ♛ 1993

F. 'Margaret' A vigorous small shrub with an abundance of crimson and violet-purple semi-double flowers.
H3

Fuchsia 'Mrs Popple'

F. **'Margaret Brown'** A dwarf, erect, compact plant with attractive large flowers, of which the calyces are rich crimson and the petals magenta.
H3

F. **'Mrs Popple'** A small, large-flowered, hardy hybrid with spreading, scarlet sepals, violet petals, and long, protruding stamens and style.
H3 ♔ 1993

F. **'Mrs W P Wood'** The single flowers of this small shrub are very freely borne; they have a pale pink calyx with slender, upturned petals, and a white corolla.
H3 ♔ 1993

Fuchsia 'Pixie'

F. **'Pixie'** An upright, bushy shrub to about 90cm (3ft), with yellowish green foliage. The single flowers have a carmine tube and sepals and have a mauve-purple, carmine-veined corolla.
H3

F. ***procumbens*** A trailing, small-leaved

Fuchsia 'Prosperity'

Fuchsia 'Tennessee Waltz'

species with small, erect flowers. The calyx tube is yellow, the sepals violet and green, the stamens red and blue, and the petals are absent. It has quite large magenta fruits. New Zealand. Introduced c1854.
H2

F. **'Prosperity'** A beautiful, small, upright shrub of vigorous growth. The large flowers are double, and have a white corolla veined with pink and a deep rose-pink calyx. It is one of the more spectacular hardy fuchsias.
H3 ♔ 1993

F. **'Riccartonii'**, syn. *F. magellanica* 'Riccartonii'. This common, hardy shrub can attain 4m (12ft) and is often used as a hedging plant in mild districts. It has a deeper-coloured calyx and broader sepals than *F. magellanica*.
H3 ♔ 1993

F. **'Snowcap'** A dwarf shrub with flowers 5cm (2in) long. The sepals and tube are red and the petals are white, veined with red.
H3

F. **'Tennessee Waltz'** A low, elegantly arching shrub. The bold corolla is violet and the calyx deep glossy rose-scarlet. In cultivation 1950.
H3

Fuchsia 'Tom Thumb'

F. **'Tom Thumb'** The profusely borne flowers of this dwarf shrub have rose-scarlet calyces and violet petals.
H3 ♔ 1993

G

Garrya *Garryaceae*

A genus of about 13 species of evergreen shrubs, native of Central and South America, with leathery leaves and long, slender, silky catkins. The male and female flowers are on separate plants. Garryas are excellent for growing in maritime exposure and atmospheric pollution and good on north- or east-facing walls. They thrive on all types of well-drained soil but need protection in cold areas. The only pruning required is to remove dead wood.

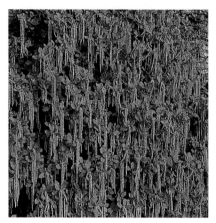

Garrya elliptica

G. elliptica The male plant of this species is a magnificent evergreen large shrub or small tree, draped during the latter half of winter with long, greyish green catkins. The female plant is also effective with its long clusters of attractive deep purple-brown fruits in summer. California, Oregon.

Garrya elliptica 'James Roof'

Introduced 1828 by David Douglas. H4

G. e. 'James Roof' A strong, vigorous male plant making a large shrub or small tree with large, leathery leaves and catkins as much as 20cm (8in) long.
H4 ♆ 1993

× Gaulnettya *Ericaceae*

The following are evergreen hybrids between the closely related Gaultheria shallon *and* Pernettya mucronata *and are of garden origin. Other hybrids between the two genera have occurred in the wild in New Zealand and the United States. According to some authorities,* Pernettya *is now merged into* Gaultheria *and these two plants should be* Gaultheria × wisleyensis *'Pink Pixie' and 'Wisley Pearl' respectively. They require a lime-free soil, preferably containing a large proportion of organic matter, and some shade. Popular plants for their foliage, flowers and fruits.*

× *Gaulnettya* 'Pink Pixie'

× *Gaulnettya* 'Wisley Pearl'

× **G. 'Pink Pixie'** A dwarf, suckering shrub, blooming in late spring with white flowers tinged with pink that are followed by purplish red fruits. Raised 1965 by Hillier Nurseries' propagator Peter Dummer through back-crossing 'Wisley Pearl' with *Gaultheria shallon*.
H4

× **G. 'Wisley Pearl'** A small shrub with dull, dark green leaves. Branches become laden in autumn and winter with short but crowded bunches of large, red fruits.
H4

Gaultheria *Ericaceae*

A genus of 150 evergreen species in all, thriving in moist, lime-free, preferably peaty soil and a shady position. They occur mainly in the Andes, but also in North America, eastern Asia and Australasia. They are mostly tufted shrubs, spreading by underground stems. The white, urn-shaped flowers are normally borne in late spring or early summer and are followed by fleshy, coloured fruits.

G. adenothrix A dainty, dwarf, creeping shrub, forming a low carpet of zig-zag, red-brown, hairy stems with small, leathery, dark green leaves. The flowers are white, blushed pink, and are borne from late spring to midsummer. They are followed by crimson fruits. Japan. Introduced 1915.
H4

Gaultheria cuneata

G. cuneata A dwarf, compact shrub with narrow leaves and white flowers from late spring to early summer. The white fruits have an antiseptic odour when crushed. A

delightful species. China. Introduced 1909 by Ernest Wilson.
H4 ♒ 1993

G. hispida A small shrub with bristly young shoots. The oblong leaves are over 6cm (2¹/₂in) long and the white flowers, produced in panicles at the branch ends from late spring to early summer, are followed by succulent white fruits. Australia, Tasmania. In cultivation 1927.
H4

G. hookeri A dwarf, densely spreading shrub with bristly, arching stems. The leathery, glandular-toothed leaves are more or less elliptic and 5–7.5cm (2–3in) long. The white flowers are in dense clusters in the axils of the leaves and at the ends of the branches, and are borne in late spring; the fruits are an exquisite shade of blue. Himalaya, W China. Introduced 1907 by Ernest Wilson.
H4

G. itoana A rare, creeping species, forming close mats of bright green, pernettya-like foliage. The flowers, borne from late spring to early summer, are white or pink and the fruits white. Taiwan. Introduced shortly before 1936.
H4

Gaultheria miqueliana

G. miqueliana A neat, dwarf shrub, usually not above 30cm (1ft) high, with shining green, oblong leaves. The short racemes of white flowers are borne in early summer and are followed by white or pink edible fruits. Japan. Introduced 1892.
H4

G. procumbens (Checkerberry) A creep-

Gaultheria procumbens

ing shrub, making carpets of dark green leaves among which, in autumn and winter, the bright red, aromatic fruits display themselves with freedom. The flowers, borne in summer, are white or palest pink. E North America. Introduced before 1762.
H4 ♒ 1993

G. pyroloides A dwarf, creeping shrub, forming mats of short stems and bright green, more or less rounded, net-veined (reticulate) leaves 2.5cm (1in) long. The pinkish, urn-shaped flowers are in short, leafy racemes from late spring until midsummer, and the fruits are blue-black. It is an interesting shrub, recalling *Salix reticulata* in leaf. Himalaya. In cultivation 1933.
H4

Gaultheria shallon

G. shallon A vigorous species, forming thickets up to 1.7m (5½ft) high. It provides excellent ground cover in a large garden, but its large size should be borne in mind for one that is on the small side. The leaves

are broad and leathery, and the flowers, which bloom from late spring to early summer, are pinkish white. The fruits, borne in large clusters, are dark purple. W North America. Introduced 1826.
H4

G. tricophylla A charming tufted shrublet with tiny leaves. The pink flowers are produced from late spring to early summer and are followed by large, highly attractive, eggshell-blue fruits. Himalaya, W China. Introduced 1897.
H4

G. × wisleyensis 'Pink Pixie' See × *Gaulnettya* 'Pink Pixie'.

G. × w. 'Wisley Pearl' See × *Gaulnettya* 'Wisley Pearl'.

Gelsemium *Loganiaceae*

A genus of two or three species of tender, evergreen, twining shrubs with attractive flowers. The following requires a sunny, sheltered wall in a mild area. It grows in any reasonably fertile soil.

G. sempervirens (Yellow jessamine) A species with stems up to 6m (18ft) long, bearing glossy green leaves and fragrant, yellow, funnel-shaped flowers 2.5cm (1in) long during late spring and early summer. S United States.
H2 ♒ 1993

Genista *Leguminosae*

For genus information see Cytisus, *page 260.*

G. aetnensis (Mount Etna broom) A large,

Genista aetnensis

elegant deciduous shrub or small tree, with slender, green, leafless shoots. The fragrant yellow flowers are borne in abundance in mid- to late summer. Sardinia and Sicily. H4 ♔ 1993

G. delphinensis This tiny decumbent deciduous shrub is one of the best species for the rock garden. It has deep yellow flowers in terminal or axillary clusters in mid- to late summer. It is like a miniature *G. sagittalis*. S France.
H4 ♔ 1993

Genista hispanica

G. hispanica (Spanish gorse) One of the best plants for sunny sites, dry banks and poorish soils, this deciduous shrub makes dense, prickly mounds 60cm (2ft) high that are unfailingly covered in late spring and early summer with masses of yellow flowers. SW Europe. Introduced 1759.
H4

Genista lydia

G. lydia An outstanding deciduous dwarf

shrub. Its elegantly slender, pendulous branches are smothered in a mass of golden flowers in late spring and early summer. E Balkans. Introduced 1926.
H4 ♔ 1993

Genista pilosa

G. pilosa A deciduous dwarf shrub, up to 45cm (18in), producing cascades of golden yellow flowers in late spring. The forms named 'Lemon Spreader' and 'Vancouver Gold' seem to be little different from the typical plant. W and C Europe, including a few parts of England and Wales.
H4

G. p. 'Goldilocks' A vigorous selection with ascending branches, reaching up to 60cm (2ft) high. It bears its golden yellow flowers on short stalks profusely over a long period. In cultivation 1970.
H4

Genista sagittalis

G. sagittalis A deciduous dwarf shrub with broadly winged, prostrate branches,

giving an evergreen appearance. It has yellow flowers in early summer and is a good plant for dry walls. C and S Europe. In cultivation 1588.
H4

Genista tenera 'Golden Shower'

G. tenera 'Golden Shower' A vigorous, large, arching deciduous shrub with masses of brilliant yellow, fragrant flowers in early summer. Grows to a height of 3m (10ft). Long grown incorrectly as *G. cinerea*.
H4 ♔ 1993

Genista tinctoria

G. tinctoria 'Plena' A free-flowering, dwarf, semi-prostrate deciduous form of the European dyer's greenweed with double yellow flowers from early summer to early autumn. It is an ideal dwarf shrub for use in the rock garden.
H4 ♔ 1993

G. t. 'Royal Gold' A small, free-flowering deciduous shrub, with stems which become thickly covered with rich yellow flowers

Genista tinctoria 'Royal Gold'

throughout the summer.
H4 🏆 1993

Gingko *Ginkgoaceae*

A genus of one remarkable deciduous coniferous species. It is the sole survivor of an ancient family of plants whose ancestors were widespread about

Gingko biloba

160 million years ago. It is of great botanical and geographical interest. After several decades, fruits are borne which consist of a nut inside an offensive-smelling pulp, but the beauty of the tree far outweighs this. It was once thought to have been extinct for a very long time. It is regarded as sacred by Buddhists and is often found planted near Buddhist temples.

G. biloba (Maidenhair tree) A medium-sized to large tree of conical habit when young. It is easily recognized by its peculiar, fan-shaped, undivided leaves that turn a beautiful clear yellow before falling in autumn. It is magnificent either as a single specimen or, where space permits, in a group. A hardy tree, it is suitable for most soils and tolerant of industrial areas. China. Introduced about 1727.
H4 🏆 1993

G. b. 'Saratoga' A fast-growing, medium-sized, broadly conical male tree with excellent rich yellow autumn colour.
H4

G. b. 'Tremonia' A narrowly columnar form. Raised 1930 in the Dortmund Botanic Garden.
H4

G. b. 'Variegata' The leaves of this form are streaked creamy white. Slow-growing and prone to reversion. In cultivation 1855.
H4

Gleditsia *Leguminosae*

A genus of about 12 species of deciduous, spiny trees, natives of North America and Asia and with one species in Argentina. Their foliage is extremely

Gleditsia triacanthos detail

beautiful and the mature trunks often bear formidable thorns. They succeed in all types of well-drained soil and tolerate atmospheric pollution. No pruning is required.

G. triacanthos (Honey locust) This elegant large tree with frond-like leaves is very tolerant of industrial atmospheres. A large specimen is effective when strung with its long, shining, brown seed pods in the autumn. C and E United States. Introduced 1700.
H4

Gleditsia triacanthos 'Elegantissima'

G. t. 'Elegantissima' A beautiful, slow-growing, dense, bushy shrub with fern-like foliage. It can grow to 3.5–4.5m (11–15ft).
H4

Gleditsia triacanthos detail

G. t. 'Ruby Lace' A medium-sized tree selected in America for its deep bronze-red young foliage. In cultivation 1961.
H4

G. t. 'Shademaster' A large, vigorous, thornless tree with ascending branches and dark green leaves that persist well into autumn. In cultivation 1961.
H4

Gleditsia triacanthos 'Sunburst'

G. t. 'Sunburst' A striking medium-sized tree with thornless stems and fern-like bright yellow-green young leaves that contrast delightfully with the older, dark green foliage. In cultivation 1953.
H4 ♔ 1993

Grevillea *Proteaceae*

A genus of about 250 species of beautiful evergreen trees and shrubs, almost all of which are native to Australia or Tasmania. The flowers, which are a little like those of honeysuckle but smaller and with showy, protruding styles, are produced over a long period. Good drainage is essential, and overhead shade and chalk soils should be avoided. Pruning is not required.

G. 'Canberra Gem' A vigorous, rounded, medium-sized shrub up to about 2.5m (8ft) high and potentially equally as much wide. It has aromatic foliage and clusters of waxy, bright pink flowers.
H3

Grevillea juniperina 'Sulphurea'

G. juniperina 'Sulphurea' A beautiful, small to medium-sized shrub for mild districts, with terminal clusters of bright yellow flowers in summer and bright green, needle-like leaves.
H3 ♔ 1993

Grevillea rosmarinifolia

G. rosmarinifolia This is a lovely medium-sized shrub for mild areas, where it can grow to as much as 1.8m (6ft) tall. The strikingly eye-catching crimson flowers are borne in long terminal clusters from spring through to summer and the needle-like leaves are dark green. SE Australia. Introduced c1822.
H3 ♔ 1993

Grindelia *Compositae*

A genus of about 60 species of evergreen and deciduous sub-shrubs and herbaceous plants, natives of west North America and South America.

Grindelia chiloensis

G. chiloensis A surprisingly hardy, handsome small evergreen sub-shrub. It has hoary, narrow leaves, toothed at the margin, and large, cornflower-like yellow flowers borne singly on tall, stout stems from early summer to mid-autumn. It requires full sun and very well-drained soil. Argentina. Introduced c1850.
H3

Griselinia *Cornaceae*

A small genus of about six species of evergreen trees and shrubs which are natives of New Zealand, Chile and southern Brazil.

G. littoralis This densely leafy large shrub,

Griselinia littoralis

which is tree-like in mild places, is an excellent hedge plant for seaside exposure. The leaves are leathery and bright apple green; the flowers are insignificant. It succeeds in all types of fertile soil but is liable to frost damage in cold, inland areas. New Zealand. Introduced c1850.
H3 🏆 1993

G. l. 'Dixon's Cream' A medium-sized shrub, one of several forms with leaves splashed and otherwise marked with creamy white. Others include 'Luscombe's Gold and 'Bantry Bay' and similar sports have occurred in New Zealand. They are all prone to reversion.
H3

G. l. 'Variegata' A medium-sized shrub with conspicuous white variegated foliage.
H3

Gymnocladus *Leguminosae*

A genus of deciduous trees with a single species in North America and three in eastern Asia. They are related to Gleditsia *and have bipinnate leaves, inconspicuous flowers and seeds in pods. They will grow in any well-drained soil.*

Gymnocladus dioica

G. dioica (Kentucky coffee tree) This medium-sized, slow-growing tree is one of the most handsome of all hardy trees. The young twigs are such a light grey as to be almost white, and are especially noticeable in winter. The large, compound leaves are pink-tinted when unfolding and turn clear yellow before falling. E and C United States. Introduced before 1748.
H4

H

Hakea *Proteaceae*

A remarkable genus of about 100 species of evergreen shrubs or small trees native to Australia and Tasmania. A few are hardy and make excellent subjects for sunny, dry positions. They are not good on chalk soils.

Hakea lissosperma

H. lissosperma A tall, erectly branched, columnar shrub, somewhat like a young Scots pine. The rigid, grey-green, needle-like, sharply pointed leaves are 2.5–7.5cm (1–3in) long, narrowed at the base and held more or less erect on the shoots. Showy white flowers are produced in clusters in the leaf axils from mid- to late spring. It has previously been listed as *H. sericea*. This splendid plant is perfectly hardy at the Hillier Gardens and Arboretum, where it was 5.5m (18ft) high in 1990. A native of SE Australia and Tasmania.
H3

Halesia *Styracaceae*
Snowdrop trees, silver bells

A genus of five species of very beautiful deciduous shrubs or small trees, allied to Styrax *and native to the south-eastern United States, with one species in eastern China. The pendulous, snowdrop-like flowers are produced in clusters along naked branches in late spring, followed by small, green, winged fruits. They thrive in a moist but well-drained, lime-free soil in sun or semi-shade.*

Pruning is seldom necessary for species of Halesia *but can be done after flowering.*

Halesia carolina

H. carolina (Snowdrop tree) A large shrub, very beautiful in spring when the branches are draped with white, nodding, bell-shaped flowers in clusters of three or five. The fruits are pear-shaped and four-winged. SE United States. Introduced 1756.
H4

H. diptera var. magniflora A large, wide-spreading shrub with broad leaves, two-winged fruits and relatively large flowers. SE United States.
H4

Halesia monticola

H. monticola (Mountain snowdrop tree) A magnificent, small, spreading tree, larger than *H. carolina* and with larger flowers and fruits which have been known to develop to 5cm (2in) long. Mts of SE United States. Introduced c1897.
H4

H. m.* var. *vestita A superb variety with even larger flowers up to 3cm (1.25in) across, white but sometimes blushed with rose. The leaves are more or less downy beneath at first and then become smooth. H4 ♈ 1993

× Halimiocistus *Cistaceae*

These are pretty and interesting evergreen hybrids between Halimium *and* Cistus. *Given a position with full sun and good drainage, they survive all but the coldest winters.*

× *Halimiocistus ingwersenii*

× ***H. ingwersenii*** A freely growing, dwarf, spreading shrub with pure white flowers borne over a long period in summer, and linear, dark green, hairy leaves. Portugal. Introduced 1929.
H4

Halimiocistus sahucii

× ***H. sahucii*** A dwarf, spreading shrub with linear leaves and pure white flowers, borne

from late spring to early autumn. S France. Introduced 1929.
H4 ♈ 1993

× ***H. wintonensis*** A beautiful dwarf shrub with grey leaves. The saucer-shaped flowers, borne from late spring to early summer, are 5cm (2in) across, pearly white and with a feathered and pencilled zone of crimson-maroon, contrasting with yellow stains at the base of the petals. Originated 1910 in the Hillier Nurseries, England.
H3 ♈ 1993

× ***H. w.* 'Merrist Wood Cream'** In this beautiful dwarf form the base colour of the flowers is creamy yellow. A sport found 1978 at Merrist Wood Agricultural College, England.
H3 ♈ 1993

Halimium *Cistaceae*

The seven evergreen species in this genus are from the Mediterranean region and western Asia. They are mostly low, spreading, evergreen shrubs, akin to Helianthemum. *They require full sun and good drainage and are subject to injury by severe frost. Pruning is not usually necessary.*

Halimium commutatum

H. commutatum A dwarf, semi-erect shrub with linear leaves and golden yellow flowers 2.5cm (1in) across, produced in early summer. Mediterranean region.
H3

H. lasianthum A low, spreading shrub, ultimately growing up to 60cm–1m (2–3ft) high, with greyish leaves and golden yellow flowers with a dark blotch at the base of each petal borne in late spring. S Portugal,

Halimium lasianthum

S Spain. Introduced 1780.
H3 ♈ 1993

H. ocymoides A charming, compact shrub of 60cm–1m (2–3ft), with small grey leaves and bright yellow flowers with blackish brown basal markings throughout the summer. Portugal, Spain. In cultivation 1800.
H3 ♈ 1993

***H. o.* 'Susan'** A more compact form with relatively broad leaves.
H3 ♈ 1993

Halimodendron *Leguminosae*

A genus of one deciduous species, related to Caragana, *which will succeed in any well-drained soil and in an open position.*

H. halodendron (Salt tree) An attractive, spiny, silvery-leaved shrub up to 1.7m (5ft). The leaves have 2–3 pairs of slender, grey-woolly leaflets and a terminal spine. In early to midsummer it bears masses of purplish pink pea flowers. It is an excellent seaside plant from dry salt-fields. Siberia, SE Russia, SW Asia. Introduced 1779.
H4

Hamamelis *Hamamelidaceae*
Witch hazel

The witch hazels are a most distinct and beautiful genus of deciduous shrubs or small trees that mostly flower in the winter. There are five or six species in eastern North America and Asia. In most cases the spider-like, yellow or reddish flowers appear on the leafless branches from early

winter to early spring. The curious, strap-shaped petals withstand the severest weather without injury, and the hazel-like foliage is usually most attractively coloured in autumn. On the whole they prefer moisture-retentive, neutral or slightly acid soils, but can grow over chalk as long as the soil is deep. Pruning is simply a matter of removing any dead wood.

H. × intermedia (*H. japonica* × *H. mollis*) These are large shrubs of variable nature often with large leaves and occasionally strong-scented flowers, almost always grown as one of the following:

Hamamelis × *intermedia* 'Advent'

H. × i. 'Advent' A large shrub with ascending branches and medium-sized, fragrant, bright yellow flowers 2–3cm (³/₄–1¹/₄in) across. The petals are tinged with red at the base and the calyces are purplish. They are abundantly produced from the very beginning of winter.
H4

Hamamelis × *intermedia* 'Arnold Promise'

H. × i. 'Arnold Promise' A vigorous, large, wide-spreading bush with freely borne, medium-sized, bright yellow flowers. Raised 1928 at the Arnold Arboretum, Jamaica Plain, Massachusetts.
H4 ♔ 1993

Hamamelis × *intermedia* 'Barmstedt Gold'

H. × i. 'Barmstedt Gold' A vigorous and upright large shrub with faintly scented deep golden yellow flowers over 3cm (1¹/₄in) across.
H4

Hamamelis × *intermedia* 'Carmine Red'

H. × i. 'Carmine Red' A large, strong-growing shrub of rather spreading habit. The large, almost round leaves are dark, shining green on their upper surfaces, turning yellow in autumn. The flowers are over 3cm (1¹/₄in) across, pale bronze and suffused at their tips with copper, so as to appear red. Raised at Hillier Nurseries.
H4

H. × i. 'Diane' One of the best red-

Hamamelis × *intermedia* 'Diane'

flowered seedlings yet raised, and superior in this respect to 'Ruby Glow'. The flowers are of medium size. The large leaves colour a rich red in autumn.
H4 ♔ 1993

H. × i. 'Hiltingbury' A large, spreading shrub. The large leaves give a brilliant display of autumn tints of orange, scarlet and red. The flowers are medium to large, pale copper, and suffused with red. Raised at Hillier Nurseries, England.
H4

Hamamelis × *intermedia* 'Jelena'

H. × i. 'Jelena' A superb large hamamelis of vigorous, spreading habit, with large, broad, softly hairy leaves that turn orange, red and scarlet in autumn. The flowers are over 3cm (1¹/₄in) across, in dense clusters, and yellow suffused with a rich coppery-red, so as to appear orange.
H4 ♔ 1993

H. × i. 'Moonlight' A large shrub with ascending branches. The flowers are

Hamamelis × intermedia 'Moonlight'

medium to large with folded and crimped petals. They are pale sulphur-yellow with a claret tinge at the base and have a strong, sweet scent. It is as effective a shrub as *H. mollis* 'Pallida' but its narrower, paler, more crimped petals distinguish it. The autumn colour is yellow.
H4

Hamamelis × intermedia 'Orange Beauty'

Hamamelis × intermedia 'Primavera'

***H.* × *i.* 'Orange Beauty'** A large shrub of broad, spreading habit and orange-yellow, early flowers over 3cm (1¼in) across.
H4

***H.* × *i.* 'Primavera'** A broadly upright large shrub, producing its medium-sized bright yellow flowers with purplish red bases rather later than most.
H4

***H.* × *i.* 'Ruby Glow'** A strong-growing, erect shrub with medium-sized coppery red flowers and rich autumn colour.
H4

***H.* × *i.* 'Sunburst'** An upright shrub with yellow autumn foliage. The pale yellow, faintly scented flowers are over 3cm (1¼in) across. In many ways an improvement on 'Moonlight', but unfortunately spoilt by poor foliage.
H4

Hamamelis × intermedia 'Vesna'

***H.* × *i.* 'Vesna'** A vigorous and upright large shrub, with strongly fragrant deep orange-yellow flowers well over 3cm (1¼in) across. The hanging petals are flushed red at the base and the calyx is deep red.
H4

***H.* × *i.* 'Westerstede'** A vigorous, upright large shrub with large, light yellow, faintly scented flowers over 3cm (1¼in) across.
H4

H. mollis (Chinese witch hazel) Perhaps the handsomest of all the witch hazels, and certainly the most popular. It is a large shrub with softly hairy, rounded leaves and clusters of sweetly fragrant, golden yellow, broad-petalled flowers over 3cm (1¼in) across from early winter to early spring.

Hamamelis mollis

The autumn colour is yellow. This species must be grown as a named, vegetatively propagated clone, otherwise you are likely to obtain a hybrid. Hillier Nurseries' clone is now called 'Jermyns Gold'. China. Introduced 1879 by Maries and early 20th century by Ernest Wilson.
H4 ♛ 1993

Hamamelis mollis 'Brevipetala'

***H. m.* 'Brevipetala'** A large, upright form, with yellow autumn colour and thick clusters of deep yellow, short-petalled flowers that appear orange from a distance. They have a heavy, sweet perfume. This form is spoilt by poor foliage.
H4

***H. m.* 'Goldcrest'** A large shrub selected for its strongly and sweetly scented flowers of rich golden yellow, suffused with claret at their bases. The red blush is also on the backs of the rolled petals in the buds and creates a characteristic orange-cluster effect. The flowers are over 3cm (1¼in)

Hamamelis mollis 'Goldcrest'

across and generally appear later than in the other forms of the species. The autumn foliage colour is yellow.

H4

H. m. 'Pallida' Deservedly one of the most popular witch hazels, this large shrub has sulphur-yellow flowers over 3cm (1¼in) across held in densely crowded clusters

Hamamelis mollis 'Pallida'

Hamamelis vernalis 'Sandra'

along the naked stems. The scent, although strong and sweet, is nevertheless delicate. The autumn foliage colour is yellow.

H4 ♈ 1993

H. vernalis 'Sandra' A form of the Ozark witch hazel in which the young, unfolding leaves are suffused with plum-purple, becoming green and purple-flushed on the undersides. In autumn, the whole bush ignites into orange, scarlet and red. The very small flowers are cadmium yellow. Originated 1962 at Hillier Nurseries.

H4 ♈ 1993

H. virginiana (Virginian witch hazel) This is the commercial source of witch hazel and is a large shrub, occasionally a broad-crowned small tree. Its main use is as an understock for witch hazels with larger, more ornamental flowers. E North America. Introduced 1736.

H4

Hebe *Scrophulariaceae*

A genus of 100 or more species of evergreen shrubs, occasionally trees, formerly included in Veronica. *Most of them are natives of New Zealand, with a few in Australia and South America. Their flowering period is spring to autumn and they are invaluable for planting at the seaside. Most of those that do not thrive inland can safely be planted along coasts where the prevailing winds are from warmer seas, even in exposed places where few other shrubs will survive. They grow well in all types of well-drained soil. Many hebes benefit from being lightly clipped over in spring and leggy specimens can be cut hard back, although this must not be done to* H. salicifolia *or the whipcord hebes.*

Hebe albicans

H. albicans A splendid dwarf shrub of dense, rounded habit and bloomy foliage. The white flowers are borne in dense spikes during summer, and it is perfectly hardy and most ornamental. New Zealand. Introduced c1880.

H4 ♈ 1993

Hebe 'Alicia Amherst'

H. 'Alicia Amherst' A magnificent hybrid of *H. speciosa* with long racemes of deep purple-blue flowers in late summer. Raised 1911.

H2 ♈ 1993

Hebe 'Amy'

H. 'Amy' A small, rounded but upright, compact shrub, with leaves tinted purple when young and holding the colour for a long period before becoming glossy dark green. Clusters of violet-purple flowers are borne during summer.

H3

H. andersonii 'Variegata' A highly attractive medium-sized shrub with 10cm

(4in) leaves broadly margined and splashed with creamy white. Vigorous and fast-growing, it is well worth overwintering as cuttings if there is a danger of frosts.
H3

Hebe ochracea

H. *armstrongii* A dwarf 'whipcord' species which is commonly grown in gardens under the name of *H. ochracea*.

Hebe 'Autumn Glory'

H. 'Autumn Glory' A small shrub of loose habit with short, dense racemes of intensely violet flowers in continuous display throughout late summer and autumn. The small round leaves are deep green and tinted purple. In cultivation 1900.
H3

H. 'Baby Marie' A very dainty shrub reaching only 30 × 45cm (12 × 18in) and making excellent ground cover. During mid- to late spring its fresh green foliage is almost completely hidden by masses of tiny white flowers. For best results plant in free-draining soil in a sunny position.
H4

H. 'Blue Clouds' A small shrub with dark glossy green leaves, purplish in winter. Long spikes of wisteria-blue flowers are borne over a long period in summer and autumn. A seedling of 'Mrs Winder'.
H3 ♕ 1993

Hebe 'Bowles' Hybrid'

H. 'Bowles' Hybrid' A charming, dwarf shrub which is most suitable for the rock garden. The flowers, both in spring and again in summer, crowd the short branches in pretty a pretty display of mauve racemes.
H3

Hebe brachysiphon

H. *brachysiphon* A popular shrub, growing to 1.5m (5ft) or more and producing white flowers profusely in early or midsummer. New Zealand. Introduced 1868.
H4

H. 'Caledonia' A small, compact and rounded shrub with red-tinted young leaves. Spikes of violet flowers are borne from spring to autumn.
H4

H. 'Carnea Variegata' An attractive shrub which grows to about 1.2m (4ft) high with long racemes of rose-pink flowers that fade to white and are plentifully produced from late spring to late summer. The leaves are grey-green, margined with creamy white. In cultivation 1945.
H3

H. *carnosula* A dwarf to prostrate shrub with small, bloomy, shell-like leaves and white flowers in mid- to late summer. It is suitable for the rock garden and makes excellent ground cover. New Zealand.
H4

H. 'County Park' A dwarf, spreading shrub suitable for ground cover. The leaves are grey-green, margined with red and flushed pink in winter. The violet flowers are borne in short racemes in summer.
H3

H. 'Cranleighensis' A small shrub with glossy leaves that are red-purple beneath when young. Long spikes of pink flowers are borne in summer.
H3

Hebe cupressoides

H. *cupressoides* Normally a small shrub, but occasionally reaching as much as 2m (6½ft), this species has a very distinctive appearance. The long, slender, green or grey branches are remarkably like those of a cypress (*Cupressus*). The flowers are small, pale blue, and quite freely produced in early to mid summer. New Zealand.
H4

H. c. 'Boughton Dome' A dense, dwarf, compact, rounded bush with white flowers. H3–4 ♔ 1993

H. 'Emerald Green', syn *H.* 'Green Globe' A bun-shaped compact shrub to 30cm (1ft) high with upright green shoots and tiny, densely arranged, glossy leaves. Small white flowers are borne in summer. Found 1970 in the wild in New Zealand and possibly a hybrid. H3 ♔ 1993

Hebe × *franciscana* 'Blue Gem'

H. × *franciscana* 'Blue Gem' A small, compact, dome-shaped shrub with dense racemes of bright blue flowers. This commonly planted species is one of the hardiest hebes, excellent as a low hedge, and highly resistant to salt winds. Raised 1868. H3 ♔ 1993

Hebe × *franciscana* 'Variegata'

H. × *f.* 'Variegata' An impressive small shrub with abundant leaves broadly edged with creamy white. It is commonly seen in

London window boxes. H2 ♔ 1993

H. *glaucophylla* 'Variegata' A small, neat shrub with slender, wiry shoots and white flowers in mid- to late summer. The leaves are greyish green, margined with creamy white. H3

H. 'Gloriosa' A most attractive *H. speciosa* hybrid. It is a small, compact shrub with bright pink flowers in conspicuous long racemes from midsummer onwards. H2

Hebe 'Great Orme'

H. 'Great Orme' A compact bush to 1m (3ft) high. The leaves are lance-shaped and 5–7.5cm (2–3in) long, and the bright pink flowers are borne in long, tapering racemes from midsummer. H3 ♔ 1993

H. 'Green Globe' See *H.* 'Emerald Green'.

H. 'Hagley Park' A dwarf, upright shrub with glossy green, red-margined, bluntly toothed leaves. The rose-purple flowers are borne in large panicles in early summer. Raised in the Christchurch Botanic Gardens, New Zealand. H3

H. 'Highdownensis' A small, spreading, tender shrub with glossy leaves and dark stems. Slender spikes of deep purple-blue flowers open in summer. H3

H. *hulkeana* Perhaps the most beautiful hebe species in cultivation. It is a small shrub of loose habit, occasionally reaching 1.7m (5.5ft) against a sheltered wall. It has

Hebe hulkeana

glossy green, toothed, ovate leaves and large clusters of delicate lavender-blue flowers in late spring and early summer. Prune lightly after flowering to remove the flower heads. New Zealand. In cultivation c1860. H3 ♔ 1993

Hebe 'La Seduisante'

H. 'La Seduisante' A most attractive *H. speciosa* hybrid. It is a small shrub with large racemes of bright crimson flowers from midsummer onwards and dark glossy green leaves flushed with purple when they are young. H2 ♔ 1993

H. 'Lindsayi' A very hardy shrub to about 1m (3ft) high and wide. The green leaves are rather rotund and the pink flowers are held in short but showy racemes from early summer. H4

H. *lycopodioides* A dwarf shrub with slender, erect, four-sided, yellow-green stems. The leaves are scale-like, each with a sharp,

horn-like point, densely clothing the branches. The white flowers are borne in midsummer. New Zealand.
H4

Hebe macrantha

H. macrantha A very valuable dwarf shrub, notable for its leathery, toothed leaves and pure white flowers, which are as much as 2cm (³/₄in) across. Mountains of New Zealand.
H3 ♔ 1993

H. 'Margaret' (PBR 3838) A compact, hardy shrub with bright green leaves, producing a profusion of sky-blue flowers on short spikes in late spring or early summer, followed by several flushes in late summer and autumn. As the flowers age they fade to pale blue and then white, producing a bicolour effect.
H3

Hebe 'Marjorie'

H. 'Marjorie' A remarkably hardy hebe, forming a neat bush about 1m (3ft) high

with racemes 5–7cm (2–3in) long of light violet and white flowers from midsummer to early autumn.
H3

H. 'Midsummer Beauty' A handsome small to medium-sized shrub with noticeably reddish undersides to the leaves. The flowers are in long, lavender racemes throughout summer. Moderately hardy.
H3 ♔ 1993

Hebe 'Mrs Winder'

H. 'Mrs Winder' A small to medium-sized, moderately hardy hybrid with purple foliage of which the colour becomes deeper in winter. The late-summer bright blue flowers also sometimes occur in winter.
H4 ♔ 1993

H. 'Nicola's Blush' A dwarf shrub, flowering profusely over a long period from summer to autumn. The pale pink flowers fade to white.
H3

H. ochracea A dwarf, densely branched

Hebe 'James Stirling'

shrub with erect, glossy, whipcord-like stems of a characteristic ochre or old gold colour. The white flowers appear in mid- to late summer. This plant is commonly found in gardens under the name *H. armstrongii*, which has greener branches and sharply keeled and pointed leaves. New Zealand.
H4

H. o. 'James Stirling' A dwarf form with stouter branches and bright ochre-gold foliage. It lacks the grace of the typical form.
H4 ♔ 1993

H. 'Pewter Dome' A low-growing shrub, making a dense, dome-shaped bush which is covered with grey-green leaves and short spikes of white flowers in early summer. A hybrid of *H. albicans*.
H4 ♔ 1993

Hebe pimelioides 'Glauco-caerulea'

H. pimelioides 'Glauco-caerulea' A dwarf with, small, glaucous-blue leaves and violet-blue flowers in early to midsummer.
H4

Hebe pinguifolia 'Pagei'

H. p. **'Quicksilver'** A dwarf, spreading shrub with tiny, silvery blue leaves that contrast with the dark shoots and pale lilac flowers.
H4 ♔ 1993

H. pinguifolia **'Pagei'** This is a prostrate shrub with wide mats of small, bloomy-grey leaves that remain attractive throughout the year. The short spikes of small pure white flowers are borne freely in late spring. It provides an excellent ground-cover or rock-garden plant.
H4 ♔ 1993

Hebe pinguifolia 'Sutherlandii'

H. p. **'Sutherlandii'** This form differs from 'Pagei' in its much more dense, more upright habit, making a compact, rounded, dwarf bush with grey-green foliage.
H4

H. **'Purple Pixie'** A dense bush reaching a maximum of 50cm (20in) across and 70cm (28in) high. The dark green leaves are narrowly oval, 2.5cm (1in) long and 1cm (½in) wide. The flowers are similar in colour to 'Autumn Glory' and are borne in racemes 3–5cm (1½–2in) long from June to August and sometimes to the first frosts. A chance seedling; the parent may be 'Great Orme'.
H3

H. **'Purple Queen'** This outstanding *H. speciosa* hybrid is a small shrub with large racemes of purple flowers in summer. There seems to be little difference between it and 'Amy'.
H2

H. **'Purple Tips'**, syn. *H. speciosa* 'Tricolor' A small shrub which is a sport of 'La Seduisante'. Its leaves are rose-purple on

the back when young and open to grey-green with deep green veins, broadly margined with creamy white and becoming rose-tinted during winter. The flowers are magenta-purple, fading to white, in long clusters. They are borne from late summer onwards. In cultivation 1926.
H2

Hebe rakaiensis

H. rakaiensis A dwarf, very hardy shrub forming dense, compact mounds of crowded stems with small, neat, pale green leaves. The white flowers are borne in short racemes in early to midsummer. A splendid ground-cover plant in full sun. Sometimes found wrongly labelled in gardens as *H. subalpina*. New Zealand.
H4 ♔ 1993

H. recurva A small, slender-branched, open, rounded shrub up to 1m (3ft). The leaves are narrow, lance-shaped and bloomy on the upper sides, and the white flowers are in slender racemes in late sum-

Hebe recurva 'Boughton Silver'

mer. The clone in general cultivation is known as 'Aoira'. New Zealand. Introduced 1923.
H3

H. r. **'Boughton Silver'** A compact small shrub with silvery blue leaves.
H3 ♔ 1993

Hebe 'Red Edge'

H. **'Red Edge'** A dwarf shrub with blue-grey leaves densely arranged and narrowly margined with red, particularly in winter. The flowers, borne in summer, are lilac, becoming white.
H3 ♔ 1993

H. **'Rosie'** (PBR 4492) A dwarf shrub with profuse spikes of clear pink flowers with purple anthers, borne over a long period in summer and autumn. The best dwarf pink hebe.
H3

H. salicifolia A medium-sized shrub for maritime areas. The leaves are lance-shaped and bright green, and the flowers, borne in long slender racemes from early to

Hebe 'Simon Delaux'

late summer, are white or blushed with lilac. A parent of many hybrids. New Zealand, S Chile.

H3

H. **'Sapphire'** A small, upright shrub with slender, red-tinged leaves and long spikes of rose-purple flowers during summer and autumn.

H3

Hebe 'Spender's Seedling'

Hebe vernicosa

H. **'Simon Delaux'** A small, rounded shrub with rich crimson flowers in large racemes from late summer onwards. One of the best of the *H. speciosa* hybrids.

H2 ♔ 1993

H. speciosa **'Tricolor'** See *H.* 'Purple Tips'.

H. **'Spender's Seedling'** A small, very hardy, free-flowering shrub with fragrant

Hebe topiaria

white flowers produced over a long period during summer.

H4 ♔ 1993

H. **'Spring Glory'** An attractive small spreading shrub bearing deep purple flowers in summer. It does best in full sun and well-drained soil.

H3

H. subalpina A small, dense, very hardy shrub with a rounded outline. It is similar to *H. rakaiensis* and often confused with it, but is distinguished by having larger leaves and glabrous seed capsules. White flowers are borne in early to midsummer.

H4

H. topiaria A small shrub to 1m (3ft) with yellow-green leaves and short clusters of white flowers in summer. New Zealand.

H4

H. vernicosa A very hardy dwarf shrub of spreading habit, with small, bright glossy green leaves. The flowers are white but may be pale lilac at first and are borne in slender spikes up to 5cm (2in) long in late spring. New Zealand.

H4

H. **'Watson's Pink'** A small, tender shrub with slender leaves and spikes of bright pink flowers throughout summer.

H3

H. **'White Gem'** A dwarf, compact, hardy shrub rarely over 45cm (18in), producing a profusion of white flowers in early summer. It is a hybrid of *H. brachysiphon*, from which it differs in being dwarfer and having smaller, paler leaves and earlier flowering on shorter racemes.

H4

H. **'Wingletye'** A prostrate shrub of compact habit, suitable for the rock garden. The leaves are small and glaucous. Ascending shoots bear racemes of deep mauve flowers in early summer.

H4

H. **'Youngii',** syn. *H.* 'Carl Teschner' A hardy, dwarf, compact shrub, prostrate at first but becoming more dome-shaped, with small dark green leaves and abundantly produced short racemes of violet flowers with white throats in early to midsummer. A splendid, free-growing ground-cover plant.

H4 ♔ 1993

HEDERA

Araliaceae Ivy

Hedera hibernica

THE IVIES are very widely grown and are valued for their ability to hide tree stumps, sheds, ugly walls and almost anything else that is better hidden. Although the genus comprises only 11 species there are many distinct ivies from which gardeners can choose, with a variety of leaf size, shape and colour.

The reputation of ivies for causing damage is only partly founded in fact. They are not parasitic and do not interfere with the systems of trees upon which they may support themselves. However, the wind resistance of their mass of evergreen foliage may be the last straw that causes the host tree to fall, though such trees are usually doomed anyway and their demise is merely accelerated by the presence of the ivy. Any tree that is overwhelmed by ivy to the extent that its growing points are smothered is likely to be senescent. On the plus side, ivy does provide a habitat for wildlife.

It is on the whole inadvisable to grow ivy on a house wall consisting of porous brick as, no matter how sound it may appear to be, the plant will find its way into the smallest fault. Few walls from which ivy has been stripped show no damage at all, and those of Rhuddlan Castle in North Wales, which date from the 13th century, are still sound above the level of the ivy that was removed shortly after World War II. Below, the masonry has been destroyed up to a depth of 30cm (12in).

The variation in forms of *Hedera helix* is very wide indeed, not only in foliage colour and leaf shape, but also in the sizes of the plants. Some are capable of ascending into very large trees, while others, such as 'Conglomerata', are small enough for the rock garden. When it comes to the leaves, there are greens, yellows, silver and cream in an almost infinite range of arrangements, while some ivies are crested, crisped or simply wavy. There are no other self-clinging climbers to be compared to the ivies.

The plants have two distinct stages in their growth. In the initial, climbing phase, the leaves, particularly in *H. helix*, are markedly different from those of the flowering shoots that develop in the arborescent phase. They are the 'typical' ivy-shaped leaves, whereas the later ones are often unlobed and heart-shaped at the base. The flowers are small and inconspicuous, borne in greenish umbels and replaced by berry-like fruits that are usually black.

There is an important role for ivies as ground cover, particularly as they will survive quite happily beneath trees and shrubs where nothing, not even grass, will grow. Although they can spread very rapidly it is not a difficult task to keep them in bounds, and ivies on walls or trees that are becoming too bulky can be clipped over quite hard without their resenting it.

Harmful if eaten/may cause skin allergy.

Hedera *Araliaceae*
Ivy

Hedera canariensis

H. algeriensis A large, strong-growing species, with large, dark green leaves up to 15 or even 20cm (6–8in) across. The leaves on the climbing shoots are kidney-shaped, while those on the flowering shoots are rounded and heart-shaped at the base. They are bright green in summer, often turning deep bronze with green veins in winter. Usually grown as *H. canariensis*. N Africa. In cultivation 1833.
H3–4

Hedera algeriensis 'Gloire de Marengo'

H. a. 'Gloire de Marengo' An attractive and colourful large form perfect for patio or walls. The large leaves are deep green in the centre, merging into silvery grey and margined with white. Less hardy than green-leaved forms and popular as a house plant. H3 ♀ 1993

Hedera algeriensis 'Margino-maculata'

H. a. 'Margino-maculata' The leaves of this large climber are a mixture of both deep green and pale green mottled with cream, often producing shoots bearing leaves that are similar to 'Gloire de Marengo' but with a mottled margin. In the open the leaves become heavily mottled with cream. It is often grown as a house plant. In cultivation 1942.
H3 ♀ 1993

Hedera azorica

H. azorica A distinct and hardy large species with broad, matt, light green leaves. Those in the climbing shoots have 5–7 blunt lobes. Azores.
H4

H. canariensis See *H. algeriensis*.
H. colchica (Persian ivy) A large, handsome, strong-growing species with the largest leaves in the genus. They are ovate or elliptic and 15–20cm (6–8in) long or more on the climbing shoots, somewhat smaller and more oblong in shape on the

flowering shoots; all are dark green and leathery. Caucasus. In cultivation 1850.
H4 ♀ 1993

H. c. 'Dentata' A spectacular large climber with leaves even larger and rather more irregular in outline than those of the typical species. They are slightly softer in outline and have occasional teeth.
H4 ♀ 1993

Hedera colchica 'Dentata Variegata'

H. c. 'Dentata Variegata' A most ornamental large ivy with large, broad, often elongated leaves that are bright green shading to grey, and notably margined with creamy yellow when young and with cream when mature. It is hardier than *H. algeriensis* 'Gloire de Marengo' and just as effective.
H4 ♀ 1993

H. c. 'Paddy's Pride' See *H. c.* 'Sulphur Heart'.

H. c. 'Sulphur Heart', syn. *H. c.* 'Paddy's Pride' A large, impressive variegated ivy with large, broad leaves that are boldly

Hedera colchica 'Sulphur Heart'

marked with an irregular central splash of yellow, merging into pale green and finally deep green. Occasionally almost the entire leaf is yellow. On old leaves the yellow splash becomes pale yellow-green.
H4 ♥ 1993

H. helix (Common ivy) One of the most adaptable and variable of all plants, the common ivy makes an excellent ground cover and is useful in situations where little else will grow. The leaves of the climbing shoots are variable and may be three- to five-lobed, while the leaves borne on the flowering shoots are entire and ovate to rhomboidal. The following forms have green leaves unless otherwise stated. Europe, Asia Minor to N Iran.
H4

Hedera helix 'Adam'

***H. h.* 'Adam'** The leaves of this large climber are rather small, shallowly three-lobed, green and grey-green in the centre, and are narrowly margined with creamy yellow. In cultivation 1968.
H4

***H. h.* 'Angularis Aurea'** A large climber with broad, glossy leaves flushed with bright yellow. Not suitable for ground cover.
H4 ♥ 1993

***H. h.* 'Atropurpurea'** The leaves of this large form are entire or with two short lateral lobes. They are dark purplish green, darker in winter, often with bright green veins. In cultivation 1884.
H4 ♥ 1993

***H. h.* 'Buttercup'** The best golden form of the common ivy. It is a slow-growing medium-sized form with rich yellow leaves,

Hedera helix 'Buttercup'

becoming yellowish green or pale green with age. In cultivation 1925.
H4 ♥ 1993

***H. h.* 'Caenwoodiana'** See *H. h.* 'Pedata'.

Hedera helix 'Cavendishii'

***H. h.* 'Cavendishii'** A pretty medium-sized form with small, angular, green leaves mottled with grey and broadly margined with cream. In cultivation 1867.
H4 ♥ 1993

***H. h.* 'Chicago Variegated'** See *H. h.* 'Harald'.

***H. h.* 'Congesta'** An upright, small, non-climbing form similar to 'Erecta' but more congested in habit and with smaller leaves. In cultivation 1887.
H4 ♥ 1993

***H. h.* 'Conglomerata'** A dense, slow-growing form with stiffly erect stems, making a low hummock. The leaves are with or without lobes and have distinctly wavy margins. It is excellent for the rock garden.
H4

Hedera helix 'Erecta'

***H. h.* 'Erecta'** A slow-growing dwarf form with stiffly erect shoots. The leaves are three-lobed and arrow-shaped. It is good against a boulder on a rock garden or a tree stump. In cultivation 1898.
H4 ♥ 1993

***H. h.* 'Glacier'** The leaves of this medium-sized climber are silvery grey with narrow

Hedera helix 'Glacier'

Hedera helix 'Goldchild'

white margins. In cultivation 1950.
H4 ♔ 1993

H. h. 'Goldchild' The young leaves are bright green, pale green in the centre, and with a broad golden yellow margin. Later they are blue-green and grey-green with a margin of creamy yellow. A small, very attractive ivy best as a house plant.
H3–4 ♔ 1993

Hedera helix 'Goldheart'

H. h. 'Goldheart' This is a most striking medium-sized ivy of neat growth. The leaf has a large, bright, central splash of yellow. Although this is a very popular ivy, it can revert badly after a few years.
H4

Hedera helix 'Green Ripple'

H. h. 'Green Ripple' An attractive medium-sized form with small, pale-veined, jaggedly lobed leaves; the central lobe is long and tapering.
H4

H. h. 'Harald', syn. H. h. 'Chicago Varie-

gated' A medium-sized form with leaves shallowly five-lobed, green and grey-green in the centre and margined with cream. In cultivation 1958.
H4

Hedera helix 'Ivalace'

H. h. 'Ivalace' A small, compact ivy with bright green, shallowly five-lobed leaves, stiffly curled at the margins. It is very good for ground cover. In cultivation 1955.
H4 ♔ 1993

Hedera helix 'Kolibri'

H. h. 'Kolibri' A striking medium-sized ivy with dark green leaves that are broadly and brightly blotched and streaked with cream. It is best grown under cover.
H3–4 ♔ 1993

H. h. 'Little Diamond' A dwarf, bushy, dense plant. The leaves are diamond-shaped, entire or three-lobed, green mottled with grey and with a cream margin. In cultivation 1976.
H3–4 ♔ 1993

Hedera helix 'Little Diamond'

Hedera helix 'Manda's Crested'

H. h. 'Manda's Crested' An attractive medium-sized ivy, suitable for ground cover. The leaves have five pointed lobes that point upwards while the sinuses point down, creating a wavy-edged effect. They turn bronze in winter. In cultivation 1940.
H4 ♔ 1993

H. h. 'Midas Touch' A medium-sized climber with golden yellow leaves splashed with lime green and dark green; some are edged with bright green.
H3–4 ♔ 1993

H. h. 'Parsley Crested' A distinct and unusual medium-sized form with pale green, often rounded leaves that are attractively twisted and crimped at the margins. In cultivation 1956.
H4

H. h. 'Pedata', syn. H. h. 'Caenwoodiana' A medium-sized form with small leaves divided into narrow lobes, of which the middle one is longest. In cultivation 1863.
H4 ♔ 1993

Hedera helix 'Parsley Crested'

H. h. 'Persian Carpet' A large, vigorous form good for ground cover or a wall, with green shoots and light green, shallowly lobed leaves.
H4

H. h. 'Sagittifolia' The leaves of this large form are bluntly three-lobed and arrow-shaped. *H. h.* 'Königer's Auslese' is often sold under this name. In cultivation 1872.
H4

Hedera helix 'Sagittifolia Variegata'

H. h. 'Sagittifolia Variegata' A large form with grey-green leaves margined with white. In cultivation 1965.
H4

H. h. 'Shamrock' (Clover-leaf ivy) A very distinct medium-sized form with small, bright green leaves that are entire to deeply three-lobed at the base, turning bronze in winter. In cultivation 1954.
H4 ♇ 1993

H. h. 'Sicilla' A form with crisped leaf margins similar to 'Parsley Crested' but

with the edges coloured creamy white.
H4

H. h. 'Spetchley' A dense, prostrate and congested form, with very small leaves. It is good for a rock garden, low wall or tub.
H4 ♇ 1993

H. h. 'Tricolor' A pretty medium-sized form with small, greyish green leaves, margined with white and edged with rose-red in winter.
H4

H. hibernica (Irish ivy) This is the common ivy of the West of England and the only species native to Ireland. It is closely related to *H. helix* but often produces large leaves which, in the commonly grown forms are large, dark green, usually five-lobed and 7.5–15cm (3–6in) wide. It is a large, vigorous ivy, particularly suited to being grown as ground cover. Also native to Atlantic coasts of Spain and Portugal.
H4 ♇ 1993

H. h. 'Deltoidea' A small form with neat,

Hedera hibernica 'Deltoidea'

Hedera nepalensis

close growth. The green leaves have two basal lobes that are rounded and overlapping. They become bronzed in winter. In cultivation 1872.
H4

H. nepalensis (Himalayan ivy) A large, strong-growing species with greyish green, taper-pointed leaves up to 13cm (5in) long.
H3–4

H. pastuchowii A large vigorous species with leaves that may be entire, heart-shaped or shallowly lobed or toothed. They are blackish green in colour with pale green veins, and the midrib is red beneath. Best grown against a wall. N Iran. Introduced 1972 to Hillier Nurseries, England, by Roy Lancaster and Mrs Ala.
H4

Hedera rhombea

H. rhombea (Japanese ivy) The Japanese equivalent of *H. helix*, differing from the common species in its ovate or triangular-ovate leaves that sometimes have two shallow lobes.
H4

Hedysarum *Leguminoseae*

A large genus of about 100 species of perennials and deciduous shrubs found throughout northern temperate regions. The following is easily cultivated, given full sun and any average, well-drained soil. It can become leggy, in which case the old stems can be completely removed and the strong, younger ones cut back by half in spring.

H. multijugum A small shrub of lax habit, with sea-green, pinnate leaves and long racemes of rose-purple pea flowers throughout the summer and occasionally into autumn. Mongolia. Introduced 1883. H4

Heimia *Lythraceae*

*A genus of three species of deciduous shrubs related to loosestrife (*Lythrum*). They are natives of the Americas. The following succeeds in any well-drained soil in sun, and pruning is a matter of removing crowded growths at the base in spring.*

H. salicifolia An interesting shrub of 1.2m (4ft), with narrow leaves and small yellow flowers 1.5cm (¹/₂in) across which are produced in the leaf axils from midsummer to early autumn. Central and South America. Introduced in 1821.
H4

Helianthemum *Cistaceae*
Rock rose

There are more than 100 species of these mainly dwarf, evergreen shrubs, which have a wide distribution in temperate areas. Those in cultivation, which are mainly hybrids, are excellent, vivid plants for dry, sunny situations and produce multitudes of brilliantly coloured flowers throughout the summer. They are not fussy about soil and should be cut back after their first flush of flowers to encourage bushiness and further flowering during the same season.

Helianthemum lunulatum

H. lunulatum A dainty, cushion-like alpine with yellow flowers, each petal of which has a small orange spot at its base,

borne in early to midsummer. NW Italy. H4

H. nummularium 'Amy Baring' A compact dwarf shrub with green foliage and deep buttercup-yellow flowers. Found in the French Pyrenees by Mrs Amy Doncaster and named by A. K. Bulley.
H4 ♛ 1993

HYBRIDS
The colourful plants generally seen in cultivation are mainly hybrids developed from a group of three species: *H. appeninum*, *H. nummularium* and *H. croceum*. Between them they have produced a great variety of attractive silver- and green-leaved plants with flowers ranging in colour from orange, yellow or white to rose, red and scarlet, both single and double. All the following are low-growing, more or less prostrate, and spread to 30–45cm (12–18in) across. All are H4. The 'Ben' cultivars are named after Scottish mountains.

H. 'Afflick' Bright, deep orange-bronze flowers with a bronze-copper centre; green foliage.
H. 'Ben Dearg' Deep copper-orange flowers with a darker centre; green foliage.
H. 'Ben Fhada' Golden yellow flowers with an orange centre, grey-green foliage.
H. 'Ben Hope' Carmine flowers with a deep orange centre; green foliage

Helianthemum 'Ben Ledi'

H. 'Ben Ledi' Bright, deep tyrian-rose flowers; dark green foliage.
H. 'Ben More' Bright, rich orange flowers with a darker centre; dark green foliage.

Helianthemum 'Ben More'

H. 'Ben Nevis' Deep buttercup-yellow flowers with a bronze-crimson centre; green foliage.

Helianthemum 'Cerise Queen'

H. 'Cerise Queen' Scarlet double flowers and green foliage.

Helianthemum 'Fire Dragon'

H. 'Fire Dragon' Bright orange-scarlet

flowers and grey-green foliage. It is also known as 'Mrs Clay'.
♔ 1993

H. **'Henfield Brilliant'** Bright orange flowers and green foliage.
♔ 1993

H. **'Jubilee'** Drooping, primrose-yellow, double flowers and green foliage.
♔ 1993

H. **'Mrs Clay'** See *H*. 'Fire Dragon'.

Helianthemum 'Mrs C. W. Earle'

H. **'Mrs C. W. Earle'** Scarlet double flowers with a yellow basal flush set off by dark green foliage.
♔ 1993.

H. **'Praecox'** Lemon-yellow flowers; a dense habit with grey foliage.

Helianthemum 'Raspberry Ripple'

H. **'Raspberry Ripple'** Deep reddish pink flowers with white-tipped petals; dark green foliage.

H. **'Red Orient'** See *H*. 'Supreme'.

H. **'Rhodanthe Carneum'** Pale, showy pink flowers with an orange centre; silver-grey foliage.

Helianthemum 'Rose of Leeswood'

H. **'Rose of Leeswood'** Rose-pink double flowers; green foliage.

H. **'Sudbury Gem'** Deep pink flowers with a flame centre; grey-green foliage.

H. **'Supreme'**, syn. *H*. 'Red Orient' Crim-

Helianthemum 'Sudbury Gem'

Helianthemum 'The Bride'

son flowers and grey-green foliage.

H. **'The Bride'** Creamy white flowers with a bright yellow centre; silver-grey foliage.
♔ 1993

H. **'Wisley Pink'** Soft pink flowers and grey foliage.
♔ 1993

Helianthemum 'Wisley Primrose'

H. **'Wisley Primrose'** Primrose-yellow flowers with a deeper centre; light grey-green foliage. An unusually vigorous form.
♔ 1993

H. **'Wisley White'** Pure white single flowers with a centre composed of golden anthers; narrow grey leaves.

Helichrysum *Compositae*

A genus of about 500 species of perennials and evergreen shrubs, widely distributed in the Old World, particularly in South Africa and Australia. Among the shrubby members are some interesting, mainly low-growing, often aromatic plants with attractive foliage. Most are reasonably hardy in full sun and a well-drained, poorish soil.

H. ***italicum*** A dwarf shrub with long, narrow, grey leaves and terminal long-stalked clusters of bright yellow flowerheads in summer. It is one of the best of all silvery grey shrubs. Mediterranean region.
H3 ♔ 1993

H. i. **subsp** *serotinum* (Curry plant) A dense, dwarf shrub with narrow, sage-green leaves with a strong smell that is supposed to be like that of curry. It bears heads of yellow flowers in midsummer. S Europe.
H3

Helichrysum petiolare

H. petiolare A dwarf, often trailing shrublet forming mounds of white woolly stems and long-stalked, ovate, grey, woolly leaves. The yellow flowers are borne in late summer. It is a tender species, usually grown as an annual, but may overwinter in milder areas if given good drainage and overhead protection. South Africa. H1–3 ♔ 1993

Helichrysum splendidum

H. selago See *Ozothamnus selago*

H. splendidum A small, globular shrub of about 1m (3ft), producing white woolly shoots densely covered with silvery grey leaves. Clusters of small, yellow everlasting flowers appear from midsummer to autumn and may remain into the middle of winter. It is surprisingly hardy. South Africa. H3 ♔ 1993

Heptacodium jasminoides

Heptacodium *Caprifoliaceae*

A genus of two species of deciduous Chinese shrubs, related to Abelia.

H. jasminoides (Seven Son Flower of Zhejiang) A vigorous and very hardy large deciduous shrub of upright habit, with peeling bark. Bold, three-veined leaves are retained until late autumn or early winter, and small, fragrant, white flowers are borne in whorls at the ends of the shoots in late summer and autumn. Given good weather, the calyx enlarges and turns bright red after flowering. E China (Zhejiang). Introduced 1981 to the Hillier Gardens and Arboretum. H4

Hibiscus *Malvaceae*

A large genus of about 200 species of perennials and deciduous shrubs and trees, widely distributed in tropical and subtropical regions. Just a few species are hardy in cool-temperate climates, but they include some of the most effective shrubs for late summer and early autumn, as long as they are planted in full sun. They should have a rich, fertile soil, and in colder areas you should mulch the roots to protect them from freezing of the soil and grow them in the shelter of a warm wall. Any shoots that are over-long can be cut back lightly in spring, and old specimens can be cut back hard at the same time.

H. sinosyriacus A hardy, handsome, vigorous species, more spreading than *H. syriacus* and with larger, sage-green leaves, but enjoying the same conditions. The single

Hibiscus sinosyriacus 'Lilac Queen'

flowers are similar but a little larger. It is grown exclusively as named clones, which include:

H. s. 'Autumn Surprise' A medium-sized shrub. The flower petals are white with an attractively feathered cerise base. H4

H. s. 'Lilac Queen' A medium-sized shrub, the flowers of which have lilac petals with a garnet-red base. H4

H. syriacus No late-flowering shrub is more beautiful than the cultivars of this shrubby 'mallow'. The large, usually single, trumpet-shaped flowers open in succession between midsummer and mid-autumn depending on the weather. They make medium to large-sized shrubs of upright habit and may occasionally reach the dimensions of small trees. The following are recommended. E Asia. H4

H. s. 'Blue Bird' A medium-sized shrub

Hibiscus syriacus 'Blue Bird'

Hibiscus syriacus 'Diana'

with violet-blue single flowers with a darker eye. The best single blue. H4 ♈ 1993

H. s. 'Diana' A medium-sized shrub with pure white, single, large flowers with crimped petals, occasionally with a few petaloids in the centre. The best white. Raised 1963 at the US National Arboretum, Washington DC. H4 ♈ 1993

Hibiscus syriacus 'Hamabo'

H. s. 'Hamabo' A medium-sized shrub with pale blush-pink, single, large flowers each with a crimson eye. One of the best cultivars and not to be confused with *H. hamabo*, which is a tender species with yellow, red-centred flowers. H4 ♈ 1993

H. s. 'Helene' The large flowers of this medium-sized shrub are 9cm (3^1/$_2$in) across, often semi-double, white, flushed pink when opening, and with the outer petals streaked with deep pink. They also have attractively feathered deep maroon blotches at the base and white petaloid stamens at the centre. A sister seedling of 'Diana'. H4

H. s. 'Lady Stanley' A medium-sized shrub with white, almost double flowers shaded blush pink, with a maroon base. In cultivation 1875. H4

H. s. 'Pink Giant' A medium-sized shrub bearing clear pink single flowers with a deep red eye. It was raised by crossing 'Red Heart' and 'Woodbridge' and has larger flowers than the latter. They have a dark

Hibiscus syriacus 'Pink Giant'

Hibiscus syriacus 'Red Heart'

band near the apex of each basal blotch, and are distinctly feathered. H4 ♈ 1993

H. s. 'Red Heart' A medium-sized shrub with large white single flowers with a bright red eye. H4 ♈ 1993

H. s. 'Russian Violet' The single flowers

Hibiscus syriacus 'Woodbridge'

of this medium-sized shrub are large and luminous lilac-pink, with a deep red centre. H4

H. s. 'William R Smith' A medium-sized shrub with pure white, single, large flowers. In cultivation 1916. H4

H. s. 'Woodbridge' A medium-sized shrub bearing single, large, rich rose-pink flowers with a carmine centre. The basal blotches are not feathered. H4 ♔ 1993

Hippophäe *Elaeagnaceae*

A genus of three species of hardy deciduous shrubs or small trees, native of Eurasia, with attractive orange berries on female plants.

Hippophäe rhamnoides

H. rhamnoides (Sea buckthorn) A tall shrub or small tree that succeeds in almost any soil and is a first-class plant for resisting salt-laden sea winds. It is attractive in summer with its narrow, silvery leaves, and in winter with its orange-yellow berries that contain an intensely acrid, yellow juice that inhibits birds from eating them. Pheasants are said to take them, but a fine specimen on an English shooting estate was never touched. Plant in groups of both sexes to obtain fruits. E Asia, Europe, including the British Isles. H4 ♔ 1993

Hoheria *Malvaceae*

A genus of five species of beautiful evergreen and deciduous shrubs or small trees belonging to the

mallow family. They all have honey-scented white flowers and bear them with great freedom in mid- to late summer. The evergreen species need a specially selected site or wall protection except in mild districts, and the same applies to the deciduous ones at the limits of their hardiness range. The leaves of juvenile plants are often deeply toothed and lobed and smaller than those of adult plants. Hoherias are best in a deep soil rich in humus and in sun or dappled shade, but the more nutritious the soil, the more likely it is that growth may be soft and susceptible to frost. Dead or damaged wood can be pruned out in spring. All the species are from New Zealand.

H. angustifolia An elegant, small, evergreen, columnar tree with roundish to narrowly lance-shaped leaves up to 5cm (2in) long. Juvenile plants are dense and bushy with slender, interlacing branches and minute, shallowly toothed leaves. Masses of small white flowers cover the plant in the middle of summer. H3

Hoheria glabrata

H. glabrata (Mountain ribbonwood) A magnificent deciduous large shrub or small tree, possibly a little hardier than *H. lyallii*. In early to midsummer its branches are festooned with fragrant, almost translucent, white flowers. In cultivation 1871. H4 ♔ 1993

H. 'Glory of Amlwch' A large shrub or small to medium-sized deciduous tree that retains its leaves during mild winters. The flowers are pure white, over 3.5cm (1½in) across and densely crowded on the stems. H3 ♔ 1993

Hoheria 'Glory of Amlwch'

Hoheria lyallii

H. lyallii (Mountain ribbonwood) A beautiful but variable large shrub or small tree. The juvenile leaves are green and adult ones grey. Clusters of cherry-blossom-like white flowers crowd the branches in midsummer, normally later than *H. glabrata*. H4 ♔ 1993

H. sexstylosa (Lacebark) This splendid, free-flowering, tall, vigorous evergreen

Hoheria sexstylosa

shrub or small tree blooms in late summer or autumn and has narrow, glossy green leaves. The fragrant flowers are over 2.5cm (1in) across. In young trees the leaves are extremely variable.
H3 ♔ 1993

***H. s.* 'Stardust'** A form with a compact, upright habit, glossy leaves and very profusely borne flowers.
H3

Holboellia *Lardizabalaceae*

A genus of about five species of luxuriant, evergreen, twining plants with attractive foliage. Natives of the Himalaya and China. They will grow in any fertile soil in sun and shade but need sun if they are to flower and fruit. Weak growths can be removed in spring.

H. coriacea A vigorous, reasonably hardy species up to 6m (20ft) or more. The leaves consist of three glossy green leaflets and the flowers, which appear in mid- to late spring, are separately male and female; the males are purplish, borne in terminal clusters, and the females are greenish white in axillary clusters. The fruits is a purplish, fleshy pod up to 7.5cm (3in) long, filled with rows of black seeds. C China. Introduced 1907 by Ernest Wilson.
H3–4

Holodiscus *Rosaceae*

A genus of about eight species of hardy, spiraea-like deciduous shrubs from western North America to Colombia. The following can be grown in sun

Holodiscus discolor

or light shade in any average soil, provided it is not liable to dry out. Pruning is done in spring, but only to remove dead or overcrowded branches.

H. discolor (Ocean spray) A handsome and elegant shrub to 3.5m (11ft) high, blooming in the middle of summer, when its long, drooping, feathery panicles of creamy white flowers are most prominent. The leaves are greyish white and woolly beneath. W North America. Introduced 1827 by David Douglas.
H4

Humulus *Cannabidaceae*

A genus of three species of perennial climbers from Europe and Asia. The following is herbaceous and grows in any fertile soil.

H. lupulus (Hop) The fruit of this large climber is used for making beer. The twining stems may reach 3-6m (10-12ft) long and produce rough, hairy, deeply three- to

Fruit of *Humulus lupulus*

five-lobed and coarsely toothed leaves; the cone-shaped fruit is borne in clusters in late summer and early autumn.
H4

***H. l.* 'Aureus'** A magnificent medium-sized form with yellow leaves which is best grown in full sun on a pergola, pole, tripod or arch.
H4 ♔ 1993

Humulus lupulus 'Aureus'

341

HYDRANGEA

Hydrangeaceae

THERE ARE A GREAT many more kinds of hydrangea than the justifiably popular 'mopheads', whose rounded inflorescences, in shades of pink, red, blue and white, are to be seen in so many gardens. In addition to these striking plants, whose drifts of bright colour are among the most effective features of late summer and early autumn, there are some intriguing and beautiful evergreen and deciduous species as well as other groups of hybrids, including the graceful 'lacecaps'.

The flowerheads of hydrangeas consist of florets, of which there are two kinds. Fertile florets are usually tiny and bear male and female flower parts, while sterile florets have none and consist mainly of large, coloured sepals. Mophead hydrangeas – often called hortensias – have flowerheads almost entirely made up of the latter, while lacecaps are like most of the species in that the fertile florets form the centre of the flattish inflorescence and are surrounded by an outer ring of sterile ones. The colours of hydrangea flowers change in autumn; whites can turn to light lime-green and light blues to an eau-de-nil hue. Others can adopt deep, russet red and purple shades. Their texture changes, too, becoming something like the finest, softest kid, particularly when cut and dried. At this stage they make very long-lasting material for floral arrangements.

Among the species, plants vary from dwarf ones for the smallest gardens, such as *Hydrangea involucrata* 'Hortensis', which is about 1m (3ft) high with pink, green and cream flowers, to *H. aspera* subsp *sargentiana*, whose bristly stems rise to over 3m (10ft) and whose rosy lilac flowerheads, as much as 23cm (9in) across, stand just above the large, velvety, jungly leaves. *H. paniculata*

Hydrangea arborescens has large flowerheads up to 15cm (6in) across

has pyramidal (rather than flattened or ball-shaped) flowerheads, and its different forms exploit varying proportions of sterile and fertile florets in frothy masses of creamy white. It is one of several species that are notably distinctive, including the climbing *H. petiolaris* and *H. quercifolia*, whose white, conical flowerheads and magnificent autumn tints deserve a good deal more recognition than they receive. The climbing species attach themselves to trees or walls by means of aerial roots. They are splendid plants which withstand atmospheric pollution and are equally happy in sun or semi-shade in all types of soil.

CARE AND CULTIVATION

Hydrangeas are not difficult to grow, but prefer good soil to which generous amounts of organic matter have been added. *H. macrophylla*, of which the lacecaps and mopheads are forms, and *H. serrata* will take a good deal of sun and also thrive beautifully in dappled shade for part of the day. Many others require rather more in the way of shade, but with them all that is essential is to make sure that they do not suffer from dryness at the root.

The mophead hydrangeas are ideal for seaside plantings. In shallow chalk soils *H. macrophylla* and its forms may become chlorotic; this can be counteracted by generous mulching and feeding. It is not true, as is often claimed, that iron nails and the like will turn a pink hydrangea blue, but colour control can be achieved in soils that are just slightly alkaline by providing free aluminium in the form of a blueing powder. Some forms are more likely to react to blueing powder than others, and results are very seldom if ever satisfactory with strong pinks and reds.

Although the plants are perfectly hardy, late spring frosts can wreak havoc among the forming flowers, hence the hardiness rating. If you live in an area which is prone to such late frosts, take the same precautions as you would for other tender plants or crops when bad weather is forecast.

Dead-heading and pruning are best carried out simultaneously in early spring. The old flowerheads should be cut to the first pair of strong buds, and dead, weak and crowded stems, as well as one or two of the very oldest, should be removed by cutting them out at their bases. This will encourage the production of strong new shoots that will quickly flower.

SHRUBS

H. arborescens A small deciduous shrub of loose, bushy growth, with ovate, slender-pointed, serrated leaves. The flowers are in corymbs up to 15cm (6in) across, bearing several long-stalked, creamy white marginal ray-florets. They appear in succession from midsummer to early autumn. Introduced 1736.
H4

H. a. 'Annabelle' A small, loose, bushy shrub with ovate, slender-pointed, serrated leaves. The flowers are huge, spectacular, rounded heads of white, sterile florets and are up to 30cm (1ft) across.
H4 ♀ 1993

H. a. 'Grandiflora' A small shrub that is the most commonly cultivated form, with large, globular heads of creamy white, sterile florets from midsummer to early autumn. Introduced 1907.
H4 ♀ 1993

H. aspera A magnificent but variable large-leaved deciduous species of medium size which bears large heads of pale porcelain-blue flowers in early and midsummer. Himalayas, W and C China, Taiwan.
H3

H. a. Kawakamii Group A small to medium-sized shrub flowering very late. The deep violet flowerheads with their white sterile florets open during autumn.
H3

H. a. 'Macrophylla' A magnificent medium-sized form of this variable species, in which the leaves and flowerheads are even larger than usual. The latter are pale porcelain blue with a ring of lilac-pink or white ray florets.
H3 ♀ 1993

H. a. subsp. sargentiana A noble medium-sized to large shrub. Its shoots are thickly clothed with a curious, moss-like covering of stiff hairs and bristles, and the leaves are very large and velvety. The very large, flat flowerheads are borne in mid- to late summer and are bluish, with white ray-florets. It is suitable for a sheltered shrub border or woodland and is winter hardy, but requires shade and wind protection. China. Introduced 1908 by Ernest Wilson.
H3 ♀ 1993

Hydrangea arborescens 'Annabelle'

Hydrangea arborescens 'Grandiflora'

Hydrangea aspera subsp. *sargentiana*

Hydrangea aspera Villosa Group

Hydrangea heteromalla

H. a. Villosa Group Close to the typical form but less coarse and with smaller leaves and flowerheads. It is one of the loveliest of the later-flowering hydrangeas and is a medium-sized shrub of spreading habit, with stems, leaves and flower stalks densely clothed in long, soft hairs. The large flowerheads are lilac-blue with prettily toothed margins to the sepals. It requires semi-shade. W China. Introduced 1908. H3 ♔ 1993

Hydrangea 'Ayesha'

H. 'Ayesha', syn. *H.* 'Silver Slipper' A most distinct and unusual deciduous hydrangea of puzzling origin but great beauty. It is often included in the hortensias, but is quite different from the usual mophead. The leaves are bold and glossy green above. The rather flattened, dense, faintly fragrant flowerheads, borne in late summer, are composed of thick-petalled, cup-shaped florets resembling those of a large lilac. They are greyish lilac or pink, depending on soil, and eventually fade to a stunning shade that is somewhere between eau-de-nil and turquoise. H3–4 ♔ 1993

H. heteromalla A very variable medium-sized to large deciduous shrub or small tree. The leaves are dark green above and white beneath. The flowers, borne in broad corymbs in midsummer, are white with conspicuous marginal ray-florets, which age to deep pink. Himalayas, N and W China. Introduced 1821. H4

H. h. 'Bretschneideri' A medium-sized shrub with broad, flattened, white lacecap

Hydrangea heteromalla 'Jermyns Lace'

flowerheads. It has dark brown peeling bark and the leaves are white beneath. China. Introduced 1882. H4 ♔ 1993

H. h. 'Jermyns Lace' A vigorous, large shrub with broad, lacecap heads, the white outer florets turning to pink. H4

H. h. 'Snowcap' A superb, large, stately shrub with large, heart-shaped leaves and white flowers in large, flattened corymbs 20–25cm (8–10in) across. It is hardy and tolerant of wind, sun and drought. H4

H. involucrata A pretty deciduous dwarf species with blue or rosy lilac flowers surrounded by white or variously tinted ray-florets, borne in mid- to late summer. Japan, Taiwan. In cultivation 1864. H3–4

Hydrangea involucrata 'Hortensis'

H. i. 'Hortensis' A remarkable and attractive hydrangea, 1–1.2m (3–4ft) or so

high, with double, creamy white florets that become rose-tinted in open situations. H3–4 ♔ 1993

HORTENSIA
These and the lacecaps that follow are all treated botanically as cultivars of *H. macrophylla*, although some are probably of hybrid origin. In all alkaline soils it is impossible to retain blue shades without treatment, and where the alkalinity is more than slight, purple shades will result, tending towards red the more alkaline the soil. Unless otherwise stated, all are small shrubs. All are deciduous and H3–4

H. m. 'Altona' Rose-coloured, large florets, blues well when treated. Best in shade. ♔ 1993

Hydrangea macrophylla 'Ami Pasquier'

H. m. 'Ami Pasquier' A dwarf shrub with deep red flowerheads. ♔ 1993

Hydrangea m. 'Generale Vicomtesse de Vibraye'

H. m. **'Ayesha'** See *H.* 'Ayesha'

H. m. **'Europa'** Deep pink flowerheads with large florets.
♆ 1993

H. m. **'Generale Vicomtesse de Vibraye'** Vivid rose-purple flowerheads; light blue on acid soils or when treated.
♆ 1993

H. m. **'Hamburg'** Deep rose or purplish large florets.

H. m. **'King George'** Large, rose-pink florets with serrated sepals.

Hydrangea m. 'Madame Emile Mouillère'

H. m. **'Madame Emile Mouillère'** Large florets with serrated sepals, white with a pink or blue eye. Perhaps the best white-flowered cultivar and certainly one of the most popular.
♆ 1993

H. m. **'Masja'** A shrub with a compact habit and red flowerheads.

H. m. **'Miss Belgium'** A dwarf shrub with rosy red flowers.

Hydrangea macrophylla 'Westfalen'

H. m. **'Nigra'** A distinct cultivar with stems black or almost so; the florets are rose or occasionally blue. In cultivation 1870.
♆ 1993

H. m. **'Parzival'** Rose-madder to crimson-pink or purple to deep blue flowers. Best in light shade.
♆ 1993

H. m. **'Silver Slipper'** See *H.* 'Ayesha'.

H. m. **'Westfalen'** Vivid crimson to violet flowerheads.
♆ 1993.

LACECAPS

H. m. **'Blue Wave'** A strong-growing shrub of medium size with beautifully shaped heads of blue fertile flowers surrounded by numerous large ray-florets, varying in colour from pink to blue. In suitable acid soils the colour is a vivid gentian blue. The sepals are noticeably wavy-edged. Best in semi-shade.
♆ 1993

H. m. **'Geoffrey Chadbund'** The lacecap flowers of this medium-sized shrub are brick red on alkaline or neutral soils, purple on acid ones.
♆ 1993

H. m. **'Lanarth White'** A medium-sized shrub of compact growth, with large, flattened heads of bright blue or pink fertile flowers surrounded by a ring of white ray-florets. A superb cultivar.
♆ 1993

Hydrangea macrophylla 'Libelle'

H. m. **'Libelle'** A very beautiful medium-sized hydrangea with heads of blue fertile flowers surrounded by pure white sterile florets. In cultivation 1964.

H. m. **'Maculata'**, syn *H. m.* 'Variegata' A medium-sized, erect shrub. The flowerheads have a few small, white ray-florets, but this hydrangea is grown mainly for its attractive leaves, which have a broad, creamy white margin.

Hydrangea macrophylla 'Mariesii'

H. m. **'Mariesii'** A medium-sized shrub with wide, flat heads of rosy pink flowers, with very large ray-florets. When grown on a suitable soil the flowers turn a very rich blue. Japan. Introduced 1879.

H. m. **'Tricolor'** A choice, strongly growing medium-sized cultivar with leaves that are most attractively variegated green, grey and pale yellow. The flowers are pale pink to white, large, and freely produced.
♆ 1993

H. m. **'Variegata'** See *H. m.* 'Maculata'.

H. m. **'Veitchii'** A medium-sized shrub with rich dark green leaves, growing best in semi-shade. The flowers are in flattened

Hydrangea macrophylla 'White Wave'

corymbs, the sterile outer florets white, fading to pink. It is a very hardy plant which is lime-tolerant.
♔ 1993

H. m. 'White Wave' A small but strongly growing shrub with flattened heads of bluish or pinkish fertile flowers, surrounded by large, beautifully formed, pearly white ray-florets. It is free-flowering when grown in an open position.
♔ 1993

H. paniculata A medium-sized to large deciduous shrub with both fertile and large, creamy white sterile florets in dense, terminal panicles in late summer to autumn. To obtain really large panicles, the laterals should be cut back to within 5–7.5cm (2–3in) of the previous year's growth in early spring. This does not apply to 'Praecox', and some gardeners prefer to prune only every other year or one year in three for the sake of a more shapely bush, although smaller panicles will result. Best in part shade and a well-fed soil. The following forms are recommended. Japan, China, Taiwan. Introduced 1861.
H4

Hydrangea paniculata 'Floribunda'

H. p. 'Floribunda' A medium-sized to large shrub producing long, narrow panicles with numerous white ray-florets, flowering from just after the middle of summer. In cultivation 1867.
H4 ♔ 1993

H. p. 'Grandiflora' One of the showiest of large, hardy shrubs. The massive panicles of large numbers of small, white, sterile florets, appearing in summer to autumn,

Hydrangea paniculata 'Grandiflora'

become deep pink. They are excellent winter decoration when dried. Japan. Introduced c1867 by Siebold.
H4 ♔ 1993

Hydrangea paniculata 'Greenspire'

H. p. 'Greenspire' Similar to 'Kyushu' but with green sterile flowers becoming tinged with pink.
H4

H. p. 'Kyushu' An upright, medium-sized to large shrub with dark glossy green, taper-pointed leaves and panicles liberally sprinkled with sterile flowers.
H4 ♔ 1993

H. p. 'Pink Diamond' A medium-sized to large shrub with large heads of sterile florets, white becoming pink. They are similar to but larger than 'Unique'.
H4

H. p. 'Praecox' The earliest-flowering form, with smaller panicles of toothed ray-florets. Flowering is generally just before the middle of summer. It is hardy in the

coldest areas. Hard pruning of this medium-sized to large cultivar in the early part of the year will prevent flowering.
H4 ♔ 1993

Hydrangea paniculata 'Tardiva'

H. p. 'Tardiva' A medium-sized to large shrub that flowers late, from the end of summer or early autumn. The large heads have numerous ray-florets.
H4

Hydrangea paniculata 'Unique'

H. p. 'Unique' Similar to 'Grandiflora' but with even larger flowerheads.
H4 ♔ 1993

H. quercifolia A medium-sized deciduous shrub valued mainly for its magnificent autumn tints. The leaves are large, and strongly lobed much like an American oak. Large, white, sterile flowers are carried in conical heads in late summer. SE United States. Introduced 1803.
H4 ♔ 1993

H. q. 'Snowflake' A striking medium-

Hydrangea quercifolia

sized form in which several series of bracts are produced in each flower, creating a double appearance.
H4

***H. q.* 'Snow Queen'** (PBR 3750) A medium-sized shrub bearing upright panicles of large, white florets that turn pink. The dark green leaves are bronze-red in autumn.
H4

H. serrata A charming deciduous shrub which rarely exceeds 1m (3ft). The flattened flowerheads consist of blue or white fertile flowers, surrounded by a pretty circle of white, pink or bluish ray-florets that often deepen to crimson in autumn. Flowering begins in mid- to late summer. A variable species. The following forms are recommended. Japan, Korea. Introduced 1843.
H4

***H. s.* 'Blue Deckle'** A small, compact and slow-growing lacecap type with clear, blue to pink, toothed ray-florets.
H4

Hydrangea serrata 'Bluebird'

***H. s.* 'Bluebird'** A small, robust shrub with stout shoots and abruptly pointed leaves. The blue fertile flowers are borne in slightly dome-shaped heads, surrounded by large ray-florets that are reddish purple on chalk soils and a lovely sea-blue in acid ones.
H4 ♔ 1993

***H. s.* 'Diadem'** A very hardy, compact small shrub with vivid blue or pink flowers. The leaves redden in full sun.
H4

***H. s.* 'Grayswood'** A small shrub with flattened heads of blue fertile flowers, surrounded by a ring of white ray-florets, changing to rose then deep crimson.
H4 ♔ 1993

***H. s.* 'Preziosa'** A handsome small shrub with purplish red stems up to 1.5m (5ft) high and leaves that are purple-tinged when young. Attractive, globular heads of large, rose-pink florets deepen to reddish purple in autumn.
H4 ♔ 1993

Hydrangea serrata 'Preziosa'

Hydrangea serrata 'Rosalba'

***H. s.* 'Rosalba'** A small shrub which has larger leaves than the other cultivars. The violet-blue flowers are surrounded by ray-florets that are white or pale pink at first, quickly turning to crimson.
H4 ♔ 1993

CLIMBERS

Hydrangea petiolaris

H. petiolaris (Climbing hydrangea) A strong-growing deciduous species that reaches 18–25m (60–80ft) in suitable trees and is excellent on a north-facing or otherwise shady wall. It can also be grown as a shrub. The flowers are in flattened clusters 15–25cm (6–10in) wide and are dull greenish white with several large, white, aterile florets along the margin of the cluster. They are produced in early summer. It may need support at first until the aerial roots become active. Japan, Korea. Introduced 1865.
H3 ♔ 1993

H. seemanii A large, vigorous evergreen climber supporting itself by aerial roots. It has leathery leaves and bears rounded heads of white flowers with white marginal florets in late summer. A tender species suitable for a mild area or a wall or tree trunk in a sheltered position.
H3

H. serratifolia A large evergreen species with leathery leaves and small, cream flowers in crowded, columnar panicles up to 15cm (6in) long in late summer. Best against a wall in sun or shade. Chile. Introduced 1925/27 by Harold Comber.
H3–4

Hypericum *Guttiferae*

A genus of altogether about 370 species of perennials and evergreen and deciduous shrubs and trees. The shrubby hypericums thrive in almost any well-drained soil and are very desirable shrubs, producing their prominent, bright yellow flowers in great abundance in summer and autumn. They are happy in full sun or semi-shade. Many of the Asiatic species have been misnamed in cultivation, and those described below are in accordance with research carried out by Dr Robson of the Natural History Museum, London. Some species, particularly H. calycinum *and* H. × inodorum, *are increasingly susceptible to rust.* H. calycinum *is best cut to ground level every other spring; a tool such as a brushcutter/strimmer can be used. Apart from that, most shrubby hypericums require little or no pruning.*

H. androsaemum (Tutsan) A good shade-bearing deciduous shrub, seldom more than 75cm (30in) high, flowering freely and continuously in summer. The flowers are rather small but with conspicuous anthers, followed in autumn by erect, red, berry-like capsules that finally turn black. 'Gladys Brabazon' is a poor variegated form. W and S Europe (including Ireland and W Britain), North Africa, W Asia. In cultivation before 1600.
H4

Hypericum calycinum

H. calycinum (Rose of Sharon) A dwarf evergreen shrub with large leaves and large golden flowers. It is excellent as ground cover in dry and shaded places but if left unchecked it can become a weed. It is occa-

sionally naturalized. It suffers badly from rust and the problem is increasing. Bulgaria, N Turkey. Introduced 1676.
H4

Hypericum coris

H. coris A dwarf or prostrate evergreen shrublet, rarely more than 15cm (6in) in cultivation. It has slender stems and slender, linear leaves arranged in whorls of 3–6. The golden yellow flowers, 1–2cm ($\frac{1}{2}$–$\frac{3}{4}$in) across, are borne in terminal panicles up to 12cm (5in) long in summer. It is ideal for the rock garden, scree or dry wall. C and S Europe. In cultivation 1640.
H4

H. × cyathiflorum 'Gold Cup' A graceful small deciduous shrub with attractive lanceolate leaves arranged along the branches in two opposite rows. The flowers are deep yellow, cup-shaped, and 6cm (2$\frac{1}{2}$in) across.
H4

Hypericum forrestii

H. forrestii A neat, hardy deciduous

shrub, usually 1–1.2m (3–4ft) high. The leaves persist into the early winter and provide rich autumn tints. The saucer-shaped, golden yellow flowers, 5–6cm (2–2$\frac{1}{2}$in) across, rounded in bud, are profusely borne throughout summer and autumn. SW China, NE Burma. Introduced 1906 by George Forrest.
H4 ♈ 1993

Hypericum 'Hidcote'

H. 'Hidcote' A superb, hardy, small to medium-sized semi-evergreen shrub of compact habit, about 2m (6$\frac{1}{2}$ft) high and 2.5m (8ft) wide. The golden yellow, saucer-shaped flowers, which are among the largest of any hardy hypericum, are produced with abandon from midsummer to mid-autumn. It is one of the most popular of all flowering shrubs. Origin is uncertain, but it probably arose at Hidcote Manor, Gloucestershire, England.
H4 ♈ 1993

H. × inodorum This erect, smallish decid-

Hypericum × inodorum 'Elstead'

uous shrub with small yellow flowers and red fruits is variable and is usually grown as one of its named clones. However, 'Albury Purple' is subject to mildew, 'Elstead' suffers badly from rust, and 'Summergold', which has yellow foliage, burns badly in sun. SW Europe, naturalized in Britain. In cultivation 1850.
H4

Hypericum kouytchense

H. kouytchense A small, deciduous or semi-evergreen, rounded, compact shrub with ovate leaves. The golden yellow flowers are up to 6cm (2¹/₂in) across and have conspicuously long stamens. They are freely borne from the early part of summer until mid-autumn and are followed by bright red seed capsules. China.
H4 ♔ 1993

Hypericum × moserianum

H. × moserianum A first-rate dwarf to small deciduous shrub, usually not more than 50cm (18in) high, making excellent

ground cover. The arching stems are reddish and the flowers are 5–6cm (2–2¹/₂in) across with reddish anthers contrasting with the gold petals from the middle of summer to mid-autumn.
H4 ♔ 1993

Hypericum × moserianum 'Tricolor'

H. × m. 'Tricolor' A dwarf to small deciduous shrub with leaves prettily variegated in white, pink and green. It succeeds best when growing fast in a sheltered position or under glass.
H4

H. olympicum A dwarf erect or hummock-forming deciduous sub-shrub with small, bloomy-green leaves. The flowers are bright yellow and borne in clusters at the ends of the slender, radiating shoots in summer. A perfect rock-garden plant. Balkans, Turkey. Introduced 1675.
H4 ♔ 1993

H. o. 'Citrinum' A dwarf shrub with stems bearing terminal clusters of pale sulphur-

Hypericum olympicum 'Citrinum'

Hypericum 'Rowallane'

yellow flowers 3.5cm (1¹/₂in) across.
H4 ♔ 1993

H. 'Rowallane' This magnificent small to medium-sized semi-evergreen shrub is the finest of the genus but needs a sheltered site. The firm-textured, beautifully moulded flowers are widely bowl-shaped, 5–7.5 cm (2–3in) across, and of an intensely rich golden yellow. It has a graceful habit and is up to 2m (6¹/₂ft) high in mild areas. It has been wrongly labelled *H. rogersii*.
H3 ♔ 1993

I

Idesia *Flacourtiaceae*

A genus of one deciduous species, related to Azara.

I. polycarpa A medium-sized tree with large, ovate, long-stalked leaves that are bloomy on their undersides. The tiny, yellowish-green flowers are borne in large panicles at the ends of the shoots in summer, but not on young trees, so it is not a tree for a small garden. Large bunches of bright red berries resembling peas are borne on female trees in autumn. It grows best in a deep, neutral or somewhat acid soil, but does quite well over chalk as long as there is about 75cm (30in) of good soil. It is hardiest where summers are long and hot. The only pruning needed is the removal of dead or diseased wood. Japan, China. Introduced c1864 by Richard Oldham.
H4

ILEX

Holly *Aquifoliaceae*

ILEX IS A large genus from which you could make a wide selection and still leave some of the most delectable trees and shrubs in cultivation unexplored. There are evergreen and – surprisingly, perhaps – decidous hollies. Some are typically prickly, others have not as much as a single prickle, and a few have prickles all over the upper surfaces of their leaves. There are hollies of all shades of green and variegation tends to be regular and attractive, and often pleasingly subtle.

Of course, it is primarily for berries that *Ilex* takes its place among the foremost woody plant genera. It is a mistake to make too much of them at the expense of other characteristics when choosing hollies, but those with the most long-lasting, profusely borne or brilliantly red winter berries are inevitably the most sought after.

However, since an evergreen holly is a feature for 12 months of the year, and possibly important to the garden architecturally, you should always look at the whole plant when making a choice. Size is a consideration, and there are hollies for the smallest garden as well as the largest. Habit – dense and bushy or graceful and tree-like – is another point to bear in mind, and so is individual leaf shape and colour. Seemingly minor details like the colours of the leaf stalks can be most effective, especially as a bush begins to mature.

Neither is it essential that holly berries should be red. There are some with highly ornamental yellow berries and others whose fruits are shining black. However, you should take care to make sure that there is a male holly reasonably near, and if there is not you should grow one, or the females will not bear fruit. A little extra care is needed in consulting the plant lists, as sometimes the male hollies have feminine

Ilex × *altaclarensis* 'Camelliifolia'

cultivar names, while some females sound decidedly masculine. For example, *Ilex aquifolium* 'Golden Queen' is male, while *I.* × *altaclarensis* 'Golden King' is female. It is perhaps unfortunate, but the names, once given, must remain.

The most attractive evergreen hollies are the English holly *I. aquifolium* and its hybrid *I.* × *altaclarensis* which, although perfectly hardy in Britain, do not like the cold winters of North America. Here, the less glossy American holly *I. opaca* will have to do; in turn, it does not do well in Britain and requires a continental climate to thrive.

CARE AND CULTIVATION
The great majority of hollies adapt to most soils, including soft, chalky limestones, but are happiest in moist but well-drained, loamy ground. There are, however, a few species that require a neutral to acid soil,

and these include the North American deciduous species *I. verticillata*. All hollies are indifferent to sun or shade.

Be vigilant with variegated hollies, maintaining a watch for emerging green shoots, which should be cut out as soon as possible. Reversion is most common when plants are young, but it can occur later and a reverted branch can rapidly take over if it is missed. Apart from this and hollies grown for hedges, pruning is rarely necessary. Bushes that habitually bear large quantities of attractive berries are not at all damaged by frequent cropping but are all the better for the occasional rest.

Should you need to move a holly it is best to choose a moist spell in late spring, but if the season is dry it would be as well to leave it for a year. Well-rooted and balled nursery stock can be moved throughout the dormant season.

I. × *altaclerensis* A number of recognizably similar but nevertheless variable hybrid evergreen hollies, mostly large shrubs or small to medium-sized, vigorous trees with handsome, usually large leaves. Most are excellent for tall hedges or screens and they are quite tolerant of air pollution and seaside exposure. The name derives from *Alta Clera* (Highclere), the Hampshire home of the earls of Carnarvon. H4

I. × *a.* **'Belgica Aurea'**, syn. *I.* × *a.* 'Silver Sentinel' One of the handsomest variegated hollies, this is a vigorous, erect, female large shrub or medium-sized tree with firm, flat, sparsely spiny leaves that are often 8–10cm (3–4in) long. The leaves are an attractive deep green with pale green and grey mottling and irregular but prominent creamy white or creamy yellow margins. H4 ♛ 1993

I. × *a.* **'Camelliifolia'** A beautiful, pyramidal, large-fruiting female holly with purple stems. The long, large, mainly spineless and quite camellia-like leaves of this large shrub or medium-sized tree are reddish purple when young and a lovely shining dark green in maturity. In cultivation 1865. H4 ♛ 1993

I. × *a.* **'Golden King'** This large shrub or medium-sized tree is one of the best hollies with gold variegation. The broad, almost spineless leaves are green with a bright yellow margin. Despite its name it is female. Found 1884 in Edinburgh. H4 ♛ 1993

I. × *a.* **'Hodginsii'** A strong, vigorous clone with purple stems. Some of the large, dark green, rounded or oval leaves are boldly spiny while others have few spines, the latter more prevalent on older plants. It makes a large shrub or a good medium-sized specimen tree for a lawn and is especially suitable for coastal and industrial areas. Although usually male, there is a female form. H4 ♛ 1993

I. × *a.* **'Lawsoniana'** A very colourful female holly with large, generally spineless leaves, splashed with yellow in the centre. Reverting shoots may occur and should be removed. It makes a large shrub or medium-sized tree. H4 ♛ 1993

Ilex × *altaclerensis*

Ilex × *altaclerensis* 'Belgica Aurea'

Ilex × *altaclerensis* 'Camelliifolia'

Ilex × *altaclerensis* 'Golden King'

Ilex × *altaclerensis* 'Lawsoniana'

I. × a. **'Silver Sentinel'** See *I. × a.* 'Belgica Aurea'.

Ilex × altaclerensis 'Wilsonii'

I. × a. **'Wilsonii'** A compact, dome-shaped female clone with green stems and large, evenly spiny, prominently veined leaves. It makes a large shrub or medium-sized tree with large, scarlet fruits and is deservedly popular. Raised early 1890s by Fisher, Son and Sibray.
H4 ♔ 1993

Ilex aquifolium

I. aquifolium (Common holly) Although capable of reaching 18–21m (60–70ft) in favourable conditions, it is usually a large shrub or small tree. There are innumerable evergreen cultivars with different habits and varying shapes and colourings of leaves. The colouring of the berries is also variable, but in the forms listed below is red unless otherwise stated. The sex of seed-raised plants will not be ascertained for a number of years. The typical form and many of the cultivars are good for hedge-making and excellent in industrial and sea-side areas. W and S Europe (including Britain and Ireland), North Africa, W Asia. In cultivation since ancient times.
H4 ♔ 1993

I. a. **'Amber'** A female large shrub or small tree with green leaves and attractive, large, bronze-yellow fruits. Selected before 1955 at Hillier Nurseries.
H4

I. a. **'Argentea Marginata'** A handsome, free-fruiting female large shrub or small tree with green stems and white-margined leaves. The young growth is shrimp-pink.
H4 ♔ 1993

Ilex aquifolium 'Argentea Marginata Pendula'

I. a. **'Argentea Marginata Pendula'** (Perry's silver weeping holly) A small, graceful female tree with weeping branches, forming a compact mushroom of leaves with white margins. It fruits freely.
H4

I. a. **'Bacciflava'** (Yellow-fruited holly) A green-leaved female large shrub or small tree bearing heavy crops of bright yellow fruits. 'Fructu-Luteo' is similar.
H4

I. a. **'Ferox'** (Hedgehog holly) A male cultivar, lower- and slower-growing than most, which makes an excellent hedge. The upper surfaces of the small leaves are puckered and almost covered with short, sharp spines. In cultivation since at least the seventeenth century.
H4

I. a. **'Ferox Argentea'** (Silver hedgehog holly) A medium-sized male shrub with a

Ilex aquifolium 'Ferox Argentea'

very effective combination of rich purple twigs and leaves with creamy white margin and spines. In cultivation 1662.
H4 ♔ 1993

I. a. **'Ferox Aurea'** (Gold hedgehog holly) The leaves of this medium-sized male shrub have a distinguishing central, deep gold or yellow-green blotch.
H4

I. a. **'Flavescens'** A female holly with leaves suffused canary-yellow, shaded old gold. It is especially effective on a dull winter afternoon or in spring when the young leaves appear. It does best in full sun.
H4

I. a. **'Fructu-Luteo'** See *I. a.* 'Bacciflava'.

Ilex aquifolium 'Golden Milkboy'

I. a. **'Golden Milkboy'** A striking male holly with large, spine-edged leaves that are green with a large splash of gold in the centre. Reverting shoots should be removed. It makes a large shrub or a small tree.
H4 ♔ 1993

I. a. **'Golden Queen'** An eye-catching large shrub or small tree with green young shoots and broad, spiny, dark green leaves with pale green and grey shading and a broad yellow margin. As discussed in the introduction to this section, despite its name, it is male.
H4 ♛ 1993

I. a. **'Golden van Tol'** A female large shrub or small tree with particularly attractive gold-margined leaves. It is a sport of 'J.C. van Tol'.
H4

Ilex aquifolium 'Green Pillar'

I. a. **'Green Pillar'** An erect, narrow female form with upright branches and dark green, spiny leaves. An excellent specimen tree and suitable for growing in tubs. It is good for hedging, with very little cutting required.
H4 ♛ 1993

I. a. **'Handsworth New Silver'** An attractive purple-stemmed free-fruiting

Ilex aquifolium 'Handsworth New Silver'

female holly, distinguished by its comparatively long, deep green leaves which have a grey mottle and a broad, creamy margin. It makes a large shrub or small tree.
H4 ♛ 1993

Ilex aquifolium 'J.C. van Tol'

I. a. **'J.C. van Tol'** A superb female cultivar with dark, shining, almost spineless green leaves and large, regular crops of red fruits. A large shrub or small tree, it is self-pollinating and does not need a male tree for berry production.
H4 ♛ 1993

Ilex aquifolium 'Madame Briot'

I. a. **'Madame Briot'** An attractively purple-stemmed female holly with large, strongly spiny green leaves mottled and margined with dark yellow. It makes a large shrub or small tree.
H4 ♛ 1993

I. a. **'Myrtifolia'** A neat male large shrub or small tree with purple shoots and small, dark green leaves that are variably edged

with sharp spines and may even be spineless.
H4

Ilex aquifolium 'Myrtifolia Aureomaculata'

I. a. **'Myrtifolia Aureomaculata'** A dense, compact male large shrub or small tree with small, evenly spined dark green leaves with pale green shading and an irregular splash of gold in the centre.
H4 ♛ 1993

I. a. **'Pendula'** An elegant, free-fruiting small female tree, forming a dense mound of weeping stems thickly clothed with dark green, spiny leaves.
H4

Ilex aquifolium 'Pyramidalis'

I. a. **'Pyramidalis'** A free-fruiting female form with green stems and bright green, slightly spiny leaves. It is conical in its youth and broadens as it matures into a large shrub or small tree.
H4 ♛ 1993

I. a. **'Pyramidalis Fructu-Luteo'** A female form similar to 'Pyramidalis' but

with profusely borne bright yellow berries.
H4 🏆 1993

Ilex aquifolium 'Silver Milkmaid'

I. a. **'Silver Milkmaid'** An attractive large shrub or small tree with strongly spiny dark green leaves with a central blotch of creamy white. It is female, and so are plants previously grown as 'Silver Milkboy'. Reverting shoots should be removed.
H4 🏆 1993

I. a. **'Silver Queen'** A striking male holly with blackish-purple young shoots and broadly ovate, dark green leaves faintly marbled with grey and bordered with cream. The young leaves are shrimp-pink. It makes a large shrub or small tree.
H4 🏆 1993

I. cornuta A dense, slow-growing evergreen species, rarely reaching 2.5m (8ft) high, with peculiar rectangular, mainly five-spined leaves. It has large, red fruits, but they are seldom freely produced. It does not perform well in the British Isles. The following form is recommended. China, Korea. Introduced 1846.
H4

I. c. **'Burfordii'** A free-fruiting, compact small to medium-sized form with shining green leathery leaves which, apart from a short terminal spine, are entire. It is extensively planted as an evergreen hedge in the United States, where it can reach 4m (12ft). It is a female form.
H4

I. crenata (Japanese holly) A tiny-leaved, slow-growing evergreen holly, reaching 4–6m (12–20ft), with small, shining, black berries. It is variable, especially in cultiva-

tion, and it is probably better to plant one of the cultivars, as you then know what to expect. The following forms are recommended. Korea, Japan. Introduced 1864.
H4

Ilex crenata 'Convexa'

I. c. **'Convexa'** A free-fruiting, small, bushy female shrub with glossy, puckered or convex leaves. It makes a superb low hedge. In cultivation 1919.
H4 🏆 1993

Ilex crenata 'Golden Gem'

I. c. **'Golden Gem'** A small, compact shrub with a flattened top and yellow leaves. It is particularly attractive in winter and spring. It is female but very shy-flowering, so does not bear many berries.
H4 🏆 1993

I. c. **'Helleri'** Perhaps the most attractive dwarf, small-leaved form, making a low, dense, flattened hummock. It is female.
H4 🏆 1993

I. c. **'Mariesii'** A dwarf, most unholly-like

Ilex crenata 'Mariesii'

female shrub of very slow growth, with crowded, tiny, round leaves. It is ideal for trough or bonsai culture. In the open ground it eventually makes a stiffly upright shrub of about 2m (6ft) and is most attractive when bearing black berries in winter. A male plant with larger leaves and faster growth has also been grown under this name. Introduced 1879 by Maries.
H4

I. c. **'Variegata'** A small female shrub with leaves irregularly blotched with gold.
H4

I. × *koehniana* **'Chestnut Leaf'** A large evergreen shrub or small tree with purple-flushed young shoots. The large yellowish green leaves are boldly margined with strong, spiny teeth. Both male and female forms exist, but it is to the female form, which bears large, red berries, that the AGM has been awarded.
H4 🏆 1993

I. latifolia (Tarajo) A small evergreen tree

Ilex latifolia

or large shrub, usually about 7m (22ft) in cultivation. It is a magnificent species with leaves that rival those of *Magnolia grandiflora* for size and are dark glossy green, leathery, oblong and with short spines. It succeeds best in a sheltered position as, although it is quite hardy, it is tender when young. Its orange-red fruits are often abundantly produced. Japan, China. Introduced 1840.
H4

I. l. **'Lydia Morris'** A medium-sized, compact, conical shrub with polished, strongly spiny leaves. It is female and has large red fruits.
H4

I. × *meservae* (Blue holly) A group of hybrid evergreen hollies which are bushy, small to medium-sized shrubs up to 2m (6ft) with angled, purplish shoots and softly spiny, dark, glossy, blue-green leaves. They are best in a continental climate, but the Royal Horticultural Society has awarded the AGM to two of the forms in cultivation. Originally raised in New York to produce an ornamental holly for the parts of eastern North America where *I. aquifolium* is not hardy.
H4

Ilex × meservae 'Blue Angel'

I. × *m.* **'Blue Angel'** A slow-growing, compact small to medium-sized female shrub with dark purple stems and red berries. The least hardy form.
H4 🏆 1993

I. × *m.* **'Blue Prince'** A small to medium-sized male shrub with purple-tinged stems and red berries.
H4

I. × *m.* **'Blue Princess'** A small to

medium-sized female form with glossy foliage and good crops of red berries.
H4 🏆 1993

Ilex pernyi

I. pernyi A distinguished large evergree shrub or small tree with small, peculiarly spined, almost triangular-shaped leaves. The fruits are small and bright red. C and W China. Introduced 1912.
H4

I. verticillata (Winterberry) A large deciduous shrub with leaves turning yellow in autumn. The fruits are bright red and long-persisting. It is not suitable for chalky or otherwise limy soils. It is best grown in a continental climate. E North America. Introduced 1736.
H4

Illicium *Illiciaceae*

The genus consists of about 40 species of aromatic evergreen trees and shrubs native to east and South-East Asia and warmer parts of America. It is the only genus in the family and is related to Magnolia. *Its members thrive under conditions congenial to rhododendrons, although they are tolerant of a little lime.*

I. anisatum A medium-sized to large, slow-growing, aromatic shrub. The leaves are more or less oval, abruptly pointed, thick and fleshy and glossy deep green. The pale yellow, many-petalled flowers are about 2.5cm (1in) across and borne, even on young plants, in spring. Japan, China. Introduced 1790.
H4

Illicium floridanum

I. floridanum A medium-sized, aromatic shrub with glossy, leathery leaves and maroon-purple, many-petalled flowers in late spring and early summer. S United States. Introduced 1771.
H4

Indigofera *Leguminosae*

This is a very large genus of about 700 species of deciduous shrubs and perennials, found mainly in tropical and sub-tropical regions. The following are very attractive shrubs of which the flower clusters are produced from the leaf axils of growing shoots, which means that they flower continuously throughout summer and autumn. All of them have elegant pinnate leaves and prefer full sun. They thrive on all types of soil and are especially good in dry situations. Some may be cut back by cold in really severe winters, but this is no bad thing as they respond by throwing up a thicket of strong shoots the following spring. Old or poorly shaped specimens can be hard pruned to give the same

Indigofera amblyantha

effect. *The commercial source of indigo is the tender* I. tinctoria.

I. amblyantha A splendid medium-sized shrub with 12–20cm (5–8in) racemes of delightfully shrimp-pink flowers. China. Introduced 1908 by William Purdom. H4 ♛ 1993

I. decora A rare and pretty dwarf shrub with long racemes of pink pea-flowers. China, Japan. Introduced 1846. H4

I. d. f. alba An attractive dwarf form with white flowers. Introduced c1878. H4

Indigofera heterantha

I. heterantha A small to medium-sized shrub with bright purplish rose flowers and particularly elegant foliage, growing to 90cm–1.2m (3–4ft) in the open but much higher against a wall. Plants named *I. divaricata* are probably just geographical variants of this species. NW Himalaya. In cultivation 1840. H4 ♛ 1993

I. potaninii A splendid, medium-sized shub similar in many ways to *I. amblyantha* but slightly smaller in size with slightly shorter racemes of clear pink flowers. In cultivation 1925. H4

I. pseudotinctoria A vigorous species reaching about 1.5m (5ft) in height and bearing pink flowers in dense clusters up to 10cm (4¹⁄₂in) long. This plant is related to *I. amblyantha*. China. Introduced 1897 by Augustine Henry. H4

Indocalamus *Gramineae*

A genus of about 15 evergreen species of bamboo, natives of China, of which only the following is generally grown. It enjoys a moist soil and is good in shade. It will grow in good soil over chalk.

I. tessellatus This remarkable species forms dense thickets of slender, bright green canes up to 2m (6ft) tall. The shining green leaves, up to 60cm (2ft) long by 5–10cm (2–4in) wide, are the largest of all found on hardy bamboos and such is their collective weight that the canes tend to bend down, giving the clump almost a dwarf habit. China. Introduced 1845. H3–4

Itea *Grossulariaceae*

A genus of about 10 species of evergreen and deciduous shrubs and small trees native to east Asia from the Himalaya to the Philippines, with one species in east North America. The following are attractive and unusual summer-flowering shrubs that thrive in semi-shade, though the evergreen species will take full sun against a south- or west-facing wall as long as the soil is not too dry.

Itea ilicifolia

I. ilicifolia A lax, evergreen, holly-like shrub to 3m (10ft) or more in height. It is particularly charming in late summer, when it is laden with long, drooping, catkin-like clusters of pleasantly fragrant greenish white flowers. C China. Introduced before 1895 by Augustine Henry. H3 ♛ 1993

I. virginica A small, attractive, erectly

Itea virginica

branched, deciduous shrub with upright, cylindrical clusters of fragrant cream flowers in midsummer. The foliage often turns rich red in autumn. It prefers a moist, acid soil. E United States. Introduced 1744. H4

J

Jasminum *Oleaceae*

There are more than 200 species of Jasminum and they include evergreen and deciduous shrubs and climbers, found in the tropical and temperate regions of the Old World. The climbers are very popular, but those that will grow as self-supporting shrubs are not well enough appreciated or widely enough planted.

CLIMBERS

The climbing jasmines are easily grown in most fertile soils with a sunny position. Excellent for training up walls or pergolas. The hardy species withstand industrial pollution. Apart from *J. officinale* and *J. polyanthum*, which need thinning after flowering, no pruning is necessary.

J. angulare A choice but tender medium-sized evergreen species with thickish, dark green leaves with three leaflets. The sweetly scented white flowers, 5cm (2in) long, are borne in large panicles in late summer. Suitable for the mildest places only, but a beautiful conservatory plant. S Africa. H2–3

J. azoricum A beautiful medium-sized evergreen twining species with attractive clusters of sweetly scented white flowers, purple-flushed in bud, that open in summer and winter. Only really suitable for the mildest places or in the conservatory. Madeira, where it is very rare. Introduced in the seventeenth century.
H2–3

Jasminum beesianum

J. beesianum A vigorous deciduous plant up to 3.5m (11ft) with fragrant, rather small flowers of an unusual deep velvet red, but sometimes pinkish crimson. They appear in late spring and early summer and are followed by shining black berries that last well into winter. SW China. Introduced 1907.
H4

Jasminum mesnyi

J. mesnyi (Primrose jasmine) A most beautiful evergreen species with bright yellow flowers 4cm (1½in) long. They are semi-double and produced in succession from

Jasminum officinale

early to late spring. It is best grown against a sunny wall in mild areas, where it can reach 4m (12ft); alternatively it can be grown in the conservatory. China. Introduced 1900 by Ernest Wilson.
H2–3 ♔ 1993

J. officinale (Common white jasmine, poet's jasmine) A strong-growing deciduous climber reaching 6–9m (20–28ft) in a suitable tree. The leaves are pinnate and have 5–9 leaflets; the deliciously fragrant white flowers are borne in terminal clusters from early summer to early autumn. In cold districts it needs a sheltered corner. It should be thinned out after flowering. Caucasus to China. Introduced 1548.
H4 ♔ 1993

J. o. f. affine A superior medium-sized to large form with slightly larger flowers that are usually tinged with pink on the outside. Sometimes known as 'Grandiflorum', which leads to confusion with *J. grandiflorum*, a tender species for the greenhouse.
H4

Jasminum officinale 'Argenteovariegatum'

J. o. 'Argenteovariegatum' A very striking medium-sized form with grey-green leaves margined with creamy white which complement the flowers.
H4 ♔ 1993

J. o. 'Aureum' The leaves of this medium-sized form are variegated and suffused with yellow. Effective and free-flowering.
H4

J. o. 'Fiona Sunrise' (*J. o.* 'Frojas' PBR 5488) A striking new form resembling the typical species in the fragrant white flowers it produces in summer but supplemented with bright golden yellow foliage.
H4

Jasminum polyanthum

J. polyanthum A beautiful, vigorous, twining evergreen species up to 7m (22ft), related to the common jasmine but tender. The intensely fragrant white flowers, flushed rose on the outside, are borne in panicles from late spring to late summer – earlier under glass. It needs a warm wall or trellis in mild places but is excellent in the conservatory as long as it is pruned regularly. The shoots should be thinned but not shortened. China. Introduced 1891.
H2 ♛ 1993

J. sambac (Arabian jasmine) The evergreen leaves of this attractive medium-sized climber are glossy and undivided and the very fragrant white flowers, which flush

Jasminum × stephanense

with pink as they age, are continuously produced from early spring to late summer or all year round when grown in a conservatory. For a warm, sheltered, sunny position in the mildest areas or in the conservatory. Possibly originally from India.
H2–3

J. × stephanense A vigorous deciduous climber up to 7m (22ft) with fragrant pale pink flowers in early and midsummer and slender green angular shoots. The leaves on young shoots are often flushed with creamy yellow. It is the only known hybrid jasmine and is very beautiful where there is enough space for it to develop fully, such as over an outbuilding. China. Found 1887.
H4 ♛ 1993

J. suavissimum A tall-growing deciduous conservatory species with slender twining stems and sweetly fragrant white flowers in loose panicles in late summer that will perfume the whole conservatory. Australia.
H2–3

SHRUBS

All the hardy shrubby species have yellow flowers and are more or less deciduous in hard winters, though their green stems create an evergreen effect. They will grow in any reasonable garden soil.

Jasminum humile 'Revolutum'

J. humile 'Revolutum' A quite remarkable and very beautiful medium-sized shrub with deep green, persistent leaves usually made up of 5–7 leaflets. These create a splendid setting for the comparatively large, deep yellow, slightly fragrant flowers that

are borne in domed heads during summer. China. Introduced 1814.
H4 ♛ 1993

Jasminum nudiflorum

J. nudiflorum (Winter jasmine) One of the most tolerant and beautiful of winter-flowering shrubs, with bright yellow flowers on the naked green branches from late autumn to late winter. It makes strong, angular growths up to 4m (12ft) long and is excellent for covering walls and banks. When grown as a wall shrub, the long growths can be cut back immediately after flowering. It is deciduous. W China. Introduced 1844 by Robert Fortune.
H4 ♛ 1993

J. n. 'Aureum' A medium-sized shrub bearing leaves that are blotched with, or almost entirely, yellow. In cultivation 1889.
H4

Jasminum parkeri

J. parkeri A dwarf or prostrate deciduous shrub, normally forming a low, 30cm (1ft)

mound of densely crowded, greenish stems, bearing small pinnate leaves and, in summer, tiny yellow flowers. It is particularly suitable for the rock garden. W. Himalaya. Introduced 1923.
H4

Jovellana *Scrophulariaceae*

A genus of about six species of perennials and evergreen and deciduous sub-shrubs related to Calceolaria *and native to New Zealand and Chile. They can be grown in the open in the warmer parts of cool-temperate areas in sun or semi-shade and any good soil. They make little thickets, and any dead stems should be cut away at ground level.*

J. sinclairii A dwarf deciduous species, suitable for a very mild rock garden, with white or pale lavender purple-spotted flowers in early summer. New Zealand. Introduced 1881.
H2

Jovellana violacea

J. violacea A small evergreen shrub with erect branches and small, neat leaves. The pale violet flowers with yellow throats and darker markings are produced in early to midsummer. Chile. Introduced 1853.
H3 ♧ 1993

Juglans *Juglandaceae*
Walnut

The walnuts are a genus of around 20 species of deciduous trees from North and South America and from south-east Europe to South-East Asia. They

are mostly fast-growing ornamental trees and are not particular about the soil, though they should not be planted where they may be subject to late frosts. The pinnate, ash-like leaves are large and beautiful in some species.

Juglans ailanthifolia

J. ailanthifolia Erect, medium-sized tree with large, handsome leaves often as much as 1m (3ft) long. Japan. Introduced 1860.
H4

J. elaeopyren, syn. *J. major* A very handsome medium-sized tree with leaves turning butter-yellow in autumn. New Mexico, Arizona, W Mexico. Introduced c1894.
H4

J. major See *J. elaeopyren.*

Juglans nigra

J. nigra (Black walnut) A large, noble, fast-growing tree with deeply furrowed bark and large leaves. The fruits, generally in pairs, are large and round. E and C United States. In cultivation 1686.
H4 ♧ 1993

Juglans regia

J. regia (Common walnut) A slow-growing, medium-sized to large tree with a characteristically rounded head. It has been cultivated in Europe for many centuries and the timber is highly prized and very valuable. Where fruit is the main consideration, plant selected clones such as 'Broadview' and 'Buccaneer' which have been selected for their early and good quality fruiting and have to be vegetatively propagated. SE Europe, Himalayas, China.
H4 ♧ 1993

J. r. 'Laciniata' (Cut-leaved walnut) A form with rather pendulous branches and deeply cut leaflets. In 1994 a tree at one of the Hillier Nurseries in England had reached a height of 16m (52ft).
H4

Juniperus *Cupressaceae*
Juniper

A genus of about 60 species of evergreen coniferous trees and shrubs, from prostrate alpines to dense, bushy shrubs and conical or columnar trees. They are native to most of the northern hemisphere, and extend from inside the Arctic Circle to Mount Kenya on the Equator; they are probably the most widely distributed of all trees and shrubs in nature. The leaves of juvenile plants are awl-shaped and usually pointed while those of adult plants are normally scale-like and crowded, although in some species they retain their juvenile form. Juniper fruits are usually rounded or egg-shaped, becoming fleshy and berry-like.

Junipers are very versatile and include plants for most soils and situations. They are among the most suitable conifers for calcareous soils. The range of their foliage colour is from green to yellow, grey and steel blue. The prostrate forms are excellent ground cover.

J. chinensis (Chinese juniper) An extremely variable species. In cultivation it is typically a tall, dense, greyish tree with both adult and juvenile foliage. Its many cultivars are far more frequently grown. The following are recommended. China, Japan. Introduced before 1767.
H4

Juniperus chinensis 'Aurea'

J. c. 'Aurea' (Young's golden juniper) A tall, slow-growing, conical or columnar tree with golden foliage that can burn in full sun. It has both adult and juvenile foliage. Raised c1855 as a sport in Surrey.
H4 ♔ 1993

J. c. 'Blue Alps' A vigorous, large shrub with striking steel-blue foliage. Austria. Found 1968.
H4

Juniperus chinensis 'Kaizuka'

J. c. 'Kaizuka' A large, erect shrub, eventually becoming a small tree, with long, spreading branches clothed with characteristic dense clusters of scale-like bright green foliage. It is a very distinct form, ideal in a large garden as an isolated lawn specimen. Japan. Introduced c1920.
H4 ♔ 1993

J. c. 'Obelisk' A medium-sized, erect, columnar shrub. The foliage is bluish green with densely packed, awl-shaped leaves. Raised 1930 in Holland.
H4 ♔ 1993

J. c. 'Pyramidalis' A dense and slow-growing, medium-sized columnar bush with almost entirely juvenile, prickly, bloomy leaves on ascending branches. Japan. Introduced 1843 by Siebold.
H4 ♔ 1993

J. c. 'Stricta' A large, compact, conical shrub with erect branches. The foliage is juvenile, soft to the touch and blue-grey. In cultivation 1949.
H4

J. c. 'Variegata' Usually a large conical bush of dense, compact habit with leaves that are mostly juvenile, blue-grey, with scattered sprays of white variegation. Japan. Introduced c1860.
H4

J. communis (Common juniper) A variable species which may be prostrate or dwarf but usually makes a medium-sized to large shrub. It has silver-backed leaves that are awl-shaped, prickly, and arranged in whorls of three. The fruits are rounded, berry-like, black and covered with a bluish bloom. They are sometimes used to flavour gin. It is one the three native conifers of the British Isles and probably has a wider distribution than any other tree or shrub. The following forms are recommended. North America, Europe, Asia, Korea, Japan.
H4

J. c. 'Compressa' A gem for the rock garden or scree. It is a dwarf, compact, slow-growing column something like a miniature Irish juniper and almost never exceeds 1m (3ft) in height. It is more effective when planted in a group. In cultivation 1855.
H4 ♔ 1993

Juniperus communis 'Depressa Aurea'

J. c. 'Depressa Aurea' A dwarf, wide-spreading form about 60cm (2ft) high. The leaves and young shoots are golden yellow in early summer, paling to green. It is unfortunately very prone to the disease needle blight. In cultivation 1887.
H4

J. c. 'Gold Cone', syn. *J. c.* 'Suecica Aurea' An erect, slow-growing medium-sized shrub with steeply ascending branches and golden yellow foliage during the summer, paling to green in winter.
H4

J. c. 'Golden Rod' A small, slender, columnar shrub with bright yellow young foliage that turns green in winter.
H4

J. c. 'Green Carpet' A dense, low-growing and wide-spreading shrub with bright green foliage. Norway. Found before 1975.
H4 ♔ 1993

J. c. 'Hibernica' (Irish juniper) A dense-growing, compact, slenderly columnar form 3m (9ft) or occasionally 5m (15ft) high,

Juniperus communis 'Hibernica'

with densely arranged leaves. It is a very popular conifer, excellent for formal gardens and to some extent the counterpart of the Italian cypress of warmer climates, though never as tall. In cultivation 1838. H4 ♇ 1993

J. c. **'Hornibrookii'** A dwarf, creeping ground cover form that takes on the shape

Juniperus communis 'Hornibrookii'

Juniperus communis 'Repanda'

of the object over which it creeps. The leaves are quite small, loosely spreading, sharply pointed and silvery white beneath. Ireland. In cultivation 1923. H4

J. c. **'Repanda'** A dwarf, carpeting shrub with densely packed, semi-prostrate stems and foliage that becomes slightly bronze in winter. It makes excellent ground cover in full sun. Ireland. In cultivation 1934. H4 ♇ 1993

J. c. **'Sentinel'** A very narrowly columnar form with densely packed, erect branches. The deep bluish green leaves contrast well with the reddish purple shoots. It reaches 4m high and 50cm wide (12ft × 20in) in 30 years. Raised before 1961 in Canada. H4

J. c. **'Suecica Aurea'** See *J. c.* 'Gold Cone'.

Juniperus conferta

J. conferta (Shore juniper) A prostrate species, making large patches of bright green, prickly leaves with a white band on the upper surface. It has round, purplish black, bloomy berries. It is a first-class ground cover conifer, its one drawback being a vulnerability to needle blight. Japan. Introduced 1915 by Ernest Wilson. H4

J. c. **'Blue Pacific'** The leaves of this prostrate form are broader, less prickly and darker green. H4

J. davurica **'Expansa Aureospicata'** A slow-growing dwarf shrub with rigid, almost horizontal branches and juvenile foliage that is greyish green with scattered

Juniperus davurica 'Expansa Variegata'

yellow splashes. In cultivation 1940. H4

J. d. **'Expansa Variegata'** Similar in habit and foliage but with scattered cream sprays. It is sometimes listed as a form of *J. chinensis*. In cultivation 1933. H4

J. drupacea (Syrian juniper) A striking and distinctive narrowly columnar small tree, with short branches densely crowded with sharply pointed, awl-shaped leaves. SW Asia, Greece. Introduced c1854. H4

J. **'Grey Owl'** A splendid, vigorous medium-sized shrub with widely spreading branches held out like arms and soft, silvery grey foliage. It is possibly a hybrid of *J. virginiana*. Originated 1938. H4 ♇ 1993

Juniperus 'Holger'

J. **'Holger'** A small, spreading, hybrid shrub with bloomy blue foliage that is creamy yellow when young. See also *J.*

'Hunnetorp'. Raised 1946 in Sweden.
H4 ♔ 1993

Juniperus horizontalis

J. horizontalis (Creeping juniper) A dwarf or prostrate shrub with long, sometimes procumbent branches, forming carpets several metres (yards) across. The leaves on cultivated plants are mostly juvenile and clothe the branchlets densely with glaucous green, grey-green or blue, often turning plum-purple in winter. It is one of the best species for ground cover. The following forms are recommended. North America. In cultivation 1830.
H4

***J. h.* 'Andorra Compact'** Similar to but an improvement on 'Plumosa'. It is of denser habit and has bronze-purple foliage in winter. In cultivation 1955.
H4

***J. h.* 'Bar Harbor'** A prostrate form which has widespread, closely ground-hugging branches. The foliage is a most attractive glaucous grey-green. In cultivation 1930.
H4

***J. h.* 'Blue Chip'** A prostrate form with foliage that is bright blue throughout the year. Raised 1940 in Denmark.
H4

***J. h.* 'Blue Rug'** See *J. h.* 'Wiltonii'.

***J. h.* 'Emerald Spreader'** A very low-growing plant, forming dense mats of bright green foliage. In cultivation 1973.
H4

***J. h.* 'Hughes'** A vigorous form with ascending branches and grey-green foliage. Raised 1979 in the United States.
H4

***J. h.* 'Plumosa'** A dense, procumbent, compact form with ascending, feathery branches up to 60cm (2ft) high. The awl-shaped leaves are usually grey-green, becoming an attractive purple-tinted shade in winter. In cultivation 1919.
H4 ♔ 1993

***J. h.* 'Prince of Wales'** A low-growing, dense form that makes mats up to 15cm (6in) high. The foliage is bright green tinged with blue and flushed with purple in winter. Found 1931 in Alberta.
H4

***J. h.* 'Wiltonii'**, syn. *J. h.* 'Blue Rug' One of the best forms, with long, prostrate branches that form flattened, glaucous-blue carpets. In cultivation 1914.
H4 ♔ 1993

***J.* 'Hunnetorp'** A sister seedling of 'Holger', under which name it has been distributed. It differs in its foliage, which is glaucous blue throughout its life.
H4

Juniperus × *media* 'Blaauw'

J.* × *media These hybrids are very variable and the following examples are among the best cultivars available.

***J.* × *m.* 'Blaauw'** A strong-growing shrub up to 1.5m (5ft), with strongly ascending main branches and shorter outer ones, all densely clothed with feathery sprays of mainly scale-like, greyish blue leaves. In cultivation 1924.
H4 ♔ 1993

Juniperus × *media* 'Carberry Gold'

***J.* × *m.* 'Carberry Gold'** A prostrate shrub with striking foliage which remains bright creamy yellow all year round.
H4

Juniperus × *media* 'Gold Coast'

***J.* × *m.* 'Gold Coast'** A flat-topped, low-growing and wide-spreading form with golden foliage.
H4

***J.* × *m.* 'Hetzii'** A medium-sized to large wide-spreading shrub similar to 'Pfitzeriana' but with stems that are more ascending. The glaucous, mainly adult foliage is also softer to the touch. In cultivation 1920. H4

J. × m. 'Kuriwao Gold' A large, dense, columnar shrub with yellow-green foliage and spreading, bright yellow shoots. H4

Juniperus × media 'Mint Julep'

J. × m. 'Mint Julep' A spreading, flat-topped bush with arching shoots. It resembles 'Pfitzeriana' but has bright green foliage. In cultivation 1960. H4

Juniperus × media 'Old Gold'

J. × m. 'Old Gold' A sport of 'Pfitzeriana Aurea', from which it differs in its more compact habit and darker gold foliage that does not fade in winter. In cultivation 1958. H4 ♀ 1993

J. × m. 'Pfitzeriana' (Pfitzer juniper) One of the most popular and commonly planted of all conifers. It is eventually a medium-sized, wide-spreading shrub with stout,

ascending branches that are held out like arms and droop at the tips. The leaves are mainly green and scale-like but there are scattered sprays of juvenile leaves with glaucous upper surfaces, particularly in the centre of the bush. An excellent conifer either as a lawn specimen or when used to break up the regular outline of a border or bed. Ideal for covering unsightly structures. Its origin is uncertain. In cultivation 1896. H4 ♀ 1993

Juniperus × media 'Pfitzeriana Aurea'

J. × m. 'Pfitzeriana Aurea' The terminal shoots and foliage of this medium-sized shrub are suffused with golden yellow in summer and become yellowish green in winter. A sport of 'Pfitzeriana' which originated 1923 in the United States. H4

J. × m. 'Pfitzeriana Compacta' A sport of 'Pfitzeriana' but more dense and compact and with a preponderance of juvenile awl-shaped leaves. In cultivation 1930. H4 ♀ 1993

J. × m. 'Pfitzeriana Glauca' A little denser than 'Pfitzeriana', with mainly awl-shaped, grey-glaucous leaves. In cultivation 1940 in the United States. H4

J. × m. 'Plumosa Aurea' A most attractive medium-sized shrub with ascending branches that arch at their tips and are densely clothed with feathery sprays of yellow, scale-like leaves that ripen to bronze-gold in winter. In cultivation 1885. H4 ♀ 1993

J. × m. 'Sulphur Spray' A sport of 'Hetzii', which it resembles in habit but for

Juniperus × media 'Sulphur Spray'

being slower growing. It eventually reaches about 2m (6ft) high and wide. The foliage is a striking pale sulphur-yellow. In cultivation 1962. H4 ♀ 1993

J. procumbens (Creeping juniper) A dwarf, procumbent species with long, stiff branches, forming carpets up to 30cm (1ft) high in the centre and several metres (yards) across. The tightly packed branches are crowded with awl-shaped, glaucous-green, sharply pointed leaves. It is an excellent ground cover for an open, sunny position on a well-drained soil. A native of Japan. Introduced 1843. H4

Juniperus procumbens 'Nana'

J. p. 'Nana' A more compact plant with shorter branches. Japan. Introduced c1900. H4 ♀ 1993

J. recurva (Drooping juniper) A large shrub or small tree, broadly conical, with stringy, shaggy bark and drooping branch-

lets. The leaves are awl-shaped, held in threes; they are green or greyish green, usually with white bands above. It is an extremely variable species. The following forms are recommended. Himalaya. Introduced 1825.
H4

J. r. 'Castlewellan' A small, loose, open tree with lax branches like fishing rods. The branchlets droop in long, slender sprays of soft, thread-like foliage.
H4

J. r. var. coxii An elegant small tree with gracefully drooping branchlets that are longer and more pendulous than the typical form. The leaves are also more loosely arranged and are sage-green. Upper Burma. Introduced 1920 by E H M Cox and Reginald Farrer.
H4

J. r. 'Embley Park' See *J. squamata* 'Embley Park'.

J. sabina An extremely variable juniper which, in its typical form, is a low, spreading shrub. It has a pungent, disagreeable, catty odour. Harmful if eaten, except exclusively juvenile forms. Mountains of S and C Europe to the Caucasus.
H4

Juniperus sabina 'Tam no Blight'

J. s. 'Tam no Blight' A form of *J. sabina* var. *tamariscifolia*. The name actually means 'Tamariscifolia that does not suffer from blight', referring to the disease that often affects the commonly grown form of that plant. It is little different in other respects, and forms a wide-spreading, flat-topped bush with horizontal branches and bright

green leaves that are mainly awl-shaped. An extremely popular juniper of architectural value. In cultivation 1970.
H4

J. scopulorum (Rocky Mountain juniper) A small, conical, cypress-like tree, often with several main stems. The bark is red-brown and shredding. It is grown in gardens in the many forms to which the species has given rise. The following are recommended. Rocky Mountains from British Columbia to Arizona, Texas and New Mexico. Introduced 1839.
H4

J. s. 'Blue Heaven' A small conical tree with striking blue foliage.
H4 ♔ 1993

J. s. 'Moonglow' A small, compact, conical tree with blue-grey foliage.
H4

J. s. 'Skyrocket', syn. *J. virginiana* 'Skyrocket' A spectacular, extremely narrowly columnar tree. Hillier Arboretum's tallest

Juniperus scopulorum 'Springbank'

specimen was 5m (15ft) high and 30cm (1ft) in diameter in 1970, and 7.5m (23ft) tall after 26 years. The foliage is blue-grey. It is one of the narrowest of all conifers and an excellent plant for breaking up low or horizontal planting schemes. It is prone to attack by the juniper webber moth, whose caterpillars feed on the leaves beneath a tent of webbing. The browning and dying of the leaves is at its worst in early summer, but a contact insecticide, applied weekly in late summer and early autumn, is usually effective. In cultivation 1949.
H4

J. s. 'Springbank' A small, erect tree of columnar habit with ascending and spreading branches, slender branchlets and silvery grey-green foliage.
H4

J. squamata An extremely variable species from prostrate shrubs to small trees. All forms have nodding tips to the shoots and short, awl-shaped, channelled leaves that are white or pale green above. In gardens it is always seen as one of its forms or cultivars. The following are recommended. Wide distribution throughout Asia. Introduced 1824.
H4

Juniperus squamata 'Blue Carpet'

J. s. 'Blue Carpet' A low-growing form with spreading branches, a depressed centre and blue-grey foliage.
H4 ♔ 1993

J. s. 'Blue Spider' A dwarf shrub, similar to 'Blue Carpet' but highest in the centre and with silvery blue foliage. In cultivation 1980.
H4

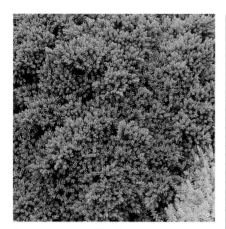
Juniperus squamata 'Blue Star'

J. s. 'Blue Star' A low-growing, dense, dwarf shrub that makes a compact, dwarf bun with comparatively large, silvery blue, awl-shaped leaves.
H4 ♛ 1993

Juniperus squamata 'Chinese Silver'

J. s. 'Chinese Silver' A beautiful, medium-sized to large, multi-stemmed, dense but somewhat shapeless shrub with down-turning terminal shoots. The awl-shaped leaves are of an eye-catching intense, silvery blue-green.
H4

J. s. 'Embley Park', syn. *J. recurva* 'Embley Park' A distinctive, small, spreading shrub with reddish brown, ascending branches clothed with rich grass-green, awl-shaped leaves.
H4

J. s. 'Loderi' A slow-growing, dense, usually conical shrub, eventually reaching 3m (9ft). The branchlets nod at their tips and are densely set with short, awl-shaped

Juniperus squamata 'Loderi'

leaves marked with two white bands above. Raised 1925 by Sir Edmund Loder at Leonardslee, Sussex.
H4

J. s. 'Meyeri' A popular and easily recognized juniper of semi-erect habit, with stout, ascending, angular branches and densely packed, glaucous blue, awl-shaped leaves. Although regarded as a small to medium-sized shrub it will eventually become large. The characteristic tendency of the species to retain its old, brown leaves is pronounced in this form and can give a rather untidy appearance. It is prone to attack by juniper webber moth (see under *J. scopulorum* 'Skyrocket'). China. Introduced 1914 by Frank N. Meyer.
H4

J. virginiana (Pencil cedar) One of the hardiest conifers, forming a medium-sized tree but always grown as one of its cultivars.
H4

J. v. 'Burkii' An excellent, dense, columnar, medium-sized form with ascending branches and both scale-like and awl-shaped, steel-blue leaves that are bronze-purple in winter. In cultivation 1932.
H4

J. v. 'Canaertii' A small, conical, fairly dense tree with bright green foliage. It is very attractive when dotted with small, cobalt-blue to purple-bloomed, violet fruits.
H4

J. v. 'Glauca' A dense, columnar form with spreading branches clothed with silvery grey, mainly scale-like leaves. A most attractive small to medium-sized tree.
H4

Juniperus virginiana 'Burkii'

J. v. 'Skyrocket' See *J. scopulorum* 'Skyrocket'.

K

Kadsura *Schisandraceae*

A genus of about 20 species of evergreen twining plants from east and South-East Asia.

K. japonica A slender climber up to 3.5m (11ft) with dark green leaves that often turn an attractive red in autumn. The fragrant flowers are solitary, cream, 2cm (³/₄in) across, and appear in summer and early autumn. The berries are scarlet and borne in clusters. It needs a warm, sheltered wall and is best in mild places. Japan, China, Taiwan. Introduced 1860.
H3

K. j. 'Variegata' The leaves of this small

to medium-sized form have a broad margin of creamy yellow.
H3

Kalmia *Ericaceae*

A genus of seven species of mainly evergreen shrubs, natives of North America but for one from Cuba. They are charming shrubs that flower in spring and early summer and luxuriate under conditions similar to those required by Rhododendron. *The flowers are saucer-shaped. For maximum flowering, plant in full sun or dappled shade and moist, acid soil. Pruning is generally unnecessary, but old specimens of* K. angustifolia *can be cut hard back and will regenerate if fed. Harmful if eaten.*

K. angustifolia 'Rubra' (Sheep laurel) An evergreen shrub up to 1m (3ft) high, slowly spreading and forming thickets. The deep green leaves are variable in shape, and the flowers, borne in early summer, are deep rosy red. This species and its forms are highly poisonous. E North America. Introduced 1736.
H4 ♛ 1993

Kalmia latifolia

K. latifolia (Calico bush, mountain laurel) A magnificent, rhododendron-like, evergreen shrub of medium size. Apart from roses and rhododendrons, it is possibly the best early-summer shrub for acid soils. The glossy leaves are 5–13cm (2–5in) long and make a pleasing setting for the clusters of bright pink, saucer-shaped flowers that are richer sugar-pink when in bud. A large number of selections are being given culti-

var names in the United States but their performance in Britain is uncertain. E North America. Introduced 1734.
H4 ♛ 1993

Kalmia latifolia 'Ostbo Red'

K. l. 'Ostbo Red' A large shrub with flowers bright red in bud, opening to pale pink. It was the first red-budded kalmia. Selected in the 1940s in the United States.
H4 ♛ 1993

K. polifolia (Eastern bog laurel) A dwarf, wiry evergreen shrub up to about 0.6m (2ft) high with narrow leaves that are dark shining green above and glaucous beneath, borne in pairs or threes. The bright rose-purple flowers are in large, terminal clusters in mid-spring. In the wild it is found in swamps and bogs. E North America. Introduced 1767.
H4

Kalmiopsis *Ericaceae*

A genus of one evergreen spring-flowering species which is related to Rhodothamnus *and most frequently grown for its flowers.*

K. leachiana A choice, rare, beautiful, dwarf shrub with pink, kalmia-like flowers which are borne in terminal leafy clusters from early to late spring. It is best grown in a moist, peaty soil in the rock garden or an alpine house or frame. It can be grown in full sun if the soil is moist enough; if not, it should be given semi-shade. From rocky ledges in the mountains of Oregon. Introduced 1931.
H4 ♛ 1993

Kalmiopsis leachiana

Kalopanax *Araliaceae*

A genus of one species of deciduous tree.

Kalopanax pictus

K. pictus A small to medium-sized tree in cultivation, superficially like an *Acer*. The branches and sucker growths have scattered, stout prickles, and the leaves, over 30cm (1ft) across in young plants, have 5–7 lobes. The small clusters of white flowers are borne in large, flattish heads, 30–60cm (1–2ft) across in autumn. It prefers a deep, moisture-retentive soil in sun or part shade. Japan, E Russia, Korea, China. Introduced 1865.
H4

Kerria *Roseaceae*

A genus of one deciduous species, related to Rhodotypos.

K. japonica A graceful suckering shrub reaching 1.8m (6ft) high against a wall. In

Kerria japonica

mid- to late spring, or earlier in a mild season, its branches are wreathed with rich yellow flowers. Its green stems are effective in winter. It is best in a moist well-drained soil with enough shade to prevent the flowers bleaching. Pruning is seldom necessary. China. Introduced 1834.
H4

Kerria japonica 'Golden Guinea'

Kerria japonica 'Pleniflora'

K. j. 'Flore Pleno' See *K. j.* 'Pleniflora'.
K. j. 'Golden Guinea' A medium-sized shrub with very large, single yellow flowers. H4 ♓ 1993
K. j. 'Picta' See *K. j.* 'Variegata'.
K. j. 'Pleniflora', syn. *K. j.* 'Flore Pleno' The well-known double yellow-flowered form, taller and more vigorous and erect than the single-flowered form. Green shoots and bright green leaves. China. Introduced 1804 by William Kerr.
H4 ♓ 1993
K. j. 'Variegata', syn. *K. j.* 'Picta' A pleasing and elegant form of lower, spreading habit, with leaves variegated in creamy white. It grows to about 1.5m (5ft). In cultivation 1844.
H4

Koelreuteria *Sapindaceae*

A genus of three species of deciduous trees, natives of China and Taiwan, of which only the one is widely cultivated. It is easily grown on all soils and flowers and fruits best in hot summers. It is tolerant of drought, poor conditions and wind, but not salty winds. Pruning is best avoided.

Koelreuteria paniculata

K. paniculata (Golden rain tree, pride of India) This is the best-known species and is an attractive, broad-headed tree 9–12m (28–40ft) high, with pinnate leaves. Each leaf has 9–15 leaflets that are broadest below the middle. Large panicles of small yellow flowers, mid- to late summer, are followed by bladder-like fruits. Leaves turn yellow in autumn. China. Introduced 1763.
H4 ♓ 1993

K. p. 'Fastigiata' A rare and remarkable, slow-growing form of narrowly columnar habit, eventually becoming 8m (25ft) high by 1m (3ft) wide.
H4

Kolkwitzia *Caprifoliaceae*

A genus of a single deciduous species, related to Abelia. Grows on all kinds of soils.

Kolkwitzia amabilis

K. amabilis (Beauty bush) Medium-sized dense, twiggy shrub. In late spring and early summer its drooping branches are draped with bell-shaped flowers that are soft pink with a yellow throat. China. Introduced 1901 by Ernest Wilson.
H4
K. a. 'Pink Cloud' A beautiful medium-sized shrub. Flowers deeper pink than the type. Selected and raised 1946 at the Royal Horticultural Society's garden, Wisley.
H4 ♓ 1993

Kolkwitzia amabilis 'Pink Cloud'

L

+ Laburnocytisus *Leguminosae*

A graft hybrid (chimaera) between Cytisus *and* Laburnum, *of which only the following form is known. Usually grown for its flowers.*

+ *L. adamii* A remarkable small deciduous tree with laburnum forming the core and broom the outer envelope. It is better described as odd rather than beautiful. Some branches bear the yellow flowers of the laburnum, while other branches have the dense, congested clusters of the purple-flowered broom (*Cytisus purpureus*). In addition, most branches produce intermediate flowers of a striking coppery pink. Cultivation is as for *Laburnum*. Originated 1825 in the nurseries of M. Adam near Paris.
H4

Laburnum *Leguminosae*

A genus of two species of small, ornamental deciduous trees that are easily grown in almost all kinds of soil. The yellow pea-flowers are produced in drooping racemes during late spring and early summer. If pruning is necessary (which it seldom is) it should be done in late summer. Spur-pruning of laburnums grown in arches is best carried out in early winter. **CAUTION:** *Toxic if eaten.*

Laburnum alpinum

L. alpinum (Scotch laburnum) A small, broad-headed tree with long, drooping clusters of fragrant yellow flowers in early

Laburnum × watereri 'Vossii'

summer. The leaves have three leaflets and are deep shining green above, paler and with a few hairs beneath. The seed pods are flattened and shining. C and S Europe. In cultivation 1596.
H4

L. a. 'Pendulum' A slow-growing form developing a low, dome-shaped head of stiffly weeping branches.
H4

L. × watereri 'Vossii' A lovely, very free-flowering small tree with glossy leaves and long racemes of yellow flowers in early summer, though it does not produce a heavy seed crop.
H4 🏆 1993

Lapageria *Philesiaceae*

A genus of one evergreen climbing species.

L. rosea (Chilean bellflower) One of the most beautiful of all climbers and the national flower of Chile, this plant has twin-

Lapageria rosea

ing stems that reach 3–5m (10–15ft) on a suitable wall. The leaves are leathery and the rose-crimson, fleshy, bell-shaped flowers, 7.5cm (3in) long by 5cm (2in) wide, are single or in pendulous clusters during most of the summer and autumn. It needs a lime-free, cool, moist soil in full or part shade. It is best on a sheltered wall and is an excellent conservatory plant but detests long exposure to strong sunlight. Chile, Argentina. Introduced 1847.

H2 🏆 1993

L. r. var. albiflora A small to medium-sized climber with white flowers.

H2

L. r. 'Flesh Pink' A small to medium-sized form with flesh-pink flowers.

H2 🏆 1993

L. r. 'Nash Court' A small to medium-sized climber with soft pink flowers marbled with deeper pink.

H2 🏆 1993

Larix *Pinaceae*
Larch

A small genus of generally fast-growing, deciduous coniferous trees. The branches are set in irregular whorls that end in long, slender, flexible branchlets which, on older trees, tend to droop or hang gracefully. On the old wood, the leaves are in dense rosettes of short spurs, while on the younger wood they are spirally arranged. They are generally bright green or occasionally blue-green in spring and summer and turn butter-yellow or old gold in autumn. The cones remain intact for a long time after shedding their seed and are often cut as indoor decoration. Larches are adaptable to most soils except those on wet sites and shallow soils over chalk. There is no more refreshing spring feature than their awakening buds, nor a more mellow shade than their autumn colour.

Larix decidua

L. decidua (European larch) A large tree with a slender, conical crown when young. The branches and branchlets droop in old specimens. The rosette leaves are up to

3.5cm (1¹/₂in) long and light green, and the egg-shaped red-brown cones are of much the same length. European Alps, Carpathians. Introduced 1620.

H4 🏆 1993

L. × eurolepis (*L. decidua × L. kaempferi*) (Dunkeld larch, hybrid larch) A vigorous large tree, more important commercially than horticulturally, as it produces high-grade timber and is disease resistant. Originated 1904 in Perthshire.

H4

Larix kaempferi

L. kaempferi (Japanese larch) A vigorous larch making a large tree with reddish shoots and sea-green leaves up to 3.5cm (1¹/₂in) long and broader than those of *L. decidua*. Japan. Introduced 1861.

H4 🏆 1993

L. k. 'Diana' A gracefully branched upright tree with contorted branchlets and fresh green foliage. Found 1974 in Germany.

H4

Larix kaempferi 'Pendula'

L. k. 'Pendula' A beautiful, tall, elegant tree with long, weeping branchlets. In cultivation 1896.

H4

Larix kaempferi 'Wolterdingen'

L. k. 'Wolterdingen' A dense, dwarf, bun-shaped bush with blue-grey foliage. Found 1970 in Germany.

H4

Laurelia *Atherospermataceae*

A genus of three species of evergreen trees from Chile, Argentina and New Zealand.

Laurelia sempervirens

L. sempervirens (Chilean laurel) A large shrub or small to medium-sized, lime-tolerant tree. The leathery leaves are bright matt green and have an aroma very similar to that of *Laurus nobilis*. It is remarkably hardy as long as it has close shelter. Chile. Introduced before 1868.

H3

Laurus *Lauraceae*
Laurel

There are only two species of true laurels. They are evergreen shrubs or small trees with small, yellowish green flowers clustered on the branches in mid-spring or earlier in a mild season. On female trees they are followed by shining black fruits.

Laurus nobilis

L. nobilis (Bay laurel, sweet bay) The tree that produces the bay leaves used in cookery. Not only is the foliage highly aromatic, but the plant is greatly tolerant of being clipped and makes fine-shaped small to medium-sized specimen trees, topiary and hedges. Salt resistant and valuable as a seaside hedge in mild places. A good, moisture-retentive, fertile soil is the best recipe, and clipping should be done in summer. Susceptible to frost but, given shelter, is much less so than commonly supposed. Mediterranean region. In cultivation 1562. H4 ♛ 1993

Laurus nobilis 'Aurea'

L. n. 'Angustifolia' A remarkably hardy form with long, narrow, pale green, wavy-edged leaves with a leathery texture. H4

L. n. 'Aurea' A large shrub or small tree with golden yellow leaves that are particularly attractive in winter and spring. H4 ♛ 1993

Lavandula *Labiatae*
Lavender

A genus of about 20 species of aromatic evergreen shrubs and herbaceous perennials, natives of the Mediterranean region. Lavender is perhaps the most highly prized of all aromatic shrubs and is a favourite for dwarf hedges, associating well with stonework or formal rose beds and making an attractive component of grey or blue borders. It succeeds in all types of well-drained soil and is best grown in full sun. It is excellent in coastal regions. It is dried to fill sachets and cushions. The heights given include the flower spike.

Lavandula angustifolia

L. angustifolia (Old English lavender) The garden forms are usually listed under the name of this species but they are in fact hybrids between *L. angustifolia* and *L. latifolia* and include back-crosses. Both species come from the Mediterranean region and have been cultivated since the middle of the sixteenth century. Flowers are borne on dense spikes on long, slender stems. Not generally long-lived so need to be replaced after about a decade, as they become over-woody and unattractive after that time, even if trimmed back every other year or so. H4

L. a. 'Alba' A robust form with long, narrow, grey-green leaves and erect stems from 90cm–1.2m (3–4ft) high. The white flowers open in the latter half of summer. H4

L. a. 'Folgate' A compact lavender with narrow, grey-green leaves and stems 60–80cm (24–32in) high. The lavender-blue flowers open towards the end of the first half of summer. In cultivation 1933. H4

Lavandula angustifolia 'Grappenhall'

L. a. 'Grappenhall' A robust form with comparatively broad, grey-green leaves and strong stems 90cm–1.2m (3–4ft) high. The flowers are lavender-blue, opening in the latter half of summer. H4

Lavandula angustifolia 'Hidcote'

L. a. 'Hidcote' A compact lavender with narrow, grey-green leaves and stems 60–80cm (24–32in) high. The violet flowers are in dense spikes and open towards the

end of the first half of summer. It is one of the best and most popular lavenders, but has to be grown from cuttings from the true plant: seed from named clones such as this does not come true.
H4 ☙ 1993

L. a. 'Hidcote Pink' A compact shrub, growing to 60cm (2ft). It is similar to 'Hidcote' but has pale pink flowers. In cultivation 1962.
H4

L. a. 'Munstead' A compact form with narrow, grey-green leaves and stems 60–75cm (24–30in) high. The dense spikes of tiny, tubular flowers are bluer than most and open towards the end of the first half of summer. In cultivation 1916.
H4

Lavandula angustifolia 'Nana Alba'

L. a. 'Nana Alba' A dwarf, compact form with comparatively broad, grey-green leaves and stems up to 30cm (1ft). The flowers are white and open towards the end of the first half of summer.
H4

L. a. 'Rosea' A compact lavender with narrow leaves, more green than grey, and stems 60–75cm (24–30in) high. The lavender-pink flowers open in midsummer. It is used in making eau-de-cologne. In cultivation 1949.
H4

L. a. 'Twickel Purple' A compact form with comparatively broad grey leaves and stems 60–75cm (24–30in) high. The flowers are lavender-blue and open towards the end of the first half of summer.
H4 ☙ 1993

Lavandula angustifolia 'Rosea'

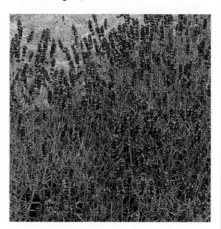

Lavandula angustifolia 'Vera'

L. a. 'Vera' (Dutch lavender) A robust form with comparatively broad grey leaves and stems 1–1.2m (3–4ft) high. The lavender-blue flowers open in the latter half of summer.
H4 ☙ 1993

L. lanata A small and attractive white-woolly shrub which produces long-stalked

Lavandula stoechas

spikes of fragrant, bright violet flowers from midsummer to early autumn. Spain.
H3

L. stoechas (French lavender) A dwarf, intensely aromatic shrublet with narrow, greyish leaves. The dark purple flowers are borne in dense, congested, terminal heads during summer and are topped by prominent purple bracts. It requires a warm, dry, sunny position. Mediterranean region. In cultivation since the mid-sixteenth century.
H3 ☙ 1993

L. s. var. leucantha A dwarf shrub with white flowers and bracts.
H3

Lavandula stoechas subsp. pedunculata

L. s. subsp. pedunculata The flower spikes of this grey-leaved dwarf form are shorter and borne on long stalks. The ear-like purple bracts, 5cm (2in) long, give rise to the common name 'papillon', French for butterfly. Spain, Portugal.
H3 ☙ 1993

Lavatera Malvaceae

A genus of some 25 species of herbaceous plants and deciduous shrubs, native to Europe, western Asia, Australia and California. The shrubby mallows have typical mallow flowers and palmate leaves. They are excellent for gardens near the sea and do well in all types of soil, preferably in full sun.

L. maritima An elegant species, growing to 1.5–2m (5–6ft) against a sunny wall. The stems and palmate leaves are greyish and downy; the large, saucer-shaped flowers, pale lilac with purple veins and eye, are produced continuously from midsummer to late autumn. It needs a warm, sheltered position with every possible protection from cold winds. N Africa.

H2–3 ♔ 1993

L. olbia 'Rosea' See *L. thuringiaca* 'Rosea'.

L. thuringiaca (*olbia* HORT.) An elegant species growing to 1.5–1.8m (5–6ft) high. Both stems and leaves are greyish and downy. Large saucer-shaped flowers are produced from summer to late autumn. The following forms are recommended. C and S Europe to W Himalayas.

H3–4

Lavatera thuringiaca 'Barnsley'

L. t. 'Barnsley' A splendid medium-sized shrub that originated as a sport of *L. t.* 'Rosea'. The flowers are very pale pink, almost white, with a red eye. It is now one of the most popular of all garden shrubs. Any reversions must be removed.

H3–4 ♔ 1993

L. t. 'Blushing Bride' A form with all the

Lavatera thuringiaca 'Burgundy Wine'

good qualities of 'Barnsley' and without its tendency to revert. The very pale pink to white flowers with a red centre are borne over a long period during summer.

H3–4

L. t. 'Burgundy Wine' A medium-sized shrub with deep purplish pink flowers.

H3–4

L. t. 'Candy Floss' A medium-sized shrub with very pale pink flowers.

H3–4

Lavatera thuringiaca 'Ice Cool'

L. t. 'Ice Cool' A small shrub, of rather weaker constitution than others. It bears white flowers with a slight green cast.

H3–4

L. t. 'Pink Frills' A beautiful form with small semi-double pink flowers on slender spikes. It is compact and upright in habit with an eventual size of approximately 1.2 x 1.2m (4 x 4ft).

H3–4

L. t. 'Kew Rose' A medium-sized shrub,

Lavatera thuringiaca 'Rosea'

more vigorous than 'Rosea', with darker, purplish stems and large, bright pink flowers. Previously grown as *Lavatera olbia*.

H3–4

L. t. 'Rosea', syn. *L. olbia* 'Rosea' A medium-sized shrub with deep pink flowers.

H3–4 ♔ 1993

Ledum *Ericaceae*

A genus of about four species of low-growing, evergreen shrubs from swampy moors in northern latitudes. All have neat foliage, usually covered below with a white or rust-coloured woolly felt, and terminal clusters of white flowers. They need a moist, lime-free soil.

Ledum groenlandicum

L. groenlandicum (Labrador tea) A dwarf, upright shrub occasionally as much as 1m (3ft) high. The white flowers are produced from mid-spring to early summer. Best known species of the genus. North America, Greenland. Introduced 1763.

H4

L. g. 'Compactum' A compact form, developing into a neat shrub 30–45cm (12–18in) high, with broader leaves in shorter branches and smaller flower clusters than the typical form.

H4

Leiophyllum *Ericaceae*

A genus of only one evergreen species.

L. buxifolium (Sand myrtle) A neat, compact, rounded, dwarf shrub with box-like leaves that are smooth on both surfaces and

Leiophyllum buxifolium

clusters of white flowers, pink in the bud, in late spring and early summer. It is an attractive species needing lime-free, moist soil. E North America. Introduced 1736 by Peter Collinson.

H4 ♛ 1993

Leonotis *Labiatae*

There are about 15 species of Leonotis, *including annuals, perennials and deciduous shrubs, native to tropical and southern Africa. The following is an easily grown shrub in all types of soil but only barely suitable for outdoor cultivation on a sunny wall in the very mildest places. It is, however, excellent for a conservatory.*

Leonotis leonurus

L. leonurus (Lion's ear) A small, square-stemmed shrub with downy, lance-shaped leaves and bright orange-scarlet, two-lipped flowers 5cm (2in) long in autumn. South Africa. Introduced 1712.

H1–2

Leptospermum *Myrtaceae*

A genus of some 30 species of attractive, small-leaved, evergreen shrubs or small trees, mainly natives of Australia, with a few found in New Zealand, New Caledonia and Malaysia. They are related to the myrtles. In warm maritime and mild localities many form large shrubs up to 4m (12ft) high or more, but elsewhere most need the protection of a wall. They flower in late spring and early summer and do best in full sun in well-drained acid or neutral soils. Bushiness is maintained if you pinch out the shoot tips after flowering.

L. humifusum An extremely hardy prostrate shrub, forming an extensive carpet of reddish stems and small, blunt, leathery leaves that turn bronze-purple in very cold weather. Small white flowers stud the branches of mature specimens in early summer. Tasmania. Introduced 1930 by Harold Comber.

H3 ♛ 1993

Leptospermum lanigerum

L. lanigerum A beautiful, medium-sized shrub with long, silvery leaves, often bronzed towards autumn. It bears its white flowers in early summer. Australia, Tasmania. Introduced 1774.

H3 ♛ 1993

L. l. 'Silver Sheen' A medium-sized shrub selected from plants previously grown as *L. cunninghamii*, with attractive, silvery grey leaves and reddish stems. It flowers in midsummer, several weeks later than the typical *L. lanigerum*. It is exceptionally hardy.

H3

Leptospermum scoparium

Leptospermum scoparium 'Keatleyi'

L. scoparium (Manuka, ti-tree) A variable, white-flowered species ranging from a medium-sized to large shrub. It has given rise to many forms. Australia, Tasmania, New Zealand. Introduced 1772.

H3

L. s. 'Keatleyi' An outstanding medium-sized shrub with large, waxy-petalled, soft pink flowers and silky, crimson young foliage. New Zealand. Introduced before 1926 by Captain Keatley.

H3 ♛ 1993

L. s. 'Kiwi' A dwarf, dense form with freely produced, deep pink flowers and bronze foliage. A seedling of 'Nanum'. Raised in New Zealand.

H3 ♛ 1993

L. s. 'Nanum' A charming dwarf form reaching about 30cm (1ft), with rose-pink flowers produced with great freedom. An excellent alpine-house shrub. Raised before 1940 in New Zealand.

H3

L. s. 'Nicholsii' The flowers of this medium-sized shrub are carmine-red and the foliage is dark, purplish bronze. In cultivation 1904.
H3 ♔ 1993

L. s. 'Red Damask' A small shrub with very double, deep red, long-lasting flowers like tiny roses all along the shoots. Raised 1944 in California.
H3 ♔ 1993

Lespedeza *Leguminoseae*
Bush clover

A genus of about 40 species of perennials and deciduous shrubs from North America, eastern Asia and Australia. The cultivated species are useful, late-flowering shrubs with profusely borne racemes of small pea-flowers along the shoots, which are bowed by their weight. The leaves of all of them have three leaflets. They are easily grown and thrive on all types of soil.

L. bicolor A medium-sized, semi-erect shrub with bright rose-purple flowers borne in racemes in late summer. Korea, Manchuria, China, Japan. Introduced 1856 by Maximowicz.
H4

L. kiusiana A very attractive small shrub with soft green, clover-like leaves and light rose-purple flowers in large, compound, leafy panicles in late summer. The identity and origin of this plant are uncertain.
H4

L. thunbergii One of the best autumn-flowering shrubs, with arching stems 1.2–1.5m (4–5ft) long that are bowed to the ground in early autumn by the weight of the huge terminal panicles of rose-purple pea-flowers. Japan, China. Introduced 1837.
H4 ♔ 1993

Leucothoë *Ericaceae*

A genus of a little over 40 species of evergreen and deciduous shade-bearing shrubs native to North America and Japan. They require lime-free, peaty or otherwise moisture-retentive organic soils. Old or weak growth or shoots that are too vigorous can be pruned after flowering.

L. davisiae A pretty evergreen shrub, usu-

Leucothoë fontanesiana 'Scarletta'

Leucothoë davisiae

ally less than 1m (3ft) high, with dark green, glossy leaves and erect clusters of pure white flowers in early summer. California. Introduced 1853 by William Lobb.
H4

L. fontanesiana A small to medium-sized elegant deciduous shrub, forming excellent ground cover for acid soils and growing to as much as 2m (6ft) high. The gracefully arching stems carry lance-shaped leathery green leaves which in autumn and winter become flushed with beetroot red or bronze-purple, especially in exposed positions. The short, drooping clusters of pitcher-shaped white flowers appear all along the stems in late spring. For many years this plant has been grown as *L. catesbaei*, a name that properly belongs to a dif-

Leucothoë fontanesiana 'Rainbow'

ferent species. SE United States. Introduced 1793.
H4 ♛ 1993

***L. f.* 'Rainbow'** The leaves of this small to medium-sized shrub are variegated with cream, yellow and pink. It arose as a seedling on one of the Hillier Nurseries.
H4

***L. f.* 'Rollisonii'** A selection with narrower leaves, making the flower clusters appear even more prominent.
H4 ♛ 1993

***L. f.* 'Scarletta'** A form with glossy red young foliage, turning dark green, then red-purple in autumn and winter.
H4

Leycesteria *Caprifoliaceae*

A genus of six species of hollow-stemmed deciduous shrubs, native to the Himalaya and China.

Leycesteria formosa

L. formosa A medium-sized, erect shrub with stout, hollow, sea-green shoots covered at first with a bluish bloom. The white flowers are among claret-coloured bracts carried in dense, terminal, drooping clusters from early summer to early autumn. They are followed by large, shining, reddish purple berries that are attractive to pheasants. It is suitable for any type of soil, including poor ones, and tolerates lime, coastal planting and atmospheric pollution. If it is cut to the ground in spring the resulting shoots will be bright, fresh green, but then the shrub should be fed or given a rich mulch.
H4

Ligustrum *Oleaceae*
Privet

A genus of about 50 species of evergreen and deciduous shrubs native to the Himalaya, east and South-East Asia and Australia, with one species in Europe and North Africa. They are mostly fast-growing and tolerant of almost any soil as well as managing in sun or shade. Many produce attractive, often fragrant, white flowers, and the evergreens are very commonly used for hedging. Specimens grown particularly for thier flowers should be fed if their soil is on the poor side. Hedges should be clipped 2–3 times a year and old, untidy hedges can be cut hard back, provided that they are fed and watered. Harmful if eaten.

L. chenaultii A remarkable, semi-evergreen, large shrub or small tree worthy of a place in every large garden. The conspicuously beautiful slender leaves are up to 15cm (6in) long and 6cm (2½in) across, and the attractive white flowers are in large, lilac-like trusses in late summer. SW China. Introduced 1908 by Ducloux.
H4

L. japonicum (Japanese privet) A compact, medium-sized, dense, evergreen shrub with shining, olive-green, camellia-like foliage and large panicles of attractive white flowers in late summer. An excellent plant for use as screening or hedging. N China, Korea, Taiwan, Japan. Introduced 1845 by Siebold.
H4

Ligustrum japonicum 'Rotundifolium'

***L. j.* 'Rotundifolium'** A very slow-growing, rigid, compact small form with round,

leathery, black-green leaves. Japan. Introduced 1860 by Robert Fortune.
H4

Ligustrum lucidum

L. lucidum A large evergreen shrub or small to medium-sized tree with large, glossy green, long-pointed leaves and handsome panicles of white flowers in autumn. It occasionally makes a beautiful, symmetrical tree 12m (40ft) or more high with an attractively fluted trunk. China. Introduced 1794.
H4 ♛ 1993

Ligustrum lucidum 'Excelsum Superbum'

***L. l.* 'Excelsum Superbum'** A most strikingly variegated large shrub or small to medium-sized tree with bright green leaves marked with pale green and edged with yellow or greenish yellow.
H4 ♛ 1993

***L. l.* 'Latifolium'** An effective large shrub or small to medium-sized tree with large, camellia-like leaves.
H4

Ligustrum lucidum 'Tricolor'

L. l. 'Tricolor' The leaves of this large shrub or small to medium-sized tree are rather narrow, deep green and prominently marked with grey-green, edged with creamy yellow or nearly white, and tinged with pink when young. In cultivation 1895. H4

L. ovalifolium (Oval-leaf privet) This is the ubiquitous evergreen hedging privet, one of the most commonly cultivated shrubs. If left unpruned it will reach a large size, but the resultant flowers, borne in summer, have an unpleasant smell. It tolerates most soils and aspects and only loses its leaves where winters are cold. Japan. In cultivation 1885. H4

L. o. 'Argenteum' A medium-sized shrub of which the leaves have a creamy margin. H4

Ligustrum ovalifolium 'Aureum'

L. o. 'Aureum' (Golden privet) A brightly coloured medium-sized shrub with rich yel-

Ligustrum quihoui

low, green-centred leaves that are often completely yellow. In cultivation 1862. H4 ♔ 1993

L. quihoui An elegant medium-sized deciduous shrub, one of the best of the genus for producing attractive flowers, which in its case are white, held in trusses up to 50cm (20in) long, headily perfumed,

Ligustrum sinense

and borne in late summer and early autumn. China. Introduced 1862. H4 ♔ 1993

L. sinense This large shrub is perhaps the most free-flowering of the deciduous privets. It is a large, spreading shrub or small tree with downy stems, oval leaves, and white flowers produced in long, dense sprays in midsummer, followed by large numbers of rich black-purple fruits. Introduced 1852 by Robert Fortune. H4

L. s. 'Variegatum' A large, attractive shrub that will light the darkest corner with its softly grey-green, white-margined leaves and white flowers. H4

Ligustrum sinense 'Vicaryi'

L. s. 'Vicaryi' A medium-sized semi-evergreen shrub with leaves suffused with golden yellow, turning bronze-purple in winter. It is said to be a hybrid between *L ovalifolium* 'Aureum' and *L. vulgare*. In cultivation c1920. H4

L. vulgare (Common privet) Despite its vernacular name this is not the almost universal hedging plant but is so-called because it is a native of Britain, occurring chiefly in chalk areas. The leaves are lance-shaped and dark green, and the off-white, strongly scented, tubular summer flowers are followed by long clusters of particularly conspicuous, round black fruits in the autumn. It makes a medium-sized semi-evergreen shrub. Europe, North Africa, SW Asia. In cultivation 1884. H4

Lindera *Lauraceae*

Altogether there are about 80 species of evergreen and deciduous aromatic trees and shrubs in this genus, related to the sweet bay (Laurus nobilis). They are natives mainly of south and east Asia, with two species in North America. They require lime-free soil and semi-shade. Prune out dead wood in spring.

L. benzoin (Spice bush) A medium-sized to large deciduous shrub with large, ovate leaves that turn clear yellow in autumn. The small, greenish yellow, spring flowers are followed on female plants by red berries. SE United States. Introduced 1683. H4

Lindera obtusiloba

L. obtusiloba A magnificent, medium-sized to large deciduous shrub of erect or compact habit. The large, three-nerved, broad leaves are sometimes three-lobed at the tip and the foliage turns in autumn from its bright summer green to a glorious butter-yellow with rich pink tints. The flowers, borne in early spring, are the colour of newly made mustard. Japan, China, Korea. Introduced 1880.
H4 ♕ 1993

Linnaea *Caprifoliaceae*

A genus of one evergreen species, named in honour of Carolus Linnaeus (1707–78), botanist and begetter of the binomial system of plant names.

L. borealis (Twinflower) A charming shrublet with slender stems carpeting the ground and forming extensive colonies in the moist, acid soils it requires. The small, delicate, nodding, pinkish, bell-like flowers are carried in pairs on thread-like stems from early summer to near its end. Found throughout the northern hemisphere, including the E Highlands of Scotland, where it is rare.
H4

Linum *Linaceae*

A genus of about 200 species of annuals, perennials and small evergreen and deciduous shrubs with a wide distribution. They are attractive plants with uniquely silky flowers, and the following requires full sun and good drainage.

Linum arboreum

L. arboreum (Tree flax) A spreading evergreen shrub, 22–60cm (9–24in) high, suitable for a larger rock garden. It has narrow, bloomy leaves and golden yellow flowers in loose terminal clusters during summer. E Mediterranean region. In cultivation 1788.
H4 ♕ 1993

Liquidambar *Hamamelidaceae*

A genus of four species of deciduous trees with maple-like, alternate leaves that usually colour well in autumn, changing to a brilliant red well before most other leaf changes. They are not suitable for shallow, chalky soils. Liquidambars can be vulnerable to frost in their first three years, so protect them while they are young and never plant them in frost pockets.

L. formosana Monticola Group A per-

Liquidambar formosana Monticola group

fectly hardy form of a beautiful large tree, with remarkably large, normally three-lobed leaves that colour richly in autumn. China. Introduced 1908 by Ernest Wilson.
H4

L. orientalis A slow-growing deciduous large bush or small bushy tree. The small, hairless leaves are deeply five-lobed and attractively tinted in autumn. In warm, dry climates it reaches large tree size. Asia Minor. Introduced c1750.
H4

Liquidambar styraciflua

L. styraciflua A large deciduous tree, beautiful at all times but especially in autumn when, if planted in a deep, fertile, moisture-retentive but well-drained soil, the deeply lobed, shining green, maple-like leaves assume their gorgeous crimson colouring. In winter, the corky bark of the older twigs is often a feature. It is occasionally taken for a maple (*Acer*) but its alternate leaves soon identify it. Autumn colour is variable on seed-raised plants. E United States. Introduced in the 17th century. H4

_L. s._ 'Lane Roberts' A selected clone and one of the most reliable for its autumn colour, which is rich, black-crimson-red, like the embers of a coal fire. The bark of this large tree is comparatively smooth. H4 ♔ 1993

_L. s._ 'Moonbeam' The leaves of this tree are creamy yellow, eventually green, turning red, yellow and purple in autumn. H4

_L. s._ 'Silver King' A large tree with leaves attractively margined with cream and flushed rose in late summer and autumn. Previously listed as 'Variegata'. H4

_L. s._ 'Variegata' A large tree with leaves striped and mottled yellow. Previously listed as 'Aurea'. H4

_L. s._ 'Worplesdon' The leaves of this large tree are divided into long, narrow lobes which turn an attractive orange and yellow in the autumn. H4 ♔ 1993

Liriodendron _Magnoliaceae_
Tulip tree

There are two species in this genus, one in China and one in North America. They are large, fast-growing deciduous trees, succeeding in all types of fertile soil, and bearing large curiously shaped leaves with three lobes, the central one of which looks as if it has been cut in half with an inward curve of the knife. The foliage turns clear yellow in autumn.

L. tulipifera (Tulip tree) A beautiful large tree with its odd-looking leaves turning a rich butter-yellow colour in autumn. The

Liquidambar styraciflua 'Lane Roberts'

Liquidambar styraciflua 'Worplesdon'

Liquidambar styraciflua 'Silver King'

Liriodendron tulipifera

Liriodendron tulipifera 'Fastigiatum'

strange flowers, appearing in early and midsummer, are like very short-stemmed tulips, yellow-green and banded with orange at the base of the petals. They are not produced on young trees. E North America. In cultivation 1688.
H4 ♔ 1993

Liriodendron tulipifera 'Aureomarginatum'

L. t. 'Aureomarginatum' A striking large tree with leaves bordered with bright yellow, turning greenish yellow by late summer. In cultivation 1903.
H4 ♔ 1993

L. t. 'Fastigiatum' An erect, broadly columnar, medium-sized tree, magnificent for planting where height is required in a confined space.
H4 ♔ 1993

Lithodora *Boraginaceae*

A genus of seven species of dwarf evergreen shrubs, natives of Europe and south-west Asia. The

following are low-growing, blue-flowered shrubs, especially delightful in the rock garden but not exclusive to it. They are hardy, especially if they are given first-class drainage. L. diffusa *requires a lime-free soil.*

L. diffusa A prostrate shrub which forms large mats to 1m (3ft) wide or more, covered with lovely blue blooms in late spring and early summer.
H4
L. d. 'Grace Ward' A form with masses of larger deep blue flowers.
H4 ♔ 1993
L. d. 'Heavenly Blue' This form is the most common one in cultivation. The name is self-explanatory.
H4 ♔ 1993

Lithodora oleifolia

L. oleifolia A choice and rare semi-prostrate shrub for a sheltered rock garden or alpine house. It has rich sky-blue, bell-shaped flowers from early summer to early autumn. E. Pyrenees. Introduced 1900.
H4 ♔ 1993

Lomatia *Proteaceae*

A genus of about 12 species of striking Australian and South American evergreen trees and shrubs. They are attractive both in foliage and flower and deserve to be better known and more widely planted. They are hardy or nearly so in all but the coolest areas and succeed best in semi-shade. They should be given a peaty, acid soil, and are not suitable for planting over chalk or where the soil is heavily charged with lime. Old growth may be removed from the base to allow room for new shoots.

L. ferruginea A magnificent foliage plant, this species makes a large shrub or small tree with large, deep green, much divided, fern-like leaves and red-brown, velvety stems. The buff and scarlet flowers are borne in short clusters in midsummer. It is hardy only in mild places. Chile, Argentina. Introduced 1846 by William Lobb.
H2–3
L. myricoides A hardy, long-lived species, making a well-furnished, wide-spreading shrub 2–2.5m (6–8ft) high. The leaves are long, narrow and toothed towards the tips, and the attractive flowers are similar to those of a grevillea, white, highly fragrant and open in midsummer. It is an excellent evergreen for the flower arranger. SE Australia. Introduced 1816.
H4

Lomatia silaifolia

L. silaifolia A small, spreading shrub with ascending stems, finely divided deep green leaves and large panicles of cream flowers in midsummer each with four narrow twisted petals. The leaves are less finely divided than those of the very similar *L. tinctoria*. Both species have been successfully grown in Great Britain for many years. E Australia. Introduced 1792.
H3
L. tinctoria A small, suckering shrub forming a dense thicket. Leaves are pinnate or doubly pinnate, with long, narrow segments. Flowers, borne in long, spreading clusters at the ends of shoots in midsummer, are sulphur-yellow in bud, turning cream. Tasmania. Introduced 1822.
H3

LONICERA

Honeysuckle *Caprifoliaceae*

Lonicera japonica 'Halliana'

ALTOGETHER there are some 180 species of evergreen and deciduous shrubs and climbers in this genus but it is best known for the climbing honeysuckles, which are some of the loveliest and most popular of all twining plants. They are all worthy of a place in the garden, although none can surpass the fragrance of the common European hedgerow species, *L. periclymenum*.

Fragrance is the first quality that comes to mind when considering climbing honeysuckles, but in this they are deceptive. Although their scents are delicious, there are times when the plants seem to sulk and withhold them. On dull or wet days or when the temperature is unseasonably low you can sniff away at a mile of hedgerow and never detect a hint of perfume, and the same is true for honeysuckles in the garden. Nevertheless, they are by no means to be downgraded because of this and their scents are the more welcome during the greater number of days when they are freed to waft on the warm summer air.

Honeysuckles have a reputation for strangling their support plants with their twining stems but the evidence for this is scanty and it is often the case that the plant was going to die anyway. In fact they are at their best when allowed to scramble over bushes or into small trees. Any artificial support such as a pergola, arch or ornamental well-head will soon become a major floral feature and gardeners with fertile imaginations will find all sorts of other ways in which these beautiful plants can be used to their best advantage. Some can even be grown as small standards.

CARE AND CULTIVATION

Some honeysuckles have a tendency to flower best with their heads in full sun but most enjoy part or even full shade, and all prefer their roots to be in shade. Shadiness inhibits the aphid attacks that can disfigure plants grown in hot positions. Their soil should be enriched with organic matter and not allowed to become too dry in summer. An annual mulch of leafmould is ideal, but do not use manures as they cause the foliage to proliferate at the expense of flowers. As far as soil types go, honeysuckles are happy in almost all of them.

It is a good idea to shorten the stems of young plants in order to promote early branching and ultimately a generous framework for the maximum possible display. Once this is achieved, pruning is a matter of keeping the plants within their required bounds and thinning them out occasionally when there is an excessive amount of old wood and the framework is in danger of being lost. Pruning should be done immediately after flowering, with the exception of those honeysuckles that flower in late summer, which should be pruned in early spring.

A judicious selection of honeysuckles from those described below can provide flowers from late spring to mid-autumn, with a peak in early to midsummer.

CLIMBERS

L. × ***americana*** A magnificent, extremely free-flowering deciduous climber that reaches a height of 9m (20ft). The 5cm (2in) long, fragrant white flowers soon turn to pale and finally deep yellow, heavily tinged with pink-purple outside. They are in whorls at the ends of the shoots and provide one of the most spectacular floral displays of midsummer. In cultivation before 1730. H4 ♔ 1993

L. × ***brownii*** (Scarlet trumpet honeysuckle) A deciduous or semi-evergreen medium-sized climber. It is moderately vigorous and has attractive orange-scarlet flowers in whorls at the ends of the branches in late spring and again in late summer. The following forms are recommended. Garden origin before 1850. H4

L. × *b.* **'Dropmore Scarlet'** A taller-growing form, with clusters of bright scarlet, tubular flowers from midsummer to mid-autumn. This is the commonest form of the hybrid in cultivation but is very susceptible to aphid attack. *L. sempervirens*, which is similarly coloured but untroubled by aphids, is a better plant. H4

L. × *b.* **'Fuchsioides'** This variety is hardly distinguishable from the typical form. H4

L. ***caprifolium*** (Italian honeysuckle, perfoliate honeysuckle) A fairly vigorous deciduous climber up to 6m (18ft). The upper pairs of leaflets are fused so that the stem appears to perforate a single, round leaf (perfoliate). The flowers are 4–5cm (1.5–2in) long, fragrant, cream, and very occasionally tinged with pink on the outside. They are in whorls at the ends of the shoots in early and midsummer and are followed by orange-red berries. Europe, Asia Minor. Long in cultivation. H4 ♔ 1993

L. c. **'Pauciflora'** The flowers of this medium-sized variety are rose-flushed on the outside. H4

L. ***etrusca*** A large and very vigorous deciduous honeysuckle with fragrant flowers that open cream, often flushed with red,

Lonicera × americana

Lonicera × brownii 'Dropmore Scarlet'

Lonicera × brownii 'Fuchsioides'

Lonicera caprifolium

Lonicera etrusca

Lonicera henryi

Lonicera japonica 'Aureoreticulata'

Lonicera japonica 'Halliana'

and deepen to yellow. They are in whorls at the ends of the shoots in early to midsummer, though not on young plants. The uppermost leaves are perfoliate. It is a superb species but is at its best where the climate is not too wet. Mediterranean. Introduced 1750.
H4

L. e. 'Donald Waterer' The young shoots of this large climber are red instead of purplish, and the flowers are red outside and white inside, becoming orange-yellow. French Pyrenees. Found 1973 by Donald Waterer.
H4

L. e. 'Superba' A large, vigorous variety with red young shoots and red flowers, white inside, turning orange-yellow.
H4

L. giraldii An evergreen species forming a dense tangle of slender, hairy stems to 2m (6ft). The leaves, heart-shaped at the base, are densely velvety. The flowers are purplish red with yellow stamens, yellowish downy on the outside, and in terminal clusters in early to midsummer. The berries are purplish black.
H4

L. × heckrottii A large, shrubby deciduous plant with some climbing branches. The fragrant flowers are yellow heavily flushed with purple, and are abundantly borne at the ends of the shoots from midsummer to late summer or early autumn. The name 'American Beauty' has been proposed for it. The following is recommended.
H4

L. × h. 'Gold Flame' Regarded by some as the only clone of the cross and by others as a separate one. The latter view is based on several differences, the more important ones from the gardener's point of view being that it is more of a climber and has brighter flowers. The typical form.
H4

L. henryi A vigorous, more or less evergreen medium-sized species with yellow flowers stained with red, borne in terminal clusters in early to midsummer. They are followed by black berries. W China. Introduced 1908 by Ernest Wilson.
H4

L. japonica A rampant evergreen or semi-evergreen species reaching 6–9m (20–28ft) on a support. The ovate to oblong leaves are often lobed on young or vigorous shoots. The fragrant flowers, 2.5–4cm (1–1½in) long, are white changing to yellow with age. They are produced continuously from early summer onwards. It is an excellent climber for climbing or creeping over unsightly garden objects. Japan, Korea, Manchuria, China. Introduced 1806.
H4

L. j. 'Aureoreticulata' A delightful form in which the small, neat, bright green leaves have a conspicuous pattern of golden netveining. Introduced before 1862 by Robert Fortune.
H4

L. j. **'Halliana'** A vigorous climber with white flowers changing to yellow and bright green leaves. Considered by some authorities to be the typical form.
H4 🏆 1993

L. j. **'Hall's Prolific'** A vigorous climber which flowers profusely even when young. Selected in Holland from plants grown as 'Halliana'.
H4

L. j. **var.** *repens* A distinct variety in which the leaves and shoots are flushed with purple and the flowers are flushed with purple on the outsides. It is highly fragrant. Japan, China. Introduced in the early 19th century.
H4

L. periclymenum (Common honeysuckle, woodbine) A vigorous medium-sized deciduous species common in Europe, including Britain and Ireland. The flowers are up to 5cm (2in) long, strongly and sweetly fragrant, cream inside darkening with age and purplish or yellowish outside. Flowering is from early summer to early autumn and red berries follow. The following forms are recommended. Europe and Morocco.
H4

L. p. **'Belgica'** (Early Dutch honeysuckle) The flowers of this medium-sized climber are reddish purple on the outside, fading to yellowish, and are produced in late spring and early summer and again in late summer. In cultivation since the seventeenth century.
H4 🏆 1993

L. p. **'Graham Thomas'** A medium-sized form in which the flowers are white in bud

Lonicera periclymenum 'Harlequin'

and become yellow when open. They are borne over a long period, particularly if the plant is hard pruned in spring. Found 1960 in Warwickshire by Graham Thomas when garden advisor to the National Trust.
H4 🏆 1993

L. p. **'Harlequin'** (*L. p.* 'Sherlite' PBR 4196) A medium-sized form bearing leaves with bright cream margins.
H4

L. p. **'Munster'** A medium-sized climber with flowers deep pink in bud, opening to white streaked with pink, fading to cream.
H4

Lonicera periclymenum 'Serotina'

L. p. **'Serotina'** (Late Dutch honeysuckle) A medium-sized form with flowers rich reddish purple outside, appearing from mid-summer to mid-autumn.
H4 🏆 1993

L. sempervirens (Trumpet honeysuckle) A high-climbing, usually semi-evergreen species with flowers to 5cm (2in) long, rich orange-scarlet outside, yellow within, in whorls towards the ends of the shoots in summer. A striking and very hardy species that does not seem to be troubled by aphids like *L.* × *brownii* 'Dropmore Scarlet'. E United States. Introduced 1656.
H4 🏆 1993

L. s. **f.** *sulphurea* A large climber with yellow flowers.
H4

L. splendida A rather fastidious evergreen or sometimes semi-evergreen species with blue-bloomy leaves and fragrant flowers up to 5cm (2in) long. They are reddish purple outside and yellowish white within, borne

Lonicera splendida

in dense terminal clusters in summer. It needs to be grown in a mild area. Spain. Introduced 1880.
H2–3

L. × *tellmanniana* A superb medium-sized deciduous hybrid with flowers 5cm (2in) long, rich coppery yellow, flushed red in bud. They are borne in large terminal

Lonicera × tellmanniana

Lonicera tragophylla

clusters in early to midsummer. It grows best in semi- to full shade. Raised before 1927 at the Royal Hungarian Horticultural School, Budapest.
H4 ♔ 1993

L. tragophylla A very beautiful and showy medium-sized deciduous climber with flowers 6–9cm (2½–3½in) long. They are bright golden yellow and in large terminal clusters in early to midsummer. It needs almost complete shade and is best grown into a tree. W China. Introduced 1900 by Ernest Wilson.
H4 ♔ 1993

SHRUBS

The shrubby honeysuckles are very different in appearance from the climbing ones. Their flowers are in pairs and are followed by berries. They are all easily grown in any ordinary soil. Old flowering shoots can be thinned out and cut back immediately after flowering to within a few centimetres (inches) of the old wood.

Lonicera chaetocarpa

L. chaetocarpa A pretty, erect deciduous shrub about 2m (6ft) high, with bristly stems and leaves. The comparatively large, primrose-yellow flowers are accompanied by large, eye-catching bracts and appear in late spring and early summer. It has bright red berries. W China. Introduced 1904 by Ernest Wilson.
H4

L. fragrantissima A partially evergreen, medium-sized shrub with sweetly fragrant cream flowers in late winter and spring.

Lonicera fragrantissima

Red berries follow in late spring. China. Introduced 1845 by Robert Fortune.
H4

L. involucrata A vigorous, spreading, distinctive deciduous shrub of medium size, flowering in early summer. The yellow flowers are each accompanied by two prominent red bracts that persist while the

Lonicera involucrata

Lonicera involucrata var. ledebourii

shining black berries form. It is robust and adaptable and grows well in seaside gardens and industrial areas. W North America. Introduced 1824.
H4

L. i. var. ledebourii The flowers of this medium-sized shrub are orange-yellow, tinged with red. Californian coast. Introduced 1838.
H4

L. korolkowii A very attractive, vigorous, large deciduous shrub of graceful, arching habit. It is given a strikingly grey-blue appearance by the down on the shoots and leaves and has pink flowers in early summer, followed by red berries. Turkestan. In cultivation 1880.
H4

L. nitida A dense, small-leaved evergreen species reaching 1.5–1.8m (5–6ft) in height. It is fast-growing and responds well to clipping, making it good for hedging. The flowers are very insignificant. W China. Introduced 1908 by Ernest Wilson.
H4

Lonicera nitida 'Baggesen's Gold'

L. n. 'Baggesen's Gold' 'Ernest Wilson' is the commonest form of the species but this runs it a close second as a first-class medium-sized hedging shrub with a dense habit and small leaves which are yellow in summer and turn yellow-green in autumn.
H4 ♔ 1993

L. n. 'Elegant' A small, dense, spreading shrub with arching branches and small, ovate, matt green leaves. Now considered to be a hybrid with *L. pileata*.
H4

L. n. 'Ernest Wilson' This is the hedging 'nitida' of the trade. It has a spreading, slightly arching habit and tiny, almost oval leaves. Flowers and fruits are not often produced, especially when it is clipped. H4

L. n. 'Maigrün' A small, dense, spreading bush with pale young leaves contrasting with the dark green older ones in spring. H4

Lonicera pileata

L. pileata A small to medium-sized, semi-evergreen, horizontally branched shrub, suitable for underplanting and ground cover, particularly in shade. The leaves are small, long-elliptic and bright green, and the young, light green ones contrast prettily with the older, darker leaves in spring. It bears clusters of translucently violet berries. China. Introduced 1900 by Ernest Wilson. H4

L. × purpusii (*L. fragrantissima × L. standishii*) A vigorous, medium-sized deciduous hybrid

Lonicera × purpursii

with highly fragrant cream flowers in winter. H4

L. × p. 'Winter Beauty' A back-cross of *L. × purpusii* with *L. standishii*. It is a medium-sized shrub that flowers when young and often from the very beginning of winter almost to the middle of spring. Raised 1966 at Hillier Nurseries by Alf Alford. H4 ♈ 1993

L. pyrenaica A choice deciduous shrubby honeysuckle, about 1m (3ft) high, with small, sea-green leaves and nodding, comparatively large, funnel-shaped, cream and pink flowers in late spring and early summer. Orange-red berries follow. Pyrenees and Balearic Isles. Introduced 1739. H4

Lonicera setifera

L. setifera A rare and beautiful medium-sized deciduous shrub with erect, bristly stems. The tubular, sweetly scented, daphne-like white and pink flowers appear in short clusters on the bare stems during winter and early spring, and even earlier if the weather is mild. The berries are red and bristly. Himalaya, China. Introduced 1924 by Frank Kingdon-Ward. H4

L. standishii A charming, deciduous or semi-evergreen, medium-sized, winter-flowering species, resembling *L. fragrantissima*. The fragrant flowers are white blushed with pink and have noticeable yellow anthers. The berries, borne in early summer, are red. Introduced 1845 by Robert Fortune. H4

L. syringantha A graceful, medium-sized,

Lonicera standishii

rounded deciduous shrub with an intricate branch structure. The leaves are small, sea green, and borne in threes on strong shoots. The fragrant tubular flowers are soft lilac, and appear in late spring and early autumn. Red berries are sometimes borne. China, Tibet. Introduced c1890. H4

L. tatarica A vigorous, variable deciduous shrub up to 3m (10ft) high with masses of pink flowers in late spring and early summer, followed by red berries. C Asia to Russia. Introduced 1752. H4

L. t. 'Arnold Red' A form with rose-pink flowers and larger berries than the typical species. Originated 1945 in the Arnold Arboretum. H4

L. t. 'Hack's Red' A first-class medium-sized selection with rose-pink flowers. H4

Lophomyrtus

L. bullata See *Myrtus bullata*.

Luculia *Rubiaceae*

A genus of five species of beautiful evergreen shrubs or small trees from the temperate Himalaya and west China. They are mainly suitable as winter-flowering shrubs for the conservatory or for outdoor culture in the very mildest gardens.

L. gratissima A semi-evergreen, free-flowering shrub with sweetly fragrant rich almond-pink flowers in many-flowered

Luculia gratissima

trusses in winter. Potentially its height is about 5m (15ft) but this is never attained outside and seldom under glass. Himalaya. Introduced 1816.

H1–2 🏆 1993

Luma

L. apiculata See *Myrtus luma*.
L. chequen See *Myrtus chequen*.

Lupinus *Leguminosae*
Tree lupin

Most lupins, of which there are more than 200 species in the Americas and the Mediterranean region, are herbaceous perennials, but some are deciduous shrubs.

Lupinus arboreus

L. arboreus (Yellow tree lupin) A fairly short-lived, more or less evergreen, fast-growing shrub to about 2m (6ft). The flowers are normally yellow, but from seed they may be blue or lavender. They are delicately scented and are produced in dense clusters continuously through the summer. It thrives in full sun in any well drained position and naturalizes itself in sandy or pebbly soils, particularly by the sea. California. In cultivation 1793.

H4 🏆 1993

Lycium *Solanaceae*

A genus of about 100 species of rambling, often spiny deciduous shrubs widely distributed throughout the world. They require full sun and will grow in any dry, poor soil.

Lycium barbarum

L. barbarum (Duke of Argyll's tea tree, matrimony vine) A vigorous, medium-sized shrub with long, usually spiny, scrambling, arching stems. The purple funnel-shaped flowers are borne in clusters in the leaf axils from early summer to early autumn, followed by small, egg-shaped, orange or scarlet berries. It is excellent by the sea. China. Introduced 1700.

H4

Lyonia *Ericaceae*

A genus of about 35 species of attractive evergreen and deciduous shrubs or occasionally small trees, closely related to Pieris *and requiring a lime-free soil. They have a wide range of distribution, from the United States to the Himalayas.*

L. ligustrina (Male berry) A deciduous, extremely hardy, small to medium-sized shrub with more or less oval leaves and panicles of pitcher-shaped white flowers in mid- to late summer. It thrives in a moist, peaty or sandy loam. E United States. Introduced 1748.

H4

Lyonothamnus *Rosaceae*

A genus of one evergreen species.

L. floribunda subsp. **aspleniifolius** A small, graceful, fast-growing tree, soon forming a remarkable slender trunk like a miniature redwood, with attractive, predominantly chestnut bark that shreds and peels attractively. The leaves are fernily pinnate with the leaflets divided into oblong lobes that are glossy green above and hairy-grey below. The creamy white flowers are borne in early summer in slender, spiraea-like panicles. It needs the shelter of a warm wall even in the milder areas. Santa Catalina and other offshore islands of California. Introduced 1900.

H2–3

M

Maackia *Leguminosae*

A genus of about eight species of very hardy, attractive, slow-growing small deciduous trees related to Cladrastis *but differing in the solitary, exposed leaf buds, opposite leaflets and densely packed, more-or-less erect clusters of flowers. They are natives of east Asia. They succeed in most soils including deep soil over chalk and require a sunny position.*

M. amurensis A small tree with pinnate leaves and white flowers, tinged palest slate-blue, in erect racemes in early and mid-summer, even on young plants. Manchuria. Introduced 1864.

H4

M. chinensis A small, broad-headed tree which produces dull white pea-flowers in summer. The dark bluish young shoots are particularly outstanding in late spring. China. Introduced 1908.

H4

MAGNOLIA

Magnoliaceae

MAGNOLIAS ARE invariably associated in the mind with large, exotic blooms, heavy scents, and some of the most romantic of all trees and shrubs. This is not a mistaken view, but there is such a wide variety of magnolias that it is difficult to generalize about them except to say that they are always beautiful. Those with not very conspicuous flowers – and they are few – are worth growing in large gardens for their stature and foliage, while the magnolias that flower intermittently for a long period in summer make up for the few flowers they carry at any one time by the magnificence of their blooms when they do appear and the nobility of their foliage. The rest – by far the majority – are simply stunning.

Magnolia is an ancient genus and its species are found wild from the Himalayas and eastern and South-East Asia to North and Central America. Their simple flower formation undoubtedly contributes to their limpid loveliness, which is appreciated by gardeners throughout the temperate regions of the world.

FORMS AND FLOWERS

Magnolias vary from tall forest trees to medium-sized or fairly small shrubs and may be deciduous or evergreen. Generally speaking, you can expect the deciduous ones to flower on naked branches before the leaves appear (and therefore in spring), and the evergreens to come into bloom in summer and early autumn. This is only a guide, as some deciduous magnolias, such as a few cultivars of *M.* × *soulangeana*, flower at the same time as the leaves unfold. On the whole, forms that flower before the leaves are the most effective.

Flowering of the large tree magnolias is usually delayed until they attain considerable size, but again this varies. Grown from

Magnolia campbellii 'Charles Raffill'

seed, the magnificent *M. campbellii* is likely to be 30 years old before it starts to bloom (though grafted clones will flower in half that time), while *M. c.* var. *mollicomata* will flower when it is 10–15 years old. With seedlings of the evergreen *M. grandiflora* flowering is again long delayed, but for the less patient, vegetatively propagated cultivars such as *M. g.* 'Goliath' and 'Exmouth' produce their beautifully scented flowers early in their lives. The smaller magnolias, particularly *M. stellata* and its forms and its excellent hybrids with *M. kobus*, which go under the name *M.* × *loebneri*, are first-class shrubs or small trees for small or medium-sized gardens. In recent years they have been included in the range of exciting developments in which ever more magnolias are being raised.

SOIL AND PLANTING

Most magnolias dislike lime in the soil, but *M. acuminata, delavayi, grandiflora, kobus,* × *loebneri stellata* and *wilsonii* are lime-tolerant to a degree which is to some extent dependent on the depth of the soil and its moisture-retentive properties. For example, *M. grandiflora* will grow on soft, chalky limestones as long as there is a good depth of soil. *M. soulangeana* is moderately lime tolerant.

There is no difficulty with heavy clay soils – indeed, magnolias do very well in them. On the other hand, it is good practice to make it easier for their soft roots to make headway early on by providing a richly organic soil at planting time. This is best done by cultivating a square metre (yard) of ground in which peat, garden compost, well-rotted manure or composted straw can be liberally mixed with the soil. Root damage at an early stage in the life of a magnolia is usually fatal in the long term, with plants that initially look strong and healthy slowly 'going backwards' and making annual extension growth that eventually dwindles to nothing. Reputable nurseries ensure that their root-balled specimens are in good condition, but if you buy a magnolia in the general market it is best to choose one that has been container grown throughout its life and not allowed to become potbound. You should be prepared to find the care needed to produce a healthy, robust, ongoing magnolia reflected in its price. A cheap magnolia is unlikely to be a good buy.

HARDINESS AND SHELTER

Early frost destroys the flowers of the early spring-flowering tree species such as *M. campbellii*, and their only protection is to be grown in mild areas, but others grown in shelter from icy winds and away from frost pockets will succeed where the climate is quite cold. The main enemy of flowering is a mild early spring followed by sudden late frosts, although the plants themselves are hardy.

Evergreen magnolias, which often have large leaves, must be sheltered from gales all year round in order to avoid them being damaged. They are also vulnerable to being broken by the weight of snow. *M. grandiflora*, for instance, is hardly subject to snow in its home range, and is capable of reaching heights of 30m (100ft) or more. Where snowfalls occur, however, it rarely attains the stature of a tall tree and is more often seen as a large shrub, chiefly because of the detrimental effects of snow damage. For this reason, snow should be shaken from the branches of evergreen magnolias as soon as possible. *M. grandiflora* is often – and very effectively – grown on a wall, where it avoids this peril. All magnolias benefit from semi-shade, but where it is not possible most of the deciduous ones and some of the evergreens, especially *M. grandiflora* and its cultivars, will take a considerable amount of sun. Trees planted in open positions are, however, more vulnerable to damaging winds and frosts.

M. acuminata (Cucumber tree) A fast-growing large deciduous tree with a spreading habit with age. The flowers, not produced on young trees, open with the greenish, metallic blue and yellow leaves in early summer but are insignificant. Its fruits are cucumber-shaped. E United States and SE Canada. Introduced 1736.
H4

Magnolia 'Ann'

M. **'Ann'** A medium-sized to large upright deciduous shrub. The flowers appear in mid-spring before the leaves and have eight deep reddish pink, upright tepals, paler on the inside. It requires a lime-free soil.
H4 ♛ 1993

Magnolia 'Betty'

M. **'Betty'** A vigorous, medium-sized deciduous shrub with large flowers to 20cm (8in) across that have up to 19 tepals, purplish red outside, white within and borne in mid-spring. It requires a lime-free soil.
H4 ♛ 1993

M. campbellii This, regarded by many as one of the most beautiful trees in the world, becomes a large tree on acid, lime-free soils in mild, sheltered places and bears enormous goblet-shaped flowers on leafless branches, rose pink outside and pale within, that spread wide after a while like water-lilies. Unfortunately, flowers are not normally produced until the tree is 20–30 years old or even more in some cases (records show that one planted in 1864 eventually flowered in 1900, but it still blooms magnificently every year). It is better to acquire young plants of vegetatively propagated forms that flower at an earlier age, say 12 years. They are mostly fairly hardy, but where spring frosts are prevalent their flowers, produced in late winter or early spring, may be destroyed. It is a deciduous species. Himalayas, SW China. Introduced 1864.
H3–4

M. c. **'Charles Raffill'** A large, vigorous hybrid between the typical form and *M. c.* subsp. *mollicomata*, inheriting the habit of the latter of flowering early in life, between 10 to 15 years old. The large flowers are deep rose-pink in bud and when expanded are rose-purple on the outside and white with a pinkish purple flush on the inside.
H3–4 ♛ 1993

Magnolia campbellii 'Darjeeling'

M. c. **'Darjeeling'** A superb clone with flowers of the darkest, richest rose. Hilliers' stock was vegetatively propagated from the original tree which grows in the Darjeeling Botanic Gardens, India.
H3–4

M. c. **'Kew's Surprise'** This large tree is

one of Charles Raffill's seedlings. The flowers are larger than those of 'Charles Raffill' and the outside of the petals is of a richer pink colouring. Raised at Caerhays Castle, Cornwall.
H3–4

Magnolia campbellii var. mollicomata

M. c. subsp. mollicomata This is similar in many ways to the typical form but is hardier and flowers at an earlier age, sometimes 10–15 years. It is usually about two weeks later in flowering and thus stands a better chance of escaping frost damage to the blooms, which are like large, pink to rose-purple water-lilies. SE Tibet, N Burma, Yunnan. Introduced 1924 by George Forrest.
H3–4

M. c. 'Werrington' A form of *M. c.* subsp. *mollicomata*. Like 'Lanarth', it has very large cyclamen-purple flowers with even darker stamens but has a better constitution.
H3–4

Magnolia cylindrica

M. cylindrica A very rare large deciduous shrub or small tree. The white flowers are very similar to those of *M. denudata* but more elegant, appearing on the naked stems in mid-spring. It requires acid soil. E China. In cultivation before 1936.
H3–4 🏆 1993

Magnolia dawsoniana

M. dawsoniana A rare and magnificent large evergreen shrub or small tree with leathery, bright green leaves almost 15cm (6in) long. Its large, pale rose flowers, suffused with purple on the outside and held horizontally, are borne in early spring but not on young trees. It requires an acid soil. China. Introduced 1908 by Ernest Wilson.
H3–4

Magnolia delavayi

M. delavayi With the exception of *Rhododendron sinograande* and its allies and *Trachycarpus fortunei*, this magnificent species probably has the largest leaves of any evergreen tree or shrub grown in cool-

temperate areas. It is a large shrub or bushy tree (eventually a medium-sized, broad-headed tree) up to 14m (46ft), with leaves that are matt sea-green and paddle-shaped. The parchment-coloured, slightly fragrant flowers appear a few at a time in late summer, each one lasting for about two days. Away from the mildest, most sheltered spots it needs the protection of a wall. It does well in soils over chalk. China. Introduced 1899 by Ernest Wilson.
H3

Magnolia denudata

M. denudata (Lily tree, yulan) A large shrub or small, rounded deciduous tree, usually below 9m (28ft) in height. The fragrant, pure white, cup-shaped flowers open in profusion in early spring and have thick, fleshy tepals. It requires an acid soil. E China. Introduced 1789.
H4 🏆 1993

M. 'Elizabeth' A particularly remarkable small, conical deciduous tree. The clear,

Magnolia 'Elizabeth'

pale primrose-yellow, fragrant, cup-shaped flowers open before the leaves in mid- or late spring. It requires an acid soil. Raised at the Brooklyn Botanic Garden by Eva Maria Spherbes and selected 1978.
H4 🏆 1993

***M.* 'Eric Savill'** A small, upright deciduous tree with large, cup-shaped flowers, rich pink outside and nearly white inside, borne in mid-spring before the leaves appear. It requires an acid soil.
H4

Magnolia 'Galaxy'

***M.* 'Galaxy'** A vigorous small conical deciduous tree with striking purple-pink to red, tulip-shaped flowers in mid- to late spring. It flowers when fairly young. It requires a lime-free soil.
H4 🏆 1993

Magnolia grandiflora

M. grandiflora This magnificent evergreen species is generally grown as a wall shrub, for which purpose it is ideal, but is hardy in the open if sheltered and planted in full sun. In areas of heavy snowfall, however, its branches are liable to breakage and it fails to reach its stature as a tree, remaining shrubby but still fairly large and round-headed. The leaves are large, leathery and sometimes decoratively brown-felted on the undersides. It is an excellent species for growing in maritime regions. The main drawback of the species is that it takes many years for it to flower. There are, however, a few cultivars that flower early in their lives. The highly scented, creamy white flowers can be up to 25cm (10in) across and are produced from midsummer to early autumn. It is lime tolerant, even over chalk, as long as there is a good depth of loamy soil. SE United States. Introduced 1734.
H4

***M. g.* 'Exmouth'** A splendid clone with large, polished leaves that are soft green above and felted with reddish brown on the undersides. The felt gradually disappears.

Magnolia grandiflora 'Exmouth'

Magnolia grandiflora 'Goliath'

The flowers, appearing at an early age, are about 25cm (10in) across and richly fragrant. In cultivation 1768.
H4 🏆 1993

***M. g.* 'Goliath'** An excellent large shrub or small tree with shorter, broader leaves than the type, dark glossy green above and with no felting on the lower surfaces. The globular flowers are very large and are produced when the plant is young. Selected before 1910 in Guernsey.
H4 🏆 1993

***M. g.* 'Little Gem'** A form of American origin that makes a compact large shrub or small tree of narrowly columnar habit. The flowers and leaves are smaller than usual, the latter being dark glossy green above with a deep brown felt beneath. Planted as a hedge in gardens in the SE United States. Selected 1952.
H4

Magnolia grandiflora 'Samuel Sommer'

***M. g.* 'Samuel Sommer'** A very hardy, wind-resistant large shrub or small tree, good for an open position. Dark green, glossy leaves have deep brown felty undersides. The huge flowers up to 35cm (14in) across are borne early in the plant's life
H4

***M.* 'Heaven Scent'** A magnificent small to medium-sized deciduous tree. The flowers, borne in mid- to late spring, are richly scented and narrowly cup-shaped, with pale pink tepals that are heavily flushed with deep pink towards the base and have a distinct magenta-pink stripe on the back. It requires an acid soil.
H4 🏆 1993

M. hypoleuca A handsome, strongly growing, medium-sized deciduous tree, often with purple-tinged young shoots. The very large leaves, broadest above the middle, are held in whorls at the ends of the shoots. The strongly fragrant cream flowers, borne in late spring and early summer, are 20cm (8in) across and have a central ring of crimson stamens. The fruit clusters are attractive and large. It requires an acid soil. Japan. Introduced 1880.
H4 ♔ 1993

M. 'Iolanthe' A vigorous, upright deciduous hybrid, forming an ungainly small to medium-sized tree. The very large, cup-shaped, rose-pink flowers are cream inside and are borne in spring when the tree is still young. It requires an acid soil. Raised 1974 in New Zealand by Felix Jury.
H4 ♔ 1993

M. 'Jane' A medium-sized, compact upright, deciduous shrub suitable for gardens with limited space. The fragrant, cup-shaped flowers open in mid- to late spring from narrow, erect, red-purple buds and the tepals are red-purple outside and white within. It requires an acid soil.
H4 ♔ 1993

Magnolia 'Judy'

M. 'Judy' A medium-sized upright deciduous shrub with small, slender, candle-like flowers that are red-purple outside and creamy white inside. They are borne in mid- to late spring. It requires an acid soil.
H4 ♔ 1993

M. 'Kewensis' A small, slender, broadly conical deciduous tree with fragrant white flowers 6cm (2½in) long, very freely borne

Magnolia 'Kewensis'

in mid-spring before the leaves appear. It is slightly lime tolerant. Originated 1938 at Kew Gardens.
H4

M. kobus A very hardy deciduous large shrub or small tree that does not produce its slightly fragrant, white flowers until it is about 12–15 years old. They are borne in spring. For an excellent, white-flowered magnolia of this type that will flower at a much younger age, grow well even on chalk soils, *M. × loebneri* 'Merrill' is recommended. Japan. Introduced 1865.
H4

Magnolia liliiflora 'Nigra'

M. liliiflora **'Nigra'** A wide-spreading but compact medium-sized deciduous shrub with broad, shining green leaves and erect flowers like slender tulips, gradually opening wide. They are deep vinous purple outside, creamy white stained with purple inside, and are borne freely over a long period during late spring and summer. It

requires an acid soil. Japan. Introduced 1861 by J. G. Veitch.
H4 ♔ 1993

M. × loebneri (*M. kobus* × *M. stellata*) Excellent variable deciduous hybrids having the best features of both parents. They are large shrubs or small trees wih strap-like tepals, fragrant in mid-spring. They flower profusely even when young and will grow on any reasonable soil, including chalk. The following forms are recommended. Originated before 1910.
H4

Magnolia × loebneri 'Leonard Messel'

M. × l. **'Leonard Messel'** A magnificent tall shrub or small tree with fragrant lilac-pink flowers, deeper in bud.
H4 ♔ 1993

Magnolia × loebneri 'Merrill'

M. × l. **'Merrill'** A vigorous small tree with large, white, fragrant flowers.
H4 ♔ 1993 .

M. macrophylla An awe-inspiring small

tree when seen alone, ideally in a site sheltered from the prevailing winds but open to the sun and backed by dark evergreens. It has larger leaves than any other deciduous tree or shrub hardy in cool-temperate areas. The leaves are rather thin, blue-grey-bloomy beneath and sometimes more than 60cm (2ft) in length. The very large (30cm/12in), fragrant flowers are the colour of parchment and have purple markings in the centre. They appear in early summer. It requires an acid soil. SE United States. Introduced 1800.
H4

M. 'Manchu Fan' A splendid small to medium-sized deciduous tree with large, goblet-shaped flowers that have nine broad, creamy tepals, the inner ones of which are flushed purplish pink at the base. They are borne in spring. It is similar to 'Sayonara' but the flowers are less goblet-shaped and less flushed with green at the base. It requires an acid soil.
H4

M. 'Maryland' (*M. grandiflora* × *M. virginiana*) (Freeman Hybrids) A large evergreen shrub or small tree with rich glossy green leaves which are thinly felted beneath and which produces large, white, lemon-scented, globular flowers in summer that open widely in summer. It tolerates lime.
H4 ♈ 1993

Magnolia officinalis var. biloba

M. officinalis var. biloba A very rare and distinct small to medium-sized deciduous tree. It has large leaves, broadest above the middle and as much as 50cm (20in) long; they are pale green above, bloomy and

finely downy beneath, and deeply notched at the apex. The parchment-coloured flowers, borne in early summer, have maroon centres and are fragrant. It requires an acid soil. Introduced 1936 to British gardens from the Botanic Garden, Lushan, China, by Hillier Nurseries.
H4 ♈ 1993

M. 'Peppermint Stick' A strong-growing, medium-sized, deciduous conical tree with narrowly columnar flower buds up to 11cm (4¹/₂in) long. There are nine cream tepals, flushed with pink at the base and with a central deep pink line; the outer ones spread with age, while the inner ones, heavily flushed with deep pink towards the base, remain erect. They appear in spring. It requires an acid soil.
H4 ♈ 1993

M. 'Pinkie' A medium-sized deciduous shrub with cup-shaped flowers up to 18cm (7in) across that have 9–12 tepals, pale red-purple becoming pink outside, white

Magnolia 'Pinkie'

Magnolia × proctoriana

within. They appear in mid- to late spring. It requires an acid soil.
H4 ♈ 1993

M. × proctoriana (*M salicifolia* × *M. stellata*) A large, very free-flowering deciduous shrub with white flowers. These have 6–12 tepals and appear in spring. It requires an acid soil. Garden origin 1928.
H4 ♈ 1993

Magnolia 'Randy'

M. 'Randy' A medium-sized, upright deciduous shrub with large, pink flowers that open widely from slender, red-purple buds in mid- to late spring. It requires an acid soil.
H4 ♈ 1993

M. 'Ricki' A medium-sized deciduous shrub with large flowers, deep purplish pink in bud, up to 15cm (6in) across when open. There are 15 rather narrow tepals, shading from pink to deep rose-purple at the bases of the outside surfaces. They are borne in mid- to late spring. It requires an acid soil.
H4 ♈ 1993

Magnolia 'Royal Crown'

M. **'Royal Crown'** A small deciduous tree with large, 12-tepalled flowers that are purplish pink in the bud and open before the leaves to white inside, shading to white at the tips outside. They appear in mid- to late spring. It requires an acid soil.
H4

Magnolia salicifolia

M. **salicifolia** A large deciduous shrub or small, broadly conical tree with slender branches. The leaves are usually narrow and willow-like and the flowers, usually produced on young plants, are white, fragrant and mostly have six narrow tepals. They are produced on the leafless stems in early to mid-spring. The leaves, bark and wood are pleasantly lemon-scented if bruised. It requires an acid soil. Japan. Introduced 1892.
H4 ♔ 1993

M. s. **'Jermyns'** A slow-growing, shrubby form with broader leaves and larger flowers that appear later than those of the typical

Magnolia sargentiana var. robusta

species. It is one of the best flowering clones of this beautiful magnolia.
H4

M. **sargentiana var. robusta** A noble, medium-sized deciduous tree with flowers fully 23cm (9in) in diameter, produced in early to mid-spring before the leaves but not until tree size is reached. They are rosy crimson without and paler within. It requires an acid soil. China. Introduced 1908 by Ernest Wilson.
H3–4

Magnolia 'Sayonara'

M. **'Sayonara'** A small deciduous tree with a profusion of white, goblet-shaped, nine-tepalled flowers 10cm (4in) across in mid-spring. They are lightly flushed with pink and cool green at the base, while the inner tepals are heavily blushed with pink above the middle. It requires an acid soil.
H4 ♔ 1993

Magnolia sieboldii

M. **sieboldii** A large, wide-spreading

deciduous shrub with fragrant white flowers that are nodding and egg-shaped in bud, but then turn more or less to the horizontal as they open to a wide dish shape. They appear intermittently from late spring to late summer. The crimson fruit clusters are very eye-catching indeed. It requires an acid soil. Japan, Korea. Introduced 1865.
H4 ♔ 1993

Magnolia sinensis

M. **sinensis** A large, wide-spreading deciduous shrub resembling *M. wilsonii* but easily distinguished by its broader leaves and wider, more strongly lemon-scented, white, nodding flowers, 10–13cm (4–5in) wide with a contrasting central cone of red stamens. They appear with the leaves in early summer. It is lime tolerant. W China. Introduced 1908 by Ernest Wilson.
H4 ♔ 1993

M. × **soulangeana** (*M. denudata* × *M. liliiflora*) The most popular and most well-known of the larger magnolias, often seen as a large, many-stemmed shrub, but also as a large, single-trunked tree. It is deciduous. There are many named clones, all of which flower in mid-spring when still young, and they are excellent for difficult clay soils and polluted atmospheres, but not for shallow chalk soils, although they are moderately tolerant of lime. The plant usually grown under this name is in fact 'Etienne Soulange-Bodin'.
H4

M. × *s.* **'Alexandrina'** One of the most popular clones, this vigorous, erect and free-flowering large shrub or tree, has large, erect white flowers heavily flushed pink-

Magnolia × soulangeana 'Alexandrina'

Magnolia × soulangeana 'Brozzonii'

purple at the base. In cultivation 1831.
H4 ♔ 1993

***M. × s.* 'Brozzonii'** An aristocratic plant with large, elongated, white flowers, shaded purple at the base. One of the largest-flowered and the latest of the group to bloom. In cultivation 1873.
H4 ♔ 1993

Magnolia × soulangeana 'Lennei'

***M. × s.* 'Etienne Soulange-Bodin'** The typical form, usually grown as *M. × soulangeana*. It has large, tulip-shaped white flowers, stained purple at the base.
H4 ♔ 1993

***M. × s.* 'Lennei'** A vigorous, spreading, multi-stemmed shrub with a tendency to flop about. It has large leaves and enormous, goblet-shaped flowers with thick, fleshy tepals that are a beautiful rosy purple outside and creamy white stained with soft purple inside. The flowers appear quite late in the middle of spring and carry on into late spring, and sometimes there is a second flush of bloom in autumn.
H4 ♔ 1993

***M. × s.* 'Lennei Alba'** A form with ivory-white cup-shaped flowers, similar to *M. denudata*. In cultivation 1905.
H4 ♔ 1993

***M. × s.* 'Picture'** A vigorous, erectly branched large shrub or large tree with large leaves and long, erect flowers that are wine-purple on the outside and white inside. It flowers when quite young. Found 1930 in a Japanese garden.
H4

Magnolia × soulangeana 'Rustica Rubra'

***M. × s.* 'Rustica Rubra'** A vigorous large shrub excellent for general planting with oval leaves and cup-shaped flowers of rich, rosy red. A seedling of 'Lennei'.
H4 ♔ 1993

Magnolia × soulangeana 'Lennei Alba'

M. × s. **'San Jose'** A vigorous but somewhat tender large shrub with large flowers that are deep pink outside and cream inside. Raised 1938 in California.
H3 ♔ 1993

M. × s. **'Sundew'** A large shrub with large, creamy flowers flushed with pink at the base. In cultivation 1966.
H4

M. sprengeri **'Claret Cup'** A small to medium-sized deciduous tree, occasionally up to 13m (43ft), with fragrant, purplish pink flowers that are white flushed with pink on the inside. They appear in early to mid-spring. The leaves are up to 18cm (7in) long and have a wedge-shaped base. It requires an acid soil in a mild environment.
H3

M. stellata A slow-growing, rounded deciduous shrub, usually wider than high, seldom more than 3m (9ft) in height. The abundant silky hairy winter buds open to fragrant, white, narrow many-tepalled flowers borne over a long period in mid-spring. It will tolerate some lime as long as there is plenty of organic matter in the soil. Japan. Introduced 1862.
H4 ♔ 1993

M. s. **'Rosea'** The flowers of this form are flushed with pink, deeper in bud.
H4

M. s. **'Royal Star'** A shrub with very large flowers, produced later than most other forms. They are pink-tinged in the bud and open white, with numerous tepals. Raised 1947 on Long Island.
H4

M. s. **'Water Lily'** An outstanding shrub

Magnolia stellata

with larger flowers and even more numerous tepals. Japan.
H4 ♔ 1993

Magnolia 'Susan'

M. **'Susan'** A medium-sized upright deciduous shrub with six-tepalled flowers, deep red-purple in the bud, showing paler inside when open. They are borne in mid- to late spring. It requires an acid soil.
H4 ♔ 1993

Magnolia × thompsoniana

M. × thompsoniana A large, wide-spreading deciduous shrub like *M. virginiana* but with larger leaves, up to 25cm (10in) long, that persist into early winter. The large, fragrant flowers, the colour of parchment, are carried intermittently in summer even on young plants. It requires an acid soil. Garden origin 1808.
H4

M. tripetala (Umbrella tree) A very hardy deciduous tree, sometimes as much as 12m (40ft) high, with an open head of branches.

Magnolia tripetala

The leaves are 30–50cm (12–20in) long and 15–25cm (6–10in) wide. The cream flowers, 18–25cm (7–10in) across, are strongly and pungently scented and borne in late spring and early summer. They are followed by attractive, cone-shaped, red fruit-clusters. It requires an acid soil. E United States. Introduced 1752.
H4

Magnolia × veitchii 'Peter Veitch'

M. × veitchii **'Peter Veitch'** As soon as this first class potentially medium-sized to large deciduous tree reaches small tree size it begins to bear lovely white goblet-shaped flowers flushed with purple-pink on the naked branches in mid-spring. It requires an acid soil.
H4

M. virginiana (Swamp bay, sweet bay) A partially evergreen large shrub or small tree with fragrant, cream, rather small, globular flowers from early to late summer. The leaves are up to 13cm (5in) long and are

Magnolia 'Wada's Memory'

Magnolia wilsonii

glossy green above and blue-white beneath. It requires an acid soil. E United States. In cultivation in the late seventeenth century and probably the first magnolia to be grown in England.
H4

M. 'Wada's Memory' This delightful deciduous magnolia probably had the same parents as 'Kewensis'. Its attractively floppy white flowers are larger than those of *M. kobus* and are borne in mid-spring in large numbers, even while the plant is still young. It is a large shrub or small to medium-sized conical tree requiring an acid soil.
H4 ♔ 1993

M. watsonsii See *M.* × *wieseneri*.

M. × wieseneri, syn. *M. watsonsii* A splendid deciduous shrub or small bushy tree with leathery leaves. The upward-facing flowers open from early to midsummer from attractive rounded white buds and are creamy white with prominent, rosy crimson anthers and pink sepals. They are saucer-shaped, 13cm (5in) wide, and have an

Magnolia × wieseneri

extremely powerful fragrance. Japan. Garden origin c1889.
H4

M. wilsonii A large, wide-spreading deciduous shrub with fairly slim, pointed leaves and pendulous, saucer-shaped, fragrant, white flowers with crimson stamens in early summer. It is a lovely species, differing from *M. sinensis* in having narrower

leaves and rather smaller flowers. It is best in a partially shaded place and is moderately lime tolerant. W China. Introduced 1908 by Ernest Wilson.
H4 ♔ 1993

M. 'Yellow Bird' A large deciduous shrub or small tree raised in America where the greenish yellow flowers are prominent on leafless branches. In this country the flowers appear with or slightly after the leaves and tend to be lost among the foliage. Further breeding will no doubt overcome this fault.
H4

× Mahoberberis *Berberidaceae*

These tough evergreen shrubs are hybrids between Mahonia *and* Berberis. *They will grow in any soil and any exposure.*

× **M. aquisargentii** A really splendid and remarkable medium-sized, dense, upright shrub. The leaves vary in shape and are either slender-stalked, up to 21cm (8in) long and regularly spine-toothed, or short-stalked and edged with vicious spines 2cm (³/₄in) long. Some leaves are compound, with two leaflets at their base. All are shining dark green above and paler underneath. The soft yellow flowers, in clusters at the ends of the shoots, are borne in spring and are followed by black berries. Of garden origin in Sweden.
H4

× **M. a. 'Magic'** A medium-sized upright shrub with spiny foliage and dense clusters of bright yellow flowers in spring.
H4

Mahonia

Berberidaceae

Mahonia × media 'Charity'

During recent decades mahonias have become more widely recognized as great assets to the garden, particularly in winter and spring. They are spiny-leaved evergreen shrubs, closely related to *Berberis* but readily distinguished by the absence of spines on their stems and by their leaves, which are generally pinnate but in some species are trifoliolate (having three leaflets). The 'typical' mahonia leaf has between 13 leaflets (the average for *M. japonica*) and 41 (the maximum for *M. lomariifolia*). Each leaflet is furnished with holly-like spines.

Many mahonias are magnificently archi-tectural shrubs, unique in appearance and important centres of attention in winter. Their winter and spring appeal is all the stronger because that is when the majority flower, and the conspicuous racemes or panicles of blossoms, which are usually yellow and often scented, make a striking feature early in the year.

It is not always appreciated that *Mahonia* can be divided roughly into two groups – the taller, more vigorous species from Asia, and the shorter, more spreading ones from America. The former prefer partly shaded positions, preferably provided by trees or other, larger shrubs, while the American mahonias thrive in drier soils and more sun.

This particular cultural distinction is not a strong one, however, and in general mahonias will grow well on any soil from peaty loam to chalk. Some are very tough indeed, and the American *M. aquifolium* thrives in sun and also in that position of despair for many gardeners, dry shade.

They vary a little in hardiness, but most of those that are listed below will tolerate con-siderable periods at temperatures of −15°C (5°F), provided they receive some shelter from wind. The main exception is *M. lomari-ifolia*, whose hardiness is on the whole con-fined to maritime areas, but whose hybrids with *M. japonica* – collectively *M. × media* – will take more cold than their parent.

The larger mahonias can reach heights of 3–5m (10–15ft) or even more, and indi-vidual leaves may be 60cm (2ft) long. Whether their multiple inflorescences are stiffly erect, as in *M. × media* 'Winter Sun', or elegantly pendent as in *M. japonica*, they are dramatic shrubs of great presence whose charms are extended by their clus-ters of blue-black, occasionally red or yel-low berries.

American species, such as *M. pinnata*, *M. repens* and particularly *M. aquifolium*, make first-class, almost impenetrable ground cover, spreading as they do by suckers. They do not become invasive in any real sense, however, as any superfluous suckers are easily removed.

The larger mahonias do not require reg-ular pruning, but weak stems should be removed in order to make room for stronger ones. After a particularly severe winter, you may find it necessary to prune away any stems with wind-burnt foliage or any that are showing signs of more than a little die-back. Apart from such things, mahonias are trouble-free.

Mahonia aquifolium

M. aquifolium (Oregon grape) A small shrub, valuable for under-planting whether in sun or shade. The polished green leaves are pinnate, with 5–13 leaflets (the odd one is at the end); they often turn red in winter. The rich yellow flowers, opening in early spring, are borne in erect racemes, which in turn are in clusters. The decorative berries produced are blue-black. W North America. Introduced 1823.
H4

Mahonia aquifolium 'Apollo'

M. a. 'Apollo' A splendid, vigorous form, making a dense, low-growing, spreading bush. The leaves are deep green with reddish stalks and the bright yellow flowers are in large, dense clusters.
H4 ♛ 1993

M. a. 'Atropurpurea' A shrub with leaves that turn rich reddish purple in winter and early spring. In cultivation 1915.
H4

M. a. 'Moseri' A form with most attractive

Mahonia aquifolium 'Moseri'

bronze-red leaves that turn to apple-green and finally dark green. It has rather a weak constitution, however. In cultivation 1895.
H4

M. a. 'Smaragd' A spreading shrub with dark green, glossy leaves that are bronze when young. The bright yellow flowers are borne in large clusters. In cultivation 1979.
H4

Mahonia fremontii

M. fremontii A very beautiful small to medium-sized shrub for a well-drained site in full sun. The blue-green pinnate leaves are composed of small, bloomy, crisped and spiny leaflets. Small clusters of yellow flowers in late spring and early summer are followed by inflated, dry, yellowish or red berries. SW United States.
H4

M. japonica This beautiful medium-sized species is deservedly one of the most popular and ornamental of all evergreen shrubs. It has magnificent deep green leaves made

up of 7–19 leaflets and terminal clusters of long, pendulous racemes of fragrant, lemon-yellow flowers from mid-winter to early spring. China.
H4 ♛ 1993

Mahonia japonica

M. j. 'Bealei' This form differs mainly in having shorter, stiffer, more or less erect racemes and broad-based, often overlapping leaflets. Confusion sometimes exists between this and the typical form, and some authorities place it in a species of its own (*M. bealei*) but it is in fact much more rare in cultivation. W China. Introduced c1849 by Robert Fortune.
H4

Mahonia lomariifolia

M. lomariifolia An imposing species but only hardy enough for milder areas with adequate protection. It is a large shrub with stout erect branches that are closely set with long leaves made up of 15–19 pairs of rigid, narrow leaflets. The rich yellow flowers are

borne during winter in dense clusters of erect racemes, with each being 15–25cm (6–10in) long and carrying as many as 250 small flowers on each blossom. W China, Burma. Introduced 1931.
H3 ♛ 1993

M. × *media* (*M. japonica* × *M. lomariifolia*) This cross is represented in gardens by several named clones. They are magnificent shrubs with yellow flowers from late autumn to mid-winter that are usually slightly fragrant. The following are recommended.
H4

Mahonia × media 'Buckland'

M. × *m.* **'Buckland'** A handsome medium-sized shrub with leaves like those of *M. japonica*, tinted in autumn, and long, spreading racemes of flowers.
H4 ♛ 1993

M. × *m.* **'Charity'** A superb, medium-sized to large, upright, stately shrub with leaves 50–60cm (20–24in) long, bearing two ranks of long, spiny leaflets. The

Mahonia × media 'Lionel Fortescue'

slightly fragrant deep yellow flowers are in long, spreading and ascending racemes that are in large terminal clusters in autumn and early winter.
H4 ♛ 1993

M. × *m.* **'Lionel Fortescue'** A medium-sized shrub with large numbers of upright racemes of bright yellow, fragrant flowers.
H4 ♛ 1993

M. × *m.* **'Underway'** A relatively compact medium-sized shrub with 17–21 leaflets. The bright yellow flowers are in long, upright racemes.
H4 ♛ 1993

Mahonia × media 'Winter Sun'

M. × *m.* **'Winter Sun'** A medium-sized shrub bearing erect racemes densely packed with fragrant yellow flowers.
H4 ♛ 1993

M. nervosa A relatively dwarf, suckering species with lustrous leaves that often turn red in winter. The yellow flowers are borne in racemes 15–20cm (6–8in) long in late spring and the berries are blackish blue. It is not the best of mahonias on chalk. W North America. Introduced 1822.
H4

M. pinnata (HORT.) See *M.* × *wagneri* 'Pinnacle'.

M. repens **'Rotundifolia'** A small, distinctive shrub with oval or rounded, sea-green, spineless leaves and large plumes of rich yellow flowers in late spring, followed by bloomy, black berries. It is probably a hybrid. In cultivation 1875.
H4

M. trifoliolata **var.** *glauca* An attractive medium-sized shrub for a well-drained,

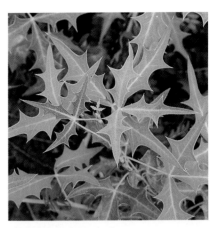
Mahonia trifoliolata var. glauca

sunny position against a warm wall, where it will grow to 4–5m (12–15ft). The leaves have three spiny, conspicuously veined, bloomy leaflets. The clusters of yellow flowers, appearing in spring, are followed by berries resembling redcurrants. SW United States. Introduced 1839.
H3–4

Mahonia × wagneri 'Pinnacle'

M. × *wagneri* **'Pinnacle'** A vigorous, upright, small to medium-sized shrub with bright green leaves that are bronze when young, and showy clusters of bright red flowers in late spring. It is a selection from plants previously grown as *M. pinnata*, the true plant of which is rare in cultivation.
H4 ♛ 1993

M. × *w.* **'Undulata'** A small to medium-sized shrub, taller than *M. aquifolium*, with lustrous, dark green leaves and undulate margins to the leaflets. The deep yellow flowers are borne in spring.
H4 ♛ 1993

MALUS

Rosaceae Flowering crab apple

Malus 'Eleyi'

THE GENUS *Malus* includes the orchard apple, of which there are said to be about 1000 varieties. Certainly there are over 500 known dessert, cooking and cider apple varieties in cultivation, from which the genus derives great economic importance. However, from a gardener's point of view it is the crab apples that come to the fore, as they are among the very best of all small trees, providing a wealth of late spring flowering to rival that of the Japanese cherries and a variety of conspicuous fruits which, while often edible only in the strictest sense, are highly attractive.

Flowering and fruiting are not the only talents of crab apples. Many of them are gloriously fragrant when in flower, and this applies right across the colour range of white through shades of rose-pink to deep burgundy red. Others, notably *M. tschonoskii* and *M. transitoria*, are among the best small trees for autumn colour, and for that alone deserve considerably more recognition than is usually given to them.

Some crabs are dual purpose in so far as their fruits can be used to make jelly, which has a natural flavour that does not cloy. Of these, *M.* 'John Downie' is probably the most familiar, but others outstanding for culinary use include *M.* 'Crittenden', 'Dartmouth' and 'Golden Hornet'.

M. 'Crittenden' is an example of a crab apple with fruit lasting throughout autumn and well into winter. Trees grown for their ornamental fruit are always the more welcome if their fruit remains on them for a long time, and this can be a major factor in choosing trees – especially for smaller gardens, in which each one has to justify its presence. Other varieties that are long-fruiting include *M.* 'Almey', 'Golden Hornet', 'Red Jade', 'Red Sentinel', 'Rudolph' and 'Wintergold'.

CARE AND CULTIVATION

Crab apples also very easy to accommodate. There are few gardens that do not have room for a small one such as the weeping *M.* 'Red Jade' or the arching *M. floribunda*, and any reasonably fertile, decently drained soil will suit them. In fact, you should avoid giving them too rich a soil, as they are then likely to produce growth at the expense of flowering. They enjoy sunny positions, but will flower and fruit well if they are in the dappled shade of other trees for part of the day.

Pruning is a matter merely of removing dead and diseased wood or any branches that are crossing or damaged, and this should be done in winter. In general, although crab apples may suffer from apple diseases such as canker and scab, they are trouble-free, long-lived and unfailingly beautiful trees to have in the garden.

M. **'American Beauty'** A vigorous small to medium-sized tree with bronze-red leaves that become bronze-green. It has double, deep red flowers and few fruits. It is resistant to scab. In cultivation 1978. H4

M. × *atrosanguinea* A small, mushroom-shaped tree with glossy green leaves. The flowers are crimson in bud and open to rose, and the small fruits are yellow with a red cheek. It is similar to *M. floribunda* but has darker flowers. In cultivation 1898. H4

M. **baccata var. mandshurica** An extremely hardy, round-headed, medium-sized tree with fragrant white flowers in mid- to late spring. The small, berry-like fruits are red or yellow. NE Asia. Introduced 1824. H4

M. **'Butterball'** A small, spreading tree with slightly drooping branches and pink-budded flowers that open blush-white. The fruits are yellow with an orange flush, and about 2.5cm (1in) across. It is probably closely related to 'Golden Hornet'. In cultivation 1961. H4

M. **coronaria 'Charlottae'** An excellent small tree with large, lobed leaves that colour richly in the autumn. The large, fragrant flowers, semi-double, shell-pink and violet-scented, are produced towards the end of spring and into early summer. After a hot summer it can fruit profusely. H4

M. **'Crittenden'** A small, compact tree with attractive pale pink flowers. It has particularly heavy crops of bright scarlet fruits that persist throughout autumn and winter. H4

M. **'Dartmouth'** An attractive small tree with abundant white flowers and equally plentiful reddish purple, bloomy fruits. Raised before 1883. H4

M. **'Echtermeyer'** A graceful, low and wide-spreading tree with elegant weeping branches clothed in purplish or bronze-green leaves. The flowers are rose-crimson, deeper in colour in bud, and are followed in autumn by reddish purple fruits. Unfortunately it is prone to mildew. See *M.* 'Royal

Malus 'American Beauty'

Malus baccata var. mandshurica

Malus 'Butterball'

Malus 'Crittenden'

Malus 'Dartmouth'

Fountain'. In cultivation 1914.
H4

M. 'Eleyi' A small tree with deep rosy crimson flowers, dark purplish shoots and leaves, crimson flowers and very decorative, purplish red fruits in autumn. It is similar to the newer 'Profusion', but like other dark-coloured crabs is susceptible to disease.
H4

Malus 'Evereste'

M. 'Evereste' A conical small tree with dark green leaves that are sometimes slightly lobed. The flowers, 5cm (2in) across, are red in bud and later become white. The fruits are up to 2.5cm (1in) across and are orange or orange-yellow. In cultivation 1980.
H4 ♔ 1993

Malus floribunda

M. floribunda (Japanese crab) A most popular large shrub or small tree with long, arching branches. It is remarkably beautiful when the crimson buds open to white or

pale blush. The fruits are small and yellow. This is one of the earliest-flowering crabs. Japan. Introduced 1862.
H4 ♔ 1993

Malus 'Golden Hornet'

M. 'Golden Hornet' A small tree with white flowers followed by large crops of bright yellow fruits that are retained until late in the year. It is one of the best fruiting crabs for general planting. In cultivation before 1949.
H4 ♔ 1993

M. 'Hillieri' A most attractive late-flowering medium-sized shrub or sometimes a small tree. The semi-double flowers are crimson in bud and open to bright pink, wreathing the arching stems with clusters of 5–8. In cultivation before 1928.
H4

M. hupehensis A freely growing small tree with stiff, ascending branches. The fragrant flowers are soft pink in bud, opening white, and produced in great abundance in late

Malus 'John Downie'

spring and early summer. The small fruits are usually deep red. China, Japan. Introduced 1900 by Ernest Wilson.
H4 ♔ 1993

M. 'John Downie' Perhaps the best fruiting crab. The late-spring flowers are white, and the fruits are comparatively large, conical, bright orange and red, and have a refreshing flavour. It makes a small tree. Raised 1875.
H4 ♔ 1993

Malus 'Katherine'

M. 'Katherine' A small tree with a regular, densely branched, globular head. Deep pink buds open to semi-double pink flowers that are over 5cm (2in) in diameter and gradually fade to white. Even though the flowers have many petals they are still capable of setting the bright red, yellow-flushed small fruits. In cultivation c1928.
H4 ♔ 1993

M. 'Lemoinei' This fine small tree has an erect habit and relatively large, deep wine-

red flowers. Unfortunately, it is prone to bark-split. Garden origin 1922.
H4

M. 'Liset' A small, dense, rounded tree with purplish young foliage and rose-red flowers that open from deep crimson buds and are followed by glossy crimson fruits. Raised before 1935 in Holland.
H4

Malus 'Neville Copeman'

M. 'Neville Copeman' A seedling of *M.* 'Eleyi' that develops into a small tree with green leaves that are shaded with purple throughout the summer. The flowers are light purple and followed by somewhat conical, orange-red fruits.
H4 ♔ 1993

M. 'Pink Perfection' A broadly upright small tree with large, fragrant, double pink flowers opening from red buds.
H4

M. 'Prince George' A slow-growing small tree with large, fully double light pink scented flowers in early summer.
H4

M. 'Profusion' Together with 'Liset' and 'Lemoinei', this is among the crab apples with wine-coloured flowers and a tendency towards purple tinting of the leaves that are prone to apple canker and mildew. This is the best of them, bearing its wine-red flowers in great profusion in fragrant clusters of 6–7 blooms, each of which is about 4cm (1½)in across. The fruits are small and dark red, and the young leaves are coppery crimson. In cultivation 1938.
H4

M. 'Red Jade' A lovely small shrub or tree

Malus 'Red Jade'

with weeping branches and bright green young leaves. The flowers are white and pink; the persistent fruit is red and the size of cherries.
H4

M. 'Red Profusion' A small tree of open but upright habit. The flowers, borne in great profusion right across the length of the branches, are an attractive rose-red turning pink, and slightly fragrant. The hairy, slightly lobed leaves are bronze-red turning bronze-green with age; the fruits are small and glossy crimson.
H4

M. 'Red Sentinel' An excellent small fruiting tree with white flowers and large clusters of deep red fruits that remain on the branches throughout winter.
H4 ♔ 1993

Malus × *robusta* 'Red Siberian'

M. × *robusta* 'Red Siberian' An attractive small hybrid tree with masses of more or less globular cherry-like, red fruits with-

out calyces, and white or pinkish flowers.
H4 ♔ 1993

M. × *r.* 'Yellow Siberian' A form similar to 'Red Siberian' but the fruits are yellow.
H4 ♔ 1993

M. 'Royal Beauty' A small weeping tree with slender, hanging, reddish purple stems and leaves that are also reddish purple when young, becoming dark green but purplish beneath with age. The flowers are deep red-purple and the fruits are dark red. In cultivation 1980.
H4 ♔ 1993

M. 'Royalty' A small, fairly upright tree with tapered, glossy, dark purple leaves that turn red in autumn. The large, purplish crimson flowers are somewhat hidden in the foliage; the fruits are dark red. Raised 1953 in Canada.
H4

M. 'Rudolph' A small, upright tree with bronze-red leaves that change to dark bronze-green. The flowers are rose-red, deeper in bud, and almost 4cm (2in) across. The fruits are orange-yellow and remain on the tree for a long time. Raised 1954 in Canada.
H4

Malus sargentii

M. sargentii This species makes a shrub of up to 2m (6½ft) high with leaves that are often three-lobed. In spring it is smothered in pure white flowers with golden anthers, and in autumn with small, bright red, cherry-like fruits. Japan. Introduced 1892.
H4

M. 'Snowcloud' A small, upright tree with young leaves bronze-green, turning to

dark green. Pale pink buds open to long-lasting, white, semi-double to double flowers 4cm (1¹/₂in) across. The yellow fruits are sparsely borne. Raised before 1978 in the United States.
H4

Malus toringoides

M. toringoides A very beautiful, small, shrubby tree with graceful, slender, wide-spreading branches and deeply lobed leaves. The slightly fragrant creamy white flowers are borne in late spring and are followed by rounded or pear-shaped red and yellow fruits. It also has very attractive autumn tints. W China. Introduced 1904 by Ernest Wilson.
H4

M. transitoria A small tree resembling the above species but more elegant, with smaller, more narrowly lobed leaves and smaller, rounded, yellow fruits. Its autumn colour is very beautiful. NW China. Introduced 1911.
H4 ♛ 1993

M. trilobata This species makes an erect tree reaching about 13m (45ft) high. It is fairly rare and so distinct that it is sometimes listed in a separate genus (*Eriolobus*). Its deeply three-lobed leaves are maple-like and attractively red in autumn. The flowers are large and white, and the green fruits have a red flush after hot summers. Mediterranean region. In cultivation 1877.
H4

M. tschonoskii An attractive, strongly growing, erect, conical tree up to 12m (40ft) high. During the spring the leaves appear silvery, becoming grey-green in summer.

The flowers are white tinged pink and the round fruits are yellowish green, tinged with reddish purple. It is one of the best of all trees for autumn colour, with bold foliage in yellow, orange, purple and scarlet. Japan. Introduced 1897 by Siebold.
H4 ♛ 1993

Malus 'Van Eseltine'

M. 'Van Eseltine' A small, distinctively columnar tree with stiffly erect branches. The semi-double flowers, up to 5cm (2in) across, are rose-scarlet in bud and open shell-pink, clouded with white on the inner petals. The fruits are yellow. An excellent crab for a small garden. In cultivation 1930.
H4

M. 'Wintergold' A shapely, small, round-headed tree with white, pink-budded flowers and an abundance of clear yellow fruits that are borne well into winter. In cultivation 1946.
H4

M. 'Wisley' A vigorous small tree with

Malus 'Wisley'

bronze-red leaves and large, wine-red, slightly scented flowers, followed by large, purple-red fruits.
H4

Mandevilla *Apocynaceae*

A genus of about 100 evergreen and deciduous species, most of which are twining climbers. They are members of the periwinkle from tropical America.

Mandevilla × amabilis 'Alice du Pont'

M. × amabilis 'Alice du Pont' See *M. × amoena* 'Alice du Pont'.

M. × amoena 'Alice du Pont', syn. *M. × amabilis* 'Alice du Pont' A vigorous evergreen climber with glossy dark green, deeply veined leaves and racemes of large, funnel-shaped, pink flowers that deepen in colour as they age. They are borne over a long period from spring to autumn. For the conservatory.
H1 ♛ 1993

M. laxa, syn. *M. suaveolens* (Chilean jasmine) An elegant, sun-loving deciduous climber with long slender stems 3–4.5m (10–13ft) or more. The leaves are heart-shaped and slender-pointed. The fragrant white flowers, 5cm (2in) across, are borne in clusters from the leaf joints in summer. Its sweetly scented flowers are so attractive that it is well worth attempting to grow it on a sunny wall outside in mild areas; otherwise it is probably best grown in the conservatory. Bolivia, N Argentina. Introduced 1837 by H. J. Mandeville.
H2–3

M. suaveolens See *M. laxa*.

Margyricarpus *Rosaceae*

A genus of one evergreen species, related to
Acaena *and* Alchemilla.

M. pinnatus (Pearl berry) A charming,
prostrate or slightly erect, white-berrying
shrub with finely cut, deep green leaves.
The flowers are insignificant. It will grow in
any well-drained soil and is suitable for the
rock garden but should be protected from
long frosts in winter. Chilean Andes. Introduced 1829.
H3–4

Maytenus *Celastraceae*

*This is a large genus of more than 200 evergreen
trees and shrubs from tropical and sub-tropical
regions. Only one or two species are hardy in cool-
temperate gardens.*

M. boaria A large, evergreen shrub or

Maytenus boaria

small tree with slender branches and narrow, elliptic, finely toothed leaves. The
flowers are small and insignificant, but the
plant is grown for its foliage and gently
weeping habit. Any well-drained soil will
suffice. Chile. Introduced 1829.
H4

Medicago *Leguminoseae*

*A genus of more than 50 evergreen and deciduous
species, mainly of annual and perennial clover-like
plants, natives of Europe, west Asia and Africa.
They enjoy any well-drained soil in sun.*

M. arborea (Moon trefoil, tree medick) A
small, semi-evergreen shrub with clusters of
yellow pea-flowers produced continuously,
though often sparsely, from late spring to
early autumn. The seed pods resemble snail
shells. In mild areas it is excellent in maritime exposure or with the shelter of a warm
wall. Mediterranean region. Introduced
1596.
H2–3

Melaleuca *Myrtaceae*

*A genus of about 150 evergreen species, related to
and resembling* Callistemon. *They are tender
natives of Australia and South-East Asia and can
be grown out of doors only in such extremely mild
areas as the far south-west of Ireland and the west
of Scotland. In parts of the south-eastern United
States some of the very large species have actually
become serious environmental pests. Those
described here require full sun and do not tolerate
chalk soils.*

Melaleuca hypericifolia

M. gibbosa A small to medium-sized (but
usually small), wiry shrub with small,
crowded leaves and light purple flowers in
short, dense bottlebrushes at the ends of the
shoots in summer. Tasmania, Australia.
H1–2
M. hypericifolia A large, graceful shrub
(but small when grown out of doors), with
small leaves like those of a hypericum. The
flowers, borne in summer, are red. Australia. Introduced 1792.
H1–2

Melia *Meliaceae*

*A genus of three species of sun-loving, deciduous
large shrubs or small trees from Asia and
Australia, of which there is one that sometimes
succeeds in the mildest areas. It will grow in any
well-drained friable soil.*

M. azedarach (Bead tree) A large shrub or
small tree best against a warm, sheltered
wall or under glass. It has large, elegant,
doubly pinnate leaves and small, fragrant,
lilac flowers borne in loose panicles in summer. In warm countries, clusters of yellow,
bead-like fruits are produced in autumn
and remain on the plant long after the
leaves have fallen. It is commonly planted
as a street tree in the Mediterranean region
and requires sun to ripen its growth. Asia to
Australia. In cultivation in England since
the sixteenth century.
H1–2

Melianthus *Melianthaceae*

*A genus of about six species of sun-loving,
evergreen sub-shrubs from South Africa. The
following can be grown in the mildest areas but
even so may be herbaceous in the colder winters. It
will grow in any well-drained friable soil.*

M. major A particularly handsome foliage
plant with spreading, hollow stems clothed
in blue-grey, deeply toothed, pinnate leaves
up to 45cm (18in) long. It lends a striking,
sub-tropical effect wherever it is placed in
the garden. The tubular flowers are brownish crimson and borne in dense, erect terminal panicles up to 15cm (6in) long in
summer. It is hardy in the very mildest

Melianthus major

areas where it can grow to a height of 2m (6½ft) or more. It is sometimes used with great effect in sub-tropical bedding. S Africa. Introduced 1688.
H3 🏆 1993

Meliosma *Sabiaceae*

A genus of about 25 species of evergreen and deciduous trees and shrubs native to Asia and Central and South America. The following species will grow in any well-drained friable soil.

Meliosma veitchiorum

M. veitchiorum A small deciduous tree of architectural quality, remarkable for its very large, pinnate, red-stalked leaves, stout, rigid branches and prominent winter buds. The creamy white, fragrant flowers are borne in panicles 30–45cm (12–18in) long in late spring. The fruits are violet. It is extremely scarce. W and C China. Introduced 1901 by Ernest Wilson.
H4

Menziesia *Ericaceae*

A genus of about seven species from North America and eastern Asia. They are small, slow-growing, deciduous shrubs resembling Enkianthus *and need a lime-free soil and protection from late frosts. The flowers are at the ends of the shoots, similar to those of* Daboecia *but waxy.*

M. ciliicalyx A beautiful small shrub with more or less oval leaves with eyelashed edges. The nodding, pitcher-shaped flowers are borne in clusters in late spring and vary from cream to soft purple. Japan. Introduced 1915.
H4

M. c. var. purpurea A superb, slow-growing variety with slightly larger, rose-purple flowers borne slightly later.
H4

Mespilus *Rosaceae*
Medlar

A genus of one deciduous species.

Mespilus germanica

M. germanica The medlar is grown for its ornamental properties as well as its fruits, which when picked over-ripe make a delicious jelly, as long as a source of pectin such as lemon-pips is included in the boil. It is a wide-spreading small tree and makes a fine architectural specimen. The large white flowers are produced in late spring and early summer and followed by large brown fruits. Native from SE Europe to C Asia but long cultivated.
H4

Mespilus germanica 'Nottingham'

M. g. 'Nottingham' The most widely grown of the few forms of medlar selected for their fruit-bearing potential. They are less thorny than the wild trees and have considerably larger leaves.
H4

Metasequoia *Taxodiaceae*

A genus of one deciduous species, thought to have been long extinct until found in a Chinese village in 1941, until when it had been known only from fossils. It is similar in general appearance to Taxodium.

Metasequoia glyptostroboides

M. glyptostroboides (Dawn redwood) A strong, vigorous tree, conical when young, with shaggy, cinnamon-brown bark. The leaves are linear, flattened, and borne in two opposite ranks on short, deciduous branchlets so that the whole resembles a pinnate leaf. They are bright larch-green in summer and become tawny pink and old

gold in autumn. It thrives best in moist but well-drained conditions and is slower growing on chalk. It is very hardy and tolerates industrial atmospheres, but young shoots may be burnt in frost pockets where late frosts occur. It grows magnificently in North America but a half-century's experience shows that while it thrives in southern Britain it does not grow well in Scotland. China. Introduced 1947 to the Arnold Arboretum, Massachusetts; to Britain a year later. Seed sent from China during the early 1980s has produced trees which are now about 5–5.5m (15–18ft). Seedling trees from both sendings developed the buttressed trunks characteristic of the species, but buttresses are not made by trees that have been vegetatively propagated.
H4 ♔ 1993

Metasequoia glyptostroboides 'Emerald Feathers'

M. g. 'Emerald Feathers' A fine tree of regular, conical habit with lush green foliage, tinted in autumn.
H4

Metrosideros *Myrtaceae*

A genus of about 50 species of handsome evergreen trees, shrubs and aerial-rooted climbers. They are related to Callistemon *and are native to Australasia, Malaysia and southern Africa. The brilliant bottle-brush flowers are spectacular. In the British Isles the following can be grown outside only in the Scilly Isles and favoured parts of Ireland. It requires a very well-drained, hot site.*

M. excelsa The New Zealand Christmas

Metrosideros excelsa

tree is a noble and picturesque tree in the North Island, where it is known as the Pohutukawa. Its branches are smothered in summer with large, crimson, bottle-brush flowers. It can become a large tree in the right conditions. Introduced 1840.
H2

M. e. 'Variegata' The leaves of this form have broad creamy margins.
H2

Michelia *Magnoliaceae*

A genus of about 45 species of evergreen trees or shrubs closely related to Magnolia *but with the flowers borne mainly in the axils of the leaves. They are natives of tropical and sub-tropical South-East Asia and suitable only for the milder lime-free areas.*

Michelia doltsopa

M. doltsopa A magnificent, small to medium-sized, semi-evergreen tree with leathery leaves, 15–18cm (6–7in) long,

glaucous beneath. The flowers are formed in the autumn and open in spring. They are multi-petalled, white and heavily scented. It can be grown only in the mildest areas. Himalayan region. Introduced c1918 by George Forrest.
H3

Microbiota *Cupressaceae*

A genus of one evergreen species, related to Juniperus.

Microbiota decussata

M. decussata A densely branched, prostrate, very hardy shrub with wide-spreading branches bearing small, almost scale-like leaves, although awl-shaped leaves are present on some branches. They are pale green in summer, turning bronze-red or purple in winter. It has very small, berry-like fruits in autumn. It is an excellent conifer for the rock garden. E Siberia. Found 1921.
H4 ♔ 1993

Microcachrys *Podocarpaceae*

A genus of one evergreen species, related to Podocarpus.

M. tetragona A splendid, quite hardy, dwarf bush with snake-like, four-angled, arching branches clad with minute, scale-like leaves arranged in four ranks. The fruits are egg-shaped, bright red, fleshy and translucent. In the wild it is rare, restricted to the summits of two mountains in Tasmania. Introduced 1857.
H3–4

Mimulus *Scrophulariaceae*

A large genus of about 150 species, mainly annuals and herbaceous perennials, but including one or two woody evergreen plants that can be grown in favoured, sunny positions. They are mostly from North America.

M. aurantiacus (Shrubby musk) A pretty, sticky-stemmed, small shrub for full sun in mild places, especially near the sea, growing to about 1.2m (4ft) high. The flowers are orange, or may be yellow shot with salmon, and are borne throughout summer and autumn. California, Oregon. Introduced late eighteenth century.
H2–3 ♀ 1993
M. a. var. puniceus A form differing mainly in its smaller, brick-red or orange-red flowers. California.
H2–3

Mitraria *Gesneriaceae*

A genus of one evergreen species.

Mitraria coccinea

M. coccinea A low, spreading or scrambling shrub with small, oval and toothed glossy leaves and comparatively large, bright orange-scarlet, tubular flowers borne singly in the leaf axils from late spring throughout the summer. It is a charming plant for a partially shaded, sheltered position in a mild area but unsuitable for shallow soils over chalk. Given a suitable host it will climb for a short distance. Chile. Introduced 1846 by William Lobb.
H3

Moltkia *Boraginaceae*

A genus of six species of herbaceous perennials and evergreen and deciduous sub-shrubs native to southern Europe and south-west Asia. They will grow in any fertile well-drained soil in full sun.

M. × intermedia A dwarf evergreen sub-shrub, domed in habit and reaching 30 × 50cm (12 × 20in). The leaves are dark green and very narrow; the bright blue, open funnel-shaped flowers are profusely borne on spikes in summer.
H4 ♀ 1993
M. petraea A deciduous sub-shrub that forms a neat dwarf bush up to 45cm (18in) high. The tubular flowers are pink in bud, opening violet-blue in midsummer. Balkan peninsula. Introduced c1840.
H4

Morus *Moraceae*
Mulberry

A genus of seven species of deciduous trees and shrubs from the Americas, Africa and Asia, generally forming small, picturesque trees. They will grow in any well-drained soil but respond well to richer soils, manuring and mulching. They do well by the sea and in towns. You should take special care when planting them as their fleshy roots are brittle.

M. alba (White mulberry) A small to medium-sized rugged tree with heart- or lance-shaped leaves, often up to 15cm (6in) wide, which are the traditional food of silkworms. The whitish fruits change to reddish

Morus alba 'Pendula'

pink or nearly black in some forms and are sweetly edible. C Asia to China. Probably in England by 1596.
H4
M. a 'Pendula' A striking small weeping tree with closely packed, perpendicular branches. Ornamental when in full fruit.
H4

Morus nigra

M. nigra (Black mulberry) A small, very long-lived, architectural tree with a wide-spreading head, becoming interestingly gnarled as it ages. The leaves are heart-shaped and the fruits are a dark, almost black red and have a pleasant taste. W Asia. In cultivation in Britain for many centuries.
H4 ♀ 1993

Muehlenbeckia *Polygonaceae*

A genus of about 15 species of creeping or climbing deciduous plants from Australasia and South America. They are of little beauty in flower but are interesting covering plants. They grow in any soil in sun or semi-shade.

M. axillaris A slow-growing, prostrate species forming dense carpets of intertwining, thread-like stems with small, almost round leaves barely 5mm (¼in) long. It has tiny, yellow-green flowers in summer and white fruits. Useful as a ground cover on rock gardens and screes. New Zealand, Australia, Tasmania.
H4
M. complexa A twining species with slender, dark, interlacing stems occasionally up to 6m (18ft) or more, forming dense, tan-

gled curtains or carpets. The leaves are 3–20mm (¹⁄₈–³⁄₄in) long and vary from round to fiddle-shaped. The minute greenish flowers in autumn are followed in female plants by small, white, fleshy fruits. New Zealand. Introduced 1842.
H3

Mutisia *Compositae*
Climbing gazania

A genus of about 60 species of erect or climbing South American evergreens. They climb by means of leaf tendrils and can be grown on a wall, pergola or arch, but are perhaps best planted near a small bushy tree so that their stems can grow into and be supported by it. They need a warm, sunny position in a rich but well-drained soil. The colourful gazania-like flowerheads are produced singly on long stalks.

M. decurrens A rare climbing species up to 3m (9ft) with narrow, oblong, stalkless leaves 7.5–13cm (3–5in) long. The daisy-like flowers are 10–13cm (4–5in) wide with brilliant orange or vermilion petals, borne continuously throughout the summer. It is a superb species but difficult to establish and succeeds best in a warm, sheltered position such as a partially shaded, west-facing wall and in a rich, friable, sandy loam. Chile. Introduced 1859.
H3

M. ilicifolia A vigorous species with stems 3–5m (9–15ft) long. The stalkless leaves are strongly toothed, dark green above and pale woolly beneath. The lilac-pink flowers are 5–7.5cm (2–3in) wide and are borne in summer and early autumn. Chile. Introduced 1832.
H3

M. oligodon A very beautiful, suckering species with straggling stems that are not too difficult to establish if grown into a sparsely branched shrub but barely reach 1.5m (4¹⁄₂ft). The leaves are coarsely toothed and heart-shaped at the base, and the flowers, which are 5–7.5cm (2–3in) across, have salmon-pink petals and appear throughout the summer and intermittently into autumn. It needs a sunny site and can look quite dead in winter. Chile. Introduced 1927.
H3

Myrica *Myricaceae*

A genus of about 50 species of interesting aromatic evergreen and deciduous shrubs widely distributed throughout the world.

Myrica gale

M. gale (Bog myrtle, sweet gale) A small, dense, deciduous shrub with warm golden-brown male and female catkins on separate plants in mid- to late spring. The whole plant is strongly aromatic. It can be grown in wet, acid, boggy places where few other plants can exist and in the coldest environments. Weak growth should be cut away at ground level in spring. Europe (including Britain and Ireland), NE Asia, North America. In cultivation 1750.
H4

Myrsine *Myrsinaceae*

A genus of five species of evergreen trees and shrubs which, having fairly inconspicuous flowers, are grown for their foliage and decorative fruit and are primarily of botanical interest. They are moderately lime tolerant but not suitable for shallow, chalky soil. They require a sunny position.

M. africana A small shrub with aromatic, myrtle-like, evergreen leaves, which bears axillary clusters of tiny, reddish brown flowers in late spring after which the female plants produce blue-black, pea-like berries. This a very slow-growing plant. Azores, Himalayas, Far East and parts of Africa. Introduced 1691.
H3

Myrteola

M. nummularia See *Myrtus nummularia*.

Myrtus *Myrtaceae*
Myrtle

An easily cultivated and effective group of evergreen shrubs or trees which are currently undergoing review, so that authorities recognize anything between two and six or more species. They are mainly for mild climates and succeed best in full sun on any well-drained soil, including chalk, although one or two perform perfectly well in part shade. They are excellent in exposed, coastal places.

Myrtus communis

Myrtus communis 'Variegata'

M. bullata, syn. *Lophomyrtus bullata* A large bush or small tree with distinct, round, leathery, coppery green or reddish brown, puckered leaves. The late-summer white flowers are followed by blackish red berries. Only suitable for the mildest areas. New

Zealand. In cultivation 1854.

H2–3

M. chequen, syn. *Luma chequen* A small, densely leafy tree with white flowers in summer and autumn. The leaves are aromatic, bright green and undulate. Chile. Introduced 1847 by William Lobb.

H3

M. communis (Common myrtle) Although on the tender side, this species tends to be hardier near the sea. It is an aromatic, densely leafy shrub which will reach 3–4m (10–12ft) against a sunny wall. The white flowers are borne profusely in mid- to late summer and are followed by purple-black berries. It is naturalized throughout the Mediterranean region and has been cultivated in England since the 16th century.

H3 ♛ 1993

***M. c.* 'Flore Pleno'** An uncommon form with double flowers.

H3

***M. c.* 'Jenny Reitenbach'** See *M. c.* subsp. *tarentina*.

M. c.* subsp.** ***tarentina, syn. *M. c.* 'Jenny Reitenbach' A very pretty, compact small to medium-sized shrub with small, narrow leaves and white berries. The pink-tinged flowers are profusely borne in autumn. Mediterranean.

H3 ♛ 1993

***M. c.* 'Variegata'** The leaves of this medium-sized shrub are mainly grey-green, narrowly margined with cream. A variegated form of *M. c.* subsp. *tarentina* is also in cultivation.

H3

M. luma, syn. *Luma apiculata* A lovely species reaching the size of a small tree in mild places but often with multiple trunks. The cinnamon-coloured outer bark of even quite young trees peels off in patches, exposing the equally beautiful, cream-coloured inner surface. The oval, sharply pointed leaves are dark green, and the delicate white flowers bedeck the branches in late summer and autumn. The red and black fruits, produced only after a warm

summer and autumn, are edible and sweet. It may self-sow abundantly in favoured spots, becoming naturalized as it does so. Chile. Introduced 1843.

H3 ♛ 1993

***M. l.* 'Glanleam Gold'** The leaves of this large shrub or small tree have a bright creamy yellow margin and are pink-tinged when young.

H3

M. nummularia, syn. *Myrteola nummularia* This tiny, prostrate shrublet, the hardiest myrtle, has wiry, reddish stems and neat, rounded leaves borne in two opposite ranks. The white flowers are borne at the ends of the stems in late spring or early summer and are followed by pink berries. Argentina, Chile, Falklands. Introduced before 1927.

H4

M. ugni, syn. *Ugni molinae* (Chilean guava) A slow-growing, small to medium-sized, leathery leaved, rather stiffly erect shrub, with nodding, waxy, pink bell-shaped flowers in late summer and deliciously edible, aromatic, mahogany berries. Chile. Introduced 1844 by William Lobb.

H3

N

Nandina *Berberidaceae*

A genus of just one deciduous species that looks a little like bamboo but is related to Berberis. *It is grown for its foliage and flowers.*

Myrtus luma

Nandina domestica

N. domestica (Sacred bamboo) A decorative, bamboo-like, medium-sized shrub with long, erect, unbranched stems. The large, compound, green leaves are attractively tinged with purplish red in spring and autumn. The small white flowers are borne in large terminal clusters during summer. Red berries are produced only after very hot summers. It is hardy in all but the coldest districts. It should be given a sheltered position in full sun in any well-drained soil. C China, Japan. Introduced 1804.
H3–4

Nandina domestica 'Firepower'

N. d. **'Firepower'** A small shrub similar to 'Nana Purpurea' but with yellow-green foliage in summer that turns brilliant orange-red in winter.
H3–4

Nandina domestica 'Nana Purpurea'

N. d. **'Nana Purpurea'** A small shrub of more compact habit than the species and with simpler leaves and broader leaflets.

The young foliage is reddish purple throughout the season.
H3–4

N. d. **'Richmond'** A vigorous medium-sized form with an abundance of red fruits during winter.
H3–4

Neillia *Rosaceae*

A genus of about 10 species of deciduous shrubs related to Spiraea. *They are very easily grown in all but the driest soils.*

Neillia thibetica

N. thibetica A most attractive, medium-sized shrub with erect, downy stems, slenderly pointed, often three-lobed leaves, and slender terminal clusters of tubular pink flowers in late spring and early summer. After flowering, cut all the old flowering stems to ground level in order to promote new young growth. W China. Introduced 1904 by Ernest Wilson.
H4

Nerium *Apocynaceae*

A genus of two species of tender, ornamental, sun-loving evergreen shrubs that tolerate lime but not shallow, chalky soils.

N. oleander The oleander is a well-known, superb medium-sized shrub with erect branches, long, lance-shaped leaves and flowers like large periwinkles. There are now many named forms chosen for colours from white to scarlet, single to double or semi-double flowers; a few have variegated

Nerium oleander

leaves. Flowering is from early summer to mid-autumn. It can be overwintered out of doors in the British Isles but only in the very mildest places, and then even though it forms flower buds the blooms do not develop. It is much better grown in a tub as a conservatory plant and put outside in full sun during the summer months. CAUTION: toxic if eaten. Mediterranean region, SW Asia. Introduced 1596.
H2

Nothofagus *Fagaceae*
Southern beech

A genus of about 20 species of ornamental, fast-growing evergreen and deciduous trees or large shrubs from South America and Australasia, and valued for their shape and their foliage. They are related to Fagus *but normally have small leaves closely spaced along the branchlets. They vary in hardiness and many are poor resisters of wind. They do not survive on chalk soils.*

Nothofagus antarctica

Nothofagus dombeyi

small to medium-sized evergreen tree with dark green and doubly toothed roundish leaves only 12mm (½in) long. The bark of the young wood is like that of a cherry. New Zealand.
H3

N. nervosa, syn. *N. procera* A fast-growing large deciduous tree with large, prominently veined leaves around 4–10cm (1½ – 4in) long, rather like those of a hornbeam. It is usually richly coloured in autumn. Chile, Argentina. Introduced 1913.
H4

N. obliqua (Roblé beech) A large, elegant, very fast-growing deciduous tree, making a handsome specimen in a few years. Its leaves are broad, 5–7.5cm (2–3in) long, and irregularly toothed. Chile, Argentina. Introduced 1902.
H4

N. procera See *N. nervosa*.

N. solanderi var. cliffortioides (Mountain beech) An elegant, small to medium-

Nothofagus solanderi var. cliffortioides

N. antarctica (Antarctic beech) An elegant, fast-growing, medium-sized deciduous tree broadly conical in shape. The small, rounded and heart-shaped leaves are irregularly toothed, dark green and glossy, and turn yellow in autumn. The trunk and main branches are often curiously twisted. Chile. Introduced 1830.
H4

Nothofagus betuloides

N. betuloides A medium-sized to large densely leafy evergreen tree, columnar when young. The shining dark green leaves are roundish, usually less than 2.5cm (1in) long, and closely arranged on the branchlets. Chile, Argentina. Introduced 1830.
H3

N. dombeyi A medium-sized to large, vigorous evergreen tree. The leaves are 2.5–4cm (1–1½in) long, doubly toothed and dark, shining green. It is fairly hardy but may lose its leaves in cold winters. Chile, Argentina. Introduced 1916.
H3

N. fusca (Red beech) This species is rather tender when young but develops into a beautiful, reasonably hardy, small to medium-sized evergreen tree. The rounded or oval coarsely toothed leaves, 2.5–4cm (1–1½in) long, often turn copper in autumn. The bark on old trees becomes flaky. New Zealand.
H3

N. menziesii (Silver beech) A graceful

sized, fast-growing evergreen tree with very small leaves that have curled edges and a raised tip. New Zealand.
H3

Notospartium *Leguminosae*

A genus of three species of leafless broom-like shrubs from New Zealand. They enjoy full sun in any well-drained soil and are only injured in the coldest winters.

N. carmichaeliae (Pink broom) A charming, medium-sized, graceful shrub with arching, leafless stems wreathed in lilac-pink pea flowers in the middle of summer. This is a scarce plant.
H3–4

Nyssa *Nyssaceae*

A genus of about five species of deciduous trees, natives of east North America and east Asia, noted for their rich autumn colours. They need moist, lime-free soil and are best planted when small, as they resent disturbance.

Nyssa sinensis

N. sinensis A rare, magnificent large shrub or small tree with fairly narrow leaves up to 15cm (6in) long. The young growths are red throughout the growing season and in autumn the leaves change to many shades of red. China. In cultivation 1902.
H4 ♔ 1993
N. sylvatica (Tupelo) A handsome, slow-growing, medium-sized to large tree with a broadly columnar outline. The leaves are variable in shape but more or less oval,

Nyssa sylvatica

pointed, up to 15cm (6in) long, dark glossy green, occasionally dull green above. The foliage of this dense-headed tree turns rich scarlet, orange and yellow in autumn. S Canada to S Mexico. Introduced 1750.
H4 ♔ 1993
N. s. 'Jermyns Flame' A form bearing relatively large leaves with striking autumn colours of red, yellow and orange. Selected 1985 by John Hillier from plants in the Hillier Gardens and Arboretum.
H4

O

Oemleria *Rosaceae*

A genus of only one deciduous species, related to Prunus but quite different. It produces suckers and growth can be restricted if desired by removing these and cutting back old shoots in late winter.

O. cerasiformis (Oso berry) A suckering shrub, making a thicket of erect stems 2–2.5m (6–8ft) or so high, with hanging racemes of fragrant, white, currant-like flowers in late winter and early spring. The fruits are plum-like, brown at first and then purple when ripe; as male and female flowers are borne on separate plants, the fruits can only be obtained if plants of both sexes are grown. The leaves are sea-green and emerge early, with the flowers. It grows in all kinds of fertile soil but may suffer from chlorosis in very poor, shallow chalk soils. California. Introduced 1848.
H4

Olea *Oleaceae*
Olive

A genus of about 20 species of tender evergreen trees and shrubs with opposite, leathery leaves. They are natives of warm regions of the Old World and one or two species survive in very mild gardens in the British Isles especially if they are grown in the protection of a south or west-facing wall in full sun. They also prefer fertile and deep, well-drained soil.

Olea europaea

O. europaea A large shrub or small tree with grey-green leaves, bloomy beneath, and clusters of small, fragrant, white flowers in late summer. Culinary olives and good olive oils are obtained from named cultivars but these are not to be expected in specimens growing in the open in cool-temperate gardens. Mediterranean region.
H2

Olearia *Compositae*
Daisy bush

A genus of about 130 species of attractive, evergreen, easily grown, wind-resisting and sun-loving shrubs. Several are less than fully hardy but in general they are first-class in maritime areas. They all have daisy-like flowerheads and their average height range is 1.2–2.5m (4–8ft). Straggly specimens can be hard pruned in mid-spring; any tidying-up pruning should be done after flowering. Olearias succeed in any well-drained soil and are highly recommended for chalky ones. An individual daisy 'flower' is technically a flower head, and the flowerheads are usually in clusters called corymbs.

Olearia avicennifolia 'White Confusion'

O. avicennifolia 'White Confusion' A medium-sized to large shrub with pointed leaves that are whitish or buff underneath and slightly wavy. The wide corymbs of sweetly scented white flowerheads are borne in great numbers in summer. It makes a fine, dense hedge.
H3–4

O. chathamica A beautiful small shrub up to 1.2m (4ft), similar to 'Henry Travers' but with broader green leaves. The flowerheads, up to 5cm (2in) across, are solitary and borne on long stalks. They are pale violet with purple centres and appear in early summer. Chatham Isles. Introduced 1910.
H3

Olearia × haastii

O. × haastii A rounded, medium-sized bush with small leaves that are white-felted beneath. It becomes smothered with fragrant white flowerheads in mid- to late summer. It is hardy in all but the coldest places, tolerant of urban pollution, and a

well-proven hedging plant. New Zealand. Introduced 1858.
H3–4

O. 'Henry Travers', syn. *O. semidentata* (HORT.) This is one of the loveliest of all shrubs for the more favoured coastal gardens. It is a medium-sized shrub with slender, grey-green leaves that are silvery beneath. The large, pendent, aster-like flowerheads are lilac with purple centres and appear in early summer. Introduced 1908 to Ireland.
H3 ♛ 1993

Olearia ilicifolia

O. ilicifolia A dense, medium-sized shrub with thick, leathery, grey-green leaves that are sharply toothed and whitish-felted beneath. The fragrant white flowerheads are borne in early summer and the whole plant has a musky aroma. It is one of the best of the hardier species. New Zealand.
H3–4

O. lacunosa A medium-sized to large but slow-growing shrub with stout, white-woolly stems. The leaves are rigid, long and narrow, up to 17cm (7in) long by 1cm (½in) across, and are covered with loose white flock on the upper surfaces at first, before becoming dark green with a pale midrib. The undersurfaces are persistently silver. The white flowerheads are small and rarely produced in gardens. New Zealand.
H3

O. macrodonta (New Zealand holly) A strong-growing and handsome shrub reaching 3m (10ft) or more, with sage-green, holly-like leaves 6–9cm (2½– 3½in) long and silvery white beneath. The fragrant

Olearia macrodonta

white flowerheads are borne in broad corymbs in early summer. It is one of the best screening or hedging plants for exposed coastal gardens. The whole plant has a slight musky aroma. New Zealand.
H3 ♛ 1993

O. m. 'Major' A form with larger leaves and flower clusters.
H3

O. × mollis A small, rounded, compact shrub with wavy-edged, silvery grey, slightly toothed leaves up to 4cm (1½in) long. White flowerheads are borne in large corymbs in late spring. It is one of the hardiest olearias.
H3–4

Olearia nummulariifolia

O. nummulariifolia One of the more hardy species, this is a medium-sized, stiffly branching, unusual-looking shrub, with small, thick, yellow-green leaves crowding the stems. The small, fragrant white flowerheads are borne in the angles of the leaves in midsummer. Some plants grown under this name are hybrids. New Zealand. H3-4

O. × *oleifolia* **'Waikariensis'** A small, attractive shrub with lance-shaped leaves measuring about 5 × 1.5cm (2 × ½in). They are glossy green above and white beneath with a buff midrib. The white flowers are in clusters in the angles of the leaves in mid- to late summer. New Zealand. Introduced early 1930s. H4

O. paniculata A large shrub or small tree with distinctive, bright olive-green, wavy leaves, reminiscent of *Pittosporum tenuifolium*. Although the flowerheads are not very conspicuous, they are borne in late autumn and early winter and are fragrant. In mild maritime areas it is used as a hedge. New Zealand. Introduced 1816. H3

O. phlogopappa **Splendens group** These are particularly lovely forms of the

Olearia paniculata

Olearia phlogopappa Splendens group

variable Tasmanian daisy bush. They are popular medium-sized shrubs with aromatic, toothed leaves thickly crowding the stems and flowerheads of blue, lavender or rose 2cm (1in) across in late spring. Introduced 1930. H2-3

O. ramulosa A small, twiggy shrub with slender, arching stems and small, linear leaves. The small white flowerheads crowd the stems in late summer. Tasmania, S Australia. In cultivation 1872. H3

O. × *scilloniensis* A compact, rounded, grey-leaved shrub sometimes reaching 2.5m (8ft) but usually considerably smaller. It is an exceedingly free-flowering hybrid, literally covering itself with froths of white bloom in late spring. Garden origin 1910 at Tresco Abbey, Isles of Scilly. H3 ♛ 1993

O. semidentata See *O.* 'Henry Travers'.

Olearia solanderi

O. solanderi A dense, heath-like shrub of medium size that gives a yellowish effect, rather like *Cassinia fulvida*. Its leaves are needle-like, 6mm (¼in) long and in clusters. The small, white, sweetly scented flowerheads are borne in late summer. Unless in a mild place, it needs the protection of a wall. New Zealand. H3

O. stellulata A variable, rather lax, small to medium-sized shrub a little like *O. phlogopappa* but taller, longer-leaved, and not as compact. The white flowerheads are borne in panicles in late spring. Tasmania. H3

Olearia stellulata

O. traversii This is considered to be one of the best and fastest growing evergreens for windbreaks in mild maritime areas, growing to 6m (20ft) even in exposed positions on sandy soils. The shoots are four-angled and white-felted. The leaves are broad, leathery and polished green above, silvery white beneath. The flowerheads, produced in summer, are insignificant. Chatham Isles. Introduced 1887. H3

O. virgata **var.** *lineata* A large, very graceful, loose shrub with slender, pendulous branches and narrow leaves. The summer flowers are insignificant. New Zealand. H4

O. viscosa A small to medium-sized shrub up to 2m (6½ft) with sticky young shoots and shiny green, lance-shaped leaves that are silvery white beneath. It has broad corymbs of attractive white flowerheads in mid- and late summer. A very free-flowering form introduced by Sir Harold Hillier

Olearia 'Zennorensis'

in 1977 is proving particularly hardy. Tasmania, SE Australia.

H3

O. 'Zennorensis' A form of *O. × mollis*, this is a striking foliage plant up to 2m (6½ft) with narrow, pointed, sharply toothed leaves about 10cm (4in) long and 12mm (½in) wide, dark olive green above and white beneath. The young stems and leaf stalks are heavily coated with pale brown wool. A first-class shrub for the less cold garden, especially in a maritime exposure, but do not expect flowers. Garden origin at Zennor, Cornwall.

H3 ♔ 1993

Ononis *Leguminoseae*

A genus of about 75 species of deciduous shrubs and herbaceous plants that are often spiny. They have a wide distribution from Europe to North Africa and western Asia, and are good dwarf plants for the border or rock garden. They all have leaves with three leaflets and pea-shaped flowers. They need full sun, and do well on any well-drained soil including shallow ones over chalk.

Ononis fruticosa

O. fruticosa A splendid small shrub forming a compact mound up to 1m (3ft) high, long grown for its display of bright rose-pink flowers in small clusters throughout summer. W Mediterranean region. In cultivation 1680.

H4

Orixa *Rutaceae*

A genus of one deciduous species.

O. japonica A pungently aromatic, dioecious, medium-sized shrub with bright green leaves that change to palest lemon or white in autumn, contrasting with the more prevalent reds and purples. It thrives in any well-drained soil. Japan, China, Korea. Introduced 1870.

H4

Osmanthus *Oleaceae*

A genus of about 14 species of evergreen shrubs and trees, natives of the United States, Asia and the Pacific Islands. The following are attractive, often very beautiful, frequently holly-like shrubs that do well in almost all soils. Their flowers are small, white or cream and usually have a sweet fragrance that carries for a considerable distance. They will grow in sun or semi-shade and all the pruning that is necessary is to remove growths that may have been damaged in winter or have become straggling or leggy.

O. armatus A large, handsome shrub of dense habit with thick, rigid leaves up to 15cm (6in) long, armed with stout, often hooked, spiny teeth. It is autumn-flowering and its white blooms are sweetly scented. W China. Introduced 1902 by Ernest Wilson.

H4

Osmanthus × burkwoodii

O. × burkwoodii This is a first-class, hardy, compact shrub that slowly grows to about 2.5–3m (8–10ft). Its oval leaves are 2.5–5cm (1–2in) long, dark shining green, leathery and toothed and contrast nicely with the highly fragrant white flowers which are profusely borne in mid-spring.

Osmanthus decorus

Raised 1930 by Burkwood and Skipwith.

H4 ♔ 1993

O. decorus, syn. *Phillyrea decora* A very distinct dome-shaped bush up to 3m (10ft), usually wider than high, with comparatively large, glossy green, leathery leaves. The clusters of small, fragrant, white flowers are borne freely in spring and followed by purplish black fruits like miniature plums. W Asia. Introduced 1866.

H4

Osmanthus delavayi

O. delavayi One of the most beautiful of the smaller evergreen shrubs. It has small leaves and slowly grows to 2m (6½ft) high and more in width. Its fragrant, white, jasmine-like flowers are borne very freely in mid-spring. China. Introduced 1890 by the Abbé Delavay.

H4 ♔ 1993

O. × fortunei A large, vigorous shrub of dense habit with large, broad, polished dark green leaves with prominently veined upper

Osmanthus × fortunei

sides and a spiny edge so that they look much like those of a holly. On mature plants they often become spineless. The autumn-borne flowers are white and sweetly scented. Japan. Introduced 1862 by Robert Fortune.
H4

O. heterophyllus A fairly slow-growing, holly-like shrub, occasionally a small tree, with entire or coarsely spine-toothed leaves of a dark, shining green. The white flowers appear in autumn and are sweetly scented. It can be distinguished from a holly by its leaves, which are opposite rather than alternately deployed. It makes a fine hedge. The following are recommended. Japan. Introduced 1856.
H4

Osmanthus heterophyllus 'Aureomarginatus'

***O. h.* 'Aureomarginatus'** A medium-sized shrub of which the leaves are margined with deep yellow. In cultivation 1877.
H4

***O. h.* 'Goshiki'** A striking medium-sized form in which the leaves are mottled with yellow and are tinged with bronze when young. The name means 'five-coloured'.
H4

Osmanthus heterophyllus 'Gulftide'

***O. h.* 'Gulftide'** A dense medium-sized bush with leaves somewhat lobed or twisted

Osmanthus heterophyllus 'Purpureus'

Osmanthus heterophyllus 'Variegatus'

and strongly spiny. It is a remarkable and worthwhile shrub.
H4 ♛ 1993

***O. h.* 'Purpureus'** The growths of this form are at first purple, later turning green with a purple tinge. Raised 1860 at Kew.
H4

***O. h.* 'Variegatus'** A medium-sized shrub bearing leaves bordered with cream.
H4 ♛ 1993

Osmanthus serrulatus

O. serrulatus A medium-sized, slow-growing, compact, rounded shrub with large, fairly slender, glossy dark green leaves that are sharply toothed or smooth, purple-red when young. The clusters of fragrant white flowers are in the leaf axils in spring. Himalayas. Introduced 1910.
H3–4

O. suavis An erect shrub up to 4m (12ft), related to *O. delavayi* but with sharply toothed, shining green leaves 8cm (3in) long. Its white flowers, borne in spring, are fragrant. It is reasonably hardy in a sheltered position. Himalayas.
H3–4

O. yunnanensis A remarkable large shrub or small tree with lance-shaped, dark olive-green leaves up to 15cm (6in) long, varying from wavy and toothed to flat and smooth, both on the same plant. The ivory-cream flowers are intensely fragrant and appear during late winter. Given a sheltered position, it has proved hardy in the Hillier Arboretum over many years and a number of exceptionally cold winters. China. Introduced 1923 by George Forrest.
H3

Ostrya *Carpinaceae*

A small genus of medium to large deciduous trees resembling hornbeams and notable in autumn when bedecked with their hop-like fruits. The following are easily grown in any fertile soil.

Ostrya carpinifolia

O. carpinifolia (Hop hornbeam) A round-headed, medium-sized tree with double-toothed leaves 8–13cm (3–5in) long that turn clear yellow in autumn. The fruits are 3.5–5cm (1½–2in) long with each nutlet contained in a flat, bladder-like husk. It is enchanting in spring, when the many branches are strung with numerous long, drooping male catkins. S Europe, W Asia. Introduced 1724.
H4

Ostrya virginiana (1 of 2)

O. virginiana (Ironwood) A rare and attractive small tree of elegant, rounded or conical habit, differing from the above in minor details and with rich, warm, yellow autumn colour. E North America. Introduced 1692.
H4

Othonna *Compositae*

A genus of about 150 species of evergreen and deciduous shrubs and herbaceous plants that are native in the main to tropical and southern Africa. The following species needs a warm position in full sun and a well-drained soil.

Othonna cheirifolia

O. cheirifolia A dwarf evergreen shrub with spreading stems and short, ascending branches, clothed with distinctive, paddle-shaped, grey-green leaves. The golden-yellow flowerheads are borne singly at the ends of the shoots in spring and summer and intermittently through autumn and winter. Algeria, Tunisia. Introduced 1752.
H3

Oxydendrum *Ericaceae*

A genus of one deciduous species.

O. arboreum (Sorrel tree) A beautiful large shrub or small tree grown for its exquisite crimson and yellow autumn colouring. White flowers are borne in slender, drooping racemes produced in clusters from the tips of the shoots in mid- to late summer. The leaves are pleasantly, if acidly, flavoured. It thrives under conditions suitable for rhododendrons, doing well in semi-shade or sun if it has a lime-free soil. E United States. Introduced 1752.
H4

Oxydendrum arboreum

Oxypetalum *Asclepiadaceae*

From a gardener's point of view there is but one species of interest in this genus of herbacious twining climbers with a total of about 100 in all, and even this is placed by most authorities in the genus Tweedia. It may be grown outside only in the very mildest places but makes an exceptionally attractive conservatory climber. It will grow in any reasonable and well-drained soil.

Oxypetalum caeruleum

O. caeruleum, syn. *Tweedia caerulea* A beautiful deciduous sub-shrub with twining stems and oblong or heart-shaped, sage-green leaves and remarkable flowers that are powder-blue at first and slightly tinged with green, turning purplish and finally lilac. They are freely borne in erect clusters of a few flowers each in summer. To encourage branching it is a good idea to pinch the tips out of the shoot during early growth. South America. Introduced 1832.
H2–3 ♆ 1993

Ozothamnus *Compositae*

A genus of 50 evergreen, summer-flowering shrubs related to Helichrysum *and sometimes so named. Woody perennial herbs, requiring full sun and a well-drained position.*

Ozothamnus ledifolius

O. ledifolius A small, dense, globular, aromatic shrub with yellow-backed, incurved leaves and comparatively large flowers with inner bracts that have notably white, spreading tips and are reddish in bud. The seedheads are honey-scented. Tasmania. Introduced 1930.
H4 ♛ 1993

Ozothamnus rosmarinifolius

O. rosmarinifolius A medium-sized shrub with white-woolly stems and slender, dark green, warty leaves. The dense corymbs of red buds are spectacular for ten days or more before they open to white, scented flowers. Given sun and a well-drained soil it is one of the hardiest species.

Tasmania, E Australia. Introduced 1827.
H4
O. r. 'Silver Jubilee' A form with silvery grey leaves.
H4 ♛ 1993
O. selago, syn. *Helichrysum selago* A dwarf shrublet with slender, erect or ascending stems that are rather stiffly held and much branched. The tiny, green, scale-like leaves are closely adpressed to the stems and they are smooth on the outside but coated with white on the inside, and this gives the stems a chequered appearance. Small, creamy flowerheads are borne at the tips of the shoots in early spring. It may be grown in a rock garden, trough or alpine house for best effect. New Zealand.
H4

P

Pachysandra *Buxaceae*

A genus of four or five evergreen and deciduous species of dwarf shrubs or sub-shrubs, natives of North America and east Asia, which are suitable for ground cover in moist, shaded sites. They do not do well in shallow soils over chalk.

Pachysandra terminalis

P. terminalis A dwarf, evergreen, carpeting shrublet for covering bare places under trees. The leaves are clustered at the ends of the stems and are somewhat diamond-shaped and toothed in the upper half. Spikes of greenish white flowers are produced at the ends of the previous year's

shoots in late winter and early spring. Japan. Introduced 1882.
H4 ♛ 1993

Pachysandra terminalis 'Variegata'

P. t. 'Variegata' The leaves of this form are attractively variegated white.
H4 ♛ 1993

Paeonia *Paeoniaceae*
Peony

There are 30 or so species in this genus, mainly herbaceous perennials that are natives of temperate regions of Europe, Asia and North America. The deciduous shrubby members, known as tree peonies, come from west China and south-east Tibet and are represented in gardens by just a few species and their varieties and hybrids. However, the term is most frequently applied to those that have originated from P. suffruticosa, *which have been bred and cultivated for many centuries in China and latterly in the West. Among the most gorgeously coloured of all shrubs, they are uninjured by severe winters, though spring frosts may damage their precocious young growths. This can be prevented to a large extent by erecting a sacking or close-mesh netting screen on a framework of bamboos and positioning it over the plants during frosty spring nights. The protection can be removed when the frost has dispersed in the morning. Some species, including* P. delavayi *and* P. lutea, *have splendid architectural foliage. Given full sun and a sheltered site, tree peonies will thrive in any well-drained soil.*

P. delavayi A handsome, suckering shrub up to 2m (6½ft) high. Its flowers, borne in late spring, are deepest crimson with golden

Paeonia delavayi

anthers and are followed by large, black-seeded fruits surrounded by brightly coloured, persistent sepals. The large, deeply cut leaves make this a notable foliage shrub, and it is excellent on chalky soils. W China. Introduced 1908.
H4 ♛ 1993

P. × lemoinii 'Chromatella' A hybrid between *P. lutea* and *P. suffruticosa* with large, double, sulphur-yellow flowers in late spring and early summer. It grows to about 1.5–2m (5–6½ft) high, appreciates a rich soil, and does well on chalk.
H4

P. × l. 'Souvenir de Maxime Cornu' A medium-sized shrub with very large, double flowers, bright yellow with carmine edges and fragrant.
H4

Paeonia lutea

P. lutea A bold shrub reaching about 2m (6½ft) in height with foliage similar to that of *P. delavayi* but with bright yellow, cup-shaped flowers 6cm (2½in) across in early to midsummer. It is shy-flowering, however. China. Introduced 1886.
H4

Paeonia lutea var. ludlowii

P. l. var. ludlowii This splendid, free-flowering medium-sized shrub has larger, beautiful golden yellow, saucer-shaped flowers. First collected in Tibet.
H4 ♛ 1993

Paeonia suffruticosa

P. suffruticosa (Moutan peony) A branching shrub up to 2m (6½ft) high with large flowers as much as 15cm (6in) or even more across in late spring. Perhaps the most celebrated form is 'Rock's Variety', which has large, single, slightly pink-blushed flowers that pass to silver white and are marked at the base of each petal with a maroon splash. Due to the difficulty in propagation it is rare. There are now several moutans available ranging in colour from white through pink to red and usually with semi-double or double flowers. Many have romantic Japanese names that complement their beauty. They are usually offered by colour and flower shape.
H4

Pandorea *Bignoniaceae*

A genus of about six species of evergreen twining plants, natives of South-East Asia and Australia. The following require warm, sheltered positions in very mild places and are best grown in the conservatory.

P. jasminoides (Bower plant) A beautiful climber with pinnate leaves consisting of 5–9 slender-pointed leaflets. The attractive funnel-shaped flowers, 4–5cm (1½–2in) long, are white stained with crimson markings in the throat. They are borne in panicles in summer. E Australia.
H1

P. j. 'Rosea Superba' A form with large, bell-shaped pink flowers, darker in the throat and with purple spots, produced from spring to summer.
H1 ♛ 1993

Parahebe *Scrophulariaceae*

A genus of about 30 species of semi-woody, dwarf deciduous plants that were formerly included in Veronica *and are native to New Zealand. They are good rock-garden plants and grow in all types of garden soil.*

P. catarractae A small-leaved dwarf plant that forms low, spreading mounds and is

Parahebe catarractae 'Diffusa'

excellent ground cover in full sun. The flowers are white to rose-purple with a central zone of crimson, and are borne in erect clusters in late summer. Blue-flowered forms are often grown. New Zealand.
H3 ♔ 1993

P. c. 'Delight' The flowers of this form are white with heliotrope veining; they are borne profusely over a long period.
H3 ♔ 1993

P. c. 'Diffusa' A form with smaller leaves, densely mat-forming, and with white flowers that are veined with rose-pink.
H3

P. c. 'Miss Willmott' A shrub bearing flowers veined with mauve.
H3

P. decora A creeping sub-shrub that forms low hummocks. It has tiny, rounded leaves with just one or two pairs of teeth, and the flowers are white or pink in long-stalked clusters in summer. New Zealand.
H3

Parahebe lyallii

P. lyallii A low, prostrate shrublet with small, rounded or ovate, leathery leaves. The flowers are white prettily veined with pink and have blue anthers; they are borne in slender racemes from mid- to late summer. New Zealand. Introduced 1870.
H3

P. l. 'Mervyn' A dwarf, spreading shrub with small, red-edged leaves and clusters of lilac-blue flowers in summer. It is probably a hybrid of *P. lyallii*.
H3

P. perfoliata (Digger's speedwell) A dwarf sub-shrub, usually herbaceous, with erect

Parahebe perfoliata

stems to about 30–45cm (12–18in) high. The leaves are perfoliate, the stem appearing to pass through a pair of fused leaves, and are most attractively grey-green. The violet-blue flowers are borne in long racemes in late summer. It is an unusual plant for sunny, well-drained spots in mild areas. Australia. Introduced 1834.
H3–4 ♔ 1993

Parasyringa *Oleaceae*

A genus of one evergreen species, related to Ligustrum *and* Syringa.

P. sempervirens A striking small to medium-sized evergreen shrub with dark green, leathery, rounded leaves. The small white flowers are produced in dense, broad clusters in late summer and early autumn. It enjoys any good garden soil. W China. Introduced 1913.
H4

Parrotia *Hamamelidaceae*

A genus of one deciduous species.

P. persica A large shrub or small tree of wide-spreading habit. The bark of older trees flakes delightfully much like that of the London plane and the leaves turn crimson and gold in autumn, often starting in late summer and before almost any other tree

Parrotia persica

or shrub. The flowers consist of clusters of crimson stamens like tiny paintbrushes and appear in winter and early spring. It is one of the finest trees for autumn colour and is remarkably lime tolerant for a member of the *Hamamelidaceae* family, growing even on chalk. N Iran to the Caucasus. In cultivation 1840.
H4 ♔ 1993

Parrotiopsis *Hamamelidaceae*

A genus of one deciduous species.

P. jaquemontiana A large, erect shrub with rounded leaves that usually turn yellow in autumn. The flower clusters have conspicuous white bracts, rather like those of *Cornus florida*, and are seen in mid- to late spring and intermittently throughout the summer. It is best in an acid or neutral soil but will tolerate some lime and can be grown over chalk as long as the soil is at least 60cm (2ft) deep. W Himalayas. Introduced 1879.
H4

Parthenocissus *Vitaceae*

A genus of about ten deciduous species of high-climbing vines, related to Vitis and attaching themselves by means of leaf tendrils that twine or bear adhesive pads. The self-clinging species are excellent on walls and tree trunks. The leaves are often richly coloured in autumn. The attractive fruits are produced only after a hot, dry summer. Plant in a moisture-retentive soil enriched with well-rotted organic matter. Prune away from windows, roof eaves and so on in early winter.

Parthenocissus henryana

P. henryana A beautiful, self-clinging species with 3–5 narrow leaflets originating from a central point. They are dark green or bronze, with a silvery white veining that shows up better when the plant is growing in part shade, and turn red in autumn. The fruits are dark blue. It is best grown on a wall. First discovered 1885. C China. Introduced 1900 by Ernest Wilson.
H4 ♔ 1993

Parthenocissus quinquefolia

P. quinquefolia (Virginia creeper) A tall-growing, more or less self-clinging vine, excellent for high walls, towers, trees and so on. The leaves usually have five stalked leaflets that are dull green but turn brilliant orange and scarlet in autumn. The fruits are blue-black. This is the true Virginia creeper: the plant still commonly and incorrectly given the name is *P. tricuspidata*, the Boston ivy. E United States.
H4 ♔ 1993

P. tricuspidata (Boston ivy) A vigorous,

Parthenocissus tricuspidata

self-clinging vine with extremely variable leaves that are conspicuously three-lobed in old plants. They turn rich crimson and scarlet in autumn. The fruits are dark blue and bloomy. It is very beautiful on the walls of buildings. Japan. Introduced 1862 by J. G. Veitch.
H4 ♔ 1993

P. t. 'Veitchii' A selected form with slightly smaller ovate or trifoliate leaves, purple when young.
H4

Passiflora *Passifloraceae*
Passion flower

There are about 350 evergreen and deciduous species in this fascinating genus. They are mainly climbers that attach themselves to supports by twining tendrils, and most are natives of tropical South America. The majority are too tender to be planted out of doors in cool-temperate gardens but those that are hardy enough can be ranked among the most beautiful and exotic of flowering creepers and succeed best on a sunny, sheltered, south-facing wall.

The beautiful and intriguing flowers are usually borne singly on long stalks. Each has a tubular calyx with five lobes or sepals, and these are often the same size and shape as the petals. Sepals and petals are collectively referred to as tepals. Inside the tepals are rings of thread-like coloured filaments, and these are collectively referred to as the corona. The five stamens are on a long central column and are topped by the ovary and its three nail-like stigmas.

The flower was used by Spanish missionaries to South America to illustrate the story of the Passion of Christ. The three stigmas represented the three nails, the five anthers the five wounds, the corona the crown of thorns or the halo of glory, the ten tepals the ten apostles (Peter and Judas were not present during the Passion), and the lobed leaves and whip-like tendrils stood for the hands and scourges of His persecutors.

Passion fruits vary in size and shape and contain many seeds in an edible, jelly-like pulp. Out of doors they are produced only after a long, hot summer, during which there was a minimum temperature of 16°C (60°F) during flowering. Commercial passion-fruit production is possible only in hot countries.

Pruning is usually unnecessary in the open, as

the frost is likely to do it for you. Under glass, a framework of branches should be established, to which the plant is pruned back in spring. This main pruning is supplemented by pinching back during the growing season.

P. alata A large, vigorous, deciduous climber with stout four-angled shoots and ovate leaves up to 15cm (6in) long. The fragrant flowers, borne from spring to summer, are 12cm (5in) across, the sepals green to white beneath and pale crimson above, the petals brilliant crimson and the filaments with purple, red and white bands. For a conservatory only.
H1

P. × allardii A strong-growing deciduous climber with large, three-lobed leaves. The flowers are 9–11.5cm (3½–4¾in) across with white, pink-shaded tepals and a white and deep cobalt-blue corona. They appear throughout summer and autumn. In milder areas it may be grown outside. Raised at the University Botanic Garden, Cambridge.
H2–3

P. 'Amethyst' See *P. amethystina*.

Passiflora amethystina

P. amethystina, syn. *P. 'Amethyst'*, *P. 'Lavender Lady'* A large, vigorous, deciduous climber with three-lobed leaves. The flowers are 8cm (3in) across with a green bell-shaped calyx and pointed sepals that are blue inside, deeper blue petals and dark purple filaments. They are produced from spring to summer. For a conservatory only.
H1

P. antioquiensis A beautiful medium-sized deciduous climber with some leaves

Passiflora antioquiensis

lance-shaped and others deeply three-lobed. The flowers are pendulous, 10–13cm (4–5in) across, rich rose-red with a small violet corona, and borne in late summer and autumn. It can be grown outside in the mildest, most sheltered places but is otherwise a plant for the conservatory. Colombia. Introduced 1858.
H2 ♔ 1993

Passiflora caerulea

P. caerulea (Blue passion flower) A vigorous, even rampant medium-sized climber in the short term, and evergreen out of doors in very mild winters. The leaves have 5–7 lobes and the slightly fragrant flowers are 7.5–10cm (3–4in) across with white or pink-tinged tepals; the corona has the outer filaments blue at the tips, white in the middle and purple at the base. Flowering is continuous throughout summer and autumn, often until the first frosts. The fruits are ovoid, orange-red, and remain a long time on the plant. It is hardy on a

warm, sunny wall in milder areas. S Brazil, Argentina. Introduced 1609.
H3 ♔ 1993

Passiflora caerulea 'Constance Elliott'

P. c. 'Constance Elliott' A superb clone with ivory-white flowers.
H3 ♔ 1993

Passiflora × caerulea racemosa

P. × caeruleoracemosa A rampant climber when established and very free-flowering. It has deeply five-lobed deciduous leaves and remarkable singly borne flowers with the tepals flushed deep violet, the corona deep violet-purple, the column apple-green and the stigmas purple and green. It is suitable for only the mildest places or a large conservatory.
H1–2 ♔ 1993

P. edulis A tender, vigorous deciduous climber with ovate, deeply three-lobed leaves. The flowers are 6cm (2½in) across, with white tepals, green without, the corona with curly white filaments, banded with purple. They are produced throughout summer. The yellow or dull purple fruits are cultivated in warmer countries for their edible pulp but are produced only in the mildest gardens. Brazil. Introduced 1810. H1–2

P. 'Exoniensis' A beautiful deciduous hybrid with downy stems and deeply three-lobed downy leaves. The pendulous flowers are 10–13cm (4–5in) across and have a 6cm (2in) tube, with rose-pink tepals and a small, whitish corona. They appear in summer. For the conservatory only. Raised c1870 by Messrs Veitch of Exeter.
H1–2 ♛ 1993

Passiflora 'Incense'

P. 'Incense' A large, vigorous deciduous climber with violet-mauve, lace-like flowers 12cm (5in) across, gathered in the centre to produce a banding effect of alternate white and deep purple. They have an exquisite sweet-pea fragrance and are borne in early to midsummer. The fruits are edible but slightly acid. For a conservatory only.
H1 ♛ 1993

P. 'Lavender Lady' See *P. amethystina*.

P. mollissima A vigorous deciduous climber with downy shoots and deeply three-lobed leaves that are densely hairy beneath. The pendulous flowers are up to 7.5cm (3in) across, with a tube 7–8cm (2¾–3¼in) long. The petals and sepals are pink and the corona purple. The yellow fruits are edible. South America. In cultivation 1843.
H1 ♛ 1993

P. quadrangularis A vigorous deciduous climber with four-angled stems and unlobed leaves up to 20cm (8in) long. The fragrant flowers are 8cm (3¼in) across, greenish outside, white, pink or red within, the corona banded with reddish purple, blue and white. The edible yellow fruits are 20–30cm (8–12in) long.
H1

P. 'Star of Bristol' A large, slender, vigorous deciduous climber with three to five-lobed leaves. The summer flowers have green sepals that are purple above and mauve petals; the filaments are mauve banded lilac. For a conservatory only.
H2 ♛ 1993

Passiflora racemosa

P. racemosa (Red passion flower) A medium-sized deciduous climber with three-lobed leaves and vivid scarlet flowers with purple, white-tipped outer filaments, borne in terminal, drooping clusters in midsummer. It is a magnificent species but needs to be grown in the conservatory. Brazil. Introduced 1815.
H2 ♛ 1993

P. umbilicata A fast-growing medium-sized deciduous species with small violet flowers and round, yellow fruits. It is one of the hardiest and thrives in the open in mild areas. Bolivia, Paraguay, N Argentina. Introduced 1954.
H2–3

Paulownia *Scrophulariaceae*

A genus of about six species of deciduous trees from east Asia. The cultivated species are among the grandest of ornamental flowering trees and are notable for their foxglove-like flowers which do not appear on very young trees and for their large, velvety leaves, which on vigorous, stooled plants are enormous. The flowers are in erect panicles, formed in autumn, but opening the following spring. Frosts can destroy the flower buds, and the flowers should if possible be looked down upon, so a sunny position but one with close shelter from strong winds is advisable. Paulownias enjoy all kinds of deep, well-drained soils.

P. fargesii The species that properly bears this name is a magnificent tree of 18–21m (60–70ft) that seems better adapted to fickle early springs than the better-known *P. tomentosa*. It also flowers when comparatively young. The heliotrope flowers are fragrant, speckled with dark purple in the throat, and have a creamy basal stain. It should not be confused with a lilac-flowered form of *P. tomentosa*, which is sometimes mistakenly given the same name. W China. Introduced c1896.
H4

Paulownia tomentosa

P. tomentosa A round-topped tree sometimes reaching 9–12m (28–40ft). The flowers are a slightly darker heliotrope than those of *P. fargesii* and make a marvellous display in late spring as long as they come through the winter. Alternatively, you can grow young plants and prune them to the ground in spring, thinning the suckers that result to a single shoot. If well fed, the shoot can reach 2.5–3m (8–10ft) in a single season and will bear huge leaves up to 60cm (2ft) or more across. China. Introduced 1834 via Japan.
H3 ♛ 1993

Paxistima *Celastraceae*

A genus of two species of interesting, dwarf, evergreen shrubs with tiny leaves and quadrangular stems, best in a moist, shady position but unsuitable for shallow chalk soils.

P. canbyi A dwarf shrub with narrow leaves and small, greenish flowers appearing in summer, followed by white fruits. It makes an unusual hedge or ground cover. E United States. In cultivation 1800. H4

Penstemon *Scrophulariaceae*

A large genus of about 250 species of evergreen and deciduous sub-shrubs, herbaceous plants and a few small shrubs, mainly from the north-west of North America and from Mexico. The hardy, woody ones are excellent rock garden plants in full sun and with good drainage.

Penstemon davidsonii

P. davidsonii A dwarf or prostrate, evergreen shrublet for the rock garden. It has short-stalked, shallowly toothed leaves and plentiful erect clusters of remarkably large tubular red-purple flowers in late spring and early summer. NW North America. In cultivation 1902.
H4 ♈ 1993

P. fruticosus var. scouleri A charming dwarf deciduous sub-shrub with narrow, lance-shaped leaves and large, lilac-coloured blossoms in erect racemes in early summer. A good rock-garden plant. W North America. Introduced 1828.
H4 ♈ 1993

Penstemon fruticosus var. scouleri

P. f. 'Albus' A form with white flowers.
H4 ♈ 1993

Penstemon heterophyllus 'Blue Gem'

P. heterophyllus 'Blue Gem' A dwarf, erect deciduous shrublet with long, narrow leaves and lovely, azure-blue flowers in long racemes during summer. California.
H4

Penstemon newberryi

P. newberryi Plants under this name are usually f. *humilior*, a deciduous dwarf shrub for the rock garden, similar to *P. davidsonii* but with longer, pointed leaves and scarlet to deep rose-pink flowers in profusion in early summer. W United States.
H4 ♈ 1993

P. pinifolius A dwarf, evergreen shrub with very slender, needle-like, pointed leaves. The bright scarlet, tubular flowers end in five-pointed lobes and are borne in terminal spikes in late summer. A first-class rock-garden plant. SW North America.
H4

P. rupicola A dwarf, mat-forming deciduous shrub with small blue-green leaves and dense racemes of deep pink flowers in late spring to summer. W North America.
H4 ♈ 1993

Pernettya *Ericaceae*

A genus of about 20 species of evergreen shrubs, closely related to and by many authorities now included in Gaultheria, *although they are likely to be found offered for sale under* Pernettya *for some years to come. Their native range extends from Mexico to the Strait of Magellan and there are a few species in Tasmania and New Zealand. They are tolerant of shade but fruit best in sun and should be provided with a lime-free soil. Pruning is unnecessary.*

P. mucronata The showiest in fruit of all dwarf evergreens and one of the hardiest of South American shrubs. It forms dense thickets of wiry stems about 60–90cm (2–3ft) high and has a profusion of small, white, heather-like flowers in late spring and early summer, followed by dense clusters of long-persistent, marble-like berries that range from pure white to mulberry-purple. It is best to plant it in groups of three or more which should include a proven male form such as 'Thymifolia', otherwise you may not see many berries. It is tolerant of shade but fruits best in sun and should be provided with a lime-free soil. In large gardens it makes excellent ground cover. Pruning is unnecessary. The following forms are recommended. Chile to Strait of Magellan. Introduced 1828.
H4

Pernettya mucronata 'Bell's Seedling'

P. m. 'Bell's Seedling' A hermaphrodite form with attractive reddish young stems and dark, shining leaves. The berries are large and dark red.
H4 ♔ 1993

P. m. 'Cherry Ripe' Similar to 'Bell's Seedling' but with medium-sized to large, bright cherry-red berries.
H4

Pernettya mucronata 'Crimsonia'

P. m. 'Crimsonia' A selection with white flowers and very large crimson fruits. In cultivation 1968.
H4 ♔ 1993

P. m. 'Lilian' This selection has white flowers and very large, lilac-pink berries. In cultivation1968.
H4

P. m. 'Mulberry Wine' The young stems of this shrub are green rather than reddish. The large berries are magenta ripening to deep purple.
H4 ♔ 1993

Pernettya mucronata 'Mulberry Wine'

Pernettya mucronata 'Pink Pearl'

P. m. 'Pink Pearl' A selection with medium-sized, lilac-pink berries.
H4 ♔ 1993

Pernettya mucronata 'Sea Shell'

P. m. 'Sea Shell' A selection with medium-sized to large berries that are shell pink deepening to rose.
H4 ♔ 1993

P. m. 'Thymifolia' A charming, neat male form with small leaves. It is smothered in white flowers in early summer.
H4

P. m. 'White Pearl' A selection which develops medium-sized to large berries of gleaming white.
H4

P. m. 'Wintertime' A selection with large, pure white berries.
H4 ♔ 1993

Perovskia *Labiatae*

A genus of seven species of late-flowering, aromatic evergreen and deciduous sub-shrubs with deeply toothed or finely cut aromatic leaves, native to an area from central Asia to the Himalayas. They associate well with lavender and other blue and grey plants in the border and succeed in sun in all types of well-drained soil. For the most striking foliage effects, they can be cut down close to ground level in spring.

Perovskia atriplicifolia 'Blue Spire'

P. atriplicifolia 'Blue Spire' A deciduous shrub to about 1.5m (5ft) high with deeply cut, grey foliage, whitish stems and an abundance of large panicles of lavender-blue flowers in late summer.
H4 ♔ 1993

Persicaria *Polygonaceae*

A genus mainly consisting of herbaceous perennials, containing several garden favourites previously under Polygonum. *The following is the best-known of the shrubby deciduous species. They will grow in any reasonably moisture-*

retentive soil, but do not like one that is very fertile. They prefer sun and require pruning only if they are becoming too invasive.

P. vacciniifolia, syn. *Polygonum vaccini-ifolium* A prostrate, mat-forming shrub with slender stems and small, glossy green leaves that are bluish bloomy beneath. The bright rose-pink flowers are borne in slender, erect spikes in late summer and autumn. It is a first-rate rock garden plant for a sunny position. Himalayas. Introduced 1845.
H4 ♔ 1993

Petteria *Leguminosae*

A genus of one deciduous species.

Petteria ramentacea

P. ramentacea (Dalmatian laburnum) An unusual, upright shrub with laburnum-like leaves. It reaches 1.7–2.5m (5½–8ft) in height and bears erect racemes of yellow scented flowers, also laburnum-like, at the ends of the current season's growth in early summer. The seeds, as in laburnum, are poisonous. It requires full sun in any well-drained soil. W Former Yugoslavia, N Albania. Introduced 1838.
H4

Phellodendron *Rutaceae*

A genus of about 10 species of small to medium-sized, wide-spreading deciduous trees from east Asia, resembling Ailanthus in their large, handsome, pinnate leaves and graceful habit. They grow well on all types of garden soil, including chalk, and their attractive, aromatic leaves turn

clear yellow before falling. The small, yellow-green flowers, which are very attractive to bees, are followed by small black fruits.

P. amurense (Amur cork tree) A small to medium-sized tree with corky bark in maturity and 24–38cm (10–15in) long, bright green leaves with 5–11 leaflets. The winter buds are silvery and silky. NE Asia. Introduced 1885.
H4

Philadelphus *Philadelphaceae*
Mock orange

These shrubs, often mistakenly called 'syringa' (the botanical name for lilac), consist in nature of about 65 deciduous species from north-temperate regions. They give a good floral display even on the poorest chalk soils and their flowers, arriving in early to midsummer, are usually fragrant and white. The 'orange' scent is redolent of orange blossom rather than of oranges, as is sometimes expected. Old flowering shoots should be thinned and cut back to within a short distance of the old wood immediately after flowering. The usual height is 1.5–2.5m (5–8ft).

P. 'Avalanche' A small, semi-erect shrub with small leaves and masses of small, single, richly fragrant flowers in summer, so plentifully borne that they weigh down the branches. In cultivation 1896.
H4

Philadelphus 'Beauclerk'

P. 'Beauclerk' A splendid medium-sized shrub with single, broad-petalled flowers 6cm (2½in) across. They are milk-white

with a zone of light cerise round the stamens and highly fragrant.
H4 ♔ 1993

Philadelphus 'Belle Etoile'

P. 'Belle Etoile' A beautiful, compact shrub up to 2m (6½ft) high. It has single white flowers, 5cm (2in) wide, with a maroon flush at the centre. They are delightfully fragrant. In cultivation 1930.
H4 ♔ 1993

P. 'Boule d'Argent' A small shrub with large, double, pure white flowers that are freely produced in dense clusters. They are slightly fragrant. In cultivation 1893.
H4

P. 'Bouquet Blanc' A small shrub with double, orange-scented flowers in large, crowded clusters. In cultivation 1903.
H4

P. 'Buckley's Quill' A broadly upright, medium-sized shrub with large white double flowers. Raised in Canada.
H4

Philadelphus 'Burfordensis'

P. **'Burfordensis'** A magnificent and particularly attractive, erect, medium-sized shrub raised by Sir William Lawrence with large, single, white, cup-shaped flowers with bright yellow stamens. Originated 1920 as a sport of 'Virginal'.
H4

Philadelphus coronarius

P. **coronarius** A strongly growing, medium-sized shrub with creamy white, richly scented flowers. Of the species, it is the most commonly grown and is especially suitable for very dry soils.
H4

Philadelphus coronarius 'Aureus'

P. c. **'Aureus'** The best philadelphus for out-of-flower effectiveness, with bright yellow leaves that become greenish yellow as they age.
H4 ♔ 1993

P. c. **'Variegatus'** Leaves have a creamy white margin. In cultivation 1770.
H4 ♔ 1993

Philadelphus coronarius 'Variegatus'

P. *delavayi* **'Nyman's Variety'** A large, vigorous shrub with large leaves which are grey-felted on the undersides, and heavily scented white flowers with particularly attractive deep purple calyces, borne in dense racemes.
H4

P. **'Erectus'** A small, erect shrub with small leaves and flowers. It is extremely free-flowering and richly scented. In cultivation 1890.
H4

P. **'Frosty Morn'** A small shrub with fragrant double flowers. In cultivation 1953.
H4

Philadelphus 'Innocence'

P. **'Innocence'** A medium-sized shrub with single, white, fragrant flowers, borne with extraordinary freedom. The leaves often have a cream variegation. In cultivation 1927.
H4

P. *intectus* A very vigorous large shrub,

outstanding when laden with masses of slightly fragrant white flowers. SE United States. In cultivation before 1890.
H4

Philadelphus 'Manteau d'Hermine'

P. **'Manteau d'Hermine'** A popular, almost dwarf, compact shrub of about 0.75–1.2m (2½–4ft) with fragrant, creamy, double flowers.
H4 ♔ 1993

P. *microphyllus* A very dainty, small-leaved species, making a twiggy bush about 1–1.2m (3–4ft) high. The very small single flowers are richly fragrant. SW United States. Introduced 1883.
H4

P. **'Silberregen'**, syn. 'Silver Showers' A dense small shrub with small, pointed leaves and profusely borne, single, white, fragrant flowers.
H4

P. **'Silver Showers'** See P. 'Silberregen'.

P. **'Sybille'** A superb small shrub with

Philadelphus 'Virginal'

arching branches and single, almost square, purple-stained, orange-scented flowers. In cultivation 1913.
H4 🏆 1993

P. 'Virginal' A strongly growing, erectly branched shrub reaching 3m (10ft) tall, with white, strongly scented flowers, 2.5–3.5cm (1–1¹/₂in) across. It is still probably the best double-flowered cultivar.
H4 🏆 1993

Philesia *Philesiaceae*

A genus of one evergreen species, related to Lapageria.

P. magellanica One of the choicest, most remarkable and beautiful of all dwarf shrubs. It is suckering and forms wide thickets of wiry stems with narrow, rigid leaves and tubular, crimson flowers 5cm (2in) long in summer and autumn. It needs a moist, peaty, semi-shady site in well-drained soil and a sheltered position. S Chile. Introduced 1847 by William Lobb.
H3–4

Phillyrea *Oleaceae*

A genus of four species of handsome evergreen shrubs or small trees, allied to Osmanthus. *They succeed in all types of soil and in sun or semi-shade. They require little pruning.*

Phillyrea angustifolia

P. angustifolia A compact, rounded, medium-sized bush with narrow dark green leaves. The flowers are small, fragrant, creamy yellow and borne in clusters in late

spring and early summer. It is an excellent shrub for seaside exposure. N Africa, S Europe. In cultivation before 1597.
H4

P. a. f. rosmarinifolia A most attractive, neat, compact form with even narrower leaves than the species.
H4

P. decora See *Osmanthus decorus.*

Phillyrea latifolia

P. latifolia An elegant, olive-like large shrub or small tree suitable for planting where the similar-looking holm oak (*Quercus ilex*) would grow too large. Its branches are bowed by the weight of luxuriant masses of small, glossy, dark green leaves. The flowers appear in late spring and are dull white, followed by tiny black fruits that are only produced in a continental-type climate. S Europe, Asia Minor. In cultivation 1597.
H4

Phlomis *Labiatae*

A genus of about 100 species of low-growing evergreen shrubs, sub-shrubs and herbaceous perennials, usually densely hairy or woolly and with attractive flowers in whorls. They are widely distributed in Europe and Asia and require full sun and good drainage.

P. chrysophylla An attractive small shrub with sage-like foliage that takes on a yellow tinge after midsummer. The golden-yellow flowers are borne in early summer. Flowering is best when the summer is particularly hot. Lebanon.
H3 🏆 1993

Phlomis chrysophylla

P. 'Edward Bowles' A small to medium-sized hybrid sub-shrub with large, hoary, heart-shaped leaves and whorls of sulphur-yellow flowers with a distinctly paler upper lip in late summer and autumn.
H4

Phlomis fruticosa

P. fruticosa (Jerusalem sage) A small grey-green shrub that is hardy in all but the coldest places. Its whorls of bright yellow flowers are attractive in summer and it is a good plant for a sunny bank. Mediterranean region. In cultivation 1596.
H3 🏆 1993

P. italica A most desirable dwarf shrub, not much more than 30cm (12in) high, with white-hairy stems and leaves and terminal spikes of pale lilac flowers in summer. Balearic Isles. In cultivation 1750.
H3–4

P. lanata A dense, dwarf, mound-forming shrub with yellow-woolly shoots asnd small, sage-green, ovate leaves up to 3cm (1¹/₄in)

Phlomis lanata

long, with the veins on the upper surfaces deeply impressed. The flowers are golden-yellow with brownish hairs and are borne in whorls in summer. Crete.
H3–4

P. longifolia A very attractive small shrub with white-woolly young stems and bright green, deeply veined, almost triangular leaves that are heart-shaped at the base. The terminal clusters of deep golden-yellow flowers are borne in summer. SW Asia.
H3–4

Phormium *Phormiaceae*

A genus of two species of New Zealand evergreens with handsome, sword-like leaves. They play much the same architectural role in the garden as yuccas and associate well with them. They thrive in a wide variety of soils and are among the best plants for maritime exposure and for industrial areas. They are more or less hardy but are very much at their best where the climate is mild. Many of the more recently raised forms are hybrids between the two species, and one or two of them should be considered quite tender. Strictly speaking, phormiums are not shrubs but evergreen perennials.

P. 'Apricot Queen' A shrub of low, weeping habit, with soft yellow leaves that are flushed with apricot and margined with dark green and bronze.
H3

P. 'Bronze Baby' The leaves of this small shrub are bronze, drooping at the tips.
H3

P. cookianum A smaller species than *P. tenax* and with thinner, greener leaves that

are more lax and flexible. The yellowish flowers are borne in panicles up to 1m (3ft) long in summer. Introduced 1848.
H3 🏆 1993

Phormium cookianum 'Cream Delight'

P. c. 'Cream Delight' The leaves of this form have a broad, cream central band and narrower stripes of cream towards the margin. Raised before 1978 in New Zealand.
H3 🏆 1993

P. c. 'Tricolor' Leaves brightly edged with creamy yellow and narrowly margined with red. Found 1880s in New Zealand.
H3 🏆 1993

P. 'Dark Delight' A form up to 1m (3ft) high, with broad, upright, dark purple-bronze leaves with reddish midribs.
H3

Phormium 'Dazzler'

P. 'Dazzler' A striking plant up to 1m (3ft) high, with deep red-purple leaves striped with rose-red in the centre.
H3

Phormium 'Maori Chief'

P. 'Maori Chief' The leaves of this small shrub are upright, drooping at the tips and variegated with attractive shades of scarlet, crimson and bronze.
H3

P. 'Maori Maiden' A small shrub with leaves to 90cm (3ft) long, drooping at the tips. They are bronze-green striped with rose red.
H3

P. 'Maori Queen' A small shrub bearing upright leaves with drooping tips which appear with a striking combination of bronze-green and rose-red stripes.
H3

Phormium 'Maori Sunrise'

P. 'Maori Sunrise' A low-growing form with slender, arching leaves that are pale red to pink, margined with bronze.
H3

P. tenax (New Zealand flax) A most striking large evergreen shrub with dramatically effective foliage, forming clumps of rigid,

Phormium tenax

leathery, sword-like leaves 1–3m (3–10ft) long and with bronze-red flowers in panicles up to 4m (12ft) or more in summer. It is a superb architectural plant and can be grown in all types of fertile soil. It is highly resistant to sea winds and industrial pollution and its leaves contain one of the toughest and finest fibres known. In western Ireland it is used as a highly effective coastal windbreak where little else will grow and has naturalized itself, sometimes where the original house for which it provided shelter has long fallen into ruin. New Zealand. Introduced 1789.
H4 ♛ 1993

P. t. 'Duet' A small shrub with upright or slightly spreading leaves up to 1m (3ft) in length, margined with creamy white.
H4 ♛ 1993

P. t. 'Nanum Purpureum' A compact dwarf shrub with slender, red-purple leaves up to 45cm (18in) long.
H4 ♛ 1993

Phormium tenax 'Purpureum'

P. t. 'Purpureum' A large shrub with bronze-purple leaves up to 2m (6½ft) long; a striking plant that contrasts well with plants with grey foliage.
H4 ♛ 1993

Phormium tenax 'Sundowner'

P. t. 'Sundowner' A medium-sized shrub with bronze-green leaves up to 1.5m (5ft) long with a deep rose-red margin.
H3 ♛ 1993

P. t. 'Variegatum' A medium-sized shrub with creamy margined leaves.
H3–4 ♛ 1993

P. t. 'Veitchii' Similar to 'Variegatum' but with creamy yellow stripes in the centre of the leaves.
H 3–4

Phormium 'Yellow Wave'

P. 'Yellow Wave' A small shrub with drooping leaves to 1m (3ft) long with a greenish yellow band variously striped with green. Raised c1967 in New Zealand.
H3 ♛ 1993

Photinia *Rosaceae*

A genus of about 40 evergreen and deciduous large shrubs or trees from east and South-East Asia and the Himalayas. The genus Stranvaesia *is now included in* Photinia. *The white flowers are borne in clusters, usually in spring, and they are followed in autumn by bright red fruits. The foliage of some deciduous species colours vividly before falling, and in some evergreens the unfolding leaves rival those of the most showy pieris. The deciduous species are inclined to be intolerant of limy soils, while the evergreens are lime tolerant. Unfortunately, with the exception of* P. davidiana, *the evergreen species seldom flower or fruit with any sort of freedom and seem to need more sun and warmth than is usual.*

P. beauverdiana A highly desirable small deciduous tree up to 6m (20ft) high. As spring passes into summer it becomes covered with wide clusters of hawthorn-like flowers and in autumn it is bedecked with dark red fruits and richly tinted leaves. It is moderately lime tolerant. C and W China. Introduced 1908 by Ernest Wilson.
H4 ♛ 1993

P. davidiana, syn. *Stranvaesia davidiana* A very vigorous evergreen large shrub or small tree with erect branches and dark green, lance-shaped, leathery, untoothed leaves. The round, brilliant crimson fruits are borne in pendent bunches. The oldest leaves turn bright red in autumn in contrast to the younger ones, which are still green. This species is, unfortunately, susceptible to fireblight. W China. Introduced 1917.
H4

Photinia davidiana 'Palette'

P. d. 'Fructuluteo' A selection tree with bright yellow fruits.
H4

P. d. 'Palette' A slow-growing form with leaves blotched and streaked with cream and tinged with pink when young. Raised before 1980 in Holland.
H4

P. d. 'Prostrata' A low-growing, more or less prostrate form.
H4

P. d. Salicifolia group The most commonly cultivated form, differing from the typical one only in slightly narrower leaves with more veins. W China. Introduced 1907 by Ernest Wilson.
H4

P. × fraseri A variable hybrid that makes a large, vigorous, evergreen shrub with dark glossy green, leathery leaves that are bright coppery red when young. The forms of this hybrid have proved very hardy.
H4

Photinia × fraseri 'Birmingham'

Photinia × fraseri 'Red Robin'

P. ×f. 'Birmingham' A clone with generally obovate, abruptly pointed leaves, bright coppery red when young. Tends towards the *P. Glabra* parent. Raised 1940 in the United States.
H4

P. ×f. 'Red Robin' A spectacular shrub with sharply toothed leaves and brilliant red young growths, equal to the best forms of *Pieris formosa*. Raised in New Zealand.
H4 ♔ 1993

P. ×f. 'Robusta' A strong-growing shrub tending towards the *P. Serratifolia* parent with thick, leathery leaves and coppery red young growths. It is the hardiest of the three. Raised in Australia.
H4 ♔ 1993

P. glabra 'Parfait' A small to medium-sized evergreen shrub with bronze young leaves margined pink and becoming green flecked with grey-green, with a narrow, creamy margin. It is a weak grower.
H4

Photinia glabra 'Rubens'

P. g. 'Rubens' A choice medium-sized shrub with brilliant, sealing-wax-red young leaves.
H4

P. 'Redstart', syn. × *Stranvinia* 'Redstart' A vigorous, large, evergreen shrub or small tree with bright red young foliage. The leaves are dark green and the white flowers are borne in early summer in dense, domed clusters with reddish purple stalks. The fruits are orange-red, flushed with yellow. Raised 1969 by Hillier Nurseries' propagator Peter Dummer.
H4 ♔ 1993

P. serratifolia A very handsome, large, evergreen shrub or small tree with oblong, dark green, leathery and coarsely toothed leaves up to 15cm (6in) long. The young leaves are bright coppery red all the way through its long growing season. The white flowers are in large clusters in the second half of spring and are at their best following a hot summer. The hawthorn-like fruits are red. It is one of the most splendid lime-tolerant evergreens.
H4

P. villosa A deciduous species, forming a large shrub or small, broad-headed tree. It has hawthorn-like flowers in late spring, followed by small, egg-shaped, bright red fruits and is highly effective in autumn, when its foliage turns to scarlet and gold. It does not thrive on shallow, chalky soils. Japan, Korea, China. Introduced 1865.
H4 ♔ 1993

Phygelius *Scrophulariaceae*

A genus of two species of attractive, evergreen or semi-evergreen, penstemon-like sub-shrubs from South Africa. P. capensis is remarkable as one of the very few South African shrubs that are to any extent hardy in the cooler temperate climates. They reach their greatest height against a sunny wall but look well almost anywhere in a shrub or herbaceous border. They are best in full sun and grow well in any type of well-drained soil as long as it is not too dry. In colder areas it is as well to mulch the root area heavily in autumn for protection. The old, soft top growth can be cut away in spring, as can any dead wood.

Phygelius aequalis

P. aequalis A small sub-shrub, growing to about 1m (3ft), with four-angled stems. The tubular flowers, 2.5–4cm (1–1½in) long, are slightly down-curved and evenly lobed at the mouth. They are pale dusky pink to red with a yellow throat, and are produced in late summer and early autumn on one side of the stem. It is not as hardy as the other species and needs the protection of a wall for survival.

H3

Phygelius aequalis 'Yellow Trumpet'

P. a. 'Yellow Trumpet' A striking form with pale, creamy yellow flowers and broad, light green leaves. South Africa. Introduced 1973 by B.L. Butt and Sir Harold Hillier.

H3

P. capensis (Cape figwort) A small shrub, occasionally growing to 2m (6½ft) in mild areas. The flowers are tubular, nodding and turning back towards the stem when open, and unevenly lobed at the mouth. They are orange-red to deep red with a yellow throat, elegantly borne on all sides of the stems in tall, open panicles in summer and autumn. In cultivation 1855.

H3 ♛ 1993

P. c. 'Coccineus' The plants that were originally given this name had rich red flowers, but the ones that are grown now have large, rich orange-red flowers.

H3

P. × rectus A group of hybrids between *P. aequalis* and *P. capensis*. The F₁ hybrids have pendulous flowers with a more or less straight tube, while back-crosses tend more to one or other of the parents. Several forms have been raised in various colours and are about 1–1.5m (3–4ft) tall.

H3

Phygelius × rectus 'African Queen'

P. × r. 'African Queen', syn. 'Indian Chief' An F₁ hybrid, this is a small shrub with pale red flowers. It was the first hybrid. See 'Winchester Fanfare'.

H3

P. × r. 'Devil's Tears' A small shrub that is a back-cross between 'Winchester Fanfare' and *P. capensis* 'Coccineus'. The tall and open flowers are deep reddish pink, deeper in bud, and have orange-red lobes. Raised 1985 by Hillier Nurseries' propagator Peter Dummer.

H3

P. × r. 'Indian Chief' See *P. × r.* 'African Queen'.

P. × r. 'Moonraker' A back-cross between 'Winchester Fanfare' and *P. aequalis* 'Yellow Trumpet'. It is like 'Yellow Trumpet' but has almost straight flowers on all sides of the

Phygelius × rectus 'Moonraker'

stems. It makes a small shrub. Raised 1985 by Peter Dummer.

H3

Phygelius × rectus 'Salmon Leap'

P. × r. 'Salmon Leap' From the same back-cross as 'Devil's Tears', this small shrub is distinguished from the other because it has orange flowers with deeper lobes. Raised 1985 by Peter Dummer at the Hillier Nurseries, England.

H3

Phygelius × rectus 'Winchester Fanfare'

P. × r. 'Winchester Fanfare' A cross between *P. aequalis* 'Yellow Trumpet' and *P. capensis* 'Coccineus'. It has straight, tubular but pendulous flowers and is a dusky reddish pink colour with scarlet lobes. It is similar to 'African Queen' but has a different flower colour and its broader triangular leaves are inherited from 'Yellow Trumpet'. Raised 1974 by Peter Dummer at the Hillier Nurseries, England.

H3

× Phylliopsis *Ericaceae*

An evergreen hybrid that occurred at Hillier Nurseries between two genera of dwarf shrubs (Kalmiopsis × Phyllodoce). It needs a lime-free, peaty soil in semi-shade.

× *P. hillieri* 'Pinocchio' A delightful dwarf shrub with small, glossy green leaves and deep pink, bell-shaped flowers about 1cm (½in) across, freely borne in long, slender racemes over a long period in spring and again in autumn.
H4

Phyllodoce *Ericaceae*

A genus of about six species of dainty, dwarf, heath-like evergreen shrubs from north-temperate and Arctic regions. Flowering is from mid-spring to midsummer. They thrive in cool, moist, but fairly open positions and lime-free soil.

P. aleutica A dwarf, carpeting shrublet, 15–23cm (6–9in) high. It has pitcher-shaped, creamy or pale yellow flowers in flat terminal clusters in late spring and early summer. Arctic. Introduced 1915.
H4

Phyllodoce caerulea

P. caerulea A dwarf, cushion-forming shrublet up to 15cm (6in) with pitcher-shaped, bluish purple flowers in terminal clusters in late spring and early summer. Arctic and sub-Arctic regions, including Perthshire, Scotland. In cultivation 1800.
H4

***P. × intermedia* 'Fred Stoker'** A vigor-ous dwarf hybrid, forming mats up to 30cm (12in) high and as much as four times as wide. Its pitcher-shaped flowers are light purple and puckered at the mouth. A form of the wild hybrid from W North America.
H4

P. nipponica One of the most perfect rock-garden shrublets for a peaty soil. It is a dwarf, erect, neat, compact species 15–23cm (6–9in) high with bell-shaped white or pinkish flowers that appear in terminal clusters in late spring. N Japan. Introduced 1915.
H4

Phyllostachys *Gramineae*

A genus of 60 tall, graceful evergreen bamboos that are less invasive than many in Pleioblastus, *from which they differ most markedly in the zig-zag stems which are flattened or shallowly grooved on alternate sides between the joints. The branches are usually in pairs at each joint. They are moisture-lovers but will grow in good soils over chalk. They are natives of China.*

Phyllostachys aurea

P. aurea A most graceful bamboo, forming large clumps 2.5–3.5m (8–11ft) high. The canes are bright green at first, maturing to pale creamy yellow, dull yellow in full sun. The leaves are 7.5–18cm (3–7in) long. There is a curious swelling beneath each joint. China. Introduced before 1870.
H4 ♔ 1993

P. bambusoides A very hardy, highly ornamental bamboo that eventually forms large clumps. The canes are 3–4.5m (10–13ft) high, deep shining green at first,

Phyllostachys bambusoides

becoming brown at maturity. The leaves are 5–19cm (2–7in) long and up to 3cm (1¼in) wide. China. Introduced 1866.
H4

***P. b.* 'Castillonis'** A form with golden yellow stems striped with a distinctive green in the grooves.
H4 ♔ 1993

P. edulis A strong-growing bamboo with bright green canes up to 4.5m (13ft) high that turn dull yellow in late summer and autumn. The young shoots are edible. The leaves are 7.5 × 10cm (3 × 4in) long and 2cm (¾in) wide. It is best grown in a sheltered position. China.
H4

Phyllostachys flexuosa

P. flexuosa A graceful bamboo, 2.5–3m (8–10ft) high, with slender, somewhat wavy canes that are bright green at first and become darker at maturity. In time, large thickets are formed. The leaves are 5–13cm (2–5in) long and 1–2cm (½–¾in) wide. The

shoots are noticeably zig-zag at the bases. It is excellent as a screening plant. N China. Introduced 1864.
H4

P. nigra (Black bamboo) A beautiful, clump-forming, gracefully arching plant. The canes are normally 2.5–3.5m (8–11ft), green in the first year, becoming mottled with dark brown or black and finally an even jet black. In colder gardens the canes often remain a mottled, brownish green. The leaves are 5–13cm (2–5in) long and 6–12mm ($\frac{1}{4}$–$\frac{1}{2}$in) wide. This distinctive and attractive species enjoys a sunny position. China. Introduced 1827.
H4 ♔ 1993

P. n. 'Boryana' An elegant bamboo with luxuriant masses of arching, leafy stems. The canes are 2.5–4m (8–12ft) high, green at first, changing to yellow and splashed with purple. The leaves are 5–9cm (2–3$\frac{1}{2}$in) long by 6–12mm ($\frac{1}{4}$–$\frac{1}{2}$in) wide. Originated in Japan.
H4

Phyllostachys nigra var. *henonis*

P. n. var. henonis A handsome plant with tall, graceful canes to 4m (12ft) high, swathed in dark green clouds of shining leaves. The canes are bright green at first, maturing to brownish yellow. The leaves are 7.5–11cm (3–4$\frac{1}{2}$in) long by 1–2cm ($\frac{1}{2}$–$\frac{3}{4}$in) wide. It is one of the best bamboos for planting in a lawn or similar prominent position. In cultivation c1890.
H4 ♔ 1993

P. viridi-glaucescens A graceful, hardy, clump-forming species with canes 4–6m (12–20ft) high, green at first, changing to

Phyllostachys viridi-glaucescens

dull yellowish green in late summer and autumn. The leaves are 7.5–15cm (3–6in) long, 1–2cm ($\frac{1}{2}$–$\frac{3}{4}$in) wide, brilliant green above and blue-bloomy beneath. In ideal positions it forms a thicket, but is otherwise a fine specimen in isolation. E China. Introduced 1846.
H4 ♔ 1993

× Phyllothamnus *Ericaceae*

An evergreen hybrid between Phyllodoce *and* Rhodothamnus *suitable for a lime-free, moist, peaty or leafy soil.*

×**P. erectus** A dwarf shrublet 30–45cm (12–18in) high with stems crowded with narrow leaves and shallowly funnel-shaped, delicate rose flowers, produced in flat clusters in mid- to late spring.
H4

Physocarpus *Rosaceae*

A genus of about 10 species of tall deciduous shrubs that grow well in open, moist positions but tend to become chlorotic on dry, shallow chalk soils. They are natives of North America, Mexico and north-east Asia.

P. opulifolius (Nine bark) A vigorous, medium-sized shrub that will grow well in most situations. The bark peels in attractive curls and the leaves are three-lobed. The flowers are white tinged with pink and are in dense clusters along the stems in early summer. E North America.
H4

Physocarpus opulifolius 'Dart's Gold'

P. o. 'Dart's Gold' A small, compact shrub, an improvement on 'Luteus' on account of its brighter yellow foliage and especially because it retains its attractive colour much longer.
H4 ♔ 1993

Physocarpus opulifolius 'Luteus'

P. o. 'Luteus' The young growths of this medium-sized shrub are clear yellow and very effective when the shrub is planted as a contrast among others with purple leaves. In cultivation 1969.
H4

Picea *Pinaceae*
Spruce

A genus of about 35 species of conifers, found throughout the north-temperate regions. They are evergreen trees, usually conical, with branches borne in whorls. The leaves are short and needle-like, flattened or square in section and arranged spirally or in two ranks. They are an extremely ornamental group of trees and thrive in a variety of soils, but cannot be recommended for really poor, shallow, chalky or dry soils, nor for planting in exposed places. The principal foliage colours are from green to grey and there are many dwarf forms.

P. abies (Common spruce, Norway spruce) This is the traditional Christmas tree as known in Britain and Ireland and elsewhere, although other conifers, especially firs, are also used for the purpose. It is a large tree with orange or reddish brown shoots and shining dark green leaves up to 2.5cm (1in) long that densely clothe the upper sides of the branchlets. It has given rise to many dwarf forms, most of which are extremely slow-growing and ideal for the rock garden. Widely distributed in N and C Europe. Introduced 1500.
H4

P. a. 'Acrocona' A large, spreading bush or small tree with semi-pendulous branches that usually end in a precocious cone, even when the tree is young. In cultivation 1890.
H4

Picea abies 'Gregoryana'

P. a. 'Gregoryana' A dense, dwarf bush that develops into a somewhat billowy, rounded, flat-topped dome. Its radially arranged, sea-green leaves are eye-catching. A specimen at the Hillier Gardens and Arboretum was 0.5 ¥ 1.2m (20in ¥ 4ft) after 30 years. In cultivation 1862.
H4

P. a. 'Inversa' An unusual form, most often seen as a large shrub with depressed branches. In cultivation 1855.
H4

Picea abies 'Inversa'

Picea abies 'Little Gem'

P. a. 'Little Gem' A dwarf, slow-growing, globular bun-shaped shrub with tiny, densely crowded leaves.
H4 ♛ 1993

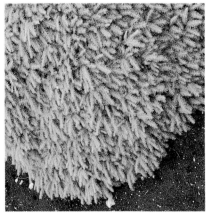

Picea abies 'Nidiformis'

P. a. 'Nidiformis' A very popular and commonly planted form, making a dwarf, dense, flat-topped bush with the branches forming a series of tight, horizontal layers with a depressed centre, likened to a bird's nest. It will reach 0.6 ¥ 1.8m (2 ¥ 6ft) after 30 years. In cultivation 1907.
H4 ♛ 1993

P. a. 'Ohlenforffii' A small, conical, dense shrub with yellow-green, rather small leaves recalling those of *P. orientalis*. It will reach 1.7 ¥ 1.2m (5½ ¥ 4ft) after 30 years. In cultivation 1845.
H4

P. a. 'Repens' A slow-growing, dwarf, flat-topped bush with branches in layers. It is a low, wide-spreading form suitable for the large rock garden. In cultivation 1898.
H4

Picea breweriana

P. breweriana (Brewer's weeping spruce) Perhaps the most beautiful of all the spruces and one of the most popular of all conifers. It is a small to medium-sized, broadly conical tree with spreading or decurved branches from which hang slender, tail-like branchlets 1.7–2.5m (5½–8ft) long. The leaves are up to 3cm (1¼in) long, shining dark blue-green above and marked with two white bands beneath. The cones are up to 10cm (4in) long, green at first, turning purple later. NW California, SW Oregon. Introduced 1897.
H4 ♛ 1993

P. glauca A large tree of dense, conical habit with decurved branches ascending at the tips. The densely arranged, four-angled leaves, up to 2cm (¾in) long, emit a foetid aroma when bruised. The cones are up to 6cm (2½in) long. It is a form of the white spruce, a very hardy species. The following

forms are recommended. Canada, NE United States. Introduced 1700.
H4

P. g. 'Echiniformis' A dwarf, slow-growing, globular, dense bush with glaucous grey-green leaves that point forwards, making it feel prickly to the touch. A first-class miniature conifer for the rock garden. In cultivation 1855.
H4 ♔ 1993

P. g. var. *albertiana* 'Alberta Globe' A form of very dense habit, making a compact, rounded bun. Raised in Holland. In cultivation 1968.
H4

P. g. var. a. 'Conica' An extremely popular, perfectly cone-shaped bush with bright grass-green leaves. In 30 years it will be a symmetrical, pointed cone 2m (6½ft) high and 1.2m (4ft) at the base. Found 1904 in the wild in Alberta.
H4 ♔ 1993

Picea likiangensis

P. likiangensis A most ornamental, vigorous, medium-sized tree. The upper branches have ascending terminal shoots, and the leaves are flattened, 1–2cm (½–¾in) long, green or bluish green above, bloomy beneath, loosely packed on the upper surfaces of the branchlets. The cones are 10cm (4in) long, reddish pink when young, and freely produced. In mid- to late spring it is spectacularly beautiful when laden with its male flowers and brilliant red young cones. W China. In cultivation 1910.
H4

P. mariana (Black spruce) A medium-sized, narrowly conical tree with dark bluish green leaves densely crowding the upper surfaces of the branchlets. The following form is recommended. NW America. In cultivation 1700.
H4

Picea mariana 'Nana'

P. m. 'Nana' A slow growing, dwarf, dense, mound-forming bush with grey-green leaves. It is ideal for the rock garden. In cultivation 1884.
H4 ♔ 1993

P. omorika (Serbian spruce) One of the most beautiful and adaptable spruces. It quickly forms a tall, graceful, slender, medium to large tree with relatively short, drooping branches that curve upwards at the tips. The leaves are dark green above, bloomy beneath, and densely arranged on the upper surfaces of the branchlets; on young plants they are narrower, sharply pointed and more spreading on the shoots. The cones are up to 6cm (2½in) long and bluish black when young. It is one of the

Picea omorika 'Pendula'

Picea omorika

best spruces for industrial areas and chalk soils. Balkans. Introduced 1889.
H4 ♔ 1993

P. o. 'Nana' A small or medium-sized, densely conical, compact bush with conspicuous white bands on the leaves. At the Hillier Gardens and Arboretum a specimen was 1.2 ¥ 1.2m (4 ¥ 4ft) after 15 years. In cultivation 1930.
H4

P. o. 'Pendula' A beautiful, medium-sized slender tree with drooping, slightly twisted branches and bloomy upper leaf surfaces. In cultivation 1920.
H4 ♔ 1993

P. orientalis (Oriental spruce) A large, densely branched, broadly conical tree with branches to the ground. Dark green leaves with blunt tips are densely pressed on to the upper surfaces of the branchlets. Cones up to 9cm (3½in) long and purple when young. Asia Minor, Caucasus. Introduced c1839.
H4 ♔ 1993

P. o. **'Aurea'** The young shoots of this medium-sized tree are creamy yellow, becoming golden yellow then green. Spectacular in spring. In cultivation 1873. H4 ♔ 1993

P. o. **'Skylands'** A beautiful, slow-growing small tree similar to 'Aurea' but golden yellow throughout the year. H4

P. pungens (Colorado spruce) A medium-sized to large conical tree with rigid, sharply pointed, green to grey leaves up to 3cm (1¼in) long that spread all round the branchlets but are denser on top. The typical form is seldom grown because of the popularity of the glaucous (blue-leaved) forms, of which there are a considerable number. The following are recommended. SW United States. Introduced 1862. H4

P. p. **Glauca Group** A medium-sized to large tree with glaucous leaves tending to lose intensity with age, those at the base of the branches being greyish green or green. It is variable. The most glaucous cultivated forms are usually small to medium-sized trees. The following are recommended. H4

Picea pungens 'Globosa'

P. p. **'Globosa'** (Glauca Group) A dwarf, flat-topped, globular, dense bush with glaucous blue leaves. In cultivation 1937. H4 ♔ 1993

P. p. **'Hoopsii'** (Glauca Group) An excellent small to medium-sized tree of densely conical habit and with vividly glaucous blue leaves. In cultivation 1958. H4 ♔ 1993

Picea pungens 'Koster'

P. p. **'Koster'** (Glauca Group) The most popular form of blue spruce for growing in the garden. A small to medium-sized, dense, conical tree with intensely silver-blue leaves. In cultivation 1885. H4 ♔ 1993

P. p. **'Moerheimii'** (Glauca Group) A small to medium-sized tree of dense, conical habit with intensely glaucous blue leaves. It is one of the most satisfactory of the group. In cultivation 1912. H4

P. p. **'Procumbens'** (Glauca Group) A dwarf shrub with low spreading branches and pendulous branchlets. Glaucous blue leaves. Reversions should be removed. In cultivation 1910. H4 ♔ 1993

P. p. **'Spekii'** (Glauca Group) A small to medium-sized conical tree with glaucous blue leaves. In cultivation c1925. H4

P. p. **'Thomsen'** (Glauca Group) A beautiful small to medium-sized, conical tree which displays strikingly silver-blue leaves. In cultivation 1928. H4

P. purpurea (Purple-coned spruce) A small to medium-sized tree previously regarded as a variety of *P. likiangensis*. It has a narrower, more pointed upper crown and the upper branches have erect terminal shoots. The leaves are also darker green, smaller, and more closely pressed to the upper surfaces of the branchlets. The cones are smaller and violet-purple. China. Introduced 1910. H4 ♔ 1993

Picea purpurea

P. sitchensis (Sitka spruce) A fast-growing, large to very large, broadly conical tree of economic importance. This prickly-leaved spruce thrives on damp sites and is one of the most important forestry trees in Britain. California to Alaska. Introduced 1831 by David Douglas. H4

P. smithiana (West Himalayan spruce) A large, extremely beautiful tree with branches that are upwardly curved at the tips and bear long, pendulous branchlets. The leaves are up to 4cm (1½in) long, dark green, needle-like and flexible, spreading all round the branchlets. The young green cones up to 17cm (7in) long, become purplish. Young plants are occasionally subject to injury by late spring frosts but established trees are fairly hardy and develop into specimens second only in elegance to *P. breweriana*. W Himalaya. Introduced 1818. H4 ♔ 1993

Picrasma *Simaroubaceae*

A genus of six species of deciduous trees and shrubs related to Ailanthus *and natives in the main of tropical areas.*

P. quassioides A remarkably hardy small tree, grown mainly for its brilliant orange and scarlet autumn foliage. The tiny yellow-green flowers in late spring and early summer are followed by small red fruits. It is lime-tolerant but does best in neutral or acid soils in sun or semi-shade. Japan, Korea, China, Himalaya. H4

PIERIS

Ericaceae

MANY gardeners, on seeing a plant of *Pieris* 'Forest Flame' in its spring growth for the first time, express great disappointment that they do not have the necessary acid soil in which to grow it. This is a pity, as in fact it is quite possible to enjoy its remarkable, brilliant red new growths in a container filled with ericaceous soil.

Pieris is an evergreen genus in the great family *Ericaceae*, most of which are lime-haters, but generally have the compact, fibrous root systems that take well to container culture. In *Pieris* there is a wide range of attractive attributes, of which coloured new growth, in anything from glossy chestnut to flaming coral-scarlet, is often, but by no means always, the most significant.

In the open ground (though only after many years) most pieris are capable of becoming small, bushy trees or large, dense shrubs which cover themselves with a frothy wealth of urn-shaped flowers in multiple racemes reminiscent of lily-of-the-valley, especially when planted in dappled shade. These are usually white, but a rapid increase in the number of cultivars has seen pink and even rich rose to dusky red appearing much more commonly. The flowers are often scented, in *P. japonica* notably and sweetly so, while in others the fragrance is more subtle.

The buds are formed in autumn. Forms of *P. japonica* whose inflorescences are borne on dark terracotta-red stems and which have calyces of the same colour are highly ornamental throughout the winter and may in fact flower in late winter where the climate is mild, although flowering is generally a spring event.

Spring flowering brings with it the peak of beauty in the genus, when richly coloured, often flamboyantly red new shoots contrast brilliantly with massed white flowers. However, a shrub as gorgeous in its new spring clothing of foliage as *P.* 'Bert Chandler' should not be shunned because it is one of the few that hardly ever flowers. If you have room, it is one of the glories of the woodland.

The spring growths of pieris are vulnerable to late frosts, and all forms of *P. formosa* especially should be protected from cold winds and preferably given light overhead shade. All is not lost, however, if the crop of new shoots is damaged by frost, as they are almost always renewed from latent buds in the stems after a short recovery interval. These growths will colour as well as those that were lost, although they may be shorter. In some, for example *P.* 'Forest Flame' and 'Wakehurst', the colour fades from the initial coral-pink or scarlet to a creamy white, after which the leaves gradually become suffused with the green colour they will bear for the rest of their lives.

CARE AND CULTIVATION

Although they are hardy pieris do benefit from shelter, not only to protect the new growths but also because the budding inflorescences may drop if they are frosted, and this may well happen as early as late autumn. Mulching with well-rotted leaf-mould or other organic matter protects the roots from frost as well as feeding the plants.

Some of the more vigorous kinds send out the occasional very strong shoot. It is best to prune this back in the early spring to keep the shape of the bush as required.

Pieris 'Firecrest'

Pieris *Ericaceae*

Pieris 'Bert Chandler'

P. 'Bert Chandler' An unusual small shrub reaching about 1.5m (5ft) high with bright salmon-pink young foliage that changes to creamy yellow, then white and finally to green. Given an open position, the leaves are attractively creamy yellow throughout the winter. It rarely flowers. Raised 1936 in Australia.
H4

P. 'Firecrest' A vigorous large shrub with bright red young foliage similar to 'Forest Flame', but with broader, more deeply veined leaves. It is also hardier than 'Forest Flame'. Large white flowers are borne in dense panicles in spring.
H4 ♛ 1993

P. 'Flaming Silver' A small shrub with bright red young leaves that show no variegation at first but soon develop striking silvery white margins that are pink at first. The flowers are creamy white. It is a sport of 'Forest Flame'. Raised in Holland.
H4 ♛ 1993

P. 'Forest Flame' A superb large shrub, immensely popular with those who can give it the right conditions. The leaves pass from red through pink and creamy white before becoming green. The white flowers are

Pieris 'Flaming Silver'

Pieris 'Forest Flame'

massed in large, drooping panicles at the ends of the shoots.
H4 ♛ 1993

P. formosa 'Jermyns' A superb shrub for milder places. The young leaves are deep wine red and become glossy green. The long, pendulous flower panicles are present over a long winter period and are an attractive red in all parts except the white flowers themselves, which open in spring.
H3 ♛ 1993

P. f. 'Wakehurst' A most lovely shrub in mild places, strong and vigorous, with relatively short, broad leaves. The vivid red young foliage contrasts beautifully with the glistening white flowers.
H3 ♛ 1993

P. japonica A medium-sized shrub with attractive, glossy foliage, coppery when young, and white, waxy flowers borne in drooping panicles. Japan, E China, Taiwan. In cultivation 1870.
H4

Pieris formosa 'Jermyns'

Pieris formosa 'Wakehurst'

Pieris japonica 'Blush'

P. j. 'Blush' A form with attractive dark glossy foliage that is coppery when young. The white, waxy flowers open from rose-pink buds in a deep purplish pink inflorescence.
H4 ♔ 1993

P. j. 'Christmas Cheer' A very hardy shrub with white flowers flushed deep rose at the tips, creating a delightfully bicolored effect. The flowers have a crimped appearance and are abundantly produced even on young plants, often appearing in winter. The flower stalks are deep rose.
H4

P. j. 'Daisen' From Mount Daisen in Japan. The pink flowers are deeper pink in the bud. In cultivation 1967.
H4

P. j. 'Debutante' A unusual low-growing form, making a compact mound. The white flowers are in dense, strictly upright panicles. Yakushima Island.
H4 ♔ 1993

P. j. 'Dorothy Wyckoff' The leaves of this form are dark green, deeply veined, turning bronze in cold weather. The inflorescence is rich purplish red during winter and the flowers open to white from pale pink buds and contrast with the deep red calyces. Raised 1960 in the United States.
H4

Pieris japonica 'Flamingo'

P. j. 'Flamingo' A form with flowers deep red in bud, borne in large panicles, and opening deep pink before fading to rose-pink and eventually becoming striped with white. Raised 1961 in the United States.
H4

Pieris japonica 'Grayswood'

P. j. 'Grayswood' A compact small shrub with narrow, dark green leaves and panicles with long, spreading and drooping branches bearing many densely packed small white flowers.
H4 ♔ 1993

P. j. 'Little Heath' Similar to 'White Rim'

Pieris japonica 'Little Heath'

but more dwarf and compact and with smaller leaves. It usually flowers sparsely but can be free flowering if grown in a position with enough light. The buds are pink. It occasionally sports to 'Little Heath Green'.
H4 ♔ 1993

Pieris japonica 'Little Heath Green'

P. j. 'Little Heath Green' A compact, dwarf shrub that forms a mound and has small green leaves that are bronze-red when young. It rarely if ever flowers.
H4 ♔ 1993

P. j. 'Mountain Fire' The young leaves of this small to medium-sized shrub are red, turning to deep, glossy, chestnut brown. The flowers are white.
H4 ♔ 1993

P. j. 'Pink Delight' A small to medium-sized shrub with long, drooping panicles of pale pink flowers, white at the base and fading to white.
H4 ♔ 1993

Pieris japonica 'Pink Delight'

Pieris japonica 'Purity'

P. j. 'Purity' A small, compact shrub with fairly upright trusses of relatively large snow-white flowers. The young foliage is pale green.
H4 ♔ 1993

P. j. 'Red Mill' A very hardy small to medium-sized shrub with dark green leaves that are a brilliant bronze-red when young,

Pieris japonica 'Red Mill'

gradually fading to green. The white flowers are carried in drooping panicles.
H4

Pieris japonica 'Scarlett O'Hara'

P. j. 'Scarlett O'Hara' A small to medium-sized shrub with an abundance of dense, hanging clusters of pure white flowers that open early. The young growths are bronze.
H4

P. j. Taiwanensis Group There is no absolute distinction between the plants from Japan and Taiwan but the latter tend to have matt green, more leathery leaves with fewer teeth and the panicles are less drooping. The young growths are bronze or bronze-red. Taiwan. Introduced 1918 by Ernest Wilson.
H4

P. j. 'Valley Rose' The flowers of this small to medium-sized shrub are deep pink in bud, opening rose-pink and streaked with white at the base, fading to white.

Pieris japonica Taiwanensis Group

Pieris japonica 'Valley Rose'

They are in large, hanging clusters and freely borne. This form is rather like 'Blush' in flower but without the attractively coloured young inflorescence. The young foliage is pale green.
H4

P. j. 'Valley Valentine' A small to medium-sized shrub with deep, dusky red

Pieris japonica 'Valley Valentine'

flowers, hardly fading at all, and white at the base. They are borne in large, drooping clusters and tend to be lost among the dark foliage.

H4 ♔ 1993

Pieris japonica 'White Rim'

***P. j.* 'White Rim'** A slow-growing shrub with its leaves prettily variegated with creamy white and flushed with pink when young. This is one of the most attractive of all silver-variegated shrubs and has been mistakenly known in the nursery trade as 'Variegata' for a very long time.

H4 ♔ 1993

Pileostegia *Hydrangeaceae*

A genus of three species of east Asian evergreen shrubs that climb by aerial roots. The following species, the only one in general cultivation, needs a wall or tree trunk in sun or shade and will grow in all types of fertile soil. Prune woody stems in spring if required.

Pileostegia viburnoides

P. viburnoides A rather slow-growing plant, reaching 6m (18ft). Its leaves are leathery, slender and strongly veined, and the creamy white flowers are borne in crowded clusters in late summer and autumn. It is one of the best evergreen climbers for growing on any aspect, including shady or north-facing walls. Himalayas. Introduced 1908 by Ernest Wilson.

H4 ♔ 1993

Pimelea *Thymelaeaceae*

A genus of about 80 species of shrubs from Australasia. They are small-leaved evergreens, closely related to Daphne *and needing much the same treatment. They are not recommended for shallow, chalky soils.*

P. prostrata A pretty, interesting, carpeting species with prostrate or nearly prostrate branches clothed with small, grey-green leaves. The fragrant white flow-

Pimelea prostrata

ers are borne in clusters in summer and followed by fleshy, white berries. It is an excellent plant for a scree. New Zealand.

H3

Pinus *Pinaceae*
Pine

A genus of more than 100 species of evergreen trees, widely distributed in the temperate regions of the northern hemisphere, South to Central America and Indonesia. Young trees are normally conical and broaden as they age, becoming bushy or flat-topped. The leaves are long and needle-like, in bundles of 2–5. Cones vary from rounded and conical to banana-shaped and ripen at the end of the second year. In most species the seeds are released as soon as they ripen, but in some they are retained in closed cones for many years until, in nature, they are acted upon by the heat of forest fires, which causes them to open and release their seeds. This mechanism ensures the maximum chance for the forest to renew itself.

Some pines succeed on the poorest soils, whether alkaline or acid, but as a rule those with their needles in bundles of five are not satisfactory on shallow chalk soils. Some species make excellent windbreaks, especially near the sea. All of them dislike shade and very few will tolerate smoke-polluted air. Several dwarf or slow-growing forms have appeared in cultivation, many of them eminently suitable for the rock garden.

P. aristata (Bristlecone pine) A large shrub or small tree with leaves in fives, up to 4cm (1½in) long, flecked with white resin and closely pressed to the branchlets. The cones are up to 9cm (3½in) long and their scales have slender-spined, bristle-like bosses. In the wild, trees up to 2000 years old have been recorded. (See also *P. longaeva.*) Rocky Mountains of the United States. Introduced 1863.

H4

P. armandii (Armand's pine) A medium-sized tree with leaves in fives and 10–15cm (4–6in) long. The cones are in twos and threes, barrel-shaped, up to 19cm (7in) long, becoming pendulous. Himalayan region and Taiwan.

H4

P. bungeana (Lace-bark pine) A small to medium-sized tree or large shrub, typically

Pinus armandii

Pinus contorta

Pinus bungeana

branching from or near the base. On trees in cultivation the smooth grey-green bark flakes away, creating a beautiful patchwork of white, yellow, purple, brown and green. The leaves are in threes, 5–10cm (2–4in) long and rigid; the cones are up to 7cm (3in) long. Discovered 1831 by Dr Bunge in a temple garden near Beijing and introduced 1846 by Robert Fortune.
H4

P. cembra (Arolloa pine) A small to medium-sized tree with, in cultivation, a characteristically dense, conical or columnar habit. The leaves are in fives, 5–8cm (2–3in) long, densely crowded, and dark blue-green with blue-white inner surfaces. The cones are deep blue, up to 8cm (3in) long; they never open and the seeds are released only when attacked by rot, squirrels or birds. A formal-looking tree and most ornamental. Mountains of C Europe and N Asia. In cultivation 1746.
H4 ♛ 1993

P. contorta (Beach pine) A medium-sized to large tree, occasionally a large bush, with short branches. The leaves are in pairs, up to 5cm (2in) long, twisted and yellowish green. The cones are paired or in clusters, 5cm (2in) long, spiny, and open when mature. It will not grow in chalky or limy soils but enjoys light, stony or sandy soil and is used for dune-fixing near the sea. W North America. Introduced 1831 by David Douglas.
H4

Pinus contorta subsp. latifolia

P. c. subsp. latifolia (Lodgepole pine) A medium-sized tree, less vigorous than the type and with slightly broader leaves and larger cones, which open in the wild only as a result of forest fire. The Native Americans used it as the central pole of their huts, hence its common name. W North America. Introduced 1853 by John Jeffrey.
H4

P. c. 'Spaan's Dwarf' A small, slow-grow-

ing form with numerous upright, spreading shoots densely clothed with short, dark green leaves.
H4

P. coulteri (Big-cone pine) A remarkable, striking, medium-sized to large tree with very stout shoots. The leaves are in threes, up to 30cm (1ft) long, stiff and curved, pale bluish grey-green. The cones, which are not often borne in Britain, are very large, up to 35cm (14in) long, and remain a long time on the tree. They weigh up to 3kg (6½lb) when fresh and are the largest of any conifer. S California, N Mexico. Discovered 1832 by Dr Coulter and introduced the same year by David Douglas.
H4 ♛ 1993

P. densiflora (Japanese red pine) A medium-sized to large tree with leaves in pairs, up to 12cm (5in) long and twisted. The cones are in twos or threes and 5cm (2in) long. It has similar bark to the Scots pine (*P. sylvestris*). It requires a lime-free soil. Introduced 1852.
H4

P. d. 'Oculus-draconis' (Dragon's-eye pine) A curious form with branchlets, when viewed from above, showing alternate yellow and green rings of needles, hence the name. In cultivation 1890.
H4

P. d. 'Umbraculifera' A miniature tree of extremely slow growth. It has an umbrella-like head of branches and bears tiny cones. The largest specimen at the Hillier Gardens and Arboretum attained 2 × 2.5m (6 × 8ft) in 30 years. In cultivation 1890.
H4

Pinus densiflora 'Umbraculifera'

Pinus jeffreyi

P. jeffreyi A large, imposing tree with a conical or spire-like crown. The leaves are in threes, up to 22cm (9in) long, dull bluish green or pale grey, crowded towards the ends of the branchlets. The cones are 13–20cm (5–8in) long and spiny. It differs from *P. ponderosa* in its black or purple-grey bark and stouter, longer, bluish leaves. SW United States. Introduced c1852.
H4 ♔ 1993

P. koraiensis (Korean pine) A medium-sized, loose, conical tree. The leaves are usually in fives, up to 12cm (5in) long, stiff and rough to the touch, and blue-green. The cones are up to 14cm (5½in) long. E Asia. Introduced 1861 by J. G. Veitch.
H4

P. k. 'Compacta Glauca' A strong-growing, compact form with short, stout branches and attractive, densely packed, blue-bloomy leaves. In cultivation 1949.
H4

P. leucodermis (Bosnian pine) A very distinct, medium-sized tree with smooth, greenish grey bark, an egg-shaped outline and a dense habit. The leaves are in pairs, up to 9cm (3½in) long, rigid and erect and dark, almost black-green. The cones are up to 7.5cm (3in) long and bright blue in the first year. It is particularly suitable for dry soils and shallow ones over chalk. Italy, Balkans. Introduced 1864.
H4 ♔ 1993

P. l. 'Satellit' A narrowly conical form with leaves densely clustered and pressed against the shoots on the young growths. In later life it is more spreading.
H4

Pinus leucodermis 'Schmidtii'

P. l. 'Schmidtii' A slow-growing, dwarf or small form that develops into a dense, compact mound. Previously listed as 'Pygmy'.
H4 ♔ 1993

P. longaeva This species, first described only in 1970, is closely related to *P. aristata* but does not have the white specks of resin on its leaves. It is also a bristlecone pine but is mentioned here chiefly because specimens in the White Mountains of California have been proved to be up to 5000 years old. These are among the oldest living plants, although some single specimens of *Gaylussacia brachycera* have been found in New Jersey – some believe there is a colony occupying as much as 4 hectares (9 acres) – which are twice as old.
H4

P. montezumae (Montezuma pine) A magnificent, medium-sized to large tree with rough, deeply fissured bark and a large, domed crown. The leaves are usually in fives but vary from three to eight on some

Pinus montezumae

trees. They are 18–25cm (7–10in) long, bluish grey, spreading and drooping. The cones are 7.5–25cm (3–10in) long. It is a bold, imposing and remarkably beautiful tree that is reasonably hardy if given shelter. Mountains of Mexico. Introduced 1839.
H3

Pinus mugo

P. mugo (Mountain pine) A very hardy, small, medium-sized or large shrub or small tree with leaves in pairs. It is very variable in the wild and has given rise to several dwarf forms that succeed on almost all soils, including chalk and limestone. C Europe.
H4

P. m. 'Gnom' A small, compact selection that forms a dense, dark green, globular mound. In cultivation 1937.
H4

P. m. 'Mops' A dwarf, globular, dense, slow-growing bush. It is ideal for the rock garden or scree. In cultivation 1951.
H4 ♔ 1993

Pinus mugo 'Gnom'

Pinus mugo var. pumilio

curved or twisted, dark bluish grey or yellowish grey-green. The cones are up to 9cm (4in) long and often remain unopened on the branches for many years. In the wild the cones have been known to stay intact for 30–40 years until liberated by forest fires. This pine is suitable for exposed areas but requires a lime-free soil. California. Introduced 1848.
H4 ♆ 1993

Pinus nigra

Pinus mugo 'Mops'

Pinus mugo 'Winter Gold'

P. nigra (Austrian pine) A commonly planted and familiar large tree with dark, rough bark and a dense head of large branches. The leaves are in pairs, 8–12cm (3–5in) long and densely crowded on the branches. It and all its forms are excellent for maritime areas and do well in most soils. It thrives better than any other pine in chalky soils and bleak exposures and makes an excellent windbreak. SE Europe. Introduced 1835.
H4 ♆ 1993

Pinus mugo 'Ophir'

Pinus muricata

Pinus nigra 'Hornibrookiana'

P. m. 'Ophir' A compact, bun-shaped dwarf shrub with golden yellow winter foliage.
H4

P. m. var. pumilio A dwarf form that is often prostrate but occasionally reaches a height of 2m (6ft). Alps of C Europe.
H4 ♆ 1993

P. m. 'Winter Gold' A dwarf, spreading bush of open habit. The foliage is golden yellow in winter.
H4

P. muricata (Bishop pine) A picturesque medium-sized to large tree with a dense, rather flat head of branches. The leaves are in pairs, up to 15cm (6in) long, stiff and

P. n. 'Hornibrookiana' A dwarf, very slow-growing form that makes a round, low mound. Originated before 1932.
H4

P. n. subsp. laricio, syn. *P. nigra* var. *maritima* (Corsican pine) A large tree with a straight main stem to the top. It is more open than the Austrian pine and has fewer, shorter and more level branches. Its needles are not as stiff and they are grey-green and less densely arranged. It will grow in almost any soil. S Italy and Corsica. Introduced 1759 by Philip Miller.
H4 ♈ 1993

P. nigra var. maritima See *P. n.* subsp. *laricio*.

Pinus parviflora

P. parviflora (Japanese white pine) A small to medium-sized tree, conical when young, flat-topped in maturity. The leaves are in fives, 5–7.5cm (2–3in) long, slightly curved and deep blue green with blue-white inner surfaces. The cones are 5–8cm (2–3in) long. Japan. Introduced 1861 by J. G. Veitch.
H4 ♈ 1993

P. p. 'Adcock's Dwarf' A slow-growing, eventually medium-sized shrub of rather compact, upright habit. The leaves are up to 2.5cm (1in) long, greyish green, and produced in congested bunches at the tips of the shoots. Raised 1961 at Hillier Nurseries by Graham Adcock and in 1990 was 2.5m (8ft) high and 1.3m (4ft) across.
H4 ♈ 1993

P. p. 'Tempelhof' A vigorous form with glaucous blue foliage.
H4

Pinus parviflora 'Adcock's Dwarf'

Pinus parviflora 'Tempelhof'

Pinus patula

P. patula An extremely beautiful, small to medium-sized, graceful tree with reddish bark, long, spreading branches and pendulous, glaucous green young shoots. The leaves are bright green, usually in threes, occasionally in fours or fives, and are up to 30cm (1ft) long. This lovely tree will grow uninjured in all but the coldest areas. It

requires a lime-free soil. Mexico.
H3 ♈ 1993

P. pinaster (Bournemouth pine, maritime pine) A sparsely branched, medium-sized or occasionally large tree with a bare stem and thick, reddish brown or deep purple bark furrowed into small squares. The leaves are in pairs, up to 25cm (10in) long, rigid, curved and dull grey. The cones are up to 18cm (7in) long, rich shining brown, often remaining on the tree for several years. It is an excellent species for sandy soils and seaside districts, especially in the warmer parts of Britain, and is the main source of turpentine and resin in W France. Mediterranean region. In cultivation since the sixteenth century.
H4 ♈ 1993

Pinus pinea

P. pinea (Stone pine, umbrella pine) A very distinct, small to medium-sized tree with a characteristically dense, flat-topped or umbrella-shaped head. The leaves are in pairs, up to 15cm (6in) long, stiff and slightly twisted and sharply pointed. The stalked cones are up to 15cm (6in) long and the seeds are large and edible. It is particularly good in sandy soils and maritime areas. Mediterranean region.
H4 ♈ 1993

P. ponderosa (Western yellow pine) A large, striking tree with a tall, clear trunk, scaly cinnamon bark and spreading or drooping branches. The leaves are in threes, up to 25cm (10in) long, stiff and curved and crowded at the ends of the branchlets. The cones are armed with small spines and are up to 16cm (6in) long. It is a

Pinus ponderosa

Pinus radiata

Pinus strobus 'Nana'

variable species. W North America. Introduced 1826 by David Douglas.
H4 🏆 1993

P. pumila 'Glauca' A form of the very variable Dwarf Siberian pine, forming a bushy, small to medium-sized shrub with bright grey-blue foliage that should be grown in a lime-free soil. The leaves are in fives.
H4 🏆 1993

Pinus pumila 'Glauca'

P. radiata (Monterey pine) A large tree with deeply fissured bark and a dense head of branches. The leaves are in threes, up to 15cm (6in) long, and are bright green and densely crowded on the branchlets. The cones are up to 15cm (6in) long, borne in whorls along the branches and often remaining intact for many years. It is an attractive, very fast-growing tree for mild inland areas and near the coast. In an open situation it tends to bear branches almost to ground level; if grown among other trees it

forms a long, fairly straight trunk. It is excellent for withstanding sea winds but requires a lime-free soil. California. Introduced 1833 by David Douglas.
H3–4 🏆 1993

Pinus strobus

P. strobus (Weymouth pine, white pine) A large tree, conical when young and with a rounded head when older. The leaves are in fives, up to 15cm (6in) long and somewhat bloomy green. The cones are up to 20cm (8in) long, pendent, on slender stalks liberally flecked with resin. Ornamental habit and fast growth. E North America. In cultivation since the mid-sixteenth century.
H4

P. s. 'Nana' A small form that develops into a dense bush. There are several slight variations of this form, some of which are more vigorous and grow larger.
H4 🏆 1993

P. s. 'Nivea' An attractive medium-sized form in which the glaucous leaves are

tipped with milky white, giving the whole tree an unusual silvery appearance.
H4

P. sylvestris (Scots pine) A large, tall-stemmed tree that may sometimes be low, picturesque and spreading. It is easily recognized by its characteristic and most attractive reddish young bark. The leaves are in pairs, up to 10cm (4in) long, twisted, and grey-green or blue-green. The cones are up to 7.5cm (3in) long on short stalks. It can be grown in all kinds of soils but does not reach its maximum size or age on damp, acid soils or shallow ones over chalk. Siberia to Scotland.
H4 🏆 1993

Pinus sylvestris

P. s. 'Aurea' A slow-growing small tree with leaves that are a striking golden yellow in winter.
H4 AGM 1993

P. s. 'Beuvronensis' A miniature Scots pine, forming a small, compact, dome-

Pinus sylvestris 'Aurea'

Pinus sylvestris 'Beuvronensis'

Pinus sylvestris 'Fastigiata'

Pinus sylvestris 'Moseri'

Pinus sylvestris 'Watereri'

Pinus thunbergii

shaped shrublet. It is a superb subject for the rock garden. In cultivation 1891.
H4 ☖ 1993

P. s. 'Edwin Hillier' A beautiful form with silvery blue-green leaves and reddish stems. It is referred to in some publications as 'Argentea' but has no connection with *P.s.* f. *argentea*, which is from the Caucasus. Selected 1926 by Edwin Hillier.
H4

P. s. 'Fastigiata' A remarkable form with the distinctive shape of a Lombardy poplar. In cultivation 1856.
H4

P. s. 'Gold Coin' A slow-growing small tree similar to 'Aurea' but with deep yellow foliage in winter.
H4

P. s. 'Moseri' A very slow-growing, dense, globular or ovoid, miniature tree with leaves that turn yellow or yellow-green in winter. In cultivation 1900.
H4 ☖ 1993

P. s. 'Watereri' A slow-growing, medium-sized bush or rarely a small tree, conical at first, later becoming rounded. The original plant, which dates from about 1865, is about 8m (25ft) high.
H4

P. thunbergii (Black pine) A distinct and splendid large tree with stout, twisted branches. The rigid, twisted needles, 7–18cm (3–7in) long, are in pairs, and the cones, up to 6cm (3in) long, are borne singly or in clusters. The black pine is one of the most important timber trees in Japan, where it often occurs by the coast. In cultivation it makes a good windbreak in maritime areas and grows well in poor, sandy soils. Japan, Korea. Introduced 1852.
H4

P. wallichiana (Bhutan pine) An elegant, large, broad-headed tree that retains its lower branches when growing in an isolated position. The needles are in fives, up to 20cm (8in) long, blue-green, slender and drooping with age. The stalked cones are solitary or in bunches, banana-shaped and 15–25cm (6–10in) long. This graceful species is moderately lime-tolerant but will not grow on shallow soils over chalk. Himalayas. Introduced c1823.
H4

Pinus wallichiana

P. w. 'Umbraculifera' A small, dome-shaped, glaucous, slow-growing, dense bush. It has long needles that are often kinked.
H4

Piptanthus *Leguminosae*

A genus of two species of large shrubs, one evergreen and one deciduous, with leaves made up of three leaflets and with showy yellow pea flowers. They grow well in any well-drained soil, including chalk.

P. laburnifolius See *P. nepalensis*.

Piptanthus nepalensis

P. nepalensis, syn. *P. laburnifolius* (Evergreen laburnum) An attractive, almost evergreen shrub 2.5–3.5m (8–11ft) high, with large, bright yellow, laburnum-like flowers in late spring. In severe winters it loses its leaves. It can be grown in the open as a specimen shrub but is excellent on a wall.

An earlier-flowering, more silky-leaved form from Bhutan is slightly more tender. Himalayas. Introduced 1821.
H3–4

Pistacia *Anacardiaceae*

A genus of nine species of evergreen and deciduous shrubs or occasionally small trees, related to Rhus *and found in warm-temperate regions of the northern hemisphere. The following is the only hardy species and even so will not tolerate the coldest parts of cool-temperate areas. It is best in sun and succeeds in all types of soil.*

Pistacia chinensis

P. chinensis (Chinese pistachio) A hardy, large deciduous shrub with elegant, glossy green, pinnate leaves that assume gorgeous colours in autumn. The greenish, inconspicuous unisexual flowers are in dense clusters and the fruits, which are seldom formed, are small, reddish at first and then blue. China. Introduced 1897.
H4

Pittosporum *Pittosporaceae*

A large genus of some 200 species of evergreen shrubs or small trees, most of which are suitable only for mild areas where they will grow well, especially near the sea. They come from Australasia, south and South-East Asia and tropical and South Africa. Several have small, scented flowers but are chiefly grown for their highly attractive, unusual and distinctive foliage, which is excellent for cutting. They enjoy all types of well-drained soil and are better off if given some shelter from wind. No pittosporum is hardy in the

coldest areas, but P. dallii *comes closest to being fully hardy in cool-temperate or mild continental climates.*

P. crassifolium 'Variegatum' One of the hardiest species, with leaves 5–7.5cm (2–3in) long, more or less oval, thick and leathery. In this form they are grey-green, attractively margined with light cream. The flowers, borne in terminal clusters, are deep purple. A large shrub or small tree, it makes an excellent dense screen or shelter-belt in mild coastal areas.
H3

Pittosporum dallii

P. dallii A large, spreading shrub or occasionally a rounded, small tree. The shoots and leaf stalks are dark reddish purple and the elliptic to lance-shaped leaves are leathery and usually jagged-toothed (occasionally entire) and matt green. The fragrant cream flowers with protruding stamens are borne in small clusters in summer. New Zealand, rare in the wild.
H3–4

P. eugenioides 'Variegatum' A very pretty and elegant medium-sized shrub for mild climates. Its undulating leaves, 5–10cm (2–4in) long are margined with cream and pleasantly aromatic. In cultivation 1882.
H3 ♛ 1993

P. 'Garnettii' A medium to large, conical to broadly columnar shrub with grey-green leaves irregularly margined with cream and marked, flushed or spotted with pink to red from late summer through winter.
H3 ♛ 1993

Pittosporum 'Garnettii'

Pittosporum tenuifolium

P. tenuifolium A charming large shrub or small tree of columnar habit, with bright, pale green, wavy leaves, prettily set on black twigs. It is one of the hardier species, extensively used as cut evergreen for floristry, and is a good edging plant in mild places. The small, chocolate-purple, honey-scented flowers appear in late spring to summer. New Zealand.
H3 ♔ 1993

P. t. 'Abbotsbury Gold' A form similar to 'Eila Keightley' but with the variegation most apparent on young foliage and becoming indistinct. Reputed to have arisen as a sport 1970 at Abbotsbury, England, but this is doubtful.
H3

P. t. 'Eila Keightley' syn. 'Sunburst' The leaves of this form are blotched in the centres with bright greenish yellow and this variegation is most noticeable on older foliage. Discovered 1964 as a sport.
H3

P. t. 'Gold Star' A compact form making a medium-sized shrub. The leaves have a conspicuous blotch of bright yellow-green in the centre, becoming dark green.
H3

Pittosporum tenuifolium 'Irene Paterson'

P. t. 'Irene Paterson' A most attractive, slow-growing form reaching about 2.5m (8ft) high. Its young leaves emerge cream, becoming deep green marbled with white, and developing a pink tinge in winter. Later summer growth is pale green. New Zealand. In cultivation 1970.
H3 ♔ 1993

P. t. 'Purpureum' A medium-sized shrub with pale green leaves turning to deep bronze-purple.
H3

Pittosporum tenuifolium 'Silver Queen'

P. t. 'Silver Queen' A neat and handsome specimen shrub with leaves suffused with silvery grey, narrowly margined with white.
H3 ♔ 1993

Pittosporum tenuifolium 'Purpureum'

P. t. 'Sunburst' See **'Eila Keightley'**.

P. t. 'Tom Thumb' A dense, rounded dwarf shrub with leaves that are green and become deep reddish purple. The colour is brighter and redder than that of 'Purpureum'. Raised c1960 in New Zealand.
H3 ♔ 1993

P. t. 'Warnham Gold' The young leaves of this medium-sized shrub are greenish yellow, maturing to golden yellow, particularly attractive in autumn and winter. Raised 1959 in Sussex.
H3 ♔ 1993

P. tobira A rather slow-growing species, eventually making a large shrub with leaves broadest towards the ends, bright glossy green and growing in whorls, among which are orange-scented flowers in summer, creamy white at first then turning yellow. It is an excellent wall shrub and is very drought-resistant. China, Taiwan, Japan. Introduced 1804.
H3 ♔ 1993

Pittosporum tenuifolium 'Tom Thumb'

Pittosporum tenuifolium 'Warnham Gold'

P. t. 'Variegatum' A medium-sized shrub bearing grey-green leaves with an irregular but conspicuous bright cream margin. If grown under glass, it often flowers in winter. It is extensively grown in the southern US as a low, clipped hedge, being particularly valued for its drought resistance. H3

Pittosporum tobira

Plagianthus *Malvaceae*

A genus of two species of graceful deciduous trees or shrubs native to New Zealand. They succeed in mild areas in all types of fertile soils.

P. regius (Ribbonwood) A graceful, slender, small to medium-sized tree with toothed leaves. The individual white flowers are inconspicuous but are borne in large panicles in late spring. Juvenile plants form dense bushes of slender, interlacing branches with toothed or lobed leaves. It is a curious tree that passes through several distinct stages of growth. Introduced 1870. H3

Platanus *Platanaceae*

A genus of about six species of magnificent, maple-like deciduous trees with attractive flaking bark. Apart from P. orientalis *and one species from South-east Asia they are North American. They can be grown in all types of fertile soil but do not grow very large on chalk and may become chlorotic if the chalky soil is very shallow.*

P. × acerifolia *See P. × hispanica.*

Platanus × hispanica

P. × hispanica, syn. *P. × acerifolia* (London plane) A large, noble tree with attractive mottled or patchwork flaking bark and large palmate leaves. The rounded, burr-like fruit clusters are in strings of 2–6 and hang like baubles on the branches from early summer right through until the following spring. Pollution tolerant.
H4 ♈ 1993
P. × h. 'Suttneri' A striking large form with large leaves boldly variegated with cream or white.
H4
P. orientalis (Oriental plane) A large, stately, long-lived tree that develops a wide-spreading head of branches. The bark is attractively dappled and flaking, and the

Platanus orientalis

leaves are deeply five-lobed with the leaves reaching halfway or more to the base. The bristly fruit clusters are 2–6 on a stalk. It is a magnificent large tree and reaches a great age. SE Europe. In cultivation in England in the early sixteenth century.
H4 ♆ 1993

P. o. 'Digitata' A large tree with leaves deeply divided into 3–5 finger-like lobes.
H4

P. o. var. insularis (Cyprian plane) A small tree with smaller, variably shaped leaves, usually deeply divided into narrow lobes and wedge-shaped at the base.
H4

Platycarya *Juglandaceae*

A genus of one deciduous species, related to Pterocarya.

P. strobilacea A beautiful small tree with pinnate leaves made up of 7–15 stalkless,

lance-shaped, toothed leaflets. The flowers are small, with the males in cylindrical catkins and the females in erect, green clusters like cones at the ends of the current year's growth in late summer. It has distinctive, cone-like fruits. It is better in warmer, dryer areas and does not survive very low temperatures, although it can be regarded

Platycarya strobilacea

as hardy. It will grow in any good, preferably deep soil. Far East. Introduced 1845 by Robert Fortune.
H4

Pleioblastus *Gramineae*

A genus of mostly smaller to medium-sized evergreen bamboos with underground running stems. Many species form extensive patches or thickets and should be planted only where there is enough space. They are moisture-lovers but will grow on good soil over chalk. The genus includes many species previously in Arundinaria.

Pleioblastus auricomus

P. auricomus, syn. *Arundinaria viridi-striata, A. auricoma* A hardy species with erect, purplish green canes up to 1–2m (3–6ft) high, forming small patches. The leaves are variable in size, up to 20cm (8in) long and 4cm (1½in) wide, dark green and striped with rich yellow, often more yellow than green. It is the best of the variegated bamboos, quite small when grown in shade and an excellent tub plant. Old canes can be cut to ground level in autumn to encourage bright young foliage. Japan. Introduced c1870.
H4 ♆ 1993

P. hindsii, syn. *Arundinaria hindsii* A strong-growing species that forms dense thickets of erect, olive-green canes 2.5–3.5m (8–11ft) high. The leaves are variable in size, up to 23cm (9in) long and 2.5cm (1in) wide, rich sea-green and thickly clustered towards the summits of the canes. It thrives in sun or dense shade and makes an excellent hedge or small screen. Japan. Introduced 1875.
H4

P. humilis **'Gauntlettii',** syn. *Arundinaria* 'Gauntlettii' A small, clump-forming bamboo with bright green, later dull purple canes up to 80cm (32in) high. The leaves are 7.5–18cm (3–7in) long by 1–2cm (¹/₂–³/₄in) wide. It is an uncommon bamboo of obscure, possibly Japanese, origin.
H4

P. pumilus, syn. *Arundinaria pumila* A very hardy, dwarf bamboo forming dense carpets of slender, dull purple canes 30–80cm (12–32in) high, with conspicuously hairy joints. The leaves are 5–18cm (2–7in) long by 1–2cm (¹/₂–³/₄in) wide. It is a far-creeping plant, useful as ground cover but only where there is plenty of space. Japan. Introduced late 19th century.
H4

P. pygmaeus, syn. *Arundinaria pygmaea* A dwarf species forming carpets of slender stems up to 25cm (10in) long, taller in shade. The leaves are up to 13cm (5in) long by 2cm (³/₄in) wide. An excellent ground-cover plant where there is enough space. Japan. Introduced c1870.
H4

P. simonii, syn. *Arundinaria simonii* A vigorous bamboo of erect habit, forming dense clumps or patches of tall, olive-green canes up to 4.5m (13ft) or more. The first-year canes are liberally dusted with a white bloom. The leaves are 7.5 × 30cm (3–12in) long by 1–3cm (¹/₂–1¹/₂in) wide. The leaf undersurface is green on one side and greyish green on the other. It is a hardy species with luxuriant foliage, useful as a hedge or screen. China. Introduced 1862.
H4

Pleioblastus variegatus

P. variegatus, syn. *Arundinaria fortunei* A low, tufted species forming dense thickets of erect, zig-zag, pale green canes 0.8–1.2m (32in–4ft) high. The leaves are 5–20cm (2–8in) long by 1–2.5cm (¹/₂–1in) wide, dark green with white stripes that fade to pale green. It is the best of the white-variegated bamboos and suitable for the rock garden or a tub. Japan. Introduced 1863.
H4 ♈ 1993

Plumbago *Plumbaginaceae*

A genus of about 15 species of deciduous shrubs, annuals and herbaceous plants from warm temperate and tropical regions. The following is valued as a conservatory plant, where it makes a superb display when given support.

P. auriculata, syn. *P. capensis* An extremely beautiful deciduous shrub, best treated as if it were a climber. It bears an extraordinary profusion of sky-blue, somewhat phlox-like flowers on the current season's growth throughout summer and autumn and sometimes into early winter. It should have a sunny position in a rich compost and be watered freely during the growing season. It is important to keep it cool in winter and early spring. S Africa, naturalized in S Europe.
H1–2 ♈ 1993

P. capensis See *P. auriculata.*

Podocarpus *Podocarpaceae*

There are about 90 species of these evergreen coniferous trees and shrubs, mainly confined in the wild to the southern hemisphere in warm-temperate and tropical countries. Their leaves are variable in shape and usually spirally arranged. The fruits are usually red, fleshy and berry-like. The flowers are insignificant. Several species are suitable for milder areas and a few may be classed as hardy. They succeed in most types of soil, whether acid or alkaline, and tolerate shade.

P. alpinus A remarkably hardy dwarf species, forming a low, densely branched mound or creeping carpet. Sometimes it is a small bush of upright or pendulous habit. The leaves are yew-like, narrow, blue-green or grey-green and crowd the stems. It can

Podocarpus alpinus

be grown in the rock garden or as ground cover. SE Australia, Tasmania.
H4

P. andinus (Chilean yew) A large shrub or small to medium-sized tree resembling a yew. The leaves are linear, up to 2.5cm (1in) long, bright green above and twisted to show the bloomy green undersurfaces. The fruits are bloomy black, like small damsons. It grows well on good soils over chalk. Andes of S Chile. Introduced 1860 by Robert Pearce.
H3–4

Podocarpus macrophyllus

P. macrophyllus One of the hardiest species, forming a large shrub or small tree of very distinct appearance. The leaves are 10–13cm (4–5in) long – even reaching 18cm (7in) on vigorous plants – and 12mm (¹/₂in) wide, bright green above, arranged in dense spirals on the stems. It is not suitable for calcareous soils. China, Japan.
H4

Podocarpus nivalis

P. nivalis (Alpine totara) One of the hardiest species, succeeding in quite cold places and doing well on chalky or limy soils. It makes a spreading mound of prostrate and short, upright stems that are densely branched and covered with small, narrow, leathery, olive-green leaves up to 2cm (³/₄in) long. It makes excellent ground cover. New Zealand.
H4

Podocarpus salignus

P. salignus A most attractive, elegant, large shrub or small tree with drooping branches and long, narrow, bright shiny green leaves, 5–15cm (2–6in) long and curved like scimitars. A well-grown specimen creates an almost tropical effect with its lush piles of glossy, evergreen, willow-like foliage. It is hardy in mild gardens when given the protection of other evergreens. Chile. Thrives in sun or shade and on most friable, well-drained soils.
H3

Poliothyrsis *Flacourtiaceae*

A genus of one deciduous species grown for its foliage and flowers, related to Idesia.

P. sinensis An interesting, hardy large shrub or small tree with slender-pointed leaves 10–15cm (4–6in) long. They are red-tinged and downy on both sides when young and become dark green, smooth and red-stalked. The unisexual flowers are fragrant, whitish in bud and open creamy yellow in panicles up to 25cm (10in) long in mid- to late summer. It flowers best in hot summers. It is quite hardy and succeeds in all types of fertile soil, preferring a sunny position but tolerating semi-shade. Introduced 1908 by Ernest Wilson.
H4

Polygala *Polygalaceae*

A very large genus of annuals, perennials and evergreen and deciduous shrubs with colourful pea-type flowers. They are found in many parts of the world. The shrubby species thrive in most kinds of soil but not shallow ones over chalk.

Polygala chamaebuxus

P. chamaebuxus A dwarf evergreen alpine shrublet that forms large tufts rarely more than 15cm (6in) high. The flowers are cream with bright yellow at the tips and are freely borne from mid-spring to early summer. It does well in a cool, moist position in the rock or peat garden. A common plant in the European alps. In cultivation 1658.
H4 ♔ 1993

P. c. var. grandiflora A very beautiful form, strikingly coloured with purple wing petals and yellow keel.
H4 ♔ 1993

P. dalmaisiana A small, almost continuously flowering deciduous shrub for the conservatory with bright purple pea-flowers. Its parents are both from South Africa. It requires a minimum temperature of 2°C (36°F).
H1 ♔ 1993

Polygala myrtifolia

P. myrtifolia One of the parents of the above, this is an erect deciduous shrub of about 1.5m (5ft) high with greenish white flowers veined with purple. *P. m.* var. *grandiflora* has larger flowers of rich purple in summer. For the conservatory or a very sheltered spot in a mild area. South Africa.
H2–3

Polygonum

P. baldschuanicum See *Fallopia baldschuanica*.
P. vacciniifolium See *Persicaria vacciniifolia*.

Poncirus *Rutaceae*

A genus of one deciduous species related to Citrus.

P. trifoliata (Japanese bitter orange) A slow-growing, medium-sized shrub with green stems armed with stout spines. The leaves are made up of three leaflets. In spring it is very beautiful when covered with

Poncirus trifoliata in autumn

Populus alba

Populus alba 'Richardii'

white, orange blossom-scented flowers almost the size of those of *Clematis montana* and exquisitely lovely when in late bud. The fruits are green and ripen to yellow, resembling miniature oranges. It makes an impenetrable barrier. It is hardy and grows well in all types of well-drained soil, preferably in full sun. N China. Introduced 1850. H4

Populus *Salicaceae*
Poplar

A genus of about 35 deciduous species, found wild throughout the northern temperate regions of the world. You should treat poplars with caution, as they are very fast-growing and their roots rapidly invade drains and disturb foundations if they are planted near houses. The problems can be especially severe if the soil is clay. In large gardens they are perfectly safe and make dramatic, if not extremely long-lived, additions to the tree-cover. Few poplars will grow on chalky soils or those that are very wet, but apart from that they are not fussy; many are tolerant of atmospheric pollution and several are excellent near the sea. The balsam poplars have pleasantly aromatic young leaves and many of the black poplars have copper-coloured growths in spring. Long catkins drape the branches of many of these attractive trees. Some species and their hybrids, however, especially the balsam poplars, are susceptible to canker, a disease in which branches die back and crack, oozing a bacterial slime. Black poplars, including the Lombardy poplar (Populus nigra 'Italica'), are resistant to canker.

P. alba A large, suckering tree with white-woolly undersurfaces to the green leaves, particularly noticeable in breezy weather. The leaves are variable in shape, some irregularly lobed and others larger and distinctly three to five-lobed like a maple; they turn yellow in autumn. It is an excellent tree in exposed sites, especially in coastal areas where, if cut back severely and kept as a shrub, it is highly effective with stooled, coloured-stemmed willows. Good on chalk. Europe and Asia, naturalized in Britain. H4

P. a. 'Pyramidalis' A large tree with erect branches, resembling the Lombardy poplar but slightly broader. In cultivation 1841. H4

***P. a.* 'Raket'** A very narrow tree with upright branches. Raised before 1956 in Holland.
H4

***P. a.* 'Richardii'** A smaller-growing, less vigorous tree or large shrub with bright golden yellow leaves that are white on their undersides. A delightful form and very effective from a distance. In cultivation 1910.
H4

***P.* 'Balsam Spire'** A large, narrow, female poplar, extremely fast-growing, with white-backed leaves and pleasantly aromatic buds in spring.
H4 ♔ 1993

Populus balsamifera

P. balsamifera (Balsam poplar) A large tree with erect branches, grown mainly for the balsam odour of its unfolding leaves. Its buds are large and sticky. North America. Introduced before 1689.
H4

P. × canadensis A large group of vigorous hybrids, known collectively as the hybrid black poplars. The following are recommended for large gardens.
H4

***P. × c.* 'Eugenei'** A large, narrow male tree with short, ascending branches and coppery young leaves.
H4

Populus × canadensis 'Robusta'

***P. × c.* 'Robusta'** A large, vigorous, male tree with an open crown and a straight bole all the way up. The young leaves are an attractive coppery red. Raised 1895 in France.
H4

***P. × c.* 'Serotina Aurea'** (Golden poplar) A large tree with leaves clear golden yellow in spring and early summer, becoming yellowish green and then golden yellow in autumn.
H4 ♔ 1993

***P. × candicans* 'Aurora'** A highly varie-

Populus × canadensis 'Serotina Aurea'

gated form of the Ontario poplar. It is a medium-sized tree with broad, ovate leaves that are cream well into late summer and often pink-tinged before turning green. The best results are obtained by hard pruning in late winter. In the first year after transplanting it is unlikely to show the variegation. This is the tree that has been wildly over-planted, particularly in Ireland and in parts of the United States, where it is derided as the potato-chip tree.
H4

P. × canescens (Grey poplar) A medium-sized to large suckering tree sometimes forming thickets. Mature specimens develop an attractive creamy grey trunk. The leaves are variable in shape, being rounded or triangular. It is one of the best poplars for chalk soils, giving yellow and sometimes red autumn colour. The woolly, crimson male catkins, up to 10cm (4in) long, are most decorative. Europe, including Britain.
H4

P. lasiocarpa A magnificent medium-sized tree with bright green, red-veined leaves that also have red stalks and are often as much as 30cm (12in) long and 23cm (9in) wide. It is imposing even when young. China. Introduced 1900 by Ernest Wilson.
H4 AGM 1993

P. nigra (Black poplar) A large, heavy-branched tree with a characteristically burred trunk. The leaves are slender-pointed and bright, shining green. Europe and W Asia.
H4

P. n.* var. *betulifolia (Manchester poplar)

Populus × candicans 'Aurora'

Populus tremula 'Pendula'

A bushy-headed large tree with downy shoots and young leaves. It is tolerant of industrial pollution. Native to E and C England.
H4 🏆 1993

P. n. 'Italica' (Lombardy poplar) The most instantly recognizable of all trees, this makes a tall, narrow column with close,

Populus nigra 'Italica'

erect branches. It is particularly suitable for making a tall screen and may be seen as such at many fruit farms. Introduced 1758.
H4 🏆 1993

P. n. 'Lombardy Gold' A striking tree with golden yellow foliage, discovered as a sport on a mature Lombardy poplar in 1974. By 1990 it had reached more than 12m (40ft) at RHS Wisley.
H4

P. szechuanica var. tibetica One of the most ornamental poplars, with large leaves resembling *P. lasiocarpa*. It has reached 24m (79ft) in the Hillier Gardens and Arboretum. W China. Introduced 1904.
H4

P. tremula (Aspen) A medium-sized, suckering tree with prominently toothed leaves that are late to appear and hang late in autumn, when they turn to clear butter-yellow. The slender leaf stalks allow the leaves to tremble and quiver in the slightest breeze. The long, grey catkins drape the

branches in late winter and early spring. Europe, Asia, North Africa.
H4 🏆 1993

P. t. 'Pendula' (Weeping aspen) One of the most effective small weeping trees, especially attractive in late winter when it bears an abundance of long, purplish grey, male catkins.
H4

P. trichocarpa (Black cottonwood) The fastest and tallest growing balsam poplar, reaching a height of over 30m (100ft) and up to twice that in the wild. The bark of young trees peels. The buds are large and sticky, and the pale leaves, net-veined beneath, are strongly balsam-scented as they unfold; they turn rich yellow in autumn. Unfortunately, as with most balsam poplars, it is liable to develop canker. W North America. Introduced 1892.
H4

Potentilla *Rosaceae*

A large genus, consisting of about 500 species, most of which are herbaceous and natives of north-temperate regions. The shrubby potentillas are very hardy, dwarf to medium-sized deciduous shrubs that thrive in any soil (although one that is too rich will tend to produce growth at the expense of flowers). The flowers are like small single roses and are displayed over a long season that begins in late spring and early summer and in some forms lasts well into late autumn. Although they are shade-tolerant, they should be grown in full sun for the best results with the exception of those with red, pink or orange flowers, which tend to fade, sometimes badly, in hot sun. Species with flowers of these colours are much better when shaded during the hottest part of the day.

Pruning consists of removing weak or very old growth at soil level and cutting back the strongest growths by about one-third. Really old bushes can be pruned for renewal by being cut back hard, and all pruning should be done in spring.

The cultivars are at one time or another treated by botanists as all belonging to the one species, P. fruticosa.

P. arbuscula **'Beesii'** A delightful dwarf shrub that displays its golden flowers in mounds of silvery foliage.
H4 ♛ 1993

Potentilla davurica 'Abbotswood'

P. davurica **'Abbotswood'** A dwarf, spreading shrub with dark foliage and white flowers that are plentifully and continuously produced.
H4 ♛ 1993

P. d. **'Abbotswood Silver'** A sport of the above with the leaflets narrowly margined with cream. Prune non-variegated shoots to prevent reversion to green.
H4

P. d. **'Manchu'** A charming form which is a mound-forming shrub and carries a continuous succession of white flowers on mats of greyish foliage.
H4

P. d. **Rhodocalyx group** A small, upright shrub of subtle, gentle quality, the aristocrat of a popular group. The rather small, cup-shaped, white flowers have reddish calyces and nod on slender stems.
H4

P. d. **var.** *veitchii* A small, graceful bush about 1m (3ft) high with arching branches and pure white flowers. W and C China. Introduced 1900 by Ernest Wilson.
H4

P. **'Dart's Golddigger'** A splendid, dense, compact, dwarf shrub with light grey-green foliage and large, butter-yellow flowers. In cultivation 1970.
H4

P. **'Daydawn'** A small shrub with flowers of an unusual shade of peach-pink suffused with cream. A sport of 'Tangerine' and best in a little shade.
H4 ♛ 1993

P. **'Eastleigh Cream'** A small, dense shrub that spreads to form a low mound. The leaves are green and the flowers cream and 2.5cm (1in) across. Raised 1969 at Hillier Nurseries at Eastleigh.
H4

P. **'Elizabeth'** A magnificent hybrid that makes a dome-shaped bush 1m × 1.2m (3 × 4ft), studded from late spring to early autumn with large, rich, canary-yellow flowers. It was wrongly distributed throughout European nurseries as *P. arbuscula*. Raised 1950 in Hillier Nurseries and named after Sir Harold Hillier's younger daughter.
H4 ♛ 1993

P. **'Floppy Disc'** A small shrub with semi-double pink flowers. Introduced by Liss Forest Nurseries.
H4

P. fruticosa **var.** *grandiflora* A shrub of up to 1.5m (4ft). It has strong, erect growth, sage-green leaves and dense clusters of large, canary-yellow flowers. A seedling of this plant named 'Jackman's Variety' is basically identical.
H4

P. **'Goldfinger'** A dwarf, compact shrub with pinkish shoots and blue-green leaves, usually with five leaflets. It has an abundance of large, richly golden yellow flowers. Raised c1970 in Holland.
H4 ♛ 1993

P. **'Goldstar'** A rather upright shrub to 80cm (32in) with very large, deep yellow flowers up to 5cm (2in) across, borne over a long period. In cultivation 1976.
H4

P. **'Hopley's Orange'** A dwarf, spreading shrub with bright orange flowers.
H4

P. **'Jackman's Variety'** See *P. fruticosa* var. *grandiflora*.

Potentilla 'Katherine Dykes'

P. **'Katherine Dykes'** A shrub up to 2m (6ft) with abundant primrose-yellow flowers in summer. In cultivation 1925.
H4 ♛ 1993

P. **'Longacre'** A dense, dwarf, mat-forming shrub with large, bright, almost sulphur-yellow flowers. In cultivation 1956.
H4 ♛ 1993

P. **'Maanelys'**, syn. 'Moonlight' A small shrub with a continuous succession of soft yellow flowers from late spring to late autumn. Raised 1950 in Scandinavia.
H4 ♛ 1993

P. **'Moonlight'** See 'Maanelys'.

P. parvifolia **'Gold Drop'** A dwarf, compact shrub with small, neat leaves and small, bright golden yellow flowers. It is often grown wrongly under the name *P. fruticosa farreri*. In cultivation 1953.
H4

P. p. **'Klondike'** A first-rate dwarf shrub, similar to 'Gold Drop' but with larger flowers. In culitvation 1950.
H4 ♛ 1993

P. **'Pretty Polly'** A low, spreading shrub with medium-sized, pale pink flowers.
H4

P. **'Primrose Beauty'** A small, spreading, free-flowering shrub with arching branches, grey-green foliage and primrose-yellow flowers with deeper yellow centres.
H4 ♛ 1993

P. 'Princess' (*P. f.* 'Blink' PBR 2098) A compact, dwarf shrub of spreading habit bearing flowers of a delicate pale pink with yellow centres and on some occasions a few extra petals.
H4

P. 'Red Ace' (PBR 1116) A compact dwarf shrub forming a dense mound of bright green foliage, the leaves usually having five narrow leaflets. The flowers are bright orange-red with cream on the backs of the petals. Unless it is grown in partial shade, the flowers revert to yellow. In cultivation 1973.
H4

P. 'Red Robin' ('Marrob' PBR 4147) A low, spreading shrub with red flowers, slightly deeper than 'Red Ace'
H4

P. 'Royal Flush' (PBR 1673) A seedling of 'Red Ace' with deep pink flowers. In cultivation 1980.
H4

P. 'Ruth' A small, upright shrub with nodding, slightly cup-shaped flowers that are creamy yellow at first, becoming white. The calyces are flushed with red. Raised 1960 at Hillier Nurseries and named after Sir Harold Hillier's elder daughter.
H4

Potentilla 'Sunset'

P. 'Sunset' A small shrub with flowers that vary between deep orange and brick red. It is a sport of 'Tangerine' and is best grown in semi-shade.
H4

P. 'Tangerine' A dwarf, wide-spreading shrub that forms a dense mound. The

Potentilla 'Tilford Cream'

colour of the flowers is a pale coppery yellow, which is developed best on plants growing in semi-shade.
H4 ♛ 1993

P. 'Tilford Cream' A dense, dwarf bush, broader than it is tall, with rich green foliage and large, creamy flowers about 3.5cm (1¹/₂in) across.
H4 ♛ 1993

P. 'Vilmoriniana' A splendid shrub with erect branches, growing to 2m (6ft). It has very silvery leaves and cream flowers, and is the best tall, erect potentilla.
H4

P. 'William Purdom' A small, semi-erect shrub to 1.5m (4ft) with plentiful, light yellow flowers.
H4

Prostanthera *Labiatae*
Mint bush

A genus of about 50 species of beautiful, small to medium-sized, free-flowering, aromatic, evergreen shrubs native to Australasia. They are ideal for the cool conservatory or in a warm, sheltered corner in the milder counties but are inclined to become chlorotic on a shallow, chalky soil. Established specimens are best pruned back hard immediately after flowering.

P. 'Chelsea Pink' A small shrub, similar to *P. rotundifolia*. It has aromatic, grey-green leaves that are wedge-shaped at the base and the pretty flowers are pale pink with purple anthers. It is sometimes known as *P. rotundifolia* 'Rosea'.
H2–3

Prostanthera cuneata

P. cuneata A hardy dwarf shrub of spreading habit, with small, dark glossy green leaves. The flowers are white, flushed with lilac and marked with purple inside. Flowering is in late spring. Australia, Tasmania. In cultivation 1886.
H4 ♛ 1993

P. lasianthos Erect, medium to large shrub with lanceolate leaves and racemes of white flowers, tinted with purple, in spring. Australia, Tasmania. In cultivation 1808.
H3-4

P. melissifolia var. parvifolia A small, shrub with bright lilac flowers almost 2.5cm (1in) across, borne freely in early summer.
H2

Prostanthera rotundifolia

P. rotundifolia A beautiful, small to medium-sized, dense shrub, with tiny, rounded leaves. The attractive heliotrope pink-purple flowers cover the branches in summer and their massed effect is stunning.
H2 ♛ 1993

PRUNUS

Rosaceae

THIS enormous genus is unsurpassed for economic value, giving us peaches, nectarines, plums, apricots, damsons, cherries, sloes, and the blackthorn sticks called shillelaghs that earn considerable foreign currency from tourists to Eire. It is also a source of some of the most decorative of trees and shrubs, and these may be not unreasonably divided between the Japanese cherries and the rest. However, in the face of the sumptuous display put on by the former, it is sometimes forgotten that *P. subhirtella* 'Pendula Rosea' is one of the most exquisitely beautiful of all spring-flowering trees, and that *P.* 'Spire' is a street tree with few, if any, peers. There are many others that should not be overlooked, and in general they have a dainty charm that contrasts interestingly with the glamour of the Japanese cherries.

It would be difficult to imagine shrubs more different from the cherries of Kyoto's blossom time than the common or cherry laurels, *P. laurocerasus*. They were the making of many a Victorian suburban garden and are still of the greatest value as interesting evergreen foliage shrubs, not the least of their attractions being their conspicuous cherry-like fruits. They are almost indestructible, standing up to wind, a considerable amount of cold, and atmospheric pollution.

There are many cultivars, all of which share a capacity for tolerating dry shade and the drips from overhead trees. While you might imagine that one cherry laurel looks much like another, you would be wrong. There is, for example, a wealth of difference between the low profile and narrow, glossy leaves of *P. l.* 'Otto Luyken' and the lush, jungly *P. l.* 'Magnoliifolia', whose foliage, for size, rivals that of some of the larger-leaved rhododendrons. They are not

at their best on shallow chalk soils, where their place can be taken with distinction by the Portugal laurel, *P. lusitanica*, which is a large shrub or small tree of the most remarkable hardiness for an evergreen, and which will tolerate degrees of cold and wind chill that may inflict bad damage on *P. laurocerasus*.

The cherry plum, myrobalan or mirabelle – *P. cerasifera* – has many garden forms that are treasured for their white or pink flowers that appear early in the year, usually just before the leaves or as they are emerging. One of them, *P. c.* 'Pissardii', known as the purple-leaved plum, is a highly popular garden tree, with red-purple foliage of a daintiness not all that often seen among trees and shrubs with this colour. In

Prunus spinosa

fact bronze or purple leaves are something of a theme among cultivars of this easily grown species.

Indeed, most of these 'other' members of the genus present no problem to gardeners with sunny positions for the deciduous kinds and partial shade for the evergreens. With the exception of the cherry laurels (which will, however, grow where chalk is overlaid by a substantial depth of soil), they thrive in virtually all kinds of soils and are particularly happy on those that contain lime or chalk. They are remarkably free of troubles caused by pests or diseases.

THE ORNAMENTAL CHERRIES
'Cherry blossom time' is one of the most beautiful periods of the year wherever the flowering cherries are planted. The most celebrated are the Japanese Sato Zakura, the garden cherries that have been developed and cultivated for more than a thousand years. Extremely ornamental, intriguingly varied in character and easily grown, they were introduced to Britain in the early twentieth century by a naval officer, Captain Collingwood Ingram – 'Cherry' Ingram.

Among the Sato Zakura are trees as different in habit as *P.* 'Amanogawa', which is as erect and columnar as a small Lombardy poplar, and 'Mount Fuji', which has a flat head of horizontal branches. Flowers may be single, as in 'Tai Haku', the great white cherry, in which their size and dazzling whiteness provides the dramatic effect, or fully double and frilled, as in 'Ichiyo'; between the two lies a variety of floral form which ensures that the fascination of Japanese cherries is never likely to pall.

As far as colour goes the palette is not a wide one, but the subtle variations on a theme of white, pink and soft rose have been brought to perfection by the centuries of careful breeding, and in many cases are enhanced by the bronze, copper or buff tones of the emerging foliage. Later, when their virtuoso spring performance is a memory, their fine autumn foliage colour creates a symphony of yellow and tawny orange.

The flowering season for Japanese cherries is not as short as many observers and gardeners might suppose, and spans roughly an eight-week period around mid-spring. Each one occupies part of the season, and therefore they can be described as early, mid or late.

The Sato Zakura, like other cherries, succeed on all types of well-drained soils, including soft limestones and chalk. During the dormant season the buds may be damaged by birds, in which case it is advisable to use a repellent. Pruning of any kind is rarely necessary, but when unavoidable is best carried out in late summer so that the cuts heal before winter.

Physical damage to the trees and their roots can readily allow the ingress of honey fungus, and care should be taken with gardening operations beneath their canopies. Bacterial canker, while a troublesome disease of edible cherries, is not nearly as significant among ornamental ones.

Prunus *Rosaceae*

Prunus 'Accolade'

P. 'Accolade' (*P. sargentii* × *P. subhirtella*) An outstanding cherry, growing to a small deciduous tree with spreading branches and semi-double, pink flowers 4cm (1½in)

across in pendulous clusters. It is very free-flowering in early to mid-spring.
H4 ♔ 1993

Prunus × *amygdalo-persica* 'Pollardii'

P. × **amygdalo-persica 'Pollardii'** A hybrid between the peach and the almond. It is a beautiful small deciduous tree with larger, more richly pink flowers than the almond. They are single and borne in mid-spring. It is susceptible to peach leaf curl, against which a traditional copper fungicide should be used.
H4

Prunus avium 'Plena'

P. avium (Gean, wild cherry) A medium-sized to large deciduous tree with smooth grey bark that turns to mahogany red and peels and becomes deeply fissured with age. The white, cup-shaped single flowers are in clusters and open with the leaves in mid- to late spring. The fruits are small, reddish purple and shiny, and the autumn foliage is crimson. Most of the sweet cherries are

derived from this species. Europe (including Britain and Ireland), W Asia.
H4 ♔ 1993

P. a. 'Plena' (Double gean) One of the loveliest of all flowering trees. Its branches are wreathed in masses of drooping white double flowers. In cultivation since 1700.
H4

P. besseyi (Western sand cherry) A small deciduous shrub with greyish green leaves that turn rusty purple in autumn. Clusters of tiny white single flowers are massed along the branches in late spring. The fruits, rounded and black with a purplish bloom, are rarely produced in Britain and Ireland. C United States. Introduced 1892.
H4

P. × **blireana** A beautiful large deciduous shrub or small tree with metallic-coppery purple leaves and slightly fragrant, rose-pink double flowers, over 2.5cm (1in) across, opening just before the leaves in mid-spring. Garden origin 1895.
H4 ♔ 1993

Prunus cerasifera

P. cerasifera (Cherry plum, myrobalan) A small deciduous tree with greenish young shoots. The myriad small single flowers crowd the twigs in early spring, sometimes earlier or later. Mature trees sometimes bear red cherry-plums. It is an excellent shrub for a dense hedge. In cultivation during the sixteenth century.
H4

P. c. 'Hessei' A medium-sized, shrubby form with leaves that are pale green at first and then become bronze-purple with irregular creamy to yellowish or pink edges. The

Prunus cerasifera 'Hessei'

snow-white flowers crowd the branches towards mid-spring.
H4

Prunus cerasifera 'Nigra'

P. c. 'Nigra' A most effective small tree, flowering prolifically in early to mid-spring with pink blossoms that fade to blush. The leaves and stems are blackish purple. It is an excellent hedging plant. In cultivation 1916.
H4 ♛ 1993

P. c. 'Pissardii' (Purple-leaved plum) A very popular form with dark red young foliage that turns to deep purple. It flowers in great profusion towards the middle of spring, with blossoms that are pink in bud, opening white. The purple fruits are only occasionally produced. It is an excellent hedging plant.
H4

P. c. 'Rosea' The leaves of this small tree are bronze-purple at first, becoming bronze-green and then green in late sum-

Prunus cerasifera 'Pissardii'

mer. The small flowers are clear salmon-pink, paling with age, and crowd the slender purple stems before the leaves emerge and after both 'Nigra' and 'Pissardii'.
H4

Prunus cerasus 'Rhexii'

P. cerasus 'Rhexii' A form of the sour cherry, this small, bushy deciduous tree has

showy double white flowers 2.5–4cm (1–1¹/₂in) across in mid- to late spring. In cultivation since the sixteenth century.
H4

P. × cistena, syn. *P.* 'Crimson Dwarf' (Purple-leaf sand cherry) A beautiful deciduous shrub up to 2m (6ft) high with red leaves and single white flowers in mid-spring and black-purple fruits. An excellent hedging plant. Garden origin before 1910 in the US.
H4

P. 'Collingwood Ingram' A small deciduous tree resembling 'Kursar' but with more deeply coloured flowers in early to mid-spring. It is a seedling of 'Kursar'. Belgium, selected by Jelena de Belder.
H4

P. 'Crimson Dwarf' see *P. × cistena*.

Prunus dulcis

P. dulcis (Common almond) One of the best spring-flowering trees. It is small and has lance-shaped, long-pointed, finely toothed deciduous leaves and single pink flowers, 2.5–5cm (1–2in) across, in early to mid-spring. It is susceptible to peach leaf curl, for which a traditional copper fungicide is recommended. Commercial edible almonds are mainly produced in S Europe. Native from N Africa to W Asia but extensively grown and naturalized in the Mediterranean region. In cultivation since the sixteenth century or earlier.
H4

P. d. 'Macrocarpa' A small tree with very pale pink or white flowers up to 5cm (2in) across. It is one of the best of the edible forms and has large fruits.
H4

Prunus glandulosa 'Alba Plena'

Prunus incisa

Prunus 'Kursar'

P. glandulosa 'Alba Plena' A very beautiful small deciduous shrub that is a form of the Chinese bush cherry. Each shoot is weighed down in mid-spring with a wealth of quite large double white flowers. It grows best in a warm, sunny position. In cultivation 1852.
H4 ♔ 1993
P. g. 'Rosea Plena' A form with bright pink flowers. In cultivation 1774.
H4 ♔ 1993
P. 'Hally Jolivette' A large deciduous shrub or small, graceful tree Its slender, willowy stems are covered in spring with small, semi-double, blush-white flowers that continue over a long period. Raised by Dr Karl Sax at the Arnold Arboretum, Boston, and named after his wife.
H4
P. 'Hillieri' A hybrid of *P. sargentii* raised before 1928 at Hilliers Nurseries. The original is now a broad-crowned deciduous tree more than 10m (30ft) high and in spring its single flowers give the impression of a soft pink cloud. In favourable positions the autumn colour is gorgeous.
H4
P. × hillieri 'Spire' See *P.* 'Spire'.
P. incisa (Fuji cherry) A lovely deciduous species, generally shrubby but occasionally a small tree, blooming very profusely in early spring. The leaves are small, beautifully tinted in autumn, and the single flowers are small, white, tinged with pink in bud and appearing pink at a distance. The small purple-black fruits are only occasionally produced. Japan. In cultivation 1910.
H4

P. i. 'Kojo Nomai' A slow-growing small shrub with zig-zag shoots and pale pink flowers.
H4

Prunus incisa 'Praecox'

P. i. 'Praecox' A winter-flowering shrub or small tree with white flowers, opening from pale pink buds.
H4 ♔ 1993
P. jamasakura, syn. *P. serrulata* var. *spontanea* (Hill cherry) A medium-sized, spreading deciduous tree with bronze young foliage and single pink flowers borne in mid- to late spring. It is a beautiful cherry that has inspired Japanese poets and artists and is a prototype of many of the Japanese cherries. It is extremely variable, with the best forms having rich coppery red young foliage and pure white flowers. The fruits are dark purplish crimson and the leaves have good autumn tints. Japan. Introduced c1914.
H4

P. 'Kursar' A very beautiful small deciduous tree. The single flowers, though small, are rich deep pink and are produced in great profusion towards mid-spring with or just before the appearance of the reddish bronze young leaves. Raised by Capt. Collingwood Ingram.
H4 ♔ 1993

Prunus laurocerasus

P. laurocerasus (Cherry laurel, common laurel) A vigorous, wide-spreading, evergreen shrub to about 6m (20ft) or more in height and as much or more across. The leaves are large, leathery, and dark, shining green. It is mainly grown for screening but is attractive in mid-spring when it has erect clusters of small, single, white flowers that are followed by cherry-like fruits, red at first and finally black. It is not at its best on shallow chalk soils. There are few other evergreens more tolerant of shade and drip from overhanging trees than the laurel in its many forms. Pruning can be carried out

either in spring or late summer, and old specimens or hedges that have grown too large can be cut hard into the old wood in spring. Harmful if eaten. E Europe, Asia Minor, naturalized in the British Isles. Introduced 1576.
H4

***P. l.* 'Castlewellan'** See *P. l.* 'Marbled White'.

***P. l.* 'Cherry Brandy'** A dense small shrub making a low mound only 60cm (2ft) high. The bronze young foliage later becomes green.
H4

***P. l.* 'Green Carpet'** A dwarf form that grows wide and flat and has narrow, dark green leaves. It is excellent for growing as ground cover. The correct name is probably 'Grüner Teppich'.
H4

***P. l.* 'Magnoliifolia'** An imposing evergreen with glossy leaves up to 30cm (12in) long and 10cm (4in) wide, making it the largest-leaved laurel. In cultivation 1869.
H4

Prunus laurocerasus 'Marbled White'

***P. l.* 'Marbled White'**, syn. 'Castlewellan' A slow-growing, dense bush, eventually quite large. The leaves are green and greygreen, marbled through with white, and variable in shape. It was originally grown as 'Variegata'. In cultivation 1811.
H4

***P. l.* 'Mischeana'** A most ornamental plant, slowly forming a dense, rather flattopped mound of dark, lustrous green, oblong leaves. It makes a fine medium-sized lawn specimen and is attractive when the

short racemes of white flowers pack the stems in spring. In cultivation 1898.
H4

***P. l.* 'Mount Vernon'** A slow-growing, dwarf shrubby laurel, making a dense mound about 30cm (12in) high covered with glossy, dark green leaves.
H4

Prunus laurocerasus 'Mount Vernon'

***P. l.* 'Otto Luyken'** A low, compact shrub with erect stems and narrow, shining green leaves. It is outstanding both for its foliage and white flowers. Raised 1940.
H4 ♚ 1993

***P. l.* 'Reynvaanii'** A small, slow-growing, compact form with stiff branches and white flowers. In cultivation 1913.
H4

***P. l.* 'Rotundifolia'** A bushy form, excellent for hedging. The leaves are half as broad as long. In cultivation 1865.
H4

***P. l.* 'Schipkaensis'** A very hardy, freeflowering, narrow-leaved form of spreading habit. Bulgaria. Introduced 1888.
H4

***P. l.* 'Zabeliana'** A low, horizontally branched form with long, narrow, willowlike leaves and profusely borne flowers. It is excellent ground cover, even in problem areas such as under the shade and drip of trees, and can be put to good use in the

Prunus laurocerasus 'Otto Luyken'

Prunus laurocerasus 'Zabeliana'

Prunus lusitanica

same way as the Pfizer juniper for breaking up the outline of a particularly long border. In cultivation 1898.

H4

P. lusitanica (Portugal laurel) A large evergreen shrub or small to medium-sized tree and a beautiful specimen when allowed to develop naturally. The ovate leaves are dark green with reddish stalks, and the small, white, hawthorn-scented single flowers are borne in long racemes in early summer. The fruits are small and red, gradually turning to dark purple. It is hardier than the cherry laurel and happy even on shallow chalk soils, where it can be planted instead of *P. laurocerasus*. Spain, Portugal. Introduced 1648.

H4 ♔ 1993

P. l. subsp. azorica A magnificent large evergreen shrub or small tree, which is unexpectedly very hardy, given its provenance. It has thicker and larger, bright green leaves than the species. They are red-

Prunus lusitanica subsp. azorica

dish when unfolding and have reddish stalks. Azores. Introduced 1860.

H4 ♔ 1993

P. l. 'Myrtifolia' A dense cone up to 5m (15ft), with polished, dark green leaves, smaller and neater than those of the type. In cultivation 1892.

H4

Prunus lusitanica 'Myrtifolia'

Prunus lusitanica 'Variegata'

P. l. 'Variegata' An attractive medium-sized to large shrub with its leaves margined with white, sometimes pink-flushed in winter. In cultivation 1865.

H4

P. maackii 'Amber Beauty' A small deciduous tree that is a form of Manchurian cherry with amber-coloured, flaking bark and a narrow crown. The small white single flowers are borne in clusters on the previous year's shoots in mid-spring.

H4

P. mume (Japanese apricot) A delightful small deciduous tree with green young shoots and single, almond-scented, pink flowers that pale as they age. They appear in early spring. China, Korea, extensively cultivated in Japan. Introduced 1844.

H4

P. m. 'Alboplena' A form with semi-double white flowers.

H4

P. m. 'Alphandii', syn. *P. m.* 'Flore Pleno' A beautiful form with double pink flowers. In cultivation 1902.

H4

Prunus mume 'Beni-shidare'

P. m. 'Beni-shidare' A striking form with strongly fragrant, double, cup-shaped, rich madder-pink flowers, darker in bud and paling slightly with age.

H4

P. m. 'Flore Pleno' See *P. m.* 'Alphandii'.

P. m. 'Omoi-no-mama' A charming small tree with semi-double, cup-shaped, usually white flowers. Occasional petals and sometimes whole flowers are pink.

H4

***P. nipponica* var. *kurilensis* 'Ruby'** A bushy, slow-growing large deciduous shrub or small tree with erect branches that bear a mass of pale pink single flowers with noticeably purplish red calyces towards mid-spring. In cultivation 1958.
H4

Prunus 'Okame'

P. 'Okame' A small deciduous tree and a very lovely one, with masses of carmine-rose single flowers opening throughout the early part of spring. The foliage is attractively tinted in autumn. A first-class Capt. Collingwood Ingram hybrid.
H4 ♛ 1993

Prunus padus

P. *padus* (Bird cherry) A deciduous small to medium-sized tree, widely distributed in the northern hemisphere. Bears abundant white, almond-scented single flowers in late spring after the leaves; the small black fruits are bitter. Europe, N Asia to Japan.
H4

Prunus padus 'Albertii'

P. p. 'Albertii' A strong-growing, very free-flowering form. In cultivation 1902.
H4

Prunus padus 'Colorata'

P. p. 'Colorata' A remarkable tree with dark purplish shoots, coppery purple young foliage and pale pink flowers. The leaves in summer are sombre green with purple-tinged veins and under-surfaces. 'Purple Queen' is very similar. Sweden.
H4 ♛ 1993
P. p. 'Grandiflora' See *P. p.* 'Watereri'.
P. p. 'Watereri', syn. *P. p.* 'Grandiflora' A form with flower clusters up to 20cm (8in) long. In cultivation 1914.
H4 ♛ 1993
P. 'Pandora' A small deciduous tree with ascending branches generously bedecked with pale shell-pink single flowers 2.5cm (1in) across in early spring or later. The leaves are bronze-red when unfolding and often colour richly in autumn.
H4 ♛ 1993

Prunus padus 'Watereri'

P. *persica* (Peach) A large deciduous shrub or small, bushy tree with pale pink single flowers. They are smaller than those of the almond and appear 2–3 weeks later. It is doubtful whether it is worth growing the peach as an outdoor ornamental because of its susceptibility to peach leaf curl. The disease can be treated with a copper fungicide

Prunus 'Pandora'

but is most disfiguring. Probably native to China but in cultivation since ancient times. H4

Prunus persica 'Klara Mayer'

P. p. 'Klara Mayer' A large shrub or small tree with double, peach-pink flowers: the best double peach for general planting. In cultivation 1890.
H4

P. 'Pink Shell' One of the loveliest cherries in a genus full of floral treasures. It is a small, elegant deciduous tree with slender, spreading branches that droop beneath a wealth of delicate, cup-shaped, shell-pink single blossoms that blend beautifully with the pale green of the emerging leaves towards mid-spring.
H4 ♀ 1993

P. prostrata (Rock cherry) A dwarf, spreading deciduous shrub that usually forms a delightful, low, gnarled hummock up to 70cm (28in) high by 2m (6ft) wide in 25 years. The bright pink single flowers are borne all along the wiry stems in mid-spring. SE Europe, Mediterranean, W Asia. Introduced 1802.
H4

P. pumila var. depressa A prostrate form of the sand cherry (see also *P. besseyi*). Less than 15cm (6in) high, it is good for ground cover and is studded with white single flowers in late spring. It is deciduous. United States. Introduced 1864.
H4

P. sargentii Considered by many people to be the loveliest of all cherries, this is a round-headed small deciduous tree with chestnut-brown bark and bronze-red young

Prunus pumila var. *depressa*

Prunus sargentii

foliage. The single pink flowers open in early spring or a little later. It is one of the first trees to colour in autumn, when its leaves assume glorious tones of orange and crimson. It is one of the few cherries that bullfinches seem to ignore. Japan, Korea. Introduced 1890.
H4 ♀ 1993

Prunus sargentii 'Rancho'

P. s. 'Rancho' A small to medium-sized tree with a narrowly upright habit. Some plants grown under this name are just poor forms of *P. sargentii*. Raised before 1962 in the United States.
H4

P. × schmittii A fast-growing, medium-sized, narrowly conical deciduous tree with a polished brown trunk that is a greater attraction than the pale pink single flowers in mid-spring. Garden origin 1923.
H4

Prunus serrula

P. serrula A small but vigorous deciduous tree of which the main attraction is the striking glistening surface of its polished, red-brown, mahogany-like new bark. The leaves are narrow and willow-like, and the small, white, single flowers are produced at the same time as the leaves towards late spring. W China. Introduced 1908 by Ernest Wilson.
H4 ♀ 1993

Prunus serrulata var. *hupehensis*

P. serrulata var. hupehensis (Chinese hill cherry) This is considered to be the prototype of the cultivated double white cherry. It is a medium-sized deciduous tree with ascending branches and clusters of white or blush flowers in mid- to late spring. The young leaves are bronze and the autumn foliage is attractively coloured. C China. Introduced 1900 by Ernest Wilson. H4

P. s. var. spontanea See *P. jamasakura*.

Prunus 'Shosar'

P. 'Shosar' A strong-growing, somewhat fastigiate medium-sized deciduous tree with single, clear pink flowers early in the season. It usually has good autumn colour. H4

P. 'Snow Goose' A small deciduous tree with ascending branches crowded in mid-spring with pure white, well-formed single flowers. It is a seedling of the same parentage as 'Umineko' but has a broader crown and larger leaves that unfold after the flowers. 'Snow Goose' is the better grower. H4

P. spinosa (Blackthorn, sloe) A large, dense deciduous shrub or small, bushy tree with dark spiny branches, crowded in early spring with small white single flowers. The fruits are like small damsons, blue-bloomy at first and shining black later. Its fruits are used in preserves and for making sloe gin, while its branches are made into walking sticks and the traditional Irish shillelaghs. It can be a liability in gardens as its spines are likely to inflict festering wounds. Europe, N Africa, W Asia. H4

Prunus 'Snow Goose'

Prunus spinosa

P. s. 'Purpurea' A neat, compact bush with rich purple leaves. H4

P. 'Spire', syn. *P. × hillieri* 'Spire' A vase-shaped tree reaching a height of 10m (30ft) and, eventually, a width of 7m (22ft). The single flowers, borne in mid-spring, are soft pink and the leaves have rich autumn tints. H4 ♛ 1993

P. subhirtella A small to medium-sized deciduous tree with a profusion of small pale pink single flowers in early spring. It includes among its forms some of the most delightful of early spring-flowering trees and in a good year most of these also produce attractive autumn tints. Unknown in the wild and probably of hybrid origin. Introduced 1894. H4

P. s. 'Autumnalis' (Autumn cherry) A small tree up to 7.5m (24ft), with semi-double white flowers at intervals from late autumn to early spring. Flowers may be found on it on almost any winter's day when there is a mild spell, and a few cut sprays are a welcome interior decoration. In cultivation 1900. H4 ♛ 1993

P. s. 'Autumnalis Rosea' A small tree similar in many ways to 'Autumnalis' but with blush-pink flowers. H4 ♛ 1993

Prunus 'Spire' in autumn

Prunus subhirtella 'Autumnalis Rosea'

P. s. 'Fukubana' This very striking small tree with its profusion of semi-double, rose-madder flowers is the most colourful of this group, collectively known as the spring cherries. Introduced 1927 from California by Capt. Collingwood Ingram.
H4 ♆ 1993

P. s. 'Pendula' A lovely slender weeping tree of medium size, reminiscent of the most graceful forms of weeping birch. It bears inconspicuous tiny blush flowers in mid-spring. Introduced 1862.
H4

P. s. 'Pendula Plena Rosea' A weeping shrub or small tree with semi-double flowers like rosettes. They are rose-madder and similar to those of 'Fukubana' but slightly paler. Introduced 1928 by Capt. Collingwood Ingram.
H4

P. s. 'Pendula Rosea' (Weeping spring cherry) A small, weeping, mushroom-shaped tree. The flowers are rich pink in

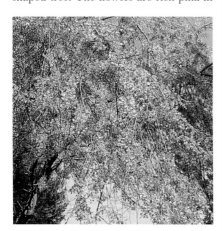
Prunus subhirtella 'Pendula Rosea'

bud and become pale blush, wreathing the graceful, drooping branches. It is often grown as *P. subhirtella* 'Pendula', a name that properly applies to the form with inconspicuous flowers.
H4 ♆ 1993

Prunus subhirtella 'Pendula Rubra'

P. s. 'Pendula Rubra' A small tree with deep rose flowers, carmine in bud, borne all along the long, pendulous branches.
H4 ♆ 1993

Prunus subhirtella 'Stellata'

P. s. 'Stellata' A very beautiful form with larger, clear pink, star-shaped spring flowers in crowded clusters along the branches. Introduced c1955.
H4

P. tenella 'Fire Hill' An outstanding small deciduous shrub with erect stems wreathed in brilliant rose-red single flowers in mid-spring; perhaps the best dwarf almond. From wild forms of *P. tenella*. Balkan Alps.
H4 ♆ 1993

Prunus tenella 'Fire Hill'

Prunus triloba 'Multiplex'

P. triloba 'Multiplex' A medium-sized to large deciduous shrub with small, coarsely toothed, three-lobed leaves. The flowers are large, double, rosette-shaped and clear rose-pink, and are produced freely towards mid-spring. It makes a splendid wall shrub if the old flowering shoots are pruned back immediately after flowering. China. Introduced 1855 by Robert Fortune.
H4 ♆ 1993

P. 'Umineko' A narrowly growing, upright small deciduous tree with single white flowers that are produced with the leaves, which colour beautifully in autumn. See also *P.* 'Snow Goose'.
H4

P. verecunda 'Autumn Glory' A form of the Korean hill cherry, this is a medium-sized deciduous tree with prolific blush single flowers in spring. Selected by Capt. Collingwood Ingram for its consistent, deep crimson and bright red autumn colours.
H4

Prunus 'Umineko'

P. virginiana 'Shubert' A small, conical deciduous tree with green young foliage that quickly changes to reddish purple. It bears small white single flowers in late spring. In cultivation 1950.
H4

Prunus × yedoensis

P. × yedoensis (Tokyo cherry, Yoshino cherry) A graceful small to medium-sized deciduous tree with arching branches. It is highly valued for its profusion of almond-scented blushed single flowers towards mid-spring. Japan, unknown in the wild. Introduced 1902.
H4 ♔ 1993

P. × y. 'Ivensii' A small, vigorous, weeping tree with long, tortuous branches and long, slender, drooping branchlets which are transformed into snowy white cascades of delicately fragrant blossom in early to mid-spring. Raised 1925 at Hillier Nurseries from seed of the type.
H4

Prunus × yedoensis 'Ivensii'

P. × y. 'Shidare Yoshino' A small tree with long, elegant arching branches that often weep to the ground and which carry pale pink flowers in mid-spring.
H4

P. × y. 'Tsubame' A small tree with slightly weeping spreading branches and white flowers.
H4

JAPANESE CHERRIES OF GARDEN ORIGIN – THE SATO ZAKURA

The flowering season of the Sato Zakura lasts from the latter part of early spring to the middle of late spring. The cherries are early, middle or late within that season.

Prunus 'Amanogawa'

P. 'Amanogawa' A small, narrowly columnar deciduous tree with strongly erect branches and dense, upright clusters of fragrant, semi-double, shell-pink flowers. Mid to late.
H4 ♔ 1993

Prunus 'Asano'

P. 'Asano' A small deciduous tree with ascending branches and dense clusters of deep pink, very double flowers. The young leaves are greenish bronze. It is in effect an upright form of 'Cheal's Weeping'. Mid. Introduced 1929 by Capt. Collingwood Ingram.
H4

P. 'Cheal's Weeping' A small deciduous tree with arching or drooping branches, very attractive when wreathed in the clear deep pink, very double flowers. The young leaves are bronze-green and later become green and glossy. It is often wrongly referred to as 'Kiku-shidare Sakura'. Mid.
H4 ♔ 1993

P. 'Choshu-hizakura' A beautiful small deciduous tree with single, deep pink flowers and attractive purplish brown calyces. The young leaves are reddish brown or coppery red. Mid. Previously listed as 'Hisakura'.
H4

P. **'Fugenzo'** In some respects this small deciduous tree resembles 'Kanzan', but is smaller and has a broader, flat-topped head. The flowers are large, double, rose-pink and borne in drooping clusters and the young leaves are coppery red. Very late. H4

P. **'Hisakura'** See under 'Choshu-hiza-kura' and 'Kanzan'.

P. **'Hokusai'** A vigorous, wide-spreading small deciduous tree with its branches hidden in spring by the generous clusters of large, semi-double, pale pink flowers. The young leaves are a brownish bronze. It is one of the most popularly grown of the Japanese cherries. Mid. H4

P. **'Ichiyo'** A beautiful small deciduous tree with ascending branches and double, shell-pink flowers with a circular, frilled appearance, borne in long-stalked corymbs. The young leaves are bronze-green. Mid. H4 ♛ 1993

Prunus 'Cheal's Weeping'

P. **'Jo-nioi'** A strongly growing, spreading small deciduous tree with single, white, deliciously scented blossoms wreathing the branches in spring, the white petals contrasting with the purple-brown sepals. The young leaves are pale golden brown. Mid. Introduced c1910. H4

P. **'Kanzan'** One of the most popular and most commonly planted ornamental cherries. It is a strong-growing, medium-sized deciduous tree with characteristically stiffly ascending branches at first, spreading when the tree is older. The flowers are large, showy, double, and purplish pink. The young leaves are coppery red or reddish brown. It is often wrongly grown as 'Hisakura' (see under 'Choshu-hizakura') but it is taller and has double flowers that appear a week later. Mid. H4 ♛ 1993

P. **'Kiku-shidare Sakura'** See under *P.* 'Cheal's Weeping'.

Prunus 'Ichiyo'

Prunus 'Jo-nioi'

P. **'Mikuruma-gaeshi'** A distinctive small deciduous tree with long, ascending, rather gaunt, short-spurred branches along which large, mostly single, blush-pink flowers are densely packed. The young leaves are bronze-green. Mid. H4

P. **'Mount Fuji'** This beautiful cherry is one of the most distinctive. It is a small, vigorous deciduous tree with widely spreading, horizontal or slightly drooping branches that often reach to the ground. The flowers are very large, single or semi-double, fragrant, snow white, and burst from the soft green young foliage in long, drooping clusters. The leaves are distinctively fringed. It has long been grown as 'Shirotae', which is similar. Mid. Introduced c1905. H4 ♛ 1993

P. **'Ojochin'** A striking small deciduous tree, easily distinguished by its large leaves and single flowers 5cm (2in) across, which are pink in bud and open blush. They are profusely borne in long-stalked clusters of as many as seven or eight. The young leaves are bronze-brown, becoming rather tough and leathery when mature. Mid. Introduced before 1905. H4

P. **'Pink Perfection'** A most striking small deciduous tree with a habit intermediate between 'Shogetsu', its seed parent, and 'Kanzan', which was probably its pollen parent. Its flowers are bright rosy pink in bud and open double, paler pink; they are carried in drooping clusters. The young leaves are bronze. It is less startling than 'Kanzan'. Mid to late. Introduced 1935. H4 ♛ 1993

P. **'Shimidsu'** See *P.* 'Shogetsu'.

P. **'Shirofugen'** A strongly growing, widely spreading deciduous tree up to 10m (30ft). The flowers are large, double, dull purplish pink in bud, opening white then fading to purplish pink. They are in long-stalked clusters and contrast superbly with the copper young leaves. The blossoms are very late and long-lasting. Introduced 1900. H4 ♛ 1993

P. **'Shirotae'** See *P.* 'Mount Fuji'.

P. **'Shogetsu'**, syn. *P.* 'Shimidsu' One of the loveliest Japanese cherries. It is a small deciduous tree with spreading branches forming a broad, flattened crown. The large, slightly frilled, double flowers are pink in bud and open to pure white, hanging all along the branches in long-stalked clusters. The young leaves are green. Mid to late.

H4 ♔ 1993

P. 'Tai Haku' (Great white cherry) A superb, robust deciduous tree up to 12m (40ft). The flowers are very large, single, dazzling white and enhanced by the coppery red of the young leaves. It is one of the finest cherries and perhaps the best of the whites. Mid. Introduced 1900.

H4 ♔ 1993

P. 'Taki-nioi' A strong, vigorous, medium-sized deciduous tree with spreading branches. The honey-scented, single white flowers are rather small but are profusely borne and contrast effectively with the reddish bronze young leaves. Late.

H4

P. 'Ukon' A robust, spreading small to medium-sized deciduous tree with semi-double, pale yellowish flowers, tinged green and occasionally pink-flushed, freely borne and very effective against the brownish bronze young leaves. Mature leaves turn rusty red or purplish brown in autumn. Mid. Introduced 1905.

H4 ♔ 1993

P. 'Yedo-Zakura' A small, upright deciduous tree with semi-double flowers, carmine in bud and almond-pink when open. The young leaves are coppery gold. Mid. Introduced 1905.

H4

Pseudolarix *Pinaceae*

A genus of one deciduous coniferous species.

P. amabilis (Golden larch) A beautiful, hardy, slow-growing, medium-sized tree of broadly conical habit. The long, larch-like, light green leaves, up to 6cm (2½in) long, turn clear golden yellow in autumn. On a mature tree the cones stud the long, slender branches and are reddish brown when ripe. It requires a moist lime-free soil and grows best in a continental climate. China. Introduced 1852 by Robert Fortune.

H4 ♔ 1993

Pseudolarix amabilis

Pseudopanax *Araliaceae*

A genus of about six species of evergreens, mainly from New Zealand. They have remarkable variable leaves that are often sword-shaped but are of different shapes according to the age of the plant, with distinct foliage stages punctuating its life. The flowers are small, greenish and insignificant, and it is chiefly for their remarkable foliage that these plants are valued in gardens. They are hardy in very mild places and grow in all types of well-drained soil. Some make good house plants.

P. crassifolius (Lancewood) A small, evergreen tree with leaves that vary remarkably with the age of the plant. There are four distinct phases: first, they are 2.5–5cm (1–2in) long and more or less diamond-shaped; next, unbranched young trees have sword-shaped, sharply toothed leaves, usually 60cm (2ft) long but sometimes more; in stage three (when branching starts), many leaves have 3–5 leaflets with no stalks, while some have the second-stage shape but are shorter; in the fourth stage, rarely seen in cultivation, the leaves are around 15cm (6in) long and simple. Stage two leaves have red midribs and purple under-surfaces. New Zealand. Introduced 1846.

H3

P. ferox (Toothed lancewood) A small, slender-stemmed tree like *P. crassifolius* but with the leaves simple at all stages though varying from 15cm (6in) to 60cm (2ft) in length. The leaves on young plants are pendent, greyish green, and have strongly hooked teeth. New Zealand.

H3

Pseudopanax ferox

P. lessonii 'Gold Splash' Usually a large shrub, sometimes a small tree, with bright green leaves brightly blotched with yellow. They are made up of 3–5 leathery leaflets that can be either toothed or entire. New Zealand.

H1–2

Pseudopanax lessonii 'Gold Splash'

Pseudosasa *Gramineae*

A small genus of evergreen bamboos from eastern Asia that tolerate damp, even wet conditions.

Pseudosasa japonica

P. japonica, syn. *Arundinaria japonica* An adaptable, hardy bamboo and the one most commonly planted in Britain. It forms dense thickets of olive-green canes, 3–4.5m (10–13ft) and occasionally up to 6m (20ft) high, arching at the summits and bearing lush masses of dark glossy green leaves 18–30cm (7–12in) long by 2.5cm (1in) wide. The greyish under-surface of the leaf has a characteristic greenish marginal strip. Branches are borne singly from each of the upper joints. Japan, S Korea. Introduced 1850.
H4 ♔ 1993

Pseudotsuga *Pinaceae*

This genus has a handful of coniferous species of broadly conical, evergreen trees with whorled branches. The leaves are linear, soft to the touch and marked with two bloomy bands on their lower sides. The cones are pendulous. Most of the species dislike chalky and excessively limy soils and thrive best in those that are moist but well-drained.

P. menziesii (Oregon Douglas fir) A fast-growing large and stately tree. The lower branches of large specimens are downswept and the bark is corky, thick and deeply furrowed. The leaves are up to 3cm (1¼in) long, in two horizontal ranks, and are fragrant when crushed. The cones are up to 10cm (4in) long. It will not grow on chalk

soils. W North America. Introduced 1827 by David Douglas.
H4 ♔ 1993

P. m. 'Fletcheri' A slow-growing, shrubby form developing into an irregular, flat-topped though globular bush that eventually reaches 1.5–2m (5–6½ft) in height. The needle-like leaves are blue-green, 2–2.5cm (¾–1in) in length and loosely arranged. Originated 1906.
H4

H4 ♔ 1993

Pseudowintera *Winteraceae*

A New Zealand genus of three evergreen species related to Drimys. *They are not suitable for shallow chalk soils.*

P. colorata (Pepper tree) A small to medium-sized shrub, unusual in the colouring of its aromatic, oval, leathery leaves. These are pale yellow-green above, flushed pink and edged and blotched with dark crimson-purple, and blue-bloomy beneath. The small, greenish yellow flowers are occasionally followed by dark red to black fruits, but only where the summers are warm. It grows best when sheltered by other shrubs and trees. New Zealand.
H3

Ptelea *Rutaceae*

A genus of 11 North American aromatic deciduous shrubs or small trees, of which the hop tree is the best-known. They are suitable for all types of fertile soil and require full sun or light shade.

P. trifoliata (Hop tree) A large shrub or low, spreading tree. It produces domed clusters of small, star-shaped yellowish flowers which open in early summer and are probably the most fragrant among hardy trees, as scented as any honeysuckle. They are followed by dense green clusters of persistent, winged, elm-like fruits. E North America, Mexico. Introduced 1704.
H4 ♔ 1993

Ptelea trifoliata 'Aurea'

P. t. 'Aurea' A form with soft yellow leaves, contrasting well with shrubs with purple or dark green foliage.
H4 ♔ 1993

Pterocarya *Juglandaceae*
Wing nut

A genus of about ten species of fast-growing, wide-crowned deciduous trees of the walnut family, with handsome, pinnate, ash-like leaves and catkin-like flower clusters. They come mainly from China. Wing nuts succeed in all types of fertile soil. Persistent suckering demands constant removal of the suckers, as they can make over 1m (3ft) in a season.

P. fraxinifolia A large, wide-spreading tree, occasionally forming thickets of suckering stems, and usually with a short trunk and deeply furrowed bark. The leaves are 30–60 cm (1–2ft) long and composed of many oblong, toothed leaflets. The pendu-

lous catkins of flowers are lime-green, the females up to 50cm (20in) long, and drape the branches in summer, It is hardy and fast-growing and happiest in a moist, loamy soil, which makes it particularly suitable for planting near a water feature. Caucasus to N Iran. Introduced 1782.
H4 🏆 1993

Pterocarya × rehderiana

P. × rehderiana (*P. fraxinifolia × P. stenoptera*) A large suckering tree that is intermediate in character between its parents and a little hardier than either, and bears its long catkins for several months. A tree in the Hillier Gardens and Arboretum reached 16m (52ft) in less than 40 years. Raised 1879 in the Arnold Arboretum, Boston.
H4

P. stenoptera A large, vigorous tree with leaves 25–40cm (10–16in) long. The female catkins are 20cm (8in) long. China. Introduced 1860.
H4

Pterostyrax *Styracaceae*

A genus of four species of interesting, large, Asiatic deciduous shrubs or small trees with halesia-like leaves and long panicles of small flowers. They succeed in any good, deep soil, even over chalk, though they do not do well where a chalky soil is shallow. Pruning for shape can be done after flowering if necessary.

P. corymbosa A rare, large, spreading shrub or small tree with bristle-toothed, ovate leaves and broad, nodding clusters of fragrant white flowers in late spring and early summer. It bears winged fruits. China, Japan. Introduced 1850.
H4

Pterostyrax hispida

P. hispida (Epaulette tree) A large shrub or small tree with more or less oval leaves and fragrant white flowers in early to midsummer. They are borne in drooping panicles up to 23cm (9in) long and are followed by spindle-shaped ribbed fruits. Japan, China. Introduced 1875.
H4 🏆 1993

Punica *Punicaceae*

A genus of two deciduous species, only one of which is in general cultivation.

P. granatum 'Flore Pleno' A showy form of the pomegranate, with double orange-red flowers in late summer to early autumn. It is a medium-sized shrub or small, bushy tree, needing a warm sunny wall and good drainage, and only suitable for milder

Punica granatum

places. The shining green, oblong leaves are coppery when young and yellow in autumn. The fruits are only borne after a long, hot summer.
H3 🏆 1993

P. g. 'Nana' A charming dwarf form 15–23cm (6–9in) high. It has narrow leaves and profusions of orange-scarlet flowers. It is suitable for a sunny site in a rock garden. In cultivation 1806.
H3

Pyracantha *Rosaceae*
Firethorn

These are relatives of Cotoneaster but easily distinguished from them by their thorny branches and toothed leaves. They are often grown as evergreen wall shrubs and will reach a height of 5m (15ft) or more. They are less tall but equally effective when grown as freestanding shrubs. On a wall their long growths should be cut back immediately after flowering. Their masses of white

hawthorn-like flowers open in early summer and their red, orange or yellow berries in autumn and winter. All of them are hardy and include some of the best evergreen flowering and berrying shrubs for north and east-facing walls. They are tolerant of all exposures and pollution and grow well in all kinds of fertile soil. The one great drawback that attends Pyracantha *is the susceptibility to fireblight and canker, one or other of which is sooner or later almost certain to affect them, even though young, fast-growing plants in the nursery*

Arboretum in Washington DC. There is little evidence yet, however, to suggest how resistant some of these forms will eventually turn out to be in other climates, such as those of Britain and Ireland. The most reliable pyracanthas have received the AGM of the RHS.

Pyracantha atlantioides

P. atlantioides A large robust shrub, occasionally a small tree and a splendid species with large, oval, dark glossy green leaves. Unfortunately very susceptible to fireblight. H4

P. coccinea 'Lalandei' Once the most popular pyracantha but now very susceptible to canker and fireblight. H4

P. 'Golden Charmer' A vigorous medium-sized to large shrub with long, arching branches and finely toothed, bright glossy leaves. Large, round, orange-yellow berries ripen early and are profusely borne. In cultivation 1960. H4

Pyracantha coccinea 'Lalandei'

Pyracantha 'Golden Charmer'

P. 'Golden Dome' A splendid small shrub that makes a dense mound of arching branches and dark green leaves. An abundance of massed white flowers in early summer are followed by an equally abundant crop of small, deep yellow berries. Selected before 1973 at Hillier Nurseries. H4

P. 'Harlequin' An unusual variegated small to medium-sized shrub with pink-flushed leaves margined with cream. It does best on a wall but so far it does not inspire great confidence and may turn out to be a poor plant. H4

P. 'Mohave' A popular dense medium-sized to large shrub with bright orange-red

Pyracantha 'Mohave'

Pyracantha 'Navaho'

Pyracantha 'Orange Glow'

berries. Highly prone to scab. 'Mohave Silver', is a variable variegated form.
H4

P. **'Navaho'** A small to medium-sized, dense, spreading shrub with narrow, almost untoothed leaves up to 6 × 1cm (2 × ½in). The small but firm, distinctly flattened berries are orange, becoming orange-red and borne in dense clusters. Raised 1966 at the National Arboretum, Washington, DC, in 1966.
H4

P. **'Orange Charmer'** A large shrub resembling 'Orange Glow' but with deeper orange, more flattened berries. In cultivation 1962.
H4

P. **'Orange Glow'** A vigorous, dense, medium-sized shrub. The branches are covered in autumn with bright orange-red berries that last well into winter and beyond.
H4 ♔ 1993

P. **'Red Column'** A dense, bushy, medium-sized upright shrub with reddish shoots and ovate to elliptical, sharply toothed, glossy leaves. The dense clusters of scarlet berries ripen early.
H4

P. rogersiana A large, dense, free-fruiting shrub with small lanceolate bright green leaves and bright reddish orange berries. W China. Introduced 1911.
H4 ♔ 1993

P. r. **'Flava'** A form that produces bright yellow berries.
H4 ♔ 1993

P. **'Sappho Orange'** (*P.* 'Cadange' PBR 4511) A medium-sized upright shrub with dark green leaves, an abundance of deep orange berries and resistance to scab and canker. It is suitable for a container.
H4

P. **'Sappho Red'** (*P.* 'Cadrou' PBR 4512) A medium-sized upright shrub with glossy dark green leaves and profuse, flattened,

carmine-red berries which ripen to orange. It is good for hedging and resistant to scab and fireblight.
H4

P. **'Sappho Yellow'** (*P.* 'Interrada' PBR 4510) A form of the two previous plants with attractive yellow berries.
H4

Pyracantha 'Sappho Yellow'

Pyracantha 'Soleil d'Or'

P. 'Soleil d'Or' A medium-sized, upright shrub with reddish stems and dark green, broadly elliptical leaves. Golden yellow berries 1cm (½in) across are borne in large clusters. The flowers are white. Raised 1970 in France.
H4

P. 'Sparkler' A most strikingly variegated form with leaves heavily mottled with white and tinged with pink in autumn and winter. Unfortunately it is particularly tender and best grown under glass.
H3

P. 'Teton' A large, vigorous, upright shrub with reddish shoots and small, bright glossy green, wavy-edged leaves. The profusely borne berries are small and yellow-orange. It is highly resistant to fireblight. Raised at the US National Arboretum, Washington, DC, in 1963.
H4

P. 'Watereri' A very free-berrying, compact medium-sized shrub with clusters of

Pyracantha 'Watereri'

white flowers followed by bright red fruits.
H4 ♔ 1993

Pyrus *Rosaceae*
Pear

A genus of about 20 species of deciduous trees and shrubs that are natives of the temperate regions of the Old World. The ornamental pears are small to medium-sized, deep-rooted trees with green to silvery grey leaves and white flowers in mid-spring. They are quite tolerant of both drought and wet and are well suited to cold areas. They also stand up well to atmospheric pollution and succeed in all types of fertile soil, though they do best in a good loam in full sun. Pear diseases such as fireblight and scab are more of a problem with culinary pears than with ornamental forms of Pyrus.

P. betulifolia A slender, graceful, small, fast-growing tree. The leaves are more or less rounded, slenderly pointed, strongly toothed and greyish green, becoming green and glossy. The brown fruits are the size of a large pea. N China. Introduced 1882.
H4

P. calleryana 'Chanticleer' A vigorous, dense, narrow, medium-sized cultivar without the thorns borne by the species. It flowers profusely in late to mid-spring and in some years colours beautifully in autumn.
H4 ♔ 1993

P. communis The common pear. A medium-sized tree with oval or rounded glossy leaves, often attractive in autumn. In mid-spring it is smothered with white blossom and later with sweet pears.
H4

P. c. 'Beech Hill' A narrow, medium-sized tree with upright branches. The autumn leaf colour is orange-yellow and can be quite brilliant. It seldom fruits.
H4

P. nivalis A small tree with stout ascending branches. In mid-spring an[d]

... when over-ripe. A most attractive silver-foliage tree. S Europe. Introduced 1800.
H4

Pyrus nivalis

P. salicifolia 'Pendula' Deservedly the best-known of the ornamental pears. It is a form of the willow-leaved pear, a small, very elegant tree with silvery, willow-like leaves and steeply weeping branches. The creamy white flowers go well with the foliage and are often followed by brown, top-shaped fruits.
H4 ♔ 1993

QUERCUS

Fagaceae Oak

THE OAKS constitute a genus of roughly 600 species of evergreen and deciduous trees and – occasionally – shrubs. It may well come as a surprise to some that they are so diverse in form and habit and that, as well as being some of the noblest of all trees, there are oaks that are suitable for much smaller gardens than might be supposed.

The typical lobed oak leaf is by no means universal. The two British species, *Q. robur* and *Q. petraea*, have it, and so does the familiar American red oak (*Q. rubra*), but many have small, unlobed, simple leaves, while others, for example the Black Jack oak (*Q.*

marilandica), are lobed but in such a way as to appear quite different from the traditional oak leaf.

In general, the warmer the summer the better oaks will grow. There is a distinct thinning-out of species as you proceed north in the northern hemisphere (to which they are confined in nature), and a given species is likely to perform less well the further north you attempt to grow it. There is an east-west factor, too, as is evinced by *Q. petraea*, which grows better in the damper, cooler west of Britain than the English oak, *Q. robur*, which prefers the east. On the

other hand it is interesting that some Mediterranean oaks, notably the evergreen *Q. ilex*, grow larger and more lush in the climate of Britain than in their native ranges.

American oaks grown in Britain tend to miss the warm summers and to be less robust than at home, but European species mostly do very well in the Eastern United States, with *Q. petraea* standing up to the cold of the Great Lakes area. American oaks are, in general, the best for autumn colour, although the quite fierce reds of some of them become muted when grown in cooler, equable climates. Almost any soil will suit some oak or other, but the genus as a whole enjoys deep, rich soils that are well-drained but at the same time moisture-retentive. The American red and white oaks are not tolerant of lime, but most of the others are. Only a few, however, will grow well on shallow soils over chalk, *Q. canariensis* being one example.

CARE AND CULTIVATION

It is best to provide oaks with open sites but with some degree of protection from wind. This is not a universal guide, though, as such a diverse genus cannot be summed up quite so neatly. *Q. ilex*, for example, forms a first-class, ultra-long-lived windbreak against salty gales, although it requires 'nurses' (usually conifer species) until it is established. However, the best specimens of this and others are likely to be among other trees.

There are many pests and quite a few diseases that attack oaks, but on the whole the trees are capable of tolerating almost all of them and shrugging them off. Nevertheless, it is essential to prevent or repair gale and other damage, otherwise more serious problems such as honey fungus and heart rots may ensue.

Quercus coccinea 'Splendens'

Quercus *Fagaceae*
Oak

Q. acutissima A medium-sized, freely growing deciduous tree with narrowly oblong leaves like those of a sweet chestnut. They are bright, polished green, margined with bristly-tipped teeth, and persist into winter. Japan, Korea, China. Introduced 1862 by Richard Oldham.

H4

Q. alnifolia (Golden oak of Cyprus) A rare, slow-growing, medium-sized to large evergreen shrub. More or less rounded, hard-textured leaves are hooded at the apex, dark glossy green above and yellow-felted beneath. It is hardy in sheltered gardens away from the coldest areas. Cyprus. Introduced 1815.

H3–4

Q. canariensis (Algerian oak) A large, deciduous tree with very dark grey, deeply fissured bark and a dense, rounded head of branches, though much narrower as a young tree. The large, more or less oval, shallowly lobed leaves are dark shining green above, paler beneath, and remain on the tree until late winter. It is a fast-growing tree that succeeds equally well on clay or shallow chalky soil and is easily recognized in winter by its bold, persistent foliage. N Africa, Portugal, Spain. Introduced c1845.
H4 ♔ 1993

Q. castaneifolia 'Green Spire' A broadly columnar form of the chestnut oak, this is a medium-sized to large deciduous tree with oblong or narrowly oval leaves, tapered at both ends and margined with triangular, sharply-pointed teeth. Raised c1948 by Hillier Nurseries.

H4

Q. cerris (Turkey oak) A fine large tree and one of the fastest growing, excellent in chalky soils and near the sea. The oval or oblong deciduous leaves are coarsely toothed or shallowly lobed and slightly rough to the touch. S Europe, Asia Minor. Introduced 1735.
H4 ♔ 1993

Q. c. 'Variegata' A most effective variegated tree bearing leaves with a cream margin. Any reversion should be cut out.

H4

Quercus cerris

Quercus cerris 'Variegata'

Quercus coccinea

Q. coccinea (Scarlet oak) A large deciduous tree with attractive, broad, dark green, deeply lobed leaves, each lobe furnished with several bristle-tipped teeth. In autumn the leaves turn to a glowing scarlet, branch by branch. In general it is one of the finest trees for autumn colour but in mild localities with unusually equable climates the

colour may be quite disappointing. It requires a lime-free soil. The following form is recommended. SE Canada, E United States. Introduced 1691.

H4

Q. c. 'Splendens' A vegetatively propagated form that was selected for the richness of its scarlet autumn colouring.
H4 ♔ 1993

Q. ellipsoidalis A medium-sized to large deciduous tree, related to *Q. palustris*, usually with a short trunk and spreading head. The deeply lobed leaves on slender stalks turn deep crimson-purple in autumn, equal to the best forms of *Q. coccinea*. It requires a lime-free soil. C North America. Introduced 1902.

H4

Quercus frainetto 'Hungarian Crown'

Q. frainetto 'Hungarian Crown' This was the name proposed by Hilliers for the tree widely grown in Britain and continental Europe as *Q. frainetto*, the Hungarian oak, and under which it has been awarded the Award of Garden Merit. It is a magnificent, large, fast-growing deciduous tree with fissured bark and upright branches making a broadly oval head. The leaves are deeply and regularly lobed with large, oblong lobes, and are occasionally as much as 20cm (8in) long. It is a tree for all types of soil, including chalk, and deserves much wider planting. The species was from SE Europe, introduced 1838.
H4 ♔ 1993

Q. × hispanica 'Lucombeana' (Lucombe oak) A large, partially evergreen, ornamental tree something like the turkey oak

Quercus coccinea 'Splendens'

Quercus ilex

Quercus libani

Quercus × ludoviciana

(*Q. cerris*) with pale grey, shallowly fissured, slightly corky bark and long leaves that mostly fall around the New Year. Raised 1762 from a cross between the turkey oak and the cork oak.

H4 ♛ 1993

Q. ilex (Evergreen oak, holm oak) A large evergreen tree with attractive corrugated bark and a rounded head of branches. The leaves are leathery, dark glossy green and variable in shape and size depending on age and growing conditions. It thrives in all kinds of well-drained soil and is particularly valuable near the coast where it can be used to make a magnificent, rigid hedge that is resistant to sea winds; it is not recommended for the coldest inland areas. It responds well to clipping and tolerates shade. Mediterranean and SW Europe. In cultivation in the British Isles since the sixteenth century.

H4 ♛ 1993

Q. × kewensis A small to medium-sized, semi-evergreen or evergreen vigorous tree with a dense, compound head and small, dark green, angularly lobed leaves. Raised 1914 at Kew.

H4

Q. libani (Lebanon oak) A small, elegant deciduous tree with slender branches and long-persistent, slender, glossy-green leaves that are margined with bristle-tipped teeth. Syria, Asia Minor. Introduced c1855.

H4

Q. × ludoviciana A most attractive, large, vigorous, semi-evergreen tree with deeply and irregularly lobed, shining green leaves that have rich autumn tints. It requires a lime-free soil. SE United States. Introduced 1880.

H4

Q. macranthera A splendid, fast-growing, medium-sized deciduous tree with strikingly large, strongly lobed leaves that are up to 15cm (6in) long. It differs from other similar species in its stout twigs, which, like the winter buds and leaf undersurfaces, are clothed in pale grey, velvety tomentum. It can be grown well in deep soils over chalk and often hybridizes in cultivation with *Q. robur*. Caucasus, N Iran. Introduced 1873.

H4

Q. marilandica (Black Jack oak) A remarkable, small, slow-growing deciduous

481

tree of low, spreading habit. The leaves are broadest above the middle, sometimes triangular, tapered to the base and more or less three-lobed at the broad end. They are up to 18cm (7in) long and often as much across, glossy green above, tawny yellow beneath, and turn yellow or brown in autumn. E United States. It requires a lime-free soil. In cultivation 1739.
H4

Quercus myrsinifolia

Q. myrsinifolia A small, very hardy, densely branched, evergreen tree of compact habit. The smooth, shining leaves are lance-shaped with finely tapered points. They are purple-red when unfolding becoming dark green above, paler beneath. It requires a lime-free soil. China, Japan. Introduced 1854 by Robert Fortune.
H4

Q. palustris (Pin oak) A free-growing, large, dense-headed deciduous tree with slender branches. The leaves are deeply

Quercus palustris

and sharply lobed, shining green on both surfaces and smaller than those of *Q. coccinea* but often turning the same rich scarlet in autumn. It requires a lime-free soil. SE Canada, E United States. Introduced 1800. H4 ♔ 1993

Q. petraea (Sessile oak) One of the two native British species, replacing *Q. robur* in

Quercus petraea

Quercus petraea 'Columna'

damper areas and moister soils. It is a large deciduous tree with often rather larger, long-stalked leaves, not auricled at the base, and stalkless fruits. It is a good tree near the coast. W, C and SE Europe, Asia Minor.
H4 ♔ 1993

Q. p. 'Columna' A densely branched, columnar tree of medium size.
H4

Q. p. 'Purpurea' A large tree with leaves similar in colour to those of the purple beech (*Fagus sylvatica* Purpurea Group).
H4

Q. phellos (Willow oak) A large deciduous tree with slender branches and narrow, willow-like leaves that are glossy green above and turn yellow and orange in autumn. The leaves are entire, but on young trees often show some lobing. It requires a lime-free soil. E United States. Introduced 1723.
H4 ♔ 1993

Quercus phillyreoides

Q. phillyreoides A rare, very hardy, large, evergreen shrub resembling *Phillyrea latifolia*, generally a dense, rounded bush to 5m (15ft) or more, but occasionally a small tree. It has more or less oval, leathery, glossy green leaves with small, sharp teeth, usually bronze when unfolding. China, Japan. Introduced 1861.
H4

Q. 'Pondaim' A small, rugged deciduous tree with large, sharply toothed leaves, dark glossy green above and grey beneath. Raised c1960 in Holland.
H4

Q. pyrenaica (Pyrenean oak) A medium-sized to large deciduous tree with a wide-

Quercus phellos

Quercus robur fastigiata 'Koster'

spreading head of pendent branches and pale grey bark that is deeply fissured into knobbly squares. The leaves, glossy green above and grey-felted below, vary in size and shape and have long, narrow, usually pointed lobes. Long, drooping, attractive male catkins in early summer turn from grey to gold. SW Europe, N Italy. Introduced 1822.

H4

Q. robur (Common oak, English oak) Claimed as the national oak by several countries, this is better known in Britain than *Q. petraea*. It is a large, long-lived deciduous tree that develops a broad head of rugged branches if it is in an open position. The leaves are stalkless or nearly so, auricled at the base and shallowly lobed. The acorns are one to several on a slender stalk. Europe, Caucasus, Asia Minor, N Africa.
H4 ♔ 1993

Q. r. 'Atropurpurea' A curious, slow-growing, medium-sized form with leaves

and shoots a rich wine-purple, becoming greyish purple at maturity.
H4

Q. r. 'Concordia' (Golden oak) A small, rounded, very slow-growing tree with golden yellow leaves in spring and summer. Raised 1843 in Belgium.
H4

Quercus robur

Q. r. fastigiata 'Koster' (Cypress oak) A large, imposing, columnar tree that makes a splendid specimen where space is restricted.
H4 ♔ 1993

Q. r. 'Pendula' (Weeping oak) A small to medium-sized tree with pendulous branches.
H4

Q. rubra (Red oak) A large, fast-growing deciduous tree with large, more or less oval, markedly lobed leaves that generally turn red and finally russet-brown before falling, though the foliage of some trees turns ruby red or mixed yellow and brown. Its branches are stouter and more horizontal than those of *Q. coccinea* and its leaves are less deeply lobed and are matt rather than glossy. It requires a lime-free soil. E North America. Introduced 1724.
H4 ♔ 1993

Q. r. 'Aurea' A small to medium-sized tree with bright yellow leaves in spring. To avoid scorching, it needs shelter and partial

Quercus rubra

Quercus rubra 'Limelight'

shade. It requires a lime-free soil.
H4

Q. r. 'Limelight' This name has been proposed by Hilliers for the tree that is grown as 'Aurea' in continental Europe, which does not scorch in full sun. It requires a lime-free soil.
H4

Q. rysophylla A strong-growing, evergreen, notably large-leaved tree with elliptical leaves that are dark glossy green above and conspicuously wrinkled beneath. They are as much as 25cm (10in) long and 8cm (3in) wide, auricled at the base and shallowly lobed to toothed. This remarkable tree is proving hardy, although its ultimate height is not yet known. Introduced 1979 from the Horsetail Falls above Monterrey, Mexico, by Sir Harold Hillier.
H3–4

Quercus shumardii

Q. shumardii A small to medium-sized deciduous tree with particularly attractive, deeply cut leaves that turn a beautiful red or golden brown in the autumn months. It requires a lime-free soil. S and C United States. Introduced 1897.
H4

Q. suber (Cork oak) Normally a short-stemmed, wide-spreading, evergreen tree of small size but occasionally found to reach a

Quercus suber

height of 20m (70ft). Its bark is thick, rugged and deeply corky and provided a rich source of commercial cork when grown in plantations, particularly in Portugal. It can withstand considerable frost if it is not of very long duration but will not cope at all with frosty winds. S Europe, N Africa. In cultivation 1699.
H3

Quercus × turneri

Q. × turneri (Turner's oak) A distinctive, small to medium-sized, semi-evergreen tree with a compact, rounded head of dark green leaves with 4–6 broad teeth on each margin. In autumn those leaves on the inner parts of the branches are shed, while the ones that are towards the ends are retained, giving the tree the appearance of having an outer 'shell' of foliage in winter. It is good on limy soils.
H4

Q. velutina 'Rubrifolia' A large deciduous tree that is one of the most striking of all oaks with its enormous, hooded leaves measuring up to 40cm (16in) long and 23cm (9in) wide. They are deeply and irregularly lobed, dark green and glossy above, pale and downy beneath. In autumn the foliage is warm reddish brown and yellow. It requires a lime-free soil.
H4

Q. wislizeni An evergreen slow-growing, large shrub or small rounded tree. The polished, leathery leaves are holly-like and oblong to ovate with slender spiny teeth at the margins; they are almost stalkless. California, Mexico. Introduced 1874.
H3-4

R

Rehderodendron *Styraceae*

A genus of nine or ten species of deciduous trees from south-west China, known only since 1930. They require an acid soil.

R. macrocarpum A small tree with more or less elliptical, finely toothed leaves, 7.5–10cm (3–4in) long, that become attractively tinted before falling. The cup-shaped, slightly fragrant flowers are white tinged with pink, with prominent yellow anthers, and are produced in hanging clusters as the leaves emerge. Fruits are oblong, ribbed and bright red. It is a magnificent species, equal in garden merit to the best *Styrax*. China (Mount Omei). Introduced 1934.
H4

Rhamnus *Rhamnaceae*

A large genus of about 125 species of evergreen and deciduous trees and shrubs. Widely distributed, mainly in north-temperate regions, the species are largely grown for their foliage effect. The inconspicuous flowers are small but numerous and borne in axillary clusters. Rhamnus will grow in all types of soils in sun or semi-shade. Harmful if eaten.

Rhamnus alaternus 'Argenteovariegata'

R. alaternus 'Argenteovariegata' A deciduous plant that is one of the best of all variegated shrubs and much sought after by flower arrangers for its green, marbled grey leaves with an irregular, creamy margin. It thrives in dry shade, but needs shelter as it is a little tender. The species was introduced early in the seventeenth century from the Mediterranean region and Portugal. Makes an excellent seaside plant.
H4 ♔ 1993

Rhamnus cathartica

R. cathartica (Common buckthorn) A large deciduous shrub or small tree with spiny branches that are quite attractive in autumn when laden with shining, dark fruits. Europe (including the British Isles).
H4

R. frangula (Alder buckthorn) A large deciduous shrub or small tree with ovate green leaves which turn yellow in autumn. The fruits are red, changing to black, and make the plant highly ornamental. Europe (including the British Isles).
H4

R. imeretina The most outstanding of the buckthorns. It is a medium-sized to large deciduous shrub with stout shoots and large, handsome, corrugated leaves that are dark green above, downy beneath, and usually become bronze-purple in autumn. Some leaves may be as much as 30–35cm (12–14in) long and 10–15cm (4–6in) wide. It is a splendid shrub for a damp, shaded site. W Caucasus. Introduced 1858.
H4

Rhaphiolepis *Rosaceae*

A genus of about 15 species from eastern Asia. They are rather slow-growing, evergreen shrubs with firm, leathery leaves and require a warm, sunny position in a well-drained, fertile soil.

R. × delacourii 'Coates' Crimson' A rounded shrub, usually less than 2m (6½ft) high, with rose-crimson flowers in erect terminal clusters from late spring to summer. It is an attractive wall shrub but is not hardy in cold areas. Raised 1952 in California.
H3

Rhaphiolepis × delacourii 'Spring Song'

R. × d. 'Spring Song' A small to medium-sized form bearing apple-blossom-pink flowers from late spring to summer.
H3

Rhaphiolepis umbellata

R. umbellata A delightful, dense, slow-growing, rounded shrub, to 1.2m (4ft) in the open and higher against a wall. The leaves are thick and leathery. Terminal clusters of fragrant, white flowers from late spring to summer followed by black-bronze fruits. Will survive outside except in colder areas, but received award for its value under glass. Japan, Korea. Introduced 1862.
H3–4 ♔ 1993

RHODODENDRON

Ericaceae

THE GENUS *Rhododendron* is a very large one indeed and includes some of the most breathtakingly beautiful of all ornamental plants. Rhododendrons range from large trees to tiny, prostrate mats; their evergreen or deciduous leaves vary from the size of paddle-blades to less than the span of a finger-nail; and their flowers range in colour through almost the entire spectrum, with some of the most brilliant hues occurring in the azaleas.

The larger ones – those of more than about 2m (7ft) in height – may seem of most interest to gardeners who have considerable space in which they can develop, but a judicious choice of just one or two can be made for gardens of medium size. Where choice is limited you should look for plants with foliage that is attractive all year round. Rhododendron leaves can be extremely dull, but they can also be a highly effective asset to your garden design, not only because of their imposing shapes but also because of their texture and posture, and often the contrasting buff, brown, white or silver undersides.

Of the larger species and hybrids, individual specimens are so striking that you can plant just one of a kind, whereas smaller ones are better in groups. In general, hybrids are a better proposition for reliable yearly flowering; many species are spectacular in a good year but may rest occasionally. Many people prefer what they perceive as a greater simplicity and naturalness in the species, although others would say that among the enormous range of rhododendron hybrids there are many that look just as natural as any species.

Some of the most exciting programmes of hybridization have been carried out among the smaller species. Sometimes quite strong colours have been used, notably vivid reds, soft but vivid orange, and yellow. There is scope for perpetrating colour clashes if you are not careful, but if you choose wisely you can create some of the most gorgeous effects of spring and early summer. You can plant for obvious, dramatic, up-front colour, or you can provide exquisite surprises as when, for instance, the sumptuousness of *R. yakushimanum* 'Koichiro Wada', a plant at the lower end of this somewhat arbitrary size category, is encountered in a leafy bay among other shrubs. On the whole, the smaller species are less given to occasional shy-flowering than the large ones, and among the hybrids of this size range – approximately 1–2m (3–7ft) high – are some of the most deservedly popular rhododendrons of all.

For some gardeners, the dwarf rhododendrons are the most desirable. There is an intimacy about them and a delicate charm that can capture the heart of anyone with a love of small plants, and their toughness and bold but dainty flowering also contribute to making them undying favourites of all who can grow them. That means just about everyone, as they are the ideal plants

Rhododendron luteum growing with bluebells

for a raised bed or tub, and one or two are small enough even for a trough. They make natural-looking associations with other members of the *Ericaceae*, such as *Pieris* and *Gaultheria*, and combine well with camellias and other rhododendrons as long as they are at a distance – plant them too close and they will be swamped.

When planted on a larger scale they are best in groups, and an undulating patchwork of colours can be made, much as with heathers. There are few sights as breathtaking in spring as drifts of mature dwarf rhododendrons in a woodland glade. On the other hand, in the intimate setting of a raised bed or peat wall, just one plant of *R. calostrotum* subsp. *keleticum* is beautiful enough on its own.

When you are choosing dwarf rhododendrons, it is a mistake to concentrate entirely on flowers. These small plants are just as likely to have attractive leaves as large ones; it is merely a matter of scale. For example, *R. lepidostylum* grows to no more than 1m

(3ft) tall at maturity, but its unusual steely blue-green foliage is a conspicuous feature in its own right quite apart from the pale yellow flowers. Turn over the leaves of *R. haematodes* and you will find the undersides covered in a thick, soft, russet felt.

Even those who classify rhododendrons are hard put to state exactly what distinguishes an azalea, although everyone is agreed on what you can say in general terms – those of interest to gardeners. This is that azaleas are either deciduous or lose their spring leaves while retaining tufts of smaller ones at the tips of the shoots through the winter (and are thus imperfectly evergreen); that their flowers are always at the ends of the branches and the inflorescence is an umbel; and that the flowers are usually zygomorphic, which is to say that they are symmetrical only from side to side and not from top to bottom.

Nowadays, evergreen azaleas appear in gardens almost exclusively in the guise of hybrids, and the great majority of decidu-

ous ones are also hybrids. However, one or two deciduous species of azalea, such as the very fragrant *R. luteum* and *R. occidentale* and the beautiful evergreen *R. kaempferi*, retain their positions in the front rank of shrubs and are described among the species of *Rhododendron*.

Evergreen azaleas flower in mid- and late spring – the majority late – and are capable of completely hiding themselves under their freely produced blossoms. Individual flowers are normally single, but certain clones have 'hose-in-hose' flowers (one flower inside another). Their average height is 0.6–1.2m (12in–4ft).

The average height of deciduous azaleas is 1.5–2.5m (5–8ft). The flowers are normally trumpet-shaped and single, although a few have double flowers. Colours range from the delicate pastel shades of the Occidentale Hybrids to the riotous reds, flames and golds of the Mollis Azaleas and Knap Hill Hybrids. Ghent and Occidentale Azaleas are deliciously fragrant, particularly in the evening, and many are among the best shrubs of all for autumn colour.

CARE AND CULTIVATION
In the past too much emphasis was laid on a need for shade and it is now realized that if rhododendrons are given good light they form more shapely specimens and flower more freely. Dappled shade is ideal. The exceptions are the Hardy Hybrids (this is a specific and not a general term, denoted by the symbol HH), which can be grown in full sun and exposure. The soil must be lime-free, friable and moist but well-drained, and should preferably contain as much organic matter as possible.

The maintenance of all rhododendrons is simple and consists mainly of regular mulching with decaying leaves, peat, spent hops, or any organic matter of that nature. The fine, fibrous roots form a wide mat near the surface and should not be disturbed by forking. Deadheading is a good idea, although it becomes less practicable as large rhododendrons grow larger. If Hardy Hybrids become straggly or too large, they can be pruned hard – which is to say anything down to 30cm (12in) from the ground – in mid-spring, but you will need there-

Rhododendron 'Blue Peter'

after to take care that no suckers are allowed to develop if the plants have been grafted on to *R. ponticum* or any other understock.

Rhododendrons may be moved at any time of the year, as long as the weather is temperate. It is as well nevertheless to be fairly accurate about the positioning of large ones, as they can quickly become heavy and awkward to move later if you get it wrong. Dwarf rhododendrons can be moved about almost at will; many experts lift them while they are in flower, pot them up and win prizes with them at shows.

Any rhododendron grown in a pot or container needs to be watched carefully, as it must never be allowed to become dry. It will be more sensitive than some other plants to extremes of heat and cold, and will not welcome an unbalanced diet. Liquid feeds and slow-release fertilizers should be applied at half the generally recommended rate. Overwatering should be avoided.

Rhododendron fulvum

Larger species and hybrids

Apart from the Hardy Hybrids the larger rhododendrons, particularly the large-leaved ones, appreciate shelter from wind and hot sun and a certain amount of shade from trees suits them perfectly. They are impractical in tubs, but gardeners who have a slight trace of lime in the soil may still be able to grow large rhododendrons by counteracting it with regular applications of sequestered iron (Sequestrene).

Smaller species and hybrids

As a general rule, the smaller the leaf of a rhododendron, the more exposure to sun and wind it can take. This is because the larger species are plants of tall woodland in nature, the habitat of dwarf ones is high moorland, and the smaller rhododendrons are more or less transitional.

It follows, too, that the smaller leaves are not as susceptible to physical wind damage, but they are still vulnerable up to a point and appreciate some shelter. They will take more sun than their larger counterparts, but still appreciate relief during the hotter part of the day. They can also tolerate slightly drier conditions.

Dwarf species and hybrids

Most of these plants are capable of growing in full sun as long as the soil never becomes dry. In places with hotter summers and in those that suffer from frosty winds, protection must be given in the form of shade and shelter respectively. Some species which in nature grow in the wetter areas where they receive little sun really do need shade. They include *R. forrestii*, *R. lepidostylum* and *R. chamaethomsonii*.

Azaleas

Evergreen azaleas will thrive in full sun if their roots are kept moist, but they should have some shelter from cold winds and a few with flowers that tend to bleach should be given partial shade if possible. In the flowering season their blossom is often produced with such freedom that the foliage is barely visible. Deciduous azaleas grow well in moist woodland or, on a smaller scale, in a moisture-retaining soil with a little, preferably dappled, shade.

R. adenogynum A small to medium-sized evergreen shrub with leathery leaves covered in tawny, suede-like felt beneath. The flowers are funnel-shaped, deep rose in bud, opening white and shaded rose in mid- to late spring. China, Tibet. Introduced 1910 by George Forrest.
H3

Rhododendron albrechtii

R. albrechtii (Azalea) A very beautiful, medium-sized, deciduous shrub with leaves turning yellow in autumn. Deep rose-pink flowers, 12cm (5in) across, appear with or before the leaves in mid- to late spring. Japan. Introduced 1914 by Ernest Wilson.
H4 ♛ 1993

R. amagianum, syn. *Azalea amagiana* An outstanding medium-sized to large deciduous shrub with broad leaves in clusters of three at the ends of the branches. Flowers are funnel-shaped, orange-red, 3–4 in the truss. Borne early to midsummer. Japan.
H4

Rhododendron atlanticum

R. ambiguum An attractive medium-sized to large evergreen shrub with leaves 5–7.5cm (2–3in) long and clusters of 3–6, funnel-shaped, greenish yellow flowers with green spots in mid- to late spring. China. Introduced 1904 by Ernest Wilson.
H4

R. annae A medium-sized to large evergreen shrub with rather small, narrow leaves and bell-shaped flowers, white to rose-flushed and sometimes with purple spots, in early to midsummer. China, Upper Burma.
H3–4

R. anthopogon A dwarf, compact evergreen shrub with narrowly tubular flowers in tight, terminal clusters, varying from cream to pink, in mid-spring. Himalayan region. Introduced 1820.
H4

R. arborescens (Azalea) A large deciduous shrub with more or less oval, glossy green leaves that are usually prettily tinted in autumn. The fragrant, funnel-shaped flowers are white, occasionally pink-flushed, and the red style is long and protruding. They are borne in early and midsummer. E North America. Introduced 1818.
H4

R. arboreum A magnificent large evergreen shrub or small to medium-sized tree that needs the shelter of other trees. The leaves, up to 20cm (8in) long, are silvery white to dark russet-brown beneath, and the bell-shaped flowers, 5cm (2in) long, vary from white to blood red. It is hardy but flowers very early in mid- to late winter and is ruined by frost in cold areas. Himalayan region. Introduced c1810.
H4

R. a. subsp. cinnamomeum A form bearing leaves with a thick cinnamon or rust-coloured woolly covering underneath. The flowers may be anything from red or pink to white.
H4

R. a. 'Sir Charles Lemon' See *R.* 'Sir Charles Lemon' under Hybrids.

R. a. 'Tony Schilling' A form with deep pink flowers that have darker spots.
H4 ♕ 1993

R. argyrophyllum 'Chinese Silver' A beautiful, large but slow-growing, densely leafy evergreen shrub with long leaves that are intensely silver beneath. It has pink flowers, slightly darker on the lobes and 5cm (2in) across, in late spring.
H4 ♕ 1993

R. atlanticum (Azalea) A charming, small, deciduous shrub with bright green leaves and fragrant, funnel-shaped flowers, white or white-flushed with pink and occasionally with a white blotch. They are borne in late spring. E United States. Introduced 1916.
H4

R. augustinii A large, small-leaved evergreen shrub which, in its most beautiful blue-flowered forms, is one of the finest of all rhododendrons. It flowers in mid- to late spring. China. Introduced 1899 by Farges.
H4

R. a. 'Electra' A magnificent shrub. Clusters of violet-blue flowers with greenish yellow blotches. Raised 1937 at Exbury.
H4 ♕ 1993

R. auriculatum A large evergreen shrub or sometimes a small tree that flowers remarkably late, normally in mid- to late summer but even later in some years. The large, white, funnel-shaped flowers are richly scented and borne in huge trusses. China. Introduced 1901 by Ernest Wilson.
H4

R. austrinum (Azalea) A small to medium-sized deciduous shrub with funnel-shaped, creamy yellow to orange flowers up to 3.5cm (1½in) long, often tinged or striped with purple, that open with or before the leaves in spring. Deep South of the United States.
H4 ♕ 1993

R. baileyi A small to medium-sized evergreen shrub, grows to 2m (6½ft) high, with saucer-shaped, red-purple flowers, usually with darker markings, in late spring. The young shoots and the undersides of the small leaves are coated with reddish brown scales. Himalayan region. Introduced 1913.
H4

Rhododendron augustinii 'Electra'

Rhododendron auriculatum

Rhododendron augustinii

R. bakeri (Azalea) A dwarf to medium-sized deciduous shrub with terminal clusters of funnel-shaped flowers from orange to yellow or red in early summer. SE United States.
H4

R. barbatum A beautiful large evergreen shrub or small tree with attractively peeling bark and bell-shaped, glowing red flowers in dense, globular heads in early spring. Himalayan region. In cultivation 1829.
H3–4

R. beanianum A medium-sized open evergreen shrub with chestnut-brown wool on the undersides of the leaves and loose trusses of bell-shaped, waxy flowers that are usually red but sometimes pink. They are borne in early to late spring. N India, Upper Burma.
H3

R. brachyanthum subsp. *hypolepidotum* A neat dwarf or small evergreen shrub which produces aromatic leaves that are very scaly beneath, and bears bell-shaped, pale yellow flowers in early to midsummer. Himalayan region.
H4

R. brachycarpum An attractive, hardy evergreen shrub of medium size with leaves covered with fawn or brownish wool on the undersides. The funnel-shaped flowers are cream flushed with pink and are borne in early to midsummer. Japan, Korea.
H4

R. bureaui A medium-sized evergreen shrub with dark glossy green leaves covered beneath with a rich red wool. The bell-shaped flowers are rose with crimson markings, borne in a tight truss of 10–15 in mid- to late spring. This outstanding species is well worth growing for the attractive colours of its young growths, which vary between pale fawn and warm, rusty red. China. Introduced 1904 by Ernest Wilson.
H4 ♔ 1993

R. burmanicum A small evergreen shrub

Rhododendron burmanicum

with scaly dark green leaves and funnel-shaped, greenish yellow, fragrant flowers, aging white, to 5cm (2in) long, in early to mid-spring. Mt Victoria, C Burma.
H3 ♔ 1993

R. calendulaceum (Azalea) A medium-sized to large deciduous shrub with leaves that turn orange or red in autumn. The flowers are funnel-shaped, 5cm (2in) across, varying from yellow to orange or scarlet (the name means 'like a marigold') but always richly coloured. They are borne in late spring to early summer. One of the most vividly coloured of all wild azaleas. E North America. Introduced 1806.
H4

Rhododendron calophytum

R. calophytum One of the noblest of the Chinese species and one of the hardiest of those with large leaves, this is a large shrub or small tree with rosettes of long, narrow evergreen leaves getting broader above the middle. It bears large trusses of white or

Rhododendron bureaui

pink bell-shaped flowers, with maroon basal blotches, in early to mid-spring. China. Introduced 1904 by Ernest Wilson. H4 ♔ 1993

R. calostrotum A most attractive dwarf evergreen shrub with grey-green foliage and comparatively large, flat, magenta-crimson flowers in late spring and early summer. A fine species for the rock garden. The following forms are recommended. China, Burma. Introduced 1919.
H4

***R. c.* 'Gigha'** A splendid selection with deep claret flowers contrasting with the grey-green young leaves.
H4 ♔ 1993

R. c.* subsp. *keleticum A dwarf shrub that forms mats or hummocks of small leaves from which the saucer-shaped, purple-crimson flowers arise singly or in pairs. Himalayan region. Introduced 1919 by George Forrest.
H4 ♔ 1993

R. campanulatum A large evergreen shrub with the unfolding leaves covered with a a fawn or rust-coloured suede-like indumentum. The bell-shaped flowers vary from pale rose to lavender-blue and are borne in mid- to late spring. The following forms are recommended. Himalayan region. Introduced 1825 by Wallich.
H4

R. c.* subsp. *aeruginosum A slow-growing, compact shrub with striking, metallic blue-green young growths. Himalayan region.
H4

Rhododendron campylocarpum subsp. caloxanthum

***R. c.* 'Knap Hill'** A form which puts forth blue flowers.
H4 ♔ 1993

R. campylocarpum* subsp. *caloxanthum A charming, small to medium-sized, free-flowering evergreen shrub with small, rounded leaves and clusters of citron-yellow flowers tipped with orange-scarlet in the bud. Himalayan region. Introduced 1919 by Reginald Farrer.
H3–4

R. campylogynum A delightful dwarf evergreen shrub with small leaves glaucous beneath and long-stalked, nodding, rose-purple to almost mahogany, bell-shaped, waxy flowers, produced when the plant is still only a few centimetres high. It flowers in late spring and early summer and is ideal for the rock garden. Himalayan region. Introduced 1912 by George Forrest.
H3–4

***R. c.* 'Bodnant Red'** A form which produces rich red flowers.
H3–4

***R. c.* Charopoeum group** The leaves and flowers are larger than those of the species.
H3–4

***R. c.* Cremastum group** A dwarf shrub of erect habit, with the leaves green beneath instead of blue-bloomy.
H3–4

***R. c.* 'Crushed Strawberry'** A form with flowers a pleasant shade of crushed strawberry. Selected c1955 at Hillier Nurseries.
H3–4

***R. c.* Myrtilloides group** A charming shrublet with smaller, delightful, waxy, plum-purple flowers.
H3–4

R. camtschaticum A dwarf, spreading, deciduous, twiggy shrublet up to 30cm (12in) high with comparatively large, saucer-shaped, rose-purple flowers in late spring. The lower side of the flower is split almost to the base. The leaves, which are 5cm (2in) long, colour attractively in autumn. It needs an open, well-drained situation. Alaska, Kamchatka, Japan. Introduced 1799.
H4

R. cerasinum A medium-sized to large evergreen shrub with elliptical leaves 5–10cm (2–4in) long and drooping trusses

of long, bell-shaped flowers from white with a marginal band of cherry-red to self red or crimson. They are borne in late spring. Himalayan region.
H4

Rhododendron cerasinum

Rhododendron chamaethomsonii

R. chamaethomsonii A dwarf, more or less prostrate evergreen shrub displaying trusses of 5-6 bell-shaped, crimson or rose-crimson flowers in early to mid-spring. W China, E Tibet.
H4

R. charitopes A charming small evergreen shrub, very occasionally growing to as much as 1.2m (4ft) high, with bell-shaped flowers in mid- to late spring that are apple-blossom-pink and speckled with crimson. Himalayan region. Introduced 1924 by George Forrest.
H4

R. c.* subsp. *tsangpoense A variable, dwarf to small, aromatic shrub that flowers very freely, producing semi-bell-shaped

blooms that vary from crushed strawberry to deep crimson or violet in late spring to early summer. Tibet.
H4

Rhododendron ciliatum

R. ciliatum A beautiful, dome-shaped evergreen shrub about 1.2–1.5m (4–5ft) high with peeling bark and bristle-edged leaves. The fragrant, bell-shaped flowers are rose-lilac, borne on still young plants in early to mid-spring. Himalayan region. Introduced 1850 by Sir Joseph Hooker.
H3–4 ♔ 1993

Rhododendron cinnabarinum

R. cinnabarinum Although this is a beautiful medium-sized to large evergreen shrub with tubular flowers of an unusual cinnabar-red and is one of the most choice of the Himalayan species, it and most of its forms have become highly prone to powdery mildew, which rapidly defoliates and destroys the shrubs. The leaves are obovate-elliptic and scaly. It flowers in late

spring to early summer. Himalayan region. Introduced 1849 by Sir Joseph Hooker.
H4

R. c. Conroy group A form which is not badly affected by powdery mildew. It bears loose, flat-topped trusses of pendent, narrowly trumpet-shaped, waxen flowers, light orange with a rose tinge, in late spring.
H4 ♔ 1993

R. c. subsp. xanthocodon A form with clusters of waxy, yellow, bell-shaped to funnel-shaped flowers in late spring and early summer. It flowers best in some shelter and is less susceptible to powdery mildew. Himalayan region. Introduced 1924 by Frank Kingdon-Ward.
H4 ♔ 1993

R. concinnum Pseudoyanthinum group A lovely, medium-sized to large evergreen shrub with elliptical leaves and clusters of funnel-shaped, deep ruby-red or purple-red flowers in mid- to late spring.
H4 ♔ 1993

R. dalhousiae var. rhabdotum A medium-sized to large evergreen shrub with bristly shoots and deeply veined leaves. The highly fragrant, lily-like, creamy white flowers, brightly streaked outside with crimson, are borne in late spring. Himalayas.
H2 ♔ 1993

Rhododendron dauricum

R. dauricum A charming semi-evergreen shrub of medium size with elliptical leaves 2–3cm (about 1in) long and trusses of 1–3 funnel-shaped, bright rose-purple flowers from mid-winter to early spring. NE Asia. In cultivation 1870.
H4

R. d. 'Hiltingbury' A compact form with leaves that turn bronze in cold weather.
H4

R. d. 'Midwinter' A deciduous or semi-evergreen form with phlox-purple flowers.
H4 ♔ 1993

Rhododendron davidsonianum

R. davidsonianum A medium-sized to large evergreen shrub with lance-shaped leaves. The funnel-shaped flowers are borne in clusters at the ends of the shoots and in the joints of the leaves. They are variable in colour from soft pink to purplish rose and are sometimes spotted. They are borne in mid- to late spring. China. Introduced 1904 by Ernest Wilson.
H3–4 ♔ 1993

R. decorum A large and beautiful evergreen species with glabrous more or less oblong leaves up to 15cm (6in) long and large, funnel-shaped, fragrant flowers in lax trusses appearing in late spring to early summer. They are white or shell-pink and

Rhododendron decorum

sometimes spotted. China, NE Burma. Introduced 1901 by Ernest Wilson.

H3–4   ’

R. dichroanthum A slow-growing, dome-shaped evergreen shrub 1.2–2m (4–6½ft) high with 5–10cm (2–4in) long leaves that have a white to grey woolly coating beneath. The flowers are variably coloured but are usually deep orange, bell-shaped, and borne in loose trusses in late spring and early summer. The calyx is large and fleshy and of the same colour as the corolla. It is a parent of many hybrids. China. Found 1906 by George Forrest.

H4

Rhododendron edgeworthii

R. edgeworthii A medium-sized evergreen shrub with branches coated in soft fawn or brown indumentum, which is also on the undersides of the dark green bullate leaves. The flowers are funnel-shaped, white or slightly pink, and richly scented. Some forms of this beautiful species can be grown in the open in very mild areas, where it forms a small, rather straggly shrub. China, Tibet, Upper Burma. Introduced 1904 by George Forrest.

H2–3 ♔ 1993

R. faberi A large shrub or small tree with young shoots clothed in woolly rust-red indumentum. The evergreen leaves are up to 15cm (6in) or more long and pale to rust-brown beneath. The white, bell-shaped flowers are borne in loose trusses in late spring. China.

H4

R. falconeri This magnificent rhododendron can be grown out of doors where there is ample shelter from nearby trees and makes a large evergreen shrub or small tree with very large, broadly obovate leaves with deeply impressed veins and a rusty indumentum beneath. It has huge, dome-shaped trusses of waxy, creamy yellow, purple-blotched, bell-shaped flowers in mid- to late spring. Himalayan region.

Rhododendron falconeri

Introduced 1850 by Sir Joseph Hooker.

H3–4 ♔ 1993

R. f. subsp. eximium A magnificent large shrub or small tree on which the young growths and leaves are covered with orange-brown felt, scurfy on the upper sides of the leaves. The leaves are up to 30cm (12in) long and 7.5cm (3in) wide and the pink or rose bell-shaped flowers are 5cm (2in) long. NE India.

H3–4

R. fastigiatum A dense, small, dome-shaped evergreen bush 60cm–1m (2–3ft) high with small, scaly leaves that are sea-green when young. The funnel-shaped lavender-purple flowers are borne in mid- to late spring. China. Introduced 1906 by George Forrest.

H4 ♔ 1993

R. ferrugineum (Alpen rose) A small, flattish-dome-shaped or spreading evergreen shrub with leaves that are reddish beneath. The flowers are rose-crimson, tubular, and

Rhododendron ferrugineum

borne in small trusses in early summer. Pyrenees and Alps. In cultivation 1740. H4

R. flavidum A pretty, erect evergreen shrub 0.6–1m (2–3ft) high with small, glossy, aromatic leaves and funnel-shaped primrose-yellow flowers in early spring. China. Introduced 1905 by Ernest Wilson. H4

R. formosum A medium-sized evergreen shrub with glossy green, pointed leaves that are margined when young with long bristles. The broadly funnel-shaped flowers, more than 5cm (2in) long, are white or slightly pink with a yellow throat and are highly fragrant. They open in late spring and early summer. Himalayan region. H2–3 ♥ 1993

R. forrestii Repens group A choice, creeping, prostrate evergreen shrub, forming mats of dark green leaves that are pale or glaucous green below. The surprisingly large, bell-shaped, bright scarlet flowers are borne singly or in pairs in mid- to late spring. It requires moist soil and partial shade. Himalayan region. H4

R. fortunei subsp. discolor A large evergreen shrub with leaves up to 20cm (8in) long and funnel-shaped, fragrant, pink flowers with seven-lobed corollas borne in huge trusses that give a magnificent display in early to midsummer. China. Introduced 1900 by Ernest Wilson. H4 ♥ 1993

R. fulgens A medium-sized evergreen shrub with broad leaves that have a reddish brown felt beneath. The tight, rounded

Rhododendron fulgens

trusses consist of 10–12 bell-shaped, bright scarlet flowers. The young shoots are adorned with crimson bracts and the bark of some forms peels attractively. Himalayan region. Introduced 1850 by Sir Joseph Hooker. H4

Rhododendron fulvum

R. fulvum A large evergreen shrub or small tree with large, polished, dark green leaves that are cinnamon-felted beneath. The flowers, borne in early to mid-spring, are bell-shaped, blush to deep rose and may have a crimson blotch. Himalayan region. Introduced 1912 by George Forrest. H4 ♥ 1993

R. glaucophyllum A small, aromatic evergreen shrub with lance-shaped leaves, white beneath. The bell-shaped flowers are pale old rose to lilac and the calyx is large and leafy. They are borne in mid- to late spring. Himalayan region. Introduced 1850 by Sir Joseph Hooker. H3–4

R. griersonianum A splendid and striking, medium-sized evergreen shrub with lance-shaped leaves, matt green above and buff-woolly beneath. The brilliant geranium-scarlet, narrowly bell-shaped flowers are unique among rhododendrons and appear in early summer. A prolific parent of hybrids including 'May Day' and 'Matador'. China, N Burma. Introduced 1917 by George Forrest. H3–4

R. haematodes Generally considered one of the finest Chinese rhododendrons, this is a compact, small to medium-sized, slow-

growing evergreen bush with dark green leaves that are thickly rufous-felted beneath. The flowers are bell-shaped and brilliant dark crimson, appearing in late spring and early summer. China. Introduced 1911 by George Forrest. H4

R. hanceanum Nanum group A slow-growing, dainty evergreen shrub making a neat hummock up to 35cm (14in) high with funnel-shaped cream or pale yellow flowers about 2.5cm (1in) long. A choice dwarf shrub for the rock garden. China. H4

R. hippophaeoides 'Haba-shan' A small, erect, leafy evergreen shrub with large trusses of lavender flowers in early to mid-spring. Tolerant of wet conditions. H4 ♥ 1993

R. hodgsonii A large shrub or small tree with very handsome evergreen foliage. The leaves are up to 30cm (12in) long and 13cm (5in) wide, dark green above and grey or fawn beneath. The bell-shaped flowers are dark magenta and carried in large trusses in mid-spring. Himalayan region. Introduced 1850 by Sir Joseph Hooker. H4

Rhododendron impeditum

R. impeditum A dwarf alpine evergreen shrub, usually much less than 1m (3ft) high. It has tiny leaves and makes a low, tangled mound of scaly branches. The flowers are funnel-shaped, light purplish blue, and borne in mid- to late spring. It is highly suitable for the rock garden. China. Introduced 1911 by George Forrest. H4 ♥ 1993

R. indicum 'Balsaminiflorum' A dwarf, dense, semi-evergreen bush with leaves that often turn crimson or purple in autumn. The double, salmon-pink flowers are single or in pairs and appear in early summer. It is a form of the Indian azalea.
H3

R. insigne A slow-growing evergreen species that eventually becomes a large shrub. It has leathery leaves that are rich glossy green above and silvery beneath when young and take on a metallic lustre. The bell-shaped flowers, borne in late spring to early summer in large trusses, are soft pink with dark markings. China. Introduced 1908 by Ernest Wilson.
H4 ♔ 1993

R. johnstoneanum A large evergreen shrub with somewhat rounded leaves that have bristly margins. The large, fragrant, funnel-shaped flowers are borne in late spring in clusters of three or four and are cream or pale yellow with red spots and a yellow blotch. Manipur. Introduced 1882.
H3 ♔ 1993

R. j. Parryae group A form with scaly dark green leaves that are glaucous beneath. It produces broadly funnel-shaped flowers that are white blotched with orange and very fragrant. They are borne in mid- to late spring.
H1–2 ♔ 1993

R. kaempferi (Azalea) A very beautiful and hardy deciduous or semi-evergreen shrub of medium size. The funnel-shaped flowers are in clusters of 2–4, and vary in colour from fawn to salmon-red, orange-red and scarlet. They appear in late spring

to early summer. It is a parent of many of the Kurume azaleas. Japan. Introduced 1892 by Professor Sargent.
H4 ♔ 1993

R. k. 'Mikado' A form bearing flowers of an exquisite shade of apricot-salmon towards midsummer.
H4

R. keiskii A most attractive, free-flowering, semi-evergreen, dwarf species for the rock garden. The lance-shaped leaves are 2.5–7.5cm (1–3in) long and the flowers are lemon-yellow, widely funnel-shaped and borne in trusses of 3–5 in early to late spring. Japan. Introduced 1908.
H4

R. k. 'Yaku Fairy' A very dwarf or prostrate form from the island of Yakushima.
H4 ♔ 1993

R. kiusianum (Kyushu azalea) A dense, dwarf, evergreen or semi-evergreen shrub, occasionally up to 1m (3ft), with small, oval leaves. The funnel-shaped flowers are in clusters of 2–5 and vary from salmon-red to crimson or purple, although they are usually lilac-purple. They are borne in late spring to early summer. This is one of the species from which the Kurume azaleas were developed. Restricted to the tops of high mountains on Kyushu Island. Introduced 1918 by Ernest Wilson.
H4 ♔ 1993

R. k. 'Hillier's Pink' A lovely form with clear lilac-pink flowers. Raised 1957 by Hillier Nurseries.
H3–4

R. lepidostylum A dwarf deciduous or semi-evergreen shrub, occasionally as much

as 1m (3ft) high. The small, bristly, ovate leaves are eye-catchingly steely blue-green on their upper surfaces until winter. The flowers are funnel-shaped, pale yellow, single or in pairs, appearing in late spring and early summer. It is a choice shrub for the peat or shady rock garden and is the most blue-leaved of the dwarf rhododendrons. China. Introduced 1924 by George Forrest.
H4 ♔ 1993

R. lepidotum 'Reuthe's Purple' See R. 'Reuthe's Purple' under Hybrids.

Rhododendron leucaspis

R. leucaspis A dwarf evergreen shrub, occasionally 1m (3ft) high, with hairy leaves. The lovely, saucer-shaped flowers, in clusters of 2–3, are 5cm (2in) wide and milky white with contrasting chocolate-brown anthers. It needs a sheltered site because it flowers in late winter and early spring and the flowers may be destroyed by frost, and it is probably best grown in an alpine house or a well-ventilated cold greenhouse. Burma-Tibet frontier. Introduced 1925 by Frank Kingdon-Ward.
H2 ♔ 1993

R. lindleyi A large, open evergreen shrub with bluish leaves, glaucous and scaly beneath, and very strongly fragrant, widely funnel-shaped, creamy flowers that are 10cm (4in) across, sometimes edged with pink, and blotched with orange or yellow at the base. They are borne in mid- to late spring. Himalayan region.
H2–3 ♔ 1993

R. lutescens 'Bagshot Sands' A large-flowered, primrose-yellow form of this variable but lovely species. It is a medium-sized

Rhododendron kaempferi

Rhododendron lutescens 'Bagshot Sands'

Rhododendron luteum

Rhododendron maddeni

to large evergreen shrub that requires shelter because of its early flowering in late winter to mid-spring. The blooms are funnel-shaped and the young growths are deep bronze-red.
H4 ♔ 1993

R. luteum, syn. *Azalea pontica* The well-known fragrant yellow azalea. It is a medium-sized, deciduous shrub occasionally growing up to 3.5m (11ft) high and equally as much across. The leaves turn to rich shades of crimson, purple and orange in autumn. The funnel-shaped, yellow, richly fragrant flowers are borne in a rounded truss in late spring. Caucasus, E Europe. Introduced 1793.
H4 ♔ 1993

R. macabeanum A magnificent species for woodland conditions, forming a large, rounded evergreen shrub or small tree with handsome leaves up to 30cm (12in) long that are shiny above and grey-white-woolly underneath. The large trusses of bell-shaped, pale yellow, purple-blotched flowers are borne in early to mid-spring, but not until the plant is several years old. In some forms the flowers are deep canary yellow. Assam, Manipur. Introduced c1928 by Frank Kingdon-Ward.
H3–4 ♔ 1993

R. maculiferum subsp. **anhweiense** A medium-sized evergreen shrub with oval-lance-shaped leaves 5–7.5cm (2–3in) long and rounded heads of bell-shaped white flowers, usually with a pink flush and reddish purple spots. They are borne in mid- to late spring. China.
H4 ♔ 1993

R. maddeni A large evergreen shrub or small tree with highly fragrant white or pink flowers. It is rather tender in its typical state, and the following subspecies is hardier. Himalayan region. Introduced 1850 by Sir Joseph Hooker.
H2–3 ♔ 1993

R. m. subsp. **crassum** A medium-sized to large shrub with thick, rigid leaves that are rusty-scaly below. The sweetly scented flowers are funnel-shaped, 5–7.5cm (2–3in) long, and vary from white to pink, with or without a yellow blotch. They are produced in early to midsummer. This is a beautiful rhododendron and is well worth growing as a conservatory shrub in colder areas.

Himalayan region. Introduced 1906 by George Forrest.

H3 ♔ 1993

Rhododendron makinoi

R. makinoi A medium-sized evergreen shrub with young growths appearing in late summer, clothed in white or tawny, woolly indumentum. The leaves are narrowly lance-shaped, rather wrinkled above and tawny-woolly beneath. The flowers, borne in early summer, are bell-shaped, pink, and sometimes have crimson dots. Japan.

H4 ♔ 1993

Rhododendron minus Carolinianum group

R. minus Carolinianum group A very attractive, free-flowering evergreen shrub up to 2m (6½ft) high with tubular, soft rose-purple flowers in late spring and early summer. N. Carolina, USA. Introduced 1812.

H4

R. morii A rare and beautiful Taiwanese rhododendron, making a large evergreen shrub or small tree with oblong-lance-shaped leaves up to 13cm (5in) long and bell-shaped, white flowers with a ray of crimson spots borne in mid- to late spring. Introduced 1918 by Ernest Wilson.

H4 ♔ 1993

R. moupinense A delightful, early-flowering, small evergreen shrub with bristly branchlets. The flowers are funnel-shaped, white, pink or deep rose, sometimes spotted red, and sweetly scented. It flowers in late winter and early spring and should have some shelter, particularly against early morning frost while in flower. China.

H3–4 ♔ 1993

R. mucronulatum A slender, medium-sized, normally deciduous shrub with ellip-tic-lanceolate leaves up to 5cm (2in) long. The large, funnel-shaped, bright rose-purple flowers are borne from mid-winter to early spring.

R. m. 'Cornell Pink' A form which produces clear pink flowers.

H4 ♔ 1993

R. m. 'Winter Brightness' The flowers of this form are a deeper purple-rose than those of the species.

H4 ♔ 1993

R. nakaharae (Azalea) An attractive, rare, dwarf, creeping evergreen shrub, suitable for rock gardens. Its leaves are small, lance-shaped and persistent. The flowers, which are funnel-shaped and up to 2.5cm (1in) long, are of an unusual dark brick-red and are borne in clusters in early to midsummer or even later. A number of named forms are increasingly becoming available. Taiwan.

H4

R. neriiflorum Euchaites group A medium-sized evergreen shrub with narrow leaves that are gleaming white beneath. Trusses of bell-shaped, fleshy, crimson-scarlet flowers appear in mid-spring: the calyx is large and has the same colour as the corolla. China. Introduced 1913.

H4

R. niveum An attractive large evergreen shrub that needs woodland conditions. The leaves, up to 15cm (6in) long, are more or less lance-shaped and are covered with a white, suede-like indumentum that persists and turns pale brown on the undersurfaces. The flowers are bell-shaped, smoky blue to rich purple, and are borne in tight, globular

Rhododendron neriiflorum Euchaites group

Rhododendron niveum

heads in mid- to late spring. Its colour needs careful placing. Himalayan region. Introduced 1849 by Sir Joseph Hooker.

H4 ♔ 1993

R. n. 'Clyne Castle' A large evergreen shrub with larger leaves than the species and rich purple flowers.

H4

Rhododendron nuttallii

R. nuttallii A superb species but too tender for all but the mildest places. It is a medium-sized to large evergreen shrub with leaves up to 20cm (8in) long, wrinkled above and enchantingly metallic-purple when unfolding. The fragrant, funnel-shaped, lily-like flowers are 13cm (5in) or more long and are borne in loose trusses of 3–9 in mid- to late spring; they are yellow or white flushed with yellow within and are tinged with pink on the lobes. It is an ideal conservatory shrub. Himalayan region. Introduced 1850.
H1–2 ♛ 1993

R. occidentale (Azalea) A medium-sized, deciduous, summer-flowering shrub with more or less oval, glossy green leaves that turn yellow, scarlet or crimson in autumn. The flowers normally appear with the leaves in early summer and are widely funnel-shaped, fragrant, and cream to pale pink with pale yellow or orange-yellow basal stains. It is a parent of many beautiful

Rhododendron oreotrephes

hybrids. W North America. Introduced 1851 by William Lobb.
H4 ♛ 1993

R. orbiculare An outstanding species forming a symmetrical, dome-shaped evergreen bush up to 3m (10ft) high. The leaves are rounded and heart-shaped and the flowers are bell-shaped, seven-lobed and rose-pink, sometimes with a bluish tinge. They are borne in early to mid-spring. China. Introduced 1904 by Ernest Wilson.
H4

R. oreodoxa var. fargesii A medium to large evergreen shrub with oblong-elliptic, funnel-shaped flowers 5cm (2in) long, deep rose-pink on the outside and paler within. They are borne about eight in a truss in early to mid-spring. China. Introduced c1901 by Ernest Wilson.
H4 ♛ 1993

R. oreotrephes A free-flowering, large shrub with glaucous young growths and leaves that are usually oblong-elliptic and glaucous beneath. The flowers, borne in mid- to late spring, are generally funnel-shaped and vary from mauve or mauve-pink to purple or rose, with or without crimson spots. It is semi-deciduous in cold gardens. China. Introduced 1910 by George Forrest.
H4

Rhododendron orbiculare

R. orthocladum var. **microleucum** A dwarf, rock garden evergreen shrub with small, funnel-shaped, white flowers borne in great profusion in mid-spring. The leaves are greyish. China.
H4

R. pachysanthum A medium-sized evergreen shrub which produces oblong leaves up to 9cm (3½in) long, with silvery or brownish tomentose on their upper surfaces when young and densely so beneath. The flowers are in large trusses of up to 20 in early to mid-spring and are broadly bell-shaped, white to pale pink, and sometimes spotted inside. Taiwan. Introduced 1972 by John Patrick.
H4 ♔ 1993

R. pemakoense A beautiful, very dwarf, suckering, evergreen alpine species with small leaves and comparatively large, funnel-shaped, lilac-pink or purple flowers in early to mid-spring. It flowers freely as long as the buds escape damage by frost.

Himalayan region. Introduced 1924 by Frank Kingdon-Ward.
H4

R. polycladum Scintillans group 'Policy' A small, upright evergreen shrub with funnel-shaped, lavender-blue flowers in mid- to late spring. This plant has been known until recently as *R. scintillans* FCC. China. Introduced 1913 by George Forrest.
H4 ♔ 1993

R. ponticum The commonest and most extensively planted rhododendron in Britain and Ireland, where it has become so successfully naturalized as to be a pestiferous weed, particularly in the national parks. It is a large evergreen shrub with mauve to lilac-pink flowers and is one of the few shrubs that will grow even under beech trees. No environmentalist would regard its planting as justifiable, however. Portugal to Caucasus. Introduced 1763.
H4

R. p. 'Variegatum' One of the few varie-

Rhododendron ponticum 'Variegatum'

gated rhododendrons, with leaves margined with cream.
H4

R. prinophyllum See *R. roseum*.

R. prunifolium (Azalea) A remarkable, late-flowering, medium-sized to large deciduous shrub with elliptical leaves up to 13cm (5in) long. The flowers, which appear after the leaves in mid- to late summer, are funnel-shaped and normally brilliant orange-red. Georgia-Alabama border. Introduced 1918 by Professor Sargent.
H4

Rhododendron pseudochrysanthum

R. pseudochrysanthum A slow-growing, medium-sized, dome-shaped, compact evergreen shrub. The ovate-elliptic leaves are 5–7.5cm (2–3in) long and have a woolly covering when young. The flowers, borne in mid-spring, are bell-shaped, pale pink or white, with darker lines and spots. Taiwan. Introduced 1918 by Ernest Wilson.
H4 ♔ 1993

Rhododendron ponticum

R. quinquefolium (Azalea) An exquisitely beautiful, medium-sized to large deciduous shrub with broadly ovate to diamond-shaped leaves in whorls of four or five at the ends of the shoots. They are green, bordered with reddish brown when young, and colour richly in autumn. Pendulous flowers appear in small clusters after the leaves in mid- to late spring and are saucer-shaped, 4–5cm (almost 2in) across, and pure white with green spots. Japan. Introduced 1896. H4 ♔ 1993

Rhododendron racemosum

R. racemosum A variable species, normally a dense, small to medium-sized evergreen shrub with oblong-elliptical, leathery leaves that are glaucous beneath and funnel-shaped, pale to bright pink flowers that arise in racemes from the leaf axils all along the branches in early to mid-spring. The following forms are recommended. China. Introduced c1889.
H4

R. r. 'Forrest's Dwarf' A dwarf form with red branchlets and bright pink flowers, ideal for the rock garden. China. Collected 1921 by George Forrest.
H4

R. r. 'Rock Rose' An extremely floriferous, small and compact form with bright pink flowers.
H4 ♔ 1993

R. reticulatum (Azalea) A medium-sized to large deciduous shrub with leaves somewhat diamond-shaped, notably net-veined beneath, purplish when young and turning wine-purple in autumn. The flowers, which appear alone or in pairs before the leaves in

mid- to late spring, are funnel-shaped and bright purple. Japan. Introduced 1865.
H4 ♔ 1993

R. rex A large evergreen shrub or small tree with large, shining dark green leaves covered with grey to pale buff felt beneath. Bell-shaped flowers, borne in large trusses in mid- to late spring, are rose or white, with a crimson basal stain and spots. China.
H4

R. r. subsp. *arizelum* A form with magnificent large leaves covered beneath with cinnamon indumentum. The flowers are borne in mid-spring in compact heads of creamy yellow bells, sometimes rose-tinted, and with a dark crimson blotch. A rhododendron for moist, woodland conditions. Himalayan region.
H3–4

Rhododendron rex subsp. fictolacteum

R. r. subsp. *fictolacteum* One of the hardiest of the large-leaved rhododendrons. The shoots are covered with cinnamon felting, and the leaves, which are as much as 30cm (12in) long, are brown-felted on their lower sides. The bell-shaped flowers, cream with a crimson blotch, are borne in large trusses. Himalayan region. Introduced 1885 by the Abbé Delavay.
H4

R. r. 'Quartz' A form with pale pink flowers, blotched and speckled with crimson.
H4 ♔ 1993

R. roseum, syn. *R. prinophyllum* (Azalea) A lovely medium-sized to large deciduous shrub with more or less oval leaves and clove-scented, funnel-shaped, pale to deep pink scented flowers that appear with them

in late spring. E North America. Introduced 1812 or earlier.
H4 ♔ 1993

Rhododendron roxieanum Oreonastes group

R. roxieanum Oreonastes group A small to medium-sized evergreen shrub with very narrow leaves 5–10cm (2–4in) long, coated beneath with a fawn or rust-red indumentum. The bell-shaped flowers are cream, usually flushed with rose, and borne 10–15 in a tight truss in mid- to late spring. Well worth growing for its leaves alone. Himalayan region.
H4 ♔ 1993

R. rubiginosum A free-flowering, large evergreen shrub with aromatic leaves 4–6cm ($1^{1}/_{2}$–$2^{1}/_{2}$ in) long, covered with rust-coloured scales beneath. The flowers, borne in mid- to late spring, are funnel-shaped, pink or rosy lilac, with brown spots. Himalaya and China. Introduced 1889 by the Abbé Delavay.
H4

Rhododendron russatum

R. russatum A first-rate garden plant up to 1–1.2m (3–4ft) high. The evergreen leaves are about 2.5cm (1in) long and the flowers are funnel-shaped and deep blue-purple in the most desirable forms. They are borne in mid- to late spring. China. Introduced 1917 by George Forrest. H4 ♛ 1993

R. saluenense A small, densely matted evergreen shrub of variable habit. The small, ovate-elliptic, aromatic leaves are hidden in mid- to late spring by clusters of funnel-shaped, rose-purple or purplish crimson flowers. SE Himalayas. Introduced 1914 by George Forrest. H4

R. s. subsp. chameunum A dwarf evergreen shrub with erect stems and bristle-clad branchlets. The flowers are saucer-shaped with wavy margins, rose-purple with crimson spots, and borne in loose clusters of up to six in mid- to late spring. SE Himalayas. H4 ♛ 1993

R. sanguineum A very variable dwarf or small evergreen shrub with bell-shaped, bright crimson flowers in trusses of 3–6 in late spring, not produced on young plants. There are several different forms of this plant in cultivation. Himalayan region. Introduced 1917 by George Forrest. H4

R. sargentianum A dwarf, twiggy, evergreen shrub of compact habit with small leaves that are aromatic when bruised. The small, tubular flowers, borne in mid- to late spring, may be white but are lemon-yellow in the best forms. It is a gem for a cool spot

on the rock garden but is not an easy plant to grow. China. Introduced 1903–4 by Ernest Wilson. H4 ♛ 1993

Rhododendron schlippenbachii

R. schlippenbachii (Azalea) Although winter hardy, this beautiful azalea is subject to damage by late spring frosts. A medium to large, deciduous shrub of rounded habit with large leaves in whorls of five at the ends of the branches, suffused with purplish red when young, turning to orange, yellow and crimson in autumn. The flowers appear with or before the leaves in mid- to late spring and are saucer-shaped, 7.5cm (3in) across, and pale pink to rose-pink, occasionally white. Korea, Manchuria. Introduced 1893 by James Veitch. H4 ♛ 1993

R. sinogrande A large evergreen shrub or small tree for woodland. It is magnificent as a foliage plant and has shining, dark green leaves as much as 80cm (32in) long and

30cm (12in) wide. The lower surface has a silvery or silvery fawn indumentum. The flowers, creamy white with a crimson blotch, are borne in huge trusses in mid-spring as the plant reaches maturity. Himalayan region. Introduced 1913 by George Forrest. H3 ♛ 1993

R. smirnowii A hardy, compact, slow-growing, medium to large evergreen shrub with leaves up to 15cm (6in) long, grey or pale brown-felted beneath. The bell-shaped flowers are rose-purple or rose-pink and are borne in late spring and early summer. NE Turkey, Georgia. Introduced 1886. H4

R. souliei A beautiful, hardy, medium-sized evergreen shrub with leaves that are almost round and 5–7.5cm (2–3in) long. The saucer-shaped, white or soft pink flowers are borne in late spring to early summer. China. Introduced 1903 by Ernest Wilson. H4

R. spinuliferum A quite remarkable medium-sized evergreen shrub with lance-shaped, puckered leaves that are 5–7.5cm (2–3in) long and, like the stems, softly downy. The flowers are borne in mid-spring in erect clusters in the axils of the upper leaves and are tubular, 2.5cm (1in) long, and red with protruding stamens. China. Introduced 1907. H3

Rhododendron sutchuenense

R. sutchuenense An outstanding large evergreen shrub with stout shoots and drooping leaves up to 30cm (12in) long. In good seasons its floral display in late winter

Rhododendron smirnowii

1.5m (5ft), with narrow, lance-shaped leaves that are an attractive plum-purple beneath when young. The bell-shaped flowers vary in colour from pink to carmine-rose and are profusely borne in mid- to late spring. Himalayan region. Introduced 1921 by George Forrest. H3 ♛ 1993

R. thomsonii A well-known species, eminently desirable but unfortunately prone to powdery mildew. It is a large evergreen shrub or small tree with smooth plum- or cinnamon-coloured bark and rounded or oval leaves. The bell-shaped flowers are held in loose trusses and are deep blood-red with large, cup-shaped, apple-green calyces that are attractive when flowering has finished. It flowers consistently and freely in early to mid-spring and thus benefits from an annual feed and mulch. Himalayas. Introduced 1850 by Sir Joseph Hooker. H3

Rhododendron trichanthum

and early spring is magnificent, with loose trusses of bell-shaped flowers 7cm (3in) long, varying from palest pink to rosy lilac, with purple spots. China. Introduced 1900 by Ernest Wilson. H4

R. taliense A medium-sized evergreen shrub with dark green leaves, densely

brown-felted beneath. The flowers are bell-shaped, cream to yellow, sometimes flushed pink with red spots and borne in trusses of up to 20 in mid- to late spring. China. Introduced c1910 by George Forrest. H4

R. tephropeplum A dwarf or small evergreen shrub, occasionally growing up to

R. trichanthum A large evergreen shrub with bristly branches and widely funnel-shaped flowers that are usually dark violet-purple, sometimes paler, and held 3–5 in a truss in late spring and early summer. China. Introduced 1908 by Ernest Wilson. H4

R. trichostomum A small, twiggy, aromatic evergreen shrub with small, narrow leaves about 2.5cm (1in) long and tight, terminal heads of tubular, daphne-like flowers that may be white, pink or rose, appearing in late spring to early summer. China. Introduced 1908 by Ernest Wilson. H4

Rhododendron taliense

Rhododendron tephropeplum

Rhododendron trichostomum

R. triflorum A slender, medium-sized to large evergreen shrub with attractive peeling bark. The flowers are funnel-shaped, lemon-yellow with a ray of green spots, and borne in trusses of three in late spring and early summer. Himalaya. Introduced 1850 by Sir Joseph Hooker.
H4

Rhododendron vaseyi

R. vaseyi (Azalea) A beautiful, medium-sized to large, deciduous shrub with narrowly oval leaves up to 13cm (5in) long, often turning fiery red in autumn. The flowers appear before the leaves in mid- to late spring and are widely funnel-shaped, up to 5cm (2in) across, pale pink, rose-pink or white with orange-red spots. North Carolina. Introduced c1880.
H4 ♔ 1993

R. veitchianum A tender, small to medium-sized evergreen shrub with relatively large, widely funnel-shaped, fragrant, deeply five-cleft white flowers with a faint

green cast and crinkled petals in late spring to early summer. It is suitable only for the conservatory. Burma, Laos, Thailand. Introduced 1850 by Thomas Lobb.
H1 ♔ 1993

R. v. Cubittii group A medium-sized to large shrub of spreading habit with leaves margined with bristles and scaly beneath. The flowers, borne in early to mid-spring, are broadly funnel-shaped, fragrant and deep pink, sometimes blotched with orange-yellow.
H2 ♔ 1993

R. viscosum, syn. *Azalea viscosa* (Swamp honeysuckle) A medium-sized, deciduous, bushy shrub with small leaves that are dark green above and glaucous green beneath. The spicily fragrant white flowers appear after them in early to midsummer and are 2.5–3.5cm (1–1½in) across, sticky on the outside and sometimes stained pink. E North America. Introduced 1734.
H4

Rhododendron wardii

R. wardii A compact, medium-sized to large evergreen shrub with rather rounded leaves 5–10cm (2–4in) long. The flowers, borne in late spring in loose trusses, are saucer-shaped and clear yellow, sometimes with a crimson basal blotch. It is subject to powdery mildew. China, Tibet. Introduced 1913 by Frank Kingdon-Ward.
H4

R. williamsianum A charming dwarf to small evergreen shrub with a maximum height of about 1–1.5m (3–5ft). It has small, round, heart-shaped leaves and attractive bronze young growths. The delightful bell-

Rhododendron williamsianum

shaped shell-pink flowers are borne in mid-spring. China. Introduced 1908 by Ernest Wilson.
H4 ♔ 1993

R. yakushimanum An evergreen species much used in recent years by hybridists seeking hardy, small, compact rhododendrons for the smaller gardens of today. It is only found wild on the windswept, rain-drenched mountain peaks of Yakushima Island, Japan. Introduced 1934.
H4

Rhododendron yakushimanum 'Koichiro Wada'

R. y. 'Koichiro Wada' A dome-shaped, dense bush up to 1.2m (4ft) high and rather more in width. The young growths are silvery and the leathery leaves, recurved at the margins, are dark, glossy green above and densely fawn-felted beneath. The bell-shaped flowers are borne in late spring in a compact truss, rose in bud, opening to apple-blossom-pink and finally turning white. The best form from the original col-

lecting of the species, it won the RHS First Class Certificate in 1947. It is named after a well-known Japanese nurseryman.
H4 ♔ 1993

R. *yunnanense* 'Openwood' A hardy and exceedingly free-flowering shrub up to 4m (12ft) high, deciduous in cold or exposed gardens. The flowers, borne in late spring, are funnel-shaped and mauve-lavender, speckled with red.
H4 ♔ 1993

HYBRIDS

Flowering seasons are indicated as follows:

Early	Mid-spring
Mid	Late spring to early summer
Late	The latter part of early summer onwards

R. 'Aladdin' A very beautiful medium-sized evergreen shrub with large, widely expanded, brilliant salmon-cerise flowers in loose trusses. Late.
H3

R. 'Albatross Townhill Pink' A large evergreen shrub or small tree with large leaves and richly fragrant, trumpet-shaped flowers borne in enormous trusses. They are deep pink in bud, opening shell-pink. Mid. Introduced 1930.
H3

R. 'Albatross Townhill White' A large evergreen shrub or small tree that is a lovely form of the Albatross group with shorter leaves and white flowers that are pale yellowish green within. Mid. Introduced 1945.
H3

Rhododendron 'Alice'

R. 'Alice' (Hardy Hybrid) A large, vigorous and upright evergreen shrub, with funnel-shaped, rose-pink flowers with lighter centres in tall, conical trusses. Mid. Introduced 1910.
H4 ♔ 1993

R. 'Alison Johnstone' A dainty medium-sized evergreen shrub with oval leaves and trusses of slender-tubed flowers that are greenish in bud and open to pale yellow, flushed with orange or pink. It is prone to powdery mildew. Mid. Introduced 1945.
H4

R. 'Alpine Glow' A large, handsome evergreen shrub with long, rich green leaves and widely funnel-shaped, sweetly scented flowers 10cm (4in) across in large trusses. They are delicate pink with a deep crimson blotch at the base. Mid. Introduced 1933.
H4 ♔ 1993

R. 'Angelo' A group of magnificent hybrids. 'Exbury Angelo' is a large evergreen shrub or small tree with handsome foliage and huge, shapely trusses of large, fragrant, trumpet-shaped, white flowers 14cm (5½in) across with green markings. Mid. Introduced 1933.
H3

Rhododendron 'Anna Baldsiefen'

R. 'Anna Baldsiefen' A dwarf, compact, upright evergreen shrub with light green leaves that become bronze-red in winter and are up to 2.5cm (1in) long. The vivid phlox-pink funnel-shaped flowers are profusely borne, 3cm (1¼in) across, with deeper coloured, wavy margins. Early. Introduced 1964.
H4 ♔ 1993

Rhododendron 'Anna Rose Whitney'

R. 'Anna Rose Whitney' A vigorous, medium-sized evergreen shrub with leaves up to 11cm (4½in) long and dense, rounded trusses of widely funnel-shaped flowers, 10cm (4in) across, deep rose-pink, spotted with brown on the upper lobes. Mid. Introduced 1954.
H4 ♔ 1993

R. 'Arctic Tern' A vigorous, compact, free-flowering, upright, dwarf evergreen shrub up to 60cm (2ft) high, with leaves 3.5cm (1½in) long. The flowers are 1cm (½in) long, white tinged with green, and borne in compact, globular trusses. It has been suggested that a *Ledum* species may have been involved in the parentage. Mid. Introduced 1982.
H4 ♔ 1993

R. 'Argosy' A vigorous large evergreen shrub or small tree with handsome large leaves and highly fragrant, trumpet-shaped, white flowers with a ray of dull crimson at the throat. Late. Introduced 1933.
H3–4 ♔ 1993

R. 'Arthur Bedford' A charming, large, free-flowering evergreen shrub, possibly a hybrid of *R. ponticum*, with compact, conical trusses of pale mauve blooms that are spotted with dark rose-madder inside. Mid. Introduced 1936.
H4

R. 'Arthur J. Ivens' A medium-sized, dome-shaped evergreen bush which displays the leaf shape and attractively copper-tinted young foliage of *R. williamsianum*, one of its parents. The flowers are shallowly bell-shaped, 7.5cm (3in) across, deep pink in bud and opening rose-pink with two small crimson flashes. Early. Raised 1938 by Hillier Nurseries and named after a former manager.

H4

R. **'Arthur Stevens'** A lovely, rounded, medium-sized evergreen shrub with young shoots, leaf stalks and buds bright yellow. The loose trusses of bell-shaped flowers are pale pink fading to white, with a deep rose-red basal stain. Mid. Raised 1960 by Hillier Nurseries and named after the rhododendron foreman of the time.

H3 ♔ 1993

Rhododendron Augfast group

R. **Augfast group** A small, dense, rounded evergreen shrub with small, scattered leaves and small, funnel-shaped flowers in terminal clusters. Forms vary from dark lavender-blue to heliotrope. Early. Introduced 1921.

H4

R. **Avalanche group** A large evergreen shrub with bold foliage and large trusses of

Rhododendron Avalanche group

enormous, fragrant, widely funnel-shaped, snow-white flowers that are pink-flushed in bud and have a red basal stain within. The red leaf stalks and bracts contrast superbly with the white of the flowers. Early. Introduced 1933.

H4 ♔ 1993

R. **'Azor'** A large evergreen shrub with trusses of large, trumpet-shaped flowers of soft salmon pink. Late. Introduced 1927.

H3–4

Rhododendron 'Baden-Baden'

R. **'Baden-Baden'** A dwarf, compact evergreen shrub with small, dark glossy green, rather twisted leaves and profusely borne deep waxy red flowers. Mid. Introduced before 1972.

H4

R. **'Bagshot Ruby'** A vigorous medium-sized evergreen shrub with dense, rounded trusses of widely funnel-shaped, ruby-red flowers. Mid. Introduced 1916.

H4 ♔ 1993

R. **'Bambi'** A small, *R. yakushimanum* hybrid of compact habit which produces dark green, deeply veined evergreen leaves that are felted with pale brown when young. The flowers are red in bud and open pale pink flushed with yellow. Mid. Introduced c1964.

H3

R. **'Bashful'** A medium-sized *R. yakushimanum* hybrid of wide-spreading habit, with narrow, red-tinged evergreen leaves that are silvery when young. The flowers are light pink with a rust-red blotch and fade to white. Mid. Introduced 1971.

H4 ♔ 1993

Rhododendron 'Bashful'

Rhododendron 'Beatrice Keir'

R. **'Beatrice Keir'** A large evergreen shrub with handsome foliage and large trusses of funnel-shaped, lemon-yellow flowers. Early. Introduced 1974.

H3 AGM 1993

R. **'Beauty of Littleworth'** (Hardy Hybrid) A most striking large evergreen shrub with immense conical trusses of

Rhododendron 'Beauty of Littleworth'

white, crimson-spotted flowers, raised in 1900 and still one of the best hardy hybrids. Mid. Introduced c1900.
H4 ♛ 1993

Rhododendron 'Belle Heller'

R. 'Belle Heller' A small, compact evergreen shrub with dark green leaves and large, dense, conical trusses of white flowers with a gold flash. Mid. Introduced 1958. H4

Rhododendron 'Betty Wormald'

R. 'Betty Wormald' (Hardy Hybrid) A magnificent medium-sized to large evergreen shrub which bears immense trusses of large, widely funnel-shaped, wavy-edged flowers that are rich crimson in bud and open to deep rose-pink, lighter in the centre, and with a broad pattern of blackish crimson markings within. Mid. Introduced before 1922.
H4 ♛ 1993

R. 'Biskra' A large, slender, floriferous evergreen shrub with rather flat trusses of

pendent, narrowly funnel-shaped, vermilion flowers. Early. Introduced 1934. H3

Rhododendron 'Blewbury'

R. 'Blewbury' A small, compact evergreen shrub with narrow, pointed leaves with loose, pale brown felt underneath. The flowers are bell-shaped, white with reddish purple spots. Mid. Introduced 1968.
H4 ♛ 1993

Rhododendron 'Bluebird'

R. 'Bluebird' A neat, dwarf, small-leaved evergreen shrub suitable for the rock garden. The lovely violet-blue flowers are borne in small, compact trusses. Early. Introduced 1930.
H4 ♛ 1993

R. 'Blue Chip' A dwarf evergreen shrub with dark green leaves which are scaly beneath and violet-purple, widely funnel-shaped, deeply five-lobed flowers. Early to mid. Introduced before 1978.
H4

R. 'Blue Diamond' A slow-growing, compact evergreen bush up to 1m (3ft) high or more, with terminal clusters of rich lavender-blue, saucer-shaped flowers in tight clusters. It is now being superseded by other cultivars. Early to mid. Introduced 1935.
H4

Rhododendron 'Blue Peter'

R. 'Blue Peter' (Hardy Hybrid) A vigorous, upright, very free-flowering medium-sized evergreen shrub with flowers in compact, conical trusses. They are funnel-shaped, frilled at the margins, and cobalt-violet, paling to white at the throat, with a ray of maroon spots. Mid. Introduced 1930.
H4 ♛ 1993

R. 'Blue Star' A dwarf evergreen shrub with mauve-blue flowers 3cm (1¼in) across. Early. Introduced 1961.
H4

R. 'Blue Tit' A dense evergreen shrub up to 1m (3ft) high and as much in width. The small, widely funnel-shaped flowers are in clusters at the tips of the branchlets and are a lovely lavender blue that intensifies with age, as it does in 'Blue Diamond'. A first-class shrub for the rock garden. Early. Introduced 1933.
H4

R. 'Boddaertianum' (Hardy Hybrid) A large, fast-growing evergreen shrub that develops into a small tree. Flowers are in a compact, rounded truss and are widely funnel-shaped, lavender-pink in bud, opening very pale pink or nearly white with a wide ray of crimson-purple markings. They are 6cm (2½in) across. Early. Introduced 1863.
H4 ♛ 1993

R. 'Bo-Peep' A small, slender evergreen shrub with widely funnel-shaped, primrose-yellow flowers that have two broad bands of pale orange spots and streaks. They are 4cm (1½in) across and are borne singly or in pairs in early spring. It is a very free-flowering shrub and a fine sight when in full flower. Introduced 1934.
H4 🏆 1993

Rhododendron 'Bow Bells'

R. 'Bow Bells' A charming, bushy evergreen shrub with bright coppery young growths. The flowers are widely bell-shaped, deep cerise in bud, opening to soft pink within and rich pink on the outside. They are borne in loose trusses. Early to mid. Introduced 1934.
H4 🏆 1993

Rhododendron 'Bric-a-brac'

R. 'Bric-a-brac' A small, neat, free-flowering evergreen shrub bearing white, wide-open flowers 6cm (2½in) across with chocolate-coloured anthers. Although

hardy, it should have a sheltered position to protect its flowers, which appear in early spring or even earlier in a mild season. Introduced 1934.
H4 🏆 1993

Rhododendron 'Britannia'

R. 'Britannia' (Hardy Hybrid) A superb, slow-growing, medium-sized evergreen shrub, forming a compact, rounded bush generally broader than high. The pretty flowers are gloxinia-shaped, glowing red, and carried in compact trusses backed by bold, handsome foliage. It resists wind well. Mid. Introduced 1921.
H4 🏆 1993

R. 'Brocade' A small evergreen dome-shaped shrub, very much like 'Arthur J. Ivens' in habit and foliage. Its bell-shaped, frilly-margined flowers are borne in loose trusses and are vivid carmine in bud, opening to peach-pink. Early to mid. Introduced 1934.
H4 🏆 1993

R. 'Bruce Brechtbill' A medium-sized evergreen shrub which is a sport of 'Unique', which it closely resembles, except that the flowers are rich pink with a yellow throat. Early to mid. Introduced 1970.
H4

R. 'Buttermint' A compact dwarf evergreen shrub with dark glossy green leaves that are bronze when young. Bright yellow, bell-shaped flowers edged with deep pink open from orange-red buds. It is a beautiful rhododendron but bud-tender. Mid. Introduced 1979.
H4

R. 'C.I.S' A vigorous, free-flowering, medium-sized evergreen shrub with flowers in compact globular trusses. They are widely funnel-shaped with wavy margins and are 6cm (2½in) across. The buds are red and open orange-yellow, flushed and veined with red, and speckled with orange-brown in the throat. The initials stand for Claude I. Sersanous, once President of the American Rhododendron Society. Mid. Introduced 1952.
H4

R. Carita group A beautiful Exbury hybrid that is a medium-sized evergreen shrub bearing well-filled trusses of large, bell-shaped flowers of the palest shade of lemon, with a small basal blotch of cerise within. Early.
H4

R. 'Carita Golden Dream' A form with flowers of deep cream, flushed and shaded with pink, becoming ivory white at maturity. Early. Introduced 1935.
H4 🏆 1993

Rhododendron 'Bruce Brechtbill'

Rhododendron 'Carita Inchmery'

Rhododendron 'Caroline Allbrook'

R. 'Carita Inchmery' A form with flowers red in bud, opening to pink with a fawn-yellow centre, usually with six lobes. Early. Introduced 1935.
H4 ♛ 1993

Rhododendron 'Carmen'

R. 'Carmen' A dwarf or prostrate evergreen shrub which bears waxy, bell-shaped, glistening dark crimson flowers. Mid. Introduced 1935.
H4 ♛ 1993

R. 'Caroline Allbrook' A vigorous *R. yakushimanum* hybrid that makes a small compact, spreading evergreen shrub with dark green leaves growing up to 11cm (4¹/₂in) long and widely funnel-shaped flowers with very wavy margins. They are lavender-pink with a paler centre, borne in compact, globular trusses, and fade with age. Mid. Introduced 1975.
H4 ♛ 1994

R. 'Cary Ann' A compact, small evergreen shrub with dark green leaves and dense,

rounded trusses of coral-pink flowers. Mid. Introduced 1962.
H4

R. 'Charlotte de Rothschild' A tall evergreen hybrid like 'Sir Frederick Moore' with long leaves and large, compact, rounded trusses of clear pink flowers spotted with chocolate. Mid. Introduced 1935.
H4 ♛ 1993

Rhododendron 'Charlotte de Rothschild'

R. 'Chevalier Felix de Sauvage' (Hardy Hybrid) A very old hybrid and still among the best. It is a medium-sized to large, evergreen shrub of dense habit with trusses of deep rose-pink, dark-blotched flowers 6cm (2¹/₂in) across and wavy at the margins. Mid. Introduced 1970.
H4 ♛ 1993

R. 'Choremia' A compact, medium-sized evergreen shrub with dark green leaves that are silvery grey beneath. The waxy, bell-shaped red flowers open in early to mid-spring. Introduced 1933.
H3

R. 'Chikor' A choice dwarf evergreen shrub with small leaves and clusters of yellow flowers. Mid.
H4

R. 'Chink' An early-flowering dwarf evergreen shrub bearing lax trusses of drooping, bell-shaped flowers of an unusual chartreuse-green, with occasional darker spotting on the lower lobe. Introduced 1961.
H4

Rhododendron 'Christmas Cheer'

R. 'Christmas Cheer' (Hardy Hybrid) An old evergreen hybrid of rather dense, compact habit with flowers that are pink in the bud and fade to white. It normally flowers in early spring, occasionally late winter, and its name refers to the erstwhile practice of forcing it for Christmas decoration. Occasionally, however, it will flower in the garden at Christmas if the weather is exceptionally mild. Introduced 1908.
H4

R. 'Chrysomanicum' A small, compact, spreading evergreen shrub with glossy dark

green leaves and primrose-yellow flowers. Early. Introduced 1947.
H2 ♈ 1993

Rhododendron Cilpinense group

R. Cilpinense group A beautiful, free-flowering evergreen hybrid, forming a neat, rounded bush up to 1m (3ft) high, with glossy green, bristle-margined leaves. The flowers are in loose trusses, shallowly bell-shaped, sparkling white, flushed with pink but deeper in the bud. They open in early spring. Introduced 1927.
H4 ♈ 1993

Rhododendron Cinnkeys group

R. Cinnkeys group A choice evergreen hybrid of upright habit with oval, glossy green leaves. The tubular flowers are bright orange-red, shading to pale apricot on the lobes, and are produced in dense, drooping clusters. Mid. Introduced 1926.
H4

R. 'Conroy' See *R. cinnabarinum* Conroy Group.

R. 'Corona' (Hardy Hybrid) A medium-sized evergreen shrub that forms a most charming, slow-growing, compact mound with funnel-shaped, rich coral-pink flowers, 5cm (2in) across, in rather elongated trusses. Mid. Introduced before 1911.
H4 ♈ 1993

R. 'Countess of Haddington' A beautiful but tender, small to medium-sized evergreen shrub of rather straggling habit. The leaves are usually in terminal clusters of five, glaucous green and dotted with glands beneath. The richly fragrant, trumpet-shaped flowers are in umbels of 2–4, and are white, flushed with pale rose. It is a charming shrub for the conservatory. Early. Introduced 1862.
H2 ♈ 1993

Rhododendron 'Cowslip'

R. 'Cowslip' A small, neat, rounded evergreen shrub with bell-shaped flowers 5–6cm (2–2½in) across, cream or pale primrose with a pale pink flush when young. They are carried in loose trusses in mid-season. Introduced 1937.
H4

R. 'Crest' A magnificent medium-sized evergreen hybrid with reddish purple shoots and large trusses of bell-shaped, primrose-yellow flowers with a slight darkening in the throat. They are orange in bud and are 10cm (4in) across when open. Mid. Introduced 1953.
H4 ♈ 1993

R. 'Curlew' A most attractive dwarf, spreading evergreen shrub with small, dark green leaves and profusely borne, widely funnel-shaped flowers 5cm (2in) across, pale

Rhododendron 'Curlew'

yellow marked with greenish brown. It is best in a cool position. Mid. Introduced 1970.
H4 ♈ 1993

R. 'Cynthia' (Hardy Hybrid) One of the best rhododendrons for general planting, as it thrives in a great variety of situations. A large, vigorous, dome-shaped evergreen

Rhododendron 'Cynthia'

shrub with magnificent conical trusses of widely funnel-shaped, rose-crimson flowers, with a ray of blackish crimson markings within. Mid. Introduced before 1870. H4 ♔ 1993

Rhododendron 'David'

R. 'David' A medium-sized evergreen shrub which produces compact trusses of funnel-shaped, frilly-margined, deep blood-red flowers, slightly spotted within. Mid. Introduced 1939. H4 ♔ 1993

R. 'Day Dream' A beautiful, open, spreading medium-sized evergreen hybrid with large, loose trusses of broadly funnel-shaped flowers that are rich crimson in bud and open pink flushed with crimson before fading to cream, flushed with pale pink on the tube. Mid. Introduced 1936. H4 ♔ 1993

R. 'Doc' A small, compact *R. yakushimanum* hybrid that is a free-flowering evergreen shrub with dull green leaves and funnel-shaped, wavy-margined flowers 4cm (1½in) across, borne in globular trusses. They are rose-pink with deeper edges and spots, fading to cream. Mid. Introduced 1972. H4 ♔ 1993

R. 'Doncaster' (Hardy Hybrid) A small evergreen shrub, broadly dome-shaped in habit, with somewhat glossy, very dark green, leathery leaves that are held very stiffly on the shoots. The flowers are in a dense truss, funnel-shaped, brilliant red with a ray of black markings within. Unfortunately this very popular hybrid is now prone to bud blast. Mid. H4

Rhododendron 'Doncaster'

Rhododendron 'Dopey'

R. 'Dopey' A small to medium-sized *R. yakushimanum* hybrid that makes a compact evergreen shrub with bell-shaped, wavy-edged, bright orange-red flowers, paler towards the margins and spotted with orange-brown. They are freely borne in globular trusses. Mid. Introduced 1970. H4 ♔ 1993

Rhododendron 'Dora Amateis'

R. 'Dora Amateis' A mound-forming medium-sized evergreen shrub with flowers freely produced in open clusters. They are funnel-shaped, 5cm (2in) across, pale pink in bud, opening to white and faintly spotted with yellow. Early. Introduced 1955. H4 ♔ 1993

R. 'Dusky Maid' A tall, erect, robust evergreen bush with tight, rounded trusses of very attractive, dark dusky red flowers. Mid to late. Introduced 1936. H4

Rhododendron 'Earl of Donoughmore'

R. 'Earl of Donoughmore' A medium-sized evergreen hybrid of *R. griersonianum* bearing bright red flowers with an orange glow. Mid. Introduced 1953. H4 ♔ 1993

R. 'Egret' A compact and free-flowering, dwarf evergreen shrub of neat habit, with widely funnel-shaped flowers 2cm (¾in) across, white with a green cast. They are borne in open trusses 7cm (3in) across. Mid. Introduced 1982. H4 ♔ 1993

R. 'Eider' A vigorous, compact yet wide-spreading small evergreen shrub hardier than *R. leucaspis*, one of its parents. The widely funnel-shaped white flowers 5cm (2in) across are freely borne in compact rounded trusses 7cm (3in) acrossand are long-lasting. Mid. Introduced 1979. H4

R. 'El Camino' A vigorous large evergreen shrub with dark green leaves and very large, wavy-edged, glowing red flowers with darker spots. Mid. Introduced 1976. H4

Rhododendron 'Elisabeth Hobbie'

R. 'Elisabeth Hobbie' A dwarf evergreen shrub with loose umbels of 6–10 translucent, scarlet, bell-shaped flowers. Early. Introduced 1945.

H4 ♀ 1993

Rhododendron 'Elizabeth'

R. 'Elizabeth' A dwarf or small spreading evergreen shrub with rich, dark red trumpet-shaped flowers, 7.5cm (3in) across, carried in clusters of five or six. It is prone to powdery mildew. Early. Introduced 1939.
H4

R. 'Elizabeth Lockhart' A small, mound-forming evergreen shrub with deep bronze-purple oval to oblong leaves and loose clusters of bell-shaped, deep red flowers. Early. Introduced 1965.
H4

R. 'Emasculum' A medium-sized, upright evergreen shrub with leaves only 3cm (1¼in) long and flowers borne in pairs or singly. They are broadly funnel-shaped, 4cm (1½in) across and mauve-pink in bud,

opening to very pale lilac pink. The stamens are present but much reduced in size, hence the name. Early.
H4 ♀ 1993

Rhododendron 'Fabia'

R. 'Fabia' A most beautiful, widely dome-shaped evergreen bush bearing loose, flat trusses of funnel-shaped scarlet flowers, which are shaded with orange in the tube and freely speckled with brown markings. Mid. Introduced 1934.

H4 ♀ 1993

Rhododendron 'Faggetter's Favourite'

R. 'Faggetter's Favourite' A tall evergreen shrub with fine foliage and large trusses of sweetly scented, shell-pink flowers with white shading. Mid. Introduced 1933.
H4 ♀ 1993

R. 'Fastuosum Flore Pleno' (Hardy Hybrid) A large, dome-shaped evergreen bush with lax trusses of semi-double flowers with wavy margins. They are pale bluish mauve with a ray of brown-crimson mark-

Rhododendron 'Fastuosum Flore Pleno'

ings within. Mid. Introduced before 1846.
H4 ♀ 1993

R. Flava group A compact, small evergreen *R. yakushimanum* hybrid with dark glossy green leaves and bell-shaped pale yellow flowers, blotched with red, that are borne in dense, dome-shaped trusses. There are several cultivars, of which one of the best is 'Volker'.
H4

Rhododendron 'Fragrantissimum'

R. 'Fragrantissimum' A beautiful, medium-sized evergreen hybrid with attractive, dark green, corrugated leaves. The extremely fragrant, widely funnel-shaped flowers are in terminal umbels of four; they are up to 7.5cm (3in) long, white flushed with pale rose without and greenish within at the base. The stamens have brown anthers. It is early and tender and is best in the conservatory except in the mildest areas. Introduced 1868.
H2–3 ♀ 1993

R. **'Frank Galsworthy'** A medium-sized evergreen shrub with narrow, slightly twisted leaves. The funnel-shaped flowers are deep purple with a large blotch of yellow and white, and white anthers. They are borne in dense, rounded trusses. Late.
H4 ♔ 1993

R. **'Fred Wynniatt'** A large evergreen shrub with large, maize-yellow flowers flushed with pink, borne in flat-topped trusses. Mid. Introduced 1964.
H4 ♔ 1993

R. **'Furnivall's Daughter'** Similar to 'Mrs Furnivall' but stronger-growing and with larger leaves and flowers. The flowers are widely funnel-shaped, light rose pink with a bold splash of dark markings. Mid to late. Introduced 1957.
H4 ♔ 1993

R. **'Fusilier'** A magnificent, dense, medium-sized evergreen bush. Long, narrow leaves are brown-felted beneath, and large trusses of brilliant red, funnel-shaped flowers 8cm (3in) wide with darker spots on all the lobes. Mid. Introduced 1938.
H4 ♔ 1993

R. **'Gartendirektor Glocker'** A compact, small, domed evergreen shrub with rounded leaves that are deep blue-green when young. The deep rose-red, funnel-shaped flowers are in loose trusses. Mid. Introduced 1952.
H4

R. **'George Johnstone'** A medium-sized evergreen shrub with aromatic leaves and loose trusses of bright orange, bell-shaped flowers. Early to mid. Introduced 1968.
H3–4 ♔ 1993

Rhododendron 'Ginny Gee'

R. **'Ginny Gee'** An excellent dwarf, free-flowering evergreen shrub of compact habit. The widely funnel-shaped, pale pink flowers are deeper in the bud and fade to near-white, edged with pink. Early to mid. Introduced 1979.
H4 ♔ 1993

R. **'Golden Orfe'** A medium-sized to large evergreen shrub resembling *R. cinnabarinum,* with tubular orange-yellow flowers 5cm (2in) long. Mid. Introduced 1965.
H4 ♔ 1993

R. **'Golden Oriole'** A small, upright evergreen shrub with red young shoots and leaves to 5cm (2in) long with bristled margins. The funnel-shaped flowers are borne in twos and threes, and are primrose-yellow with two patches of orange spots inside. When newly opened they contrast prettily with the bright pink bud scales at their bases. Early. Introduced 1964.
H3 ♔ 1993

R. **'Golden Oriole Talavera'** A small evergreen shrub similar to 'Golden Oriole' but with clear, pale yellow flowers. Early. Introduced 1964.
H3 ♔ 1993

Rhododendron 'Golden Torch'

R. **'Golden Torch'** A small, compact evergreen shrub with leaves up to 6cm (2½in) long and bell-shaped flowers 5cm (2in) wide. They are salmon-pink in bud opening to pale yellow and are borne in compact trusses. Mid. Introduced 1972.
H4 ♔ 1993

R. **'Goldkrone'** A small, compact evergreen mound with large trusses of golden-yellow, funnel-shaped flowers, profusely

borne over a long period. One of the best small yellows. Mid. Introduced 1983.
H4

R. **'Goldsworth Orange'** A low evergreen bush with large trusses of pale orange flowers, tinged with apricot-pink. It is still popular but its colour is somewhat muddy and there are better rhododendrons in its range. Late. Introduced 1938.
H4

Rhododendron 'Gomer Waterer'

R. **'Gomer Waterer'** (Hardy Hybrid) A very beautiful, medium-sized, dense evergreen bush with large, leathery leaves and fragrant flowers in large, dense, rounded trusses. They are 8cm (3in) wide, funnel-shaped but deeply divided, and white flushed with pale mauve towards the edges, with a mustard basal blotch. Mid to late. Introduced before 1900.
H4 ♔ 1993

R. **'Grace Seabrook'** A vigorous, tough, medium-sized evergreen shrub with dark green pointed leaves and deep red flowers with paler margins in compact, broadly conical trusses. Early to mid. Introduced 1965.
H4

R. **'Gristede'** A compact dwarf evergreen shrub resembling 'Blue Diamond', with glossy green leaves and clusters of funnel-shaped, violet-blue flowers. Early to mid. Introduced 1977.
H4

R. **'Grosclaude'** A neat, compact evergreen hybrid producing lax trusses of bell-shaped, waxen, wavy-margined, blood-red flowers which have darker spots inside. The

Rhododendron 'Grosclaude'

calyx is coloured the same as the petals. Mid. Introduced 1941.

H4 🏆 1993

Rhododendron 'Grumpy'

R. 'Grumpy' A small, compact *R. yakushimanum* hybrid that makes a spreading evergreen shrub with funnel-shaped flowers borne in rounded trusses. They are 5cm (2in) wide, cream tinged with pale pink at the margins and spotted with orange-yellow. It is a rather shy-flowering shrub. Mid. Introduced 1971.

H4

R. 'Hachmann's Polaris' A small *R. yakushimanum* hybrid that makes a compact evergreen mound with hairy leaves The light, rosy pink flowers whci are edged with fuchsia-purple, are carmine in bud. Mid. Introduced 1963.

H4

R. 'Halfdan Lem' A vigorous, medium-sized evergreen shrub which has dark green, somewhat twisted leaves and bright red flowers borne in large trusses. Mid. Introduced 1974.

H4

R. 'Hampshire Belle' A very distinctive, small, compact, upright evergreen shrub which has slender leaves growing up to 8 × 1cm (3 × ½in). The flowers, borne in dense, hemispherical trusses of about 18, are funnel-shaped, 5cm (2in) wide, and pink in bud, opening to lilac-pink that fades to white in the centre, heavily blotched with red. Discovered 1970 as a seedling in the Hillier Gardens and Arboretum by the head gardener, Bill George.

H4

R. 'Harvest Moon' A lovely medium-sized evergreen hybrid with bell-shaped cream flowers marked with a broad ray of carmine spots inside. Mid. Introduced 1938.

H4

Rhododendron 'Halfdan Lem'

R. 'Hélène Schiffner' A small, dense, rounded evergreen bush which bears rounded trusses of widely funnel-shaped flowers. They are mauve in bud and open to pure white, occasionally with an inconspicuous ray of greenish or yellow markings inside. Mid. Introduced 1893.

H4 🏆 1993

R. 'Hoppy' A vigorous, compact *R. yakushimanum* hybrid that makes a free-flowering small evergreen shrub. The funnel-shaped flowers, pale lilac fading to white spotted with yellow, are 5cm (2in) across. They are borne in compact trusses up to 18cm (7in) wide. Mid. Introduced 1972.

H4

Rhododendron 'Hotei'

R. 'Hotei' A compact, medium-sized evergreen shrub with deep yellow, widely bell-shaped flowers. Mid. Introduced 1964.

H4 🏆 1993

Rhododendron 'Hugh Koster'

R. 'Hugh Koster' (Hardy Hybrid) A sturdy, leafy, medium-sized evergreen bush with stiff, erect branches. It bears funnel-shaped flowers which are borne in well-formed trusses, and are glowing red, with black markings within. This is a fine hybrid that is something like 'Doncaster', except the flowers are slightly lighter and the leaves are a little wavy at the margins. Mid. Introduced 1915.

H4 🏆 1993

R. 'Humming Bird' A small, compact, dome-shaped evergreen bush of distinctive appearance. The half-nodding, widely bell-shaped flowers are carmine, and are shaded with glowing scarlet inside the tube. Early. Introduced 1955.

H3

Rhododendron 'Humming Bird'

Rhododendron 'Idealist'

Rhododendron Intrifast group

Rhododendron 'Hydon Dawn'

R. 'Hydon Dawn' A compact dwarf *R. yakushimanum* hybrid that makes an evergreen shrub with leaves cream-felted beneath when young. The flowers are 5cm (2in) across, funnel-shaped with wavy margins, and borne in compact trusses. They are light pink with paler margins and reddish brown spots. Mid. Introduced 1969. H4 ♔ 1993

R. 'Hydon Hunter' A vigorous *R. yakushimanum* hybrid that makes a compact small evergreen shrub with funnel-shaped flowers over 5cm (2in) across, borne in compact, domed trusses. They are white, flushed with pink and spotted with yellow. Mid. Introduced 1972. H4 ♔ 1993

R. 'Idealist' A very free-flowering large evergreen shrub or small tree with flowers in large, compact, clustered trusses that appear to weigh down the branches. They are widely funnel-shaped with 5–7 lobes, up to 8cm (3in) across, and coral pink in bud,

opening to pale creamy yellow with lines of reddish markings at the base. Early to mid. Introduced 1941. H4 ♔ 1993

Rhododendron 'Ilam Violet'

R. 'Ilam Violet' A very free-flowering small, upright evergreen shrub with deep violet-blue widely funnel-shaped flowers with wavy margins. They are 4cm (1¹/₂in) wide and borne in globular trusses. Early to mid. Introduced 1947. H4

R. 'Impi' A medium-sized upright evergreen shrub. The funnel-shaped flowers, which are borne in small trusses, are 5cm (2in) across, nearly black in bud and open to a very deep wine-crimson, faintly spotted with black within. The colour is brilliant when seen lit from behind. Late. Introduced 1945. H4 ♔ 1993

R. Intrifast group A dwarf, dense evergreen shrub with innumerable clusters of

small, violet-blue flowers. Mid. H4

R. 'Isabel Pierce' A stiffly branched, large evergreen shrub with long, narrow leaves and rose-red flowers fading to pink with deeper margins, noticeably blotched and spotted. They are borne in large trusses. Mid. Introduced 1975. H4 ♔ 1993

Rhododendron 'Jacksonii'

R. 'Jacksonii' (Hardy Hybrid) A broadly dome-shaped, slow-growing, medium-sized evergreen bush. The flowers, borne in well-formed trusses, are widely funnel-shaped and bright rose pink, with maroon markings and paler spotting within. It tolerates industrial pollution and often succeeds where other rhododendrons fail. Early. Introduced 1835. H4

R. 'Jalisco Eclipse' A medium-sized evergreen shrub with primrose-yellow flowers, streaked with crimson on the outside,

blotched and spotted with crimson at the base inside. The calyx is yellow, edged with red. Late. Introduced 1942.
H4

R. 'Jalisco Elect' A medium-sized evergreen shrub with primrose-yellow flowers with paler lobes. The margins are slightly frilled, and they are marked with brownish red spots within. The calyx is yellow. Late. Introduced 1942.
H4 ♛ 1993

R. 'James Barto' A compact small evergreen shrub which bears funnel-shaped, slightly fragrant pink flowers. Early to mid. Introduced 1953.
H4

R. 'James Burchett' A vigorous, large, evergreen shrub of dense habit with dark green leaves. The flowers are white and flushed with mauve with a bronze-green flare. They are held in compact trusses. Late. Introduced 1960.
H4 ♛ 1993

Rhododendron 'Jenny'

R. 'Jenny' A prostrate evergreen shrub with large, deep red, bell-shaped flowers. Mid. Introduced 1939.
H4 ♛ 1993

R. 'Jervis Bay' A superb, rounded, medium-sized evergreen shrub which has dark green leaves, and widely funnel-shaped flowers which are borne in firm, rounded trusses. They are golden yellow tinged with orange in bud, and open to primrose-yellow with a large maroon blotch at the base and maroon markings inside. Mid. Introduced 1951.
H4 ♛ 1993

Rhododendron 'Kate Waterer'

R. 'Kate Waterer' (Hardy Hybrid) A medium-sized to large, dense evergreen shrub with funnel-shaped flowers up to 6cm (2¹/₂in) wide. They are rose-crimson becoming clear rose and have a ray of greenish yellow spots on a white background on the upper lobe. Mid. Introduced before 1876.
H4 ♛ 1993

Rhododendron 'Kilimanjaro'

R. 'Kilimanjaro' A superb evergreen hybrid with compact, globular trusses of funnel-shaped, currant-red, wavy-edged flowers, spotted with chocolate inside. Mid to late. Introduced 1943.
H3–4 ♛ 1993

R. 'Kluis Sensation' A hardy medium-sized evergreen shrub with bright scarlet flowers that have darker spots on the upper lobes. Mid. Introduced 1948.
H4 ♛ 1993

R. 'Lady Alice Fitzwilliam' A beautiful but tender medium-sized evergreen shrub with dark green, deeply veined leaves. The

highly fragrant funnel-shaped flowers are 10cm (4in) across, white flushed with pink with yellow markings in the throat. Ideal for the conservatory. Mid. Introduced 1881.
H2–3 ♛ 1993

Rhododendron Lady Chamberlain group

Rhododendron Lady Rosebery group

R. Lady Chamberlain and Lady Rosebery groups These most lovely evergreen rhododendrons have clusters of drooping, waxy, long, narrowly bell-shaped flowers in shades of mandarin red, pink and buff-orange They are so prone to mildew that they cannot be recommended for planting in gardens at present. Introduced 1930.
H3

R. 'Lady Clementine Mitford' (Hardy Hybrid) A large evergreen shrub with its widely funnel-shaped flowers held in firm trusses. They are peach-pink shading to white in the centre, with a V-shaped pattern of pink, olive green and brown markings within. Mid to late. Introduced 1870.
H4 ♛ 1993

R. **'Lady Eleanor Cathcart'** (Hardy Hybrid) A magnificent, large, dome-shaped evergreen shrub or small tree with handsome and very distinctive long, dark grey-green leaves, rusty beneath and pointing downwards. They are attractively felted when young. The widely funnel-shaped flowers which are borne in rounded trusses are bright clear rose with slightly darker veins and an outstanding maroon basal blotch within. Mid to late. Introduced before 1844.
H4 ♈ 1993

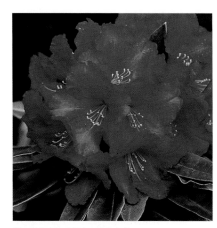

Rhododendron 'Lamplighter'

R. **'Lamplighter'** A vigorous large evergreen shrub of open habit with narrow, pointed, dark green leaves and bright red flowers borne in large trusses. Mid. Introduced 1955.
H4 ♈ 1993

R. **'Lavender Girl'** A vigorous, free-flowering, compact evergreen hybrid with dome-shaped trusses of fragrant, funnel-

Rhododendron 'Lavender Girl'

shaped flowers. They are lilac-mauve in bud and open pale lavender, darker at the margins, with a pinkish yellow throat. Mid. Introduced 1950.
H4 ♈ 1993

Rhododendron 'Lee's Dark Purple'

R. **'Lee's Dark Purple'** (Hardy Hybrid) A compact, rounded evergreen bush with widely funnel-shaped flowers which are borne in dense, rounded trusses. They are royal purple with a ray of greenish brown to ochre markings within. Mid. Introduced before 1851.
H4

R. **'Lem's Cameo'** A medium-sized upright evergreen shrub which has dark, matt green leaves up to 16cm (6in) long that are bronze when young. It bears funnel-shaped flowers up to 9cm (3½in) wide. They are red in bud, opening cream and apricot flushed with red and spotted with pink. They are borne in rounded trusses. Mid. Introduced 1962.
H4 ♈ 1993

R. **'Lem's Monarch'** A vigorous, large evergreen shrub with thick-textured, pointed leaves. The flowers are pale pink at first fading to white, edged with pink and held in very large, conical trusses. Mid. Introduced 1971.
H4 ♈ 1993

R. **'Lionel's Triumph'** An outstanding medium-sized evergreen hybrid with large trusses of bell-shaped yellow flowers, spotted and blotched with crimson at the base within. The flowers are 10cm (4in) across. Early to mid. Introduced 1954.
H3–4

Rhododendron 'Lionel's Triumph'

R. **'Lodauric Iceberg'** A large evergreen shrub or small tree with nodding trusses of richly scented, trumpet-shaped, pure white flowers 13cm (5in) across, with two streaks of brownish crimson at the base within. Late. Introduced 1936.
H4 ♈ 1993

Rhododendron 'Loderi King George'

R. **'Loderi King George'** Probably the best of the Loderi group and the best hybrid rhododendron. It is a strong-growing, large, rounded evergreen shrub or small tree with enormous trusses of very large, lily-like, trumpet-shaped, richly scented flowers 13–15cm (5–6in) across. They are soft pink in bud and open to pure white with a basal flash of green markings within. Early to mid. Introduced 1901.
H4 ♈ 1993

R. **'Loderi Pink Diamond'** A large evergreen shrub or small tree with flowers similar to 'Loderi King George' but slightly smaller and delicate pink with a basal flash

Rhododendron 'Loderi Pink Diamond'

of crimson, passing to green flushed with brown. Early to mid. Introduced 1901.
H4 ♛ 1993

R. 'Loderi Venus'. A large evergreen shrub or small tree with flowers deep pink in bud, opening to strong rose pink and passing to pale pink with a very faint greenish flash at the base within. Early to mid. Introduced 1901.
H4 ♛ 1993

Rhododendron 'Loder's White'

R. 'Loder's White' (Hardy Hybrid) A large, dome-shaped evergreen shrub unconnected with the Loderi group. It is clothed in handsome foliage and its flowers, borne in a magnificent conical truss, are widely funnel-shaped, mauve-pink in bud, opening to pure white edged with pink and marked with a few scattered crimson spots. Mid. Introduced before 1884.
H4 ♛ 1993

R. 'Lord Roberts' (Hardy Hybrid) A large evergreen shrub of erect growth with

flowers borne in dense, rounded trusses. They are funnel-shaped and dark crimson with an extensive V-shaped pattern of black markings. Mid to late.
H4

Rhododendron 'Madame de Bruin'

R. 'Madame de Bruin' (Hardy Hybrid) A vigorous, leafy, medium-sized evergreen hybrid with conical trusses of cerise-red flowers. Mid. Introduced 1904.
H4

Rhododendron 'Madame Masson'

R. 'Madame Masson' (Hardy Hybrid) A medium-sized evergreen shrub with trusses of white flowers, deeply cut into five lobes, with a striking yellow basal blotch within. Mid. Introduced 1849.
H4

R. 'Mandalay' A small, compact evergreen shrub with deeply veined, dark green leaves. The tubular flowers are brilliant, waxy red. Mid. Introduced 1947.
H4

Rhododendron 'Mariloo'

R. 'Mariloo' A large, handsome woodland rhododendron which bears bold evergreen foliage, and large trusses of lemon-yellow flowers which are flushed green. Early to mid. Introduced 1941.
H3–4

Rhododendron 'Marinus Koster'

R. 'Marinus Koster' A magnificent, hardy evergreen shrub with flowers 10cm (4in) wide, profusely borne in large trusses. They are deep pink in bud, gradually fading to white after opening and shading to pink at the margins, with a large purple blotch within. Mid. Introduced 1937.
H4 ♛ 1993

R. 'Marion Street' A vigorous, small evergreen *R. yakishimanum* hybrid with dark green leaves up to 10cm (4in) long, brown-felted beneath. The flowers are widely funnel-shaped, up to 7cm (3in) across, and pale pink, edged and flushed white, fading to white. Mid. Introduced 1965.
H4 ♛ 1993

Rhododendron 'Marion Street'

R. 'Markeeta's Prize' A medium-sized to large evergreen shrub with scarlet flowers that have darker spots. They are freely borne in large, flat-topped trusses. Mid. Introduced 1967.
H4 ☙ 1993

R. 'Mary Fleming' A very hardy, compact, dwarf evergreen shrub with foliage that turns bronze in cold weather. The flowers are buff-yellow flushed with pink at the margins and are borne in small clusters. Early to mid. Introduced 1967.
H4

R. 'Matador' A large, spreading evergreen shrub with leaves that are densely covered with rusty hairs beneath. The flowers, borne in large, loose trusses, are 5cm (2in) across and brilliant, dark orange-red. Early to mid. Introduced 1945.
H4 ☙ 1993

R. 'May Day' A magnificent, comparatively low, wide-spreading evergreen shrub with loose trusses of slightly drooping,

Rhododendron 'May Day'

funnel-shaped flowers that are brilliant signal-red or orange-red, with large calyces of the same colour. The leaves are felted with fawn beneath. Mid. Introduced 1937.
H4 ☙ 1993

R. 'Merganser' A vigorous dwarf evergreen shrub with many funnel-shaped, pale primrose-yellow flowers 3cm (1¼in) wide, borne in compact trusses 6cm (2½in) across. Early to mid. Introduced 1967.
H4 ☙ 1993

R. 'Michael Waterer' (Hardy Hybrid) A slow-growing medium-sized evergreen shrub with funnel-shaped red flowers which fade to rose-crimson. They are borne in well-formed trusses. Mid to late. Introduced before 1894.
H4 ☙ 1993

R. 'Michael's Pride' A small to medium-sized evergreen shrub with lily-like, creamy yellow, waxy, fragrant flowers opening from lime-green buds. The young foliage is bronze. Early. Introduced 1964.
H2 ☙ 1993

R. 'Moerheim' A dwarf, compact evergreen shrub with glossy green leaves that turn maroon in winter. The clusters of small, aster-violet flowers are freely borne. Mid. Introduced 1966.
H4 ☙ 1993

Rhododendron 'Moerheim's Pink'

R. 'Moerheim's Pink' A small, dome-shaped, dense evergreen bush with funnel-shaped flowers that are deep pink in bud. They open to pale lilac, are spotted rose inside and have slightly frilled lobes. Mid. Introduced 1973.
H4

Rhododendron 'Moonshine Crescent'

R. 'Moonshine Crescent' A medium-sized evergreen shrub which produces clear yellow flowers. They are borne in compact, dome-shaped trusses. Early to mid. Introduced 1962.
H4

Rhododendron 'Morning Cloud'

R. 'Morning Cloud' A dwarf, compact evergreen shrub. The leaves have a woolly felting beneath and the flowers are white, heavily flushed with rich pink fading to cream. They are borne in rounded trusses. Mid to late. Introduced 1970.
H4 ☙ 1993

R. 'Morgenrot', syn. *R.* 'Morning Red' A small, *R. yakushimanum* hybrid of compact habit. This is a rounded evergreen shrub which produces dark green leaves and flowers that are deep red in bud, open rose-red, and are borne in large trusses. Mid. Introduced 1983.
H4 ☙ 1993

R. 'Morning Red' See *R.* 'Morgenrot'.

Rhododendron 'Mother of Pearl'

R. 'Mother of Pearl' A medium-sized to large evergreen shrub that is a sport of 'Pink Pearl'. The flowers are rich pink in bud, open to a delicate blush and fade to white with a few external pink streaks. Mid. Introduced before 1914.
H4

Rhododendron 'Mount Everest'

R. 'Mount Everest' A large, vigorous evergreen shrub that is very free-flowering. It has conical trusses of narrow, bell-shaped, pure white flowers with red speckling in the throat. Early. Introduced 1930.
H4

R. 'Mrs A.T. de la Mare' (Hardy Hybrid) A vigorous, upright, medium-sized evergreen shrub of compact upright habit, with compact dome-shaped trusses of funnel-shaped, frilly-margined flowers, profusely borne. They are pink-tinged in bud, opening to white with greenish yellow spotting in the throat. Mid.
H4 ♥ 1993

Rhododendron 'Mrs Charles E. Pearson'

R. 'Mrs Charles E. Pearson' (Hardy Hybrid) A robust, erect, medium-sized evergreen shrub which has erect branches and bears conical trusses of widely funnel-shaped flowers 10cm (4in) across. They are mauve-pink in bud, opening to pale pinkish mauve that fades eventually to near-white. There is also a ray of brown markings

Rhododendron 'Mrs A.T. de la Mare'

within. Mid. Introduced 1909.
H4 ♥ 1993

R. 'Mrs Davies Evans' (Hardy Hybrid) A vigorous, free-flowering, upright but compact medium-sized evergreen hybrid with flowers in a globular truss. They are funnel-shaped with frilly margins, imperial purple, with a white basal blotch and yellow spots inside. Mid. Introduced before 1915.
H4 ♥ 1993

R. 'Mrs Furnivall' A magnificent, large, densely growing evergreen bush that produces compact trusses of widely funnel-shaped, light rose pink flowers with an eye-catching blush of brown and crimson markings inside. It is considered by many to be one of the finest hardy hybrids ever produced. Mid to late. Introduced 1920.
H4 ♥ 1993

R. 'Mrs G.W. Leak' (Hardy Hybrid) A splendid, large, dense evergreen shrub with somewhat lax trusses of widely funnel-shaped flowers 8cm (3in) wide. They are

Rhododendron 'Mrs Furnivall'

Rhododendron 'Mrs G.W. Leak'

mottled light rose pink, darkening in the tube and with a splash of blackish brown and crimson markings inside. The nectaries are blood red. Although the flowers are beautiful, this rhododendron presents problems in maintaining healthy foliage. Mid. Introduced 1916.
H4

Rhododendron 'Mrs Lionel de Rothschild'

R. 'Mrs Lionel de Rothschild' A compact, erect, medium-sized evergreen shrub with large, firm trusses of fleshy, widely funnel-shaped flowers that are white, edged with apple-blossom pink and marked with a ray of dark crimson. Mid. Introduced 1931. H4 ♔ 1993

R. 'Mrs P. D. Williams' A medium-sized free-flowering evergreen shrub with flowers in compact, flattened trusses. They are ivory white with a large brown blotch on the upper lobe. Mid to late.
H4 ♔ 1993

R. 'Mrs R. S. Holford' (Hardy Hybrid) A vigorous medium-sized to large evergreen shrub that tends to become leggy with age. Its widely funnel-shaped flowers, borne in large trusses, are salmon-rose with a small pattern of crimson spots within. Mid to late. Introduced 1866.
H4 ♔ 1993

Rhododendron 'Mrs P. D. Williams'

R. 'Mrs T. H. Lowinsky' A vigorous, tall, hardy evergreen shrub with open funnel-shaped flowers 7.5cm (3in) across. They are lilac, whitish towards the centre, and heavily spotted with orange-brown. Mid. Introduced before 1917.
H4 ♔ 1993

R. 'Naomi Astarte' A large evergreen shrub or small tree with large, shapely trusses of fragrant, widely expanded flowers that are pink, shaded with yellow and with a yellow throat. Unfortunately, all the Naomi group are subject to powdery mildew. Early to mid.
H3–4

R. 'Naomi Exbury' A large evergreen

shrub or small tree with lilac flowers tinged with yellow. It is prone to powdery mildew. Early to mid. Introduced 1926.
H3–4

R. 'Nobleanum Album' (Hardy Hybrid) A dense, compact, medium-sized evergreen bush with white flowers borne in firm trusses. They are widely funnel-shaped, pink in bud, and have purplish spots inside and reddish purple nectaries, faintly marked with a small ray of yellowish green. They open in mid-winter to early spring.
H4

R. 'Nobleanum Coccineum' (Hardy Hybrid) A large, conical evergreen bush with trusses of bell-shaped, deep rose flowers, marked with a few dark crimson spots at the base within. They are borne in mid-winter to early spring. Introduced 1832.
H4

R. 'Nobleanum Venustum' (Hardy Hybrid) A densely leafy, broadly dome-shaped evergreen bush up to 2m (6½ft) high and 3m (10ft) wide. The funnel-shaped flowers borne in neat trusses are pink shading to white at the centre with a small pattern of dark crimson markings at the base within and crimson nectaries. They usually appear in late winter, but may open in early winter in a mild season. Introduced 1829.
H4

Rhododendron 'Nova Zembla'

R. 'Nova Zembla' An excellent and very hardy medium-sized evergreen shrub with deeply veined leaves and deep red flowers with a dark blotch, borne in compact trusses. Mid. Introduced 1902.
H4

R. **'Odee Wright'** A small to medium-sized, neat evergreen shrub with dark, glossy green leaves. The flowers are widely funnel-shaped with frilled lobes, pale yellow, tinged with pink and spotted with red. Mid. Introduced 1964.
H4 ♔ 1993

R. **'Old Copper'** A medium-sized to large, upright evergreen shrub with large, bell-shaped flowers in loose trusses. They are an unusual coppery colour and open from red buds. Mid to late. Introduced 1958.
H4

R. **'Old Port'** (Hardy Hybrid) A vigorous, leafy, dome-shaped evergreen bush with very glossy foliage. The flowers, up to 6cm (2¹⁄₂in) wide and borne in dense trusses, are widely funnel-shaped with frilled lobes and of a rich plum colour with a well-defined pattern of blackish crimson markings. Mid to late. Introduced 1865.
H4

R. **'Olive'** A free-flowering, small to medium-sized, upright evergreen shrub with its flowers in twos and threes. They are funnel-shaped, mauve-pink with deeper spots and up to 4cm (1¹⁄₂in) wide. Very early. Introduced 1936.
H4

R. **'Oudjik's Sensation'** A small evergreen shrub which produces bronze-tinged foliage and bell-shaped flowers, strikingly bright pink with a few spots in the upper lobe, borne in open, flat-topped trusses. Mid. Introduced 1965.
H4

R. **'P.J. Mezitt'** See *R.* 'Peter John Mezitt'.

Rhododendron 'Olive'

R. **'Patty Bee'** A compact and vigorous dwarf evergreen shrub with dark green leaves 4.5cm (1³⁄₄in) long that turn bronze in winter. It displays pale yellow flowers which are funnel-shaped with wavy margins and are borne in compact trusses. Early. Introduced 1977.
H4 ♔ 1993

Rhododendron 'Oudjik's Sensation'

Rhododendron 'Peter John Mezitt'

R. **'Penheale Blue'** A small, compact, rounded evergreen shrub with leaves up to 2.5cm (1in) long. The widely funnel-shaped flowers are freely borne in dense clusters; they are 3.5cm (1¹⁄₂in) wide and deep violet-blue flushed with red. It is one of the best blues. Early. Introduced 1975.
H4 ♔ 1993

Rhododendron 'Percy Wiseman'

R. **'Percy Wiseman'** A small, compact *R. yakushimanum* hybrid that makes an evergreen shrub with dark glossy green leaves and funnel-shaped flowers 5cm (2in) wide. They are cream flushed with pink, fading to creamy white, and are borne in globular trusses. Mid. Introduced 1971.
H4 ♔ 1993

R. **'Peter John Mezitt'**, syn. 'P. J. Mezitt' A small, free-flowering evergreen shrub with broad, elliptical leaves up to 5cm (2in) long, blackish green above, purplish in cold weather, and with a bronze lustre beneath. The saucer-shaped flowers, borne in small, dense clusters, are lilac, with two patches of pink spots. It is extremely hardy in North America. Early. Introduced 1943.
H4 ♔ 1993

R. **'Peter Koster'** (Hardy Hybrid) A handsome, sturdy, bushy evergreen shrub with trumpet-shaped flowers in a firm trusses. They are rosy crimson paling towards the margins, and darker in bud. Mid to late. Introduced 1909.
H4 ♔ 1993

R. **'Pink Cherub'** A vigorous but compact *R. yakushimanum* hybrid that makes a small evergreen shrub with flowers that are very freely borne in large, rounded trusses. They

Rhododendron 'Pink Cherub'

Rhododendron 'Pink Pebble'

Rhododendron 'Princess Anne'

are funnel-shaped, wavy-margined, salmon-pink in bud, and open to whitish with a fuschia-purple flush. Reverses are rich rose. Introduced 1969.
H4 ♔ 1993

R. 'Pink Drift' A neat, dwarf evergreen shrub resembling an evergreen azalea with small, aromatic leaves and clusters of soft lavender-rose flowers. It is suitable for the rock garden. Mid. Introduced 1955.
H4

Rhododendron 'Pink Pearl'

R. 'Pink Pearl' (Hardy Hybrid) One of the most popular of all rhododendrons. It is a strong-growing evergreen shrub, eventually tall and bare at the base. The flowers, borne in magnificent, large, conical trusses, are widely funnel-shaped, rose in bud, opening to deep lilac-pink. They fade to white at the margins and have a well-defined ray of crimson-brown markings. Mid. Introduced before 1897.
H4

R. 'Pink Pebble' A free-flowering, dense, small evergreen shrub with loose trusses of widely bell-shaped, rose-pink flowers opening from red buds. Mid. Introduced 1954.
H4 ♔ 1993

R. 'Polar Bear' A superb late-flowering evergreen hybrid making a large shrub or small tree. The richly fragrant flowers, borne in large trusses, are trumpet-shaped, like pure white lilies, with a green flash within. However, it does not flower when young and requires woodland conditions. Late. Introduced 1926.
H4 ♔ 1993

R. Praecox group An extremely popular small, compact, partially deciduous shrub with leaves that are aromatic when crushed. The flowers are in twos and threes at the tips of the shoots and are widely funnel-shaped, rosy purple and slightly darker on the outside. They are borne in late winter to early spring. Introduced c1855.
H4 ♔ 1993

R. 'Princess Alice' A small, evergreen shrub of compact habit with highly fragrant flowers that are white, flushed with pink and pink in bud, in clusters of three. It is on the tender side but can be grown out of doors in mild areas with shelter or on a wall. Mid. Introduced 1863.
H2 ♔ 1993

R. 'Princess Anne' A very attractive dwarf evergreen shrub of dense habit with light matt green leaves and pale yellow flowers from greenish buds, funnel-shaped and 3cm (1¼in) wide. Early to mid. Introduced 1974.
H4 ♔ 1993

Rhododendron 'Professor Hugo de Vries'

R. 'Professor Hugo de Vries' A large evergreen shrub with flowers in large, conical trusses. They are widely funnel-shaped, rich rose in bud opening to lilac-rose, with a ray of reddish brown markings on a light ground. Mid.
H4 ♔ 1993

R. 'Ptarmigan' A free-flowering, very

Rhododendron 'Ptarmigan'

dwarf, spreading evergreen shrub with flowers usually in threes, saucer-shaped, 3cm (1¹/₄in) wide and pure white. Early. Introduced 1966.
H4 🏆 1993

Rhododendron 'Purple Splendour'

R. 'Purple Splendour' (Hardy Hybrid) A sturdy evergreen bush with widely funnel-shaped flowers in neat trusses, rich purplish blue, with a distinct ray of black embossed markings in a purplish brown background. Mid to late. Introduced before 1900.
H4 🏆 1993

Rhododendron 'Queen Elizabeth II'

R. 'Queen Elizabeth II' A medium-sized evergreen shrub with slender leaves and seven-lobed, pale greenish yellow flowers that are widely funnel-shaped and 11cm (4¹/₂in) wide, borne in trusses of up to 12. Mid. Introduced 1968.
H4 🏆 1993

R. 'Queen of Hearts' A striking medium-sized evergreen shrub, producing dome-

Rhododendron 'Queen of Hearts'

shaped trusses of a deep, glowing crimson, and speckled white within. Early to mid. Introduced 1949.
H4 🏆 1993

R. Racil group A small, free-flowering evergreen shrub with clusters of funnel-shaped flowers 2.5cm (1in) across, pink in bud, opening lilac-pink, darker on the margins. Early. Introduced 1937.
H4

R. 'Ramapo' A dwarf, very hardy, compact evergreen shrub. Attractive blue-grey young foliage. Clusters of small, violet-purple flowers are freely borne. It does best in sun. Early to mid. Introduced 1940.
H4 🏆 1993

R. 'Razorbill' A most ornamental dwarf evergreen shrub reaching 60cm (2ft) high, with tubular flowers that are deep pink in bud and open to rose-pink outside, paler inside. They are held upright in dense trusses. Early to mid. Introduced 1976.
H4 🏆 1993

Rhododendron 'Razorbill'

Rhododendron 'Red Carpet'

R. 'Red Carpet' A dwarf evergreen shrub with particularly striking bright red, bell-shaped flowers 5.5cm (2¹/₄in) wide with wavy margins. They are borne in lax trusses. Mid. Introduced 1967.
H4 🏆 1993

R. 'Renoir' A compact, upright small evergreen shrub with rich rose flowers borne in

Rhododendron 'Renoir'

rounded trusses. spotted crimson, fading to nearly white. Mid to late. Introduced 1963. H4 ♔ 1993

R. 'Reuthe's Purple', syn. *R. lepidotum* 'Reuthe's Purple' A dwarf evergreen shrub with saucer-shaped, deep rose-purple flowers in small trusses of 1–3. It is very free-flowering. Late. Introduced 1968. H4 ♔ 1993

R. Riplet group A small evergreen shrub with rounded trusses of bell-shaped, rich rose flowers, white in the throat with crimson spots. Early to mid. Introduced 1963. H4 ♔ 1993

Rhododendron 'Robert Keir'

R. 'Robert Keir' A large evergreen shrub with dark green foliage and dense, rounded trusses of pale yellow flowers flushed with pink. Mid. Introduced 1951. H4 ♔ 1993

R. 'Romany Chai' A lovely medium-sized evergreen shrub, the name meaning 'Gypsy Children', with large, compact trusses of rich terracotta flowers with a dark maroon basal blotch. Mid to late. Introduced 1912. H4 ♔ 1993

R. 'Romany Chal' Gypsy Girl, a tall evergreen bush with lax trusses of bell-shaped, cardinal red flowers with a black ray within. Mid to late. Introduced 1932. H4

R. 'Roza Stevenson' A superb large evergreen shrub with saucer-shaped flowers 10–12cm (4–5in) across, borne in attractive trusses. They are deep lemon-yellow, darker in bud. Mid. Introduced 1970. H4 ♔ 1993

Rhododendron 'Saffron Queen'

R. 'Saffron Queen' A beautiful medium-sized evergreen shrub with glossy green leaves and tubular, sulphur-yellow flowers that are spotted with a darker tone on the upper lobes. Mid. Introduced 1948. H3

R. 'Saint Breward' A beautiful, small, rounded evergreen shrub bearing tight, globular trusses of shallowly bell-shaped, soft lavender-coloured flowers, darker at the margins and with pale blue anthers. Early to mid. Introduced 1963. H4

R. 'Saint Merryn' A free-flowering dwarf evergreen shrub with dark glossy green leaves and broadly funnel-shaped, wavy-margined flowers of deep violet-blue, darker at the margins and borne in trusses 5cm (2in) across. Mid. Introduced 1971. H4 ♔ 1993

R. 'Saint Minver' A small, compact evergreen shrub with clusters of violet-blue flowers. Early to mid. Introduced 1973. H4 ♔ 1993

R. 'Saint Tudy' A small, dense, bushy evergreen shrub with dense trusses of shallowly bell-shaped, lobelia-blue flowers. Early to mid. Introduced 1962. H4 ♔ 1993

R. 'Sapphire' A dwarf, small-leaved evergreen shrub of open habit, resembling *R.*

Rhododendron 'Sapphire'

Rhododendron 'Saint Breward'

Rhododendron 'Sappho'

impeditum, with pale lavender-blue flowers. Early. Introduced 1969.
H4 🏆 1993

R. 'Sappho' (Hardy Hybrid) A very freely growing large evergreen bush, rounded or dome-shaped, with dark glossy green leaves and handsome conical trusses of widely funnel-shaped flowers, mauve in bud, that open to pure white with a highly conspicuous blotch of rich purple overlaid with black. Mid. Introduced before 1867.
H4 🏆 1993

R. Sarled group A dwarf evergreen shrub suitable for the rock garden, with tiny leaves and rounded trusses of small flowers that are pink in the bud and open to cream. Mid. Introduced 1942.
H4

Rhododendron 'Scarlet Wonder'

R. 'Scarlet Wonder' A very hardy, dwarf evergreen shrub that forms a neat mound of dense foliage. The flowers are trumpet-shaped with frilly margins, ruby-red, and borne in loose trusses at the ends of the shoots. Mid. Introduced 1965.
H4 🏆 1993

R. 'Sennocke' A dense, dwarf evergreen bush with deep waxy red, funnel-shaped flowers. Mid.
H4 🏆 1993

R. 'Seta' An exceedingly pretty, medium-sized evergreen shrub of erect habit with umbels of unspotted, narrowly bell-shaped flowers that are white at the base, shading to vivid pink in the lobes. It is one of the first hybrids to flower, in early to mid-spring. Introduced 1933.
H3 🏆 1994

Rhododendron 'Seta'

Rhododendron 'Seven Stars'

R. 'Seven Stars' A large, vigorous *R. yakushimanum* hybrid. It is a free-flowering evergreen shrub which bears bell-shaped, wavy-margined flowers that are white, flushed with pink and reddish in bud. Mid. Introduced 1966.
H4 🏆 1993

R. 'Shamrock' A dwarf evergreen shrub

Rhododendron 'Shamrock'

which bears pale yellow flowers opening from yellow-green buds. Early to mid. Introduced 1978.
H4

R. 'Silver Cloud' A dwarf *R. yakushimanum* hybrid that makes an evergreen shrub of dense, rounded habit with dark green leaves and pale purple, frilly-margined flowers, darker outside, spotted with yellow green. Mid. Introduced 1963.
H4

R. 'Silver Sixpence' An upright, small evergreen shrub with cream flowers spotted with yellow. The buds are green, tinged with mauve. Mid. Introduced 1975.
H4 🏆 1993

Rhododendron 'Sir Charles Lemon'

R. 'Sir Charles Lemon', syn. *R. arboreum* 'Sir Charles Lemon' A magnificent large evergreen shrub or small tree with leaves that are rusty brown beneath. The white flowers are borne in dense trusses. Early.
H3 🏆 1993

R. 'Snipe' A dwarf, dense evergreen shrub with pale green leaves and pale pink to white flowers, flushed with violet and purple and with deeper spots. Early to mid. Introduced 1978.
H4 🏆 1993

R. 'Snow Lady' A compact, small evergreen shrub of spreading habit, with bristly leaves up to 7.5cm (3in) long and fragrant white flowers borne in lax trusses. Mid. Introduced 1955.
H4 🏆 1993

R. 'Snow Queen' A lovely large evergreen bush with profusely borne dome-shaped trusses of large, funnel-shaped, pure white

Rhododendron 'Snow Queen'

flowers opening from dark pink buds, each with a small basal blotch within. Mid. Introduced 1926.
H4 🏆 1993

R. **'Songbird'** A charming small evergreen shrub with clusters of violet bell-shaped flowers. Early. Introduced 1954.
H4

R. **'Souvenir d'Anthony Waterer'** A vigorous, upright, large evergreen shrub with dark rose-red flowers with a prominent yellow eye, borne in domed trusses. Mid. Introduced before 1924.
H4 🏆 1994

R. **'Souvenir de Dr S. Endtz'** A compact medium-sized evergreen bush with flowers

Rhododendron 'Souvenir de Dr S. Endtz'

in dome-shaped trusses. They are widely funnel-shaped, rich rose in bud, opening to rich, mottled pink, paler in the centre and marked with a ray of crimson, nectaries crimson. Mid. Introduced 1927.
H4 🏆 1993

R. **'Streatley'** A small *R. yakushimanum* hybrid evergreen shrub with white flowers that are flushed with rose pink and spotted with red. The buds are magenta. Mid. Introduced 1965.
H4 🏆 1993

Rhododendron 'Surrey Heath'

R. **'Surrey Heath'** A small *R. yakushimanum* hybrid that makes a bushy, spreading evergreen shrub with narrow leaves that are slightly woolly above when young. The funnel-shaped flowers, borne in globular trusses, are 4.5cm (1³/₄in) wide and pale rose pink, deeper at the margins. Mid. Introduced 1975.
H4 🏆 1993

R. **'Susan'** A tall, bushy evergreen hybrid

Rhododendron 'Songbird'

Rhododendron 'Susan'

with large trusses of bluish mauve flowers, darker at the margins and spotted with purple. Early to mid. Introduced 1930.
H4 ♔ 1993

Rhododendron 'Temple Belle'

Rhododendron 'Sweet Simplicity'

R. 'Sweet Simplicity' A medium-sized, bushy evergreen shrub with large, glossy leaves. It bears ruffled white flowers with pink edges and olive spots, which are borne in rounded trusses. Mid to late. Introduced before 1922.
H4 ♔ 1993

R. 'Taurus' A stout-branched, large evergreen shrub with prominently veined leaves. The vivid red, widely funnel-shaped flowers, which have frilled margins, are borne in large, rounded trusses. Early to mid. Introduced 1972.
H4 ♔ 1993

R. 'Teal' A dwarf, rather upright evergreen shrub with pale green leaves more than 5cm (2in) long and bark that peels with age. The flowers, up to 3.5cm (1³⁄₄in) wide, are broadly bell-shaped and primrose-yellow. Mid. Introduced 1977.
H4 ♔ 1993

R. 'Temple Belle' A charming neat rounded evergreen shrub which is similar to R. orbiculare, one of its parents. It bears rounded leaves that are attractively glaucous on the undersides. The flowers are held in a loose cluster and are bell-shaped, of uniform rose-pink without markings. Early to mid. Introduced 1916.
H3 ♔ 1993

R. 'Tessa Roza' A small evergreen bush up to 1m (3ft) high with deep, slightly purplish pink flowers borne in loose, flat-

tened umbels. Early. The cross was made 1928 and it was introduced 1953.
H4 ♔ 1993

R. 'The Honourable Jean Marie de Montague' A vigorous, medium-sized evergreen shrub with dark green leaves and bell-shaped flowers with wavy margins. They are 8cm (3in) across, deep red with darker spots in the throat, and borne in neat, domed trusses up to 15cm (6in) wide. Mid. Introduced 1921.
H4 ♔ 1993

R. 'The Master' A medium-sized evergreen shrub with huge, globular trusses of large, funnel-shaped pink flowers with a dark red blotch. Mid. Introduced 1955.
H4 ♔ 1993

R. 'Thunderstorm' A medium-sized evergreen shrub with glossy dark green leaves. It produces dark red, wavy-edged flowers which have darker spots and white stamens and are borne in neat, dome-shaped trusses. Mid to late. The cross was made 1930.
H4 ♔ 1993

R. 'Tidbit' A small, dense, spreading evergreen shrub with bell-shaped, wavy-margined flowers that are straw-yellow, red in the throat. They are borne in compact, domed trusses. Mid. Introduced 1957.
H4

R. 'Titian Beauty' A small, compact R. yakushimanum hybrid that makes a fairly upright evergreen shrub with dark green leaves lightly covered beneath with thin, brown felt. The flowers are waxy red. Mid. Introduced 1971.
H4 ♔ 1993

Rhododendron 'Tortoiseshell Champagne'

R. 'Tortoiseshell Champagne' A medium-sized evergreen shrub with rich yellow, funnel-shaped flowers, fading to pale yellow tinged with pink at the margins of the lobes. Mid to late. Introduced 1945.
H4 ♔ 1993

R. 'Tortoiseshell Orange' A medium-sized evergreen shrub with large, deep orange flowers. Mid to late. Introduced 1945.
H4 ♔ 1993

R. 'Tortoiseshell Wonder' A medium-sized evergreen shrub with salmon-pink flowers. Mid to late. Introduced 1945.
H4 ♔ 1993

R. 'Trude Webster' A strong-growing, medium-sized to large evergreen shrub, the winner of several awards in North America. The flowers are clear pink, white on the lobes with darker spots, and are borne in very large, rounded trusses. Mid to late. Introduced 1961.
H4

Rhododendron 'Tortoiseshell Wonder'

Rhododendron 'Virginia Richards'

Rhododendron 'Tyermannii'

R. 'Tyermannii' An upright medium-sized, evergreen shrub with glossy leaves and fragrant lily-like flowers, cream fading to white inside, tinged green and brown outside. It is tender. Mid. Introduced 1925. H2 ♀ 1993

R. 'Unique' A leafy, dense, medium-sized evergreen bush with dome-shaped trusses

Rhododendron 'Unique'

of funnel-shaped flowers. They are cream with a faint blush and marked with scattered, faint crimson spots. Early to mid. Introduced 1934.
H4 ♀ 1993

R. 'Vanessa Pastel' A spreading, shapely, medium-sized evergreen bush with loose trusses of soft rose-pink flowers, flushed with buff and with a deep crimson eye. Mid to late. Introduced 1946.
H4 ♀ 1993

R. 'Venetian Chimes' A vigorous, small *R. yakushimanum* hybrid evergreen shrub with bell-shaped flowers 5cm (2in) wide in compact, globular trusses. They are brick red, flushed with scarlet towards the base and spotted with blackish red. Mid to late. Introduced 1971.
H4

R. 'Veryan Bay' A medium-sized evergreen shrub of compact habit with shell-pink flowers borne in profusion. The foliage is greyish. It is ideal for smaller gardens. Mid.
H4 ♀ 1993

R. 'Vintage Rosé' A small *R. yakushimanum* hybrid evergreen shrub with leaves up to 10cm (4in) long with a thick felting beneath. The flowers are funnel-shaped with wavy margins, 6cm (2½in) wide, and rose-pink, deeper in the centre. They are borne in large conical trusses. Mid to late. Introduced 1974.
H4 ♀ 1993

R. 'Virginia Richards' A small evergreen shrub of vigorous upright habit with funnel-shaped flowers in large, globular trusses up to 16cm (6in) wide. They have wavy mar-

gins and are pale orange in the centre, flushed with rose-pink at the margins and deeper at the base with red spots inside. It is a popular rhododendron and lovely when in flower but very prone to powdery mildew. Mid. Introduced 1962.
H4

Rhododendron 'Vulcan'

R. 'Vulcan' A medium-sized evergreen shrub with funnel-shaped, wavy-margined, bright red flowers in dome-shaped trusses. Mid. Introduced 1938.
H4 ♀ 1993

R. 'W.F.H.' A small, spreading evergreen shrub with clusters of brilliant scarlet, funnel-shaped flowers. Mid. Introduced 1941.
H4 ♀ 1993

R. 'White Swan' A large, upright evergreen shrub with grey-green leaves. The flowers, borne in large trusses, are pale pink, fading to white marked with green. Mid to late. Introduced 1937.
H4 ♀ 1993

R. 'Wigeon' A free-flowering dwarf evergreen shrub with open funnel-shaped blooms 4cm (1½in) across. They have wavy margins and are deep lavender-pink with dark spots, borne in dome-shaped trusses. Mid. Introduced 1982.
H4

R. 'Wilgen's Ruby' A popular and very hardy medium-sized evergreen shrub with large, rounded trusses of deep red, funnel-shaped flowers with darker spots. Mid to late. Introduced 1951.
H4 ♛ 1993

R. 'Willbrit' A small evergreen shrub with dark green leaves that are reddish when young. The deep pink, bell-shaped flowers, paler at the margin, are borne in open trusses. Mid to late. Introduced 1960.
H4

R. 'Windlesham Scarlet' A vigorous, medium-sized evergreen shrub bearing dome-shaped trusses of widely bell-shaped, deep crimson flowers with frilly margins and black speckling inside. Mid to late. Introduced 1950.
H4 ♛ 1993

R. 'Windsor Lad' A hybrid of *R. ponticum*, forming a medium-sized evergreen shrub. It bears widely funnel-shaped flowers that open from purple buds to lilac-purple with a prominent green patch. Mid to late. Introduced 1958.
H4

R. 'Winsome' A beautiful hybrid, making a small evergreen bush with deep coppery young growths. The leaves are thinly covered with a rusty felt on the undersides. The funnel-shaped flowers, borne in loose, pen-

dent clusters, are scarlet in bud, opening rose-pink, reddish towards the base. Mid. Introduced 1939.
H4 ♛ 1993

R. 'Wishmoor' A neat, small *R. yakushimanum* hybrid evergreen shrub which bears seven-lobed flowers 8cm (3in) wide, orange-red in the bud, opening to pale primrose-yellow, deeper in the throat. Mid. Introduced 1972.
H4 ♛ 1993

Rhododendron 'Woodcock'

R. 'Woodcock' A distinctive, small, rounded evergreen shrub with rich green, deeply veined leaves up to 10cm (4in) long with recurved margins. The funnel-shaped, clear pale pink flowers have a few red spots and are in flat-topped trusses of about 10. The buds are deep strawberry-pink. Mid. Introduced 1972.
H4 ♛ 1993

R. 'Wren' A prostrate, mound-forming dwarf evergreen shrub with glossy leaves,

reddish young growths and clear yellow flowers. Early to mid. Introduced 1983.
H4

R. 'Yaku Princess' A small, very hardy *R. yakushimanum* hybrid making a dense, rounded evergreen shrub. The leaves have a pale brown felt on their undersides. The flowers are apple-blossom pink with greenish spots, borne in dense, rounded trusses. Mid to late. Introduced 1977.
H4

Rhododendron 'Yellow Hammer'

R. 'Yellow Hammer' A charming, rather slender small to medium-sized evergreen shrub with pairs of flowers at the ends of the shoots and in the axils of the leaves. They are so narrowly bell-shaped as to be almost tubular, and bright yellow. Early. Introduced before 1931.
H4 ♛ 1993

AZALEODENDRONS

Azaleodendrons are hybrids between deciduous azaleas and evergreen rhododendrons. They are very hardy small to medium-sized evergreen or semi-evergreen shrubs, flowering in late spring and early summer.

R. 'Galloper Light' A scarce, leafy semi-evergreen bush with loose trusses of funnel-shaped flowers in late spring to early summer that are cream in the tube and shade to soft salmon-pink in the lobes. A chrome-yellow blotch adds to the general effect of creamy pink.
H4

Rhododendron 'Winsome'

Rhododendron 'Glory of Littleworth'

R. 'Glory of Littleworth' A superb small azalea-like semi-evergreen shrub of stiff, erect habit. The more or less oblong leaves, 7.5–11cm (3–4½in) long, are often curled and wavy. The fragrant flowers, borne in late spring are funnel-shaped, cream at first, becoming milk-white with a conspicuous coppery blotch.
H4

R. 'Hardijzer Beauty' A small, compact, evergreen shrub with dense trusses of purple flowers in late spring.
H4 ♔ 1993

R. 'Martha Isaacson' A medium-sized evergreen shrub with tubular-funnel-shaped, slightly fragrant white flowers striped with pink, borne in late spring to early summer.
H4

R. 'Martine' A small, densely branched evergreen shrub with bright glossy green leaves and funnel-shaped, shell-pink flowers that are produced abundantly in late spring to early summer.
H4

R. 'Ria Hardijzer' A small evergreen shrub with rich purple flowers, spotted inside, in trusses of 5–10. They appear in late spring to early summer.
H4

DECIDUOUS HYBRID AZALEAS

These are fairly twiggy shrubs 1.5–2.5m (5–8ft) tall or more, usually with trumpet-shaped single flowers, although a few are double. The colour range is a glorious one, from soft pastels to riotous reds and outrageous orange. Some are outstandingly fragrant, and many have flamboyantly coloured leaves in autumn. All deciduous azaleas require a lime-free soil to which good quantities of well-rotted organic matter have been added.

Ghent hybrids (Gh) have fragrant, long-tubed flowers looking something like those of honeysuckle and their season is around the end of spring. On average they are 1.8–2.5m (6–8ft).

Knap Hill Hybrids (Kn) have trumpet-shaped, usually scentless flowers in late spring and are often brilliantly coloured. Shrubs of this group raised at Exbury, Hampshire, England, are called Exbury azaleas (Kn-Ex). Their average height is 1.8–2.5m (6–8ft)

Mollis Azaleas (M) have large, scentless flowers in handsome trusses, usually in the latter part of the middle of spring, before the leaves emerge. Their average height is 1.2–1.8m (4–6½ft).

Occidentale Hybrids (O) have delicate, pastel-coloured, fragrant flowers at the end of spring, two weeks or so later than the Mollis azaleas. Their average height is 1.8–2.5m (6–8ft)

Rustica Hybrids (R) are sweetly scented, double-flowered azaleas, opening in late spring and early summer. Their average height is 1.2–1.5m (4–5ft).

R. 'Aida' (R) Fragrant double flowers of deep peach-pink with a deeper flush. Introduced 1888.
H4

R. 'Annabella' (Kn) Orange and yellow

Rhododendron 'Annabella'

buds open to golden yellow, overlaid and flushed with orange-rose. Introduced 1947.
H4 ♔ 1993

R. 'Ballerina' (Kn-Ex) Large, white, frilly-edged flowers with an orange flush, flesh-pink in bud.
H4

R. 'Balzac' (Kn-Ex) Fragrant nasturtium-red flowers with an orange flash.
H4

R. 'Berryrose' (Kn-Ex) Rose-pink flowers with a yellow flash and coppery young foliage.
H4 ♔ 1993

R. 'Bouquet de Flore' (Gh) Fragrant, vivid red flowers blotched with yellow. Introduced 1869.
H4 ♔ 1993

Rhododendron 'Cecile'

R. 'Cecile' (Kn-Ex) Large flowers, dark salmon-pink in bud, opening to salmon pink with a yellow flare. Introduced 1947.
H4 ♔ 1993

R. 'Coccineum Speciosum' (Gh) One of the best old azaleas, with brilliant orange-red fragrant flowers. Introduced 1846.
H4 ♔ 1993

R. 'Corneille' (Gh) Fragrant cream double flowers, flushed deep pink on the outside, pink in bud. Autumn colour is good.
H4 ♔ 1993

R. 'Corringe' (Kn-Ex) Flame-coloured flowers.
H4 ♔ 1993

R. 'Daviesii' (Gh) Fragrant white flowers with a yellow flare. Autumn colour is effective. Introduced c1840.
H4 ♔ 1993

Rhododendron 'Daviesii'

Rhododendron 'Exquisitum'

Rhododendron 'Gibraltar'

Rhododendron 'Delicatissimum'

R. 'Delicatissimum' (O) Fragrant pale yellowish white flowers, flushed pink and with a yellow blotch.
H4 ♔ 1993

R. 'Diorama' (M-Kn) Deep red and fragrant flowers.
H4

R. 'Directeur Moerlands' (M) Golden yellow flowers, deeper in the throat, with an orange flare; the buds are Chinese white.
H4 ♔ 1993

R. 'Dr M. Oosthoek' (M) Deep orange-red flowers. Introduced 1920.
H4 ♔ 1993

R. 'Exquisitum' (O) Fragrant flesh-pink flowers, flushed with deep pink on the outside, with an orange flare and frilly margins. Introduced 1901.
H4 ♔ 1993

R. 'Fanny' (Gh) Fragrant deep rose-magenta flowers with a darker tube and orange flare, becoming rose with age.
H4 ♔ 1993

R. 'Fireball' (Kn-Ex) Deep orange-red flowers and deep copper-red young foliage. Introduced 1951.
H4

R. 'Fireglow' (Kn) Rich reddish orange flowers.
H4

Rhododendron 'Freya'

R. 'Freya' (R) Fragrant pale pink double flowers, tinted a rich orange-salmon. Introduced 1888.
H4

R. 'Gibraltar' (Kn-Ex) Large, flame-orange flowers with a warm yellow flash and crinkly petals; they are deep crimson-orange in bud. Introduced 1947.
H4 ♔ 1993

R. 'Ginger' (Kn-Ex) The flowers are orange-carmine in bud, opening to brilliant orange with a warm golden upper petal. Introduced 1947.
H4

R. 'Glowing Embers' (Kn-Ex) Vivid red-dish orange flowers with an orange blotch.
H4

R. 'Gog' (Kn) Orange-red flowers with a yellow flash, flushed with dark red on the outside. Introduced 1926.
H4

R. 'Golden Sunset' (Kn) Produces vivid sunset-yellow flowers.
H4

R. 'Homebush' (Kn) Rose-madder, semi-double flowers with paler shading, borne in tight, rounded heads. Introduced 1926.
H4 ♔ 1993

R. 'Hotspur' (Kn-Ex) Dazzling flame-red flowers with even darker markings on the upper petals.
H4 ♔ 1993

R. 'Hotspur Red' (Kn-Ex) Rich reddish orange flowers with an orange blotch.
H4 ♔ 1993

R. 'Irene Koster' (O) Fragrant rose-pink flowers with a small yellow blotch inside, opening late.
H4 ♔ 1993

R. 'Klondyke' (Kn-Ex) The large flowers are a wonderful, glowing orange-gold, tinted red on the back. They are flushed red in bud and the young foliage is coppery red. Introduced 1947.
H4 ♔ 1993

R. 'Magnificum' (O) Fragrant cream flowers, flushed pink with orange flare, rose in bud. Introduced 1910.
H4

R. 'Nancy Waterer' (Gh) Large, fragrant, brilliant golden yellow flowers. Introduced before 1876.
H4 ♔ 1993

Rhododendron 'Klondyke'

Rhododendron 'Nancy Waterer'

R. 'Narcissiflorum' (Gh) Double, sweetly scented pale yellow flowers, darker in the centre and on the outside. Introduced before 1871.
H4 ♔ 1993

R. 'Norma' (R) Rose-red double flowers with a salmon glow. Introduced 1888.
H4 ♔ 1993

Rhododendron 'Norma'

R. 'Orange Truffles' (Kn) Apricot flowers, illuminated chrome-yellow within, flushed nasturtium-red on the outside. They are double with frilly margins, borne in a very compact rounded truss. The young foliage is coppery red. Raised 1966 at Hillier Nurseries.

R. 'Oxydol' (Kn-Ex) White flowers with a yellow blotch. In cultivation 1947.
H4 ♔ 1993

Rhododendron 'Persil'

R. 'Persil' (Kn) White flowers with an orange-yellow flare.
H4 ♔ 1993

R. 'Pink Delight' (Kn) Deep pink flowers.
H4

R. 'Raphael de Smet' (Gh) Fragrant white double flowers, flushed with rose. Excellent autumn colour. Introduced before 1889.
H4

R. 'Rosta' (-) Fragrant, deep pink flowers with darker veins.
H4

Rhododendron 'Pink Delight'

R. 'Royal Command' (Kn-Ex) Vivid reddish orange flowers.
H4

R. 'Royal Lodge' (Kn-Ex) Deep vermilion red flowers, becoming crimson with age. Introduced 1947.
H4 ♔ 1993

Rhododendron 'Satan'

R. 'Satan' (Kn) Geranium-red flowers, darker in bud. Introduced 1926.
H4 ♔ 1993

R. 'Silver Slipper' (Kn-Ex) White flowers are flushed with pink and have an orange flare. The young foliage is copper-tinted. Introduced 1948.
H4 ♔ 1993

R. 'Spek's Orange' (M) Orange flowers, deeper in bud. It is late-flowering for a Mollis azalea.
H4 ♔ 1993

R. 'Strawberry Ice' (Kn-Ex) Flesh pink flowers, which are mottled deeper pink at the margins and with a gold flare. They are

Rhododendron 'Strawberry Ice'

deep pink in bud. Introduced 1947.
H4 ♔ 1993

***R.* 'Sugared Almond'** (Kn-Ex) Pale pink flowers. In cultivation 1951.
H4 ♔ 1993

***R.* 'Summer Fragrance'** (O) Fragrant, pale yellow flowers with a vivid yellow blotch, flowering in early summer. A small shrub with good autumn colour.
H4 ♔ 1993

***R.* 'Sun Chariot'** (Kn-Ex) Vivid yellow flowers with an orange-yellow blotch.
H4 ♔ 1993

***R.* 'Sunte Nectarine'** (Kn-Ex) Deep orange flowers, blotched with yellow.
H4 ♔ 1993

***R.* 'Tunis'** (Kn) Deep crimson flowers with an orange flare, opening from darker buds. Introduced 1926.
H4

***R.* 'Westminster'** (O) Rich almond-pink, fragrant flowers with a faint orange flash.
H4

Rhododendron 'Westminster'

Rhododendron 'Whitethroat'

***R.* 'Whitethroat'** (Kn) A compact shrub with pure white flowers with frilly margins. Introduced 1941.
H4 ♔ 1993

Rhododendron 'Wryneck'

***R.* 'Wryneck'** (Kn) Straw-yellow flowers, darker at the margins, with a deeper yellow flash. They are pinkish in bud.
H4 ♔ 1993.

EVERGREEN HYBRID AZALEAS

These are also known as Japanese azaleas. They are dwarf or small shrubs that flower in mid- to late spring so profusely that their foliage is often hidden. They do well in full sun as long as their roots are moist but in general prefer partial or dappled shade and shelter from cold winds. Their average height is 0.6–1.2m (2–4ft). The majority are single, but some are hose-in-hose doubles, in which the calyx is the same colour as the petals and in some cases the same shape,

giving the appearance of one flower sitting inside another. They require a lime-free soil to which good quantities of well-rotted organic matter have been added.

Exbury Hybrids (E) normally have large flowers up to 7.5cm (3in) wide.

Gable Hybrids (G) were developed in the United States. They have medium-sized flowers up to 6cm (2¹/₂in) wide.

Glenn Dale Hybrids (GD) were also developed in the United States. Their flowers vary from medium to very large, 5–10cm (2–4in) across.

Kaempferi Hybrids (Kf) have medium-sized flowers up to 5cm (2in) across.

Kurume Azaleas (K) originated in Japan during the 19th century. The great plant hunter Ernest Wilson was responsible for their original introduction to the West, since when many more have been raised, particularly in the United States. The flowers are small but are borne with almost unbelievable freedom.

Satsuki Hybrids (S) were introduced from Japan to America in 1938–9. The flowers are medium to large. They have a tendency to sport.

Vuyk Hybrids (V) normally have large flowers 5–7.5cm (2–3in) wide.

Wada Hybrids (W) were raised by Koichiro Wada of Yokohama, Japan, before 1940. The flowers are medium to large. A few hybrids do not fall easily into any of these groups and are designated below by (-).

***R.* 'Addy Wery'** (K) Deep vermilion red flowers. Introduced 1940.
H4 ♔ 1993

***R.* 'Aladdin'** (K) Intense geranium red flowers, fading to salmon.
H4

***R.* 'Alexander'** (-) Deep reddish orange medium-sized flowers each marked with a purplish red blotch.
H4

***R.* 'Apple Blossom'** See *R.* 'Ho-o'.

***R.* 'Atalanta'** (Kf) Soft lilac flowers.
H4

***R.* 'Azuma Kagami'** (K) Phlox-pink flowers with darker shading, hose-in-hose. This azalea reaches 1.8m (6¹/₂ft) and is best grown in shade.
H4 ♔ 1993

Rhododendron 'Atalanta'

Rhododendron 'Beethoven'

R. 'Beethoven' (V) Orchid-purple flowers with a deeper blotch and fringed petals. Introduced 1941.
H4 ♔ 1993

R. 'Betty' (Kf) Salmon-pink flowers with a deeper centre. Introduced 1922.
H4 ♔ 1993

R. 'Blaauw's Pink' (K) Salmon-pink flow-

Rhododendron 'Blaauw's Pink'

ers with paler shading, borne early.
H4 ♔ 1993

R. 'Blue Danube' (Kf) The flowers are bluish-violet – a striking colour but difficult with other evergreen azaleas.
H4 ♔ 1993

R. 'Buccaneer' (GD) A vigorous shrub with vivid reddish orange flowers.
H4

R. 'Bungo-Nishiki' (W) Orange-scarlet, semi-double flowers, borne late.
H4

R. 'Chippewa' (-) Purplish red medium-sized flowers with a darker blotch.
H4

R. 'Connie' (Kf) Reddish orange flowers.
H4

R. 'Double Beauty' (-) A low, compact shrub with purplish red large hose-in-hose flowers. In cultivation 1966.
H4

R. 'Fedora' (Kf) Pale pink flowers with a darker flash. Introduced 1922.
H4 ♔ 1993

R. 'Florida' (V) Deep red hose-in-hose flowers with some petaloid stamens. In cultivation 1962.
H4 ♔ 1993

R. 'Gaiety' (GD) Large, purplish pink flowers with a darker blotch, large.
H4

R. 'Hardy Gardenia' (-) A dwarf, spreading shrub with white, large double flowers 6cm (2½in) wide.
H4

R. 'Hatsugiri' (K) A very dwarf shrub with magenta-purple flowers.
H4 ♔ 1993

Rhododendron 'Hatsugiri'

Rhododendron 'Hino Crimson'

R. 'Hino Crimson' (K) Bright crimson flowers.
H4 ♔ 1993

R. 'Hinode Giri' (K) Bright red flowers.
H4 ♔ 1993

Rhododendron 'Hinomayo'

R. 'Hinomayo' (K) A beautiful shrub up to 1.5m (5ft) high, with clear pink flowers. Introduced c1910.
H4 ♔ 1993

R. 'Ho-o', syn. R. 'Appleblossom' (K) Pale pink flowers with a white throat.
H4

R. 'Ima Shojo' (K) Bright red, hose-in-hose flowers.
H4 ♔ 1993

R. 'Iroha Yama' (K) White flowers, with a pink flush, fading to a lavender margin and with a faint chestnut-brown eye.
H4 ♔ 1993

R. 'Ivette' (Kf) A low, compact shrub with brilliant rose-pink flowers.
H4

Rhododendron 'Iroha Yama'

Rhododendron 'Johanna'

R. 'Johanna' (-) Small to medium-sized deep red flowers.
H4

R. 'John Cairns' (Kf) Dark orange-red flowers.
H4 🏆 1993

R. 'Kermesinum' (-) A low, compact shrub with small, vivid purplish red flowers.
H4

R. 'Kirin' (K) Deep rose hose-in-hose flowers, shaded silvery rose.
H4 🏆 1993

R. 'Koningin Wilhelmina' (V) A dwarf shrub with vermilion flowers. It does best in semi-shade.
H4

R. 'Kure-no-Yuki' (K) A dwarf shrub with white hose-in-hose flowers.
H4 🏆 1003

R. 'Lemur' (-) A shrub of dwarf, prostrate habit, with deep pink medium-sized flowers and red winter buds.
H4

R. 'Leo' (**E**) A dwarf, spreading shrub with bright orange flowers, borne late.
H4

R. 'Louise Dowdle' (GD) Large flowers of brilliant rose-pink each with a deep rose blotch.
H4

R. 'Madame van Hecke' (-) Small, rosy pink flowers.
H4

R. 'Mary Helen' (-) Medium-sized white, wavy margined flowers with yellow spots.
H4

R. 'Mother's Day' (S) Rose-red flowers.
H4 🏆 1993

R. Mucronatum group (-) A lovely small evergreen or semi-evergreen shrub of wide-spreading, dome-shaped habit. The fragrant, funnel-shaped, pure white flowers are borne in late spring. Long cultivated in Japan but unknown in the wild and probably of hybrid origin. Introduced 1819.
H4

Rhododendron 'Kirin'

Rhododendron 'Mother's Day'

R. 'Naomi' (Kf) A shrub ultimately reaching 1.8m (6ft) high. The salmon-pink flowers are borne very late. Raised at Exburgh. Introduced 1933.
H4

R. 'Niagara' (GD) White flowers with a frilly margin and yellow-green blotch.
H4 🏆 1993

R. 'Obtusum Amoenum' (-) A small, densely branched, spreading evergreen or semi-evergreen shrub. The brilliant magenta or rose-purple small hose-in-hose flowers are profusely borne in spring. Introduced 1845 from Japanese gardens.
H4

R. 'Orange Beauty' (Kf) Salmon-orange flowers, best in semi-shade, as they fade badly in sun. Introduced 1920.
H4 🏆 1993

R. 'Palestrina' (V) Distinctive and attractive white flowers with a faint ray of green. Introduced 1926.
H4 🏆 1993

Rhododendron 'Palestrina'

R. 'Pippa' (-) A low, spreading shrub with large red flowers.
H4 ♛ 1993

R. 'Prinses Juliana' (V) Light orange-red flowers.
H4

R. 'Purple Splendor' (-) Medium-sized to large, vivid reddish purple flowers.
H4

R. 'Purple Triumph' (V) Deep purple flowers.
H4

R. 'Rose Greeley' (-) A shrub of low, compact, spreading habit. The fragrant hose-in-hose flowers are medium-sized and white with a green blotch.
H4

R. 'Rosebud' (K) A shrub of low, spreading habit, with rose-pink hose-in-hose flowers, borne late.
H4

R. 'Royal Pink' (Kf) Rich purplish pink flowers. In cultivation 1969.
H4

R. 'Salmon Leap' (-) Large, clear salmon-pink flowers. The leaves have a striking, silver-white margin.
H4

R. 'Santa Maria' (-) Brick red flowers.
H4

R. 'Silvester' (K) Purplish red flowers which have paler margins, borne early. In cultivation 1969.
H4

R. 'Squirrel' A dwarf, compact shrub with small, deep reddish orange flowers.
H4

R. 'Stewartsonianum' (G) Vivid red flowers. The foliage is reddish in winter.
H4 ♛ 1993

R. 'Surprise' (K) Light orange flowers. Introduced 1939.
H4

R. 'Terry' (-) Deep rose-pink flowers.
H4

R. 'Vida Brown' (K) Clear rose-pink hose-in-hose flowers.
H4

R. 'Vuyk's Rosyred' (V) Deep satiny rose flowers each with a darker flash inside. Introduced 1954.
H4 ♛ 1993

R. 'Vuyk's Scarlet' (V) Bright red flowers

Rhododendron 'Vuyk's Rosyred'

Rhododendron 'Vuyk's Scarlet'

with wavy petals. Introduced 1954.
H4 ♛ 1993

R. 'Willy' (Kf) Soft pink flowers.
H4

R. 'Wombat' (-) A prostrate shrub good for ground cover, with profusely borne medium-sized pink flowers.
H4

Rhodotypos *Rosaceae*

A genus of one deciduous species most closely related to Kerria, but with opposite leaves and white flowers.

R. scandens A free-flowering, erect shrub up to 1.2m (4ft). The paper-white flowers, 4–5cm (1¾–2in) across, appear from late spring to midsummer and are followed by shining black fruits. It can be grown in all types of soil and in sun or semi-shade. China, Korea, Japan. Introduced 1866.
H4

Rhus *Anacardinaceae*
Sumach

A genus of about 200 species of deciduous shrubs and trees that do well in any fertile soil. They are grown mainly for their striking foliage and rich autumn colours. The individual flowers are small but in several species are followed by fruits that are colourful in the mass. The sap of some species is a severe irritant to the skin of sensitive subjects and the genus also includes the poison ivy of North America. R. glabra and R. typhina make handsome foliage plants if pruned to the ground each or every other year in late winter. They will grow in any well-cultivated garden soil and are particularly well adapted to poor, sandy ones.

Rhus copallina

R. copallina (Dwarf sumach) A small to medium-sized, downy shrub. The lustrous leaves are pinnate. It bears dense, erect clusters of small, greenish yellow flowers but is mainly valued for the autumn colour of the foliage, which is rich red or purple and combines well with the red fruit clusters. E North America. Introduced 1688.
H4

R. glabra (Smooth sumach) A wide-spreading, medium-sized shrub with attractive pinnate leaves that are bloomy beneath and usually turn an intense red or orange-yellow in autumn. The erect, scarlet, hairy, plume-like fruit clusters of the female plant are also eye-catching in autumn. E North America. In cultivation 1620.
H4

R. g. 'Laciniata' The true plant has become quite rare in cultivation and most plants which are grown under this name are

Rhus glabra

Rhus trichocarpa

Rhus typhina

in actual fact the hybrid *R. × pulvinata* 'Red Autumn Lace'.
H4

R. × *pulvinata* 'Red Autumn Lace' A foliage plant with fern-like leaves with deeply cut leaflets that turn orange, yellow and red in autumn.
H4 ♛ 1993

R. *trichocarpa* A splendid large shrub or small tree with large, pinnate, downy leaves that are coppery pink when young and turn deep orange in autumn. The yellow, bristly fruits are borne in drooping clusters on female plants in autumn. Japan, Korea, China. Introduced 1894.
H4

R. *typhina* (Stag's-horn sumach) A wide-spreading, sparsely branched, irregular large shrub or small tree that develops a gaunt, flat-topped appearance, particularly noticeable in winter. When young, the branchlets are covered with a dense coat of reddish brown hairs. The large, pinnate leaves turn rich orange, yellow, red or purple in autumn. The dense, conical clusters of crimson, hairy fruits are most decorative at the end of the year. It sometimes forms small thickets of suckering stems. E North America. In cultivation 1629.
H4 ♛ 1993

R. *t*. 'Dissecta' A striking female form with deeply cut leaflets that create a fern-like effect. It has orange and yellow autumn colours.
H4 ♛ 1993

Ribes *Grossulariaceae*
Flowering currant and ornamental gooseberry

A genus of about 150 evergreen and deciduous species from temperate regions of the northern hemisphere and South America. They are mainly spring-flowering shrubs and are easily cultivated in all kinds of soil. The majority are very hardy. The leaves usually have 3–5 lobes and the flowers vary from being inconspicuous to very showy. Straggly or untidy specimens can be pruned hard immediately after flowering.

R. *alpinum* A small to medium-sized, fairly erect, neat and densely twiggy decid-uous shrub that makes a good hedge. The small flowers are greenish yellow and the

Rhus typhina 'Dissecta'

berries are red. It is highly tolerant of shade. N and C Europe.
H4

R. a. 'Aureum' A small, wide shrub with leaves that are yellow when young.
H4

Ribes gayanum

R. gayanum A small, suckering, evergreen shrub with soft green, velvety leaves. The bell-shaped, yellow flowers are honey-scented and densely packed into erect, cylindrical clusters in early summer. The berries are black. Mountains of Chile. In cultivation 1858.
H4

R. × gordonianum (*R. odoratum × R. sanguineum*) A vigorous, pleasing deciduous shrub, intermediate between its parents. The flowers are in drooping clusters, bronze-red on the outside and yellow within. The berries are black. Garden origin, 1837.
H4

Ribes laurifolium

R. laurifolium An excellent dwarf evergreen shrub with large, leathery leaves and drooping clusters of greenish white flowers in late winter and early spring. The berries are red and then blackish. On the rock garden it creates early interest. China. Introduced 1908 by Ernest Wilson.
H4

Ribes odoratum

R. odoratum (Buffalo currant) A small to medium-sized, loose, erect deciduous shrub with shining green leaves that colour richly in autumn. It has lax clusters of deliciously clove-scented, golden yellow flowers in mid-spring. The berries are black. C United States. Introduced 1812.
H4

R. sanguineum (Flowering currant) This popular medium-sized deciduous shrub has a characteristic pungent smell. The flowers vary from white to deep red and appear in mid-spring in racemes that droop at first, later becoming more upright. The berries are black and bloomy. The following forms are recommended. W North America. Introduced 1817.
H4

R. s. 'Albescens' A form with whitish flowers, tinged with pink.
H4

R. s. 'Brocklebankii' A small, slower-growing shrub with attractive golden yellow leaves and pink flowers. It tends to burn in full sun.
H4 ♔ 1993

R. s. 'King Edward VII' A small to medium-sized shrub, rather slower growing than the typical form, producing flowers

Ribes sanguineum 'Albescens'

Ribes sanguineum 'Brocklebankii'

that are intensely crimson.
H4

R. s. 'Pulborough Scarlet' A form with deep red flowers.
H4 ♔ 1993

R. s. 'Tydeman's White' This medium-sized shrub is the best white-flowered form.
H4 ♔ 1993

Ribes sanguineum 'Pulborough Scarlet'

Ribes sanguineum 'Tydeman's White'

Ribes speciosum

R. speciosum An attractive, medium-sized, semi-evergreen shrub with reddish bristly stems and fruits, and shining leaves. The beautiful, fuchsia-like, rich red flowers are borne in pendulous clusters, mid- to late spring. In cold areas it is best grown against a sunny wall. California. Introduced 1828.
H4 ♛ 1993

Richea *Epacridaceae*

A genus of some ten species of subtly attractive evergreen shrubs, natives mainly of Tasmania but with one species in south-east Australia.

R. scoparia An unusual, hardy, small, spreading shrub resembling a dwarf, shrubby monkey puzzle tree. The stems are clothed in stiff, sharply pointed leaves and the pink flowers are in erect terminal clusters 5–10cm (2–4in) long in late spring. It requires a moist, acid soil. Tasmania.
H4

Robinia *Leguminoseae*

A small genus of about eight species of fast-growing deciduous trees and shrubs, confined in the wild to the United States and Mexico. They are often referred to as acacias but that name really belongs to members of the genus Acacia, *which are mainly from Africa and Australia, and it is better to use the term 'robinias' colloquially. Robinias have attractive pinnate leaves, stems that are often spiny, and hanging racemes of pea-flowers. They will grow in ordinary soil and are especially good for dry, sunny places. They are also tolerant of atmospheric pollution. While they are small it is a good idea to prune them fairly hard after flowering to avoid damage to the brittle, rapidly extending branches.*

R. × ambigua 'Bella-rosea' An elegant small tree with rather sticky shoots and racemes of large pink flowers in early summer. Raised c1860.
H4

Robinia hispida

R. hispida (Rose acacia) A medium-sized suckering shrub with short racemes of large, deep rose flowers in late spring and early summer. It is an excellent small tree when purchased grafted on to *R. pseudoacacia* but is somewhat brittle and needs a sheltered position. It can also be grown effectively against a sunny wall. SE United States. Introduced 1743.
H4 ♛ 1993

R. h. 'Macrophylla' A medium-sized shrub or small tree with larger leaflets and flowers than the typical species, resembling a pink wisteria.
H4

R. × holdtii In habit and vigour this plant resembles *R. pseudoacacia*. It bears long, loose racemes of pale pink flowers from early to midsummer that often continue almost into autumn. They are followed by attractive red bristly seed pods. Garden origin around 1890.
H4

R. kelseyi A graceful medium-sized shrub or small tree with slender branches and elegant foliage, producing its slightly fragrant, lilac-pink flowers in early summer. E United States. Introduced 1901.
H4

R. × margaretta 'Casque Rouge' A large, suckering shrub or small tree with profusely borne, large, purplish pink flowers. Raised c1934 in the United States.
H4

R. pseudoacacia (False acacia) A large, suckering tree with rugged, furrowed bark and slightly fragrant white flowers with a yellow stain at the base of the standard

Robinia pseudoacacia

petal. They appear in early summer and are attractive to bees. E United States.
H4 ♔ 1993

R. p. 'Bessoniana' A small to medium-sized, round-headed tree, usually spineless. In cultivation 1871.
H4

Robinia pseudoacacia 'Frisia'

R. p. 'Frisia' A dramatically outstanding, small to medium-sized tree with rich golden leaves from spring to autumn, creating a brilliant splash of colour. It can be cut hard back each spring and grown as a shrub where space is at a premium. Raised 1935 in Holland.
H4 ♔ 1993

R. p. var. inermis A form that produces thornless shoots. For the mop-head acacia often grown under this name see *R. p.* 'Umbraculifera'.
H4

R. p. 'Monophylla' See *R. p.* 'Unifoliola'.

R. p. 'Pyramidalis' A slender, columnar, medium-sized tree with spineless, closely erect branches. In cultivation 1843.
H4

R. p. 'Rozynskyana' An elegant, beautiful large shrub or small spreading tree. The branches droop at the tips and bear large drooping leaves. In cultivation 1903.
H4

R. p. 'Tortuosa' A picturesque, slow-growing, small to medium-sized tree with somewhat contorted branches.
H4

R. p. 'Umbraculifera' (Mop-head acacia) A small, mop-headed tree with spineless branches that needs protection from strong

Robinia pseudoacacia 'Tortuosa'

Robinia pseudoacacia 'Umbraculifera'

winds. It rarely flowers. This tree is often grown under the name *inermis*.
H4

R. p. 'Unifoliola', syn. *R. p.* 'Monophylla' A curious form with the leaves reduced to a single large leaflet, which may be accompanied by one or two normal-sized leaflets. It makes a medium-sized to large tree. Raised c1855.
H4

R. × slavinii 'Hillieri' An elegant small tree with delicate foliage produced on a rounded head of branches. The lilac-pink flowers, borne in early summer, are slightly fragrant. It is an excellent tree for a small garden.
H4 ♔ 1993

Romneya *Papaveraceae*
Tree poppy

A genus of two species of sub-shrubby, Californian perennials with deeply cut, grey to grey-green leaves

and large, white, poppy-like flowers with a central mass of golden yellow stamens. They are sometimes difficult to establish but once settled spread by underground stems. They are best in a warm, sunny position and should not be disturbed once planted. Any soil suits them, but the deeper and better drained the better.

Romneya coulteri

R. coulteri A small to medium-sized perennial with large, solitary, fragrant flowers 10–15cm (4–6in) wide, opening from slightly conical buds from midsummer to mid-autumn. Introduced 1875.
H4 ♔ 1993

R. trichocalyx This plant closely resembles *R. coulteri* but the stems are more slender and the buds more rounded.
H4

Romneya 'White Cloud'

R. 'White Cloud' A strong-growing small to medium-sized perennial with extra-large white flowers.
H4

ROSA

Rosaceae

IT IS a strange quirk of many gardeners that although they generally regard a shrub that flowers for a month or more as highly desirable, they turn their backs on species and primary hybrid roses, a great many of which are among the most graceful and charming of all shrubs. Indeed, they are for the most part infinitely more elegant than their modern, complex counterparts, which are hardly more than flower-bearers and have little to commend them as plants in the sense of being inherently attractive in the absence of flowers.

The 'wild' roses present a very great variety of form. There are species that climb and ramble, covering banks, scrambling into trees and decorating pergolas, arches and bowers; there are shrubs that stand tall and others that arch gracefully, while still more are low, dense and bushy. The great majority of them flower for quite as long and even longer than any philadelphus, deutzia or lilac and, moreover, start to flower at a time in early to midsummer when the general transition from shrubs that flower on old wood to those that bloom on new creates a hiatus in shrub-flowering.

Their flowers lack the blowsy fulsomeness of so many modern roses and have instead a simplicity and refreshingly natural air; the colours range from luxuriantly vivid to softly pastel but are very seldom coarse or strident and rarely clash. The everlasting search for fullness of flower may seem a little pointless when you look at the dazzling simplicity of *Rosa moyesii* or the changing moods of *R. odorata* 'Mutabilis'.

The latter exemplifies yet another attraction of the wild roses: they tend to have those scents that immediately transport you back to a succession of warm summers when country lanes were rich with a heady mixture of flowery aromas and hedges buzzed with bees.

And then there are the fruits. The intense doubling of flowers reduces their ability to set seed, but the wild roses and their near hybrids experience no such difficulty and the brilliant hips, evolved by nature to be as eye-catching as possible, decorate the shrubs well into autumn and may sometimes linger like discarded, raffish jewellery well into winter.

CARE AND CULTIVATION

That wild roses are so easily grown should deter none but the most elitist of gardeners. They will grow in virtually any soil except one that is wet and highly acid – although there are even some that will tolerate such conditions if the drainage is good. They flower better in full sun, but a great many will not object to a little shade. The more ornamental species react favourably to an annual or bi-annual manuring.

Pruning is largely a matter of common sense. Once they are established very little pruning is needed except for the removal of dead wood, although older specimens that have become so tangled, dense and overcrowded that their stability is threatened should be thinned back to a firm framework. Pruning should be done immediately after flowering or, if you wish to enjoy a display of hips, in late winter.

Rosa nutkana 'Plena'

Rosa *Rosaceae*

R. 'Agnes' A medium-sized deciduous hybrid of *R. rugosa* with arching branches and densely arranged, bright green leaves. The amber-tinted, butter-yellow, fully double flowers, borne in late spring, are deliciously scented. In cultivation 1922.
H4

Rosa × alba 'Alba Maxima'

R. × *alba* 'Alba Maxima' (Jacobite rose) A small deciduous shrub with grey-green foliage and pure white, very double flowers in upright clusters and occasional red hips.
H4 🏆 1993

R. × *alba* 'Alba Semiplena' (White Rose of York) A medium-sized deciduous shrub with greyish green leaves and white, usually semi-double, richly scented flowers 7.5cm (3in) wide. The hips are oblong and red. In cultivation before 1600.
H4 🏆 1993

R. 'Albert Edwards' A medium-sized deciduous shrub with arching branches wreathed in late spring with fragrant, lemon-yellow single flowers up to 6cm (2¹/₂in) across. Raised c1938 by Hillier Nurseries and named after the rose foreman of that time.
H4

R. 'Andersonii' A medium-sized, strong deciduous shrub with arching, prickly stems and scented single flowers 5–7.5cm (2–3in) across. They are a rich, clear rose-pink, and are freely produced over a long period. The scarlet, urn-shaped hips resemble those of a dog rose. In cultivation 1912.
H4

Rosa 'Anemonoides'

R. 'Anemonoides' A lovely deciduous shrub rose, with single flowers 10cm (4in) wide, produced over several weeks. They are silver-pink and shaded with rose-pink. It is a hybrid of *R. laevigata* and requires, as does its parent, a warm, sheltered wall. Garden origin c1895.
H3–4

Rosa 'Arthur Hillier'

R. 'Arthur Hillier' A large, vigorous deciduous shrub with a multitude of large, rose-crimson single flowers in early to midsummer. They are followed in autumn by bright red, flask-shaped fruits. Occurred c1938 at Hillier Nurseries.
H4

R. banksiae (Banksian rose). A beautiful, tall-growing, semi-evergreen climber, reaching more than 7m (22ft) in a suitable position. It is a well-known and much-admired rose, but it does not flower when young. It prefers a warm wall in full sun, and plants grown in cold areas tend to suffer frost damage that reduces or prevents flowering. The single flowers are borne in late spring and early summer and have a delicate scent of violets. China.
H3

R. b. 'Alba Plena' In this form, which is the one that was originally named in honour of Lady Banks, the flowers are rosette, white, and in densely packed umbels. Introduced 1807 from a garden in Canton, China, by William Kerr.
H3

Rosa banksiae 'Lutea'

R. b. 'Lutea' (Yellow banksian rose) A most beautiful rose bearing yellow rosette flowers with a delicate fragrance. Introduced before 1824.
H3 🏆 1993

R. b. 'Lutescens' A form with single, yellow, sweetly fragrant flowers. Introduced before 1807.
H3

R. b. 'Normalis' This, the wild form, has single, cream, sweetly fragrant flowers. China. Said to have been introduced 1796 by Robert Drummond.
H3

R. 'Blanc Double de Coubert' A medium-sized deciduous hybrid of *R. rugosa* with more open, taller growth. The semi-double white flowers are blush-tinted in bud. Garden origin 1892.
H4 🏆 1993

R. bracteata (Macartney rose) A medium-sized to large evergreen shrub with prickly, rambling stems and leaves composed of 5–11 leaflets. The white, lemon-scented single flowers are 7.5–10 cm (3–4in) wide and

have golden anthers; each head is surrounded by large, downy bracts. The fruits are spherical and orange-red. It is highly ornamental but needs a warm, sunny, sheltered wall. SE China, Taiwan. Introduced 1795 by Lord Macartney.
H3–4

R. brunonii 'La Mortola' A fine selection of the Himalayan musk rose, with large, richly fragrant, white single flowers in tight clusters in early to midsummer. It is a rampant deciduous climber reaching 9–12m (28–40ft) high, but needs a sheltered position and full sun to ripen its growth.
H 3–4

R. californica 'Plena' See *R. nutkana* 'Plena'.

Rosa 'Canary Bird'

R. 'Canary Bird' A beautiful medium-sized deciduous shrub with arching stems, small, fern-like leaves and bright canary-yellow single flowers that wreathe the branches in late spring and early summer.
H4 ♔ 1993

R. canina (Dog rose) A rose familiar in Europe, where it is native, and North America, where it is naturalized. It is a medium to large deciduous shrub with strong, prickly stems, leaves with 5-7 leaflets and white to pink fragrant single flowers, followed by bright red, egg-shaped hips. It is highly variable.
H4

R. 'Cantabrigiensis' A medium-sized deciduous arching shrub with fragrant, fern-like leaves. The single flowers 5cm (2in) wide are soft yellow fading to cream.
H4

Rosa canina

Rosa 'Cantabrigiensis'

R. centifolia (Cabbage rose, Provence rose) A complex hybrid, thought to have been one of the most ancient roses but now known to have appeared in its present form in the 18th century. It is a small deciduous shrub with aromatic leaves and large, double, rose-pink, richly fragrant flowers. There are several cultivars and it is the parent of many hybrids.
H4

R. c. 'Cristata' The crested cabbage rose is a charming small shrub in which the sepals are beautifully crested to such an extent that the flower buds are completely enveloped. The flowers are large, fully double and rosy pink. Said to have been discovered 1820 in Fribourg, Switzerland.
H4 ♔ 1993

R. c. 'Muscosa' (Common moss rose) The archetypal moss rose, with a dense, moss-like, glandular-bristly covering of the upper stems, leaf stalks, flower stalks and calyces. This unusual and characteristic clothing is

Rosa centifolia 'Muscosa'

sticky to the touch and gives off a balsam-like odour when bruised. The clear pink, globular, flat-topped, very double flowers later open much wider and are richly scented. In cultivation 1720.
H4 ♔ 1993

R. chinensis A small to medium-sized deciduous shrub with stout branches and leaves with 3–5 shining leaflets. The single flowers are 5cm (2in) across, crimson or pink, occasionally white, and are produced from early to late summer, followed by scarlet fruits. First introduced in the late eighteenth and early nineteenth century in several garden forms; the wild form was not found until c1900 in C China by Dr Augustine Henry.
H4

Rosa chinensis 'Old Blush'

R. c. 'Old Blush' (Monthly rose) An important rose because it introduced remontant flowering into garden roses. It is compact, generally small, and has pink, double flowers that have the scent of sweet peas; produced over a very long period. H4

R. c. 'Mutabilis' See *R.* × *odorata* 'Mutabilis'.

Rosa chinensis 'Viridiflora'

R. c. 'Viridiflora' (Green rose) A curious small shrub with double flowers consisting of crowded, greenish, petal-like scales. H4

R. 'Complicata' A most beautiful medium-sized deciduous shrub that can clamber into trees or cover fences and hedges. It has many very large, rose-pink, white-eyed single flowers that are deliciously fragrant. It is a hybrid of *R. gallica*. H4 ♔ 1993

R. × damascena 'Versicolor' (York and Lancaster Rose) An unusual form of the Damask rose with loosely double flowers, some of which are completely white, while others may be completely pink and still others have some pink petals and some white ones; no two flowers are quite the same. It makes a small deciduous shrub. In cultivation before 1629. H4

R. 'Dupontii' A strong-growing, medium-sized deciduous shrub with large, fragrant single flowers 7.5cm (3in) wide. They are blush, fading to creamy white, and are borne in domed clusters in midsummer. Of loose habit and may need a little support. In cultivation 1817. H4

R. ecae A small, dainty deciduous shrub with prickly, slender, arching, chestnut-brown branches, along which the butter-

Rosa 'Dupontii'

Rosa ecae

cup-yellow single flowers, 2.5cm (1in) wide, are borne in very early summer. The hips are round and red. Afghanistan. Introduced 1880 by Dr Aitchison. H4

R. eglanteria, syn. *R. rubiginosa* (Eglantine, sweet briar) A medium-sized deciduous shrub with deliciously aromatic leaves and

Rosa eglanteria

clear pink, fragrant, beautifully formed single flowers 3–4cm (1¼–1½in) wide which stud the arching branches in summer. The oval, bright red hips last well into winter. It is the parent of many hybrids. Europe. H4 ♔ 1993

R. elegantula 'Persetosa' (Threepenny-bit rose) A charming deciduous rose up to 2m (7ft) high, with dainty, fern-like leaves that contrast with the coral-red buds which open to soft pink single flowers rather less than 2.5cm (1in) across. H4

R. fedtschenkoana An erect, medium-sized deciduous shrub with sea-green leaves and white single flowers, 5cm (2in) wide, produced continuously throughout the summer and followed by orange-red, bristly, pear-shaped fruits. Turkestan. H4

Rosa filipes 'Kiftsgate'

R. filipes 'Kiftsgate' An extremely vigorous deciduous rambling species, much too large for the average garden, although stunningly beautiful like a white waterfall where there is room. In midsummer each panicle, up to 45cm (18in) across, may have as many as 100 or more sweetly scented single flowers, each 2.5cm (1in) wide. The display of myriad fruits, small and bright red, is almost as spectacular. In cultivation 1938. H4 ♔ 1993

R. foetida (Austrian yellow rose) A small deciduous shrub with erect, slender stems and rich yellow single flowers 5–6cm (2–2½in) across. It should be planted in full sun and a well-drained site. It has been extremely important in the development of

many of the modern garden roses. SW Asia, naturalized in Europe. In cultivation since the sixteenth century.
H4

***R. f.* 'Bicolor'** (Austrian copper rose) A remarkably beautiful shrub that needs plenty of sun and good drainage. The petals are brilliant coppery red with a bright yellow reverse. It was also of great importance in the history of the modern rose.
H4

Rosa foetida 'Bicolor'

Rosa foetida 'Persiana'

***R. f.* 'Persiana'** (Persian yellow rose) A beautiful shrub with golden-yellow, double flowers. It is the parent of innumerable garden hybrid roses. Iran. Introduced 1837.
H4

R. forrestiana A strong-growing, medium-sized deciduous shrub with arching stems to 2m (7ft). The rose-crimson, strongly fragrant single flowers, 3–4cm (1¼–1½in) wide, are in clusters surrounded by leafy bracts and followed by bright red,

bottle-shaped hips. W China. Introduced 1918 by George Forrest.
H4

***R.* 'Fru Dagmar Hastrup'** A hybrid of *R. rugosa* which makes a dense deciduous shrub up to 2m (7ft) with lush, dark green foliage. The single flowers are pale rose-pink with cream stamens and it bears large crops of large, rich crimson hips. It makes an excellent hedge. Garden origin 1914.
H4 🏆 1993

Rosa 'Fru Dagmar Hastrup'

R. gallica A small, suckering deciduous shrub with erect, slender, thorny stems and leaves composed of 5–7 leaflets. The deep pink single flowers, 5–7cm (2–2½in) across, are followed by rounded or top-shaped brick-red fruits. C and S Europe. In cultivation for many centuries.
H4

R. g.* var. *officinalis (Apothecary's rose, red rose of Lancaster) A shrub with richly fragrant, semi-double, rosy crimson flowers

Rosa gallica var. *officinalis*

with prominent yellow anthers in early to midsummer. Its petals retain their fragrance even when dried and powdered. In cultivation since at least 1310.
H4 🏆 1993

***R. g.* 'Rosa Mundi'** See *R. g.* 'Versicolor'.

Rosa gallica 'Versicolor'

***R. g.* 'Versicolor'**, syn. *R. g.* 'Rosa Mundi' An old, well-loved rose with semi-double flowers, usually rose-red striped with white, but with a few entirely red blooms. In some seasons all the flowers may be 'self' red. It should not be confused with the York and Lancaster rose, *R. × damascena* 'Versicolor'.
H4 🏆 1993

Rosa glauca

R. glauca, syn. *R. rubrifolia* A medium-sized deciduous shrub with reddish violet, almost thornless stems and attractive foliage, bloomy purple in sun and greyish green with a burgundy tinge in shade, making them look as if they have been dipped in red wine. The small, clear pink single flowers

are followed by ovoid, dark red hips. C and S Europe. In cultivation before 1830.
H4 ♔ 1993

R. 'Golden Chersonese' A medium-sized deciduous shrub with small leaves and deep buttercup-yellow, sweetly scented single flowers wreathing the branches at the end of spring. Raised 1963 by E. F. Allen.
H4

Rosa × *harisonii* 'Harison's Yellow'

R. × harisonii 'Harison's Yellow' A small, free-flowering deciduous shrub occasionally reaching 2m (7ft). It has brilliant yellow, double flowers with a slightly unpleasant odour like that of *R. foetida*. The fruits are small and almost black.
H4 ♔ 1993

Rosa 'Helen Knight'

R. 'Helen Knight' A small deciduous shrub similar to *R. ecae* but larger and with larger flowers. Raised 1966 at the Royal Horticultural Society's Garden at Wisley.
H4

R. helenae A vigorous deciduous rambling or climbing species reaching a height of 6m (20ft) or more in a tree. The creamy white, fragrant single flowers 2–4cm (1–1½in) across are borne in dense corymbs in early summer and are followed in autumn by large, drooping bunches of narrowly ovoid, orange-red hips. W and C China. Introduced 1907 by Ernest Wilson and named after his wife, Helen.
H4

Rosa 'Highdownensis'

R. 'Highdownensis' A medium-sized deciduous shrub, something like *R. moyesii*, of which it is a seedling. It has dainty leaves and light velvety crimson single flowers 6cm (2½in) across. The large hips are flagon-shaped and orange-scarlet. Raised before 1925 by Sir Frederick Stern.
H4

R. 'Hillieri' A very beautiful deciduous seedling of *R. moyesii*. Its flowers are like those of the species but so dark a crimson as

Rosa 'Hillieri'

to be the darkest of all single roses. Raised c1924 by Hillier Nurseries.
H4

R. hugonis A most graceful deciduous shrub reaching 2m (7ft), with long, arching branches clothed with neat, fern-like leaves. During the latter part of spring the branches are wreathed with hundreds of soft yellow single flowers, 5cm (2in) wide, that are followed by small, rounded, dark red hips. It makes a good informal hedge. C China. Introduced 1899.
H4 ♔ 1993

Rosa hugonis

R. 'Lady Penzance' A medium-sized deciduous shrub with arching branches, fragrant leaves and single, copper-tinted flowers with bright yellow centres.
H4

R. laevigata 'Cooperi' (Cooper's Burmese rose) A strong-growing deciduous rambler, reaching 12m (40ft) in a warm, sheltered position. The large, slightly fragrant, pure white single flowers have golden anthers. It usually does best on a warm wall. Introduced 1921.
H4

R. longicuspis See *R. mulliganii*.

R. 'Lutea Maxima' A small deciduous shrub with few scattered thorns and bright green foliage. The buttercup-yellow single flowers are 5cm (2in) across. One of the best single yellow roses.
H4

R. 'Macrantha' A small, variable deciduous shrub with large single flowers that are pink in bud and open to clear almond-pink, changing to near-white. They are deli-

Rosa primula

Rosa 'Red Max Graf'

R. 'Rose d'Amour' (St Mark's rose) A medium-sized deciduous shrub up to 2m (6¹/₂ft) high. The double, fragrant flowers are deep pink with paler outer petals, continuing for several weeks from mid- to late summer. A vigorous, free-flowering rose. Garden origin before 1820.
H4 ⚆ 1993

Rosa 'Roseraie de l'Hay'

R. 'Roseraie de l'Hay' A deciduous hybrid of *R. rugosa* with long, pointed, purplish red buds that open to rich crimson-purple flowers 10–12cm (4–5in) across with cream stamens. The double flowers are very fragrant. A superb, vigorous rose and an excellent hedge. Garden origin 1901.
H4 ⚆ 1993

R. roxburghii (Burr rose, chestnut rose) A viciously armed, medium-sized to large deciduous shrub with 9–15 leaflets and fragrant shell-pink single flowers up to 7.5cm (3in) wide. They are followed by orange-yellow, tomato-shaped hips covered with stiff prickles. China. Introduced 1908 by Ernest Wilson.
H4

R. rubiginosa See *R. eglanteria*.
R. rubrifolia See *R. glauca*.

Rosa rugosa

R. rugosa A strong-growing, perpetual-flowering deciduous shrub with densely prickly stems up to 2m (6¹/₂ft) high. The leaflets are conspicuously veined and puckered (rugose). The purplish rose, fragrant single flowers are up to 9cm (3¹/₂in) wide, and are followed by bright red, tomato-shaped hips 2.5cm (1in) across. It forms dense thickets and makes an excellent hedge. NE Asia. Introduced 1796.
H4

R. r. 'Alba' A form with white flowers, tinted blush in bud. It is very vigorous and is exceptionally free-fruiting.
H4 ⚆ 1993

R. r. 'Rubra' A shrub with wine-crimson, fragrant flowers. Conspicuous large hips.
H4 ⚆ 1993

Rosa rugosa 'Alba'

Rosa rugosa 'Rubra'

Rosa 'Scabrosa'

R. 'Scabrosa' A vigorous medium-sized deciduous hybrid of *R. rugosa* particularly valued for its excellent foliage. The flowers, similar in shape to *R. rugosa*, are enormous deep crimson and single, and up to 14cm (5¹/₂in) wide. The fruits are large, like small tomatoes, and have persistent sepals.
H4 ⚆ 1993

Rosa sericea f. pteracantha

Rosa soulieana

Rosa virginiana

R. sericea f. pteracantha A highly distinctive deciduous rose with stems furnished with flat, broad-based, translucent, crimson thorns that are beautiful when seen in the winter sun. Annual or bi-annual pruning encourages the young shoots on which these remarkable thorns are most eye-catching. The flowers are single, four-petalled, yellowish white, and borne in late spring and early summer. Himalayas and W China. Introduced 1890.
H4

R. setipoda A medium-sized deciduous shrub with leaflets that have a briar fragrance if crushed. The clear pink single flowers, more than 5cm (2in) across, are on contrasting purplish stalks all along the branches. They are followed by large, flagon-shaped, crimson hips. W China. Introduced 1901 by Ernest Wilson.
H4

R. 'Silver Moon' A vigorous deciduous rambler up to 9m (28ft) high with large, creamy, richly scented single flowers that are butter-yellow in bud.
H4

R. soulieana A large deciduous shrub with long, climbing stems making large mounds. The leaves are grey-green and the single white flowers are up to 4cm (1½in) wide in large, domed clusters, but only on well-established, mature plants. The fruits are small, orange-red and egg-shaped. W China. Introduced 1896.
H3–4 ☻ 1993

R. stellata var. mirifica (Sacramento rose) A dwarf deciduous shrub with ivory-coloured prickles and rose-purple single

flowers that pale with age and are followed by red, top-shaped hips. It needs a sunny position in a well-drained soil. New Mexico. Introduced 1916.
H4

Rosa sweginzowii

R. sweginzowii A strong deciduous shrub 3–4m (10–12ft) high, resembling *R. moyesii*. The bright rose-pink single flowers are 4cm (1½in) wide, usually in clusters, and precede flagon-shaped, bright red hips about the same size and colour as those of *R. moyesii* but ripening earlier. NW China. Introduced 1903 by Ernest Wilson.
H4

R. villosa (Apple rose) A vigorous, medium-sized deciduous shrub with aromatic leaves and single flowers 5cm (2in) wide, carmine in bud, opening clear pink. In early autumn it has large, apple-shaped, bristly, crimson hips. C and S Europe, W Asia. Introduced 1771.
H4

R. virginiana A small, suckering deciduous shrub with leaflets that are glossy green, in autumn turning first to purple and then to orange-red, crimson and yellow. The single flowers are 5–6cm (2–2½in) wide, bright pink, deeper in bud, and appear continuously from early to late summer. The hips are small, bright red and slightly flat-

Rosa webbiana

tened. It is excellent in sandy soils, especially by the sea. E North America. Introduced before 1807.
H4 ♛ 1993

R. webbiana A graceful, slender deciduous shrub up to 2m (6½ft). The single flowers are clear almond pink, up to 5cm (2in) wide and carried to effect all along the arching stems in early summer. In late summer bottle-shaped, sealing-wax-red fruits follow. W Himalayas. Introduced 1879.
H4

Rosa 'Wedding Day'

R. 'Wedding Day' A vigorous deciduous climbing or rambling shrub reaching 10m (30ft) in a tree. The richly scented single flowers are deep yellow in bud, opening to creamy white and fading to pink; the stamens are vivid yellow. They are borne in large trusses.
H4

R. 'White Max Graf' A shrub resembling 'Max Graf' but with large, single, pure white flowers. It is prostrate or climbing to 2m (6½ft).
H4

R. wichuraiana A vigorous, semi-evergreen rambler. It has white, richly scented single flowers up to 5cm (2in) across borne in small conical clusters in late summer and followed by tiny, round, red hips. The stems root as they grow, making good ground cover, and they will climb objects such as tree stumps. Parent of the wichuraiana hybrids including 'Albéric Barbier', 'Albertine' and 'Dorothy Perkins'. E Asia. Introduced 1891 from Japan.
H4

Rosa wichuraiana

R. 'William's Double Yellow' A small deciduous hybrid of *R. pimpinellifolia* bearing fragrant yellow double flowers with a central cluster of green carpels.
H4

R. willmottiae A medium-sized deciduous shrub with gracefully arching branches and small, sea-green, fern-like leaves that are pleasantly aromatic when crushed. The single flowers are up to 4cm (1½in) wide, lilac-pink with cream anthers, and the fruits are pear-shaped and orange-red. W China. Introduced 1904 by Ernest Wilson.
H4

R. woodsii var. fendleri A first-class, dense, leafy deciduous bush about 1.5m (5ft) high with bright lilac-pink single flowers and sealing-wax-red hips that persist well into winter. W North America. In cultivation 1888.
H4

R. xanthina A beautiful, medium-sized deciduous shrub with small, dainty, fern-like leaves and semi-double, golden-yellow flowers 4cm (1½in) wide. A garden form, cultivated in China and Korea for more than 100 years.
H4

Rosmarinus *Labiatae*
Rosemary

A genus of two species of evergreen, aromatic shrubs, thriving in all well-drained soils in sun.

R. officinalis A dense shrub up to 2m (6½ft) high and wide, with grey-green leaves and, in late spring, blue flowers in

Rosmarinus officinalis

many clusters along the branches made in the previous year. It makes an informal hedge that can be lightly pruned immediately after flowering. S Europe, Asia Minor.
H4

R. o. 'Albus' A white-flowered form.
H4

R. o. 'Benenden Blue' A smaller form with very narrow, dark green leaves and bright blue flowers.
H3

R. o. 'Fastigiatus' See *R. o.* 'Miss Jessop's Upright'.

R. o. 'Miss Jessop's Upright', syn. *R. o.* 'Fastigiatus' A strong, erect, small to medium-sized shrub.
H4 ♛ 1993

Rosmarinus officinalis 'Prostratus'

R. o. 'Prostratus' A low-growing form making large, dense, prostrate mats with clusters of blue flowers in late spring and early summer. It is a little tender.
H3 ♛ 1993

R. o. 'Roseus' A small shrub with lilac-pink flowers.
H4

R. o. 'Severn Sea' A dwarf shrub with arching branches and brilliant blue flowers.
H4 ♔ 1993

Rosmarinus officinalis 'Sissinghurst Blue'

R. o. 'Sissinghurst Blue' Upright dwarf form with blue flowers. Introduced c1958.
H4 ♔ 1993

Rosmarinus officinalis 'Tuscan Blue'

R. o. 'Tuscan Blue' A small shrub with broader leaves and brighter coloured, deep blue flowers that often occur in winter.
H3

Rubus *Rosaceae*
Bramble

A large genus of 250 evergreen and deciduous species. The ornamental brambles vary greatly but share a tendency to grow well in the poorest soils and in all kinds of adverse conditions. Several have attractive flowers and foliage, others have strikingly white stems in winter, and the great majority have prickles. Those with ornamental stems should have the old flowering stems cut down to ground level each year immediately after flowering. The climbing members of the genus are fairly vigorous and have long, prickly stems. They can be trained up wooden supports or into small trees or hedges. They are grown mainly for their ornamental foliage and thrive in all types of well-drained soil.

Rubus 'Benenden'

R. 'Benenden' A beautiful deciduous hybrid, producing erect, peeling, thornless shoots up to 3m (10ft) high with three- to five-lobed leaves. The flowers are 5cm (2in) wide, glistening white with a central boss of golden-yellow stamens, produced singly all along the branches at the end of spring. Raised by Capt Collingwood Ingram 1950.
H4 ♔ 1993

R. 'Betty Ashburner' A prostrate evergreen shrub with glossy green, rounded, more or less three-lobed leaves with wavy

Rubus 'Betty Ashburner'

margins. It is a good ground-cover plant where *R. tricolor* may be too invasive.
H4

R. biflorus A vigorous medium-sized deciduous shrub with green stems covered with a vivid white, waxy bloom. The leaves have five (or occasionally three) leaflets and are white-felted beneath. The small white flowers are borne in terminal clusters in summer and followed by edible, yellow fruits. Himalayas. Introduced 1818.
H4

Rubus calycinoides

R. calycinoides A creeping alpine evergreen, forming dense mats. The leaves are small, three- to five-lobed and mallow-like, glossy green and puckered above, grey-felted below. White flowers appear in summer. It is a good plant for ground cover, even in shade. The true species is possibly not in cultivation and the plant generally grown is probably *R. pentalobus*. Taiwan.
H4

Rubus cockburnianus

R. cockburnianus A medium-sized decid-uous species with purple, arching stems overlaid with a vivid white bloom, which is outstanding in winter. The attractive, fern-like leaves have 7–9 leaflets and are white or grey beneath. The flowers are of little merit but are followed by bloomy black fruits. China. Introduced 1907 by Ernest Wilson. H4 ♛ 1993

R. c. 'Goldenvale' (PBR 4148) A form with equally striking white shoots in winter but also with the added bonus of yellow foliage in summer.
H4

Rubus crataegifolius

R. crataegifolius A dwarf deciduous shrub with arching shoots that are red-pur-ple in winter. The deeply lobed leaves turn to striking shades of orange, red and purple in autumn.
H4

R. deliciosus The arching branches of this medium-sized, thornless deciduous shrub have peeling bark. The leaves are three- to five-lobed and the flowers, 5cm (2in) wide, are like white dog roses. They open in late spring and early summer. Colorado (United States). Introduced 1870.
H4

R. flagelliflorus An evergreen climber with long, white-felted, minutely prickly stems. The leaves are broadly egg-shaped to more or less lance-shaped, up to 18cm (7in) long, shallowly lobed and toothed and felted beneath. The small white flowers are borne in clusters in early summer and are followed by black, edible fruits. It is most often grown for its striking foliage. China.

Rubus flagelliflorus

Introduced 1901 by Ernest Wilson.
H4

R. × fraseri A medium-sized, suckering deciduous shrub with palmate leaves and fragrant, rose-coloured flowers from early to late summer. It is good for shady areas under trees. Garden origin 1918.
H4

Rubus fruticosus

R. fruticosus (Blackberry, bramble) A ferocious, pestiferous weed of horticulture and agriculture, occurring in one form or another in most of the temperate world. However, it also includes the blackberries, fruiting clones of which are non-weedy and welcome in gardens. They include 'Ashton Cross', 'Oregon Thornless' and 'John

Rubus × fraseri

Innes', all of which are restrained enough for the average garden. Plant at 2.5–3m (8–10ft) centres. It is a deciduous species. H4

R. henryi var. bambusarum An evergreen climbing species with long stems, up to 6m (18ft) on a suitable support. The leaves are composed of three distinct, lance-shaped leaflets and are 10–15cm (4–6in) long, glossy dark green above, white-felted beneath. The pink flowers are borne in slender racemes in summer, followed by black fruits. China. Introduced 1900. H4

R. 'Kenneth Ashburner' A prostrate, vigorous, evergreen shrub with glossy green, pointed leaves. It is suitable for ground cover. H4

R. lineatus A deciduous or semi-evergreen shrub with rambling, silky-hairy stems, usually less than 1.2m (4ft). The leaves, which have five leaflets, are unique and beautiful; they are dark green above and covered with a shining, silvery, silky down beneath, and prickles are almost entirely absent. The white flowers are in small clusters and the small fruits are red or yellow. It needs a warm, sheltered position. E Himalayas to Malaya. Introduced 1905 by George Forrest. H3

R. microphyllus 'Variegatus' A small, deciduous suckering shrub, forming dense mounds of prickly stems and prettily three-lobed leaves that are green, mottled with cream and pink. H4

R. nepalensis A dwarf, evergreen, creeping shrub with softly bristly stems and leaves with three leaflets. The attractive, nodding, white flowers, 2.5–4cm (1–1½in) wide, are on erect, leafy shoots in early summer and are followed by edible fruits. A charming, carpeting shrub for a shady border or bank. Himalayas. Introduced 1850. H4

R. odoratus A vigorous, suckering deciduous shrub with erect, peeling, thornless stems up to 2.5m (8ft) high. The leaves are large, velvety and palmate, and the fragrant, purplish rose flowers are in branched clusters, up to 5cm (2in) wide, opening from

Rubus odoratus

early summer to early autumn. The red fruits are edible. It is an excellent, very ornamental shrub for semi-shade beneath trees. E North America. Introduced 1770. H4

R. phoenicolasius (Japanese wineberry) The reddish, glandular-bristly stems of this deciduous shrub are 2.5–3m (8–10ft) high and the leaves are large, with three leaflets that are white-felted beneath. The small, pale pink flowers are in clusters in midsummer, and the fruits are bright orange-red and sweetly edible. Japan, China, Korea. Introduced c1876. H4

R. spectabilis (Salmonberry) A vigorous, suckering deciduous shrub with erect stems 1.2–1.8m (4–6ft) high and leaves with three leaflets. The fragrant flowers are solitary or in small clusters, up to 4cm (1½in) across, bright magenta-rose, borne in mid-spring. The edible fruits are large, egg-shaped and orange-yellow. Makes good ground cover

beneath trees. W North America. Introduced 1827 by David Douglas. H4

R. s. 'Olympic Double' A striking, double-flowered form. H4

R. thibetanus 'Silver Fern' An attractive deciduous plant with semi-erect, purplish

Rubus thibetanus 'Silver Fern'

Rubus phoenicolasius

brown stems covered with a blue-white bloom. They are up to 2m (6½ft) high and bear small, fern-like leaves with 7–13 coarsely-toothed leaflets that are silvery-silky-hairy above, white or grey-felted beneath. The flowers are small and purple, and the fruits are black or red. This is a greyer form than the typical species. W China. Introduced 1904 by Ernest Wilson. H4 ♔ 1993

R. tricolor An attractive, vigorous evergreen ground-cover plant with long, trailing stems and dark, glossy leaves with white undersides. The white, 2.5cm (1in) wide flowers are borne in midsummer, and are sometimes followed by large, bright red, edible fruits. It will form a carpet even under beech trees yet with age can become 1m (3ft) high. W China. Introduced 1908 by Ernest Wilson. H4

R. ulmifolius 'Bellidiflorus' A scrambling, rambling deciduous shrub with

Rubus ulmifolius 'Bellidiflorus'

plum-coloured stems and large panicles of showy, double, pink flowers in mid- to late summer. It is too vigorous for anything but a wild garden. H4

Ruscus *Ruscaceae*

A genus of about six species of evergreen sub-shrubs occurring from Madeira to Iran and spreading by underground stems. What appear to be leaves are really flattened stems (cladodes), and the minute flowers are borne on the surfaces of these in spring, with male and female on separate plants. The females bear attractive fruits. These are good plants for dry shade in all kinds of soil.

Ruscus aculeatus

R. aculeatus (Butcher's broom) A small, erect shrub with thick clumps of green stems, 0.5–1m (1½–3ft) high, that are sturdy but flexible. The cladodes are small, sharply spine-tipped, and densely arranged on the upper parts of the stems. The berries are like bright red cherries and are sometimes abundantly borne where both sexes are grown. It grows in dense shade where little else will survive. S Europe, including S England. H4

R. hypoglossum A dwarf shrub with broad clumps of green, 'leafy' stems. The comparatively large, leaf-like cladodes have tiny green flowers on the upper surface and, on female plants, large, cherry-like fruits. It can provide excellent ground cover in shade. S Europe. In cultivation since the sixteenth century. H4

Ruta *Rutaceae*

A genus of about seven species of evergreen and deciduous shrubs and perennials with aromatic, deeply divided leaves, grown for both flowers and foliage, sometimes for medical purposes. They are native to Europe and south-west Asia. They thrive in sunny, well-drained positions in almost any soil. CAUTION: severely toxic to skin in sunlight.

Ruta graveolens 'Jackman's Blue'

R. graveolens 'Jackman's Blue' This strikingly glaucous-blue form of rue, the one almost invariably grown, is a compact and bushy deciduous shrub. Less than 1m (3ft) high, it has leaves something like the fronds of a maidenhair fern and clusters of small, mustard-yellow flowers in summer. It is a popular herb, but can cause a skin rash to develop on people who are sensitive to it. This can be extremely severe if the plant is handled in strong sunlight. S Europe. In cultivation for several centuries. H4 ♔ 1993

SALIX

Salicaceae

WILLOWS bring to mind sweeps of whippy branches sighing in the wind by a river's bank in summer, heads of bright, naked, pollarded branches glowing redly from water meadows in winter, and soft, silky catkins in spring. Romantic as these rural visions may be, they are grounded in a reality that can be transported without difficulty into the garden.

There are something like 300 deciduous species of willows in nature, from noble, quite lofty trees to small, gnarled alpine bushes or prostrate shrubs of the tundra. It is unfortunate that the variety grown in the majority of gardens is the ubiquitous weeping willow – *S. × sepulchralis* 'Chrysocoma' – which is a fine, perfectly weeping, golden tree of great merit but unexpectedly large and capable of taking up the entire area of some of the small gardens in which one sees it planted. There are so many other willows that deserve popularity but fail to attain it because among gardeners who do not know the great range of beauty of which the genus is capable the word 'willow' conjures up a tree to avoid.

Salix alba 'Britzensis'

For example, a comparatively tiny garden will contain in perfect proportion the perpendicular curtain of branches of the weeping Kilmarnock willow, *S. caprea* 'Kilmarnock', without the slightest danger of its embarking on a land-grabbing career. Still on the smallest scale, the alpine willows such as *S. helvetica, lanata, reticulata* and × *boydii* are ideal for the rock garden or some small corner where their subtle charms can be quietly appreciated.

The garden value of the coloured stems of willows is quite widely known, but perhaps we should be more aware of the variety of colours and of the species that bear them. The brilliant, coral-orange winter stems of *S. alba* 'Britzensis' are indeed popular, but so should be the purple stems of *S. irrorata*, covered in a bloominess of white in winter, and the black-damson shoots of *S. acutifolia* 'Blue Streak'. With willow wands in red, orange, purple, yellow and jade green, the bright scarlet and yellow-ochre available in *Cornus* species, the exquisite patterning of a snakebark maple and the flash of a silver birch, the winter garden can be a most cheerfully decorated place.

The male and female flowers are carried on separate plants, and it is usually the male catkins that give the best display. Flowering is one of the early events of the year, and catkins backlit by the sun of late winter and early spring are stunningly beautiful.

CARE AND CULTIVATION

The willows with coloured stems produce their best effects if they are pruned hard in alternate years in early spring, but apart from this, pruning among willows is hardly necessary. With the exception of some of the alpines, willows enjoy moist, even wet places, but they do not appreciate stagnancy. Provided they have plenty of moisture, they are indifferent to soil and will even grow in sand, though they will not thrive on shallow soils over chalk or any other soil that becomes hot and dry.

There are few problems with willows, although the weeping willow is subject to fungal attacks that cause die-back. It is not advisable to plant any but the alpine willows anywhere near drains, as the roots can invade them.

S. acutifolia **'Blue Streak'** A large, graceful shrub or small tree with lance-shaped, long-pointed leaves and slender, polished, black-purple stems overlaid with a vivid, blue-white bloom. The male catkins appear before the leaves.
H4 ♔ 1993

S. aegyptiaca (Musk willow) A large shrub, occasionally a small tree, with densely grey-downy twigs, and lance-shaped leaves that are downy beneath. Its large, bright yellow male catkins occur in late winter and early spring, making this a very beautiful, early spring-flowering tree. SW to S Asia. In cultivation 1820.
H4

S. alba (White willow) A species of water meadows and riversides, this is a large, elegant, conical tree with slender branches that droop at the tips. The lance-shaped, silkily hairy leaves are in great, billowy masses and create the characteristically silver appearance at a distance. The slender catkins appear with the young leaves in spring. A vigorous, fast-growing tree. Europe, W Asia.
H4

S. a. **'Britzensis'** (Scarlet willow) A remarkable small to medium-sized tree with brilliant orange-scarlet branches in winter, especially if it is pruned severely every second year.
H4 ♔ 1993

S. a. **var.** *caerulea* (Cricket-bat willow) A large tree with leaves that are sea-green above and a little bloomy beneath. Discovered c1700 in Norfolk.
H4

S. a. **'Liempde'** A vigorous male form with upright branches, making a narrow, conical tree.
H4

S. a. **var.** *sericea* A smaller, less vigorous, round-headed tree with silver leaves.
H4 ♔ 1993

S. a. **var.** *vitellina* (Golden willow) A smaller tree than the type with brilliant, yolk-yellow shoots that are made more showy by severe pruning every second year.
H4 ♔ 1993

S. apoda A dwarf species with ground-hugging stems and glossy green leaves. The erect, silver-furry male catkins appear all along the branches in early spring, before the leaves. They gradually become more than 2.5cm (1in) long and turn bright yellow. A good plant for the rock garden. Caucasus, Turkey. In cultivation before 1939.
H4

S. arbuscula A dwarf, creeping shrub forming close mats of green leaves that are glaucous beneath. It produces long, slender catkins as the leaves appear in spring. Scandinavia, N Russia, Scotland.
H4

Salix alba var. vitellina

Salix apoda

S. babylonica (Weeping willow) A medium-sized tree with a wide-spreading head of long, pendulous, brown branches. The leaves are long and narrow, green above and bluish grey beneath. The slender catkins appear with the young leaves in spring. It has now largely been superseded by *S. sepulchralis* 'Chrysocoma' and other similar hybrids. China. Introduced c1730.
H4

S. b. **var.** *pekinensis* **'Pendula'**, syn. *S. matsudana* 'Pendula' A very graceful tree and one of the best weeping willows, showing resistance to scab and canker.
H4

S. b. **var.** *pekinensis* **'Tortuosa'**, syn. *S. matsudana* 'Tortuosa' (Dragon's claw willow) A curious small to medium-sized tree with branches and twigs which are much twisted and contorted.
H4 ♔ 1993

S. × *balfourii* A splendid, strong-growing, medium-sized to large shrub with grey-

Salix babylonica

Salix babylonica var. pekinensis 'Tortuosa'

woolly leaves that become green and downy later. The yellowish, silky-hairy catkins with tiny red bracts appear before the leaves in mid-spring. It is good for growing in damp sites.
H4

S. bockii A small to medium-sized shrub, making a neat, spreading bush 1–1.2m (3–4ft) high. It has slender, reddish twigs and many small, greyish catkins that appear in late summer and autumn along the current year's growth. It is the only willow in gardens to flower at this time of year. W China. Introduced 1908 by Ernest Wilson.
H4

S. × boydii A dwarf, erect, extremely slow-growing, gnarled shrub with round, grey-downy leaves that become grey-green above. It rarely produces catkins but is perfect for a trough or a pocket on the rock garden. It was found just once, by William Brack Boyd and his daughter on a mountain in Angus, Scotland in the 1870s and the oldest specimens in cultivation are little more than 1m (3ft) high.
H4 ♛ 1993

S. 'Caerulea' See *S. alba* var. *caerulea*.

Salix caprea

S. caprea (Goat willow, great sallow) A common European species, known in Britain as pussy willow, and particularly noticeable in spring for its yellow male catkins and silvery female ones. It makes a large shrub or small tree. Europe, W Asia.
H4

S. c. 'Kilmarnock' (Kilmarnock willow) A small, umbrella-like, male tree with stiffly and steeply weeping branches. It rarely

Salix caprea 'Kilmarnock'

grows to as much as 3m (10ft) in height and is an ideal tree for the small garden. It has silver catkins studded with golden anthers in late winter.
H4 ♛ 1993

S. cinerea 'Tricolor' A variegated form of the grey sallow and the only form that has any particular garden merit. It is a large shrub with leaves splashed and mottled with yellow and cream.
H4

S. × cottetii A vigorous, low-growing shrub with long, trailing stems making carpets several metres (yards) across. The leaves are dark, shining green and the catkins appear before the leaves in early spring. It makes good ground cover. European Alps. In cultivation 1905.
H4

S. daphnoides (Violet willow) A fast-growing small tree with long, purple-violet shoots attractively overlaid with a white bloom. The catkins arrive before the leaves in spring. It is extremely effective if hard pruned each or every other year towards the middle of spring. N Europe, C Asia, Himalayas. In cultivation 1829.
H4

S. d. 'Aglaia' A male clone with large, handsome catkins, silvery at first and then bright yellow, in early spring. The stems are red in winter and not bloomed.
H4 ♛ 1993

S. elaeagnos (Hoary willow) A beautiful, medium-sized to large, dense, bushy shrub with leaves like rosemary but much elongated. They are greyish and hoary at first, becoming green above and white beneath,

Salix daphnoides 'Aglaia'

and are thickly deployed along the slender, reddish brown stems. Slender catkins appear with the leaves in spring. One of the prettiest willows for waterside planting. Europe, Asia Minor. Introduced c1820.
H4 ♛ 1993

Salix exigua

S. exigua (Coyote willow) A beautiful, large, erect shrub or small tree with linear, silvery-silky, minutely toothed leaves. The catkins are slender and appear with the leaves. W North America, N Mexico. Introduced 1921.
H4

S. fargesii A medium-sized to large, rather open shrub with polished, reddish brown shoots and elliptical deep glossy green leaves up to 18cm (7in) long, with impressed veins. The catkins appear with or after the leaves and the females are 10–15cm (4–6in) long. C China. Introduced 1911 by Ernest Wilson.
H4

Salix fargesii

S. × finnmarchica A dwarf shrub that forms a low, wide-spreading patch with slender, ascending shoots and small leaves. The small catkins crowd the stems before the leaves in early spring and female clones are the more attractive. It is excellent for the rock garden or as ground cover. N and C Europe.
H4

Salix fragilis

S. fragilis (Crack willow) A large tree with widely spreading branches, often seen by rivers and streams. It has rugged bark, lance-shaped green leaves and slender catkins that appear with the leaves in spring. The twigs are brittle at their joints. Europe, N Asia.
H4

S. glaucosericea An attractive grey dwarf shrub suitable for the rock garden. The leaves are narrowly elliptic to elliptic-lance-olate and are densely grey-hairy at first, becoming less so by autumn. European Alps, Pyrenees.
H4

Salix gracilistyla

S. gracilistyla A splendid, vigorous, medium-sized shrub with silky grey-downy leaves that gradually become green and smooth and remain late in autumn. The catkins appear before the leaves in early spring. The young males are covered with grey silk, through which the reddish, unopened anthers can be seen. Later they develop to become bright yellow. NE Asia. Introduced 1895.
H4

S. g. 'Melanostachys' A form outstanding for the remarkable colour combination of its catkins, which are very dark, with blackish scales and brick-red anthers, opening to yellow. They appear before the leaves. It is a male clone and known only in cultivation.
H4 ♔ 1993

S. grahamii 'Moorei' A dwarf shrub, ideal for the rock garden, forming a low, wide-spreading mound of slender stems.

The leaves are small and shining green, and the catkins appear before the leaves in spring. Discovered 1886 in Co. Donegal by Douglas Moore.
H4

Salix hastata 'Wehrhahnii'

S. hastata 'Wehrhahnii' A slow-growing, small to medium-sized shrub. In spring the stout twigs become alive with pretty, silvery grey, male catkins that later turn yellow. Switzerland. Found c1930.
H4 ♔ 1993

Salix helvetica

S. helvetica A small, bushy shrub with its leaves and catkins clothed in soft, downy hairs. The small leaves are grey-green above and white beneath, and the catkins appear with the young leaves in spring. An attractive foliage shrub for the rock garden. European Alps. In cultivation 1872.
H4 ♔ 1993

S. herbacea (Dwarf willow) A tiny, alpine species that forms mats of creeping, often

underground stems. The rounded, very small leaves are glossy green and net-veined, and borne in pairs or threes at the tips of the shoots. Catkins up to 2cm (1in) long appear with the leaves in spring. It is an interesting and unusual dwarf shrub for a moist position in the peat or rock garden. Europe, N America.
H4

S. hookeriana A medium-sized to large shrub or small tree with glossy, reddish brown branches and oblong leaves that are densely felted beneath. The catkins appear with the leaves. W North America. In cultivation 1891.
H4

Salix integra 'Hakuru Nishiki'

S. integra 'Hakuru Nishiki' An elegant large shrub or small tree with slightly drooping branches and slender catkins on the polished stems before the leaves, which are prettily blotched with white. It is ideal for waterside planting but tends to burn in full sun. Japan. Introduced 1979 by Harry van de Laar.
H4

S. irrorata A vigorous, medium-sized shrub with long shoots that are green at first and then purple, covered with a striking white bloom that is particularly eye-catching in winter. The catkins come before the leaves, the males having brick-red anthers that become yellow. SW United States. Introduced 1898.
H4

S. lanata (Woolly willow) An attractive, slow-growing shrub up to 1.2m (4ft) or occasionally more, with rounded, silvery

Salix irrorata

Salix lanata

grey, downy leaves and erect, yellowish grey, woolly catkins in spring. The female catkins elongate considerably when seeding, sometimes becoming up to 10cm (4in) long. A first-class shrub for growing in the rock garden. N Europe, including Scotland.
H4 ♔ 1993

S. magnifica A large, sparse shrub or small tree with large, magnolia-like leaves up to 20cm (8in) long and 13cm (5in) wide. Catkins are produced with the leaves in spring, and the females are often 15–25cm (6–10in) long. It is a most impressive and unusual species. W China. Introduced 1909 by Ernest Wilson.
H4 ♔ 1993

S. 'Mark Postill' A dwarf, spreading shrub with purplish brown winter shoots and stout catkins that are silvery at first and are produced over a long period with and after the leaves. Raised 1967 by Hillier Nurseries' propagator Alan Postill.
H4

S. matsudana 'Pendula' See *S. babylonica* var. *pekinensis* 'Pendula'.
S. matsudana 'Tortuosa' See *S. babylonica* var. *pekinensis* 'Tortuosa'.
S. moupinensis A beautiful, medium-sized shrub of great quality, related to and generally resembling *S. fargesii*, with which it has often been confused in gardens. It has red-brown shoots and slender erect green catkins. Its leaves, however, are slightly smaller and normally smooth. Both species are highly ornamental at all times of year. China. Introduced 1869 by Armand David and 1910 by Ernest Wilson.
H4

S. × pendulina A small to medium-sized, normally female, weeping tree similar to *S. babylonica* but with a better constitution. Originated in the early nineteenth century in Germany.
H4

S. × p. 'Elegantissima' (Thurlow weeping willow) A form with a widely spreading head of strongly weeping branches, sometimes to be found in cultivation under the name *S. babylonica*, of which it is a hybrid. Catkins are produced with the leaves.
H4

Salix pentandra

S. pentandra (Bay willow) A beautiful small to medium-sized tree with glossy twigs and attractive, lustrous, bay-like leaves that are pleasantly aromatic when unfolding or crushed. The catkins are produced with the leaves in spring, and the males are bright yellow. Found growing wild in N British Isles.
H4

S. purpurea A graceful, medium-sized to large shrub with long, arching, often purplish shoots. The narrowly oblong leaves are dull green above, paler or glaucous beneath. Slender catkins are produced all along the shoots in spring before the leaves. Europe (including the British Isles), C Asia. H4

S. p. **'Nana'** A dwarf, compact, slender-branched shrub that makes a good hedge on a damp site. H4

Salix purpurea 'Pendula'

S. p. **'Pendula'** An attractive form with long, pendulous branches. When trained as a standard it forms a charming, small, weeping tree. H4 ♔ 1993

S. repens **var.** *argentea* A pretty, prostrate shrub with silvery-silky leaves. When trained as a standard it makes an effective, miniature weeping tree. W coast of Europe. H4 ♔ 1993

Salix repens var. argentea

S. r. **'Voorthuizen'** A charming little plant with slender, prostrate stems, small silky leaves and tiny female catkins. Suitable for the small rock garden or scree. H4

S. reticulata A dwarf shrub with prostrate stems forming dense mats. The small, rounded, dark green leaves are attractively net-veined, and erect catkins appear after the leaves. It is dainty and pretty and just right for a moist ledge in the rock garden. Arctic and mountain areas of N America, Europe, N Asia. In cultivation 1789. H4 ♔ 1993

Salix retusa

S. retusa A prostrate species forming extensive carpets of creeping stems and small, notched, shiny green leaves. The catkins are erect, very small, and appear with the leaves. Europe. Introduced 1763. H4

S. × *rubens* **'Basfordiana'** A medium-sized to large tree with long, narrow leaves

Salix × rubens 'Basfordiana'

and bright orange-red twigs in winter. It is male, and has long, slender, yellow catkins with the leaves in spring. Ardennes. Introduced c1863. H4 ♔ 1993

S. × *rubra* **'Eugenei'** A slender, conical, small tree with erect branches and subtly attractive, grey-pink male catkins. H4

S. × *sepulcralis* **'Chrysocoma'** Possibly the most beautiful hardy weeping willow. It is a medium-sized, wide-spreading tree with vigorous, arching branches that end in slender, golden-yellow, weeping branchlets, ultimately of great length. The leaves are slender, and the catkins, which are both male and female, appear with the leaves in mid-spring. It is not suitable, however, for the small gardens in which it is so often planted and it is subject to scab and canker, though these can be controlled by spraying. In cultivation 1888. H4 ♔ 1993

S. × *s.* **'Erythroflexuosa'** A curious, ornamental small tree. The vigorous, orange-yellow, pendulous shoots are twisted and contorted, as are the narrow leaves. Argentina. H4

S. **'Stuartii'** A dwarf, gnarled shrublet, with yellow shoots and orange buds that are outstanding in winter. It is a hybrid of *S. lanata* and has smaller leaves and larger catkins than that species. H4

S. subopposita A rare and very distinct dwarf shrub with slender, erect stems and small leaves that are almost opposite (rather than spirally arranged, as in the genus as a whole). The catkins come before the leaves in early spring, and the males have brick-red anthers that turn yellow. This unusual willow has something of the appearance of a hebe. Japan, Korea. H4

S. udensis **'Sekka'** A large shrub or small tree with curiously recurved and flattened stems and slender, pointed leaves. It is a male clone, with large catkins that appear before the leaves. The stems, which are sought after by flower arrangers, can be encouraged by hard pruning. H4

Salix uva-ursi

S. uva-ursi (Bearberry willow) A prostrate shrub forming dense carpets of creeping stems clothed with small, glossy leaves. The catkins appear with the young leaves. It is a grand plant for the rock garden. Canada, NE United States. Introduced 1880.
H4

S. viminalis (Common osier) A large shrub or small tree with long, straight shoots and long, finely tapering leaves with a covering of silky hairs beneath. The catkins appear before the leaves. It is often seen beside rivers, streams and lakes and has been long cultivated for basket-making. Europe, NE Asia, Himalayas.
H4

S. yezoalpina A prostrate shrub with long, trailing stems and attractive, long-stalked, rounded or obovate glossy green leaves with veins in a conspicuous net pattern. The catkins appear with the leaves in spring. It is a rare alpine species suitable for the rock garden or scree and is now considered to be a variety of *S. nakamurana*. Japan.
H4

Salvia *Labiatae*

A large genus of about 900 semi-evergreen and deciduous species of aromatic, flowering plants, mainly consisting of herbs and sub-shrubs, of which all but S. officinalis *are more or less tender. They need a warm, dry, well-drained position in full sun, and a surprising number will flourish and come through quite sharp winters as long as these conditions are met and they have shelter from winds. The two-lipped flowers are often brightly, even dramatically coloured, and the more tender kinds are excellent cool house or conservatory subjects as long as they are not allowed to become drawn and lanky. Flowering is usually in late summer and autumn and can go on for several weeks; in mild areas some species will flower right through into early winter. Old plants can be pruned severely if required. It is a good idea to take a few cuttings of the more tender salvias; taken in late summer, they will produce flowering plants the following year.*

Salvia elegans

S. elegans (Pineapple sage) A small deciduous species up to 1m (3ft), suitable for a sunny wall, with softly downy, heart-shaped leaves that are scented of pineapple, and loose, leafy panicles of magenta-crimson flowers throughout summer. Mexico. In cultivation before 1873.
H3

Salvia fulgens

S. fulgens (Mexican red sage) A small, upright deciduous species up to 1m (3ft) tall with heart-shaped leaves and long clusters of showy, densely hairy, scarlet flowers, 5cm (2in) long, in late summer. Mexico. Introduced 1829.
H3 ♔ 1993

S. gesneriiflora A small deciduous species related to *S. fulgens* but with even larger, showier flowers of intense scarlet. Texas, Mexico. Introduced 1840.
H3

Salvia guaranitica

S. guaranitica A small deciduous sub-shrub with erect stems up to 1.5m (5ft). It has softly downy, heart-shaped leaves and long racemes of deep azure-blue flowers about 5cm (2in) long during summer and autumn. South America. Introduced 1925.
H4 ♔ 1993

S. interrupta A small, hairy deciduous sub-shrub up to 1m (3ft). The leaves vary from entire, with two basal lobes, to pinnate, with two pairs of leaflets. Violet-purple flowers with a white throat are borne in loose terminal panicles from late spring to midsummer. Morocco. Introduced 1867.
H3

S. involucrata A small deciduous species with ovate, long-pointed leaves and spike-like racemes of rose-magenta flowers that are sticky to the touch. Late summer to autumn. Mexico. Introduced 1824.
H3 ♔ 1993

S. lavandulifolia A dwarf deciduous species with narrow, grey, downy leaves and spike-like racemes of blue-violet flowers in early summer. Spain.
H3–4

S. microphylla var. neurepia A deciduous sub-shrub reaching 1.2m (4ft) high,

Salvia involucrata

Salvia lavandulifolia

Salvia microphylla var. *neurepia*

with showy, bright rosy red flowers in late summer and autumn. Mexico.
H3

S. *officinalis* (Common sage) The well-known, dwarf, semi-evergreen species long cultivated as a herb. The leaves are grey-green and strongly aromatic. The flowers are bluish purple and borne during sum-

Salvia officinalis

mer. Europe. Cultivated in England since 1597 and probably before.
H4

S. o. 'Icterina' A low, spreading form with leaves variegated with green and gold.
H4 ♕ 1993

S. o. 'Purpurascens' (Purple-leaved sage) The stems and young foliage of this form

Salvia officinalis 'Icterina'

Salvia officinalis 'Tricolor'

are suffused with purple. It is particularly effective in coloured foliage groups.
H4 ♕ 1993

S. o. 'Tricolor' A distinct, compact form with grey-green leaves splashed with cream and suffused with purple and pink. It is unlike the other forms in being rather tender, but it is well worth planting each year.
H3

Sambucus *Caprifoliaceae*
Elder

A genus of about 20 species of deciduous shrubs, small trees and perennial herbs, widely distributed in temperate and sub-tropical regions. The cultivated species are hardy and will grow in almost all soils and situations. Few can rely on their flowers for showiness, but many have highly ornamental foliage and fruits. They all have pinnate leaves and serrated leaflets. If you wish to encourage the production of large flowerheads or lush foliage, cut back the lateral branches to within a short distance from the previous year's growth in early spring. Ideal subjects for the wild garden.

Sambucus canadensis 'Maxima'

S. *canadensis* 'Maxima' A handsome form of the American elderberry, this is a strong shrub of medium to large size. The leaves have 5–11 (usually 7) leaflets and are 30–45cm (12–18in) long. The enormous flowerheads are 30cm (12in) or more across and the rose-purple flower stalks, which remain after the flowers have fallen, are an added attraction. It is a bold shrub that should be pruned each spring to encourage production of new shoots.
H4

Sambucus nigra

Sambucus nigra 'Guincho Purple'

Sambucus nigra 'Pulverulenta'

S. nigra (Common elder) A large shrub or small tree that is familiar to Europeans as a native. It has rugged bark and leaves with 5–7 leaflets. The flattened heads of cream, sweetly fragrant flowers are borne in early summer and followed by heavy bunches of shining black fruits. The flowers and fruits are used in the making of country wines. It grows well in extremely chalky places. Europe, North Africa and W Asia. Long cultivated.
H4

Sambucus nigra 'Aurea'

S. n. 'Aurea' (Golden elder) The leaves of this form are attractive golden yellow, deepening with age. It is one of the hardiest and best golden-foliaged shrubs available. In cultivation 1883.
H4 ♔ 1993

S. n. 'Aureomarginata' The leaflets of this form have an irregular, bright yellow margin.
H4

S. n. 'Guincho Purple' In this form the leaves are green when young and become deep blackish purple then red in autumn. The flowers are pink in bud, opening to white flushed with pink, and the stalks are stained with purple.
H4 ♔ 1993

Sambucus nigra f. *laciniata*

S. n. f. laciniata (Fern-leaved elder) An attractive large shrub with finely divided, fern-like leaves.
H4 ♔ 1993

S. n. 'Marginata' The leaflets of this large shrub have an irregular cream margin.
H4

S. n. 'Pulverulenta' A slow-growing but most effective medium-sized shrub with white-striped and -mottled leaves.
H4

S. n. 'Pyramidalis' A stiff, erect medium-sized or large shrub, wider above than below, with densely clustered leaves.
H4

Sambucus nigra 'Pyramidalis'

S. racemosa (Red-berried elder) A medium-sized to large shrub with leaves that have 5–7 coarsely toothed leaflets. The yellowish white flowers are in conical heads and crowd the branches in mid-spring followed by dense clusters of bright scarlet berries which ripen in summer. Used as game cover in parts of England and Scotland. Europe, W Asia. In cultivation in England since the sixteenth century. The following forms are recommended.
H4

S. r. 'Plumosa Aurea' A colourful medium-sized shrub with beautiful, deeply cut, golden foliage. It is one of the elite of golden-leaved shrubs, fairly slow growing and best in light shade to avoid sun-scorch. The flowers are rich yellow.
H4

S. r. 'Sutherland Gold' An excellent plant, like 'Plumosa Aurea' but more coarsely textured and less liable to scorch in the sun.
H4 ♔ 1993

Sambucus racemosa 'Plumosa Aurea'

Santolina chamaecyparissus

Sambucus racemosa 'Sutherland Gold'

S. r. 'Tenuifolia' A small, slow-growing shrub forming a low mound of arching branches and with finely divided, fern-like leaves. It is as beautiful as a cut-leaved Japanese maple and a good substitute on chalky soils. A good rock-garden plant. H4 ♔ 1993

Santolina *Compositae*
Lavender cotton

Low-growing, mound-forming, evergreen sub-shrubs with dense, grey, green or silvery, finely divided foliage and dainty, button-like flowerheads on tall stalks in midsummer. They need a sunny position in any well-drained soil. They are natives of the Mediterranean region and there are about five species in all.

S. chamaecyparissus A charming dwarf species, particularly valued for its woolly, silvery-hued, feathery foliage. Its flower-heads are bright lemon-yellow. S France,

Pyrenees. In cultivation in England since the sixteenth century.
H4 ♔ 1993
S. c. 'Nana' A more dwarf, denser, more compact form, ideal for the rock garden.
H4 ♔ 1993

Santolina chamaecyparissus 'Nana'

S. pinnata A dwarf sub-shrub related to *S. chamaecyparissus* but differing in its longer, finely divided leaves and off-white flower-heads. Italy.
H4
S. p. subsp. neapolitana A dwarf sub-shrub similar to *S. chamaecyparissus* but rather looser in growth and with longer, more feathery leaves. The flowers are bright lemon-yellow. Italy.
H4 ♔ 1993
S. p. 'Edward Bowles' A charming form, similar to 'Sulphurea' but with foliage that is more grey-green and flowerheads of much paler yellow, almost cream.
H4

Santolina chamaecyparissus 'Edward Bowles'

S. p. 'Sulphurea' A form with grey-green foliage and pale yellow flowerheads.
H4
S. rosmarinifolia A dwarf species with thread-like vivid green leaves. The flower-heads are bright lemon-yellow. SW Europe. In cultivation 1727.
H4

Santolina rosmarinifolia 'Primrose Gem'

565

S. r. 'Primrose Gem' A lovely form only 30cm (12in) high, with pale primrose-yellow flowerheads. Originated before 1960 at Hillier Nurseries.
H4 ♔ 1993

Sapium *Euphorbiaceae*

A genus of 100 or more species of deciduous trees and shrubs, almost all from the tropics. They will grow in any well-drained fertile soil and prefer a sunny position.

S. japonicum A rare small tree or shrub that has proved hardy at Hillier Nurseries. It has greyish branches and smooth, dark green, more or less elliptic, entire leaves that turn glowing crimson in autumn. The inconspicuous flowers appear in early summer in slender, axillary, greenish yellow, catkin-like clusters. The seed capsules are like large capers, three-lobed, green and finally brown. Japan, China, Korea.
H3–4

Sarcococca *Buscaceae*
Christmas box

A genus of about 14 species, native to eastern and South East Asia. They are shade-bearing dwarf to small shrubs, with glossy evergreen foliage. The small, white, fragrant male flowers open during late winter, with the tiny female ones occurring in the same cluster. They succeed in any fertile soil and are especially happy on chalk soils. With one or two exceptions, they slowly reach 1.2–1.5m (4–5ft). They are excellent for cutting, as their foliage is attractive all year round, the flowers are powerfully scented, and they last well in a vase, though they should not be overdone when in flower, as their perfume may then be too strong.

S. confusa A dense, spreading, hardy small shrub with elliptic, taper-pointed leaves and highly fragrant, white flowers with cream anthers. It has black berries. China. In cultivation 1916.
H4 ♔ 1993
S. hookeriana A rare, erectly growing small species with lance-shaped leaves, white flowers and black berries. Himalayas.
H4 ♔ 1993
S. h. var. digyna A slightly hardier small

Sarcococca confusa

Sarcococca hookeriana

Sarcococca hookeriana var. digyna

form with leaves that are more slender. The true plant has female flowers with two stigmas rather than three.
H4 ♔ 1993
S. h. 'Purple Stem' An attractive small shrub with the young stems, leaf stalks and midribs flushed with purple.
H4

Sarcococca hookeriana 'Purple Stem'

Sarcococca hookeriana var. humilis

S. h. var. humilis A dwarf, dense shrub that suckers to form clumps and is seldom more than 60cm (2ft) high. The male flowers have pink anthers and the berries are black. China. Introduced 1907.
H4 ♔ 1993
S. orientalis A strong-growing, upright small shrub with leaves that are three-

Sarcococca orientalis

veined, wedge-shaped at the base and pointed. The flowers are fragrant and the fruits black. E China. Introduced 1980 by Roy Lancaster.
H4

S. ruscifolia var. *chinensis* A small, fairly slow-growing shrub similar in general appearance to *S. confusa*, but with dark red berries. C and W China.
H4 ♛ 1993

Sasa *Gramineae*

A genus of between 40 and 50 species of small, thicket-forming evergreen bamboos, natives of Japan, Korea and China. They have a typically low habit and relatively broad leaves. They are moisture-lovers but will grow effectively on good soil over chalk.

S. palmata A rampant, large-leaved bamboo that forms extensive thickets of green canes 2–2.5m (7–8ft) high. The leaves are up to 35cm (14in) long by 9cm (3½in) wide and the margins often wither during a hard winter. Although too invasive for the small garden it is an excellent shelter plant where there is enough space for it. Japan. Introduced 1889.
H4 ♛ 1993

Sasa ramosa

S. ramosa A dwarf, creeping species that quickly makes extensive carpets of bright green foliage. The canes are 0.4–1.1m (16in–3½ft) high, bright green at first, becoming deep olive-green, bearing a solitary branch from each joint. The leaves are 5–15cm (2–6in) long by 1–2cm (½–¾in)

wide and downy on both surfaces. It is too rampant for most gardens but makes an excellent ground cover plant where little else will grow, even in dense shade. Japan. Introduced 1892.
H4

Sasa veitchii

S. veitchii A small, dense species forming large thickets of deep purplish green, later purple, canes 0.6–1.2m (2–4ft) high. The leaves are 10–25cm (4–10in) long by 2.5–6cm (1–2½in) wide, withering and becoming pale straw-coloured or whitish along the margins in autumn, providing an attractive variegated effect that lasts throughout the winter. Invasive. Japan. Introduced 1880.
H3–4

Sassafras *Lauraceae*

A genus of three species of deciduous trees needing a lime-free soil and a slightly sheltered position.

S. albidum An attractive and distinct, aromatic, medium-sized, suckering tree. It is broadly conical and has zig-zag branches that show up well in winter. The leaves vary in shape and may have one or two conspicuous lobes or none at all. Some of the leaves have much the same outline as those of a fig (*Ficus carica*). They are dark green above, paler beneath and change to red and gold in autumn. The flowers, which appear in late spring, are not of any great account. The young growth is vulnerable to frost. E United States. Introduced 1633.
H4

Sassafras albidum

Saxegothaea *Podocarpaceae*

There is just one evergreen coniferous species in this genus, which was named after Albert of Saxe-Coburg-Gotha, Prince Consort of Queen Victoria.

S. conspicua (Prince Albert's yew) An unusual large shrub or small tree of loose

Saxegothaea conspicua

habit, with laxly spreading branches arranged in whorls of three or four and drooping branchlets. The linear leaves are up to 2cm (¾in) long, dark green, and marked with two blue bands beneath. They are rather twisted and are arranged on the lateral branches in two ranks. The fruits are up to 2cm (¾in) across, soft and prickly. It will grow in any fertile friable soil and does best in shade. Chile, Patagonia. Introduced 1847 by William Lobb.
H4

Schima *Theaceae*

A small genus of uncommon evergreen trees and shrubs, requiring a lime-free soil in a sheltered position. Now usually regarded as consisting of one variable species.

S. argentea A medium-sized to large, erect, bushy shrub with leaves that taper to both ends and are shiny dark green above and usually bloomy beneath. The flowers are cream, like small camellias, about 4cm (1½in) wide, and produced on the young wood in late summer. This distinct and most attractive member of the camellia family has reached 5m (15ft) at the Hillier Gardens and Arboretum in 40 years. China, Assam, Taiwan.
H3

Schisandra *Schisandraceae*

A genus of some 25 species of evergreen and deciduous twining shrubs from Asia, with one species in North America. They are charming plants of considerable quality and bear their clusters of flowers in the axils of the leaves, after which female plants bear long, pendulous spikes of attractive berries. They are suitable for growing on walls or fences or over shrubs and into trees and will grow well in any fertile, well-drained but moisture-retentive soil, preferably out of the hottest sun. Any pruning that is necessary for the removal of dead wood or for training should be done in late winter or early spring.

S. grandiflora A medium-sized deciduous climber with fairly leathery leaves, 7.5–10cm (3–4in) long and with conspicuous veins. The flowers, 2.5–3cm (1–1¼in)

across, are white or pale pink, borne on drooping stalks in late spring and early summer. The berries are scarlet. Himalayas.
H3–4

S. propinqua var. chinensis A hardy medium-sized deciduous climber with short-stalked, orange flowers in late summer and autumn. The leaves are long persistent and the berries are scarlet. China. Introduced 1907.
H4

Schisandra rubriflora

S. rubriflora A medium-sized deciduous climber closely related to *S. grandiflora* but with deep crimson flowers on pendulous stalks in late spring. The berries are scarlet. Himalayan region. Introduced 1908.
H3–4

S. sphenanthera A strong-growing medium-sized deciduous climber with leaves broadest above the middle and flowers of a distinct shade of orange-red, verging on terracotta, that are borne on slender stalks in late spring and early summer. The berries are scarlet. China. Introduced 1907 by Ernest Wilson.
H4

Schizophragma *Hydrangeaceae*

A genus of four species of deciduous ornamental climbers that support themselves by means of aerial roots. The small, creamy flowers are densely borne in large, flattened heads, each of which is attended by several large, cream, sterile flowers. They will grow in all types of soil and are suitable for shady walls, though flowering best in sun. They are most

effective when allowed to climb a large tree or an old stump. Although eventually tall, they are slow starters and need a fair amount of cultural encouragement in the early years.

Schizophragma hydrangeoides

S. hydrangeoides A superb climber, reaching 12m (40ft) or more. The leaves are coarsely toothed and the flowerheads are 20–25cm (8–10in) across with white or ivory bracts 2.5–4cm (1–1½in) long. Japan.
H4

Schizophragma hydrangeoides 'Roseum'

S. h. 'Roseum' A lovely form with rose-blushed bracts.
H4

S. integrifolium A climber of much the same size as *S. hydrangeoides* but with smooth-edged leaves or just a few small, narrow teeth. The flowerheads are often as much as 30cm (1ft) across and the bracts can be 6–9cm (2½–3½in) long. They are borne freely in midsummer. It is a magnificent species, larger in all its parts than *S.*

Schizophragma integrifolium

hydrangeoides. A native of C China. Introduced 1901 by Ernest Wilson.
H4 ⚲ 1993

Sciadopitys *Taxodiaceae*

A genus of one evergreen coniferous species.

Sciadopitys verticillata

S. verticillata (Umbrella pine) A slow-growing, hardy tree of medium size. It is dense and conical when young, usually with a single trunk, sometimes with several main stems. The bark peels to reveal the reddish brown new bark. The branches are horizontal and bear lush clusters of rich, glossy green foliage. The apparently single linear leaves, up to 13cm (5in) long, are in fact fused pairs and are arranged in dense whorls like the spokes of an umbrella. The attractive cones, 6–10cm (2½–4in) long, are green at first and ripen to brown in the second year. Japan. Introduced 1861
H4 ⚲ 1993

Semiarundinaria *Gramineae*

A small genus of evergreen bamboos native to eastern Asia. They are moisture-lovers but will grow on good soil over chalk.

Semiarundinaria fastuosa

S. fastuosa A hardy, vigorous, stiffly erect bamboo that forms tall, dense clumps of deep glossy green canes 4.5–7.5m (13–24ft) high, which are useful as stakes. The leaves are 10–25cm (4–10in) long and up to 2.5cm (1in) wide. It is a distinctively handsome species that makes an excellent screen or tall hedge. Japan. Introduced 1892.
H4 ⚲ 1993

Senecio *Compositae*

A very large genus of 1500 or more species of annuals and perennials, shrubs and climbers, widely distributed throughout the world. S. scandens is the only hardy climber likely to be met with in cultivation. The shrubby members are mostly evergreen and bear heads or panicles of white or yellow daisy flowers in summer. They are all sun-lovers and are excellent by the sea. However, with rare exceptions the woody species will not tolerate low continental temperatures, although they resist wind well. Most of those listed below are from New Zealand.

S. bidwillii A striking, dwarf, evergreen, alpine shrub of compact, rigid habit that very slowly reaches 0.75m (30in). The more or less elliptical leaves, up to 2.5cm (1in) long, are remarkably thick, shining green above and covered beneath, like the stems, in a soft white or buff, woolly felt. The flow-

ers are not very decorative. New Zealand.
H3–4

S. compactus A small, compact evergreen shrub up to 1m (3ft) high, making a dense, broad mound. The oval leaves are up to 5cm (2in) long, wavy-edged and white-felted beneath, as are the shoots and flower stalks. The flowerheads are bright yellow. It is subject to injury in severe winters. See also *S.* Dunedin Hybrids. One locality in North Island of New Zealand.
H3

Senecio 'Drysdale'

S. 'Drysdale' A small evergreen shrub similar to 'Sunshine' but with slightly larger flowers and scalloped leaves.
H3–4

S. Dunedin Hybrids This name encompasses various hybrids and back-crosses that have occurred between *S. compactus*, *S. greyi* and *S. laxifolius* and are now more commonly grown than any of the parents. The most frequently seen, previously grown as

Senecio elaeagnifolius

S. greyi and *S. laxifolius*, both of which are extremely rare in cultivation, has been named 'Sunshine'.
H3–4

S. elaeagnifolius A medium-sized, rigid, dense evergreen shrub with oval, leathery leaves 7.5–15cm (3–6in) long. They are glossy above, and their undersides are thickly buff-felted, as are the young shoots and flower stalks. The flowerheads are not very ornamental. It is an excellent coastal shrub. New Zealand.
H3–4

S. greyi See *S.* 'Sunshine' and *S.* Dunedin Hybrids.

Senecio heritieri

S. heritieri A small, loosely growing evergreen shrub with broad leaves 10–15cm (4–6in) long. The young stems and the leaf undersides are covered with a dense white felt. The flowerheads are white and crimson with purple centres, violet-scented, recalling the popular cineraria, and are borne in large panicles from late spring to midsummer. It is suitable only for the mildest areas or the conservatory. Tenerife. Introduced 1774.
H2–3

S. laxifolius See *S.* 'Sunshine'.

S. 'Moira Read' A small evergreen shrub also similar to 'Sunshine' but with the leaves blotched with creamy yellow.
H3–4

S. monroi A small, dense shrub often forming a broad dome, easily recognized by its oblong or oval, conspicuously undulate leaves that are covered beneath, like the young shoots and flower stalks, with a dense

Senecio monroi

white felt. The yellow flowerheads are in dense terminal clusters. New Zealand.
H3 ♔ 1993

S. reinoldii (Muttonbird scrub) A medium-sized, dense, rounded evergreen shrub with thick, leathery, rounded leaves 5–13cm (2–5in) long, shining green above and felted below. The flowers are yellowish and not outstanding. It is nevertheless one of the best shrubs for windswept gardens by the sea and will take the full blast of the ocean. New Zealand.
H3

Senecio reinoldii

S. scandens A fairly vigorous, semi-evergreen, semi-woody climber with stems up to 4m (18ft) long. The conspicuous small, bright yellow, short-rayed flowerheads are produced in large panicles in autumn. It is best planted where it can scramble over bushes and into small, densely branched trees. It needs a sunny, sheltered site and, although in cold areas it

is frequently cut to the ground in winter, it will normally spring again from the base. E Asia. Introduced 1895.
H3

Senecio 'Sunshine'

S. 'Sunshine' A grey shrub, making a mound up to 1m (3ft) high and 2m (6½ft) wide. The evergreen leaves are silvery grey when young and become green above. The flowerheads are yellow and borne in large, dome-shaped clusters.
H3–4

Senecio viravara

S. viravara A strikingly beautiful, lax, silvery white, medium-sized evergreen shrub with finely divided pinnate leaves. Its branches have a climbing tendency and this, together with its tender nature, demands a sunny wall. The flowers, borne in summer, are not very ornamental, and it is grown for the superb effect of its foliage. Argentina. Introduced 1893.
H3

Senna *Leguminosae*

A large genus of about 240 species of deciduous trees, shrubs and herbs with a wide tropical and sub-tropical distribution. The leaves are evenly pinnate and the pods produce the senna of medicinal use. The following requires a warm, sheltered, sunny site or (more usually) a conservatory.

Senna × floribunda

S. × **floribunda** A handsome, vigorous shrub for a wall. Its leaves have 4–5 pairs of leaflets and the flowers, which are large and rich, deep yellow, are borne in terminal clusters in late summer and autumn. It is widely naturalized in warm parts of the world. In cultivation c1800.
H2

Sequoia *Taxodiaceae*

A genus of one evergreen coniferous species.

S. sempervirens (Californian redwood) A very large tree, over 100m (330ft) high in its native forest but usually up to 30m (100ft) in gardens. It has a thick, fibrous, reddish brown outer bark that is soft and spongy. The branches are slightly drooping, yew-like, and bear linear-oblong leaves in two ranks. The redwood is the world's tallest living tree and one of the most long-lived, with a specimen having been dated at 2,200 years. In cultivation it is hardy in Britain and Ireland but can be burned brown by cold winter winds, after which it recovers. In the southern end of its native range, where there is little rain, it depends on

Sequoia sempervirens

coastal fog for moisture, and does best in cultivation in moist, humid areas. It will, however, grow on chalk soils as long as there is a reasonable layer – about 60cm (2ft) deep – of loamy soil above the chalk.
H4 🏆 1993

S. s. 'Adpressa', syn. *S. s.* 'Albospica' The tips of the young shoots are cream. It is

Sequoia sempervirens 'Adpressa'

Sequoia sempervirens 'Prostrata'

often grown as a dwarf shrub but unless frequently cut back will eventually make a large tree.
H4

S. s. 'Albospica' See *S. s.* 'Adpressa'.

S. s. 'Prostrata' A most remarkable dwarf form with spreading branches that are thickly clothed with comparatively broad, glaucous green, two-ranked leaves.
H4

Sequoiadendron

A genus of one evergreen coniferous species.

Sequoiadendron giganteum

S. giganteum (Big tree, wellingtonia) A very large tree in the wild and a large one in cultivation. It has deeply furrowed, reddish brown outer bark, similar to that of *Sequoia sempervirens*. When young it is densely branched and conical; later the branches are more widely spaced and conspicuously down-swept. Sometimes the trunk is clear

of branches for a considerable distance from the ground. The leaves, which persist for up to four years, are awl-shaped, up to 12mm (½in) long, and spirally arranged. In California it grows on the western slopes of the Sierra Nevada and, although never as tall as the redwood, it attains greater girths, and the 'General Sherman' tree, 84m (275ft) high and with a girth of 25m (82ft), is the world's largest living thing. The oldest authenticated felled specimen was about 3,200 years old, and this puts the wellingtonia among the oldest living things as well. In moist temperate gardens it is the largest tree of all and will grow in almost all conditions. This applies in most of Western Europe and in New Zealand. In North America, however, it will hardly grow at all away from its extremely limited native range.
H4 ♔ 1993

Sequoiadendron giganteum 'Pendulum'

S. g. 'Pendulum' A tree of unique appearance, often assuming the most fantastic shapes, but usually forming a tall, narrow column with long branches hanging almost parallel with the trunk.
H4

Shibataea *Gramineae*

A small genus of low-growing evergreen bamboos from China and Japan. They are moisture-lovers but will grow on good soil over chalk.

S. kumasasa A very distinct, dwarf, compact bamboo. The canes, which are 50–80cm (20–32in) high, zig-zag character-istically and are almost triangular in outline. They are pale green at first, maturing to a dull, brownish tone. The leaves are 5–10cm (2–4in) long by 2–3cm (¾–1¼in) wide. It is a charming species, forming dense, leafy clumps, that is especially happy in a moist soil. Japan. Introduced 1861.
H4

Sinarundinaria

A genus of some 50 evergreen bamboos, natives of China and the Himalayas. They are moisture-lovers but will grow on good soil over chalk.

S. anceps See *Yushania anceps*.

Sinarundinaria nitida

S. nitida, syn. *Arundinaria nitida* This beautiful, clump-forming species is often confused with *Thamnocalamus spathaceus* but has purple-flushed canes and narrower leaves. It is one of the most elegant and ornamental of all bamboos, with canes 3–4m (10–12ft) high or more, arching at the summits under the weight of foliage. The leaves are 5–8cm (2–3in) long by 6–12mm (¼–½in) wide, thin and delicate. It thrives best in a little shade and makes an excellent specimen plant. It may also be grown in a large tub. China. In cultivation 1889.
H4 ♔ 1993

Sinocalycanthus *Calycanthaceae*

A genus of one deciduous species closely related to Calycanthus *and originally included in it.*

S. chinensis A shrub reaching about 3m (10ft) in height with leaves up to 15cm (6in) long, glossy green turning yellow in autumn. The nodding flowers, 7cm (2½in) across, are borne singly at the ends of the shoots in early summer. They are composed of two whorls of about ten tepals, the outer ones white, sometimes flushed pink, the inner ones smaller, pale yellow, and white at the base with maroon markings. E China. Introduced 1983.
H4

Skimmia *Rutaceae*

A genus of four species of slow-growing, aromatic, evergreen shrubs or trees, natives of the Himalaya and east Asia. All those listed below, with the exception of S. japonica *subsp.* reevesiana, *bear male and female flowers on separate plants and you will need both sexes if the brightly coloured berries, which persist throughout the winter, are to be produced. They are tolerant of shade and industrial pollution and are ideal for seaside gardens. Any good soil, preferably on the light side but fairly rich, will suit them.*

S. anquetilia A small shrub that has previously been distributed as *S. laureola* female. The true *S. laureola* has been introduced but is very rare in cultivation. *S. anquetilia* has pungently aromatic leaves, greenish yellow flowers and bright red fruits; the true *S. laureola* is small and creeping, with cream or greenish white flowers and black berries. Himalayas. Introduced 1841.
H4

S. × confusa 'Kew Green' A small, mound-forming male shrub with broad

Skimmia × *confusa* 'Kew Green'

Skimmia japonica 'Nymans'

leaves. It is the best of the genus for flower, having very large clusters of highly fragrant, creamy blooms.
H4 ♔ 1993

S. japonica A variable, small, dome-shaped shrub with leathery leaves and dense terminal panicles of white, often fragrant flowers in mid- to late spring. On female plants they are followed by clusters of globular, bright red fruits where both sexes are grown. It is most adaptable and equally at home on chalk or acid soils. The following forms are recommended.
H4

Skimmia japonica 'Fragrans'

S. j. 'Fragrans' A free-flowering male clone bearing dense panicles of white flowers with a scent of lily-of-the-valley.
H4 ♔ 1993

S. j. 'Fructu-albo' A rather weak, low-growing, compact female clone with small leaves and white flowers.
H4

S. j. 'Nymans' An extremely free-fruiting form with comparatively large fruits.
H4 ♔ 1993

S. j. 'Red Riding Hood' A dwarf, mound-forming shrub with small leaves. It is a female with red berries.
H4

Skimmia japonica subsp. *reevesiana* 'Robert Fortune'

S. j. subsp. *reevesiana* 'Robert Fortune' This name applies to the commonly grown clone deriving from the original introduction. It is a dwarf shrub, rarely reaching the height of 1m (3ft), and forms a low, compact mound. The leaves are narrowly elliptic, often with a pale margin. The flowers are hermaphrodite, white, and in short terminal panicles in late spring. The matt, bright red berries are egg-shaped, and last throughout the winter and usually until the flowers appear again in spring. Unlike other forms of *S. japonica*, this plant will not grow very well on chalky soils. S China,

SE Asia. Introduced 1849.
H4 ♔ 1993

S. j. 'Rogersii' A dense, dwarf, slow-growing female with curved or twisted leaves and large red fruits.
H4

S. j. 'Rogersii Nana' A free-flowering male clone, similar to 'Rogersii' but even more dwarf, slower growing and with smaller leaves.
H4

Skimmia japonica 'Rubella'

S. j. 'Rubella' A small male shrub with large, open panicles of red buds throughout the winter, opening in early spring into white, yellow-anthered flowers. It is of great value in the winter garden.
H4 ♔ 1993

S. j. 'Ruby King' A small male shrub with narrow, taper-pointed, dark green leaves and large, conical panicles of flowers from deep red buds. Male.
H4

S. j. 'Veitchii' A vigorous female clone with distinctly broad leaves and large bunches of brilliant orange-red fruits. It is usually grown as 'Foremanii'.
H4

Smilax *Smilacaceae*

A large genus of 200 or more species of evergreen and deciduous plants, the majority of them climbing. Their often prickly stems are tough and wiry, and they support themselves by means of tendrils. They are normally grown for their rich, often glossy green foliage and are excellent for covering stumps, low walls and so on. In most the flowers are of little beauty. They will grow in sun or shade in any ordinary soil.

S. china A deciduous shrub with rounded, prickly, scrambling stems. The leaves are variable, usually roundish ovate with a heart-shaped base, often turning red in autumn. Greenish yellow flowers are borne in late spring, followed by bright red fruits. China, Japan, Korea. Introduced 1759.
H4

Solanum *Solanaceae*

A very large genus of about 1500 species, mainly herbaceous plants but also encompassing some semi-evergreen or deciduous climbers, shrubs and sub-shrubs, widely distributed throughout the world and including several, such as the potato (S. tuberosum), *that are economically important. The climbing members of the genus make spectacular wall climbers for sheltered gardens, requiring full sun but not fastidious as to soil.*

S. crispum 'Glasnevin' A vigorous, semi-evergreen climber with scrambling, normally herbaceous stems up to 6m (18ft) long. The flowers are very slightly fragrant, a little more than 2.5cm (1in) across, and similar to those of a potato but rich purple-blue with a bright yellow beak of stamens. In loose clusters, they are borne very freely over a long season from midsummer well into autumn. It is beautiful when trained on a wall or allowed to scramble over a fence or shed. It is hardier than *S. jasminoides* and grows very well indeed in a chalk soil.
H3 ♆ 1993

Solanum jasminoides 'Album'

S. jasminoides 'Album' A fast-growing, semi-evergreen climber with twining stems up to 9m (28ft) long in mild areas. The flowers are 2cm (³⁄₄in) across, white with a staminal beak, and profusely borne in loose clusters from midsummer until the frosts. It needs the protection of a sunny wall.
H3 ♆ 1993

Solanum laciniatum

S. laciniatum (Kangaroo apple) A beautiful deciduous sub-shrub with purple stems up to 2m (6¹⁄₂ft) high. The leaves are lance-shaped and deeply cut into irregular lobes. The very attractive flowers, violet with a yellow beak, are borne in loose clusters during summer. They are followed by small, egg-shaped fruits that change from green to

Solanum crispum 'Glasnevin'

yellow. It is a vigorous species for the very mildest areas, where it sometimes seeds itself. It can be grown in the conservatory, but it should be noted that this plant is poisonous in all its parts. Australia.
H2–3

Sollya *Pittosporaceae*

A genus of three species of extremely beautiful evergreen climbers from south-west Australia only suitable for the mildest locations or the conservatory. They require a sunny, sheltered position and a well-drained soil.

S. heterophylla A beautiful plant with slender stems up to 2m (6½ft) or more. The leaves are usually ovate to lanceolate, 2.5–5cm (1–2in) long. Nodding clusters of sky-blue flowers are freely borne during summer and autumn. Introduced 1830.
H1–2

Sophora *Leguminoseae*

A genus of about 80 species of evergreen and deciduous sun-loving trees, shrubs and herbaceous perennials. The following are much valued for their elegant pinnate leaves and bright floral display. They grow well in all well-drained, fertile soils.

Sophora davidii

S. davidii A medium-sized to large deciduous shrub with grey-downy later spiny branches. The leaves have 7–10 pairs of leaflets, and the small, bluish white pea-flowers are borne in short, terminal clusters in early summer. China. Introduced 1897.
H4

Sophora japonica

S. japonica (Japanese pagoda tree) A medium-sized to large, normally rounded deciduous tree with leaves up to 30cm (1ft) long, composed of 9–15 leaflets. The creamy pea-flowers are in large terminal clusters in late summer and autumn, but are not borne on young trees. China. Introduced 1753.
H4 ♛ 1993

S. j. 'Pendula' A picturesque small weeping tree with stiffly drooping branchlets. It is an admirable lawn specimen and also forms a natural arbour.
H4

S. j. 'Regent' A vigorous medium-sized shrub with dark glossy green leaves that flowers at a relatively early age.
H4

Sophora microphylla 'Sun King'

S. microphylla 'Sun King' (*S. m.* 'Hilsop' PBR 5683) Although the species is a large evergreen shrub, this is a more bushy and very hardy form with small, pinnate leaves

and somewhat elongated, large, bright yellow flowers in early to late spring. At the Hillier Gardens and Arboretum in England it has survived several cold winters in exposed positions.
H4

S. prostrata A small evergreen shrub, occasionally prostrate in habit but usually forming a broad, rounded hummock of wiry, interlacing stems. The leaves have between 6 and 8 pairs of tiny leaflets. The small, brownish yellow to orange pea-flowers are borne singly or in clusters of 2–3 in late spring. New Zealand.
H3–4

Sophora tetraptera

S. tetraptera (Kowhai) A large evergreen shrub or small tree, best grown against a sunny wall. The spreading or drooping branches are covered when young with a yellow down and the leaves have 10–20 pairs of leaflets. The flowers are pea-shaped but somewhat tubular, bright yellow, up to

5cm (2in) long, and in drooping clusters in late spring. The seed pods look like rows of beads. New Zealand. Introduced 1772. H3–4 🏆 1993

S. t. 'Grandiflora' A form with large leaflets and slightly larger flowers. H3–4

Sorbaria *Rosaceae*

A genus of four to five handsome, vigorous deciduous shrubs with elegant pinnate leaves that distinguish them from Spiraea. *They have white or creamy flowers in terminal panicles during summer and early autumn, and even in winter their brownish or reddish stems and seedheads are attractive. They thrive in most soils, flowering best in full sun. The old flowering stems can be hard pruned in late winter or early spring to encourage production of strong, vigorous shoots.*

S. aitchisonii A most elegant medium-sized shrub with long, spreading branches

that are reddish when young. The leaves have 11–23 sharply toothed and tapered leaflets and the creamy flowers are borne in large, conical panicles in mid- to late summer. Afghanistan. Introduced 1895. H4 🏆 1993

S. arborea, syn. *S. kirilowii* A large, robust shrub with strong, spreading, arching stems

Sorbaria arborea

and large leaves composed of 13–17 lance-shaped slender-pointed leaflets which are downy beneath. The white flowers are borne in large, conical panicles at the ends of the current year's growths in mid- to late summer. C and W China. Introduced 1908 by Ernest Wilson. H4

S. kirilowii See *S. arborea*.

Sorbaria sorbifolia

S. sorbifolia A small to medium-sized, suckering shrub with erect stems and leaves made up of 13–25 sharply pointed leaflets. The flowers are borne in narrow, stiffly erect panicles in mid- to late summer. N Asia. Introduced 1759. H4

Sorbaria aitchisonii

Sorbaria tomentosa

S. tomentosa A large, strong, spreading shrub bearing large leaves composed of 11–23 deeply toothed leaflets, and yellowish white flowers. Himalayas. H4

SORBUS

Rosaceae

IF YOU are looking for a good tree for a small garden, it pays to choose from among those that are ornamental for a large part of the year; space is too precious for it to be taken up by trees that spend much of their time being quite ordinary and put on a display for only about a month. Eleven months of dullness is something to be avoided at all costs. *Sorbus* provides a wide and fascinating range of deciduous trees for all sizes of gardens, most of them easily grown in any good, fertile soil. There are, however, distinct groups in the genus, and it is as well to look at them separately in order to see what they have to offer.

The best-known group is the one called Aucuparia, which consists of the trees known in Britain as mountain ash (in Australia this name belongs to *Eucalyptus regnans*, an example of how misleading the use of common names can be). These have pinnate leaves with numerous leaflets and present a delightful, ferny aspect all the time they are in leaf. They often colour deliciously in autumn. Their clusters of off-white flowers are quite attractive and are succeeded by berries that range from bright red, pink and orange to yellow and white. They are often coloured by late summer and the amber, yellow and, especially, white ones may remain on the trees well into late autumn or even winter. They are mainly ill at ease and short-lived on chalk but thrive in moist, acid soils.

The second group, called Aria and also known as whitebeams, are quite different and have simple rather than pinnate leaves. These are usually toothed and sometimes lobed and are often silvery or white on their undersides, a characteristic that gives them their common name and a beautiful effect of rippling silver in a breeze. While they are not as spectacular in fruit, the bunches of red to brown fruits are attractive, and the autumn colour of the foliage ranges from eye-catching to dramatic. This group is generally first-class on chalk and in maritime exposure.

The third group, Micromeles, is similar to the Aria group except in botanical details, but these are sufficient to give some botanists cause to consider separating it into a distinct genus.

CARE AND CULTIVATION

Sorbus, like so many other genera in the *Rosaceae* family, is susceptible to the bacterial disease fireblight, the signs of which are shrivelled flowers and leaves and shoots that die back, possibly exuding a slime. The only solution is to dig out and burn the affected plant.

Any dead wood should be cut out as soon as possible, as the coral-spot fungus may quickly enter and spread to healthy parts of the tree. Certain strains of mistletoe take to *Sorbus* as a host, but this is not a common occurrence and usually has no noticeable effect upon the tree.

Sorbus vilmorinii

Sorbus *Rosaceae*

S. alnifolia (Micromeles Section) A small to medium-sized tree with a dense head of purplish brown branches. The leaves are oval-shaped and are strongly veined and double-toothed, like those of a hornbeam. The small, oval fruits are bright red, and the leaves take on rich scarlet and orange tints in autumn. Japan, Korea, China. Introduced 1892.
H4

Sorbus aria

S. aria (Whitebeam) A small to medium-sized tree, usually with a rounded head of branches. The more or less oval leaves are greyish white at first, later bright green above but vividly silver-white beneath, turning to gold and russet in autumn, when bunches of deep crimson fruits are shown to their best advantage. It grows well on chalk and is one of the best trees for windswept or maritime areas and potentially polluted industrial environments. The following are recommended for gardens.
H4

S. a. 'Chrysophylla' A form with leaves yellowish throughout summer (particularly effective in late spring) and becoming rich butter-yellow in autumn.
H4

S. a. 'Decaisneana' See *S. a.* 'Majestica'.

S. a. 'Lutescens' A form in which the upper surfaces of the young leaves are covered with a dense, creamy felt, becoming grey-green by late summer. It is an outstanding tree in spring.
H4 ♔ 1993

Sorbus aria 'Chrysophylla'

Sorbus aria 'Lutescens'

Sorbus aria 'Majestica'

S. a. 'Magnifica' An upright tree with large, glossy green leaves and large clusters of red fruits.
H4

S. a. 'Majestica', syn. *S. a.* 'Decaisneana' A handsome tree with larger, elliptic leaves 10–15cm (4–6in) long and larger fruits.
H4 ♔ 1993

Sorbus aucuparia

S. aucuparia (Mountain ash, rowan) A small to medium-sized tree of which the leaves have 11–19 sharply toothed leaflets. The fruits, which are bright red and carried in large, dense bunches in late summer and autumn, are soon greedily devoured by birds. It is an easily grown species but not long-lived on very shallow chalk soils. On the other hand, it is highly tolerant of extreme acidity. Europe, including Britain and Ireland.
H4

S. a. 'Aspleniifolia', syn. *S. a.* 'Laciniata' An elegant tree with deeply cut and toothed leaflets that give the leaves a fern-like effect.
H4

Sorbus aucuparia 'Beissneri'

S. a. 'Beissneri' An interesting tree with a dense head of erect branches. The young shoots and sometimes the leaf stalks are dark, coral-red. The leaves are yellowish green, particularly when young, and the leaflets vary in shape, many having an

attractive, fern-like appearance. The trunk and main branches are warm copper or russet. In cultivation 1899.
H4

S. a. 'Cardinal Royal' An upright tree with a profusion of bright red berries.
H4

Sorbus·aucuparia 'Edulis'

S. a. 'Edulis' A strong-growing, extremely hardy tree with larger leaves and broader, longer leaflets than usual. Its fruits are also larger, sweetly edible, and carried in heavier bunches. Originated c1800.
H4

Sorbus aucuparia 'Fastigiata'

S. a. 'Fastigiata' A remarkable, slow-growing, columnar shrub or small tree up to rather more than 5m (15ft), with stout, closely erect stems. The leaves are large and have 11–15 dark green leaflets. The fruits are sealing-wax-red, large, and in densely packed bunches.
H4

S. a. 'Fructu-luteo' The fruits of this tree are amber-yellow and much longer lasting than most other forms.
H4 ♔ 1993

S. a. 'Laciniata' See *S. a.* 'Aspleniifolia'.

S. a. 'Sheerwater Seedling' A vigorous, upright, small tree with a compact, egg-shaped head of ascending branches and large clusters of orange-red fruits.
H4 ♔ 1993

Sorbus cashmiriana

S. cashmiriana (Aucuparia Section) A beautiful, small, open tree with leaves consisting of 17–19 strongly serrated leaflets. The flowers are soft pink in late spring, and the fruits are gleaming white and 12mm (½in) across. It is a distinctive species with its loose, drooping clusters of fruits remaining long after the leaves have fallen. Kashmir. In cultivation 1934.
H4 ♔ 1993

S. 'Chinese Lace' (Aucuparia Section) A small, upright tree of which the leaves have deeply cut and divided leaflets that give a charming, lacy effect. They turn purple in autumn. The fruits are dark red.
H4

S. commixta (Aucuparia Section) A small, variable tree that is columnar when young and broadens a little at maturity. Its leaves have 11–15 slender-pointed, serrated leaflets that are coppery when young, becoming glossy green and then colouring richly and brilliantly in autumn, in shades of vivid yellow and red. Where there is room, it is an excellent small tree for group planting. Japan, Korea. In cultivation 1880.
H4

Sorbus commixta

S. c. 'Embley' A superb small tree whose leaves consistently turn to a glowing red in autumn, colouring generally later and remaining on the branches longer than other forms. It has large, heavy bunches of glistening, orange-red fruits.
H4 ♔ 1993

S. domestica (Service tree) A medium-sized tree with open, spreading branches, rough, scaly bark and sticky, shining winter buds. The pinnate leaves are composed of 13–21 leaflets and turn orange-red or yellow in autumn; the pear- or apple-shaped fruits are 2.5–3cm (1–1¼in) long and are green tinged with red. S and E Europe. Long cultivated.
H4

Sorbus 'Eastern Promise'

S. 'Eastern Promise' (Aucuparia Section). A small, oval-headed, upright tree. Its pinnate leaves have 15-19 leaflets that are dark green and arise from a reddish main axis. In autumn they turn to purple and then fiery orange. The deep rose-pink fruits are borne in dense, hanging clusters that weigh down the branches.

H4

Sorbus 'Ethel's Gold'

S. 'Ethel's Gold' (Aucuparia Section) A small tree with bright green, sharply serrated leaflets and bunches of golden-amber fruits that persist into winter if the birds allow. Originated before 1959 at Hillier Nurseries and was named after Sir Harold Hillier's mother.

H4

S. folgneri (Micromeles Section) A graceful, variable small tree, usually with spreading or arching branches. The leaves are oval or narrowly so, double-toothed, dark green above, white or grey-felted beneath, often assuming rich autumn colours. The fruits are variable in size and shape and are dark red or purplish red, borne in drooping clusters. C China. Introduced 1901.

H4

S. f. 'Lemon Drop' A small tree with glossy, bright yellow fruits. Originated before 1950 at Hillier Nurseries.

H4

S. forrestii A graceful small tree related to *S. hupehensis*. It has blue-green leaves, usually with 13–15 oblong leaflets, and small, white, long-lasting fruits tinged with pink on the calyx. An excellent small garden tree. China. Introduced 1921 by George Forrest but not named until 1980.

H4

S. 'Golden Wonder' (Aucuparia Section) A small, upright tree. Its leaves have 13–15 deep blue-green, sharply toothed leaflets

that turn yellow and red in autumn. Golden-yellow fruits are borne in large clusters in late summer and early autumn.

H4

S. harrowiana (Aucuparia Section) A most remarkable and distinct large shrub or small tree with stout, ascending branches. The leaves are 20–30cm (8–12in) long, with 2–4 pairs of stalkless leaflets and a long-stalked terminal leaflet: the leaflets are 15–18cm (6–7in) long and up to 5cm (2in) wide. The small, dull white flowers are borne in large, flattened corymbs, and followed by equally small, pink or pearly white fruits. China. Trees from Forrest's 1912 seed did not survive years with severe winters, even in the mildest places, while those from Kingdon Ward's later reintroduction came through the notoriously hard British winters of 1962/3 and the 1980s. For this reason, hardiness ratings would be unreliable and are not given.

Sorbus × hostii

S. × hostii (Aria Section) A large shrub or small tree. The leaves are more or less oval, sharply toothed, green above and grey-downy beneath. The pale pink flowers are followed by early-ripening, bright red fruits. Europe. In cultivation 1820.

H4

S. hupehensis (Aucuparia Section) A small but strongly growing tree, developing a bold, compact head of ascending, purple-brown branches. The leaves are large, distinctively blue-green and easily recognizable from a distance. There are 11–17 leaflets and the fruits are white or sometimes tinged with pink. They are borne in

Sorbus hupehensis

loose, drooping bunches that last into late winter. The leaves turn glorious red in autumn. W China (Hupeh). Introduced 1910 by Ernest Wilson.

H4 ♔ 1993

Sorbus hupehensis var. obtusa

S. h. var. obtusa A most attractive form with pink fruits and leaves usually with 11 leaflets. Various selections have been made and named, including 'Pink Pagoda', 'Rosea' and 'Rufus', all of them have pink fruits and they can be difficult to distinguish from the type.

H4 ♔ 1993

S. hybrida 'Gibbsii' (Aria Section) A small tree to about 7m (22ft) with broad, ovate leaves, divided at the base into 1–2 pairs of long leaflets and with a widely rounded apex. They are green above and grey-woolly below. The fruits are spherical, red, and 12mm (½in) or a little more across, in large clusters.

H4 ♔ 1993

Sorbus hybrida 'Gibbsii'

S. insignis (Aucuparia Section) A magnificent small tree for a reasonably sheltered site. It has stout, stiffly ascending branches and pinnate leaves, up to 25cm (10in) long, composed of 11–15 leaflets that stay on the tree for a long period and turn red in early winter. The small, oval, pink fruits are borne in large heads and persist into the early part of spring; they seem to hold little attraction for birds. Himalayan region. Introduced 1928.
H4

Sorbus intermedia

S. intermedia (Aria Section) (Swedish whitebeam) A small to medium-sized tree with a dense, usually rounded head of branches and leaves lobed in the lower half, coarsely toothed beyond, dark green and glossy above and grey-woolly beneath. The orange-red fruits are 12mm (½in) wide and held in bunches. The following form is recommended. N Europe.
H4

S. i. 'Brouwers' A selected form with ascending branches making an oval crown. H4 ⚊ 1993

Sorbus 'Joseph Rock'

S. 'Joseph Rock' (Aucuparia Section) An outstanding small tree which has an erect head of branches. Its leaves have 15–19 leaflets that turn red, orange, copper and purple in autumn. The clusters of round fruits are creamy yellow at first and deepen to amber-yellow, remaining on the branches well after leaf fall. Unfortunately, very susceptible to fireblight. Although its actual origin remains a mystery, it could be a form of a variable Chinese species.
H4 ⚊ 1993

Sorbus × kewensis

S. × kewensis (Aucuparia Section) A first-class, hardy, free-fruiting small tree. The orange-red fruits are in large, heavy bunches and provide an autumn feast for the eyes. Raised at Kew Gardens.
H4 ⚊ 1993

Sorbus koehniana

S. koehniana (Aucuparia Section) A medium-sized shrub or small, elegant tree. Its leaves have 17–33 narrow, toothed leaflets and the small, porcelain-white fruits are in slender, drooping clusters. Best as a shrub. C China. Introduced 1910 by Ernest Wilson.
H4 ⚊ 1993

Sorbus latifolia

S. latifolia (Aria Section) (Service tree of Fontainbleau) A small to medium-sized tree with downy young shoots and shaggy, peeling bark. The leaves are ovate or broadly elliptic, sharply lobed, glossy green above and felted beneath. The fruits are globular and russet-yellow with large, brownish speckles. Portugal to Germany.
H4

S. 'Leonard Messel' A sadly rather neglected form, this makes a splendid small tree with upright branches that make a dense, oval crown. The large leaves, which usually have 9–11 blue-green leaflets on a

Sorbus 'Leonard Messel'

Sorbus reducta

Sorbus scalaris

Sorbus sargentiana

Sorbus 'Sunshine'

pink rachis, turn red and purple in autumn. The distinctive, bright pink fruits are borne in broad, hanging clusters. Raised 1949 by Col. L. C. R. Messel.
H4

S. *megalocarpa* (Micromeles Section) A remarkable large shrub with large, more or less oval leaves that sometimes turn crimson in autumn. The large flower buds open before the leaves in spring, and form large, domed heads of cream flowers. (Avoid the temptation to cut these for decoration, as their smell is most disagreeable.) The fruits are big, about 2.5cm (1in) across, brown, and of no great beauty. W China. Introduced 1903 by Ernest Wilson.
H4

S. 'Pearly King' (Aucuparia Section) A small tree with ferny leaves consisting of 13–17 narrow, sharply toothed leaflets. The fruits are 15mm (⅝in) across, rose at first, changing to white with a pink flush, and in large, loose, pendulous bunches. It is a hybrid of *S. vilmorinii*. Originated at Hillier Nurseries, England.
H4

S. *reducta* (Aucuparia Section) An unusual dwarf to small, suckering shrub making thickets of slender, erect stems 0.6–1m (2–3ft) high. The leaves have red stalks and 13–15 leaflets that turn bronze and reddish purple in autumn. The fruits are globular and white, flushed with rose. Some plants under this name are similar in leaf and fruit but grow on a single stem and do not sucker. China, N Burma. Introduced 1943 by Frank Kingdon-Ward.
H4 ♔ 1993

S. *sargentiana* (Aucuparia Section) A magnificent species that slowly develops into a tree up to 9m (28ft) high and as much across. The leaves are large and attractive, up to 30cm (1ft) long, and composed of 7–11 slender-pointed leaflets, each 7.5–13cm (3–5in) long. The small, scarlet fruits, late to ripen, are in large, rounded heads up to 15cm (6in) across. The foliage turns rich red in autumn. The winter buds are large, sticky and crimson. W China. Introduced 1908 by Ernest Wilson.
H4 ♔ 1993

S. 'Savill Orange' (Aucuparia Section) A small tree with dense clusters of large, orange-red berries. It is a seedling of *S. aucuparia* 'Fructu-luteo'. Originated c1970 in the Valley Gardens, Windsor Great Park.
H4

S. *scalaris* (Aucuparia Section) A small, tree with side-spreading branches and neat, frond-like leaves composed of 21–33 narrow leaflets that turn rich red and purple late in autumn. The fruits are small, red, and densely packed in flattened heads. China. Introduced 1904 by Ernest Wilson.
H4 ♔ 1993

S. sp. 'Ghose' A superb small upright tree, something like *S. insignis* but hardier. It is possibly a new species. The large leaves, dark matt green above, glaucous beneath and rusty pubescent, consist of 15–19 sharply serrated leaflets. The fruits are rose-red, small, but produced in large, densely packed bunches that remain late on the branches. Himalayas. Introduced by Hillier Nurseries.
H4

S. 'Sunshine' (Aucuparia Section) A small tree, erect when young. The leaves have 7–8 pairs of leaflets and the fruits, which are golden-yellow in large clusters, colour before those of 'Joseph Rock', of which it is a seedling. Raised 1968 at Hillier Nurseries.
H4

S. thibetica 'John Mitchell' (Aria Section) A handsome, medium-sized to large tree, eventually developing a broad, rounded head. The mature leaves are large, about 15cm (6in) long by as much across. They are dark glossy green above and white-felted beneath. The fruit is gold to red, borne in bunches.
H4 ♛ 1993

Sorbus × thuringiaca 'Fastigiata'

S. × thuringiaca 'Fastigiata' A most distinctive small tree with an egg-shaped head of closely packed, ascending branches. The leaves are narrow, divided at the base into 1–3 pairs of leaflets, dull green above and grey-felted below. The fruits are scarlet with a few brown flecks.
H4

Bark of Sorbus torminalis

S. torminalis (Aria Section) (Chequer tree, wild service tree) An attractive medium-sized tree with ascending branches. The leaves are maple-like, ovate, sharply and conspicuously lobed, glossy dark green above, and turning bronze-yellow in autumn. The fruits are elongated and russet-brown. Europe (including England), Asia Minor, N Africa.
H4

S. ursina (Aucuparia Section) A small, erect tree with stout, ascending branches and red buds. The leaves have 15–21 net-veined leaflets and the fruits are white or pink-tinted and in dense bunches. A very distinct and beautiful species. Himalayas. Introduced 1950 by Col. Donald Lowndes.
H4

S. vestita (Aria Section) (Himalayan white-beam) A medium-sized tree, erect when young, spreading when older. The leaves are 15–25cm (6–10in) long, green above and silvery white or buff beneath. The fruits are green, speckled and flushed with warm brown, resembling small crab apples or miniature pears. A magnificent species with bold foliage and quite one of the most handsome of all hardy trees. Himalayas. Introduced 1820.
H4

Sorbus vilmorinii

S. vilmorinii (Aucuparia Section) A beautiful medium-sized shrub or small tree. The fern-like leaves, often in clusters, are composed of 11–31 small leaflets that turn red and purple in autumn. The loose, drooping clusters of fruits are rose-red at first, gradually passing through shades of pink to white, flushed with light rose. It is a charming species, eminently suitable for the smaller garden. W China. Introduced 1889 by the Abbé Delavay.
H4 ♛ 1993

S. wardii (Aria Section) A rare tree with stiff, erect branches, giving it a columnar habit. The elliptic to obovate leaves are green and ribbed above, thinly hairy beneath; young leaves are grey-downy. The globular fruits, borne in loose corymbs, are amber speckled greyish brown. A specimen in the Hillier Gardens and Aboretum is growing strongly and is over 9m (28ft) high. It is a splendid silvery whitebeam for gardens where space is limited. Bhutan, Tibet. Introduced by Frank Kingdon-Ward.
H4

S. 'White Wax' (Aucuparia Section) A small tree with a conical head of branches. The leaves are fern-like with up to 23 oblong, sharply toothed leaflets and the pure white fruits, 1cm (½in) across, are borne in drooping clusters.
H4

S. 'Wilfred Fox' (Aria Section) A handsome hybrid tree, broadly columnar when young, eventually a roundheaded tree 12m (40ft) high. The elliptic leaves are 15–20cm (6–8in) long, shallowly lobed and doubly serrated; they are dark glossy green above, greyish white tomentose below. The marble-like fruits are green at first, turning to deep amber speckled grey. It is named after the creator of Winkworth Arboretum.
H4

S. 'Winter Cheer' (Aucuparia Section) A small to medium-sized, open-branched tree. The large, flat bunches of fruit are a warm chrome yellow at first, ripening to orange-red. They begin to colour in early autumn and last well into winter. Raised 1959 by Hillier Nurseries.
H4

Spartium *Leguminosae*

A genus of one deciduous species, closely related to Cytisus *and* Genista.

S. junceum (Spanish broom) A strongly growing shrub of loose habit, with erect, green, rush-like stems up to 3m (10ft) high and small, inconspicuous leaves. The quite large, fragrant, yellow pea-flowers, 2.5cm (1in) long, are in loose, terminal clusters throughout summer and early autumn. It thrives in a well drained, sunny position

Spartium junceum

Spiraea 'Arguta'

Spiraea × billardii 'Triumphans'

Spiraea fritschiana

Spiraea japonica 'Albiflora'

and is an excellent seaside shrub. Specimens in sheltered gardens are apt to become tall and leggy, but they can be pruned hard in early spring as long as care is taken not to cut into the old, hard wood. It is a wonderful shrub when kept low and bushy by winds from the sea. Mediterranean region. Introduced c1548.

H4 1993

Spiraea *Rosaceae*

A varied genus of deciduous hardy flowering shrubs, many of which have attractive foliage and are graceful in habit. There are about 70 species in north-temperate regions. They are easily grown in any ordinary soil and a sunny position, although a few turn yellow and fail in very shallow chalk soils. Those such as S. japonica that flower on the current year's shoots can be pruned to the ground in early spring, while those like S. veitchii which flower on the previous year's shoots may need to be thinned out and to have their old flowering shoots cut to within a short distance of the old wood immediately after flowering. Any untidy specimens of S. 'Arguta' and S. thunbergii can be pruned back hard immediately after flowering.

S. 'Arguta' (Bridal wreath) A dense, medium-sized shrub with graceful, slender branches and pure white flowers in small clusters all along the branches in mid- to late spring. One of the most effective and free-flowering of the early spiraeas, but *S. × cinerea* 'Grefsheim' is considered to be a better plant. In cultivation before 1884.
H4

S. betulifolia A dwarf shrub, occasionally 1m (3ft) high, forming mounds of reddish brown branches and rounded leaves. White flowers in dense, dome-shaped clusters 2.5–6cm (1–2½in) across are borne in early summer. Small enough for large rock gardens. NE Asia, Japan. Introduced c1812.
H4

S. × billardii 'Triumphans' A beautiful, medium-sized shrub with erect stems bearing oblong to lance-shaped sharply-toothed leaves, with greyish hairs, and dense, conical panicles of purplish rose flowers in summer. It is not happy on shallow, chalky soils.
H4

S. cantoniensis 'Flore Pleno' A widespreading, graceful shrub up to 2m (6½ft) high with slender, arching branches, lance-shaped leaves and double, white flowers in rounded clusters along the branches in early summer.
H4

S. × cinerea 'Grefsheim' A small, densely branched shrub with downy, arching stems and narrow leaves. The small white flowers are profusely produced in dense clusters all along the branches towards the latter part of spring.
H4 1993

S. fritschiana A small, mound-forming shrub with blue-green leaves and flowers that are white tinged with pink, held in broad, dense terminal corymbs in early summer. Korea. Introduced 1976 by Carl Miller and Sir Harold Hillier.
H4

S. japonica 'Albiflora' A dwarf shrub of compact habit with white flowers in dense, terminal clusters from midsummer onwards. Introduced before 1868.
H4

S. j. 'Anthony Waterer' An excellent dwarf shrub for the front of the border or

Spiraea japonica 'Anthony Waterer'

Spiraea japonica 'Crispa'

Spiraea japonica 'Gold Mound'

for mass effect. The flowers are bright crimson, borne from midsummer onwards; the foliage is occasionally variegated with cream and pink.
H4 ♀ 1993

S. j. 'Bullata' A dwarf, slow-growing shrub with small, broad leaves that are puckered on their upper surfaces. The rose-crimson flowers are borne in terminal, flat-topped clusters in summer. Garden origin, Japan. In cultivation before 1881.
H4

Spiraea japonica 'Candlelight'

S. j. 'Candlelight' A dwarf, compact, bushy shrub with buttery yellow young leaves that gradually turn deeper and make a good foil for the pink flowers from midsummer onwards. It has good autumn leaf colour and is free from reversion.
H4

S. j. 'Crispa' A dwarf shrub with dark, glossy green leaves, that are reddish purple when young. They are deeply and sharply

toothed. The pink flowers are borne in large, flattened heads from midsummer onwards.
H4

S. j. 'Dart's Red' A similar plant to 'Anthony Waterer' with flattened heads of deep red flowers but without the white-variegated foliage.
H4

Spiraea japonica 'Firelight'

S. j. 'Firelight' The young leaves of this dwarf shrub with arching branches are rich orange-red, deeper than 'Gold Flame', of which it is a seedling. They turn bright orange-yellow and then pale green. The deep rose-pink flowers are borne from midsummer, and the autumn colour is a stunning fiery red. It is free from reversion.
H4

S. j. 'Gold Mound' A dwarf, compact shrub with yellow foliage and small heads of pink flowers from midsummer onwards.
H4 ♀ 1993

S. j. 'Golden Dome' A compact, dome-shaped dwarf shrub with foliage that is golden yellow in spring and early summer. Flattened heads of pink flowers are borne from midsummer onwards.
H4

Spiraea japonica 'Goldflame'

S. j. 'Goldflame' A very popular dwarf shrub. The young leaves emerge reddish orange in spring and become bright yellow, eventually turning green. The flowers are deep rose-red. All-green shoots should be removed.
H4 ♀ 1993

S. j. 'Little Princess' This shrub forms a low, dwarf mound with rose-crimson flowers from midsummer onwards.
H4

S. j. 'Macrophylla' Not the form to choose for flowers but perhaps the best spiraea for autumn colour. The large, bullate leaves are reddish purple when young.
H4

Spiraea japonica 'Little Princess'

S. j. 'Nana' A superb dwarf shrub forming a dense mound 45–60cm (18in–2ft) high and rather more across. It is spectacular when closely studded with tiny heads of rose-pink flowers from midsummer onwards and is worthy of a position in the smallest garden. Where there is enough space it should be mass-planted. H4 ♔ 1993

Spiraea japonica 'Shiburi'

S. j. 'Shiburi', syn. *S. j.* 'Shirobana' An unusual dwarf form producing a mixture of deep pink and white flowers on both the same and different heads. They are borne from midsummer onwards. H4 ♔ 1993

S. j. 'Shirobana' See *S. j.* 'Shiburi'.
S. nipponica One of the best shrubs for early-summer flowers. It is strong-growing and medium-sized with a dense, bushy habit having long, arching stems and leaves that are almost round. The clusters of small white flowers crowd the upper sides of the stout branches and each flower lies immediately above a green bract. Japan. Introduced c1885 by Siebold. H4

S. n. 'Rotundifolia' A strong-growing form with broader leaves and slightly larger flowers than the type. It is excellent on chalky soils. Introduced 1830. H4

Spiraea nipponica 'Snowmound'

S. n. 'Snowmound' A small, dense, mound-forming shrub with white flowers that crowd the upper sides of the branches in early summer to the extent that they are almost entirely hidden. Japan. H4 ♔ 1993

Spiraea prunifolia 'Plena'

S. prunifolia 'Plena' A dense shrub with arching branches up to 2m (6½ft) high. The ovate leaves turn orange or red in autumn. The white, double flowers are in tight, button-like clusters along the branches in mid- to late spring. It was introduced from Japan in about 1845, before the inferior single form was discovered, and for that reason is sometimes listed simply as *S. prunifolia*, while the single is named f. *simpliciflora*. H4

Spiraea thunbergii

S. thunbergii A popular, small to medium-sized, spreading, dense shrub with white flowers in numerous clusters along the branches in early and mid-spring, often entirely hiding the wiry stems. The earliest of the spiraeas to bloom. China, naturalized in Japan. Introduced c1863 from Japan. H4 ♔ 1993

Spiraea × vanhouttei

S. × vanhouttei A vigorous medium-sized shrub up to 2m (6½ft) high, with gracefully arching branches. The leaves are more or less rhomboidal, sometimes with 3-5 lobes, and the white flowers are borne in dense umbels along the branches in early summer. Garden origin before 1886. H4 ♔ 1993

S. × v. 'Pink Ice' A small shrub with the foliage conspicuously flecked with creamy white. Although quite widely sold, it is perhaps a little freakish and may be merely temporarily fashionable.
H4

S. veitchii A strong-growing shrub up to 3m (10ft) high with long, arching branches and leaves 2.5–5cm (1–2in) long. The white flowers are borne in dense, domed clusters all along the branches in early to mid-summer. A superb species and highly desirable where there is enough space. C and W China. Introduced 1900 by Ernest Wilson.
H4

Stachyurus *Stachyuraceae*

The only genus in its family, consisting of five or six deciduous species native to eastern Asia, only two of which are reliably hardy. The stiffly pendulous flower clusters are formed in the leaf axils before the leaves fall in autumn, but the flowers do not open until the early spring. Stachyurus will grow in all fertile soils and in sun or semi-shade. It is good practice to remove old or weak shoots at ground level, as new shoots are readily produced from the base.

Stachyurus chinensis

S. chinensis A medium-sized to large shrub with purplish branchlets and fairly slender leaves. The drooping flower clusters are 10–13cm (4–5in) long and consist of 30–35 soft yellow, cup-shaped flowers. China. Introduced 1908 by Ernest Wilson.
H4

S. c. 'Magpie' The leaves of this medium-sized shrub are grey-green above with an

irregular cream margin, splashed with pale green and tinted with rose-pink. It tends to produce shoots with all-white foliage. Originated c1945 at Hillier Nurseries.
H4

Stachyurus praecox

S. praecox A medium-sized to large shrub with reddish brown branchlets. The leaves are more or less elliptical and are larger and broader than those of *S. chinensis*. The flower clusters are stiffly drooping, 4–7cm (1½–3in) long and consist of 15–24 cup-shaped, pale yellow flowers. They open about two weeks earlier than *S. chinensis*, in early spring or even earlier in mild weather. Japan. Introduced 1864.
H4 ♔ 1993

Staphylea *Staphyleaceae*
Bladder nut

A genus of 11 deciduous species, natives of temperate regions of the northern hemisphere. Their seeds are in curious, inflated, bladder-like capsules with 2–3 cells. They are easily grown in any fertile soil in sun or semi-shade and need no regular pruning if given enough room to develop. Old, overgrown or untidy specimens may be cut back hard in winter.

S. colchica A strong-growing shrub with erect branches, reaching 3.5m (11ft) high. The leaves have 3–5 leaflets and the white flowers are in erect panicles up to 13cm (5in) long in late spring. The bladders are up to 10cm (4in) long. Caucasus. Introduced 1850.
H4 ♔ 1993

Staphylea colchica 'Hessei'

S. c. 'Hessei' An attractive form with pretty flowers which are flushed with red-purple.
H4

Staphylea holocarpa 'Rosea'

S. holocarpa 'Rosea' A lovely large shrub or small tree. In mid- to late spring its branches are strung with drooping clusters of soft pink flowers. The bronze young

Staphylea pinnata

leaves age blue-green. In cultivation 1908. H4

S. pinnata A large, vigorous, erect shrub with leaves of 3–7 (usually 5) leaflets and white flowers in long, narrow, drooping panicles in late spring and early summer. Europe, Asia Minor. In cultivation 1596. H4

Stauntonia *Lardizabalaceae*

A genus of about six species of evergreen, twining shrubs closely related to Holboellia *and needing a warm, sheltered wall in full sun or semi-shade. They will thrive in ordinary soil.*

Stauntonia hexaphylla

S. hexaphylla A strong climber up to 10m (30ft) or more, with large leaves composed of 3–7 stalked, leathery, dark green leaflets. The fragrant flowers are 2cm (³/₄in) across, with male and female in separate clusters. They are white, tinged with violet, and appear in spring. The egg-shaped, pulpy, purple fruits, 2.5–5cm (1–2in) long, are edible but are only produced after a warm, dry summer. E Asia. Introduced 1874. H3

Stephanandra *Rosaceae*

A genus of four species of shrubs native to eastern Asia and deciduous in Britain. Although they are of only subtle beauty in flower, their graceful habit and very attractive foliage qualify them for a place in the garden, where they are happy in most soils in sun or semi-shade. The leaves are often richly tinted in autumn. Untidy specimens may be pruned back hard in early spring.

S. incisa A small to medium-sized shrub of dense habit which has slender, warm-brown zig-zag stems. The leaves are up to 7.5cm (3in) long, ovate, incisely toothed and lobed. The greenish white flowers are borne in crowded, small panicles in the early days of summer. Japan, Korea. Introduced 1872. H4

Stephanandra incisa 'Crispa'

S. i. 'Crispa' A dwarf shrub with crinkled leaves, forming dense, low mounds. It makes good ground cover, especially in full exposure. H4

Stephanandra tanakae

S. tanakae An elegant medium-sized shrub which produces long, arching rich brown stems. The toothed leaves are more or less triangular, growing up to 13cm (5in) long, with 3–5 lobes. They produce good autumn colours of red, orange and yellow. The flowers are a little larger than those of

S. incisa but are not at all showy. Japan. Introduced 1893. H4

Stranvaesia

S. davidiana See *Photinia davidiana*.

Stewartia

See *Stuartia*.

Stuartia *Theaceae*

A small genus of evergreen and deciduous ornamental shrubs and trees allied to Camellia. *They need a semi-shaded position and a moist, loamy, lime-free soil and revel in a position among trees. All have white or cream flowers which soon fall but are produced in a continuous succession over several weeks in mid- to late summer. They also have rich autumn colour and older specimens have beautiful trunks and flaking bark. They resent being moved once planted and prefer to have their roots shaded from the hot sun. Over-shading can give rise to dead wood at the base, and the removal of this is virtually the only pruning that is required.*

Stuartia malacodendron

S. malacodendron A large, beautiful deciduous shrub or occasionally a small tree, which produces solitary flowers in the leaf axils; they are white, 6–9cm (2¹/₂–3in) wide, with purple stamens. It is most lovely when the flowers stud the branches in mid- to late summer. SE United States. In cultivation 1742. H4

S. monadelpha A large deciduous shrub or small tree with attractive autumn colour. The white flowers are solitary, 2.5–4cm (1–1½in) across, with spreading petals. The stamens have violet anthers. Japan, Korea. In cultivation 1903.
H4

S. pseudocamellia A small to medium-sized deciduous tree with attractive, dark red, peeling bark. The solitary white flowers are 5–6cm (2–2½in) wide, cup-shaped, with bright yellow anthers, and the leaves turn yellow and red in autumn. Japan.
H4 ♛ 1993

S. p. var. koreana A splendid tree with exceptionally bright autumn colour. The flowers are similar to the species but open wider with spreading petals. Korea. Introduced 1917 by Ernest Wilson.
H4 ♛ 1993

S. serrata A small deciduous tree with warm brown stems and leathery leaves. The cup-shaped, solitary flowers are 5–6cm

Stuartia serrata

(2–2½in) wide, white stained with red on the outside at the base, and with yellow anthers. They open in early summer, before the other species. It has rich autumn colour. Japan. In cultivation before 1915.
H4

S. sinensis A large deciduous shrub or small tree with smooth, yellow bark that

peels in autumn to reveal the new grey bark. The solitary white flowers are up to 5cm (2in) wide and are cup-shaped and fragrant. It has rich autumn colour. C China. Introduced 1901 by Ernest Wilson.
H4

Styrax *Styracaceae*

A genus of some 120 species of evergreen and deciduous trees and shrubs, widely distributed in temperate and tropical regions of the northern hemisphere. The cultivated species are distinguished and beautiful, thriving in most loamy, lime-free soils in sun or semi-shade, and are small enough for quite restricted gardens. If any pruning becomes necessary, it should be done in summer. Their pure white flowers, which appear in late spring and summer, have given rise in North America to the name 'snowbell'.

S. hemsleyana An attractive, open-branched small deciduous tree with broad,

Stuartia monadelpha

Stuartia pseudocamellia

Stuartia pseudocamellia var. *koreana*

almost round leaves 10–13cm (4–5in) long. The flowers are white with a central cone of yellow anthers and are borne in long, lax racemes in early summer. Similar to *S. obassia*, but with less downy leaves. C and W China. Introduced 1900 by Ernest Wilson. H4 ♔ 1993

Styrax japonica

S. japonica A most beautiful large decidu-ous shrub or small tree with wide-spread-ing, almost horizontal, fan-like branches, often drooping at the tips. The leaves are fairly narrow and pointed and the bell-shaped fragrant white flowers, with a yellow beak of stamens, hang all along the under-sides of the branches in early summer. It is the most widely grown species and deservedly so, as it combines daintiness and elegance with a hardy constitution. It is best planted where the flowers can be admired from beneath. Japan, Korea. Introduced 1862 by Richard Oldham. H4 ♔ 1993

Styrax obassia

S. j. 'Pink Chimes' A very free-flowering form with pale pink flowers that are deeper at the base. Raised before 1976 in Japan. H4

S. obassia A beautiful large deciduous shrub or small, round-headed tree with handsome, broad, almost rounded leaves 10–20cm (4–8in) long. The fragrant, bell-shaped flowers are 2.5cm (1in) long and borne in long, lax, terminal racemes in early summer. Japan. Introduced 1879 by Charles Maries. H4 ♔ 1993

Sycopsis *Hamamelidaceae*

A genus of seven species of evergreen shrubs and trees, natives of the Himalayas. There is only one species in general cultivation. It prefers moisture-retentive, neutral or slightly acid soils, but can grow over chalk as long as the soil is deep.

Sycopsis sinensis

S. sinensis A medium-sized to large shrub or small tree. The leaves are somewhat puckered and leathery. The flowers have no petals and consist of small clusters of yellow, red-anthered stamens, enclosed by choco-late-brown, woolly scales. They open in late winter and early spring. C China. Intro-duced 1901 by Ernest Wilson. H4

Symphoricarpos *Caprifoliaceae*

A genus of about 17 species of deciduous shrubs from North America and Mexico and with one species in China. The flowers are bell-shaped but small and of no decorative merit; the plants are

grown mainly for their often abundant display of white or rose berries, which appear in autumn and generally last well into winter, as they are left untouched by birds. Several are excellent for hedging and all grow well in shade, even among the roots and under the drip of overhanging trees. They are quite hardy and will grow in all types of soils. Untidy specimens may be pruned back hard in early spring.

Symphoricarpos albus var. laevigatus

S. albus var. laevigatus (Snowberry) A strong-growing shrub forming dense thick-ets up to 2m (6½ft) high. The elliptical leaves are up to 7.5cm (3in) long and the berries, borne in great profusion in autumn, are reminiscent of glistening white marbles. This is the common snowberry of English plantations; *S. albus* itself, a smaller shrub, is rare in cultivation. H4

S. × chenaultii 'Hancock' A dense, dwarf, wide-spreading shrub with pinkish berries, that are purplish red on the exposed side, forming excellent ground cover, especially under trees. H3

S. Doorenbos Hybrids A very useful group of attractive hybrids. Raised in Hol-land by Mr Doorenbos.

S. Doorenbos Hybrid 'Magic Berry' A small, compact, spreading shrub with large quantities of rose-pink berries. H4

S. Doorenbos Hybrid 'Mother of Pearl' A small, dense shrub with heavy crops of white, rose-flushed berries. H4

S. Doorenbos Hybrid 'White Hedge' A

Symphoricarpos Doorenbos Hybrid 'Magic Berry'

small, strong, upright shrub that freely produces erect clusters of small white berries. H4

S. orbiculatus 'Albovariegatus' See *S. o.* 'Taff's Silver Edge'.

S. o. 'Argenteovariegatus' See *S. o.* 'Taff's Silver Edge'.

S. o. 'Foliis Variegatis' A graceful small shrub grown for its small, oval leaves that are irregularly margined with yellow. If planted in shade it throws reverted branches, which should be removed. H4

S. o. 'Taff's Silver Edge', syns. *S. o.* 'Albovariegatus', 'Argenteovariegatus' A small shrub in which the leaves are margined with white. H4

Symplocos *Symplocaceae*

A large genus of about 250 species of evergreen and deciduous trees and shrubs, widely distributed in tropical and sub-tropical regions, excluding Africa. Only one is generally hardy. It requires a lime-free soil and, if it is to bear fruits, a warm, sunny position.

S. paniculata A deciduous medium-sized twiggy shrub or small tree with small, white, fragrant flowers borne in panicles in late spring and early summer. They are followed (particularly after a hot summer and if two or more are planted in order to achieve fertilization) by brilliant ultramarine autumn fruits that persist into winter. Himalayas to Japan. Introduced 1871. H4

Syringa *Oleaceae*
Lilac

A genus of extremely popular, hardy, deciduous shrubs and small trees that include some of the most elegant, colourful and deliciously fragrant of the woody plants that flower in late spring and early summer. The species, which are all single-flowered, are less well-known than the considerable number of large-flowered garden lilacs, and their fine qualities deserve much wider recognition. Lilacs are happy in most well-drained soils, especially chalky ones, and revel in full sun. Pruned by removing their old flowering wood immediately after flowering; summer pinching of extra-strong shoots is desirable. Overcrowding of the branches sets up the conditions in which mildew thrives, and a little judicious thinning from time to time is good practice. Where the soil is shallow or otherwise on the poor side, lilacs will respond well to mulching and feeding. 'Syringa' is often misleadingly used as a common name for Philadelphus.

Syringa × chinensis 'Saugeana'

S. × chinensis 'Saugeana' A dense, bushy, medium-sized shrub with ovate leaves and large, drooping panicles of fragrant, lilac-red flowers in late spring. Raised c1809. H4

S. × hyacinthiflora 'Esther Staley' A large shrub with red buds that open to single pink flowers towards the latter part of spring. In cultivation 1948. H4 ♔ 1993

S. × josiflexa 'Bellicent' A large shrub with deep green leaves and enormous panicles of clear rose-pink flowers. It is the best

Syringa × hyacinthiflora 'Esther Staley'

Syringa × josiflexa 'Bellicent'

Syringa julianae

form of this excellent hybrid. H4 ♔ 1993

S. julianae A choice, free-flowering, graceful shrub about 2m (6½ft) high and wide. It has privet-like leaves that are grey-downy on their undersides. The flowers are fragrant, pale lilac, from darker buds, and borne in slender, upright panicles in late

spring and early summer. W China. Introduced 1900 by Ernest Wilson.
H4

S. laciniata A graceful small shrub with three- to nine-lobed leaves and small panicles of lilac flowers in late spring. Turkey. Introduced in the seventeenth century.
H4

Syringa meyeri 'Palibin'

S. meyeri 'Palibin' A slow-growing, eventually medium-sized shrub of dense habit. The pale lilac-pink flowers are borne in numerous elegant panicles, even on young plants. This is a lovely lilac that is suitable for the small garden.
H4 ♟ 1993

Syringa microphylla 'Superba'

S. microphylla 'Superba' A very pretty, small-leaved shrub up to 2m (6¹/₂ft) high. The rosy pink flowers are abundantly borne in late spring and then intermittently until mid-autumn.
H4 ♟ 1993

S. patula 'Miss Kim' A small to medium-sized shrub with fragrant single flowers, purple in bud and on first opening, fading to blue-ice white. They are borne in late spring to early summer. The leaves are dark green with wavy edges. A selection from wild source seed of *S. patula*, collected 1947 in Korea.
H4 ♟ 1993

S. × persica (Persian lilac) A charming, slenderly branched shrub of up to 2.5m (8ft) high, rounded and bushy. The leaves are lance-shaped and the fragrant flowers are borne in small panicles in late spring.
H4 ♟ 1993

Syringa × persica 'Alba'

S. × p. 'Alba' A form with white flowers.
H4 ♟ 1993

S. × prestoniae A race of extremely hardy, late-flowering lilacs, collectively known as Canadian Hybrids. They are medium-sized to large shrubs with large panicles of flowers in late spring and early summer. Reddish purple is the dominant colour.
H4

S. × p. 'Audrey' A form that produces deep pink flowers in the early part of summer. In cultivation 1927.
H4

S. × p. 'Elinor' A form with flowers dark purplish red in bud, opening to pale lavender. They are borne in fairly erect panicles. In cultivation 1934.
H4 ♟ 1993

S. × p. 'Isabella' A form in which the mallow-purple flowers are borne in fairly erect panicles. In cultivation 1927.
H4

Syringa × prestoniae 'Elinor'

S. × p. 'Royalty' A form with attractive violet-purple flowers.
H4

S. reflexa A distinctive, large shrub of considerable quality, with large, oval, rough-textured leaves up to 20cm (8in) long. The flowers are rich purplish pink outside, whitish within, and are densely packed in long, drooping panicles appearing at the end of spring and the beginning of summer. It is one of the best of the species lilacs and very free flowering. C China. Introduced 1904 by Ernest Wilson.
H4 ♟ 1993

S. × swegiflexa 'Fountain' A beautiful, medium-sized, compact shrub with long, drooping panicles of pale pink, fragrant flowers in late spring and early summer.
H4

Syringa sweginzowii 'Superba'

S. sweginzowii 'Superba' A vigorous, elegant, medium-sized shrub with flesh-pink, sweetly fragrant flowers borne in loose, long panicles in late spring and early summer. W China. Introduced 1894. H4

Syringa yunnanensis 'Rosea'

S. _yunnanensis_ 'Rosea' A superior form of the Yunnan lilac, this is a beautiful medium-sized to large shrub with attractive foliage and rose-pink fragrant flowers in long, slender panicles in early summer. Selected at Hillier Nurseries. H4

CULTIVARS OF *SYRINGA VULGARIS*

Syringa vulgaris, the common lilac, is a large, vigorous, suckering shrub. Its flowers are richly scented and borne in dense, erect panicles in late spring. This European species has been the parent of a vast range of garden lilacs which are medium-sized to large shrubs or occasionally small trees, flowering in late spring and early summer. Their colours range from white and creamy yellow to red, blue and purple and may be single or double. All are sweetly scented. Far too many cultivars with little to distinguish them have been named, and the following list includes only the best of them. After transplanting it takes 2–3 years before full flower and size of truss are achieved. All the following are large shrubs and H4.

SINGLE

S. 'Congo' Rich lilac-red flowers in large, compact panicles, paling with age. In cultivation 1896.

S. 'Firmament' Clear lilac-blue flowers, borne early. In cultivation 1932. 1993

Syringa vulgaris 'Congo'

S. 'Massena' Deep reddish purple flowers with large florets, borne in broad panicles. In cultivation 1923.

S. 'Maud Notcutt' Pure white flowers in large panicles up to 30cm (1ft) long. In cultivation 1956.

S. 'Primrose' Pale primrose-yellow only faintly scented flowers which are borne in

Syringa vulgaris 'Firmament'

small, dense panicles. Originated 1949 as a sport in Holland.

S. 'Sensation' Purplish red florets edged with white, in large panicles. It is inclined to revert and lose its variegation. In cultivation 1938.

S. 'Souvenir de Louis Späth' Gorgeous wine-red flowers in long slender panicles. It

Syringa vulgaris 'Massena'

Syringa vulgaris 'Maud Notcutt'

Syringa vulgaris 'Sensation'

is perhaps the most popular lilac and is certainly one of the most consistent and reliable. In cultivation 1883.
♈ 1993

S. **'Vestale'** Pure white flowers in broad, densely packed panicles; a magnificent lilac. In cultivation 1910.
♈ 1993

DOUBLE

S. **'Charles Joly'** Dark purplish red flowers, borne late. A reliable and popular lilac. In cultivation 1896.
♈ 1993

S. **'Katherine Havemeyer'** Purple-lavender flowers, fading to pale lilac-pink, in broad, compact panicles. It is a first-class lilac. In cultivation 1922.
♈ 1993

S. **'Madame Antoine Buchner'** Rose-pink to rosy mauve flowers, borne late in loose, narrow panicles. In cultivation 1900.
♈ 1993

Syringa vulgaris 'Madame Lemoine'

S. **'Madame Lemoine'** Flowers creamy yellow in bud, opening to pure white. An old and popular lilac. In cultivation 1890.
♈ 1993

S. **'Michel Buchner'** Pale rosy lilac flowers are borne in large, dense panicles. In cultivation 1885.

S. **'Mrs Edward Harding'** Claret-red

Syringa vulgaris 'Mrs Edward Harding'

flowers, shaded pink, very free-flowering and borne late. A superb and popular lilac. In cultivation 1922.
♈ 1993

S. **'Paul Thirion'** Flowers carmine in bud, opening to claret-rose and finally lilac pink. They are borne late. In cultivation 1915.

S. **'Président Grévy'** Lilac-blue flowers in massive panicles. In cultivation 1886.

Syringa vulgaris 'Président Grévy'

Syringa vulgaris 'Souvenir de Louis Späth'

T

Tamarix *Tamaricaceae*
Tamarisk

A genus of about 50 species of deciduous shrubs or small trees, native to Europe, Asia and North Africa. They are outstandingly capable of resisting the strongest winds and will tolerate salt to the extent of surviving on the edges of storm beaches. As long as they are in full sun and in any soil apart from a shallow one over chalk they will thrive inland. They are graceful and in some cases showy, with slender, whippy branches and plume-like foliage. The tiny pink flowers are borne in slender racemes towards the ends of the branches, and these combine into large, feathery flower trusses that make a brave splash of colour. Deprived in garden settings of the natural pruning effect of wind, the plants can become straggly, and pruning is necessary in order to maintain balance. Species that flower on growths of the current year should be pruned in late winter or early spring, while those that flower on the previous year's wood should be pruned immediately after flowering.

T. gallica A large, spreading shrub or small tree, with dark purple-brown branches and sea-green foliage. The pink flowers appear during summer and are crowded into lax, cylindrical racemes on shoots of the current year. SW Europe. Naturalized along the English coast.
H4

T. ramosissima A large shrub or small tree with reddish brown branches and pink

Tamarix ramosissima

flowers in slender racemes in summer. They are borne on shoots of the current year. W and C Asia. Introduced c1885. H4

Tamarix ramosissima 'Rubra'

T. r. 'Rubra' A splendid large shrub or small tree which is distinguished by darker flowers than the species.
H4 ♔ 1993

Tamarix tetrandra

T. tetrandra A large shrub with long, dark branches and green leaves. Light pink flowers in long panicles open in late spring or early summer on the previous year's wood. SE Europe, W Asia. Introduced 1821.
H4 ♔ 1993

Taxodium *Taxodiaceae*

A genus of three species of deciduous coniferous trees. The linear leaves are either flattened or awl-shaped, arranged in two opposite ranks on short branchlets that are themselves deciduous and look like pinnate leaves. These beautiful North and Central American trees can be successfully grown in all soils other than chalk or limestone and are remarkable for growing in waterlogged conditions (where, however, they should be mound-planted).

Taxodium ascendens 'Nutans'

T. ascendens 'Nutans' A beautiful, tall, columnar tree with shortly spreading or ascending branches. The thin, crowded branches are erect at first, later nodding, and clothed with adpressed, awl-shaped leaves up to 5mm (¼in) long and rich brown in autumn. In cultivation 1789.
H4 ♔ 1993

T. distichum (Bald cypress, swamp cypress) A strikingly beautiful tree and the most suitable conifer for wet soils. It is a large tree with fibrous, reddish brown bark and a strongly buttressed trunk. The leaves, which are 1–1.5cm (½–¾in) long, turn bronze-yellow in autumn. When grown near water, large specimens produce 'knees' – above-ground growths from the

roots that look like termite hills. It is the dominant tree in the Everglades of Florida. Introduced c1640 by John Tradescant.
H4 ♈ 1993

Taxus *Taxaceae*
Yew

A genus of about seven species of evergreen coniferous trees and shrubs widely distributed in north-temperate regions. They have linear leaves, either in two ranks or arranged radially, which are marked by two yellowish green or greyish brown bands on their undersides. The fruits, borne on female plants, have a brightly coloured, fleshy cup (aril) that contains a single seed. The cup itself is the only part of a yew that is not poisonous. The yews are of great garden value and given good drainage are tolerant of most soils and situations, including dry chalk and heavy shade. They make good hedges and topiary. CAUTION: toxic if eaten.

Taxus baccata

T. baccata (Common yew, English yew) This is a small to medium-sized tree or large shrub with dark, almost black-green leaves up to 3cm (1¼in) long. The aril is red. It is usually found in the wild on chalk formations and there are many garden forms. Europe, W Asia, Algeria.
H4 ♈ 1993

T. b. 'Adpressa Variegata' A large shrub or small tree with leaves only 1cm (½in) long. It is a male form with unfolding leaves of old gold, passing to yellow, confined to the margins as the leaves age to green. Usually grown wrongly under the name 'Adpressa Aurea'. In cultivation 1866.
H4 ♈ 1993

T. b. 'Amersfoort' A curious, small to medium-sized, open shrub with stiffly ascending branches clothed with small, radially arranged leaves. It is most unlike a yew and recalls *Olearia nummulariifolia*.
H4

Taxus baccata Aurea group

T. b. Aurea group (Golden yew) A large, compact shrub with golden-yellow leaves that turn green by their second year. This name is used to cover all gold-margined forms, the most popular of which is 'Elegantissima'. In cultivation 1855.
H4

T. b. 'Dovastoniana' A very distinct, wide-spreading, small, elegant tree with tiers of long, horizontal branches and long, weeping branchlets. The leaves are blackish green and it is normally female. In cultivation 1777.
H4 ♈ 1993

T. b. 'Dovastoniana Aurea' Similar in habit to 'Dovastoniana' but with its leaves

Taxus baccata 'Dovastoniana Aurea'

margined with bright yellow. It is a male form. In cultivation 1891.
H4 ♈ 1993

T. b. 'Elegantissima' The most popular of the golden yews. It is a dense-growing, large bush with ascending branches and yellow young leaves that later pass to straw-yellow with the colour confined to the mar-

Taxus baccata 'Elegantissima'

Taxus baccata 'Fastigiata'

gin. It is a female form. In cultivation 1852. H4 ♔ 1993

***T. b.* 'Fastigiata'** (Irish yew) A large female shrub of erect habit, making a dense, compact, broad column of closely packed branches. As a young specimen it is narrowly columnar. The leaves are black-green and radially arranged. Originally found 1778 in County Fermanagh, Ireland. H4 ♔ 1993

Taxus baccata 'Fastigiata Aureomarginata'

***T. b.* 'Fastigiata Aureomarginata'** (Golden Irish yew) A male form similar to 'Fastigiata' except that the leaves have yellow margins. In cultivation 1880. H4 ♔ 1993

***T. b.* 'Fructo Luteo'** See *T. b.* 'Lutea'.

***T. b.* 'Lutea'**, syn. *T. b.* 'Fructo Luteo' (Yellow-berried yew) An attractive form in which the yellow berries are often abundant and quite spectacular against the dark foliage. In cultivation c1817. H4

Taxus baccata 'Nutans'

***T. b.* 'Nutans'** A flat-topped bush with leaves irregular in shape, often small and scale-like. At Hillier Nurseries a specimen attained 1 × 0.8m (3ft × 32in) after 30 years. H4

***T. b.* 'Repandans'** A low-growing, often semi-prostrate, female bush with long, spreading branches that droop at the tips. A

Taxus baccata 'Repandans'

Taxus baccata 'Repens Aurea'

splendid ground-cover plant that does well in sun or intense shade. In cultivation 1887. H4 ♔ 1993

***T. b.* 'Repens Aurea'** A low, spreading, female bush with leaves margined with yellow when young, turning to cream later. It loses its colour when in deep shade. H4 ♔ 1993

Taxus baccata 'Semperaurea'

***T. b.* 'Semperaurea'** A slow-growing male bush of medium size with short, crowded, ascending branches well clothed with foliage. The unfolding leaves are old gold, becoming and retaining a rusty yellow colour. In cultivation 1908. H4 ♔ 1993

Taxus baccata 'Standishii'

***T. b.* 'Standishii'** A small, dense, columnar female form of 'Fastigiata Aureomarginata' with erect, slow-growing branches and radially arranged, golden yellow leaves. The best of its colour and habit. H4 ♔ 1993

***T. b.* 'Summergold'** A low shrub with broadly spreading branches. The foliage is yellow in summer and becomes green, margined with yellow. It does not burn when exposed to full sun.
H4

***T.* × *media* 'Hicksii'** A broadly columnar medium-sized to large female bush that makes an excellent hedge. It is similar to *T. baccata* 'Fastigiata' but has longer leaves, up to 3cm (1¼in).
H4 ♔ 1993

Tecomaria *Bignoniaceae*

A genus of one evergreen climbing species related to Campsis.

T. capensis (Cape honeysuckle) A vigorous, self-clinging or twining climber up to 5m (15ft) high. The leaves are pinnate and consist of 5–9 toothed leaflets. The brilliant scarlet, trumpet-shaped flowers are 5cm (2in) long and are in terminal racemes in late summer. It is suitable only for the mildest places and requires a warm, sunny wall in a sheltered position and any good, well-drained soil. In colder districts it makes an excellent conservatory climber. E and S Africa. Introduced 1823.
H2–3

Telopea *Proteaceae*

A small Australasian genus of three or four evergreen species, most of which need a warm climate. The species below enjoys moist but well-drained acid soil.

Telopea truncata

T. truncata (Tasmanian waratah) A medium-sized to large evergreen shrub or occasionally a small tree. The flowers are rich crimson, in dense terminal heads in early summer. For its genus it is remarkably hardy, and at its hardiest when planted among other evergreens. Tasmania. Introduced 1930 by Harold Comber.
H3–4

Tetracentron *Tetracentraceae*

A genus of one deciduous species.

T. sinense A large shrub or small to medium-sized tree. The leaves are ovate or heart-shaped, with long, slender points, and are tinted red when young. The flowers are minute, yellowish, and drape the leafy branches in summer with dense, pendulous catkins. It prefers neutral or acid soil although it has grown happily for a long time on the chalk in the Hillier Nurseries at Winchester. Himalayan region. Introduced 1901 by Ernest Wilson.
H4

Tetradium *Rutaceae*

A genus of nine species of trees with pinnate leaves, now including Euodia. *They are related to* Phellodendron. *Those in cultivation are deciduous trees that succeed on all types of soil.*

Tetradium daniellii

T. daniellii, syn. *Euodia daniellii* A variable, fast-growing, small to medium-sized tree with large pinnate leaves and domed clusters of small, white, pungently scented flow-

ers with yellow anthers, which are borne in late summer and early autumn. Red to purplish or black fruits follow. China, Korea. Introduced 1905.
H4

Teucrium *Labiatae*

A genus of about 100 species of herbaceous perennials, shrubs and sub-shrubs, widely distributed but concentrated in the Mediterranean region. The shrubby members are grown for flower and foliage and require a sunny, well-drained position. They all have square stems and two-lipped flowers.

Teucrium chamaedrys

T. chamaedrys (Wall germander) A dwarf, bushy, aromatic evergreen sub-shrub with a creeping rootstock and erect, hairy stems, densely clothed with small, prettily toothed leaves. The flowers are rose-pink with darker veins, produced in whorls from midsummer to early autumn. It is suitable for growing in walls. Europe.
H4

T. fruticans (Shrubby germander) A small evergreen shrub with its stems and the undersides of its leaves covered with a dense, white felt. The pale blue flowers are borne in terminal racemes in summer. It needs a sunny, well-drained position with the shelter of a wall. S Europe, N Africa. Introduced 1714.
H3

***T. f.* 'Azureum'** A slightly more tender form with darker blue flowers that contrast better with the foliage.
H3 ♔ 1993

T. subspinosum A very dwarf, grey, spiny shrublet of unusual appearance, with small, mauve-pink flowers produced in summer. An excellent plant for the rock garden or scree. Majorca.
H4

Thamnocalamus *Gramineae*

A genus of six evergreen species of bamboo, natives of China, the Himalayas and Africa. They are moisture-lovers but will grow on good soil over chalk.

T. spathaceus, syn. *Arundinaria murielae* An elegant species, forming graceful, arching clumps 2.5–3.5m (8–11ft) or more high. The canes are bright green at first, maturing to dull yellow-green. The leaves are 6–10cm (2½–4in) long by 1–2cm (½–¾in) wide and bright pea-green. This beautiful bamboo is undoubtedly one of the best species in cultivation. China. Introduced 1913 by Ernest Wilson.
H4 ♔ 1993

Thamnocalamus spathiflorus

T. spathiflorus, syn. *Arundinaria spathiflora* A beautiful, clump-forming species of neat, erect habit. The densely packed canes can reach 4.5m (13ft) high but are more usually 2.5–3m (8–10ft). They are bright green, ripening to a pinkish purple shade on the exposed sides, and white bloomy during their first season. The leaves are 7.5–15cm (3–6in) long by 6–12mm (¼–½in) wide. A lovely bamboo; thrives in a little shade and shelter. NW Himalaya. Introduced 1882.
H4

Thuja *Cupressaceae*
Arbor-vitae

A genus of six species of hardy, evergreen coniferous trees and shrubs. They differ from Chamaecyparis *in the usually aromatic foliage and the formation of the cones. Most form attractively conical trees with small, scale-like, overlapping leaves in four ranks, borne in large, flattened, fan-like sprays. The thujas will thrive in almost any soil, provided it is well-drained. Two species (*T. occidentalis *and* T. plicata*) are invaluable for hedges and screens, and a good number of cultivars are dwarf or slow-growing enough for the rock garden. There are several excellent coloured forms. Harmful if eaten.*

T. koraiensis (Korean arbor-vitae) A striking species, usually densely shrubby, but occasionally a small tree with decurved branches and dark brown, peeling bark. The foliage is in large, flattened, frond-like

Thuja occidentalis 'Aureospicata'

sprays, green or sea-green above, white beneath, and pungently aromatic when crushed. Korea. Introduced 1917.
H4

T. occidentalis (American arbor-vitae) An extremely hardy, medium-sized, columnar tree with reddish brown, peeling bark. The branches are spreading, upwardly curved at the tips. The leaves, which have conspicuous resin glands, are dark green above, pale green beneath, and borne in numerous flattened sprays. They usually turn bronze in winter. The foliage is pleasantly fruity-smelling when crushed. E North America. In cultivation 1534.
H4

T. o. 'Aureospicata' A large, erect tree with young shoots becoming yellow, intensified in winter to a rich old gold.
H4

Thuja occidentalis 'Danica'

T. o. 'Danica' A dwarf, dense, compact, globular bush with its foliage held in erect, flattened sprays.
H4 ♔ 1993

T. o. 'Emerald' See *T. o.* 'Smaragd'.

T. o. 'Europe Gold' A large shrub or small tree of narrowly conical habit and golden-yellow foliage.
H4

T. o. 'Golden Globe' A small, dense, rounded shrub with year-round golden-yellow foliage. In cultivation 1965.
H4

T. o. 'Hetz Midget' An extremely slow-growing, dwarf, globular bush. Perhaps the smallest form of all. In cultivation 1928.
H4

Thuja occidentalis 'Europe Gold'

Thuja occidentalis 'Golden Globe'

Thuja occidentalis 'Hetz Midget'

T. o. **'Holmstrup'** A slow-growing, medium-sized to large, narrowly conical bush of dense, compact habit. It has rich green foliage on display throughout the year, held in vertically arranged sprays. In cultivation 1951.
H4 ♔ 1993
T. o. **'Holmstrup Yellow'** A sport of

'Holmstrup' with golden-yellow foliage. Raised before 1951 in Denmark.
H4
T. o. **'Little Gem'** A dense, dwarf, globular, slightly flat-topped bush with deep green foliage in crowded, crimped sprays. In cultivation 1891.
H4
T. o. **'Lutea Nana'** A small, conical, dense bush with foliage which is yellow-green in summer and deep golden yellow in winter. In cultivation 1891.
H4 ♔ 1993
T. o. **'Malonyana'** A striking, small to medium-sized tree of narrow, columnar habit, with leaves uniformly rich green in short, dense, crowded sprays.
H4
T. o. **'Rheingold'** A slow-growing ovoid or conical bush, eventually growing into a medium-sized to large shrub. The foliage is mainly adult, and rich deep gold, shading to amber. It is a very popular plant, provid-

Thuja occidentalis 'Rheingold'

ing perhaps the richest patch of radiant old gold to be found in the garden in the dead of winter. Young plants with juvenile foliage will in time revert to the form described here. It is indistinguishable from 'Ellwangeriana Aurea'.
H4 ♔ 1993
T. o. **'Smaragd'**, syn. *T. o.* 'Emerald' A narrowly conical small tree with bright green foliage.
H4 ♔ 1993

Thuja occidentalis 'Sunkist'

T. o. **'Sunkist'** A dense, small, broadly conical, round-topped bush with golden-yellow foliage in summer.
H4
T. o. **'Wansdyke Silver'** An attractive small, slow-growing bush of conical habit with foliage brightly variegated with cream. In cultivation 1966.
H4
T. o. **'Wareana Lutescens'** A slow-growing, very compact, conical bush with short,

thickened sprays of pale yellow foliage. In cultivation 1884.
H4

T. o. 'Woodwardii' A dense, ovoid bush, taller than broad, eventually reaching 1m (3ft) in height, with typical *T. occidentalis* foliage that remains green in winter.
H4

T. o. 'Yellow Ribbon' A medium-sized shrub, narrowly conical in shape and with bright yellow foliage.
H4

T. orientalis (Chinese arbor-vitae) A large shrub or small tree of dense, conical or columnar habit when young. The branches are erect and the leaves are borne in frond-like, vertical sprays. It is distinct in its rather formal habit, the aroma of its foliage, which is less noticeable than in the other species, and in details of its cones. There are several forms suitable for the rock garden. China. Introduced c1690.
H4

T. o. 'Aurea Nana' A dwarf, globular, dense bush with crowded, vertically arranged sprays of light yellow-green foliage. In cultivation 1804.
H4 ♉ 1993

T. o. 'Conspicua' A medium-sized to large, dense, compact, conical shrub with foliage of a gold colour retained longer than most. In cultivation 1804.
H4

T. o. 'Elegantissima' A medium-sized to large bush of dense, columnar habit and attractive golden yellow foliage, tinged with old gold, that becomes green in winter. In cultivation 1858.
H4 ♉ 1993

T. o. 'Meldensis' A dwarf, densely globular bush with semi-juvenile foliage that is sea-green in summer and turns to a warm yellow-brown in winter. Raised 1852.
H4

T. o. 'Rosedalis' A dense, ovoid bush with soft juvenile foliage. In early spring it is bright canary yellow; it changes by mid-summer to sea-green, and by winter into bloomy plum-purple. In 15 years it is likely to reach 80cm (32in) high. Its soft-to-the-touch foliage and spring colour distinguish it from 'Meldensis'. In cultivation 1923.
H4

Thuja orientalis 'Elegantissima'

Thuja occidentalis 'Rosedalis'

T. plicata (Western red cedar) A large, fast-growing tree with shredding bark and spreading branches. The leaves are bright glossy green above, faintly bloomy beneath, in large, drooping sprays. They have a pleasant, fruity odour when crushed. It makes a splendid hedge or screen and stands up well to clipping. It is also tolerant

Thuja plicata

of shade and chalk soils. W North America. Introduced 1853 by William Lobb.
H4 ♉ 1993

Thuja plicata 'Aurea'

T. p. 'Aurea' An outstanding medium-sized tree with rich old gold foliage, at its best in winter after frost.
H4 ♉ 1993

Thuja plicata 'Cuprea'

***T. p.* 'Cuprea'** A dense, very slow-growing, small conical bush, with the growths tipped in various shades of deep cream to old gold. Splendid for the rock garden.
H4

***T. p.* 'Fastigiata'** A tall, narrowly columnar form with densely arranged, slender, ascending branches. It is excellent as a single specimen tree or for hedging, when a minimum of clipping is necessary. In cultivation 1867.
H4 ♛ 1993

***T. p.* 'Irish Gold'** A large tree similar to 'Zebrina' except that the foliage is more strongly flecked with deeper yellow.
H4 ♛ 1993

Thuja plicata 'Rogersii'

***T. p.* 'Rogersii'** A slow-growing, compact, dwarf, conical bush with densely crowded gold and bronze foliage. It will grow to about 1.2 × 1m (4 × 3ft) in 30 years. In cultivation c1928.
H4

Thuja plicata 'Zebrina'

***T. p.* 'Semperaurescens'** An extremely vigorous large tree with its leaves and shoots tinged with golden-yellow, becoming bronze-yellow by winter. Ideal for use as a tall screen. In cultivation 1923.
H4

***T. p.* 'Stoneham Gold'** A slow-growing but eventually large shrub of dense, nar-

Thuja plicata 'Stoneham Gold'

rowly conical habit. The foliage is bright gold, tipped with coppery bronze. It is a superb plant for the large rock garden. In cultivation 1948.
H4 ♛ 1993

***T. p.* 'Zebrina'** A conical tree with sprays of green foliage banded with creamy yellow. It is a strong-growing, large tree and certainly one of the best variegated conifers, the variegations being so densely crowded as to give a yellow effect to the whole tree. In cultivation 1868.
H4

Thujopsis *Cupressaceae*

A genus of one evergreen coniferous species, differing from Thuja *in having broader, flatter branchlets and larger leaves.*

T. dolobrata A distinctive and attractive large shrub or small to medium-sized tree of dense, broadly conical habit. The branch-

Thujopsis dolobrata 'Aurea'

lets are flattened and bear sprays of large, four-ranked, scale-like leaves that are shining dark green above and are marked with silver-white bands beneath. It produces cones up to 2cm (1in) long. It thrives in all kinds of well-drained soil, including shallow chalk soils. Japan. Introduced 1853.
H4 ♇ 1993

T. d. 'Aurea' A large shrub or small to medium-sized tree with leaves suffused with golden yellow. A splendid conifer that deserves to be planted more frequently. In cultivation 1866.
H4

T. d. 'Nana' A dwarf, compact, spreading, flat-topped bush. A superb little conifer for the rock garden. Introduced 1861.
H4

Tibouchina *Melastomataceae*

A large genus of about 350 species of evergreen and deciduous shrubs and sub-shrubs native to tropical America. None are hardy but several may be grown in conservatories.

T. semidecandra See *T. urvilleana*

T. urvilleana, syn. *T. semidecandra* (Glory bush) A large evergreen shrub with four-angled stems and velvety-hairy, prominently veined leaves. The large, vividly royal purple flowers are produced continuously throughout summer and autumn. Old plants may become straggly and should be pruned in early spring to avoid this. It is an excellent conservatory plant. S Brazil. Introduced 1864.
H1 ♇ 1993

Tibouchina urvilleana

Tilia *Tiliaceae*
Lime, linden

A genus of about 45 species of deciduous trees from many parts of the north-temperate regions. They are easily grown and many of them develop into stately, noble trees. They will grow in all types of fertile soils and in all situations. Unless otherwise stated, all those below have small, fragrant, creamy yellow flowers quite freely borne in clusters in midsummer. If you keep bees, do not grow T. tomentosa and its forms, as the flowers are toxic to them, and do not plant T. platyphyllos where its branches may eventually overhang parked cars, as aphids feeding on it drop a sticky honeydew.

T. americana (American lime, basswood) A medium-sized tree with broad leaves up to 30cm (1ft) long. They are coarsely toothed and green on both sides. Its large leaves make it a striking tree, but like the American beech it is not at its best in Britain and Ireland. Its leaves tend to become shredded if it is exposed to strong winds. Introduced 1752.
H4

Tilia cordata

T. cordata (Small-leaved lime) A medium-sized to large, rounded tree with heart-shaped, 5–7.5cm (2–3in) long, leathery leaves, glossy dark green above and pale green below with reddish brown axillary tufts. The spreading flower clusters appear towards the latter part of summer, and the ivory flowers are sweetly scented. Europe, including England and Wales.
H4 ♇ 1993

T. c. 'Greenspire' A fast-growing, upright selection from the United States, making a narrowly oval crown. In cultivation 1961.
H4 ♇ 1993

Tilia × euchlora

T. × euchlora A medium-sized tree with almost round leaves that are shining dark green above and paler beneath. It is an elegant tree when young, with glossy leaves and arching branches, and becomes dense and twiggy with pendulous lower branches when mature. It is a clean lime, as it is free from aphids, but its flowers tend to have a narcotic effect on bees. In cultivation 1860.
H4 ♇ 1993

Tilia × europaea

T. × europaea (Common lime) A large, vigorous, long-lived tree with glabrous, greenish, zigzag shoots. The broadly ovate or rounded leaves are heart shaped at the base and sharply toothed. Easily recognized by its densely suckering habit. Honeydew from aphids is a problem in summer.
H4

T. × e. 'Pallida' (Kaiser linden) The lime of Berlin's Unter den Linden. The ascending branches form a broadly conical crown and the leaves are yellowish green beneath. H4

Tilia × europaea 'Wratislaviensis'

T. × e. 'Wratislaviensis' The leaves of this large tree are golden-yellow when young and become green with age. It is a splendid tree in which the young growths give the effect of a halo. H4 ♛ 1993

T. 'Harold Hillier' A handsome, vigorous, medium-sized, narrowly conical tree. The leaves vary in length up to 15cm (6in) and are maple-like, with three lobes, edged with bristle-tipped teeth. The autumn colour is a beautiful butter-yellow. Raised 1973 by Nigel Muir. H4

T. henryana A very rare, autumn-flowering tree with wonderful broad fringed leaves often brightly edged with carmine

Tilia henryana

when young. Unfortunately, although medium-sized in the wild, it is very slow growing indeed in cultivation. China. H4

T. mongolica (Mongolian lime) A small, compact, rounded tree of dense, twiggy growth, with reddish shoots. The pretty, ivy-like leaves are up to 7.5cm (3in) long, on red stalks. They are coarsely toothed with 3-5 lobes, especially on young trees, and turn bright yellow in autumn. Russia, Mongolia, N China. Introduced 1880. H4 ♛ 1993

T. oliveri An elegant, medium-sized to large tree with shoots that are inclined to be pendulous. The leaves are dark green above and silvery white beneath. It is free from aphids. C China. Introduced 1900 by Ernest Wilson. H4

T. 'Petiolaris' See *T. tomentosa* 'Petiolaris'.

T. platyphyllos (Broad-leaved lime) A large, vigorous tree with roundish leaves

Tilia platyphyllos

Tilia platyphyllos 'Aurea'

that are sharply toothed, shortly downy above and densely so beneath. The flowers appear towards the middle of summer. It suckers slightly and has aphid problems. Europe, possibly native in parts of England. H4

T. p. 'Aurea' The young shoots of this large tree are yellow, becoming olive-green. They are particularly notable in winter. H4

T. p. 'Laciniata' A small to medium-sized tree of dense, conical habit, with leaves deeply and irregularly cut into rounded and tail-like lobes. H4

T. p. 'Prince's Street' A vigorous, upright large tree, with young shoots which are bright red in winter. H4

T. p. 'Rubra' (Red-twigged lime) The young shoots of this medium-sized tree are bright brownish red, particularly effective in winter. H4 ♛ 1993

Tilia tomentosa

T. tomentosa A handsome but variable large tree of stately habit. The erect branches carry short-stalked rounded, sharply toothed leaves, dark green above and silver-felted beneath, particularly effective when disturbed by a breeze. It is free from aphids but the flowers are toxic to bees. SE and EC Europe. Introduced 1767. H4

T. t. 'Brabant' A large, upright tree that develops a dense, broadly conical crown. Selected in Holland. In cultivation 1970. H4 ♛ 1993

T. t. 'Chelsea Sentinel' A form resembling 'Petiolaris' in its long-stalked leaves and attractively weeping branches but is distinctly columnar.
H4

Tilia tomentosa 'Petiolaris'

T. t. 'Petiolaris' (Weeping silver lime) One of the most beautiful of all large, weeping trees. It has graceful, downward-sweeping branches and the leaves are long-stalked, rounded, toothed, dark green above and white-felted beneath, making them especially attractive when ruffled by a breeze. The flowers are richly scented but narcotic to bees. A tree of uncertain origin. In cultivation 1840.
H4 ♔ 1993

Toona *Meliaceae*

A genus of six species of evergreen and deciduous trees from China, South East Asia and north Australia, distinct from Cedrela, *which is now confined to eight species occurring in the tropical regions of the Americas. They thrive in most fertile well-drained soils with plenty of sun. The following is rather like a more refined* Ailanthus altissima.

T. sinensis, syn. *Cedrela sinensis* A medium-sized, fast-growing deciduous tree with handsome, large, pinnate leaves that are often bronze when young. It has fragrant white flowers in panicles often as much as 30cm (1ft) long, and lovely yellow tints in autumn. China. Introduced 1862.
H4

T. s. 'Flamingo' The young foliage of this medium-sized tree is brilliant pink, turning to cream, then green.
H4

Torreya *Taxaceae*

A genus of about seven species of evergreen coniferous trees and shrubs, natives of east Asia and North America. The leaves are linear, rigid and spine-tipped, marked with two glaucous bands beneath, spirally arranged on leading shoots, and on the lateral shoots twisted to appear in two ranks. The fruits are plum-like and fleshy, each containing a single seed. They are excellent trees on chalk soils and bear shade well.

T. californica (Californian nutmeg) A small to medium-sized, broadly conical tree, well furnished to ground level, like a majestic yew. The leaves are rigid, up to 7.5cm (3in) long, shining dark green above and spine-tipped. The fruits are egg-shaped, green and streaked with purple when ripe. California. Introduced 1851 by William Lobb.
H4

Trachelospermum *Apocynaceae*

There are about 20 species in this genus, of which all but one native of the south-east United States are from east and South East Asia. These beautiful, self-clinging, evergreen, twining climbers should be grown on a sunny, sheltered wall in mild areas or otherwise in the conservatory. Their attractive, sweetly scented, jasmine-like flowers are borne in mid- to late summer. When cut, the stems exude a milky sap. The soil should be well-drained and reasonably moisture-retentive.

T. asiaticum The hardiest species and a very beautiful one. It is densely leafy, up to 6m (20ft) high and as much across, with fragrant flowers 2cm (³/₄in) across, cream with a buff-yellow centre, changing to yellow. It is hardier, neater and more compact than *T. jasminoides*. Japan, Korea.
H2–3 ♔ 1993

T. jasminoides A lovely, rather slow-growing climber up to 7m (22ft) high and wide. The highly fragrant flowers are 2.5cm (1in) across and white, becoming cream

with age. China, Taiwan. Introduced 1844 by Robert Fortune.
H2–3 ♔ 1993

T. j. 'Japonicum' A taller-growing selection with larger leaves than the typical form. When established it will clothe a wall as effectively as ivy. The leaves often colour richly in winter.
H2–3

Trachelospermum jasminoides 'Variegatum'

T. j. 'Variegatum' The leaves of this form are margined and splashed with cream, often suffused with crimson in winter.
H2–3 ♔ 1993

T. j. 'Wilsonii' An unusual form in which the leaves vary from ovate to slenderly lance-shaped. They are attractively veined and often turn crimson in winter. China. Introduced by Ernest Wilson.
H2–3

Trachycarpus *Palmae*

A genus of four species of evergreen palms with very large, fan-shaped leaves, natives of the Himalayas and east Asia. The following species is much more hardy than generally supposed but needs a sheltered position to protect its leaves from being shredded by strong winds.

T. fortunei (Chusan palm) A remarkable small to medium-sized palm, ultimately 12m (40ft) after many decades. It develops a single trunk, thickly clothed with the fibrous remains of the old leaf bases, as neatly and precisely woven as if done by hand. The leaves are large, fan-shaped, 1–1.5m (3–5ft) wide, and on long, stout

Trachycarpus fortunei

stalks in a cluster from the top of the trunk. They persist for many years. The small, yellow flowers are borne in large, terminal, curving panicles in early summer. The fruits are like blue-black marbles. In very favoured gardens it may seed itself quite freely. China (Chusan Island). Introduced 1830 by Philipp von Siebold and 1849 by Robert Fortune.
H3–4 ♡ 1993

Trochodendron *Trochodendraceae*

A genus of one evergreen species.

Trochodendron aralioides

T. aralioides A large but slow-growing shrub or small tree with a spreading head. It has aromatic bark and long-stalked, leathery leaves, broadest above the middle, bright apple-green or yellowish green and scalloped at the margins. They are held in beautiful spiral whorls. The green flowers are borne in erect terminal clusters in

spring and early summer. Flower arrangers find this shrub irresistible. It grows in most fertile soils except shallow ones over chalk and will grow in sun or shade. It is hardier than generally supposed. Japan, Taiwan, S Korea. In cultivation 1894.
H4

Tsuga *Pinaceae*

A genus of about 10 species of extremely elegant, evergreen coniferous trees of broadly conical habit, which have spreading branches and gently drooping or arching branchlets. They are natives of east Asia and North America. The leaves are short, narrow and straight and appear to be in two ranks, except in T. mertensiana, *in which they are arranged radially. They bear shade well and grow best in a moist but well-drained, loamy soil.* T. canadensis *can be grown in moderately deep soils over chalk.*

T. canadensis (Eastern hemlock) A large tree, often with several main stems from near the base. It is the best species for a limy soil. The leaves are short and marked with two white bands beneath. E North America. Introduced 1736.
H4

T. c. 'Albospica' A slow-growing compact shrub which produces leaves with creamy white growing tips.
H4

T. c. 'Aurea' A dwarf, slow-growing form with a compact conical habit. Its leaves are broad and crowded and are golden yellow when unfolding, becoming greenish yellow.
H4

Tsuga canadensis 'Cole'

Tsuga canadensis 'Jeddeloh'

T. c. 'Bennett' A slow-growing, dwarf shrub of spreading habit and dense, crowded growth. In cultivation 1920.
H4

T. c. 'Cole' A remarkable, prostrate plant which has long branches growing flattened along the ground. In time they spread out widely to form extensive carpets. Found

Tsuga canadensis 'Bennett'

Tsuga canadensis 'Pendula'

1929 in New Hampshire, USA.
H4

T. c. 'Jeddeloh' A reliably dwarf, compact bush with arching branches. Selected in W Germany. In cultivation 1965.
H4 🏆 1993

T. c. 'Pendula' A most attractive form that develops into a low mound of overlapping, drooping branches. A superb plant for a prominent position on a large rock garden. In 40 years it reached 2 × 3.5m (6 × 11ft) at Hilliers. Introduced before 1876.
H4 🏆 1993

T. heterophylla (Western hemlock) A large, fast-growing tree with gracefully spreading branches. The leaves are up to 2 cm (³/₄in) long, marked with two white bands beneath. It is a beautiful conifer, particularly when grown as a single specimen, and develops into an elegant tree with a spire-like crown. It is not suitable for limy soils but is tolerant of shade. W North America. Introduced 1851 by John Jeffrey.
H4 🏆 1993

T. h. 'Greenmantle' A graceful, tall, narrow tree producing pendulous branches which originated at Windsor Great Park. Named 1971.
H4

T. mertensiana 'Glauca' A beautiful, slow-growing, spire-like tree with glaucous leaves which are radially arranged on the branchlets. In cultivation 1850.
H4

Tweedia

T. caerulea See *Oxypetalum caeruleum*.

U

Ugni

U. molinae See *Myrtus ugni*.

Ulex *Leguminosae*
Furze, gorse, whin

A genus of about 20 species of spiny shrubs from western Europe and North Africa, some of which are naturalized in parts of the United States. They should be pot-grown, otherwise they are hard to establish. Strong-growing plants are liable to become leggy and bare at the base and may be cut to ground level after flowering. Like heather, gorse does best in poor, acid soil. It is not recommended for shallow chalk soils. In areas of high rainfall where the soil is poor and acid but well-drained, gorse is successful as a hedge, and trimming is carried out after the main flush of flowers. If the area is mild, flowering is almost continuous throughout the year.

Ulex europaeus 'Flore Pleno'

U. europaeus 'Flore Pleno' A densely branched, green, viciously spiny shrub. It is quite compact and lower than the 2m (6¹/₂ft) to which the common single form grows. The flowers are chrome-yellow, semi-double, long-lasting and caramel-scented, and almost completely cover the hummocky plants in mid- to late spring and later. In cultivation 1828.
H4 🏆 1993

U. gallii 'Mizen Head' A dwarf shrub of prostrate habit with shoots spreading along the ground and deep yellow flowers in early autumn.
H4

Ulmus *Ulmaceae*
Elm

The elm population of Britain and North America was virtually wiped out by the mid-1970s as a result of the depredations of elm bark beetles, which carry the spores of a virulent strain of fungus that blocks the conductive tissues of the trees. The disease is known as Dutch elm disease because it was initially identified in the Netherlands. Asiatic elms are resistant to it.

The disease did not disappear when the trees died. Many of them regrew from suckers and show little sign of a problem until they become large enough to have thick, rugged bark, when they can become reinfected. If an elm is infected, which is evidenced by the sudden dying-off of a branch or larger portion of the tree, immediate action should be taken. Where it is the odd branch that is affected, it may be removed and burnt; if it is more than that, the tree should be felled, burnt, and its stump de-barked or preferably removed.

Many of the elms that were previously thought of as resistant to the disease were in fact only capable of coming through the attacks of the much less virulent form that was prevalent in the 1930s and which subsequently died down.

The elms are noble trees that thrive in almost any soil and in any situation, no matter how exposed. In most cases the leaves turn golden in autumn – as they do earlier in the year if Dutch elm disease strikes them. The small, reddish flowers of the elms are borne on naked twigs in spring and the seeds, called samaras, are winged and somewhat disc-shaped.

U. glabra A large and impressive tree which usually develops a dome-shaped crown with spreading branches that are arching or pendulous at their extremities. The large, short-stalked leaves are rough to the touch and coarsely toothed. They turn yellow in autumn. The fruits are effective in early spring when they crowd the branches. It is an excellent tree for planting in exposed situations either inland or along the coast and is probably the only elm native to Britain. Europe, N and W Asia.
H4

Ulmus glabra 'Camperdownii'

U. g. 'Camperdownii' (Camperdown elm) A small, neat, compact form which is still seen unaffected by Dutch elm disease in towns. In cultivation 1850.
H4

U. g. 'Lutescens' A very beautiful, free-growing form, which has leaves that are soft cream-yellow in spring, later becoming yellowish green. It can be seen unaffected by Dutch elm disease in several parts of Britain.
H4

U. × hollandica 'Dampieri Aurea' A form of the hybrid between *U. glabra* and *U. minor*. It is a narrowly conical small tree in which the crowded, broad leaves are suffused with golden-yellow. It does not appear to be affected by Dutch elm disease.
H4

U. japonica (Japanese elm) A graceful tree that appears immune to Dutch elm disease. NE Asia, Japan.
H4

U. minor 'Dicksonii' (Dickson's golden elm) A very slow-growing medium-sized to large tree with leaves of a beautiful, bright golden-yellow. It appears to be unaffected by Dutch elm disease.
H4

U. m. 'Jaqueline Hillier' A medium-sized to large, slowish growing, suckering, dense shrub with small, double-toothed leaves. Its neat, dense, closely-packed habit lends itself to planting as a low hedge, for bonsai, or simply as an intriguing and beautiful specimen. It appears to be unaffected by Dutch elm disease.
H4

Ulmus minor 'Jaqueline Hillier'

U. parvifolia (Chinese elm) A medium-sized tree with downy young shoots. The leaves are small, leathery and glossy green, persisting halfway through the winter. The flowers are produced in early autumn. It appears to be unaffected by Dutch elm disease. N and C China, Korea, Taiwan, Japan. Introduced 1794.
H4

U. p. 'Frosty' A small, slow-growing, shrubby form in which the tiny, neatly arranged leaves have margins and teeth frosted with white.
H4

U. p. 'Geisha' A dwarf shrub with tiny, dark green leaves edged with white.
H4

U. pumila A variable species that may be anything from a large shrub to a medium-sized tree. The leaves are oval to lance-shaped and toothed. N Asia. Introduced 1770.
H4

U. 'Sapporo Autumn Gold' A fast-growing, medium-sized tree with a spreading habit which has glossy green leaves that are attractively red-tinged when young and turn yellow-green in autumn. Its resistance to the virulent strain of Dutch elm disease is to be expected from its parentage, which is Asiatic on both sides: it is a cross of *U pumilla* and *U. japonica*.
H4

Ulmus × hollandica 'Dampieri Aurea'

V

Vaccinium *Ericaceae*

A large genus of about 450 species of evergreen and deciduous shrubs with a wide distribution. They need much the same conditions as heathers, but are more tolerant of shade and moisture – in fact, some species demand such conditions. They are modestly beautiful flowering shrubs with fine autumn colour in the deciduous species and notable crops of berries. They are excellent in extremely acid soils. Pruning is rarely necessary.

Vaccinium corymbosum

V. corymbosum (High bush blueberry) A colourful, small to medium-sized shrub that forms a dense thicket of erect, branching stems. The leaves, which are up to 8cm (3in) long, turn vivid scarlet and bronze in autumn. The clusters of pale pink or white, urn-shaped flowers are borne in late spring. The berries are comparatively large, black with a blue bloom, and sweetly edible, like black grapes. It is extensively cultivated in the United States and Canada for commercial fruit production, and demand for cultivars selected for fruit quality is growing quite rapidly in Britain. E North America. Introduced 1765.
H4 ♛ 1993

V. cylindraceum A superb, semi-evergreen species, forming a medium-sized to large shrub with leaves that often stay green well into winter. The cylindrical flowers are packed into short clusters along the previous year's branchlets in late summer and

Vaccinium cylindraceum

autumn. They are red in bud, opening to pale yellow-green, tinged with red, and are followed by cylindrical, blue-black, bloomy berries. Azores.
H4 ♛ 1993

V. delavayi A neat, compact evergreen shrub, slowly reaching 60cm (2ft), densely set with small, box-like, leathery leaves. The tiny, pink-tinged flowers are in small clusters at the ends of the shoots in late spring or early summer. The rounded berries are purplish blue. China. Introduced before 1923 by George Forrest.
H4

V. floribundum A beautiful small evergreen shrub with red young growths and small, dark green leaves that are purplish red when young. They are densely set on the spray-like branches. The cylindrical, rose-pink flowers are in dense clusters in early summer, and the berries are red and edible. Although it comes from near the equator, it is remarkably hardy. Andes of Ecuador. Introduced c1840.
H3–4

V. glauco-album An attractive evergreen shrub, suckering and forming patches up to 2m (6½ft) high. The leaves are comparatively large, more or less oval, grey-green above and vividly blue-white beneath. The cylindrical, pale pink flowers are borne among rosy, silvery white bracts in clusters during late spring and early summer. The berries are black with a blue bloom and last well into winter. It may be damaged by frost in cold areas. Himalayan region. In cultivation 1900.
H3–4 ♛ 1993

Vaccinium glauco-album

V. macrocarpon (American cranberry) A prostrate evergreen shrublet with slender, wiry, creeping stems and small oval leaves. The flowers are small, drooping, pink, and with the petals curving back to reveal a beak of yellow anthers. They are carried in short clusters in summer. The fruit are called cranberries and are red, globular, edible, but acid in flavour. It needs a moist, peaty, boggy soil. Selected clones are grown in the United States for cranberries. E North America. Introduced 1760.
H4

Vaccinium moupinense

V. moupinense A neat, dwarf, evergreen shrub of dense habit, which has more or less narrow-oval leaves and urn-shaped, mahogany-red flowers borne on stalks of the same colour in dense clusters in late spring and early summer. The rounded berries are purplish black. W China. Introduced 1909 by Ernest Wilson.
H4

Vaccinium nummularia

Vaccinium vitis-idaea 'Koralle'

V. nummularia This is probably the most attractive of the dwarf species in cultivation. It is a compact, evergreen shrub with bristly-hairy, arching shoots that are neatly clothed with a double row of small, leathery, rounded leaves. The small, cylindrical, rose-red flowers are in dense clusters at the ends of the shoots in late spring and early summer and are followed by edible black berries. Although hardy only in mild areas, where it is excellent on a sheltered, shady bank that is not too dry, this choice little shrub makes an ideal alpine-house plant. Himalaya. Introduced c1850.
H3

V. ovatum (Box blueberry) An attractive evergreen shrub of medium size. The leathery leaves are bright coppery red when young and become shiny dark green, thickly crowding the downy branches. The bell-shaped, white or pink flowers are in short clusters in late spring and early summer. The berries are red at first, ripening to black. A useful evergreen for cutting. W North America. Introduced 1826 by David Douglas.
H4

V. praestans A creeping deciduous shrub forming dense patches 2.5–10cm (1–4in) high. The leaves are 2.5–5cm (1–2in) long and the bell-shaped, white to reddish flowers are borne singly or in clusters of 2–3 in early summer. The quite large, edible berries are globular, bright glossy red, fragrant, and sweet. Its leaves colour richly in autumn. Choice species for a moist, cool place. NE Asia, Japan. Introduced 1914.
H4

V. retusum A dwarf, slow-growing evergreen shrub up to 1m (3ft) tall. It has stiff, downy shoots, small, leathery, oval leaves, and small, urn-shaped, pink flowers in late spring. E Himalaya. Introduced c1882.
H4

V. vitis-idaea 'Koralle' A form of the cowberry, this is a dwarf, creeping ever-green shrub. The leaves are small and box-like and the flowers are bell-shaped, white tinged with pink, and borne in short clusters from early to late summer. The large, bright red berries are very freely borne.
H4 ♛ 1993

Vestia *Solanaceae*

A genus of one evergreen species, related to Cestrum.

V. foetida A small, erect shrub with leaves that have an unpleasant burnt rubber smell when bruised. The flowers, however, are most attractive; they are nodding, tubular, pale yellow, and profusely borne in the axils of the upper leaves from mid-spring to mid-summer. They are followed by small yellow fruits. It is suitable only for the milder areas, where it needs a warm, sunny position in a well-drained soil. Chile. Introduced 1815.
H3

Vestia foetida

VIBURNUM

Caprifoliaceae

YOU ARE unlikely to see a border consisting solely of viburnums outside a botanic garden, but were you to do so you would readily agree that this is a genus of shrubs that is outstanding in its ability to provide beauty and interest all year round.

Viburnum has about 150 species of evergreen and deciduous shrubs with a very wide distribution in north-temperate regions. That most of them have white flowers is no restriction to their versatility, as there are so many other ways in which they are beautiful. Their scent is, of course, renowned and there are few shrubs as gorgeously fragrant as the many perfumed viburnums. Their foliage is almost always an attractive feature, whether it be the glossy freshness of the evergreen *V. × burkwoodii*, the velvety softness of *V. carlesii*, the unusual, pleated foliage of *V. plicatum* and its forms, or the combination of glossiness and puckered, wrinkled surface that characterizes *V. rhytidophyllum*. Then, too, there are viburnums with a display of autumn colour to rival any Japanese maple. The deciduous *V. lantanoides* turns deep red, *V. carlesii* has a mixture of amber and soft red, and the lime-hating *V. furcatum* colours boldly over a long period in late summer and autumn.

It is not simply scent that distinguishes the flowers of viburnums but also an indefinable quality that is a combination of gentle beauty and simplicity. Look at the clusters of white, pink-budded flowers all along the upright branches of *V. farreri* and you will agree that nothing could be more perfect on a winter's day. This species, its hybrids, and all the scented viburnums should if possible be planted close to paths and preferably where the prevailing wind of the season in which they flower takes the perfumes into the garden.

On top of these excellent qualities, many viburnums are unsurpassed as berrying shrubs. The technical term for the fruit is a drupe, but the effect is of clusters or sometimes large bunches of red, blue, black or yellow berries, some of which are so long-lasting that they meet the flowers of the following year.

CARE AND CULTIVATION

Viburnums are not difficult to grow. Only one species, *V. lantanoides*, requires an absence of lime in the soil; the rest will grow in any deep, moisture-retentive soil in sun or semi-shade. None of the species listed below, however, will thrive on really poor soils. They are in general hardy, although the evergreens are for the most part a little less so than those that are deciduous. Berry production is uncertain unless more than one clone of the same species is grown or related species flower at the same time as one another. The exception to this rule is *V. opulus*, although forms of that species with nothing but sterile florets (for example *V.o.* 'Roseum') cannot bear fruits at all.

In order to keep a proper shape, avoid overcrowding. To remove dead or diseased wood, prune evergreens in late spring and deciduous viburnums immediately flowering ceases.

Viburnum opulus may suffer from black bean aphid, and an aphid that badly damages the leaves of *V. carlesii*, causing them to curl up, is quite a frequent pest. Apart from these troubles, however, viburnums are remarkably problem-free.

Viburnum × bodnantense 'Dawn'

Viburnum *Caprifoliaceae*

Viburnum betulifolium

Viburnum × bodnantense 'Charles Lamont'

Viburnum × burkwoodii 'Anne Russell'

V. *betulifolium* A large, erect shrub with coarsely toothed leaves and wide, flat heads of white flowers in early summer. It is a magnificent sight in autumn, when the long, swaying branches are heavy with innumerable bunches of fruits resembling redcurrants that persist into winter. Unfortunately, they are not freely borne on young plants. To ensure fruiting, a group of plants from different sources should be planted, and this means that it is not a shrub for smaller gardens. W and C China. Introduced 1901 by Ernest Wilson.
H4

V. × *bodnantense* A splendid, vigorous, medium-sized to large shrub with densely packed clusters of sweetly scented, rose-tinted flowers that are freely produced over several weeks from mid-autumn on, well into winter and beyond. The flowers are remarkably frost-resistant and a cheering sight on a cold winter's day. First raised 1933 at the Royal Botanic Garden, Edinburgh, and then 1935 at Bodnant Gardens.
H4

V. × *b*. 'Charles Lamont' A form with pure pink flowers like those of *V. farreri*. One of the original seedlings raised 1933 at the Royal Botanic Garden, Edinburgh.
H4 ♛ 1993

V. × *b*. 'Dawn' This was the first-named form of the cross and for many people it is the most beautiful. It has highly scented, rose-tinted flowers, darkening with age.
H4 ♛ 1993

Viburnum × bodnantense 'Deben'

V. × *b*. 'Deben' A lovely shrub with clusters of sweetly scented flowers that are pink in bud and open white during mild spells from mid-autumn to mid-spring.
H4 ♛ 1993

V. × *burkwoodii* A lovely medium-sized evergreen shrub. It inherits its attractive clusters of fragrant, pink-budded, white flowers from *V. carlesii*, which was one of its parents. The leaves are dark, shining green above and brownish grey felted beneath. Flowering is from mid-winter to late spring. Raised c1924.
H4

V. × *b*. 'Anne Russell' A lovely, more compact, less evergreen hybrid with clusters of fragrant flowers. Raised c1951.
H4 ♛ 1993

V. × *b*. 'Fulbrook' A later-flowering form with clusters of comparatively large, sweetly scented flowers that are pink in bud and open white.
H4 ♛ 1993

Viburnum × burkwoodii 'Park Farm Hybrid'

V. × *b*. 'Park Farm Hybrid' A strong-growing medium-sized shrub, rather more spreading than the others, with fragrant, quite large flowers in mid- to late spring.
H4 ♛ 1993

V. × *carlcephalum* A splendid, medium-sized, compact shrub with rounded clusters up to 13cm (5in) across of relatively large,

Viburnum carlcephalum

highly fragrant, pink-budded, white flowers in late spring. The leaves often colour richly in autumn. Raised c1932.
H4 🏆 1993

V. carlesii This is one of the most popular of all shrubs and one of the most deliciously scented. It is a medium-sized, rounded shrub with ovate, velvety-downy leaves that colour beautifully in autumn. The rounded clusters of pure white flowers, borne in mid- and late spring, are pink in bud and emit a sweet, daphne-like fragrance. The fruits are jet black. Korea. Introduced 1902.
H4

***V. c.* 'Aurora'** An outstanding selection with red buds opening to deliciously fragrant pink flowers.
H4 🏆 1993

Viburnum carlesii 'Diana'

***V. c.* 'Diana'** A strong-growing medium-sized form with perfumed flowers, first red then pink. Young foliage is tinged purple.
H4 🏆 1993

***V.* 'Chesapeake'** A small shrub, forming a mound broader than it is tall, with dark, glossy green, long-persistent leaves. The flowers are pink in bud, open white and are followed by red fruits that turn black.
H4

Viburnum cinnamomifolium

V. cinnamomifolium A large, handsome, evergreen shrub with large, leathery leaves somewhat like those of *V. davidii*. The small, dull white flowers are borne in flattish clusters 10–15cm (4–6in) across in early summer. They are followed in autumn by small, egg-shaped, shining blue-black fruits. When well grown it is an imposing shrub, needing a more sheltered position than *V. davidii* and equally happy in semi-shade. China. Introduced 1904 by Ernest Wilson.
H4 🏆 1993

V. davidii A small evergreen shrub forming a low, wide mound and creating good ground cover. The large, narrowly oval leaves are three-nerved and glossy dark green above, paler beneath. The flowers are small, dull white, in terminal clusters in early summer, and the bright turquoise-blue, egg-shaped fruits are particularly striking in winter. More than one specimen is needed to ensure pollination but male and female vegetatively propagated or specially selected clones are available. W China. Introduced 1904 by Ernest Wilson.
H4 🏆 1993

Viburnum dilatatum

V. dilatatum A medium-sized shrub with oval to fairly rounded, coarsely toothed leaves and pure white, pungently scented flowers. They are freely borne in trusses in late spring and early summer. The vivid red fruits are held in heavy bunches that often last well into winter. It seems to prefer a climate that is fairly sunny and dry. Japan. Introduced before 1875.
H4

***V.* 'Eskimo'** A small, semi-evergreen shrub from the same cross as 'Chesapeake'.

Viburnum 'Chesapeake'

Viburnum davidii

Viburnum 'Eskimo'

It has leathery leaves and compact white flowerheads, 7.5cm (3in) across, like snow-balls, borne in mid-spring, opening from buds that are creamy and tinged with pink. The fruits are red turning to black.
H4

Viburnum farreri

V. farreri, syn. *V. fragrans* A medium-sized to large shrub with stiff, erect branches but a broad, rounded outline as it ages. Its leaves are bronze when young. The flowers are in terminal and lateral clusters and are pink in bud, opening white, and deliciously scented. They appear in late autumn and continue throughout winter. The red fruits are rarely produced. N China. Introduced 1910 by William Purdom and later by Reginald Farrer.
H4 ♈ 1993

V. f. **'Candidissimum'** A distinct form with young leaves that are green, not bronze, and pure white flowers.
H4

Viburnum farreri 'Candidissimum'

Viburnum farreri 'Nanum'

V. f. **'Nanum'** A dense, dwarf form with a compact, mound-like habit. The flowers, although pleasantly scented, are sadly only sparsely produced.
H4

Viburnum foetens

V. foetens A beautiful, fragrant, medium-sized shrub of loose spreading habit with white flowers that are occasionally pink in bud opening from mid-winter to early spring. It is not an easy plant but seems to appreciate a good, deep moist loam soil in semi-shade. It will grow well on chalk. W Himalayas. In cultivation 1937.
H4

V. fragrans, syn. *V. farreri*.

V. furcatum A large shrub with fairly rounded leaves up to 15cm (6in) long that colour richly over a long period in late summer and autumn. The flowers appear in late spring and are in flattened, terminal clusters, surrounded by several ray florets in the manner of a lacecap hydrangea. The

Viburnum furcatum

fruits are red, turning black. It is a beautiful, elgantly charming species, excellent among trees or other large shrubs. Japan, Taiwan. Introduced 1892.
H4 ♈ 1993

Viburnum × globosum 'Jermyn's Globe'

V. × globosum **'Jermyn's Globe'** A small to medium-sized, evergreen, rounded, dense shrub with leathery, narrow leaves and small, white flowers in flattened clusters in late spring and often at other times of the year. The fruits are egg-shaped and bluish black. Originated 1964 as one of a batch of seedlings at Hilliers' West Hill Nursery.
H4

V. harryanum A medium-sized, dense, bushy evergreen shrub with very distinctive small, neat, almost perfectly round leaves, often in whorls of three. The small white flowers open in late spring, and the fruits are egg-shaped and shining black. China. Introduced 1904 by Ernest Wilson.
H3–4

Viburnum henryi

Viburnum japonicum

Viburnum lantanoides

V. henryi A medium-sized, eventually quite large evergreen shrub of open, erect habit. The white, fragrant flowers are borne in pyramidal panicles in early summer and are followed by ellipsoid fruits that are bright red and then black. Introduced 1901 by Ernest Wilson.
H4

Viburnum × hillieri 'Winton'

V. × hillieri 'Winton' A semi-evergreen, medium-sized shrub with spreading and ascending branches and narrowly oval leaves that are copper-tinted when unfolding and suffused with bronze-red in winter. The creamy white flowers are profusely borne in panicles in early summer and are succeeded by red fruits that turn black. The hybrid, of which this is the original, selected clone, arose 1950 at Hillier Nurseries.
H4 ♔ 1993

V. japonicum A handsome, medium-sized, evergreen shrub with firm, leathery, often puckered leaves up to 15cm (6in) long

and 10cm (4in) wide. The white, fragrant flowers are borne in dense, rounded trusses in early summer, but not on young plants. The fruits are red. Japan. Introduced c1879 by Charles Maries.
H4

Viburnum × juddii

V. × juddii A delightful, small to medium-sized, bushy shrub with freely produced terminal clusters of sweetly scented, pink-tinted flowers in mid- to late spring. It has a better constitution than *V. carlesii*, which is one of its parents, and is less prone to attack by aphids. Raised 1920 by William Judd at the Arnold Arboretum, Boston, Massachusetts.
H4 ♔ 1993

V. lantana A large native shrub that is a familiar sight in hedgerows, particularly on the chalk downs of southern England. The broadly ovate leaves and the young shoots are covered with a dense tomentum, sometimes turning a dark crimson in autumn.

The creamy white flowers appear in late spring and early summer, and are followed by oblong fruits which mature from red to black. C and S Europe, N Asia Minor, North Africa.
H4

V. lantanoides (Hobble bush) A distinctive and attractive, medium-sized shrub with fairly large, quite rounded leaves that turn deep claret in autumn. The flowers are in heads much like a lacecap hydrangea, with a conspicuous row of white, sterile florets, and appear in late spring and early summer. The fruits are red, turning to blackish purple. It enjoys woodland conditions and a lime-free soil. E North America. Introduced 1820.
H4

V. macrocephalum 'Sterile' A semi-evergreen, medium-sized, rounded shrub with flowers in large, globular heads that look like those of a mophead hydrangea. In

Viburnum macrocephalum 'Sterile'

cold districts it is best against a sunny wall. Garden origin. China. Introduced 1844 by Robert Fortune.

H4

V. odoratissimum A large, evergreen, noble shrub with striking, glossy, more or less oval, leathery leaves, the older ones of which often colour richly in winter and early spring. The fragrant white flowers are borne in large, conical panicles in summer, and the fruits are red, turning black. A magnificent species for gardens in mild areas. India to Japan. Introduced c1818.

H3

Viburnum opulus

Viburnum opulus 'Xanthocarpum'

V. opulus (Guelder rose) The species itself is a large, vigorous shrub with five-lobed, maple-like leaves that colour richly in autumn and flattened clusters of white flowers in summer, rather like those of a lacecap hydrangea. The red, translucent fruits last well into winter. It enjoys most soils but is especially happy in boggy conditions. Europe (including Britain), Asia, N Africa.

H4

***V. o.* 'Aureum'** A compact medium-sized form with bright yellow leaves that turn green. It tends to burn in full sun.

H4

***V. o.* 'Compactum'** A small, dense shrub that flowers and fruits freely.

H4 ♔ 1993

***V. o.* 'Notcutt's Variety'** A large shrub with larger flowers and fruits.

H4 ♔ 1993

***V. o.* 'Roseum'**, syn. *V. o.* 'Sterile' (Snowball tree) One of the most popular and attractive hardy flowering shrubs. The

Viburnum opulus 'Roseum'

flowers are gathered into conspicuous, creamy, globular heads. The name derives from its having been called rose elder (*Sambucus rosea*) in previous centuries; the individual florets were thought to resemble small, single roses.

H4 ♔ 1993

***V. o.* 'Sterile'** See *V. o.* 'Roseum'.

***V. o.* 'Xanthocarpum'** A medium-sized shrub with fruits pure, clear yellow at all stages, becoming a little darker and almost translucent when ripe.

H4 ♔ 1993

V. plicatum A wide-spreading, medium-sized shrub with a distinctive method of branching that gives it considerable architectural value. The branches are in layers, creating in time a most attractive tiered or wedding-cake effect. The leaves are bright green and pleated, and the inflorescences, which appear in late spring and early summer, are umbels of small, fertile, creamy flowers, surrounded by large, white, ray florets, very much like a lacecap hydrangea. They are borne in double rows along the upper sides of the branches, and form the 'icing' on the 'cake'. The fruits are red, turning black, and the leaves are often tinted red to purple in autumn. China, Japan, Taiwan. Introduced c1865.

H4

Viburnum plicatum 'Grandiflorum'

V. p. 'Grandiflorum' A medium-sized shrub similar to 'Sterile' but with larger heads of sterile white florets, flushed pink at the margins.
H4 ♛ 1993

Viburnum plicatum 'Lanarth'

V. p. 'Lanarth' A very fine medium-sized shrub, resembling 'Mariesii' but stronger in growth and less horizontally branched.
H4

V. p. 'Mariesii' A superb medium-sized shrub with tiered branches and an abundance of flowers that when open give the appearance of a snow-laden bush. The ray florets are also relatively large and the leaves colour well in autumn.
H4 ♛ 1993

V. p. 'Nanum Semperflorens', syn. *V. p.* 'Watanabe' A slow-growing, small, dense form with white flowers borne over a long period in summer and autumn. Found wild in Japan by Kanji Watanabe c1956.
H4

Viburnum plicatum 'Mariesii'

Viburnum plicatum 'Nanum Semperflorens'

Viburnum plicatum 'Pink Beauty'

V. p. 'Pink Beauty' A charming selection in which the initially white ray florets change to a delightful shade of pink as they age. It is free-fruiting.
H4 ♛ 1993

V. p. 'Rowallane' A medium-sized shrub similar to 'Lanarth' but a little less vigorous. The ray florets are larger and it usually pro-

duced a good crop of fruits, which very seldom occurs with 'Mariesii'. It has good autumn colour.
H4 ♛ 1993

Viburnum plicatum 'Shasta'

V. p. 'Shasta' A profusely flowering, widespreading form, like 'Lanarth' but with larger ray-florets. The bright red fruits later turn black. Raised 1970 in United States.
H4

Viburnum plicatum 'Sterile'

V. p. 'Sterile' (Japanese Snowball) A very popular, medium-sized, dense, spreading shrub and one of the best among the hardy ornamental shrubs. The white sterile florets are concentrated in globular heads up to 7.5cm (3in) across, borne in a double row along the length of each arching branch in late spring and early summer. It is sometimes confused in the trade with *V. opulus* 'Sterile'. Garden origin, China. Introduced 1844 by Robert Fortune.
H4

Viburnum plicatum 'Summer Snowflake'

V. p. 'Summer Snowflake' A medium-sized shrub with tiered branches and lacecap flowerheads in late spring and onwards through summer. The leaves turn red to purple in autumn.
H4

V. p. 'Watanabe' See *V. p.* 'Nanum Semperflorens'.

V. 'Pragense' A medium-sized to large, spreading, evergreen shrub with elliptic, corrugated leaves up to 10cm (4in) long, lustrous dark green above and white-felted below. The flowers open creamy white from pink buds and are borne in terminal, branched clusters in late spring.
H4 ♔ 1993

V. × rhytidophylloides 'Alleghany' A large shrub with elliptical, leathery, dark green, puckered leaves, clusters of yellowish white flowers, and brilliant red fruits that ripen to black.
H4

V. rhytidophyllum A large, fast-growing,

Viburnum rhytidophyllum

handsome, evergreen shrub with large, elliptic to oblong, corrugated leaves that are dark green above and densely grey-felted beneath. The small, creamy flowers are borne in stout, felty clusters in late spring. The fruits are oval, red, and finally black, but two or more plants are required for free fruiting. It is a magnificent foliage shrub and superb on chalk, creating the effect of a large-leaved rhododendron. China. Introduced 1900 by Ernest Wilson.
H4

Viburnum sargentii 'Onondaga'

V. sargentii 'Onondaga' A large shrub with maple-like leaves that are deep maroon when young, green when mature and reddish purple in autumn. The flowers are borne in lacecap heads, with the fertile flowers deep red in bud, surrounded by a loose ring of white, sterile flowers. Selected 1959 at the US National Arboretum in Washington state.
H4 ♔ 1993

Viburnum setigerum

V. setigerum A distinctive, medium-sized, open, somewhat lax shrub. From when they unfold in spring until early winter, the slender-pointed leaves are constantly changing colour from metallic blue-red through shades of green to orange-yellow in autumn. The trusses of white flowers in early summer are followed by clusters of large, orange-yellow, somewhat flattened, oval fruits that are finally brilliant red. China. Introduced 1901 by Ernest Wilson.
H4

Viburnum tinus

V. tinus (Laurustinus) One of the most popular evergreens, especially in its several garden forms. It is a medium-sized to large shrub with luxuriant masses of glossy green, oval leaves. The flattened clusters of white, pink-budded flowers are borne continuously from late autumn to early spring, The egg-shaped fruits are metallic blue and finally black. It is an excellent winter-flowering shrub for all but the coldest areas and makes an attractive informal hedge. It tolerates shade and seaside exposure. Mediterranean region. In cultivation since the late sixteenth century.
H4

V. t. 'Eve Price' A dense, compact, medium-sized shrub with smaller leaves than the type. It produces flowers from most attractive carmine buds which are pink-tinged when open.
H4 ♔ 1993

V. t. 'French White' A strong-growing medium-sized to large shrub which bears large heads of white flowers.
H4

Viburnum tinus 'Eve Price'

Viburnum tinus 'French White'

Viburnum tinus 'Gwenllian'

V. t. 'Gwenllian' A compact medium-sized form of compact habit with small leaves. The flowers are deep pink in bud and open to white with a flush of pink on the backs of the lobes.
H4 ♆ 1993

V. t. 'Lucidum' A vigorous medium-sized to large shrub with relatively large leaves

Viburnum tinus 'Lucidum'

and flowerheads, larger than in the type, which open white in early to mid-spring.
H4

Viburnum tinus 'Purpureum'

V. t. 'Purpureum' A medium-sized to large shrub with very dark green leaves that are purple-tinted when young.
H4

Viburnum tinus 'Variegatum'

V. t. 'Variegatum' A medium-sized shrub with leaves variegated with creamy yellow. It is not recommended for cold districts.
H3–4

V. utile A graceful, medium-sized evergreen shrub, elegant and rather sparingly branched. The long, slender stems bear narrow, glossy leaves that are white-felted on their undersides. The white, sweetly scented flowers are in dense, rounded clusters in late spring. The fruits are bluish black. It is much used by hybridists. China. Introduced 1908 by Ernest Wilson.
H4

Viburnum wrightii 'Hessei'

V. wrightii 'Hessei' A dwarf shrub with broad, ovate, prettily veined leaves and white flowers in clusters in late spring, followed by sealing-wax-red fruits that appear reliably every autumn. An excellent shrub for the front of the border.
H4

Vinca *Apocynaceae*
Periwinkle

A genus of seven species of herbaceous plants and evergreen shrubs, natives of Europe, North Africa and west and central Asia. The following are vigorous, evergreen, trailing shrubs that make extensive carpets and are ideal as ground cover in sun or shade. They grow in all fertile soils. The shoots root as they go but not very deeply, and the plants can easily be controlled by reducing the overwintered stems in late winter.

V. major (Greater periwinkle) A rampant, arching, trailing species that roots only at

Vinca major

the tips of the shoots. The leaves are up to 7.5cm (3in) long and the flowers are bright blue, 4cm (1½in) across, and borne in the leaf axils in late spring and early summer. C and S Europe, North Africa.
H4

***V. m.* 'Elegantissima'** See *V. m.* 'Variegata'.

Vinca major 'Maculata'

***V. m.* 'Maculata'** The leaves have a central splash of greenish yellow, more noticeable on young plants in open positions.
H4

***V. m.* 'Variegata'**, syn. *V. m.* 'Elegantissima' The leaves are blotched and margined with cream. The plant is as vigorous as the green form.
H4 ♔ 1993

V. minor (Lesser periwinkle) A familiar cottage garden plant with long, trailing stems that root at intervals and leaves up to 5cm (2in) long. Bright blue flowers, 2.5cm (1in) wide, borne singly on the leaf axils of

Vinca major 'Variegata'

Vinca minor

short, erect shoots, appear from mid-spring to early summer and then intermittently until autumn. Europe, W Asia.
H4

Vinca minor 'Argenteo-variegata'

***V. m.* 'Argenteo-variegata'** Leaves are variegated with cream and flowers are blue.
H4 ♔ 1993

***V. m.* 'Atropurpurea'** A form with deep plum-purple flowers.
H4 ♔ 1993

***V. m.* 'Aureovariegata'** In this form the leaves are blotched with yellow and the flowers are blue.
H4

***V. m.* 'Azurea Flore Pleno'** A form with attractive sky blue, double flowers.
H4 ♔ 1993

Vinca minor 'Gertrude Jekyll'

***V. m.* 'Gertrude Jekyll'** A form with glistening white flowers.
H4 ♔ 1993

Vinca minor 'La Grave'

***V. m.* 'La Grave'** The flowers of this form are azure blue, larger than those of the type. 'Bowles' Variety' is now regarded as a synonym of this plant.
H4 ♔ 1993

***V. m.* 'Multiplex'** A form with plum-purple, double flowers.
H4

Vitex *Verbenaceae*

Of the 250-odd species in this genus, the few that are grown in cool-temperate gardens are deciduous and are valued for their aromatic foliage and scented flowers. The more continental the climate the better, and in maritime places and islands such as those of Britain, they need good drainage and maximum sun in order to ripen their growths and maximize their flowering. They are excellent on a sunny wall. Pruning is simply a matter of removing the old flowering shoots either in late winter or very early spring.

Vitex agnus-castus

V. agnus-castus (Chaste tree) An attractive, spreading, aromatic, medium-sized shrub with pairs of leaves consisting of 5–7 short-stalked leaflets. The flowers are violet, fragrant, and in slender racemes at the ends of the current year's shoots in early to mid-autumn. Mediterranean to C Asia. In cultivation since 1570.
H4

Vitex agnus-castus f. alba

V. a. f. alba A medium-sized shrub with white flowers.
H4

Vitis *Vitaceae*
Vine

This genus consists of about 60 species, many of them primarily grown for ornamental use, which are widely distributed throughout the north-temperate regions, particularly in North America. They are climbers and support themselves by twining tendrils. They are variable in leaf, and several species give rich autumn colour. Most are vigorous and most effective when allowed to clamber into large trees or to cover large hedges or stumps; they can also be trained to cover walls, pergolas, arches and fences and will grow in any well-drained soil, preferably in a sunny position. The small, greenish flowers are in panicles or racemes in summer and are not particularly beautiful, although they are followed after hot, dry seasons by bunches of small grapes. See also Ampelopsis *and* Parthenocissus.

Vitis 'Brant'

V. 'Brant' One of the most popular of hardy, fruiting vines. It reaches a height of 9m (28ft), if provided with a suitable support, and produces cylindrical bunches of sweet, aromatic, dark purple-black grapes that are bloomy when ripe. The attractive, deeply three- to five-lobed leaves turn dark red and purple in autumn, with greenish or yellow veins. It is not a form of the common grape vine but a seedling of multiple parentage. Raised early 1860s in Canada by Charles Arnold.
H4 ♔ 1993

Vitis coignetiae

V. coignetiae This is perhaps the most spectacular of all vines and is capable of growing to the tops of lofty trees. The leaves often measure 30cm (1ft) across and are heart-shaped at the base, with 3–5 shallow lobes and with a rust-coloured felt beneath. The fruits are black with a purple bloom. The leaves turn crimson and scarlet in autumn and give a magnificent display. The best colours occur where the soil is poor or the root run is restricted, as when grown against a wall. Japan, Korea. In cultivation c1875.
H4 ♔ 1993

V. pulchra A large climber with reddish shoots and coarsely toothed leaves up to 15cm (6in) wide. The young leaves are reddish and the autumn foliage brilliant scarlet. It is possibly a hybrid of *V. coignetiae*. In cultivation 1880.
H4

V. vinifera (Grape vine) The following forms are particularly ornamental.

Vitis vinifera

Vitis vinifera 'Apiifolia'

***V. v.* 'Apiifolia'** (Parsley vine) A large, attractive plant with deeply divided leaves. H4

***V. v.* 'Fragola'** A large, unusual form with small fruits that have a distinctly musky flavour. Some palates distinguish it as of strawberries, others of gooseberries. H4

***V. v.* 'Incana'** (Dusty miller grape) The leaves of this medium-sized climber are grey-green, covered with a white, cob-webby down, and three-lobed or unlobed. It has black fruits. This vine is most effective when grown with purple-leaved shrubs. H4

Vitis vinifera 'Purpurea'

***V. v.* 'Purpurea'** (Teinturier grape) The leaves of this medium-sized climber are claret-red at first, becoming deep wine-purple. It is highly effective when grown with shrubs with silver foliage. Teinturier originally meant 'dyer'.
H4 🏆 1993

W

Wattaka

W. sinensis See *Dregea sinensis.*

Weigela *Caprifoliaceae*

A genus of about 10 species of deciduous hardy flowering shrubs from temperate-east Asia. They are very decorative and easily grown shrubs, growing to an average height of 2m (6¹/₂ft) and ideal for town gardens and other areas where there may be atmospheric pollution. The tubular, foxglove-like flowers appear in late spring and early summer all along the shoots of the previous year. Occasionally a small second crop is produced in late summer or early autumn. Any reasonably fertile soil suits these shrubs. Thin out and cut back old flowering shoots to within a short distance of the old wood immediately after flowering.

Weigela florida

W. florida A medium-sized shrub with ovate-oblong to obovate, tapering leaves. The funnel-shaped flowers are reddish or rose-pink on the outside, paler within, opening in late spring and early summer. It is probably the most popular species in cultivation and is the parent of many hybrids. Japan, Korea, N China, Manchuria. Introduced 1845 by Robert Fortune.
H4

***W. f.* 'Foliis Purpureis'** A slower-growing, dwarfer form of compact habit which has purple-flushed leaves and pink flowers.
H4 🏆 1993

***W. f.* 'Variegata'** A compact, small to medium-sized shrub with leaves edged with cream and rose-pink flowers. It is one of the best variegated shrubs for general garden planting.
H4 🏆 1993

Weigela florida 'Versicolor'

***W. f.* 'Versicolor'** A small to medium-sized shrub with creamy white flowers, changing to red. 'Dart's Colour Dream' is very similar.
H4

***W. hortensis* 'Nivea'** A beautiful, small to medium-sized shrub with leaves that are densely white-downy beneath. It bears quite large white flowers in late spring and early summer. In cultivation 1870.
H4

W. middendorffiana A small shrub with flaking bark and bell-shaped, sulphur-yellow flowers with dark orange marking on the lower lobes, produced in mid- to late spring. An ornamental, compact species

Weigela praecox 'Variegata'

best grown in a sheltered and partially shaded position. Japan, N China, Manchuria. Introduced 1850.
H4

***W. praecox* 'Variegata'** A small to medium-sized shrub with leaves variegated with creamy white and quite large, honey-scented, rose-pink flowers with yellow markings in the throat. Flowering starts just after the middle of spring.
H4 ♔ 1993

CULTIVARS AND HYBRIDS

The following are a colourful selection of hardy hybrids, flowering on the old wood in late spring and early summer and often a second time in early autumn. Pruning consists of shortening or removing the flowering stems immediately after flowering.

Weigela 'Abel Carrière'

***W.* 'Abel Carrière'** A medium-sized shrub with many large, bright rose-carmine flowers, flecked gold in the throat. Buds are purple-carmine. In cultivation 1876.
H4 ♔ 1993

Weigela 'Bristol Ruby'

***W.* 'Bristol Ruby'** A vigorous and erect medium-sized shrub with an abundance of sparkling ruby-red flowers.
H4

Weigela 'Eva Rathke'

***W.* 'Eva Rathke'** A slow-growing, compact, medium-sized shrub bearing bright red-crimson flowers with straw-coloured anthers that are borne over a long season.
H4

***W.* 'Evita'** A dwarf, spreading shrub with bright red flowers over a long period.
H4

***W.* 'Fiesta'** A medium-sized shrub with lax growth and flowers of a shining uniform red, produced very freely.
H4 ♔ 1993

***W.* 'Looymansii Aurea'** The foliage of this medium-sized shrub is light golden yellow, enhanced in spring by the pink flowers. It is best in partial shade.
H4

***W.* 'Majestueux'** An erect and early flowering medium-sized shrub, with masses of large, madder-pink flowers flushed with carmine in the throat.
H4

Weigela 'Mont Blanc'

Weigela 'Rubidor'

W. **'Mont Blanc'** A vigorous medium-sized shrub with large, white, fragrant flowers. It is perhaps the best of the whites. In cultivation 1898.
H4 ♕ 1993

W. **'Newport Red'** A superb medium-sized shrub, similar to 'Eve Rathke' but with larger flowers of a lighter red.
H4

W. **'Rubidor'** A small shrub with yellow or green leaves with a broad yellow margin and carmine flowers. It is likely to burn if planted in full sun.
H4

W. **'Victoria'** A small, upright shrub with deep bronze-purple foliage and purple-pink flowers.
H4

Wisteria *Leguminosae*

A genus of about six species of deciduous twiners, natives of east Asia and North America. These are among the most beautiful of all climbers, lavishly draping themselves with their distinctive long racemes of white, pink, blue or mauve pea-flowers in late spring and early summer, and often producing a few later in the year. The pinnate leaves are also very attractive.

Wisterias should be planted in full sun, and if the soil is chalky, some good loamy soil should be added to it. They are excellent for walls and pergolas and for growing into trees, and may even be carefully trained into small standards. Large, vigorous specimens may require an annual hard pruning in late winter to keep them within bounds, and this can be followed in late summer by a second pruning that consists of shortening the leafy shoots to five or six buds. Pruning early in the life of the plant should, however, be concentrated on forming a strong framework of primary branches.

Cultivars have proliferated in recent years and there has been a tendency for named forms to arrive from the Far East with little to distinguish them from the established ones. It is as well to take some pains to make certain that you are obtaining value for money. If there is any doubt, you can rely on those cultivars and other forms that have been distinguished by the Award of Garden Merit. To avoid disappointment only buy plants that have been vegetatively propagated (usually grafted), as seedlings may well not flower for many years. Harmful if eaten.

W. ***floribunda*** (Japanese wisteria) A lovely climber up to 4m (12ft) or more with leaves consisting of 13–19 leaflets and fragrant, violet-blue or bluish purple flowers in slender racemes 13–25cm (5–10in) long that emerge with the leaves and open from the base upwards. The stems twine in a clockwise direction. The following forms are recommended. Japan. Introduced 1830 by Philipp von Siebold.
H4

Wisteria floribunda 'Alba'

W. f. **'Alba'** The flowers are white with a lilac tint on the keel. They are borne in racemes 45–60cm (18–24in) long.
H4 ♕ 1993

W. f. **f.** ***macrobotrys*** A group of forms with racemes to 0.3–1m (1–3ft) or more. 'Multijuga', the most common, has fragrant, lilac flowers tinged blue-purple. Best grown on a wooden bridge, pergola or arch to allow for the long flower clusters.
H4 ♕ 1993

Wisteria floribunda f. macrobotrys

Wisteria floribunda 'Rosea'

W. f. **'Rosea'** The flowers of this form are pale rose, tipped with purple, in long racemes.
H4 ♕ 1993

W. f. **'Violacea Plena'** A form with double, violet-blue flowers.
H4

W. ***sinensis*** (Chinese wisteria) This is per-

Wisteria sinensis

haps the most popular of the wisterias and it is one of the noblest of all climbers, reaching 18–30m (60–100ft) in a suitably large tree. The elegant leaves have 9–13 elliptic to elliptic-oblong leaflets. The fragrant, mauve or deep lilac flowers, 2.5cm (1in) long, are borne before the leaves appear in late spring. They are produced in racemes 20–30cm (8–12in) long on which all the flowers open simultaneously and are followed by velvety seed pods. The stems twine in an anti-clockwise direction. A large specimen in full flower against an old house wall is one of the wonders of spring. Unlike *W. floribunda*, it often has a small second flush of flowers later in the summer. China. First introduced in 1816 from a garden in Canton.
H4 🏆 1993

Wisteria sinensis 'Alba'

W. s. **'Alba'** A form with white flowers.
H4 🏆 1993

W. s. **'Black Dragon'** The flowers are double and dark purple, but most if not all the plants in cultivation appear to be *W. floribunda* 'Violacea Plena'.
H4

W. s. **'Caroline'** A form with deep blue-purple, very fragrant flowers.
H4

W. s. **'Plena'** This form produces double, rosette-shaped flowers, which are an attractive lilac colour.
H4

Wisteria venusta

W. venusta A strong-growing climber reaching up to 9m (28ft) or more. The leaves consist of 9–13 ovate to oval, downy leaflets and in late spring and early summer it bears slightly fragrant white flowers, which are the largest in the genus. They are in racemes which are 10–15cm (4–6in) long. The seed pods are velvety. Introduced before 1912 from Japan, where it is known only in cultivation.
H4

Xanthoceras *Sapindaceae*

A genus of one deciduous species that is related to Koelreuteria, but quite different in its general appearance.

Xanthoceras sorbifolium

X. sorbifolium A beautiful large shrub or small tree with pinnate leaves composed of 9–17 leaflets, and flowers 2.5cm (1in) wide, borne in late spring in erect clusters rather like those of a horse chestnut. Although it requires sun and warmth to ripen its growths and flower well, it is worth every effort for its sweetly scented white flowers, which are white with a carmine eye which fades to soft carmine. It can be grown in all types of fertile soil and does especially well on chalk. N China. Introduced 1866.
H3–4 🏆 1993

Xanthorhiza *Ranunculaceae*

A genus of one deciduous species. Although it is related to the buttercup family it is very different in general appearance from other family members.

Xanthorhiza simplicissima

X. simplicissima (Yellow root) A small, suckering shrub that eventually makes a thicket of erect stems up to 1m (3ft) high. It has very attractive pinnate leaves, composed of 3–5 oval to lance-shaped, deeply toothed, bright green leaflets, turning to burnished bronze, often with a purple tinge, in autumn. The tiny, delicate, deep purple flowers appear in loose, drooping panicles with the leaves in early to mid-spring. The roots and inner bark are bright yellow. It thrives in moist clay but dislikes shallow soils over chalk. Overgrown plants can be cut right back to the ground in spring and mulched. E United States. Introduced 1776.
H4

Y

Yucca *Agavaceae*

These remarkable evergreens, with rosettes or clumps of narrow, usually rigid leaves and tall, candelabrum-like panicles of large, drooping, bell-shaped, lily-like flowers, are of great architectural value and rare beauty. They help to create a sub-tropical effect in the cool-temperate garden. There are about 40 species native to Central America, Mexico and the southern United States. Several species are hardy in all but really cold conditions and prefer a hot, dry, well-drained position in full sun. They are well suited to gardens near the sea and some make good container specimens.

Yucca filamentosa

Y. filamentosa A stemless species with dense clumps of spreading or erect, lance-shaped, slightly bloomy leaves. Along the leaf margins are many curly white threads. The creamy flowers, each 5–7.5cm (2–3in) long, are borne in erect, conical panicles 1–2m (3–6¹⁄₂ft) high in mid- to late summer, even on young plants. SE United States. In cultivation 1675.
H4 ♛ 1993

Y. f. 'Bright Edge' A small shrub with leaves that have a narrow, golden-yellow margin. It is slightly tender.
H3 ♛ 1993

Y. f. 'Variegata' The leaves of this small shrub are margined with cream. It is slightly tender.
H3 ♛ 1993

Y. flaccida A stemless, low-growing yucca

Yucca filamentosa 'Bright Edge'

Yucca filamentosa 'Variegata'

forming tufts of long, lance-shaped leaves. The terminal part of each leaf bends downwards and the margins are well-furnished with thin, curly white threads. The flowers are creamy, 5–6.5cm (2–2¹⁄₂in) long, and borne in erect, downy panicles 0.6–1.2m (2–4ft) high in mid- to late summer. It spreads by short growths at the base. The

following forms are recommended. SE United States. Introduced 1816.
H3–4

Yucca flaccida 'Golden Sword'

Y. f. 'Golden Sword' A striking form in which the leaves have a broad central band of creamy yellow.
H3 ♔ 1993

Yucca flaccida 'Ivory'

Yucca glauca

Y. f. 'Ivory' A small shrub producing large panicles of creamy white flowers stained with green.
H3–4 ♔ 1993

Y. glauca A low-growing, short-stemmed species with a compact, rounded head of linear, greyish green leaves that are margined with white and edged with a few threads. The greenish white flowers, 5–7.5cm (2–3in) long, are borne in an erect raceme 1–1.5m (3–4½ft) high in mid- to late summer. The species is hardy, but young plants do not flower.
H4

Yucca gloriosa

Y. gloriosa (Adam's needle) A shrub reaching 2.5m (8ft) or so, with a stout stem and few or no branches. The leaves are very stiff and the sharp spine-tips are potentially dangerous if near a garden thoroughfare or where there are children. They are bloomy green, up to 60cm (2ft) long by 7.5–10cm (3–4in) wide, and are produced in a dense,

terminal head. The creamy flowers, sometimes tinged with red on the outside, are carried in an erect, crowded, conical panicle, 1–2m (3–6½ft) high or more, from midsummer to early autumn. SE United States. In cultivation c1550.
H4 ♔ 1993

Yucca gloriosa 'Variegata'

Y. g. 'Variegata' The leaves of this form are dramatically but quite subtly margined and striped with creamy yellow, fading to cream on older leaves.
H4 ♔ 1993

Yucca recurvifolia

Y. recurvifolia A medium-sized species, usually with a short stem and several branches. The tapered leaves, 0.6–1m (2–3ft) long, are blue-bloomy at first and become green as they age. All but the central, upper leaves are characteristically downward-curved. The creamy flowers are in dense, erect panicles 0.6–1m (2–3ft) or more high in late summer. It is the best

species for town gardens. It differs from *Y. gloriosa* in the recurved leaves, which are not as sharply pointed. SE United States. Introduced 1794.
H4 🏆 1993

Yucca whipplei

Y. whipplei A stemless species that develops into a dense, globular clump of long, narrow, rigid, spine-tipped leaves that are finely toothed and blue-bloomy. The large, fragrant flowers are greenish white, edged with purple. They are in a densely packed panicle at the end of an erect, 2–3.5m (6½–11ft) scape (stalk) in late spring and early summer. Although it can withstand frost, this magnificent species can be recommended only for sunny places in very mild areas; it needs a very well-drained position. California. Introduced 1854.
H2–3

Yushania *Gramineae*

A genus of two evergreen species of bamboo from east Asia.

Y. anceps, syn. *Arundinaria anceps, Sinarundinaria anceps* A beautiful but rampant species, ideal for screens and hedges in large gardens. The mature canes are also useful for staking and other tasks. They are straight, erect, deep glossy green and reach a height of 3–3.5m (10–11ft) or more in mild places. The arching tips bear masses of glossy green leaves, 10–15cm (4–6in) long and 12mm (½in) wide. N Himalayas. Introduced 1865.
H4 🏆 1993

Z

Zanthoxylum *Rutaceae*

A genus of about 200 species of deciduous trees and shrubs largely found in warm regions of the world. Most have spiny branches and aromatic leaves. The flowers are small but the compound leaves are always attractive and in some species are as beautiful as the fronds of a fern, while in others they have the spectacular appeal of the tree of heaven, Ailanthus altissima. *The fruits may be jet black or bright red. They are easily grown in any ordinary soil in sun or shade.*

Z. americanum (Prickly ash, toothache tree) A large, rather gaunt shrub or short-stemmed tree with short, stout spines and leaves that are composed of 5–11 more or less oval leaflets. The small, yellowish green flowers are in short clusters in spring and are followed by dense gatherings of jet-black fruits. The twigs and fruits are said to have been chewed by the Native Americans to alleviate toothache: the acrid juice has a numbing effect. It is very hardy. E North America. Introduced c1740.
H4

Zanthoxylum piperitum

Z. piperitum (Japan pepper) A neat, medium-sized shrub with pairs of flattened spines and attractive pinnate leaves composed of 11–23 stalkless, broadly lance-shaped or fairly oval leaves. Small, greenish yellow flowers, produced on the old wood in late spring or early summer, are followed

by small, reddish fruits with black seeds used as a pepper in Japan. Leaves turn a rich yellow in autumn. Japan, Korea, Manchuria, China. In cultivation 1877.
H4

Zauschneria *Onagraceae*

A genus of four species of dwarf deciduous subshrubs or perennials. They require a warm, sunny and, most importantly, well-drained position and make excellent subjects for the rock garden. Although not rated as very hardy, experience shows that they can in fact be grown in areas where the cold is considerable, as long as they do not have to tolerate wet, sticky soil. Known as Californian fuchsias, they are not fuchsias at all but belong to the same plant family.

Z. californica 'Dublin', syn. *Z. c.* 'Glasnevin' A bushy sub-shrub with several erect stems that are clothed with narrow, downy, grey-green leaves. The tubular, fuchsia-like flowers are red with a scarlet tube and are borne in long, loose spikes over a very long period from late summer to mid-autumn.
H3 🏆 1993

Z. c. 'Glasnevin' See *Z. c.* 'Dublin'.

Zauschneria californica subsp. *mexicana*

Z. c. subsp. mexicana A similar plant to the above, but with broader, green leaves.
H3

Z. cana, syn. *Z. microphylla* A dwarf sub-shrub with linear grey leaves and loose spikes of red, scarlet-tubed flowers in late summer and autumn. California.
H3

Z. microphylla See *Z. cana*.

Zelkova *Ulmaceae*

A genus of five species of smooth-barked deciduous trees or, rarely, shrubs, natives of Asia with one species found in Crete. They are allied to the elms, Ulmus, but do not suffer from Dutch elm disease. They thrive in deep, moist, loamy soils and are fairly tolerant of shade. The small, greenish flowers and the fruits that follow them are unremarkable and of little ornamental value; nevertheless the zelkovas are trees of considerable quality, and they are as useful and attractive in the garden as the deciduous nothofagus.

Z. carpinifolia A large, long-lived, slow-growing tree which grows up to 30m (100ft) in height. The bark is smooth and grey like a beech (*Fagus*) but flakes with age. The trunk is generally short, soon giving way to numerous erect, crowded branches that form a characteristically dense, conical head, much loved by children for climbing. In old trees the trunk is often buttressed.

The dark green leaves which grow up to 7.5cm (3in) long, are more or less elliptical, coarsely toothed and rough to the touch. They are borne on hairy shoots and turn an attractive orange-brown in autumn Caucasus. N Iran. Introduced 1760.
H4

Z. serrata A medium-sized, occasionally

Zelkova serrata

large, graceful, wide-spreading tree with a rounded crown and smooth, grey, later flaking bark. The leaves are more or less slenderly oval, up to 12cm (5in) long and edged with slender-pointed, coarse teeth. In autumn they turn bronze or red. Japan, Korea, Taiwan, China. Introduced 1861.
H4 ♔ 1993

Z. × verschaffeltii This is normally a splendid, large shrub or small, bushy tree of graceful habit which produces slender shoots and more or less oval conspicuously-toothed leaves that are rough to the touch. In cultivation 1886.
H4

Zenobia *Ericaceae*

A genus of one deciduous or semi-evergreen species.

Zenobia pulverulenta

Z. pulverulenta A ravishingly beautiful small shrub of loose, slightly arching habit with bloomy young shoots and lovely, blue-grey, bloomy, more or less oblong, shallowly-toothed leaves. The bloom on these tends to be more conspicuous on the young leaves and gradually fades as they become older. The white, bell-shaped flowers, fairly similar to those of a large lily-of-the-valley, are aniseed-scented and held in pendulous clusters in early to midsummer. It requires a lime-free soil and preferably semi-shade. It is one of the most beautiful of shrubs that flower in early summer and for some unfathomable reason is widely and unjustifiably neglected. E United States. Introduced 1801.
H4

Zelkova carpinifolia

INDEX

THIS IS AN INDEX OF COMMON NAMES, GARDENING TERMS AND TECHNIQUES. BOTANICAL NAMES MAY BE ACCESSED VIA THE PLANT DIRECTORY AND ARE INDEXED HERE ONLY WHEN A MENTION OCCURS OUTSIDE THE PLANT DIRECTORY, PLANT SELECTOR AND GUIDE TO PLANT CHARACTERISTICS. ITALIC PAGE NUMBERS REFER TO PHOTOGRAPHS AND ILLUSTRATIONS

PICTURE ACKNOWLEDGEMENTS

The roman numerals i to vii following a page reference identify the position of the photograph on the page. Starting at the top of the left-hand column with i, the numerals are allocated in sequential order running vertically from the top to the bottom of each column. For example, on page 269 shown below, the top picture in the left column is 269i, the centre column picture is 269iv and the bottom right picture is 269vi.

Andrew Lawson 19; 38; 48; 55; 60ii; 119i; 120ii; 125v; 128iv; 129i; 133iv; 136ii; 137ii; 141i, iii, v; 143iv; 144iii; 145ii; 146ii, iv; 147v; 153ii; 161iv; 162ii; 164i, iii; 167ii, iii; 168ii, v, vi; 169iv, v; 172i, ii; 185iv; 186i; 187i, v; 188vi; 189iv; 191v; 192i; 193iv, v; 197i; 200iii, vi; 204i, iv; 205iv; 215iv; 216i; 217iii; 219vii; 222i; 223ii, iv; 224iv; 225iii; 226i, iii, iv; 227iv; 229v; 231ii; 235iv; 237i; 238i, ii; 241iii; 242iii; 245i, iii; 254iii; 255ii; 264i; 265v; 266i; 267i; 273v; 279i; 291iii; 293iii; 296iii; 299ii; 300i, vi; 302iv; 304ii; 305ii, iv; 307iv; 308iii; 316i; 318v, vi; 325iv; 326iv, v; 329ii; 333ii, iii, iv; 334i; 335ii; 340i; 343iv, v; 347i, v; 353iii; 358i, iv; 359iii; 361i; 366i, iii; 367i, v; 369ii; 381iii, v; 382i; iii; 383iii, v; 413iii; 416ii; 418ii, v; 419i; 424ii, iii; 425iv; 428vi; 430iii; 432i; 433ii; 434iii; 438ii; 445iv; 446vii; 447v; 451iv; 452iii; 453i; 456ii; 457i, ii; 458i, ii; 459i; 466vi; 467ii; 470i, vi; 472iii; 474iii; 484ii; 485ii; 486i; 487i; 489iii; 495i; 499ii; 503i; 506v; 525ii; 537ii, iv; 538iii; 539iii, v; 542iii; 544i, iv; 545i, iii; 546iii, iv; 550ii; 551iii; 554i, ii; 558ii, iv; 560i, iii; 562ii, iii, iv; 563i, iv, vi; 564i, ii; 566v; 568i; 570i; 574ii; 575i, ii; 576iii; 577i; 579iv; 581iii; 584ii; 585vi; 591iv; 593iv; 595i; 596v; 597i; 598iii; 600iv, v; 603iv; 607i; 610ii; 611i; 612iii; 614i, iii; 617vii; 618v; 619vi; 620i; 621iv; 622i; 624i, iii; 625ii; 626iv

Brian Carter/Garden Picture Library 119iv; 128ii; 133ii; 139iv; 154i; 174i; 177i; 179i; 180i; 184ii; 185v; 186iii; 193iii; 201ii; 231iv; 245v; 262iv; 264iii; 268iv; 276ii; 277iv; 283iv; 300v; 309iii, iv; 314iii; 320iii; 321i; 322iii; 324vi; 328vi; 336iii; 338i; 340iii, iv; 347iv; 348i, iii; 351ii; 369iii; 370iii; 389v; 391i; 392iii; 398iv; 402iv; 406i; 411v; 413i; 414v; 415iv; 419ii; 420i, iv; 426iv; 432ii; 442v; 444iii; 448iii; 449v; 450iii; 455iv; 460i; 462ii; 466ii; 468ii, vi; 470ii; 473i; 491ii; 497i; 498ii; 501iii; 505iii; 506ii; 507i; 510i, v; 513iv; 514i; 517ii; 518i; 519iv; 520i, ii; 521ii; 522v; 523ii; 526i; 529i; 530ii; 531iii; 532i; 533iv; 535iii; 536i; 537iii; 539ii; 540iv; 543v; 544iii; 546i; 548iii; 549ii; 555iii; 565vi; 567i, iv; 570v; 574i; 584iii; 587ii; 593iii; 594i; 595v; 596iii; 597v; 598i; 599ii; 603ii; 615v; 616ii; 618iv

Brigitte Thomas/Garden Picture Library 18; 31i, ii; 64; 67; 116-7; 120i, iv, v; 133vi; 202iv; 385ii; 446v; 463ii; 475ii; 551i; 622v

Bob Challinor/Garden Picture Library 221i; 299i, 536ii

Christopher Fairweather/Garden Picture Library 161i; 183ii; 189v; 206i; 245ii; 246i; 303iii; 332iii; 391iii; 423ii; 439i; 442vi; 460iv; 499iii; 501ii; 503iv, v; 514ii; 516v; 522iv, vi; 525i; 607ii; 618i; 623iv

Christopher Gallagher/Garden Picture Library 17

Clay Perry/Garden Picture Library 24

Clive Nichols 618ii

Clive Nichols/Garden Picture Library 269v; 278iii; 356ii; 426iii; 579iii

David Askham/Garden Picture Library 243i; 386ii; 478ii; 516v; 520v; 581v; 582iii; 608i

David England/Garden Picture Library 269i; 336ii; 337ii, iv; 558i

David Russell/Garden Picture Library 122iii; 125vi; 220ii; 225ii; 231iii; 263ii; 268i; 299iv; 355ii; 384iv; 385i; 411iv; 539iv; 592ii

Densey Clyne/Garden Picture Library 185i; 547iii

Didier Willery/Garden Picture Library 62; 129iv; 131iv; 136iii; 138ii; 143ii; 156iii; 160iv; 161ii; 163iv; 183iv; 193ii; 197iv; 208iii; 242i; 243v; 258iii; 259iii; 263iv; 271i; 272vi; 273iii, vi; 299iii; 344i; 345iv; 379ii; 395iv; 402iii; 428ii; 435iii; 458iii; 463iv; 466v; 467v; 468i; 471i; 474ii; 492iii; 499i; 531ii; 543iii; 550v; 554iii; 559iii, v; 561i; 564iv; 578iv; 581ii; 582iv; 590iv; 592iii; 594iv; 604ii, iii; 608ii; 612vi; 617ii; 623i; 629iii

Eric Crichton 142ii; 147ii; 149iii; 159iii; 163v; 170iii; 173ii; 174ii, v; 175ii; 178i; 185ii; 188v; 193i; 195iv; 206iv; 215iii; 223i; 230v; 235iii; 239ii; 244iii; 252iii; 259iv; 260i; 261ii; 262v; 266iii; 270iii; 274iii; 277i; 283iii; 285ii; 286iii; 288v; 290iii; 291i, v; 293iv; 298i; 303iv; 304iii; 305iii; 312i; 316v; 317iii; 320iii; 324v; 325ii; 328iii; 330ii; 335v; 336iii; 337i, vi; 341ii, iii; 342i; 343i; 345iii; 348iv; 349iv; 350i; 351i; 358v; 365i; 368i, iii; 370iv; 371iii; 373ii; 376i; 377ii; 380i; 381ii; 383ii; 384i; 387i; 390ii; 394iii; 399v; 400i; 403iv; 404iv; 408ii, iii; 409iii; 414iii; 416iii, iv; 418i, iii; 419iv; 420iii, v; 421ii; 425ii, iii; 427i, iv; 431i; 434i; 436iii, iv; 442iv; 443iii; 449iii, vi; 451i; 452i; 454ii; 461i; 462iv; 463iii; 466iii; 468iii, iv; 469iii; 471ii, iv, v; 472i; 476ii; 485iii, iv; 488i; 490iii; 492v; 493iii; 494ii; 496i; 500i; 504i; 505i; 507ii; 508iv; 509i; 512ii, iii; 513i; 518iii, iv; 519ii; 521iii; 526v; 528iii; 535v; 536iii; 538iv; 541i; 542ii; 545ii; 546ii; 547v; 549i; 550iii; 552i; 553iii; 557ii; 559ii; 563ii; 565iii; 569i; 570iv; 575iv; 578i; 580ii; 586iv; 587iii; 588ii; 590ii; 593ii; 594v, vi; 596ii; 597iii; 601i; 603iii; 606i; 614iv; 615; 620vi; 621ii, v; 623iii; 627iv; 629ii

Garden Picture Library 234iii

Harry Smith Collection 124iv; 125iv; 127i; 130i; 131vi; 132ii; 135iii; 136iv, v; 138iv; 139iv; 141ii; 146iii; 147iv; 154ii; 163i; 164ii, v, vi; 166i; 168i, iii; 171i; 172iv; 175iii; 176ii, iv; 184v; 185iii, vi; 186iv; 187ii; 188ii, iii; 190v; 192iv; 196i; 199ii; 204iii; 206ii; 215ii; 217ii; 218v; 219ii; 220iii; 233iv; 234i, iii; 235i; 236iii; 247iii; 248iv, v; 250i; 252v; 253iii, v; 254ii; 261iii; 262i, iii; 264ii; 265ii; 267iv; 269iii; 270iv; 271ii; 272i, iv; 273ii; 274iii, iv; 275ii; 278i; 279iii; 280ii; 284v; 285iii, vi; 288vi; 289v; 297iii; 301iii; 302vi; 305i; 306i; 309ii; 310i, ii, iii; 311iv; 313v; 315iii; 317i; 325iii; 327i, iv; 330iii; 336i, iv; 337iii; 338ii; 341i; 343iii; 355iv; 359iv; 371i; 373i, iii; 384iii; 386i; 388i; 389iii, iv; 390i, iii; 391ii; 393ii, v; 394i, ii, v; 395iii, v; 399iii; 402i; 403i, iii; 404i; 407ii, iii; 409i; 411i, ii; 415i; 416i; 429iii; 435iv; 440iii; 441iii, vi; 442vii; 455iii; 456iii; 463v; 467iii, iv; 469i; 475iii; 479i; 480i; 482ii, iv; 488ii; 489ii; 490i; 491i, iii; 492i, ii; 493i, ii; 494i; 496iii; 497iii; 498i; 500ii, iii; 502i, ii, iii; 503ii; 504ii; 506i, iii; 507iv; 508i, ii, iii; 509ii; 511vi; 513iii; 514iv, vi; 515i, ii, iii, iv, v; 516i; 517iii, v; 518v; 519iii; 521i; 522iii; 523vi; 524i, ii, iii, v; 525v; 526ii; 528i, ii; 531iv; 534ii; 535ii; 539i; 552ii; 553iv; 555i; 559i; 561ii, iii; 563vii; 570iii; 573ii; 576iv; 581vi; 582ii; 583; 589ii; 595ii; 610iii; 613ii, v, vi; 617iv; 619v; 620v; 623v

Henj Dijkman/Garden Picture Library 476i

Howard Rice/Garden Picture Library 160i; 205i; 225v; 251i; 254iv; 311v; 357i;

538iii; 556i; 557i; 564v; 591v; 615iv

Jane Legate/Garden Picture Library 617iii

Jerry Pavia/Garden Picture Library 236i; 283ii; 366ii; 525iv; 610i

Jill Hedges Garden Archive 3; 5

Joanne Pavia/Garden Picture Library 240iv

John Ferro Sims/Garden Picture Library 462ii; 578vi

John Glover 20i,ii; 21; 27; 35; 36i, ii; 39; 71; 79; 83; 84; 85ii, iii; 88i, ii, iii; 95i, ii, iii; 98i, ii, iii; 102i, ii, iii; 103i, ii, iii; 105i, ii

John Glover/Garden Picture Library 16; 122v; 127iv; 131i; 132i, iv; 133i; 134i; 137i, iii; 140i; 141iv; 142i; 143i; 146i, v; 148i; 160iii; 161v; 162i; 176i; 177ii; 178iii; 179ii; 181i, 184i, iv; 188iv; 191ii; 194iii; 195i; 200v; 205ii; 216ii; 219i; 223iii; 225i; 230i; 242ii; 246iv; 248ii; 250ii; 254i; 262ii; 265i, iii; 266iii, iv; 267ii; 269vi; 271iii; 275iv; 281i; 283v; 284i, iv, vi; 285v; 288ii, iii, vii; 290ii; 292ii; 294i; 301ii; 304iii; 316ii; 318iv; 321iii; 323iii; 324iv; 326i; 328i; 332iv; 334ii, vi; 338iii; 346i, iii; 361iii; 364iii; 367iii; 370ii; 372ii; 376iv; 383i; 388iii; 389i, ii, vi; 392i, iv; 393i, iii; 395iii; 396iii; 398v; 401v; 406ii, iii; 411iii; 418iv; 421i; 427iii; 440i; 441ii; 443i; 460iii; 462iii; 463i; 464ii, v; 466i; 467vi; 469ii; 470iii, iv, v; 472ii; 476iv, v; 478iii; 483i; 484iii; 496ii; 497iv; 505ii, iv, v, vi; 510iii; 511ii, iii, iv; 513ii; 521iv; 523iii, iv; 525iii; 527ii; 529ii; 532ii; 545iv; 547iv; 560ii; 561iv; 566iii, vi; 568ii; 573iv; 580i; 581iv; 586i, iii, v, vi; 587iv, v; 588iv; 591i; 592i; 593i; 597iv; 601iv; 604v; 605i; 612ii; 613i; 614ii, v, vi; 620iv; 621iii, iv; 622ii; 624iv; 625i; 626i, iii; 627vi; 628ii; 629i

John Hillier 143ii; 286vi; 398i; 399v; 405i; 416iv; 555i; 566iv; 569iv,v; 576i; 579i; 588i

Jonathan Weaver/Garden Picture Library 523i

J S Sira/Garden Picture Library 140iii, iv; 169i, ii, iii; 190vii; 191i, iii; 220iv; 224i; 245iv; 279iv; 315i; 323vi; 324iii; 346iv; 369i; 396ii; 397i; 401iv; 420iii; 423i, v; 424i; 425i; 437i; 441iv; 442i; 443ii; 444iii; 449ii; 475i; 476iii; 506iv; 538v; 548i; 574iii; 581i; 594ii; 598ii; 603ii; 612i; 627iii

Juliette Wade/Garden Picture Library 130iii; 159ii; 160v; 162iii; 224iii; 243iv; 268iii; 495ii

Karin Craddock/Garden Picture

Library 295ii; 587i

Lamontagne/Garden Picture Library 127ii; 130ii; 184iii, vi; 190ii; 192ii; 196iv; 202i; 226ii; 248iii; 255i; 302ii; 345iii; 384v; 391iv; 435ii; 494iii; 543iv; 544v; 547ii; 595iii

Linda Burgess/Garden Picture Library 318iii; 452iv; 459ii; 624ii

Marijke Heuff/Garden Picture Library 28; 227iii; 578v; 620iv

Mayer/Le Scanff/Garden Picture Library 347ii; 558iii

Mel Watson/Garden Picture Library 460ii

Michael Howes/Garden Picture Library 23

Neil Holmes/Garden Picture Library 29; 139iii; 156i; 157i; 158i, ii; 162iv; 170ii; 171iv; 216v; 218iii; 234ii; 241iii; 323ii; 325v; 326ii; 329iv, v; 358iii; 371ii; 383iv; 464i; 467i; 477ii; 478i; 523v; 565i; 594iii

Nigel Kemp/Garden Picture Library 309v

Noel Kavanagh/Garden Picture Library 42; 392v; 543ii

Philippe Bonduel/Garden Picture Library 553ii

Photos Horticultural 154iii

Reader's Digest 135ii; 136i; 140ii; 156v; 158iv; 175i; 195iii; 200ii; 201iii; 236ii; 244iv; 255v; 261i; 264iv; 336v; 337v; 344iv; 345i; 346ii; 348iv, v; 349iii; 352i, v; 353vi; 359ii; 361ii; 362iii; 365ii; 379iii; 398i, vi; 405ii; 406v; 415v; 427ii; 428i

Robert Estall/Garden Picture Library 448iv

Roger Hyam/Garden Picture Library 14-15; 471iii; 497ii

Ron Evans/Garden Picture Library 501i; 578iii

Ron Sutherland/Garden Picture Library 247ii; 309i; 484i; 628i

Stephen Jury/Garden Picture Library 547i

Steven Wooster/Garden Picture Library 37; 75; 125i; 257iii

Sue Atkinson 198i

Sunniva Harte/Garden Picture Library 430i; 433i; 543i

Vaughan Fleming/Garden Picture Library 426i; 446vi; 596i

Zara McCalmont/Garden Picture Library 357iii